Koren Talmud Bavli
THE NOÉ EDITION

BAVA BATRA

Steinsaltz Center

KOREN

תלמוד בבלי

KOREN TALMUD BAVLI

THE NOÉ EDITION

בבא בתרא

BAVA BATRA

Daf 108a through Daf 139b

COMMENTARY BY

Rabbi Adin Even-Israel Steinsaltz

EDITOR-IN-CHIEF

Rabbi Dr Tzvi Hersh Weinreb

SENIOR CONTENT EDITOR

Rabbi Dr Shalom Z Berger

EXECUTIVE EDITOR

Rabbi Joshua Schreier

•

STEINSALTZ CENTER

KOREN PUBLISHERS JERUSALEM

Supported by the Matanel Foundation

Koren Talmud Bavli, The Noe Edition
Vol. 23f: Tractate Bava Batra, Daf 108a through Daf 139b
Paperback, ISBN,978-965-7766-13-2

First Hebrew/English paperback edition, 2021

Koren Publishers Jerusalem Ltd.
PO Box 4044, Jerusalem 91040, ISRAEL
PO Box 8531, New Milford, CT 06776, USA
www.korenpub.com

Steinsaltz Center

Steinsaltz Center is the parent organization of institutions established by Rabbi Adin Even-Israel Steinsaltz

PO Box 45187, Jerusalem 91450 ISRAEL
Telephone: +972 2 646 0900, Fax +972 2 624 9454
www.steinsaltz-center.org

הִנֵּה יָמִים בָּאִים, נְאֻם אֲדֹנָי יֱהוִֹה, וְהִשְׁלַחְתִּי רָעָב בָּאָרֶץ,
לֹא־רָעָב לַלֶּחֶם וְלֹא־צָמָא לַמַּיִם, כִּי אִם־לִשְׁמֹעַ אֵת דִּבְרֵי יהוה.

Behold, days are coming – says the Lord God – I will send a hunger to the land, not a hunger for bread nor a thirst for water, but to hear the words of the Lord. (AMOS 8:11)

The Noé edition of the Koren Talmud Bavli
with the commentary of Rabbi Adin Even-Israel Steinsaltz
is dedicated to all those who open its covers
to quench their thirst for Jewish Knowledge,
in our generation of Torah renaissance.

This beautiful edition is for the young, the aged,
the novice and the savant alike,
as it unites the depth of Torah knowledge
with the best of academic scholarship.

Within its exquisite and vibrant pages,
words become worlds.

It will claim its place in the library of classics,
in the bookcases of the Beit Midrash,
the classrooms of our schools,
and in the offices of professionals and business people
who carve out precious time to grapple with its timeless wisdom.

For the Student and the Scholar

DEDICATED BY LEO AND SUE NOÉ

Steinsaltz Center

Executive Director, Steinsaltz Center

Rabbi Meni Even-Israel

Managing Editor

Rabbi Jason Rappoport

Senior Content Editor

Rabbi Dr. Shalom Z. Berger

Editors

Rabbi Dr. Joshua Amaru, *Coordinating Editor*
Rabbi Yehoshua Duker, *Final Editor*
Rabbi Avishai Magence, *Content Curator*
Yedidya Naveh, *Content Curator*
Tal Avrahami
Menucha Chwat
Rabbi Adin Krohn
Betzalel Philip Edwards
Rabbi Yonatan Shai Freedman
Raphael Friedman
Rabbi Ayal Geffon
Rabbi Uri Goldstein
Nechama Greenberg
Rabbi Tzvi Chaim Kaye
Rabbi Yonatan Kohn
Catriel Lev
Elisha Loewenstern
Adina Luber
Rabbi Simcha Mirvis
Rabbi Jonathan Mishkin
Rabbi David Sedley
Avi Steinhart
Rabbi David Strauss
Rabbi Yitzchak Twersky

Copy Editors

Aliza Israel, *Coordinator*
Ita Olesker
Debbie Ismailoff
Shira Finson
Ilana Sobel
Deena Nataf
Eliana Kurlantzick Yorav
Erica Hirsch Edvi
Nava Wieder
Sara Henna Dahan
Shalom Dinerstein

Language Consultants

Dr. Stephanie E. Binder, *Greek & Latin*
Rabbi Yaakov Hoffman, *Arabic*
Dr. Shai Secunda, *Persian*
Shira Shmidman, *Aramaic*

KOREN

Design & Typesetting

Dena Landowne Bailey, *Typesetting*
Tani Bayer, *Jacket Design*
Raphaël Freeman, *Design & Typography*

Images

Eliahu Misgav, *Illustration & Image Acquisition*
Daniel Gdalevich, *Illustration & Image Acquisition*

Introduction by the Publisher

The Talmud has sustained and inspired Jews for thousands of years. Throughout Jewish history, an elite cadre of scholars has absorbed its learning and passed it on to succeeding generations. The Talmud has been the fundamental text of our people.

Beginning in the 1960s, Rabbi Adin Even-Israel Steinsaltz שליט״א created a revolution in the history of Talmud study. His translation of the Talmud, first into modern Hebrew and then into other languages, as well the practical learning aids he added to the text, have enabled millions of people around the world to access and master the complexity and context of the world of Talmud.

It is thus a privilege to present the *Koren Talmud Bavli*, an English translation of the talmudic text with the brilliant elucidation of Rabbi Steinsaltz. The depth and breadth of his knowledge are unique in our time. His rootedness in the tradition and his reach into the world beyond it are inspirational.

Working with Rabbi Steinsaltz on this remarkable project has been not only an honor, but a great pleasure. Never shy to express an opinion, with wisdom and humor, Rabbi Steinsaltz sparkles in conversation, demonstrating his knowledge (both sacred and worldly), sharing his wide-ranging interests, and, above all, radiating his passion. I am grateful for the unique opportunity to work closely with him, and I wish him many more years of writing and teaching.

Our intentions in publishing this new edition of the Talmud are threefold. First, we seek to fully clarify the talmudic page to the reader – textually, intellectually, and graphically. Second, we seek to utilize today's most sophisticated technologies, both in print and electronic formats, to provide the reader with a comprehensive set of study tools. And third, we seek to help readers advance in their process of Talmud study.

To achieve these goals, the *Koren Talmud Bavli* is unique in a number of ways:

- The classic *tzurat hadaf* of Vilna, used by scholars since the 1800s, has been reset for greater clarity, and opens from the Hebrew "front" of the book. Full *nikkud* has been added to both the talmudic text and Rashi's commentary, allowing for a more fluent reading with the correct pronunciation; the commentaries of *Tosafot* have been punctuated. Upon the advice of many English-speaking teachers of Talmud, we have separated these core pages from the translation, thereby enabling the advanced student to approach the text without the distraction of the translation. This also reduces the number of volumes in the set. At the bottom of each *daf*, there is a reference to the corresponding English pages. In addition, the Vilna edition was read against other manuscripts and older print editions, so that texts which had been removed by non-Jewish censors have been restored to their rightful place.

- The English translation, which starts on the English "front" of the book, reproduces the *menukad* Talmud text alongside the English translation (in bold) and commentary and explanation (in a lighter font). The Hebrew and Aramaic text is presented in logical paragraphs. This allows for a fluent reading of the text for the non-Hebrew or non-Aramaic reader. It also allows for the Hebrew reader to refer easily to the text alongside. Where the original text features dialogue or poetry, the English text is laid out in a manner appropriate to the genre. Each page refers to the relevant *daf*.

- Critical contextual tools surround the text and translation: personality notes, providing short biographies of the Sages; language notes, explaining foreign terms borrowed from Greek, Latin, Persian, or Arabic; and background notes, giving information essential to the understanding of the text, including history, geography, botany, archaeology, zoology, astronomy, and aspects of daily life in the talmudic era.

- Halakhic summaries provide references to the authoritative legal decisions made over the centuries by the rabbis. They explain the reasons behind each halakhic decision as well as the ruling's close connection to the Talmud and its various interpreters.

- Photographs, drawings, and other illustrations have been added throughout the text – in full color in the Standard and Electronic editions, and in black and white in the Daf Yomi edition – to visually elucidate the text.

This is not an exhaustive list of features of this edition, it merely presents an overview for the English-speaking reader who may not be familiar with the "total approach" to Talmud pioneered by Rabbi Steinsaltz.

Several professionals have helped bring this vast collaborative project to fruition. My many colleagues are noted on the Acknowledgments page, and the leadership of this project has been exceptional.

RABBI MENACHEM EVEN-ISRAEL, DIRECTOR OF THE STEINSALTZ CENTER, was the driving force behind this enterprise. With enthusiasm and energy, he formed the happy alliance with Koren and established close relationships among all involved in the work.

RABBI DR. TZVI HERSH WEINREB שליט״א, EDITOR-IN-CHIEF, brought to this project his profound knowledge of Torah, intellectual literacy of Talmud, and erudition of Western literature. It is to him that the text owes its very high standard, both in form and content, and the logical manner in which the beauty of the Talmud is presented.

RABBI JOSHUA SCHREIER, EXECUTIVE EDITOR, assembled an outstanding group of scholars, translators, editors, and proofreaders, whose standards and discipline enabled this project to proceed in a timely and highly professional manner.

RABBI MEIR HANEGBI, EDITOR OF THE HEBREW EDITION OF THE STEINSALTZ TALMUD, lent his invaluable assistance throughout the work process, supervising the reproduction of the Vilna pages.

RAPHAËL FREEMAN, EXECUTIVE EDITOR OF KOREN, created this Talmud's unique typographic design which, true to the Koren approach, is both elegant and user friendly.

It has been an enriching experience for all of us at Koren Publishers Jerusalem to work with the Steinsaltz Center to develop and produce the *Koren Talmud Bavli*. We pray that this publication will be a source of great learning and, ultimately, greater *avodat Hashem* for all Jews.

Matthew Miller, Publisher
Koren Publishers Jerusalem
Jerusalem 5772

Contents

For the vocalized Vilna Shas layout, please open as a Hebrew book.

Introduction to **Perek VIII**

And the Lord spoke to Moses, saying: The daughters of Zelophehad speak right: You shall give them a possession of an inheritance among their father's brothers; and you shall pass the inheritance of their father to them. And you shall speak to the children of Israel, saying: If a man dies, and has no son, then you shall pass his inheritance to his daughter. And if he has no daughter, then you shall give his inheritance to his brothers. And if he has no brothers, then you shall give his inheritance to his father's brothers. And if his father has no brothers, then you shall give his inheritance to his kinsman that is next to him of his family, and he shall possess it. And it shall be to the children of Israel a statute of judgment, as the Lord commanded Moses.

(Numbers 27:6–11)

If a man has two wives, the one beloved, and the other hated, and they have borne him children, both the beloved and the hated; and if the firstborn son is hers that was hated; then it shall be, in the day that he causes his sons to inherit that which he has, that he may not make the son of the beloved the firstborn before the son of the hated, who is the firstborn; but he shall acknowledge the firstborn, the son of the hated, by giving him a double portion of all that he has; because he is the first fruits of his strength, the right of the firstborn is his.

(Deuteronomy 21:15–17)

The topic of this chapter is inheritance. Although the Torah delineates who a person's heirs are and the order in which the inheritance is apportioned, several details, e.g., a husband's right to inherit from his wife, and whether an heir's heir inherits in a case where the heir is already dead, are not explicit and are inferred by the Talmud from the verses. In addition, the chapter examines whether an inheritor can deviate from the Torah's laws of inheritance by bequeathing his property to other people. Even if it is possible to do so, the question remains as to whether or when it is appropriate.

An additional issue is primogeniture, a firstborn son's right to a double portion of the inheritance. The chapter analyzes the definition of a firstborn in this regard, whether a firstborn receives a double portion only of his father's inheritance or whether he receives a double portion of his mother's inheritance as well, and whether he receives a double portion of the entire inheritance or only of a certain part of it.

The chapter also discusses a father's credibility in identifying a person as his child or as his firstborn son, thereby including him in the inheritance.

Besides one's heirs, there are others who have the right to collect from an estate debts or monetary obligations after the death of the owner. For example, a widow has the right to collect her marriage contract or money for her sustenance. The relationship between these collectors and the heirs is discussed in this chapter and the next.

Another aspect of inheritance involves a situation where the inheritance has not yet been divided between the heirs and remains the common property of the sons or daughters. The Talmud discusses the management of the property in this case, i.e., the rights and obligations of each partner.

מתני׳ יֵשׁ נוֹחֲלִין וּמַנְחִילִין, וְיֵשׁ נוֹחֲלִין וְלֹא מַנְחִילִין, מַנְחִילִין וְלֹא נוֹחֲלִין, לֹא נוֹחֲלִין וְלֹא מַנְחִילִין.

MISHNA There are family members who both **inherit** from **and bequeath** to each other upon their respective deaths; **and there are** those who **inherit** from certain relatives **but do not bequeath** to them; and there are those who **bequeath** to certain relatives **but do not inherit** from them; and there are those who, despite being relatives, **do not inherit** from **nor bequeath** to one another.

וְאֵלּוּ נוֹחֲלִין וּמַנְחִילִין: הָאָב אֶת הַבָּנִים, וְהַבָּנִים אֶת הָאָב, וְהָאַחִין מִן הָאָב – נוֹחֲלִין וּמַנְחִילִין. הָאִישׁ אֶת אִמּוֹ, וְהָאִישׁ אֶת אִשְׁתּוֹ, וּבְנֵי אֲחָיוֹת – נוֹחֲלִין וְלֹא מַנְחִילִין. הָאִשָּׁה אֶת בָּנֶיהָ, וְהָאִשָּׁה אֶת בַּעְלָהּ, וַאֲחֵי הָאֵם – מַנְחִילִין וְלֹא נוֹחֲלִין. וְהָאַחִין מִן הָאֵם – לֹא נוֹחֲלִין וְלֹא מַנְחִילִין.

The mishna lists those referred to above. **And these** both **inherit and bequeath: A father** with regard to his **sons,**[H] **and sons** with regard to their **father, and paternal brothers;**[N] all **inherit** from one another **and bequeath** to each other. **A man** with regard to **his mother,**[N] **and a man** with regard to **his wife, and sons of sisters,**[N] i.e., nephews born to the sisters of the deceased, all **inherit** from their respective relatives **but do not bequeath** to them. **A woman** with regard to **her sons, and a woman** with regard to **her husband, and maternal uncles,** all **bequeath** to their respective relatives **but do not inherit** from them. **And maternal brothers,** despite being blood relatives, **do not inherit** from each other **nor** do they **bequeath** to one another, as they are not considered relatives for the purpose of inheritance.

גמ׳ מַאי שְׁנָא דְּקָתָנֵי ״הָאָב אֶת הַבָּנִים״ בְּרֵישָׁא? לִיתְנֵי ״הַבָּנִים אֶת הָאָב״ בְּרֵישָׁא! חֲדָא, דְּאַתְחוּלֵי בְּפוּרְעָנוּתָא לָא מַתְחְלִינַן,

GEMARA The Gemara begins by clarifying the order of the list in the mishna. **What is different,** i.e., what is the reason, **that** the mishna **teaches: A father** with regard to his **sons,** as **the first** example? **Let it teach: Sons** with regard to their **father,** as **the first** example. The Gemara explains why this would be preferable: **One** reason is **that we do not** want to **begin with a calamity,**[N] as the death of a son during his father's lifetime is a calamity; therefore, it would have been appropriate to begin with the example of sons inheriting from their father.

HALAKHA

A father with regard to his sons – הָאָב אֶת הַבָּנִים: If a man dies and leaves a son, his son inherits his estate; if a son dies and had no offspring, his father inherits from him (Rambam *Sefer Mishpatim, Hilkhot Naḥalot* 1:1–2; *Shulḥan Arukh, Ḥoshen Mishpat* 276:1).

NOTES

And paternal brothers – וְהָאַחִין מִן הָאָב: The inheritance that paternal brothers inherit from one another is not direct. Rather, when one dies without sons, his property is inherited by his father. If the father is deceased, he inherits while in the grave, as it were, and his inheritance is then bequeathed to his sons, the paternal brothers of the one now deceased (Rashbam). Maternal brothers do not inherit from one another since, as the Gemara explains later (110b), the mother herself does not inherit from her son.

Tosafot ask: Why did the mishna omit paternal uncles from the order of inheritance, even though it is explicitly mentioned in the Torah that they inherit from their brother's son? They answer that it is unnecessary to mention paternal uncles here since their status as heirs is implied in the mishna's previous statements indirectly: If there are no sons, the father inherits from the deceased, and the father's brothers inherit from the father. Therefore, it is clear that the paternal uncles can inherit from their nephew.

The Rashba suggests that the mishna did not include any of the obvious *halakhot* that are mentioned explicitly in the Torah, but only ones derived from the verses or *halakhot* that contain some novelty. The mishna, therefore, emphasizes that only paternal brothers inherit from the deceased, while maternal brothers do not, a detail that is not explicit in the Torah.

A man with regard to his mother – הָאִישׁ אֶת אִמּוֹ: A son inherits his mother's property, but if he dies, his mother does not inherit from him. Rather, the inheritance passes to his paternal relatives, since for the purpose of inheritance only the relatives of the father are deemed significant, as the Gemara will clarify later (109b).

And sons of sisters – וּבְנֵי אֲחָיוֹת: This means that the nephew of the deceased, who is the son of his sister, inherits from his uncle. If the uncle died and left no sons, his sister, who is the mother of his nephew, inherits from him, and if she is no longer living, her son inherits via her inheritance.

We do not want to begin with a calamity – דְּאַתְחוּלֵי בְּפוּרְעָנוּתָא לָא מַתְחְלִינַן: The circumstance in which a father inherits from his son includes two calamities: First, the fact that the son died in the father's lifetime; and second, the son must have died childless; otherwise, his children would precede his father in the order of inheritance (Rashbam).

וְעוֹד, כְּדִכְתִיב: ״אִישׁ כִּי יָמוּת וּבֵן אֵין לוֹ״!

And furthermore, the verse first states that a son inherits from his father, **as it is written** in the portion concerning inheritance: **"If a man dies,**[N] **and has no son,** then you shall pass his inheritance to his daughter" (Numbers 27:8).

וְתַנָּא, אַיְּידֵי דְּאָתְיָא לֵיהּ מִדְּרָשָׁא חֲבִיבָא לֵיהּ.

The Gemara answers: **And** as for the ***tanna*** of the mishna who listed the father inheriting first, **since** the *halakha* that a father inherits from his son **is learned through a derivation**[N] and is not explicitly mentioned in the verse, this *halakha* is **dear to him;** therefore, he listed it first.

וּמַאי דְּרָשָׁא? דְּתַנְיָא: ״שְׁאֵרוֹ״ – זֶה הָאָב, מְלַמֵּד שֶׁהָאָב קוֹדֵם לָאַחִין; יָכוֹל יְהֵא קוֹדֵם לַבֵּן? תַּלְמוּד לוֹמַר: ״הַקָּרוֹב״ – קָרוֹב קָרוֹב קוֹדֵם.

And what is the **derivation? As it is taught** in a *baraita* concerning the verse: "And if his father has no brothers, then you shall give his inheritance to his kinsman who is next to him of his family, and he shall inherit it" (Numbers 27:11): **"His kinsman"; this** is referring to **the father,**[N] and the Torah **teaches that the father precedes the brothers**[H] of the deceased in inheriting from him. One **might** have thought that the father of the deceased **should precede the son** of the deceased in inheriting from him; **the verse** therefore **states: "Next [*hakkarov*]** to him," teaching that the **closer [*karov*]** one is to the deceased, the **earlier**[N] one is in the order of inheritance, and a son of the deceased is considered to be a closer relative to the deceased than the father of the deceased.

וּמָה רָאִיתָ לְרַבּוֹת אֶת הַבֵּן וּלְהוֹצִיא אֶת הָאָח? מְרַבֶּה אֲנִי אֶת הַבֵּן, שֶׁכֵּן קָם תַּחַת אָבִיו לִיעָדָה וְלִשְׂדֵה אֲחוּזָּה.

The Gemara asks: **And what did you see to include the son** as the closer relative than the father **and to exclude the brother?** The Gemara answers: **I include the son, as he stands in place of his father to designate**[N] a Hebrew maidservant[H] as a wife for himself, which a brother cannot do. **And** similarly, he stands in place of his father **with regard to an ancestral field.**[NH] If a son redeems a field consecrated by his father, it is considered as though the father himself redeemed it and the field returns to the family in the Jubilee Year. By contrast, if the brother of the one who consecrated it redeems the field, it does not return to the family (see Leviticus 27:16–21).

אַדְּרַבָּה, מְרַבֶּה אֲנִי אֶת הָאָח, שֶׁכֵּן קָם תַּחַת אָחִיו לְיִבּוּם! כְּלוּם יֵשׁ יִבּוּם אֶלָּא בְּמָקוֹם שֶׁאֵין בֵּן, הָא בְּמָקוֹם שֶׁיֵּשׁ בֵּן – אֵין יִבּוּם.

The Gemara asks: **On the contrary, I** should **include the brother** as the closer relative, **as he stands in his brother's place with regard to levirate marriage,**[NBH] and a son does not. The Gemara answers: This is not a valid claim, as **is there levirate marriage except in a case where there is no son? In a case where there is a son, there is no levirate marriage.** This indicates that a son stands in place of the deceased before a brother even with regard to levirate marriage.

NOTES

As it is written, if a man dies, etc. – כְּדִכְתִיב, אִישׁ כִּי יָמוּת וכו׳: The verse indicates that if a man does have a son, the son inherits from him. The *halakha* that the son inherits from his father is thereby implicitly written before any of the other *halakhot* of inheritance (Rashbam).

Is learned through a derivation – אָתְיָא לֵיהּ מִדְּרָשָׁא: Since the *halakha* that a father inherits from his son is not explicitly stated in the Torah but is derived from a verse, as explained in the Gemara (109a), this *halakha* contains a novelty. *Tanna'im* are accustomed to list novel *halakhot* before known *halakhot*, even when this runs counter to the order in which they are presented in the Torah.

His kinsman, this is referring to the father – שְׁאֵרוֹ, זֶה הָאָב: This is derived in the Gemara (109b) from the verse: "She is your father's kinswoman" (Leviticus 18:12).

The closer the earlier – קָרוֹב קָרוֹב קוֹדֵם: The commentaries write that this principle is derived from the definite article "*ha*" in the phrase "*hakkarov elav*," referring to the unique relative, the one who is closest. This indicates that the closest relative is the first to inherit. A man's son is a closer relative to him than any other person, even closer than his own father, since, as it is explained later, a son stands in place of his father with regard to certain *halakhot* while a father never stands in place of his son (Rashbam).

To designate her – לִיעָדָה: One who purchases a Hebrew maidservant from her father can designate her for himself as a wife, and he even has a mitzva to do so (see Exodus 21:8–11), as the money used for her purchase also serves as her betrothal money if the master so desires. He can also decide to betroth her some time later as long as she is in his service, by saying: You are hereby betrothed to me with the money your father received for you. The verse states: "And if he designates her for his son" (Exodus 21:9), indicating that this money can be used to betroth the maidservant to the son of her master as well. It is specifically the son who stands in place of his father with regard to this *halakha*, as the father cannot designate her for anyone else, not even his brother.

And with regard to an ancestral field – וְלִשְׂדֵה אֲחוּזָּה: The Torah states that if one consecrates his ancestral field and fails to redeem it before the Jubilee Year, then even if the field is redeemed from the Temple treasury by a third party, the ownership of the field is transferred to the priests and becomes their inheritance (see Leviticus 27:20–21). The Sages taught that the son of the prior owner can redeem the field from the Temple treasury and is not considered a third party, which is not the case with regard to a brother or any other relative.

In his brother's place with regard to levirate marriage – תַּחַת אָחִיו לְיִבּוּם: The verses written concerning levirate marriage indicate that the brother actually replaces the deceased, as his firstborn from his brother's wife is considered the son of the deceased (see Deuteronomy 25:6). Levirate marriage is performed only by a brother, not by any other relative, not even the father of the deceased.

BACKGROUND

Levirate marriage – יִבּוּם: A man whose brother died without children is commanded by Torah law to marry his deceased brother's widow or grant her *ḥalitza* (see Deuteronomy 25:5–10). As long as neither levirate marriage nor *ḥalitza* has taken place, it is prohibited for her to marry another man. By Torah law, levirate marriage is effected by the act of sexual intercourse alone. The Sages instituted the practice of levirate betrothal, in which the deceased husband's brother betroths the widow before performing levirate marriage. After this betrothal is performed, sexual intercourse consummates the marriage between the deceased's brother and the widow, and she is thereafter considered his wife in all respects. Nowadays, in most Jewish communities the brother-in-law is instructed to free his brother's widow of her bond through *ḥalitza*, and he is not permitted to marry her through levirate marriage.

HALAKHA

Teaches that the father precedes the brothers – מְלַמֵּד שֶׁהָאָב קוֹדֵם לָאַחִין: If a man dies without having had a son or a daughter, his father inherits from him. If his father is no longer alive, the brothers of the deceased inherit from him (Rambam *Sefer Mishpatim*, *Hilkhot Naḥalot* 1:3; *Shulḥan Arukh*, *Ḥoshen Mishpat* 276:1).

To designate her – לִיעָדָה: A master can designate his maidservant to marry his son, just as he can designate her to marry himself, with the money he paid her father serving as the betrothal money. At the time of designation, he says: You are hereby betrothed to my son with the money your father received from me (Rambam *Sefer Kinyan*, *Hilkhot Avadim* 4:7 and *Leḥem Mishne* there).

And with regard to an ancestral field – וְלִשְׂדֵה אֲחוּזָּה: If one consecrated his ancestral field and his son redeemed it, it returns to the father at the Jubilee Year. If it was redeemed by his daughter or by another relative, and the one who consecrated the field did not, in turn, redeem it from them, it is transferred to the priests at the Jubilee Year and never returns to its owner (Rambam *Sefer Hafla'a*, *Hilkhot Arakhin VaḤaramim* 4:20).

In his brother's place with regard to levirate marriage – תַּחַת אָחִיו לְיִבּוּם: One whose paternal brother died and left no offspring is commanded to marry his brother's wife in levirate marriage or to perform with her the ritual through which he frees her of her levirate bonds [*ḥalitza*], whether she was married or betrothed to the deceased (Rambam *Sefer Nashim*, *Hilkhot Yibbum VaḤalitza* 1:1; *Shulḥan Arukh*, *Even HaEzer* 156:1).

טַעֲמָא דְּאִיכָּא הַאי פִּירְכָא, הָא לָאו הָכִי – הֲוָה אָמִינָא אָח עֲדִיף; תֵּיפּוֹק לֵיהּ

The Gemara comments: **The reason** that a son is considered to be a closer relative than a brother **is** specifically **due to this refutation,** that where there is a son there is no levirate marriage. This indicates that **without this** refutation **I would say** that **a brother is superior** to a son in terms of how close a relative he is. The Gemara therefore asks: Why not **derive** that a son is closer to the deceased than a brother

Perek **VIII**
Daf **109** Amud **a**

דְּהָכָא תַּרְתֵּי וְהָכָא חֲדָא!

from the fact **that here,** there are **two** examples of the superiority of a son, designation and an ancestral field, **and here,** there is only **one** demonstration of the superiority of a brother, levirate marriage?

שְׂדֵה אֲחוּזָּה גּוּפָהּ מֵהַאי טַעֲמָא הוּא דְּקָא קַיְימָא לֵיהּ לְתַנָּא: כְּלוּם יֵשׁ יִבּוּם אֶלָּא בְּמָקוֹם שֶׁאֵין בֵּן, הָא יֵשׁ בֵּן – אֵין יִבּוּם.

The Gemara answers: With regard to **an ancestral field itself, the** ***tanna*** **establishes his** ruling **from this** same **reason: Is there levirate marriage except in a case where there is no son? In a case where there is a son, there is no levirate marriage.** The determination that the redemption of the ancestral field by a son is in place of the redemption of the field by the father, whereas the redemption of the field by a brother is not, is based on the reasoning that the *halakha* of levirate marriage is not an indication that a brother is a closer relative than a son. Therefore, the *halakha* of an ancestral field cannot be regarded as a second example of the son's superiority, as it stems from the first example, that of levirate marriage.

אֵימָא: ״שְׁאֵרוֹ״ – זֶה הָאָב, מְלַמֵּד שֶׁהָאָב קוֹדֵם לַבַּת; יָכוֹל יַקְדִּים לַבֵּן? תַּלְמוּד לוֹמַר: ״הַקָּרוֹב״ – קָרוֹב קָרוֹב קוֹדֵם!

The Gemara suggests an alternative derivation: Why should the father of the deceased inherit before only the brothers? **Say** that he should inherit before the daughter of the deceased as well by interpreting the verse as follows: **"His kinsman"** (Numbers 27:11), **this** is referring to **the father,** and the Torah **teaches that the father precedes the daughter** of the deceased in inheriting from him. One **might** have thought that the father of the deceased **should precede the son** of the deceased in inheriting from him. **The verse** therefore **states: "Next** [*hakkarov*] to him," teaching that the **closer** [*karov*] one is to the deceased, the **earlier** one is in the order of inheritance.

כֵּיוָן דִּלְעִנְיַן יִבּוּם – בֵּן וּבַת כִּי הֲדָדֵי נִינְהוּ, לְעִנְיַן נַחֲלָה נַמִי – בֵּן וּבַת כִּי הֲדָדֵי נִינְהוּ.

This suggestion is rejected: **Since with regard to the matter of levirate marriage a son and a daughter are equivalent,**[H] as levirate marriage is not performed if the deceased had either a son or a daughter, it stands to reason that **with regard to the matter of inheritance as well, a son and a daughter are equivalent**[H] in that the father does not precede the daughter.

וְאֵימָא: ״שְׁאֵרוֹ״ – זֶה הָאָב, מְלַמֵּד שֶׁהָאָב קוֹדֵם לַאֲחֵי הָאָב; יָכוֹל יַקְדִּים לָאַחִין? תַּלְמוּד לוֹמַר: ״הַקָּרוֹב״ – קָרוֹב קָרוֹב קוֹדֵם!

The Gemara suggests an alternative derivation: Why should the father of the deceased inherit before the brothers of the deceased? **Say** that he should inherit only before his own brothers by interpreting the verse as follows: **"His kinsman"** (Numbers 27:11), **this** is referring to **the father,** and the Torah **teaches that the father precedes the father's brothers** in inheriting from the deceased. One **might** have thought that the father of the deceased **should precede the brothers** of the deceased in inheriting from him. **The verse states: "Next** [*hakkarov*] to him," teaching that the **closer** [*karov*] one is to the deceased, the **earlier** one is in the order of inheritance.

אֲחֵי הָאָב לָא צְרִיכִי קְרָא; אֲחֵי הָאָב מִכֹּחַ מַאן קָא אָתוּ? מִכֹּחַ אָב, קָאֵי אָב קָא יָרְתִי אֲחֵי הָאָב?!

The Gemara responds: **A verse is not necessary** to teach that the father of the deceased inherits before **the father's brothers,** for the following reason: **By whose virtue do the father's brothers come** to inherit from the deceased? **By virtue** of the **father,** as their right to inherit is a result of their being brothers of the father of the deceased. Could it be that while the **father is still alive, his brothers should inherit?** The Gemara therefore concludes that the father precedes the brothers of the deceased.

HALAKHA

With regard to the matter of levirate marriage a son and a daughter are equivalent – **לְעִנְיַן יִבּוּם בֵּן וּבַת כִּי הֲדָדֵי נִינְהוּ**: If one died and left offspring, whether a son or a daughter, or if the son or daughter had died but left descendants, the deceased's wife is exempt from levirate marriage (Rambam *Sefer Nashim, Hilkhot Yibbum VaHalitza* 1:3; *Shulḥan Arukh, Even HaEzer* 156:2).

With regard to the matter of inheritance…a son and a daughter are equivalent – **לְעִנְיַן נַחֲלָה...בֵּן וּבַת כִּי הֲדָדֵי נִינְהוּ**: If one died and did not leave a son, or his son had died with no surviving descendants, his daughter or her offspring inherit his estate (Rambam *Sefer Mishpatim, Hilkhot Naḥalot* 1:3; *Shulḥan Arukh, Ḥoshen Mishpat* 276:1).

וְהָא קְרָאֵי לָאו הָכִי כְּתִיבִי, דִּכְתִיב: "וְאִם אֵין אַחִים לְאָבִיו" וגו׳! קְרָאֵי שֶׁלֹּא כְּסִדְרָן כְּתִיבִי.

The Gemara challenges: **But the verses are not written that way, as it is written:** "And if he has no brothers, then you shall give his inheritance to his father's brothers" (Numbers 27:10), and only later is it written: **"And if his father has no brothers,** then you shall give his inheritance to his kinsman who is next to him" (Numbers 27:11), indicating that the father, whose right to inherit is derived from the term "kinsman," inherits only after the brothers of the deceased and his own brothers. The Gemara explains: The **verses are not written in order,** since as explained earlier, it is not reasonable that the father's brothers inherit before the father. Therefore, it must be that the inheritance of the father is not written in its proper place, and he may inherit even before the brothers of the deceased.

וְהַאי תַּנָּא מַיְיתֵי לַהּ מֵהָכָא: דְּתַנְיָא, אֶת זוֹ דָּרַשׁ רַבִּי יִשְׁמָעֵאל בְּרַבִּי יוֹסֵי: "אִישׁ כִּי יָמוּת וּבֵן אֵין לוֹ" וגו׳ – בִּמְקוֹם בַּת אַתָּה מַעֲבִיר נַחֲלָה מִן הָאָב, וְאִי אַתָּה מַעֲבִיר נַחֲלָה מִן הָאָב בִּמְקוֹם אַחִין.

§ The Gemara records an additional derivation for the *halakha* that the father precedes the brothers of the deceased. **And this** *tanna* **cites it from here, as it is taught** in a *baraita*: **Rabbi Yishmael, son of Rabbi Yosei, taught this** *halakha*: It is written: **"If a man dies, and has no son,** then you shall pass his inheritance to his daughter" (Numbers 27:8). In the rest of the passage the verse employs the phrase "and you shall give." It is only in this verse that it employs the phrase "and you shall pass." Based on this, Rabbi Yishmael teaches that **in a case** where there is **a daughter, you pass an inheritance** to her **from** one who appears to have precedence, namely, **the father, and** by inference, **you do not pass** the **inheritance from the father in a case** where there are **brothers** of the deceased.

וְאֵימָא: בִּמְקוֹם בַּת אַתָּה מַעֲבִיר נַחֲלָה מִן הָאַחִין,

The Gemara asks: **But** why not **say** that **in a case** where there is **a daughter, you pass** the **inheritance** to her **from the brothers,**

Perek **VIII**
Daf **109** Amud **b**

NOTES

But you do not pass, etc. – ׳וְאִי אַתָּה מַעֲבִיר וכו: This would mean that in any case a father would precede a daughter in the order of inheritance. The Rashbam writes that the Gemara does not mean to say that this is indicated in the verse, as it could very well be that the inheritance is passed to a daughter even from the father of the deceased. Rather, since the father is considered a closer relative to the deceased than a daughter, and the verse does not preclude the possibility that he inherits before her, the Gemara suggests that this may, in fact, be the *halakha*.

וְאִי אַתָּה מַעֲבִיר נַחֲלָה מִן הָאָב אֲפִילּוּ בִּמְקוֹם בַּת! אִם כֵּן, לָא נִכְתּוֹב רַחֲמָנָא "וְהַעֲבַרְתֶּם"!

but you do not pass[N] **an inheritance from the father even in a case** where there is **a daughter,** so that the father precedes the daughter in the order of inheritance? The Gemara answers: **If so, the Merciful One would not write: "Then you shall pass** the inheritance to his daughter" (Numbers 27:8). This indicates that the logical order of inheritance is being overridden, as the fact that the daughter precedes the brothers of the deceased is due to her being a closer relative of his. It is obvious that the Torah intends that she precede even the father.

וּלְמַאן דְּנָפְקָא לֵיהּ מִ"וְּהַעֲבַרְתֶּם", הַאי "שְׁאֵרוֹ" מַאי עָבֵיד לֵיהּ? מִיבְּעֵי לֵיהּ לְכִדְתַנְיָא: "שְׁאֵרוֹ" – זוֹ אִשְׁתּוֹ, מְלַמֵּד שֶׁהַבַּעַל יוֹרֵשׁ אֶת אִשְׁתּוֹ.

Having quoted two derivations for the *halakha* that the father precedes the brothers, the Gemara proceeds to discuss them and asks: **And according to the one who derives it from** the term: **"And you shall pass," what does he do with this** term: **"His kinsman,"** which was said to refer to the father? The Gemara answers: **He requires it for that which is taught** in a *baraita*: **"His kinsman." This** is referring to **his wife,** and the Torah **teaches that a husband inherits** from **his wife.**

וּלְמַאן דְּנָפְקָא לֵיהּ מִ"שְּׁאֵרוֹ", הַאי "וְהַעֲבַרְתֶּם" מַאי עָבֵיד לֵיהּ? מִיבְּעֵי לֵיהּ לְכִדְתַנְיָא, רַבִּי אוֹמֵר: בְּכוּלָּן נֶאֱמַר בָּהֶן נְתִינָה, וְכָאן נֶאֶמְרָה בָּהֶן הַעֲבָרָה – שֶׁאֵין לְךָ שֶׁמַּעֲבִיר נַחֲלָה מִשֵּׁבֶט לְשֵׁבֶט אֶלָּא בַּת, הוֹאִיל וּבְנָהּ וּבַעְלָהּ יוֹרְשִׁין אוֹתָהּ.

The Gemara asks: **And according to the one who derives it from** the term: **"His kinsman," what does he do with this** term: **"And you shall pass"? He requires it for that which is taught** in a *baraita*, that **Rabbi** Yehuda HaNasi **says: In** the context of **all** of the relatives listed in the passage detailing the laws of inheritance, it **is stated concerning them** with the terminology of **giving, and** only **here,** in the context of daughters, it **is stated concerning them** with the terminology of **passing.** This teaches us **that you have no one who passes an inheritance** of land in Eretz Yisrael **from one tribe to another except for a daughter, since her son and husband inherit** from **her.**

וּמִמַּאי דִּ״שְׁאֵרוֹ״ זֶה הָאָב? דִּכְתִיב: ״שְׁאֵר אָבִיךָ הִוא״, אֵימָא: ״שְׁאֵרוֹ״ – זוֹ הָאֵם, דִּכְתִיב: ״שְׁאֵר אִמְּךָ הִוא״!

§ The Gemara returns to discuss the interpretation of the term: "His kinsman" (Numbers 27:11). **And from where** does one know to derive **that** with regard to the term: **"His kinsman** [*she'ero*]," this is referring to **the father, as it is written** in the context of forbidden sexual relations: **"She is your father's kinswoman** [*she'er*]" (Leviticus 18:12)?[N] Perhaps one should **say** instead: **"His kinswoman,"** this is referring to **the mother, as it is** also **written: "For she is your mother's kinswoman** [*she'er*]" (Leviticus 18:13).

אָמַר רָבָא, אָמַר קְרָא: ״מִמִּשְׁפַּחְתּוֹ וְיָרַשׁ אֹתָהּ״ – מִשְׁפַּחַת אָב קְרוּיָה מִשְׁפָּחָה, מִשְׁפַּחַת אֵם אֵינָהּ קְרוּיָה מִשְׁפָּחָה, דִּכְתִיב: ״לְמִשְׁפְּחֹתָם לְבֵית אֲבֹתָם״.

Rava said in response that **the verse states:** "Then you shall give his inheritance to his kinsman who is next to him **of his family, and he shall inherit it"** (Numbers 27:11), emphasizing that "kinsman" is referring specifically to someone who is of his family, and it is **the father's family** that **is called** one's **family,** while one's **mother's family**[H] **is not called** one's **family.** Proof for this is found in another verse, **as it is written: "By their families, by their fathers' houses"** (Numbers 1:2).

וּמִשְׁפַּחַת אֵם אֵינָהּ קְרוּיָה מִשְׁפָּחָה? וְהָא כְּתִיב: ״וַיְהִי נַעַר מִבֵּית לֶחֶם יְהוּדָה מִמִּשְׁפַּחַת יְהוּדָה וְהוּא לֵוִי וְהוּא גָר שָׁם״; הָא גּוּפָא קַשְׁיָא, אָמַרְתְּ ״וְהוּא לֵוִי״ – אַלְמָא מִלֵּוִי אָתֵי, ״מִמִּשְׁפַּחַת יְהוּדָה״ – אַלְמָא מִיהוּדָה אָתֵי; אֶלָּא לָאו דַּאֲבוּהּ מִלֵּוִי וְאִימֵּיהּ מִיהוּדָה, וְקָאָמַר: ״מִמִּשְׁפַּחַת יְהוּדָה״!

The Gemara raises a difficulty: **And is** one's **mother's family** indeed **not called** one's **family? But it is written** in the episode of Micah forming an idol to be worshipped: **"And there was a young man of Bethlehem in Judah of the family of Judah who was a Levite, and he sojourned there"** (Judges 17:7). The Gemara explains the difficulty: **This matter itself** is **difficult. You said: "Who was a Levite,"** as **apparently he came from** the tribe of **Levi,** but the verse says: **"Of the family of Judah,"** so **apparently he came from** the tribe of **Judah. Rather, is it not that his father** was **from** the tribe of **Levi and his mother** was **from** the tribe of **Judah, and** yet the verse **says** that he was: **"Of the family of Judah"?** This appears to prove that one's mother's family is also called his family.

אָמַר רָבָא בַּר רַב חָנָן: לָא, גַּבְרָא דִּשְׁמֵיהּ לֵוִי. אִי הָכִי, הַיְינוּ דְּקָאָמַר מִיכָה: ״עַתָּה יָדַעְתִּי כִּי יֵיטִיב ה׳ לִי כִּי הָיָה לִי הַלֵּוִי לְכֹהֵן״? אִין, דְּאִיתְרְמֵי לֵיהּ גַּבְרָא דִּשְׁמֵיהּ לֵוִי.

Rava bar Rav Ḥanan said in response: **No,** the verse speaks of **a man whose name** was **Levi,** but his father was of the tribe of Judah. The Gemara asks: **If that is so,** how **is that which Micah said** when that man agreed to serve as his priest: **"Now I know that the Lord will do me good, seeing that I have a Levite as my priest"** (Judges 17:13), understood? It is understood only if he was an actual Levite, not if he was from the tribe of Judah and named Levi. Rava bar Rav Ḥanan responded: **Yes,** it is understood. Micah understood the fact **that a man whose name** is **Levi happened upon him**[N] as an auspicious sign.

וְכִי לֵוִי שְׁמוֹ? וַהֲלֹא יְהוֹנָתָן שְׁמוֹ, שֶׁנֶּאֱמַר: ״וִיהוֹנָתָן בֶּן גֵּרְשׁוֹם בֶּן מְנַשֶּׁה הוּא וּבָנָיו הָיוּ כֹהֲנִים לְשֵׁבֶט הַדָּנִי״! אֲמַר לֵיהּ: וְלִיטַעֲמִיךְ, וְכִי בֶּן מְנַשֶּׁה הוּא? וַהֲלֹא בֶּן מֹשֶׁה הוּא, דִּכְתִיב: ״בְּנֵי מֹשֶׁה גֵּרְשׁוֹם וֶאֱלִיעֶזֶר״!

The Gemara asks further: **But** is it **so** that **his name** was indeed **Levi; but wasn't Jonathan his name, as it is stated: "And Jonathan, the son of Gershom, the son of Manasseh, he and his sons were priests to the tribe of the Danites"** (Judges 18:30)? Rava bar Rav Ḥanan **said to him: And according to your reasoning,** that his name was not Levi but he was from the tribe of Levi, there is also a difficulty from that same verse: **But is it so that he was the son of Manasseh;**[N] **but wasn't he the son of Moses, as it is written: "The sons of Moses: Gershom and Eliezer"** (I Chronicles 23:15)?

אֶלָּא, מִתּוֹךְ שֶׁעָשָׂה מַעֲשֵׂה מְנַשֶּׁה – תְּלָאוֹ הַכָּתוּב בִּמְנַשֶּׁה; הָכָא נַמִי, מִתּוֹךְ שֶׁעָשָׂה מַעֲשֵׂה מְנַשֶּׁה דְּאָתֵי מִיהוּדָה – תְּלָאוֹ הַכָּתוּב בִּיהוּדָה.

Rava bar Rav Ḥanan explains the verse: **Rather,** although he was the son of Moses, **because he acted** as **Manasseh** the king of Judah, who was notorious for idol worship, **acted, the verse linked him to Manasseh**[N] by calling him "the son of Manasseh." **Here too,** in the verse from which you seek to prove that one's mother's family is called one's family, **since he acted** as **Manasseh, who came from** the tribe of **Judah, acted, the verse linked him to Judah** by stating that he was "of the family of Judah," but he was, in fact, a Levite.

NOTES

She is your father's kinswoman – שְׁאֵר אָבִיךָ הִוא: This phrase appears in the book of Leviticus, in the passage that lists those with whom sexual intercourse is forbidden. The verse is written in the context of the prohibition of intercourse with one's father's sister. The phrase is superfluous in that context, since it is stated beforehand that the reason that sexual intercourse with any of the listed relatives is forbidden is that they are kinsmen. Therefore, the Torah must have mentioned this phrase in connection with a father for another matter with regard to which the designation of "kinsman" is relevant, namely the laws of inheritance (*Tosefot Yom Tov*; see Rashash).

That a man whose name is Levi happened upon him – דְּאִיתְרְמֵי לֵיהּ גַּבְרָא דִּשְׁמֵיהּ לֵוִי: Micah gloated about having found a young man with the name of the priestly tribe, as if he were an actual priest (Rashbam). The Ritva explains that Micah was glad because others would think the young man was actually a Levite, due to his name.

But is it so that he was the son of Manasseh, etc. – וְכִי בֶּן מְנַשֶּׁה הוּא וכו׳: Despite the fact that the Torah already teaches that Gershom was the son of Moses, the Gemara cites a verse from the book of Chronicles here because it mentions Shebuel, whom the Sages identify as Jonathan, son of Gershom, son of Moses (Maharsha).

The verse linked him to Manasseh – תְּלָאוֹ הַכָּתוּב בִּמְנַשֶּׁה: There is proof that he was not actually the son of Manasseh: According to the Masoretic text the letter *nun* in the name Manasseh is suspended, which hints that it does not belong in the word. Without the *nun* the word would be read as Moshe, or Moses (see Rashbam).

HALAKHA

One's mother's family – מִשְׁפַּחַת אֵם: One's mother's family is not called one's family. Therefore, a mother does not inherit from her son or daughter, and brothers who share the same mother but not the same father do not inherit from one another (Rambam *Sefer Mishpatim*, *Hilkhot Naḥalot* 1:6 and *Sefer Kedusha*, *Hilkhot Issurei Bia* 19:15; *Shulḥan Arukh*, *Ḥoshen Mishpat* 276:4).

LANGUAGE

Battled [*pitpet*] – פטפט: It appears that the word *pitpet* in this context is unrelated to the common Hebrew meaning of that word, chatter. Rather, it is related to the Aramaic word *pitput*, legs upon which vessels rest. It may also be related to the Greek πούς, *pous*, which means leg or foot. Accordingly, the word *pitpet* would mean to step on something with one's foot; in other words, to vanquish or conquer (see Rabbeinu Gershom Meor HaGola).

אמר רבי יוחנן משום רבי שמעון בן יוחי: מכאן שתולין את הקלקלה במקולקל. רבי יוסי בר חנינא אמר, מהכא: "וגם הוא טוב תאר מאד ואתו ילדה אחרי אבשלום", והלא אדניה בן חגית ואבשלום בן מעכה! אלא, מתוך שעשה מעשה אבשלום דמרד במלכות – תלאו הכתוב באבשלום; הכא נמי, מתוך שעשה מעשה מנשה – תלאו הכתוב במנשה.

In connection with this, **Rabbi Yoḥanan says in the name of Rabbi Shimon ben Yoḥai: From here** it is learned **that corruption is linked to one who is corrupt,**[N] as this man was linked to Manasseh and Judah despite having no familial connection to them. **Rabbi Yosei bar Ḥanina says:** That concept can be seen **from here,** in the matter of Adonijah, the son of David: **"And he was also a very handsome man; and she gave birth to him after Absalom,"** (I Kings 1:6) **but Adonijah wasn't the son of Haggith and Absalom was the son of Maachah,** so why does the verse state: "And she gave birth to him after Absalom," as if they were sons of the same mother? **Rather, since Adonijah acted** in a manner fit for **Absalom, who** also **rebelled against the monarchy, the verse linked him to Absalom,** referring to him as his full brother. **Here too,** with regard to Jonathan, **since he acted** as **Manasseh acted, the verse linked him to Manasseh.**

אמר רבי אלעזר: לעולם ידבק אדם בטובים, שהרי משה שנשא בת יתרו – יצא ממנו יהונתן, אהרן שנשא בת עמינדב – יצא ממנו פנחס.

§ In connection with the story of Jonathan, son of Manasseh, the Gemara cites a related statement. **Rabbi Elazar says: A person should always cleave to good**[NH] people, meaning one should marry a woman from a good family, as this is beneficial for the offspring of that marriage. **As** in the case of **Moses, who married a daughter of Yitro,** who was a priest of idolatry, **Jonathan,** who was also a priest of idolatry, **descended from him,** while in the case of **Aaron, who married the daughter of Amminadab,** who was of distinguished lineage in the tribe of Judah, **Pinehas descended from him.**

ופנחס לאו מיתרו אתי? והא כתיב: "ואלעזר בן אהרן לקח לו מבנות פוטיאל לו לאשה", מאי לאו דאתי מיתרו שפיטם עגלים לעבודה זרה? לא, דאתי מיוסף שפטפט ביצרו.

The Gemara asks: **And did Pinehas not** also **come from Yitro? But it is written: "And Elazar, Aaron's son, took one of the daughters of Putiel as a wife;** and she bore him Pinehas" (Exodus 6:25). **What,** is it **not** stating **that** Pinehas **came from** the family of **Yitro,**[N] who was also called Putiel because he **fattened** [*pittem*] **calves for idol worship?** The Gemara answers: **No,** it is stating **that he came from Joseph, who battled** [*shepitpet*][L] **with his desire** by resisting the advances of Potiphar's wife.

והלא שבטים מבזים אותו ואומרים: ראיתם בן פוטי זה, בן שפיטם אבי אמו עגלים לעבודה זרה, יהרוג נשיא שבט מישראל?!

The Gemara asks: **But didn't the tribes denigrated him** after he killed Zimri (see Numbers, chapter 25), **and would say** of him: **Have you seen this son of Puti, the son of** he **whose mother's father fattened calves for idol worship? Should** such a man **kill a prince of a tribe of Israel?**

NOTES

Corruption is linked to one who is corrupt – תולין את הקלקלה במקולקל: The Maharsha adds an explanation of the choice of the name Manasseh in this context: Although there were other kings who worshipped idols, the name Manasseh, as written in Hebrew, includes the letters of the name of Moses. Additionally, as explained later (110a), Manasseh repented and returned to God wholeheartedly (see II Chronicles, chapter 33), as did Jonathan.

A person should always cleave to good – לעולם ידבק אדם בטובים: Because it is unseemly that a man as great and righteous as Moses would have such a descendant, the Sages explain that it was due to the fact that Jonathan descended from Yitro's family on his mother's side. Although Yitro himself repented and abandoned idol worship, his family is not considered one of respectable lineage, so that one of the descendants could have become corrupted by worshipping idols (Maharal).

Is it not stating that Pinehas came from Yitro, etc. – לאו דאתי מיתרו וכו׳: Since the name Putiel is mentioned only once in the Bible, as the grandfather of Pinehas, the Sages understood that Putiel was not that person's real name but a name used to describe him. It can be assumed that Putiel is merely the nickname of one who is mentioned elsewhere in the Bible (*Torat Ḥayyim*).

HALAKHA

A person should always cleave to good – לעולם ידבק אדם בטובים: It is fitting for a man to marry a woman from a good family. This is why the Sages say (*Pesaḥim* 49b): A person should always be willing to sell all he has in order to marry the daughter of a Torah scholar. If he cannot find the daughter of a Torah scholar he should marry the daughter of one of the great people of the generation, who are pious although they are not Torah scholars. If he cannot find the daughter of one of the great people of the generation, he should marry the daughter of one of the heads of the congregation. If he cannot find the daughter of one of the heads of the congregation he should marry the daughter of one of the charity collectors. If he cannot find the daughter of one of the charity collectors he should marry the daughter of one of the schoolteachers.

He should not marry the daughter of an ignoramus, and one should not marry his daughter off to an ignoramus unless they are punctilious in their performance of the mitzvot (Rambam *Sefer Kedusha, Hilkhot Issurei Bia* 21:32; *Shulḥan Arukh, Even HaEzer* 2:6).

אֶלָּא, אִי אֲבוּהָ דְּאִמֵּיהּ מִיּוֹסֵף – אִמָּהּ דְּאִמֵּיהּ מִיִּתְרוֹ, אִי אֲבוּהָ דְּאִמֵּיהּ מִיִּתְרוֹ – אִמָּהּ דְּאִמֵּיהּ מִיּוֹסֵף. דַּיְקָא נַמִי, דִּכְתִיב: ״מִבְּנוֹת פּוּטִיאֵל״, תַּרְתֵּי שְׁמַע מִינָּהּ.

Rather, this is how the matter should be resolved: **If his mother's father**[N] came **from** the family of **Joseph, his mother's mother** came **from** the family of **Yitro, and if his mother's father** came **from** the family of **Yitro, his mother's mother** came **from** the family of **Joseph,** so while his mother was descended from Joseph on one side and from Yitro on the other, Pinehas was a more distant relative to Yitro than Jonathan was. Based on this conclusion, the language of the verse **is also precise, as it is written:** "And Elazar, Aaron's son, took **one of the daughters of Putiel**" (Exodus 6:25).[N] **Conclude from** the wording of the verse that Pinehas was descended from **two** men who were referred to as Puti: Yitro and Joseph.

אָמַר רָבָא: הַנּוֹשֵׂא אִשָּׁה צָרִיךְ שֶׁיִּבְדּוֹק בְּאַחֶיהָ, שֶׁנֶּאֱמַר: ״וַיִּקַּח אַהֲרֹן אֶת אֱלִישֶׁבַע בַּת עַמִּינָדָב אֲחוֹת נַחְשׁוֹן״, מִמַּשְׁמַע שֶׁנֶּאֱמַר ״בַּת עַמִּינָדָב״, אֵינִי יוֹדֵעַ שֶׁאֲחוֹת נַחְשׁוֹן הִיא? מַה תַּלְמוּד לוֹמַר ״אֲחוֹת נַחְשׁוֹן״? מִכָּאן, שֶׁהַנּוֹשֵׂא אִשָּׁה צָרִיךְ שֶׁיִּבְדּוֹק בְּאַחֶיהָ. תָּנָא: רוֹב בָּנִים דּוֹמִין לַאֲחֵי הָאֵם.

Rava says: One who marries a woman needs to first **examine her brothers** so that he will know in advance what character his children will have, **as it is stated: "And Aaron took Elisheva, the daughter of Amminadav, the sister of Nahshon"** (Exodus 6:23). **By inference from that which is stated: "The daughter of Amminadav," do I not know that she is the sister of Nahshon,** as Nahshon was the son of Amminadav? **What is the meaning** when **the verse states: "The sister of Nahshon"? From here** one learns **that one who marries a woman needs to examine her brothers.** The reason is as the Sages **taught: Most sons resemble the mother's brothers.**

״וַיָּסוּרוּ שָׁמָּה וַיֹּאמְרוּ מִי הֱבִיאֲךָ הֲלֹם וּמָה אַתָּה עֹשֶׂה בָּזֶה וּמַה לְּךָ פֹה״, אָמְרוּ לוֹ: לָאו מִמֹּשֶׁה קָא אָתֵית, דִּכְתִיב בֵּיהּ: ״אַל תִּקְרַב הֲלֹם״? לָאו מִמֹּשֶׁה קָא אָתֵית דִּכְתִיב בֵּיהּ: ״מַה זֶּה בְיָדֶךָ״? לָאו מִמֹּשֶׁה קָא אָתֵית דִּכְתִיב בֵּיהּ: ״וְאַתָּה פֹּה עֲמֹד עִמָּדִי״? תֵּעָשֶׂה כּוֹמֶר לַעֲבוֹדָה זָרָה?!

In connection with the Gemara's mention of Jonathan, who served as a priest for Micah, the Gemara quotes additional statements of the Sages concerning that episode. Describing when the men from the tribe of Dan passed through Micah's house, the verse states: **"And they turned aside there and said to him: Who brought you here [*halom*], and what [*ma*] are you doing in this place, and what do you have here [*po*]?"** (Judges 18:3). The Sages interpret their multiple questions. **They said to him: Do you not come from Moses, about whom it is written: "Do not draw close to here [*halom*]"** (Exodus 3:5)? **Do you not come from Moses, about whom it is written: "What [*ma*] is that in your hand"** (Exodus 4:2)? **Do you not come from Moses, about whom it is written: "But as for you, stand here [*po*] with me"** (Deuteronomy 5:27)? **Shall you,** a descendant of our teacher Moses, **become a priest for idol worship?**

אָמַר לָהֶן, כָּךְ מְקוּבְּלַנִי מִבֵּית אֲבִי אַבָּא: לְעוֹלָם יַשְׂכִּיר אָדָם עַצְמוֹ לַעֲבוֹדָה זָרָה וְאַל יִצְטָרֵךְ לַבְּרִיּוֹת.

Jonathan **said to them: This is the tradition that I received from the house of my father's father: A person should always hire himself**[H] out **to idol worship and not require** the help **of people** by receiving charity, and I took this position in order to avoid having to take charity.

וְהוּא סָבַר: לַעֲבוֹדָה זָרָה מַמָּשׁ; וְלָא הִיא, אֶלָּא עֲבוֹדָה זָרָה – עֲבוֹדָה שֶׁזָּרָה לוֹ, כִּדְאָמַר לֵיהּ רַב לְרַב כָּהֲנָא: נְטוֹשׁ נְבֵילְתָּא בְּשׁוּקָא וּשְׁקוֹל אַגְרָא, וְלָא תֵּימָא: גַּבְרָא רַבָּא אֲנָא וְזִילָא בִּי מִילְּתָא.

The Gemara comments: **And he,** Jonathan, **thought** that this referred **to actual idol worship,**[N] **but** that **is not so,** that was not the intent of the tradition. **Rather,** here the term **idol worship,** literally: Strange service, is referring to **service,** i.e., labor, **that is strange,** i.e., unsuitable, **for him.** In other words, one should be willing to perform labor that is difficult and humiliating in his eyes rather than become a recipient of charity. **As Rav said to Rav Kahana,** his student: **Skin a carcass in the market and take payment, but do not say: I am a great man**[N] **and this matter is beneath me.**

NOTES

If his mother's father, etc. – אִי אֲבוּהָ דְּאִמֵּיהּ וכו׳: Accordingly, Pinehas' mother was descended from both Yitro and Joseph. The commentaries ask: If Pinehas is also a descendant of Yitro, why did Rabbi Elazar state that it was due to Pinehas' lineage that he was praiseworthy? The Rashbam writes that Pinehas was more distantly related to Yitro than Jonathan, who was Yitro's great-grandson. *Tosafot* explain that Pinehas was a descendant of Yitro on his maternal grandmother's side and a descendant of Joseph on his maternal grandfather's side, while Yitro was Jonathan's paternal grandfather, and a paternal connection has a stronger influence. The Ritva writes that in any case, Pinehas' father Elazar did not marry a daughter of Yitro, as Moses did, but a Jewish woman.

As it is written, one of the daughters of Putiel – דִּכְתִיב מִבְּנוֹת פּוּטִיאֵל: The commentaries disagree as to what precisely is the derivation from the verse. Rabbeinu Gershom and others say that Pinehas' lineage is derived from the wording: "Of the daughters of," written in the plural. The verse did not simply write: The daughter of. This indicates that she was descended from two different families. The Rashbam explains that it is derived from the fact that the name "Putiel" is written plene, with the letter *yod*, as it could have been written defective, without the letter *yod*, thereby alluding to the fattening of calves and also to battling with one's desire. The Ritva writes that Putiel is read *puti eleh*, which means: These Putis.

Actual idol worship – עֲבוֹדָה זָרָה מַמָּשׁ: Micah's priest understood this statement to mean that one should hire himself out even as a priest for idol worship as long as he is doing so for his livelihood only and he does not actually believe in the power of the idol (Rashbam).

I am a great man – גַּבְרָא רַבָּא אֲנָא: The Rashbam explains that a Torah scholar should not be concerned that he is causing a desecration of God's name by performing degrading tasks, since there is no shame in sustaining oneself by performing menial tasks in public. It is explained in the Jerusalem Talmud, and decided by the halakhic authorities as well, that a judge who is appointed by the community should have others serving him and should not perform menial tasks in public. By contrast, when a Torah scholar needs to perform labor in order to earn a livelihood, it is fitting that he do so in order that he not become a burden upon the community, especially if he performs the labor in private and if it is not degrading (see *Einayim LaMishpat*).

Another aspect of this *halakha* has been widely discussed: May a Torah scholar accept financial support from the community? The Rambam in his Commentary on the Mishna (*Avot* 4:5) and in other places is of the opinion that this is strictly prohibited, but in reality it has been the custom in all Jewish communities for Torah scholars to accept financial support due to the critical importance of Torah scholarship (Rambam *Sefer HaMadda*, *Hilkhot Talmud Torah* chapter 1 and *Kesef Mishne* there; see *Shulḥan Arukh*, *Yoreh De'a* 255 and commentaries there).

HALAKHA

A person should always hire himself, etc. – לְעוֹלָם יַשְׂכִּיר אָדָם עַצְמוֹ וכו׳: One should always distance himself from receiving charity and should be willing to live a life of discomfort in order to avoid being dependent on others. The Sages instructed: Make your Shabbat like a weekday, i.e., do not purchase more expensive foods for Shabbat, and do not be beholden to other beings (*Shabbat* 118a). Even if one is a respected Torah scholar and becomes impoverished, he should practice a trade, even a lowly one, in order to avoid accepting charity. If one was appointed a judge and a leader in the community, it is forbidden for him to perform such labor in the presence of three or more people, in order that he not degrade himself in their presence (Rambam *Sefer HaMadda*, *Hilkhot Talmud Torah* 3:10–11; *Sefer Zera'im*, *Hilkhot Mattenot Aniyyim* 10:18; and *Sefer Shofetim*, *Hilkhot Sanhedrin* 25:4; *Shulḥan Arukh*, *Yoreh De'a* 255:1 and *Ḥoshen Mishpat* 8:4, and in the comment of Rema; see Rambam *Sefer HaMadda*, *Hilkhot Talmud Torah* :9).

כֵּיוָן שֶׁרָאָה דָּוִד שֶׁמָּמוֹן חָבִיב עָלָיו בְּיוֹתֵר, מִינָּהוּ עַל הָאוֹצָרוֹת, שֶׁנֶּאֱמַר: ״וּשְׁבֻאֵל בֶּן גֵּרְשׁוֹם בֶּן מְנַשֶּׁה נָגִיד עַל הָאוֹצָרוֹת״. וְכִי שְׁבוּאֵל שְׁמוֹ? וַהֲלֹא יְהוֹנָתָן שְׁמוֹ! אָמַר רַבִּי יוֹחָנָן: שֶׁשָּׁב לָאֵל בְּכָל לִבּוֹ.

The Gemara continues its discussion of that episode. Later, **when King David saw that money was excessively precious to** Jonathan, **he appointed him** as director **of the treasuries** of the Temple, **as it is stated: "And Shebuel, the son of Gershom, the son of Moses, was ruler over the treasuries"** (I Chronicles 26:24). The Gemara asks: **And was his name** really **Shebuel; but wasn't his name Jonathan?**[N] **Rabbi Yoḥanan says:** He is called Shebuel in order to allude to the fact **that** he repented and **returned to God** [*shav la'el*][N] **with all his heart.**

״וְהַבָּנִים אֶת הָאָב״. מְנָלַן? דִּכְתִיב: ״אִישׁ כִּי יָמוּת״ וגו׳, טַעְמָא דְּאֵין לוֹ בֵּן, הָא יֵשׁ לוֹ בֵּן – בֵּן קוֹדֵם. אֲמַר לֵיהּ רַב פָּפָּא לְאַבַּיֵי, אֵימָא: אִי אִיכָּא בֵּן – לֵירוֹת בֵּן, אִיכָּא בַּת – תֵּירוֹת בַּת, אִיכָּא בֵּן וּבַת – לָא הַאי לֵירוֹת וְלָא הַאי לֵירוֹת!

§ The mishna teaches in the list of those who inherit from and bequeath to each other: **Sons** with regard to **their father.** The Gemara asks: **From where do** we derive this *halakha* that sons inherit the entire estate and daughters do not receive a share along with them? **As it is written: "If a man dies,** and has no son, then you shall pass his inheritance to his daughter" (Numbers 27:8). **The reason** the inheritance would be passed to a daughter is **that he has no son, but if he has a son, the son takes precedence. Rav Pappa said to Abaye:** Why not say the following: **If there is** only **a son, let** the **son inherit** the father's estate; if **there is** only **a daughter, let** the **daughter inherit** the father's estate; and if **there is** both **a son and a daughter, neither this one should inherit nor that one should inherit.**

וְאֶלָּא

Abaye asked Rav Pappa: **And rather,**

Perek **VIII**
Daf **110** Amud **b**

מַאן כּו׳ לֵירוֹת? אַטּוּ בַּר קַשָּׁא דְּמָתָא לֵירוֹת?! הָכִי קָא אָמִינָא: אִיכָּא בֵּן וּבַת – לָא הַאי לֵירוֹת כּוּלֵּיהּ, וְלָא הַאי לֵירוֹת כּוּלֵּיהּ, אֶלָּא כִּי הֲדָדֵי לֵירְתוּ!

who then **should inherit? Is that to say that the ruler**[N] **of the city should inherit?** Rav Pappa said to him: **This is what I** meant to say: If **there is a son and a daughter, this** one **should not inherit all of** the estate, **and that** one **should not inherit all of** the estate, **but they should inherit it** in **equal** portions **to one another.**[N]

אֲמַר לֵיהּ אַבַּיֵי: וְאִצְטְרִיךְ קְרָא לְאַשְׁמוּעִינַן הֵיכָא דְּלֵית לֵיהּ אֶלָּא חַד בְּרָא לֵירְתִינְהוּ לְכוּלְּהוּ נִכְסֵי? וְדִלְמָא הָא קָא מַשְׁמַע לָן, דְּבַת נַמִּי בַּת יְרוּשָּׁה הִיא! הַהוּא, מִ״וְּכָל בַּת יֹרֶשֶׁת נַחֲלָה״ נָפְקָא.

Abaye said to him: But is the verse necessary in order **to teach us that when he has only one child,** that child **should inherit all of his property?** If you say that the right of the son and daughter to the inheritance is equal, then the verse: "If a man dies, and has no son" (Numbers 27:8), which teaches that when there is no son his daughter inherits, is superfluous. Rav Pappa responded: **And perhaps this** verse **teaches us this: That a daughter is also subject to** receiving **inheritance.** The Gemara replies: No, the verse does not need to teach us this, since **that** *halakha* **is derived from** the verse: **"And every daughter who possesses an inheritance"** (Numbers 36:8), which clearly states that a daughter is subject to receiving inheritance.

רַב אַחָא בַּר יַעֲקֹב אָמַר, מֵהָכָא: ״לָמָּה יִגָּרַע שֵׁם אָבִינוּ מִתּוֹךְ מִשְׁפַּחְתּוֹ כִּי אֵין לוֹ בֵּן״, טַעְמָא דְּאֵין לוֹ בֵּן, הָא יֵשׁ לוֹ בֵּן – בֵּן קוֹדֵם.

Rav Aḥa bar Ya'akov said: The *halakha* that a son inherits his father's estate and precedes a daughter is derived **from here,** in the passage in the Torah where the daughters of Zelophehad request their father's inheritance in Eretz Yisrael. They said to Moses: **"Why should the name of our father be done away from among his family, because he has no son?"** (Numbers 27:4). Rabbi Aḥa ben Ya'akov infers: **The reason** they requested the inheritance is **that,** as they said: He **has no son.** One can infer: **But if he has a son,** the **son takes precedence** and the daughters would not have requested an inheritance.

NOTES

But wasn't his name Jonathan – וַהֲלֹא יְהוֹנָתָן שְׁמוֹ: As no other son of Gershom is mentioned in the Bible other than Shebuel, it is clear that he is the same person mentioned elsewhere as Jonathan (Rashbam).

That he returned to God – שֶׁשָּׁב לָאֵל: In order to explain the statement in the book of Judges that Jonathan and his descendants served as priests for the tribe of Dan until the exile of the Jewish people from Eretz Yisrael, it states in the Jerusalem Talmud that when King David died and King Solomon appointed others over the treasury, Jonathan reverted to his sinful ways and resumed his position as a priest for the tribe of Dan (Rashbam).

NOTES

Is that to say that the ruler [*bar kasha*], etc. – אַטּוּ בַּר קַשָּׁא וכו׳: The *Arukh* suggests two definitions of the term *bar kasha*: One, the tax collector of the city, and the other, the ruler of the city (see Rashbam).

They should inherit it equal to one another – כִּי הֲדָדֵי לֵירְתוּ: The verse "If a man dies, and has no son, then you shall pass his inheritance to his daughter," does not mean to say that the son precedes the daughter; rather, if there is only a daughter she precedes all other relatives (Ritva).

וְדִלְמָא בְּנוֹת צְלָפְחָד הוּא דְּקָאָמְרָן הָכִי, נִיתְּנָה תּוֹרָה וְנִתְחַדְּשָׁה הֲלָכָה! אֶלָּא, מְחַוַּורְתָּא כִּדְשַׁנִּין מֵעִיקָּרָא.

The Gemara raises a difficulty: **But perhaps it was the daughters of Zelophehad who said this,** i.e., that they were entitled to an inheritance only because their father had no son. They thought that this was the *halakha* based on the custom at that time, but after God spoke to Moses, the **Torah was given and a *halakha* was initiated** that a daughter's right to inherit is equal to that of the son. The Gemara accepts this difficulty and states: **Rather, it is clear** that the source for this *halakha* is **as we answered initially,** i.e., as Abaya derived from the verse of: "If a man dies, and has no son, then you shall pass his inheritance to his daughter" (Numbers 27:8).

רָבִינָא אָמַר, מֵהָכָא: ״הַקָּרֹב אֵלָיו״, הַקָּרוֹב – קָרוֹב קוֹדֵם.

Ravina said: The source for the *halakha* that a son precedes a daughter is **from here: "Who is next to him [*hakkarov elav*]"** (Numbers 27:11), teaching that the **closer [*karov*]** one is to the deceased, the **earlier** one is in the order of inheritance, and a son of the deceased is considered to be a closer relative to the deceased than the daughter.

וּמַאי קוּרְבָה דְּבֵן מִבַּת, שֶׁבֵּן קָם תַּחַת אָבִיו לִיעָדָה וְלִשְׂדֵה אֲחוּזָּה? יְעָדָה – בַּת לָאו בַּת יְעָדָה הִיא, שְׂדֵה אֲחוּזָּה נַמִּי – מֵהַאי פִּירְכָא גּוּפַהּ הוּא, דְּהָא קַיְימָא לֵיהּ לְתַנָּא: כְּלוּם יֵשׁ יִבּוּם אֶלָּא בִּמְקוֹם שֶׁאֵין בֵּן! אֶלָּא, מְחַוַּורְתָּא כִּדְשַׁנִּין מֵעִיקָּרָא.

The Gemara asks: **And what** demonstrates the **closeness of a son more than** that of **a daughter? That a son stands in place of his father to designate** a Hebrew maidservant as a wife for himself **and with regard to an ancestral field.** The Gemara rejects this: This is not a valid proof, as **designation** cannot demonstrate that a son is a closer relative; **a daughter is not subject to designation,** because she obviously cannot marry the Hebrew maidservant. With regard to **an ancestral field as well, the *tanna* establishes his** ruling that a son is a closer relative than others **from this** same **refutation: Is there levirate marriage except in a case where there is no son?** And this applies also where there is no daughter. **Rather, it is clear** that the source for this *halakha* is **as we answered initially.**

וְאִי בָּעֵית אֵימָא, מֵהָכָא: ״וְהִתְנַחַלְתֶּם אֹתָם לִבְנֵיכֶם אַחֲרֵיכֶם״, בְּנֵיכֶם – וְלֹא בְּנוֹתֵיכֶם. אֶלָּא מֵעַתָּה, ״לְמַעַן יִרְבּוּ יְמֵיכֶם וִימֵי בְנֵיכֶם״, הָכִי נַמִּי בְּנֵיכֶם וְלֹא בְּנוֹתֵיכֶם?

And if you wish, say instead that the *halakha* that a son precedes a daughter is derived **from here,** in the passage in the Torah addressing the inheritance of slaves, which states: **"And you may make them an inheritance for your sons [*livneikhem*] after you"** (Leviticus 25:46). One can infer: **"Your sons," but not your daughters.** The Gemara asks: **If that is so,** then when the verse states: **"That your days may be multiplied, and the days of your sons [*beneikhem*]"** (Deuteronomy 11:21), should one infer that **this too** means: **"Your sons," but not your daughters?** Is it not obvious that daughters are also worthy of receiving the blessing of longevity?

בְּרָכָה שָׁאנֵי.

The Gemara answers: **A blessing is different.**[N] In a verse that speaks of blessings, the term *beneikhem* should be understood in its broader sense, as "your children." In a verse that speaks of a *halakha*, it is to be understood in the narrower sense of "your sons."

״וְהָאַחִין מִן הָאָב נוֹחֲלִין וּמַנְחִילִין״ וכו׳. מְנָלַן? אָמַר רַבָּה: אָתְיָא אַחֲוָה אַחֲוָה מִבְּנֵי יַעֲקֹב, מָה לְהַלָּן מִן הָאָב וְלֹא מִן הָאֵם, אַף כָּאן מִן הָאָב וְלֹא מִן הָאֵם.

§ The mishna teaches: **And paternal brothers**[H] **inherit** from one another **and bequeath** to each other. **From where do we** derive this *halakha*? **Rabba said:** It is **derived from** a verbal analogy between the word: **Brothers,** stated with regard to inheritance, and the word: **Brothers,** found in the verses concerning **Jacob's sons.** When Jacob's sons speak to Joseph, they state: "We, your servants, are twelve brothers, the sons of one man in the land of Canaan" (Genesis 42:13), and in the passage discussing inheritance the verse states: "And if he has no brothers, then you shall give his inheritance to his father's brothers" (Numbers 27:10). **Just as there,** in the verse concerning Jacob's sons, the word brothers is referring to **paternal** brothers **and not maternal** brothers, as the twelve of them shared only the same father, **so too here,** where this term is used with regard to inheritance, the verse is referring to **paternal** brothers **and not maternal** brothers.

וְלָמָּה לִי? ״מִמִּשְׁפַּחְתּוֹ וְיָרַשׁ אֹתָהּ״ כְּתִיב; מִשְׁפַּחַת אָב קְרוּיָה מִשְׁפָּחָה, מִשְׁפַּחַת אֵם אֵינָהּ קְרוּיָה מִשְׁפָּחָה!

The Gemara asks: **But why do I** need this proof from the verse concerning Jacob's sons? **It is written** in the passage concerning inheritance: "Then you shall give his inheritance to his kinsman who is next to him **of his family, and he shall inherit it"** (Numbers 27:11). When the term "family" is used in the Bible, one's **father's family is called** one's **family,** while one's **mother's family is not called** one's **family,** so that in all matters of inheritance, it is the patrilineal relatives who are taken into account.

NOTES

A blessing is different – בְּרָכָה שָׁאנֵי: Blessings should be understood as applying broadly to all of the Jewish people. Therefore, when the Torah states *beneikhem* in the context of a blessing it does not intend to limit the blessing to males. Moreover, there is no such thing as half a blessing, so it is obvious that it applies to one's sons and daughters (Rashbam). The Ritva adds that this blessing is mentioned in the context of the performance of the mitzva of *mezuza*, which is incumbent upon males and females equally, so it is logical that the blessing applies to all.

HALAKHA

And paternal brothers – וְהָאַחִין מִן הָאָב: If a man dies without any offspring and his father is also no longer alive, his paternal brothers inherit from him (Rambam *Sefer Mishpatim, Hilkhot Naḥalot* 1:3; *Shulḥan Arukh, Ḥoshen Mishpat* 276:1).

אִין הָכִי נַמִי, וְכִי אִיתְּמַר דְּרַבָּה – לְעִנְיַן יִבּוּם אִיתְּמַר.

The Gemara answers: **Yes, it is indeed so** that the verbal analogy is not needed to teach the *halakha* of inheritance, **and when Rabba's** explanation **was stated,** it **was stated with regard to the matter of levirate marriage,** teaching that levirate marriage is performed only by a paternal brother but not by a maternal brother.

״וְהָאִישׁ אֶת אִמּוֹ״ וכו׳. מְנָא הָנֵי מִילֵּי? דְּתָנוּ רַבָּנַן.

§ The mishna teaches: **And a man** with regard to **his mother** inherits from her relatives but does not bequeath to her. The Gemara asks: **From where are these matters** derived? The Gemara answers: **As the Sages taught:**

Perek **VIII**
Daf **111** Amud **a**

PERSONALITIES

Rabbi Zekharya ben HaKatzav – רַבִּי זְכַרְיָה בֶּן הַקַּצָּב: Rabbi Zekharya ben HaKatzav was one of the early *tanna'im*, and he lived in Jerusalem while the Second Temple still stood. The exact period in which he lived is unknown, but it appears he was already active when Rabban Yoḥanan ben Zakkai was the leader of the Jewish people, as statements are recorded in Rabbi Zekharya ben HaKatzav's name from that time. It seems that he lived a long life, and he testified, along with the disciples of Rabban Yoḥanan, before the Sanhedrin when it relocated to Yavne. It is known that Rabbi Zekharya was a priest, and he had to divorce his wife because he was stringent with regard to an ordinance of the Sages in the matter of priestly lineage.

״וְכָל בַּת יֹרֶשֶׁת נַחֲלָה מִמַּטּוֹת בְּנֵי יִשְׂרָאֵל״ – הֵיאַךְ בַּת יוֹרֶשֶׁת שְׁנֵי מַטּוֹת? אֶלָּא זוֹ שֶׁאָבִיהָ מִשֵּׁבֶט אֶחָד וְאִמָּהּ מִשֵּׁבֶט אַחֵר, וּמֵתוּ, וִירֵשְׁתָן.

The verse states: **"And every daughter who possesses an inheritance from the tribes of the children of Israel"** (Numbers 36:8). Noting the plural in the phrase "from the tribes of the children of Israel," the *baraita* asks: **How can a daughter inherit** land from **two tribes? Rather, this** is referring to a daughter **whose father is from one tribe but her mother** is **from another tribe, and they** both **died, and she inherited** from both of **them.** Therefore, it can be seen in this verse that a daughter inherits from her mother.

וְאֵין לִי אֶלָּא בַּת, בֵּן מִנַּיִן? אָמַרְתָּ קַל וָחוֹמֶר: וּמַה בַּת שֶׁהוּרַע כֹּחָהּ בְּנִכְסֵי הָאָב – יָפֶה כֹּחָהּ בְּנִכְסֵי הָאֵם, בֵּן שֶׁיָּפֶה כֹּחוֹ בְּנִכְסֵי הָאָב – אֵינוֹ דִּין שֶׁיָּפֶה כֹּחוֹ בְּנִכְסֵי הָאֵם? וּמִמָּקוֹם שֶׁבָּאתָ: מַה לְּהַלָּן בֵּן קוֹדֵם לְבַת, אַף כָּאן בֵּן קוֹדֵם לְבַת.

The *baraita* continues: **I have** derived **only** that **a daughter** inherits from her mother; **from where** do I derive that **a son** inherits from his mother as well? **You can say an *a fortiori* inference: And just as a daughter, whose power is diminished with regard to** her **father's property** in that she does not inherit it when there is a son, yet her power **is enhanced with regard to** her **mother's property** in that she inherits it; with regard to **a son, whose power is enhanced with regard to** his **father's property** in that he is first in the order of inheritance, **is it not logical that his power is enhanced with regard to** his **mother's property?** The *baraita* continues: **And from the place that you came,** i.e., from the inference that was just stated, one can say the following: **Just as there,** with regard to a father's property, **a son precedes a daughter, so too here,** with regard to a mother's property, **a son precedes a daughter.** This is the opinion of the first *tanna*.

רַבִּי יוֹסֵי בְּרַבִּי יְהוּדָה וְרַבִּי אֶלְעָזָר בְּרַבִּי יוֹסֵי אָמְרוּ מִשּׁוּם רַבִּי זְכַרְיָה בֶּן הַקַּצָּב: אֶחָד הַבֵּן וְאֶחָד הַבַּת שָׁוִין בְּנִכְסֵי הָאֵם. מַאי טַעֲמָא? דַּיּוֹ לַבָּא מִן הַדִּין לִהְיוֹת כַּנִּדּוֹן.

The *baraita* continues: **Rabbi Yosei, son of Rabbi Yehuda, and Rabbi Elazar, son of Rabbi Yosei, said in the name of Rabbi Zekharya ben Hakatzav:**[P] **Both the son and the daughter are equal with regard to the mother's property. What is the reason** for his ruling? **It is sufficient for the** conclusion that **emerges from** an *a fortiori* **inference to be like** its **source.** According to this principle, a *halakha* derived by means of an *a fortiori* inference cannot go beyond the *halakhot* of the source from which it is derived. Since the *halakha* that a son inherits from his mother was derived via an *a fortiori* inference from the *halakha* that a daughter inherits from her mother, it cannot be that this inference should lead to the conclusion that a son precedes a daughter in inheriting from their mother.

וְתַנָּא קַמָּא לָא דָּרֵישׁ ״דַּיּוֹ״? וְהָא ״דַּיּוֹ״ דְּאוֹרַיְיתָא הוּא!

The Gemara asks: **And doesn't the first *tanna*** also **interpret** verses employing the principle of: **It is sufficient** for the conclusion that emerges from an *a fortiori* inference to be like its source? **But the principle of: It is sufficient,** which limits the extent of *a fortiori* inference, **is found in the Torah,** so how could he disagree with it?

דְּתַנְיָא: מִדִּין קַל וָחוֹמֶר כֵּיצַד? ״וַיֹּאמֶר ה׳ אֶל מֹשֶׁה וְאָבִיהָ יָרֹק יָרַק בְּפָנֶיהָ הֲלֹא תִכָּלֵם שִׁבְעַת יָמִים״, קַל וָחוֹמֶר לַשְּׁכִינָה אַרְבָּעָה עָשָׂר!

As it is taught in a *baraita* that explains the hermeneutical principles: **How** does **an** ***a fortiori*** **inference** work? The verse states with regard to Miriam, after she spoke ill of her brother Moses: **"And the Lord said to Moses: If her father had but spit in her face, should she not hide in shame seven days?"** (Numbers 12:14). The verse is saying that if a father spits in the face of his daughter and reprimands her, she would feel shame for seven days. By **an** ***a fortiori*** inference it is derived that Miriam, who suffered the more severe reprimand **of the Divine Presence**,[N] should be ostracized for **fourteen** days. Why then, was Miriam ostracized for only seven days?

אֶלָּא דַּיּוֹ לַבָּא מִן הַדִּין לִהְיוֹת כַּנִּדּוֹן!

Rather, it is sufficient for the conclusion that **emerges from** an *a fortiori* **inference to be like** its **source**, so her punishment cannot be for longer than the punishment of one who is reprimanded by a father. In any event, the principle the begins with: It is sufficient, can be seen in this verse, so how does the first *tanna* rule that a son precedes a daughter with regard to a mother's property?

בְּעָלְמָא דָּרֵישׁ ״דַּיּוֹ״, וְשָׁאנֵי הָכָא, דְּאָמַר קְרָא: ״מִמַּטּוֹת״, מַקִּישׁ מַטֵּה הָאֵם לְמַטֵּה הָאָב, מַה מַּטֵּה הָאָב – בֵּן קוֹדֵם לְבַת, אַף מַטֵּה הָאֵם – בֵּן קוֹדֵם לְבַת.

The Gemara answers: **Generally,** the first *tanna* also **interprets** verses employing the principle that begins with: **It is sufficient, but it is different here** with regard to inheritance, **as the verse states:** "And every daughter who possesses an inheritance **from the tribes** of the children of Israel" (Numbers 36:8). The verse **juxtaposes the tribe of the mother to the tribe of the father.** Therefore, the first *tanna* holds that **just as** with regard to the **tribe of the father,** i.e., inheriting from one's father, **a son precedes a daughter, so too,** with regard to the **tribe of the mother,** i.e., inheriting from one's mother, **a son precedes a daughter.**

רַב נִיתַּאי סְבַר לְמֶעְבַּד עוּבְדָא כְּרַבִּי זְכַרְיָה בֶּן הַקַּצָּב, אֲמַר לֵיהּ שְׁמוּאֵל: כְּמַאן, כִּזְכַרְיָה? אֶפֶס זְכַרְיָה. רַבִּי טַבְלָא עֲבַד עוּבְדָא כְּרַבִּי זְכַרְיָה בֶּן הַקַּצָּב, אֲמַר לֵיהּ רַב נַחְמָן: מַאי הַאי? אֲמַר לֵיהּ, דְּאָמַר רַב חִינָּנָא בַּר שְׁלַמְיָא מִשְּׁמֵיהּ דְּרַב: הֲלָכָה כְּרַבִּי זְכַרְיָה בֶּן הַקַּצָּב. אֲמַר לֵיהּ: זִיל אַהְדַּר בָּךְ, וְאִי לָא – מַפֵּיקְנָא לָךְ רַב חִינָּנָא בַּר שְׁלַמְיָא מֵאוּנַיךְ.

The Gemara relates: **Rav Nittai thought to perform an action,** i.e., issue a ruling, **in accordance with** the opinion of **Rabbi Zekharya ben HaKatzav,** who taught that a son and daughter are equal with regard to inheriting from their mother. **Shmuel said to him: In accordance with whose** opinion do you wish to issue this ruling, **in accordance with** the opinion of **Zekharya? Zekharya is nil** [***afes***],[L] i.e., his statement was not accepted as *halakha.* **Rabbi Tavla performed an action,** i.e., issued a ruling, **in accordance with** the opinion of **Rabbi Zekharya ben HaKatzav. Rav Naḥman said to him: What is this?** Rabbi Tavla **said to him: As Rav Ḥinnana bar Shelamya says in the name of Rav:** The *halakha* **is in accordance with** the opinion of **Rabbi Zekharya ben HaKatzav.** Rav Naḥman **said to him: Go retract your ruling, and if** you do **not, I will take Rav Ḥinnana bar Shelamya out of your ear,**[N] i.e., I will punish you severely for ruling against the accepted *halakha.*

LANGUAGE

Nil [*afes*] – אֶפֶס: According to the Rashbam, the word *afes* is the same Hebrew word for lost or gone, as in the phrase in the verse: "Our money is gone [*afes*]" (Genesis 47:15).

NOTES

An ***a fortiori*** **inference to one reprimanded by the Divine Presence** – קַל וָחוֹמֶר לַשְּׁכִינָה: The early commentaries discuss the following question: Why should the *a fortiori* inference teach that the ostracism of one who was reprimanded by the Divine Presence be specifically fourteen days? Some add: Why not permanent ostracism?

Rabbeinu Tam, cited in *Tosafot* as well as in *Sefer HaYashar*, explains this in accordance with the Gemara (*Nidda* 31a) that states that while every child inherits physical characteristics from both his mother and his father, it is God who gives life to the child. Therefore, God is deserving of double the honor of a parent. Others explain that the *a fortiori* inference teaches that some minimal amount of days should be added beyond the seven days resulting from the father's reprimand. Since the *halakhot* of a leper require ostracism of at least one week, Miriam, who became a leper, would have been required to remain isolated for more time than that. Less than a week is not regarded as a significant amount of time with regard to a leper, so it follows that she would be ostracized for a second week (Rabbeinu Ḥayyim HaKohen; see *Tosafot Yeshanim* and Ritva).

Other early commentaries say that none of these explanations are necessary, as it is the way of the Sages to phrase an *a fortiori* inference in a way that doubles the number mentioned in the source of the inference (Ramban; Ran).

I will take Rav Ḥinnana bar Shelamya out of your ear – מַפֵּיקְנָא לָךְ רַב חִינָּנָא בַּר שְׁלַמְיָא מֵאוּנַיךְ: This expression appears several times in the Talmud. Both the Rashbam and Rashi explain that it is a threat to excommunicate the person until he retracts his ruling. Rabbeinu Gershom explains that it is a threat to confiscate the person's money because his ruling caused a litigant to pay money he did not owe. Other commentaries explain that this is a means of intimidation, intended to cause the person to change his mind and retract his ruling.

רַב הוּנָא בַּר חִיָּיא סָבַר לְמֶעְבַּד עוּבְדָא כְּרַבִּי זְכַרְיָה בֶּן הַקַּצָּב, אֲמַר לֵיהּ רַב נַחְמָן: מַאי הַאי? אֲמַר לֵיהּ, דְּאָמַר רַב הוּנָא אָמַר רַב: הֲלָכָה כְּרַבִּי זְכַרְיָה בֶּן הַקַּצָּב. אֲמַר לֵיהּ: אֶשְׁלַח לֵיהּ? אִיכְסִיף. אֲמַר לֵיהּ: הָשְׁתָּא כִּי נָח נַפְשֵׁיהּ דְּרַב הוּנָא, אִיתְרִיסַתְּ לְקִבְלִי.

The Gemara relates further: **Rav Huna bar Ḥiyya thought to perform an action,** i.e., issue a ruling, **in accordance with** the opinion **of Rabbi Zekharya ben HaKatzav. Rav Naḥman said to him: What is this?** Rav Huna bar Ḥiyya **said to him: As Rav Huna says** that **Rav says:** The ***halakha*** **is in accordance with** the opinion of **Rabbi Zekharya ben HaKatzav.** Rav Naḥman **said to him: Shall I send** a messenger **to** Rav Huna to ask him if that is indeed what he said? Rav Huna bar Ḥiyya **was embarrassed,**[N] as he was not certain that Rav Huna actually said this ruling. Rav Naḥman **said to him: Now, if Rav Huna were** to have **died, you would have been brazen** enough to say **before me** that this is what he said, but since he is still alive, you cannot be so brazen.

וְאִיהוּ כְּמַאן סְבָרָהּ? כִּי הָא דְּרַב וּשְׁמוּאֵל דְּאָמְרִי תַּרְוַיְיהוּ: אֵין הֲלָכָה כְּרַבִּי זְכַרְיָה בֶּן הַקַּצָּב.

The Gemara asks: **And he,** Rav Naḥman, **in accordance with whose** opinion **does he hold?** As there were various sages who ruled in accordance with the opinion of Rabbi Zekharya ben HaKatzav, why did Rav Naḥman not agree? The Gemara answers: He holds **in accordance with this** statement **of Rav and Shmuel, who both say:** The ***halakha*** **is not in accordance with** the opinion **of Rabbi Zekharya ben HaKatzav.**

מִסְתַּמֵּיךְ וְאָזֵיל רַבִּי יַנַּאי אַכִּתְפָּא דְּרַבִּי שִׂמְלַאי שַׁמָּעֵיהּ, וְאָתֵי רַבִּי יְהוּדָה נְשִׂיאָה לְאַפַּיְיהוּ. אֲמַר לֵיהּ: בַּר אֱינָשׁ דְּאָתָא לְקִיבְלָנָא, הוּא יָאֵי וְגוּלְתֵיהּ יָאֵי. כִּי מְטָא לְגַבֵּיהּ גְּשָׁשָׁהּ, אֲמַר לֵיהּ: דֵּין שִׁיעוּרֵיהּ כַּשַּׂק.

The Gemara relates: **Rabbi Yannai,** who had already grown old and whose eyes were dim, **would walk leaning on the shoulder of Rabbi Simlai, his attendant, and Rabbi Yehuda Nesia**[P] **came toward them.** Rabbi Simlai **said to** Rabbi Yannai: The **person who is coming toward us is handsome and his cloak** is **handsome.**[N] **When** Rabbi Yehuda Nesia **reached him,** Rabbi Yannai **felt** his cloak **and said to** Rabbi Simlai: Concerning **this** cloak, **its measurement** with regard to the *halakhot* of ritual impurity **is like the** measurement of **sackcloth,**[N] meaning it was a cloak of inferior quality, as it was thick and rough.

בְּעָא מִינֵּיהּ: מִנַּיִן לְבֵן שֶׁקּוֹדֵם לְבַת בְּנִכְסֵי הָאֵם? אֲמַר לֵיהּ, דִּכְתִיב: "מַטּוֹת", מַקִּישׁ מַטֵּה הָאֵם לְמַטֵּה הָאָב, מַה מַּטֵּה הָאָב – בֵּן קוֹדֵם לְבַת, אַף מַטֵּה הָאֵם – בֵּן קוֹדֵם לְבַת. אֲמַר לֵיהּ: אִי מַה מַּטֵּה הָאָב – בְּכוֹר נוֹטֵל פִּי שְׁנַיִם, אַף מַטֵּה הָאֵם – בְּכוֹר נוֹטֵל פִּי שְׁנַיִם!

When Rabbi Yehuda Nesia met Rabbi Yannai he **asked him: From where** is it derived **that a son precedes a daughter with regard to the mother's property?**[H] Rabbi Yannai **said to him: As it is written:** "And every daughter who possesses an inheritance from the **tribes** of the children of Israel" (Numbers 36:8). The verse **juxtaposes** the **tribe of the mother** to the **tribe of the father.** This teaches that **just as** with regard to the **tribe of the father a son precedes a daughter, so too,** with regard to the **tribe of the mother, a son precedes a daughter.** Rabbi Yehuda Nesia **said to him: If** so, if these two *halakhot* are in fact juxtaposed, the following should also be derived: **Just as** with regard to the inheritance of **the father's tribe a firstborn takes a double** portion, **so too,** with regard to inheritance from **the mother's tribe,** when he inherits from his mother **a firstborn takes a double** portion.

NOTES

He was embarrassed – אִיכְסִיף: The Rashbam explains that Rav Huna bar Ḥiyya in fact thought he had heard this from Rav Huna, but he was concerned that Rav Huna may have retracted his ruling. Alternatively, Rav Huna bar Ḥiyya began to doubt whether that was indeed the ruling he heard from him, and perhaps Rav Huna would deny having issued it. The Ritva explains that he was concerned that Rav Huna may have made the statement offhand, not as an actual halakhic ruling, or that Rav Huna would forget that he had said these words.

By contrast, Rabbeinu Gershom explains that Rav Huna did not, in fact, state this ruling, but Rav Huna bar Ḥiyya quoted it in his name in order to buttress his ruling. He was embarrassed because he knew Rav Huna would eventually deny having said it.

His cloak [*gulteih*] is handsome – גּוּלְתֵיהּ יָאֵי: The Rashbam explains that *gulteih* means a cloak, while the Ri Migash says it is a type of hat. With regard to the statement itself, it is possible that Rabbi Simlai's intention was merely to describe Rabbi Yehuda Nesia's clothing. Others explain that Rabbi Yannai meant to say that Rabbi Yehuda Nesia was dressed in the garb of a Torah scholar. The Meiri writes that he may have been indicating that the man was wise and also had sterling character traits, as these attributes are likened to a person's clothing, which is visible to others.

Its measurement is like the measurement of sackcloth – שִׁיעוּרֵיהּ כַּשַּׂק: Rabbi Yannai meant that the cloth was thick and of low quality, like sackcloth. Therefore, with regard to the *halakhot* of becoming susceptible to ritual impurity, the measurement of a garment that renders it susceptible is four handbreadths by four handbreadths and not three by three, as in the case of articles of clothing (Rashbam). The Meiri explains that the statement was meant metaphorically: Rabbi Yannai discerned immediately from the conduct of Rabbi Yehuda Nesia that he was not a distinguished man, and the statement that his clothing was like sackcloth is an allusion to his character in general.

PERSONALITIES

Rabbi Yehuda Nesia – רַבִּי יְהוּדָה נְשִׂיאָה: This appears to be Rabbi Yehuda Nesia II, grandson of the first Rabbi Yehuda Nesia, who in turn was the grandson of Rabbi Yehuda HaNasi, the redactor of the Mishna. He was not as great a scholar as his forefathers. It is possible that in his time the leadership of the community was already separate from the leadership of the yeshiva, so that he was not the head of the yeshiva, and that role was fulfilled by Rabbi Yoḥanan.

The role of the *Nasi* was mainly ceremonial and political. Nevertheless, this Rabbi Yehuda Nesia was a Torah scholar and learned from Rabbi Yoḥanan and Reish Lakish and their students. His Torah statements are mentioned periodically in the Babylonian Talmud and even more so in the Jerusalem Talmud. He was succeeded by his son, Rabban Gamliel V.

HALAKHA

A son precedes a daughter with regard to the mother's property – בֵּן שֶׁקּוֹדֵם לְבַת בְּנִכְסֵי הָאֵם: If a mother dies, her son or his offspring inherit her property. If she had no sons or offspring of sons, her daughter or her daughter's offspring inherit her property. This is due to the fact that, as Rav and Shmuel rule later, the *halakha* is not in accordance with the opinion of Rabbi Zekharya ben HaKatzav (Rambam *Sefer Mishpatim, Hilkhot Naḥalot* 1:3; *Shulḥan Arukh, Ḥoshen Mishpat* 276:1, 4).

אֲמַר לֵיהּ לְשַׁמָּעֵיהּ: גּוֹד, לֵית דֵּין צָבֵי לְמֵילַף. וְטַעְמָא מַאי? אֲמַר אַבָּיֵי, אָמַר קְרָא: ״בְּכֹל אֲשֶׁר יִמָּצֵא לוֹ״, לוֹ – וְלֹא לָהּ.

He said to his attendant: Take me away from here, as **this** man, Rabbi Yehuda Nesia, **does not desire to learn**[N] but is instead raising difficulties that are easily resolved. **And what is the reason** he does not receive a double portion? **Abaye said: The verse** concerning the double portion received by a firstborn son **states:** "By giving him a double portion **of all that he has**" (Deuteronomy 21:17), indicating that he receives a double portion in all that **he** has, **but not** in all that **she** has.

וְאֵימָא: הָנֵי מִילֵּי בָּחוּר שֶׁנָּשָׂא אַלְמָנָה, אֲבָל בָּחוּר שֶׁנָּשָׂא בְּתוּלָה הָכִי נָמֵי דְּשָׁקֵיל!

The Gemara asks: **And** why not **say** that **this statement** applies in the case of **a bachelor who married a widow,** i.e., a man who marries a woman who already has children from another man, so that the firstborn son is his firstborn but not hers, **but** in the case of **a bachelor who married a virgin, so too the** *halakha* will be **that** their firstborn son **will take** a double portion of his mother's inheritance?

אָמַר רַב נַחְמָן בַּר יִצְחָק, אָמַר קְרָא: ״רֵאשִׁית אֹנוֹ״, אוֹנוֹ – וְלֹא אוֹנָהּ.

Rav Naḥman bar Yitzḥak said: There is a different derivation teaching that *halakha*, as the same **verse states:** "For he is **the first fruits of his strength** [*ono*]" (Deuteronomy 21:17), indicating that the *halakha* of the double portion is stated with regard to **his strength, but not her strength,** thereby excluding a son who is the firstborn of his mother alone.

הַהוּא מִבָּעֵיא לֵיהּ לְבָא אַחַר נְפָלִים דְּלֶהֱוֵי בְּכוֹר לְנַחֲלָה – מִי שֶׁלִּבּוֹ דָּוֶה עָלָיו, יָצָא זֶה שֶׁאֵין לִבּוֹ דָּוֶה עָלָיו!

The Gemara challenges: But **that** verse **is required to** derive the *halakha* of a child who **came** into the world **after** his mother gave birth to **non-viable newborns**[H] who did not reach the full term of nine months. This verse teaches **that** such a firstborn son **should be a firstborn with regard to inheritance,** even though he is not a firstborn with regard to the mitzva to redeem one's firstborn son. How is this *halakha* derived from the verse? The term "his strength [*ono*]" is understood as referring to acute mourning [*aninut*], in the following manner: A firstborn son for the purpose of inheritance of land is only **one whose** father's **heart is pained about him** when he dies, i.e., a son who lives beyond birth, **excluding this** non-viable newborn **whose** father's **heart is not pained about him** when he dies. Therefore, the next viable son to be born after a non-viable newborn is considered the firstborn.

אִם כֵּן, לֵימָא קְרָא כִּי הוּא ״רֵאשִׁית אוֹן״, מַאי ״אוֹנוֹ״? שְׁמַע מִינַּהּ תַּרְתֵּי.

The Gemara answers: **If so,** that the sole purpose of the term: "His strength" is to teach that *halakha*, **let the verse say: For he is the first fruit of strength** [*on*], omitting the possessive "his," represented by the letter *vav*. **What** is derived from the more expanded term: **"His strength** [*ono*]," which indicates specifically the father's strength? **Conclude two** conclusions **from it,** both with regard to mourning and with regard to the status of the firstborn as the father's heir specifically.

וְאַכַּתִּי אֵימָא: הָנֵי מִילֵּי אַלְמוֹן שֶׁנָּשָׂא בְּתוּלָה, אֲבָל בָּחוּר שֶׁנָּשָׂא בְּתוּלָה הָכִי נָמֵי דְּשָׁקֵיל!

The Gemara raises a difficulty: **But** one can **still say** that **this statement** applies in a case of **a widower who married a virgin,** so that he already has a firstborn from his previous marriage who is the first fruit of his strength. And the son born to him and his second wife is not the first fruit of his strength, and it is this type of firstborn who does not inherit a double portion of his mother's estate. **But** in a case of **a bachelor who married a virgin, so too the** *halakha* will be **that** their shared firstborn son **will take** a double portion of his mother's inheritance.

אֶלָּא אָמַר רָבָא, אָמַר קְרָא: ״לוֹ מִשְׁפַּט הַבְּכֹרָה״, מִשְׁפַּט הַבְּכוֹרָה לָאִישׁ, וְלֹא מִשְׁפַּט הַבְּכוֹרָה לָאִשָּׁה.

Rather, Rava said: There is a different derivation teaching that *halakha*, as the same **verse states: "The right of the firstborn is his"** (Deuteronomy 21:17). The emphasis on "his" indicates that **the primogeniture** applies specifically **to a man,**[H] **and the primogeniture does not** apply **to a woman,** whether the woman is the one inheriting or is the legator.

NOTES

Does not desire to learn – לֵית דֵּין צָבֵי לְמֵילַף: Rabbi Yannai means that because Rabbi Yehuda Nesia asked an unimportant question, it demonstrates that his intention was not to learn but to provoke (see Rashbam).

HALAKHA

Came into the world after non-viable newborns – בָּא אַחַר נְפָלִים: A son born after a non-viable newborn is considered a firstborn with regard to inheritance. This applies even if the head of the non-viable newborn, or even his entire body, emerged when he was still alive. The *Sma* notes that the viable son is not considered a firstborn with regard to redemption (Rambam *Sefer Mishpatim, Hilkhot Naḥalot* 2:10; *Shulḥan Arukh, Ḥoshen Mishpat* 277:6).

The primogeniture applies to a man – מִשְׁפַּט הַבְּכוֹרָה לָאִישׁ: A firstborn receives a double portion of his father's property but not of his mother's, even if he is the firstborn of both his parents. He and his brothers share their mother's property equally (Rambam *Sefer Mishpatim, Hilkhot Naḥalot* 2:8; *Shulḥan Arukh, Ḥoshen Mishpat* 278:1).

וְהָאִישׁ אֶת אִשְׁתּוֹ״ וכו׳. מְנָהָנֵי מִילֵּי? דְּתָנוּ רַבָּנַן: ״שְׁאֵרוֹ״ – זוֹ אִשְׁתּוֹ, מְלַמֵּד שֶׁהַבַּעַל יוֹרֵשׁ אֶת אִשְׁתּוֹ. יָכוֹל אַף הִיא תִּירָשֶׁנּוּ? תַּלְמוּד לוֹמַר: ״וְיָרַשׁ אוֹתָהּ״, הוּא יוֹרֵשׁ אוֹתָהּ, וְאֵין הִיא יוֹרֶשֶׁת אוֹתוֹ.

§ The mishna teaches: **And a man** with regard to **his wife**[N] inherits but does not bequeath. The Gemara asks: **From where are these matters** derived? The Gemara explains: **As the Sages taught** in a *baraita*: The verse concerning inheritance states: "And if his father has no brothers, then you shall give his inheritance to **his kinsman** [*she'ero*] who is next to him of his family, and he shall inherit it" (Numbers 27:11). **This** kinsman is **one's wife,** and the Torah **teaches that a husband inherits** from **his wife,**[H] as the Gemara will explain later. One **might** have thought that **she would also inherit** from **him;** therefore, **the verse states: "And he shall inherit it,"** with the word "it" written in the feminine "*otah*," which can also be translated as: Her. This teaches that it is **he who inherits** from **her, but she does not inherit** from **him.**[H]

וְהָא קְרָאֵי לָאו הָכִי כְּתִיבִי! אָמַר אַבַּיֵי, תְּרֵיץ הָכִי: ״וּנְתַתֶּם אֶת נַחֲלָתוֹ לַקָּרוֹב אֵלָיו, שְׁאֵרוֹ וְיָרַשׁ אוֹתָהּ״.

The Gemara questions this explanation: **But the verses are not written like this.** The verse states that "his kinsman" inherits from the deceased, so that if that term is referring to one's wife, a wife should inherit from her husband. **Abaye said: Answer like this,** i.e., as if the verse were split into two parts. The first part is: **Then you shall give his inheritance to he who is next to him,** which is a general statement with regard to the inheritance of relatives. The second is: **His kinsman, and he shall inherit it,** meaning that a husband inherits from his kinsman, referring to his wife.

אֲמַר רָבָא: סַכִּינָא חֲרִיפָא מְפַסְקָא קְרָאֵי? אֶלָּא אֲמַר רָבָא, הָכִי קָאָמַר: ״וּנְתַתֶּם אֶת נַחֲלַת שְׁאֵרוֹ לוֹ״. קָא סָבַר: גּוֹרְעִין וּמוֹסִיפִין וְדוֹרְשִׁין.

Rava said: Does **a sharp knife cut verses?** How can you split the verse, rearrange it and omit letters from its words? Abaye's derivation rearranges the words and omits the letter *lamed* from the term "to his kinsman [*leshe'ero*]." **Rather, Rava said: This** is what the verse **is saying: And you shall give the inheritance of his kinsman** [*she'ero*] **to him.** The letters should be arranged differently, removing the letter *lamed* from the word *leshe'ero* and the letter *vav* from the word *naḥalato* and combining them to form the word *lo*, meaning: To him. Accordingly, the verse teaches that a husband inherits from his wife. The Gemara explains that Rava **holds that** the Sages **subtract and add and interpret homiletically,**[N] meaning that letters can be removed from words and appended to each other, and a *halakha* can be derived from the new word formed by the combination of letters.

וְהַאי תַּנָּא מַיְיתֵי לָהּ מֵהָכָא, דְּתַנְיָא: ״וְיָרַשׁ אוֹתָהּ״ – מְלַמֵּד שֶׁהַבַּעַל יוֹרֵשׁ אֶת אִשְׁתּוֹ, דִּבְרֵי רַבִּי עֲקִיבָא.

The Gemara comments: **And this** *tanna* **cites** the *halakha* that a husband inherits from his wife **from here, as it is taught** in a *baraita*: **"And he shall inherit it,"** with the word "it" written in the feminine "*otah*," which can also be translated as: Her. This **teaches that a husband inherits** from **his wife;** this is **the statement of Rabbi Akiva,** similar to the derivation cited in the *baraita* above.

רַבִּי יִשְׁמָעֵאל אוֹמֵר: אֵינוֹ צָרִיךְ, הֲרֵי הוּא אוֹמֵר: ״וְכָל בַּת יֹרֶשֶׁת נַחֲלָה מִמַּטּוֹת בְּנֵי יִשְׂרָאֵל לְאֶחָד מִמִּשְׁפַּחַת״ וגו׳, בְּהַסָּבַת הַבַּעַל הַכָּתוּב מְדַבֵּר;

The *baraita* quotes another *tanna*. **Rabbi Yishmael says:** This derivation **is not necessary,**[N] as the verse **states: "And every daughter who possesses an inheritance from the tribes of the children of Israel** shall be wife **to one of the family** of the tribe of her father" (Numbers 36:8). The purpose of this mitzva was so that the land she inherited from her father's tribe will not be transferred to another tribe upon her death. **The verse speaks of a transfer** of inheritance from one tribe to another **by means of the husband,** i.e., she must not marry a man from another tribe so that the land will not be transferred to that tribe when her husband inherits from her upon her death. This indicates that a husband inherits from his wife.

NOTES

And a man with regard to his wife – וְהָאִישׁ אֶת אִשְׁתּוֹ: The Rashbam and other early commentaries write that the *halakha* that a husband inherits from his wife is not due to their family tie but due to a Torah edict. Therefore, even if the wife has a son, her husband, not her son, inherits from her. It appears from the Gemara's discussion here that there is no clear proof from the verses themselves that a husband inherits from his wife.

The Rambam writes that it is *midivrei Soferim*, a *halakha* of the Sages. Although it is at times unclear what the Rambam means when using this term, as he does not always mean that it is by rabbinic law but merely that it is not explicitly mentioned in the Torah, the *Kesef Mishne* provides a proof that the Rambam is of the opinion that the *halakha* that a husband inherits from his wife is indeed by rabbinic law. By contrast, the Ra'avad and other authorities are of the opinion that it is by Torah law. The Ramah explains that according to the *tanna* of this *baraita*, the *halakha* that a husband inherits from his wife is a *halakha* transmitted to Moses from Sinai.

Subtract and add and interpret homiletically – גּוֹרְעִין וּמוֹסִיפִין וְדוֹרְשִׁין: The Ramah explains that this method of interpretation is employed with regard to *halakhot* that were transmitted to Moses from Sinai whose sources are unknown.

The early commentaries are puzzled by Rava's interpretation, as he had just challenged Abaye's interpretation, saying that one cannot cut up verses with a knife, as it were, then he proceeded to do the same. The Rashbam explains that the main thrust of Rava's interpretation is not the adding and subtracting of letters but offering an alternative understanding. This is similar to the explanation of Rabbeinu Hananel, who says that subtracting and adding homiletically does not mean that the actual verse is modified. Rather, the Gemara is saying that this interpretation of the verse is possible only in the original Hebrew, but the verse cannot be translated in a manner that adheres to both the straightforward meaning and the homiletical interpretation.

In an alternative explanation, the Rashbam writes that Rava is in fact adding and subtracting, but his modification of the verse is not as extreme as Abaye's. As long as one does not transpose entire words, but merely transposes letters, it is considered adding and subtracting, which is acceptable. The Ri Migash explains that Abaye's interpretation of the verse is vastly more radical than that of Rava in that he not only deletes letters and transposes words, he also divides the verse into two topics, one topic of passing the inheritance to a relative and the other of the husband's right to inherit from his wife. By contrast, Rava keeps the verse as discussing a single topic, does not transpose words, and does not even delete letters from the verse.

Is not necessary – אֵינוֹ צָרִיךְ: Rabbi Yishmael, in accordance with his general methodology, is of the opinion that the Torah speaks in the language of people. This means that the methodology that utilizes changing the order of letters or words is inappropriate. He holds that the *halakha* with regard to the husband's inheritance can be derived from several verses in the Bible itself. Although the *halakha* is not written explicitly, one can discern that it is an assumption underlying the entire passage detailing the *halakhot* of inheritance of land.

HALAKHA

A husband inherits from his wife – הַבַּעַל יוֹרֵשׁ אֶת אִשְׁתּוֹ: A husband inherits from his wife. This includes her usufruct property, even if the husband is not entitled to receive the profits (*Sma*), as well as her guaranteed property. He takes precedence over any other relative. According to the Rambam, the husband's right to inherit from his wife is by rabbinic law, but the Sages reinforced their ordinances by imposing upon them the severity of Torah law (*Beit Yosef*; *Derisha*). The Ra'avad holds that the husband's right to inherit from his wife is by Torah law (Rambam *Sefer Mishpatim*, *Hilkhot Naḥalot* 1:8, 6:8 and *Sefer Nashim*, *Hilkhot Ishut* 12:3, 9, 22:1; *Shulḥan Arukh*, *Even HaEzer* 57:1, 69:3, 90:1.

But she does not inherit from him – וְאֵין הִיא יוֹרֶשֶׁת אוֹתוֹ: A wife does not inherit from her husband (Rambam *Sefer Mishpatim*, *Hilkhot Naḥalot* 1:8).

וְאוֹמֵר: ״וְלֹא תִסֹּב נַחֲלָה לִבְנֵי יִשְׂרָאֵל מִמַּטֶּה אֶל מַטֶּה״; וְאוֹמֵר: ״וְלֹא תִסֹּב נַחֲלָה מִמַּטֶּה לְמַטֶּה אַחֵר״;

Rabbi Yishmael continues: **And** another verse **states: "So shall no inheritance of the children of Israel transfer from tribe to tribe"** (Numbers 36:7), **and** another verse **states: "So shall no inheritance transfer from one tribe to another tribe"** (Numbers 36:9), also indicating that a husband inherits from his wife.

וְאוֹמֵר: ״וְאֶלְעָזָר בֶּן אַהֲרֹן מֵת וַיִּקְבְּרוּ אֹתוֹ בְּגִבְעַת פִּנְחָס בְּנוֹ״, וְכִי מִנַּיִן לְפִנְחָס שֶׁלֹּא הָיָה לוֹ לְאֶלְעָזָר? אֶלָּא, מְלַמֵּד שֶׁנָּשָׂא פִּנְחָס אִשָּׁה וּמֵתָה וִירָשָׁהּ;

Rabbi Yishmael continues: **And** the verse in the Prophets **states: "And Elazar, the son of Aaron, died; and they buried him in the Hill of Pinehas his son,** which was given him in Mount Ephraim" (Joshua 24:33). **And from where** did **Pinehas have**[N] land **that** his father, **Elazar, did not have? Rather,** this **teaches that Pinehas married a woman** who inherited her father's land, **and she died and he inherited** from **her** so that he had his own land. This also indicates that a husband inherits from his wife.

וְאוֹמֵר: ״וּשְׂגוּב הוֹלִיד אֶת יָאִיר וַיְהִי לוֹ עֶשְׂרִים וְשָׁלֹשׁ עָרִים בְּאֶרֶץ הַגִּלְעָד״,

Rabbi Yishmael continues. **And** the verse in the Writings **states: "And Seguv begot Yair, who had twenty-three cities in the land of Gilead"** (1 Chronicles 2:22).

NOTES

From where did Pinehas have, etc. – מִנַּיִן לְפִנְחָס וכו׳: Even assuming that Eretz Yisrael was divided according to those who entered the land and not according to those who left Egypt (see 117a), one cannot say that Pinehas, who was an adult when the Jews entered Eretz Yisrael, received land in his own right. This is due to the fact that Pinehas was a priest, and the priests received their inheritance in specially designated cities. No priestly city was located within the land of the tribe of Ephraim. Therefore, if Pinehas had land, it could have been only from another source of inheritance (Ra'avad).

Perek **VIII**
Daf **112** Amud **a**

וְכִי מִנַּיִן לְיָאִיר שֶׁלֹּא הָיָה לוֹ לִשְׂגוּב? מְלַמֵּד שֶׁנָּשָׂא יָאִיר אִשָּׁה וּמֵתָה וִירָשָׁהּ.

And from where did **Yair have**[N] land **that** his father, **Seguv, did not have?** Rather, this **teaches that Yair married a woman** who inherited her father's land, **and she died and he inherited** from **her** so that he had his own land. This also indicates that a husband inherits from his wife.

מַאי ״וְאוֹמֵר״? וְכִי תֵּימָא: בְּסִבַּת הַבֵּן קָא קָפֵיד קְרָא, אֲבָל בַּעַל לָא יָרֵית – תָּא שְׁמַע: ״וְלֹא תִסֹּב נַחֲלָה לִבְנֵי יִשְׂרָאֵל מִמַּטֶּה לְמַטֶּה״;

The Gemara proceeds to explain this *baraita*. **What** is the meaning of: **And it states?** Why is it necessary to provide additional proofs beyond the first verse? The Gemara explains: The first verse seems to prove the *halakha* that a husband inherits from his wife. **And if you would say** that the **verse** that rules that a woman who inherited land from her father cannot marry a man from another tribe is not concerned that he will inherit from her, but rather the verse **is concerned about a transfer** of inheritance from one tribe to another by means of **the son** who will inherit from his mother, as he belongs to his father's tribe, **but a husband does not inherit** from his wife; therefore, **come** and **hear** another verse that is seemingly superfluous: **"So shall no inheritance of the children of Israel transfer from tribe to tribe"** (Numbers 36:7). This teaches that a transfer of land could occur by means of the husband inheriting from her.

וְכִי תֵּימָא: לַעֲבוֹר עָלָיו בְּלָאו וַעֲשֵׂה – תָּא שְׁמַע: ״לֹא תִסֹּב נַחֲלָה מִמַּטֶּה לְמַטֶּה אַחֵר״;

And if you would say that this verse is also concerned with the transfer of the inheritance by means of the son, and that the seemingly superfluous verse is stated for another purpose, i.e., in order to establish that a woman who inherited land from her father and marries a man from another tribe **will violate for that** act **a prohibition,** namely: "So shall no inheritance of the children of Israel transfer," **and a positive mitzva,** namely: "Shall be wife to one of the family of the tribe of her father"; therefore, **come** and **hear** another verse that is seemingly superfluous: **"So shall no inheritance transfer from one tribe to another tribe"** (Numbers 36:9), which teaches that a transfer can occur by means of the husband inheriting from his wife.

וְכִי תֵּימָא: לַעֲבוֹר עָלָיו בִּשְׁנֵי לָאוִין וַעֲשֵׂה – תָּא שְׁמַע: ״וְאֶלְעָזָר בֶּן אַהֲרֹן מֵת״ וגו׳;

And if you would say that this verse is also concerned with the transfer of the inheritance by means of the son, and that the seemingly superfluous verse is stated for another purpose, i.e., in order to establish that a woman who inherited land from her father and marries a man from another tribe **violates for that** act **two prohibitions and a positive mitzva;** therefore, **come** and **hear** another proof that a husband inherits from his wife, from the verse: **"And Elazar, the son of Aaron, died"** (Joshua 24:33).

NOTES

And from where did Yair have, etc. – וְכִי מִנַּיִן לְיָאִיר וכו׳: *Tosafot* ask: If Eretz Yisrael was divided according to those who initially entered the land (see 117a), it is possible that Yair, who was of that generation, would have his own inheritance of land that he did not receive from his father. Why does the Gemara not consider this possibility? The Ramah suggests that Yair was actually born after the Jews entered Eretz Yisrael.

וְכִי תֵּימָא: אֶלְעָזָר הוּא דִּנְסִיב אִיתְּתָא, וּמֵתָה וְיָרְתָהּ פִּנְחָס – תָּא שְׁמַע: "וּשְׂגוּב הוֹלִיד אֶת יָאִיר" וגו׳.

And if you would say that Pinehas did not inherit this land from his wife, but from his mother, as **it was Elazar,** his father, **who married a woman** who inherited land, **and she** subsequently **died, and** her son **Pinehas inherited** from **her** so that this verse proves the inheritance of a son and not that of a husband; therefore, **come** and **hear** a proof from the verse: **"And Seguv begot Yair"** (I Chronicles 2:22).

וְכִי תֵּימָא: הָתָם נַמִי הָכִי הוּא – אִם כֵּן תְּרֵי קְרָאֵי לָמָּה לִי?

And if you would say: That is the case **there as well,** that it was Yair who inherited it from his deceased mother, **if so, why do I** need **two verses** to teach the same *halakha*? This concludes the Gemara's explanation of the *baraita*.

אֲמַר לֵיהּ רַב פַּפָּא לְאַבַּיֵי: מִמַּאי? דִּלְמָא לְעוֹלָם אֵימָא לָךְ: בַּעַל לָא יָרֵית, וּקְרָאֵי בְּסִבַּת הַבֵּן כִּדְשַׁנֵּינַן, וְיָאִיר – דִּזְבֵין מִיזְבַּן, וּפִנְחָס נַמִי – דִּזְבֵין מִיזְבַּן!

Rav Pappa said to Abaye: From where do you know that this is how the verse should be understood? **Perhaps I** could **actually say to you: A husband does not inherit** from his wife, **and the verses are** concerned **about a transfer** of inheritance from one tribe to another by means of **the son, as we explained,** teaching that one who does so violates two prohibitions and a positive mitzva. **And** with regard to **Yair,** one could say **that he purchased** it from a third party and did not inherit it. **And** with regard to **Pinehas as well,** one could say **that he purchased** it from a third party.

אֲמַר לֵיהּ: פִּנְחָס דִּזְבֵין מִיזְבַּן לָא מָצֵית אָמְרַתְּ, דְּאִם כֵּן, נִמְצֵאת שָׂדֶה חוֹזֶרֶת בַּיּוֹבֵל, וְנִמְצָא צַדִּיק קָבוּר בְּקֶבֶר שֶׁאֵינוֹ שֶׁלּוֹ.

Abaye **said to him: You cannot say that Pinehas purchased** the land where he buried his father, **as if so,** the **field would return** to its original owner **in the Jubilee** Year (see Leviticus, chapter 25), **and it would be found** that this **righteous man,** i.e., Elazar, **is buried**[N] **in a** grave in land **that is not his.**

אֶלָּא אֵימָא: דְּנָפְלָה לֵיהּ מִשְּׂדֵה חֲרָמִים!

Rav Pappa asked further: **Rather, say that** in his capacity as a priest **he came into** possession of this land **as a dedicated field.**[N] Pinehas, as a priest, may have owned the land by that means. Therefore, one can still say that a husband does not inherit from his wife, and the verses are concerned about a transfer of inheritance from one tribe to another by means of the son.

אֲמַר אַבַּיֵי: סוֹף סוֹף הָא קָא מִתְעַקְּרָא נַחֲלָה מִשִּׁבְטָא דְּאִימָּא לְשִׁבְטָא דְּאַבָּא.

Abaye said: Even if you say that her son and not her husband inherits from her, **ultimately** the **inheritance is uprooted**[N] **from the tribe of the mother and is moved to the tribe of the father,** and the prohibition against her marrying a man from another tribe is not effective in achieving its goal. The verse speaks of a woman who inherited the land from her mother who is of a different tribe from her father (see 111a). Even if she marries a man from her own tribe, the inheritance will be transferred from her mother's tribe to that of her, the woman's, husband, as even if the woman's son inherits, he is of his father's tribe.

NOTES

It would be found that this righteous man is buried, etc. – **נִמְצָא צַדִּיק קָבוּר וכו׳**: It is mentioned in several places (see, e.g., 100a) that people took great care to make sure they were buried in the graves of their ancestors and not in land belonging to strangers. See the Responsa of the *Ḥatam Sofer*, who writes that this Gemara is the source for the statement that one should purchase a burial plot for himself so as not to be buried in property that is not his own. With regard to Elazar, although he was not buried in his own land, since he was buried in his son's land it is not considered a disgrace (*Tosafot Yeshanim*).

As a dedicated field – **מִשְּׂדֵה חֲרָמִים**: If one dedicates an item to God and does not explicitly state that he is consecrating it for the purpose of Temple maintenance, it becomes the property of the priests, as the verse states: "Everything devoted in Israel shall be yours" (Numbers 18:14). This type of consecrated property is referred to in the Mishna as *ḥermei kohanim* (*Arakhin* 28b).

The Rashbam offers another explanation: The Gemara is referring to an ancestral field that was consecrated but was not redeemed before the Jubilee Year. It is then given to the priests. This explanation is opposed by the Ramban, who proves from *Seder Olam* that the Jubilee Year was not practiced until after the death of Elazar.

Ultimately the inheritance is uprooted – **סוֹף סוֹף הָא קָא מִתְעַקְּרָא נַחֲלָה**: The early commentaries disagree with regard to the meaning of this passage. There are two basic versions of the text, and the text here combines elements of both and can be interpreted in either direction (see Rabbeinu Gershom). All agree that Abaye's statement assumes that the biblical passage concerning the transfer of inheritance is discussing a woman who inherits land from two tribes, as the *baraita* (111a) explained. The disagreement is: In reference to what inheritance did Abaye made his statement?

The Ri Migash here, as well as the Rashbam on 112b, is of the opinion that Abaye's statement is not meant as a response to Rav Pappa's statement but rather raises an independent difficulty concerning the verses. When a woman inherits from two tribes, a transfer of land is inevitable whether her husband or her son inherit from her. Even if she marries a man from her father's tribe, because her mother is from another tribe, the land from her mother's tribe is eventually transferred away from its original tribe. This explanation accords with the standard version of the text, which reads: Abaye said.

Another version of the text reads: Abaye said to him, meaning, he said to Rav Pappa. According to this version, Abaye's statement is a continuation of the discussion between Abaye and Rav Pappa, and Abaye is responding to Rav Pappa's suggestion that the verse is dealing with the transfer by means of the son. Abaye claims that if in fact the verse speaks of transfer via the husband, it is possible to prevent the transfer of the inheritance beyond what occurred when this woman's mother married a man from another tribe, as Rav Ashi will later explain. But if it speaks of transfer via the son, the inheritance will be transferred in any case, because the son's lineage follows that of his father exclusively. This is the explanation of *Tosafot*, Rabbi Avraham *Av Beit Din*, *Ba'al HaMaor*, and Rabbeinu Gershom, according to the standard version of his commentary.

וּמִמַּאי? וְדִלְמָא שָׁאנֵי הָתָם, שֶׁכְּבָר הוּסְבָה! אֲמַר לֵיהּ: שֶׁכְּבָר הוּסְבָה לָא אָמְרִינַן.

Rav Pappa rejects this: **And from where** do you raise your challenge? **But perhaps** it **is different there, as** the inheritance **had already been transferred** by the mother of the woman when she married the father, so that the Torah is no longer concerned with the continued transfer. When the parents of this now-deceased woman married, the land that her mother would eventually inherit was already thought of as being transferred away from the ownership of her mother's tribe. Therefore, the fact that even if this woman's son inherits from her, the fact that the land will permanently belong to a member of her husband's tribe is of no concern. Abaye **said to him: We do not say,** i.e., employ, the logic of: **As it had already been transferred,** since as long as this woman owned it, it still belonged to a person of the first tribe.

אֲמַר לֵיהּ רַב יֵימָר לְרַב אַשִׁי: אִי אָמְרַתְּ בִּשְׁלָמָא שֶׁכְּבָר הוּסְבָה, הַיְינוּ דְּמִתּוֹקְמָא קְרָא בֵּין בְּסִבַּת הַבֵּן בֵּין בְּסִבַּת הַבַּעַל,

Rav Yeimar said to Rav Ashi:[N] Even according to Abaye, who holds the verses teach that the husband inherits, there is still a difficulty. **Granted, if you say** the logic of: **As it has already been transferred, this is** how it can be understood **that the verse is established** as referring to both scenarios: The verse can be understood **either with regard to a transfer** by means of **the son** or **with regard to a transfer** by means of **the husband.** In both of these scenarios, the daughter's marriage to a man from her father's tribe is effective in ensuring that land she will inherit will not leave the tribe, because if she inherited it from her father it remains within the same tribe, and if she inherited it from her mother it had already been transferred when her mother married her father.

אֶלָּא אִי אָמְרַתְּ לָא אָמְרִינַן שֶׁכְּבָר הוּסְבָה, כִּי מִינַּסְבָא לְאֶחָד מִמִּשְׁפַּחַת מַטֵּה אָבִיהָ מַאי הָוֵה? הָא מִתְעַקְרָא נַחֲלָה מִשִּׁבְטָא דְאִימָּא לְשִׁבְטָא דְאַבָּא!

But if you say that **we do not say** the logic of: **As it has already been transferred,** then even **when she gets married to one of the family of the tribe of her father, what of it? But an inheritance is uprooted from the tribe of** her **mother,** who had inherited land from her, the mother's, father, **to the tribe of** her **father,** as her husband is from her father's tribe.

דְּמַנְסְבִינַן לָהּ לְגַבְרָא, דַּאֲבוּהִי מִשִּׁבְטָא דַּאֲבוּהָ וְאִימֵּיהּ מִשִּׁבְטָא דְאִימָּהּ.

Rav Ashi said to him: There is a way that the transfer to another tribe can be avoided: **Where we marry her to a man**[N] **whose father** is **from her father's tribe and his mother is from her mother's tribe,** the transfer is avoided as the land retains the exact status as it had when it was in the woman's possession.

Perek **VIII**
Daf **112** Amud **b**

אִי הָכִי, הַאי "לְאֶחָד מִמִּשְׁפַּחַת מַטֵּה אָבִיהָ וְאִמָּהּ" מִיבָּעֵי לֵיהּ! אִי כְּתִיב הָכִי, הֲוָה אָמִינָא אֲפִילּוּ אִיפְּכָא, קָא מַשְׁמַע לַן.

The Gemara asks: **If so,** if a daughter who inherits land from both of her parents must marry a man whose father is from her father's tribe and whose mother is from her mother's tribe, **this** verse: "Shall be a wife to one of the family of the tribe of her father" (Numbers 36:8), **should have** said: Shall be a wife **to one of the family of the tribe of her father and her mother.** The Gemara replies: **If** it **were written like this, I would say** that **even the opposite** is permitted, that she may marry a man whose mother is from her father's tribe and whose father is from her mother's tribe. As long as she marries someone who is connected to both tribes, it is permitted. The verse therefore **teaches us** that the opposite is not permitted.

תַּנְיָא בְּסִבַּת הַבֵּן, וְתַנְיָא בְּסִבַּת הַבַּעַל. תַּנְיָא בְּסִבַּת הַבֵּן: "וְלֹא תִסֹּב נַחֲלָה לִבְנֵי יִשְׂרָאֵל מִמַּטֶּה אֶל מַטֶּה" – בְּסִבַּת הַבֵּן הַכָּתוּב מְדַבֵּר;

The Gemara comments: Concerning the marriage of a woman who inherited land, it **is taught** in a *baraita* **with regard to the transfer** of the inheritance **by means of the son, and it is taught** in a *baraita* **with regard to the transfer** of the inheritance **by means of the husband.** The Gemara presents the *baraitot*: A *baraita* **is taught with regard to the transfer** of the inheritance **by means of the son,** as follows: **"So shall no inheritance of the children of Israel transfer from tribe to tribe"** (Numbers 36:7); that **verse speaks of** the transfer of the inheritance **by means of the son.** The Torah prohibits the woman from marrying a man from a different tribe since her son will inherit from her and thereby the inheritance will transfer away from its original tribe.

NOTES

Rav Yeimar said to Rav Ashi – אֲמַר לֵיהּ רַב יֵימָר לְרַב אַשִׁי: It appears that Rav Yeimar's statement is merely a repetition of Abaye's question; this is how the Ri Migash explains it. The Rashbam explains that Abaye was uncertain whether one says the logic of: As it has already been transferred, but Rav Yeimar was definitive in the matter.

We marry her to a man, etc. – מַנְסְבִינַן לָהּ לְגַבְרָא וכו׳: The Ri Migash notes that even though if the husband were to predecease the wife, in which case her son will inherit from her, and in this case both of the son's parents are from the same tribe, nevertheless, the fact that his maternal grandmother is from the other tribe is sufficient to render this as not being an absolute transfer.

אַתָּה אוֹמֵר: בְּסִבַּת הַבֵּן, אוֹ אֵינוֹ אֶלָּא בְּסִבַּת הַבַּעַל? כְּשֶׁהוּא אוֹמֵר "וְלֹא תִסֹּב נַחֲלָה מִמַּטֶּה לְמַטֶּה אַחֵר" – הֲרֵי בְּסִבַּת הַבַּעַל אָמוּר, הָא מָה אֲנִי מְקַיֵּים "וְלֹא תִסֹּב נַחֲלָה לִבְנֵי יִשְׂרָאֵל מִמַּטֶּה אֶל מַטֶּה" – בְּסִבַּת הַבֵּן הַכָּתוּב מְדַבֵּר.

Do you say that this is **with regard to the transfer** of the inheritance **by means of the son, or is it only with regard to the transfer** of the inheritance **by means of the husband? When it says: "So shall no inheritance transfer from one tribe to another tribe"** (Numbers 36:9), the verse is **speaking with regard to** the **transfer** of the inheritance **by means of the husband. How do I realize** the meaning of the verse: **"So shall no inheritance of the children of Israel transfer from tribe to tribe"** (Numbers 36:7)? That **verse speaks of** the **transfer** of the inheritance **by means of the son.**

Perek **VIII**
Daf **113** Amud **a**

תַּנְיָא אִידָּךְ: "וְלֹא תִסֹּב נַחֲלָה מִמַּטֶּה לְמַטֶּה אַחֵר" – בְּסִיבַּת הַבַּעַל הַכָּתוּב מְדַבֵּר;

It **is taught** in **another** *baraita*:[N] **"So shall no inheritance transfer from one tribe to another tribe"** (Numbers 36:9); **the verse speaks** of the **transfer** of the inheritance **by means of the husband.** The Torah prohibits the woman from marrying a man from a different tribe since her husband will inherit from her, thereby transferring her inheritance away from its original tribe.

אַתָּה אוֹמֵר: בְּסִיבַּת הַבַּעַל, אוֹ אֵינוֹ אֶלָּא בְּסִיבַּת הַבֵּן? כְּשֶׁהוּא אוֹמֵר: "וְלֹא תִסֹּב נַחֲלָה לִבְנֵי יִשְׂרָאֵל מִמַּטֶּה אֶל מַטֶּה" – הֲרֵי הַסִיבַּת הַבֵּן אָמוּר, הָא מָה אֲנִי מְקַיֵּים "וְלֹא תִסֹּב נַחֲלָה מִמַּטֶּה לְמַטֶּה אַחֵר" – בְּסִיבַּת הַבַּעַל הַכָּתוּב מְדַבֵּר.

Do you say that this is **with regard to** the **transfer** of the inheritance **by means of the husband, or is it only with regard to** the **transfer** of the inheritance **by means of the son? When it says: "So shall no inheritance of the children of Israel transfer from tribe to tribe"** (Numbers 36:7), the verse is **speaking with regard to** the **transfer** of the inheritance **by means of the son. How do I realize** the meaning of the verse: **"So shall no inheritance transfer from one tribe to another tribe"** (Numbers 36:9)? That **verse speaks of** the **transfer** of the inheritance **by means of the husband.**

דְּכוּלֵּי עָלְמָא מִיהַת, "מִמַּטֶּה לְמַטֶּה אַחֵר" – בְּסִיבַּת הַבַּעַל הַכָּתוּב מְדַבֵּר, מַאי מַשְׁמַע? (סִימָן) אָמַר רַבָּה בַּר רַב שֵׁילָא, אָמַר קְרָא: "אִישׁ". תַּרְוַיְיהוּ "אִישׁ" כְּתִיב בְּהוּ!

The Gemara comments: **In any event, according to everyone,**[N] i.e., according to both *baraitot*, the phrase in **the verse "from one tribe to another tribe" speaks of** the **transfer** of the inheritance **by means of the husband.** The Gemara asks: **From where is this inferred?** The Gemara supplies **a mnemonic.**[N] **Rabba bar Rav Sheila said** that the latter part of **the verse states:** "So shall no inheritance transfer from one tribe to another tribe; for the tribes of the children of Israel shall cleave **each one** [*ish*] to its own inheritance," alluding to the transfer by means of the husband, as the word "*ish*" means husband, in the context of: "Elimelech the husband [*ish*] of Naomi" (Ruth 1:3). The Gemara asks: But the word **"*ish*" is written in both**[N] of the verses. Therefore, both verses should be interpreted with regard to the transfer of the inheritance by means of the husband.

NOTES

It is taught in another *baraita*, etc. – תַּנְיָא אִידָּךְ וכו׳: This version of the text is the same as the one the Rashbam, the Ramah, and the Rid had. According to this version, there are two *baraitot* that both arrive at the same conclusion, that the first verse (Numbers 36:7) speaks of a transfer due to the son and the second verse (Numbers 36:9) speaks of a transfer due to the husband. The difference between the *baraitot* is that the first *baraita* assumes that the phrase "another tribe" indicates that the second verse is referring to the husband, and the first verse must then refer to the son, while the second *baraita* begins with the assumption that each of the verses would in and of itself refer to the son, as he is a closer relative, and the second, superfluous verse must then refer to the husband.

In any event, according to everyone – דְּכוּלֵּי עָלְמָא מִיהַת: As explained in the previous note, the inference that the verse: "So shall no inheritance transfer from one tribe to another tribe" (Numbers 36:9), is referring to the husband is correct only according to the first *baraita*. Accordingly, the Rashbam explains that while the entire sentence: In any event, according to everyone, the verse "from one tribe to another tribe" speaks of transfer of the inheritance by means of the husband, is true of both *baraitot*, the subsequent question: From where is this inferred, is asked only according to the first *baraita*.

The Gemara supplies a mnemonic [*siman*] – סִימָן: The term mnemonic seems out of place here, as there is no mnemonic presented in the Gemara. Indeed, there are some manuscripts in which it does not appear. The *Masoret HaShas* understands that the word *siman* is actually the name of a Sage, as a similar name, Simon, frequently appears in midrashic sources and in the Jerusalem Talmud. Others suggest that there was a mnemonic recorded in the Gemara here but it was later deleted. The Ya'avetz attempts to reconstruct the mnemonic, and suggests that it was: *Aleph, yod, mem, mem*; which is a mnemonic for the words *ish*, *yidbeku*, *matot*, *mimateh*, which are words from the verses from which the Sages derive the *halakhot* of the transfer of inheritance.

***Ish* is written in both, etc.** – אִישׁ תַּרְוַיְיהוּ אִישׁ כְּתִיב בְּהוּ וכו׳: Both verses include the word "*ish*" and the word "cleave"; how is it that the Gemara seems not to know this at the outset? *Tosafot* comment that the *amora'im* did not always remember biblical verses by heart. *Tosefot Rosh* explains similarly. The Rashbam is of the opinion that the *amora'im* were certainly proficient in all biblical verses and were aware that those words appeared in the first verse as well. Nevertheless, they thought the verse referred to the transfer of inheritance by means of a son, and the words "*ish*" and "cleave" were written to teach some other *halakhot*. The Gemara then challenges that this assumption cannot be the basis for inferring that the verse is referring to the transfer of inheritance by means of a husband (see Ritva).

אֶלָּא אֲמַר רַב נַחְמָן בַּר יִצְחָק, אָמַר קְרָא: "יִדְבְּקוּ". תַּרְוַיְיהוּ "יִדְבְּקוּ" כְּתִיב בְּהוּ!

Rather, Rav Naḥman bar Yitzḥak said a different explanation. **The verse states: "Shall cleave,"** and this term alludes to marriage, as in the context of: "And he shall cleave to his wife" (Genesis 2:24). The Gemara raises a difficulty: But the term **"shall cleave" is written in both of** the verses. Therefore, both verses should be interpreted with regard to the transfer of the inheritance by means of the husband.

אֶלָּא אֲמַר רָבָא, אָמַר קְרָא: "יִדְבְּקוּ מַטּוֹת". רַב אַשִׁי אֲמַר, אָמַר קְרָא: "מִמַּטֶּה לְמַטֶּה אַחֵר", וּבֵן לָאו אַחֵר הוּא.

Rather, Rava said a different explanation: The **verse states: "The tribes** of the children of Israel **shall cleave,"** and tribes cleave to one another through marriage. **Rav Ashi said** another explanation: The **verse states: "From one tribe to another tribe," and a son is not** considered **"another,"** as he is an extension of his mother.

אָמַר רַבִּי אַבָּהוּ אָמַר רַבִּי יוֹחָנָן אָמַר רַבִּי יַנַּאי אָמַר רַבִּי, וּמָטוּ בָּהּ מִשְּׁמֵיהּ דְּרַבִּי יְהוֹשֻׁעַ בֶּן קָרְחָה: מִנַּיִן לְבַעַל שֶׁאֵינוֹ נוֹטֵל בְּרָאוּי כְּבְמוּחְזָק? שֶׁנֶּאֱמַר: "וּשְׂגוּב הוֹלִיד אֶת יָאִיר וַיְהִי לוֹ עֶשְׂרִים וְשָׁלוֹשׁ עָרִים בְּאֶרֶץ הַגִּלְעָד", מִנַּיִן לְיָאִיר שֶׁלֹּא הָיָה לוֹ לִשְׂגוּב? אֶלָּא, מְלַמֵּד שֶׁנָּשָׂא שְׂגוּב אִשָּׁה וּמֵתָה בְּחַיֵּי מוֹרִישֶׁיהָ, וּמֵתוּ מוֹרִישֶׁיהָ וִירָשָׁהּ יָאִיר;

§ **Rabbi Abbahu says** that **Rabbi Yoḥanan says** that **Rabbi Yannai says** that Rabbi Yehuda HaNasi **says, and** some **determined it** was **in the name of Rabbi Yehoshua ben Korḥa: From where** is it derived **that a husband** who inherits from his wife does not **take in** inheritance the property **due**[H] to the deceased **as** he does the property she **possessed?**[N] Instead of the husband inheriting the property that was due to her, that property is inherited by her other relatives, such as her son, or other relatives of her father. **As it is stated: "And Seguv begot Yair, who had twenty three cities in the land of Gilead"** (1 Chronicles 2:22). The Gemara asks: **From where** did **Yair have** land **that** his father, **Seguv, did not have? Rather,** this **teaches that Seguv married** a **woman and she died in the lifetime of her** potential **legators, and her legators** then **died, and Yair,** her son, not Seguv, her husband, **inherited** these inheritances from **her.**

וְאוֹמֵר: "וְאֶלְעָזָר בֶּן אַהֲרֹן מֵת וַיִּקְבְּרוּ" וגו׳, מִנַּיִן לְפִנְחָס שֶׁלֹּא הָיָה לוֹ לְאֶלְעָזָר? מְלַמֵּד שֶׁנָּשָׂא אֶלְעָזָר אִשָּׁה וּמֵתָה בְּחַיֵּי מוֹרִישֶׁיהָ, וּמֵתוּ מוֹרִישֶׁיהָ וִירָשָׁהּ פִּנְחָס.

And it is stated: "And Elazar, the son of Aaron, died; and they buried him in the Hill of Pinehas his son" (Joshua 24:33). **From where** did **Pinehas have** land **that** his father, **Elazar, did not have?** Rather, this **teaches that Elazar married a woman and she died in the lifetime of her** potential **legators, and her legators** then **died, and Pinehas** her son, not Elazar her husband, **inherited** the property from **her.**

וּמַאי "וְאוֹמֵר"? וְכִי תֵּימָא: יָאִיר דַּהֲוָה נְסֵיב אִיתְּתָא וּמֵתָה וִירִתָהּ – תַּלְמוּד לוֹמַר: "וְאֶלְעָזָר בֶּן אַהֲרֹן מֵת"; וְכִי תֵּימָא: דְּנָפְלָה לֵיהּ בִּשְׂדֵה חֲרָמִים – אָמַר קְרָא: "בְּנוֹ", נַחֲלָה הָרְאוּיָה לוֹ, וִירָשָׁהּ בְּנוֹ.

And what is the meaning of: **And it is stated?** Why is it necessary to provide an additional proof beyond the first verse? The Gemara explains. **And if you would say:** In the verse concerning Seguv and Yair, it is **Yair,** not Seguv, **who married a woman and she died and he inherited** from **her,** and he did not inherit from his mother, **the verse states: "And Elazar, the son of Aaron, died;** and they buried him in the Hill of Pinehas his son" (Joshua 24:33), teaching that Pinehas inherited the land of those from whom his mother inherited, and Elazar did not. **And if you would say that** this land **came into** the possession of Pinehas **as a dedicated field,** as he was a priest, and he did not inherit it from his mother, **the verse states: "His son,"**[N] indicating that it was **an inheritance that was fitting for him,** i.e., Elazar, had his wife not predeceased her legators, **and his son inherited it.**

"וּבְנֵי אֲחוֹת". תָּנָא: בְּנֵי אָחוֹת, וְלֹא בְּנוֹת אָחוֹת.

§ The mishna teaches: **And sons of sisters,**[H] i.e., nephews born to the sisters of the deceased, inherit from their maternal uncles but do not bequeath to them. **It is taught** in a *baraita*: This *halakha* applies to **sons of sisters but not** to **daughters of sisters.**

NOTES

A husband does not take in inheritance the property due to the deceased as he does the property she possessed – **בַּעַל שֶׁאֵינוֹ נוֹטֵל בְּרָאוּי כְּבְמוּחְזָק:** The Gemara is referring to property that his wife would have received as an inheritance but which she did not inherit in her lifetime since she predeceased her legators. In this event, her husband does not inherit the property when her relatives eventually die. Rather, if she left descendants, they inherit the property, and if she had none, a relative of her legator inherits it.

Tosafot comment: Since her son would inherit this property while her husband would not, it should follow that her son, as her closer relative, should precede her husband in inheriting her own property as well. They explain that the inheritance a husband receives of his wife's property is not an indication that he is a closer relative but is an independent *halakha*, which applies only with regard to certain types of property.

The verse states, his son – **אָמַר קְרָא, בְּנוֹ:** The Rashbam explains that the phrase written with regard to Pinehas' inheritance: "Which was given him in Mount Ephraim" (Joshua 24:33), indicates that this land was given to him by an order of the court, even though Elazar had a potential right to inherit it. Rabbeinu Hananel explains that this is derived from the phrase "Pinehas his son." As it is known that Pinehas was Elazar's son, the phrase seems redundant. Its role is to teach that Elazar had a potential right to inherit that property, but he did not inherit it because a husband does not inherit property merely due his wife. Therefore, it was inherited by her son. The Ri Migash explains this matter similarly.

HALAKHA

That a husband does not take in inheritance the property due – **לְבַעַל שֶׁאֵינוֹ נוֹטֵל בְּרָאוּי:** A husband who inherits from his wife inherits only the property she possessed at the time of her death, but he does not inherit property that was due to her, such as the inheritance from her father when she has no brothers, in the event that she predeceased her father (Rambam *Sefer Mishpatim, Hilkhot Naḥalot* 1:11 and *Sefer Kinyan, Hilkhot Zekhiya UMattana* 12:12; *Shulḥan Arukh, Even HaEzer* 90:1 and *Ḥoshen Mishpat* 248:9).

And sons of sisters – **וּבְנֵי אָחוֹת:** If a man died without descendants and without a father, a paternal brother, or their offspring, the inheritance goes to the paternal sister of the deceased and her offspring (Rambam *Sefer Mishpatim, Hilkhot Naḥalot* 1:3; *Shulḥan Arukh, Ḥoshen Mishpat* 276:1).

לְמַאי הִלְכְתָא? אֲמַר רַב שֵׁשֶׁת: לְקַדֵּם.

With regard to what *halakha* was this said? It is obvious that in principle daughters have the right to inherit from their maternal uncle, as the mother inherits from him. **Rav Sheshet said:** It is said **to** teach that where there are sons as well, they **precede**[H] the daughters in inheriting from their maternal uncle.

תָּנֵי רַב שְׁמוּאֵל בַּר רַב יִצְחָק קַמֵּיהּ דְּרַב הוּנָא: "וְיָרַשׁ" – מַקִּישׁ יְרוּשָּׁה שְׁנִיָּה לִירוּשָּׁה רִאשׁוֹנָה, מַה יְּרוּשָּׁה רִאשׁוֹנָה – בֵּן קוֹדֵם לְבַת, אַף יְרוּשָּׁה שְׁנִיָּה – בֵּן קוֹדֵם לְבַת.

Rav Shmuel bar Rav Yitzḥak taught a *baraita* **before Rav Huna:** At the end of the passage discussing inheritance of land, the verse states: "Then you shall give his inheritance to his kinsman who is next to him of his family, **and he shall inherit**[N] it" (Numbers 27:11). The verse **juxtaposes a secondary inheritance,**[N] that of one inheriting from other relatives, **to a primary inheritance,** that of a child inheriting from a parent. This teaches that **just as** with regard to **a primary inheritance a son precedes a daughter, so too,** with regard to **a secondary inheritance a son precedes a daughter.**

תָּנֵי רַבָּה בַּר חֲנִינָא קַמֵּיהּ דְּרַב נַחְמָן: "וְהָיָה בְּיוֹם הַנְחִילוֹ אֶת בָּנָיו" – בַּיּוֹם אַתָּה מַפִּיל נְחָלוֹת, וְאִי אַתָּה מַפִּיל נְחָלוֹת בַּלַּיְלָה. אֲמַר לֵיהּ אַבַּיֵי: אֶלָּא מֵעַתָּה, דְּשָׁכֵיב בִּימָמָא הוּא דְּיָרְתִי לֵיהּ בְּנֵיהּ, מַאן דְּשָׁכֵיב בְּלֵילְיָא לָא יָרְתִי לֵיהּ בְּנֵיהּ?!

§ **Rabba bar Ḥanina taught** a *baraita* **before Rav Naḥman:** A verse in the passage concerning the double portion inherited by a firstborn states: **"Then it shall be on the day that he causes his sons to inherit** that which he has" (Deuteronomy 21:16). The addition of the phrase "on the day" teaches that **it is** specifically **during the day** that **you may distribute inheritances, but you may not distribute inheritances at night. Abaye said to him:** That cannot be the *halakha*, as, **if that is so,** it ought to be **that** only **one who dies during the day is** the one from **whom his children inherit,** but with regard to **one who dies at night, his children do not inherit from him,** and this is not the case.

דִּלְמָא דִּין נְחָלוֹת קָא אָמְרַתְּ, דְּתַנְיָא: "וְהָיְתָה לִבְנֵי יִשְׂרָאֵל לְחֻקַּת מִשְׁפָּט" – אוּרְעָה כָּל הַפָּרָשָׁה כּוּלָּהּ לִהְיוֹת דִּין;

Abaye suggests a different interpretation of Rabba bar Ḥanina's statement: **Perhaps you said** a distinction between day and night with regard to the **adjudication of inheritances,** as judges are permitted to sit only during the day. A proof for this distinction is **as it is taught** in a *baraita*: A verse in the passage concerning inheritance states: **"And it shall be for the children of Israel a statute of judgment"** (Numbers 27:11), teaching that **the entire portion was placed** [*ure'a*][L] together **to be** considered a matter of **judgment,**[N] subject to the procedural rules of a court matter.

וּכְדְרַב יְהוּדָה. דְּאָמַר רַב יְהוּדָה: שְׁלֹשָׁה שֶׁנִּכְנְסוּ לְבַקֵּר אֶת הַחוֹלֶה – רָצוּ כּוֹתְבִין, רָצוּ עוֹשִׂין דִּין, שְׁנַיִם – כּוֹתְבִין וְאֵין עוֹשִׂין דִּין; וְאָמַר רַב חִסְדָּא: לֹא שָׁנוּ אֶלָּא בַּיּוֹם,

Abaye continues: **And** this is **in accordance with** the statement **of Rav Yehuda, as Rav Yehuda says:** In a case where there were **three** men **who entered**[H] a room **to visit a sick person** and the sick person desired to write a will in order to distribute his property following his death, if the visitors **wish** to do so **they may write** his will and sign it as witnesses. And if **they wish, they may act** in **judgment,** i.e., they may act as a court in the matter, since there are three of them. Therefore, they can determine that the will has the validity of an act of court and transfer the property to the heirs in their capacity as a court. But if only **two** came to visit the sick person, **they may write** the will and sign it as witnesses, **but they may not act** in **judgment,** since three are required to form a court. **And Rav Ḥisda says:** This *halakha* was **taught only** in a case where the three came to visit him **during the day,**

HALAKHA

To precede – לְקַדֵּם: Males and their descendants precede females with regard to inheritance in any case where they are equally close to the deceased. Therefore, a nephew precedes his sister with regard to inheriting from their uncle (Rambam *Sefer Mishpatim*, *Hilkhot Naḥalot* 1:1 and *Maggid Mishne* there; *Shulḥan Arukh*, *Ḥoshen Mishpat* 276:4).

NOTES

And he shall inherit, etc. – וְיָרַשׁ וכו׳: The Rashbam explains that the conjunctive letter *vav* in the term "and he shall inherit [*veyarash*]" teaches that even this inheritance, which appears last in the order of inheritance, follows the same principles as the ones preceding it. Each stage in the order of inheritance begins with the conjunctive *vav*, demonstrating that it is connected to the principle mentioned at the outset, that a son precedes a daughter.

A secondary inheritance – יְרוּשָּׁה שְׁנִיָּה: The Rashbam explains that the primary inheritance is the son's inheritance from a parent, as he precedes all other heirs, including a daughter. The secondary inheritance is one inherited by the brothers of the deceased, who follow the son in the order of inheritance. Accordingly, the next heirs on the list would be called the tertiary, quaternary, and so forth.

Others explain that a primary inheritance is that which the children inherit from their parent, and all other inheritances are called secondary inheritances (Ri Migash; Rabbi Avraham *Av Beit Din*). *Tosafot* explain that all inheritances mentioned explicitly in the Torah are called primary inheritances, while secondary inheritances are those that do not appear explicitly in the Torah, including that of a grandson or granddaughter descended either from the son or the daughter of the deceased, whose right to inherit is discussed later in this chapter (115a).

To be considered a matter of judgment – לִהְיוֹת דִּין: The Rashbam explains that the novelty here is that the division of an inheritance is not akin to a division of property by partners, which does not require court supervision. Therefore, it must be done only during the daytime. *Tosafot*, citing Rabbeinu Yitzhak of Dampierre, disagree with the Rashbam. According to their interpretation, the novelty is that if three people are present at the time the sick person declares his will, they are considered judges even though they were not formally appointed as such, and, as they constitute an official court, none of the heirs can contest their decision or insist that the matter be adjudicated in another court. Rabbi Avraham *Av Beit Din* explains the matter differently. He holds that a more general principle is being taught here: The *halakha* that requires adjudication of inheritances to take place during the daytime applies equally to all matters of judgment.

LANGUAGE

Was placed [*ure'a*] – אוּרְעָה: Based on the context, the term *ure'a* means that a certain matter was categorized deliberately in a certain fashion. Some explain the literal meaning of the word *ure'a* as placed or timed, that this passage was placed together with a certain term, in this case, judgment. Others explain that it means to publicize or notify.

HALAKHA

Three who entered, etc., – שְׁלֹשָׁה שֶׁנִּכְנְסוּ וכו׳: If two men visited a sick person and he declared before them how he wished to bequeath his property, they may write his will but they cannot adjudicate the matter. If there were three visitors and the sick person stated an irrevocable declaration of his will, then they may either write his will as witnesses or adjudicate the matter, meaning that they have the authority to distribute the property to each heir according to his portion and rule concerning any uncertainties that arise with regard to the conditions of the will. None of the heirs can contest their authority and insist on transferring the case to the jurisdiction of another court.

This *halakha* applies when the sick person stated his will during the day, but if he did so at night, the visitors are authorized only to write the will but not to act as judges, as judicial deliberations cannot take place at night. The Rema writes that if they did adjudicate at night their judgment stands, but the *Shakh* disagrees (Rambam *Sefer Shofetim*, *Hilkhot Sanhedrin* 3:5–6; *Shulḥan Arukh*, *Ḥoshen Mishpat* 5:2, and in the comment of Rema, 7:5, 253:1).

אֲבָל בַּלַּיְלָה, אֲפִילּוּ שְׁלֹשָׁה – כּוֹתְבִין וְאֵין עוֹשִׂין דִּין; מַאי טַעְמָא? דַּהֲווּ לְהוּ עֵדִים, וְאֵין עֵד נַעֲשֶׂה דַּיָּין. אֲמַר לֵיהּ: אִין, הָכִי נַמִי קָאָמִינָא.

but if they came **at night**,[H] **even** if **three** men came to visit the sick person, **they may write** the will and sign it as witnesses **but they may not act in judgment.**[N] **What is the reason** that they may not act in judgment the next day? It is **because they are** already **witnesses** to the will of the deceased, **and** there is a principle that **a witness cannot become a judge**,[HN] i.e., one who acts as a witness in a particular matter cannot become a judge with regard to that same matter? Rabba bar Ḥanina **said to** Abaye: **Yes,** it **is indeed so;** this is what **I was saying.**

אִיתְּמַר: קִנְיָן, עַד אֵימָתַי חוֹזֵר? רַבָּה אָמַר: כָּל זְמַן שֶׁיּוֹשְׁבִין; רַב יוֹסֵף אָמַר: כָּל זְמַן שֶׁעוֹסְקִין בְּאוֹתוֹ עִנְיָן.

§ After mentioning Rav Yehuda's ruling the Gemara cites a related dispute. **It was stated:** With regard to **a transaction, until when** may one of the parties **renege**[HN] on the transaction? **Rabba says: As long as they are seated** in the same location they may renege on the transaction. **Rav Yosef says: As long as they are dealing with that matter,** i.e., they are still discussing that transaction, they may renege on it.

אָמַר רַב יוֹסֵף: כְּוָותִי דִּידִי מִסְתַּבְּרָא, דְּאָמַר רַב יְהוּדָה: שְׁלֹשָׁה שֶׁנִּכְנְסוּ לְבַקֵּר אֶת הַחוֹלֶה – רָצוּ כּוֹתְבִין, רָצוּ עוֹשִׂין דִּין; וְאִי סָלְקָא דַּעְתָּךְ כָּל זְמַן שֶׁיּוֹשְׁבִין, לֵיחוּשׁ דִּלְמָא הָדַר בֵּיהּ!

Rav Yosef said: It stands to reason in accordance with my opinion, as Rav Yehuda says: In a case where there were **three** men **who entered** a room **to visit a sick person** and the sick person desires to write a will in order to distribute his property following his death, if the visitors **wish** to do so **they may write** his will and sign it as witnesses. And if **they wish, they may act** in **judgment. And if it enters your mind** that one may renege on a deal **as long as they are seated** in the same location, then **let us be concerned** that **perhaps he will renege on** his decision. How can the visitors act in judgment in a case where the matter has not been resolved, as the sick person may still change his mind?

אָמַר רַב אַשִׁי: אֲמַרִיתַהּ לִשְׁמַעְתָּא קַמֵּיהּ דְּרַב כָּהֲנָא: וּלְרַב יוֹסֵף מִי נִיחָא? וְלֵיחוּשׁ דִּלְמָא הָדַר בֵּיהּ! אֶלָּא מַאי אִית לָךְ לְמֵימַר? דִּיסַלִּיקוּ

Rav Ashi said: I stated this *halakha* before Rav Kahana and I asked him: **And according to** the opinion of **Rav Yosef, does it work out well? But** even according to his opinion there **should be a concern** that **perhaps he will renege on** his decision, as Rav Yosef holds that one may renege on a transaction as long as the two parties are still dealing with that matter. **Rather, what have you to say?** That according to Rav Yosef, Rav Yehuda's ruling applies **where they withdrew**

NOTES

They may write but they may not act in judgment – כּוֹתְבִין וְאֵין עוֹשִׂין דִּין: The witnesses cannot adjudicate the matter, because cases of monetary law may be adjudicated only during the daytime. The Rashbam explains that since they could not have served as judges at the time of the declaration of the sick man, they assumed the role of witnesses, and they cannot later serve as judges in this matter. By contrast, *Tosafot* explain that they cannot judge the matter on the following day based on what they had heard from the sick man the previous night, as that would mean that the statement of the sick man had the status of testimony, which cannot be accepted at night.

A witness cannot become a judge – אֵין עֵד נַעֲשֶׂה דַּיָּין: The Rashbam and others maintain that the principle that a witness cannot become a judge applies not only to one who actually provided testimony but even to one who witnessed something related to the case and intended to testify or who was summoned to court to testify. *Tosafot* and most authorities hold that only one who actually testified is disqualified from serving as a judge in the matter. The *Rid* writes that even a witness who testified may serve as a judge in the matter, provided it is determined that his testimony is not needed.

With regard to a transaction, until when may one of the parties renege – קִנְיָן, עַד אֵימָתַי חוֹזֵר: Even if a formal act of acquisition has already been performed, the parties involved can still add stipulations to the agreement, or even renege on the transaction entirely (Rashba). The Ramban cites Rav Yehuda of Barcelona, who cites other early commentaries who hold that this is stated specifically with regard to the discussion at hand, that of a sick person declaring how his property should be distributed after his death, as it is common for people to change their minds in these matters. By contrast, Rabbeinu Tam holds that this applies to any transaction, even one that has already been formalized with an act of acquisition.

The majority of halakhic authorities rule in accordance with the opinion of Rav Yehuda of Barcelona himself, who holds that one can renege on a transaction after an act of acquisition has been performed only if the act of acquisition was done by means of a cloth, a symbolic act in which one of the participants raises a cloth to indicate acceptance of the agreement. If an act of acquisition such as pulling or lifting was performed, one cannot renege. Rabbeinu Yona explains that the reason for this distinction is that when one performs a physical act of acquisition with the item he has full intent to carry out the transaction. When an acquisition by means of a cloth is performed, the act functions as more of a formality and one may not have resolved to complete the transaction. The Sages therefore provided a small window of time for one to renege on his decision. Rabbeinu Yona rules this way but adds that reneging will be effective only if done within the time needed for speaking a short phrase, meaning almost immediately.

HALAKHA

But at night, etc. – אֲבָל בַּלַּיְלָה וכו׳: Three men who witness an event are able to act as judges with regard to that matter even if they had intended to act as witnesses, provided that the event was witnessed during the day. If they witnessed it at night they cannot judge the matter based on their own knowledge, as a witness cannot become a judge. Nevertheless, they may judge the case on the basis of testimony provided by others unless they were specifically summoned to testify (Ramban). *Tosafot* rule that even if they were summoned to testify, they may still judge the matter on the basis of the testimony of others (Rambam *Sefer Shofetim*, *Hilkhot Edut* 5:8; *Shulḥan Arukh*, *Ḥoshen Mishpat* 7:5).

A witness cannot become a judge – אֵין עֵד נַעֲשֶׂה דַּיָּין: One who acted as a witness in a matter cannot later adjudicate it as a judge, regardless of whether it is a case of monetary or capital law. This ruling applies only to cases that require testimony and adjudication by Torah law; in a matter where the requirement for testimony and judges is by rabbinic law, a witness can become a judge. Therefore, one who testifies that a bill of divorce was written and signed before him or one who is signed on a promissory note may judge a case involving these documents (Rambam *Sefer Shofetim*, *Hilkhot Edut* 5:8–9, 7:6; *Shulḥan Arukh*, *Ḥoshen Mishpat* 7:5, and in the comment of Rema).

With regard to a transaction, until when can one of the parties renege – קִנְיָן, עַד אֵימָתַי חוֹזֵר: If one sells an item or gives a gift to another, if the mode of acquisition is by means of a cloth, either party may renege on the deal as long as the matter is still being discussed, even if the transaction has already been formalized. The *halakha* is in accordance with the opinion of Rav Yosef. If the transaction is completed through any of the other modes of acquisition, such as taking possession, pulling, passing, lifting, or payment, neither party can renege on the deal if they did not do so within the time required to speak a short phrase (Rambam *Sefer Kinyan*, *Hilkhot Mekhira* 5:10; *Shulḥan Arukh*, *Ḥoshen Mishpat* 195:6).

מֵעִנְיָנָא לְעִנְיָנָא, הָכִי נַמִי – דְּקָמוּ וַהֲדַר יָתִיבוּ. וְהִלְכְתָא כְּוָותֵיהּ דְּרַב יוֹסֵף: בְּשָׂדֶה, עִנְיָן, וּמֶחֱצָה.

from discussing that **matter to** discuss a different **matter,** so he can no longer renege on his decision. **So too,** according to Rabba, one can explain that Rav Yehuda was referring to a case **where they arose and then sat** down again. Although no support for Rav Yosef's opinion was adduced from Rav Yehuda's ruling, the Gemara nevertheless states: **And the *halakha* is in accordance with** the opinion **of Rav Yosef**[N] in the disputes concerning the division of **a field,** discussed above (12b), reneging while they are discussing the same **matter,** discussed here, **and a half** of one's property, discussed below (143a).

״הָאִשָּׁה אֶת בְּנָהּ״ וכו׳. הָא תּוּ לָמָּה לִי? הָא תְּנָא לֵיהּ רֵישָׁא: הָאִישׁ אֶת אִמּוֹ וְהָאִישׁ אֶת אִשְׁתּוֹ!

§ The mishna teaches that **a woman** bequeaths to **her son,** her husband, and her maternal uncles, but she does not inherit from them. The Gemara asks: **Why do I need this as well? But it is** already **taught** in **the former clause: A man** inherits from **his mother and a man** inherits from **his wife.** The *halakha* stated in this clause seems to be the same as that of the other clause.

הָא קָא מַשְׁמַע לָן, דְּאִשָּׁה אֶת בְּנָהּ דּוּמְיָא דְּאִשָּׁה אֶת בַּעְלָהּ: מָה אִשָּׁה אֶת בַּעְלָהּ – אֵין הַבַּעַל יוֹרֵשׁ אֶת אִשְׁתּוֹ בַּקֶּבֶר, אַף אִשָּׁה אֶת בְּנָהּ – אֵין הַבֵּן יוֹרֵשׁ אֶת אִמּוֹ בַּקֶּבֶר לְהַנְחִיל לָאַחִין מִן הָאָב.

The Gemara answers: **This teaches us**[N] **that** the *halakha* of a **woman** who bequeaths to **her son is similar to that** of **a woman** who bequeaths to **her husband: Just as** with regard to **a woman** who bequeaths to **her husband, the husband does not inherit** property through **his wife** while he is **in the grave,**[HN] i.e., if a husband predeceases his wife, then his relatives, such as children from another marriage, do not inherit the wife's property through him but rather the wife's own relatives inherit her property, **so too,** the same *halakha* applies with regard to **a woman** who bequeaths to **her son,** that **the son does not inherit** property through **his mother** while he is **in the grave**[HN] in order **to bequeath to his paternal brothers.** In both cases, the woman's own relatives inherit her property.

אָמַר רַבִּי יוֹחָנָן מִשּׁוּם רַבִּי יְהוּדָה בֶּן רַבִּי שִׁמְעוֹן: דְּבַר תּוֹרָה – הָאָב יוֹרֵשׁ אֶת בְּנוֹ וְאִשָּׁה יוֹרֶשֶׁת אֶת בְּנָהּ, שֶׁנֶּאֱמַר: ״מַטּוֹת״, מַקִּישׁ מַטֵּה הָאֵם לְמַטֵּה הָאָב, מַה מַּטֵּה הָאָב – אָב יוֹרֵשׁ אֶת בְּנוֹ, אַף מַטֵּה הָאֵם – אִשָּׁה יוֹרֶשֶׁת אֶת בְּנָהּ.

§ With regard to the *halakha* that a mother inherits from her son, the Gemara notes that **Rabbi Yoḥanan says in the name of Rabbi Yehuda ben Rabbi Shimon: By Torah law a father inherits** from **his son,**[N] **and a woman inherits** from **her son**[N] if the father is no longer alive, **as it is stated** with regard to a woman receiving inheritance: "And every daughter who possesses an inheritance from the **tribes** of the children of Israel" (Numbers 36:8). Since the plural term "tribes" includes both her father's tribe and her mother's tribe, the verse **juxtaposes** the **tribe of the mother to the tribe of the father,** in that **just as** with regard to **the father's tribe a father inherits** from **his son, so too,** with regard to **the mother's tribe, a woman inherits** from **her son** if the father is deceased.

NOTES

And the *halakha* is in accordance with the opinion of Rav Yosef, etc. – וְהִלְכְתָא כְּוָותֵיהּ דְּרַב יוֹסֵף וכו׳: Although the *halakha* is usually in accordance with the opinion of Rabba in his disputes with Rav Yosef, it is in accordance with Rav Yosef's opinion in these three cases. The early commentaries note that the issue of a half is not, in fact, subject to a dispute between Rabba and Rav Yosef. Rather, Rav Yosef stated a ruling that Abaye questions, and Rav Yosef responds to Abaye. Accordingly, the Ramban suggests that it was known that Abaye's questions were asked in the name of Rabba. *Tosafot* explain that since it is known that Rav Yosef was ill and began to forget his studies as he aged, it might have been assumed that the *halakha* is not in accordance with his opinion even when his ruling is not disputed. The Gemara therefore states explicitly that the *halakha* is in accordance with his opinion in this case.

Since the Gemara emphasizes that the *halakha* is in accordance with Rav Yosef's opinion in these cases in particular, there is discussion among the early commentaries whether the *halakha* is in accordance with Rabba's opinion in all other cases (Rif; *Tosafot*), or only those found in this tractate, with the *halakha* being decided at times in accordance with the opinion of Rav Yosef in other tractates (Rabbi Avraham *Av Beit Din*; Rabbi Yitzḥak Karkusha). The Ramban suggests that, in general, the *halakha* in all other cases is decided in accordance with the opinion of Rabba, although there are exceptions to this principle, as is the case with regard to many principles throughout the Talmud.

HALAKHA

The husband does not inherit property through his wife while in the grave – אֵין הַבַּעַל יוֹרֵשׁ אֶת אִשְׁתּוֹ בַּקֶּבֶר: The Rambam writes that if a husband predeceases his wife, his relatives do not inherit her property through him when she dies; rather, the wife's own relatives inherit her property. This *halakha* is not found in the *Shulḥan Arukh*, which does quote the *halakha* stated in the Gemara (113a) that a husband does not inherit the property of his deceased wife's relatives even though she would have done so had she been alive, and appears to have understood this Gemara as referring to that *halakha* (Rambam *Sefer Mishpatim, Hilkhot Naḥalot* 1:11–12; *Shulḥan Arukh, Even HaEzer* 90:1).

The son does not inherit property through his mother while in the grave – אֵין הַבֵּן יוֹרֵשׁ אֶת אִמּוֹ בַּקֶּבֶר: If a childless son predeceases his mother, his paternal brothers do not inherit her property through him based on the fact that he would have inherited her property had he been alive. Rather, the property is inherited by her relatives (Rambam *Sefer Mishpatim, Hilkhot Naḥalot* 1:13, 5:6; *Shulḥan Arukh, Ḥoshen Mishpat* 276:5, 280:10).

NOTES

This teaches us – הָא קָא מַשְׁמַע לָן: Since the mishna repeats these *halakhot*, the association and comparison between the inheritance of the husband and the inheritance of the son is emphasized. The maternal uncles are mentioned here along with these inheritors to keep to a parallel structure (Rashbam).

The husband does not inherit property through his wife while in the grave – אֵין הַבַּעַל יוֹרֵשׁ אֶת אִשְׁתּוֹ בַּקֶּבֶר: The precise meaning of this statement is the subject of dispute among the early commentaries. Some explain that it is a reference to the *halakha* mentioned on 113a, and they understand it to mean that a husband does not inherit property due to his deceased wife as he does the property she possessed. That is, if she predeceases her relatives, the husband does not inherit their property through his deceased wife. Rather, the property is inherited by her own relatives (Rashbam; Rabbeinu Ḥananel; Rabbeinu Gershom Meor HaGola).

Many other commentaries disagree with this explanation, as the statement of the Gemara would then be imprecise, as a son does inherit property due to his deceased mother as he does the property she possessed. They therefore explain that the meaning here is that if the husband predeceases his wife, his relatives do not inherit her property through him when she dies (*Tosafot*; Ri Migash; Ramah; Ramban). This is a dispute between the halakhic authorities as well, as the Rambam adopts the opinion of his teacher, the Ri Migash, while the *Tur* and *Shulḥan Arukh* mention only the halakhic conclusion that emerges from the Rashbam's understanding. The Gemara here is translated according to the understanding of *Tosafot*.

The son does not inherit property through his mother while in the grave – אֵין הַבֵּן יוֹרֵשׁ אֶת אִמּוֹ בַּקֶּבֶר: The meaning here is that if a son predeceases his mother, his paternal brothers do not inherit his mother's property through him, even though they would have inherited it upon his death had she predeceased him. Rather, the mother's own relatives inherit her property, provided that her son had no children of his own (Rashbam).

A father inherits from his son – הָאָב יוֹרֵשׁ אֶת בְּנוֹ: The same applies to his daughter (Rashbam) and any other descendants he may have, provided they have no children of their own.

A woman inherits from her son – אִשָּׁה יוֹרֶשֶׁת אֶת בְּנָהּ: A woman inherits the property of her children if their father has died and the children are childless (Rashbam). *Tosafot* is perplexed by this opinion in the Gemara, as it would then turn out that inheritance can be transferred from tribe to tribe through a mother inheriting from a child, while the verses seem to indicate that this can occur only when a daughter inherits from her parents. Furthermore, the Torah states explicitly that the father's relatives inherit. *Tosafot* therefore explain that the Gemara is referring specifically to the estate of the child of a female convert. If he has no other relatives, his property is inherited by his mother.

אֵיתִיבֵיהּ רַבִּי יוֹחָנָן לְרַבִּי יְהוּדָה בֶּן שִׁמְעוֹן: הָאִשָּׁה אֶת בְּנָהּ, וְהָאִשָּׁה אֶת בַּעְלָהּ, וַאֲחֵי הָאֵם – מַנְחִילִין וְלֹא נוֹחֲלִין! אֲמַר לֵיהּ: מִשְׁנָתֵנוּ, אֵינִי יוֹדֵעַ מִי שְׁנָאָהּ.

Rabbi Yoḥanan raised an objection to the opinion of **Rabbi Yehuda ben Shimon** from the mishna, which teaches: **A woman** with regard to **her son, a woman** with regard to **her husband, and maternal uncles** all **bequeath** to their respective relatives **but do not inherit** from them. The mishna states explicitly that a mother does not inherit her son's property. Rabbi Yehuda ben Shimon **said to him:** With regard to **our mishna, I do not know who taught it,**[N] i.e., I am not aware of any *tanna* who concurs with its ruling and it is not the accepted *halakha*.

וְלֵימָא לֵיהּ: רַבִּי זְכַרְיָה בֶּן הַקַּצָּב הִיא, דְּלָא דָּרֵישׁ ״מַטּוֹת״!

The Gemara asks: **But let** Rabbi Yoḥanan **say to** Rabbi Yehuda ben Shimon that the mishna **is** written in accordance with the opinion of **Rabbi Zekharya ben HaKatzav, who,** as noted on page 111a, **does not derive** the *halakha* that sons precede daughters with regard to the inheritance of their mother from the word **"tribes."** Since Rabbi Yehuda ben Shimon's ruling is based on a derivation from the word "tribes," it stands to reason that Rabbi Zekharya disagrees with Rabbi Yehuda ben Shimon, and the ruling of the mishna is in accordance with Rabbi Zekharya's opinion.

לָא מִיתּוֹקְמָא מַתְנִיתִין כְּרַבִּי זְכַרְיָה בֶּן הַקַּצָּב. דְּקָתָנֵי: וּבְנֵי אָחוֹת; וְתָנָא: בְּנֵי אָחוֹת – וְלֹא בְּנוֹת אָחוֹת; וַאֲמַרִינַן: לְמַאי הִלְכְתָא? וַאֲמַר רַב שֵׁשֶׁת: לְקַדֵּם;

The Gemara answers: **The mishna cannot be interpreted in accordance with** the opinion of **Rabbi Zekharya ben HaKatzav, as it teaches: And the sons of a sister** inherit but do not bequeath, and a Sage **taught** that the mishna is referring only to **sons of a sister**[N] **and not** to **daughters of a sister, and we say: With regard to what *halakha*** is there a distinction between the sons and daughters of a sister? **And Rav Sheshet said:** The distinction is meant **to** teach that where there are sons as well, they **precede** the daughters in inheriting from their maternal uncle.

וְאִי סָלְקָא דַּעְתָּךְ מַתְנִיתִין רַבִּי זְכַרְיָה בֶּן הַקַּצָּב הִיא, הָא אָמַר: אֶחָד הַבֵּן וְאֶחָד הַבַּת שָׁוִין בְּנִכְסֵי הָאֵם.

The Gemara continues: **And if it enters your mind** that **the mishna is** written in accordance with the opinion of **Rabbi Zekharya ben HaKatzav, doesn't he say: Both the son and the daughter are equal with regard to the mother's property,** as they inherit equally? The mishna stands in contraposition to Rabbi Zekharya's ruling, and therefore it cannot be written in accordance with his opinion.

וְתַנָּא דִּידַן, מִמָּה נַפְשָׁךְ? אִי דָּרֵישׁ ״מַטּוֹת״ – אִשָּׁה נַמִּי תִּירַשׁ אֶת בְּנָהּ, אִי לָא דָּרֵישׁ ״מַטּוֹת״ – בֵּן דְּקוֹדֵם לְבַת בְּנִכְסֵי הָאֵם מְנָא לֵיהּ?

The Gemara asks: **And the *tanna* of our** mishna, **whichever** way **you look at it, is inconsistent: If he interprets** the word **"tribes,"** then **a woman also should inherit** from **her son,**[H] as noted above (114b). **And if he does not interpret** the word **"tribes,"** then **from where is it** clear **to him** that **a son precedes a daughter with regard to the property of the mother?** Both *halakhot* are derived from the same source, so how can the *tanna* accept one and reject the other?

לְעוֹלָם דָּרֵישׁ ״מַטּוֹת״, וְשָׁאנֵי הָכָא, דְּאָמַר קְרָא: ״וְכָל בַּת יֹרֶשֶׁת נַחֲלָה״, יוֹרֶשֶׁת – וְאֵינָהּ מוֹרֶשֶׁת.

The Gemara explains: **Actually,** the *tanna* of the mishna **interprets** the word **"tribes," but it is different here,** with regard to a woman inheriting from her son, **as the verse states: "And every daughter** who **possesses** [*yoreshet*] **an inheritance**[N] from the tribes" (Numbers 36:8), which teaches that a daughter **inherits** [*yoreshet*] from two tribes, **but** she **does not bequeath** to two tribes. She bequeaths only to her father's tribe.

מתני׳ סֵדֶר נְחָלוֹת כָּךְ הוּא: ״אִישׁ כִּי יָמוּת וּבֵן אֵין לוֹ וְהַעֲבַרְתֶּם אֶת נַחֲלָתוֹ לְבִתּוֹ״ – בֵּן קוֹדֵם לַבַּת, כָּל יוֹצְאֵי יְרֵיכוֹ שֶׁל בֵּן קוֹדְמִין לַבַּת. בַּת קוֹדֶמֶת לָאַחִין, יוֹצְאֵי יְרֵיכָהּ שֶׁל בַּת קוֹדְמִין לָאַחִין. אַחִין קוֹדְמִין לַאֲחֵי הָאָב, יוֹצְאֵי יְרֵיכָן שֶׁל אַחִין קוֹדְמִין לַאֲחֵי הָאָב.

MISHNA The **order** of precedence with regard to **inheritances is this:**[H] The verse states: **"If a man dies, and has no son, then you shall pass his inheritance to his daughter"** (Numbers 27:8). This teaches that **a son precedes a daughter.** Additionally, **all descendants of a son precede a daughter. A daughter precedes the brothers** of the deceased. Additionally, the **descendants of a daughter precede the brothers** of the deceased. **Brothers** of the deceased **precede the uncles** of the deceased. Additionally, the **descendants of the brothers precede the uncles.**

NOTES

I do not know who taught it – אֵינִי יוֹדֵעַ מִי שְׁנָאָהּ: The Rashbam and others explain that according to Rabbi Yehuda ben Rabbi Shimon, the ruling of the mishna is not relied upon because it includes an inherent contradiction, as noted in the Gemara. Rabbeinu Gershom Meor HaGola writes that Rabbi Yehuda ben Rabbi Shimon could not identify another *tanna* who held in accordance with this mishna and therefore rejected its ruling.

And a Sage taught, sons of a sister – וְתָנָא בְּנֵי אָחוֹת: The word taught [*tana*] indicates that this particular statement was meant to accompany the text of the mishna (see Rashbam).

Who possesses an inheritance – יֹרֶשֶׁת נַחֲלָה: The Rashbam explains that the word "possesses [*yoreshet*]" is apparently superfluous, as the verse could have stated: And every daughter subject to inheritance. The verse includes this word to convey the fact that a daughter only inherits from two tribes, i.e., those of her father and mother, but she does not bequeath to two tribes but to her father's tribe alone. Accordingly, a mother's property may be transferred from her own tribe to her husband's tribe through her daughter, while a father's property is not transferred to his wife's tribe through his children, as she does not inherit their estate.

HALAKHA

A woman also should inherit from her son – אִשָּׁה נַמִּי תִּירַשׁ אֶת בְּנָהּ: A mother does not inherit the property of her children. The Rambam writes that this is known through tradition (Rambam *Sefer Mishpatim, Hilkhot Naḥalot* 1:2 and *Leḥem Mishne* there; *Shulḥan Arukh, Ḥoshen Mishpat* 276:4).

The order with regard to inheritances is this, etc. – סֵדֶר נְחָלוֹת כָּךְ הוּא וכו׳: A son and his descendants precede all others with regard to the inheritance of the deceased. If the son died with no offspring, the deceased's daughter and her descendants inherit. If she died with no offspring, the father of the deceased inherits. If the father has died, the deceased's brothers and their descendants inherit. If there are no brothers or descendants of brothers, then the deceased's sister and her descendants inherit. If the deceased had no sister, or if the sister died without descendants, then the deceased's paternal grandfather and his descendants, i.e., the deceased's uncles and aunts, inherit. If all these are no longer alive, then the deceased's paternal great-grandfather and his descendants inherit. This process may continue from generation to generation as far back as Jacob our Patriarch, until a fitting heir is found (Rambam *Sefer Mishpatim, Hilkhot Naḥalot* 1:1–4; *Shulḥan Arukh, Ḥoshen Mishpat* 276:1).

זֶה הַכְּלָל: כָּל הַקּוֹדֵם בְּנַחֲלָה – יוֹצְאֵי יְרֵיכוֹ קוֹדְמִין. וְהָאָב קוֹדֵם לְכָל יוֹצְאֵי יְרֵיכוֹ.

This is the principle: Concerning **anyone who precedes** another **with regard to inheritance, his descendants precede** the other as well, **and a father** who inherits **precedes all of his descendants.**[N]

גמ׳ תָּנוּ רַבָּנַן: "בֵּן" – אֵין לִי אֶלָּא בֵּן; בֶּן הַבֵּן, אוֹ בַּת הַבֵּן, אוֹ בֶּן בַּת הַבֵּן, מִנַּיִן? תַּלְמוּד לוֹמַר: "אֵין לוֹ" – עַיֵּין עָלָיו.

GEMARA **The Sages taught:** The verse states: "If a man dies, and has no **son,** then you shall pass his inheritance to his daughter" (Numbers 27:8). **I have** derived **only** that **a son** precedes others with regard to the inheritance of the deceased; **from where** do I derive that **a son of a son, or a daughter of a son, or a son of a daughter of a son** also precedes the deceased's other relatives? **The verse states:** "If a man dies, and **he has no** [*ein lo*][L] son." The word *ein* is written *aleph*, *yod*, *nun*. Therefore, the Sages read it as if it states: **Investigate with regard to him** [*ayyein alav*],[N] to search for descendants of his son, and give the inheritance to them if they are found.

"בַּת" – אֵין לִי אֶלָּא בַּת; בַּת הַבַּת, וּבֶן הַבַּת, וּבַת בֶּן הַבַּת, מִנַּיִן? תַּלְמוּד לוֹמַר: "אֵין לוֹ" – עַיֵּין עָלָיו.

The next verse states: "And if he has no **daughter,** then you shall give his inheritance to his brothers" (Numbers 27:9). **I have** derived **only** that **a daughter** precedes others, except a son and his descendants, with regard to the inheritance of the deceased, **from where** then do I derive that **a daughter's daughter, or a son of a daughter, or a daughter of a son of a daughter** also precede the deceased's other relatives? **The verse states:** "And if he **has no** [*ein lo*] daughter." The word *ein* is written *aleph*, *yod*, *nun*. Therefore, the Sages read it as if it states: **Investigate with regard to him** [*ayyein alav*], to search for descendants of his daughter, and give the inheritance to them if they are found.

NOTES

And a father precedes all of his descendants – וְהָאָב קוֹדֵם לְכָל יוֹצְאֵי יְרֵיכוֹ: The exception to this is that the children of the deceased precede the father of the deceased, despite being the descendants of the father.

***Ein lo*, investigate with regard to him [*ayyein alav*]** – אֵין לוֹ עַיֵּין עָלָיו: That is, investigate whether he has a living son or a deceased son who has descendants who stand in his stead. The Rashbam explains that this interpretation is based on the fact that the word *ein* could have been written without the letter *yod* (see *Kiddushin* 4a). The addition of the *yod* indicates that it may be expounded to mean investigate [*ayyein*].

LANGUAGE

Has no [*ein lo*] – אֵין לוֹ: The word *ein* has two meanings. The first is: That which exists but is not present, as in: The child is not [*hayyeled einennu*] (Genesis 37:30). The second, which usually appears as *ayin*, is referring to that which does not exist at all. The interpretation here is that a son does not inherit his parent's property only where he is considered to no longer exist at all, as he has absolutely no descendants and is himself deceased.

הָא כֵּיצַד? נַחֲלָה מְמַשְׁמֶשֶׁת וְהוֹלֶכֶת עַד רְאוּבֵן. וְלֵימָא: עַד יַעֲקֹב! אֲמַר אַבַּיֵי: גְּמִירִי, דְּלָא כָּלֶה שִׁבְטָא.

The Gemara asks: **How so,**[N] i.e., how is the investigation performed when he has no offspring at all? The Gemara answers: The family lineage that determines the **inheritance is successively examined**[H] **up to Reuben,** son of Jacob, i.e., the heirs are determined by investigating the family genealogy, and that investigation can extend all the way to Reuben, son of our forefather Jacob. The Gemara asks: **And let it say: Until Jacob** himself, rather than until Reuben, since if none of Reuven's descendants survive, one would have to examine Jacob's descendants. **Abaye said** in reply: It **is learned** as a tradition **that a tribe will not be eliminated**[N] entirely, and some descendants will always remain.

HALAKHA

Inheritance is successively examined – נַחֲלָה מְמַשְׁמֶשֶׁת: The estate of one who has no living descendants is inherited by his father, or his father's descendants if the father is no longer alive. If the father also has no living descendants, then the inheritance is transferred to the deceased's paternal grandfather and his descendants, and so on, as far back as the tribe's patriarch, until the appropriate heir is located (Rambam *Sefer Mishpatim*, *Hilkhot Naḥalot* 1:3; *Shulḥan Arukh*, *Ḥoshen Mishpat* 276:1).

BACKGROUND

An act of the Sadducees – מַעֲשֵׂה צְדוּקִין: The conflicts between the Sages and the Sadducees manifested themselves in both ideological and political areas. The Sadducees did not believe in the World-to-Come and rejected the halakhic traditions espoused by the Sages, choosing to interpret the Torah according to their own rationale and understanding. Although the Sadducees themselves resorted to the enactment of various ordinances and devised their own interpretations of verses, these were not rooted in any tradition. Additionally, though the Sadducees constituted only a minority of the population, they enjoyed a good deal of political influence, as they were close with the later Hasmonean kings. They used this influence to exacerbate the conflict between the kings and the Sages, and to lessen the influence of the latter. As a result, the Sages responded in kind and rejected all Sadducee practices, even those acceptable from a purely halakhic perspective.

NOTES

How so – הָא כֵּיצַד: Some understand this term to be a continuation of the previous statement and interpret it as an *a fortiori* inference: If the heir of an inheritance can be determined by tracing his lineage as far back as Reuben, certainly the deceased's own descendants are able to inherit (see Ritva). By contrast, the Rashbam explains that this is not a direct continuation of the previous statement. Rather, the Gemara has already assumed that an heir is to be determined by both the deceased's descendants and patrilineal relatives, and is asking by which means this is accomplished.

That a tribe will not be eliminated – דְּלָא כָּלֶה שִׁבְטָא: An allusion to this phrase is found in the verse: "For I, the Lord, change not; and you, O sons of Jacob, are not consumed" (Malachi 3:6). Just as God will never change, so too, the sons of Jacob will never be consumed or rendered extinct. It is thereby guaranteed that at least one descendant of each of Jacob's children will remain for eternity (Rabbeinu Barukh; Rashbam, citing Rabbeinu Ḥananel).

There are those who question this assertion in light of the fact that Sennacherib had already exiled ten tribes of Israel, who then presumably became assimilated into foreign nations. In *Margaliyyot HaYam* (*Sanhedrin* 110b), it is noted that recent archeological findings, such as those unearthed by cuneiform tablets, reveal evidence that not all of the members of the tribes were exiled, and many of them assimilated into the tribes of Judah and Benjamin. There is a verse that supports this idea, referring to members of some of the ten tribes even long after the exile (see II Chronicles 30:11). It is noted in *Margaliyyot HaYam* that the Gemara here also seems to provide evidence for the limited nature of the exile.

אָמַר רַב הוּנָא אָמַר רַב: כָּל הָאוֹמֵר תִּירַשׁ בַּת עִם בַּת הַבֵּן, אֲפִילּוּ נָשִׂיא שֶׁבְּיִשְׂרָאֵל – אֵין שׁוֹמְעִין לוֹ, שֶׁאֵינָן אֶלָּא מַעֲשֵׂה צְדוֹקִין. דְּתַנְיָא: בְּאַרְבָּעָה וְעֶשְׂרִים בְּטֵבֵת תָּבְנָא לְדִינָנָא; שֶׁהָיוּ צְדוֹקִין אוֹמְרִין: תִּירַשׁ הַבַּת עִם בַּת הַבֵּן;

§ **Rav Huna says that Rav says:** With regard to **anyone who says** that a **daughter** of the deceased **should inherit** the estate of her father along **with the daughter of the son**[H] of the deceased, **even** if he is **a prince of the Jewish people,**[N] one **should not listen to him, as this is nothing other than an act of the Sadducees,**[B] and runs counter to the ruling of the mishna that the descendants of a son inherit before a daughter. **As it is taught** in a *baraita* in *Megillat Ta'anit*, which describes various minor holidays on which it is forbidden to fast or eulogize: **On the twenty-fourth of Tevet, we returned to our law,** i.e., the *halakha* was reestablished in accordance with the opinion of the Sages after having been dictated by the Sadducees. **As the Sadducees would say: A daughter should inherit** the estate of her father along **with the daughter of the son** of the deceased.

נִטְפַּל לָהֶן רַבָּן יוֹחָנָן בֶּן זַכַּאי, אָמַר לָהֶם: שׁוֹטִים, מִנַּיִן זֶה לָכֶם? וְלֹא הָיָה אָדָם שֶׁהֶחְזִירוֹ דָּבָר, חוּץ מִזָּקֵן אֶחָד שֶׁהָיָה מְפַטְפֵּט כְּנֶגְדּוֹ וְאוֹמֵר: וּמַה בַּת בְּנוֹ הַבָּאָה מִכֹּחַ בְּנוֹ, תִּירָשֶׁנּוּ. בִּתּוֹ הַבָּאָה מִכֹּחוֹ, לֹא כָּל שֶׁכֵּן?

The *baraita* continues: **Rabban Yoḥanan ben Zakkai**[P] **joined them** to discuss their ruling, and **said to them: Imbeciles, from where do you** derive **this** ruling? **And there was no person that answered him anything, except for one old man who was chattering at him and saying** that it is an *a fortiori* inference: **And just as a daughter of the** deceased's **son, who comes** to claim her inheritance from her grandfather **by virtue of his son, inherits** her grandfather's property, so too, with regard to the deceased's own **daughter, who comes** to inherit **by virtue of** the deceased, **all the more so** is it **not** clear that she should inherit his property?

קָרָא עָלָיו אֶת הַמִּקְרָא הַזֶּה: ״אֵלֶּה בְנֵי שֵׂעִיר הַחֹרִי יֹשְׁבֵי הָאָרֶץ לוֹטָן וְשׁוֹבָל וְצִבְעוֹן וַעֲנָה״, וּכְתִיב: ״אֵלֶּה בְנֵי צִבְעוֹן וְאַיָּה וַעֲנָה״! אֶלָּא, מְלַמֵּד שֶׁבָּא צִבְעוֹן עַל אִמּוֹ וְהוֹלִיד עֲנָה.

Rabban Yoḥanan ben Zakkai **recited this verse about him: "These are the sons of Seir the Horite, the inhabitants of the land: Lotan and Shobal and Zibeon and Anah"** (Genesis 36:20), **and it is written: "And these are the children of Zibeon: Aiah and Anah"** (Genesis 36:24). The first verse portrays Zibeon and Anah as brothers, while the second states that they are father and son. **Rather,** this **teaches that Zibeon engaged in sexual intercourse**[N] **with his mother and begot Anah,** so that he was both Anah's father and his brother. From the fact that the first verse equates Zibeon and Anah by referring to both of them as Seir's sons despite Anah being a grandson of Seir, it is clear that grandchildren are equal to children, contrary to the Sadducees' assertion.

וְדִלְמָא תְּרֵי עֲנָה הָווּ! אֲמַר רַבָּה: אָמִינָא מִלְּתָא דְּלָא אֲמָרָהּ שָׁבוּר מַלְכָּא, וּמַנּוּ? שְׁמוּאֵל; אִיכָּא דְּאָמְרִי, אֲמַר רַב פַּפָּא: אָמִינָא מִלְּתָא דְּלָא אֲמָרָהּ שָׁבוּר מַלְכָּא, וּמַנּוּ? רַבָּה; אָמַר קְרָא: ״הוּא עֲנָה״ – הוּא עֲנָה דְּמֵעִיקָּרָא.

The Gemara interrupts the recounting of the *baraita* and questions Rabban Yoḥanan ben Zakkai's inference: **But perhaps there were two** people named **Anah,** so that one Anah was Zibeon's son, and the other his brother? **Rabba said: I will state a matter** that even **King Shapur**[NB] **did not state. And who is** this King Shapur? This cannot be a reference to Shapur, king of Persia; rather, it must be a moniker for someone else. He is **Shmuel,** whose legal rulings were accepted by the public like the edicts of a king by his subjects. **Some state** a different version, that it was **Rav Pappa who said: I will state a matter** that even **King Shapur did not state. And who is** this King Shapur? He is **Rabba. The verse** goes on to **state: "This is Anah"** (Genesis 36:24), indicating that **he is** the same **Anah** mentioned **initially,** earlier in the verse. Accordingly, there was only one Anah, who was both Zibeon's brother and Zibeon's son.

PERSONALITIES

Rabban Yoḥanan ben Zakkai – רַבָּן יוֹחָנָן בֶּן זַכַּאי: Rabban Yoḥanan ben Zakkai headed the Sanhedrin after the destruction of the Second Temple. He was one of the greatest leaders in the history of the Jewish people. The youngest of Hillel the Elder's students, Rabban Yoḥanan ben Zakkai lived to an old age and served as the leader of the Jewish people for many years. The Sages said of him that there was not a single area of Torah that he neglected. Despite his prominence, he was a modest individual who greeted every individual he met, including gentiles in the marketplace.

Even while the Temple stood he was acknowledged as a leading Torah scholar, and most of the Sages of that generation were his students. When the Great Revolt erupted, Rabban Yoḥanan was strongly opposed to it, and attempted to resolve the conflict peacefully. As one of the leaders of besieged Jerusalem, he was aware that the city would soon fall, and he succeeded in escaping with the help of several of his students in order to appear before the Roman general Vespasian, who received him warmly. When his prediction that Vespasian would be appointed emperor was fulfilled, Vespasian rewarded him by allowing him to establish a new center of Torah study and leadership in the city of Yavne. Rabban Yoḥanan took this opportunity to save the life of Rabban Gamliel as well.

In Yavne, Rabban Yoḥanan succeeded in instituting a wide range of ordinances that offered hope for Jewish continuity in the absence of the Temple, as well as ordinances that served to commemorate the Temple and heralded its ultimate rebuilding. The results of his efforts are integral to the modern practice of halakhic Judaism. His students taught Torah throughout Eretz Yisrael following the destruction of the Temple, and he served as a mentor for Rabban Gamliel of Yavne, who succeeded him as the acting *Nasi*.

HALAKHA

Anyone who says that a daughter should inherit along with the daughter of the son, etc. – כָּל הָאוֹמֵר תִּירַשׁ בַּת עִם בַּת הַבֵּן וכו׳: The inheritance of one who has left behind a daughter as well as a direct female descendant of a son is bequeathed exclusively to the latter. The *halakha* is the same with regard to siblings, as the daughter of the deceased's brother precedes his sister (Rambam *Sefer Mishpatim, Hilkhot Naḥalot* 1:4; *Shulḥan Arukh, Ḥoshen Mishpat* 276:2).

NOTES

Even a prince of the Jewish people – אֲפִילּוּ נָשִׂיא שֶׁבְּיִשְׂרָאֵל: The Rashbam understands this phrase to mean that even if a respected and authoritative scholar issues such a ruling based on an *a fortiori* inference, his ruling is not accepted (see Rambam *Sefer Shofetim, Hilkhot Mamrim* 2:1). Some explain that this phrase is referring to one who is on his deathbed and declares that his estate should be divided equally between his daughter and his son's daughter. The Gemara teaches that although Rabbi Yoḥanan ben Beroka rules that one may bequeath his inheritance to whomever he chooses (see 130a), in this case the father's directives are ignored in order to repudiate the Sadducee practice. The Rashbam rejects this explanation. Other commentaries offer a third explanation: If a leader of the Jewish people wishes to enact a temporary ordinance due to unique circumstances that will allow a daughter to inherit equally with a son's daughter, one does not listen to him (*Tosafot*; Rid; Meiri).

This teaches that Zibeon engaged in sexual intercourse, etc. – מְלַמֵּד שֶׁבָּא צִבְעוֹן וכו׳: The Rashbam adds that since Anah is described as a son of Seir and is included in the list of "the inhabitants of the land," it is apparent that he was among Seir's heirs. Accordingly, it can be seen that a son of a son inherits equally with his uncles. *Tosafot* are perplexed by this proof, as it relates only to the son of a son, and the subject of discussion is the daughter of a son. Rabbeinu Tam therefore writes that Anah was actually the name of a woman, Seir's granddaughter.

King Shapur – שָׁבוּר מַלְכָּא: The Rashbam explains that Shmuel was referred to as King Shapur because he was like a king with regard to monetary law, since his rulings were followed in that domain. The same can be applied to Rabba, as the *halakha* is almost always decided in accordance with his opinion against his disputant, Rav Yosef.

BACKGROUND

Act of the Sadducees – מַעֲשֵׂה צְדוֹקִין: See facing page (page 112).

King Shapur – שָׁבוּר מַלְכָּא: Even in antiquity it was common to assign sobriquets to well-known people, to such an extent that some became known by those names alone. The honorifics of Rabbi, for Rabbi Yehuda HaNasi, and Rav, for Rav Abba, are examples of this. This practice continued in the time of the early commentaries, with Rabbeinu Tam, whose given name was Ya'akov, being one prominent example. The name King Shapur in the Talmud is generally used to refer to Shmuel, one of the reasons being that he developed a friendship with a Persian king with this name.

Relief of King Shapur I of Persia

אָמַר לֵיהּ: רַבִּי, בְּכָךְ אַתָּה פּוֹטְרֵנִי? אָמַר לוֹ: שׁוֹטֶה,

The *baraita* continues: The Sadducee **said to** Rabban Yoḥanan ben Zakkai: **My teacher, you dismiss me with this**[N] retort? I agree that the son of a son precedes a daughter, as the verse you quoted suggests; I am asserting that a daughter inherits together with the daughter of a son, and the verse you quoted has no bearing on that claim. Rabban Yoḥanan ben Zakkai **said to him: Imbecile,**

NOTES

You dismiss me with this – בְּכָךְ אַתָּה פּוֹטְרֵנִי: According to the Rashbam, the Sadducee rejected Rabban Yoḥanan ben Zakkai's proof because it related only to a son of a son, whereas the Sadducee was discussing the daughter of a son. Rabbeinu Tam, who holds that Anah was in fact Zibeon's daughter, explains that the proof was dismissed because it proves only that a daughter of a son inherits along with the deceased's sons, but not that she would precede the deceased's daughter in the event that there was no living son. The Ran suggests that the Sadducee held that the verse might refer to Anah as Seir's son only because a grandfather may at times affectionately refer to a grandson as his own child, so this verse has no bearing on the laws of inheritance. The Maharsha explains that the Sadducee held that *halakhot* cannot be derived from the narrative portions of the Torah.

NOTES

That her right is enhanced with the brothers – שֶׁכֵּן יָפֶה כֹּחָהּ בִּמְקוֹם הָאַחִין: This claim would be accepted even by the Sadducees because this *halakha* is stated explicitly in the Torah and is not based on the Sages' interpretations, since Zelophehad's daughters inherited their grandfather's property along with their uncles (Rashbam).

וְלֹא תְּהֵא תּוֹרָה שְׁלֵמָה שֶׁלָּנוּ כְּשִׂיחָה בְּטֵלָה שֶׁלָּכֶם; מַה לְּבַת בְּנוֹ – שֶׁכֵּן יָפֶה כֹּחָהּ בִּמְקוֹם הָאַחִין, תֹּאמַר בְּבִתּוֹ – שֶׁהוּרַע כֹּחָהּ בִּמְקוֹם אַחִין! וְנִצְּחוּם, וְאוֹתוֹ הַיּוֹם עֲשָׂאוּהוּ יוֹם טוֹב.

but will our perfect Torah not be as worthy **as your frivolous speech,** as your inference is fallacious: **What** is notable **about** the inheritance of **a daughter of** the deceased's **son?** It is notable **in that her right is enhanced** in that she inherits from her paternal grandfather together **with the brothers**[N] of her father. Would you **say** that the same applies **with regard to** the deceased's **daughter, whose right** to inherit **is diminished** in that she does not inherit from her father together **with** her **brothers?** The Sadducee's *a fortiori* inference is thereby disproved. The Gemara concludes: **And** since the Sadducees had no counterargument, the Sages **were victorious over them, and they established that day,** the twenty-fourth of Tevet, as a minor **festival** to celebrate the establishment of the *halakha* in accordance with the opinion of the Sages.

״וַיֹּאמְרוּ יְרֻשַּׁת פְּלֵיטָה לְבִנְיָמִן וְלֹא יִמָּחֶה שֵׁבֶט מִיִּשְׂרָאֵל״

Having discussed the *halakha* of a son's daughter's right to inheritance, the Gemara cites a verse that relates to the matter. After the incident known as: The concubine in Gibeah, the men of the tribe of Benjamin numbered only six hundred, and each of these men had inherited large plots of land from their deceased relatives. The verse states: **"And they said: They that are escaped must be as an inheritance for Benjamin, that a tribe be not blotted out from Israel"** (Judges 21:17).

אָמַר רַבִּי יִצְחָק דְּבֵי רַבִּי אַמִי: מְלַמֵּד, שֶׁהִתְנוּ עַל שֵׁבֶט בִּנְיָמִין שֶׁלֹּא תִּירַשׁ בַּת הַבֵּן עִם הָאַחִין.

Rabbi Yitzḥak of the house of Rabbi Ami says: This **teaches that** the elders of that generation **stipulated with regard to the tribe of Benjamin that a daughter of a son shall not inherit with the brothers** of her father. Since the daughter of a son who inherits her grandfather's property may later bequeath it to her husband, who may be from another tribe, the elders instituted this temporary ordinance in order to ensure that other tribes would not inherit large quantities of land belonging to the tribe of Benjamin, lest the tribe of Benjamin be left with little land of its own.

אָמַר רַבִּי יוֹחָנָן מִשּׁוּם רַבִּי שִׁמְעוֹן בֶּן יוֹחַאי: כָּל שֶׁאֵינוֹ מַנִּיחַ בֵּן לְיוֹרְשׁוֹ – הַקָּדוֹשׁ בָּרוּךְ הוּא מָלֵא עָלָיו עֶבְרָה. כְּתִיב הָכָא: ״וְהַעֲבַרְתֶּם אֶת נַחֲלָתוֹ״, וּכְתִיב הָתָם: ״יוֹם עֶבְרָה הַיּוֹם הַהוּא״.

§ The Gemara presents a related statement. **Rabbi Yoḥanan says in the name of Rabbi Shimon ben Yoḥai:** Concerning **anyone who does not leave** behind **a son to inherit** from **him, the Holy One, Blessed be He, is filled with wrath** [*evra*] **toward him,** as **it is written here:** "If a man die, and he has no son, **then you shall pass his inheritance** [*veha'avartem*] to his daughter" (Numbers 27:8), **and it is written there: "That day is a day of wrath** [*evra*]" (Zephaniah 1:15). The words "*veha'avartem*" and "*evra*" share common root letters, whereby Rabbi Shimon ben Yoḥai interprets that God's wrath may be the result of the inheritance passing to a daughter rather than a son.

"אֲשֶׁר אֵין חֲלִיפוֹת לָמוֹ וְלֹא יָרְאוּ אֱלֹהִים" – רַבִּי יוֹחָנָן וְרַבִּי יְהוֹשֻׁעַ בֶּן לֵוִי, חַד אָמַר: כׇּל שֶׁאֵינוֹ מַנִּיחַ בֵּן, וְחַד אָמַר: כׇּל שֶׁאֵינוֹ מַנִּיחַ תַּלְמִיד.

The Gemara presents a related statement. Concerning the verse: "God shall hear, and humble them, even He that is enthroned of old, Selah; **those that have no exchange, and fear not God**" (Psalms 55:20), **Rabbi Yoḥanan and Rabbi Yehoshua ben Levi** each interpret the verse in a different manner. **One says** that this is a reference to **anyone who does not leave** behind **a son**[N] to inherit from him, as he does not leave anyone to serve in exchange, i.e., as a replacement, for him; **and one says** that this is a reference to **anyone who does not leave** behind **a student**[N] to serve in exchange for him.

תִּסְתַּיֵּים רַבִּי יוֹחָנָן דְּאָמַר תַּלְמִיד, דְּאָמַר רַבִּי יוֹחָנָן: דֵּין גַּרְמֵיהּ דַּעֲשִׂירָאָה בִּיר, תִּסְתַּיֵּים דְּרַבִּי יוֹחָנָן דְּאָמַר תַּלְמִיד.

The Gemara suggests: **It may be concluded** that it was **Rabbi Yoḥanan who says** that the verse is referring to one who does not leave behind **a student, for Rabbi Yoḥanan,** whose ten sons died in his lifetime, **said** to those he would console: **This is the bone of my tenth son,** to encourage them not to succumb to their sorrow. Since Rabbi Yoḥanan knew that he would not leave any sons to inherit his property, it is reasonable to assume that he interpreted the verse as meaning that God is full of wrath toward one who does not leave behind a student. The Gemara comments that **it may be concluded that** it was **Rabbi Yoḥanan who says** that the verse is referring to one who does not leave behind **a student.**

וּמִדְּרַבִּי יוֹחָנָן אָמַר תַּלְמִיד, רַבִּי יְהוֹשֻׁעַ בֶּן לֵוִי אָמַר בֵּן?

The Gemara notes: **And from this, that Rabbi Yoḥanan** is the one who **says** that the verse is referring to one who does not leave behind **a student,** it follows that **Rabbi Yehoshua ben Levi says** the verse is referring to one who does not leave behind **a son.**

וְהָא רַבִּי יְהוֹשֻׁעַ בֶּן לֵוִי לָא אָזֵיל לְבֵי טַמְיָא אֶלָּא לְבֵי מַאן דִּשְׁכִיב בְּלָא בְּנֵי, דִּכְתִיב: "בְּכוּ בָכֹה לַהֹלֵךְ", וְאָמַר רַב יְהוּדָה אָמַר רַב: לַהוֹלֵךְ בְּלֹא בֵּן זָכָר! אֶלָּא, רַבִּי יְהוֹשֻׁעַ בֶּן לֵוִי הוּא דְּאָמַר תַּלְמִיד.

The Gemara asks: **But** this cannot be, as **Rabbi Yehoshua ben Levi would not go to a house of mourning** [*bei tamya*][L] to console the bereaved so as not to interrupt his studies, **except to the house of one who died without any sons, as it is written:** "Weep not for the dead, neither bemoan him; but **weep sore for him that goes away**" (Jeremiah 22:10), **and Rabbi Yehuda says** that **Rav says** that the verse is referring **to** one who **departs** from this world **without** leaving behind **a male child.** From the fact that Rabbi Yehoshua ben Levi would console specifically one who died without leaving a son, it is apparent that he does not hold that God is full of wrath toward such an individual. **Rather,** it must be that **Rabbi Yehoshua ben Levi is** the Sage **who says** that the verse is referring to one who does not leave behind **a student.**

וּמִדְּרַבִּי יְהוֹשֻׁעַ בֶּן לֵוִי הוּא דְּאָמַר תַּלְמִיד, רַבִּי יוֹחָנָן אָמַר בֵּן;

The Gemara notes: **And from this that Rabbi Yehoshua ben Levi is** the one **who says** that the verse is referring to one who does not leave behind **a student,** it follows that **Rabbi Yoḥanan says** it is referring to one who does not leave behind **a son.**

קַשְׁיָא דְּרַבִּי יוֹחָנָן אַדְּרַבִּי יוֹחָנָן! לָא קַשְׁיָא: הָא דִּידֵיהּ, הָא דְּרַבֵּיהּ.

The Gemara asks: This poses **a difficulty** from one statement **of Rabbi Yoḥanan,** that the verse is referring to one who does not leave behind a son, **to** another statement **of Rabbi Yoḥanan,** as he would say: This is the bone of my tenth son. The Gemara answers: It is **not difficult: This** statement, with regard to the bone of his son, **is his,** while **that** statement, with regard to the verse, **is his teacher's.**

NOTES

Who does not leave behind a son – שֶׁאֵינוֹ מַנִּיחַ בֵּן: The Ramah writes that this reference applies only to one who intentionally refrained from fathering children, and it is for this reason that God is filled with wrath toward him. Others note that based on the continuation of the Gemara discussing Rabbi Yoḥanan, it seems that even one whose children have died is included in this category.

Who does not leave behind a student – שֶׁאֵינוֹ מַנִּיחַ תַּלְמִיד: This phrase refers to one who refused to teach Torah to others (Rabbeinu Gershom Meor HaGola).

LANGUAGE

House of mourning [*bei tamya*] – בֵּי טַמְיָא: Several interpretations of this term have been suggested. Some write that the word *tamya* means bones in Aramaic, and the term therefore literally means: House of bones, referring to the bones of the deceased. The *ge'onim* and several early authorities had a variant reading of the text in other sections of the Talmud in which this place was referred to as *bei ta'ama*, the house of the reason. Rav Hai Gaon explains that this latter designation arose from a ceremony in which people would accept the judgment of Heaven. An attendant would turn to visitors and announce: Let the Rabbis ask the reason for which the mourners are in mourning, to which those assembled would respond: Blessed is the True Judge. Alternatively, it was called a house of the reason because it is a place where people seek to console the mourners by attempting to explain the tragedy that befell them.

(סִימָן: הֲדַד עָנִי וְחָכָם.)

§ The Gemara continues with three homiletic interpretations by Rabbi Pineḥas ben Ḥama, and provides **a mnemonic**[B] to facilitate the memorization of these expositions: **Hadad, poverty, and sage.**

דָּרַשׁ רַבִּי פִּנְחָס בֶּן חָמָא, מַאי דִּכְתִיב: "וַהֲדַד שָׁמַע בְּמִצְרַיִם כִּי שָׁכַב דָּוִד עִם אֲבוֹתָיו וְכִי מֵת יוֹאָב שַׂר הַצָּבָא", מִפְּנֵי מָה בְּדָוִד נֶאֶמְרָה בּוֹ שְׁכִיבָה, וּבְיוֹאָב נֶאֶמְרָה בּוֹ מִיתָה? דָּוִד שֶׁהִנִּיחַ בֵּן – נֶאֶמְרָה בּוֹ שְׁכִיבָה, יוֹאָב שֶׁלֹּא הִנִּיחַ בֵּן – נֶאֶמְרָה בּוֹ מִיתָה.

The Gemara presents the first homiletic interpretation: **Rabbi Pineḥas ben Ḥama interpreted** a verse **homiletically: What** is the meaning of that **which is written: "And when Hadad heard in Egypt that David slept with his fathers, and that Joab the captain of the host was dead"** (I Kings 11:21)? **For what** reason is it that **in** the case of King **David, sleeping was stated with regard to his** demise, **and in the case of Joab, death was stated with regard to his** demise? He answers: Concerning King **David, who left a son** behind, **sleeping was stated with regard to his** demise, as it was not a complete death, while concerning **Joab, who did not leave a son** behind, **death was stated with regard to his** demise, as he left no son to succeed him.

וְיוֹאָב לֹא הִנִּיחַ בֵּן? וְהָכְתִיב: "מִבְּנֵי יוֹאָב עֹבַדְיָה בֶּן יְחִיאֵל"! אֶלָּא, דָּוִד שֶׁהִנִּיחַ בֵּן כְּמוֹתוֹ – נֶאֶמְרָה בּוֹ שְׁכִיבָה, יוֹאָב שֶׁלֹּא הִנִּיחַ בֵּן כְּמוֹתוֹ – נֶאֶמְרָה בּוֹ מִיתָה.

The Gemara asks: **And** is it so that **Joab did not leave a son** behind; **but isn't it written: "Of the sons of Joab: Obadiah, son of Jehiel"** (Ezra 8:9)? **Rather,** concerning King **David, who left a son as** great as **himself, sleeping was stated with regard to his demise,** but concerning **Joab, who did not leave a son** as great as **himself, death was stated with regard to his** demise.

דָּרַשׁ רַבִּי פִּנְחָס בֶּן חָמָא: קָשָׁה עֲנִיּוּת בְּתוֹךְ בֵּיתוֹ שֶׁל אָדָם יוֹתֵר מֵחֲמִשִּׁים מַכּוֹת, שֶׁנֶּאֱמַר: "חָנֻּנִי חָנֻּנִי אַתֶּם רֵעָי כִּי יַד אֱלוֹהַּ נָגְעָה בִּי", וְקָא אָמְרִי לֵיהּ חַבְרֵיהּ: "הִשָּׁמֵר אַל תֵּפֶן אֶל אָוֶן כִּי עַל זֶה בָּחַרְתָּ מֵעֹנִי".

The Gemara presents the second homiletic interpretation: **Rabbi Pineḥas ben Ḥama interpreted** a verse **homiletically,** and derived that **poverty in a person's household is more difficult**[N] **than fifty plagues,**[N] **as it is stated: "Have pity upon me, have pity upon me, O you my friends; for the hand of God has touched me"** (Job 19:21), **and his friends were saying to him: "Take heed, regard not iniquity; for this have you chosen rather than poverty"** (Job 36:21). Job, who suffered many plagues, was told by his friends that his suffering was preferable to poverty.

דָּרַשׁ רַבִּי פִּנְחָס בַּר חָמָא: כָּל שֶׁיֵּשׁ לוֹ חוֹלֶה בְּתוֹךְ בֵּיתוֹ, יֵלֵךְ אֵצֶל חָכָם וִיבַקֵּשׁ עָלָיו רַחֲמִים, שֶׁנֶּאֱמַר: "חֲמַת מֶלֶךְ מַלְאֲכֵי מָוֶת וְאִישׁ חָכָם יְכַפְּרֶנָּה".

The Gemara presents the third homiletic interpretation: **Rabbi Pineḥas bar Ḥama interpreted** a verse **homiletically: Anyone who has a sick person in his home should go to a sage, and the sage** will **ask** for **mercy on** the sick person's **behalf, as it is stated: "The wrath of a king is as messengers of death; but a wise man will pacify it"** (Proverbs 16:14).

"זֶה הַכְּלָל: כָּל הַקּוֹדֵם בְּנַחֲלָה – יוֹצְאֵי יְרֵכוֹ קוֹדְמִין; וְהָאָב קוֹדֵם לְכָל יוֹצְאֵי יְרֵכוֹ". בָּעֵי רָמִי בַּר חָמָא: אֲבִי הָאָב וַאֲחִי הָאָב, כְּגוֹן אַבְרָהָם וְיִשְׁמָעֵאל בְּנִכְסֵי עֵשָׂו, אֵיזֶה מֵהֶן קוֹדֵם? אָמַר רָבָא, תָּא שְׁמַע: הָאָב קוֹדֵם לְכָל יוֹצְאֵי יְרֵכוֹ. וְרָמִי בַּר חָמָא?

§ The mishna teaches that **this is the principle:** Concerning **anyone who precedes** another **with regard to inheritance, his descendants precede** the other as well, **and a father precedes all of his descendants.**[H] **Rami bar Ḥama**[P] **raises a dilemma:** With regard to the claim of **a father of the** deceased's **father and** the claim of **the brother of the** deceased's **father, such as** the claims of **Abraham and Ishmael to the property of Esau,**[N] who was Abraham's grandson and Ishmael's nephew, **which of them precedes** the other and inherits the property? **Rava said: Come** and **hear** a proof from the mishna: **A father precedes all of his descendants,** therefore, Abraham would inherit, as Ishmael was his descendant. The Gemara asks: **And** why did **Rami bar Ḥama** have a dilemma; was he not aware of the statement of the mishna?

BACKGROUND

Mnemonic – סִימָן: Because the Talmud was studied orally for many generations, mnemonic devices were devised to facilitate the memorization of, e.g., a series of *halakhot* and the order in which they were taught.

NOTES

Poverty in a person's household is more difficult, etc. – קָשָׁה עֲנִיּוּת בְּתוֹךְ בֵּיתוֹ שֶׁל אָדָם וכו׳: Poverty is considered a particularly difficult hardship because it engenders conflict within the home (*Iyyun Ya'akov*). Alternatively, the pain of parents who see their children lacking food is unparalleled (*Ein Eliyahu*).

Than fifty plagues – מֵחֲמִשִּׁים מַכּוֹת: The number fifty is used here because Job states: "The hand of God has touched me," while the ten plagues in Egypt are described as: "The finger of God" (Exodus 8:15). If one finger is the cause of ten plagues, it follows that Job was afflicted with fifty plagues. This idea is found in the Passover Haggadah as well (Rashbam).

The property of Esau – נִכְסֵי עֵשָׂו: Though Esau had many descendants, he is used as an example when discussing one who died with no children because both he and his descendants are deemed wicked (see Rashbam).

HALAKHA

A father precedes all of his descendants – הָאָב קוֹדֵם לְכָל יוֹצְאֵי יְרֵכוֹ: The property of one who died with no descendants is inherited by his father, who precedes the brothers of the deceased (Rambam *Sefer Mishpatim*, *Hilkhot Naḥalot* 1:2; *Shulḥan Arukh*, *Ḥoshen Mishpat* 276:1).

PERSONALITIES

Rami bar Ḥama – רָמִי בַּר חָמָא: Rami bar Ḥama was an important fourth-generation Babylonian *amora*. Rami is an abbreviation of Rav Ami. He was a student of Rav Ḥisda and a study partner of Rava. Rami bar Ḥama and his brother Rav Ukva bar Ḥama married the daughters of Rav Ḥisda. In a story related earlier in this tractate (12b), Rava and Rami bar Ḥama visited Rav Ḥisda and saw his young daughter sitting on his lap. Rav Ḥisda playfully asked her which of the Torah scholars she would prefer marrying. The girl diplomatically answered that she would like to marry both, whereupon Rava responded that he would defer to his colleague. Ultimately, the daughter married Rami bar Ḥama, and after he died, married Rava. Rami bar Ḥama was known for his sharp intellect and sought to resolve all dilemmas posed to him by employing logical reasoning rather than by seeking to cite proof from the Mishna and *baraitot*, in contrast to the approach of his teacher, Rav Sheshet. The *amora* Ameimar was the son of Rami bar Ḥama's daughter.

אַגַּב חוּרְפֵּיהּ לָא עַיֵּין בַּהּ.

The Gemara answers: **Due to his keen** mind,[N] **he did not analyze** the mishna carefully.

בָּעֵי רָמִי בַּר חָמָא: אֲבִי הָאָב וְאָחִיו, כְּגוֹן אַבְרָהָם וְיַעֲקֹב בְּנִכְסֵי עֵשָׂו, אֵיזֶה מֵהֶן קוֹדֵם? אָמַר רָבָא, תָּא שְׁמַע: הָאָב קוֹדֵם לְכׇל יוֹצְאֵי יְרֵיכוֹ. וְרָמִי בַּר חָמָא? יוֹצְאֵי יְרֵיכוֹ שֶׁלּוֹ, וְלֹא יוֹצְאֵי יְרֵיכוֹ שֶׁל בְּנוֹ.

Rami bar Ḥama raised a dilemma: With regard to the claim of **a father of the** deceased's **father and** the claim of the deceased's **brother, such as** the claims of **Abraham and Jacob to the property of Esau,** who was Abraham's grandson and Jacob's brother, **which of them precedes** the other and inherits the property? **Rava said: Come** and **hear** a proof from the mishna: **A father precedes**[H] **all of his descendants,** therefore, Abraham would inherit, as Jacob was his descendant. The Gemara asks: **And** why did **Rami bar Ḥama** have a dilemma; presumably, he was aware of the statement of the mishna? The Gemara answers: Rami bar Ḥama understood that the mishna teaches that a father **precedes** only **his own** immediate **descendants, but not the descendants of his son.**

הָכִי נָמֵי מִסְתַּבְּרָא, דְּקָתָנֵי, זֶה הַכְּלָל: כׇּל הַקּוֹדֵם בְּנַחֲלָה – יוֹצְאֵי יְרֵיכוֹ קוֹדְמִין; וְאִילּוּ אִיתֵיהּ לְיִצְחָק – יִצְחָק קוֹדֵם, הָשְׁתָּא נָמֵי דְּלֵיתֵיהּ יִצְחָק – יַעֲקֹב קוֹדֵם, שְׁמַע מִינַּהּ.

The Gemara notes that **so too, it is reasonable** to understand the mishna in that manner, **as it teaches: This is the principle: Anyone who precedes** another **with regard to inheritance, his descendants precede** the other as well. **And if Isaac were** alive, **Isaac** would **precede** Abraham and inherit Esau's property. **Now, also, when Isaac is not** alive, **Jacob** should **precede** Abraham, because of the principle that the descendants of one who precedes another with regard to inheritance also precede the other. The Gemara affirms: **Conclude from** this clause of the mishna that the brother of the deceased precedes the grandfather.

מתני׳ בְּנוֹת צְלׇפְחָד נָטְלוּ שְׁלֹשָׁה חֲלָקִים בְּנַחֲלָה: חֵלֶק אֲבִיהֶן שֶׁהָיָה עִם יוֹצְאֵי מִצְרַיִם, וְחֶלְקוֹ עִם אֶחָיו בְּנִכְסֵי חֵפֶר, וְשֶׁהָיָה בְּכוֹר נוֹטֵל שְׁנֵי חֲלָקִים.

MISHNA **Zelophehad's daughters**[H] **took three portions** of land **in the inheritance** of Eretz Yisrael: **Their father's portion** that he received **because he was among those who left Egypt; and his portion** that he received **with his brothers in the property of Hepher,** their father; **and** an additional portion that he received from Hepher **because he was a firstborn,**[N] and a firstborn **takes two portions** of inheritance from his father.

NOTES

Due to his keen mind – אַגַּב חוּרְפֵּיהּ: Rabbeinu Gershom Meor HaGola explains that since Rami bar Ḥama would review his studies at a brisk pace, he did not take the time to examine the details and implications of this particular mishna. The Rashbam explains that he did not examine the first dilemma because he was less concerned with it, as his primary purpose in raising it was to introduce the second dilemma, whose resolution is not mentioned in the mishna explicitly.

And because he was a firstborn, etc. – וְשֶׁהָיָה בְּכוֹר וכו׳: It is stated in the Jerusalem Talmud that just as one's right to inheritance is not negated by his death, and his children receive the inheritance due to him from his father, the descendants of a firstborn son receive his double portion of inheritance even if he predeceased his own father. Accordingly, Zelophehad's daughters received their father's double portion of land from Hepher even though Zelophehad himself had already died. It should be noted that a firstborn inherits a double portion only from that which was in his father's possession at the time of the father's death, but not from that which his father had a legal right to but had not legally acquired (see Rashbam, *Tosafot*, and Ramban). In this case, Zelophehad was able to receive a double portion of Hepher's inheritance in Eretz Yisrael even though Hepher had not legally acquired it, because Eretz Yisrael was considered to be in the possession of the Jewish people even before they actually conquered it. As a result, Zelophehad's daughters were able to inherit a double portion from Hepher through their deceased father.

HALAKHA

A father precedes, etc. – הָאָב קוֹדֵם וכו׳: If one dies childless, his inheritance passes to his father, or, in the event of the father's death, his father's children. If the father himself also has no living descendants, then the inheritance passes to the deceased's grandfather and his descendants (Rambam *Sefer Mishpatim, Hilkhot Naḥalot* 1:3; *Shulḥan Arukh, Ḥoshen Mishpat* 276:1).

Zelophehad's daughters, etc. – בְּנוֹת צְלׇפְחָד וכו׳: If one has two sons who both predeceased him, and one of them had one daughter and the other had three sons, the granddaughter inherits half of his property and the three grandsons divide the other half. If the granddaughter's father was the firstborn, she inherits two-thirds of the property from her grandfather while the grandsons divide the other third. This is because the descendants of one who is entitled to an inheritance receive the inheritance through him (Rambam *Sefer Mishpatim, Hilkhot Naḥalot* 1:5, 2:7; *Shulḥan Arukh, Ḥoshen Mishpat* 276:3, 277:15).

NOTES

Among those who left Egypt – לְיוֹצְאֵי מִצְרַיִם: Those who left Egypt did not actually receive their portions, as nearly all of that generation died in the wilderness. Rather, the allotment was made in accordance with the census that took place in the second year after the Exodus, with each adult male receiving a plot. The land was not divided equally among the members of the generation that actually received shares of the land, but rather was divided as if it were an inheritance from their fathers. To illustrate: If one brother who left Egypt had five sons and another brother of that generation had one son, the five sons of the first brother would share a portion equal to that of the one son of the second brother.

גמ׳ תְּנַן כְּמַאן דְּאָמַר: לְיוֹצְאֵי מִצְרַיִם נִתְחַלְּקָה הָאָרֶץ;

GEMARA

The Gemara comments: In the mishna that teaches that Zelophehad and Hepher were entitled to portions in Eretz Yisrael, **we learned in accordance with** the opinion of the **one who says: Eretz** Yisrael **was divided among those who left Egypt.**[N]

דְּתַנְיָא, רַבִּי יֹאשִׁיָּה אוֹמֵר: לְיוֹצְאֵי מִצְרַיִם נִתְחַלְּקָה הָאָרֶץ, שֶׁנֶּאֱמַר: ״לִשְׁמוֹת מַטּוֹת אֲבֹתָם יִנְחָלוּ״. אֶלָּא מָה אֲנִי מְקַיֵּים ״לָאֵלֶּה תֵּחָלֵק הָאָרֶץ בְּנַחֲלָה״? ״לָאֵלֶּה״ – כָּאֵלֶּה, לְהוֹצִיא אֶת הַטְּפָלִים;

The Gemara cites a *baraita* that presents three opinions as to how Eretz Yisrael was divided. **As it is taught** in a *baraita* that **Rabbi Yoshiya says: Eretz** Yisrael **was divided among those who left Egypt, as it is stated: "According to the names of the tribes of their fathers they shall inherit"** (Numbers 26:55), which teaches that the Jewish people would inherit Eretz Yisrael according to the names of their fathers, i.e., those who left Egypt. Rabbi Yoshiya continues: **But how do I realize** the meaning of the verse: **"Unto these the land shall be divided for an inheritance"** (Numbers 26:53), which indicates that the land was to be divided among those recently counted in the wilderness, i.e., those who would enter Eretz Yisrael? He answers: **"Unto these"** teaches that the land will be divided among those who are **like these** people who were counted, in that they were adults above the age of twenty, **to exclude the children,**[N] who were not entitled to a portion in Eretz Yisrael, as they were not of age at the time of the Exodus.

רַבִּי יוֹנָתָן אוֹמֵר: לְבָאֵי הָאָרֶץ נִתְחַלְּקָה הָאָרֶץ, שֶׁנֶּאֱמַר: ״לָאֵלֶּה תֵּחָלֵק הָאָרֶץ בְּנַחֲלָה״. אֶלָּא מָה אֲנִי מְקַיֵּים ״לִשְׁמוֹת מַטּוֹת אֲבֹתָם יִנְחָלוּ״? מְשׁוּנָּה נַחֲלָה זוֹ מִכׇּל נְחָלוֹת שֶׁבָּעוֹלָם, שֶׁכׇּל נְחָלוֹת שֶׁבָּעוֹלָם – חַיִּין יוֹרְשִׁין מֵתִים, וְכָאן מֵתִים יוֹרְשִׁין חַיִּין.

The *baraita* presents a second opinion. **Rabbi Yonatan says: Eretz** Yisrael **was divided among those who entered Eretz** Yisrael, **as it is stated: "Unto these the land shall be divided for an inheritance"** (Numbers 26:53). **But how do I realize** the meaning of the verse: **"According to the names of the tribes of their fathers they shall inherit"** (Numbers 26:55)? This teaches that **this inheritance is different from all** other **inheritances in the world, for in all** other **inheritances in the world,** the **living inherit** from the **dead, but here, the dead inherit** from the **living.**[N] In other words, the portions of land received by those who entered Eretz Yisrael were transferred to their fathers who left Egypt, and then inherited by the current generation, as the Gemara will now explain.

אָמַר רַבִּי: אֶמְשׁוֹל לְךָ מָשָׁל, לְמָה הַדָּבָר דּוֹמֶה? לִשְׁנֵי אַחִין כֹּהֲנִים שֶׁהָיוּ בְּעִיר אַחַת, לְאֶחָד יֵשׁ לוֹ בֵּן אֶחָד, וְאֶחָד יֵשׁ לוֹ שְׁנֵי בָנִים, וְהָלְכוּ לַגּוֹרֶן. זֶה שֶׁיֵּשׁ לוֹ בֵּן אֶחָד – נוֹטֵל חֵלֶק אֶחָד, וְזֶה שֶׁיֵּשׁ לוֹ שְׁנֵי בָנִים – נוֹטֵל שְׁנֵי חֲלָקִים. וּמַחְזִירִין אֵצֶל אֲבִיהֶן, וְחוֹזְרִין וְחוֹלְקִין בְּשָׁוֶה.

Rabbi Yehuda HaNasi **said: I will tell you a parable. To what is this matter comparable? To two brothers** who were **priests**[N] and **who were in one town. One** brother **has one son, and one** brother **has two sons,** and the sons all **went to the threshing floor** to collect *teruma*. **This** brother, **who has one son, takes one portion** of the *teruma* from his child, **and that** brother, **who has two sons, takes two portions** from his sons. **And** the brothers then **return** with the three portions **to their father, and** then **redivide** the portions among themselves **equally,** so that each brother receives one and one-half portions. When the brothers give their shares to their children, the son of the first brother will receive all that his father had received, while the sons of the other brother will divide what their father had received.

רַבִּי שִׁמְעוֹן בֶּן אֶלְעָזָר אוֹמֵר:

The *baraita* presents a third opinion. **Rabbi Shimon ben Elazar says:**

NOTES

Like these, to exclude the children – כָּאֵלֶּה לְהוֹצִיא אֶת הַטְּפָלִים: The term "unto these" is referring to anyone who was not at least twenty years old at the time of the Exodus, or, according to Rabbeinu Gershom Meor HaGola, at the time of entry into Eretz Yisrael.

The dead inherit from the living – מֵתִים יוֹרְשִׁין חַיִּין: This means that if, for example, two brothers left Egypt and perished in the wilderness, after which five sons of one of the brothers and a single son of the other entered Eretz Yisrael together, the sons would receive one portion of land each, for a total of six portions. Those six portions would then be transferred to their fathers, who together would receive six portions of the land posthumously. The sons would then inherit these portions from their fathers so that the five sons would receive three portions of land to be divided among all of them, while the single son would receive three portions of land for himself.

Two brothers who were priests, etc. – שְׁנֵי אַחִין כֹּהֲנִים וכו׳: The Rashbam explains that the two brothers had agreed that they would equally divide the *teruma* that they receive.

לְאֵלּוּ וּלְאֵלּוּ נִתְחַלְּקָה הָאָרֶץ, כְּדֵי לְקַיֵּים שְׁנֵי מִקְרָאוֹת הַלָּלוּ; הָא כֵּיצַד? הָיָה מִיּוֹצְאֵי מִצְרַיִם – נוֹטֵל חֶלְקוֹ עִם יוֹצְאֵי מִצְרַיִם, הָיָה מִבָּאֵי הָאָרֶץ – נוֹטֵל חֶלְקוֹ עִם בָּאֵי הָאָרֶץ, מִכָּאן וּמִכָּאן – נוֹטֵל חֶלְקוֹ מִכָּאן וּמִכָּאן.

Eretz Yisrael **was divided to these and to those,**[N] **so as to uphold these two verses. How so?** If one **was from** among **those who left Egypt,**[N] **he takes his portion** along **with those who left Egypt.** If one was from among **those who entered Eretz** Yisrael, **he takes his portion** along **with those who entered Eretz** Yisrael. If one was **from** both **here and there,**[N] i.e., he was among those who left Egypt and also entered Eretz Yisrael himself, **he takes his portion from here and there,** as he is entitled to two portions.

מְרַגְּלִים – יְהוֹשֻׁעַ וְכָלֵב נָטְלוּ חֶלְקָם, מִתְלוֹנְנִים וַעֲדַת קֹרַח לֹא הָיָה לָהֶם חֵלֶק בָּאָרֶץ, הַבָּנִים נָטְלוּ בִּזְכוּת אֲבִי אֲבִיהֶן וּבִזְכוּת אֲבִי אִמּוֹתֵיהֶן.

The *baraita* continues: With regard to the twelve **spies** sent to survey Eretz Yisrael prior to the Jewish people's entry into the land, **Joshua and Caleb took** all of the spies' **portions** of the land. Additionally, the **protesters and the assembly of Korah did not have a portion of Eretz** Yisrael. Nevertheless, their **sons took** portions of the land **in the merit of their paternal grandfathers and in the merit of their maternal grandfathers** if they were among those who left Egypt. This concludes the Gemara's citation of the *baraita*.

מַאי מַשְׁמַע דְּהַאי "לִשְׁמוֹת מַטּוֹת אֲבֹתָם" בְּיוֹצְאֵי מִצְרַיִם כְּתִיב? דִּלְמָא לִשְׁבָטִים קָאָמַר לָהּ! דִּכְתִיב: "וְנָתַתִּי אֹתָהּ לָכֶם מוֹרָשָׁה אֲנִי ה'", יְרוּשָּׁה הִיא לָכֶם מֵאֲבוֹתֵיכֶם, וּלְיוֹצְאֵי מִצְרַיִם קָאָמַר לְהוּ.

The Gemara asks: **From where may** it **be inferred that this** verse, which states: **"According to the names of the tribes of their fathers** they shall inherit" (Numbers 26:55), **is written with regard to those who left Egypt; perhaps** the verse **was stated** in reference **to** the progenitors of the **tribes,** and teaches that the land should be divided among the twelve tribes? The Gemara answers: The inference is from a verse, **as it is written:** "And I will bring you in to the land, concerning which I lifted up My hand to give it to Abraham, to Isaac, and to Jacob; **and I will give it to you for a heritage: I am the Lord"** (Exodus 6:8). This verse states that Eretz Yisrael **is an inheritance for you from your forefathers, and** this verse **was told to those who left Egypt,** indicating that those who left Egypt inherit the land.

(סִימָן: לָרַב צְלָפְחָד וְיוֹסֵף אִיכְּפַל מְנַשֶּׁה יַחֲשֹׁב.)

The Gemara presents **a mnemonic** device for the following series of questions posed by Rav Pappa to Abaye relating to the division of Eretz Yisrael: **To the more; Zelophehad; and Joseph; contested; Manasseh; will count.**

אֲמַר לֵיהּ רַב פָּפָּא לְאַבַּיֵי: בִּשְׁלָמָא לְמַאן דְּאָמַר לְיוֹצְאֵי מִצְרַיִם נִתְחַלְּקָה הָאָרֶץ, הַיְינוּ דִּכְתִיב: "לָרַב תַּרְבֶּה נַחֲלָתוֹ וְלַמְעַט תַּמְעִיט נַחֲלָתוֹ",

The Gemara presents the first question. **Rav Pappa said to Abaye: Granted, according to the one who says that Eretz** Yisrael **was divided among those who left Egypt, this is** the meaning of that **which is written: "To the more you shall give the more inheritance, and to the fewer you shall give the less inheritance"** (Numbers 26:54). The verse may be understood as teaching the novelty that even though the number of Jewish people entering Eretz Yisrael differed from the number who left Egypt, the land is nevertheless divided according to the numbers at the time of the Exodus, not according to the count at the time they received the land.

NOTES

To these and to those – לְאֵלּוּ וּלְאֵלּוּ: According to this opinion, the land was divided according to the number of people who left Egypt as well as according to the number of those who entered Eretz Yisrael. Anyone who was included in either one of these groups was entitled to a portion of land, and those who were included in both received two portions. The Rashbam notes that Rabbi Shimon ben Elazar disagrees with Rabbi Yonatan and holds that there was no reversion of inheritance to the older generation. Rather, there was an additional portion that the current generation inherited from the earlier generation that left Egypt.

From among those who left Egypt, etc. – מִיּוֹצְאֵי מִצְרַיִם וכו׳: If one left Egypt at the age of twenty or older and then perished in the wilderness, his sons, even those under twenty years of age at the time the Jewish people entered Eretz Yisrael, would divide the portion to which their father had been entitled. One who left Egypt under the age of twenty or one born in the wilderness who entered Eretz Yisrael would receive his own portion of land.

From both here and there – מִכָּאן וּמִכָּאן: Since anyone who was between twenty and sixty years old at the time of the Exodus died in the wilderness, it seems that this phrase must be referring to someone whose father had left Egypt above the age of twenty, and who himself entered Eretz Yisrael over the same age. Such an individual would receive the portion to which his father was entitled for being among those who left Egypt, and receive his own portion as one who entered Eretz Yisrael (Rashbam; see Ri Migash and Ramah).

The Rashbam explains that this expression is referring to one who himself was among both those who left Egypt and those who entered Eretz Yisrael. The Rashba points out that according to the straightforward understanding of the verses, only Joshua and Caleb would be included in this category. *Tosafot* write that it is possible that God's decree, which called for the entire generation that left Egypt to die in the wilderness, applied only to those who were between the ages of twenty and sixty. Accordingly, there may have been those who were over the age of sixty at the time of the decree, and who themselves entered Eretz Yisrael around the age of one hundred, and who therefore were entitled to two portions. The Ramah writes that based on the continuation of the *baraita*, it seems that Joshua and Caleb were not entitled to a second portion for being among those who entered the land, indicating that only those who entered the land under the age of sixty received a portion.

The Ramah adds that, presumably, one who entered Eretz Yisrael under the age of twenty and whose father was not twenty years of age at the time of the Exodus would nevertheless receive a portion from his grandfather who was among those who left Egypt. In fact, this is what was done for the children of the spies.

BACKGROUND

This poses a difficulty [*kashya*] – קַשְׁיָא: The commentaries point out that the term *kashya* suggests that although the question on a statement is strong, there may be a solution to the question. By contrast, the term *teyuvta* signifies a conclusive refutation of a statement, which indicates that the statement is indefensible.

NOTES

Due to the children – מִשּׁוּם טְפָלִים: Most commentaries understand this phrase to mean that the tribe included many children who were under the age of twenty and ineligible to receive a portion of land; the tribe as a whole, therefore, would receive too small a portion of land. By contrast, the Rashbam understands that there were many underage orphans among the members of this tribe, whose grandparents' children did not enter Eretz Yisrael. Therefore, they themselves could not inherit a portion of land due to their age, and they had no means of inheriting land from their ancestors who left Egypt, because those ancestors had no descendants who returned a portion to them, as none of their descendants entered the land at the age of twenty or over.

There was not one man who did not take – לָא הֲוָה חַד דְּלָא שָׁקֵיל: The Rashbam explains that according to the opinion that Eretz Yisrael was divided among those who left Egypt, there was no one whose father left Egypt under the age of twenty and did not have some other relative from whom to receive a portion; and according to the opinion that Eretz Yisrael was divided among those who entered Eretz Yisrael, there was no one under the age of twenty who did not receive a portion from an ancestor who left Egypt through the process of the portions being returned to those who left Egypt. While there may have been those who did not receive a portion due to these reasons, i.e., a case where a father, who was still alive, received his portion instead of the son, the son in effect did receive it because he would eventually inherit it from his father.

The descendants of Joseph who cried out and their protest was not effective – בְּנֵי יוֹסֵף דִּצְוֹוחִי וְלָא אַהֲנֵי: Although the Gemara soon teaches that they were told that they could inhabit the forest, this forest was within the portion designated for them, and their petition for more land was denied (Rashbam).

Should be wary of the evil eye – לְאִיזְדַּהוּרֵי מֵעֵינָא בִּישָׁא: One who is excessively successful in a particular area, such as wealth or childbearing, evokes the jealousy of others, which can lead to the dominion of the evil eye. It is prudent for such an individual to refrain from publicizing his successes because doing so could lead to his misfortune.

אֶלָּא לְמַאן דְּאָמַר לְבָאֵי הָאָרֶץ, מַאי ״לָרַב תַּרְבּוּ נַחֲלָתוֹ״? קַשְׁיָא.

But according to the one who says that Eretz Yisrael was divided **among those who entered** Eretz Yisrael, **what** does the verse: **"To the more you shall give the more inheritance"** teach? It is obvious that larger families will receive more land due to their greater numbers. The Gemara concludes: This poses **a difficulty**[B] to one who holds that opinion.

וַאֲמַר לֵיהּ רַב פַּפָּא לְאַבַּיֵי: בִּשְׁלָמָא לְמַאן דְּאָמַר לְיוֹצְאֵי מִצְרַיִם, הַיְינוּ דְּקָא צַוְוחָן בְּנוֹת צְלָפְחָד, אֶלָּא לְמַאן דְּאָמַר לְבָאֵי הָאָרֶץ, אַמַּאי צַוְוחָן? הָא לֵיתֵיהּ דְּלִשְׁקוֹל!

The Gemara presents the second question. **And Rav Pappa said to Abaye: Granted, according to the one who says** that Eretz Yisrael was divided **among those who left Egypt, this is** why **the daughters of Zelophehad cried out** in protest of the fact that they would be denied their father's portion, to which he was entitled as one who left Egypt. **But according to the one who says** that Eretz Yisrael was divided **among those who entered Eretz** Yisrael, **why did they cry out** in protest; after all, Zelophehad **was not** there **to take** his portion, so his daughters should have no claim to the land?

אֶלָּא לַחֲזָרָה וְלִיטּוֹל בְּנִכְסֵי חֵפֶר.

Abaye answers: **Rather,** according to this opinion, the protest of Zelophehad's daughters was in reference **to the returning** of the portions from the generation that entered Eretz Yisrael to the generation that left Egypt, as described in the *baraita* above. **And** accordingly, Zelophehad's daughters demanded **to take** their portion **in** the **property of** their grandfather **Hepher,** who received land posthumously through his children, their uncles.

בִּשְׁלָמָא לְמַאן דְּאָמַר לְיוֹצְאֵי מִצְרַיִם, הַיְינוּ דְּקָא צַוְוחָן בְּנֵי יוֹסֵף, דִּכְתִיב: ״וַיְדַבְּרוּ בְּנֵי יוֹסֵף״, אֶלָּא לְמַאן דְּאָמַר לְבָאֵי הָאָרֶץ, מַאי קָא צָוְוחִי? כּוּלְּהוּ שְׁקוּל!

The Gemara presents Rav Pappa's third question: **Granted, according to the one who says** that Eretz Yisrael was divided **among those who left Egypt, this is** why **the descendants of Joseph cried out** in protest of the fact that they would receive an inadequate portion of land due to the fact that they had proliferated greatly in the wilderness. **As it is written: "And the children of Joseph spoke** to Joshua, saying: Why have you given me but one lot and one part for an inheritance, seeing I am a great people, because the Lord has blessed me thus" (Joshua 17:14). **But according to the one who says** that Eretz Yisrael was divided **among those who entered Eretz** Yisrael, **what** is the reason **they were crying out? They** were **all** entitled to **take** their own portion of land and should have had no cause for complaint.

מִשּׁוּם טְפָלִים דַּהֲווּ נְפִישִׁי לְהוּ.

The Gemara answers: They protested **due to the children,**[N] **as they had many** children who were not entitled to a portion of the land.

אֲמַר אַבַּיֵי, שְׁמַע מִינָּהּ: לָא הֲוָה חַד דְּלָא שָׁקֵיל, דְּאִי סָלְקָא דַּעְתָּךְ הֲוָה חַד דְּלָא שָׁקֵיל, אִיבָּעֵי לֵיהּ לְמִצְוַח. וְכִי תֵּימָא: דִּצְוַח וְאַהֲנֵי – כְּתָבֵיהּ קְרָא, דִּצְוַח וְלָא אַהֲנֵי – לָא כְּתָבֵיהּ קְרָא, הָא בְּנֵי יוֹסֵף דִּצְוְוחִי וְלָא אַהֲנֵי וּכְתָבִינְהוּ קְרָא.

Abaye said: Learn from the fact that the Bible records the complaints of only the daughters of Zelophehad and the descendants of Joseph that **there was not one** other individual **who did not take**[N] a portion of land; **as if it enters your mind** that **there was** even **one** other **who did not take** a portion of land, **he should have cried out** in protest. **And if you would say: The verse wrote** about one **who cried out and** his protest **was effective,** and **the verse did not write** about one **who cried out and** his protest **was not effective,** that is difficult. **But** there is the counterexample of **the descendants of Joseph, who cried out and** their protest **was not effective,**[N] **and the verse wrote** about **them.**

הָתָם עֵצָה טוֹבָה קָא מַשְׁמַע לָן, דְּאִיבָּעֵי לֵיהּ לְאִינִישׁ לְאִיזְדַּהוּרֵי מֵעֵינָא בִּישָׁא. וְהַיְינוּ דְּקָאָמַר לְהוּ יְהוֹשֻׁעַ, דִּכְתִיב: ״וַיֹּאמֶר אֲלֵיהֶם יְהוֹשֻׁעַ אִם עַם רַב אַתָּה עֲלֵה לְךָ הַיַּעְרָה״, אֲמַר לְהוּ: לְכוּ וְהַחְבִּאוּ עַצְמְכֶם בַּיְּעָרִים שֶׁלֹּא תִּשְׁלוֹט בָּכֶם עַיִן רַע.

The Gemara rejects Abaye's inference: Generally, the verse would not record an instance where one cried out if his protest was not effective, and **there,** the verse includes the protest of Joseph's descendants in order to **teach us** a measure of **good advice: That a person should be wary of the evil eye.**[N] **And this is what Joshua said to them, as it is written: "And Joshua said unto them: If you be a great people, go up to the forest,** and cut down for yourself there in the land of the Perizzites and of the Rephaim" (Joshua 17:15). Joshua **said to them: Go and conceal yourselves in the forests so that the evil eye will not have dominion over you.**

אֲמַרוּ לֵיהּ: אֲנַן מִזַּרְעָא דְּיוֹסֵף דְּלָא שָׁלְטָא בֵּיהּ עֵינָא בִּישָׁא; דִּכְתִיב: ״בֵּן פֹּרָת יוֹסֵף בֵּן פֹּרָת עֲלֵי עָיִן״, וְאָמַר רַבִּי אַבָּהוּ: אַל תִּקְרֵי ״עֲלֵי עָיִן״ אֶלָּא: עוֹלֵי עַיִן.

Joseph's descendants **said to him: We are of the descendants of Joseph,** upon **whom the evil eye had no dominion, as it is written: "Joseph is a fruitful vine, a fruitful vine by a fountain [*alei ayin*]"** (Genesis 49:22), **and Rabbi Abbahu states** a homiletic interpretation: **Do not read** it as ***"alei ayin,"***[N] **rather** read it as ***olei ayin,*** above the eye, i.e., he transcended the influence of the evil eye. Joseph's descendants were saying that they also do not need to be wary.

רַבִּי יוֹסֵי בְּרַבִּי חֲנִינָא אֲמַר, מֵהָכָא: ״וְיִדְגּוּ לָרֹב בְּקֶרֶב הָאָרֶץ״, מַה דָּגִים שֶׁבַּיָּם – מַיִם מְכַסִּים עֲלֵיהֶם וְאֵין הָעַיִן שׁוֹלֶטֶת בָּהֶם, אַף זַרְעוֹ שֶׁל יוֹסֵף – אֵין הָעַיִן שׁוֹלֶטֶת בָּהֶם.

Rabbi Yosei, son of Rabbi Ḥanina, said that a proof for the notion that the evil eye holds no sway over Joseph and his descendants, is **from here,** Jacob's blessing of Joseph's sons, Ephraim and Manasseh: "The angel who has redeemed me from all evil, bless the lads; and let my name be named in them and the name of my fathers, Abraham and Isaac; **and let them grow into a multitude [*veyidgu*] in the midst of the earth"** (Genesis 48:16). *Veyidgu* is related etymologically to the word for fish [*dag*]. **Just as** with regard to **the fish in the sea, water covers them and the evil eye has no dominion over them, so too, the seed of Joseph, the** evil **eye has no dominion over them.**

״מְרַגְּלִים – יְהוֹשֻׁעַ וְכָלֵב נָטְלוּ חֶלְקָם״. מְנָהָנֵי מִילֵּי? אֲמַר עוּלָּא, דְּאָמַר קְרָא: ״וִיהוֹשֻׁעַ בִּן נוּן וְכָלֵב בֶּן יְפֻנֶּה חָיוּ מִן הָאֲנָשִׁים הָהֵם״, מַאי ״חָיוּ״? אִילֵימָא חָיוּ מַמָּשׁ – וְהָא כְּתִיב קְרָא אַחֲרִינָא: ״וְלֹא נוֹתַר מֵהֶם אִישׁ כִּי אִם כָּלֵב בֶּן יְפֻנֶּה וִיהוֹשֻׁעַ בִּן נוּן״! אֶלָּא מַאי ״חָיוּ״? שֶׁחָיוּ בְּחֶלְקָם.

§ The Gemara analyzes the next section of the *baraita,* which states: With regard to the twelve **spies**[N] sent to survey Eretz Yisrael prior to the Jewish people's entry into the land, **Joshua and Caleb took** all of the spies' **portions** of the land. The Gemara asks: **From where is this matter** derived? **Ulla said:** It is as **the verse states: "But Joshua, son of Nun, and Caleb, son of Jephunneh, lived of those men** that went to spy out the land" (Numbers 14:38). **What** does the term **"lived"** mean? **If we say** that it means **literally** that **they lived, but** there is **another verse** that **states: "And there was not left a man of them, save Caleb, son of Jephunneh, and Joshua, son of Nun"** (Numbers 26:65), so why would the Torah state it twice? **Rather, what** does the term **"lived"** mean? **That** Joshua and Caleb **lived in** the other spies' **portion**[N] of the land.

״מִתְלוֹנְנִין וַעֲדַת קֹרַח לֹא הָיָה לָהֶן חֵלֶק בָּאָרֶץ״. וְהָתַנְיָא: מְרַגְּלִים, מִתְלוֹנְנִים וַעֲדַת קֹרַח – יְהוֹשֻׁעַ וְכָלֵב נָטְלוּ חֶלְקָם! לָא קַשְׁיָא: מָר מַקִּישׁ מִתְלוֹנְנִים לַמְרַגְּלִים, מָר לָא מַקִּישׁ מִתְלוֹנְנִים לַמְרַגְּלִים;

The *baraita* teaches that the **protesters and the assembly of Korah did not possess a portion of Eretz Yisrael.** The Gemara asks: **But isn't it taught** otherwise in a *baraita*: With regard to the **spies,** the **protesters, and the assembly of Korah, Joshua and Caleb took their portions** of the land? Apparently, the protesters and the assembly of Korah were assigned portions in Eretz Yisrael, which were then given to Joshua and Caleb. The Gemara answers: It is **not difficult:** One **Sage,** the *tanna* of the *baraita* quoted earlier, **juxtaposes** the **protesters to the spies,** teaching that just as the spies were assigned a portion of Eretz Yisrael, so were the protesters. And one **Sage,** the *tanna* of the *baraita* quoted here, **does not juxtapose** the **protesters to the spies.** Although the spies were assigned a portion, the protesters were not.

דְּתַנְיָא: ״אָבִינוּ מֵת בַּמִּדְבָּר״ – זֶה צְלָפְחָד, ״וְהוּא לֹא הָיָה בְּתוֹךְ הָעֵדָה״ – זֶה עֲדַת מְרַגְּלִים, ״הַנּוֹעָדִים עַל ה׳״ – אֵלּוּ מִתְלוֹנְנִים, ״בַּעֲדַת קֹרַח״ – כְּמַשְׁמָעוֹ;

The Gemara quotes a related *baraita.* **As it is taught** in a *baraita* that the verse quotes the daughters of Zelophehad: "Our father died in the wilderness, and he was not among the assembly of them that gathered themselves together against the Lord in the assembly of Korah, but he died in his own sin; and he had no sons" (Numbers 27:3), and the daughters of Zelophehad therefore claim they are entitled to his portion. **"Our father died in the wilderness," this** is referring to **Zelophehad. "And he was not among the assembly," this** is referring to the **assembly of spies. "That gathered themselves together against the Lord," these** are the **protesters. "In the assembly of Korah,"** this is **in accordance with its** straightforward **meaning.** It is clear from this verse that those in these categories were not entitled to a portion in Eretz Yisrael.

NOTES

Do not read it *alei ayin* – אַל תִּקְרֵי עֲלֵי עַיִן: Some versions of the text omit the homiletical revision of the verse and simply offer an alternative meaning: Do not understand the word *ayin* to mean "fountain," so that *alei ayin* means "by a fountain"; understand *"ayin"* to mean eye, so that the expression means above the eye (Ritva).

Spies, etc. – מְרַגְּלִים וכו׳: This discussion arises only according to the opinion that Eretz Yisrael was divided among those who left Egypt. According to the opinion that it was divided among those who entered Eretz Yisrael, it is obvious that the spies and protesters were not entitled to a portion in the land, as they never entered Eretz Yisrael.

That Joshua and Caleb lived in the other spies' portion – שֶׁחָיוּ בְּחֶלְקָם: The meaning here is not simply that they alone among the spies remained alive, but that they sustained themselves through the land that they received from the portions of the other spies.

מָר מַקִּישׁ מִתְלוֹנְנִים לַמְרַגְּלִים, וּמָר לָא מַקִּישׁ מִתְלוֹנְנִים לַמְרַגְּלִים.

The Gemara concludes: One **Sage juxtaposes** the **protesters to the spies,** so that Joshua and Caleb inherited the portions of both; **and** one **Sage does not juxtapose** the **protesters to the spies.**

וְאָמַר לֵיהּ רַב פָּפָּא לְאַבָּיֵי: וּלְמַאן דְּמַקִּישׁ מִתְלוֹנְנִים לַמְרַגְּלִים, אִיכְפּוּל יְהוֹשֻׁעַ וְכָלֵב וְיָרְתוּ לְכוּלַּהּ אֶרֶץ יִשְׂרָאֵל? אֲמַר לֵיהּ: מִתְלוֹנְנִים שֶׁבַּעֲדַת קֹרַח קָאָמְרִינַן.

The Gemara presents Rav Pappa's fourth question. **And Rav Pappa said to Abaye: And according to the one who juxtaposes** the **protesters to the spies,** is it reasonable that **Joshua and Caleb contested** the spies **and inherited all of Eretz Yisrael?**[N] Many of the Jewish people protested in the wilderness at one point or another, and it cannot be that Joshua and Caleb received all of their portions by virtue of not participating in the sin of the spies. Abaye **said to him: We are referring** to the **protesters who were among the assembly of Korah.**[N] This term is not referring to all those who protested, but rather to the 250 individuals who protested along with Korah, and it is their portions of land that Joshua and Caleb received.

וְאָמַר לֵיהּ רַב פָּפָּא לְאַבָּיֵי: בִּשְׁלָמָא לְמַאן דְּאָמַר לְיוֹצְאֵי מִצְרַיִם נִתְחַלְּקָה הָאָרֶץ, הַיְינוּ דִּכְתִיב: ״וַיִּפְּלוּ חַבְלֵי מְנַשֶּׁה עֲשָׂרָה״, שִׁיתָּא דְּשִׁיתָּא בָּתֵּי אָבוֹת וְאַרְבָּעָה דִּידְהוּ – הָא עֲשָׂרָה.

The Gemara returns to the *baraita* and presents the fifth question. **And Rav Pappa said to Abaye: Granted, according to the one who says** that **Eretz** Yisrael **was divided among those who left Egypt, this is as it is written** with regard to the inheritance of the tribe of Manasseh: **"And ten parts fell to Manasseh,** beside the land of Gilead and Bashan, which is beyond the Jordan; because the daughters of Manasseh had an inheritance among his sons" (Joshua 17:5–6). **Six** were the portions **of the six fathers' houses**[N] of Manasseh listed in a previous verse (Joshua 17:2), **and four** parts **of** the daughters of Zelophehad;[N] **that is ten** parts.

אֶלָּא לְמַאן דְּאָמַר לְבָאֵי הָאָרֶץ – תְּמָנְיָא הוּא דְּהָווּ, שִׁיתָּא דְּשִׁיתָּא בָּתֵּי אָבוֹת וּתְרֵי דִּידְהוּ, הָא תְּמָנְיָא!

But according to the one who says that Eretz Yisrael was divided among those **who entered Eretz** Yisrael, **there were eight** parts, as follows: **Six** were the portions **of the six fathers' houses, and two of theirs,** which they received from the estate of their grandfather Hepher, of whom Zelophehad was the firstborn; **that is eight.** Zelophehad himself, by contrast, was not entitled to a portion, as he did not enter Eretz Yisrael.

NOTES

And inherited all of Eretz Yisrael – וְיָרְתוּ לְכוּלַּהּ אֶרֶץ יִשְׂרָאֵל: The Rashbam writes that at this point, the Gemara understands that the protesters mentioned here are those who complained about a lack of water (see Exodus 15:24), which included only part of the nation (see Maharshal). Accordingly, even at this stage the Gemara does not mean to suggest that according to this opinion Joshua and Caleb would have inherited literally all of Eretz Yisrael, but rather a large portion of it. By contrast, Rabbeinu Gershom Meor HaGola explains that the Gemara is referring to protesters in a general sense, including all those who complained at any point during the Jewish people's travel through the wilderness. If so, Joshua and Caleb would have inherited all of the land, since the entire nation complained to Moses at one point or another.

The protesters who were among the assembly of Korah – מִתְלוֹנְנִים שֶׁבַּעֲדַת קֹרַח: It is not clear who are the subjects of the phrase: The protesters who were among the assembly of Korah, as one does not find the term protesters in that context. Nevertheless, the Rashbam explains that this phrase refers to Dathan and Abiram and the 250 men who supported Korah in his rebellion. A proof for this assertion is that Zelophehad's daughters refer to the rebellion as those "that gathered themselves together against the Lord," while Moses addresses Korah and his rebellion as: "You and all your assembly that are gathered together against the Lord" (Numbers 16:11). The Ri Migash explains that the reference is to all the Jewish people who, following the death of Korah and his supporters, "protested against Moses and against Aaron, saying: You have killed the people of the Lord" (Numbers 17:6). The Ritva rejects this explanation, as it does not resolve Rav Pappa's difficulty, since Joshua and Caleb would then still have taken much of Eretz Yisrael. Citing the Ra'ah, he explains that among those who participated in Korah's rebellion were individuals who also spoke against Moses following the spies' report, where the term "protest" is used (see Numbers 14:27).

Of the six fathers' houses – דְּשִׁיתָּא בָּתֵּי אָבוֹת: The verse states: "For the children of Abiezer, and for the children of Helek, and for the children of Asriel, and for the children of Shechem, and for the children of Hepher, and for the children of Shemida" (Joshua 17:2). These were the families of Manasseh who received inheritances on the western side of the Jordan River.

And four parts of the daughters of Zelophehad – וְאַרְבָּעָה דִּידְהוּ: Three of these parts are enumerated in the mishna (116b): The inheritance of Zelophehad himself, because he was among those who left Egypt; the inheritance that Zelophehad received from his father, Hepher, who was also among those who left Egypt; and an additional share of Hepher's inheritance, as Zelophehad was a firstborn. As the Gemara explains further on, the fourth part is the portion Zelophehad's estate inherited from a brother who died without children.

According to the opinion that the daughters had only two of their own parts, in accordance with the opinion that Eretz Yisrael was divided among those who entered Eretz Yisrael, the two parts are Zelophehad's two portions that he was to receive as the firstborn son of Hepher.

וליטעמיך, ולמאן דאמר ליוצאי מצרים נתחלקה הארץ, תשעה הוו! אלא מאי אית לך למימר? חד אחא דאבא הוה להו, הכי נמי – תרי אחי דאבא הוה להו;

The Gemara objects: **And according to your reasoning, but** even **according to the one who says** that **Eretz** Yisrael **was divided among those who left Egypt, there are** only **nine** parts, as the mishna (116b) states that Zelophehad's daughters took three parts. **Rather, what have you to say?** How can the mishna be reconciled with the verse? One must say that according to the opinion that Eretz Yisrael was divided among those who left Egypt, **they had one** unmentioned **paternal uncle** who died without children, and Zelophehad's estate received a share of his portion. **So too,** according to the opinion that Eretz Yisrael was divided among those who entered Eretz Yisrael, it could be said that **they had two** unmentioned **paternal uncles,** so that they received two additional portions of land.

דתניא: "נתן תתן להם" – זו נחלת אביהן, "בתוך אחי אביהן" – זו נחלת אבי אביהן, "והעברת את נחלת אביהן להן" – זו חלק בכורה;

The fact that they received a portion from an uncle may be derived from a verse. **As it is taught** in a *baraita* that the verse states: **"You shall give [*naton titten*] them**[N] a possession of an inheritance" (Numbers 27:7). **This** is referring to the **inheritance of their father.** The verse continues: **"Among their father's brothers"; this** is referring to the **inheritance of their father's father.** The verse continues: **"And you shall pass the inheritance of their father to them"; this** is referring to the **portion of the firstborn** to which Zelophehad was entitled.

רבי אליעזר בן יעקב אומר: אף חלק אחי אביהם נטלו, שנאמר: "נתן תתן". ולמאן דאמר: תרי אחי דאבא הוה להו, ההוא מ"אחזת נחלה" נפקא.

The *baraita* continues. **Rabbi Eliezer ben Ya'akov says: They also took a portion of their father's brother, as it is stated: "You shall give [*naton titten*]."**[N] The double expression indicates that they received an additional portion. The Gemara notes: **And according to the one who says** that **they had two paternal uncles,**[N] **that** additional portion **is derived from** the phrase: "You shall give them **a possession of an inheritance,"** which would be superfluous were it not to indicate an additional portion.

ואמר ליה רב פפא לאביי: קרא מאי קא חשיב? אי טפלים קא חשיב, טובא הוו! אי בתי אבות קחשיב, שיתא הוו!

The Gemara presents the sixth question. **And Rav Pappa said to Abaye:** In **the verse** quoted above, **what** portions **is it counting? If** the verse **is counting children,** i.e., the portions of those who inherited from their antecedents, as with the daughters of Zelophehad, **there were many** such portions, and the verse did not enumerate all portions inherited by all members of the tribe. And **if** the verse **is counting fathers' houses, there are** only **six,** as Hepher is included among the six enumerated in Joshua 17:2. Why, then, does the verse count the portions of the daughters of Zelophehad separately?

NOTES

As it is taught in a *baraita*, you shall give them, etc. – דתניא נתן תתן להם וכו׳: The early commentaries note that this *baraita* can be reconciled only with the opinion that holds that Eretz Yisrael was divided among those who left Egypt, as the verse speaks of Zelophehad's inheritance and he was not among those who entered Eretz Yisrael.

As it is stated: You shall give [*naton titten*] – שנאמר נתן תתן: There is a dispute between the *tanna'im* whether double expressions are to be understood as indicating inclusions or as simple conventions of language, the latter following the principle: The Torah spoke in the language of people (Rashbam). Accordingly, Rabbi Eliezer ben Ya'akov follows the opinion of Rabbi Akiva, who says that the double expressions are meant as inclusions. Some early commentaries note that according to the first *tanna*, it is unclear how to arrive at the sum of ten portions of land within the inheritance of Manasseh, as the first *tanna* does not derive from the double expression that Zelophehad's daughters inherited from an uncle. Therefore, Rabbeinu Yona suggests that this *tanna* holds that the uncle in question was still alive when Moses received this mitzva, and he died before the portion was actually divided. According to another solution, accepted by the Ritva, the first *tanna* and Rabbi Eliezer ben Ya'akov are in agreement concerning the verse's double expression.

They had two paternal uncles – תרי אחי דאבא הוה להו: According to the opinion that Eretz Yisrael was divided among those who entered Eretz Yisrael, these brothers of Zelophehad must have died after their father, Hepher. Consequently, when Hepher's portion was assigned based on his descendants who entered Eretz Yisrael, the portions of land that would have been due these deceased sons were divided in their stead among Hepher's surviving sons and Zelophehad's inheriting daughters (Rashbam).

The Ra'avad explains that these two sons of Hepher entered Eretz Yisrael but died before the land was divided. Therefore, this verse, which was spoken in the wilderness, was prophetically alluding to the fact that this would occur (see Rabbeinu Yona).

NOTES

In accordance with the one who says the land was divided among those who entered Eretz Yisrael – כְּמַאן דְּאָמַר לְבָאֵי הָאָרֶץ: As long as one had reached the age of twenty by the time they entered Eretz Yisrael, he would be entitled to his own portion of land (Rashbam). Some commentaries explain that the Gemara is referring specifically to the opinion of Rabbi Shimon ben Elazar, which is that both those who left Egypt and those who entered Eretz Yisrael were entitled to portions of the land. Accordingly, the meaning is: Although all the other people of their generation inherited their fathers' portions in addition to receiving their own, the children of the spies received land only in their own merit (Rashbam). According to this interpretation, the Gemara could not be referring to the opinion of Rabbi Yonatan, which is that the land was divided only among those who entered Eretz Yisrael, as then there would be no reason to distinguish between the children of the spies and all the other members of their generation.

Nevertheless, the wording of the Gemara seems to be referring to the opinion of Rabbi Yonatan. Rabbeinu Yona therefore explains that it is reasonable to distinguish between the children of the spies and others with regard to the concept of the returning of the portions (see 117a), according to which the portions of those entering Eretz Yisrael were returned to their antecedents who left Egypt, and then redistributed among their descendants. Because the spies were not entitled to portions of the land, this process would not take effect. Therefore, unlike the portions of their peers, the portions of the children of the spies were given directly to them.

Who was not twenty years old – דְּלָא הֲוָה בֶּן עֶשְׂרִים: The children described here must have been the grandchildren, and not the children, of the spies. According to the chronology presented in *Seder Olam*, the spies died in the second year following the Exodus, so any children they fathered would have been much older than twenty years old by the time they entered Eretz Yisrael, after the fortieth year in the wilderness. It is common for the Gemara to refer to grandchildren as children, in accordance with the principle: Grandchildren are considered like children. Accordingly, when the Gemara speaks of: Their fathers' fathers, this must mean their fathers' fathers' fathers, for the grandfathers themselves were the spies (Rashbam).

Eretz Yisrael is already in possession – אֶרֶץ יִשְׂרָאֵל מוּחְזֶקֶת הִיא: Later, the Gemara derives this principle from the verse: "And I will give it to you for a heritage [*morasha*]" (Exodus 6:8), which teaches: Eretz Yisrael has the legal status of an inheritance [*yerusha*] from your fathers (119b). In explaining this concept, some suggest that since God gave the land to the Patriarchs, the children have the status of actual inheritors and not simply potential inheritors (Rabbi Avraham *Av Beit Din*).

The Ramah explains that the difference between property due to the deceased and the property that is already possessed by the deceased is that property due to the deceased will not necessarily ever be part of the inheritance. For example, when considering the inheritance of an orphaned grandson from his paternal grandfather, it cannot be said that when the grandson's father died, the grandfather's property should be considered as the father's by dint of the fact that were the grandfather to have died first, he would have inherited it. This is because this grandfather may not own the property by the time he passes away, which is when the inheritance would pass through the father of the grandson to the grandson. By contrast, once Eretz Yisrael was granted to the Patriarchs during their lifetimes, there was no uncertainty as to whether their descendants would inherit it. Therefore, it is already considered to be in the possession of the Jewish people.

The Meiri explains that a matter promised through prophecy and the divine spirit has the status of already being possessed and is not regarded as a property due to the deceased.

לְעוֹלָם בָּתֵּי אָבוֹת קָא חָשֵׁיב, וְהָא קָא מַשְׁמַע לָן, דִּבְנוֹת צְלָפְחָד נָטְלוּ חֵלֶק בְּכוֹרָה. אַלְמָא: אֶרֶץ יִשְׂרָאֵל מוּחְזֶקֶת הִיא.

The Gemara answers: **Actually,** the verse **is counting fathers' houses. And** by also counting the inheritance of Zelophehad's daughters, the verse **teaches us this: That** the **daughters of Zelophehad took** the **portion of the firstborn** due their father. **Evidently, Eretz Yisrael is** considered already **in possession** of one who was entitled to his portion of the land, even before the land was assigned. Although a firstborn son does not take a double portion of the property due to his deceased father as he does the property his father possessed, it is considered that Hepher possessed the portion that would eventually be assigned to him, and that Zelophehad was entitled to a double portion.

אָמַר מָר: וְהַבָּנִים נָטְלוּ בִּזְכוּת אֲבִי אֲבִיהֶם וּבִזְכוּת אֲבִי אִמּוֹתֵיהֶן. וְהָתַנְיָא: בִּזְכוּת עַצְמָן! לָא קַשְׁיָא: הָא – כְּמַאן דְּאָמַר לְיוֹצְאֵי מִצְרַיִם, הָא – כְּמַאן דְּאָמַר לְבָאֵי הָאָרֶץ.

§ The Gemara continues its discussion of the *baraita*. **The Master says: And the sons** of the spies and of the protesters **took** portions of the land **in the merit of their paternal grandfathers and in the merit of their maternal grandfathers** if those grandfathers were among those who left Egypt. The Gemara asks: **But isn't it taught** in a *baraita* (*Tosefta* 7:10): The sons of the spies and of the protesters took portions **in their own merit?** The Gemara answers: This is **not difficult: This** *baraita*, which states they took portions in the merit of their grandfathers, is written **in accordance with** the opinion of the **one who says** that Eretz Yisrael was divided **among those who left Egypt;** and **that** *baraita*, which states that they took portions in their own merit, is written **in accordance with** the opinion of the **one who says** that Eretz Yisrael was divided **among those who entered Eretz** Yisrael.[N]

וְאִיבָּעֵית אֵימָא: הָא וְהָא לְבָאֵי הָאָרֶץ, וְלָא קַשְׁיָא: הָא – דַּהֲוָה בֶּן עֶשְׂרִים, הָא – דְּלָא הֲוָה בֶּן עֶשְׂרִים.

The Gemara suggests another answer. **And if you wish, say** instead: **This** *baraita* **and that** *baraita* are written in accordance with the opinion that asserts that Eretz Yisrael was divided **among those who entered Eretz** Yisrael, **and** it is **not difficult: This** *baraita* is discussing one **who was twenty** years **old** when the Jewish people entered Eretz Yisrael, and therefore he took a portion in his own merit, and **that** *baraita* is discussing one **who was not twenty** years **old.**[N]

״וְשֶׁהָיָה בְּכוֹר נוֹטֵל שְׁנֵי חֲלָקִים״. וְאַמַּאי? רָאוּי הוּא, וְאֵין הַבְּכוֹר נוֹטֵל בְּרָאוּי כְּבְמוּחְזָק! אֲמַר רַב יְהוּדָה אֲמַר שְׁמוּאֵל: בִּיתֵדוֹת אֹהָלִים.

§ The mishna teaches: **And** Zelophehad took an additional portion that he received from Hepher, **because he was a firstborn,** and a firstborn **takes two portions** of inheritance from his father. The Gemara asks: **But why** was he entitled to the double portion of the firstborn? His portion of land **is** property merely **due** to Hepher, as Hepher never actually possessed the land, **and the** *halakha* is that **a firstborn does not take** a double portion **of** property **due** to the deceased **as** he does **of** property the deceased **possessed.**[H] **Rav Yehuda says** that **Shmuel says:** This clause of the mishna is stated **with regard to tent pegs** and other assorted movable property that Hepher possessed.

מְתִיב רַבָּה, רַבִּי יְהוּדָה אוֹמֵר: בְּנוֹת צְלָפְחָד נָטְלוּ אַרְבָּעָה חֲלָקִים, שֶׁנֶּאֱמַר ״וַיִּפְּלוּ חַבְלֵי מְנַשֶּׁה עֲשָׂרָה״! אֶלָּא אֲמַר רַבָּה: אֶרֶץ יִשְׂרָאֵל מוּחְזֶקֶת הִיא.

Rabba raises an objection from a *baraita*: **Rabbi Yehuda says:** The **daughters of Zelophehad took four parts, as it is stated: "And ten parts fell to Manasseh"** (Joshua 17:5). Clearly, this is referring to portions of land, and not simply movable property. **Rather, Rabba says: Eretz Yisrael is** considered already **in possession**[N] of one who was entitled to his portion of inheritance land, even before the land was assigned.

HALAKHA

A firstborn does not take a double portion of property due to the deceased as he does of property the deceased possessed – אֵין הַבְּכוֹר נוֹטֵל בְּרָאוּי כְּבְמוּחְזָק: A firstborn does not take a double portion from properties that were due to reach the possession of his father, but only from properties that were in his father's possession at the time of his death. Therefore, if the father's estate is due to receive an inheritance from someone else after the father dies, the firstborn claims from this property only that which is equal to the portions of each of his brothers (Rambam *Sefer Mishpatim*, *Hilkhot Naḥalot* 3:1, 7; *Shulḥan Arukh*, *Ḥoshen Mishpat* 278:3, and see *Even HaEzer* 163:1).

מֵיתִיבֵי, אָמַר רַבִּי חִידְקָא: שִׁמְעוֹן הַשִּׁקְמוֹנִי הָיָה לִי חָבֵר מִתַּלְמִידֵי רַבִּי עֲקִיבָא, וְכָךְ הָיָה רַבִּי שִׁמְעוֹן הַשִּׁקְמוֹנִי אוֹמֵר: יוֹדֵעַ הָיָה מֹשֶׁה רַבֵּינוּ שֶׁבְּנוֹת צְלָפְחָד יוֹרְשׁוֹת הֵן, אֲבָל לֹא הָיָה יוֹדֵעַ אִם נוֹטְלוֹת חֵלֶק בְּכוֹרָה אִם לָאו,

The Gemara **raises an objection** from a *baraita*. **Rabbi Ḥideka said: Shimon HaShikmoni**[P] **was my colleague among the students of Rabbi Akiva, and so would Rabbi Shimon HaShikmoni say:** Even before turning to God for guidance, **Moses our teacher knew that the daughters of Zelophehad were inheritors** and that they were entitled to their father's portion, as well as his share in Hepher's portion. **But he did not know if they** were entitled to **take a portion of the firstborn** of Hepher's portion **or not.**

וּרְאוּיָה הָיְתָה פָּרָשַׁת נְחָלוֹת לִיכָּתֵב עַל יְדֵי מֹשֶׁה, אֶלָּא שֶׁזָּכוּ בְּנוֹת צְלָפְחָד וְנִכְתְּבָה עַל יָדָן.

Rabbi Ḥideka continues citing Rabbi Shimon HaShikmoni: **And** the Torah **portion** concerning the laws **of inheritances was fit**[N] **to have been written through** God initiating a commandment to **Moses,** without mentioning Zelophehad's daughters. **But** by demonstrating their desire for land in Eretz Yisrael the **daughters of Zelophehad merited** that the portion was **written through** a response to **them.**

וְיוֹדֵעַ הָיָה מֹשֶׁה רַבֵּינוּ שֶׁהַמְקוֹשֵׁשׁ בְּמִיתָה, שֶׁנֶּאֱמַר: ״מְחַלְלֶיהָ מוֹת יוּמָת״, אֲבָל לֹא הָיָה יוֹדֵעַ בְּאֵי זוֹ מִיתָה הוּא יָמוּת, וּרְאוּיָה הָיְתָה פָּרָשַׁת מְקוֹשֵׁשׁ שֶׁתִּכָּתֵב עַל יְדֵי מֹשֶׁה, אֶלָּא שֶׁנִּתְחַיֵּיב מְקוֹשֵׁשׁ וְנִכְתְּבָה עַל יָדוֹ; לְלַמֶּדְךָ,

Rabbi Ḥideka continues citing Rabbi Shimon HaShikmoni: **And Moses our teacher** similarly **knew that the** wood **gatherer,** who gathered wood on Shabbat (see Numbers 15:32–36), was to be punished **by death, as it is stated: "Every one that profanes it shall be put to death"** (Exodus 31:14), **but he did not know by which death** penalty the wood gatherer **must die. And the** Torah **portion** concerning the punishment **of the** wood **gatherer was fit**[N] **to have been written through** God initiating a commandment to **Moses,** to teach which form of court-imposed capital punishment is administered to one who violates Shabbat. **But** the wood **gatherer was** found **guilty, and** the portion was **written through** the incident involving **him.** This is **to teach you**

PERSONALITIES

Shimon HaShikmoni – שִׁמְעוֹן הַשִּׁקְמוֹנִי: This Sage, one of the students of Rabbi Akiva, is mentioned in the Talmud only here, and is also mentioned in the halakhic *midrashim*. He is known by the name of his city, Shikmona, a Mediterranean coastal city mentioned in the Mishna and also in other sources. Shikmona was so near to the city of Haifa that it eventually merged with Haifa.

NOTES

And the Torah portion of inheritance was fit, etc. – וּרְאוּיָה הָיְתָה פָּרָשַׁת נְחָלוֹת וכו׳: In other words, the laws of inheritance could have been written in the same manner as all the other laws, presented as direct instructions to Moses, unconnected to any specific incidents or halakhic inquiries. With this suggestion, the Gemara asserts that all the laws in the Torah are fundamental and germane; nothing was included or formulated merely as a response to circumstances that arose. The Ramah explains that these laws would have been presented earlier in the Torah were it not for the fact that Zelophehad's daughters merited that the portion be written in their names.

And the Torah portion of the wood gatherer was fit, etc. – וּרְאוּיָה הָיְתָה פָּרָשַׁת מְקוֹשֵׁשׁ וכו׳: Aside from the two mentioned here in the Gemara, other Torah portions also present *halakhot* as a response to an incident, such as the *halakhot* of the blasphemer (Leviticus 24:10–23), or as a response to inquiries presented to Moses, such as the *halakhot* of the second *Pesaḥ* (Numbers 9:1–14). Nevertheless, the Gemara singles out the incident of the wood gatherer because, according to the midrash, Zelophehad himself was the wood gatherer. Accordingly, the two incidents are related (Ritva).

Perek **VIII**
Daf **119** Amud **b**

שֶׁמְּגַלְגְּלִים זְכוּת עַל יְדֵי זַכַּאי וְחוֹבָה עַל יְדֵי חַיָּיב;

that merit is brought about by means of one who **is meritorious and liability by means of** one who **is liable.** Accordingly, the daughters of Zelophehad merited that the Torah portion concerning a positive matter be written through them, and the wood gatherer deserved that a portion concerning a negative matter be written through him. This concludes Rabbi Hideka's citation of Rabbi Shimon HaShikmoni.

וְאִי סָלְקָא דַּעְתָּךְ אֶרֶץ יִשְׂרָאֵל מוּחְזֶקֶת, מַאי קָא מִסְתַּפְּקָא לֵיהּ?

The Gemara states its objection: **And if it enters your mind** to say that **Eretz Yisrael** was already **in possession** of the Jewish people even before the land was assigned, **what was** Moses **uncertain** about with regard to the right of Zelophehad's daughters to collect a double portion; after all, Hepher's portion in the land was in his possession, and Zelophehad was the firstborn?

הִיא גּוּפַהּ קָא מִסְתַּפְּקָא לֵיהּ, דִּכְתִיב: ״וְנָתַתִּי אֹתָהּ לָכֶם מוֹרָשָׁה אֲנִי ה׳״, יְרוּשָּׁה הִיא לָכֶם מֵאֲבוֹתֵיכֶם, אוֹ דִּלְמָא שֶׁמּוֹרִישִׁין וְאֵינָן יוֹרְשִׁין?

The Gemara answers: **This** matter **itself** is what Moses **was uncertain** about, **as it is written: "And I will give it to you for a heritage** [*morasha*]: **I am the Lord"** (Exodus 6:8). Moses was unsure if the verse should be understood: **It is an inheritance** [*yerusha*] **for you from your fathers,** such that it is considered in the possession of those who left Egypt; **or perhaps** the verse indicates another matter, **that** the generation of those who left Egypt **bequeath** [*morishin*] the portions to others **but they do not inherit** [*yoreshin*] the portions themselves, because they are destined to die in the wilderness.

וּפַשְׁטוּ לֵיהּ: תַּרְוַיְיהוּ – יְרוּשָּׁה לָכֶם מֵאֲבוֹתֵיכֶם, וּמוֹרִישִׁין וְאֵינָן יוֹרְשִׁין. וְהַיְינוּ דִּכְתִיב: ״תְּבִאֵמוֹ וְתִטָּעֵמוֹ בְּהַר נַחֲלָתְךָ״, תְּבִיאֵנוּ לֹא נֶאֱמַר, אֶלָּא ״תְּבִאֵמוֹ״, מְלַמֵּד שֶׁמִּתְנַבְּאִין וְאֵינָן יוֹדְעִין מָה מִתְנַבְּאִין.

The Gemara continues: **And** God **resolved** the question **for him:** The verse teaches **both of them. It is an inheritance for you from your fathers** and is considered in your possession; **and** also the generation that left Egypt **bequeath but they do not inherit. And this is** the meaning of that **which is written** in the song that the Jewish people sang after the splitting of the Red Sea: **"You will bring them in, and plant them in the mountain of Your inheritance"** (Exodus 15:17). It **is not stated: You will bring us in, rather: "You will bring them in,"** which **teaches that** in their song, the Jewish people **were prophesying** that their generation would never enter Eretz Yisrael, **but they did not know what they were prophesying.**

״וַתַּעֲמֹדְנָה לִפְנֵי מֹשֶׁה וְלִפְנֵי אֶלְעָזָר הַכֹּהֵן וְלִפְנֵי הַנְּשִׂיאִם וְכָל הָעֵדָה״ – אֶפְשָׁר עָמְדוּ לִפְנֵי מֹשֶׁה כו׳ וְלֹא אָמְרוּ לָהֶן דָּבָר, וְעָמְדוּ לִפְנֵי הַנְּשִׂיאִים וְכָל הָעֵדָה?

§ The Gemara continues its discussion of the incident involving Zelophehad's daughters. The verse states: **"And they stood before Moses, and before Eleazar the priest, and before the princes and all the congregation"** (Numbers 27:2). The Gemara asks: Is it **possible** that Zelophehad's daughters **stood before Moses** and then Eleazar to ask their question, **and they said nothing to them;** and then the daughters **stood before the princes and all the congregation** to ask them? How would the princes or the congregation know an answer if Moses and Eleazar did not?

אֶלָּא סָרֵס הַמִּקְרָא וְדָרְשֵׁהוּ, דִּבְרֵי רַבִּי יֹאשִׁיָּה; אַבָּא חָנָן אָמַר מִשּׁוּם רַבִּי אֱלִיעֶזֶר: בְּבֵית הַמִּדְרָשׁ הָיוּ יוֹשְׁבִין, וְהָלְכוּ וְעָמְדוּ לָהֶן לִפְנֵי כּוּלָּן.

The Gemara answers: **Rather, transpose the verse and interpret it:**[N] First, the daughters went to the congregation and ultimately came to Moses, this is **the statement of Rabbi Yoshiya. Abba Ḥanan says in the name of Rabbi Eliezer:** Those enumerated in the verse **were** all **sitting in the house of study, and** Zelophehad's daughters **went and stood before all of them** at once. They were not asked separately; rather, the order of the verse reflects their stature.

בְּמַאי קָמִיפַּלְגִי? מָר סָבַר: חוֹלְקִין כָּבוֹד לְתַלְמִיד בִּמְקוֹם הָרַב, וּמָר סָבַר: אֵין חוֹלְקִין.

The Gemara clarifies: **With regard to what do they disagree?** One **Sage,** Abba Ḥanan, **holds** that one may **show honor to a student in the presence of the teacher,**[H] such that the verse would mention all the others even though they were in the presence of Moses; **and** one **Sage,** Rabbi Yoshiya, **holds** one may **not show** honor to a student in the presence of the teacher, such that only Moses would have been mentioned if they were all in the same place.

וְהִלְכְתָא: חוֹלְקִין. וְהִלְכְתָא: אֵין חוֹלְקִין. קַשְׁיָא הִלְכְתָא אַהִלְכְתָא! הִלְכְתָא אַהִלְכְתָא לָא קַשְׁיָא: הָא – דְּפָלֵיג לֵיהּ רַבֵּיהּ יְקָרָא, הָא – דְּלָא פָּלֵיג לֵיהּ רַבֵּיהּ יְקָרָא.

The Gemara concludes: **And the *halakha*** is that one may **show** honor to a student, **and the *halakha*** is that one may **not show** honor. The Gemara asks: This is **difficult,** as there is a contradiction between **the one *halakha* and the other *halakha*.** The Gemara answers: The contradiction between **the one *halakha* and the other *halakha*** is **not difficult,** as **this** ruling, that one may show honor, was stated **where his teacher**[N] himself **accords** the student **honor.** In such a case, others also may show the student honor. And **that** ruling, that one may not show honor, was stated **where his teacher does not accord him honor.**

NOTES

Transpose [*sares*] the verse and interpret it – סָרֵס הַמִּקְרָא וְדָרְשֵׁהוּ: The word *sares*, meaning a change in the order of the terms, is commonly employed by the Sages (see 80a). According to this interpretation, the events actually occurred in the reverse order: First, the daughters came before the whole congregation; then, before the princes; then, before Eleazar; and finally, before Moses (Rashbam). If so, the verse is written out of chronological order in order to mention them in the order of the honor due to them (Ritva).

This ruling was stated where his teacher, etc. – הָא דְּפָלֵיג לֵיהּ רַבֵּיהּ וכו׳: The fact that the teacher honors him indicates that he is not uncomfortable with the student being honored; therefore, others may honor him as well. At times it is a source of honor for the teacher that his students are themselves worthy of being honored. In particular, Moses himself was in favor of all the Jewish people receiving honor (Rashbam), as in the verse (Numbers 11:29): "Would that all the Lord's people were prophets" (Ritva).

HALAKHA

Honor to a student in the presence of the teacher – כָּבוֹד לְתַלְמִיד בִּמְקוֹם הָרַב: One does not show honor to a student in the presence of his teacher. The Rema adds that even the student of the student may not show honor to his own teacher in front of his teacher's teacher. This *halakha* does not apply if the teacher himself shows honor to his student or if the teacher is honored by the honor bestowed upon his student (later authorities, citing Rabbeinu Simḥa and Mordekhai). The Rema, citing *Shibbolei HaLeket*, writes that the prohibition is in effect only if the one bestowing honor to the student is himself a student of the teacher; others disagree (Rambam *Sefer HaMadda*, *Hilkhot Talmud Torah* 5:8; *Shulḥan Arukh*, *Yoreh De'a* 242:21).

תָּנָא: בְּנוֹת צְלָפְחָד חַכְמָנִיּוֹת הֵן, דַּרְשָׁנִיּוֹת הֵן, צִדְקָנִיּוֹת הֵן.

§ The Sages **taught: The daughters of Zelophehad are wise,**[N] **they are interpreters** of verses, and **they are righteous.**

חַכְמָנִיּוֹת הֵן – שֶׁלְּפִי שָׁעָה דִּבְּרוּ, דְּאָמַר רַבִּי שְׁמוּאֵל בַּר רַב יִצְחָק: מְלַמֵּד שֶׁהָיָה מֹשֶׁה רַבֵּינוּ יוֹשֵׁב וְדוֹרֵשׁ בְּפָרָשַׁת יְבָמִין, שֶׁנֶּאֱמַר: "כִּי יֵשְׁבוּ אַחִים יַחְדָּו", אָמְרוּ לוֹ: אִם כְּבֵן אָנוּ חֲשׁוּבִין – תְּנָה לָנוּ נַחֲלָה כְּבֵן, אִם לָאו – תִּתְיַבֵּם אִמֵּנוּ! מִיָּד: "וַיַּקְרֵב מֹשֶׁה אֶת מִשְׁפָּטָן לִפְנֵי ה'".

The Gemara proves these assertions. That **they are wise** can be seen from the fact **that they spoke in accordance with the moment,** i.e., they presented their case at an auspicious time. **As Rabbi Shmuel bar Rav Yitzḥak says:** Tradition **teaches that Moses our teacher was sitting and interpreting in** the Torah **portion about men whose married brothers had died childless, as it is stated: "If brothers dwell together,** and one of them dies, and has no child, the wife of the dead shall not be married abroad to one not of his kin; her husband's brother shall come to her, and take her for him as a wife" (Deuteronomy 25:5). The daughters of Zelophehad **said to** Moses: **If we are** each **considered like a son, give us** each **an inheritance like a son;** and **if not, our mother should enter into levirate marriage. Immediately** upon hearing their claim, the verse records: **"And Moses brought their cause before the Lord"** (Numbers 27:5).

דַּרְשָׁנִיּוֹת הֵן – שֶׁהָיוּ אוֹמְרוֹת: אִילּוּ הָיָה לוֹ בֵּן, לֹא דִּבַּרְנוּ. וְהָתַנְיָא: בַּת! אָמַר רַבִּי יִרְמְיָה: סַמֵּי מִכָּאן בַּת. אַבַּיֵּי אָמַר: אֲפִילּוּ הָיָה בַּת לַבֵּן, לֹא דִּבַּרְנוּ.

That **they are interpreters** of verses can be seen from the fact **that they were saying: If** our father **had had a son, we would not have spoken;** but because he had no son, we are filling the role of the heir. The Gemara asks: **But isn't it taught** in a *baraita*: They would say, if he had had **a daughter,** we would not have spoken? **Rabbi Yirmeya said: Delete from** the *baraita* **here** the word: **Daughter.** As they were themselves daughters, this cannot have been their claim. **Abaye said** that the *baraita* need not be emended, and should be understood as follows: **Even if** there **was a daughter of a son** of Zelophehad, **we would not have spoken,**[N] for she would have been the heir.

צִדְקָנִיּוֹת הֵן – שֶׁלֹּא נִישְּׂאוּ אֶלָּא לְהָגוּן לָהֶן. תָּנֵי רַבִּי אֱלִיעֶזֶר בֶּן יַעֲקֹב: אֲפִילּוּ קְטַנָּה שֶׁבָּהֶן לֹא נִשֵּׂאת פְּחוּתָה מֵאַרְבָּעִים שָׁנָה.

That **they are righteous** can be seen from the fact **that they did not** rush **to marry,** but **rather** waited **to** marry those **fit for them. Rabbi Eliezer ben Ya'akov teaches: Even the youngest** to be married **among them was not married** at **less than forty years** of age.[N]

אִינִי? וְהָא אָמַר רַב חִסְדָּא: נִיסֵּת פְּחוּתָה מִבַּת עֶשְׂרִים – יוֹלֶדֶת עַד שִׁשִּׁים, בַּת עֶשְׂרִים – יוֹלֶדֶת עַד אַרְבָּעִים, בַּת אַרְבָּעִים – שׁוּב אֵינָהּ יוֹלֶדֶת! אֶלָּא, מִתּוֹךְ שֶׁצִּדְקָנִיּוֹת הֵן נַעֲשָׂה לָהֶן נֵס כְּיוֹכֶבֶד, דִּכְתִיב: "וַיֵּלֶךְ אִישׁ מִבֵּית לֵוִי וַיִּקַּח אֶת בַּת לֵוִי",

The Gemara asks: **Is that so? But doesn't Rav Ḥisda say:** If a woman **marries** when she is **less than twenty** years **old,** she is able to **give birth until** she reaches the age of **sixty;** if she marries when she is **twenty** years **old** or older, she is able to **give birth until** she reaches the age of **forty;** if she marries when she is **forty** years **old** or older, she is **no longer** able to **give birth** at all. If so, how could Zelophehad's daughters have waited until the age of forty to marry? **Rather, since they are righteous women, a miracle was performed for them, like** the one done for **Jochebed. As it is written: "And a man of the house of Levi went, and took as a wife a daughter of Levi"** (Exodus 2:1).

NOTES

They are wise – חַכְמָנִיּוֹת הֵן: In other words, they conducted their affairs with sensibility, as in the given example in which they presented their case at an opportune time. Moreover, as Rashbam explains, they grounded their claim in sound logic.

Even if there was a daughter of a son of Zelophehad we would not have spoken – אֲפִילּוּ הָיָה בַּת לַבֵּן לֹא דִּבַּרְנוּ: This claim proves that they were interpreters of verses, as they understood that the formulation: "And he has no [*ein lo*] son" (Deuteronomy 25:5), teaches that the court must investigate to see if the deceased's sons have any offspring, as well (Rashbam).

Less than forty years of age – פְּחוּתָה מֵאַרְבָּעִים שָׁנָה: Some explain that they delayed marriage because they were waiting for proper husbands. This fact can be deduced from a midrashic interpretation that asserts that the incident of the wood gatherer occurred immediately after the sin of the spies, in the second year after the exodus from Egypt. According to the opinion that Zelophehad was the wood gatherer, his daughters must have all been born early in the nation's sojourn in the wilderness. If so, they were all at least close to forty years old when Moses taught the laws of inheritance, just before the Jewish people entered Eretz Yisrael. It was only thereafter that they married (*Tosafot*).

אֶפְשָׁר בַּת מֵאָה וּשְׁלֹשִׁים שָׁנָה וְקָרָא לָהּ "בַּת"? דְּאָמַר רַבִּי חָמָא בַּר חֲנִינָא: זוֹ יוֹכֶבֶד שֶׁהוֹרָתָהּ בַּדֶּרֶךְ וְנוֹלְדָה בֵּין הַחוֹמוֹת, דִּכְתִיב: "אֲשֶׁר יָלְדָה אֹתָהּ לְלֵוִי בְּמִצְרָיִם",

The Gemara asks: Is it **possible** that this is Jochebed? Jochebed was then **130 years old and** the verse **called her a daughter,** indicating one who is very young. Jochebed's age is established based on a tradition concerning the number of Jacob's descendants who came to Egypt, as follows: While the verse states that Leah had thirty-three descendants (Genesis 46:15), only thirty-two were enumerated. This was explained **as Rabbi Ḥama bar Ḥanina says: This** "daughter of Levi" is **Jochebed, whose conception** occurred **on the journey** as the family of Jacob descended to Egypt, **and she was born within the walls,** i.e., having entered Egypt, **as it is written:** "And the name of Amram's wife was Jochebed, the daughter of Levi, **who was born to Levi in Egypt**" (Numbers 26:59).

לֵידָתָהּ בְּמִצְרַיִם וְהוֹרָתָהּ שֶׁלֹּא בְּמִצְרַיִם. וְאַמַּאי קָרוּ לָהּ "בַּת"? אָמַר רַב יְהוּדָה בַּר זְבִידָא: מְלַמֵּד שֶׁנּוֹלְדוּ בָּהּ סִימָנֵי נַעֲרוּת, נִתְעַדֵּן הַבָּשָׂר, נִתְפַּשְּׁטוּ הַקְּמָטִין, וְחָזַר הַיּוֹפִי לִמְקוֹמוֹ.

One can infer from the verse: **Her birth** was **in Egypt, but her conception was not in Egypt.** Since the Jewish people were in Egypt for 210 years and Moses was eighty years old at the time of the Exodus, Jochebed must have been 130 years old when Moses was born. The Gemara therefore asks: **And why** does the verse **call her "a daughter"? Rav Yehuda bar Zevida says:** This **teaches that** her **signs of youth** miraculously **came into being** again. **The flesh became smooth, the wrinkles were straightened out, and the** youthful **beauty returned to its place.**

"וַיִּקַּח" – "וַיַּחֲזוֹר" מִיבָּעֵי לֵיהּ! אָמַר רַב יְהוּדָה בַּר זְבִידָא: מְלַמֵּד שֶׁעָשָׂה לָהּ מַעֲשֵׂה לְקוּחִין, הוֹשִׁיבָהּ בְּאַפִּרְיוֹן, וְאַהֲרֹן וּמִרְיָם מְשׁוֹרְרִים לְפָנֶיהָ, וּמַלְאֲכֵי שָׁרֵת אוֹמְרִים: "אֵם הַבָּנִים שְׂמֵחָה".

The verse concerning Amram's marriage to Jochebed states: "And a man of the house of Levi went, **and took** as a wife a daughter of Levi" (Exodus 2:1). The Gemara asks: Since Jochebed had already been married to Amram for some years, as Miriam and Aaron were already born, the verse **should have** stated: **And** he **took back**[N] as a wife. **Rav Yehuda bar Zevida says:** The wording of the verse **teaches that** Amram **performed for her** a formal **act of marriage**[N] as though he were marrying her for the first time. He **seated her in** a bridal **palanquin** [*be'appiryon*],[L] **and Aaron and Miriam** were **singing before her, and the ministering angels** were **saying: "A joyful mother of children"** (Psalms 113:9).

לְהַלָּן מְנָאָן הַכָּתוּב דֶּרֶךְ גְּדוּלָּתָן וְכָאן דֶּרֶךְ חָכְמָתָן. מְסַיְּיעָא לֵיהּ לְרַבִּי אַמִי, דְּאָמַר רַבִּי אַמִי: בִּישִׁיבָה הַלֵּךְ אַחַר חָכְמָה, בִּמְסִיבָּה הַלֵּךְ אַחַר זִקְנָה. אָמַר רַב אַשִׁי: וְהוּא דְּמַפְלִיג בְּחָכְמָה, וְהוּא דְּמַפְלִיג בְּזִקְנָה.

§ The Gemara returns to discuss Zelophehad's daughters: **Later on, the verse lists them**[N] **according to their age,** stating: "For Mahlah, Tirzah, and Hoglah, and Milcah, and Noah, the daughters of Zelophehad, were married" (Numbers 36:11), **and here** the verse lists them in a different order, **according to their wisdom:** "And these are the names of his daughters: Mahlah, Noah, and Hoglah, and Milcah, and Tirzah" (Numbers 27:1). This **supports** the ruling **of Rabbi Ami, as Rabbi Ami says: In** the context of **sitting** in judgment[H] or learning Torah, **follow** the participants' **wisdom** in determining the seating, so that the wisest is granted the highest honor, and **in** the context of **reclining** for a meal, **follow** the participants' **age. Rav Ashi says: And this** is so only **when** one is **outstanding**[N] **in wisdom,** then wisdom trumps age; **and this** is so only **when** one of the participants is **outstanding in age,** i.e., particularly old, then age trumps wisdom.

NOTES

And took…and took back – וַיִּקַּח...וַיַּחֲזוֹר: According to a fuller account presented in tractate *Sota* 12a, Amram had divorced Jochebed when Pharaoh issued the decree: "Every son that is born you shall cast into the river" (Exodus 1:22). Amram reasoned that it was futile to have children destined to be killed. Miriam then convinced Amram to remarry Jochebed.

He performed for her a formal act of marriage – עָשָׂה לָהּ מַעֲשֵׂה לְקוּחִין: Generally, one who remarries his divorcée does not conduct an elaborate wedding with an extensive guest list. Nevertheless, in this instance, Amram did arrange an elaborate wedding, as if he were marrying her for the first time. He did so in order to publicize the fact that he was remarrying her and thereby discourage others from divorcing their wives (*Tosafot Yeshanim*).

Later on the verse lists them, etc. – לְהַלָּן מְנָאָן הַכָּתוּב וכו׳: The verse in Numbers, chapter 36 speaks of the marriages of Zelophehad's daughters. Presumably, they were married according to the order they are listed in the verse, and it stands to reason that they were married in order of age. Therefore, the Gemara assumes that the verse there follows their order of birth.

And this is so when one is outstanding – וְהוּא דְּמַפְלִיג: There are two approaches to understanding this classification. Some explain that this means that the individual is outstanding relative to his peer group. The one outstanding in wisdom is among the greatest of the generation, and the one outstanding in age is exceedingly old. These individuals are deserving of extra honor (Rashbam; Ri Migash).

According to another opinion, the scholar is outstanding in wisdom relative to the oldest one present. Similarly, the elderly person is outstanding in age relative to the wisest one present (Ramah).

LANGUAGE

Palanquin [*appiryon*] – אַפִּרְיוֹן: From the Greek φορεῖον, *phoreion*, meaning a chair used for carrying people.

Men carrying a palanquin

HALAKHA

In the context of sitting in judgment, etc. – בִּישִׁיבָה וכו׳: If, in the setting of a court or engaged in Torah study, there is a young scholar who is outstanding in wisdom sitting together with an elderly scholar outstanding in age, the scholar outstanding in wisdom sits at the head of the table and is invited to speak first. If these individuals are together at an occasion for reclining, such as a wedding feast, the elderly scholar is given the greater honor.

If the young scholar is outstanding in wisdom and the elder one is not particularly old, then the outstanding scholar is given the greater honor even in a situation of reclining. Conversely, if the elder scholar is particularly old and the younger scholar is not outstanding in wisdom, the elder scholar is given the greater honor even for occasions of sitting in judgment. According to the Maharshal, this is the *halakha* only if the elder is a Torah scholar as well.

If neither individual is particularly distinguished by either wisdom or age, the elder one is given the greater honor in all matters. Here, too, the Maharshal rules that this *halakha* applies only if he is a Torah scholar. Some say that even if neither is particularly distinguished, the one greater in wisdom is afforded the greater honor in sitting in judgment, and the older one in reclining (*Shakh*, citing Ran).

The *Baḥ* learns from this Gemara that if two siblings are to be married, the older one should be married first, even if the younger one is more distinguished in scholarship (Rambam *Sefer Shofetim, Hilkhot Sanhedrin* 1:7; *Shulḥan Arukh, Yoreh De'a* 244:18).

תָּנָא דְּבֵי רַבִּי יִשְׁמָעֵאל: בְּנוֹת צְלָפְחָד שְׁקוּלוֹת הָיוּ, שֶׁנֶּאֱמַר: "וַתִּהְיֶינָה", הֲוָיָה אַחַת לְכוּלָּן.

The Gemara cites an alternative opinion: **The school of Rabbi Yishmael taught: The daughters of Zelophehad were equal** in stature, **as it is stated:** "For Mahlah, Tirzah, and Hoglah, and Milcah, and Noah, the daughters of Zelophehad, were [***vatihyena***] married." The word "*vatihyena*" demonstrates: **There was one** uniform **existence** [***havaya***], i.e., spiritual level, **for all of them.**

אָמַר רַב יְהוּדָה אָמַר שְׁמוּאֵל: בְּנוֹת צְלָפְחָד הוּתְּרוּ לְהִנָּשֵׂא לְכָל הַשְּׁבָטִים, שֶׁנֶּאֱמַר: "לַטּוֹב בְּעֵינֵיהֶם תִּהְיֶינָה לְנָשִׁים", אֶלָּא מָה אֲנִי מְקַיֵּים "אַךְ לְמִשְׁפַּחַת מַטֵּה אֲבִיהֶם תִּהְיֶינָה לְנָשִׁים"? עֵצָה טוֹבָה הִשִּׂיאָן הַכָּתוּב, שֶׁלֹּא יִנָּשְׂאוּ אֶלָּא לְהָגוּן לָהֶן.

§ **Rav Yehuda says** that **Shmuel says: The daughters of Zelophehad were permitted**[N] **to marry** members **of any of the tribes, as it is stated: "Let them be married to whom they think best"** (Numbers 36:6). **But how do I realize** the meaning of the continuation of the same verse: **"Only into the family of the tribe of their father shall they be married"** (Numbers 36:6), according to which they were permitted to marry only members of their own tribe? **The verse offered them good advice, that they should be married only** to those **fit for them,** who were often men from within the family.

מוֹתִיב רַבָּה: "אֱמֹר אֲלֵיהֶם" – לְאוֹתָן הָעוֹמְדִים עַל הַר סִינַי, "לְדֹרֹתֵיכֶם" – אֵלּוּ דּוֹרוֹת הַבָּאִים. אִם נֶאֱמַר אָבוֹת לָמָּה נֶאֱמַר בָּנִים, וְאִם נֶאֱמַר בָּנִים לָמָּה נֶאֱמַר אָבוֹת? מִפְּנֵי שֶׁיֵּשׁ בָּאָבוֹת מַה שֶּׁאֵין בַּבָּנִים, וְיֵשׁ בַּבָּנִים מַה שֶּׁאֵין בָּאָבוֹת;

Rabba raised an objection from a *baraita* taught concerning the prohibition against eating consecrated foods while in a state of ritual impurity. Moses was commanded: "Say to them: Whoever will be of all your descendants throughout your generations, who approaches to the holy things, which the children of Israel consecrate to the Lord, having his uncleanness upon him, that soul shall be cut off from before Me" (Leviticus 22:3). Which people are referred to in the phrase **"say to them"?** It is referring **to those standing at Mount Sinai.** Which people are referred to in the phrase **"throughout your generations"? These are the coming generations. If** the *halakha* **is stated to the fathers, why is** it **stated** to **the sons; and if** the *halakha* **is stated** to **the sons, why is** it **stated to the fathers?** This is **because there are** mitzvot **for the fathers that are not for the sons, and there are** mitzvot **for the sons that are not for the fathers.**

בָּאָבוֹת הוּא אוֹמֵר: "וְכָל בַּת יֹרֶשֶׁת נַחֲלָה", וְהַרְבֵּה מִצְוֹת נִצְטַוּוּ בָּנִים שֶׁלֹּא נִצְטַוּוּ אָבוֹת; הָא מִפְּנֵי שֶׁיֵּשׁ בָּאָבוֹת שֶׁאֵין בַּבָּנִים, וְיֵשׁ בַּבָּנִים מַה שֶּׁאֵין בָּאָבוֹת – הוּצְרַךְ לוֹמַר אָבוֹת הוּצְרַךְ לוֹמַר בָּנִים.

The *baraita* continues: **For the fathers,** the verse **states:** "**And every daughter who possesses an inheritance** from the tribes of the children of Israel, shall be wife to one of the family of the tribe of her father" (Numbers 36:8). This mitzva, that the woman should marry a member of her own tribe, applied only to the first generation that received tribal portions of Eretz Yisrael. **And,** by contrast, there were **many mitzvot**, e.g., all the mitzvot that applied only from the time that Eretz Yisrael was settled, which **the sons were commanded** to fulfill but **which the fathers were not commanded** to fulfill. **Because there are** mitzvot **for the fathers that are not for the sons, and there are** mitzvot **for the sons that are not for the fathers,** the verse **needed to state,** i.e., to address, the **fathers,** and it **needed to state,** i.e., to address, the **sons.**

קָתָנֵי מִיהַת: בָּאָבוֹת הוּא אוֹמֵר: "וְכָל בַּת יֹרֶשֶׁת נַחֲלָה"! הוּא מוֹתִיב לַהּ, וְהוּא מְפָרֵק לַהּ: לְבַר מִבְּנוֹת צְלָפְחָד.

Rabba states his objection: **In any event,** the *baraita* **teaches: For the fathers,** the verse **states: "And every daughter who possesses an inheritance** from the tribes of the children of Israel, shall be wife to one of the family of the tribe of her father." This indicates that this was a mitzva for that entire generation, including Zelophehad's daughters, in contrast to the statement of Shmuel. The Gemara explains: **He,** Rabba, **raised the objection, and he resolved it:** This mitzva applied to everyone **except for the daughters of Zelophehad,** who were explicitly permitted to marry members of any tribe.

אָמַר מָר: בָּאָבוֹת הוּא אוֹמֵר "וְכָל בַּת יוֹרֶשֶׁת נַחֲלָה". בָּאָבוֹת – אִין, בַּבָּנִים – לָא, מַאי מַשְׁמַע? אָמַר רָבָא, אָמַר קְרָא: "זֶה הַדָּבָר", דָּבָר זֶה לֹא יְהֵא נוֹהֵג אֶלָּא בְּדוֹר זֶה.

The Master says in the *baraita* cited above: **For the fathers,** the verse **states: "And every daughter who possesses an inheritance** from the tribes of the children of Israel, shall be wife to one of the family of the tribe of her father." **For the fathers, yes,** this is the mitzva, but **for the sons,** it is **not** so. The Gemara asks: **From where may it be inferred? Rava said** that **the verse states** there: **"This is the matter** that the Lord has commanded" (Numbers 36:6), meaning: **This matter will not be practiced except in this generation.**

NOTES

The daughters of Zelophehad were permitted – בְּנוֹת צְלָפְחָד הוּתְּרוּ: Only they were permitted, as Moses allowed them alone to marry whomever they chose. According to the *halakha* for everyone else, women who inherited from their fathers were allowed to marry only members of their own tribes.

אֲמַר לֵיהּ רַבָּה זוּטִי לְרַב אַשִׁי: אֶלָּא מֵעַתָּה, "זֶה הַדָּבָר" דִּשְׁחוּטֵי חוּץ, הָכִי נַמִי דְּלֹא יְהֵא נוֹהֵג אֶלָּא בְּדוֹר זֶה?! שָׁאנֵי הָתָם, דִּכְתִיב: "לְדֹרֹתָם".

Rabba Zuti said to Rav Ashi: If that is so, then concerning the phrase **"this is the matter"** written **with regard to** an offering **slaughtered outside** the Tabernacle (see Leviticus 17:2–3), **so too,** is it the *halakha* **that it will not be practiced except in this generation?** Certainly that is not so, as that prohibition applies in all generations. What is the difference between the two passages? Rav Ashi answered: It **is different there,** with regard to offerings slaughtered outside the Tabernacle or Temple, **as it is written: "Throughout their generations"** (Leviticus 17:7), indicating that the prohibition is in effect in all generations.

Perek **VIII**
Daf **120** Amud **b**

"זֶה הַדָּבָר" דְּרָאשֵׁי הַמַּטּוֹת, הָכִי נַמִי דְּלֹא יְהֵא נוֹהֵג אֶלָּא בְּדוֹר זֶה? אֲמַר לֵיהּ: הַהוּא יָלֵיף "זֶה" "זֶה" מֵהָתָם.

Rabba Zuti asked Rav Ashi about another instance of the same phrase. In the case of **"this is the matter"** written **with regard to** the **heads of the tribes,** in the introductory verse to the *halakhot* of vows: "And Moses spoke to the heads of the tribes of the children of Israel, saying: This is the matter that the Lord has commanded" (Numbers 30:2), is it **also** the case **that** the *halakhot* of vows **will not be practiced except in this generation?** Rav Ashi **said to him:** The *halakha* in **that** case, that of vows, **is derived through** a verbal analogy between the word **"this"** stated here, in the verse discussing vows, and the word **"this"** stated **there,** in the verse discussing offerings slaughtered outside the Tabernacle or Temple, which is applicable in all generations.

הַאי נַמִי לֵילֵיף "זֶה" "זֶה" מֵהָתָם! הַאי מַאי? בִּשְׁלָמָא הָתָם אִיצְטְרִיךְ לִגְזֵרָה שָׁוָה, הָכָא לְמַאי אִיצְטְרִיךְ? לִשְׁתּוֹק קְרָא מִינֵּיהּ וַאֲנָא יָדַעְנָא דִּלְדוֹרוֹת הוּא.

The Gemara asks: **This** *halakha,* concerning the daughter inheriting her father's portion, **let it be derived through** a verbal analogy between the word **"this"** stated here, with regard to inheritance, and the word **"this"** stated **there,** in the verse discussing offerings, **as well.** The Gemara rejects that comparison: **What is this** suggestion? **Granted, there,** i.e., with regard to offerings slaughtered outside the Tabernacle or Temple and with regard to vows, the phrase "this is the matter" **was necessary** for deriving other *halakhot* through **a verbal analogy,**[N] as will be explained later. Therefore, the term may also be employed to teach that the *halakha* applies in all generations. But **here,** with regard to a daughter's inheritance, **for what** other *halakha* **was** this phrase **necessary?** If the *halakha* truly applies for posterity, **let the verse be silent** and refrain **from** addressing when this *halakha* applies by not stating "this is the matter," **and I** would **know that it is for all generations,** as is the case with all other mitzvot.

מַאי גְּזֵרָה שָׁוָה? דְּתַנְיָא: נֶאֱמַר כָּאן "זֶה הַדָּבָר" וְנֶאֱמַר לְהַלָּן "זֶה הַדָּבָר", מַה לְּהַלָּן אַהֲרֹן וּבָנָיו וְכָל יִשְׂרָאֵל, אַף כָּאן אַהֲרֹן וּבָנָיו וְכָל יִשְׂרָאֵל; וּמַה כָּאן רָאשֵׁי הַמַּטּוֹת, אַף לְהַלָּן רָאשֵׁי הַמַּטּוֹת.

The Gemara explains: **What** is the **verbal analogy** for which the phrase was necessary? **As it is taught** in a *baraita*: **It is stated here,** with regard to vows: **"This is the matter," and it is stated there,** with regard to offerings slaughtered outside the Tabernacle or Temple: **"This is the matter." Just as there** the mitzva applies to **Aaron and his sons and all Israel, so too here,** with regard to vows, the mitzva applies to **Aaron and his sons and all Israel. And just as here** the mitzva applies to **the heads of the tribes,** as explicitly stated in the verse cited above, **so too there,** with regard to offerings slaughtered outside the Tabernacle or Temple, there is particular relevance to **the heads of the tribes.**

NOTES

Was necessary for a verbal analogy – אִיצְטְרִיךְ לִגְזֵרָה שָׁוָה: The verbal analogy is explained later in the Gemara. In any case, a verbal analogy is not employed only in one direction. Therefore, once it is established that there is a verbal analogy linking the passage of vows with the passage of offerings slaughtered outside the Tabernacle or Temple, it may be surmised that just as the prohibition of offerings sacrificed outside the Tabernacle or Temple applies permanently, so should the *halakhot* of vows apply permanently (Rashbam).

אָמַר מָר: מַה לְהַלָּן אַהֲרֹן וּבָנָיו וְכָל יִשְׂרָאֵל, אַף כָּאן אַהֲרֹן וּבָנָיו וְכָל יִשְׂרָאֵל. לְמַאי הִלְכְתָא? אֲמַר רַב אַחָא בַּר יַעֲקֹב: לוֹמַר, שֶׁהֲפָרַת נְדָרִים בִּשְׁלֹשָׁה הֶדְיוֹטוֹת.

The Gemara analyzes the cited *baraita*. **The Master says: Just as there,** with regard to offerings, the mitzva applies to **Aaron and his sons and all Israel, so too here,** with regard to vows, the mitzva applies to **Aaron and his sons and all Israel.** The Gemara asks: **With regard to what** ***halakha*** is this verbal analogy stated? **Rav Aḥa bar Ya'akov says:** This is written **to say that** the **dissolution of vows**[H] can be performed **by three**[N] **laymen**[N] with no particular expertise in the *halakhot* of vows, just as the prohibition of offerings slaughtered outside the Tabernacle or Temple applies to all of the Jewish people, including laymen.

וְהָא "רָאשֵׁי הַמַּטּוֹת" כְּתִיב בֵּיהּ! כִּדְאָמַר רַב חִסְדָּא אָמַר רַבִּי יוֹחָנָן: בְּיָחִיד מוּמְחֶה, הָכִי נַמִּי בְּיָחִיד מוּמְחֶה.

The Gemara objects: **But** the phrase **"the heads of the tribes" is written** explicitly **in** the portion of the vows, indicating that the matter is not entrusted to laymen. The Gemara answers: It is **as Rav Ḥisda says** that **Rabbi Yoḥanan says** in a different context: The mention of the heads of tribes teaches that vows may be dissolved **by a single expert**[N] halakhic authority; **so too here,** this phrase teaches that vows can be nullified **by a single expert** halakhic authority.

"וּמַה כָּאן רָאשֵׁי הַמַּטּוֹת, אַף לְהַלָּן רָאשֵׁי הַמַּטּוֹת". לְמַאי הִלְכְתָא? אֲמַר רַב שֵׁשֶׁת: לוֹמַר, שֶׁיֵּשׁ שְׁאֵלָה בְּהֶקְדֵּשׁ.

The Gemara analyzes the next clause of the cited *baraita*: **And just as here** the mitzva applies to **the heads of the tribes, so too there,** with regard to offerings slaughtered outside the Tabernacle or Temple, there is particular relevance to **the heads of the tribes.** The Gemara asks: **With regard to what** ***halakha*** are the heads of the tribes linked to the prohibition of slaughtering offerings outside the Tabernacle or Temple? **Rav Sheshet says:** This is written **to say** that **there is** a concept of **requesting** dissolution of consecration **of consecrated** property,[H] just as one can request dissolution of a vow.

וּלְבֵית שַׁמַּאי דְּאָמְרִי: אֵין שְׁאֵלָה בְּהֶקְדֵּשׁ, דִּתְנַן, בֵּית שַׁמַּאי אוֹמְרִים: הֶקְדֵּשׁ טָעוּת הֶקְדֵּשׁ, וּבֵית הִלֵּל אוֹמְרִים: אֵינוֹ הֶקְדֵּשׁ, הַאי "זֶה" וְ"זֶה" מַאי עָבְדִי לֵיהּ?

The Gemara asks: **And according to Beit Shammai, who say** that **there is no** possibility of **requesting** that a halakhic authority dissolve a vow **of consecrated** property, this cannot explain the connection of the heads of the tribes to offerings slaughtered outside the Tabernacle or Temple. **As we learned** in a mishna (*Nazir* 30b): **Beit Shammai say: Consecration** that one performed **in error**[H] is nevertheless effective as **consecration,**[N] because one's mindset does not supersede his verbal declaration; **and Beit Hillel say:** This is **not consecration.** Accordingly, in the opinion of Beit Shammai, **what do they do with this** seemingly analogous usage of **"this"** and **"this,"** in the portions of offerings slaughtered outside the Tabernacle or Temple and vows, respectively?

NOTES

Dissolution of [*hafarat*] vows can be performed by three, etc. – **הֲפָרַת נְדָרִים בִּשְׁלֹשָׁה וכו׳**: It should be noted that this language is imprecise, as the procedure known as *hafara*, generally translated as nullification, is not within the jurisdiction of the court, but within that of a husband or a father, as the Gemara later notes. Rather, the procedure described here is *hatara*, which is performed by halakhic authorities or courts and not by the father or husband, and which follows a different set of *halakhot* than the *hafara*, which is performed by the husband or father (Rashbam).

By three laymen – **בִּשְׁלֹשָׁה הֶדְיוֹטוֹת**: A number of commentaries explain how this *halakha* is derived from the language of the verse, which states: "Speak to Aaron, and to his sons, and to all the children of Israel" (Leviticus 17:2). Some explain that the general category of "all the children of Israel" includes laymen (Rabbeinu Gershom Meor HaGola; Ramah). Some understand that the verse implicitly compares all the people of Israel, including the laymen thereof, to Aaron and his sons with respect to this *halakha* (Rashbam). Others understand that although laymen are able to dissolve vows, they must have at least learned the *halakhot* relevant to this function, as was the case with the children of Israel, who learned these *halakhot* from Moses in the wilderness (Ramah; see Ritva).

Still others learn that there must be three people from the wording in the same verse: Aaron is one, his sons is two, and the children of Israel is three. Or, all of Israel is implicitly likened to Aaron and his two sons, who are three altogether (Ramban; Ritva). According to a different understanding, the requirement for three people is learned from the phrase "the heads of the tribes," which implies a generic plural number. The minimum of any plural is two, and a court cannot be composed of an even number of judges, so the minimum number is set at three (*Tosafot*, citing Rivam).

By a single expert – **בְּיָחִיד מוּמְחֶה**: A single expert can dissolve vows by himself, and he is not required to ask others to constitute a court with him. Although the verse states: "The heads of the tribes," in the plural, this may be understood as a general term including all the individuals who are within this category (Rashbam).

With regard to the single expert, some commentaries understand that the category applies only to ordained judges. Therefore, since in this era there is no ordination, no individual can dissolve vows himself, even if he is otherwise qualified (Ramah; Ramban). Others understand that the Gemara is simply using the term: Single expert, in a more general sense, referring to any exceptional halakhic authority (*Ge'onim*; Rashbam; Rambam). Contemporary practice is to conduct dissolution with three judges.

Consecration performed in error is effective consecration – **הֶקְדֵּשׁ טָעוּת הֶקְדֵּשׁ**: The dissolution of vows functions on the basis of regret, by which the individual states that he did not account for all the possible implications of his vow, or that he was not fully committed to the vow, such that the vow was predicated upon an error. Therefore, Beit Shammai, who hold that a vow of consecration takes effect even if one did not mean the words that he uttered at all, hold that there is no basis whatsoever for dissolving a consecration vow.

HALAKHA

Dissolution of vows, etc. – **שֶׁהֲפָרַת נְדָרִים וכו׳**: If one takes a vow or an oath and later regrets it, he should go to an expert halakhic authority, one who is both learned and sound in reasoning, or, as understood by one later authority, to an expert who has learned a certain tradition from his teachers and knows the concepts himself as well (*Taz*). Alternatively, one who regrets having taken a vow or oath can appear before three laymen who are learned and sound in reasoning and who would know how to identify a solution for the petitioner. As understood by one later commentary, it is sufficient that the three be capable of absorbing that which they are taught, even if they do not produce their own insights and theories, and common practice is to be lenient to such people (*Shakh*). At present, there are no experts qualified to dissolve vows alone, and even in the case of exceptional scholars, three are required (*Shakh*). The *Taz* writes that with fewer than three judges, the dissolution is considered insufficient even after the fact (Rambam *Sefer Hafla'a*, *Hilkhot Shevuot* 6:1 and *Hilkhot Nedarim* 4:5; *Shulḥan Arukh*, *Yoreh De'a* 228:1).

There is a concept of requesting dissolution of consecration of consecrated property – **יֵשׁ שְׁאֵלָה בְּהֶקְדֵּשׁ**: Just as vows that effect prohibitions can be dissolved, so too, vows of consecration can be dissolved. This holds true for both consecrations of assets for Temple maintenance and consecrations of animals earmarked as offerings. This ruling is in accordance with the opinion of Rabbi Yehoshua in tractate *Arakhin* (23a) as well as that of Beit Hillel (Rambam *Sefer Hafla'a Hilkhot Nedarim* 4:7 and *Hilkhot Arakhin VaḤaramim* 1:17; *Shulḥan Arukh*, *Yoreh De'a* 258:6, 323:1, and in the comment of Rema).

Consecration that one performed in error – **הֶקְדֵּשׁ טָעוּת**: Consecration that one performed in error is not consecration. How so? If one says: The black ox that will emerge from my house first is hereby consecrated property, and a white ox emerges, the latter is not considered consecrated property. Similarly, if someone thought that he was obligated to conduct himself as a nazirite, and he accordingly separated the requisite offerings, if it is subsequently determined that he had never committed himself to become a nazirite, the animals that he had designated may go out to pasture, for the consecration was predicated upon an error. This ruling is in accordance with the opinion of Beit Hillel (Rambam *Sefer Hafla'a*, *Hilkhot Arakhin VaḤaramim* 6:34 and *Hilkhot Nezirut* 9:8; see *Shulḥan Arukh*, *Even HaEzer* 35:9).

״זֶה הַדָּבָר״ דִּשְׁחוּטֵי חוּץ מִיבָּעֵי לֵיהּ: עַל הַשּׁוֹחֵט הוּא חַיָּיב, וְאֵינוֹ חַיָּיב עַל הַמּוֹלֵק; ״זֶה הַדָּבָר״ דְּרָאשֵׁי הַמַּטּוֹת מִיבָּעֵי לֵיהּ לְחָכָם מַתִּיר וְאֵין בַּעַל מַתִּיר, בַּעַל מֵפֵר וְאֵין חָכָם מֵפֵר.

The Gemara answers: Beit Shammai **require "this is the matter"** written **of offerings slaughtered outside** the Tabernacle or Temple to teach that **for the** act of **slaughtering, he is liable**[H] to receive excision from the World-to-Come [*karet*]; **but he is not liable** to receive *karet* **for the** act of **pinching** the neck of a consecrated bird outside the Tabernacle or Temple, which is excluded from the category of slaughtering in this mitzva. And Beit Shammai **require "this is the matter"** written of **the heads of the tribes** in the portion about vows **to** teach that only **a halakhic authority can dissolve** vows,[HN] **but a husband cannot dissolve** them. The halakhic authority can dissolve the vow for a petitioner, but a woman's husband or father cannot dissolve her vow. And, conversely, **a husband can nullify**[H] his wife's or his daughter's vows on the day that he hears the vow, regardless of her mindset, **but a halakhic authority cannot nullify** vows in this manner.

וּלְבֵית שַׁמַּאי דְּלֵית לְהוּ גְּזֵרָה שָׁוָה, הֲפָרַת נְדָרִים בִּשְׁלֹשָׁה הֶדְיוֹטוֹת מְנָא לְהוּ? נָפְקָא לְהוּ מִדְּתַנְיָא: ״וַיְדַבֵּר מֹשֶׁה אֶת מֹעֲדֵי ה׳ אֶל בְּנֵי יִשְׂרָאֵל״ – רַבִּי יוֹסֵי הַגְּלִילִי אוֹמֵר:

The Gemara asks: **But according to Beit Shammai, who do not have** this **verbal analogy,** meaning that they do not recognize as authoritative the verbal analogy that links vows to offerings slaughtered outside the Tabernacle or Temple, **from where do they** derive that **dissolution of vows** can be performed **by three laymen?** The Gemara answers: Beit Shammai **derive it from that which is taught** in a *baraita*: The verse states at the end of a passage relating to the *halakhot* of the Festivals: **"And Moses declared to the children of Israel the appointed seasons of the Lord"** (Leviticus 23:44). In explaining the verse, **Rabbi Yosei HaGelili says:**

HALAKHA

For the act of slaughtering he is liable, etc. – עַל הַשּׁוֹחֵט הוּא חַיָּיב וכו׳: If one slaughters consecrated beasts or fowl outside the Temple courtyard, although they had never reached the altar, if done intentionally, he is liable to receive *karet*; and if done unwittingly, he is liable to bring a sin-offering. If one pinches the neck of a consecrated fowl outside the Temple, he is exempt (Rambam *Sefer Avoda, Hilkhot Ma'aseh HaKorbanot* 18:3, 18).

To teach that only a halakhic authority can dissolve vows, etc. – לְחָכָם מַתִּיר וכו׳: The dissolution of vows can be performed only by a halakhic authority. Therefore, if a man says to his wife or daughter: It is dissolved for you, or: It is allowed for you, the vow is still intact because a father or husband does not dissolve vows in the manner of a halakhic authority; rather, he uproots them, with the terminology of nullification (Rambam *Sefer Hafla'a, Hilkhot Nedarim* 13:2; *Shulhan Arukh, Yoreh De'a* 234:37).

A husband can nullify, etc. – בַּעַל מֵפֵר וכו׳: The nullification of vows can be performed only by a father for his daughter or by a husband for his wife. If a halakhic authority tells one who has taken a vow: It is nullified for you, or: Your oath is uprooted, his statement is meaningless, as only a father or husband can nullify a vow. The halakhic authority must instead employ terminology of dissolution or allowance (Rambam *Sefer Hafla'a, Hilkhot Shevuot* 6:5; see *Shulhan Arukh, Yoreh De'a* 228:3).

NOTES

A halakhic authority can dissolve vows, etc. – חָכָם מַתִּיר וכו׳: There are two ways for vows to be negated. One, discussed explicitly in the Torah (Numbers, chapter 30), is the nullification of a vow. In this procedure, a husband can nullify his wife's vow, and a father can nullify the vow of his daughter, if she is an unmarried young woman. To do so, the man must declare: It is nullified for you, or: This vow is canceled, or another equivalent formulation.

A vow can also be negated in another manner, a method that has an allusion in the Torah but is not mentioned explicitly. This is the dissolution of a vow by a halakhic authority. In this method, a court or single expert authority dissolves a vow on behalf of someone if that person is found to regret having undertaken the vow; or if a person did not fully consider the implications of the vow at the time of the vow; or if the vow was taken under mistaken pretenses. This manner of cancellation is executed with the language of: It is permitted to you; it is excused for you; or the like (see Ritva).

The commentaries point to two crucial distinctions between these two methods. First, the husband's or father's nullification operates independently of the woman's mindset, as he can nullify the vow on the strength of his authority alone. This is unlike the dissolution of the vow as performed by a halakhic authority, which can be done only at the request of the one who took the vow and is predicated upon determining that individual's mindset.

The second difference between these two methods is that the husband or father nullifies a vow from this point forward, preventing the vow from continuing to be in effect. By contrast, a halakhic authority determines that the vow never took effect from the outset.

Being that these are two distinct methods, the halakhic authority or court cannot nullify or cancel anyone's vow from this point forward, therefore it would be inappropriate to employ the language: It is nullified for you. Similarly, it is not effective for a husband or father to perform a nullification with the expression: It is permitted for you, because this language is inconsistent with the process he is attempting to effect. The Ritva notes that a husband or father can execute a dissolution for his wife or daughter when collaborating with other judges, but this is not a function of his being the husband or father of the petitioner.

מוֹעֲדֵי ה׳ נֶאֶמְרוּ, שַׁבַּת בְּרֵאשִׁית לֹא נֶאֶמְרָה; בֶּן עַזַּאי אוֹמֵר: מוֹעֲדֵי ה׳ נֶאֶמְרוּ, הֲפָרַת נְדָרִים לֹא נֶאֶמְרָה.

The Festivals of the Lord were stated, but **Shabbat,** which commemorates **Creation, was not stated. Ben Azzai says: The Festivals of the Lord were stated,** but **the dissolution of vows was not stated.** This concludes the *baraita*.

רַבִּי יוֹסֵי בַּר נָתָן גָּמֵיר לַהּ לְהָא מַתְנִיתָא וְלָא יָדַע לַיהּ לְפֵרוּשַׁהּ, אֲזַל בַּתְרֵיהּ דְּרַב שֵׁשֶׁת לִנְהַרְדְּעָא וְלָא אַשְׁכְּחֵיהּ, אֲזַל בַּתְרֵיהּ לִמְחוֹזָא, אַשְׁכְּחֵיהּ, אֲמַר לֵיהּ: מַאי ״מוֹעֲדֵי ה׳ נֶאֶמְרוּ, שַׁבַּת בְּרֵאשִׁית לֹא נֶאֶמְרָה״?

The Gemara recounts: **Rabbi Yosei bar Natan learned this** *baraita* **and did not know how to explain it.** He **followed Rav Sheshet to Neharde'a** in order to ask him about it, **but** he **did not find him** there. He **followed him to Meḥoza** and **found him,** and he **said to him: What** is meant by Rabbi Yosei HaGelili's statement: **The Festivals of the Lord were stated,** but **Shabbat,** which commemorates **Creation, was not stated?** What does he mean, as Shabbat of Creation is explicitly mentioned in that section of the Torah (Leviticus 23:3)?

אֲמַר לֵיהּ: מוֹעֲדֵי ה׳ צְרִיכִין קִידּוּשׁ בֵּית דִּין, שַׁבַּת בְּרֵאשִׁית אֵינָהּ צְרִיכָה קִידּוּשׁ בֵּית דִּין; סָלְקָא דַּעְתָּךְ אָמִינָא: הוֹאִיל וּכְתִיבִי גַּבֵּי מוֹעֲדוֹת, תִּיבָּעֵי קִידּוּשׁ בֵּית דִּין כְּמוֹעֲדוֹת, קָא מַשְׁמַע לַן.

Rav Sheshet **said to him: The Festivals of the Lord require sanctification by the court.**[H] This means that the start of the month, which is dependent upon the appearance of the New Moon, which determines the Festivals, can be established only by a court composed of experts. **Shabbat,** which commemorates **Creation, does not require sanctification by the court.**[H] Shabbat is sanctified every week independent of any court action. It may **enter your mind to say: Since** Shabbat **is written adjacent to the Festivals, it should require sanctification by the court as** do the **Festivals.** Rabbi Yosei HaGelili **teaches us** that Shabbat does not require this.

מַאי ״מוֹעֲדֵי ה׳ נֶאֶמְרוּ, הֲפָרַת נְדָרִים לֹא נֶאֶמְרָה״? מוֹעֲדֵי ה׳ צְרִיכִין מוּמְחִין, הֲפָרַת נְדָרִים אֵינָהּ צְרִיכָה מוּמְחִין.

Rabbi Yosei bar Natan asked: **What** is meant by ben Azzai's statement: **The Festivals of the Lord were stated,** but **the dissolution of vows was not stated?** After all, the Torah writes explicitly about the dissolution of vows. Rav Sheshet answered him: **The Festivals of the Lord require experts**[H] to determine when the months begin and when the Festivals will be observed, but **the dissolution of vows does not require experts.**

וְהָא ״רָאשֵׁי הַמַּטּוֹת״ כְּתִיב! אָמַר רַב חִסְדָּא אָמַר רַבִּי יוֹחָנָן: בְּיָחִיד מוּמְחֶה.

The Gemara questions this explanation. **But it is written: "The heads of the tribes"** (Numbers 30:2), in the portion discussing the *halakhot* of vows. How, then, can it be said that vows can be dissolved by laymen? **Rav Ḥisda says** that **Rabbi Yoḥanan says:** The phrase teaches that vows can be dissolved **by a single expert** authority. In any event, the Gemara has established that Beit Shammai can derive that dissolution of vows can be performed by laymen in the manner stated by ben Azzai, as explained by Rav Sheshet.

HALAKHA

The Festivals of the Lord require sanctification by the court – מוֹעֲדֵי ה׳ צְרִיכִין קִידּוּשׁ בֵּית דִּין: The sanctification of the New Moon is not dictated by the precise moment of the appearance of the new moon, but by the court, such that only a day sanctified and fixed by the court has the status of the New Moon. After the day is sanctified, the court dispatches messengers to inform the communities that the new month has been sanctified, so that they will know when the Festivals will occur (Rambam *Sefer Zemanim, Hilkhot Kiddush HaḤodesh* 1:5, 7).

Shabbat, which commemorates Creation, does not require sanctification by the court – שַׁבַּת בְּרֵאשִׁית אֵינָהּ צְרִיכָה קִידּוּשׁ בֵּית דִּין: The designation of Shabbat is not entrusted to, and does not depend upon, the court. Rather, it is up to each individual to count six days from the first day of the week and observe the Shabbat on the seventh day (Rambam *Sefer Zemanim, Hilkhot Kiddush HaḤodesh* 1:5).

The Festivals of the Lord require experts – מוֹעֲדֵי ה׳ צְרִיכִין מוּמְחִין: The determination and sanctification of the New Moon and the intercalation of the year can be executed only by the Sanhedrin in Eretz Yisrael, or by a court of ordained judges in Eretz Yisrael that has been licensed for this task by the Sanhedrin. At present, when there is no Sanhedrin, the determination of months and intercalation of years is done only in accordance with the calculation that was transmitted to us (Rambam *Sefer Zemanim, Hilkhot Kiddush HaḤodesh* 5:1, see 1:17, 5:13; see *Sefer HaMitzvot*, positive mitzva 153, and Ramban's comments there).

תְּנַן הָתָם, אָמַר רַבָּן שִׁמְעוֹן בֶּן גַּמְלִיאֵל: לֹא הָיוּ יָמִים טוֹבִים לְיִשְׂרָאֵל כַּחֲמִשָּׁה עָשָׂר בְּאָב וּכְיוֹם הַכִּפּוּרִים, שֶׁבָּהֶן בְּנוֹת יְרוּשָׁלַיִם יוֹצְאוֹת בִּכְלֵי לָבָן שְׁאוּלִין, שֶׁלֹּא לְבַיֵּישׁ אֶת מִי שֶׁאֵין לוֹ. בִּשְׁלָמָא יוֹם הַכִּפּוּרִים – יוֹם סְלִיחָה וּמְחִילָה, יוֹם שֶׁנִּתְּנוּ בּוֹ לוּחוֹת אַחֲרוֹנוֹת, אֶלָּא חֲמִשָּׁה עָשָׂר בְּאָב מַאי הִיא?

§ The Gemara discusses a mishna that addresses the issue of intertribal marriages. **We learned** in a mishna **there** (*Ta'anit* 26b): **Rabban Shimon ben Gamliel said: There were no days as joyous for the Jewish people as the fifteenth of Av and as Yom Kippur, as on these** days **the daughters of Jerusalem would emerge in white garments,**[N] which each woman **borrowed** from another. Why did they borrow garments? They did this **so as not to embarrass one who did not have** her own white garments. The Gemara analyzes the mishna: **Granted** that **Yom Kippur** is a day of joy, because it is **a day of pardon and forgiveness,**[N] and moreover, it is the **day on which the last Tablets** of the Covenant **were given. But what is** the special joy of the **fifteenth of Av?**

אָמַר רַב יְהוּדָה אָמַר שְׁמוּאֵל: יוֹם שֶׁהוּתְּרוּ שְׁבָטִים לָבֹא זֶה בָּזֶה. מַאי דְּרוּשׁ? "זֶה הַדָּבָר" – דָּבָר זֶה לֹא יְהֵא נוֹהֵג אֶלָּא בְּדוֹר זֶה.

Rav Yehuda says that **Shmuel says:** This was the **day when the** members of different **tribes were permitted**[N] **to** marry into **one another's** tribe. Such marriages were restricted for the first generation to enter Eretz Yisrael, as discussed above (120a). **What** verse **did** the sages of that time **interpret**[N] in support of their conclusion that this *halakha* was no longer in effect? The verse states: **"This is the matter"** (Numbers 36:6), meaning, **this matter shall be practiced only in this generation,** in which Eretz Yisrael is being divided among the tribes.

רַבָּה בַּר בַּר חָנָה אָמַר רַבִּי יוֹחָנָן: יוֹם שֶׁהוּתַּר שֵׁבֶט בִּנְיָמִן לָבֹא בַּקָּהָל, דִּכְתִיב: "וְאִישׁ יִשְׂרָאֵל נִשְׁבַּע בַּמִּצְפָּה לֵאמֹר אִישׁ מִמֶּנּוּ לֹא יִתֵּן בִּתּוֹ לְבִנְיָמִן לְאִשָּׁה". מַאי דְּרוּשׁ? "מִמֶּנּוּ" – וְלֹא מִבָּנֵינוּ.

Rabba bar bar Ḥana says that **Rabbi Yoḥanan** offered another explanation: The fifteenth of Av was the **day when the tribe of Benjamin was permitted to enter into the congregation** of the other tribes of Israel through marriage, after the other tribes found a way to dissolve the vow that had prohibited them from marrying a member of the tribe of Benjamin in the aftermath of the episode of the concubine in Gibeah (Judges, chapters 19–20). **As it is written: "And the men of Israel had taken an oath in Mizpah, saying: None of us shall give his daughter to Benjamin as a wife"** (Judges 21:1). The Gemara asks: **What** verse **did** the sages of that time **interpret** that enabled them to dissolve this vow? The verse states: "None **of us," and not:** None **of our children;** therefore, the oath applied only to the generation that had taken the oath.

רַב דִּימִי בַּר יוֹסֵף אָמַר רַב נַחְמָן: יוֹם שֶׁכָּלוּ בּוֹ מֵתֵי מִדְבָּר, דְּאָמַר מָר: עַד שֶׁלֹּא כָּלוּ מֵתֵי מִדְבָּר

Rav Dimi bar Yosef says that **Rav Naḥman** says: The fifteenth of Av was the **day on which those designated to perish in the wilderness stopped** dying,[N] as the entire generation that had left Egypt had died due to the sin of the spies (Numbers 14:29–30). **As the Master says: As long as those designated to perish** in the **wilderness had not stopped** dying,[N]

NOTES

In white garments – בִּכְלֵי לָבָן: The Ritva explains that the young women wore white garments as a symbol of purity and freedom from the evil inclination and sin. It is for this reason that they did not hesitate to call out: Young man, please lift up your eyes (see *Ta'anit* 26b), which might otherwise have been understood as appealing to the evil inclination. This is also why it is customary to wear white clothing on Yom Kippur, to demonstrate the same purity from sin.

A day of pardon and forgiveness – יוֹם סְלִיחָה וּמְחִילָה: In addition to the essential character of Yom Kippur as a day of pardon and forgiveness, as described in the Torah (see Leviticus 16:30), the giving of the second Tablets on that day served as a symbol that the Jewish people were forgiven for the sin of the Golden Calf. Others explain that the Jewish people were forgiven for the sin of the Golden Calf in the merit of the nation's women and girls, who refrained from participating in the sin altogether. For this reason, Yom Kippur was a day of joy for the women in particular (*Allon Bakhut*; *Etz Yosef*).

When tribes were permitted – שֶׁהוּתְּרוּ שְׁבָטִים: The Sages had a tradition that this was the day on which the ban on intertribal marriage was canceled. This must have been after the Jewish people had received their inheritances, and the inheriting daughters of that generation had all married.

The Maharsha notes that this day was especially joyous for the women, as even prior to this event, the men were allowed to marry women of any tribe. The population most affected by the change was that of women inheritors, who were limited in that they were allowed to marry only within their own tribes. Similarly, the cancellation of the ban of marriage with the tribe of Benjamin was relevant to Jewish women of all tribes, who were now permitted to marry men from Benjamin, and men of all tribes were permitted to marry women of Benjamin.

What did the sages interpret – מַאי דְּרוּשׁ: Some explain that this does not mean that the authorities of the generation devised the ruling that limited the ban to the first generation. Doubtless, this was one of the details of the mitzva as Moses taught it to the nation's leaders. Rather, it means that this detail was not publicized so as not to undermine the observance of this mitzva while it was still in effect. By contrast, see *Gevurat Ari* (*Ta'anit* 30b), who explains that this interpretation was arrived at by the Sages only at a much later date than the entry to Eretz Yisrael, at which point it assumed the status of Torah law.

On which those designated to perish in the wilderness stopped dying – שֶׁכָּלוּ בּוֹ מֵתֵי מִדְבָּר: Based on a tradition recorded in *Midrash Eikha*, the Rashbam explains that from the moment that this punishment was decreed upon the Jewish people in the wake of the sin of the spies, approximately fifteen thousand men would die each year, on the ninth of Av. As the decree took effect over forty years in the desert, approximately one-fortieth, or fifteen thousand, of the 600,000 condemned would die each year. When, one year, the people did not die on the ninth of Av, the nation thought that they had miscalculated the days of the month. Once they saw the full moon on the fifteenth of Av, they were certain that the ninth of Av had passed without incident and that the decree had ended.

An alternative explanation favored in *Tosafot* is one suggested by Rabbeinu Tam, that the fifteenth of Av was the day on which the seven days of mourning for those who had died on the ninth of Av during the fortieth year concluded, such that the mourning for the victims of the decree reached an ultimate conclusion on the fifteenth of Av.

As long as those designated to perish in the wilderness had not stopped dying, etc. – עַד שֶׁלֹּא כָּלוּ מֵתֵי מִדְבָּר וכו׳: Since Moses' prophecy was interrupted throughout the period of the decree, it was a joyous event when Moses again received his prophecy on that very day. As long as the people were alienated from God, and while they were still in mourning, the Divine Presence did not rest upon Moses. This phenomenon was in accordance with the principle: The Divine Presence rests only amid joy (see *Pesaḥim* 117a). Since Moses' prophecy was exclusively for the sake of, and for the needs of, the Jewish people, his prophecy depended upon the joy of the nation as a whole, and not upon Moses' personal state (see *Tosafot*).

לֹא הָיָה דִּיבּוּר עִם מֹשֶׁה, שֶׁנֶּאֱמַר: ״וַיְהִי כַאֲשֶׁר תַּמּוּ כָּל אַנְשֵׁי הַמִּלְחָמָה לָמוּת מִקֶּרֶב הָעָם״, וּסְמִיךְ לֵיהּ: ״וַיְדַבֵּר ה׳ אֵלַי לֵאמֹר״ – אֵלַי הָיָה הַדִּיבּוּר.

God **did not speak with Moses,**[N] **as it is stated: "So it came to pass, when all the men of war were consumed and dead from among the people"** (Deuteronomy 2:16), **and juxtaposed to** that verse it is written: **"That the Lord spoke to me, saying"** (Deuteronomy 2:17). Moses indicates: Only after the last of that generation had died, **was the speech** of God directed **to me.** When the Jewish people realized that the decree had been lifted, the day was established as a permanent day of rejoicing.

עוּלָּא אָמַר: יוֹם שֶׁבִּיטֵּל בּוֹ הוֹשֵׁעַ בֶּן אֵלָה פַּרְדְּסָאוֹת שֶׁהוֹשִׁיב יָרָבְעָם עַל הַדְּרָכִים שֶׁלֹּא יַעֲלוּ יִשְׂרָאֵל לָרֶגֶל.

The Gemara continues to cite explanations for the significance of the fifteenth of Av. **Ulla says:** The fifteenth of Av was the **day when** King **Hoshea, son of Ela, removed** the **guards** [*pardesaot*][L] **that Jeroboam,** son of Nevat, **placed**[N] **on the roads so that Israel** would **not ascend** to Jerusalem **for the pilgrimage Festival.** By doing so, King Hoshea renewed the access to Jerusalem for pilgrims.

רַב מַתָּנָה אָמַר: יוֹם שֶׁנִּיתְּנוּ הֲרוּגֵי בֵיתָר לִקְבוּרָה; דְּאָמַר רַב מַתָּנָה: אוֹתוֹ הַיּוֹם שֶׁנִּיתְּנוּ הֲרוּגֵי בֵיתָר לִקְבוּרָה – תִּיקְּנוּ בְּיַבְנֶה ״הַטּוֹב וְהַמֵּטִיב״, ״הַטּוֹב״ – שֶׁלֹּא הִסְרִיחוּ, ״וְהַמֵּטִיב״ – שֶׁנִּיתְּנוּ לִקְבוּרָה.

Rav Mattana says: The fifteenth of Av was the **day when the slain** victims **of Beitar were afforded burial,** several years after they were killed and the Roman emperor Hadrian decreed that they were not to be buried (see *Gittin* 57a). **As Rav Mattana says: On the day that the slain of Beitar**[B] **were afforded burial,** the **Sages in Yavne instituted** the blessing: Blessed is He **Who is good and Who does good.**[HN] The term: **Who is good,** is to give thanks **that** the corpses **did not decompose** despite the long delay; and the term: **And Who does good,** is to give thanks **that** the slain ones **were** ultimately **afforded burial.**

רַבָּה וְרַב יוֹסֵף דְּאָמְרִי תַּרְוַיְיהוּ: יוֹם שֶׁפּוֹסְקִין בּוֹ מִלִּכְרוֹת עֵצִים לַמַּעֲרָכָה. תַּנְיָא, רַבִּי אֱלִיעֶזֶר הַגָּדוֹל אוֹמֵר: כֵּיוָן שֶׁהִגִּיעַ חֲמִשָּׁה עָשָׂר בְּאָב תָּשַׁשׁ כֹּחָהּ שֶׁל חַמָּה, וְלֹא הָיוּ כּוֹרְתִין עֵצִים לַמַּעֲרָכָה. אֲמַר רַב מְנַשֶּׁה: וְקָרוּ לֵיהּ יוֹם תְּבַר מַגָּל.

Rabba and Rav Yosef both say: The fifteenth of Av is the **day when they stop cutting wood**[N] **for the arrangement** of wood on the altar. **It is taught** in a *baraita* that **Rabbi Eliezer the Great says: Once the fifteenth of Av came, the force of the sun would weaken,**[B] **and** from this date **they would not cut** additional **wood for the arrangement,** because wood cut from then on would not dry properly and would be unfit for use in the Temple. **Rav Menashe said: And the** people **called** the fifteenth of Av: The **day of the breaking of the sickle** [*maggal*],[N] as they did not need the lumbering tools until the following year.

LANGUAGE

Guards [*pardesaot*] – פַּרְדְּסָאוֹת: In certain manuscripts and parallel texts, the word reads *parsedaot*, or *peruzdaot*. From the Latin praesidia, which means protection or guard.

BACKGROUND

The slain of Beitar – הֲרוּגֵי בֵיתָר: After his final suppression of the bar Kokheva revolt, the Roman emperor Hadrian issued a lengthy series of decrees of apostasy against the Jewish people and Judaism. One of these decrees was a prohibition against burying those slain in the war. These decrees were in force for at least three years, until Hadrian's death in 138 CE. The decrees were rescinded only in the reign of the following emperor. This annulment, along with the gradual cancellation of all the decrees, was commemorated for future generations in several ways, including the addition of the fourth blessing to Grace after Meals.

The force of the sun would weaken – תָּשַׁשׁ כֹּחָהּ שֶׁל חַמָּה: The fifteenth of Av coincides with the period on the solar calendar ranging from July 30 to August 21. Preceding this time is the period of the highest temperatures in the northern hemisphere, and the lowest moisture in the mountain regions. From August on, the force of the sun weakens, in the Gemara's language. Practically speaking, this means that temperatures decrease, and moisture increases. The wood for the arrangement on the altar needed several months of dryness before it was fit for use. Additionally, because beetles crawl about in the bark of moist cut trees, it became impractical to cut wood for the arrangement beginning at this point in the year.

HALAKHA

Who is good and Who does good – הַטּוֹב וְהַמֵּטִיב: The fourth blessing of Grace after Meals was instituted by the Sages of the Mishna at Yavne, on the day that the victims of Beitar were afforded burial. The blessing declares that God is good, because the corpses did not decompose; and that He does good, because those slain were ultimately buried (Rambam *Sefer Ahava, Hilkhot Berakhot* 1:17 2:1; *Tur, Oraḥ Ḥayyim* 189; see *Shulḥan Arukh, Oraḥ Ḥayyim* 188:1–2).

NOTES

God did not speak with Moses – לֹא הָיָה דִּיבּוּר עִם מֹשֶׁה: According to a number of commentaries, the Gemara does not mean that Moses received no prophecy at all over this period, but that the prophecy was different. The Rashbam holds that Moses did not experience the type of prophecy that he experienced at first, which is described as "face to face" (Exodus 33:11). Accordingly, although God spoke to Moses during the episode of Korah, after the incident of the spies, it was in the manner of prophecy experienced by other prophets, through the medium of an angel or the *Urim VeTummim*. Additionally, it may be that Moses received only those prophecies that were necessary for that period.

Alternatively, the Ritva suggests that God did not speak affectionately to Moses during this time, as He previously did. Finally, according to Rabbeinu Baḥyei, during the period of the decree Moses received prophecies only of the type: "The Lord said [*vayyomer*] to Moses" and not of the type: "The Lord spoke [*vayyedaber*] to Moses." It is this second type, which was restored after the end of the decree, which is considered the superior vision of a luminous crystal (Rabbeinu Baḥyei on Deuteronomy 2:16).

The guards that Jeroboam placed – פַּרְדְּסָאוֹת שֶׁהוֹשִׁיב יָרָבְעָם: Although the Bible does not explicitly mention these guards, it does describe how Jeroboam, the first king of the northern kingdom of Israel, whose separation left a distinct southern kingdom of Judea, led a conscious campaign to prevent pilgrimage to the Temple in Judean-held Jerusalem. For this reason, he erected temples and calves for worship at Dan and Beth-el. Moreover, there was war between the two kingdoms.

Concerning Hoshea, son of Ela, the verse states explicitly: "And he did that which was evil in the eyes of the Lord, yet not as the kings of Israel that were before him" (II Kings 17:2). Since the Bible describes the other kings as having not deviated from the sins of Jeroboam, the Sages learned that Hoshea canceled some of the orders that were in place prior to his reign.

The Sages in Yavne instituted, Who is good and Who does good – תִּיקְּנוּ בְּיַבְנֶה הַטּוֹב וְהַמֵּטִיב: The first three blessings of Grace after Meals have the status of a mitzva by Torah law (see *Berakhot* 48b), but this fourth blessing: Who is good and Who does good, is a rabbinic enactment (Rashbam).

Some early commentaries explain why the Sages placed this additional blessing in Grace after Meals and not in the regular order of prayers. The Ramban posits, based on a midrashic source, that Hadrian had the corpses strewn about a large vineyard of his in Eretz Yisrael. In recalling the miracle that the corpses did not decompose, the Sages instituted that this blessing be recited alongside the blessing over wine, which is recited after this blessing, upon the conclusion of Grace after Meals.

The Ritva offers an alternative approach: Grace after Meals includes blessings upon monumental matters that have no direct connection to food, including Jerusalem and the kingship of the Davidic dynasty. The Sages saw fit to add the blessing for this miracle, which they saw as having great significance. The Netziv adds that this was the first manifestation of divine providence on a national level following the destruction of the Second Temple, and was recognized as a sign that God had not abandoned the Jewish people.

The day when they stop cutting wood – יוֹם שֶׁפּוֹסְקִין בּוֹ מִלִּכְרוֹת עֵצִים: According to the Rashbam, this celebration was an expression of their joy for having completed the mitzva for a whole year. By contrast, Rabbeinu Gershom Meor HaGola contends that they were celebrating the fact that by being relieved of this seasonal responsibility, they were free to engage more in Torah study.

Sickle [*maggal*] – מַגָּל: The term *maggal*, whose primary meaning is sickle, is used in the Talmud as a term for lumbering tools in general.

מִכָּאן וְאֵילָךְ, דְּמוֹסִיף – יוֹסִיף, שֶׁאֵינוֹ מוֹסִיף – יְסִיף. מַאי "יְסִיף"? תָּנֵי רַב יוֹסֵף: תִּקְבְּרֵיהּ אִמֵּיהּ.

The Gemara adds: **From this** point **forward,** when the nights lengthen, **one who adds** [*demosif*][H] to his nightly Torah study **will add** [*yosif*] to his life, **and he who does not add,** that person is *yesif*.[N] The Gemara asks: **What** is the meaning of the term *yesif*? **Rav Yosef teaches:** It means that **his mother will bury him,** as he will die during his mother's lifetime.

תָּנוּ רַבָּנַן, שִׁבְעָה קִפְּלוּ אֶת כָּל הָעוֹלָם כּוּלּוֹ: מְתוּשֶׁלַח רָאָה אָדָם, שֵׁם רָאָה מְתוּשֶׁלַח, יַעֲקֹב רָאָה אֶת שֵׁם, עַמְרָם רָאָה אֶת יַעֲקֹב, אֲחִיָּה הַשִּׁילוֹנִי רָאָה אֶת עַמְרָם, אֵלִיָּהוּ רָאָה אֶת אֲחִיָּה הַשִּׁילוֹנִי וַעֲדַיִין קַיָּים.

§ After discussing the generation of those who died in the wilderness, the Gemara mentions a tradition that relates to that generation. **The Sages taught: Seven** people **spanned**[N] in their lifetimes **the whole world in its entirety,** i.e., their lives have spanned all of human history. **Methuselah saw Adam** in his lifetime; **Shem saw Methuselah; Jacob saw Shem; Amram saw Jacob; Ahijah the Shilonite saw Amram; Elijah**[P] **saw Ahijah the Shilonite; and** Elijah **is still alive.**

וַאֲחִיָּה הַשִּׁילוֹנִי רָאָה אֶת עַמְרָם? וְהָא כְּתִיב: "וְלֹא נוֹתַר מֵהֶם אִישׁ כִּי אִם כָּלֵב בֶּן יְפֻנֶּה וִיהוֹשֻׁעַ בִּן נוּן"!

The Gemara asks: **And** is it true that **Ahijah the Shilonite saw Amram? But it is written: "And no man among them remained, save Caleb, son of Jephunneh, and Joshua, son of Nun"** (Numbers 26:65). Since Amram died well before the Jewish people left Egypt, in order to have lived at the time of Amram, Ahijah would have had to be an adult at the time of the Exodus. How, then, could he have lived through the generation of those who died in the wilderness?

אָמַר רַב הַמְנוּנָא: לֹא נִגְזְרָה גְּזֵרָה עַל שִׁבְטוֹ שֶׁל לֵוִי, דִּכְתִיב: "בַּמִּדְבָּר הַזֶּה יִפְּלוּ פִגְרֵיכֶם וְכָל פְּקֻדֵיכֶם לְכָל מִסְפַּרְכֶם מִבֶּן עֶשְׂרִים שָׁנָה וָמָעְלָה", מִי שֶׁפְּקוּדָיו מִבֶּן עֶשְׂרִים, יָצָא שִׁבְטוֹ שֶׁל לֵוִי שֶׁפְּקוּדָיו מִבֶּן שְׁלֹשִׁים.

Rav Hamnuna says: The **decree** of death pronounced for the generation of the spies **was not decreed upon the tribe of Levi,**[N] **as it is written: "Your carcasses shall fall in this wilderness, and all those who were counted among you, according to your whole number, from twenty years old and upward"** (Numbers 14:29). The verse is interpreted: The decree applies to **one whose count** in the census **is from the age of twenty** and up, **excluding the tribe of Levi, whose count is from the age of thirty** and up. Ahijah was a Levite, and he was not subject to the decree.

וּמִשְּׁאָר שְׁבָטִים לָא עַיֵּיל? וְהָתַנְיָא: יָאִיר בֶּן מְנַשֶּׁה וּמָכִיר בֶּן מְנַשֶּׁה נוֹלְדוּ בִּימֵי יַעֲקֹב, וְלֹא מֵתוּ עַד שֶׁנִּכְנְסוּ יִשְׂרָאֵל לָאָרֶץ, שֶׁנֶּאֱמַר: "וַיַּכּוּ מֵהֶם אַנְשֵׁי הָעַי כִּשְׁלֹשִׁים וְשִׁשָּׁה אִישׁ", וְתַנְיָא: שְׁלֹשִׁים וְשִׁשָּׁה מַמָּשׁ, דִּבְרֵי רַבִּי יְהוּדָה.

The Gemara asks: **And** is it true that **no** one **from the other tribes entered** Eretz Yisrael? **But isn't it taught** in a *baraita*: **Yair, son of Manasseh, and Machir, son of Manasseh, were born in the days of Jacob, and they did not die until the Jewish people entered Eretz Yisrael, as it is stated: "And the men of Ai killed of them about thirty-six men"** (Joshua 7:5). **And** concerning this verse, **it is taught: Literally thirty-six** people were killed, this is **the statement of Rabbi Yehuda.**

אָמַר לוֹ רַבִּי נְחֶמְיָה: וְכִי נֶאֱמַר שְׁלֹשִׁים וְשִׁשָּׁה? וַהֲלֹא לֹא נֶאֱמַר אֶלָּא "כִּשְׁלֹשִׁים וְשִׁשָּׁה"! אֶלָּא זֶה יָאִיר בֶּן מְנַשֶּׁה, שֶׁשָּׁקוּל כְּרוּבָּהּ שֶׁל סַנְהֶדְרִין!

Rabbi Neḥemya said to him: But is it stated that **thirty-six** were killed? **Isn't it stated nothing other than: "About thirty-six"**[N] were killed? **Rather, this** unusual term is referring to **Yair, son of Manasseh, who** was **equivalent to the majority of the Sanhedrin,** whose maximum number of judges is seventy-one, of which thirty-six is a slight majority. Evidently, then, Yair, son of Manasseh also survived the time in the wilderness.

אֶלָּא אָמַר רַב אַחָא בַּר יַעֲקֹב: לֹא נִגְזְרָה גְּזֵירָה לֹא עַל פָּחוֹת מִבֶּן עֶשְׂרִים וְלֹא עַל יָתֵר מִבֶּן שִׁשִּׁים; לֹא עַל פָּחוֹת מִבֶּן עֶשְׂרִים – דִּכְתִיב: "מִבֶּן עֶשְׂרִים שָׁנָה וָמָעְלָה", וְלֹא עַל יָתֵר מִבֶּן שִׁשִּׁים – גָּמַר "וָמָעְלָה", "וָמָעְלָה" מֵעֲרָכִין, מַה לְהַלָּן יָתֵר מִבֶּן שִׁשִּׁים כְּפָחוֹת מִבֶּן עֶשְׂרִים, אַף כָּאן יָתֵר מִבֶּן שִׁשִּׁים כְּפָחוֹת מִבֶּן עֶשְׂרִים.

Rather, Rav Aḥa bar Ya'akov said: The **decree** of death **was not decreed** either **upon** those **less than twenty** years **old or upon** those **more than sixty** years **old** at the time of the sin of the spies. The Gemara explains: **Not upon** those **less than twenty** years **old, as it is written: "From twenty years old and upward"** (Numbers 14:29). **And not upon** those **more than sixty** years **old,** because he **learns** that there is a verbal analogy between **"and upward"** in the verse cited, and **"and upward" from the** *halakhot* of **valuations,** in the phrase: "From sixty years old and upward" (Leviticus 27:7). **Just as there,** concerning valuations, **more than sixty** years **old is comparable to less than twenty** years **old,** as there is a distinct category of those between the ages of twenty and sixty, **so too here, more than sixty** years **old is comparable to less than twenty** years **old** insofar as those older were not subject to the sentence. Yair, son of Manasseh, who was already older, did not die in the wilderness.

HALAKHA

From this point forward, one who adds, etc. – מִכָּאן וְאֵילָךְ, דְּמוֹסִיף וכו׳: One learns most of his wisdom specifically at night. Accordingly, one should add from the nighttime hours to his daily order of study of Torah, beginning on the fifteenth of Av (*Shulḥan Arukh, Yoreh De'a* 246:24, and in the comment of Rema).

NOTES

Yesif – יְסִיף: The Gemara asks about this obscure word, whose meaning is uncertain. The Rashbam notes that the Gemara does not employ the word *ye'asef*, i.e., he will be gathered, which appears many times in the Bible and which unambiguously refers to death. Rav Yosef explains that the word is related to the word *sof*, meaning end, and the Gemara is teaching that whoever does not increase his Torah study will die a premature death.

Some explain that this is a fitting punishment, by the principle of measure for measure. When someone chooses to increase his hours of sleep when the nights get longer, instead of adding the time to the productive daylight hours, the heavenly tribunal sees fit to reduce his productive time and to shorten his life in favor of eternal sleep (*Iyyun Ya'akov*).

Seven people spanned, etc. – שִׁבְעָה קִפְּלוּ וכו׳: Some commentaries offer an esoteric explanation of this statement: The seven men correspond to seven days of Creation and the seven thousand years of the world's existence (Maharal; Mabit).

Upon the tribe of Levi – עַל שִׁבְטוֹ שֶׁל לֵוִי: Ahijah the Shilonite was excluded from the decree, as he was from the tribe of Levi. Although this lineage is not explicitly mentioned in the Bible, the Rashbam notes that this is implied by the mention of Ahijah together with the Levites (I Chronicles 26:20). Taking a different approach, the Ri Migash explains that it was Amram, and not Ahijah, who lived through the wilderness and entered Eretz Yisrael; and Amram was certainly from the tribe of Levi. This interpretation, however, cannot be reconciled with the ages given for Kohath and Amram (Rashba).

Isn't it stated nothing other than: About thirty-six – וַהֲלֹא לֹא נֶאֱמַר אֶלָּא כִּשְׁלֹשִׁים וְשִׁשָּׁה: The reason why the Gemara assumes that the number thirty-six is not precise is because while it is common for the Bible to round numbers to the nearest ten or hundred, it is unusual to use a term such as "about" when referring to a specific number. Evidently, the verse is describing the worth of thirty-six, which is the smallest number that can form a majority of the great Sanhedrin.

PERSONALITIES

Elijah – אֵלִיָּהוּ: In many places in the Talmud and the midrash, Elijah the prophet appears to people, especially the Sages, and resolves their dilemmas. Elijah did not die (II Kings 2:11), and he continues to serve as an emissary of God.

אִיבַּעְיָא לְהוּ: אֶרֶץ יִשְׂרָאֵל לִשְׁבָטִים אִיפְּלוּג, אוֹ דִּלְמָא לְקַרְקַף גַּבְרֵי אִיפְּלוּג?

§ **A dilemma was raised before** the Sages: Was **Eretz Yisrael divided according to** the **tribes,**[N] meaning that each of the twelve tribes received an equal portion, and the members of each tribe divided these tribal portions according to their numbers; **or perhaps** Eretz Yisrael was **divided according to men's skulls,** meaning that a certain area of land was given to each individual, and the size of the tribal allotments was a function of the tribe's population?

NOTES

Divided according to the tribes – לִשְׁבָטִים אִיפְּלוּג: The Rashbam understands the Gemara's question as follows: Was the land divided into twelve equal parts and then subdivided within each tribe, or was it divided into the number of those entitled to portions, either those who left Egypt, or those who were entering Eretz Yisrael? If divided according to the amount of people, then each tribe would receive a portion whose size corresponds to its population relative to the total population of the nation.

The Ra'avad explains that the Gemara is not asking about the sizes of the respective tribes' inheritances. Rather, when the Gemara further on asserts that the land was divided by a lottery with the aid of the *Urim VeTummim*, it is asking whether this describes only the division of the tribal portions, or whether it relates in addition to the individuals' portions of land (*Shita Mekubbetzet*).

Perek **VIII**
Daf **122** Amud **a**

תָּא שְׁמַע: ״בֵּין רַב לִמְעָט״.

The Gemara suggests: **Come and hear** a proof. The verse states: "According to the lot shall their inheritance be divided **between the more and the fewer**" (Numbers 26:56). Evidently, whether the tribe had many or few people, the tribe as a whole received a portion equal to that of every other tribe, and each individual within the tribe received a different amount of land than those in other tribes.

וְעוֹד תַּנְיָא: עֲתִידָה אֶרֶץ יִשְׂרָאֵל שֶׁתִּתְחַלֵּק לִשְׁלֹשָׁה עָשָׂר שְׁבָטִים, שֶׁבַּתְּחִלָּה לֹא נִתְחַלְּקָה אֶלָּא לִשְׁנֵים עָשָׂר שְׁבָטִים. וְלֹא נִתְחַלְּקָה אֶלָּא בְּכֶסֶף, שֶׁנֶּאֱמַר: ״בֵּין רַב לִמְעָט״; אָמַר רַבִּי יְהוּדָה: סְאָה בִּיהוּדָה שָׁוָה חָמֵשׁ סְאִין בַּגָּלִיל.

And another proof can be seen from that which **is taught** in a *baraita*: **Eretz Yisrael is destined to be divided among thirteen tribes** during the messianic era, unlike the division in the time of Joshua. **As, initially** the land was **divided only among twelve tribes,** as the Torah does not allot a portion to the tribe of Levi. The *baraita* continues: **And** the land was **divided only with money,** such that each tribe that received a portion more valuable than average compensated another tribe that had received a portion less valuable than average, **as it is stated: "Between the more and the fewer."**[N] **Rabbi Yehuda said:** The area of land whose yield is a ***se'a***[B] of grain **in Judea** is so valuable that it is **equal** in value to the area necessary to produce **five *se'a*** of grain **in the Galilee.**

וְלֹא נִתְחַלְּקָה אֶלָּא בְּגוֹרָל, שֶׁנֶּאֱמַר: ״אַךְ בְּגוֹרָל״. וְלֹא נִתְחַלְּקָה אֶלָּא בְּאוּרִים וְתוּמִּים, שֶׁנֶּאֱמַר: ״עַל פִּי הַגּוֹרָל״.

The *baraita* continues: **And** the land was **divided only by a lottery, as it is stated: "Only by lot** shall the land be divided" (Numbers 26:55). **And** the land was **divided only with the *Urim VeTummim*,**[B] **as it is stated: "By the pronouncement of the lot"** (Numbers 26:56).

הָא כֵּיצַד? אֶלְעָזָר מְלוּבָּשׁ אוּרִים וְתוּמִּים, וִיהוֹשֻׁעַ וְכׇל יִשְׂרָאֵל עוֹמְדִים לְפָנָיו, וְקַלְפִּי שֶׁל שְׁבָטִים וְקַלְפִּי שֶׁל תְּחוּמִין מוּנָּחִין לְפָנָיו,

The *baraita* asks: **How can these** texts be reconciled? One indicates that the land was divided by lottery and the other indicates that the land was divided with the *Urim VeTummim*. The *baraita* explains: **Elazar** the High Priest **was dressed** with the ***Urim VeTummim*, and Joshua and all the Jewish people** were **standing before him, and** a lottery **receptacle** containing the names **of the tribes and** another lottery **receptacle** containing the names **of the boundaries** of the twelve different regions of Eretz Yisrael were **placed before him.**

וְהָיָה מְכַוֵּין בְּרוּחַ הַקֹּדֶשׁ וְאוֹמֵר: ״זְבוּלֻן עוֹלֶה – תְּחוּם עַכּוֹ עוֹלֶה עִמּוֹ״, טָרַף בְּקַלְפִּי שֶׁל שְׁבָטִים וְעָלָה בְּיָדוֹ זְבוּלֻן, טָרַף בְּקַלְפִּי שֶׁל תְּחוּמִין וְעָלָה בְּיָדוֹ תְּחוּם עַכּוֹ;

And Elazar **would ascertain** the assignments of land **with the Divine Spirit and say,** in accordance with the notification of the *Urim VeTummim*: The name of the tribe **Zebulun** now **emerges** from the receptacle in the lottery, and the region whose **boundary** is **Akko emerges with it** from the other receptacle. After stating this, he would **mix** the lots **in the receptacle of the tribes and** the lot of **Zebulun** would **emerge in his hand.** He would then **mix** the lots **in the receptacle of the boundaries, and the boundary** of **Akko** would **emerge in his hand.**

NOTES

As it is stated, between the more and the fewer – שֶׁנֶּאֱמַר ״בֵּין רַב לִמְעָט״: At this stage of the Gemara, this verse serves to prove that the land was divided with money, i.e., the leaders used monetary compensation to balance the inequality of the distributed inheritances between the choicest portions, which the verse calls "more," and the less desirable portions, which the verse calls "fewer" (Rashbam).

BACKGROUND

Se'a – סְאָה: A *se'a* is a biblical dry measure of volume (Genesis 18:6) and is used by the Sages as a point of reference for all measures. A *se'a* is equal to six *kav*, or twenty-four *log*. Estimates of the modern equivalent of a *se'a* range from 7.2–14.4 ℓ.

Urim VeTummim – אוּרִים וְתוּמִּים: It is unclear precisely what the *Urim VeTummim* were, due to the cryptic description of them in the Torah (Exodus 28:30). Rashi explains that this term is referring to the name of God, presumably written on parchment, which was inserted between the folds of the High Priest's breastplate. According to the Mishna (*Yoma* 71a) and Gemara (*Yoma* 73a–b), the *Urim VeTummim* were a medium through which the High Priest communicated with God, at the behest of the king or the Nasi of the Sanhedrin. In a crisis, anyone could ask for direction from God through the High Priest and the *Urim VeTummim*, provided the community required it. According to the Gemara, in the many instances in the Bible where God is consulted this was generally accomplished by using the *Urim VeTummim*. When a question was asked, certain letters on the breastplate would be illuminated, providing the proper answer. In the second Temple the *Urim VeTummim* were no longer extant (see *Sota* 48a).

וְחוֹזֵר וּמְכַוֵּין בְּרוּחַ הַקֹּדֶשׁ וְאוֹמֵר: ״נַפְתָּלִי עוֹלֶה וּתְחוּם גִּינּוֹסָר עוֹלֶה עִמּוֹ״, טָרַף בַּקַּלְפִּי שֶׁל שְׁבָטִים וְעָלָה בְּיָדוֹ נַפְתָּלִי, טָרַף בַּקַּלְפִּי שֶׁל תְּחוּמִין וְעָלָה בְּיָדוֹ תְּחוּם גִּינּוֹסָר. וְכֵן כׇּל שֵׁבֶט וְשֵׁבֶט.

And Elazar **would repeat** the process **and ascertain** the assignments **with the Divine Spirit and say:** The name of the tribe **Naftali** now **emerges, and** the region whose **boundary** is **Ginnosar emerges with it** from the other receptacle. After stating this, he would **mix** the lots **in the receptacle of the tribes and** the lot of **Naftali** would **emerge in his hand.** He would then **mix** the lots **in the receptacle of the boundaries, and** the **boundary** of **Ginnosar** would **emerge in his hand. And so** he would proceed for **each and every tribe.**

וְלֹא כַּחֲלוּקָּה שֶׁל עוֹלָם הַזֶּה חֲלוּקָּה שֶׁל עוֹלָם הַבָּא; הָעוֹלָם הַזֶּה, אָדָם יֵשׁ לוֹ שְׂדֵה לָבָן – אֵין לוֹ שְׂדֵה פַּרְדֵּס, שְׂדֵה פַּרְדֵּס – אֵין לוֹ שְׂדֵה לָבָן; לָעוֹלָם הַבָּא, אֵין לְךָ כׇּל אֶחָד וְאֶחָד שֶׁאֵין לוֹ בָּהָר וּבַשְּׁפֵלָה וּבָעֵמֶק, שֶׁנֶּאֱמַר: ״שַׁעַר רְאוּבֵן אֶחָד שַׁעַר יְהוּדָה אֶחָד שַׁעַר לֵוִי אֶחָד״; הַקָּדוֹשׁ בָּרוּךְ הוּא מְחַלֵּק לָהֶן בְּעַצְמוֹ, שֶׁנֶּאֱמַר: ״וְאֵלֶּה מַחְלְקוֹתָם נְאֻם ה׳״.

The *baraita* continues: **And unlike the division in this world,** i.e., in the time of Joshua, will be the **division** of portions **in the World-to-Come,** i.e., in the messianic era. In **this world,** if **a person has a field of grain, he does not have a field** for an **orchard;** if he has **a field for an orchard, he does not have a field of grain.** This is so because each climate and variety of soil is suitable for a different type of produce. But **in the World-to-Come, you do not have any person who does not have** a portion in Eretz Yisrael **in the mountain, and in the lowland, and in the valley, as it is stated: "The gate of Reuben, one;**[N] **the gate of Judah, one; the gate of Levi, one"** (Ezekiel 48:31), which is to say that everyone's portion will be the same. And **the Holy One, Blessed be He, will distribute it to them personally, as it is stated: "And these are their portions, says the Lord"** (Ezekiel 48:29). This is the conclusion of the *baraita.*

קָתָנֵי מִיהַת: ״שֶׁבַּתְּחִלָּה לֹא נִתְחַלְּקָה אֶלָּא לִשְׁנֵים עָשָׂר שְׁבָטִים״, שְׁמַע מִינַּהּ לִשְׁבָטִים אִיפְּלוּג, שְׁמַע מִינַּהּ.

The Gemara states its proof: **In any event,** the *baraita* **teaches: As initially,** the land was **divided only among the twelve tribes. Conclude from** the *baraita* that the land **was divided according to the tribes,**[N] and not apportioned directly to each person. The Gemara affirms: **Conclude from** the *baraita* that this is the case.

אָמַר מָר: עֲתִידָה אֶרֶץ יִשְׂרָאֵל שֶׁתִּתְחַלֵּק לִשְׁלֹשָׁה עָשָׂר שְׁבָטִים. אִידָּךְ לְמַאן? אֲמַר רַב חִסְדָּא: לַנָּשִׂיא, דִּכְתִיב: ״וְהָעֹבֵד הָעִיר יַעַבְדוּהוּ מִכֹּל שִׁבְטֵי יִשְׂרָאֵל״. אֲמַר לֵיהּ רַב פָּפָּא לְאַבָּיֵי, אֵימָא: רוֹנְגָר בְּעָלְמָא! לָא סָלְקָא דַּעְתָּךְ, דִּכְתִיב: ״וְהַנּוֹתָר לַנָּשִׂיא מִזֶּה וּמִזֶּה לִתְרוּמַת הַקֹּדֶשׁ וְלַאֲחֻזַּת הָעִיר״.

§ The Gemara returns to analyze the *baraita* just cited. **The Master says** above: **Eretz Yisrael is destined to be divided among thirteen tribes.** The Gemara asks: As to **the other,** thirteenth portion, **for whom** is it? **Rav Ḥisda said: For the king,**[H] **as it is written: "And they that serve the city, out of all the tribes of Israel, shall till it"** (Ezekiel 48:19). The verse is understood as meaning that the nation will collectively allot a portion to the king, who serves the needs of the nation. **Rav Pappa said to Abaye:** Why is the verse interpreted in this way? **Say** that the verse speaks of **mere wages** [*rongar*],[NL] so that the king has rights to collect taxes, but not an actual portion of land. The Gemara answers: That possibility should **not enter your mind, as it is written: "And the residue shall be for the prince, on the one side and on the other of the sacred offering and of the possession of the city"** (Ezekiel 48:21). Based on this latter verse, the former verse speaks of a specific tract of land.

וְלֹא נִתְחַלְּקָה אֶלָּא לִכְסָפִים, שֶׁנֶּאֱמַר: ״בֵּין רַב לִמְעָט״. לְמַאי? אִילֵימָא לְשׁוּפְרָא וְסַנְיָא – אַטּוּ בְּשׁוּפְטָנֵי עָסְקִינַן? אֶלָּא, לִקְרוֹבָה וּרְחוֹקָה.

The *baraita* also states: And the land was **divided only with money, as it is stated: "Between the more and the fewer."** With regard **to what** is this said? **If we say** it is with regard **to beauty and ugliness,** i.e., that those who receive inferior-quality land received monetary compensation from the others, **is that to say we are dealing with fools** [*beshufetanei*][L] who would agree to take inferior-quality land in exchange for more money? **Rather,** it is said **with regard to** the difference between land that is **close** to Jerusalem **and** land that is **far** from Jerusalem. Those whose property was close to Jerusalem compensated those whose property was farther away.

NOTES

The gate of Reuben, one, etc. – שַׁעַר רְאוּבֵן אֶחָד וכו׳: How does the Gemara learn about the portions of land from a verse that is speaking about the gates of Jerusalem? The Rashbam suggests that when foretelling that each tribe will have its own gate into Jerusalem, the verse describes this by repeating the word "one," indicating that each tribe will have an equal portion in the inheritance and division of the whole land. In a similar fashion, the Ramah explains that the fact that each tribe has a gate demonstrates that each tribe has an equal share of Jerusalem itself, and that is reflective of the arrangement for the whole land, of which each tribe has an equal portion.

Divided according to the tribes – לִשְׁבָטִים אִיפְּלוּג: According to most commentaries, the Gemara's conclusion is that the land was first divided into twelve portions of equal area, irrespective of each tribe's population, and each tribe was then assigned to its portion by both the lottery and the *Urim VeTummim*. Thereafter, the various discrepancies among the respective portions, considering the quality of the farmland and its proximity to Jerusalem, were evaluated. On the basis of these evaluations, those tribes that were allotted inferior portions received compensation in the form of money or additional tracts of land.

In his commentary on the Torah (Numbers 26:54), Rashi explains that the land was divided into twelve unequal portions, in accordance with the population of each tribe. The role of the lottery was to validate the prior division. This opinion is discussed at length in the commentaries of the Ramban, Rabbi Eliyahu Mizraḥi, and the Abravanel. According to the Abravanel, Rashi presumes that the land was divided to individuals, not tribes.

The Ra'avad adopts a variation of Rashi's opinion and explains that the lottery did not assign precise portions, but rather general regions. Once each tribe was assigned to its proper region, the precise borders were determined on the basis of the respective tribes' populations (see *Shita Mekubbetzet* on 117b and Abravanel's commentary on Joshua).

Wages [*rongar*] – רוֹנְגָר: According to the Rashbam, the term *rongar* is referring to hired laborers. In other words, the verse does not state that the tribes will give the king a literal tract of land. Rather, when the verse states: "Shall till it," that means they will work for the king as though they are day laborers. Alternatively, Rabbeinu Gershom Meor HaGola suggests that the term *rongar* is referring to a tract of land, but one much smaller than the tribal territories, e.g., a single city or small district.

HALAKHA

For the king – לַנָּשִׂיא: In the future, the messianic king, called the prince, will appropriate one-thirteenth of all the lands that the Jewish people will conquer. This matter is an ordained allotment for him and his descendants in perpetuity (Rambam *Sefer Shofetim, Hilkhot Melakhim UMilḥemoteihem* 4:8).

LANGUAGE

Wages [*rongar*] – רוֹנְגָר: It would seem that the correct reading of this word is rōzgār, a Middle Iranian word meaning day laborer that consists of rōz, meaning day, and the agent suffix gār.

Fools [*shufetanei*] – שׁוּפְטָנֵי: The origin of this word is not clear, although the most convincing explanation is that it is a metathetic equivalent of the Aramaic *tapshena*, meaning foolish, or stupid. The Sages employ the term to denote a senseless person who behaves in an irrational or imbalanced manner.

כְּתַנָּאֵי; רַבִּי אֱלִיעֶזֶר אוֹמֵר: בִּכְסָפִים הֶעֱלוּהָ, רַבִּי יְהוֹשֻׁעַ אוֹמֵר: בְּקַרְקַע הֶעֱלוּהָ.

The Gemara notes: There is a dispute between *tanna'im* with regard to the manner by which this compensation was given: **Rabbi Eliezer says:** The tribes **compensated** each other **with money. Rabbi Yehoshua says:** The tribes **compensated** each other **with land** by giving extra land to those whose portions were in less advantageous locations.

וְלֹא נִתְחַלְּקָה אֶלָּא בְּגוֹרָל, שֶׁנֶּאֱמַר: "אַךְ בְּגוֹרָל". תָּנָא: "אַךְ בְּגוֹרָל" – יָצְאוּ יְהוֹשֻׁעַ וְכָלֵב. לְמַאי? אִילֵימָא דְּלָא שְׁקוּל כְּלָל, הַשְׁתָּא דְּלָאו דִּידְהוּ שְׁקוּל, דִּידְהוּ מִיבַּעְיָא? אֶלָּא, שֶׁלֹּא נָטְלוּ בְּגוֹרָל, אֶלָּא עַל פִּי ה׳; יְהוֹשֻׁעַ – דִּכְתִיב: "עַל פִּי ה׳ נָתְנוּ לוֹ אֶת הָעִיר אֲשֶׁר שָׁאָל אֶת תִּמְנַת סֶרַח בְּהַר אֶפְרָיִם".

The *baraita* also states: **And** the land was **divided only by a lottery, as it is stated: "Only by lot** shall the land be divided" (Numbers 26:55). The Sages **taught:** In the phrase **"only by lot,"** the term "only" indicates that **Joshua and Caleb** are **excluded** from this proviso. The Gemara asks: With regard **to what** were they excluded? **If we say that** they did **not take** portions **at all, now** that it has already been taught that they **took** the portions of the spies (118b) **that** were **not their** own, **is** it **necessary** to teach that they took **their own** portions? It goes without saying that they did collect their portions. **Rather,** the exclusion teaches **that** they **did not take** portions **by a lottery but according to** explicit designation by **the Lord.** With regard to **Joshua,** this is **as it is written: "According to the commandment of the Lord they gave him the city that he asked, even Timnath Serah in the hill-country of Ephraim"** (Joshua 19:50).

Perek **VIII**
Daf **122** Amud **b**

כְּתִיב: "סֶרַח", וּכְתִיב: "חֶרֶס"! אָמַר רַבִּי אֶלְעָזָר: בַּתְּחִלָּה פֵּירוֹתֶיהָ כְּחֶרֶס, וּלְבַסּוֹף פֵּירוֹתֶיהָ מַסְרִיחִין; וְאִיכָּא דְּאָמְרִי: בַּתְּחִלָּה מַסְרִיחִין, וּלְבַסּוֹף כְּחֶרֶס.

The Gemara interjects: **It is written** concerning Joshua's burial: "And they buried him in the border of his inheritance in Timnath **Serah**" (Joshua 24:30), **and it is written:** "And they buried him in the border of his inheritance in Timnath **Heres**" (Judges 2:9). Why is the name changed? **Rabbi Elazar says: Initially, its fruits** were as dry **as clay** [*keḥeres*], **and ultimately,**[N] **its fruits** were so plump that they were **spoiling** [*masriḥin*]. **And there are** those **who say** the opposite: **Initially,** the fruits were **spoiling** prematurely, **and ultimately,** they lasted as long **as clay** without spoiling.

כָּלֵב – דִּכְתִיב: "וַיִּתְּנוּ לְכָלֵב אֶת חֶבְרוֹן כַּאֲשֶׁר דִּבֶּר מֹשֶׁה וַיּוֹרֶשׁ מִשָּׁם אֶת שְׁלֹשָׁה בְּנֵי הָעֲנָק". חֶבְרוֹן עִיר מִקְלָט הֲוַאי! אָמַר אַבַּיֵי: פַּרְוָורָהָא, דִּכְתִיב: "וְאֶת שְׂדֵה הָעִיר וְאֶת חֲצֵרֶיהָ נָתְנוּ לְכָלֵב בֶּן יְפֻנֶּה בַּאֲחֻזָּתוֹ".

Caleb also received his portion directly from God and not through the lottery, **as it is written: "And they gave Hebron to Caleb, as Moses had spoken; and he drove out from there the three sons of the giant"** (Judges 1:20). The Gemara asks about this verse: But **Hebron was a city of refuge**[B] that belonged to the priests, as described in the book of Joshua (21:13); how could it have been given to Caleb? **Abaye said: Its outskirts** [*parvaraha*],[L] i.e., only the fields and vineyards lying beyond the city limits, were given to Caleb. **As it is written: "But the fields of the city, and the villages thereof, they gave to Caleb the son of Jephunneh for his possession"** (Joshua 21:12).

NOTES

Initially…and ultimately – בַּתְּחִלָּה...וּלְבַסּוֹף: The Rashbam explains that initially, before this portion of land came into Joshua's possession, the produce had inferior qualities. Once the land was designated for Joshua, the produce was profoundly improved in his merit. The Ri Migash appears to suggest a different explanation: This land is renowned in that its produce, which is always inferior at its early stages of growth, becomes profoundly improved over the course of its growth.

LANGUAGE

Its outskirts [*parvaraha*] **– פַּרְוָורָהָא:** From the Middle Persian parwār, meaning surroundings, this word is written in several different forms with essentially the same definition. Two versions of the word appear in the Bible (II Kings 23:11; I Chronicles 26:18).

BACKGROUND

City of refuge – עִיר מִקְלָט: The books of Numbers (35:9–34) and Deuteronomy (19:1–13) describe the mitzva to establish cities of refuge to protect one who unwittingly committed manslaughter. The Sages explain that anyone who caused another's death must flee to a city of refuge, whereupon he is taken to be tried by the court. If he is convicted of intentional murder, he is executed. If the other person's death was a complete accident, he is released. If the court decides that he is guilty of negligent manslaughter, he must return to the city of refuge and remain there throughout the lifetime of the High Priest. If he leaves the city of refuge for any reason, he may be killed by his victim's blood redeemer. After the death of the High Priest, he may return to his own city, and the blood redeemer may not kill him. The Torah mentions the establishment of six cities of refuge, three west of the Jordan River and three east of the Jordan. The six cities were among the forty-eight cities given to the Levites. The Sages explained that the other forty-two cities given to the Levites (Numbers 35:2–8) also served as cities of refuge.

מתני׳ אֶחָד הַבֵּן וְאֶחָד הַבַּת בְּנַחֲלָה, אֶלָּא שֶׁהַבֵּן נוֹטֵל פִּי שְׁנַיִם בְּנִכְסֵי הָאָב וְאֵינוֹ נוֹטֵל פִּי שְׁנַיִם בְּנִכְסֵי הָאֵם, וְהַבָּנוֹת נִזּוֹנוֹת מִנִּכְסֵי הָאָב וְאֵינָן נִזּוֹנוֹת מִנִּכְסֵי הָאֵם.

MISHNA **Both the son and the daughter** of the deceased are included **in the** *halakhot* of **inheritance. But** the difference is **that the** firstborn **son takes a double** portion **of the property of the father,**[H] **and he does not take a double** portion **of the property of the mother. And** another difference is that **the daughters are sustained**[H] **from the property of the father** after he dies, as it is a mandatory condition of their mother's marriage contract that they are to be sustained even before the estate is disbursed to the children, **but the** daughters **are not sustained from the property of the mother,** which is all inherited by the sons.

גמ׳ מַאי "אֶחָד הַבֵּן וְאֶחָד הַבַּת לְנַחֲלָה"? אִילֵימָא דְּיָרְתִי כִּי הֲדָדֵי – הָא תְּנַן: בֵּן קוֹדֵם לְבַת, כָּל יוֹצְאֵי יְרֵיכוֹ שֶׁל בֵּן קוֹדְמִין לְבַת!

GEMARA The Gemara analyzes the mishna: **What** is meant by the first clause of the mishna: **Both the son and the daughter** of the deceased are included **in** the *halakhot* of **inheritance? If we say that** they **inherit together, didn't we learn** in a mishna (115a): **A son precedes a daughter?** Additionally, **all descendants of a son precede a daughter.** It is clear that a daughter does not inherit together with a son.

(סִימָן: נַפְשָׁם) אָמַר רַב נַחְמָן בַּר יִצְחָק, הָכִי קָאָמַר: אֶחָד הַבֵּן וְאֶחָד הַבַּת נוֹטְלִין בָּרָאוּי כִּבְמוּחְזָק.

Nafsham is **a mnemonic** for the names of the Sages cited in the following discussion: Nahman; Pappa; Ashi; Mar. **Rav Nahman bar Yitzhak says: This** is what the mishna **is saying: Both the son and the daughter take in** inheritance the property **due** to their father **as** they would take **in** inheritance the property that he had **in** his **possession.**

הָא נַמִי תָּנֵינָא: בְּנוֹת צְלָפְחָד נָטְלוּ שְׁלֹשָׁה חֲלָקִים בְּנַחֲלָה, חֵלֶק אֲבִיהֶן שֶׁהָיָה מִיּוֹצְאֵי מִצְרַיִם, וְחֶלְקוֹ עִם אֶחָיו בְּנִכְסֵי חֵפֶר!

The Gemara questions this explanation: **We** already **learn** this **as well**[N] in a mishna (116b): **Zelophehad's daughters took three portions** of land **in** the **inheritance** of Eretz Yisrael: **Their father's portion** that he received **because he was among those who left Egypt; and his portion** that he received **with his brothers in** the **property of Hepher,** their father, although Zelophehad predeceased his father and never was in possession of the inheritance from Hepher; and an additional portion that he received from Hepher because he was a firstborn. It is already taught in that mishna that property due to the deceased is inherited in the same manner as property possessed by the deceased.

וְעוֹד, מַאי "אֶלָּא"?

And furthermore, if the explanation of the mishna is as stated by Rav Nahman, **what** is meant by the phrase: **But** the difference is that the firstborn son takes a double portion of the property of the father, and he does not take a double portion of the property of the mother? According to Rav Nahman's explanation, what is the contrast between the two clauses in the mishna?

אֶלָּא אֲמַר רַב פַּפָּא, הָכִי קָאָמַר: אֶחָד הַבֵּן וְאֶחָד הַבַּת נוֹטְלִין חֵלֶק בַּבְּכוֹרָה.

Rather, Rav Pappa said: This is what the mishna **is saying: Both the son and the daughter** of the deceased **take a portion of the firstborn.**[H]

הָא נַמִי תָּנֵינָא: וְשֶׁהָיָה בְּכוֹר נוֹטֵל שְׁנֵי חֲלָקִים! וְעוֹד, מַאי "אֶלָּא"?

The Gemara questions this explanation: **We** already **learn** this in a mishna **as well** (116b), which explains the third portion taken by the daughters of Zelophehad: **And** they took an additional portion that he received from Hepher, **as he was a firstborn,** and a firstborn **takes two portions** of inheritance from his father. **And furthermore,** if the explanation of the mishna is as stated by Rav Pappa, **what** is meant by the phrase: **But** the difference is that the firstborn son takes a double portion of the property of the father, and he does not take a double portion of the property of the mother? According to this explanation as well, the first clause of the mishna has nothing to do with inheriting from the mother.

אֶלָּא אֲמַר רַב אַשִׁי, הָכִי קָאָמַר: אֶחָד בֵּן בֵּין הַבָּנִים וְאֶחָד בַּת בֵּין הַבָּנוֹת, אִם אָמַר "יִירַשׁ כָּל נְכָסַי" – דְּבָרָיו קַיָּימִין.

Rather, Rav Ashi said: This is what the mishna **is saying:** With regard to **both a son among the sons, and a daughter among the daughters, if** the father **says:** This particular child **shall inherit all my property, his statement stands.** A father can do so for any one son, or, when there are no sons, for any one daughter.

HALAKHA

That the son takes…of the property of the father, etc. – שֶׁהַבֵּן נוֹטֵל...בְּנִכְסֵי הָאָב וכו׳: A firstborn son takes a double portion only from the father's property, not from the mother's. Even if he is the firstborn of both the father and the mother, he takes only a standard portion of the mother's property (Rambam *Sefer Mishpatim, Hilkhot Nahalot* 2:8; *Shulhan Arukh, Hoshen Mishpat* 278:1).

And the daughters are sustained – וְהַבָּנוֹת נִזּוֹנוֹת: One of the conditions of a marriage contract is that the daughters are to be sustained from their father's estate after his death until they are betrothed or until they reach adulthood. The Rema adds that this condition is operative regardless of whether it was written in the marriage contract, or even if the mother did not receive a marriage contract, or where the local custom is not to write a marriage contract. Some add that this is so even if other conditions were written in the contract and this particular condition was omitted (*Helkat Mehokek*). There are also those who say that the daughters are sustained even in cases where, against local custom, the mother did not receive a marriage contract, or where the woman has relinquished her right to collect the marriage contract, or in the event of divorce, in which case the wife herself is not entitled to be sustained.

The Rema adds that the commentaries discuss the status of the daughters' dowry: Some say that this is not considered the daughters' sustenance and therefore is not taken from the father's property (*Nimmukei Yosef*), while the Maharil holds that the dowry is included in the category of sustenance (Rambam *Sefer Nashim, Hilkhot Ishut* 19:10; *Shulhan Arukh, Even HaEzer* 112:1, 113:1, and in the comment of Rema).

Both the son and the daughter take a portion of the firstborn – אֶחָד הַבֵּן וְאֶחָד הַבַּת נוֹטְלִין חֵלֶק בַּבְּכוֹרָה: If a firstborn and his only brother both predecease their father, a lone daughter of the firstborn inherits two-thirds of her grandfather's property, and a lone son of the younger brother inherits one-third of the grandfather's property (Rambam *Sefer Mishpatim, Hilkhot Nahalot* 2:7; *Shulhan Arukh, Hoshen Mishpat* 277:15, and see 276:3).

NOTES

We learn as well – הָא נַמִי תָּנֵינָא: According to that mishna, Zelophehad's daughters took a portion from among the properties of their grandfather Hepher, although Zelophehad predeceased Hepher.

Tosafot Yeshanim note that, in fact, there is no definitive proof that Zelophehad predeceased his father. Therefore, it must be that the *halakha* that the son and the daughter take in inheritance the property due to their father just as they would take in inheritance the property that he had in his possession is in fact understood from a different mishna (115a), which states that all descendants of a son precede a daughter, indicating that they have the right to any property that their father would have the right to receive.

כְּמַאן, כְּרַבִּי יוֹחָנָן בֶּן בְּרוֹקָא? הָא קָתָנֵי לַהּ לְקַמָּן, רַבִּי יוֹחָנָן בֶּן בְּרוֹקָא אוֹמֵר: אִם אָמַר עַל מִי שֶׁרָאוּי לְיוֹרְשׁוֹ – דְּבָרָיו קַיָּימִין, עַל מִי שֶׁאֵינוֹ רָאוּי לְיוֹרְשׁוֹ – אֵין דְּבָרָיו קַיָּימִין!

The Gemara asks: **In accordance with whose** opinion does Rav Ashi say this? Is it **in accordance with** the opinion of **Rabbi Yoḥanan ben Beroka?** The Gemara challenges: **But** the mishna **teaches this later** (130a), as **Rabbi Yoḥanan ben Beroka says: If** one **said about** another **who is fit to inherit** from **him** that the named individual should inherit all his property, **his statement stands,** but if one said it **about** another **who is unfit to inherit** from **him, his statement does not stand.** It is not reasonable to say that this mishna is stating the same *halakha* that is recorded in the later mishna in the name of Rabbi Yoḥanan ben Beroka.

וְכִי תֵּימָא: קָא סָתֵם לַן כְּרַבִּי יוֹחָנָן בֶּן בְּרוֹקָא – סְתָם וְאַחַר כָּךְ מַחֲלוֹקֶת הִיא, וּסְתָם וְאַחַר כָּךְ מַחֲלוֹקֶת – אֵין הֲלָכָה כִּסְתָם!

And if you would say that the ***tanna*** **here taught us an unattributed** mishna **in accordance with** the opinion of **Rabbi Yoḥanan ben Beroka,** in order to demonstrate that his opinion is accepted as *halakha*, this would not establish the *halakha* in accordance with his opinion. The reason is that this would be an instance of **an unattributed** mishna **and thereafter** a mishnaic **dispute** concerning the same matter, as in the later mishna there is a *tanna* who disagrees with the ruling of Rabbi Yoḥanan ben Beroka; **and** in an instance of **an unattributed** mishna **and thereafter** a mishnaic **dispute, the** ***halakha*** **is not in accordance with the unattributed** mishna.[N]

וְעוֹד, מַאי ״אֶלָּא״?

And furthermore, if the explanation of the mishna is as stated by Rav Ashi, **what** is meant by the clause: **But** the difference is that the firstborn son takes a double portion of the property of the father, and he does not take a double portion of the property of the mother? According to this explanation as well, the first clause of the mishna has nothing to do with inheriting from the mother.

אֶלָּא אָמַר מָר בַּר רַב אָשֵׁי, הָכִי קָאָמַר: אֶחָד הַבֵּן וְאֶחָד הַבַּת שָׁוִין בְּנִכְסֵי הָאֵם וּבְנִכְסֵי הָאָב, אֶלָּא שֶׁהַבֵּן נוֹטֵל פִּי שְׁנַיִם בְּנִכְסֵי הָאָב, וְאֵינוֹ נוֹטֵל פִּי שְׁנַיִם בְּנִכְסֵי הָאֵם.

Rather, Mar bar Rav Ashi said: This is what the mishna **is saying: Both the son and the daughter are equal** in their rights both **with regard to** the **property of the mother and with regard to** the **property of the father.** Sons and daughters can inherit from either fathers or mothers. **But** the differences are that **the** firstborn **son takes a double** portion **of the property of the father, and he does not take a double** portion **of the property of the mother,** and that the daughters are sustained from their father's estate before it is disbursed to the children, but they are not sustained from the property of their mother.

תָּנוּ רַבָּנַן: ״לָתֶת לוֹ פִּי שְׁנַיִם״ – פִּי שְׁנַיִם כְּאֶחָד. אַתָּה אוֹמֵר: פִּי שְׁנַיִם כְּאֶחָד, אוֹ אֵינוֹ אֶלָּא פִּי שְׁנַיִם בְּכָל הַנְּכָסִים? וְדִין הוּא.

§ **The Sages taught** in a *baraita*: When the verse states: **"But he shall acknowledge the firstborn, the son of the hated, by giving him a double portion of all that he has"** (Deuteronomy 21:17), this means the firstborn receives **double** the property received **by** any other **one** inheritor.[H] The *baraita* analyzes this statement: **Do you say** the firstborn receives **double** the property received **by** any **one** inheritor, **or rather, is it a double** portion **of all the property,** such that the firstborn receives two-thirds of the entire estate, which is twice the portion left for the other inheritors to divide between themselves? The *baraita* suggests: **And this** question can be resolved through **logical inference:**

NOTES

In an unattributed mishna and thereafter a dispute, the *halakha* is not in accordance with the unattributed mishna – סְתָם וְאַחַר כָּךְ מַחֲלוֹקֶת אֵין הֲלָכָה כִּסְתָם: When an unattributed opinion is presented in a mishna and subsequently it is presented as one opinion in a mishnaic dispute, the *halakha* is not in accordance with that unattributed opinion (Ritva; *Meromei Sadeh*).

Tosafot explain that this principle does not mean that the *halakha* is definitely not in accordance with the unattributed opinion, but merely that under such circumstances, the *halakha* is not in accordance with that opinion as a matter of course.

HALAKHA

Double the property received by any other one inheritor – פִּי שְׁנַיִם כְּאֶחָד: The firstborn collects double the property received by any other single inheritor. How so? If a father is survived by five sons, one of whom is a firstborn, the estate is divided into six equal parts, of which the firstborn collects two, equal to one-third of the total estate, and the other four brothers collect one-sixth each. If someone is survived by nine sons, the estate is divided into ten equal parts, of which the firstborn collects two, equal to one-fifth of the total estate. Each of the other eight brothers collects one tenth. This is the manner of division in all instances (Rambam *Sefer Mishpatim*, *Hilkhot Naḥalot* 2:1; *Shulḥan Arukh*, *Ḥoshen Mishpat* 277:1).

Perek **VIII**
Daf **123** Amud **a**

חֶלְקוֹ עִם אֶחָד וְחֶלְקוֹ עִם חֲמִשָּׁה, מָה חֶלְקוֹ עִם אֶחָד – פִּי שְׁנַיִם כְּאֶחָד, אַף חֶלְקוֹ עִם חֲמִשָּׁה – פִּי שְׁנַיִם כְּאֶחָד;

There may be times when a firstborn takes **his portion** of the inheritance, dividing the estate **with one** other brother, **and** there may be times when a firstborn takes **his portion** of the inheritance, dividing the estate **with five** brothers, and there is no indication that the Torah differentiates between the manner in which the respective firstborns collect in each scenario. Therefore, **just as** when a firstborn takes **his portion,** dividing the estate **with one** other brother, he receives **double** the property received **by one** inheritor, **so too,** when a firstborn takes **his portion** of the inheritance, dividing the estate **with five** brothers, he receives **double** the property received **by one** inheritor.

אוֹ כְּלָךְ לְדֶרֶךְ זוֹ: חֶלְקוֹ עִם אֶחָד וְחֶלְקוֹ עִם חֲמִשָּׁה, מַה חֶלְקוֹ עִם אֶחָד – פִּי שְׁנַיִם בְּכׇל הַנְּכָסִים, אַף חֶלְקוֹ עִם חֲמִשָּׁה – פִּי שְׁנַיִם בְּכׇל הַנְּכָסִים!

The *baraita* suggests the opposite logical derivation: **Or** perhaps **go this way:** There may be times when a firstborn takes **his portion** of the inheritance, dividing the estate **with one** other brother, **and** there may be times when a firstborn takes **his portion** of the inheritance, dividing the estate **with five** brothers. Therefore, **just as** when a firstborn takes **his portion**, dividing the estate **with one** other brother, he receives **a double** portion **of all the property, so too** when a firstborn takes **his portion** of the inheritance, dividing the estate **with five** brothers, he receives **a double** portion **of all the property.**

תַּלְמוּד לוֹמַר: ״וְהָיָה בְּיוֹם הַנְחִילוֹ אֶת בָּנָיו״, הַתּוֹרָה רִיבְּתָה נַחֲלָה אֵצֶל אַחִין, הָא אֵין עָלֶיךָ לָדוּן כַּלָּשׁוֹן הָאַחֲרוֹן אֶלָּא כַּלָּשׁוֹן הָרִאשׁוֹן;

As the logical inference can lead to either conclusion, the *halakha* is determined by a derivation from a verse. **The verse states: "Then it shall be, in the day that he causes his sons to inherit"** (Deuteronomy 21:16). As the next verse spells out: "But he shall acknowledge the firstborn, the son of the hated, by giving him a double portion of all that he has" (Deuteronomy 21:17), the former verse is ostensibly redundant. The additional verse is therefore understood as an inclusion: **The Torah increased inheritance with regard to** the **brothers,** indicating that the more brothers there are, the greater the portion they collect from the entire estate. **Therefore, you should not reason in accordance with the final formulation,** in which the *baraita* suggests that the firstborn inherits twice as much as all the other brothers combined, **but in accordance with the first formulation,** according to which the firstborn inherits twice as much as each other brother.

וְאוֹמֵר: ״וּבְנֵי רְאוּבֵן בְּכוֹר יִשְׂרָאֵל כִּי הוּא הַבְּכוֹר וּבְחַלְּלוֹ יְצוּעֵי אָבִיו נִתְּנָה בְּכֹרָתוֹ לִבְנֵי יוֹסֵף בֶּן יִשְׂרָאֵל וְלֹא לְהִתְיַחֵשׂ לַבְּכֹרָה״; וְאוֹמֵר: ״כִּי יְהוּדָה גָּבַר בְּאֶחָיו וּלְנָגִיד מִמֶּנּוּ וְהַבְּכֹרָה לְיוֹסֵף״,

The *baraita* reinforces this statement by citing additional verses: **And** the verse **states: "And the sons of Reuben the firstborn of Israel, for he was the firstborn; but, inasmuch as he defiled his father's couch, his birthright** [*bekhorato*] **was given to the sons of Joseph the son of Israel, yet not so that he was to be reckoned in the genealogy as firstborn"** (1 Chronicles 5:1).[N] **And** the following verse **states: "For Judah prevailed above his brothers, and the prince came of him; but the birthright** [*vehabekhora*] **was Joseph's"** (1 Chronicles 5:2).

נֶאֶמְרָה בְּכוֹרָה לְיוֹסֵף וְנֶאֶמְרָה בְּכוֹרָה לְדוֹרוֹת, מַה בְּכוֹרָה הָאֲמוּרָה לְיוֹסֵף – פִּי שְׁנַיִם כְּאֶחָד, אַף בְּכוֹרָה הָאֲמוּרָה לְדוֹרוֹת – פִּי שְׁנַיִם כְּאֶחָד;

The *baraita* derives: **Birthright,** i.e., firstborn status, **is stated** here **with regard to Joseph, and birthright is stated** in another verse concerning the double portion **with regard to** the later **generations:** "By giving him a double portion of all that he has, for he is the first-fruits of his strength, the birthright [*habekhora*] is his" (Deuteronomy 21:17). **Just as the birthright stated with regard to Joseph is double** the property received **by one** inheritor, as the Gemara will explain, **so too the birthright stated with regard to** the later **generations** is **double** the property received **by one** inheritor.

וְאוֹמֵר: ״וַאֲנִי נָתַתִּי לְךָ שְׁכֶם אַחַד עַל אַחֶיךָ אֲשֶׁר לָקַחְתִּי מִיַּד הָאֱמֹרִי בְּחַרְבִּי וּבְקַשְׁתִּי״, וְכִי בְּחַרְבּוֹ וּבְקַשְׁתּוֹ לָקַח? וַהֲלֹא כְּבָר נֶאֱמַר: ״כִּי לֹא בְקַשְׁתִּי אֶבְטָח וְחַרְבִּי לֹא תוֹשִׁיעֵנִי״! אֶלָּא, ״חַרְבִּי״ – זוֹ תְּפִלָּה, ״קַשְׁתִּי״ – זוֹ בַּקָּשָׁה.

The *baraita* cites additional related verses: **And** with regard to Jacob's bequest to Joseph, the verse **states: "Moreover I have given to you one portion above your brothers, which I took out of the hand of the Amorite with my sword and with my bow"** (Genesis 48:22). The *baraita* explains the verse: **But** is it **so that** Jacob **took** the portion **with his sword and with his bow? But isn't it already stated:** "Through You do we push down our adversaries; through Your name do we trample those that rise against us. **For I trust not in my bow, neither can my sword save me"** (Psalms 44:6–7)? **Rather,** what is the meaning of "with **my sword"? This** is referring to **prayer.**[N] What is the meaning of "with **my bow"? This** is referring to **petition.** This concludes the *baraita*.

מַאי ״וְאוֹמֵר״? וְכִי תֵּימָא: הַאי לְכִדְרַבִּי יוֹחָנָן בֶּן בְּרוֹקָא הוּא דְּאָתָא – תָּא שְׁמַע: ״וּבְנֵי רְאוּבֵן בְּכוֹר יִשְׂרָאֵל״;

The Gemara analyzes the *baraita*: **What** is the reason the *baraita* cites additional proofs, introducing them with the term: **And** the verse **states?** The Gemara explains: **And if you would say** that the proof from the verse: "Then it shall be, in the day that he causes his sons to inherit" is not valid, as perhaps **this** verse **comes to** teach the *halakha* **of Rabbi Yoḥanan ben Beroka** that a father may designate property for whichever child he desires, then **come** and **hear** a separate proof: **"And the sons of Reuben the firstborn of Israel...** his birthright was given to the sons of Joseph the son of Israel." As Joseph's birthright was that his sons received two portions, evidently the birthright of the firstborn is that he receives double the amount received by one inheritor.

NOTES

Yet not so that he was to be reckoned in the genealogy as firstborn – וְלֹא לְהִתְיַחֵשׂ לַבְּכֹרָה: According to the Rashbam, this means to say that, in any event, Reuben continues to be called the firstborn of Jacob. Rabbeinu Gershom Meor HaGola explains that although by virtue of historical fact, Reuben remains the firstborn, Jacob transferred the status of the firstborn to Joseph.

My sword, this is prayer – חַרְבִּי זוֹ תְּפִלָּה: On what basis do the Sages reinterpret the terms "sword" and "bow"? The Ya'avetz notes that the Sages' interpretation of "sword" derives from the verse: "Let the high praises of God be in their mouth, and a two-edged sword in their hand" (Psalms 149:6), which likens a sword to prayer. Furthermore, the term: "And my bow [*uvekashti*]," spelled *vav*, *vet*, *kuf*, *shin*, *tav*, *yod*, can also be read as: And my petition [*uvakashati*].

וְכִי תֵּימָא: בְּכוֹרָה מִ״בְּכוֹרָתוֹ״ לָא גָּמְרִינַן – תָּא שְׁמַע: ״וְהַבְּכֹרָה לְיוֹסֵף״;

And if you would say that this is not a proof either, as **we do not derive** the meaning of the term: **"Birthright** [*bekhora*]" (see Deuteronomy 21:17) **from** the similar but not identical term of: **"His birthright** [*bekhorato*]," **come** and **hear** a proof from the term employed in the following phrase from the verse: **"But the birthright** [*vehabekhora*] **was Joseph's."**

וְכִי תֵּימָא: יוֹסֵף גּוּפֵיהּ, מִמַּאי דְּפִי שְׁנַיִם כְּאֶחָד הֲוָה? תָּא שְׁמַע: ״וַאֲנִי נָתַתִּי לְךָ שְׁכֶם אַחַד עַל אַחֶיךָ״.

The Gemara continues to explicate the biblical citations in the *baraita*: **And if you would say** that this is not a proof either, as concerning **Joseph himself, from where** may it be learned **that** his birthright **was double** the property received **by one** inheritor? **Come** and **hear** a proof: **"Moreover I have given to you one portion above your brothers,"** indicating that Joseph received one more portion than each of the other sons of Jacob.

אֲמַר לֵיהּ רַב פַּפָּא לְאַבָּיֵי, אֵימָא: דִּיקְלָא בְּעָלְמָא! אֲמַר לֵיהּ, עָלֶיךָ אָמַר קְרָא: ״אֶפְרַיִם וּמְנַשֶּׁה כִּרְאוּבֵן וְשִׁמְעוֹן יִהְיוּ לִי״.

Rav Pappa said to Abaye: Why not **say** that the term "one portion" is referring to **a mere palm tree** or some other relatively small extra gift, instead of a full, equal share? Abaye **said to him: For you,** i.e., to answer your question, the **verse states: "Ephraim and Manasseh, even as Reuben and Simeon, shall be mine"** (Genesis 48:5). Evidently, Joseph's children together received portions equal to that of Reuben and Simeon together, i.e., two full portions.

בְּעָא מִינֵּיהּ רַבִּי חֶלְבּוֹ מֵרַבִּי שְׁמוּאֵל בַּר נַחְמָנִי: מָה רָאָה יַעֲקֹב שֶׁנָּטַל בְּכוֹרָה מֵרְאוּבֵן וּנְתָנָהּ לְיוֹסֵף? מָה רָאָה?! ״וּבְחַלְּלוֹ יְצוּעֵי אָבִיו״ כְּתִיב! אֶלָּא, מָה רָאָה שֶׁנְּתָנָהּ לְיוֹסֵף?

§ **Rabbi Ḥelbo asked Rabbi Shmuel bar Naḥmani: What did Jacob see that he took** the status as **firstborn from Reuben and gave it to Joseph?** The Gemara wonders: What does he mean, **what did** he **see?** The matter is **written** explicitly: **"But, inasmuch as he defiled his father's couch,** his birthright was given to the sons of Joseph" (I Chronicles 5:1). **Rather,** Rabbi Helbo's question was: **What did he see that he gave it** specifically **to Joseph?**

אֶמְשׁוֹל לְךָ מָשָׁל, לְמָה הַדָּבָר דּוֹמֶה? לְבַעַל הַבַּיִת שֶׁגִּידֵּל יָתוֹם בְּתוֹךְ בֵּיתוֹ, לְיָמִים הֶעֱשִׁיר אוֹתוֹ יָתוֹם וְאָמַר: אֲהֲנֵיהוּ לְבַעַל הַבַּיִת מִנְּכָסַי. אֲמַר לֵיהּ: וְאִי לָאו דַּחֲטָא רְאוּבֵן, לָא מְהַנֵּי לֵיהּ לְיוֹסֵף וְלָא מִדַּעַם?

Rabbi Shmuel bar Naḥmani answered Rabbi Ḥelbo: **I will tell you a parable. To what is this matter comparable? To a homeowner who raised an orphan in his home. Eventually, that orphan became wealthy and said: I will provide benefit to the homeowner from my property.** Similarly, since Joseph sustained Jacob in Egypt for a number of years, Jacob saw fit to repay the kindness. Rabbi Ḥelbo **said to him: And if Reuben did not sin,** would Jacob **not have provided any benefit to Joseph?** It cannot be that Jacob repaid Joseph only as a result of Reuben's sin.

אֶלָּא, רַבִּי יוֹנָתָן רַבָּךְ לָא כָּךְ אָמַר: רְאוּיָה הָיְתָה בְּכוֹרָה לָצֵאת מֵרָחֵל, דִּכְתִיב: ״אֵלֶּה תֹּלְדוֹת יַעֲקֹב יוֹסֵף״, אֶלָּא שֶׁקְּדָמַתָּה לֵאָה בְּרַחֲמִים, וּמִתּוֹךְ צְנִיעוּת שֶׁהָיְתָה בָּהּ בְּרָחֵל הֶחֱזִירָהּ הַקָּדוֹשׁ בָּרוּךְ הוּא לָהּ.

Rather, doesn't your teacher Rabbi Yonatan say like this: It was appropriate for the child receiving the status of **firstborn to emerge from Rachel, as it is written: "These are the generations of Jacob, Joseph"** (Genesis 37:2), indicating that Joseph was Jacob's primary progeny. **But Leah advanced** ahead of Rachel **with** appeals for **mercy,** i.e., with prayer, and thereby earned the status as firstborn for her firstborn. **But because of the modesty that Rachel possessed, the Holy One, Blessed be He, returned** the status as firstborn **to her.** This is why Jacob gave the status as firstborn to Joseph.

מַאי קְדָמַתָּה לֵאָה בְּרַחֲמִים? דִּכְתִיב: ״וְעֵינֵי לֵאָה רַכּוֹת״, מַאי ״רַכּוֹת״? אִילֵימָא רַכּוֹת מַמָּשׁ, אֶפְשָׁר? בִּגְנוּת בְּהֵמָה טְמֵאָה לֹא דִּבֵּר הַכָּתוּב, דִּכְתִיב: ״מִן הַבְּהֵמָה הַטְּהוֹרָה וּמִן הַבְּהֵמָה אֲשֶׁר אֵינֶנָּה טְהֹרָה״, בִּגְנוּת צַדִּיקִים דִּבֵּר הַכָּתוּב?! אֶלָּא אָמַר רַבִּי אֶלְעָזָר: שֶׁמַּתְּנוֹתֶיהָ אֲרוּכּוֹת.

The Gemara explains this answer: **What does it mean that Leah advanced** ahead of Rachel **with mercy? As it is written: "And Leah's eyes were weak** [*rakkot*]" (Genesis 29:17). **What** is the meaning of "*rakkot*"? **If we say** that her eyes were **literally weak,** is it **possible** that the verse would say that? **The verse** there **did not speak to the disparagement of** even **a non-kosher animal, as it is written: "From the pure animals and from the animals that are lacking purity"** (Genesis 7:8). The verse states: "That are lacking purity" rather than stating explicitly and disparagingly: That are impure. If that is so with regard to animals, **did the verse speak** here **to the disparagement of the righteous? Rather, Rabbi Elazar says:** The term alludes to the fact **that her gifts,** i.e., the gifts given to her descendants, e.g., the priesthood and the monarchy, **were long-lasting** [*arukkot*],[N] as they were passed down from generation to generation.

NOTES

That her gifts were long-lasting – שֶׁמַּתְּנוֹתֶיהָ אֲרוּכּוֹת: These gifts are that her descendants were the Levites and the priests, as well as the kings, all of whom are governed by an eternal covenant (Rabbeinu Gershom Meor HaGola). By contrast, the Maharsha suggests that the term *arukkot* denotes not a long period of time, but prominence. A number of other instances of this word in the Talmud reinforce this interpretation.

רַב אֲמַר: לְעוֹלָם רַכּוֹת מַמָּשׁ, וְלֹא גְּנַאי הוּא לָהּ, אֶלָּא שֶׁבַח הוּא לָהּ; שֶׁהָיְתָה שׁוֹמַעַת עַל פָּרָשַׁת דְּרָכִים בְּנֵי אָדָם שֶׁהָיוּ אוֹמְרִים: שְׁנֵי בָנִים יֵשׁ לָהּ לְרִבְקָה, שְׁתֵּי בָנוֹת יֵשׁ לוֹ לְלָבָן, גְּדוֹלָה לְגָדוֹל וּקְטַנָּה לְקָטָן.

Rav says that there is a different explanation of the verse: **Actually,** the verse means that her eyes **were literally weak, and** this is **not a denigration of her but a praise of her. As she would hear people at the crossroads,** coming from the land of Canaan, **who would say: Rebecca has two sons,** and her brother **Laban has two daughters;** the **older** daughter will be married **to** the **older** son, **and** the **younger** daughter will be married **to** the **younger** son.

וְהָיְתָה יוֹשֶׁבֶת עַל פָּרָשַׁת דְּרָכִים וּמַשְׁאֶלֶת: גָּדוֹל מַה מַּעֲשָׂיו? אִישׁ רַע הוּא, מְלַסְטֵם בְּרִיּוֹת. קָטָן מַה מַּעֲשָׂיו? ״אִישׁ תָּם יֹשֵׁב אֹהָלִים״, וְהָיְתָה בּוֹכָה עַד שֶׁנָּשְׁרוּ רִיסֵי עֵינֶיהָ.

Rav continues: **And she would sit at the crossroads and ask: What** are **the deeds of** the **older** son? The passersby would answer: **He is an evil man,** and he **robs people.** She would ask: **What** are **the deeds of** the **younger** son? They would answer: He is **"a quiet man, dwelling in tents"** (Genesis 25:27). **And** because she was so distraught at the prospect of marrying the evil brother, **she would cry** and pray for mercy **until her eyelashes fell out.** Since the weakness of her eyes was due to this cause, characterizing her eyes as weak constitutes praise. This is Leah's prayer for mercy to which Rabbi Yonatan referred.

וְהַיְינוּ דִּכְתִיב: ״וַיַּרְא ה׳ כִּי שְׂנוּאָה לֵאָה״, מַאי שְׂנוּאָה? אִילֵימָא שְׂנוּאָה מַמָּשׁ, אֶפְשָׁר? בִּגְנוּת בְּהֵמָה טְמֵאָה לֹא דִּבֵּר הַכָּתוּב, בִּגְנוּת צַדִּיקִים דִּבֵּר הַכָּתוּב?! אֶלָּא רָאָה הַקָּדוֹשׁ בָּרוּךְ הוּא שֶׁשְּׂנוּאִין מַעֲשֵׂה עֵשָׂו בְּפָנֶיהָ – ״וַיִּפְתַּח אֶת רַחְמָהּ״.

The Gemara comments: **And** her desire not to marry Esau is the basis of that **which is written: "And the Lord saw that Leah was hated,** and He opened her womb" (Genesis 29:31). **What** is the meaning of **"hated"? If we say** that she was **literally hated,**[N] is it **possible? The verse** there **did not speak to the disparagement** of even a **non-kosher animal,** so **did the verse** here **speak to the disparagement of the righteous? Rather, the Holy One, Blessed be He, saw that the behavior of Esau was hated by her,** and therefore: **"And He opened her womb."**

וּמַאי צְנִיעוּת הָיְתָה בָּהּ בְּרָחֵל? דִּכְתִיב: ״וַיַּגֵּד יַעֲקֹב לְרָחֵל כִּי אֲחִי אָבִיהָ הוּא וְכִי בֶן רִבְקָה הוּא״, וַהֲלֹא בֶּן אֲחוֹת אָבִיהָ הוּא! אֶלָּא, אֲמַר לָהּ: מִינַּסְבַתְּ לִי? אֲמַרָה לֵיהּ: אִין, מִיהוּ אַבָּא רַמָּאָה הוּא וְלָא יָכְלַתְּ לֵיהּ.

The Gemara now explains the second part of Rabbi Yonatan's explanation: **And what** was a demonstration of the **modesty that Rachel possessed? As it is written: "And Jacob told Rachel that he was her father's brother, and that he was Rebecca's son"** (Genesis 29:12). The Gemara asks: **But isn't he the son of her father's sister?** Why did he say that he was her father's brother? **Rather,** Jacob and Rachel had the following exchange: Jacob **said to** Rachel: **Will you marry me?** Rachel **said to him: Yes, but** my **father is a deceitful person, and you cannot defeat him.**

אֲמַר לָהּ: מַאי רַמָּאוּתֵיהּ? אֲמַרָה לֵיהּ: אִית לִי אַחְתָּא דְּקַשִּׁישָׁא מִינַּאי, וְלָא מַנְּסְבָא לִי מִקַּמַּהּ. אֲמַר לָהּ: אָחִיו אֲנִי בְּרַמָּאוּת. אֲמַרָה לֵיהּ: וּמִי שָׁרֵי לְהוּ לְצַדִּיקֵי לְסַגּוּיֵי בְּרַמָּאוּתָא? אִין, ״עִם נָבָר תִּתָּבָר וְעִם עִקֵּשׁ תִּתַּפָּל״. מָסַר לָהּ סִימָנִין.

Jacob **said to her: What is his** method of **deceit** of which I need be aware? Rachel **said to him: I have a sister who is older than me, and he will not marry me off before** he marries **her** off, even if he promises that he will do so. Jacob **said to her: I am his brother,** i.e., equal, **in deceit,**[N] and he will not be able to deceive me. That is why Jacob said that he was "her father's brother." Rachel **said to him: But is it permitted for the righteous to act deceitfully?** Jacob answered her: **Yes,** in certain circumstances. As the verse states concerning God: **"With the pure You show Yourself pure; and with the crooked You show Yourself subtle"** (II Samuel 22:27). Therefore, to counter Laban's deceit, Jacob **gave** Rachel secret **signs** to prove to him that she was the one marrying him.

NOTES

If we say that she was literally hated – אִילֵימָא שְׂנוּאָה מַמָּשׁ: The verse: "And he loved Rachel more than Leah" (Genesis 29:30), reinforces the understanding that Jacob indeed loved Leah, but not as much as he loved Rachel. In any case, "hated" certainly does not suggest that Jacob hated Leah in every respect, which is often indicated by the term hated.

I am his brother in deceit – אָחִיו אֲנִי בְּרַמָּאוּת: The Meiri describes how the righteous must exercise caution to conduct all of their dealings to completely avoid dishonesty or deceit. Despite this, when dealing with devious people, one may take steps to protect himself from their trickery. Such behavior is warranted even if it resembles deviousness, e.g., if one partner fails to fulfill his obligations in a certain agreement, the righteous partner need not fulfill his own obligations.

כִּי קָא מְעַיְּילִי לָהּ לְלֵאָה, סָבְרָה: הָשְׁתָּא מִיכַּסְפָא אַחְתַאי. מְסַרְתִּינְהוּ נִיהֲלָהּ. וְהַיְינוּ דִּכְתִיב: ״וַיְהִי בַבֹּקֶר וְהִנֵּה הִיא לֵאָה״, מִכְּלָל דְּעַד הָשְׁתָּא לָאו לֵאָה הִיא?! אֶלָּא, מִתּוֹךְ סִימָנִים שֶׁמָּסַר לָהּ יַעֲקֹב לְרָחֵל וּמְסַרְתָּה לְלֵאָה, לָא הֲוָה יָדַע לָהּ עַד הַהִיא שַׁעְתָּא.

Laban did in fact attempt to have Jacob marry Leah instead of marrying Rachel. **When** Laban's associates **were bringing Leah up** to the wedding canopy to marry Jacob, Rachel **thought: Now my sister will be humiliated** when Jacob discovers that she is the one marrying him. Therefore, Rachel **gave** the signs **to** Leah. **And this is as it is written: "And it came to pass in the morning that, behold, it was Leah"** (Genesis 29:25). This verse is difficult, as **by inference,** should one derive **that until now she was not Leah? Rather, through the signs that Jacob gave to Rachel and that she gave to Leah, he did not know** it was she **until that moment.** This is the modesty of Rachel to which Rabbi Yonatan was referring.

בְּעָא מִינֵּיהּ אַבָּא חֲלִיפָא קָרוֹיָא מֵרַבִּי חִיָּיא בַּר אַבָּא: בִּכְלָלָן אַתָּה מוֹצֵא שִׁבְעִים, בִּפְרָטָן אַתָּה מוֹצֵא שִׁבְעִים חָסֵר אֶחָד! אֲמַר לֵיהּ: תְּאוֹמָה הָיְתָה עִם דִּינָה, דִּכְתִיב: ״וְאֵת דִּינָה בִתּוֹ״. אֶלָּא מֵעַתָּה, תְּאוֹמָה הָיְתָה עִם בִּנְיָמִין, דִּכְתִיב:

§ The Gemara continues its discussion of Jacob's family. **Abba Ḥalifa Karoya asked Rabbi Ḥiyya bar Abba: In the total** tally of Jacob's family members who descended to Egypt, **you find seventy,** as stated in the verse: "All the souls of the house of Jacob, that came into Egypt, were seventy" (Genesis 46:27). By contrast, **in their individual** listing, when the family members of each of his sons are listed by name, **you find seventy-less-one.** How can this be resolved? Rabbi Ḥiyya bar Abba **said to him: A twin** sister **was** born **with Dinah, as it is written: "And** [*ve'et*] **his daughter Dinah"** (Genesis 46:15). The term *et* implies an unspecified additional person. Abba Ḥalifa Karoya replied: **If that is so,** one would have to say that **a twin** sister **was** born **with Benjamin, as it is written:**

״וְאֶת בִּנְיָמִין אָחִיו בֶּן אִמּוֹ״! אֲמַר: מַרְגָּלִית טוֹבָה הָיְתָה בְּיָדִי וְאַתָּה מְבַקֵּשׁ לְאַבְּדָהּ מִמֶּנִּי, הָכִי אֲמַר רַבִּי חָמָא בַּר חֲנִינָא: זוֹ יוֹכֶבֶד, שֶׁהוֹרָתָהּ בַּדֶּרֶךְ וְלֵידָתָהּ בֵּין הַחוֹמוֹת, שֶׁנֶּאֱמַר: ״אֲשֶׁר יָלְדָה אוֹתָהּ לְלֵוִי בְּמִצְרָיִם״, לֵידָתָהּ בְּמִצְרַיִם וְאֵין הוֹרָתָהּ בְּמִצְרַיִם.

"And he lifted up his eyes, and saw *et* **Benjamin his brother, his mother's son"** (Genesis 43:29), which would render the count of seventy incorrect. Rabbi Ḥiyya bar Abba **said:** There **was a goodly pearl** [*margalit*][NL] **in my hand, and you are trying to have me lose it.** He continued: **So said Rabbi Ḥama bar Ḥanina: This** missing seventieth person is **Jochebed, whose conception was on the journey,** as the family of Jacob descended to Egypt, **and she was born within the walls,** i.e., in Egypt, **as it is stated:** "And the name of Amram's wife was Jochebed, the daughter of Levi, **who was born to Levi in Egypt"** (Numbers 26:59). **Her birth was in Egypt, but her conception was not in Egypt.** Accordingly, the family had seventy persons upon arrival, but she could not have been listed as descending to Egypt.

בְּעָא מִינֵּיהּ רַבִּי חֶלְבּוֹ מֵרַבִּי שְׁמוּאֵל בַּר נַחְמָנִי, כְּתִיב: ״וַיְהִי כַּאֲשֶׁר יָלְדָה רָחֵל אֶת יוֹסֵף״ וגו׳, מַאי שְׁנָא כִּי אִתְיְלִיד יוֹסֵף? אֲמַר לֵיהּ: רָאָה יַעֲקֹב אָבִינוּ שֶׁאֵין זַרְעוֹ שֶׁל עֵשָׂו נִמְסָר אֶלָּא בְּיַד זַרְעוֹ שֶׁל יוֹסֵף, שֶׁנֶּאֱמַר: ״וְהָיָה בֵית יַעֲקֹב אֵשׁ וּבֵית יוֹסֵף לֶהָבָה וּבֵית עֵשָׂו לְקַשׁ״ וגו׳.

§ **Rabbi Ḥelbo asked Rabbi Shmuel bar Naḥmani: It is written: "And it came to pass, when Rachel gave birth to Joseph,** that Jacob said to Laban: Send me away, that I may go to my own place, and to my country" (Genesis 30:25). **What was different when Joseph was born,** that Jacob decided only then to return home? Rabbi Shmuel bar Naḥmani **said to him: Jacob our patriarch saw** prophetically **that the descendants of Esau** will be **delivered only to the hand of the descendants of Joseph, as it is stated: "And the house of Jacob shall be a fire, and the house of Joseph a flame, and the house of Esau for straw,** and they shall kindle in them, and devour them" (Obadiah 1:18). Jacob had left Eretz Yisrael to escape Esau, but he now felt confident that he could return without endangering his family.

אֵיתִיבֵיהּ: ״וַיַּכֵּם דָּוִד מֵהַנֶּשֶׁף וְעַד הָעֶרֶב לְמָחֳרָתָם״! אֲמַר לֵיהּ: דְּאַקְרְיָךְ נְבִיאֵי לָא אַקְרְיָךְ כְּתוּבֵי, דִּכְתִיב: ״בְּלֶכְתּוֹ אֶל צִקְלַג נָפְלוּ עָלָיו מִמְּנַשֶּׁה עַדְנָה וְיוֹזָבָד וִידִיעֲאֵל וּמִיכָאֵל וְיוֹזָבָד וֶאֱלִיהוּא וְצִלְּתָי רָאשֵׁי הָאֲלָפִים אֲשֶׁר לִמְנַשֶּׁה״.

Rabbi Ḥelbo **raised an objection to** Rabbi Shmuel bar Naḥmani: Concering a battle between the Jewish people and the nation of Amalek, who descend from Esau, the verse states: **"And David smote them from the twilight even to the evening of the next day"** (I Samuel 30:17). David was from the tribe of Judah, yet he was able to defeat the descendants of Esau. Rabbi Shmuel bar Naḥmani **said to him: Whoever read** and taught **Prophets to you did not read** and teach **Writings to you, as it is written: "As he went to Ziklag, there fell to him of Manasseh, Adnah, and Jozabad, and Jediael, and Michael, and Jozabad, and Elihu, and Zillethai, captains of thousands that were of Manasseh,** and they helped David against the troop" (I Chronicles 12:21–2). The verse in Writings teaches that David's campaign against Esau was led by Joseph's descendants, from the family of Manasseh.

NOTES

There was a goodly pearl, etc. – מַרְגָּלִית טוֹבָה הָיְתָה וכו׳: In other words: I had a satisfying explanation, and at first, I did not want to share it, but now I am compelled to reveal it to everyone (Rabbeinu Gershom Meor HaGola). The Rashbam explains that he was attempting to increase interest in the answer.

LANGUAGE

Pearl [*margalit*] – מַרְגָּלִית: From the Greek μαργαρίτης, *margaritēs*, meaning pearl, with the second r phoneme exchanged for an l. A similar word in Greek means precious stone, and the word *margalit* has both definitions in various places in rabbinic literature.

מְתִיב רַב יוֹסֵף: ״וּמֵהֶם מִן בְּנֵי שִׁמְעוֹן הָלְכוּ לְהַר שֵׂעִיר אֲנָשִׁים חֲמֵשׁ מֵאוֹת וּפְלַטְיָה וּנְעַרְיָה וּרְפָיָה וְעֻזִּיאֵל בְּנֵי יִשְׁעִי בְּרֹאשָׁם, וַיַּכּוּ אֶת שְׁאֵרִית הַפְּלֵטָה לַעֲמָלֵק וַיֵּשְׁבוּ שָׁם עַד הַיּוֹם הַזֶּה״. אֲמַר רַבָּה בַּר שֵׁילָא: יִשְׁעִי מִבְּנֵי מְנַשֶּׁה אָתֵי, דִּכְתִיב: ״וּבְנֵי מְנַשֶּׁה חֵפֶר וְיִשְׁעִי״.

Rav Yosef raises an objection: Another verse indicates that the descendants of Simeon also have the ability to defeat the descendants of Esau: **"And some of them, even of the sons of Simeon, five hundred men, went to Mount Seir, having for their captains Pelatiah, and Ne'ariah, and Rephaiah, and Uzziel, the sons of Ishi. And they struck the remnant of the Amalekites that escaped, and dwelled there until this day"** (I Chronicles 4:42–43). **Rabba bar Sheila said** in response: **Ishi came from** the **children of Manasseh, as it is written: And the sons of Manasseh: Hepher and Ishi.**[N]

תָּנוּ רַבָּנַן: הַבְּכוֹר נוֹטֵל פִּי שְׁנַיִם בַּזְּרוֹעַ וּבַלְּחָיַיִם וּבַקֵּיבָה, וּבְמוּקְדָּשִׁין, וּבְשֶׁבַח שֶׁשָּׁבְחוּ נְכָסִים לְאַחַר מִיתַת אֲבִיהֶן.

§ **The Sages taught** (*Tosefta* 7:4–5): **The firstborn** priest **takes a double** portion **of the foreleg, and of the jaw, and of the maw,**[H] which are given to a priest from all slaughtered non-sacred cattle, sheep, and goats (see Deuteronomy 18:3). **And** a firstborn, whether he is a priest or non-priest, takes a double portion **of** his father's **sacrificial** animals **and of the enhancement of the property** that occurred **after the death of their father.**

כֵּיצַד? הִנִּיחַ לָהֶן אֲבִיהֶן פָּרָה מוּחְכֶּרֶת וּמוּשְׂכֶּרֶת בְּיַד אֲחֵרִים, אוֹ שֶׁהָיְתָה רוֹעָה בָּאֲפָר, וְיָלְדָה – בְּכוֹר נוֹטֵל פִּי שְׁנַיִם. אֲבָל בָּנוּ בָּתִּים וְנָטְעוּ כְּרָמִים – אֵין בְּכוֹר נוֹטֵל פִּי שְׁנַיִם.

The *baraita* continues: **How so?** To what type of enhancement is this referring? If **their father left them a cow** that was **leased or rented in the possession of others, or if it was grazing in the meadow,**[N] **and it gave birth,**[HN] then the **firstborn takes a double** portion of the rental income or of the calf. **But** if the inheritors **built homes or planted vineyards** after their father's death, thereby enhancing the property, the **firstborn does not take a double** portion. This is not considered enhancement of the father's property, but profit due to their actions.

הַאי הַזְּרוֹעַ וְהַלְּחָיַיִם וְהַקֵּיבָה הֵיכִי דָמֵי? אִי דְּאָתֵי לִידֵי אֲבוּהוֹן – פְּשִׁיטָא, וְאִי דְּלָא אָתֵי לִידֵי אֲבוּהוֹן – רָאוּי הוּא, וְאֵין הַבְּכוֹר נוֹטֵל בְּרָאוּי כְּבְמוּחְזָק!

The Gemara analyzes the *baraita*: Concerning **this** right to collect a double portion of **the foreleg, and the jaw, and the maw, what are the circumstances? If** they **came into the possession of their father,** then it is **obvious** that the firstborn collects a double portion. **And if** they **did not come into the possession of their father,** then these items **are** merely property **due** to their father,[N] **and the firstborn does not take** a double portion **of** property **due** to the deceased **as** he does the property his father **possessed.**

HALAKHA

Of the foreleg, and of the jaw, and of the maw – בַּזְּרוֹעַ וּבַלְּחָיַיִם וּבַקֵּיבָה: When an associate of the priesthood slaughters an animal, the priestly gifts from that animal have a presumptive status of being owned by that priest from the moment of the slaughter. Therefore, the priest's firstborn son collects a double portion of those gifts, as the Gemara explains later (Rambam *Sefer Mishpatim*, *Hilkhot Naḥalot* 3:3; *Shulḥan Arukh*, *Ḥoshen Mishpat* 278:5 and *Sma* there).

A cow that was leased…and it gave birth, etc. – פָּרָה מוּחְכֶּרֶת...וְיָלְדָה וכו׳: If a father left his sons a leased or rented cow, or if the cow was left grazing in the meadow, and it gave birth, the firstborn takes a double portion of the cow and its calf. This is in accordance with the *baraita*, which some hold is the unanimous opinion, according to the Gemara's conclusion (*Maggid Mishne*).

The Rema writes that some say he does not take a double portion (Ra'avad; *Tur*; Rosh), as the Gemara later ascribes this *baraita* to Rabbi Yehuda HaNasi and the *halakha* is ruled contrary to his opinion (Rambam *Sefer Mishpatim*, *Hilkhot Naḥalot* 3:2; *Shulḥan Arukh*, *Ḥoshen Mishpat* 278:4).

NOTES

And the son of Manasseh: Hepher and Ishi – וּבְנֵי מְנַשֶּׁה חֵפֶר וְיִשְׁעִי: As the Ritva notes, this is not a verse from the Bible. Nevertheless, the Bible does identify Ishi as being from the tribe of Manasseh (I Chronicles 5:24), and the Gemara occasionally cites biblical verses in an approximate way, presenting the material necessary for the topic at hand. The Maharsha suggests that the Gemara is citing, in shorthand, I Chronicles (5:23–24): "And the children of the half-tribe of Manasseh dwelt in the land, from Bashan to Baal Hermon and Senir and Mount Hermon, where they increased. And these were the heads of their fathers' houses: Epher, and Ishi, and Eliel, and Azriel, and Jeremiah, and Hodaviah, and Jahdiel, mighty men of valor, famous men, heads of their fathers' houses." If so, the text of the Gemara should read Epher instead of Hepher.

Grazing in the meadow – רוֹעָה בָּאֲפָר: The significance of stating that it was grazing in the meadow is that the animal became fat over the course of its grazing and became more valuable than it had been during their father's lifetime (*Sma*).

And it gave birth – וְיָלְדָה: Some early commentaries claim that this is the *halakha* only in the case of an animal that had already been pregnant before the father's death, because the firstborn can claim a double portion only from an improvement that began during the father's lifetime. Similarly, in the case of a rented animal, it is the *halakha* only if the animal was rented before the father's death (Rid).

Others hold that this *halakha* is in effect even if the animal became pregnant after the father's death because the change occurred to the animal that their father left (Rabbeinu Yona).

And if they did not come into the possession of their father, they are property due to their father – וְאִי דְּלָא אָתֵי לִידֵי אֲבוּהוֹן רָאוּי הוּא: The Ri Migash asks: If the gifts have not been separated yet, then how may they be considered due to their father? Therefore, he deletes the words: It is due to their father, from the Gemara. Citing this opinion, the Rashba agrees that the emended text seems correct. Nevertheless, he suggests that the standard version of the text may be maintained if it is already taken for granted that this is a case in which the giver of the gifts regularly gives these gifts to a specific priest. Even if the individual regularly behaves this way, it could be argued that the inheritance is considered due to their father only as long as the gifts have not been formally separated.

הָכָא בְּמַכִּירֵי כְהוּנָּה עָסְקִינַן, וּדְאִשְׁתְּחִיט בְּחַיֵּי דַּאֲבוּהוֹן, וְקָסָבַר: מַתָּנוֹת שֶׁלֹּא הוּרְמוּ כְּמִי שֶׁהוּרְמוּ דָּמוּ.

The Gemara answers: **Here, we are dealing with associates of the priesthood,**[N] i.e., people who have an arrangement with a specific priest to give him their priestly gifts. **And** it was a case **where** the animal **was slaughtered while the father was alive, and** the *tanna* of this *baraita* **holds:** Priestly **gifts that were not** yet **separated**[H] **are considered as though they** have already been **separated.** Therefore, even though the gifts were not yet given, they were considered in the possession of the priest before his death.

מוּקְדָּשִׁין – לָאו דִּידֵיהּ נִינְהוּ!

The Gemara continues to analyze the *baraita*: Why does the firstborn take a double portion of the father's **sacrificial** animals? Isn't it so that once the father consecrates them, **they** belong to Heaven and **are not his?**

בְּקָדָשִׁים קַלִּים, וְאַלִּיבָּא דְּרַבִּי יוֹסֵי הַגְּלִילִי דְּאָמַר: מָמוֹן בְּעָלִים הוּא; דְּתַנְיָא: ״וּמָעֲלָה מַעַל בַּה׳״ – לְרַבּוֹת קָדָשִׁים קַלִּים שֶׁהֵן מָמוֹן בְּעָלִים, דִּבְרֵי רַבִּי יוֹסֵי הַגְּלִילִי.

The Gemara answers: This is stated **with regard to** a case of **offerings of lesser sanctity,** such as peace offerings, **and in accordance with** the opinion **of Rabbi Yosei HaGelili, who says:** These sacrificial animals **are** considered the **property of** their **owners,** as opposed to property of Heaven. **As it is taught** in a *baraita* that concerning one who steals another's property and takes a false oath denying he has done so, incurring the obligation to bring a guilt-offering, the verse states: **"And commits a trespass against the Lord,** and deals falsely with his neighbor" (Leviticus 5:21). The verse serves **to include offerings of lesser sanctity,**[B] **which are** the **property of** their **owners;** this is **the statement of Rabbi Yosei HaGelili.** Consequently, the firstborn collects a double portion of these as well.

הִנִּיחַ לָהֶן אֲבִיהֶן פָּרָה מוּחְכֶּרֶת וּמוּשְׂכֶּרֶת בְּיַד אֲחֵרִים, אוֹ שֶׁהָיְתָה רוֹעָה בָּאֲפָר, וְיָלְדָה – בְּכוֹר נוֹטֵל בָּהּ פִּי שְׁנַיִם. הָשְׁתָּא מוּחְכֶּרֶת וּמוּשְׂכֶּרֶת דְּלָאו בִּרְשׁוּתָא דְּמָרָהּ דִּידְהוּ קַיְימָא, אָמְרַתְּ: שָׁקֵיל, רוֹעָה בָּאֲפָר מִיבַּעְיָא?

The *baraita* states: If **their father left them a cow** that was **leased or rented in the possession of others, or if it was grazing in the meadow, and it gave birth,** then **the firstborn takes a double** portion of the rental income or calf. The Gemara asks: **Now** that in a case where the cow was **leased or rented** to others, **where** the animals **are not in their owner's possession, you say** that the firstborn **takes** a double portion, in a case where it was **grazing in the meadow, is** it **necessary** for the *baraita* to state that he receives a double portion?

הָא קָא מַשְׁמַע לָן, דְּמוּחְכֶּרֶת וּמוּשְׂכֶּרֶת דּוּמְיָא דְּרוֹעָה בָּאֲפָר, מָה רוֹעָה בָּאֲפָר – שְׁבָחָא דְּמִמֵּילָא קָא אָתֵי, וְלָא קָא חַסְרִי בָּהּ מְזוֹנָא,

The Gemara answers that **this** is what the *baraita* **teaches us:** It teaches **that** a case where the animal was **leased or rented is similar to** a case where it was **grazing in the meadow,** in that **just as** in a case where it was **grazing in the meadow, the enhancement came by itself and** the brothers **did not lose** money **for its sustenance,**

HALAKHA

Gifts that were not yet separated – מַתָּנוֹת שֶׁלֹּא הוּרְמוּ: Priestly gifts that have not yet been separated have the status of property that has already been separated, with respect to inheritance, betrothal, and tithes (Rambam *Sefer Mishpatim, Hilkhot Naḥalot* 3:3; *Sefer Nashim, Hilkhot Ishut* 5:6; and *Sefer Zera'im, Hilkhot Ma'aser* 6:21; *Shulḥan Arukh, Ḥoshen Mishpat* 278:5 and *Yoreh De'a* 61:5 and *Shakh* there).

BACKGROUND

Offerings of lesser sanctity – קָדָשִׁים קַלִּים: The offerings sacrificed in the Temple are divided into two main categories: Offerings of the most sacred order and offerings of lesser sanctity. The offerings of the most sacred order include those offered on Yom Kippur, communal sin-offerings, burnt-offerings, and sin-offerings. The offerings of lesser sanctity include peace-offerings, animal tithes, and the Paschal offering.

One of the primary differences between the two types of offerings is that offerings of the most sacred order are slaughtered only in the north of the Temple courtyard, while offerings of lesser sanctity may be slaughtered anywhere in the courtyard. The most fundamental difference between the two types of offerings is with regard to when the animal becomes sacred and when its sanctity is nullified through misuse. Offerings of the most sacred order are sacred, and their sanctity can be nullified through misuse from the moment they are consecrated. By contrast, only certain parts of the offerings of lesser sanctity are considered sacred, and their sanctity takes effect from the time they are slaughtered. Similarly, the offerings of the most sacred order may be consumed only on the day they are sacrificed and the following night, while most offerings of lesser sanctity may be consumed on the following day as well.

NOTES

Associates of the priesthood [*makkirei kehuna*] **– מַכִּירֵי כְהוּנָּה:** According to the Rashbam, the Gemara is discussing residents of a place in which the gifts are given only to a specific priest. Similarly, Rabbeinu Gershom Meor HaGola and the Ri Migash explain that the Gemara is talking about the friends of the priest, who always give the gifts to him. The Ri Migash adds that since there is a presumption that the animal's owner will give the gifts to the priest, the gifts are considered like the property of the priest already, akin to a priest's property that is being temporarily held by another, of which the firstborn certainly collects a double portion.

Tosafot suggest that although the owner of the animal has the legal right to give the gifts to another priest, until he changes his mind about giving them to the usual priest, this priest retains presumptive ownership. This is so because the owner is like one who has promised to give another a small gift, and one is not permitted to renege from such a promise.

By contrast, the Rashbam explains that from the moment the animal is slaughtered, the owner has an explicit intent to give the gifts to the priest even before the gifts are separated. Therefore, the gifts have the status of gifts held by a priest, even without having been formally separated. According to the Gemara (*Hullin* 130b), these gifts may not be taken from the priest, and he even has the right to claim them in court (see Rabbeinu Yona).

As an alternative explanation, some say that the term: *Makkirei kehuna* is related to the term: Sale [*mekher*], and not: Associate [*makkir*]. Accordingly, the Gemara is discussing a case in which a priest has purchased the right to all priestly gifts that will be given over a certain period of time. Therefore, he has presumptive ownership of those items (*Tosafot Yeshanim*).

In any case, all of these opinions apply only if the animal has already been slaughtered. Before the animal is slaughtered, the priest certainly has no right to the gifts. If the priest dies before the animal is slaughtered and his sons receive those gifts, they receive them in their own right, as the status of receiving the gifts due to the *halakha* of an associate of the priesthood is not inherited (Ri Migash).

אף מוחכרת ומושכרת – שבחא דממילא קא אתי, דלא חסרי בה מזוני.

so too in the case of a cow that was **leased or rented,** the *baraita* is referring only to a case where **the enhancement came by itself, as** the brothers **did not lose** money for **its sustenance,** since it was stipulated that the one who rented or leased it would provide its feed.

מני? רבי היא; דתניא: אין בכור נוטל פי שנים בשבח ששבחו נכסים לאחר מיתת אביהן; רבי אומר, אומר אני: בכור נוטל פי שנים בשבח ששבחו נכסים לאחר מיתת אביהן, אבל לא בשבח שהשביחו יתומים לאחר מיתת אביהן.

§ The Gemara continues its discussion of the *baraita*. In accordance with **whose** opinion is the *baraita*? **It is** in accordance with the opinion of **Rabbi** Yehuda HaNasi, **as it is taught** in a *baraita* (*Tosefta* 7:4): **A firstborn does not take a double** portion **of the enhancement of the property** that occurred **after the death of** the sons' **father.**[H] **Rabbi** Yehuda HaNasi **says: I say** that **a firstborn does take a double** portion **of the enhancement of the property** that occurred by itself **after their father's death,** e.g., the birth of a calf, **but not of the enhancement that the orphans caused after their father's death.**

ירשו שטר חוב – בכור נוטל פי שנים, יצא עליהן שטר חוב – בכור נותן פי שנים, ואם אמר: איני נותן ואיני נוטל – רשאי.

Rabbi Yehuda HaNasi continues: Therefore, if they **inherited a promissory note** indicating a debt owed to their father, the **firstborn takes a double** portion of the money when it is collected, as this is an enhancement to the estate that came by itself. The Gemara adds: In a case where **a promissory note emerged against them**[H] for their father's debt, the **firstborn gives,** i.e., repays, **a double** portion of the debt. **But if he says: I am not giving** a double portion of the debt **and I am not taking** a double portion of the estate, he is **permitted** to do so, and he is exempt from paying a double portion.

מאי טעמייהו דרבנן? אמר קרא: "לתת לו פי שנים", מתנה קרייה רחמנא, מה מתנה עד דמטיא לידיה, אף חלק בכורה – עד דמטיא לידיה.

The Gemara asks: **What is the reason** for the ruling **of the Rabbis** that the firstborn does not receive a double portion of any enhancements that occur after the death of the father? **The verse states: "Giving him a double portion"** (Deuteronomy 21:17); by employing the term "giving" **the Merciful One calls** the double portion **a gift. Just as** a recipient of a gift does not acquire **a gift unless it** first **reaches the possession of** the one giving the gift, **so too** the firstborn does not acquire **the portion of the firstborn unless it has reached the possession of** the father before he died.

ורבי אומר, אמר קרא: "פי שנים", מקיש חלק בכורה לחלק פשוט, מה חלק פשוט אף על גב דלא מטא לידיה, אף חלק בכורה – אף על גב דלא מטא לידיה.

And Rabbi Yehuda HaNasi **says** that the reason for his ruling that a firstborn receives a double portion of the enhancement is that **the verse states: "A double portion"** (Deuteronomy 21:17). It **juxtaposes the portion of the firstborn to the portion of an ordinary** son, in that **just as the portion of an ordinary** son is inherited **even** from property **that did not reach** the father's **possession** before he died, **so too, the portion of the firstborn** is inherited **even** from property **that did not reach** the father's **possession** before he died.

HALAKHA

The enhancement of the property that occurred after the death of the father – בשבח ששבחו נכסים לאחר מיתת אביהן: If the estate was enhanced after the father's death through transformation, e.g., unripe grain grew to be full ears of grain, or undeveloped dates became fully developed, the firstborn is not entitled to receive a double portion of the enhancement; rather, the enhancement is appraised by the court, and the firstborn, who already took a double portion, must return the value of the enhancement to his brothers. If the property was enhanced without transformation, e.g., a small tree grew larger, or land that yielded silt, the firstborn is entitled to a double portion. This is in accordance with the opinion of the Rabbis, according to the interpretation of Rav Pappa. If the property was enhanced due to the financial investment of the brothers, the firstborn is not entitled to a double portion (Rambam *Sefer Mishpatim, Hilkhot Naḥalot* 3:4; *Shulḥan Arukh, Ḥoshen Mishpat* 278:6).

A promissory note emerged against them, etc. – יצא עליהן שטר חוב וכו׳: If a promissory note was produced against the heirs due to their father's debt, the firstborn pays a double portion of the debt. He can declare that he relinquishes his right to a double portion of the inheritance and is likewise exempt from paying a double portion of the debt. If he does so, he pays only the portion of an ordinary brother, even if the other brothers cannot pay their shares, either because they are minors or because they are not present. This is in accordance with the explanation of the Ri Migash. The *Sma* and the Gra note that the Ra'avad maintains that the firstborn cannot later retract his declaration and claim a double portion (*Shulḥan Arukh, Ḥoshen Mishpat* 278:10, 107:1, and in the comment of Rema).

וְרַבָּנַן נַמִי, הָכְתִיב: "פִּי שְׁנַיִם"! הַהוּא, לְמֵיתְבָא לֵיהּ אַחַד מִצְרָא.

The Gemara asks: And according to the Rabbis as well, isn't the phrase "a double portion" written? The Gemara answers: That phrase can be said to teach a different *halakha*, requiring the brothers to give the firstborn both of his portions on one border,[H] i.e., adjoining, and not in separate locations.

וְרַבִּי נַמִי, הָכְתִיב: "לָתֶת לוֹ"! הַהוּא, שֶׁאִם אָמַר: אֵינִי נוֹטֵל וְאֵינִי נוֹתֵן – רַשַּׁאי.

The Gemara asks: And according to Rabbi Yehuda HaNasi as well, isn't the phrase "giving him" written? The Gemara answers: That phrase can be said to teach a different *halakha*, that if the firstborn says: I am not taking a double portion of the estate and I am not giving a double portion of the debt, he is permitted to do so. Since the inheritance is referred to as a gift, he has the right to refuse it.

אָמַר רַב פַּפָּא: דִּיקְלָא וְאַלִּים, אַרְעָא וְאַסֵּיק שִׂירְטוֹן – דְּכוּלֵּי עָלְמָא לָא פְּלִיגִי דְּשָׁקֵיל, כִּי פְּלִיגִי – בַּחֲפוּרָה וַהֲוָה שׁוּבְלֵי, שְׁלוּפָפֵי וַהֲווּ תַּמְרֵי, דְּמָר סָבַר: שְׁבָחָא דְּמִמֵּילָא, וּמָר סָבַר: אִישְׁתַּנֵּי.

The Gemara discusses several types of enhancement. Rav Pappa says:[N] With regard to a palm tree that became enhanced by growing broader after the father's death, or land that yielded silt[BN] and thereby became enhanced, everyone agrees that the firstborn takes a double portion of the enhancement. When they disagree is in a case when fodder [*baḥafura*],[N] i.e., grain that has grown stalks but is not yet ripe, becomes full ears, of grain, and when date flowers [*shelofafei*][L] become fully developed dates.[N] As one Sage, Rabbi Yehuda HaNasi, holds that since this enhancement develops by itself, the firstborn is entitled to a double portion of it, and one Sage, the Rabbis, holds that since the item transformed,[N] it is not considered the same item that was in the father's possession, and the firstborn is not entitled to a double portion of it.

אָמַר רַבָּה בַּר חָנָא אָמַר רַבִּי חִיָּיא: עָשָׂה כְּדִבְרֵי רַבִּי – עָשָׂה, כְּדִבְרֵי חֲכָמִים – עָשָׂה;

§ Rabba bar Ḥana says that Rabbi Ḥiyya says: A judge who acted, i.e., ruled, in accordance with the statement of Rabbi Yehuda HaNasi has acted legally, and one who acted in accordance with the statement of the Rabbis has also acted legally. Either way, the decision stands.

BACKGROUND

Silt – שִׂירְטוֹן: In Babylonia, a flat land whose rivers at times flood its banks, it happens that rivers wash over the fields and leave behind a certain amount of silt and waste. Although at the time it happens the silt usually damages the crops in the fields, in the long term it improves the land.

LANGUAGE

Fodder [*ḥafura*] – חֲפוּרָה: Although the exact derivation of this word is not known, some claim that it is related to the Syriac *ḥurfa*, which relates to types of green plants in general. From the context it means produce that is not fully ripe.

Date flowers [*shelofafei*] – שְׁלוּפָפֵי: The Sages equate this word to the root *shin*, *lamed*, *feh*, meaning growing and blooming (see Psalms 129:6).

HALAKHA

To give his portions on one border – לְמֵיתְבָא לֵיהּ אַחַד מִצְרָא: When land is divided among heirs, the firstborn receives a contiguous piece of land for his double portion. According to the Rambam, this is the *halakha* even if as a result the firstborn receives higher-quality land than his brothers, in which case he must compensate them financially (*Maggid Mishne*). The Rema, citing the Rosh, rules that the firstborn does not receive a contiguous piece of land if that would result in his receiving higher-quality land than his brothers (Rambam *Sefer Kinyan*, *Hilkhot Shekhenim* 12:2 and *Sefer Mishpatim*, *Hilkhot Naḥalot* 3:8; *Shulḥan Arukh*, *Ḥoshen Mishpat* 174:2).

NOTES

Rav Pappa says – אָמַר רַב פַּפָּא: According to Rabbeinu Yona and other early commentaries, Rav Pappa's assertion that the Rabbis concede that the firstborn receives a double portion of an enhancement that occurred by itself contradicts the assumption of the Gemara until this point, that this is the opinion of only Rabbi Yehuda HaNasi. They suggest that according to Rav Pappa, the *halakha* that the firstborn receives a double portion of the enhancement of a leased or rented cow that gave birth is agreed to by the Rabbis as well (Rambam, as explained in *Maggid Mishna* and *Baḥ*). Furthermore, the dispute between Rabbi Yehuda HaNasi and the Rabbis is not based on the phrase: "Giving him a double portion" (Deuteronomy 21:17), but rather the continuation of the verse: "Of all that he has," in accordance with the interpretation of the *baraita* (124b) that the firstborn receives a double portion only of property that the father possessed at the time of his death.

Land that yielded silt – אַרְעָא וְאַסֵּיק שִׂירְטוֹן: The Rashbam explains that a flood covered the land with richer soil and fertilizer. The Ramah explains (based on 82a) that the incoming soil covered the roots of the trees, enhancing their growth. Rabbeinu Ḥananel and others explain that this is referring to a depression in the ground filled with water that now became filled with soil, and is now fit to be worked and sown. The emphasis, according to all explanations, is that the land is the same land, but its value increased.

When they disagree is in a case when fodder, etc. – כִּי פְּלִיגִי בַּחֲפוּרָה וכו׳: The Ri Migash explains that because the items transformed, the Rabbis consider the value of this enhancement to be property due to the father; whereas Rabbi Yehuda HaNasi holds that since the items themselves had already existed during the lifetime of the father the enhancement is also considered property he possessed.

When date flowers become fully developed dates – שְׁלוּפָפֵי וַהֲווּ תַּמְרֵי: The Ramah asserts that according to Rabbi Yehuda HaNasi, even if the trees themselves grew only after the father's death, the firstborn receives a double portion, as the land was in the father's possession. The reason the case mentioned is one where there were undeveloped dates on the trees is to teach that even in this case, the Rabbis hold that the firstborn does not receive a double portion (see also Ritva).

Transformed – אִישְׁתַּנֵּי: The commentaries disagree as to whether, according to the opinion of the Rabbis, the firstborn loses his double portion of the initial value of the item as well, due to the transformation (Ra'avad).

מְסַפְּקָא לֵיהּ אִי הֲלָכָה כְּרַבִּי מֵחֲבֵירוֹ וְלֹא מֵחֲבֵירָיו, אוֹ הֲלָכָה כְּרַבִּי מֵחֲבֵירוֹ וַאֲפִילּוּ מֵחֲבֵירָיו.

The Gemara explains: Rabbi Ḥiyya **is uncertain**[N] as to **whether** the principle that the ***halakha*** is **in accordance with** the opinion of **Rabbi** Yehuda HaNasi in his disputes **with his colleague** applies specifically to a dispute with one other *tanna* **but not** to a dispute **with** several of **his colleagues, or** whether the principle that the ***halakha*** is **in accordance with** the opinion of **Rabbi** Yehuda HaNasi in his disputes **with his colleague** applies **even to** a dispute with several of **his colleagues,** as in this case, where the Rabbis disagree with Rabbi Yehuda HaNasi. Since he was uncertain, he left the decision to each individual judge.

אָמַר רַב נַחְמָן אָמַר רַב: אָסוּר לַעֲשׂוֹת כְּדִבְרֵי רַבִּי; קָא סָבַר: הֲלָכָה כְּרַבִּי מֵחֲבֵירוֹ וְלֹא מֵחֲבֵירָיו.

Rav Naḥman says that **Rav says:** It is **prohibited to act in accordance with the statement of Rabbi** Yehuda HaNasi. The Gemara explains: Rav **holds** that the ***halakha*** is **in accordance with** the opinion of **Rabbi** Yehuda HaNasi in his disputes **with his** single **colleague, but not** in his disputes **with** several of **his colleagues.**

וְרַב נַחְמָן דִּידֵיהּ אָמַר: מוּתָּר לַעֲשׂוֹת כְּדִבְרֵי רַבִּי; קָא סָבַר: הֲלָכָה כְּרַבִּי מֵחֲבֵירוֹ וַאֲפִילּוּ מֵחֲבֵירָיו.

And Rav Naḥman says his own statement: It is **permitted to act in accordance with the statement of Rabbi** Yehuda HaNasi.[N] The Gemara explains: **He holds** that the ***halakha*** is **in accordance with** the opinion of **Rabbi** Yehuda HaNasi not only in his disputes **with his** single **colleague, but even** in his disputes **with** several of **his colleagues.**

אָמַר רָבָא: אָסוּר לַעֲשׂוֹת כְּדִבְרֵי רַבִּי, וְאִם עָשָׂה – עָשׂוּי; קָא סָבַר: מַטִּין אִיתְּמַר.

Rava says: It is **prohibited to act in accordance with the statement of Rabbi** Yehuda HaNasi, **but if** a judge **acted** in accordance with the statement of Rabbi Yehuda HaNasi, what is done **is done** and the decision stands. The Gemara explains: **He holds** that it **was stated** that **one is inclined**[N] to follow the opinion of the Rabbis *ab initio*, but if a judge rules in accordance with the opinion of Rabbi Yehuda HaNasi, his decision stands.

NOTES

He is uncertain, etc. – **מְסַפְּקָא לֵיהּ וכו׳**: The Rashbam explains that the uncertainty was whether the principle that the *halakha* follows the opinion of Rabbi Yehuda HaNasi in his disputes with his colleague applies specifically to disputes with only one colleague or even to several of his colleagues. *Tosafot* question this interpretation, as it is an established principle in the Talmud that the *halakha* follows the opinion of Rabbi Yehuda HaNasi only in his disputes with one of his colleagues. Therefore, Rabbeinu Tam explains that the uncertainty was only with regard to this specific dispute between Rabbi Yehuda HaNasi and the Rabbis. Rabbeinu Yitzḥak of Dampierre explains that Rabbi Ḥiyya was uncertain as to whether the assumption that the *halakha* does not follow the opinion of Rabbi Yehuda HaNasi in his disputes with several of his colleagues is an established principle, or whether it was not established explicitly and any judge may choose whether to follow it (see Maharam; Maharsha).

It is permitted to act in accordance with the statement of Rabbi Yehuda HaNasi – **מוּתָּר לַעֲשׂוֹת כְּדִבְרֵי רַבִּי**: The early commentaries ask why Rav Naḥman did not use the standard formulation: The *halakha* is in accordance with the statement of Rabbi Yehuda HaNasi. Furthermore, if the *halakha* is in accordance with the opinion of Rabbi Yehuda HaNasi, it is mandatory, not only permitted, to follow his opinion. The Rashbam explains that Rav Naḥman merely formulated his statement in accordance with the formulation used previously by Rabbi Ḥiyya, i.e., a judge who acted in accordance with the statement of Rabbi Yehuda HaNasi has acted legally. The Ramban infers that Rav Naḥman did not rule in accordance with the opinion of Rabbi Yehuda HaNasi; rather, he held that a judge can choose to follow his opinion.

It was stated that one is inclined – **מַטִּין אִיתְּמַר**: The Rashbam explains that although one might be inclined to follow the opinion of the Rabbis, the *halakha* was not formally decided in accordance with their opinion. Therefore, if a judge rules in accordance with the opinion of Rabbi Yehuda HaNasi, his decision is not reversed. *Tosafot* question this interpretation, as until this point in the discussion the opinion that the *amora'im* are referring to is that of Rabbi Yehuda HaNasi, not that of the Rabbis. In fact, the Ri Migash interprets the statement to mean that one is inclined to follow the opinion of Rabbi Yehuda HaNasi, but the principle is to follow the majority opinion. Therefore, although a judge should follow the opinion of the Rabbis *ab initio*, if he rules in accordance with the opinion of Rabbi Yehuda HaNasi, his decision stands. The Ri Migash comments that Rav Hai Gaon interprets this statement in the same manner.

תָּנֵי רַב נַחְמָן בִּשְׁאָר סִפְרֵי דְּבֵי רַב: ״בְּכֹל אֲשֶׁר יִמָּצֵא לוֹ״ – פְּרָט לְשֶׁבַח שֶׁהִשְׁבִּיחוּ יוֹרְשִׁין לְאַחַר מִיתַת אֲבִיהֶן; אֲבָל שֶׁבַח שֶׁשָּׁבְחוּ נְכָסִים לְאַחַר מִיתַת אֲבִיהֶן – שָׁקֵיל, וּמַנִּי? רַבִּי הִיא.

The Gemara comments that there are conflicting opinions in halakhic midrash as to whether the *halakha* is in accordance with the opinion of Rabbi Yehuda HaNasi or in accordance with the opinion of the Rabbis, as each opinion is supported by a different version of the midrash. **Rav Naḥman taught** a *baraita* **from the other books of the school of Rav** [***debei Rav***],[N] i.e., a volume of halakhic midrash other than *Torat Kohanim*, which is a halakhic midrash on the book of Leviticus. The phrase from the verse: "By giving him a double portion **of all that he has"** (Deuteronomy 21:17), **excludes the enhancement that the heirs brought about after their father's death,** of which the firstborn is not entitled to a double portion. The Gemara infers: **But** of **the enhancement of the property** that occurred by itself **after their father's death, he does take** a double portion. The Gemara comments: **And whose** opinion is this? **It is** the opinion of **Rabbi** Yehuda HaNasi.

תָּנֵי רָמִי בַּר חָמָא בִּשְׁאָר סִפְרֵי דְּבֵי רַב: ״בְּכֹל אֲשֶׁר יִמָּצֵא לוֹ״ – פְּרָט לְשֶׁבַח שֶׁשָּׁבְחוּ נְכָסִים לְאַחַר מִיתַת אֲבִיהֶן; וְכָל שֶׁכֵּן שֶׁבַח שֶׁהִשְׁבִּיחוּ יוֹרְשִׁין לְאַחַר מִיתַת אֲבִיהֶן דְּלָא שָׁקֵיל, וּמַנִּי? רַבָּנַן הִיא.

Rami bar Ḥama taught a different version of the *baraita* **from the other books of the school of Rav: "Of all that he has" excludes** the **enhancement of the property** that occurred by itself **after their father's death,**[N] of which the firstborn is not entitled to a double portion. The Gemara infers: **And all the more so, he does not take** a double portion of the **enhancement that the heirs brought about after their father's death.** The Gemara comments: **And whose** opinion is this? **It is** the opinion of **the Rabbis.** Accordingly, there is a discrepancy between the *baraitot* as to whether the *halakha* is in accordance with the opinion of the Rabbis or Rabbi Yehuda HaNasi.

אָמַר רַב יְהוּדָה אָמַר שְׁמוּאֵל: אֵין בְּכוֹר נוֹטֵל פִּי שְׁנַיִם בְּמִלְוֶה. לְמַאן? אִילֵימָא לְרַבָּנַן? הַשְׁתָּא שְׁבָחָא דְּאִיתֵיהּ בִּרְשׁוּתֵיהּ אָמְרִי רַבָּנַן לָא שָׁקֵיל, מִלְוֶה מִבַּעְיָא?

§ **Rav Yehuda says** that **Shmuel says: A firstborn does not take a double** portion **of a loan,** i.e., of a debt that is owed to the father. The Gemara asks: **According to whom** is this *halakha* stated? **If we say** it is **in accordance with** the opinion of **the Rabbis, now** that **the Rabbis say** that a firstborn **does not take** a double portion even with regard to the **enhancement** of property **that is in the possession of** the father, is it **necessary** to state that he is not entitled to a double portion of **a loan?** The debt is not in the father's possession at the time of his death; it is merely due to him.

אֶלָּא לְרַבִּי.

Rather, it must be **in accordance with** the opinion of **Rabbi** Yehuda HaNasi. Although he holds that a firstborn is entitled to a double portion of the enhancement of the property itself, he concedes that he is not entitled to a double portion of the payment of a debt, as it was not in the possession of his father at the time of his death.

וְאֶלָּא הָא דְּתַנְיָא: יָרְשׁוּ שְׁטַר חוֹב – בְּכוֹר נוֹטֵל פִּי שְׁנַיִם בֵּין בְּמִלְוֶה בֵּין בְּרִבִּית, מַנִּי? לָא רַבִּי וְלָא רַבָּנַן!

The Gemara asks: **But** if so, in accordance with **whose** opinion is **that which is taught** in a *baraita*: If the sons **inherited a promissory note, the firstborn takes a double** portion of the payment of **both** the value of **the loan** itself **and the interest?** It is **neither** in accordance with the opinion of **Rabbi** Yehuda HaNasi, **nor** the opinion of **the Rabbis.**

NOTES

From the other books of the school of Rav [*debei Rav*] – בִּשְׁאָר סִפְרֵי דְּבֵי רַב: The expression: The books of the school of Rav, is referring to volumes of halakhic midrash on the Torah. Since the volume on Leviticus, also known as *Torat Kohanim*, received the title: The book of the school of Rav, the volumes on the other books of the Torah are referred to as the other books of the school of Rav.

The early authorities disagree with regard to the meaning of the term *bei Rav* in this context. The Rambam indicates in his introduction to the *Mishne Torah* that *bei Rav* refers to the school of Rav, who edited these volumes. Rashi interprets it in tractate *Ḥullin* (66a) to mean the study hall, and he explains that the expression refers to midrash that was familiar to everyone in the study halls.

Excludes the enhancement of the property after their father's death – פְּרָט לְשֶׁבַח שֶׁשָּׁבְחוּ נְכָסִים לְאַחַר מִיתַת אֲבִיהֶן: The Maharsha asserts that the wording of the *baraita* is inaccurate; the *halakha* that the firstborn is not entitled to a double portion of the enhancement that occurs by itself is derived from the phrase "giving him," as explained on 124a, whereas the phrase "of all that he has" is referring only to the enhancement brought about by the heirs. Rabbeinu Yona maintains that this *baraita* derives the *halakha* from "of all that he has," contrary to the derivation of the Gemara.

לְעוֹלָם לְרַבָּנַן, וְאִיצְטְרִיךְ; סָלְקָא דַּעְתָּךְ אָמִינָא: מִלְוֶה, כֵּיוָן דִּנְקִיט שְׁטָרָא – כְּמַאן דִּגְבִיָא דָּמְיָא, קָא מַשְׁמַע לָן.

The Gemara answers: **Actually,** Shmuel's statement that the firstborn is not entitled to a double portion of the payment of a debt is **in accordance with** the opinion of **the Rabbis, and it was necessary** to state it. It might **enter your mind to say** that with regard to **a loan, since** the creditor **holds** a promissory **note, it is considered as though it has** already **been collected** and is in the creditor's possession, so too, the firstborn should be entitled to a double portion even according to the opinion of the Rabbis. Therefore, Shmuel **teaches us** that the loan is not considered to be in the creditor's possession, and the firstborn is not entitled to a double portion.

שָׁלְחוּ מִתָּם: בְּכוֹר נוֹטֵל פִּי שְׁנַיִם בְּמִלְוֶה אֲבָל לֹא בְּרִבִּית.

The Gemara relates: **They sent** the following ruling **from there,** Eretz Yisrael: If the father lent money to a gentile, the **firstborn takes a double** portion of the value **of** the **loan** itself, **but not of** the **interest,** as the interest is considered property due to the father.

לְמַאן? אִילֵימָא לְרַבָּנַן, הָשְׁתָּא שְׁבָחָא דְּאִיתֵיהּ בִּרְשׁוּתֵיהּ אָמְרִי רַבָּנַן דְּלָא שָׁקֵיל, מִלְוֶה מִבַּעְיָא?

The Gemara asks: **According to whom** is this *halakha* stated? **If we say** it is **in accordance with** the opinion of **the Rabbis, now** that **the Rabbis say** that a firstborn **does not take** a double portion even with regard to the **enhancement** of property, **which is in the possession of** the father, is it **necessary** to state that they would hold that he is not entitled to a double portion of **a loan?** Since the debt is not in the father's possession at the time of his death, as it is merely due to him, the rabbis would certainly not hold that the firstborn takes a double portion of it.

אֶלָּא לְרַבִּי. וּלְרַבִּי, בְּרִבִּית לֹא? וְהָתַנְיָא, רַבִּי אוֹמֵר: בְּכוֹר נוֹטֵל פִּי שְׁנַיִם בֵּין בְּמִלְוֶה בֵּין בְּרִבִּית!

Rather, it must be **in accordance with** the opinion of **Rabbi** Yehuda HaNasi. The Gemara asks: **And according to** the opinion of **Rabbi** Yehuda HaNasi, is it so that the firstborn is **not** entitled to a double portion **of the interest? But isn't it taught** in a *baraita* that **Rabbi** Yehuda HaNasi **says: A firstborn takes a double** portion **of both** the value of **the loan** itself **and the interest?**

לְעוֹלָם רַבָּנַן הִיא, וּמִלְוֶה כְּמַאן דִּגְבִיָא דָּמְיָא.

The Gemara answers: **Actually,** the *halakha* sent from the Sages of Eretz Yisrael **is** in accordance with the opinion of **the Rabbis.**[N] **And** the Sages of Eretz Yisrael hold that the Rabbis concede that the firstborn receives a double portion of the value of the loan itself, because **a loan is considered as though it has** already **been collected** and is in the creditor's possession. By contrast, the interest on the loan is not considered as though it is already in the creditor's possession, and therefore the firstborn does not receive a double portion of its payment.

אֲמַר לֵיהּ רַב אַחָא בַּר רַב לְרָבִינָא: אִיקְלַע אַמֵימָר לְאַתְרִין, וְדָרֵישׁ: בְּכוֹר נוֹטֵל פִּי שְׁנַיִם בְּמִלְוֶה אֲבָל לֹא בְּרִבִּית. אֲמַר לֵיהּ: נְהַרְדְּעֵי לְטַעֲמַיְיהוּ,

Rav Aḥa bar Rav said to Ravina: Ameimar[P] **arrived at our locale and taught** that **a firstborn takes a double** portion **of** the value of **a loan** itself, **but not of** the **interest.** Ravina **said to him:** The Sages **of Neharde'a** conform **to their** standard line of **reasoning.**[N] Ameimar followed the opinion of Rav Naḥman, who was one of the Sages of Naharde'a, as was Ameimar.

דְּאָמַר רַבָּה: גָּבוּ קַרְקַע – יֵשׁ לוֹ, גָּבוּ מָעוֹת – אֵין לוֹ; וְרַב נַחְמָן אָמַר: גָּבוּ מָעוֹת – יֵשׁ לוֹ, גָּבוּ קַרְקַע – אֵין לוֹ.

The Gemara explains: **As Rabba says:** If the sons **collected land** as payment of a debt owed to their father, the firstborn **has** a double portion[N] of it, but if **they collected money, he does not have** a double portion. **And Rav Naḥman says** that if **they collected money, he has** a double portion,[N] but if **they collected land, he does not have** a double portion.

אֲמַר לֵיהּ אַבַּיֵי לְרַבָּה: לְדִידָךְ קַשְׁיָא, לְרַב נַחְמָן קַשְׁיָא; לְדִידָךְ קַשְׁיָא:

Abaye said to Rabba: According to your opinion it **is difficult,** and **according to** the opinion of **Rav Naḥman** it is also **difficult. According to your** opinion it **is difficult**

NOTES

Actually, it is the Rabbis – לְעוֹלָם רַבָּנַן הִיא: The majority of the commentaries maintain that this opinion is in conflict with the statement of Rav Yehuda, that a firstborn is not entitled to a double portion of a loan at all (see Rashbam; Ritva).

The Sages of Neharde'a conform to their standard line of reasoning – נְהַרְדְּעֵי לְטַעֲמַיְיהוּ: Why did Ravina assume that Ameimar followed the opinion of Rav Naḥman and not that of Rabba, who was from Pumbedita? The Rashbam explains that the phrase: The value of a loan itself, presumably is referring to money. Therefore, it is in accordance with the opinion of Rav Naḥman, that the firstborn is entitled to a double portion only if the debt is repaid with money. The Rashbam also suggests an alternative interpretation: Ravina did not mean that Ameimar holds that if the debt is repaid with land the firstborn is not entitled to a double portion, contrary to the opinion of Rabba, but rather that both Rav Naḥman and Ameimar hold that in principle, a firstborn is entitled to a double portion of payment for a loan. Therefore, the Sages of Neharde'a conform to their standard line of reasoning.

If they collected land, he has a double portion – גָּבוּ קַרְקַע יֵשׁ לוֹ: Rabbeinu Yona explains, based on the premise of the Gemara (175b), that according to this opinion, the land of a debtor is liened by Torah law. In other words, the lien on the land, which grants the creditor the legal power to repossess the land from people who purchased it from the debtor, renders it property possessed by the creditor with regard to the *halakhot* of inheritance even before it is actually collected as payment of the debt. Money, by contrast, is not liened against the debt, as it is intended to be spent. Therefore it is not considered possessed by the creditor.

If they collected money, he has a double portion – גָּבוּ מָעוֹת יֵשׁ לוֹ: The Rashbam explains that since the loan was a loan of money, the debt is considered a debt of money. The Ritva adds that in a case where the creditor collects land, it is considered as though the debtor is selling the land to the creditor in exchange for the debt.

Other early commentaries disagree with the explanation of the Rashbam, as the reference is not only to a debt as result of a loan, but also to other debts, e.g., liability for damages. *Tosafot* explain that the standard form of payment of a debt is money, and money is the manner in which the creditor expects to be paid. Therefore, the money is considered as though it is possessed by the creditor even before it is collected, whereas the land is not.

PERSONALITIES

Ameimar – אַמֵימָר: Ameimar was one of the most prominent fifth- and sixth- generation Babylonian *amora'im*. Ameimar was born and raised in Neharde'a where he studied and taught Torah, although it is likely that he studied with the rabbis of Pumbedita as well. The statements that he cites are primarily from fifth-generation *amora'im*, students of Abaye and Rava. It appears that he served as rabbi and judge in Neharde'a, where he established various rabbinic regulations, but he also wielded influence in many other places, e.g., Meḥoza. The leaders of the following generation, among them Rav Ashi, were his students. He had at least one son, named Mar, who studied with Rav Ashi while Ameimar was still alive.

מַאי שְׁנָא מָעוֹת דְּלָא? דְּלָאו הָנֵי מָעוֹת שְׁבַק אֲבוּהוֹן, קַרְקַע נַמִי – לָאו הָא קַרְקַע שְׁבַק אֲבוּהוֹן!

because **what is different** about **money,** resulting in the *halakha* **that** the firstborn is **not** entitled to a double portion of it, is **that their father did not leave** them **this** specific **money** that was collected. With regard to **land as well, their father did not leave** them **this** specific parcel of **land** when he died, as the debtor could have repaid them with a different parcel of land, or with money.

וְעוֹד, הָא אַתְּ הוּא דַּאֲמַרְתְּ: מִסְתַּבֵּר טַעְמָא דִּבְנֵי מַעֲרְבָא, דְּאִי קָדֵים סַבְתָּא וְזַבְנָא – זְבִינָה זְבִינֵי!

And furthermore, aren't you the one **who said** that **the explanation of the people of the West,** Eretz Yisrael, **is reasonable?** In a case where a married woman had been fit to inherit from her great-grandmother but then predeceased her great-grandmother, who then died, and her widower claims the inheritance in his late wife's stead, the Sages of Eretz Yisrael ruled that he is not entitled to the inheritance, as it is merely property due to his wife, and a husband does not inherit property due to be inherited by his late wife. Rabba agreed that the inheritance is considered property due to the wife, and not property possessed by her, **as if the great-grandmother would have sold it before** she died,[N] **her sale would have been** a valid **sale.** Here, too, the land should be considered property due to the father, of which a firstborn is not entitled to a double portion, since the debtor could have sold it. Therefore, Rabba's opinion is difficult.

לְרַב נַחְמָן קַשְׁיָא: מַאי שְׁנָא קַרְקַע דְּלָא? דְּלָאו הָא קַרְקַע שְׁבַק אֲבוּהוֹן, מָעוֹת נַמִי – לָאו הָנֵי מָעוֹת שְׁבַק אֲבוּהוֹן!

Abaya continues: **According to** the opinion of **Rav Naḥman** it is **difficult; what is different** about **land,** resulting in the *halakha* **that** the firstborn is **not** entitled to a double portion of it, is **that their father did not leave** them **this** specific parcel of **land.** With regard to **money as well, their father did not leave** them **this** specific **money** when he died.

וְעוֹד, הָא אָמַר רַב נַחְמָן אָמַר רַבָּה בַּר אֲבוּהּ: יְתוֹמִים שֶׁגָּבוּ קַרְקַע בְּחוֹבַת אֲבִיהֶן – בַּעַל חוֹב חוֹזֵר וְגוֹבֶה מֵהֶן!

And furthermore, doesn't Rav Naḥman say that **Rabba bar Avuh says:** With regard to **orphans who collected land**[H] **for a debt owed to their father,** their father's **creditor** can **come and seize this** land **from them,** as any land owned by the father is liened against his debts. Evidently, Rav Naḥman holds that land liened against a debt has the legal status of land that is in the possession of the creditor. If so, why does Rav Naḥman hold that a firstborn is not entitled to a double portion of land that is collected as payment of a debt?

אֲמַר לֵיהּ: לָא לְדִידִי קַשְׁיָא וְלָא לְרַב נַחְמָן קַשְׁיָא, טַעְמָא דִּבְנֵי מַעֲרְבָא קָאָמְרִינַן, וְלַן לָא סְבִירָא לַן.

Rabba **said to** Abaye: **According to my** opinion it **is not difficult, and according to** the opinion of **Rav Naḥman** it **is not difficult. We were** merely **saying,** i.e., explaining, **the reason** for the opinion **of the people of the West,** Eretz Yisrael, introduced with the phrase: They sent the following ruling from there, that a firstborn is entitled to a double portion of the payment of a debt. **But we ourselves do not hold** in accordance with that opinion.[N] Therefore, one cannot raise a contradiction from our opinions stated elsewhere to what we said in explanation of the Sages of Eretz Yisrael.

מַאי סַבְתָּא? דְּהַהוּא דַּאֲמַר לְהוּ:

Having mentioned in passing the case of the great-grandmother, the Gemara discusses that case in depth. **What** is the case of the great-**grandmother** that was mentioned by Abaye? The Gemara explains: There was **a certain** moribund person **who said to** those present:

NOTES

As if the great-grandmother would have sold it before she died, etc. – **דְּאִי קָדֵים סַבְתָּא וְזַבְנָא וכו׳**: The early commentaries question the comparison between the cases, as here the land is liened against the debt, and if the debtor sells all his land, the creditor can collect it from the purchasers. By contrast, in the case of the great-grandmother, her great-granddaughter would not inherit anything if the great-grandmother were to sell all of her property. One answer is that Abaye's objection is based on Rabba's opinion that the property of a debtor is not liened by Torah law (see 175b). Therefore, in the case of the debtor as well, if he were to sell all of his property the creditors would not collect their debt. Another explanation is that since the debtor is able to sell the land and pay with the money he receives in exchange, if money has the status of being only due to the creditor but not in his possession, the land must have the same status.

But we ourselves do not hold in accordance with that opinion – **וְלַן לָא סְבִירָא לַן**: The Gemara does not record Rabba and Rav Naḥman's own opinions. This issue is discussed by the early commentaries, who attempt to extrapolate the opinions of Rabba and Rav Naḥman from other sources, both in this tractate and in tractate *Bava Metzia* (43b). The Rashbam holds that both of them agree with the opinion of Shmuel (124b) that whether the brothers collected money or land, the firstborn is not entitled to a double portion. The majority of the early commentaries concur. Rabbeinu Tam, as presented in *Sefer HaYashar*, reaches the opposite conclusion: Both Rabba and Rav Naḥman hold that whether the brothers collected money or land, the firstborn is entitled to a double portion. Rabbeinu Tam, as cited by several early commentaries, explains that Rabba holds that in both cases the firstborn is not entitled to a double portion, and Rav Naḥman holds that in both cases he is entitled (*Tosafot*; Rabbeinu Yona; Ramban).

HALAKHA

With regard to orphans who collected land, etc. – **יְתוֹמִים שֶׁגָּבוּ קַרְקַע וכו׳**: If orphans collected land in payment of a debt owed to their father, their father's creditor can then collect the land from them. This *halakha* does not apply if they collected movable property, as the movable property of orphans cannot be collected for the debt of their father. Later, after the *ge'onim* instituted that movable property can also be collected from orphans, it has the same *halakha* as land. The *Sma* rules that if the loan was issued with a promissory note, the father's creditor can appropriate the note from the orphans as movable property and use it to collect the debt (Rambam *Sefer Mishpatim*, *Hilkhot Malve VeLoveh* 11:9; *Shulḥan Arukh*, *Ḥoshen Mishpat* 107:1).

״נִכְסַי לְסַבְתָּא וּבָתְרָהּ לְיָרְתַאי״, הֲוָיָא לֵיהּ בְּרַתָּא דַּהֲוָה נְסִיבָא, שְׁכִיבָא בְּחַיֵּי בַּעְלָהּ וּבְחַיֵּי סַבְתָּא, בָּתַר דִּשְׁכִיבָא סַבְתָּא אֲתָא בַּעַל קָא תָּבַע;

All **my property** is given **to my grandmother,**[H] **and after she** dies, it is given **to my heirs,** not inherited by her heirs. He then died. **He had a married daughter,** who **died during the lifetime of her husband and during the lifetime of** her father's **grandmother.** **After** her father's **grandmother died,** her **husband came and claimed** the inheritance, as his wife was the heir of her father, and he is his wife's heir.

אֲמַר רַב הוּנָא: ״לְיָרְתַי״ – וַאֲפִילּוּ לְיָרְתֵי יָרְתַי, וְרַב עָנָן אֲמַר: ״לְיָרְתַי״ – וְלָא לְיָרְתֵי יָרְתַי.

Rav Huna said: When her father said that his property is given: **To my heirs,** he meant: **And even to the heirs of my heirs.** Therefore, since his daughter's husband is the heir of his heir, he is entitled to the inheritance. **And Rav Anan said** that he meant: **To my heirs, but not to the heirs of my heirs.** Therefore, the husband is not entitled to the property.

שְׁלַחוּ מִתָּם: הִלְכְתָא כְּוָותֵיהּ דְּרַב עָנָן, וְלָאו מִטַּעְמֵיהּ; הִלְכְתָא כְּוָותֵיהּ דְּרַב עָנָן – דְּבַעַל לָא יָרֵית. וְלָאו מִטַּעְמֵיהּ – דְּאִילּוּ רַב עָנָן סָבַר: אַף עַל גַּב דַּהֲוָה לֵיהּ בְּרָא לִבְרַתֵּיהּ לָא יָרֵית; וְלָא הִיא, דְּאִילּוּ הֲוָה לֵיהּ בְּרָא לִבְרַתֵּיהּ – וַדַּאי יָרֵית, וּבַעַל הַיְינוּ טַעֲמָא דְּלָא יָרֵית, מִשּׁוּם דַּהֲוָה לֵיהּ רָאוּי, וְאֵין הַבַּעַל נוֹטֵל בְּרָאוּי כִּבְמוּחְזָק.

The Gemara relates: **They sent** a ruling **from there,** Eretz Yisrael: **The *halakha* is in accordance with** the opinion **of Rav Anan, but not due to his reasoning.** The Gemara explains: **The *halakha* is in accordance with** the opinion **of Rav Anan that the husband does not inherit** the property. **But not due to his reasoning, as Rav Anan holds** that **even if his daughter had a son** to inherit from her, **he** would **not inherit** the property, as her father bequeathed it only to his heirs, not to the heirs of his heirs. **And that is not so, as if his daughter had a son, he** would **certainly inherit; and this is the reason the husband does not inherit: Because** the inheritance **is considered** property **due** to the daughter, as she did not own it during her lifetime, **and a husband does not take** in inheritance property **due** to his wife **as** he does the property she **possessed.**

מִכְּלָל דְּרַב הוּנָא סָבַר: בַּעַל נוֹטֵל בְּרָאוּי כִּבְמוּחְזָק?!

The Gemara asks: **By inference, does Rav Huna,** who ruled that the husband is entitled to the inheritance, **hold** that **a husband takes** in inheritance property **due** to his wife **as** he does the property she **possessed?**

HALAKHA

My property is given to my grandmother, etc. – נִכְסַי לְסַבְתָּא וכו׳: If one said on his deathbed: My property is given to my mother, and after her, it is given to my heirs, and he had a married daughter who then predeceased her grandmother, her husband does not inherit the property from her grandmother, as she inherited it only after her death, and a husband does not inherit property due to his wife. Her child, by contrast, does inherit the property, as do his heirs after him.

If the initial owner said: The property is given to my daughter from now to take effect when my mother dies, and his daughter predeceased his mother, the daughter's husband inherits the property, even if she has children (*Sma*), in accordance with the opinion of the Sages of Eretz Yisrael and Rabba. This is in accordance with the explanation of the Rif that the statement: After you die it is given to so-and-so, is not equivalent to the statement: It is given to so-and-so from now (Rambam *Sefer Kinyan*, *Hilkhot Zekhiya UMattana* 12:13; *Shulḥan Arukh*, *Even HaEzer* 90:2 and *Ḥoshen Mishpat* 248:9, 148:7, and in the comment of Rema;).

אָמַר רַבִּי אֶלְעָזָר, דָּבָר זֶה נִפְתַּח בִּגְדוֹלִים וְנִסְתַּיֵּים בִּקְטַנִּים: כׇּל הָאוֹמֵר ״אַחֲרֶיךָ״, כְּאוֹמֵר ״מֵעַכְשָׁיו״ דָּמֵי.

Rabbi Elazar says: This matter was introduced by great Sages, namely Rav Huna, **and concluded by lesser** Sages, i.e., by me. Rabbi Elazar, humbly referring to himself as a lesser Sage, will now explain Rav Huna's statement. **Anyone who says** to another upon granting him an inheritance or a gift: **After you** die it is given to so-and-so, is considered **like one who says:** It is given to so-and-so **from now.** The first recipient merely has the right to use the property during his lifetime but did not actually become the owner. Accordingly, the inheritance was owned by the daughter in her lifetime, and the great-grandmother merely had usage rights. Therefore, it is inherited by the husband.

אָמַר רַבָּה: מִסְתַּבְּרָא טַעְמָא דִּבְנֵי מַעֲרָבָא, דְּאִי קָדֵים סַבְתָּא וְזַבְנָא – זְבִינָהּ זְבִינֵי.

Rabba said: The explanation of the people of the West, that the inheritance is considered property due to the daughter and not property possessed by her, **is reasonable,** as **if the grandmother would have sold it before** she died, **her sale would have been** a valid **sale,**[N] and the daughter would not have received it at all.

אָמַר רַב פָּפָּא, הִלְכְתָא: אֵין הַבַּעַל נוֹטֵל בְּרָאוּי כִּבְמוּחְזָק, וְאֵין הַבְּכוֹר נוֹטֵל בְּרָאוּי כִּבְמוּחְזָק, וְאֵין הַבְּכוֹר נוֹטֵל פִּי שְׁנַיִם בְּמִלְוָה – בֵּין שֶׁגָּבוּ קַרְקַע בֵּין שֶׁגָּבוּ מָעוֹת.

In conclusion, **Rav Pappa**[P] **said** that **the** ***halakha*** is that **the husband does not take** in inheritance property **due** to his wife[H] **as he** does the property she **possessed; and a firstborn does not take** a double portion of property **due** to his father[NH] **as** he does the property his father **possessed; and a firstborn does not take a double** portion **of** payment for **a loan,**[H] **whether** the brothers **collected land** or **whether they collected money.**

PERSONALITIES

Rav Pappa – רַב פָּפָּא: Rav Pappa, a fifth-generation Babylonia *amora*, was a student of both Abaye and Rava in Pumbedita. After Rava's death, Rav Pappa established an academy in Neresh, where he was joined by his close friend, Rav Huna, son of Rav Yehoshua, who was appointed as the primary lecturer. Many of Rava's students came to study under Rav Pappa, who had more than two hundred students attending his lectures.

NOTES

Her sale would have been a valid sale – זְבִינָהּ זְבִינֵי: The Rif explains that according to Rabba, when one says upon granting another an inheritance or a gift: After you die it is given to so-and-so, his statement is not understood to mean: It is given to so-and-so from now. Therefore the grandmother's sale of the property would have been valid. If he would have said explicitly that the property is given to his heirs from now, the grandmother would not have been able to sell it, and the daughter's husband would have inherited it. Other early commentaries disagree with the Rif, maintaining that Rabba agrees with the assertion that the statement: After you die it is given to so-and-so, is understood to mean: From now. He interprets it to mean: What is left of this property when you die is given to so-and-so from now. Therefore, the grandmother would have been able to sell it even if the father had stated explicitly: It is given to my heirs from now (see Ba'al HaMaor; Rabbeinu Yona).

And a firstborn does not take a double portion of property due to his father – וְאֵין הַבְּכוֹר נוֹטֵל בְּרָאוּי: Rav Pappa is apparently ruling in accordance with the opinion of the Rabbis, who disagree with Rabbi Yehuda HaNasi, including the Rabbis' assertion that even if the property becomes enhanced by itself, if it occurs through the transformation of the property, e.g., unripe grain becomes fully grown, the firstborn is not entitled to a double portion of the enhancement (see 124a). The early commentaries disagree as to whether Rav Pappa agrees with the ruling of the *amora'im* (124b) that if a judge rules according to the opinion of Rabbi Yehuda HaNasi, his decision stands (see Rashbam; Rashba).

HALAKHA

The husband does not take property due to his wife – אֵין הַבַּעַל נוֹטֵל בְּרָאוּי: A husband inherits from his wife only property she possessed during her lifetime, not property due to her, e.g., property she would have inherited had she not predeceased the owner (Rambam *Sefer Mishpatim*, *Hilkhot Naḥalot* 1:11; *Shulḥan Arukh*, *Even HaEzer* 90:1).

A firstborn does not take a double portion of property due to his father – אֵין הַבְּכוֹר נוֹטֵל בְּרָאוּי: A firstborn is entitled to a double portion only of the property that was possessed by his father at the time of his death, not property due to him. For example, if one from whom the father would have inherited property dies after the father's death, the firstborn is entitled to only a regular portion of the inheritance from that person, not a double portion (Rambam *Sefer Mishpatim*, *Hilkhot Naḥalot* 3:1; *Shulḥan Arukh*, *Ḥoshen Mishpat* 278:3).

A firstborn does not take a double portion of payment for a loan – אֵין הַבְּכוֹר נוֹטֵל פִּי שְׁנַיִם בְּמִלְוָה: A firstborn is not entitled to a double portion of payment of a debt that his father was owed, even if it was for a loan with a promissory note, whether the debtor is a Jew or a gentile, in accordance with the ruling of Rav Pappa (*Shakh*, citing Rambam). If collateral was liened to the loan, the firstborn is entitled to a double portion, as it is considered as though the debt was already collected during the lifetime of the father (Rambam *Sefer Mishpatim*, *Hilkhot Naḥalot* 3:1, and see *Hilkhot Malve VeLoveh* 7:4; *Shulḥan Arukh*, *Ḥoshen Mishpat* 278:7).

וּמִלְוֶה שֶׁעִמּוֹ – פַּלְגִי.

And as for **a loan that is with** the firstborn,[H] i.e., he had borrowed money from his father then his father died, it is uncertain whether the payment should be considered property due to the father or property possessed by him. Therefore, the firstborn and his brothers **divide**[N] the additional portion.

אָמַר רַב הוּנָא אָמַר רַב אַסִּי: בְּכוֹר שֶׁמִּיחָה – מִיחָה.

§ With regard to the *halakha* that the firstborn is not entitled to a double portion of the enhancement of the property resulting from the actions of the heirs, **Rav Huna says that Rav Asi says: A firstborn who protested**[HN] the efforts of enhancing the property before it is divided has **protested,** and if the brothers use resources from the estate to enhance it against his will, he is entitled to a double portion of the enhanced value.

אָמַר רַבָּה: מִסְתַּבֵּר טַעְמֵיהּ דְּרַב אַסִּי – בַּעֲנָבִים וּבְצָרוּם, זֵיתִים וּמְסָקוּם, אֲבָל דְּרָכוּם – לָא; וְרַב יוֹסֵף אָמַר: אֲפִילּוּ דְּרָכוּם.

Rabba said: Rav Asi's opinion is reasonable in a case where they inherited **grapes** on a grapevine **and** the brothers **harvested them**[N] against the will of the firstborn, or if they inherited **olives** on olive trees **and** the brothers **harvested them,** as in these cases, the produce itself did not change. **But if they treaded on them,** converting them into wine or oil, even if the firstborn protested their doing so, he is **not** entitled[N] to a double portion. **And Rav Yosef said: Even** if they **treaded on them,** the firstborn is entitled to a double portion.

דְּרָכוּם?! מֵעִיקָּרָא עִינְבֵי, הַשְׁתָּא חַמְרָא!

The Gemara asks: Why is he entitled to a double portion, according to Rav Yosef, even if **they treaded on them?** Since the brothers transformed the produce, as **initially** it was in the form of **grapes** and **now it is wine,** they have acquired it in the same manner that a thief acquires an item he stole. Therefore, the firstborn should have no share of the enhancement.

HALAKHA

A loan that is with the firstborn – מִלְוֶה שֶׁעִמּוֹ: If the firstborn owed money to his father, it is uncertain whether he is entitled to a double portion of the debt, as it is currently in his possession, or whether he is not entitled to a double portion, as he needs to inherit it from his father, and it was not in his father's possession. Therefore, he receives half of an additional portion. This is in accordance with the interpretation of the Rashbam and other commentaries (Rambam *Sefer Mishpatim, Hilkhot Naḥalot* 3:6; *Shulḥan Arukh, Ḥoshen Mishpat* 278:7).

A firstborn who protested – בְּכוֹר שֶׁמִּיחָה: There is a *halakha* that if a firstborn relinquishes his additional portion of some of his father's property, he has thereby relinquished his additional portion of all the property. This *halakha* applies only in a case where he did not declare otherwise, as concluded by the Gemara (126b). If he declared in the presence of two witnesses that despite having divided a certain part of the inheritance with his brothers equally, he has not relinquished his right to an additional portion of the rest of the inheritance, his declaration is effective, and he is still entitled to an additional portion of the remaining property.

Even if after the firstborn's declaration, the brothers harvested grapes from their joint vineyard and divided them equally, he has not relinquished his additional portion of the rest of the property. If they converted the grapes into wine, and he divided it with them equally without issuing another declaration with regard to his additional portion, he has relinquished his additional portion of all the property, as this is comparable to a case where he issued his declaration when they divided the grapes, and then divided olives with them equally. This is in accordance with the opinion of Rabba, according to the explanation of Rabbeinu Ḥananel of this discussion (*Maggid Mishne*).

Based on the Rashbam's explanation of the Gemara, the Rema writes that the *halakha* that a firstborn is not entitled to a double portion of the enhancement resulting from the actions of his brothers applies only in a case where the firstborn did not protest his brothers' enhancing the property. If he protested their doing so, and they enhanced it anyway, he is entitled to a double portion of the enhancement as well. If the brothers effected a change to the property, the firstborn does not receive a double portion of the enhancement, nor does he suffer a double portion of the loss if the value decreases (Rambam *Sefer Mishpatim, Hilkhot Naḥalot* 3:5; *Shulḥan Arukh, Ḥoshen Mishpat* 178:9, 178:6, and in the comment of Rema).

NOTES

Divide [*palgi*] – פַּלְגִי: Among the early commentaries there are three different interpretations of *palgi*.

The most widely accepted interpretation is that of the Rashbam, that *palgi* means divide. In other words, since it is uncertain whether the firstborn is entitled to a double portion of the debt, the additional portion is divided between the firstborn and his brothers, so that the firstborn receives half of it, and the other brothers divide the other half. For example, if there are three brothers, each brother receives a quarter of the debt, and the remaining quarter is divided so that the firstborn receives an eighth, and the remaining eighth is divided among the other two brothers equally (see the first interpretation cited by Rabbeinu Gershom Meor HaGola; the second interpretation cited by the Rif; Ri Migash; Ramah; Ra'avad).

Rabbeinu Ḥananel explains that *palgi* refers to two portions, i.e., the firstborn receives a double portion, as the money is in his possession (see the first interpretation cited in the Rif).

A third interpretation is that *palgi* means disagree, meaning that this case is subject to the dispute between the Sages of Eretz Yisrael and Rav Pappa (Rabbeinu Gershom Meor HaGola), or to the dispute between Rabbi Yehuda HaNasi and the Rabbis (*Tosefot Yeshanim*), as the first Sage of each pair of disputants holds that the firstborn receives a double portion, and the latter Sage holds that he does not.

A firstborn who protested – בְּכוֹר שֶׁמִּיחָה: The Rashbam explains that if the brothers desire to work the field and enhance it before it is divided, he may protest their doing so, and if they work it anyway, he is entitled to a double portion of the enhancement. Many other early commentaries concur. The Ran explains that this *halakha* is based on the conclusion of the Gemara that the firstborn has possession of his additional portion even before the property is divided. Therefore, once he expresses his desire to receive his portion of the additional portion, it becomes his immediately, and he then has the right to prevent his brothers from working it.

Rabbeinu Ḥananel, by contrast, interprets this discussion in the context of the subsequent discussion, namely, a firstborn's relinquishment of his additional portion. He interprets Rav Asi's statement to mean that if the firstborn declares that he has no intention to relinquish his additional portion, he need not declare this after the division of every part of the estate, even if in some parts he takes an equal portion to his brothers. Rather, his declaration at the outset is sufficient. This is apparently the Rambam's understanding of the discussion as well (see Meiri).

Grapes and harvested them – עֲנָבִים וּבְצָרוּם: The Rashbam explains that even though the brothers enhanced the value of the grapes by harvesting them, the firstborn is entitled to an additional portion of the harvested grapes, since he protested their harvesting his portion. Therefore, in accordance with the *halakha* concerning one who develops another's property without his permission, a double portion of the enhancement belongs to the firstborn, but he is obligated to compensate his brothers for their expenses in picking his grapes (Meiri).

According to the explanation of Rabbeinu Ḥananel, this means that after his brothers harvested the grapes he need not declare again that he is not relinquishing his additional portion, as his initial declaration is sufficient.

But if they treaded on them he is not entitled – אֲבָל דְּרָכוּם לָא: According to the Rashbam, since the grapes were transformed into wine, they were acquired by the brothers, and the firstborn does not receive an additional portion of their enhancement; rather, the brothers are obligated to pay him the value of the harvested grapes. It is clear that he receives his basic portion of the wine itself, like the other brothers (Ri Migash). Rabbeinu Gershom Meor HaGola adds that in contrast to harvesting the grapes, converting them into wine entails great effort and results in a major enhancement of the grapes' value. Therefore the firstborn is not entitled to a double portion of its enhanced value, even if he protested the brothers' converting the grapes to wine at the outset.

According to the explanation of Rabbeinu Ḥananel, this major change necessitates an additional declaration by the firstborn that he has not relinquished his additional portion, as his initial declaration does not apply to the produce in its new state.

כִּדְאָמַר רַב עוּקְבָא בַּר חָמָא: לִיתֵּן לוֹ דְּמֵי הֶיזֵּק עֲנָבָיו, הָכָא נַמִי – נוֹתֵן לוֹ דְּמֵי הֶיזֵּק עֲנָבָיו.

The Gemara answers: Rav Yosef did not mean that the firstborn is entitled to a double portion of the enhanced value of the wine. Rather, his intention was the same **as that which Rav Ukva bar Ḥama says** in a differnet context, that the ruling is referring **to** a case where the wine spoiled, its value decreasing to below the initial value of the grapes, in which case the brothers must **give** the firstborn **payment for** the **damage to his** additional portion of the **grapes. Here, too,** Rav Yosef meant that the brothers **must give** the firstborn **payment for** the **damage to his grapes.**[N]

הֵיכָא אִיתְּמַר דְּרַב עוּקְבָא בַּר חָמָא? אַהָא דְּאָמַר רַב יְהוּדָה אָמַר שְׁמוּאֵל: בְּכוֹר וּפָשׁוּט שֶׁהִנִּיחַ לָהֶן אֲבִיהֶן עֲנָבִים וּבְצָרוּם, זֵיתִים וּמְסָקוּם – בְּכוֹר נוֹטֵל פִּי שְׁנַיִם, אֲפִילּוּ דְּרָכוּם. דְּרָכוּם? ! מֵעִיקָּרָא עִינְבֵי הָשְׁתָּא חַמְרָא! אָמַר מָר עוּקְבָא בַּר חָמָא: לִיתֵּן לוֹ דְּמֵי הֶיזֵּק עֲנָבָיו.

The Gemara explains: **Where,** i.e., in what context, **was the statement of Rav Ukva bar Ḥama stated?** It was **in reference to that which Rav Yehuda says** that **Shmuel says:** With regard to **a firstborn and an ordinary** son **whose father left them grapes and they harvested them,** or if he left them **olives and they harvested them,** the **firstborn takes a double** portion. This is the *halakha* **even** if **they treaded** on **them.** The Gemara asks: Why is he entitled to a double portion if **they treaded** on **them; initially** they were **grapes,** and **now** it is **wine? Mar Ukva bar Ḥama says:** Shmuel did not mean that he is entitled to a double portion of the wine; rather, the reference is **to** a case where the wine spoiled, its value decreasing to below the initial value of the grapes, in which case the ordinary brother must **give** the firstborn **payment for** the **damage to his grapes.**

אָמַר רַב אַסִי: בְּכוֹר שֶׁנָּטַל חֵלֶק כְּפָשׁוּט – וִיתֵּר. מַאי וִיתֵּר? רַב פַּפָּא מִשְּׁמֵיהּ דְּרָבָא אָמַר: וִיתֵּר בְּאוֹתָהּ שָׂדֶה, רַב פַּפִּי מִשְּׁמֵיהּ דְּרָבָא אָמַר: וִיתֵּר בְּכָל הַנְּכָסִים כּוּלָּן;

§ **Rav Asi says: A firstborn who took a portion** of the property **like** that of **an ordinary** heir[H] **has relinquished** his right to an additional portion. The Gemara asks: **What** does it mean that he has **relinquished** his additional portion? **Rav Pappa says in the name of Rava** that he has **relinquished** his additional portion only **with regard to that field** that was divided, since he did not exercise his right to an additional portion, but he has not relinquished his right to receive an additional portion of the rest of the estate. **Rav Pappi**[P] **says in the name of Rava** that he has **relinquished** his additional portion **with regard to all** of **the property.**

רַב פַּפָּא מִשְּׁמֵיהּ דְּרָבָא אָמַר וִיתֵּר בְּאוֹתָהּ שָׂדֶה, קָא סָבַר: אֵין לוֹ לַבְּכוֹר קוֹדֶם חֲלוּקָּה, וּמַה דַּאֲתָא לִידֵיהּ אַחֵיל, אִידָּךְ לָא אַחֵיל;

The Gemara explains: **Rav Pappa says in the name of Rava** that he has **relinquished** his additional portion only **with regard to that field** that was divided, because he **holds** that **a firstborn does not have** a right to his additional portion **before** the **division**[N] of the property. **And** therefore, he **has waived** his additional portion of **what has** already **reached his possession,** namely, the field that was divided, but he **has not waived** his portion **of the other** fields of the estate.

וְרַב פַּפִּי מִשְּׁמֵיהּ דְּרָבָא אָמַר וִיתֵּר בְּכָל הַנְּכָסִים כּוּלָּן, קָא סָבַר: יֵשׁ לוֹ לַבְּכוֹר קוֹדֶם חֲלוּקָּה, וּמִדְּאַחֵיל בְּהָא אַחֵיל בְּכוּלְּהוּ.

And Rav Pappi says in the name of Rava that he has **relinquished** his additional portion **with regard to all of the property,** as **he holds** that **a firstborn has** a right to his additional portion **before** the **division** of the property. **And** therefore, **since** he **waived** his additional portion **in this field,** he **has waived** his portion **of all** of the property.

וְהָא דְּרַב פַּפִּי וְרַב פַּפָּא – לָאו בְּפֵירוּשׁ אִיתְּמַר אֶלָּא מִכְּלָלָא אִיתְּמַר; דְּהַהוּא בְּכוֹר דְּאָזֵיל זַבֵּין נִכְסֵי דִּידֵיהּ וּדְפָשׁוּט, אֲזוּל יַתְמֵי בְּנֵי פָשׁוּט לְמֵיכַל תַּמְרֵי מֵהַנְהוּ לָקוֹחוֹת, מַחוּנְהוּ; אָמְרִי לְהוּ קְרוֹבִים: לָא מִיסְתַּיָּיא דִּזְבַנְתִּינְהוּ לְנִכְסַיְיהוּ, אֶלָּא מִימְחָא נַמִי מַחִיתוּ לְהוּ? אֲתוּ לְקַמֵּיהּ דְּרָבָא, אֲמַר לְהוּ: לֹא עָשָׂה וְלֹא כְּלוּם;

The Gemara notes: **And this** dispute **of Rav Pappi and Rav Pappa was not stated explicitly; rather, it was stated by inference.** As there was **a certain firstborn who went** and **sold his property and** the property **of** his deceased **ordinary** brother, i.e., their respective portions of their father's property, before the property was divided. The **orphan sons of** the **ordinary** brother **went to eat dates from** the field that was now in the possession of **those purchasers,** due to their father's share in the field. The purchasers **hit them,** as though they were thieves. The **relatives** of the orphans **said to** the purchasers: **Not only did you purchase their property** illegally, **but you now hit them as well? They came before Rava, who said to them:** The firstborn **has done nothing.** His sale was not valid.

NOTES

Payment for the damage to his grapes – הֶיזֵּק עֲנָבָיו: The Rashbam explains that this is referring to a case where the value of the grapes decreased. Rabbeinu Gershom Meor HaGola explains that since some of the juice goes to waste during the treading, the brothers must pay the firstborn for those grapes. If the firstborn did not protest his brothers' treading on the grapes, and their value eventually decreases, he suffers the loss together with his brothers, just as he shares their gain in a case where the value increases.

The Rashbam adds that according to the Gemara's answer, there is no disagreement between Rabba and Rav Yosef, as Rabba referred to a case where the grapes' value increased, and Rav Yosef was referring to a case where it decreased.

According to the explanation of Rabbeinu Ḥananel, the Gemara's answer is that Rav Yosef was referring to a case where the firstborn did not know that his brothers were treading on the grapes, and he later protested their action and demanded compensation for the damage to his grapes. Therefore, his initial declaration that he is not relinquishing his additional portion is still in effect.

A firstborn does not have a right before the division – אֵין לוֹ לַבְּכוֹר קוֹדֶם חֲלוּקָּה: Since a firstborn cannot sell or give away his additional portion before the property is divided, he cannot relinquish it either.

HALAKHA

A firstborn who took a portion like that of an ordinary heir – בְּכוֹר שֶׁנָּטַל חֵלֶק כְּפָשׁוּט: If a firstborn divided part of his father's estate with his brothers, and took a portion that was equal to that of an ordinary son, he has relinquished his additional portion of the rest of the estate as well, and he receives only an ordinary portion. The ruling is in accordance with the opinion of Rav Pappi in the name of Rava (Rambam *Sefer Mishpatim, Hilkhot Naḥalot* 3:6; *Shulḥan Arukh, Ḥoshen Mishpat* 278:6).

PERSONALITIES

Rav Pappi – רַב פַּפִּי: Rav Pappi, a fourth-generation Babylonian *amora*, was a primary student of Rava. The Gemara records some of his discussions of halakhic issues with his colleagues, mainly with other students of Rava, such as Rav Huna, son of Rabbi Yehoshua, and Rav Pappa. Apparently Rav Pappi was connected to the house of the Exilarch and there were warm relations between them. Eventually he joined the Exilarch's court.

מר סבר: לא עשה כלום בפלגא, ומר סבר: בכולהו.

Rav Pappi and Rav Pappa disagree with regard to Rava's intention. One Sage, Rav Pappi, **holds that he has done nothing with regard to** his brother's **portion,**[N] as he had no right to sell it; with regard to his own additional portion, the sale was valid, as it was in his possession even before the division of the property. **And one Sage,** Rav Pappa, **holds** that he has done nothing **with regard to all** of the property,[N] as he does not possess the additional portion before the property is divided between the brothers.

שלחו מתם: בכור שמכר קודם חלוקה – לא עשה כלום. אלמא, אין לו לבכור קודם חלוקה. והלכתא: יש לבכור קודם חלוקה.

The Gemara notes that **they sent** a ruling **from there,** Eretz Yisrael: **A firstborn who sold** his additional portion **before** the **division**[H] of the property **has done nothing. Apparently,** the Sages of Eretz Yisrael hold that **a firstborn does not have** a right to his additional portion **before** the **division. But the** ***halakha*** is that **a firstborn has** a right to his additional portion **before** the **division.**

מר זוטרא מדרישבא פלג בצנא דפלפלי בהדי אחין בשוה, אתא לקמיה דרב אשי, אמר ליה: הואיל ויתרתה במקצת – ויתרתה בכל הנכסים כולן.

The Gemara relates: **Mar Zutra of** the house **of Rishba,** who was a firstborn, **divided a basket of peppers**[B] from the estate of his father **with** his **brothers equally.** He **came before Rav Ashi** to claim a double portion of the rest of the estate. Rav Ashi **said to him: Since you relinquished** your additional portion **with regard to some** of the estate, **you have relinquished** your additional portion **with regard to all of the property,** as a firstborn has a right to his additional portion before the division.

מתני׳

האומר: ״איש פלוני בני בכור לא יטול פי שנים״, ״איש פלוני בני לא יירש עם אחיו״ – לא אמר כלום, שהתנה על מה שכתוב בתורה.

MISHNA

In a case of **one who says: So-and-so, my firstborn son,**[H] **will not take a double** portion of my estate; or one who says: **So-and-so, my son, will not inherit** my estate **among his brothers, he has said nothing,**[N] as he **has stipulated counter to that which is written in the Torah.**[B]

המחלק נכסיו על פיו, ריבה לאחד ומיעט לאחד, והשוה להן את הבכור – דבריו קיימין, ואם אמר משום ירושה – לא אמר כלום. כתב בין בתחלה בין באמצע בין בסוף משום מתנה – דבריו קיימין.

With regard to **one** on his deathbed **who apportions his property**[H] **orally,** granting it to his sons as a gift, and he **increased** the portion given **to one** of his sons **and reduced** the portion given **to one** son, **or equated** the portion of **the firstborn to** the portions of the other sons, **his statement stands. But if he said** that they will receive the property not as a gift but **as inheritance, he has said nothing.** If he **wrote** in his will, **whether at the beginning, or in the middle, or at the end,** that he is granting them the property **as a gift, his statement stands.**

NOTES

He has done nothing with regard to his brother's portion – לא עשה כלום בפלגא: The Rashbam maintains that the firstborn's sale of his own basic portion is also not valid; according to Rav Pappi only his additional portion can be sold before the property is divided, as it is considered a gift and is his from when their father dies. The majority of the commentaries disagree, maintaining that one can certainly sell his own basic portion of the inheritance, and Rava's ruling means that he has done nothing with regard to his brother's portion (*Tosafot*; Ra'avad).

With regard to all of the property – בכולהו: The Rashbam explains that he cannot sell his additional portion, and certainly not his basic portion, which he cannot sell even according to Rav Pappi. *Tosafot* maintain that this refers only to his additional portion and his brother's portion, but he can sell his basic portion.

He has said nothing – לא אמר כלום: The early commentaries discuss the relationship between this mishna and the following mishna (130a), where the Gemara accepts the opinion of Rabbi Yoḥanan ben Beroka that one can bequeath his property to one of his heirs at the expense of the others by stating that a certain heir will inherit from him. Some commentaries maintain that this mishna follows the opinion of the Rabbis, who disagree with Rabbi Yoḥanan ben Beroka (Rashbam; Rashba). Others understand this mishna as representing Rabbi Yoḥanan ben Beroka's opinion as well (Ri Migash; Rav Hai Gaon). They explain that the case in this mishna is different, as the father does not explicitly bequeath the property to one of his sons, but rather attempts to deprive one of them of his portion, without explicitly designating it for someone else. With regard to the latter clause of this mishna, they explain that a father cannot reduce the portion of his firstborn son even according to the opinion of Rabbi Yoḥanan ben Beroka unless he does so by giving it as a gift to another person (see Meiri).

BACKGROUND

A basket of peppers – צנא דפלפלי: Peppers arrived in Babylonia from East Asia. As they were transported great distances they were very valuable, and a basket filled with peppers was presumably worth a significant amount of money.

Stipulated counter to that which is written in the Torah – התנה על מה שכתוב בתורה: This is referring to stipulating that a Torah obligation should not apply to a particular transaction, e.g., a creditor stipulates that the Sabbatical Year should not abrogate a debt. According to some authorities, those stipulations are binding if made in connection with monetary matters, such as in the case here of a father stipulating that his firstborn son should not receive a double portion of the inheritance. All agree that stipulations that contradict a mitzva of the Torah with regard to other matters, e.g., obligations between husband and wife, are null and void.

HALAKHA

A firstborn who sold his portion before the division – בכור שמכר קודם חלוקה: If a firstborn sells his additional portion before the brothers divide the estate, the sale is valid, as a firstborn has the right to his additional portion before the division, in accordance with the conclusion of the Gemara (Rambam *Sefer Mishpatim, Hilkhot Naḥalot* 3:6; *Shulḥan Arukh, Ḥoshen Mishpat* 178:8).

So-and-so my firstborn son – איש פלוני בני בכור: One cannot deprive his heir of his inheritance, whether via oral instruction or in writing, whether as a healthy person or on his deathbed, as that is a stipulation counter to that which is written in the Torah. Therefore, if one instructs: So-and-so, my firstborn, will not receive a double portion, or: My son so-and-so will not inherit from me with his brothers, his statement is meaningless. If he bequeaths his estate to one of his sons, ultimately causing the others to lose their portions, his bequeathal is in effect, in accordance with the Gemara (130a), where the *halakha* is decided in accordance with the opinion of Rabbi Yoḥanan ben Beroka (Rambam *Sefer Mishpatim, Hilkhot Naḥalot* 6:1–2; *Shulḥan Arukh, Ḥoshen Mishpat* 281:1, 3).

One who apportions his property, etc. – המחלק נכסיו וכו׳: One's bequeathal counter to what is written in the Torah is void if it is stated as an inheritance and valid if it is stated as a gift. Therefore, if one apportions his property, whether orally on his deathbed, or through an act of acquisition as a healthy person (*Maggid Mishne*), increasing the portions of some of his sons and reducing the portions of others, or if he renders the portion of the firstborn equal to those of his brothers, or if he grants his estate to one who is not his heir at all, if his instruction is stated as a gift, it takes effect. If it is stated as inheritance, it is disregarded. Provided the instruction is stated as a gift at some point in the will, whether at the beginning, in the middle, or at the end, it takes effect, even if inheritance is also mentioned (Rambam *Sefer Mishpatim, Hilkhot Naḥalot* 6:5; *Shulḥan Arukh, Ḥoshen Mishpat* 281:7).

גמ׳ לֵימָא, מַתְנִיתִין דְּלָא כְּרַבִּי יְהוּדָה, דְּאִי רַבִּי יְהוּדָה, הָאָמַר: בְּדָבָר שֶׁל מָמוֹן תְּנָאוֹ קַיָּים!

GEMARA

The Gemara suggests: **Let us say that the mishna is not in accordance with the opinion of Rabbi Yehuda, as if** it is in accordance with the opinion of **Rabbi Yehuda, doesn't he say** elsewhere that if one stipulates counter to that which is written in the Torah **with regard to monetary matters, his stipulation stands?**

דְּתַנְיָא: הָאוֹמֵר לְאִשָּׁה ״הֲרֵי אַתְּ מְקוּדֶּשֶׁת לִי עַל מְנָת שֶׁאֵין לִיךְ עָלַי שְׁאֵר כְּסוּת וְעוֹנָה״ – הֲרֵי זוֹ מְקוּדֶּשֶׁת, וּתְנָאוֹ בָּטֵל, דִּבְרֵי רַבִּי מֵאִיר; רַבִּי יְהוּדָה אוֹמֵר: בְּדָבָר שֶׁל מָמוֹן תְּנָאוֹ קַיָּים.

As it is taught in a *baraita* (*Tosefta, Kiddushin* 3:7): If one **says to a woman: You are hereby betrothed to me on the condition that you have no** ability to claim **from me food, clothing, and conjugal rights,**[H] **she is betrothed and his stipulation is void;**[N] this is **the statement of Rabbi Meir. Rabbi Yehuda says: With regard to monetary matters,**[N] such as food and clothing, **his stipulation stands,** despite being counter to that which is written in the Torah. According to the opinion of Rabbi Yehuda, one should be able to stipulate that his firstborn son not receive a double portion, or that one of his sons not inherit from him at all, as inheritance is a monetary matter.

אֲפִילּוּ תֵּימָא רַבִּי יְהוּדָה, הָתָם יָדְעָה וְקָא מָחֲלָה, הָכָא לָא קָא מָחֵיל.

The Gemara rejects this suggestion: **Even if you say** that the mishna is in accordance with the opinion of **Rabbi Yehuda, there,** the woman **knew** of his stipulation **and waived** her rights. Therefore, the stipulation stands. **Here,** the son whose portion was reduced **did not waive**[N] his portion. Therefore the stipulation is not valid.

אָמַר רַב יוֹסֵף: אָמַר ״אִישׁ פְּלוֹנִי בְּנִי בְּכוֹרִי הוּא״ – נוֹטֵל פִּי שְׁנַיִם, ״אִישׁ פְּלוֹנִי בְּכוֹר הוּא״ – אֵינוֹ נוֹטֵל פִּי שְׁנַיִם, דִּלְמָא בּוּכְרָא דְּאִמָּא קָאָמַר.

§ **Rav Yosef says** that if a man **says: So-and-so is my firstborn son,**[NH] the son **takes a double** portion of his inheritance based on this testimony. If he says: **So-and-so is a firstborn,** the son **does not take a double** portion, as **perhaps** the man **was saying** that the son is his **mother's firstborn** but not his own firstborn.

הַהוּא דַּאֲתָא לְקַמֵּיהּ דְּרַבָּה בַּר בַּר חָנָה, אֲמַר לֵיהּ: מוּחְזְקַנִי בָּזֶה שֶׁהוּא בְּכוֹר. אֲמַר לֵיהּ: מְנָא יָדְעַתְּ? דַּהֲוָה קָרֵי לֵיהּ אֲבוּהּ ״בּוּכְרָא סִכְלָא״. דִּלְמָא בּוּכְרָא דְּאִמָּא הוּא, דְּכׇל בּוּכְרָא דְּאִמָּא נָמֵי ״בּוּכְרָא סִכְלָא״ קָארוּ לֵיהּ.

The Gemara relates: There was **a certain** man **who came**[N] **before Rabba bar bar Ḥana and said to him: I know that this man is a firstborn.** Rabba bar bar Ḥana **said to him: From where do you know?** He answered: **Because his father would call him a foolish firstborn.** Rabba bar bar Ḥana replied: **Perhaps he is** his **mother's firstborn, as any firstborn of a mother is also called a foolish firstborn.**[N]

הַהוּא דַּאֲתָא לְקַמֵּיהּ דְּרַבִּי חֲנִינָא, אֲמַר לֵיהּ: מוּחְזְקַנִי בָּזֶה שֶׁהוּא בְּכוֹר. אֲמַר לֵיהּ: מְנָא יָדְעַתְּ? אֲמַר לֵיהּ: דְּכִי הֲווּ אָתוּ לְגַבֵּי אֲבוּהּ, אֲמַר לְהוּ: זִילוּ לְגַבֵּי שִׁכְחַת בְּרִי, דְּבוּכְרָא הוּא וּמַסֵּי רוּקֵיהּ.

The Gemara relates: There was **a certain man who came before Rabbi Ḥanina and said to him: I know that this man is a firstborn.** Rabbi Ḥanina **said to him: From where do you know?** He said to Rabbi Ḥanina: **Because when** people **would come before his father** to obtain a cure for their ailing eyes, **he would say to them: Go to my son Shikhḥat,**[L] **as he is a firstborn and his saliva heals** this ailment.

וְדִלְמָא בּוּכְרָא דְּאִמָּא הוּא! גְּמִירִי: בּוּכְרָא דְּאַבָּא – מַסֵּי רוּקֵיהּ, בּוּכְרָא דְּאִמָּא – לָא מַסֵּי רוּקֵיהּ.

The Gemara asks: **But perhaps he is** his **mother's firstborn?** The Gemara answers: It **is learned** as a tradition that **the saliva of a father's firstborn heals** this ailment but **the saliva of a mother's firstborn does not heal** this ailment.

NOTES

And his stipulation is void – וּתְנָאוֹ בָּטֵל: Why is the stipulation void, and not the betrothal? Rabbeinu Tam explains that a stipulation contrary to that which is written in the Torah is considered hyperbole, like any stipulation that cannot be fulfilled, e.g., a stipulation that a woman ascend to the sky (see *Gittin* 84a and Ramban).

With regard to monetary matters – בְּדָבָר שֶׁל מָמוֹן: According to most early commentaries, food and clothing are considered monetary matters, whereas conjugal rights are considered physical needs (Rashi; Rashbam; Rambam). The Ritva maintains, based on the Jerusalem Talmud, that all physical needs are considered monetary matters, including conjugal rights. Rather, an invalid stipulation is one that pertains to a matter that the woman cannot waive, e.g., that she will be exempt from levirate marriage or that she can be divorced without a bill of divorce (see Meiri).

Did not waive – לָא קָא מָחֵיל: The Rashbam explains that even if he did not protest, this should be attributed to his unwillingness to cause his father distress, and not to his acquiescence.

So-and-so is my firstborn son – אִישׁ פְּלוֹנִי בְּנִי בְּכוֹרִי הוּא: The Rashbam explains that since no other son is presumed to be the firstborn, the father's testimony is reliable according to all *tanna'im* (see 127b).

A certain man who came, etc. – הַהוּא דַּאֲתָא וכו׳: The Rashbam writes that this person's testimony was apparently supported by another witness, as the testimony of two witnesses is required in order to establish that one is a firstborn.

A foolish [*sikhla*] firstborn – בּוּכְרָא סִכְלָא: Although one might call his firstborn son a foolish firstborn, this is a common nickname for a person who is only his mother's firstborn. The Rashbam explains that the word *sikhla*, *shoteh* in Hebrew, is employed in this nickname the way it is employed in the expression *hadas shoteh*, meaning wild myrtle (see *Sukka* 12a); the myrtle is called *shoteh*, usually meaning incompetent, as it is not fit for the mitzva of the four species. So too, one who is his mother's firstborn but not his father's firstborn is an unfit firstborn. The Maharshal explains that this nickname is meant to tease him about the fact that he has only the obligations of a firstborn but not the rights of a firstborn, as he requires redemption but does not receive a double portion of inheritance.

LANGUAGE

Shikhḥat – שִׁכְחַת: The Talmud does not explain this name. It is possible that this child was born after the death of a brother. Consequently, he was called Shikhḥat, meaning forgetting, as he caused the mourning over his brother to be forgotten.

HALAKHA

On the condition that you have no ability to claim from me food, clothing, and conjugal rights – עַל מְנָת שֶׁאֵין לִיךְ עָלַי שְׁאֵר כְּסוּת וְעוֹנָה: If a husband stipulated with his wife at the time of betrothal that she has no rights to food or clothing, his stipulation is effective and he is not obligated to provide food or clothing. If he stipulated that he will not be required to engage in sexual intercourse with her, this stipulation is void and his obligation is in effect. This *halakha* is in accordance with the opinion of Rabbi Yehuda (Rambam *Sefer Nashim, Hilkhot Ishut* 6:9–10, 12:6–7; *Shulḥan Arukh, Even HaEzer* 38:5; see 69:6).

So-and-so is my firstborn son – אִישׁ פְּלוֹנִי בְּנִי בְּכוֹרִי הוּא: If witnesses heard one declare: So-and-so is my firstborn son, the son receives a double portion of the estate of the one who stated the declaration. If they heard him declare: My son so-and-so is a firstborn, that person does not receive a double portion, as perhaps the father meant that he is his mother's firstborn. If it is evident from the context that he meant that the son is his own firstborn, the son receives a double portion (Rambam *Sefer Mishpatim, Hilkhot Naḥalot* 2:16–17; *Shulḥan Arukh, Ḥoshen Mishpat* 277:13).

אָמַר רַבִּי אַמִי: טוּמְטוּם שֶׁנִּקְרַע וְנִמְצָא זָכָר – אֵינוֹ נוֹטֵל פִּי שְׁנַיִם, דְּאָמַר קְרָא: ״וְהָיָה הַבֵּן הַבְּכוֹר לַשְּׂנִיאָה״, עַד שֶׁיְּהֵא בֵּן מִשְּׁעַת הֲוָיָה.

§ **Rabbi Ami says:** In the case of **one whose sexual organs are** indeterminate [*tumtum*] and whose **skin became perforated**[HB] so that his genitals were exposed **and** he **was found** to be **a male,** he **does not take a double** portion of his father's estate. **As the verse states: "And if the firstborn son was** [*vehaya*] **hers that was hated"** (Deuteronomy 21:15), which is interpreted to mean that he is not considered a firstborn **unless he is** recognized as **a son,** i.e., male, **from the moment of** his coming into being [*havaya*], i.e., his birth.

רַב נַחְמָן בַּר יִצְחָק אָמַר: אַף אֵינוֹ נִידּוֹן כְּבֵן סוֹרֵר וּמוֹרֶה, דְּאָמַר קְרָא: ״כִּי יִהְיֶה לְאִישׁ בֵּן סוֹרֵר וּמוֹרֶה״, עַד שֶׁיְּהֵא בֵּן מִשְּׁעַת הֲוָיָה.

Rav Naḥman bar Yitzḥak says: A *tumtum* who was found to be male **is also not judged as a stubborn and rebellious son, as the verse states: "If there will be** [*yihyeh*] **to a man a stubborn and rebellious son"** (Deuteronomy 21:18), which is interpreted to mean that one is not judged in this manner **unless he is** recognized **as a son from the moment of** his coming into **being.**

HALAKHA

A *tumtum* whose skin became perforated, etc. – טוּמְטוּם שֶׁנִּקְרַע וכו׳: A firstborn who was born a *tumtum* and who was found to have male sexual organs when his skin eventually became perforated does not receive a double portion of the inheritance (Rambam *Sefer Mishpatim, Hilkhot Naḥalot* 2:3; *Shulḥan Arukh, Ḥoshen Mishpat* 277:4).

BACKGROUND

A *tumtum* whose skin became perforated – טוּמְטוּם שֶׁנִּקְרַע: A *tumtum* is a person born with no visible external sexual organs. Sometimes this occurs due to a significant genetic defect that causes the *tumtum* to remain in this state for his entire life. Yet at times it is caused by the underdevelopment of sex hormones, and given time, sometimes after many years, the sexual organs develop until eventually they become visible. When male sexual organs develop later, it appears as though the skin that covers the urinary orifice is perforated, revealing an underdeveloped penis beneath.

Perek **VIII**
Daf **127** Amud **a**

אֲמֵימָר אָמַר: אַף אֵינוֹ מְמַעֵט חֵלֶק בְּכוֹרָה, שֶׁנֶּאֱמַר: ״וְיָלְדָה לוֹ בָנִים״, עַד שֶׁיְּהֵא בֵּן בִּשְׁעַת לֵידָה.

Ameimar says: A *tumtum* who was found to be male **also does not reduce the** additional **portion of the firstborn.**[H] His portion is not taken into account in the calculation of the firstborn's additional portion. For example, if there are three brothers: A firstborn, an ordinary brother, and a *tumtum*, the firstborn receives one-third of the property as his additional portion, as he would if he and the ordinary brother were the only heirs, and the remaining two-thirds are divided among all three brothers. This is **because it is stated** with regard to the portion of the firstborn: **"And they have borne him sons"** (Deuteronomy 21:15), which is interpreted to mean that the brother of a firstborn does not affect his additional portion **unless he is** recognized as **a son at the moment of** his **birth.**

רַב שֵׁיזְבִי אָמַר: אַף אֵינוֹ נִימּוֹל לִשְׁמוֹנָה, דְּאָמַר קְרָא: ״אִשָּׁה כִּי תַזְרִיעַ וְיָלְדָה זָכָר...וּבַיּוֹם הַשְּׁמִינִי יִמּוֹל״, עַד שֶׁיְּהֵא זָכָר מִשְּׁעַת לֵידָה.

Rav Sheizevi says: A *tumtum* who was found to be male **is also not circumcised on the eighth** day,[HN] if his eighth day occurs on Shabbat, although the mitzva of circumcision on the eighth day generally overrides Shabbat prohibtions. **As the verse states: "If a woman bears seed and gives birth to a male** then she shall be unclean seven days; as in the days of the impurity of her sickness shall she be unclean. **And on the eighth day** the flesh of his foreskin **shall be circumcised"** (Leviticus 12:2–3), which is interpreted to mean that he is not circumcised on the eighth day, in the event that it occurs on Shabbat, **unless he is** recognized as **a male from the moment of** his **birth.**

רַב שֵׁרֵבְיָא אָמַר: אַף אֵין אִמּוֹ טְמֵאָה לֵידָה, דְּאָמַר קְרָא: ״אִשָּׁה כִּי תַזְרִיעַ וְיָלְדָה זָכָר וְטָמְאָה שִׁבְעַת יָמִים״, עַד שֶׁיְּהֵא זָכָר מִשְּׁעַת לֵידָה.

Rav Sherevya says: His mother is also not rendered **ritually** impure due to his **birth, as the verse states: "If a woman bears seed and gives birth to a male, then she shall be unclean seven days,"** which is interpreted to mean that she is not rendered impure **unless he is** recognized as **a male from the moment of** his **birth.**[N]

HALAKHA

Does not reduce the portion of the firstborn – אֵינוֹ מְמַעֵט חֵלֶק בְּכוֹרָה: A *tumtum* whose skin is perforated and is found to be a male does not reduce the additional portion of his firstborn brother. For example, if the father left a firstborn son and three other sons, and one of them is a *tumtum* whose skin is perforated and is found to be a male, the inheritance is initially regarded as though it should be divided only among the firstborn and the two ordinary brothers, and the firstborn receives a quarter of the property as his additional portion. The rest is then divided among all four brothers equally. Accordingly, the firstborn receives seven-sixteenths and the others receive three-sixteenths each (Rambam *Sefer Mishpatim, Hilkhot Naḥalot* 2:3–4; *Shulḥan Arukh, Ḥoshen Mishpat* 277:4).

Not circumcised on the eighth day – אֵינוֹ נִימּוֹל לִשְׁמוֹנָה: The Rosh rules that a *tumtum* whose skin is perforated and who is found to be a male is circumcised even on Shabbat, maintaining that Rav Sheizevi's opinion was rejected by the Gemara. The *Pilpula Ḥarifta* notes that the Rif rules that it is prohibited to circumcise him on Shabbat, as the Gemara does not deem the challenge to his opinion a conclusive refutation (*Shulḥan Arukh, Yoreh De'a* 266:10, and in the comment of Rema).

NOTES

He is also not circumcised on the eighth day – אַף אֵינוֹ נִימּוֹל לִשְׁמוֹנָה: The *Noda BiYehuda*, citing the Rambam, explains that this means that the infant does not require circumcision specifically on his eighth day at all, even if it does not occur on Shabbat; he may be circumcised at any time.

Unless he is recognized as a male from the moment of his birth – עַד שֶׁיְּהֵא זָכָר מִשְּׁעַת לֵידָה: A new mother is not ritually impure unless her infant is recognized as either a male or a female, as the Torah later states: "But if she gives birth to a female, she shall be unclean two weeks" (Leviticus 12:5). It is stated in the Torah that a woman who gives birth is ritually impure for a week if she gives birth to a male and for two weeks if she gives birth to a female. Following this is a period of thirty-three days for a male or sixty-six days for a female, during which her blood is pure (see Leviticus 12:1–5). Since the Torah is referring specifically to a case where she gives birth to a male or to a female, a case where she gives birth to a *tumtum* or a hermaphrodite, who is not recognized as a male or a female at the time of birth, is not included in these *halakhot*.

מֵיתִיבֵי: הַמַּפֶּלֶת טוּמְטוּם וְאַנְדְּרוֹגִינוֹס – תֵּשֵׁב לְזָכָר וְלִנְקֵיבָה; תְּיוּבְתֵּיהּ דְּרַב שֵׁרֶבְיָא! תְּיוּבְתָּא.

The Gemara **raises an objection** from a mishna (*Nidda* 28a): A woman **who miscarries a *tumtum* or a hermaphrodite** [*ve'androginos*][LH] **observes** the strictures of a woman who gave birth **to a male and to a female.**[N] Since it is uncertain whether the fetus is male or female, the woman must observe the *halakhot* of ritual impurity according to both possibilities. This appears to be **a conclusive refutation** of the statement **of Rav Sherevya** that a woman who gives birth to a *tumtum* is not rendered impure at all. The Gemara affirms: This is **a conclusive refutation.**

לֵימָא, תֶּיהֱוֵי תְּיוּבְתָּא דְּרַב שֵׁיזְבִי!

The Gemara asks: **Shall we say it is** also **a conclusive refutation** of the statement **of Rav Sheizevi** with regard to circumcision, as the *halakha* of circumsicion is stated together with the *halakha* of ritual impurity?

תַּנָּא סַפּוֹקֵי מְסַפְּקָא לֵיהּ וּלְחוּמְרָא.

The Gemara answers: The ***tanna*** of the mishna in tractate *Nidda* **is uncertain** whether the birth discussed in the verse includes that of a *tumtum*, **and** therefore he rules **stringently,** that she should observe the *halakhot* of ritual impurity for both possibilities. Rav Sheizevi's ruling can follow the same logic: The infant should not be circumcised on Shabbat, as it is uncertain whether the mitzva of his circumcision overrides the prohibitions of Shabbat.

אִי הָכִי, תֵּשֵׁב לְזָכָר וְלִנְקֵבָה וּלְנִדָּה מִיבָּעֵי לֵיהּ! קַשְׁיָא.

The Gemara asks: **If so,** that the *tanna* of the mishna in tractate *Nidda* is uncertain whether the birth discussed in the verse includes that of a *tumtum*, the mishna **should have** stated that the woman **observes** the strictures of a woman who gave birth **to** both **a male and to a female, and** also **as a menstruating woman.**[N] If it is uncertain whether the *halakhot* of ritual purity after birth pertain to a woman who gives birth to a *tumtum* at all, she should observe the *halakhot* of ritual impurity for any blood that emerges in the time period following the birth, as it should have the status of the blood of a menstruating woman. The Gemara concludes: This poses **a difficulty.**[N]

אָמַר רָבָא, תַּנְיָא כְּוָותֵיהּ דְּרַבִּי אַמִּי: "בֵּן" – וְלֹא טוּמְטוּם, "בְּכוֹר" – וְלֹא סָפֵק.

Rava says that **it is taught** in a *baraita* **in accordance with** the opinion **of Rabbi Ami** that a *tumtum* firstborn does not receive a double portion of the inheritance. The *baraita* states: From the phrase "the firstborn son" (Deuteronomy 21:15) it is derived that only **a son** receives a double portion, **but not a *tumtum*,** and only a definite **firstborn** receives a double portion, **but not** one about whom it is **uncertain** if he is a firstborn.

בִּשְׁלָמָא בֵּן וְלֹא טוּמְטוּם – כִּדְרַבִּי אַמִּי, אֶלָּא בְּכוֹר וְלֹא סָפֵק לְאַפּוֹקֵי מַאי?

The Gemara asks: **Granted,** the *halakha* that **a son** receives a double portion **but a *tumtum*** does **not** is understandable, as it **is in accordance with** the statement **of Rabbi Ami, but what** case **does** the *halakha* that only a definite **firstborn** receives a double portion **but not** one about whom it is **uncertain** if he is a firstborn serve **to exclude?** Why would one about whom it is uncertain if he is a firstborn receive a double portion?

LANGUAGE

Hermaphrodite [*androginos*] – אַנְדְּרוֹגִינוֹס: From the Greek ἀνδρόγυνος, *androgunos*, literally meaning man-woman, referring to one who has both male and female sexual organs.

HALAKHA

A woman who miscarries a *tumtum* or a hermaphrodite – הַמַּפֶּלֶת טוּמְטוּם וְאַנְדְּרוֹגִינוֹס: A woman who gives birth to or miscarries a *tumtum* or a hermaphrodite must observe the strictures of impurity for the birth of a male and a female, due to the uncertainty with regard to the sex of the baby (Rambam *Sefer Kedusha, Hilkhot Issurei Bia* 10:18; *Shulḥan Arukh, Yoreh De'a* 194:8).

NOTES

Observes the strictures of a woman who gave birth to both a male and to a female – תֵּשֵׁב לְזָכָר וְלִנְקֵבָה: The woman must observe the strictures of both possibilities; namely, she is considered impure for two weeks after the birth, as is the *halakha* for the birth of a female. Concerning the *halakha* that blood emerging from the cervical canal following birth, termed blood of purity, does not render the woman impure, her blood is considered blood of purity only until the fortieth day after the birth, as is the *halakha* with regard to the birth of a male (Rashbam).

To both a male and to a female, and also as a menstruating woman – לְזָכָר וְלִנְקֵבָה וּלְנִדָּה: If the mishna had considered it uncertain whether the *halakhot* of ritual purity after birth apply in this case, it would have ruled that she should not observe any period where blood emerging from her is considered blood of purity, not even during the twenty-six days from the fifteenth to the fortieth day after a woman gives birth, during which her blood is considered blood of purity whether she gave birth to a male or to a female. Her blood would be considered impure during this time as well, either as blood of menstruation or as *ziva* blood.

Difficulty – קַשְׁיָא: The *tanna* apparently holds that the infant should be circumcised on the eighth day even on Shabbat. The early commentaries note that the Gemara does not deem this a conclusive refutation, and they explain that perhaps the *tanna* inadvertently omitted the phrase: And as a menstruating woman. In practice, there is a dispute among the early authorities as to whether, as a matter of stringency, a tumtum may not be circumcised on the eighth day in the event that it is Shabbat (see Ramah and Meiri).

לְאַפּוֹקֵי מִדִּדְרַשׁ רָבָא, דִּדְרַשׁ רָבָא: שְׁתֵּי נָשִׁים שֶׁיָּלְדוּ שְׁנֵי זְכָרִים בְּמַחֲבֵא – כּוֹתְבִין הַרְשָׁאָה זֶה לָזֶה.	The Gemara answers: It serves **to exclude that which Rava taught, as Rava taught** that if **two wives** of the same husband **gave birth to two males in hiding,** so that it is unknown which son was born first, and the husband subsequently had other sons, **each** of the two possible firstborns **writes an authorization**[N] **to the other.** Since their brothers can claim against each of them individually that he is not the firstborn and does not deserve a double portion, each writes the other an authorization to collect his portion, so that they can jointly claim the additional portion in any event.
אֲמַר לֵיהּ רַב פַּפָּא לְרָבָא, וְהָא שְׁלַח רָבִין: דָּבָר זֶה שָׁאַלְתִּי לְכׇל רַבּוֹתַי וְלֹא אָמְרוּ לִי דָּבָר, בְּרַם כָּךְ אָמְרוּ מִשּׁוּם רַבִּי יַנַּאי: הוּכְּרוּ וּלְבַסּוֹף נִתְעָרְבוּ – כּוֹתְבִין הַרְשָׁאָה זֶה לָזֶה, לֹא הוּכְּרוּ – אֵין כּוֹתְבִין הַרְשָׁאָה זֶה לָזֶה!	Rav Pappa subsequently **said to Rava: But didn't Ravin send** a letter from Eretz Yisrael to Babylonia, stating: **I asked all my teachers** about **this matter and they did not tell me anything; but this is** what **they said in the name of Rabbi Yannai:** If the two sons **were** initially **recognized,** i.e., it was known which one of them was the firstborn, **and** they **were ultimately mixed,**[H] and now the firstborn cannot be identified, **each writes an authorization to the other.**[N] **If they were not** initially **recognized, each does not write an authorization to the other.**[N]
הֲדַר אוֹקֵי רָבָא אָמוֹרָא עֲלֵיהּ וּדְרַשׁ: דְּבָרִים שֶׁאָמַרְתִּי לָכֶם טָעוּת הֵן בְּיָדִי, בְּרַם כָּךְ אָמְרוּ מִשּׁוּם רַבִּי יַנַּאי: הוּכְּרוּ וּלְבַסּוֹף נִתְעָרְבוּ – כּוֹתְבִין הַרְשָׁאָה זֶה לָזֶה, לֹא הוּכְּרוּ – אֵין כּוֹתְבִין הַרְשָׁאָה זֶה לָזֶה.	**Rava then established an** ***amora*** to repeat his lesson to the masses aloud **and taught: The statements that I said to you are a mistake on my part. But this is** what **they said in the name of Rabbi Yannai:** If the two sons **were** initially **recognized and were ultimately mixed, each writes an authorization to the other.** If **they were not** initially **recognized, each does not write an authorization to the other.**
שְׁלַחוּ לֵיהּ בְּנֵי אַקְרָא דְּאַגְמָא לִשְׁמוּאֵל, יְלַמְּדֵנוּ רַבֵּינוּ: הָיוּ מוּחְזָקִין בָּזֶה שֶׁהוּא בְּכוֹר, וְאָמַר אָבִיו עַל אַחֵר ״בְּכוֹר הוּא״, מַהוּ? שְׁלַח לְהוּ: כּוֹתְבִין הַרְשָׁאָה	§ **The residents of Akra De'Agma sent** the following inquiry **to Shmuel: Teach us, our master:** If the court **had a presumption concerning this son, that he is a firstborn,**[N] **and his father says concerning another** son of his: He is his **firstborn, what is the** *halakha*? Shmuel **sent to them** in response: Both of these sons **write an authorization,**

Perek **VIII**
Daf **127** Amud **b**

זֶה לָזֶה.	**each to the other.**
מַה נַּפְשָׁךְ? אִי כְּרַבָּנַן סְבִירָא לֵיהּ – לִישְׁלַח לְהוּ כְּרַבָּנַן, אִי כְּרַבִּי יְהוּדָה סְבִירָא לֵיהּ – לִישְׁלַח לְהוּ כְּרַבִּי יְהוּדָה!	The Gemara questions this ruling: **Whichever way you** look at it, Shmuel's opinion is difficult. **If he holds in accordance with** the opinion of **the Rabbis** with regard to this issue, **he should have sent them** a response **in accordance with** the opinion of **the Rabbis,** and **if he holds in accordance with** the opinion of **Rabbi Yehuda, he should have sent them** a response **in accordance with** the opinion of **Rabbi Yehuda.** Shmuel's response is not in accordance with either tannaitic opinion.
מְסַפְּקָא לֵיהּ אִי כְּרַבִּי יְהוּדָה אִי כְּרַבָּנַן.	The Gemara answers: **He is uncertain whether** the *halakha* is **in accordance with** the opinion of **Rabbi Yehuda or in accordance with** the opinion of **the Rabbis.** Therefore he sent them a response that incorporates both opinions.
מַאי הִיא? דְּתַנְיָא: ״יַכִּיר״ – יַכִּירֶנּוּ לַאֲחֵרִים,	The Gemara explains: **What is** the dispute between Rabbi Yehuda and the Rabbis? **As it is taught** in a *baraita*: Expounding the verse: "**He shall acknowledge** the firstborn" (Deuteronomy 21:17), the Sages said: **He shall acknowledge him to others.** In other words, a father is deemed credible to tell others that this is his firstborn.

NOTES

Writes an authorization – כּוֹתְבִין הַרְשָׁאָה: Either one can then claim the additional portion from the other brothers, claiming that if he is the firstborn, he is claiming his own portion, and if the other one is the firstborn, he has his authorization to collect his brother's portion. Then, the two of them divide the additional portion.

Rav Pappa said…each writes an authorization to the other – אֲמַר לֵיהּ רַב פַּפָּא...כּוֹתְבִין הַרְשָׁאָה זֶה לָזֶה: *Tosafot* ask how a firstborn can grant another authorization to collect his additional portion before the property is divided, given the opinion of Rav Pappa himself (126a) that a firstborn does not have the right to an additional portion before the division of the property. They answer that authorization is not a conferral of rights but rather an appointment as an agent. Other early commentaries derive from here that one can grant another authorization even for rights that he cannot transfer (Ramban; Ritva, citing Ra'ah). The Rashba and Rid conclude that Rav Pappa retracted the opinion recorded on 126a.

If they were not initially recognized, each does not write an authorization to the other – לֹא הוּכְּרוּ אֵין כּוֹתְבִין הַרְשָׁאָה זֶה לָזֶה: This is because a son about whom it is uncertain from birth whether he is a firstborn does not receive a double portion, as stated in the *baraita*. If the firstborn was initially recognized, he already has the right to a double portion, and the subsequent uncertainty does not affect his essential right.

If the court had a presumption concerning this son that he is a firstborn – הָיוּ מוּחְזָקִין בָּזֶה שֶׁהוּא בְּכוֹר: The Rashbam explains that the presumption is based on circumstantial evidence, e.g., they heard the father call him a firstborn (see 126b), not based on the explicit testimony of two witnesses, as in such a case the father's testimony that another son of his is the firstborn would not be deemed credible. The Ramban, by contrast, maintains (citing *Yevamot* 47a) that even in a case where there are two witnesses that a certain son is the firstborn, the father can deprive him of his portion by testifying that he is not his son at all.

If the father calls his son a firstborn, he cannot retract his statement, as delineated in the Gemara (127b).

HALAKHA

Were recognized and were ultimately mixed, etc. – הוּכְּרוּ וּלְבַסּוֹף נִתְעָרְבוּ וכו׳: If it is uncertain whether a certain son is the firstborn, e.g., two wives of one husband gave birth concurrently, and it is unknown who gave birth first, the son does not receive a double portion of the inheritance. In a case where one of the sons was recognized as the firstborn at the time of his birth, and only afterward the two sons were intermixed, the true firstborn has the right to a double portion. Therefore, each of them writes the other an authorization to collect the additional portion for him, and they then divide it (*Sma*). This is in accordance with Rabbi Yannai's statement and Rava's conclusion (Rambam *Sefer Mishpatim, Hilkhot Naḥalot* 2:6; *Shulḥan Arukh, Ḥoshen Mishpat* 277:11).

מִכָּאן אָמַר רַבִּי יְהוּדָה: נֶאֱמָן אָדָם לוֹמַר "זֶה בְּנִי בְּכוֹר". וּכְשֵׁם שֶׁנֶּאֱמָן אָדָם לוֹמַר "זֶה בְּנִי בְּכוֹר", כָּךְ נֶאֱמָן אָדָם לוֹמַר "זֶה בֶּן גְּרוּשָׁה" וְ"זֶה בֶּן חֲלוּצָה"; וַחֲכָמִים אוֹמְרִים: אֵינוֹ נֶאֱמָן.

From here, Rabbi Yehuda says that **a man is deemed credible to say: This is my firstborn son,**[H] even if he has sons presumed to be older. **And just as a man is deemed credible to say: This is my firstborn son, so too, a man** who is a priest **is deemed credible to say** about his son: **This is a son of a divorced woman,**[N] **or: This** is **a son of a** ***yevama*** **who has performed** ***halitza*** [***halutza***],[H] in which cases he is disqualified from the priesthood due to his flawed lineage [*halal*]. **And the Rabbis say: He is not deemed credible.**

אֲמַר לֵיהּ רַב נַחְמָן בַּר יִצְחָק לְרָבָא: בִּשְׁלָמָא לְרַבִּי יְהוּדָה – הַיְינוּ דִּכְתִיב "יַכִּיר", אֶלָּא לְרַבָּנַן "יַכִּיר" לָמָּה לִי?

Rav Naḥman bar Yitzḥak said to Rava: Granted, according **to Rabbi Yehuda, this is** the reason **that it is written: "He shall acknowledge;"** he derives from these words that a father is deemed credible to attest to the identity of his sons. **But** according **to the Rabbis, why do I** need the term **"he shall acknowledge"?**

בְּצָרִיךְ הֶיכֵּרָא.

The Gemara answers: It is necessary for a case **when he requires identification,** i.e., when there is no presumption as to the identity of the firstborn. In such a situation the verse teaches that the father is deemed credible. The Rabbis disagree with Rabbi Yehuda's opinion only in a case where another son is presumed to be the firstborn.

לְמַאי הִלְכְתָא – לְמֵיתְבָא לוֹ פִּי שְׁנַיִם; לֹא יְהֵא אֶלָּא אַחֵר, אִילּוּ בָּעֵי לְמֵיתְבָא לֵיהּ בְּמַתָּנָה מִי לָא יָהֵיב לֵיהּ?!

The Gemara asks: According to the Rabbis, **with regard to what** ***halakha*** is it necessary for the verse to teach that a father's identification of his firstborn is deemed credible? If it is **with regard to giving him a double** portion, it is superfluous. **Let** the son **be only** like **another** person, i.e., one who is not an heir; **if** the father **wants to give him** a double portion of his estate **as a gift, can he not give** it to **him?** Since the father can give a double portion to the firstborn without having to testify that he is his firstborn, it cannot be that the verse is teaching us that he is deemed credible with regard to the *halakha* that a firstborn receives a double portion.

לָא צְרִיכָא, בִּנְכָסִים שֶׁנָּפְלוּ לוֹ לְאַחַר מִכָּאן.

The Gemara answers: **No,** it is **necessary with regard to property that came into** the father's possession **afterward,** after he testified that his son is his firstborn. He could not have given him this property as a gift, as at the time of his testimony, the property did not yet belong to him, and one cannot transfer ownership of an item that one does not own. Therefore, it is necessary for the verse to teach that the father's testimony is deemed credible so that the son can receive a double portion of the father's future property as well.

וּלְרַבִּי מֵאִיר דְּאָמַר: אָדָם מַקְנֶה דָּבָר שֶׁלֹּא בָּא לָעוֹלָם, "יַכִּיר" לָמָּה לִי?

The Gemara asks: **And according to Rabbi Meir,**[N] **who says** that **a person can transfer an entity that has not yet come into the world,** which would mean that one can give away his property even before it enters his possession, **why do I** need the term **"he shall acknowledge"?**

בִּנְכָסִים שֶׁנָּפְלוּ לוֹ כְּשֶׁהוּא גּוֹסֵס.

The Gemara answers: The term is necessary for a case **where property came into** the father's possession **when he was moribund,**[N] at which point he cannot transfer ownership of any of his property to others. It is with regard to such property that the verse states: "He shall acknowledge," to teach that the son who the father states is the firstborn will receive a double portion even of that property.

NOTES

And according to Rabbi Meir, etc. – **וּלְרַבִּי מֵאִיר וכו׳**: The Rashbam explains that the Gemara assumes that the opinion of the Rabbis in this *baraita* is the opinion of Rabbi Meir, because he often engages in disputes with Rabbi Yehuda.

Where property came into his possession when he was moribund – **בִּנְכָסִים שֶׁנָּפְלוּ לוֹ כְּשֶׁהוּא גּוֹסֵס**: Rabbi Meir holds that one can transfer ownership of an item that has not yet come into the world only in a case where he will be capable of transferring it when it does come into the world, and a dying person cannot transfer ownership of his property.

Why is a dying person unable to transfer ownership of his property? Some early commentaries (Rabbeinu Hananel) maintain that a dying person does not have the legal power to perform transactions. Others reject this opinion based on a *baraita* in tractate *Semahot*, where it is stated that a dying person has all the legal capacities of a living person, including assigning inheritance, giving or receiving a bill of divorce, and granting gifts. Rather, the Gemara means that often a dying person cannot transfer ownership of his property to another because he is incapable of speaking (Rashbam) or even nodding his head (Ra'avad; see *Gittin* 71a).

Tosafot comment that the Gemara could have also answered that this *halakha* is necessary with regard to property that is not likely to come into his possession, as Rabbi Meir concedes that one cannot transfer his ownership of this type of property in advance.

HALAKHA

This is my firstborn son – **זֶה בְּנִי בְּכוֹר**: A father is deemed credible to say about one of his sons, or even about one who was presumed not to be his son at all, that he is in fact his firstborn son, as the *halakha* is in accordance with the opinion of Rabbi Yehuda, as the Gemara rules (128b). Furthermore, he is deemed credible to say that someone who was presumed to be his firstborn son is actually not his firstborn, as the *halakha* is not in accordance with the opinion of Shmuel, who was uncertain about this matter. The Rema writes that once a father has claimed that a certain individual is his firstborn, he can no longer claim that someone else is (*Tur*, citing Ramban; *Beit Yosef*, citing Ran). If it has been established based on the testimony of two witnesses that a certain individual is not his son, he is not deemed credible to say that he is his son or his firstborn son (Rambam *Sefer Mishpatim*, *Hilkhot Nahalot* 2:14; *Shulhan Arukh*, *Hoshen Mishpat* 277:12).

This is a son of a divorced woman, or this is a son of a *halutza* – **זֶה בֶּן גְּרוּשָׁה וְזֶה בֶּן חֲלוּצָה**: Just as a father is deemed credible to say that his son is a firstborn, so too he is deemed credible to say that his son is a *mamzer*, or the son of a divorcée, or the son of a *halutza*. This is the *halakha* only if the son does not have any children. If the son does have children, the father's statement is not deemed credible even with regard to his son, as the *halakha* that a father is deemed credible with regard to his children is in effect only if his statement pertains solely to his son. The Rema, citing Rabbeinu Yeruham, writes that if the son was presumed to have unflawed lineage based on the testimony of his father, the father is no longer able to disqualify him (Rambam *Sefer Kedusha*, *Hilkhot Issurei Bia* 15:16; *Shulhan Arukh*, *Even HaEzer* 4:29).

NOTES

This is a son of a divorced woman – **זֶה בֶּן גְּרוּשָׁה**: The Rashbam explains that the father's credibility in this case is derived from the same verse; just as he is deemed credible to identify his son as a firstborn, so too, he is deemed credible to identify him as a *halal*. *Tosafot* question this reasoning, as the credibility of a statement that lowers the son's status by declaring him a *halal* cannot be compared to the credibility of a statement that enhances his status by declaring him a firstborn. Therefore, they explain that the father's credibility concerning the son's status as a *halal* is derived from the *halakha* that the father is deemed credible to say that his younger son is the firstborn, which perforce renders his older sons not his and therefore *mamzerim*; and if one can render his sons *mamzerim*, he can render them *halalim* as well (see Ramah).

Tosafot, citing Rabbi Eliyahu of Paris, provide another explanation: Since the verse states: "He shall acknowledge the firstborn, the son of the hated" (Deuteronomy 21:17), and the concept of a wife who is hated is expounded to mean one whose marriage is hated, i.e., forbidden by the Torah (*Yevamot* 23a), such as a divorcée married to a priest, evidently a father can identify his son as the product of a forbidden marriage. The Ritva cites the Jerusalem Talmud (*Kiddushin* 4:7) in support of this explanation.

With regard to a father who testifies that his son is a *mamzer*, some early commentaries maintain that he is deemed credible only if he does so indirectly, by testifying that his younger son is his firstborn (*Halakhot Gedolot*; Ramban, citing Rabbeinu Tam). The Ramah writes that according to this opinion, the son's status as a *mamzer* is uncertain, as perhaps his real father is a gentile or a slave, in which case he is not a *mamzer*. Other commentaries hold that the father can render his son a *mamzer* directly (*Tosafot*, citing Rabbeinu Yitzhak of Dampierre).

תָּנוּ רַבָּנַן: הָיוּ מוּחְזָקִין בּוֹ שֶׁהוּא בְּכוֹר, וְאָמַר אָבִיו עַל אַחֵר שֶׁהוּא בְּכוֹר – נֶאֱמָן; הָיוּ מוּחְזָקִין בּוֹ שֶׁאֵינוֹ בְּכוֹר, וְאָמַר אָבִיו בְּכוֹר הוּא – אֵינוֹ נֶאֱמָן;

The Sages taught in a *baraita* (*Tosefta* 7:3): If the court **had a presumption concerning** a son **that he is a firstborn, and his father said concerning another** son of his **that he is** his **firstborn,** the father's statement is **deemed credible.** If the court **had a presumption concerning** a son **that he is not a firstborn, and his father said** that **he is** his **firstborn,** the father's statement is **not deemed credible.**

רֵישָׁא – רַבִּי יְהוּדָה, וְסֵיפָא – רַבָּנַן.

The Gemara asserts that as the two *halakhot* of the *baraita* seem to contradict each other, it must be that **the first clause** represents the opinion of **Rabbi Yehuda, and the latter clause** represents the opinion of **the Rabbis.**

אָמַר רַבִּי יוֹחָנָן: אָמַר ״בְּנִי הוּא״, וְחָזַר וְאָמַר ״עַבְדִּי הוּא״ – אֵינוֹ נֶאֱמָן; ״עַבְדִּי הוּא״, וְחָזַר וְאָמַר ״בְּנִי הוּא״ – נֶאֱמָן, דִּמְשַׁמֵּשׁ לִי כְּעַבְדָּא קָאָמַר.

§ **Rabbi Yoḥanan says** that if one **says** about another: **He is my son, and then says: He is my slave,**[N][H] his latter statement is **not deemed credible.** It cannot disqualify him from marrying a Jewish woman or exclude him from his inheritance. Conversely, if he first says: **He is my slave, and then says: He is my son,**[H] his latter statement is **deemed credible,** as in his first statement he presumably **was saying: He serves me as a slave** does.

וְחִילּוּפֵיהּ אַבֵּית הַמֶּכֶס: הָיָה עוֹבֵר עַל בֵּית הַמֶּכֶס וְאָמַר ״בְּנִי הוּא״, וְחָזַר וְאָמַר ״עַבְדִּי הוּא״ – נֶאֱמָן; אָמַר ״עַבְדִּי הוּא״, וְחָזַר וְאָמַר ״בְּנִי הוּא״ – אֵינוֹ נֶאֱמָן.

And the opposite *halakha* applies **to** one **at the tax house:** If one **is passing the customs house and says** about a certain person: **He is my son,**[H] **and then** later **says: He is my slave,** his latter statement is **deemed credible,** as he presumably says that the other is his son only to evade paying a tax for possessing a slave. Conversely, if **he says** at the customs house: **He is my slave, and then** later **says: He is my son,** his latter statement is **not deemed credible,** as one would not unnecessarily render himself liable to pay a tax.

מֵיתִיבֵי: הָיָה מְשַׁמְּשׁוֹ כְּבֵן, וּבָא וְאָמַר ״בְּנִי הוּא״, וְחָזַר וְאָמַר ״עַבְדִּי הוּא״ – אֵינוֹ נֶאֱמָן; הָיָה מְשַׁמְּשׁוֹ כְּעֶבֶד, וּבָא וְאָמַר ״עַבְדִּי הוּא״, וְחָזַר וְאָמַר ״בְּנִי הוּא״ – אֵינוֹ נֶאֱמָן!

The Gemara **raises an objection** from a *baraita*: If one **was serving** another person **like a son** serves his father, **and** the person being served **came and said: He is my son, and then said: He is my slave,** his latter statement is **not deemed credible.** Additionally, if one **was serving** another person **like a slave** serves his master, **and** the one being served **came and said: He is my slave, and then said: He is my son,** his latter statement is **not deemed credible.** This contradicts Rabbi Yoḥanan's statement that if he first says that he is his slave and then says that he is his son, his latter statement is deemed credible.

אָמַר רַב נַחְמָן בַּר יִצְחָק: הָתָם דְּקָארוּ לֵיהּ ״עַבְדָּא מְצַר מְאָה״. מַאי מְצַר מְאָה? מְצַר עַבְדָּא מְאָה זוּזֵי.

Rav Naḥman bar Yitzḥak said: There, in Rabbi Yoḥanan's statement, it is a case where he is presumed to be a slave **because** everyone **calls him:**[N] **A slave** on whose **border** [*metzar*] are **one hundred.**[H] Since everyone is referring to him in this manner, the person he served cannot call into question his status as a slave by saying that he is his son. The Gemara asks: **What** does it mean that on his **border** [*metzar*] are **one hundred?** The Gemara answers: **One hundred dinars are adjacent to** [*metzar*] this **slave.** In other words, he is worth one hundred dinars.

שְׁלַח לֵיהּ רַבִּי אַבָּא לְרַב יוֹסֵף בַּר חָמָא: הָאוֹמֵר לַחֲבֵירוֹ: ״עַבְדִּי גָּנַבְתָּ״, וְהוּא אוֹמֵר: ״לֹא גָנַבְתִּי״. ״מַה טִּיבוֹ אֶצְלְךָ״? ״אַתָּה מְכַרְתּוֹ לִי,

§ **Rabbi Abba sent** several rulings from Eretz Yisrael **to**[N] **Rav Yosef bar Ḥama,**[P] including the following: In the case of **one who says to another: You stole my slave, and he says** in response: **I did not steal** him, and when the first inquires: If so, **what is the nature of his** presence **in your** possession, the latter responds: **You sold him to me,**

NOTES

And then says, he is my slave – וְחָזַר וְאָמַר עַבְדִּי הוּא: Once one provides testimony that is deemed credible and accepted, he cannot retract his statement or testify to the contrary (see 168a). Therefore, once one states that another is his son, he cannot testify that that person is in fact his slave (see Rashbam).

There because everybody calls him, etc. – הָתָם דְּקָארוּ לֵיהּ וכו׳: Since other people refer to him in a manner that is reserved for a slave, if his father does not protest, apparently he is in fact a slave (Rabbeinu Barukh). The Rashbam has a version of the text that reads: There he calls him a slave on whose border are one hundred, i.e., the father referred to him in this manner. Since he referred to him in a manner that is reserved for an actual slave, saying that he is worth a certain amount of money, he was clearly not referring only to the quality of his service.

Rabbi Abba sent to, etc. – שְׁלַח לֵיהּ רַבִּי אַבָּא וכו׳: This *halakha* is not related to the discussion and is cited only in connection with the subsequent *halakha* that Rabbi Abba sent Rav Yosef bar Ḥama, that the *halakha* is in accordance with the opinion of Rabbi Yehuda with regard to a father's testimony concerning his son (Rashbam).

HALAKHA

One says he is my son, and then says he is my slave – אָמַר בְּנִי הוּא, וְחָזַר וְאָמַר עַבְדִּי הוּא: If one said about another: This is my son, and after the time required for speaking a short phrase (*Tur*) he said: He is my slave, i.e., he is the son of a maidservant and me and is therefore a slave (*Sma*), his statement is not deemed credible (Rambam *Sefer Mishpatim, Hilkhot Naḥalot* 4:3; *Shulḥan Arukh, Ḥoshen Mishpat* 279:3).

He is my slave, and then says he is my son – עַבְדִּי הוּא, וְחָזַר וְאָמַר בְּנִי הוּא: If one said about another: He is my slave, and then said: He is my son, his latter statement is deemed credible, even if the one he speaks about serves him like a slave does, as the intention of his former statement was presumably to praise him for fulfilling all his needs and requests as does a slave (Rambam *Sefer Mishpatim, Hilkhot Naḥalot* 4:3; *Shulḥan Arukh, Ḥoshen Mishpat* 279:3).

If one was passing the customs house and says he is my son, etc. – הָיָה עוֹבֵר עַל בֵּית הַמֶּכֶס וְאָמַר בְּנִי הוּא וכו׳: If one said about another who was with him at the customs house: He is my son, and then later he said: He is my slave, his latter statement is deemed credible, as he presumably said that the other is his son only to evade paying a tax on his slave. This applies only in a case where the mother does not have the presumptive status of a Jewish woman of unflawed lineage; if she has this presumptive status, he cannot make a statement that renders her son a slave, as that would render her a maidservant. Others rule that the statement is also not deemed credible if the speaker has the presumptive status of unflawed lineage (*Sma*). If he said in the customs house that the other is his slave, and later he said that he is his son, his latter statement is not deemed credible (Rambam *Sefer Mishpatim, Hilkhot Naḥalot* 4:4; *Shulḥan Arukh, Ḥoshen Mishpat* 279:4).

Because everybody calls him a slave on whose border are one hundred – דְּקָארוּ לֵיהּ עַבְדָּא מְצַר מְאָה: In a case where one is called a slave, the son of a maidservant (*Shulḥan Arukh*, based on one version in the Rambam), or a slave worth one hundred dinars (according to the standard version of the Rambam), or any other sobriquet used exclusively for slaves, if another says that he is his slave, the speaker cannot subsequently retract his statement and say that he is actually his son. The *Tur*, citing the Rashbam, rules that one cannot say that this individual is his son after he himself called him by a sobriquet used for slaves (Rambam *Sefer Mishpatim, Hilkhot Naḥalot* 4:3; *Shulḥan Arukh, Ḥoshen Mishpat* 279:3).

PERSONALITIES

Rav Yosef bar Ḥama – רַב יוֹסֵף בַּר חָמָא: Rav Yosef bar Ḥama was a third-generation Babylonian *amora* who lived in Meḥoza and may have been the leader of that community. He was a student of Rav Sheshet, although he also retained ties with the method of Torah study and halakhic practice of other Sages. He often discussed matters of *halakha* with Rabbi Zeira. His son was Rava, who was considered to be a great Sage even during the life of his father. Occasionally, Rava would comment on his father's rulings, suggesting a different opinion, albeit in a respectful manner, and Rav Yosef would sometimes even concede the point to his son.

אַתָּה נְתַתּוֹ לִי בְּמַתָּנָה, רְצוֹנְךָ הִשָּׁבַע וְטוֹל״, וְנִשְׁבַּע – אֵינוֹ יָכוֹל לַחֲזוֹר בּוֹ.

or: **You gave him to me as a gift,** if he then adds: Although I owe you nothing, as the slave is mine, if it is **your desire, take an oath** that he is yours **and take** him;[H] **and** the claimant **takes an oath**[N] that the slave is his, the one in possession of the slave **cannot retract** his offer, although he was not obligated to make the offer.

מַאי קָא מַשְׁמַע לַן? תְּנֵינָא: אָמַר לוֹ: ״נֶאֱמָן עָלַי אַבָּא״, ״נֶאֱמָן עָלַי אָבִיךָ״, ״נֶאֱמָנִין עָלַי שְׁלֹשָׁה רוֹעֵי בָקָר״ – רַבִּי מֵאִיר אוֹמֵר: יָכוֹל לַחֲזוֹר בּוֹ, וַחֲכָמִים אוֹמְרִים: אֵינוֹ יָכוֹל לַחֲזוֹר בּוֹ!

The Gemara asks: **What is** Rabbi Abba **teaching us? We** already **learned** in a mishna (*Sanhedrin* 24a) that if one of the litigants **said to** the other: My **father is trusted** to adjudicate **for me,** or: **Your father is trusted** to adjudicate **for me,** or: These **three cattle herders**[H] who are not experts in *halakha* **are trusted** to adjudicate **for me,** and all of the individuals this litigant mentioned are legally disqualified from serving as judges, **Rabbi Meir says** that the one who stated this **can retract** his statement, **and the Rabbis say** that **he cannot retract** it, and he is obligated to have them serve as judges if the other litigant so desires. Since this *halakha* is already stated in the mishna, what novel *halakha* did Rabbi Abba teach?

הָא קָא מַשְׁמַע לַן, דְּ״בְאֶתֵּן לָךְ״ מַחֲלוֹקֶת, וַהֲלָכָה כְּדִבְרֵי חֲכָמִים.

The Gemara in tractate *Sanhedrin* records a dispute between *amora'im* as to the circumstances of the case of that mishna, with one *amora* holding that the dispute pertains only to a case where the one accepting the disqualified judge will need to forgive a debt if the judge rules in accordance with his opponent, while another *amora* holds that the dispute pertains even to a case where he will need to pay the other litigant if the judge rules in accordance with his opponent. By stating his ruling in a case where the litigant will have to give the slave to the other, Rabbi Abba **teaches us this, that the dispute** between Rabbi Meir and the Rabbis is even **in** a case where the litigant said: **I will give you**[N] what you claim if that is the ruling of these judges, and the Rabbis hold that if he subsequently wishes to retract his suggestion, he cannot do so. **And** Rabbi Abba also teaches that the ***halakha*** **is in accordance with the statement of the Rabbis.**

שְׁלַח לֵיהּ רַבִּי אַבָּא לְרַב יוֹסֵף בַּר חָמָא, הֲלָכָה: גּוֹבִין מִן הָעֲבָדִים. וְרַב נַחְמָן אָמַר: אֵין גּוֹבִין.

§ **Rabbi Abba** also **sent** a ruling **to Rav Yosef bar Ḥama** that **the *halakha*** is that the creditors of one who died **collect** the debts **from the** Canaanite **slaves** the deceased left his heirs, i.e., they take the slaves, as slaves have the same status as land in this regard. **And Rav Naḥman says** that they **do not collect**[NH] the debt by taking the slaves.

HALAKHA

If it is your desire take an oath and take him, etc. – רְצוֹנְךָ הִשָּׁבַע וְטוֹל וכו׳: If one is obligated to take an oath in a court case concerning a monetary matter, and he suggests to the other party: You take an oath, and you will be exempt from paying me, or: You take an oath, and I will pay you what you claim, if they performed an act of acquisition concerning this offer, the party that made the offer cannot retract it. If they did not perform an act of acquisition, he can retract his offer until the other party takes the oath. This is also the *halakha* with regard to an oath of inducement, i.e., an oath instituted by the Sages in a case where the defendant completely denies the claim against him (see *Beur HaGra*). The *Shakh* and the *Beur HaGra* note that according to the version of the text of the Gemara that reads only: The claimant takes an oath, not: And the claimant takes an oath, as soon as the other party accepts the offer, and the discussion of the matter is over, or the one who made the offer left the court, he cannot retract his offer (Rambam *Sefer Shofetim, Hilkhot Sanhedrin* 7:3; *Shulḥan Arukh, Ḥoshen Mishpat* 22:3).

My father is trusted…your father…three cattle herders – נֶאֱמָן עָלַי אַבָּא...אָבִיךָ...שְׁלֹשָׁה רוֹעֵי בָקָר: In a case where the litigants accepted a person to serve as their judge who is related to one of them, or who is entirely disqualified from serving as a judge (*Sma*), if they performed an act of acquisition to confirm the agreement, neither side can retract his acceptance, even if they stipulated that he would have the authority of three judges. If they did not perform an act of acquisition, they can retract their acceptance until the verdict is issued. Once the verdict is issued, the liable party cannot retract his acceptance unless the judge was clearly mistaken in his verdict (see *Sanhedrin* 24b). The Rema, citing *Tosafot*, rules that if the local rabbinical authorities are the judges, one cannot appeal their verdict even if they were mistaken, as the norm is to accept their decisions in any event (Rambam *Sefer Shofetim, Hilkhot Sanhedrin* 7:2; *Shulḥan Arukh, Ḥoshen Mishpat* 22:1, and in the comment of Rema).

They do not collect – אֵין גּוֹבִין: Canaanite slaves have the legal status of movable property with regard to payment of debts. Therefore, in principle, orphans who inherited slaves from their father are not compelled to pay their father's debts by giving the slaves to the creditors, although it is a mitzva for them to do so. The *ge'onim* instituted that creditors collect movable property from the debtor's orphans just as they collect land (Rambam *Sefer Mishpatim, Hilkhot Malve VeLoveh* 11:8, 11 and *Sefer Kinyan, Hilkhot Zekhiya UMattana* 11:13; *Shulḥan Arukh, Ḥoshen Mishpat* 107:1, 248:10).

NOTES

And the claimant takes an oath – וְנִשְׁבַּע: According to the printed version of the text, which is based on the version of Rabbeinu Ḥananel and Rabbeinu Tam, only after the claimant takes an oath can the other no longer retract his offer. According to an alternative version of the text, perhaps that of the Rif and Rashi, the Gemara states: The claimant takes an oath, without the conjunction: And. Several commentaries maintain that according to this version, as soon as the claimant accepts the offer, it takes effect, even if he did not yet take an oath. The Ri Migash claims that this inference is incorrect.

That the dispute is even in a case where the litigant said, I will give you – דִּבְאֶתֵּן לָךְ מַחֲלוֹקֶת: The novel element of this ruling is that although in principle one who commits to give an item to another person can retract his commitment until an act of acquisition is performed, in this case the Rabbis hold that even the one who possesses the property under dispute cannot retract his offer. This is inferred from the case taught by Rabbi Abba, where it is the one in possession who offers the claimant the opportunity to take the property after the latter takes an oath.

They do not collect – אֵין גּוֹבִין: The commentaries explain that although Canaanite slaves are categorized as land with regard to several matters, only property that the creditor assumes will always be accessible is liened to debts, i.e., land, as the debtor cannot hide it. This is in contrast to slaves, who, like movable items, can be hidden from the creditor. Therefore, they are not liened to the debt and can be collected only from the debtor himself, not from his heirs or from others who purchased them from the debtor.

שְׁלַח לֵיהּ רַבִּי אַבָּא לְרַב יוֹסֵף בַּר חָמָא, הֲלָכָה: שְׁלִישִׁי בְּשֵׁנִי – כָּשֵׁר. רָבָא אָמַר: אַף בְּרִאשׁוֹן.

§ **Rabbi Abba** also **sent** a ruling **to Rav Yosef bar Ḥama** that with regard to people with a common ancestor, the ***halakha*** is that the testimony of members of the **third** generation **with regard to** members of the **second**[HN] generation whose closest familial connection is through that ancestor is **valid.** For example, one can testify about his first cousin once removed, and is not disqualified as a relative. **Rava says: Even** the testimony of members of the third generation **with regard to** members of the **first** generation is valid; e.g., one can testify about his great-uncle.

מָר בַּר רַב אַשִׁי אַכְשַׁר בְּאַבָּא דְּאַבָּא. וְלֵית הִלְכְתָא כְּמָר בַּר רַב אַשִׁי.

Mar bar Rav Ashi deemed one's testimony **with regard to** his **father's father valid,** as he considered it a case of testimony of a member of the third generation with regard to a member of the first generation, which Rava deemed valid. **But the *halakha* is not in accordance with** the opinion of **Mar bar Rav Ashi.**[N]

שְׁלַח לֵיהּ רַבִּי אַבָּא לְרַב יוֹסֵף בַּר חָמָא: הָיָה יוֹדֵעַ לוֹ בְּעֵדוּת קַרְקַע עַד שֶׁלֹּא נִסְתַּמֵּא, וְנִסְתַּמֵּא – פָּסוּל.

§ **Rabbi Abba** also **sent** a ruling **to Rav Yosef bar Ḥama** concerning testimony: If one **knew** information that could serve as **testimony about** the boundary of another's **land before he became blind, and** then he **became blind,** he is **disqualified** from bearing witness in a dispute as to the boundaries of that person's properties.

וּשְׁמוּאֵל אֲמַר: כָּשֵׁר, אֶפְשָׁר דִּמְכַוֵּין מִצְרָנֵהָא, אֲבָל גְּלִימָא – לָא. וְרַב שֵׁשֶׁת אֲמַר: אֲפִילּוּ גְּלִימָא, אֶפְשָׁר דִּמְכַוֵּין מִדַּת אׇרְכּוֹ וּמִדַּת רׇחְבּוֹ, אֲבָל נַסְכָא – לָא. וְרַב פַּפָּא אֲמַר: אֲפִילּוּ נַסְכָא, אֶפְשָׁר דִּמְכַוֵּין מִדַּת מִשְׁקְלוֹתָיו.

And Shmuel said: He is fit to bear witness, as it is **possible** for him **to determine the boundaries** of the fields despite his blindness. **But** he is **not** fit to identify a movable item, e.g., **a cloak,** as he cannot see it. **And Rav Sheshet said:** He can identify **even a cloak,** as it is **possible** for him **to determine its length and its width. But** he is **not** fit to identify **a piece of silver. And Rav Pappa said:** He can identify **even a piece of silver,** as it is **possible** for him **to determine its weight.**

מֵיתִיבִי: הָיָה יוֹדֵעַ לוֹ בְּעֵדוּת עַד שֶׁלֹּא נַעֲשָׂה חֲתָנוֹ וְנַעֲשָׂה חֲתָנוֹ, פִּיקֵּחַ וְנִתְחָרֵשׁ, פִּיתֵּחַ וְנִסְתַּמֵּא, שָׁפוּי וְנִשְׁתַּטָּה – פָּסוּל;

The Gemara **raises an objection** from a *baraita* (*Tosefta, Sanhedrin* 3:5): If one **knew** information that could serve as **testimony about** another **before he became his son-in-law, and** then **he became his son-in-law,** thereby becoming a relative who is disqualified from bearing witness concerning him; or if he was **able to hear** at the time he witnessed an incident **and** then **he became deaf;** or if he was **able to see** at the time he witnessed an incident **and** then **became blind;** or if he was halakhically **competent and** then **became insane,** in all these cases, he is **disqualified** from bearing witness.

אֲבָל הָיָה יוֹדֵעַ לוֹ בְּעֵדוּת עַד שֶׁלֹּא נַעֲשָׂה חֲתָנוֹ וְנַעֲשָׂה חֲתָנוֹ וּמֵתָה בִּתּוֹ, פִּיקֵּחַ וְנִתְחָרֵשׁ וְחָזַר וְנִתְפַּקַּח, פִּיתֵּחַ וְנִסְתַּמֵּא וְחָזַר וְנִתְפַּתַּח, שָׁפוּי וְנִשְׁתַּטָּה וְחָזַר וְנִשְׁתַּפָּה – כָּשֵׁר;

The *baraita* continues: **But if he knew** information **about him** that could serve as **testimony before he became his son-in-law, and** then **he became his son-in-law, and** then **his daughter died,** so that they are no longer related; or if he was **able to hear, and** then **became deaf, and** then **again became able to hear;** or if he was **able to see, and** then **became blind, and** then **again became able to see;** or if he was halakhically **competent, and** then **became insane, and** then **again became** halakhically **competent,** in all these cases, he is **fit** to bear witness.

זֶה הַכְּלָל: כׇּל שֶׁתְּחִלָּתוֹ אוֹ סוֹפוֹ בְּפַסְלוּת – פָּסוּל, תְּחִלָּתוֹ וְסוֹפוֹ בְּכַשְׁרוּת – כָּשֵׁר;

The *baraita* concludes: **This is the principle: Anyone whose initial** state **or his ultimate** state,[N] i.e., his state at the time of the incident or at the time of his testimony in court, **is** one of **disqualification**[H] for bearing witness is **disqualified** from bearing witness. But anyone **whose initial** state **and his ultimate** state **is** one of **fitness** to bear witness is **fit** to bear witness, even if he was disqualified in the interim. This *baraita* clearly states that one who is blind is disqualified from bearing witness.

HALAKHA

The third generation with regard to the second, etc. – 'שְׁלִישִׁי בְּשֵׁנִי וכו: Those who are disqualified from bearing witness with regard to each other due to their familial relationship are as follows: A father and son, brothers or half-brothers, all of whom are considered members of the first generation; and their respective sons, who are considered members of the second generation. Testimony of members of the third generation with regard to members of the second generation is valid, in accordance with the statement of Rabbi Abba. A grandfather and grandson cannot testify concerning each other; they are equivalent to members of the first and second generations, since the *halakha* is not in accordance with the opinion of Mar bar Rav Ashi.

According to the Rif and the Rambam, testimony of a member of the third generation with regard to a member of the first generation or vice versa, e.g., a great-grandfather and great-grandson, is valid, in accordance with the opinion of Rava. The Rema rules in accordance with the opinion of Rabbeinu Tam and other authorities that this testimony is invalid; in their opinion, Rabbi Abba disagrees with Rava's ruling. The Rema cites the opinion of *Halakhot Gedolot* that this testimony is disqualified by rabbinic law (Rambam *Sefer Shofetim, Hilkhot Edut* 13:4–5; *Shulḥan Arukh, Ḥoshen Mishpat* 33:2).

NOTES

The third generation with regard to the second – שְׁלִישִׁי בְּשֵׁנִי: With regard to the *halakhot* of testimony, familial relationship is defined based on distance from a common ancestor (Rashbam). Brothers are defined as members of the first generation, first cousins are members of the second generation, and second cousins are members of the third generation.

But the *halakha* is not in accordance with Mar bar Rav Ashi – וְלֵית הִלְכְתָא כְּמָר בַּר רַב אַשִׁי: The Rashbam explains that all of one's ancestors and descendants are disqualified from bearing witness with regard to him. The other early commentaries disagree with this ruling. The Rif explains that the relationship between a father and son is equivalent to that of two members of the first generation, i.e., brothers. Therefore, the relationship between a grandfather and grandson is equivalent to that of a member of the first generation and a member of the second generation, who are disqualified from bearing witness concerning each other. The Ramah adds that the proximity of a familial relationship is defined not based on which generation one belongs to, but on the directness of the relationship. Therefore, the relationship between a father and son is comparable to the relationship between brothers.

Whose initial state or his ultimate state, etc. – 'שֶׁתְּחִלָּתוֹ אוֹ סוֹפוֹ וכו: This *halakha* is derived from the verse: "He being a witness, whether he has seen or known, if he does not utter it, then he shall bear his iniquity" (Leviticus 5:1), which is expounded to teach that the witness must be fit to provide testimony both at the time he sees the incident and at the time he utters the testimony (*Arakhin* 18a).

HALAKHA

Anyone whose initial or his ultimate state is one of disqualification, etc. – 'כׇּל שֶׁתְּחִלָּתוֹ אוֹ סוֹפוֹ בְּפַסְלוּת וכו: One cannot testify about what he witnessed when he was deaf, blind, or insane, even if at the time of his testimony he is able to hear and see and is halakhically competent. Similarly, if he was fit to testify at the time that he witnessed the incident, but by the time of the testimony he became disqualified, he cannot provide testimony, in accordance with the ruling that Rabbi Abba sent to Rav Yosef bar Ḥama. If he was fit to testify both at the time he witnessed the incident and at the time of his testimony, even if in the interim there was a period during which he was blind, deaf, or insane, his testimony is valid.

Similarly, if at the time he witnessed the incident the litigants were unrelated to him, but by the time of his testimony one of them became related to him, e.g., he became his son-in-law, or conversely, if at the time he witnessed the incident they were related, and by the time he testified they were no longer related, e.g., his daughter died and the litigant was no longer his son-in-law, in both cases, he is disqualified from providing testimony concerning him. If both at the time he witnessed the incident and at the time of the testimony they were unrelated, even if in the interim he was his son-in-law for a certain period of time, he is fit to provide testimony, as he was fit both initially and ultimately (Rambam *Sefer Shofetim, Hilkhot Edut* 14:2; *Shulḥan Arukh, Ḥoshen Mishpat* 33:13, 15, and see *Beur HaGra* there).

תְּיוּבְתָּא דְּכוּלְּהוּ, תְּיוּבְתָּא.

The Gemara concludes: **The refutation** of the opinions **of all** the *amora'im* who held that a person who became blind after witnessing a matter can, in certain cases, testify about it, is indeed **a conclusive refutation.**[B]

שְׁלַח רַבִּי אַבָּא לְרַב יוֹסֵף בַּר חָמָא: הָאוֹמֵר עַל תִּינוֹק בֵּין הַבָּנִים – נֶאֱמָן; וְרַבִּי יוֹחָנָן אָמַר: אֵינוֹ נֶאֱמָן.

§ **Rabbi Abba sent** another ruling **to Rav Yosef bar Ḥama: One who says** something **concerning** one **child among** his **sons is deemed credible, and Rabbi Yoḥanan says** that **he is not deemed credible.**

מַאי קָאָמַר? אָמַר אַבַּיֵי, הָכִי קָאָמַר: הָאוֹמֵר עַל תִּינוֹק בֵּין הַבָּנִים "יִירַשׁ כָּל נְכָסַי" – נֶאֱמָן, כְּרַבִּי יוֹחָנָן בֶּן בְּרוֹקָה; וְרַבִּי יוֹחָנָן אָמַר: אֵינוֹ נֶאֱמָן, כְּרַבָּנַן.

The Gemara asks: **What is** Rabbi Abba **saying? Abaye said** that **this** is what Rabbi Abba **is saying: One who says concerning** one **child among** his **sons: He shall inherit all my property,** is **deemed credible, in accordance with** the opinion of **Rabbi Yoḥanan ben Beroka,** who holds that one can bequeath all his property to one of his heirs (130a). **And Rabbi Yoḥanan says** that **he is not deemed credible, in accordance with** the opinion of **the Rabbis,** who disagree with Rabbi Yoḥanan ben Beroka.

מַתְקִיף לַהּ רָבָא: הַאי נֶאֱמָן וְאֵינוֹ נֶאֱמָן, יִירַשׁ וְלֹא יִירַשׁ מִבְּעֵי לֵיהּ!

Rava objects to this explanation: According to Abaye's explanation, **this** wording: Is **deemed credible, and: He is not deemed credible,** is not precise; **he should have** employed the terms: **Shall inherit, and: Shall not inherit,** as the issue is the ability of the father to specify who will inherit from him, not his credibility.

אֶלָּא אָמַר רָבָא, הָכִי קָאָמַר: הָאוֹמֵר עַל תִּינוֹק בֵּין הַבָּנִים "בְּכוֹר הוּא" – נֶאֱמָן, כְּרַבִּי יְהוּדָה; וְרַבִּי יוֹחָנָן אָמַר: אֵינוֹ נֶאֱמָן, כְּרַבָּנַן.

Rather, Rava said that **this** is what Rabbi Abba **is saying: One who says about** one **child among** his **sons** that **he is** his **firstborn** is **deemed credible, in accordance with** the opinion of **Rabbi Yehuda** (127b); **and Rabbi Yoḥanan says** that **he is not deemed credible, in accordance with** the opinion of **the Rabbis,** who disagree with Rabbi Yehuda.

שְׁלַח לֵיהּ רַבִּי אַבָּא לְרַב יוֹסֵף בַּר חָמָא: הָאוֹמֵר "תִּטּוֹל אִשְׁתִּי כְּאֶחָד מִן הַבָּנִים" – נוֹטֶלֶת כְּאֶחָד מִן הַבָּנִים. אָמַר רָבָא: וּבִנְכָסִים שֶׁל עַכְשָׁיו, וּבְבָנִים הַבָּאִין לְאַחַר מִכָּאן.

§ **Rabbi Abba sent** another ruling **to Rav Yosef bar Ḥama:** In a case of **one who says: My wife will take** a portion of my estate **like one of the sons,**[H] **she takes** a portion **like one of the sons,** as it is considered a gift. **Rava says: And** this ruling is only **with regard to** the husband's **current property,**[HN] which he can give her as a gift. The husband cannot give her a portion of his future property. **And** furthermore, the calculation of her portion must take into account not only the number of sons the husband has at the time of his statement, but also **the sons who come,** i.e., who will be born, **afterward.**

שְׁלַח לֵיהּ רַבִּי אַבָּא לְרַב יוֹסֵף בַּר חָמָא: הַמּוֹצִיא שְׁטַר חוֹב עַל חֲבֵירוֹ, מַלְוֶה אוֹמֵר "לֹא נִפְרַעְתִּי כְּלוּם", וְלֹוֶה אוֹמֵר "פָּרַעְתִּי מֶחֱצָה", וְהָעֵדִים מְעִידִין שֶׁפָּרַע כּוּלּוֹ – הֲרֵי זֶה נִשְׁבָּע וְגוֹבֶה מֶחֱצָה מִנְּכָסִים בְּנֵי חוֹרִין, אֲבָל מִמְּשׁוּעְבָּדִין לָא, דְּאָמְרִי: אֲנַן אַעֵדִים סָמְכִינַן.

§ **Rabbi Abba sent** another ruling **to Rav Yosef bar Ḥama:** In the case of **one who produces a promissory note against another,** and **the creditor says: I was not repaid anything and the debtor says: I repaid half**[H] the debt, **and the witnesses testify that** the debtor **repaid the entire** debt, then **this** debtor **takes an oath** that he repaid half, as is the *halakha* with regard to one who admits to a part of a claim, and he is exempt from paying that half. **And** the creditor **collects** the second **half**[N] **from unsold property;**[B] **but not from liened** property that was sold after the loan, as the buyers can **say: We rely on the witnesses** that the debt was repaid in its entirety.

NOTES

With regard to the husband's current property – בִּנְכָסִים שֶׁל עַכְשָׁיו: The Rashbam explains that even according to the opinion of Rabbi Meir, that one can transfer ownership of an item that has not yet come into the world, one can do so only if he specifies explicitly that he is doing so. Rabbeinu Yona adds that she receives more of the husband's property at the time of his instruction in exchange for the property he acquired afterward, which she cannot receive. The Meiri writes that she receives a portion of the appreciation of the property after the instruction.

Takes an oath and collects half – נִשְׁבָּע וְגוֹבֶה מֶחֱצָה: Rabbeinu Gershom Meor HaGola explains that the creditor takes an oath that he is owed at least half the debt, and he collects half of the debt; one who claims that another owes him money and has a promissory note to that effect is liable to take an oath before collecting the debt in the event that the defendant demands that he do so. The other early commentaries follow the explanation of the Rashbam that the debtor takes an oath that he repaid half the debt, due to his admission to part of the claim, and the creditor collects the rest.

BACKGROUND

Conclusive refutation [*teyuvta*] – תְּיוּבְתָּא: An amoraic statement can be refuted on the basis of a tannaitic source that contradicts the statement of the *amora*. The word *teyuvta* is one of several terms based on the Aramaic root *tav, vav, beit*. When one *amora* raises an objection to the opinion of another *amora* by citing a tannaitic source, the expression used is *eitivei*, an objection, e.g., X raised an objection to the statement of Y. When an *amora* raises an objection against an unattributed amoraic opinion by citing a tannaitic source, the expression employed is *meitiv*, meaning: He raises an objection. In the case cited here, where the Gemara itself raises the objection by citing a tannaitic source, the expression used is *meitivei*, meaning: An objection is raised. When there is no response to the objection, it is deemed a conclusive refutation and the term *teyuvta* is used, and often it is repeated both before and after the name of the *amora*, effectively disqualifying his opinion.

Unsold property – נְכָסִים בְּנֵי חוֹרִין: Unsold property stands in contrast to sold, liened property. If a debtor sells his previously liened property, his creditor may seize that property from the buyer. The creditor may not seize property from the current owner if the debtor possesses non-liened property from which the creditor can collect the debt, even if that land is inferior in quality to the liened property.

HALAKHA

One who says, my wife will take like one of the sons – הָאוֹמֵר תִּטּוֹל אִשְׁתִּי כְּאֶחָד מִן הַבָּנִים: If a man on his deathbed instructed that his wife or his daughter or son-in-law (Rema, citing Mordekhai) will receive a portion of the inheritance like one of his sons, she receives a portion equal to that of one of the sons. In the case of the wife, this is in addition to payment of her marriage contract. This is the *halakha* even if he had more sons after he issued this instruction, or if some of them died and he had fewer sons at the time of his death (see Rashbam), although some authorities question the latter ruling (Ra'avad). If all the sons died, she receives a portion equivalent to what one of them would have received at the time of the instruction, and the rest of the property goes to the heirs. The Rema, citing the Rashbam, rules that if a healthy man gives this instruction, it takes effect only if an act of acquisition is performed (Rambam *Sefer Kinyan, Hilkhot Zekhiya UMattana* 11:10; *Shulḥan Arukh, Even HaEzer* 108:1–3).

With regard to the husband's current property – בִּנְכָסִים שֶׁל עַכְשָׁיו: If a man on his deathbed instructs that his wife will receive a portion of the inheritance like one of his sons, she receives only a portion of the property that her husband had at the time of his instruction. She does not receive a portion of any property he acquired after his instruction, as one cannot transfer ownership of an item that has not yet come into his possession. The Rema, citing the *Beit Yosef*, notes that if it is uncertain whether certain items were in the husband's possession at the time of his instruction, the burden of proof rests upon the wife, as she is the claimant (*Shulḥan Arukh, Even HaEzer* 108:1).

The creditor says I was not repaid anything, and the debtor says I repaid half – מַלְוֶה אוֹמֵר לֹא נִפְרַעְתִּי כְּלוּם וְלֹוֶה אוֹמֵר פָּרַעְתִּי מֶחֱצָה: If a creditor claims that the debtor did not repay any of the debt, and he produces a ratified promissory note, and the debtor claims that he repaid half, and afterward (*Sma*; see *Shakh*) witnesses testify that the entire debt was repaid, in this case, the debtor takes an oath of one who admits to part of a claim and pays the half he admits he owes. The *Sma* rules that this debt is collected only from unsold property (Rambam *Sefer Mishpatim, Hilkhot Malve VeLoveh* 14:4; *Shulḥan Arukh, Ḥoshen Mishpat* 82:13).

וַאֲפִילּוּ לְרַבִּי עֲקִיבָא דְּאָמַר: מֵשִׁיב אֲבֵדָה הָוֵי – הָנֵי מִילֵּי הֵיכָא דְּלֵיכָּא עֵדִים, אֲבָל הֵיכָא דְּאִיכָּא עֵדִים – אִירְתוּתֵי אִירְתַת.

The Gemara compares this *halakha* to the case of a promissory note that states that the debtor owes the creditor: *Sela* coins, without stating how many. The creditor claims that he lent the debtor five *sela* and the debtor claims that he borrowed only three. Rabbi Akiva holds that since the wording of the promissory note indicates a minimum debt of two *sela*, and the creditor could not have collected the third *sela* without the debtor's admission, the latter's admission to a part of the claim cannot render him liable to take an oath. The Gemara states: **And even according to Rabbi Akiva, who says that** the debtor is not liable to take an oath, as with regard to the third *sela* his legal status **is** similar to that of **one who returns a lost item, this statement** applies only in a case **where there are no witnesses** to the loan. **But where there are witnesses,**[N] as is the case in Rabbi Abba's ruling, the debtor **fears**[N] denying the entire debt. Therefore he is liable to take an oath that he repaid half, as one who admits to a part of the claim.

מַתְקִיף לַהּ מָר בַּר רַב אַשִׁי: אַדְּרַבָּה, אֲפִילּוּ לְרַבִּי שִׁמְעוֹן בֶּן אֶלְעָזָר דְּאָמַר: מוֹדֶה מִקְצָת הַטַּעֲנָה הָוֵי – הָנֵי מִילֵּי הֵיכָא דְּלֵיכָּא עֵדִים דְּקָא מְסַיְּיעִי לֵיהּ, אֲבָל הֵיכָא דְּאִיכָּא עֵדִים דְּקָא מְסַיְּיעִי לֵיהּ – וַדַּאי מֵשִׁיב אֲבֵדָה הָוֵי.

Mar bar Rav Ashi objects to this: On the contrary; even according to Rabbi Shimon ben Elazar, who disagrees with Rabbi Akiva and **says** that the debtor **is considered** one who **admits to a part of the claim, this statement** applies only in a case **where there are no witnesses who support him. But** here in the case of Rabbi Abba, **where there are witnesses who support him,** testifying that he repaid the entire debt, his legal status **is certainly** that of **one who returns a lost item,** and he does not need to take an oath that he repaid half.

דָּרַשׁ מָר זוּטְרָא מִשְּׁמֵיהּ דְּרַב שִׁימִי בַּר אַשִׁי: הִלְכְתָא בְּכׇל הָנֵי שְׁמַעְתָּתָא כִּדְשָׁלַח לֵיהּ רַבִּי אַבָּא לְרַב יוֹסֵף בַּר חָמָא. אֲמַר לֵיהּ רָבִינָא לְרַב אַשִׁי: דְּרַב נַחְמָן מַאי? אֲמַר לֵיהּ: ״אֵין גּוֹבִין״ מַתְנִינַן לַהּ, וְכֵן אָמַר רַב נַחְמָן.

§ **Mar Zutra taught in the name of Rav Shimi bar Ashi: The** ***halakha*** **in all these** ***halakhot*** **is as Rabbi Abba sent to Rav Yosef bar Ḥama. Ravina said to Rav Ashi: What** about the statement with **which Rav Naḥman** disagreed, i.e., that a debt can be collected by taking the slaves the debtor left his heirs? Is the *halakha* in accordance with this ruling of Rabbi Abba as well, despite the principle that in monetary matters the *halakha* is in accordance with Rav Naḥman's opinion? Rav Ashi **said to him: We teach** a different tradition, that Rabbi Abba's statement rules that a creditor **does not collect** the debt from the slaves the debtor left his heirs, **and that Rav Naḥman said the same.**

וְאֶלָּא הִלְכְתָא לְאַפּוּקֵי מַאי?

The Gemara asks: **But** then **what** possibility **does** Mar Zutra **exclude** in ruling that **the** ***halakha*** is in accordance with Rabbi Abba's statement?

Perek **VIII**
Daf **129** Amud **a**

אִי לְאַפּוּקֵי מִדְּרָבָא – מוֹסִיף הוּא, אִי דְּמָר בַּר רַב אַשִׁי – לֵית הִלְכְתָא כְּמָר בַּר רַב אַשִׁי, אִי לְאַפּוּקֵי מִדִּשְׁמוּאֵל וְרַב שֵׁשֶׁת וְרַב פַּפָּא – הָא אִיתּוֹתְבוּ!

If his statement is said **to exclude** the statement **of Rava** that the testimony of members of the third generation concerning members of the first generation is valid, this is difficult, as Rava's statement is not in conflict with Rabbi Abba's statement that the testimony of members of the third generation with regard to members of the second generation is valid; **it merely adds** to it.[N] **If** it is said to exclude the opinion **of Mar bar Rav Ashi** that a grandfather can testify concerning his grandchild, this is also difficult, as it has already been established that **the** ***halakha*** **is not in accordance with** the opinion of **Mar bar Rav Ashi. If** it is said **to exclude** the rulings **of Shmuel and Rav Sheshet and Rav Pappa,** that a person who became blind can testify about what he saw beforehand, this too is difficult, as their rulings **were refuted** based on a *baraita*.

NOTES

But where there are witnesses – אֲבָל הֵיכָא דְּאִיכָּא עֵדִים: According to most early commentaries, the correct version of the text is: Where there is no promissory note, and: But where there is a promissory note (Rif; Ri Migash; Ramah). They explain that as opposed to the case where the promissory note merely states: *Sela* coins, indicating a debt of a minimum of only two *sela*, here the promissory note details the entire amount claimed by the creditor. Therefore the debtor's legal status is not similar to that of one who returns a lost item.

Fears – אִירְתוּתֵי אִירְתַת: The assumption is that the debtor knew that there were witnesses but did not know that they would testify that he repaid the debt. Therefore he was afraid to deny the entire debt, in case the witnesses would testify that he repaid nothing.

NOTES

It merely adds to it – מוֹסִיף הוּא: The Rashbam explains that Rabbi Abba does not necessarily disagree with Rava's opinion with regard to testimony between members of the third generation and the first generation; the reason he mentioned only that the testimony between members of the third generation and the second generation is valid is simply that that was the case he was asked about. The Ramah adds that since there is no direct contradiction between their statements, the assumption is that they are not in conflict, due to the principle that disagreements should be limited whenever possible. The Ramban explains that the Gemara's assumption that Rabbi Abba does not disagree with Rava's opinion is due to the fact that Rava's statement is an established *halakha*.

By contrast, Rabbeinu Tam maintains that Rabbi Abba would not agree with the addition of Rava; and had Mar Zutra's intention been that the *halakha* is not in accordance with Rava's opinion, he would have said explicitly that the *halakha* is not in accordance with Rava's opinion, as Rava does not disagree with Rabbi Abba's opinion directly, but rather he adds to it.

אֶלָּא, לְאַפּוּקֵי מִדְּרַבִּי יוֹחָנָן וּמֵאַתְקַפְתָּא דְּמָר בַּר רַב אַשִׁי.

The Gemara explains: **Rather,** Mar Zutra's statement is said **to exclude** the statement **of Rabbi Yoḥanan** that one cannot testify that a specific one of his sons is his firstborn, **and** to exclude **the strong objection of Mar bar Rav Ashi** to the statement of Rabbi Abba with regard to a case where a debtor admitted to part of a claim and witnesses testified that he repaid the entire debt. Despite Mar bar Rav Ashi's objection, the *halakha* is that the debtor is not liable to take an oath.

״הַמְחַלֵּק נְכָסָיו עַל פִּיו, רִיבָּה לְאֶחָד וּמִיעֵט לְאֶחָד״ כו׳. הֵיכִי דָּמֵי מַתָּנָה בַּתְּחִלָּה, הֵיכִי דָּמֵי בְּאֶמְצַע, הֵיכִי דָּמֵי בַּסּוֹף?

§ The mishna teaches: With regard to **one** on his deathbed **who apportions his property orally,** granting it to his sons as a gift, and he **increased** the portion given **to one** of his sons **and reduced** the portion given **to one** other son, or equated the portion of the firstborn to the portions of the other sons, his statement stands. But if he said that they will receive the property not as a gift but as an inheritance, he has said nothing. If he wrote in his will, whether at the beginning, or in the middle, or at the end, that he is granting them the property as a gift, his statement stands. The Gemara asks: **What are the circumstances** where it is phrased as **a gift at the beginning? What are the circumstances** where it is phrased as a gift **in the middle? What are the circumstances** where it is phrased as a gift **at the end?**

כִּי אֲתָא רַב דִּימִי אָמַר רַבִּי יוֹחָנָן: ״תִּנָּתֵן שָׂדֶה פְּלוֹנִית לִפְלוֹנִי וְיִירָשֶׁהָ״ – זוֹ הִיא מַתָּנָה בַּתְּחִלָּה, ״וְיִירָשֶׁהָ וְתִנָּתֵן לוֹ״ – זוֹ הִיא מַתָּנָה בַּסּוֹף, ״יִירָשֶׁהָ וְתִנָּתֵן לוֹ וְיִירָשֶׁהָ״ – זוֹ הִיא מַתָּנָה בְּאֶמְצַע;

When **Rav Dimi came** from Eretz Yisrael to Babylonia, he said that **Rabbi Yoḥanan says** that where one on his deathbed instructed: **Such and such a field will be given to so-and-so and he will inherit it, this is** a case where it is phrased as **a gift at the beginning.** Where he instructed: **And he will inherit it and it will be given to him, this is** a case where it is phrased as **a gift at the end.**[H] Where he instructed: **He will inherit it and it will be given to him and he will inherit it, this is** a case where it is phrased as **a gift in the middle.**

וְדַוְקָא בְּאָדָם אֶחָד וְשָׂדֶה אַחַת, אֲבָל בְּאָדָם אֶחָד וּשְׁתֵּי שָׂדוֹת, שָׂדֶה אַחַת וּשְׁנֵי בְּנֵי אָדָם – לֹא.

And the *halakha* that his statement is valid pertains **specifically** to a case where the two terms, giving and inheritance, are employed **with regard to one person and one field. But** if they are employed **with regard to one person and two fields,** e.g., if he says: Reuven will inherit this field and will be given that field, or **one field and two people,** e.g., Reuven will inherit half of this field and Shimon will be given the other half, the part that was phrased as inheritance does **not** take effect.[N] Only the part that is phrased as a gift takes effect.

רַבִּי אֶלְעָזָר אוֹמֵר: אֲפִילּוּ אָדָם אֶחָד וּשְׁתֵּי שָׂדוֹת, שָׂדֶה אַחַת וּשְׁנֵי בְּנֵי אָדָם, אֲבָל בִּשְׁתֵּי שָׂדוֹת וּשְׁנֵי בְּנֵי אָדָם – לֹא.

Rabbi Elazar says: Even in a case where the two terms are employed with regard to **one person and two fields,** or **one field and two people,** his instruction takes effect, as both terms were employed with regard to the same person or the same field. **But with regard to two fields and two people,** it does **not** take effect, as the two instructions are not connected to one another.

כִּי אֲתָא רָבִין אֲמַר: ״תִּנָּתֵן שָׂדֶה פְּלוֹנִית לִפְלוֹנִי וְיִירַשׁ פְּלוֹנִי שָׂדֶה פְּלוֹנִית״ – רַבִּי יוֹחָנָן אוֹמֵר: קָנָה, רַבִּי אֶלְעָזָר אוֹמֵר: לֹא קָנָה.

When **Ravin came** from Eretz Yisrael to Babylonia, **he said** that if one on his deathbed said: **Such and such a field will be given to so-and-so, and so-and-so,** i.e., another person, **will inherit such and such a field,** i.e., another field, **Rabbi Yoḥanan says** that even the latter person, who was designated to inherit his field, has **acquired** it. **Rabbi Elazar says:** He has **not acquired** it.

אֲמַר לֵיהּ אַבָּיֵי לְרָבִין: אַנְחַתְּתְּ לָן חֲדָא וְאַתְקַפְתְּ לָן חֲדָא; בִּשְׁלָמָא דְּרַבִּי אֶלְעָזָר אַדְּרַבִּי אֶלְעָזָר לָא קַשְׁיָא: כָּאן בְּאָדָם אֶחָד וּשְׁתֵּי שָׂדוֹת, כָּאן בִּשְׁנֵי בְּנֵי אָדָם וּשְׁתֵּי שָׂדוֹת,

Abaye said to Ravin: You have lightened our burden with **one** statement that you cited, **but you have made it difficult for us** with the other **one. Granted,** the contradiction **between** this statement **of Rabbi Elazar** that you cited and the previously cited statement **of Rabbi Elazar is not difficult. There,** in the previously cited statement, Rabbi Elazar said that the directive takes effect **with regard to** a case of **one person and two fields,** and **here** he said that the directive does not take effect **with regard to** a case of **two people and two fields.**

HALAKHA

A gift at the beginning…at the end, etc. – מַתָּנָה בַּתְּחִלָּה...בַּסּוֹף וכו׳: In a case where one bequeaths his property in a manner that is contrary to the laws of inheritance, if the bequest is phrased as a gift in any part of the statement, whether at the beginning, in the middle, or at the end, it is valid, even if it is also phrased as an inheritance (see *Sma*). For example, if one says: This field will be given to so-and-so, my son, and he will inherit it; or: So-and-so, my son, will inherit this field and it will be given to him; or: He will inherit it, and it will be given to him, and he will inherit it, in all of these cases, the bequest is valid, as it includes the phrasing of a gift. This is the *halakha* even if he pauses between parts of his statement for more than the time required for speaking a short phrase (Rema, citing *Tur*). The Rema writes that if he says: So-and-so, my son, will inherit it, and adds: It will be given to him, without connecting the two parts of the statement with the word: And, the bequest is not valid (Rambam *Sefer Mishpatim*, *Hilkhot Naḥalot* 6:6; *Shulḥan Arukh*, *Ḥoshen Mishpat* 281:7).

NOTES

But with regard to one person and two fields…it does not take effect – אֲבָל בְּאָדָם אֶחָד וּשְׁתֵּי שָׂדוֹת...לֹא: The Rashbam and the Rid explain that the part that was phrased as an inheritance does not take effect, while the part that was phrased as a gift does. Rabbeinu Gershom Meor HaGola holds that the entire statement is ineffective.

אֶלָּא דְּרַבִּי יוֹחָנָן אַדְּרַבִּי יוֹחָנָן קַשְׁיָא!

But the apparent contradiction **between** one statement **of Rabbi Yoḥanan** and the other statement **of Rabbi Yoḥanan is difficult,** as Rav Dimi cited in Rabbi Yoḥanan's name that his directive takes effect only in a case of one person and one field, and according to your citation in the name of Rabbi Yoḥanan it takes effect even in a case of two people and two fields.

אֲמוֹרָאֵי נִינְהוּ וְאַלִּיבָּא דְּרַבִּי יוֹחָנָן.

Ravin answered him: Rav Dimi and I **are** ***amora'im*****, and** we each have a different tradition **with regard to** the opinion **of Rabbi Yoḥanan.**

וְרֵישׁ לָקִישׁ אָמַר: לֹא קָנָה עַד שֶׁיֹּאמַר "פְּלוֹנִי וּפְלוֹנִי יִירְשׁוּ שָׂדֶה פְּלוֹנִית וּפְלוֹנִית שֶׁנְּתַתִּים לָהֶם בְּמַתָּנָה וְיִירָשׁוּם".

Ravin continued: **And Reish Lakish says** that one has **not acquired** the field in the case of two people and two fields **unless** the giver **says: So-and-so and so-and-so will inherit such and such a field and such and such** a field **that I have given them as a gift,**[N] **and they will inherit it.**

בִּפְלוּגְתָּא; אָמַר רַב הַמְנוּנָא: לֹא שָׁנוּ אֶלָּא אָדָם אֶחָד וְשָׂדֶה אַחַת, אֲבָל אָדָם אֶחָד וּשְׁתֵּי שָׂדוֹת, שָׂדֶה אַחַת וּשְׁנֵי בְּנֵי אָדָם – לֹא; וְרַב נַחְמָן אָמַר: אֲפִילּוּ אָדָם אֶחָד וּשְׁתֵּי שָׂדוֹת, שָׂדֶה אַחַת וּשְׁנֵי בְּנֵי אָדָם, אֲבָל שְׁתֵּי שָׂדוֹת וּשְׁנֵי בְּנֵי אָדָם – לֹא; וְרַב שֵׁשֶׁת אָמַר: אֲפִילּוּ שְׁתֵּי שָׂדוֹת וּשְׁנֵי בְּנֵי אָדָם.

This dispute between the *amora'im* of Eretz Yisrael is also the subject **of a dispute**[N] between the *amora'im* of Babylonia. **Rav Hamnuna says:** The mishna **taught** that when both giving and inheritance are mentioned one can increase the portion of one of his sons **only** with regard to a case of **one person and one field, but** with regard to **one person and two fields,** or **one field and two people,** it is **not** effective. **And Rav Naḥman says:** Even in a case of **one person and two fields,** or **one field and two people,** it is effective, **but** in a case of **two fields and two people,** it is **not. And Rav Sheshet says:** Even in a case of **two fields and two people,** it is effective.

אָמַר רַב שֵׁשֶׁת: מְנָא אָמִינָא לָהּ? דְּתַנְיָא: הָאוֹמֵר "תְּנוּ שֶׁקֶל לְבָנַי בְּשַׁבָּת", וּרְאוּיִן לִיתֵּן סֶלַע – נוֹתֵן לָהֶן סֶלַע; וְאִם אָמַר "אַל תִּתְּנוּ לָהֶן אֶלָּא שֶׁקֶל" – אֵין נוֹתְנִין לָהֶן אֶלָּא שֶׁקֶל; וְאִם אָמַר "אִם מֵתוּ

Rav Sheshet said: From where do I say this? As it is taught in a *baraita* (*Tosefta, Ketubot* 6:10): If a person on his deathbed, or **one who** is going overseas, **says** to his children's steward: **Give a shekel to my children** every **week**[H] for their needs, **and** this is a situation where, based on their needs, **they are fit** for the steward **to give them a** ***sela*****,** i.e., double the amount, **he gives them a** ***sela*****.** When the father mentioned a shekel, he presumably meant that the children should be given a sum in accordance with their actual requirements, not that specific amount. **But if** he **said: Give them only a shekel,** the steward **gives them only a shekel,** and no more. **And if he said:** If my children **die,**

NOTES

That I have given them as a gift – שֶׁנְּתַתִּים לָהֶם בְּמַתָּנָה: The Rashbam explains that the reason the statement is valid in this case, as opposed to a regular case of two people and two fields, is that giving was mentioned between the two mentions of inheritance. Since it was mentioned neither at the beginning nor at the end, it cannot be attributed to the first person mentioned or to the last. Therefore it is interpreted as referring to both.

Rabbeinu Gershom Meor HaGola explains that the element that validates this statement is the fact that the phrase: That I have given them, is stated in the past tense, meaning: That I have given them as a gift before I stated that I am bequeathing it to them as an inheritance.

The Ri Migash explains that the advantage of this phrase is that it is stated in the plural; therefore, it presumably refers to both recipients. As opposed to the Rashbam and Rabbeinu Gershom Meor HaGola, who hold that Reish Lakish's qualification pertains only to the case of two people and two fields, the Ri Migash maintains that even in a case of two people and one field, or one person and two fields, Reish Lakish holds that giving must be mentioned in the plural by saying: I have given them. He explains that the reason Reish Lakish refers specifically to a case of two people and two fields is that this is the case where it makes the most sense for the giving to be mentioned in the middle of the statement, which explains the mention of this particular case in the mishna.

The subject of a dispute – בִּפְלוּגְתָּא: The Rashbam explains that Rav Hamnuna's opinion is in accordance with that of Rabbi Yoḥanan as cited by Rav Dimi, Rav Naḥman's opinion is in accordance with that of Rabbi Elazar, and Rav Sheshet's opinion is in accordance with that of Rabbi Yoḥanan as cited by Ravin. Rabbeinu Gershom Meor HaGola maintains that the opinion of each Babylonian *amora* is in accordance with one of the opinions quoted by Ravin; Rav Sheshet's opinion is in accordance with that of Reish Lakish.

HALAKHA

Give a shekel to my children every week, etc. – תְּנוּ שֶׁקֶל לְבָנַי בְּשַׁבָּת וכו׳: In a case where a person on his deathbed instructs that his children should each receive a shekel every week, if their needs cost more than a shekel, they receive the amount that they need. This ruling follows the conclusion of the Gemara in tractate *Ketubot* (70a), as opposed to the statement of the *baraita* quoted here (Rambam *Sefer Kinyan, Hilkhot Zekhiya UMattana* 11:23; *Shulḥan Arukh, Ḥoshen Mishpat* 253:17).

Perek **VIII**
Daf **129** Amud **b**

יִירְשׁוּ אֲחֵרִים תַּחְתֵּיהֶם", בֵּין שֶׁאָמַר "תְּנוּ" בֵּין שֶׁאָמַר "אַל תִּתְּנוּ" – אֵין נוֹתְנִין לָהֶן אֶלָּא שֶׁקֶל;

others will inherit their portion **in their stead,**[H] then regardless of **whether he said: Give them** a shekel, or **whether he said: Do not give** them more than a shekel, the court **gives** his children **only a shekel** per week, so as not to reduce the share of the others, as their father clearly stated that he wishes to give his children only a specific stipend, and that he intends to leave the bulk of his property to others.

וְהָא הָכָא דִּכְשְׁתֵּי שָׂדוֹת וְכִשְׁנֵי בְּנֵי אָדָם דָּמֵי, וְקָתָנֵי דְּקָנֵי!

Rav Sheshet concludes: **And isn't** the case **here like** a case of **two fields and two people,** as the father gave part of his property to his sons as a gift, and the rest to others as an inheritance? **But it is taught that** the others **acquire** the property, although he employed only the terminology of inheritance concerning them.

הוּא מוֹתִיב לָהּ, וְהוּא מְפָרֵק לָהּ: בְּרָאוּי לְיוֹרְשׁוֹ, וְרַבִּי יוֹחָנָן בֶּן בְּרוֹקָה הִיא.

Rav Sheshet **raised the objection and he resolved it:** The term others is referring **to** those who are **fit to inherit** from **him; and** the ruling of the *baraita* **is** in accordance with the opinion of **Rabbi Yoḥanan ben Beroka,** who holds that one can bequeath his property to anyone who is fit to inherit from him. Therefore it is unnecessary for the bequest to be phrased as a gift.

HALAKHA

Others will inherit in their stead – יִירְשׁוּ אֲחֵרִים תַּחְתֵּיהֶם: If a person on his deathbed deposits his money with another and instructs him to give his children a shekel every week, as a gift and not as inheritance, and that the rest of the property should be given to someone else, the children receive only a shekel every week, even if this amount is insufficient to provide for their needs (Rambam *Sefer Kinyan, Hilkhot Zekhiya UMattana* 12:6; *Shulḥan Arukh, Ḥoshen Mishpat* 248:2).

אָמַר רַב אַשִׁי, תָּא שְׁמַע: ״נְכָסַי לְךָ, וְאַחֲרֶיךָ יִירַשׁ פְּלוֹנִי, וְאַחֲרֵי אַחֲרֶיךָ יִירַשׁ פְּלוֹנִי״, מֵת רִאשׁוֹן – קָנָה שֵׁנִי, מֵת שֵׁנִי – קָנָה שְׁלִישִׁי, וְאִם מֵת שֵׁנִי בְּחַיֵּי רִאשׁוֹן – יַחְזְרוּ נְכָסִים לְיוֹרְשֵׁי רִאשׁוֹן;

Rav Ashi said: Come and **hear** a proof for the opinion of Rav Sheshet from a *baraita* (*Tosefta* 8:4): If one states: **My property** will go **to you** after my death for your use during your lifetime, **and after you** die, **so-and-so will inherit**[H] the property, **and after** the one who inherits **after you** dies, **so-and-so will inherit** the property, then in this case, when **the first** recipient **dies, the second acquires** it, and when **the second dies, the third acquires it. And if the second dies during the lifetime of the first, the property returns** after his death **to the heirs of the first,** and does not go to the third designated recipient, as his right was to inherit it from the second one, who never received it.

וְהָא הָכָא דִּכְשְׁתֵּי שָׂדוֹת וּשְׁנֵי בְּנֵי אָדָם דָּמֵי, וְקָתָנֵי דְּקָנָה!

Rav Ashi states his proof: **And here it is** a case **like** that of **two fields**[N] **and two people,** as the bequest to the first recipient was phrased as a gift, and to the second one it was phrased as inheritance; **and** yet the *baraita* **teaches that** the second recipient **acquires** the property after the death of the first.

וְכִי תֵּימָא: הָכָא נַמִי בְּרָאוּי לְיוֹרְשׁוֹ, וְרַבִּי יוֹחָנָן בֶּן בְּרוֹקָה הִיא, אִי הָכִי, מֵת שֵׁנִי קָנָה שְׁלִישִׁי?

And if you would say that **here, too,** the *baraita* is referring **to** a case where the recipient is **fit to inherit** from **him, and** it is in accordance with the opinion of **Rabbi Yoḥanan ben Beroka, if so,** why does it state that when **the second dies, the third acquires** it?

הָא שְׁלַח רַב אַחָא בְּרֵיהּ דְּרַב עֲוְיָא: לְדִבְרֵי רַבִּי יוֹחָנָן בֶּן בְּרוֹקָה, ״נְכָסַי לְךָ וְאַחֲרֶיךָ לִפְלוֹנִי״, וְרִאשׁוֹן רָאוּי לְיוֹרְשׁוֹ – אֵין לַשֵּׁנִי בִּמְקוֹם רִאשׁוֹן כְּלוּם, שֶׁאֵין זֶה לְשׁוֹן מַתָּנָה אֶלָּא לְשׁוֹן יְרוּשָּׁה, וִירוּשָּׁה אֵין לָהּ הֶפְסֵק!

Rav Ashi explains his previous comment: **Didn't Rav Aḥa, son of Rav Avya, send** the following ruling **in accordance with the statement of Rabbi Yoḥanan ben Beroka?** If a person on his deathbed said: **My property** is given **to you, and after you to so-and-so, and the first** recipient **was fit to inherit** from **him,**[H] **the second gets nothing in place of the first,** i.e., he does not receive the property after the first one dies, **as this formulation** employed by the owner **was not one of a gift;**[N] **rather,** it was **a formulation of inheritance, and inheritance has no end,**[N] i.e., it cannot be stopped. Therefore, since the first recipient acquired it as inheritance, his heirs inherit it from him, and it cannot be taken by the second one. Therefore, the *baraita* is irreconcilable with the opinion of Rabbi Yoḥanan ben Beroka.

תְּיוּבְתָּא דְּכוּלְּהוּ. תְּיוּבְתָּא.

The Gemara affirms: **The refutation of** the opinions **of all** the Sages who disagree with the opinion of Rav Sheshet that even if one uses the two terms with regard to two fields and two people his gift to both people is effective, is **a conclusive refutation.**

לֵימָא נַמִי תֶּיהֱוֵי תְּיוּבְתֵּיהּ דְּרֵישׁ לָקִישׁ! וְתִסְבְּרָא? וְהָא אָמַר רָבָא: הִלְכְתָא כְּוָותֵיהּ דְּרֵישׁ לָקִישׁ בְּהָנֵי תְּלָת!

The Gemara suggests: **Let us say that it is also a conclusive refutation** of the opinion **of Reish Lakish,** who maintains that giving must be mentioned with regard to both recipients and both fields. The Gemara asks: **And how can you understand this? But didn't Rava say that the** ***halakha*** **is in accordance with** the opinion **of Reish Lakish**[H] **with regard to these three** issues: Acquisition of land for the rights to its produce, *ḥalitza* of a pregnant woman, and the matter of bequeathal phrased both as a gift and as inheritance?

NOTES

And here it is like two fields – וְהָא הָכָא דִּכְשְׁתֵּי שָׂדוֹת: Although all the parts of the statement refer to the same property, since it is bequeathed to the different parties for separate periods of time, it is considered like several fields (Rashbam).

As this formulation was not one of a gift, etc. – שֶׁאֵין זֶה לְשׁוֹן מַתָּנָה וכו׳: The Rashbam explains that the expression: My property is given to you, is vague. Therefore, since the designated recipient is his heir, it is interpreted as an inheritance and not as a gift. Some of the *ge'onim* maintain that even if he uses a formulation indicating a gift, since the designated recipient is his heir, the statement is interpreted as referring to inheritance and not to an actual gift.

The Rashbam adds that this *halakha* is only according to the opinion of Rabbi Yoḥanan ben Beroka. According to the opinion of the Rabbis, who hold that one cannot change the apportionment of his inheritance, the expression: My property is given to you, clearly refers to a gift.

And inheritance has no end – וִירוּשָּׁה אֵין לָהּ הֶפְסֵק: As opposed to a gift, which can be given for a limited period of time, inheritance cannot be qualified or restricted in any manner.

The early commentaries discuss the relationship between this principle and the *baraita* cited earlier concerning one who instructed that a shekel be given to his children every week, and that when they die, the rest should be given to another person. It would appear that according to the principle stated here, the children should receive the property as an inheritance, and therefore the other person should not receive anything, contrary to the ruling of the *baraita*. Since the *baraita* was established as the opinion of Rabbi Yoḥanan ben Beroka, this contradiction poses a difficulty.

The Ra'avad answers that since the property was not given directly to the children but to the steward, who was instructed to give the sons a shekel every week, it is not considered inheritance even according to the opinion of Rabbi Yoḥanan ben Beroka. Therefore, the qualification that the remainder should be given to another person is valid. The Ra'avad suggests an additional answer, according to which the father's intention was for his estate to be acquired by the other person at the outset, with the exception of the weekly shekel that was designated for the children (see Ri Migash).

The Rambam posits that the *baraita* is referring to a case where the father specified that the sons will receive the estate as a gift and not as an inheritance.

HALAKHA

My property will go to you and after you die so-and-so will inherit – נְכָסַי לְךָ וְאַחֲרֶיךָ יִירַשׁ פְּלוֹנִי: If a person on his deathbed says: My property will go to so-and-so, and after he dies, to so-and-so, and after he dies, to so-and-so, then when the first recipient dies, the property belongs to the second, and when the second dies, it belongs to the third. If the second predeceases the first, the property belongs to the heirs of the first, and the third receives nothing, as his right to receive it is only from the second (*Tur*). The Rema, citing the *Maggid Mishne*, notes that if the first predeceases the second, and the third predeceases the second, the property is inherited by the heirs of the second, and the heirs of the third receive nothing (Rambam *Sefer Kinyan*, *Hilkhot Zekhiya UMattana* 12:7; *Shulḥan Arukh*, *Ḥoshen Mishpat* 248:3).

And the first was fit to inherit from him, etc. – וְרִאשׁוֹן רָאוּי לְיוֹרְשׁוֹ וכו׳: In a case where a person on his deathbed said: My property will go to so-and-so, and after he dies, to so-and-so, if the first recipient is one of his heirs, e.g., one of his sons, the second receives nothing, even if he is also one of his heirs (Rema, citing *Maggid Mishne* and Ran). This is because property that a person wills to his heir is considered an inheritance even if the bequest is not phrased as an inheritance, and once the heir inherits it, it becomes entirely his and is inherited by his heirs after his death, as inheritance has no end. This is in accordance with the statement of Rav Aḥa, son of Rav Avya.

If the giver stipulates explicitly that he is giving the property to his heir not as inheritance, but specifically as a gift, so that he can stipulate that it will go to the second designated recipient after the first, the second receives what is left after the first dies. Consequently, if a person on his deathbed deposits his money with a steward, and instructs him to give his children a shekel every week, not as inheritance but as a gift, and to give the rest of his estate to another person, his children receive only a shekel every week, even if this amount is not sufficient for their needs, as the father's statement is valid. This is the Rambam's resolution to the apparent contradiction between the *baraita* concerning a person who instructed that his sons receive one shekel a week and the statement of Rav Aḥa, son of Rav Avya (Rambam *Sefer Kinyan*, *Hilkhot Zekhiya UMattana* 12:6; *Shulḥan Arukh*, *Ḥoshen Mishpat* 248:1, and see 248:7 and 253:6).

The ***halakha*** **is in accordance with the opinion of Reish Lakish** – הִלְכְתָא כְּוָותֵיהּ דְּרֵישׁ לָקִישׁ: If a person on his deathbed apportioned his estate to his sons in a manner that increased the portion of some of his sons and reduced the portion of others, saying: So-and-so will inherit such and such a field, and such and such a field will be given to so-and-so, and so-and-so will inherit such and such a field, in this case, all of them acquire the fields that he designated for them, despite the fact that the portions of some of the sons were phrased as gifts and the portions of others were phrased as inheritance, provided the father did not pause between the parts of his statement for more than the time required for saying a short phrase. If he paused for more than that time, the apportionment is invalid, unless he mentioned all of them in the same sentence, so that gift terminology was mentioned with regard to all of them, e.g., if he said: So-and-so and so-and-so and so-and-so will inherit field A, field B, and field C, respectively, which are given to them as gifts, and they will inherit them. The *Sma* explains that giving can be mentioned anywhere in the statement for it to be valid, whether at the beginning, in the middle, or at the end. This is in accordance with the opinion of Reish Lakish, as understood by the Ri Migash. The Rema adds that if all the fields were willed to the same person, or if the same field was willed to several people, then even if he paused for more than the time required for speaking a short phrase, the statement takes effect (Rambam *Sefer Kinyan*, *Hilkhot Naḥalot* 6:6; *Shulḥan Arukh*, *Ḥoshen Mishpat* 281:7).

לָא קַשְׁיָא: כָּאן בְּתוֹךְ כְּדֵי דִבּוּר, כָּאן לְאַחַר כְּדֵי דִבּוּר.

The Gemara answers: This is **not difficult. Here,** in the case where giving can be mentioned concerning one of the recipients and inheritance with regard to the other, it is a case where the two bequests were stated **within** the time **required for speaking**[N] a short phrase, i.e., the time it takes to greet one's teacher. According to the *halakha,* within this time a speaker can retract his statement. Therefore both bequests are considered to be part of one statement. **There,** in the case where Reish Lakish maintains that giving must be mentioned with regard to both people for it to take effect, it is a case where the final part of the statement, where he said: And they will inherit it, was **after** the time required **for speaking** a short phrase.

וְהִלְכְתָא: כָּל תּוֹךְ כְּדֵי דִבּוּר כְּדִבּוּר דָּמֵי, לְבַר מֵעֲבוֹדָה זָרָה

And the *halakha* is that the legal status of **any** statement interrupted or retracted **within** the time **required for speaking**[N] a short phrase **is like** that of continuous **speech.**[H] This is the *halakha* in all cases, **apart from idol worship,**[N] as one who accepts an idol as his god is liable to receive court-imposed capital punishment even if he retracts his statement within the time required for speaking a short phrase,

Perek **VIII**
Daf **130** Amud **a**

וְקִדּוּשִׁין.

and betrothal, as if a man betroths a woman and retracts the betrothal within the time required for speaking, his retraction is not effective.

HALAKHA

Any statement interrupted or retracted within the time required for speaking is like continuous speech – **כָּל תּוֹךְ כְּדֵי דִבּוּר כְּדִבּוּר דָּמֵי**: If one makes a statement and retracts or changes it within the time required for saying a short phrase, i.e., the amount of time it takes to say to one's teacher: *Shalom alekha, rabbi*, the retraction or change is effective. Exceptions to the rule are one who blasphemes, one who accepts an idol as his god, and one who betroths a woman or divorces her. In these cases, one cannot retract his statement even within the time required for saying this short phrase (Rambam *Sefer HaMadda, Hilkhot Avoda Zara* 2:9, 3:4; *Sefer Nashim, Hilkhot Ishut* 7:22; *Sefer Hafla'a, Hilkhot Shevuot* 2:18; and *Sefer Shofetim, Hilkhot Edut* 20:3; *Shulḥan Arukh, Yoreh De'a* 234:31–33, 340:24, *Even HaEzer* 49:2, and *Ḥoshen Mishpat* 29:1, 281:7).

NOTES

Here it is within the time required for speaking – **כָּאן בְּתוֹךְ כְּדֵי דִבּוּר**: Some of the early commentaries maintain that this answer is valid with regard to the opinions of the other *amora'im* as well. The Rid consequently emends the text of the Gemara by deleting the statement that there was a conclusive refutation; by contrast, the Ramban writes that there are many examples of discussions in the Talmud where a difficulty is resolved after it is deemed a conclusive refutation. The Rashbam and the Ramah explain that this answer is not viable for the opinions of the other *amora'im*, as they hold that in a case of two people and two fields the instruction of a person on his deathbed is invalid, regardless of any pause between the two parts of the statement.

And the *halakha* of any statement within the time required for speaking – **וְהִלְכְתָא כָּל תּוֹךְ כְּדֵי דִבּוּר**: The Sages determined that this is the time it takes to say three words, i.e., *Shalom alekha, rabbi*, meaning: Greetings to you, my teacher.

The *halakha* concerning the time required for speaking a short phrase is summarized by the Rashbam: If one makes two statements within the time required for speaking a short phrase, they are considered as having been stated continuously. Therefore, if both statements are valid, they both take effect. If only one of them is valid, as is the case here, where giving and inheritance are mentioned consecutively, the one that is valid takes effect and the other does not. In a case where each statement is independently valid but the statements contradict each other, there are different opinions among the Sages as to whether the court recognizes the first statement or the last statement, or, in a monetary matter, whether the case is considered uncertain and the money is divided between the disputants or whether the money remains in the possession of the one currently in possession of it.

The early authorities disagree as to whether this principle is by Torah law or by rabbinic law. Rabbeinu Tam maintains that it was instituted by the Sages so that one whose teacher passes while he is in the process of completing a business transaction will be able to greet him without worrying about not being able to complete the transaction. Although the principle applies in cases where this reason is not applicable, that is because it was instituted as a principle, and no distinction was drawn between cases. This also seems to be the opinion of Rabbi Avraham *Av Beit Din*, who reasons that once the Sages ruled that it is permitted for one to pause in the middle of the recitation of *Shema* to respond to the greeting of his teacher, they ruled that this is not considered an interruption in other matters. Other early commentaries argue that the principle is implemented in matters of Torah law as well, and even produces leniencies in those matters. Therefore they assert that the principle is by Torah law (*Tosafot* on *Nedarim* 97a).

Apart from idol worship – **לְבַר מֵעֲבוֹדָה זָרָה**: In *Piskei HaRid* it is explained that this is referring to one who slaughters an animal as an offering to an idol and immediately retracts his intention. The Rashbam and Rabbeinu Gershom Meor HaGola maintain that this is referring to one who dedicates an item for idol worship and immediately retracts his dedication. *Tosafot* argue that dedication of an item for idol worship is halakhically meaningless, and therefore interpret this *halakha* differently: It refers to one who accepts an idol as his god; he is liable to receive court-imposed capital punishment even if he retracts his acceptance immediately.

מתני׳ הָאוֹמֵר ״אִישׁ פְּלוֹנִי יִירָשֵׁנִי״ בִּמְקוֹם שֶׁיֵּשׁ בַּת, ״בִּתִּי תִּירָשֵׁנִי״ בִּמְקוֹם שֶׁיֵּשׁ בֵּן – לֹא אָמַר כְּלוּם, שֶׁהִתְנָה עַל מַה שֶּׁכָּתוּב בַּתּוֹרָה; רַבִּי יוֹחָנָן בֶּן בְּרוֹקָה אוֹמֵר: אִם אָמַר עַל מִי שֶׁרָאוּי לְיוֹרְשׁוֹ – דְּבָרָיו קַיָּימִין, וְעַל מִי שֶׁאֵין רָאוּי לוֹ לְיוֹרְשׁוֹ – אֵין דְּבָרָיו קַיָּימִין.

MISHNA In a case of **one who says: So-and-so will inherit** from **me,**[H] **in a case where there is a daughter,** or: **My daughter will inherit** from **me, in a case where there is a son, he has said nothing, as he has stipulated counter to that which is written in the Torah** concerning the order of inheritance. **Rabbi Yoḥanan ben Beroka says: If he said** this **about one fit to inherit** from **him,**[H] **his statement stands, but** if it was **about one for whom** it was **not fit to inherit** from **him, his statement does not stand.**

גמ׳ טַעְמָא דְּאַחֵר בִּמְקוֹם בַּת וּבַת בִּמְקוֹם בֵּן, הָא בֵּן בֵּין הַבָּנִים וּבַת בֵּין הַבָּנוֹת – דְּבָרָיו קַיָּימִין; אֵימָא סֵיפָא, רַבִּי יוֹחָנָן בֶּן בְּרוֹקָה אוֹמֵר: אִם אָמַר עַל מִי שֶׁרָאוּי לְיוֹרְשׁוֹ – דְּבָרָיו קַיָּימִין; הַיְינוּ תַּנָּא קַמָּא!

GEMARA The Gemara infers from the mishna that **the reason** the first *tanna* rules that his bequeathal is invalid is **that** he bequeathed his estate to **another** in a case **where** he had **a daughter, or** to his **daughter where** he had **a son, but** if he bequeathed his entire estate to one **son** among his other **sons, or** to one **daughter among** his other **daughters, his statement stands.** The Gemara questions this inference: **Say the latter clause** of the mishna: **Rabbi Yoḥanan ben Beroka says** that **if he said** this **about one fit to inherit** from **him, his statement stands. This is** identical to the opinion of **the first *tanna*.** What information does this statement of Rabbi Yoḥanan ben Beroka add? With regard to what case do they disagree?

וְכִי תֵּימָא: רַבִּי יוֹחָנָן בֶּן בְּרוֹקָה אֲפִילּוּ אַחֵר בִּמְקוֹם בַּת וּבַת בִּמְקוֹם בֵּן קָאָמַר – וְהָתַנְיָא, רַבִּי יִשְׁמָעֵאל בְּנוֹ שֶׁל רַבִּי יוֹחָנָן בֶּן בְּרוֹקָה אוֹמֵר: לֹא נֶחְלְקוּ אַבָּא וַחֲכָמִים עַל אַחֵר בִּמְקוֹם בַּת וּבַת בִּמְקוֹם בֵּן, שֶׁלֹּא אָמַר כְּלוּם.

The Gemara continues: **And if you would say** that **Rabbi Yoḥanan ben Beroka is saying** that one's statement stands **even** in a case where he bequeathed his estate to **another where** he had **a daughter or** to **a daughter where** he had **a son,** as although he bequeathed it to one who is not currently his heir, the beneficiary would be fit to inherit from him if the current heirs die, and this would be contrary to the opinion of the first *tanna*, this is difficult. **And isn't it taught** in a *baraita* (*Tosefta* 7:18) **that Rabbi Yishmael, son of Rabbi Yoḥanan ben Beroka, says: My father and the Rabbis did not disagree about** a case where one bequeathed his estate to **another where** he had **a daughter or** to **a daughter where** he had **a son;** in a case such as this, my father concedes **that he has said nothing.**

עַל מָה נֶחְלְקוּ? עַל בֵּן בֵּין הַבָּנִים וּבַת בֵּין הַבָּנוֹת, שֶׁאַבָּא אוֹמֵר: יִירַשׁ, וַחֲכָמִים אוֹמְרִים: לֹא יִירַשׁ!

Rabbi Yishmael continues: **With regard to what** case **do they disagree?** They disagree **with regard to** a case where he bequeathed his entire estate to one **son among** his other **sons, or** to one **daughter among** his other **daughters, as my father says** that the son or daughter **inherits** the entire estate, **and the Rabbis say** that **he does not inherit** it.

אִיבָּעֵית אֵימָא: מִדְּקָאָמַר ״לֹא נֶחְלְקוּ״, מִכְּלָל דְּתַנָּא קַמָּא סָבַר נֶחְלְקוּ.

The Gemara explains: **If you wish, say** that **from** the fact **that** Rabbi Yishmael **is saying** that **they did not disagree** about a case where one bequeathed his estate to another where he had a daughter or to a daughter where he had a son, **by inference, the first *tanna*** of that *baraita*, to whom he was responding, **holds** that they did **disagree** in this case.

אִיבָּעֵית אֵימָא: כּוּלֵּיהּ דְּרַבִּי יוֹחָנָן בֶּן בְּרוֹקָה הִיא, וְחַסּוּרֵי מִחַסְּרָא וְהָכִי קָתָנֵי: הָאוֹמֵר ״אִישׁ פְּלוֹנִי יִירָשֵׁנִי״ בִּמְקוֹם שֶׁיֵּשׁ בַּת, ״בִּתִּי תִּירָשֵׁנִי״ בִּמְקוֹם שֶׁיֵּשׁ בֵּן – לֹא אָמַר כְּלוּם; הָא בַּת בֵּין הַבָּנוֹת וּבֵן בֵּין הַבָּנִים, אִם אָמַר יִירַשׁ כׇּל נְכָסָיו – דְּבָרָיו קַיָּימִין, שֶׁרַבִּי יוֹחָנָן אוֹמֵר: אִם אָמַר עַל מִי שֶׁרָאוּי לְיוֹרְשׁוֹ – דְּבָרָיו קַיָּימִין.

And **if you wish, say** instead that the **entire** mishna **is** stating the opinion **of Rabbi Yoḥanan ben Beroka,**[N] **and** the mishna **is incomplete, and this** is what **it is teaching:**[B] With regard to **one who says: So-and-so will inherit** from **me,** in a case **where there is a daughter,** or: **My daughter will inherit** from **me,** in a case **where there is a son, he has said nothing, but** if he bequeathed his property to one **son among** his other **sons, or** one **daughter among** his other **daughters,** then **if he said** that the son or daughter **will inherit all his property, his statement stands, as Rabbi Yoḥanan** ben Beroka **says: If he said** this **about one fit to inherit him,** that he should inherit all of his property, **his statement stands.**

אָמַר רַב יְהוּדָה אָמַר שְׁמוּאֵל: הֲלָכָה כְּרַבִּי יוֹחָנָן בֶּן בְּרוֹקָה. וְכֵן אָמַר רָבָא: הֲלָכָה כְּרַבִּי יוֹחָנָן בֶּן בְּרוֹקָה.

§ As for the halakhic ruling, **Rav Yehuda says** that **Shmuel says:** The ***halakha*** is **in accordance with** the opinion of **Rabbi Yoḥanan ben Beroka. And Rava says as well** that the ***halakha*** is **in accordance with** the opinion of **Rabbi Yoḥanan ben Beroka.**

HALAKHA

So-and-so will inherit from me, etc. – אִישׁ פְּלוֹנִי יִירָשֵׁנִי וכו׳: One cannot bequeath his estate to a person who is not his heir or deprive his heir of the inheritance, whether through an act of acquisition during a time of health or through instruction while on his deathbed, whether orally or with a written will, as one cannot stipulate counter to that which is written in the Torah. For example, if one who has a son bequeaths his estate to his daughter, or one who has a daughter but no sons bequeaths his property to another relative, his bequeathal is ineffective. If it is worded as a gift, his statement is effective (*Sma*). This is in accordance with the Gemara's conclusion that the entire mishna is the opinion of Rabbi Yoḥanan ben Beroka, and that it is the accepted *halakha* (Rambam *Sefer Mishpatim, Hilkhot Naḥalot* 6:2 and *Sefer Nashim, Hilkhot Ishut* 12:9; *Shulḥan Arukh, Ḥoshen Mishpat* 281:1).

If he said this about one fit to inherit from him, etc. – אִם אָמַר עַל מִי שֶׁרָאוּי לְיוֹרְשׁוֹ וכו׳: If one has several heirs, e.g., several sons, daughters, or brothers, and instructs while on his deathbed, whether orally or in writing, that a specific one of his heirs will receive the entire inheritance, or that some of his heirs will receive more than others (Rema, citing *Tur*), his statement stands. This is the *halakha* only in a case where he does not explicitly state that he is reducing or eliminating the portions of the other heirs. If he does state this explicitly, his statement is ineffective, in accordance with the opinion of the Ri Migash that the previous mishna also accords with the opinion of Rabbi Yoḥanan ben Beroka (Rambam *Sefer Mishpatim, Hilkhot Naḥalot* 6:2; *Shulḥan Arukh, Ḥoshen Mishpat* 281:1, 3).

NOTES

The entire mishna is the opinion of Rabbi Yoḥanan ben Beroka – כּוּלֵּיהּ דְּרַבִּי יוֹחָנָן בֶּן בְּרוֹקָה הִיא: With regard to the previous mishna (126b), which states that one cannot increase or reduce the portion of one of his heirs, some of the commentaries hold that it is in accordance with the opinion of the Rabbis, who disagree with Rabbi Yoḥanan ben Beroka; others maintain that it is consistent with the opinion of Rabbi Yoḥanan ben Beroka, reasoning that he concedes that one cannot explicitly exclude one of his heirs from the inheritance or deprive his firstborn of his double portion (see Rambam's Commentary on the Mishna and Meiri). Accordingly, the Gemara's assumption that other Rabbis disagree with Rabbi Yoḥanan ben Beroka is not derived from the previous mishna, but rather from the fact that the *halakha* in the mishna is mentioned in his name and not as an unattributed *halakha* (Rashba).

BACKGROUND

The mishna is incomplete and this is what it is teaching – חַסּוּרֵי מִחַסְּרָא וְהָכִי קָתָנֵי: This method of explanation is often found in the Gemara. The addition introduced by the Gemara is an elaboration upon that which is written in the mishna, based on various difficulties raised in the Gemara that render the mishna in its present form incoherent or inconsistent with another authoritative source. The addition provides the necessary clarification.

NOTES

He may not make the son of the beloved the firstborn – לֹא יוּכַל לְבַכֵּר: The early commentaries infer from this verse that even according to the opinion of Rabbi Yoḥanan ben Beroka, one cannot deprive his firstborn of his double portion.

אֲמַר רָבָא: מַאי טַעְמֵיהּ דְּרַבִּי יוֹחָנָן בֶּן בְּרוֹקָה? אָמַר קְרָא: "וְהָיָה בְּיוֹם הַנְחִילוֹ אֶת בָּנָיו", הַתּוֹרָה נָתְנָה רְשׁוּת לָאָב לְהַנְחִיל לְכָל מִי שֶׁיִּרְצֶה.

Rava said: What is the reason for the opinion **of Rabbi Yoḥanan ben Beroka? The verse states: "Then it shall be, in the day that he causes his sons to inherit"** (Deuteronomy 21:16), which is interpreted to mean that **the Torah gave the father permission to bequeath** his estate **to whomever he wishes** among his sons.

אֲמַר לֵיהּ אַבַּיֵי: הָא מִ"לֹּא יוּכַל לְבַכֵּר" נָפְקָא!

Abaye said to him: Isn't **this** *halakha* **derived from** the continuation of the verse: **"He may not make** the son of the beloved **the firstborn,**[N] before the son of the hated, who is the firstborn"? From the prohibition against depriving the firstborn of his double portion it can be inferred that one can change the apportionment of the inheritance of his other sons.

הַהוּא מִיבָּעֵי לֵיהּ לְכִדְתַנְיָא, אַבָּא חָנָן אָמַר מִשּׁוּם רַבִּי אֱלִיעֶזֶר:

The Gemara answers: **That** clause in the verse is **necessary for that which is taught** in a *baraita*: **Abba Ḥanan says in the name of Rabbi Eliezer:**

Perek **VIII**
Daf **130** Amud **b**

HALAKHA

He may not make the son of the beloved the firstborn – לֹא יוּכַל לְבַכֵּר: If one states that his firstborn will inherit only the portion of an ordinary son, or that he will not receive a double portion, or that he will not inherit a double portion, his statement is ineffective, as the Torah states: "He may not make the son of the beloved the firstborn." The Rema, citing the Maharik, adds that in a locale where the norm is that the firstborn does not receive a double portion, this norm should not be followed, as it contradicts Torah law (Rambam *Sefer Mishpatim*, *Hilkhot Naḥalot* 6:3; *Shulḥan Arukh*, *Ḥoshen Mishpat* 281:4).

מַה תַּלְמוּד לוֹמַר "לֹא יוּכַל לְבַכֵּר"?

Why must **the verse state: "He may not make** the son of the beloved **the firstborn"** (Deuteronomy 21:16)?[H]

לְפִי שֶׁנֶּאֱמַר: "וְהָיָה בְּיוֹם הַנְחִילוֹ אֶת בָּנָיו", שֶׁיָּכוֹל, וַהֲלֹא דִּין הוּא: וּמָה פָּשׁוּט שֶׁיִּפָּה כֹּחוֹ, שֶׁנּוֹטֵל בְּרָאוּי כְּבְמוּחְזָק – הַתּוֹרָה נָתְנָה רְשׁוּת לָאָב לְהַנְחִיל לְכָל מִי שֶׁיִּרְצֶה, בְּכוֹר שֶׁהוּרַע כֹּחוֹ, שֶׁאֵינוֹ נוֹטֵל בְּרָאוּי כְּבְמוּחְזָק – לֹא כָּל שֶׁכֵּן? תַּלְמוּד לוֹמַר: "לֹא יוּכַל לְבַכֵּר".

Abba Ḥanan explains: It is necessary **because** it **is stated** previously in the verse: **"Then it shall be, in the day that he causes his sons to inherit," as** one **might** have thought: **Could this not** be derived through an *a fortiori* **inference,** as follows: **And if** with regard to **an ordinary** son, one who is not a firstborn, **whose power is enhanced** in **that he takes** in inheritance the property **due** the deceased **as** he does the property the deceased **possessed** at the time he died, nevertheless, **the Torah gave the father permission to bequeath** his estate **to whichever** of his sons **he wishes,** depriving his other sons of their portions, then with regard to **a firstborn, whose power is diminished** in **that he does not take** a double portion of the property **due** his father **as** he takes of the property the deceased **possessed** at the time of his death, is it **not** clear **all the more so** that his father can deprive him of the double portion he receives as a firstborn? Therefore, **the verse states: "He may not make** the son of the beloved **the firstborn."**

וְיֹאמַר: "לֹא יוּכַל לְבַכֵּר", מַה תַּלְמוּד לוֹמַר "וְהָיָה בְּיוֹם הַנְחִילוֹ אֶת בָּנָיו"?

Abba Ḥanan continues: **And let** the verse **state** only the prohibition of: **"He may not make** the son of the beloved **the firstborn." Why** must **the verse state: "Then it shall be, in the day that he causes his sons to inherit"?**

שֶׁיָּכוֹל, וַהֲלֹא דִּין הוּא: וּמָה בְּכוֹר שֶׁהוּרַע כֹּחוֹ, שֶׁאֵינוֹ נוֹטֵל בְּרָאוּי כְּבְמוּחְזָק – אָמְרָה תוֹרָה: "לֹא יוּכַל לְבַכֵּר", פָּשׁוּט שֶׁיִּפָּה כֹּחוֹ, שֶׁנּוֹטֵל בְּרָאוּי כְּבְמוּחְזָק – לֹא כָּל שֶׁכֵּן?

It is necessary **because** one **might** have thought: **Could this not** be derived through an *a fortiori* **inference,** as follows: **And if** with regard to **a firstborn, whose power is diminished** in **that he does not take** a double portion of the property **due** his father **as** he takes of the property the deceased **possessed,** nevertheless **the Torah states: "He may not make** the son of the beloved **the firstborn,"** i.e., the firstborn may not be deprived of his double portion, then with regard to **an ordinary** son, **whose power is enhanced** in **that he takes** in inheritance the property **due** the deceased **as** he does the property the deceased **possessed,** is it **not** clear **all the more so** that his father cannot deprive him of his portion of the inheritance?

תַּלְמוּד לוֹמַר: "וְהָיָה בְּיוֹם הַנְחִילוֹ אֶת בָּנָיו", הַתּוֹרָה נָתְנָה רְשׁוּת לָאָב לְהַנְחִיל לְכָל מִי שֶׁיִּרְצֶה.

Therefore, **the verse states: "Then it shall be, in the day that he causes his sons to inherit,"** indicating that **the Torah gave the father permission to bequeath** his estate **to whichever** of his sons **he wishes.** Consequently, the prohibition "he may not make the son of the beloved the firstborn" is not available to prove that one may bequeath his estate to whichever of his sons he wishes.

אָמַר רַבִּי זְרִיקָא אָמַר רַבִּי אַמִּי אָמַר רַבִּי חֲנִינָא אָמַר רַבִּי: הֲלָכָה כְּרַבִּי יוֹחָנָן בֶּן בְּרוֹקָה. אֲמַר לֵיהּ רַבִּי אַבָּא: "הוֹרָה" אִיתְּמַר.

§ The Gemara resumes discussion of the halakhic ruling: **Rabbi Zerika says** that **Rabbi Ami says** that **Rabbi Ḥanina says** that Rabbi Yehuda HaNasi **says:** The ***halakha*** **is in accordance with** the opinion of **Rabbi Yoḥanan ben Beroka. Rabbi Abba said to** Rabbi Zerika: **It was stated** that Rabbi Yehuda HaNasi **ruled** in an actual case in accordance with the opinion of Rabbi Yoḥanan ben Beroka.

בְּמַאי קָמִיפַּלְגִי? מָר סָבַר: הֲלָכָה עֲדִיפָא, וּמָר סָבַר: מַעֲשֶׂה רַב.

The Gemara asks: **With regard to what** principle **do they disagree?** Since both Rabbi Zerika and Rabbi Abba agree that the *halakha* is in accordance with the opinion of Rabbi Yoḥanan ben Beroka, why did Rabbi Abba state that Rabbi Yehuda HaNasi ruled as much in an actual case? The Gemara answers: One **Sage,** Rabbi Zerika, **holds** that a ruling in principle is **a preferable** source for a ***halakha,*** rather than a ruling from an incident; **and** one **Sage,** Rabbi Abba, **holds** that a specific **incident** ruled upon by **a Sage** is a preferable source.

תָּנוּ רַבָּנַן: אֵין לְמֵדִין הֲלָכָה לֹא מִפִּי תַלְמוּד וְלֹא מִפִּי מַעֲשֶׂה – עַד שֶׁיֹּאמְרוּ לוֹ הֲלָכָה לְמַעֲשֶׂה. שָׁאַל וְאָמְרוּ לוֹ הֲלָכָה לְמַעֲשֶׂה – יֵלֵךְ וְיַעֲשֶׂה מַעֲשֶׂה, וּבִלְבַד שֶׁלֹּא יְדַמֶּה.

The Gemara examines which source is preferable. **The Sages taught** in a *baraita*: **One may derive the** ***halakha*** **neither from a statement**[N] **nor from an incident**[N] where one saw a ruling issued in a certain manner, **unless** the Sages explicitly **tell him** that it is the **practical** ***halakha.***[N] If he **asked** the Sages **and they told him** the **practical** ***halakha,*** **he may go and act** upon the ruling in those circumstances, **provided that he does not compare** between cases and apply the ruling to other circumstances.

מַאי "וּבִלְבַד שֶׁלֹּא יְדַמֶּה"? וְהָא כׇּל הַתּוֹרָה כּוּלָּהּ דַּמּוּיֵי מְדַמִּינַן לַהּ!

The Gemara asks: **What is the meaning of the statement: Provided that he does not compare? But don't we compare** cases throughout **the entire Torah?** The main method of halakhic derivation is through comparing cases where the *halakha* was already established to cases where the *halakha* is unclear.

אֲמַר רַב אַשִׁי, הָכִי קָאָמַר: וּבִלְבַד שֶׁלֹּא יְדַמֶּה בִּטְרֵפוֹת;

Rav Ashi said that **this** is what the *baraita* **is saying: Provided that he does not compare between** various cases of **animals with wounds that will cause them to die within twelve months** [***tereifot***], which are forbidden for consumption. In general, one may compare cases, but with regard to the definition of a *tereifa*, one may not compare.

דְּתַנְיָא: אֵין אוֹמְרִים בִּטְרֵפוֹת זוֹ דּוֹמָה לָזוֹ; וְאַל תִּתְמַהּ, שֶׁהֲרֵי חוֹתְכָהּ מִכָּאן וּמֵתָה, חוֹתְכָהּ מִכָּאן וְחָיְתָה.

This is **as it is taught** in a *baraita*: **With regard to** ***tereifot,*** **one does not say: This** wound **is similar to that** wound. Every type of wound has its own *halakhot*. **And do not wonder** about this principle, **as there are** organs with regard to which one **cuts it from here,** i.e., one side, **and** the animal **dies** within twelve months, but one **cuts it from there,** i.e., another side, **and it lives.**

אֲמַר לֵיהּ רַבִּי אַסִי לְרַבִּי יוֹחָנָן: כִּי אָמַר לָן מָר "הֲלָכָה הָכִי", נַעֲבֵיד מַעֲשֶׂה? אֲמַר: לָא תַּעֲבִידוּ עַד דְּאָמֵינָא "הֲלָכָה לְמַעֲשֶׂה".

Rabbi Asi said to Rabbi Yoḥanan: When the Master, i.e., Rabbi Yoḥanan, **says to us: This is the** ***halakha,*** **should we act** upon the ruling? Rabbi Yoḥanan **said: Do not act** upon the ruling **unless I say** that it is **a practical** ***halakha.***

אֲמַר לְהוּ רָבָא לְרַב פַּפָּא וּלְרַב הוּנָא בְּרֵיהּ דְּרַב יְהוֹשֻׁעַ: כִּי אָתֵי פְּסָקָא דְּדִינָא דִּידִי לְקַמַּיְיכוּ וַחֲזִיתוּ בֵּיהּ פִּירְכָא – לָא תִּקְרְעוּהוּ עַד דְּאָתֵיתוּ לְקַמַּאי, אִי אִית לִי טַעְמָא – אָמֵינָא לְכוּ, וְאִי לָא – הָדַרְנָא בִּי. לְאַחַר מִיתָה – לָא מִיקְרַע תִּקְרְעוּהוּ, וּמִגְמַר נַמִי לָא תִּגְמְרוּ מִינֵּיהּ; לָא מִיקְרַע תִּקְרְעִינֵיהּ – דְּאִי הֲוַאי הָתָם, דִּלְמָא הֲוָה אָמֵינָא לְכוּ טַעְמָא,

Rava said to Rav Pappa and to Rav Huna, son of Rav Yehoshua: When a legal ruling of mine comes before you and you perceive a refutation of it, do not tear it up until you come before me to discuss it. **If I have a valid explanation, I will tell you, and if not, I will retract** my ruling. If a ruling of mine comes before you **after** my **death,** when you can no longer discuss it with me, **do not tear it up, but do not learn from it either,** i.e., do not rule in accordance with it. **Do not tear it up, as had I been there, perhaps I would have told you** a valid **explanation** that you would have accepted;

NOTES

One may derive the ***halakha*** **neither from a statement [*talmud*]** – אֵין לְמֵדִין הֲלָכָה לֹא מִפִּי תַלְמוּד: The *baraita* is not referring to the Gemara, which was written much later. Rabbeinu Ḥananel and several other commentaries interpret *talmud* as referring to the halakhic decisions of the later *tanna'im* that were not included in the *mishnayot* and *baraitot*, e.g.: And the *halakha* is in accordance with Rabbi So-and-so's opinion (see *Nidda* 7b and Rashi there). The Rashbam explains that one may not issue a ruling based on the conclusion of a discussion in the study hall, as the conclusion would have been examined more thoroughly had it been referring to a practical case.

The Ri Migash has a different version of the text, which reads: From a student [*talmid*]. The Meiri explains that one may not issue a ruling based on a student's account of his teacher's statement, as the account might not be precise.

Nor from an incident – וְלֹא מִפִּי מַעֲשֶׂה: Rabbeinu Gershom Meor HaGola and Rabbi Binyamin Musafya interpret this as a continuation of the previous clause, i.e., neither rulings nor incidents mentioned in the statements of the *tanna'im* may be relied upon for the purpose of deriving the *halakha*, unless it is confirmed by the Sages in the study hall that it is the accepted *halakha*. The Meiri, citing the Ri Migash, explains that the ruling of a student issued in a particular instance cannot be relied upon unless it is confirmed that he heard it from his teacher, who told him that this is the practical *halakha*. By contrast, the Rashbam and the Ramah interpret this as a separate clause relating to one who witnesses the practical ruling of a Sage.

NOTES

Unless the Sages tell him the practical ***halakha*** – עַד שֶׁיֹּאמְרוּ לוֹ הֲלָכָה לְמַעֲשֶׂה: According to this principle, the halakhic conclusions of the Talmud would seemingly be deemed unreliable, as most of them are not referred to as: Practical *halakhot*. The early commentaries all maintain that the *halakhot* of the Talmud are, in fact, binding in practice. This applies not only to the explicit halakhic rulings of the Talmud, but also to *halakhot* that are inferred from incidents that appear in the Talmud, as well as to implicit halakhic presumptions (see *Sanhedrin* 33a). The Ri Migash explains that the Talmud was written for the purpose of ruling the practical *halakha* and is the result of thorough examination and discussion spanning several generations. The Ramah adds that by transcribing these *halakhot*, Rav Ashi and Ravina, the primary redactors of the Talmud, indicated that they are practical *halakha*. Furthermore, according to the principle that Rav Ashi and Ravina mark the conclusion of instruction (see *Bava Metzia* 86a), the Sages in later generations do not have the authority to rule against the Talmud.

מִגְמַר נַמִּי לָא תִּגְמְרוּ מִינֵּיהּ – דְּאֵין לַדַּיָּין אֶלָּא מַה שֶּׁעֵינָיו רוֹאוֹת.

but **do not learn from it either, as a judge has only what his eyes see**[N] as the basis for his ruling. One must rule according to his own understanding.

בָּעֵי רָבָא: בְּבָרִיא הֵיאָךְ? כִּי קָאָמַר רַבִּי יוֹחָנָן בֶּן בְּרוֹקָה – בִּשְׁכִיב מְרַע, דְּבַר אוֹרוּתֵי הוּא, אֲבָל בְּבָרִיא – לָא. אוֹ דִּלְמָא אֲפִילּוּ בְּבָרִיא נַמִּי?

§ **Rava raises a dilemma: In** the case of **a healthy person**[H] who bequeaths his estate to one of his sons, **how** should the court rule? Should it be reasoned that **when Rabbi Yoḥanan ben Beroka says** that the bequeathal is valid, he said so specifically **with regard to** the case of **a person on his deathbed, since he is capable of bequeathal,** as the verse: "In the day that he causes his sons to inherit" (Deuteronomy 21:16), from which the validity of this bequeathal is derived, is referring specifically to the time of one's death; **but in** the case of **a healthy person,** he did **not** say his ruling? **Or perhaps** he stated his ruling **even in** the case of **a healthy person.**[N]

אֲמַר לֵיהּ רַב מְשָׁרְשִׁיָּא לְרָבָא: תָּא שְׁמַע, דְּאָמַר לוֹ רַבִּי נָתָן לְרַבִּי: שְׁנִיתֶם מִשְׁנַתְכֶם כְּרַבִּי יוֹחָנָן בֶּן בְּרוֹקָה, דִּתְנַן: לֹא כָּתַב לָהּ ״בְּנִין דִּיכְרִין דְּיֶהֱוְיָן לַיךְ מִינַּאי, אִינּוּן יִרְתוּן כְּסַף כְּתוּבְּתֵיךְ יוֹתֵר עַל חוּלְקֵיהוֹן דְּעִם אֲחוּהוֹן״ – חַיָּיב, שֶׁתְּנַאי בֵּית דִּין הוּא!

Rav Mesharshiyya said to Rava: Come and **hear** a resolution of your dilemma from a *baraita*, **as Rabbi Natan said to Rabbi** Yehuda HaNasi: **You taught** in **your Mishna in accordance with** the opinion of **Rabbi Yoḥanan ben Beroka, as we learned** in a mishna (*Ketubot* 52b): If the husband **did not write for her** in her marriage contract: Any **male children**[HB] **you will have from me will inherit the money of your marriage contract in addition to their portion** of the inheritance **that** they receive together **with their brothers,** he is nevertheless **obligated** as though he had written it, **as it is a stipulation of the court**[N] and consequently takes effect even if it is not explicitly stated. This mishna is in accordance with the opinion of Rabbi Yoḥanan ben Beroka that one may add to the share of some of his sons at the expense of the others.

וְאָמַר לוֹ רַבִּי: ״יִסְבּוּן״ תְּנַן.

And Rabbi Yehuda HaNasi **said to him:** We did not learn that the male children she has from him will inherit the money of the marriage contract; that version is not accurate. Rather, **we learned** that **they will take** the money of the marriage contract, as a gift. When a bequeathal is worded in this manner, it is valid in any event, as stated in the previous mishna (126b).

וְאָמַר רַבִּי: יַלְדוּת הָיְתָה בִּי וְהֵעַזְתִּי פְּנֵי בְּנָתָן הַבַּבְלִי; אֶלָּא דְּקַיְימָא לָן: בְּנִין דִּכְרִין לָא טָרְפָא מִמְּשַׁעְבְּדֵי, אִי סָלְקָא דַּעְתָּךְ ״יִסְבּוּן״ תְּנַן, אַמַּאי לָא טָרְפָא מִמְּשַׁעְבְּדֵי? אֶלָּא שְׁמַע מִינָּהּ: ״יִרְתוּן״ תְּנַן.

The *baraita* continues: **And Rabbi** Yehuda HaNasi later retracted his response, and **said:** My response was because of **immaturity that I had in me, and I was insolent in the presence of** Rabbi **Natan the Babylonian** by responding in a manner that is incorrect. It is incorrect for the following reason: **But since we maintain** that concerning an obligation detailed in a marriage document ensuring inheritance rights of a woman's **male children,** the beneficiaries **do not repossess liened** property[H] that has been sold, one can infer that they do not receive the money as a gift. As, **if it enters your mind** that **we learned** in the mishna that **they will take** the money as a gift, **why don't they repossess liened** property? The gift was given to them before the property was sold to others. **Rather, conclude from** this claim that **we learned** in the mishna that **they will inherit** the money.

NOTES

As a judge has only what his eyes see – דְּאֵין לַדַּיָּין אֶלָּא מַה שֶּׁעֵינָיו רוֹאוֹת: In other words, do not rule according to my ruling; rather, use your own judgment (Rashbam). Rabbeinu Gershom Meor HaGola explains that Rava is referring here to himself, meaning: I may have been mistaken, as I ruled according to my judgment at the time, and perhaps on another occasion I would have ruled differently.

Even in the case of a healthy person – אֲפִילּוּ בְּבָרִיא נַמִּי: The practical ramifications of this possibility are discussed by the early commentaries. Rabbeinu Yona maintains that if it were to be accepted that the statement of Rabbi Yoḥanan ben Beroka applies to a healthy person as well, he would be able to bequeath his property orally, just as a person on his deathbed can, and he can change his mind until he dies. He explains that although in principle oral transfer of ownership is the right of a person on his deathbed exclusively, if the gift is worded as bequeathal, others can transfer property in this manner as well (see Rashbam and Rashba). The Ri Migash holds that an oral statement would not suffice and that an act of acquisition would be necessary. He suggests a more moderate ramification: If one transfers ownership of his property to one of his sons using the phrase: From today and after my death (see 136a), the transfer is effective even if it is worded as an inheritance and not as a gift, despite the fact that a healthy person generally cannot transfer property employing the terminology of inheritance.

As it is a stipulation of the court – שֶׁתְּנַאי בֵּית דִּין הוּא: The Sages instituted this stipulation so that people would give their daughters large dowries, out of confidence that the money would remain in the possession of their own descendants.

HALAKHA

In the case of a healthy person – בְּבָרִיא: If a healthy person gives an instruction to increase or reduce the share of his firstborn son or of any of his other heirs, his instruction is ineffective. This is because the dilemma of Rava is left unresolved in the Gemara, and therefore the inheritance cannot be appropriated from the legal heirs, as they have the presumptive right to the property by Torah law. The *Tur* notes that this is the *halakha* only if one employs the terminology of inheritance, but if he employs the terminology of a gift, his statement stands (Rambam *Sefer Mishpatim, Hilkhot Naḥalot* 6:4; *Shulḥan Arukh, Ḥoshen Mishpat* 281:5).

Did not write for her, any male children, etc. – לֹא כָּתַב לָהּ בְּנִין דִּיכְרִין וכו׳: It is stipulated in the marriage contract that the husband's male children whose mother died in their father's lifetime inherit payment of the sum written in her marriage contract in addition to their share of his estate. This stipulation is implemented even if it is not written, as it is a stipulation of the court (Rambam *Sefer Nashim, Hilkhot Ishut* 12:2, 19:1–2; *Shulḥan Arukh, Even HaEzer* 69:2, 111:1).

Do not repossess liened property – לָא טָרְפָא מִמְּשַׁעְבְּדֵי: A son who inherits the right to receive payment of the marriage contract of his mother, who died in his father's lifetime, does not repossess liened property that has been sold. Rather, he collects it only from unsold property, like all other heirs (Rambam *Sefer Nashim, Hilkhot Ishut* 19:9; *Shulḥan Arukh, Even HaEzer* 111:13).

BACKGROUND

Marriage contract concerning male children – כְּתוּבַּת בְּנִין דִּיכְרִין: Most *ge'onim* agree that the stipulation of the marriage contract concerning male children was no longer in effect in their time. They explain that as a considerable number of different *halakhot* apply to this condition, many of which depend on an accurate assessment of the value of the estate, the courts preferred not to get entangled in the ensuing uncertainties. The main reason for the lapse of this enactment is that it became customary to provide daughters with very large dowries, which meant that sons inherited virtually nothing. Although not all authorities accept that the stipulation was no longer in effect by the time of the *ge'onim*, they agree that the stipulation of the marriage contract concerning male children should be limited to land, despite the ordinance of the *ge'onim* that the sums detailed in the marriage contract and its stipulations can generally be collected from movable property.

מַאן שָׁמְעַתְּ לֵיהּ דְּאִית לֵיהּ הַאי סְבָרָא – רַבִּי יוֹחָנָן בֶּן בְּרוֹקָה, וּשְׁמַע מִינָּהּ: אֲפִילּוּ בְּבָרִיא.

Rav Mesharshiyya concludes: **Of whom have you heard that he holds this opinion** that one can add to the inheritance of some of his sons at the expense of the others? It is the opinion of **Rabbi Yoḥanan ben Beroka, and conclude from** the mishna in *Ketubot* that his ruling applies **even with regard to a healthy person,** as one does not write a marriage contract on his deathbed. This resolves Rava's dilemma.

אֲמַר לֵיהּ רַב פַּפָּא לְאַבַּיֵי: בֵּין לְמַאן דְּאָמַר "יִסְבּוּן", וּבֵין לְמַאן דְּאָמַר "יָרְתוּן", הָא אֵין אָדָם מַקְנֶה דָּבָר שֶׁלֹּא בָּא לָעוֹלָם!

Rav Pappa said to Abaye:[N] How can one prove that the mishna in tractate *Ketubot* is in accordance with the opinion of Rabbi Yoḥanan ben Beroka? **Whether according to the one who says** that the correct version of the mishna is: **They will take, and whether according to the one who says** the correct version of the mishna is: **They will inherit,** the mishna is difficult, for the following reason: **A person cannot transfer ownership of an entity that has not yet come into the world.**[N] How can the husband confer rights to his property to children that have yet to be born?

וַאֲפִילּוּ לְרַבִּי מֵאִיר דְּאָמַר: אָדָם מַקְנֶה דָּבָר שֶׁלֹּא בָּא לָעוֹלָם, הָנֵי מִילֵּי לְדָבָר שֶׁיֶּשְׁנוֹ בָּעוֹלָם, אֲבָל לְדָבָר שֶׁאֵינוֹ בָּעוֹלָם לָא!

Rav Pappa explains: **And even according to Rabbi Meir, who says** that **a person can transfer ownership of an entity that has not** yet **come into the world, this statement** applies specifically in a case where he transfers the item **to an entity,** i.e., a person, **that is in the world; but** with regard to transferring ownership of an item **to an entity that is not** yet **in the world,** e.g., to his children that have yet to be born, this statement does **not** apply. Therefore, the ruling of the mishna is difficult according to all opinions.

אֶלָּא, תְּנַאי בֵּית דִּין שָׁאנֵי, הָכָא נַמִּי – תְּנַאי בֵּית דִּין שָׁאנֵי!

Rav Pappa explains: **Rather,** evidently **a stipulation of the court is different.** Since this clause of the marriage contract was instituted by rabbinic ordinance, it is not subject to the standard *halakhot* of transferring property, and one can transfer ownership of an item to an entity that is not yet in the world. Accordingly, **here too,** with regard to the dispute between Rabbi Yoḥanan ben Beroka and the Rabbis, **a stipulation of the court is different,** and even according to the Rabbis, who disagree with the opinion of Rabbi Yoḥanan ben Beroka, one can bequeath the money of his wife's marriage contract to the male children she will have from him in any manner he chooses. Consequently, there is no proof that the mishna is in accordance with the opinion of Rabbi Yoḥanan ben Beroka.

אֲמַר לֵיהּ: מִשּׁוּם דְּקָא מַפֵּיק לָהּ בִּלְשׁוֹן "יָרְתוּן".

Abaye **said to him:** The assertion that the mishna is in accordance with the opinion of Rabbi Yoḥanan ben Beroka is **due to** the fact **that it expresses** this bequeathal **with the wording: They will inherit,**[N] as opposed to: They will take. This indicates that a person can normally apportion his inheritance to his sons in any manner he wishes, in accordance with the opinion of Rabbi Yoḥanan ben Beroka.

הֲדַר אֲמַר אַבַּיֵי: לָאו מִילְּתָא הִיא דַּאֲמַרִי, דִּתְנַן: לֹא כָּתַב לָהּ "בְּנָן נוּקְבָן דְּיֶהֶוְיָין לִיכִי מִינַּאי יֶהֶוְיָין יָתְבָן בְּבֵיתִי וְיִתְזָנָן מִנִּכְסַאי עַד דְּתִילַּקְחָן לְגוּבְרִין" – חַיָּיב, שֶׁהוּא תְּנַאי בֵּית דִּין;

Abaye then said: That which I said is not correct. The expression: They will inherit, is appropriate even according to the Rabbis, who disagree with Rabbi Yoḥanan ben Beroka, **as we learned** in the continuation of that mishna that even if the husband **did not write for** his wife: Any **female children**[H] **you will have from me will sit in my house and be sustained from my property until they are taken by men,** i.e., until they are married, he **is** nevertheless **obligated** as though he had written it, **as it too is a stipulation of the court.**

וַהֲוָה לֵיהּ בְּמַתָּנָה וְלָזֶה בִּירוּשָּׁה, וְכׇל לָזֶה בִּירוּשָּׁה וְלָזֶה בְּמַתָּנָה – אֲפִילּוּ רַבָּנַן מוֹדוּ.

And since these two clauses are written adjacent to each other in the marriage contract, **it is** effectively **a case** where one bequeaths his estate to two people: **To this** one, the daughters, **as a gift, and to that** one, the sons, **as an inheritance. And in any** case where one bequeaths his estate **to this person as an inheritance and to that** person **as a gift, even the Rabbis concede** that the bequest is valid even if it is to people who are not his heirs, as it is considered a gift with regard to both recipients.

אֲמַר לֵיהּ רַב נַחוּמִי, וְאִית דְּאָמַר רַב חֲנַנְיָה בַּר מִנְיוּמִי לְאַבַּיֵי:

Rav Naḥumi, and some say it was **Rav Ḥananya bar Minyumi, said to Abaye:**

NOTES

Rav Pappa said to Abaye, etc. – אֲמַר לֵיהּ רַב פַּפָּא לְאַבַּיֵי וכו׳: The connection between the ensuing discussion and the one up to this point is a subject of analysis among the early commentaries, and their varying interpretations carry halakhic ramifications. Several commentaries hold that Rava's dilemma has been resolved, the conclusion being that the ruling of Rabbi Yoḥanan ben Beroka applies in the case of a healthy person as well. The discussion initiated by Rav Pappa pertains only to the interpretation of the mishna in tractate *Ketubot*, which, according to the assumption of both Rabbi Natan and Rabbi Yehuda HaNasi, accords with the opinion of Rabbi Yoḥanan ben Beroka, provided that the correct version of that mishna is: They will inherit (Rashbam; Ba'al HaMaor). The Ramban notes that Rav Se'adya Gaon and Rabbeinu Ḥananel rule in accordance with this interpretation.

Other commentaries hold that according to Rav Pappa there is no evidence that Rabbi Yoḥanan ben Beroka's ruling pertains to a healthy person as well, as the stipulation in a marriage contract concerning male children is a stipulation of the court, and is unrelated to the *halakhot* of inheritance (see *Tosafot* and Rashbam Commentary). According to this opinion, there is no clear resolution to Rava's dilemma. This is also the opinion of Rav Hai Gaon, the Rif, and the Ri Migash.

An entity that has not come into the world – דָּבָר שֶׁלֹּא בָּא לָעוֹלָם: The Ri Migash explains that the sum of the marriage contract is considered such an entity, since as long as the wife is still alive, it does not yet belong to the husband and he is therefore unable to bequeath it to his sons. The Rashbam and other commentaries interpret this sentence as merely an introduction to Rav Pappa's main point, that the money is being transferred to an entity that is not yet in the world, i.e., his sons that will be born to him.

That it expresses this with the wording, they will inherit – דְּקָא מַפֵּיק לָהּ בִּלְשׁוֹן יָרְתוּן: The Rashbam explains that the seemingly unnecessary use of the term inherit suggests an inclination toward the opinion of Rabbi Yoḥanan ben Beroka, who allows for a similar type of bequeathal. Other early commentaries cite another interpretation of the Rashbam: When the term inherit is used, it is unnecessary for the stipulation to be based on the special authority of the court, as by the time inheritance will take effect, i.e., after the husband's death, the sons are already in existence. Therefore, it can be proven from the wording of the mishna that it is in accordance with the opinion of Rabbi Yoḥanan ben Beroka, and that this ruling applies in the case of a healthy person as well (see *Tosafot* and Ramban).

HALAKHA

Did not write for his wife, any female children, etc. – לֹא כָּתַב לָהּ בְּנָן נוּקְבָן וכו׳: It is stipulated in the marriage contract that any female children the couple has together are entitled to their sustenance from the husband's property until their betrothal or until they reach adulthood. This is the *halakha* even if this was not stated in the marriage contract, or if it was the local custom not to write a marriage contract at all, as it is a stipulation of the court. In *Ḥelkat Meḥokek* it is added that even if other stipulations were written and this one was not, it is implemented. In a case where the local custom is to write a marriage contract but the children are unable to bring the marriage contract to the court, the Rambam and the *Tur* rule that the daughters do not receive sustenance, as perhaps their mother waived payment of her marriage contract. The Ra'avad rules that even if she waived payment of her marriage contract, her daughters receive sustenance (Rambam *Sefer Nashim, Hilkhot Ishut* 19:10; *Shulḥan Arukh, Even HaEzer* 69:1–2, 112:1, and see *Ḥelkat Meḥokek* and *Beit Shmuel* there).

NOTES

The daughters are sustained only after their father's death – בָּנוֹת לֹא יִזּוֹנוּ אֶלָּא לְאַחַר מִיתַת אֲבִיהֶן: Although in practice a father is coerced by the court to sustain his children, the terms of the marriage contract do not obligate him to do so.

מִמַּאי דִּבְחַד בֵּי דִינָא אִיתְקוּן? דִּלְמָא בִּתְרֵי בֵּי דִינָא אִיתְקוּן!

From where do you conclude **that** both clauses, the one for the benefit of the sons and the one for the benefit of the daughters, **were instituted by one court** and are therefore each read in light of the other? **Perhaps they were instituted by two** different **courts** and are unrelated to each other. Accordingly, the wording of the gift and the wording of the inheritance are not part of the same statement.

לָא סָלְקָא דַּעְתָּךְ, דְּקָתָנֵי רֵישָׁא, זֶה מִדְרָשׁ דָּרַשׁ רַבִּי אֶלְעָזָר בֶּן עֲזַרְיָה לִפְנֵי חֲכָמִים בְּכֶרֶם בְּיַבְנֶה: הַבָּנִים יִירְשׁוּ וְהַבָּנוֹת יִזּוֹנוּ, מָה הַבָּנִים אֵינָן יוֹרְשִׁין אֶלָּא לְאַחַר מִיתַת אֲבִיהֶם, אַף בָּנוֹת לֹא יִזּוֹנוּ אֶלָּא לְאַחַר מִיתַת אֲבִיהֶן;

The Gemara answers: This possibility should **not enter your mind,** as the **former clause** of that mishna **teaches** (*Ketubot* 49a): A father is not obligated to provide his daughter's sustenance. **This interpretation was interpreted** by **Rabbi Elazar ben Azarya before the Sages of the vineyard in Yavne:**[B] Since the Sages instituted that after the father's death, **the sons inherit** the sum of money specified in their mother's marriage contract, **and the daughters are sustained** from their father's estate, these two *halakhot* are equated: **Just as the sons inherit only after their father's death,** not during his lifetime, **so too, the daughters are sustained** from their father's property **only after their father's death.**[N]

אִי אָמְרַתְּ בִּשְׁלָמָא בְּחַד בֵּי דִינָא אִיתְקוּן, הַיְינוּ דְּיָלְפִינַן תַּקָּנָה מִתַּקָּנָה, אֶלָּא אִי אָמְרַתְּ בִּתְרֵי בֵּי דִינָא אִיתְקוּן, הֵיכִי יָלְפִינַן תַּקָּנָה מִתַּקָּנָה!

The Gemara explains: **Granted, if you say** that the two clauses **were instituted by one court, this is** the reason **that we derive** the *halakhot* of one **ordinance from** the *halakhot* of the other **ordinance,** under the assumption that a court institutes ordinances in a consistent manner. **But if you say** that they **were instituted by two** distinct **courts** operating in different periods, **how can we derive** the *halakhot* of one **ordinance from** the *halakhot* of the other **ordinance?**

מִמַּאי? דִּלְמָא לְעוֹלָם אֵימָא לָךְ: בִּתְרֵי בֵּי דִינָא אִיתְקוּן, וּבֵי דִינָא בָּתְרָא תְּקוּן כְּבֵי דִינָא קַמָּא, כִּי הֵיכִי דְּלָא תִּקְשֶׁה תַּקַּנְתָּא אַתַּקַּנְתָּא.

The Gemara rejects this explanation: **From where** is it assumed that they were instituted by one court? **Actually, I will say to you** that **perhaps** the two clauses **were instituted by two** separate **courts, and** nevertheless Rabbi Elazar ben Azarya derived the *halakhot* of one ordinance from the *halakhot* of the other ordinance, because **the latter court** presumably **instituted** its ordinance **in accordance with** the format of **the former court, so that** one should **not ask** about contradictions between one **ordinance and** the other **ordinance.** With regard to the *halakhot* of inheritance, there is no reason to read the two clauses in light of the other.

אָמַר רַב יְהוּדָה אָמַר שְׁמוּאֵל: הַכּוֹתֵב כָּל נְכָסָיו לְאִשְׁתּוֹ – לֹא עֲשָׂאָהּ אֶלָּא אַפּוֹטְרוֹפָּא.

§ **Rav Yehuda says** that **Shmuel says:** A person on his deathbed **who writes** a document granting **all his property to his wife**[H] **has merely rendered her a steward.** The assumption is that he did not intend to deprive his heirs of their entire inheritance. Rather, he intended to appoint her as a steward in charge of the property, so that the heirs will honor her.

BACKGROUND

The vineyard in Yavne – כֶּרֶם בְּיַבְנֶה: The great yeshiva in Yavne, which served as a meeting place of the Sages and the seat of the Nasi after the destruction of the Second Temple, is commonly referred to as *kerem beYavne* or the vineyard in Yavne. According to the Jerusalem Talmud (Berakhot 4:1) the place was called a vineyard because the students would sit in rows, evoking the rows of grapevines in a vineyard. Since the majority of that generation's leading Sages were gathered there, their decisions were decisive in safeguarding the continued existence of the Jewish people. The place is held in high esteem, and the *halakhot* taught in this vineyard [*matnita dekarma*] have special authority.

HALAKHA

A person on his deathbed who writes a document granting all his property to his wife – הַכּוֹתֵב כָּל נְכָסָיו לְאִשְׁתּוֹ: If a person on his deathbed writes a document granting all of his property to his wife, he has merely rendered her a steward in charge of his property for his heirs. According to the Rambam, this is the *halakha* even if an act of acquisition was performed; other authorities disagree. If he left any amount of his property for his heirs, whether land or movable property, the wife acquires the property that he granted to her in the document (Rambam *Sefer Kinyan, Hilkhot Zekhiya UMattana* 6:4; *Shulḥan Arukh, Even HaEzer* 107:1 and *Ḥoshen Mishpat* 246:12, and see 246:7).

פְּשִׁיטָא, בְּנוֹ הַגָּדוֹל – לֹא עֲשָׂאוֹ אֶלָּא אַפּוֹטְרוֹפּוֹס; בְּנוֹ הַקָּטָן מַאי?

The Gemara discusses similar cases: It is **obvious** that if one writes a document granting all his property to **his adult son,**[N] he does not intend to give him the entire inheritance, but to have him distribute it among his brothers. Rather, **he has merely rendered him a steward** [***apotropos***].[L] If he writes it to **his minor son,**[H] **what** is the *halakha*? Is it still assumed that his intention is to appoint him as a steward, or is that implausible since a minor boy is not yet capable of assuming this position and therefore the father apparently intended to bequeath to him the entire inheritance?

אִיתְּמַר, רַב חֲנִילָאי בַּר אִידִי אָמַר שְׁמוּאֵל: אֲפִילּוּ בְּנוֹ קָטָן הַמּוּטָּל בַּעֲרִיסָה.

It **was stated** that **Rav Ḥanilai bar Idi** says that **Shmuel says** that **even** if one wrote a document granting all his property to **his minor son who is lying in** his **crib,** he does not receive the entire inheritance. Rather, the father presumably intended to appoint him as a steward when he reached adulthood, so that the other heirs would honor him.

פְּשִׁיטָא, בְּנוֹ וְאַחֵר – אַחֵר בְּמַתָּנָה וּבְנוֹ אַפּוֹטְרוֹפּוֹס. אִשְׁתּוֹ וְאַחֵר – לְאַחֵר בְּמַתָּנָה וְאִשְׁתּוֹ אַפּוֹטְרוֹפּוֹס.

The Gemara states: It is **obvious** that if one wrote a document granting all his property to **his son and another**[NH] person, he intended to give **the other** person half the property **as a gift, and** to appoint **his son a steward** to oversee the property of his brothers, with whom he shares the other half. Similarly, if he wrote a document granting all his property to **his wife and another**[H] person, he intended to give **the other** person half the property **as a gift, and** to appoint **his wife a steward** to oversee the other half of the property for his sons.

אִשְׁתּוֹ אֲרוּסָה וְאִשְׁתּוֹ גְּרוּשָׁה – בְּמַתָּנָה.

Furthermore, it is obvious that if one wrote a document granting all his property to **his betrothed**[B] **wife,** whom he did not yet wed, **or** to **his** former **wife,** whom he had **divorced,**[H] he intended to give it to them **as a gift,** as he had no reason to have his heirs honor them.

HALAKHA

His adult son…his minor son, etc. – **בְּנוֹ הַגָּדוֹל...בְּנוֹ הַקָּטָן וכו׳**: If a person on his deathbed writes a document granting all his property to one of his sons, the son receives only his standard portion of the inheritance, and he is rendered a steward with regard to the rest of it. This is the *halakha* even if he is still an infant, and even if the document is formulated in the manner of a will (Rabbeinu Yona). If he specifies that it is a complete transfer of ownership and not merely an appointment of stewardship, or if it is evident from the wording of the document that his intention is to give an actual gift, the property belongs to the son (Ri Migash). The Rema, citing the Rashbam, writes that if the document is worded not as a gift but rather as a bequest, the son receives the entire inheritance in any event. In any case of uncertainty with regard to the father's intention, the burden of proof rests upon the son designated in the document. If an act of acquisition was performed, the Ra'avad and the Rashba hold that the property belongs to the son, as such an act is unnecessary for appointment of stewardship. Rabbeinu Yona maintains that the act was performed merely to reinforce the appointment.

If he has daughters and wrote a document granting his property to his son, or if he has only daughters and wrote a document granting his property to one of them, or if he has no children and wrote a document granting his property to one of several heirs, it is considered a proper gift, even if he did not leave any property of his out of the gift. This is in accordance with the opinion of the Rif, that because this *halakha* was instituted as though without a reason, it cannot be expanded to cases that were not explicitly mentioned (Rambam *Sefer Kinyan, Hilkhot Zekhiya UMattana* 6:2, and see *Sefer Mishpatim, Hilkhot Naḥalot* 6:2; *Shulḥan Arukh, Ḥoshen Mishpat* 246:4, 7).

His son and another – **בְּנוֹ וְאַחֵר**: If one writes a document his deathbed granting all his property to one of his sons and another person jointly, the other person receives half the property as a gift, and the rest is divided among one's sons. The son to whom he wrote the property is appointed as a steward for the portions of his brothers (Rambam *Sefer Kinyan, Hilkhot Zekhiya UMattana* 6:6; *Shulḥan Arukh, Ḥoshen Mishpat* 246:9–10).

His wife and another – **אִשְׁתּוֹ וְאַחֵר**: If one writes a document granting all his property to his wife and another person jointly, the other person receives half the property and his wife is appointed as a steward for the other half (Rambam *Sefer Kinyan, Hilkhot Zekhiya UMattana* 6:7; *Shulḥan Arukh, Even HaEzer* 107:8).

His betrothed wife or to his wife whom he divorced – **אִשְׁתּוֹ אֲרוּסָה וְאִשְׁתּוֹ גְּרוּשָׁה**: If one writes a document granting all his property to his betrothed or to his divorcée, even if he left nothing for his heirs, the gift is valid and the property belongs to her. The Rema, citing the *Tur*, writes that if he left nothing out of the gift, she loses her right to receive payment of her marriage contract (Rambam *Sefer Kinyan, Hilkhot Zekhiya UMattana* 6:5; *Shulḥan Arukh, Even HaEzer* 107:2).

NOTES

His adult son, etc. – **בְּנוֹ הַגָּדוֹל וכו׳**: The *ge'onim* and the early commentaries discuss the apparent contradiction between this *halakha* and the ruling of Rabbi Yoḥanan ben Beroka in the mishna (130a) that if a person instructs that his property be given to one of his sons, he inherits it. Rabbeinu Gershom Meor HaGola explains that the mishna is referring specifically to one who states orally that his estate should be given to his son, whereas this *halakha* refers to one who writes a document. Rabbeinu Ḥananel explains this distinction: Since a person on his deathbed need not write his will, by writing it he indicates his intention that the instruction be publicized, so that everyone will recognize his son as the steward in charge of the property and honor him (see Ramban).

The Rashbam (130a) suggests that in the case of the mishna the instruction is worded as a conferral of inheritance rights, whereas in this case it is worded as a gift. Several other commentaries concur. According to the Rosh, citing Rabbeinu Ḥananel, and the Rid, this *halakha* is referring to a case where the entire estate is willed to the son, whereas the mishna is referring to a case where some of it was granted to the other heirs. The Ba'al HaMaor writes that the case in this *halakha* is where the other sons are minors who need a steward to take care of their property; whereas in the case of the mishna, the other heirs are adults.

His son and another – **בְּנוֹ וְאַחֵר**: The majority of commentaries explain that this is a case where he wrote a document granting all his property to his son and another person together, so that each receives half. Since in the document he wrote that he granted to his son the entire part of the estate that he left for his sons, this is considered like a case where he wrote a document granting all his property to one of his sons, and the son is therefore rendered a steward. By contrast, the Rashbam interprets this statement as referring to two separate cases. It refers to a situation where he wrote a document granting his property to his son, in which case it is obvious that he intended to appoint him as a steward, and one where he wrote a document granting his property to another person, who is not his relative, in which case he clearly intended to grant him ownership of the property.

LANGUAGE

Steward [*apotropos*] – **אַפּוֹטְרוֹפּוֹס**: From the Greek ἐπίτροπος, *epitropos*, meaning an appointee or trustee. It generally refers to a person who has the right to manage the properties or affairs of another.

BACKGROUND

Betrothed – **אֲרוּסָה**: Betrothal is the first of two stages in the process of a Jewish marriage. The bond created by betrothal requires the woman to be divorced before she can remarry another man. Furthermore, once she is betrothed, sexual intercourse with other men constitutes adultery and is punishable by death. A betrothed couple may not yet live together as husband and wife, and most of the couple's mutual obligations do not yet apply.

Marriage takes effect by means of the wedding ceremony, when the bride and groom come together under the bridal canopy, symbolizing their union. This immediately confers upon the couple the privileges and the responsibilities associated with marriage, including all monetary rights and obligations. After marriage, if one spouse dies, all the *halakhot* of mourning for a close relative apply to the surviving spouse. If the wife of a priest dies, it is permitted for him to become ritually impure to bury her. While today betrothal and marriage are performed in a single ceremony, in talmudic times there was usually a yearlong gap between the two.

אִיבַּעְיָא לְהוּ: בַּת אֵצֶל הַבָּנִים, וְאִשָּׁה אֵצֶל הָאַחִים, וְאִשָּׁה אֵצֶל בְּנֵי הַבַּעַל, מַהוּ?

A dilemma was raised before the Sages: If one wrote a document granting all his property to his **daughter before his sons,**[HN] in a case where he has sons who would inherit from him, **or** to his **wife before** his **brothers,**[H] **or** to his **wife before the husband's sons** who are not her sons, **what is** the *halakha*? Is it assumed that his intention was to appoint her as a steward or to give her the property as a gift?

אֲמַר רָבִינָא, מִשְּׁמֵיהּ דְּרָבָא: בְּכוּלְּהוּ לֹא קָנָה, לְבַר מֵאִשְׁתּוֹ אֲרוּסָה וְאִשְׁתּוֹ גְּרוּשָׁה; רַב עֲוִירָא מִשְּׁמֵיהּ דְּרָבָא אֲמַר: בְּכוּלְּהוּ קָנֵי, לְבַר מֵהָאִשָּׁה אֵצֶל הָאַחִין וְאִשָּׁה אֵצֶל בְּנֵי הַבַּעַל.

Ravina said in the name of Rava that **in all of** these cases the recipient **did not acquire** the property. Rather, he or she was merely appointed a steward, **except for** the cases of **his betrothed wife and** his former **wife** whom he **divorced.** By contrast, **Rav Avira said in the name of Rava** that **in all of** these cases the recipient **acquired** the property, **except for** the cases of his **wife before** his **brothers and** his **wife before the husband's sons,** where he clearly intended only to appoint her as a steward.

NOTES

His daughter before his sons, etc. – בַּת אֵצֶל הַבָּנִים וכו׳: The dilemma is explained by the Rashbam as follows: On the one hand, there is no explicit Torah commandment for brothers to honor their sister or their sister-in-law, or for sons to honor their father's widow who is not their mother. Therefore, it can be reasoned that he did not intend to lead the heirs to honor her by appointing her as a steward. On the other hand, perhaps he wanted to guarantee that his daughter or wife be honored for her own benefit, although there is no mitzva to honor them.

HALAKHA

His daughter before his sons – בַּת אֵצֶל הַבָּנִים: The Rambam writes that if one with sons writes a document granting all his property to his daughter as a gift, the gift is valid and the property belongs to her, in accordance with the Rif's version of the text, in which this case is not discussed. Other authorities rule that she does not receive ownership of the property, even if he words it as a gift and not as a bequest (Rema, citing Rosh and Ramah). This is in accordance with the standard version of the text and in accordance with the opinion of Ravina (Rambam *Sefer Kinyan*, *Hilkhot Zekhiya UMattana* 6:3; *Shulḥan Arukh*, *Ḥoshen Mishpat* 246:6).

His wife before his brothers – אִשָּׁה אֵצֶל הָאַחִים: If a person writes a document granting all his property to his wife, she is rendered a steward for the heirs, whether they are her children, his children from another woman, his brothers, or any other of his relatives. This is in accordance with Rava's opinion, as understood by both Rav Avira and Ravina (Rambam *Sefer Kinyan*, *Hilkhot Zekhiya UMattana* 6:4; *Shulḥan Arukh*, *Even HaEzer* 107:1).

Perek **VIII**
Daf **132** Amud **a**

בָּעֵי רָבָא: בְּבָרִיא הֵיאָךְ? בִּשְׁכִיב מְרַע הוּא דְּנִיחָא לֵיהּ דְּלִישְׁתַּמְעוּן מִלָּה, אֲבָל בְּבָרִיא – הָא קָאֵי אִיהוּ. אוֹ דִּלְמָא בָּרִיא נַמִי נִיחָא לֵיהּ דְּלִישְׁתַּמְעוּן מִלָּה מֵהָשְׁתָּא?

With regard to the *halakha* that a person on his deathbed who wrote a document granting all his property to his wife has appointed her as a steward, **Rava raises a dilemma: In** the case of **a healthy person, what is** the *halakha*?[NH] Should it be reasoned that specifically **in** the case of **a person on his deathbed it** is assumed that he intended to appoint his wife as a steward, **as it is preferable for him that her word be heard** and she is honored after his death, **but in** the case of **a healthy person, he is** still **standing** and can ensure that his wife is honored, so he apparently intended to actually give her all of his property? **Or perhaps** should it be reasoned that **in** the case of **a healthy person as well, it is preferable that** his wife's **word be heard** and she be given honor **from now?**

תָּא שְׁמַע: הַכּוֹתֵב פֵּירוֹת נְכָסָיו לְאִשְׁתּוֹ – גּוֹבָה כְּתוּבָּתָהּ מִן הַקַּרְקַע; לְמֶחֱצָה לְשָׁלִישׁ וְלִרְבִיעַ – גּוֹבָה כְּתוּבָּתָהּ מִן הַשְּׁאָר.

The Gemara suggests: **Come** and **hear** a resolution of the dilemma from a *baraita*: If **one writes** a document that **the profits of his property** should go **to his wife** in the event that he dies or divorces her, **she collects** payment of **her marriage contract,** which he wrote her at the time of their marriage, **from the land** itself. The profits are hers as a result of his gift. Similarly, if he wrote a document granting her **one-half, one-third, or one-quarter** of his property, **she collects** payment of **her marriage contract from the rest** of his property, which he did not give her as a separate gift.

כָּתַב כׇּל נְכָסָיו לְאִשְׁתּוֹ, וְיָצָא עָלָיו שְׁטַר חוֹב – רַבִּי אֱלִיעֶזֶר אוֹמֵר: תִּקְרַע מַתְּנָתָהּ וְתַעֲמוֹד עַל כְּתוּבָּתָהּ, וַחֲכָמִים אוֹמְרִים: תִּקְרַע כְּתוּבָּתָהּ וְתַעֲמוֹד עַל מַתְּנָתָהּ, וְנִמְצֵאת קֵרַחַת מִכָּאן וּמִכָּאן;

The *baraita* continues: If one **wrote** a document granting **all his property to his wife, and** subsequently **a promissory note emerged against him** for a loan he took while they were married but before he gave her this gift, **Rabbi Eliezer says** that **she** should **tear up her** deed of **gift**[N] **and remain with her marriage contract,** so that the creditor will not be able to collect the property she received, as her marriage contract preceded the promissory note. **And the Rabbis say: She** must **tear up her marriage contract**[N] **and remain with her** deed of **gift,** as by accepting the gift of all her husband's property she waived her right to receive payment of her marriage contract. Since the promissory note preceded the deed of gift, the creditor receives the property, **and** the wife **is found** to be **bald from here and from there,** i.e., she receives neither her gift nor her marriage contract.

NOTES

In the case of a healthy person what is the *halakha* – בְּבָרִיא הֵיאָךְ: The Ran maintains that this is referring to a case where he writes: All my property is given to my wife from now and after my death; see the mishna on *daf* 136a. The Rashbam writes that this is referring even to a standard deed of gift written by a healthy person, which takes effect immediately.

She should tear up her deed of gift, etc. – תִּקְרַע מַתְּנָתָהּ וכו׳: This means she should forgo the gift and exercise her right to collect the land as payment of her marriage contract, as she did not waive this right when she received the gift. The Ramah explains that the court actually tears up the deed of gift, so that in the event the husband acquires additional land she will not claim that she has a right to this land due to the gift.

She must tear up her marriage contract – תִּקְרַע כְּתוּבָּתָהּ: The Rashbam explains that while she cannot collect payment of her marriage contract from the property her husband owned at the time of the gift, if he acquires additional property, she can receive payment of her marriage contract from that, as any property acquired by the husband is liened to his wife's marriage contract. Other commentaries maintain that the wife waived her right to receive payment of her marriage contract entirely, as she realized upon receiving the gift that he had no more property with which to pay her (Ri Migash).

HALAKHA

In the case of a healthy person what is the *halakha* – בְּבָרִיא הֵיאָךְ: If a healthy person writes a document granting his property to his wife or son or other people detailed in the Gemara, the recipient is rendered a steward with regard to the property, as in the case of a person on his deathbed. This is because Rava's dilemma was not resolved, and the other heirs have the presumptive right to the property (Rambam *Sefer Kinyan*, *Hilkhot Zekhiya UMattana* 6:4; *Shulḥan Arukh*, *Even HaEzer* 107:1 and *Ḥoshen Mishpat* 246:4).

וְאָמַר רַבִּי יְהוּדָה הַנַּחְתּוֹם: מַעֲשֶׂה וְאֵירַע הַדָּבָר בְּבַת אֲחוֹתִי כַּלָּה, וּבָא מַעֲשֶׂה לִפְנֵי חֲכָמִים וְאָמְרוּ: תִּקְרַע כְּתוּבָּתָהּ וְתַעֲמוֹד עַל מַתְּנָתָהּ, וְנִמְצֵאת קֵרַחַת מִכָּאן וּמִכָּאן;

And Rabbi Yehuda the baker[P] **said:** There was **an incident where this matter occurred to my sister's daughter** who is my **daughter-in-law** [*kalla*],[N] that my son wrote such a document to her, **and the incident came before the Sages. And they said** that **she must tear up her marriage contract and remain with her** deed of **gift, and she is found** to be **bald from here and from there.**

טַעְמָא דְּיָצָא עָלָיו שְׁטַר חוֹב, הָא לֹא יָצָא עָלָיו שְׁטַר חוֹב – קָנְיָא; וּבְמַאי? אִילֵימָא בִּשְׁכִיב מְרַע – וְהָא אָמְרַתְּ: לֹא עֲשָׂאָהּ אֶלָּא אַפּוֹטְרוֹפּוֹס! אֶלָּא לָאו בְּבָרִיא.

The Gemara infers: **The reason** she loses her gift **is that a promissory note emerged against him, but if a promissory note did not emerge against him, she acquires** the gift of his property. **And with regard to what** case is this stated? **If we say** it is **with regard to a person on his deathbed, but didn't you say** previously that in such a case **he merely rendered her a steward? Rather, is it not with regard to a healthy person?** Accordingly, Rava's dilemma is resolved: If a healthy person writes a document granting all his property to his wife, it is hers.

לְעוֹלָם בִּשְׁכִיב מְרַע, וְרַב עֲוִירָא מוֹקֵי לַהּ בְּכוּלְּהוּ, רָבִינָא מוֹקֵי לַהּ בְּאִשְׁתּוֹ אֲרוּסָה וְאִשְׁתּוֹ גְּרוּשָׁה.

The Gemara rejects this proof: **Actually,** the *halakha* of the *baraita* is stated **with regard to a person on his deathbed; and Rav Avira would interpret** the *baraita* as referring **to all of** the cases mentioned above in which, in his opinion, the wife acquires the property and is not appointed as a steward. And **Ravina would interpret** it specifically **in reference to** a case where one wrote a document granting all his property to **his betrothed wife or his former wife, whom he divorced,**[N] where he concedes that she acquires the property.

אָמַר רַב יוֹסֵף בַּר מִנְיוּמִי אָמַר רַב נַחְמָן, הֲלָכָה: תִּקְרַע כְּתוּבָּתָהּ וְתַעֲמוֹד עַל מַתְּנָתָהּ, וְנִמְצֵאת קֵרַחַת מִכָּאן וּמִכָּאן.

Rav Yosef bar Minyumi says that Rav Naḥman says: The *halakha* is in accordance with the opinion of the Rabbis. **She** must **tear up her marriage contract**[H] **and remain with her** deed of **gift, and she is found** to be **bald from here and from there.**

לְמֵימְרָא, דְּלָא אָזֵיל רַב נַחְמָן בָּתַר אוּמְדָּנָא?

The Gemara asks: **Is this to say that Rav Naḥman does not follow** the principle of **assessing** intention, meaning that even if one did not state something explicitly, the court assesses what his intention was and decides the *halakha* based on that assessment? Clearly, upon accepting the gift the wife did not intend to waive payment of her marriage contract and thereby be left with nothing in the event that her husband's creditor produces a promissory note that predates her gift.

וְהָתַנְיָא: הֲרֵי שֶׁהָלַךְ בְּנוֹ לִמְדִינַת הַיָּם, וְשָׁמַע שֶׁמֵּת בְּנוֹ, וְעָמַד וְכָתַב כׇּל נְכָסָיו לַאֲחֵרִים, וְאַחַר כָּךְ בָּא בְּנוֹ – מַתְּנָתוֹ מַתָּנָה; רַבִּי שִׁמְעוֹן בֶּן מְנַסְיָא אוֹמֵר: אֵין מַתְּנָתוֹ מַתָּנָה, שֶׁאִילּוּ הָיָה יוֹדֵעַ שֶׁבְּנוֹ קַיָּים לֹא כְּתָבָן; וְאָמַר רַב נַחְמָן: הֲלָכָה כְּרַבִּי שִׁמְעוֹן בֶּן מְנַסְיָא!

But isn't it taught in a *baraita* (*Tosefta, Ketubot* 5:9): In a case **where one's son went overseas and he heard that his son died,** and then he **arose and wrote** a document granting **all his property to others,**[H] **and then his son came back, his gift** to the other people **is** a valid **gift. Rabbi Shimon ben Menasya says: His gift is not** a valid **gift, as had he known that his son** was **alive he would not have written** a document granting **them** his property. **And Rav Naḥman says** that the *halakha* **is in accordance with** the opinion of **Rabbi Shimon ben Menasya.** Apparently, Rav Naḥman follows the principle of assessing intention.

PERSONALITIES

Rabbi Yehuda the baker – רַבִּי יְהוּדָה הַנַּחְתּוֹם: Rabbi Yehuda the baker lived in the generation of Rabbi Akiva and may have been one of his students. His statements are mentioned in both the Babylonian Talmud and the Jerusalem Talmud. Little is known of his personal life, although apparently he was a baker. He was one of the Sages executed by the Romans for transgressing Hadrian's decrees against the observance of Judaism. Although an attempt was made to save him from his fate, the effort failed, and the one who tried to save him was executed as well. It is related that that the Romans did not allow his body to be buried, but ordered that it be left exposed to rot, causing shock among the onlookers.

NOTES

To my sister's daughter who is my daughter-in-law [*kalla*] – בְּבַת אֲחוֹתִי כַּלָּה: The Rashbam and several other commentaries explain that his niece became his daughter-in-law, as she married his son. Rabbeinu Gershom Meor HaGola interprets the word *kalla* here as bride, meaning that this happened to his niece when she was betrothed. Her betrothed wrote a document granting her all of his property and died before they were married.

His former wife whom he divorced – אִשְׁתּוֹ גְּרוּשָׁה: The Ritva, citing his teacher, writes that the *baraita* is not referring to the case of a divorcée, as she certainly does not waive payment of her marriage contract. Rather, the *baraita* is referring to the case of a betrothed wife, and a divorcée is included in the statement only because it is the typical formulation cited elsewhere.

HALAKHA

The *halakha* is that she must tear up her marriage contract, etc. – הֲלָכָה תִּקְרַע כְּתוּבָּתָהּ וכו׳: If a wife receives all her husband's property as a gift, she loses her right to receive payment of her marriage contract. Therefore, if a promissory note that is dated prior to the gift emerges against him, the creditor collects the debt from the property, and the wife does not receive payment of the marriage contract or the gift, in accordance with the ruling of Rav Naḥman. This is due to the assessment that she presumably intended to waive her lien on the property in exchange for the benefit she derived from the public knowledge of her husband's gift to her. The Rashbam notes that if he later acquires other property, she receives payment of her marriage contract from that property (Rambam *Sefer Kinyan, Hilkhot Zekhiya UMattana* 6:8; *Shulḥan Arukh, Even HaEzer* 107:3).

Where one's son went overseas…and wrote a document granting all his property to others – הֲרֵי שֶׁהָלַךְ בְּנוֹ לִמְדִינַת הַיָּם...וְכָתַב כׇּל נְכָסָיו לַאֲחֵרִים: If one's son went overseas, and he heard that his son died, and he wrote a document granting all his property to another as a gift, and then his son returned, the gift is canceled, as it is assumed that the father would not have given the other all his property had he known that his son was still alive. This is in accordance with the opinion of Rav Naḥman, who rules in accordance with the opinion of Rabbi Shimon ben Menasya. If he left some of his property out of the gift, the gift stands (Rambam *Sefer Kinyan, Hilkhot Zekhiya UMattana* 6:1; *Shulḥan Arukh, Ḥoshen Mishpat* 246:1).

NOTES

She has lost her marriage contract – אִבְּדָה כְּתוּבָּתָהּ: In this case as well, the Rashbam holds that she loses only her right to collect the property that her husband gave the sons, but that she can still collect property that he acquires afterward, whereas the Ri Migash maintains that she has waived her right entirely.

And she is silent – וְהִיא שׁוֹתֶקֶת: Her silence is interpreted as consent to the transaction. The Rashbam maintains that this is only because he gave her a share of the property as well. Otherwise, she can claim that she did not consent to the transaction, and remained silent only so as not to displease her husband at the time (see Ba'al HaMaor).

To a case where he says to her, take this land for your marriage contract – בְּאוֹמֵר לָהּ טְלִי קַרְקַע זוֹ בִּכְתוּבָּתֵךְ: The Rashbam explains that the opinion of Rabbi Yosei, son of Rabbi Ḥanina, is the most lenient toward the husband, as he holds that even if the wife was not present at all when the husband distributed the property, and he gives her a parcel of land at a later date, stating that he is giving it to her as full payment of her marriage contract, and she does not protest, she is considered to have consented to the distribution. Other commentaries interpret the opinion of Rabbi Yosei, son of Rabbi Ḥanina, as more stringent toward the husband than that of Shmuel, as he requires that the husband state upon giving her the land that only this parcel of land and not what he gave his sons is for her marriage contract, and then the wife accepts it or remains silent (see Rabbeinu Yona).

שָׁאנֵי הָתָם, דְּנִיחָא לָהּ דְּתֵיפּוֹק עֲלָהּ קָלָא דִּכְתַבִינְהוּ נִיהֲלָהּ לְהָנְהוּ נְכָסִים.

The Gemara answers: **There,** in the case of one who writes a document granting all his property to his wife, it **is different, as** it is **beneficial to her that it be publicized that he wrote** a document granting **her** all of **that property,** and she was willing to risk not receiving payment of her marriage contract to gain this benefit.

תְּנַן הָתָם: הַכּוֹתֵב נְכָסָיו לְבָנָיו, וְכָתַב לְאִשְׁתּוֹ קַרְקַע כׇּל שֶׁהוּא – אִבְּדָה כְּתוּבָּתָהּ. מִשּׁוּם דִּכְתַב לָהּ קַרְקַע כׇּל שֶׁהוּא אִבְּדָה כְּתוּבָּתָהּ?

§ **We learned** in a mishna **there** (*Pe'a* 3:7): If a man **writes** a document granting **his property to his sons, and he wrote** a document granting **any amount of land to his wife, she has lost** her right to receive payment of **her marriage contract.**[N] The Gemara questions this: **Because he wrote** a document granting **her any amount of land, she has lost** her right to receive payment **of her marriage contract?** Why should this be?

אָמַר רַב: בִּמְזַכֶּה לָהֶן עַל יָדָהּ. וּשְׁמוּאֵל אָמַר: בִּמְחַלֵּק לְפָנֶיהָ וְהִיא שׁוֹתֶקֶת. רַבִּי יוֹסֵי בְּרַבִּי חֲנִינָא אָמַר: בְּאוֹמֵר לָהּ "טְלִי קַרְקַע זוֹ בִּכְתוּבָּתֵךְ".

Rav says: This mishna is referring **to** a case where the husband **transfers ownership** of his property **to** his sons **through** his wife's participation in a formal act of acquisition. Not only did she not protest the transfer of property to the sons, but she facilitated the transaction. Clearly, she agreed to waive payment of her marriage contract. **And Shmuel says:** It is referring not only to a case where she actually participates in the act of acquisition, but also **to** a case where he **distributes** the property to his sons **in her presence, and she is silent**[N] and does not ask about her marriage contract. **Rabbi Yosei, son of Rabbi Ḥanina, says:** It is referring **to** a case where **he says to her: Take** only **this** parcel of **land for your marriage contract.**[N]

Perek **VIII**
Daf **132** Amud **b**

וּמִקּוּלֵּי כְתוּבָּה שָׁנוּ כָּאן.

And the Sages **taught here** one **of the leniencies** that apply to **a marriage contract.**[N] This manner in which the wife loses her right to receive payment of her marriage contract is a leniency for the husband, as an ordinary creditor does not lose money he is owed in this fashion.

תְּנַן, רַבִּי יוֹסֵי אוֹמֵר: אִם קִבְּלָה עָלֶיהָ, אַף עַל פִּי שֶׁלֹּא כָּתַב לָהּ – אִבְּדָה כְּתוּבָּתָהּ; מִכְּלָל דְּתַנָּא קַמָּא סָבַר: כְּתִיבָה וְקַבָּלָה בָּעֵי!

The Gemara questions this statement: **We learned** in the same mishna that **Rabbi Yosei says** that **if she accepted** the distribution **upon herself, even if he did not write** a document granting **her** any amount of land, **she has lost** her right to receive payment **of her marriage contract. By inference,** it can be stated **that the first *tanna* holds** that both his **writing** a document granting her a piece of land **and** her **acceptance** of the distribution **are necessary** for her to lose her right, contrary to the interpretation of all three *amora'im*, i.e., Rav, Shmuel, and Rabbi Yosei, son of Rabbi Ḥanina, all of whom assumed that she need not affirmatively accept the distribution and that her silence is sufficient.

NOTES

One of the leniencies that apply to a marriage contract – מִקּוּלֵּי כְתוּבָּה: This leniency refers not to one of the specific explanations of Rav, Shmuel, or Rabbi Yosei, son of Rabbi Ḥanina, but to the ruling of the mishna that the wife can lose her right to payment of her marriage contract in this manner, as one who gives property to his creditor as a gift is not exempt from repaying the debt. Another leniency that applies to a marriage contract is that whereas a standard creditor collects the amount owed him from intermediate-quality land, a wife collects from inferior-quality land. The reason for these leniencies is that as opposed to a standard creditor, who performed a favor for the debtor by lending him money, women generally want to get married no less than a man does (see *Ketubot* 86b). Since there is no need to impose conditions upon the collection of the marriage contract to encourage marriage, payment of a marriage contract is treated more leniently than is a standard debt.

וְכִי תֵּימָא: כּוּלָּהּ רַבִּי יוֹסֵי הִיא – וְהָא תַּנְיָא, אָמַר רַבִּי יְהוּדָה: אֵימָתַי? שֶׁהָיְתָה שָׁם וְקִבְּלָה עָלֶיהָ, אֲבָל הָיְתָה שָׁם וְלֹא קִבְּלָה עָלֶיהָ, קִבְּלָה עָלֶיהָ וְלֹא הָיְתָה שָׁם – לֹא אִבְּדָה כְּתוּבָּתָהּ! תְּיוּבְתָּא דְּכוּלְּהוּ. תְּיוּבְתָּא.

And if you would say that the entire mishna **is the opinion of Rabbi Yosei,** who holds that either the husband's writing a deed of gift or the wife's acceptance of the distribution is sufficient, **but isn't it taught** in a *baraita* that **Rabbi Yehuda said:** According to the first *tanna*, **when**[N] does she lose her right to receive payment of her marriage contract? In a case **where she was there** at the time of the distribution **and accepted it; but if she was there but did not accept** it, or **accepted** it **but was not there, she has not lost** her right to receive payment of **her marriage contract,** as she can claim that her acquiescence was only to please her husband and was not sincere. The Gemara concludes: The **refutation** of the opinions **of all** the interpretations of the *amora'im* **is** indeed **a conclusive refutation.**

אֲמַר לֵיהּ רָבָא לְרַב נַחְמָן: הָא רַב, הָא שְׁמוּאֵל, הָא רַבִּי יוֹסֵי בְּרַבִּי חֲנִינָא, מָר מַאי סְבִירָא לֵיהּ? אֲמַר לֵיהּ, שֶׁאֲנִי אוֹמֵר: כֵּיוָן שֶׁעֲשָׂאָהּ שׁוּתָּף בֵּין הַבָּנִים – אִבְּדָה כְּתוּבָּתָהּ.

Rava said to Rav Naḥman: This is the opinion **of Rav; this is** the opinion **of Shmuel;** and **this is** the opinion **of Rabbi Yosei, son of Rabbi Ḥanina. What does the Master hold** in this matter? Rav Naḥman **said to him: As I say, that once he rendered her a partner**[H] in the property **among the sons,**[N] **she lost** her right to receive payment of **her marriage contract.**

אִיתְּמַר נַמִי, אָמַר רַב יוֹסֵף בַּר מִנְיוּמִי אָמַר רַב נַחְמָן: כֵּיוָן שֶׁעֲשָׂאָהּ שׁוּתָּף בֵּין הַבָּנִים – אִבְּדָה כְּתוּבָּתָהּ.

Rav Naḥman's opinion **was also stated** as a halakhic ruling: **Rav Yosef bar Minyumi says** that **Rav Naḥman says** that **once he rendered her a partner** in the property **among the sons, she lost** her right to receive payment of **her marriage contract.**

בָּעֵי רָבָא: בְּבָרִיא הֵיאָךְ? מִי אָמְרִינַן: בְּשָׁכִיב מְרַע הוּא דְּיָדְעָה דְּלֵית לֵיהּ וְקָמָחֲלָה, אֲבָל בְּבָרִיא סָבְרָה: הָדַר קָנֵי. אוֹ דִּלְמָא הָשְׁתָּא מִיהַת לֵית לֵיהּ? תֵּיקוּ.

Rava raises a dilemma: In the case of **a healthy person, what** is the *halakha*?[H] **Do we say** that the wife loses her right to receive payment of her marriage contract only **in** the case of **a person on his deathbed, as she knew that he had no** other property **and** nevertheless **waived** payment of the marriage contract, **but in** the case of **a healthy person,** she might have **reasoned** that **he will then acquire** other property from which she will be able to collect payment of her marriage contract, and that is why she accepted the distribution of the property? If so, she did not waive her right to receive payment of her marriage contract. **Or perhaps,** should it be reasoned that since **in any event, now he has no** other property, her acceptance should be interpreted as waiving her right? The Gemara concludes: The dilemma **shall stand** unresolved.

NOTES

Rabbi Yehuda said, when, etc. – אָמַר רַבִּי יְהוּדָה אֵימָתַי וכו׳: Why does the Gemara assume that Rabbi Yehuda was explaining the opinion of the first *tanna* and not disagreeing with it?

The Rashbam answers that there is a principle that whenever Rabbi Yehuda opens his response to a previously mentioned statement with the term: When, his intent is to explain the previous statement.

Other early commentaries argue that this principle applies only to *mishnayot*, while this statement of Rabbi Yehuda appears in a *baraita*. Furthermore, according to a different version of the text, Rabbi Yehuda's statement opens not with the term: When, but with the question: In what case is this statement said? This sentence indicates the opposite, i.e., that Rabbi Yehuda's intent is to disagree with the previous statement (see Rabbeinu Yona, *Tosefot HaRosh*, and Ritva).

Another answer suggested is that since Rabbi Yehuda evidently disagrees with Rabbi Yosei, maintaining that both the husband's writing the document and the wife's acceptance are necessary, it is more reasonable to assume that his opinion is that of the first *tanna* than to assume that the entire mishna is stating Rabbi Yosei's opinion (Rabbeinu Yona).

Once he rendered her a partner among the sons – כֵּיוָן שֶׁעֲשָׂאָהּ שׁוּתָּף בֵּין הַבָּנִים: The Rashbam explains that she presumably waived her right to receive payment of her marriage contract due to the honor he bestowed on her by giving her a portion in his estate.

The early commentaries discuss the relationship between Rav Naḥman's opinion and those of the *tanna'im* and *amora'im* mentioned previously. The Rashbam, citing Rashi, writes that Rav Naḥman's statement is an explanation of Shmuel's opinion, that if the husband distributes the property in his wife's presence and she remains silent, this suffices for her to lose her right to receive payment of her marriage contract. This is in accordance with the opinion of Rabbi Yosei that either his writing a document or her acceptance of the distribution is sufficient (see Rabbeinu Yona).

The Ritva argues that according to the Rashbam's own opinion, Rav Naḥman ruled in accordance with the opinion of Rabbi Yosei, son of Rabbi Ḥanina, who in his opinion is the most lenient toward the husband.

The Rosh holds that Rav Naḥman is more lenient toward the husband than all of the aforementioned *amora'im*, as he holds that even if the wife was not present during the distribution and the husband did not tell her that he is giving her the parcel of land for her marriage contract, as long as she finds out and does not protest, she has lost her right to receive payment of her marriage contract. Conversely, Rabbeinu Ḥananel maintains that Rav Naḥman ruled in accordance with the opinion of the first *tanna* in the mishna, that both his writing of the document and her acceptance of the distribution are necessary, as she can enter a partnership only with explicit consent.

Another opinion, cited by Rabbeinu Yona, is that if the wife receives an equal portion of the property, her silence is sufficient. If her share is not equal to that of the other heirs, Rav Naḥman holds that her explicit consent is necessary, in accordance with the opinion of the first *tanna*.

HALAKHA

Once he rendered her a partner, etc. – כֵּיוָן שֶׁעֲשָׂאָהּ שׁוּתָּף וכו׳: If a person on his deathbed wrote, or said (*Helkat Meḥokek*), that all his property is given to his children, and wrote a document granting any amount of land to his wife as well, if she found out about it and did not protest, she has lost her right to receive payment of her marriage contract, though not of her dowry (Rema, citing *Maggid Mishne*), as she became a partner in the inheritance. This is in accordance with the Rosh's interpretation of Rav Naḥman's ruling, which is based on several factors: That if the husband gives the wife a parcel of land, her explicit acquiescence is not required, in accordance with Rabbi Yosei's opinion; that her presence during the distribution is not required, contrary to Shmuel's opinion; and that the husband does not need to tell her that he is giving her the parcel of land for her marriage contract, contrary to the opinion of Rabbi Yosei, son of Rabbi Ḥanina (Rambam *Sefer Kinyan, Hilkhot Zekhiya UMattana* 6:9; *Shulḥan Arukh, Even HaEzer* 106:1).

In the case of a healthy person, what is the *halakha* – בְּבָרִיא הֵיאָךְ: If a healthy person distributed his property to his children and wrote a document granting his wife a parcel of land, the *halakha* is that she has lost her right to receive payment of her marriage contract. This is because Rava's dilemma was not resolved, and the property cannot be appropriated from the heirs due to the uncertainty (Rambam *Sefer Kinyan, Hilkhot Zekhiya UMattana* 6:9; *Shulḥan Arukh, Even HaEzer* 106:1).

הַהוּא דַּאֲמַר לְהוּ: ״פַּלְגָּא לִבְרַת, וּפַלְגָּא לִבְרַת, וְתִילְתָּא לְאִיתְּתַ בְּפֵירֵי״; אִיקְּלַע רַב נַחְמָן לְסוּרָא, עוּל לְגַבֵּי רַב חִסְדָּא, אֲמַר לֵיהּ: כִּי הַאי גַּוְונָא מַאי? אֲמַר לֵיהּ, הָכִי אָמַר שְׁמוּאֵל: אֲפִילּוּ לֹא הִקְנָה לָהּ אֶלָּא דֶּקֶל אֶחָד לְפֵירוֹתָיו – אִבְּדָה כְּתוּבָּתָהּ.

§ There was **a certain** man on his deathbed **who said to** the people surrounding him: Give **one-half** of my estate **to** my **daughter, and one-half to** my other **daughter, and one-third of the produce to** my **wife. Rav Naḥman**[P] **happened** to come **to Sura. He entered** the study hall **to** see **Rav Ḥisda,**[P] **who said to him:** In **a case like this, what** is the *halakha*? Rav Naḥman **said to him** that **this** is what **Shmuel says: Even if he transferred to her** ownership **only one palm tree for its produce,**[N] **she has lost** her right to receive payment of **her marriage contract.**

אֲמַר לֵיהּ: אֵימוּר דְּאָמַר שְׁמוּאֵל הָתָם – דְּאַקְנֵי לָהּ בְּגוּפָהּ דְּאַרְעָא, הָכָא פֵּירָא הוּא! אֲמַר לֵיהּ: מִטַּלְטְלֵי קָא אָמְרַתְּ? מִטַּלְטְלֵי וַדַּאי לָא קָא אָמִינָא.

Rav Ḥisda **said to him: Say that Shmuel said** his statement that she loses her right **there,** in a case where he gave her a palm tree for its produce, **because he transferred** rights **in the land itself to her ownership,** as the palm tree is connected to the ground. But **here,** in this case, **it is** only **produce** that he gave her, without any share in the land itself. Perhaps she does not lose payment of her marriage contract. Rav Naḥman **said to him: You say** that he gave her only **movable property? I certainly did not** mean to **say** that she loses her right even if he gave her only **movable property**[NH] such as produce. Rather, she receives payment of her marriage contract.

הַהוּא דַּאֲמַר לְהוּ: ״תִּלְתָּא לִבְרַת, וְתִלְתָּא לִבְרַת, וְתִלְתָּא לְאִיתְּתַ״, שְׁכִיבָא חֲדָא מִבְּנָתֵיהּ; סָבַר רַב פַּפִּי לְמֵימַר: לָא שָׁקְלָא אֶלָּא תִּלְתָּא,

There was **a certain** man on his deathbed **who said to** the people surrounding him: Give **one-third** of my property **to** my **daughter, and one-third to** my other **daughter, and one-third to** my **wife. One of his daughters died** before he did, and her portion consequently returned to his possession. **Rav Pappi thought to say** that the wife **takes only one-third.** She cannot receive payment of her marriage contract from the two-thirds bequeathed to the daughters, as by entering a partnership with the daughters in ownership of the property, she waived payment of her marriage contract.

PERSONALITIES

Rav Naḥman – רַב נַחְמָן: Rav Naḥman bar Ya'akov was a second- and third-generation Babylonian *amora*. While he cites statements in the names of both Rav and Shmuel, his primary teacher was Rabba bar Avuh, Rav's student. While he never formally headed one of the Babylonian academies, nevertheless, many of the Sages of the following generation were his students, including the prominent *amora* Rava.

Rav Ḥisda – רַב חִסְדָּא: One of the most prominent second-generation Babylonian *amora'im*, Rav Ḥisda, a priest, was one of Rav's younger students. After Rav's death, he remained a disciple-colleague of Rav's student, Rav Huna. Throughout his life, Rav Ḥisda showed high regard for the statements of Rav and constantly tried to learn additional matters of Torah cited in his name. Although he was poor as a youth, he became wealthy and lived most of his life in comfort, although he was very generous toward others. He was devoted to his students, his sons, and his daughters, guiding them along the proper path in both spiritual and worldly matters.

NOTES

Even if he transferred to her only one palm tree for its produce – אֲפִילּוּ לֹא הִקְנָה לָהּ אֶלָּא דֶּקֶל אֶחָד לְפֵירוֹתָיו: Even if he did not give her the land itself but only the rights to its produce, she loses her right to receive payment of her marriage contract. This is the *halakha* despite the fact that if the tree dies she will remain with nothing, neither the tree itself nor the right to plant another one in its place.

I certainly did not say only movable property – מִטַּלְטְלֵי וַדַּאי לָא קָא אָמִינָא: Rav Naḥman had assumed that the husband gave her one-third of the produce that is still connected to the ground and is not yet ready to be harvested; this is considered a portion of the land, thereby rendering the wife a partner in the inheritance. By contrast, produce that was already harvested or that is ready to be harvested is considered movable property and is not liened to the marriage contract. Therefore it is not assumed that upon receiving the gift the wife waived the payment of the rest of her marriage contract (Ramah). The Ramah concludes that once the *ge'onim* instituted that one's movable property is also liened to payment of his wife's marriage contract, she also loses her right to receive payment of the marriage contract if he gives her movable property.

HALAKHA

Movable property – מִטַּלְטְלֵי: In a case where one distributed all his property to his children, then even if he wrote a document granting his wife only produce that is connected to the ground, or one palm tree for its produce, she has become a partner in the inheritance and has lost her right to receive payment of her marriage contract, in accordance with Shmuel's statement. If he wrote a document granting her only movable property, her right remains. Some authorities hold that following the ordinance of the *ge'onim* that payment of a marriage contract is collectable from movable property as well, even if the husband wrote a document granting her only movable property, she has lost her right to receive payment of her marriage contract (*Beit Yosef*). The *Darkhei Moshe* holds that movable property is not a significant enough gift to induce the wife to waive her right to receive payment of her marriage contract (Rambam *Sefer Kinyan*, *Hilkhot Zekhiya UMattana* 6:9–10; *Shulḥan Arukh*, *Even HaEzer* 106:1–2).

אֲמַר לֵיהּ רַב כָּהֲנָא: אִילּוּ הֲדַר קָנֵי, מִי לָא שָׁקְלָא? וְכֵיוָן דְּאִילּוּ הֲדַר קָנֵי שָׁקְלָא, הָשְׁתָּא נַמִּי שָׁקְלָא.

Rav Kahana said to him: If the husband had **then acquired** other property, **would she not have taken** it as payment of her marriage contract? **And since if he** would have **then acquired**[H] other property **she would have taken** it as payment of her marriage contract, **now she also takes** the deceased daughter's share as payment of her marriage contract.

הַהוּא דְּפַלְגִינְהוּ לְנִכְסֵיהּ לְאִתְּתֵיהּ וְלִבְנֵיהּ, שַׁיֵּיר חַד דִּיקְלָא; סָבַר רָבִינָא לְמֵימַר: לֵית לָהּ אֶלָּא חַד דִּיקְלָא. אֲמַר לֵיהּ רַב יֵימָר לְרָבִינָא: אִי לֵית לָהּ, חַד דִּיקְלָא נַמִּי לֵית לָהּ! אֶלָּא, מִיגּוֹ דְּנָחֲתָא לְדִיקְלָא, נָחֲתָא נַמִּי לְכוּלְּהוּ נִכְסֵי.

There was **a certain** person **who divided his property between his wife and his son, leaving out a single palm tree. Ravina thought to say** that the wife **has only** the **single palm tree** as future payment of her marriage contract, which was presumably left out of the distribution for this reason. **Rav Yeimar said to Ravina: If she does not have** the right to collect payment of her marriage contract from all of his property, as she presumably waived that right when he gave her the gift of some of his property, **she does not have** the right to collect it from the **single palm tree either** and it belongs to the heirs. Rav Yeimar presents a different ruling: **Rather, since** the *halakha* is that **she** does **descend to** collect the **palm tree,**[H] **she** therefore **descends to** collect **all of the property as well,** i.e., she receives payment of her marriage contract from all the property.

אָמַר רַב הוּנָא: שְׁכִיב מְרַע שֶׁכָּתַב כָּל נְכָסָיו לְאַחֵר – רוֹאִין: אִם רָאוּי לְיוֹרְשׁוֹ – נוֹטְלָן מִשּׁוּם יְרוּשָּׁה, וְאִם לָאו – נוֹטְלָן מִשּׁוּם מַתָּנָה.

§ **Rav Huna says:** With regard to **a person on his deathbed who wrote** a document granting **all his property to another,** the court **investigates** the legal status of the recipient: **If he is fit to inherit from him,**[N] e.g., if he is one of his sons, **he takes** the property **as an inheritance, and if not, he takes it as a gift.**

אֲמַר לֵיהּ רַב נַחְמָן: גַּנָּבָא גַּנּוּבֵי לָמָּה לָךְ? אִי סְבִירָא לָךְ כְּרַבִּי יוֹחָנָן בֶּן בְּרוֹקָה, אֵימָא: הֲלָכָה כְּרַבִּי יוֹחָנָן בֶּן בְּרוֹקָה, דְּהָא שְׁמַעְתְּתִיךְ כְּרַבִּי יוֹחָנָן בֶּן בְּרוֹקָה הוּא דְּאָזְלָא!

Rav Naḥman said to him: Why should you steal this *halakha* and not attribute it to its source? **If you hold in accordance with** the opinion of **Rabbi Yoḥanan ben Beroka, say** explicitly that **the** ***halakha*** **is in accordance with** the opinion of **Rabbi Yoḥanan ben Beroka, as your halakhic statement follows** the opinion of **Rabbi Yoḥanan ben Beroka** that a person can bequeath his property to any of his heirs.

דִּלְמָא כִּי הָא קָאָמְרַתְּ; דְּהַהוּא דַּהֲוָה קָא שָׁכֵיב, וַאֲמַרוּ לֵיהּ: נִכְסֵיהּ לְמַאן, דִּלְמָא לִפְלָנְיָא? וַאֲמַר לְהוּ: אֶלָּא לְמַאן? וַאֲמַרְתְּ לָן עֲלָהּ: אִם רָאוּי לְיוֹרְשׁוֹ – נוֹטְלָן מִשּׁוּם יְרוּשָּׁה, וְאִם לָאו – נוֹטְלָן מִשּׁוּם מַתָּנָה? אֲמַר לֵיהּ: אִין, הָכִי קָאָמִינָא.

Perhaps this is what you meant to **say:**[N] **There was a certain** childless person **who was dying, and** those around him **said to him: To whom** should **his,** i.e., your, **property** be given? **Perhaps** it should be given **to so-and-so? And he said to them: Rather, to whom** if not him? **And you,** Rav Huna, meant to **say to us: If** that person **is fit to inherit** from **him,**[H] **he takes it as an inheritance, and if not, he takes it as a gift.** Rav Huna **said to him: Yes, that is what I was saying.**[N]

HALAKHA

If he would have then acquired, etc. – **אִילּוּ הֲדַר קָנֵי וכו׳:** If a husband rendered his wife a partner in his inheritance, though she cannot collect payment of her marriage contract from the property that he distributed to his children, she can collect it from property he acquired afterward, even if he reacquired some of the same property that he distributed to his children due to the death of one of his children, in accordance with Rav Kahana's statement (Rambam *Sefer Kinyan, Hilkhot Zekhiya UMattana* 6:9; *Shulḥan Arukh, Even HaEzer* 106:1, 107:3).

Since she does descend to collect the palm tree, etc. – **מִיגּוֹ דְּנָחֲתָא לְדִיקְלָא וכו׳:** If one wrote a document granting all his property to his wife and children, with the exception of any parcel of land that he did not distribute, the wife maintains her right to receive payment of her marriage contract. This is because she can claim that the reason she did not protest the distribution is that she would anyway collect the remaining piece of land first as the payment of her marriage contract, and once she collects that land, she can collect from the distributed property as well. Following the ordinance of the *ge'onim* that payment of a marriage contract is collected from movable property as well, the wife maintains her right to receive payment even if only movable property was left out of the distribution (Rambam *Sefer Kinyan, Hilkhot Zekhiya UMattana* 6:10; *Shulḥan Arukh, Even HaEzer* 106:2).

If he is fit to inherit from him, etc. – **אִם רָאוּי לְיוֹרְשׁוֹ וכו׳:** If a person on his deathbed said: My property will go to so-and-so, or if he was asked whether his property should be given to a certain person and he responded: To whom else if not him, if this person is his son, the son is rendered a steward, as the Gemara ruled earlier (131b, and see *Shakh*). If the owner has no sons, and the recipient is his heir, he acquires the property as an inheritance. If he is not his heir, he acquires it as a gift. The difference between acquiring it as an inheritance and as a gift is in a case where the owner added: And after that one dies, the property will go to so-and-so, who is not the heir of the recipient. If he acquires it as a gift, after his death it is acquired by the second person; but if he acquires it as an inheritance, this addition is meaningless, as inheritance has no end. This is in accordance with Rav Huna's statement as it was interpreted by Rava. The Rema adds, citing Maharil, that if the owner stated explicitly that he is giving it to him as a gift, even if he is his heir, he acquires it as a gift (Rambam *Sefer Kinyan, Hilkhot Zekhiya UMattana* 9:5–6, and see *Maggid Mishne* there; *Shulḥan Arukh, Ḥoshen Mishpat* 253:6–7).

NOTES

If he is fit to inherit from him, etc. – **אִם רָאוּי לְיוֹרְשׁוֹ:** The Rashbam explains that this is a case where the owner did not clarify whether he intended to give him the property as a gift or as an inheritance. Therefore, if the recipient is his legal heir, e.g., one of his sons, it is considered an inheritance, as he would have inherited a share of the property even without this instruction. If he is not his heir, he assumedly intended to give it to him as a gift.

Perhaps this is what you meant to say – **דִּלְמָא כִּי הָא קָאָמְרַתְּ:** In other words, your intention was not to teach the halakhic principle of Rabbi Yoḥanan ben Beroka, but rather to rule in a specific case (Rashbam). Rabbi Gedalya Lifschitz explains that the recipient was a relative of the owner and it was unclear whether he had any closer relatives. Therefore Rav Huna ruled that if a closer relative is found, the property is a gift, and if not, it is an inheritance. Accordingly, the case is unrelated to the principle of Rabbi Yoḥanan ben Beroka, and Rav Huna did not rule in accordance with it.

Yes, that is what I was saying – **אִין, הָכִי קָאָמִינָא:** The novel element of this ruling is that although the benefactor did not state the name of the one to whom he wants to give his property, his statement is interpreted as referring to that person (Ri Migash).

לְמַאי הִלְכְתָא? סָבַר רַב אַדָּא בַּר אַהֲבָה קַמֵּיהּ דְּרָבָא לְמֵימַר: אִם רָאוּי לְיוֹרְשׁוֹ – אַלְמְנָתוֹ נִזּוֹנֵית מִנְּכָסָיו, וְאִם לָאו – אֵין אַלְמְנָתוֹ נִזּוֹנֵית מִנְּכָסָיו.

The Gemara asks: **With regard to what *halakha*** is there a difference whether he receives it as an inheritance or as a gift? **Rav Adda bar Ahava,** who was **in the presence of Rava, thought** that it would be correct **to say: If he is fit to inherit** from **him,** the giver's **widow is sustained from his property,**[N] as she has the right to be sustained from the inheritance; **and if not,** and the property was given as a gift, **his widow is not sustained from his property.**

אֲמַר לֵיהּ רָבָא: מִיגְרַע גָּרְעָא? הָשְׁתָּא בִּירוּשָּׁה דְּאוֹרַיְיתָא אָמְרַתְּ: אַלְמְנָתוֹ נִזּוֹנֵית מִנְּכָסָיו, בְּמַתָּנָה דְּרַבָּנַן לֹא כָּל שֶׁכֵּן?

Rava said to him: Can the widow's right be **diminished** by the gift? **Now that you say with regard to inheritance,** which is granted **by Torah law,** that **his widow is sustained from his property, with regard to** the **gift** of a person on his deathbed, which is effective without any formal act of acquisition **by rabbinic law,**[NH] **all the more so** is it **not** clear that the widow has sustenance rights?

אֶלָּא אֲמַר רָבָא: כִּדְשְׁלַח רַב אַחָא בַּר רַב עַוְיָא: לְדִבְרֵי רַבִּי יוֹחָנָן בֶּן בְּרוֹקָה, ״נְכָסַי לְךָ וְאַחֲרֶיךָ לִפְלוֹנִי״, אִם הָיָה רִאשׁוֹן רָאוּי לְיוֹרְשׁוֹ – אֵין לַשֵּׁנִי בִּמְקוֹם רִאשׁוֹן כְּלוּם, שֶׁאֵין לְשׁוֹן מַתָּנָה אֶלָּא לְשׁוֹן יְרוּשָּׁה, וִירוּשָּׁה אֵין לָהּ הֶפְסֵק.

Rather, Rava said that the difference whether it is inheritance or a gift is **in accordance with** the ruling that **Rav Aḥa bar Rav Avya sent: According to the statement of Rabbi Yoḥanan ben Beroka,** in the case of one who said: **My property** is given **to you, and after you to so-and-so, and the first** recipient **was fit to inherit** from **him, the second gets nothing in place of the first,** i.e., he does not receive the property after the first one dies, **as this formulation** employed by the owner was **not** one **of a gift. Rather,** it was **a formulation of inheritance, and inheritance has no end,** i.e., it cannot be stopped. Therefore, since the first recipient acquired it as an inheritance, his heirs inherit it from him, and it cannot be taken by the second.

אֲמַר לֵיהּ רָבָא לְרַב נַחְמָן: וְהָא אַפְסְקָהּ! הוּא סָבַר: יֵשׁ לָהּ הֶפְסֵק, וְרַחֲמָנָא אָמַר: אֵין לָהּ הֶפְסֵק.

Rava said to Rav Naḥman: But he ended it. The one who bequeathed it to him ended his inheritance in advance by stating that after the first dies, the property will be given to the second. The Gemara answers: **He thought** that inheritance **has an end; but the Merciful One states** that **it has no end.**

NOTES

The giver's widow is sustained from his property – אַלְמְנָתוֹ נִזּוֹנֵית: It is stipulated in a marriage contract that after the husband's death, the wife continues to receive sustenance from the husband's property. If the property was sold or given away, she cannot repossess it, as sustenance is not a fixed amount of money and cannot be taken into account by the purchasers. This is also the *halakha* with regard to the daughters' sustenance.

The gift, which is by rabbinic law – מַתָּנָה דְּרַבָּנַן: By Torah law, a formal act of acquisition is required in order for a transaction to take effect, and it cannot take effect after the owner's death. The Sages instituted that a person on his deathbed can gift his property orally, and the gift takes effect after his death. The reason for this is to minimize the aggravation of one in a precarious position.

HALAKHA

His widow is sustained from his property…by rabbinic law – אַלְמְנָתוֹ נִזּוֹנֵית מִנְּכָסָיו...דְּרַבָּנַן: If a person on his deathbed gave all his property to another, the amount of the property that is necessary for the sustenance of his widow and daughters is withheld from the recipient. Property is also withheld for payment of the wife's marriage contract to their shared male offspring, as stipulated in her marriage contract. This is because the property is liened as a result of these obligations at the moment the giver dies, whereas the recipient acquires the gift only after his death (see *Sma*). If the deceased left out of the gift enough of his property to cover these obligations, they are not collected from the property that was given away (Rambam *Sefer Nashim, Hilkhot Ishut* 19:13; *Shulḥan Arukh, Even HaEzer* 111:17 and *Ḥoshen Mishpat* 252:1).

Perek **VIII**
Daf **133** Amud **b**

הַהוּא דַּאֲמַר לֵיהּ לְחַבְרֵיהּ: ״נְכָסַי לְךָ וְאַחֲרֶיךָ לִפְלוֹנִי״, וְרִאשׁוֹן רָאוּי לְיוֹרְשׁוֹ הֲוָה. שְׁכֵיב רִאשׁוֹן, אֲתָא שֵׁנִי קָא תָּבַע;

There was a **certain** person **who said to another: My property** is given **to you, and after you, to so-and-so, and the first one was fit to inherit** from **him.** After **the first died, the second came and claimed** the property.

סָבַר רַב עִילִישׁ קַמֵּיהּ דְּרָבָא לְמֵימַר: שֵׁנִי נָמֵי שָׁקֵיל, אֲמַר לֵיהּ: דַּיָּינֵי דַּחֲצַצְתָּא הָכִי דָּיְינִי, לָאו הַיְינוּ דִּשְׁלַח רַב אַחָא בַּר רַב עַוְיָא?

Rav Ilish, who was **in the presence of Rava, thought to say** that **the second also takes**[N] a share of the property; he divides it with the heirs of the first. Rava **said to him: Judges of compromise,**[N] who as a matter of course divide disputed property between the parties, **rule in this manner.** But **isn't this** identical to the case concerning **which Rav Aḥa bar Rav Avya sent** a ruling that the second receives nothing?

אִכְסִיף. קָרֵי עֲלֵיהּ: ״אֲנִי ה׳ בְּעִתָּהּ אֲחִישֶׁנָּה״.

Rav Ilish **was embarrassed** by his mistake. To comfort him, Rav **read** the following verse **about him: "I, the Lord, will hasten it in its time"** (Isaiah 60:22),[N] as if to say: It was due to Divine Providence that I was here to correct you before your mistaken ruling was implemented.

NOTES

The second also takes – שֵׁנִי נָמֵי שָׁקֵיל: This wording indicates that Rav Ilish's suggestion was that the heirs of the first and the second should divide the property (Rabbeinu Gershom Meor HaGola; see Rashbam). By contrast, Rabbeinu Ḥananel had a version of the Gemara that did not include the word: Also, and maintains that Rav Ilish held that the second should receive all the property, as the giver instructed.

Judges of compromise [*ḥatzatzta*] – דַּיָּינֵי דַּחֲצַצְתָּא: Rabbeinu Gershom Meor HaGola and the Rashbam interpret the word *ḥatzatzta* to mean compromise, referring to judges who as a matter of course compromise between the two parties, giving each one half the amount, because they do not know the *halakha*. Rabbeinu Ḥananel interprets the phrase to mean judges of graves (see *Arukh*). The Maharsha explains this interpretation as follows: Although the giver, who is in the grave, assumed that inheritance can be halted, that is not the *halakha*. Another explanation, in accordance with Rabbeinu Ḥananel's interpretation, is that these are judges who know nothing, like the dead (Rabbi Gedalya Lifschitz).

NOTES

I the Lord will hasten it in its time – אֲנִי ה׳ בְּעִתָּהּ אֲחִישֶׁנָּה: The Rashbam explains that Rav Ilish was embarrassed because the incident indicated that he probably erred in other cases as well, when Rava was not present to correct him. Therefore, Rava comforted him by saying that it was due to Divine Providence that he happened to be present specifically when Rav Ilish made a mistake, so that he could prevent him from issuing an erroneous ruling.

Rabbeinu Ḥananel (cited in Ritva and *Tosefot HaRosh*) suggests a different interpretation: Rava said to Rav Ilish that he need not be distressed by his error, as he is still young, and in time he will master the *halakha*. The Maharal explains that Rava meant that even if one is sufficiently wise and knowledgeable, Heaven prevents him from reaching the correct conclusion until the appropriate time comes.

מתני׳ הַכּוֹתֵב אֶת נְכָסָיו לַאֲחֵרִים וְהִנִּיחַ אֶת בָּנָיו – מַה שֶּׁעָשָׂה עָשׂוּי, אֶלָּא אֵין רוּחַ חֲכָמִים נוֹחָה הֵימֶנּוּ; רַבָּן שִׁמְעוֹן בֶּן גַּמְלִיאֵל אוֹמֵר: אִם לֹא הָיוּ בָנָיו נוֹהֲגִים כַּשּׁוּרָה – זָכוּר לְטוֹב.

MISHNA With regard to **one who wrote** a document granting **his property to others** as a gift **and left his sons** with nothing,[H] **what he did is done,** i.e., it takes effect; **but the Sages are displeased with him. Rabban Shimon ben Gamliel says: If** he did so because **his sons were not acting properly, he is remembered** positively.[N]

גמ׳ אִיבַּעְיָא לְהוּ: מִי פְּלִיגִי רַבָּנַן עֲלֵיהּ דְּרַבָּן שִׁמְעוֹן בֶּן גַּמְלִיאֵל, אוֹ לָא?

GEMARA A dilemma was raised before the Sages: **Do the Rabbis disagree with Rabban Shimon ben Gamliel,** maintaining that depriving one's children of their inheritance is inappropriate in any event, **or not?**

תָּא שְׁמַע: דְּיוֹסֵף בֶּן יוֹעֶזֶר הָיָה לוֹ בֵּן שֶׁלֹּא הָיָה נוֹהֵג כַּשּׁוּרָה, הֲוָה לֵיהּ עִילִּיתָא דְּדִינָרֵי, קָם אַקְדְּשָׁהּ. אֲזַל נְסֵיב בַּת גָּאדֵיל כְּלִילֵי דִּינַּאי מַלְכָּא, אוֹלִידָה דְּבֵיתְהוּ, זְבֵין לַהּ בִּינִיתָא, קַרְעָהּ אַשְׁכַּח בַּהּ מַרְגָּלִיתָא.

The Gemara suggests: **Come and hear,** as **Yosef ben Yo'ezer**[P] **had a son who was not acting properly.** Yosef ben Yo'ezer **had a vessel** [*illiyyata*][N] full **of dinars,** and **he arose and consecrated it** to the Temple treasury, depriving his son of his inheritance. His son **went and married the daughter of King Yannai's crown weaver.** After the son's **wife gave birth, he bought her a fish** [*binita*].[L] **He tore its** stomach open and **found a pearl in it.** He decided to sell it.

אֲמַרָה לֵיהּ: לָא תַּמְטְיֵיהּ לְמַלְכָּא, דְּשָׁקְלִי לַהּ מִינָּךְ בִּדְמֵי קַלִּילֵי, זִיל אַמְטְיֵיהּ לְגַבֵּי גִּזְבָּרֵי. וְלָא תְּשַׁיְּימָהּ אַתְּ, דַּאֲמִירָתוֹ לַגָּבוֹהַּ כִּמְסִירָתוֹ לְהֶדְיוֹט, אֶלָּא לְשַׁיְּימוּהָ אִינְהוּ.

His wife **said to him: Do not bring it to** the treasury of **the king** to sell it, **as they will take it from you for an insignificant** sum **of money.** Rather, **go bring it to the** Temple **treasurers.**[N] **And do not appraise it yourself,**[HN] **as declaration to the Most High is equivalent to transfer to an ordinary** person, and if you offer to sell it for an amount less than its worth, you will not be able to change your mind. **Rather, let them appraise it.**

אַמְטְיֵיהּ, שָׁמוּהָ בִּתְלֵיסַרֵי עִלְיָאתָא דְּדִינָרֵי. אָמְרִי לֵיהּ: שְׁבַע אִיכָּא, שִׁית לֵיכָּא. אֲמַר לְהוּ: שְׁבַע הָבוּ לִי, שִׁית הֲרֵי הֵן מוּקְדָּשׁוֹת לְשָׁמַיִם.

He brought it to the Temple treasury, and **they appraised it as** having the value of **thirteen vessels** [*illiyyata*] full **of dinars.** The treasurers **said to him: There are seven** *illiyyata* of dinars at our disposal to pay you for the pearl, but **there are not** an additional **six. He said to** the treasurers: **Give me the seven** in exchange for the pearl, and as for the additional **six** that you owe me, **they are hereby consecrated to Heaven.**

עָמְדוּ וְכָתְבוּ: ״יוֹסֵף בֶּן יוֹעֶזֶר הִכְנִיס אַחַת, וּבְנוֹ הִכְנִיס שֵׁשׁ״. וְאִיכָּא דְּאָמְרִי: ״יוֹסֵף בֶּן יוֹעֶזֶר הִכְנִיס אַחַת, וּבְנוֹ הוֹצִיא שֶׁבַע״;

The treasurers **arose and wrote:**[N] **Yosef ben Yo'ezer bestowed one** *illiyyata* to the Temple treasury, **and his son bestowed six. And there are** those **who say** that they wrote: **Yosef ben Yo'ezer bestowed one** *illiyyata* to the Temple treasury, **and his son removed seven,** which he received for the pearl.

HALAKHA

One who wrote his property to others as a gift and left his sons with nothing – הַכּוֹתֵב אֶת נְכָסָיו לַאֲחֵרִים וְהִנִּיחַ אֶת בָּנָיו: If one gives his entire estate to others, leaving his heirs with nothing, the Sages are displeased with his action but the gift is valid. This is in accordance with Shmuel's statement, according to which the Rabbis disagree with the opinion of Rabban Shimon ben Gamliel, and their opinion is accepted. The Rema, citing the Mordekhai, adds that if one instructs that his estate be allotted in the best possible manner, it should be given to his heirs, as there is no better designation for the property. It is even better to give the property to the heirs than for it to be consecrated, as is evident from the incident involving Yosef ben Yo'ezer and his son (Rambam *Sefer Mishpatim*, *Hilkhot Naḥalot* 6:11; *Shulḥan Arukh*, *Ḥoshen Mishpat* 252:2, 282:1).

Go bring it to the Temple treasurers, and do not appraise it yourself, etc. – אַמְטְיֵיהּ לְגַבֵּי גִּזְבָּרֵי וְלָא תְּשַׁיְּימָהּ אַתְּ וכו׳: If one sells an item to the Temple treasury and is asked by the treasurer for how much money he is willing to sell it, and he quotes a certain amount, he cannot change his mind. This is the *halakha* even if it is actually worth more than the amount he quoted. The reason is that declaration to the Most High is equivalent to transfer to an ordinary person (Rambam *Sefer Kinyan*, *Hilkhot Mekhira* 9:1; *Shulḥan Arukh*, *Yoreh De'a* 258:13).

PERSONALITIES

Yosef ben Yo'ezer – יוֹסֵף בֶּן יוֹעֶזֶר: Yosef ben Yo'ezer of Tzereida was the first of the pairs of Sages (see *Avot* 1:4), and was a student of Antigonus of Sokho. During that period, Sages were not granted honorary titles, but were known by their first name alone. Based on the accounts of the Talmud, Yosef ben Yo'ezer lived in an era when Hellenists controlled Jerusalem. He was executed, probably by the wicked priest Alkimos, his sister's son, dying a martyr's death. Together with his counterpart, Yosei ben Yoḥanan, he decreed that lands outside Eretz Yisrael and glass vessels be considered impure. Additionally, testimony is provided in tractate *Eduyyot* concerning his lenient rulings with regard to several *halakhot*, to such an extent that he was called: Yosef the Lenient. The Sages of the Mishna discussed his statements at length (see *Pesaḥim* 14a), and said that his death brought an end to the clusters [*eshkolot*], i.e., scholars with expertise in all areas of the Torah.

LANGUAGE

Fish [*binita*] – בִּינִיתָא: This noun, close to the Arabic بني, *bunnā*, is apparently a particular kind of fish, perhaps a kind of carp, and indeed the Arabs living in Israel call carp *bini*.

Carp

NOTES

If his sons were not acting properly, he is remembered positively – אִם לֹא הָיוּ בָנָיו נוֹהֲגִים כַּשּׁוּרָה זָכוּר לְטוֹב: The Rif has a version of the text that reads: If his sons were not acting properly toward him (see Rambam and *Shulḥan Arukh*). In other words, even if they were acting properly with respect to God, if they were not acting properly toward him, that is sufficient grounds for depriving them of the inheritance (see *Sma*).

Vessel [*illiyyata*] – עִילִּיתָא: Rabbeinu Tam asserts that although the word *illiyyata* usually means the loft of a house, here it refers to a vessel used for drawing wine. Other commentaries concur.

To the Temple treasurers – לְגַבֵּי גִּזְבָּרֵי: Precious stones were needed for the breastplate and the ephod of the High Priest (Rashbam).

And do not appraise it yourself – וְלָא תְּשַׁיְּימָהּ אַתְּ: There are early commentaries that hold that the woman's instruction was halakhically incorrect, as if one pledges a certain item to the Temple treasury, and its value rises, he is not obligated to sell it for the price he had stated. Others claim that she was correct, as until the official market value changes, one must fulfill his pledge in accordance with the value he had stated (Ritva; see Rambam).

They arose and wrote, etc. – עָמְדוּ וְכָתְבוּ וכו׳: Where did they write it? One suggestion is that they wrote it in the account book of the Temple treasury, where they would record the expenses and revenues of the Temple. Accordingly, the Gemara's inference is from the manner in which it was written. Another suggestion is that it was written specially to teach the moral ramifications of Yosef ben Yo'ezer's act (Rashbam). The Ritva explains that they wrote it in a book of dedication, where all those who would dedicate to the Temple were honored (Ritva; Responsa of the Rashba).

מִדְּקָא אָמְרִי ״הִכְנִיס״, מִכְּלָל דְּשַׁפִּיר עֲבַד. אַדְּרַבָּה, מִדְּקָא אָמְרִי ״הוֹצִיא״, מִכְּלָל דְּלָאו שַׁפִּיר עֲבַד! אֶלָּא מֵהָא לֵיכָּא לְמִשְׁמַע מִינָּהּ.

The Gemara infers: **From the fact that they said** approvingly that Yosef ben Yo'ezer's son **bestowed** seven, **by inference, he acted well** when he left him out of his inheritance. The Gemara responds: **On the contrary; from the fact that** according to the second account, **they said** disparagingly that he **removed** seven, **by inference,** Yosef ben Yo'ezer **did not act well** when he left him out of his inheritance, as he caused money to be removed from the Temple treasury. **Rather, no** inference is **to be learned from this** story with regard to the dilemma as to whether the Rabbis agree with the opinion of Rabban Shimon ben Gamliel, as the two accounts contradict each other on this matter.

מַאי הָוֵי עֲלַהּ? תָּא שְׁמַע, דַּאֲמַר לֵיהּ שְׁמוּאֵל לְרַב יְהוּדָה: שִׁינָּנָא, לָא תֶּיהֱוֵי בֵּי עֲבוּרֵי אַחְסַנְתָּא, וַאֲפִילּוּ מִבְּרָא בִּישָׁא לִבְרָא טָבָא, וְכׇל שֶׁכֵּן מִבְּרָא לִבְרַתָּא.

The Gemara asks: **What** halakhic conclusion **was** reached **about** this matter? **Come** and **hear, as Shmuel said to Rav Yehuda:** ***Shinnana*,**[B] **do not be in a house where inheritance is transferred**[HN] away from its rightful heir, **even** if it is transferred **from a wicked son to a good son,**[N] **and all the more so** if it is transferred **from a son to a daughter.** Evidently, the Rabbis hold that inheritance should not be transferred in any case.

תָּנוּ רַבָּנַן: מַעֲשֶׂה בְּאָדָם אֶחָד שֶׁלֹּא הָיוּ בָּנָיו נוֹהֲגִין כַּשּׁוּרָה, עָמַד וְכָתַב נְכָסָיו לְיוֹנָתָן בֶּן עוּזִּיאֵל. מֶה עָשָׂה יוֹנָתָן בֶּן עוּזִּיאֵל? מָכַר שְׁלִישׁ, וְהִקְדִּישׁ שְׁלִישׁ, וְהֶחֱזִיר לְבָנָיו שְׁלִישׁ.

§ **The Sages taught:** There was **an incident involving one man whose children did not act properly. He arose and wrote** a document transferring all **his property**[N] **to Yonatan ben Uzziel,**[P] one of the Sages, as a gift. **What did Yonatan ben Uzziel do? He sold a third** of the property for his needs, **and consecrated a third**[N] of the property, **and returned** the remaining **third to** the man's **children.**

בָּא עָלָיו שַׁמַּאי בְּמַקְלוֹ וְתַרְמִילוֹ. אָמַר לוֹ: שַׁמַּאי, אִם אַתָּה יָכוֹל לְהוֹצִיא אֶת מַה שֶּׁמָּכַרְתִּי וּמַה שֶּׁהִקְדַּשְׁתִּי – אַתָּה יָכוֹל לְהוֹצִיא מַה שֶּׁהֶחֱזַרְתִּי,

Shammai[P] **came to** Yonatan ben Uzziel **with his staff and traveling bag**[N] to protest his giving part of the property to the man's children against the deceased's wishes. Yonatan ben Uzziel **said to him: Shammai, if you can repossess** the property **that I sold**[N] from the purchasers **and** the property **that I consecrated** from the Temple treasury, **you can repossess what I returned** to the man's children as well;

NOTES

Do not be in a house where inheritance is transferred – לָא תֶּיהֱוֵי בֵּי עֲבוּרֵי אַחְסַנְתָּא: In other words, do not participate in such a transfer, even if it is from one child to another, and certainly if it is to someone to whom the person is not related at all, as the Sages disapprove of this behavior. The Meiri writes that it is a custom of the pious to refrain from participating in such an event.

Even from a wicked son to a good son – וַאֲפִילּוּ מִבְּרָא בִּישָׁא לִבְרָא טָבָא: The early commentaries explain that one cannot know which of his children will have more righteous descendants. Due to the possibility that the wicked son will have descendants that are more righteous than those of the righteous son, he should not be deprived of his inheritance.

He arose and wrote a document transferring all his property, etc. – עָמַד וְכָתַב נְכָסָיו וכו׳: The Rashbam explains this incident in the context of the topic under discussion, namely, a person who decides to grant his property to another party, depriving his legal heirs of their inheritance. Other commentaries interpret the story differently, based on the comparison on 134a to the incident in Beit Ḥoron, where one gave his property to another in order to enable his relative to derive benefit from it despite a prior vow prohibiting him from doing so. They explain that the man in this story took a vow prohibiting his children from deriving benefit from his property, as he was angry about their behavior. Before his death he regretted his vow and wanted to leave them some of the inheritance, so he transferred his property to Yonatan ben Uzziel, assuming that this pious man would give some of the property to his children (Rabbi Avraham *Av Bet Din*, citing Rabbi Yitzḥak, son of Rabbi Reuven of Barcelona; see *Tosafot*).

He sold a third and consecrated a third – מָכַר שְׁלִישׁ וְהִקְדִּישׁ שְׁלִישׁ: The Rashbam writes that he did so in order to prove that the property is his own and he can use it in any way he wishes; he can therefore give a portion to the children as well.

With his staff and traveling bag – בְּמַקְלוֹ וְתַרְמִילוֹ: The Rashbam interprets this to mean that he came ready to protest Yonatan ben Uzziel's action. The Ramah writes that he brought these items in order to appropriate the property that was given to the man's children; he brought the staff to threaten them with it, and the bag to collect the money.

The early commentaries disagree as to what Shammai's claim was. The Rashbam maintains that Shammai held that the gift was designated for Yonatan ben Uzziel's benefit, and he had no right to give it to the man's children. He was therefore obligated to repossess the property, as it is a mitzva to fulfill the statement of the dead. Rabbi Avraham *Av Bet Din*, who holds that the purpose of the gift was to circumvent a prior vow, explains that according to Shammai, Yonatan ben Uzziel's action was tantamount to artifice, as in the incident in Beit Ḥoron.

If you can repossess the property that I sold, etc. – אִם אַתָּה יָכוֹל לְהוֹצִיא אֶת מַה שֶּׁמָּכַרְתִּי וכו׳: In other words, since you acknowledge that my sale and consecration are valid, you clearly recognize that the property was given to me unconditionally and I can do whatever I want with it. Therefore, my gift to the children is also valid. The difference between this case and the incident in Beit Ḥoron is that in the latter case, the gift was explicitly conditional, whereas in this case, it was not (Rashbam).

BACKGROUND

***Shinnana* – שִׁינָּנָא:** According to many commentaries, Rashi among them, *shinnana* means sharp, and it is an honorific that Shmuel conferred upon Rav Yehuda, his most prominent student. The *ge'onim* explain, based on old Aramaic vernacular, that *shinnana* means the one with the large teeth, and that was Rav Yehuda's nickname.

HALAKHA

Do not be in a house where inheritance is transferred – לָא תֶּיהֱוֵי בֵּי עֲבוּרֵי אַחְסַנְתָּא: It is a custom of the pious not to serve as a witness of the transfer of a person's estate away from the rightful heir, in accordance with Shmuel's directive to Rav Yehuda. This applies even to the transfer of the share of a son who does not act properly to his brother who acts properly and is a scholar (Rambam *Sefer Mishpatim*, *Hilkhot Naḥalot* 6:11; *Shulḥan Arukh*, *Ḥoshen Mishpat* 282:1).

PERSONALITIES

Yonatan ben Uzziel – יוֹנָתָן בֶּן עוּזִּיאֵל: Very little is known about Yonatan ben Uzziel, who was the greatest student of Hillel the Elder. His greatest project, for which he is most remembered, was the translation of the books of the Prophets from Hebrew into Aramaic. It was apparently a loose translation that included much interpretation and explanation. Although there were previous translations into Greek, his translation was the first that also served as a kind of commentary, whose methodology was accepted and adopted by the Torah scholars of the Jewish people. It is not clear whether the translation carrying his name today is his translation or whether it is merely based on his translation.

Shammai – שַׁמַּאי: Shammai, occasionally referred to as Shammai the Elder, was the counterpart of Hillel the Elder, as they constituted the last of the pairs of the early tannaitic period, approximately one hundred years prior to the destruction of the Temple, at the beginning of Herod's reign. Hillel was the *Nasi* and Shammai served as president of the court. Little is known about Shammai's personal life. He was apparently an architect or builder by trade, as he is depicted on several occasions as standing with a builder's cubit, which was a common measuring stick, in his hand.

Shammai and Hillel were noted as having different personalities. Shammai took a severe approach and held others to a high standard in terms of their actions and motivation (see, e.g., *Shabbat* 31a). Nevertheless, it was Shammai who coined the phrase: One should receive all people with a pleasant countenance (*Avot* 1:15). Hillel, by contrast, treated himself and others in an easygoing manner and exhibited extreme flexibility to avoid conflict. While Shammai and Hillel themselves engaged in only a handful of halakhic disputes, *tanna'im* who studied at the academies they established, known as Beit Shammai and Beit Hillel, did not fully understand the opinions of their teachers and engaged in many more disputes (see *Sanhedrin* 88b).

אם לָאו – אִי אַתָּה יָכוֹל לְהוֹצִיא מַה שֶּׁהֶחֱזַרְתִּי. אָמַר: הֵטִיחַ עָלַי בֶּן עוּזִּיאֵל! הֵטִיחַ עָלַי בֶּן עוּזִּיאֵל!

but **if not,** as the property is mine and I have the right to do with it whatever I want, **you cannot repossess what I returned** to the man's children either. Shammai then **said: Ben Uzziel reprimanded me; ben Uzziel reprimanded me,** and I have no response.

מֵעִיקָּרָא מַאי סָבַר? מִשּׁוּם מַעֲשֶׂה דְּבֵית חוֹרוֹן;

The Gemara asks: **What did** Shammai **hold initially,** causing him to protest Yonatan ben Uzziel's behavior? The Gemara answers: He protested **due to the incident** that happened **in the city of Beit Ḥoron.**

דִּתְנַן: מַעֲשֶׂה בְּבֵית חוֹרוֹן בְּאֶחָד שֶׁהָיָה אָבִיו מוּדָּר הֵימֶנּוּ הֲנָאָה, וְהָיָה מַשִּׂיא בְּנוֹ, וְאָמַר לַחֲבֵירוֹ: הֲרֵי חָצֵר וּסְעוּדָה נְתוּנִין לְךָ בְּמַתָּנָה, וְאֵינָן לְפָנֶיךָ אֶלָּא כְּדֵי שֶׁיָּבֹא אַבָּא וְיֹאכַל עִמָּנוּ בַּסְּעוּדָה.

As we learned in a mishna (*Nedarim* 48a): **An incident** occurred **involving someone in** the city of **Beit Ḥoron whose father had vowed not to derive benefit from him, and the** son **was marrying off his** own **son** and wanted his father to be able to participate in the wedding meal. **And** he therefore **said to another:** The **courtyard** where the wedding will take place **and** the wedding **meal are hereby given to you as a gift, but they are** given **to you only so that my father will come and eat with us at the meal.** The son wanted to circumvent the prohibition imposed by the vow and enable his father to participate in the meal, so he transferred ownership to someone else for that purpose.

אָמַר לוֹ: אִם שֶׁלִּי הֵן – הֲרֵי הֵן מוּקְדָּשִׁין לַשָּׁמַיִם! אָמַר לוֹ: לֹא נָתַתִּי לְךָ אֶת שֶׁלִּי שֶׁתַּקְדִּישֵׁם לַשָּׁמַיִם! אָמַר לוֹ: לֹא נָתַתָּ לִי אֶת שֶׁלְּךָ אֶלָּא שֶׁתְּהֵא אַתָּה וְאָבִיךָ אוֹכְלִין וְשׁוֹתִין וּמְרַצִּין זֶה לָזֶה, וִיהֵא עָוֹן תָּלוּי בְּרֹאשׁוֹ!

The recipient **said to him: If they are mine, they are** all **hereby consecrated to Heaven,** i.e., the Temple, and are forbidden to everyone. The son **said to him** in anger: **I did not give you my** property **so that you should consecrate them to Heaven.** The recipient **said to him: You gave me your** property **only** so **that you and your father would eat and drink and** thereby **appease each other, and the sin** of transgressing the vow would **be hung on his,** i.e., my, **head,** as I enabled the transgression.

אָמְרוּ חֲכָמִים: כׇּל מַתָּנָה שֶׁאֵינָהּ שֶׁאִם הִקְדִּישָׁהּ מוּקְדֶּשֶׁת – אֵינָהּ מַתָּנָה.

The mishna continues: In reference to this incident, **the Sages said: Any gift that is not** so absolute **that if** the recipient **were to consecrate it,**[H] the gift **would be consecrated, is not a gift.** In other words, in order for it to be a gift the recipient must have the ability to consecrate it. Similarly, Shammai had initially reasoned that the gift to Yonatan ben Uzziel was not a valid gift, as its sole purpose was so that the property should not fall into the possession of the man's children. Once he discovered that Yonatan ben Uzziel consecrated part of the gift, he realized that it was, in fact, a valid gift, with which the recipient could do whatever he pleased.

תָּנוּ רַבָּנַן: שְׁמוֹנִים תַּלְמִידִים הָיוּ לוֹ לְהִלֵּל הַזָּקֵן, שְׁלֹשִׁים מֵהֶן רְאוּיִם שֶׁתִּשְׁרֶה עֲלֵיהֶן שְׁכִינָה כְּמֹשֶׁה רַבֵּינוּ, שְׁלֹשִׁים מֵהֶן רְאוּיִם שֶׁתַּעֲמוֹד לָהֶן חַמָּה כִּיהוֹשֻׁעַ בִּן נוּן, עֶשְׂרִים בֵּינוֹנִיִּים. גָּדוֹל שֶׁבְּכוּלָּן יוֹנָתָן בֶּן עוּזִּיאֵל, קָטָן שֶׁבְּכוּלָּן רַבָּן יוֹחָנָן בֶּן זַכַּאי.

§ Apropos Yonatan ben Uzziel, the Gemara cites that **the Sages taught: Hillel the Elder**[P] **had eighty students. Thirty of them** were sufficiently **worthy that the Divine Presence should rest upon them**[N] as it did upon **Moses our teacher, thirty of them** were sufficiently **worthy that the sun should stand still for them** as it did for **Joshua bin Nun,** and **twenty** were on **an intermediate** level between the other two. **The greatest of all** the students was **Yonatan ben Uzziel, and the least of them** was **Rabban Yoḥanan ben Zakkai.**

HALAKHA

Any gift that is not so absolute that if the recipient were to consecrate it, etc. – **כׇּל מַתָּנָה שֶׁאֵינָהּ שֶׁאִם הִקְדִּישָׁהּ וכו׳**: Any gift that the recipient cannot consecrate is not a gift. For example, if one says to another: I hereby give you my meal so that so-and-so, who is prohibited to derive benefit from me due to a vow, will eat with you, the subject of the vow is prohibited to partake of the meal, as it is evident from the giver's statement that he does not have intention to transfer the meal to the recipient unconditionally (Rambam *Sefer Hafla'a, Hilkhot Nedarim* 7:16; *Shulḥan Arukh, Yoreh De'a* 221:9).

NOTES

That the Divine Presence should rest upon them – **שֶׁתִּשְׁרֶה עֲלֵיהֶן שְׁכִינָה**: The reason they did not actually achieve this level of prophecy is that the generation was not worthy of it (Rashbam).

PERSONALITIES

Hillel the Elder – **הִלֵּל הַזָּקֵן**: Hillel, referred to as the Elder due to his position in the Sanhedrin, was born in Babylonia and lived in Jerusalem during the time of King Herod and the Roman Emperor Augustus, about a hundred years before the destruction of the Second Temple. He and his colleague Shammai were the last of the pairs of *tanna'im* who played a role in establishing the Mishna. When approached by a potential convert whom Shammai had rejected because he wished to learn the entire Torah on one leg, Hillel offered him the maxim: That which is hateful to you, do not do to your fellow. That is the whole Torah, and the rest is its interpretation; go and learn.

According to tradition, Hillel arrived in Eretz Yisrael to study at age forty in a state of poverty, but his perseverance brought him to the attention of Shemaya and Avtalyon, the heads of the academy, who welcomed him into the study hall. Ultimately, studying under those Sages enabled him to settle questions whose solutions were unknown to others, and he was appointed head of the Sanhedrin. The Gemara compares Hillel to Ezra the Scribe, crediting him with reestablishing Torah at a period in history when it was being forgotten (*Sukka* 20a).

אָמְרוּ עָלָיו עַל רַבָּן יוֹחָנָן בֶּן זַכַּאי, שֶׁלֹּא הִנִּיחַ מִקְרָא וּמִשְׁנָה, תַּלְמוּד, הֲלָכוֹת וַאֲגָדוֹת, דִּקְדּוּקֵי תוֹרָה וְדִקְדּוּקֵי סוֹפְרִים, וְקַלִּין וַחֲמוּרִין, וּגְזֵרוֹת שָׁווֹת, וּתְקוּפוֹת, וְגַמַטְרִיאוֹת, וּמִשְׁלוֹת כּוֹבְסִים וּמִשְׁלוֹת שׁוּעָלִים, שִׂיחַת שֵׁדִים וְשִׂיחַת דְּקָלִים, וְשִׂיחַת מַלְאֲכֵי הַשָּׁרֵת, וְדָבָר גָּדוֹל וְדָבָר קָטָן;

The Sages said about Rabban Yoḥanan ben Zakkai that he did not neglect Bible and Mishna; Talmud;[N] *halakhot* and *aggadot*; minutiae of the Torah[N] and minutiae of the scribes;[N] and the hermeneutical principles of the Torah with regard to *a fortiori* inferences; and verbal analogies; and the calculation of the calendric seasons;[N] and numerical values of Hebrew letters [*gimatriyot*];[NL] and parables of launderers, which are folktales that can be used to explain the Torah, and parables of foxes.[N] In addition, he did not neglect esoteric matters, including the conversation of demons, and the conversation of palm trees,[N] and the conversation of ministering angels, and more generally, a great matter and a small matter.

דָּבָר גָּדוֹל – מַעֲשֵׂה מֶרְכָּבָה, וְדָבָר קָטָן – הֲוָיוֹת דְּאַבַּיֵי וְרָבָא; לְקַיֵּים מַה שֶּׁנֶּאֱמַר: ״לְהַנְחִיל אוֹהֲבַי יֵשׁ וְאוֹצְרֹתֵיהֶם אֲמַלֵּא״.

The Gemara elaborates: A great matter is referring to the secrets of the Design of the Divine Chariot (see Ezekiel, chapter 1), the conduct of the transcendent universe, and a small matter is, for example, *halakhot* that were ultimately formulated in the framework of the discussions of Abaye and Rava.[N] He did not neglect any of these disciplines, so as to fulfill that which is stated: "That I may cause those that love me to inherit substance and that I may fill their treasuries" (Proverbs 8:21), as Rabban Yoḥanan was filled with the disciplines of Torah and wisdom.

וְכִי מֵאַחַר דְּקָטָן שֶׁבְּכוּלָּם כֵּן, גָּדוֹל שֶׁבְּכוּלָּם – עַל אַחַת כַּמָּה וְכַמָּה! אָמְרוּ עָלָיו עַל יוֹנָתָן בֶּן עוּזִּיאֵל, בְּשָׁעָה שֶׁיּוֹשֵׁב וְעוֹסֵק בַּתּוֹרָה – כׇּל עוֹף שֶׁפּוֹרֵחַ עָלָיו נִשְׂרַף.

The Gemara adds: And if the least of them was so prolific, the greatest of them was all the more so prolific. The Gemara relates that the Sages said of Yonatan ben Uzziel, the greatest of Hillel's students, that when he would sit and engage in Torah study, the sanctity that he generated was so intense that any bird that would fly[N] over him would be incinerated.

מתני׳ הָאוֹמֵר ״זֶה בְּנִי״ – נֶאֱמָן, ״זֶה אָחִי״ – אֵינוֹ נֶאֱמָן, וְיִטּוֹל עִמּוֹ בְּחֶלְקוֹ.

MISHNA One who says: This is my son, is deemed credible. One who says: This is my brother,[H] is not deemed credible with regard to his other brothers' obligation to share the inheritance with the subject of his statement. When one claims that this man is his brother, this claim is accepted with regard to the speaker's own portion, and the man in question takes a share of their father's inheritance with him, i.e., from his portion.[H]

מֵת – יַחְזְרוּ נְכָסִים לִמְקוֹמָן.

If the man in question dies, the property he received from the father's inheritance shall return to its place,[N] i.e., to the possession of the brother who testified on his behalf, from whose portion he received a share.

NOTES

Talmud – תַּלְמוּד: This clearly does not refer to the Gemara, which was written many generations later. Rather, it refers to the essential activity in which the Sages were involved, namely, comparing different statements of the Sages of the Mishna and explaining them (Rashbam; see 130b).

Minutiae of the Torah – דִּקְדּוּקֵי תוֹרָה: The Rashbam interprets this as referring to *halakhot* derived from single letters in the Torah, e.g., the conjunctive prefix *vav*, or the definite article *heh*. Rabbeinu Gershom Meor HaGola maintains that this refers to the details of the spelling of words of the Torah, e.g., where the vowel letter *vav* is written and where it is not.

Minutiae [*dikdukei*] of the scribes – דִּקְדּוּקֵי סוֹפְרִים: The Rashbam follows Rashi's explanation (see *Sukka* 28a) that this refers to rabbinic decrees issued as preventive measures against sin. Rashi explains that the Sages would scrutinize [*dikdeku*] people's behavior to correct their actions and distance them from sin.

Calculation of the calendric seasons – תְּקוּפוֹת: This is the calculation of the timing of the solar and lunar orbits, necessary in order to set the Jewish calendar.

Numerical values [*gimatriyot*] – גַּמַטְרִיאוֹת: The Rashbam interprets this as homiletic interpretation of verses based on the first letter of each word of the verse. According to Rashi, these interpretations are based on a substitution cipher for the Hebrew alphabet in which *alef* is substituted for *tav* and *beit* for *shin*, and so on. Other homiletic interpretations based on the numerical value of letters are also included in *gimatriyot*.

Parables of foxes – מִשְׁלוֹת שׁוּעָלִים: People would tell parables about various animals, among them foxes and lions. Several of these parables are cited in tractate *Sanhedrin*.

The conversation of palm trees – שִׂיחַת דְּקָלִים: The Rashbam explains that Rabban Yoḥanan ben Zakkai knew the matters spoken about trees, similar to what is stated with regard to Solomon: "And he spoke of trees, from the cedar that is in Lebanon even unto the hyssop that springs out of the wall" (I Kings 5:13). Rabbeinu Gershom Meor HaGola explains that he knew spells that would help trees grow or wither. Rav Hai Gaon explains that there was a method to divine esoterica from the motion of palm leaves, which appear to be speaking with each other (see *Arukh*; Rashba; Ritva).

A small matter is the discussions of Abaye and Rava – דָּבָר קָטָן הֲוָיוֹת דְּאַבַּיֵי וְרָבָא: The talmudic discussions are referred to as a small matter because they are trivial in comparison to the Design of the Divine Chariot. The reference to Abaye and Rava, who lived many generations after Rabban Yoḥanan ben Zakkai, is discussed in the early commentaries. The Rashba explains that Rabban Yoḥanan ben Zakkai perceived the fundamental roots of the *halakhot* that were later discussed by Abaye and Rava.

The Ritva interprets the expression: A small matter, as referring to the statements of the *amora'im*, in contradistinction to those of the *tanna'im*, as the *amora'im* would discuss the *mishnayot* at length because their understanding fell short of that of the *tanna'im*. Accordingly, Rabban Yoḥanan ben Zakkai would clarify his own statements so that there would be no need for such discussions.

Any bird that would fly, etc. – עוֹף שֶׁפּוֹרֵחַ וכו׳: *Tosafot* (*Sukka* 28a) explain that when he studied Torah, it was as though his words were transmitted at Mount Sinai with the Torah, which was given during a fiery event. Therefore any bird that flew over him was incinerated. In *Derekh Emuna* this description is explained allegorically: Yonatan ben Uzziel's mind was so sharp that any doubt of his conclusions would immediately vanish.

The property shall return to its place – יַחְזְרוּ נְכָסִים לִמְקוֹמָן: The Ramah explains that even according to the assumption that he is their brother, the other brothers do not receive a portion of his inheritance, since they were supposed to give him a share of their portion, and they did not. Therefore, they do not deserve an additional share of the inheritance of the man in question.

LANGUAGE

Numerical value [*gimatriyya*] – גִּימַטְרִיָּה: From the Greek γεωμετρία, *geometria*, literally, land measurement. The Greeks used it as a term for mathematics in general and engineering in particular. In rabbinic literature it also refers to mathematical calculations in general, though it was designated for performing calculations using the numerical value of the letters in particular.

HALAKHA

This is my son…this is my brother – זֶה בְּנִי...זֶה אָחִי: If one claims that a specific person is his son or his brother (see *Maggid Mishne*), even if they are not presumed to be related, the court accepts his claim with regard to inheritance, whether he makes this claim when he is healthy or on his deathbed (Rambam *Sefer Mishpatim*, *Hilkhot Naḥalot* 4:1; *Shulḥan Arukh*, *Ḥoshen Mishpat* 279:1).

And he takes a share with him, from his portion – וְיִטּוֹל עִמּוֹ בְּחֶלְקוֹ: If there are two brothers, Reuven and Shimon, whose father died, and they are not known to have any other brothers, and Reuven claims that a third person, Levi, is their brother as well, and Shimon claims not to have any knowledge on the matter, in such a case Shimon receives half the inheritance, since as far as he is concerned there are only two brothers (*Sma*). Reuven receives a third, as he admits that there are three brothers; and Levi receives the remaining sixth.

If Levi subsequently dies, the sixth that he received is inherited by Reuven. If Levi had other property, Reuven and Shimon divide it between them, as Reuven admits that Levi is Shimon's brother as well. The Rema, citing the Ramah, adds that only the actual property that Levi received from their father's property or property Levi received in exchange for that property is inherited by Reuven. Any other property of Levi is divided equally (Rambam *Sefer Mishpatim*, *Hilkhot Naḥalot* 4:8; *Shulḥan Arukh*, *Ḥoshen Mishpat* 280:2).

נָפְלוּ לוֹ נְכָסִים מִמָּקוֹם אַחֵר – יִירְשׁוּ אֶחָיו עִמּוֹ.

If **property came into** the man in question's possession **from somewhere else,** other than from the father, and the man in question died, all of **the brothers of** the one who testified **shall inherit with** the one who testified, as according to his claim they too are the heirs of the deceased.

גמ׳ ״זֶה בְּנִי״ נֶאֱמָן, לְמַאי הִלְכְתָא? אָמַר רַב יְהוּדָה אָמַר שְׁמוּאֵל: לְיוֹרְשׁוֹ, וְלִפְטוֹר אֶת אִשְׁתּוֹ מִן הַיִּבּוּם.

GEMARA The mishna teaches that one who says: **This is my son, is deemed credible. With** regard to what ***halakha*** is this stated? **Rav Yehuda says** that **Shmuel says:** It is stated **with regard to inheriting** from **him,** i.e., the son inherits from the speaker, **and with regard to rendering his wife exempt from levirate marriage.**[B] Because he claims that the person in question is his son, his wife is not required to enter into levirate marriage after his death, as he has a child.

BACKGROUND

Levirate marriage – יבום: A man whose brother died without children is obligated by Torah law to marry his deceased brother's widow or free her by means of a *ḥalitza* ceremony (see Deuteronomy 25:5–10). As long as neither levirate marriage nor *ḥalitza* has taken place, it is prohibited for her to marry another man. According to the Torah, levirate marriage is effected by the act of sexual intercourse. The Sages, however, instituted the practice of *ma'amar*, in which the deceased husband's brother betroths the widow, even though this betrothal is not effective by Torah law without intercourse. Conjugal relations consummate the marriage between the deceased's brother and the widow and she is thereafter considered his wife in all respects. A bill of divorce would be necessary to formalize a divorce between them. Nowadays, the brother-in-law is required to free his brother's widow of her obligation through *ḥalitza*, and he is not permitted to marry her through levirate marriage.

Perek **VIII**
Daf **134** Amud **b**

לְיוֹרְשׁוֹ, פְּשִׁיטָא! לִפְטוֹר אֶת אִשְׁתּוֹ מִן הַיִּבּוּם אִצְטְרִיכָא לֵיהּ.

The Gemara asks: Isn't it **obvious** that his claim is deemed credible **with regard to** someone **inheriting** from **him?**[N] Since he could have given this person his property as a gift, it need not be stated that his claim is accepted with regard to his inheritance. The Gemara responds: **It was necessary for** the mishna to state that his claim is deemed credible **with regard to rendering his wife exempt from levirate marriage**[H] despite the fact that it is not in his power to render her exempt, but the *halakha* of inheritance is not a novelty.

הָא נַמִי תְּנֵינָא: מִי שֶׁאָמַר בִּשְׁעַת מִיתָתוֹ ״יֵשׁ לִי בָּנִים״ – נֶאֱמָן, ״יֵשׁ לִי אַחִים״ – אֵינוֹ נֶאֱמָן!

The Gemara asks: **We** already **learned this** in a mishna (*Kiddushin* 64a) **as well: One who said at the time of his death: I have children,** is **deemed credible,** and his wife is thereby exempt from levirate marriage. If he said: **I have brothers,**[H] and his wife therefore must enter levirate marriage, **he** is **not deemed credible.**

הָתָם דְּלָא מוּחְזַק לָן בְּאָח, הָכָא – אַף עַל גַּב דְּמוּחְזַק לֵיהּ בְּאָח.

The Gemara answers: **There,** in that mishna, it is a case **where he is not presumed by us to have a brother.**[N] Therefore, his wife is already presumed to be exempt from levirate marriage, and his claim that he has a son merely substantiates this presumption. **Here,** the mishna adds a novelty that **even if he is presumed to** have **a brother,** his claim that he has a son is accepted, and his wife is thereby exempted from levirate marriage.

אָמַר רַב יוֹסֵף אָמַר רַב יְהוּדָה אָמַר שְׁמוּאֵל: מִפְּנֵי מָה אָמְרוּ: ״זֶה בְּנִי״ – נֶאֱמָן? הוֹאִיל וּבַעַל שֶׁאָמַר ״גֵּרַשְׁתִּי אֶת אִשְׁתִּי״ – נֶאֱמָן.

Rav Yosef says that **Rav Yehuda says** that **Shmuel says: For what** reason **did** the Sages **say** that one who says: **This is my son,** is **deemed credible? Since**[B] **a husband who says: I divorced my wife,** is **deemed credible,** and his wife is thereby exempt from levirate marriage, he is deemed credible with regard to this claim as well.

HALAKHA

With regard to rendering his wife exempt from levirate marriage – לִפְטוֹר אֶת אִשְׁתּוֹ מִן הַיִּבּוּם: If a husband claims that a specific person is his child, or that he has children in general, contrary to the presumption that he has no children (*Maggid Mishne*; see *Beit Shmuel*), his claim is accepted inasmuch as his wife is exempt from levirate marriage. It is added in *Beit Shmuel* that if there are witnesses that he has a brother, his claim that he has children is not accepted (Rambam *Sefer Nashim, Hilkhot Yibbum VaḤalitza* 3:1; *Shulḥan Arukh, Even HaEzer* 156:6).

I have brothers – יֵשׁ לִי אַחִים: If a husband who is not presumed to have brothers claims that he has brothers, his claim is not accepted, as his intention is presumably to prohibit his wife from remarrying after his death (Rambam *Sefer Nashim, Hilkhot Yibbum VaḤalitza* 3:2; *Shulḥan Arukh, Even HaEzer* 157:6).

BACKGROUND

Since – הוֹאִיל: The principle: Since, etc., and other similar principles, are employed in various areas of *halakha*. The fundamental principle is that conditions that may develop in the future are taken into consideration in determining the *halakha* in the present. Not all of the talmudic Sages agreed that the *halakha* may be determined based upon potential future developments, and therefore not all of them accepted these principles.

NOTES

Isn't it obvious that his claim is deemed credible with regard to inheriting from him – לְיוֹרְשׁוֹ פְּשִׁיטָא: The Rashbam explains that he could have given this person his property as a gift. He therefore concludes that the father's claim is accepted only with regard to the property he had until his claim, as he could not have given him his future property. This is not to be confused with a father who testifies that a certain son of his is his firstborn and therefore receives a double portion of his inheritance; in that case the son receives a double portion of the father's future property as well, due to a Torah edict that a father's testimony is deemed credible with regard to clarifying the identity of his firstborn son. *Tosafot* concur. Other authorities maintain that in the case here as well, the father's claim is accepted with regard to future property (*Sefer Hashlama*, citing Ra'avad; Rosh, citing Maharam of Rothenburg; Rashba). They explain that this case is included in the same Torah edict as clarifying the identity of his firstborn son; alternatively, they maintain that this case is more obvious than the case of testimony concerning a firstborn, and a Torah edict is not needed (see Rashba).

There it is a case where he is not presumed by us to have a brother, etc. – הָתָם דְּלָא מוּחְזַק לָן בְּאָח וכו׳: The Gemara does not mean that the mishna in tractate *Kiddushin* necessarily refers to such a case, as there is no proof of this; rather, it means that the mishna tolerates such an interpretation, and therefore the mishna here is necessary to teach that the husband's claim is accepted even in a case where he is presumed to have a brother (Ritva; see Rashbam). The Rashbam limits the acceptance of the husband's claim to a case where it contradicts a presumption; if it contradicts explicit testimony of witnesses, his claim is rejected.

אֲמַר רַב יוֹסֵף: מָרֵיהּ דְּאַבְרָהָם, תָּלֵי תַּנְיָא בִּדְלָא תַּנְיָא!

As Rav Yosef forgot some of his Torah knowledge due to an illness, he questioned the accuracy of his citation of Rav Yehuda. **Rav Yosef said: Master of Abraham!** This reasoning **makes** that which **is taught** in the Mishna **dependent upon that which is not taught,** as the credibility of one who claims: This is my son, is stated in the mishna, while the *halakha* that a husband's claim that he divorced his wife is accepted is the statement of an *amora*.

אֶלָּא אִי אִתְּמַר הָכִי אִיתְּמַר, אָמַר רַב יְהוּדָה אָמַר שְׁמוּאֵל: מִפְּנֵי מָה אָמְרוּ: ״זֶה בְּנִי״ – נֶאֱמָן? הוֹאִיל וּבְיָדוֹ לְגָרְשָׁהּ.

Rather, if this explanation **was stated, it was stated like this: Rav Yehuda says** that **Shmuel says: For what** reason **did** the Sages **say** that one who says: **This is my son,** is **deemed credible** with regard to rendering his wife exempt from levirate marriage? **Since it is in his power to divorce her** and thereby render her exempt from levirate marriage, he is deemed credible with regard to this claim as well.

אֲמַר רַב יוֹסֵף, הַשְׁתָּא דְּאָמְרַתְּ: אָמְרִינַן ״הוֹאִיל״, בַּעַל שֶׁאָמַר ״גֵּרַשְׁתִּי אֶת אִשְׁתִּי״ – נֶאֱמָן, הוֹאִיל וּבְיָדוֹ לְגָרְשָׁהּ.

Rav Yosef said in addition: **Now that you said** that **we say** that the husband is deemed credible **since** he has the power to divorce her, **a husband who says: I divorced my wife,** is also **deemed credible, since it is in his power to divorce her** at any time.

כִּי אֲתָא רַב יִצְחָק בַּר יוֹסֵף אָמַר רַבִּי יוֹחָנָן: בַּעַל שֶׁאָמַר ״גֵּרַשְׁתִּי אֶת אִשְׁתִּי״ – אֵינוֹ נֶאֱמָן. מְנַפֵּחַ רַב שֵׁשֶׁת בִּידֵיהּ: אֲזַל לֵיהּ ״הוֹאִיל״ דְּרַב יוֹסֵף.

When Rav Yitzḥak bar Yosef came from Eretz Yisrael to Babylonia, he said that **Rabbi Yoḥanan says: A husband who says: I have divorced my wife,** is **not deemed credible.**[N] **Rav Sheshet waved his hand** disparagingly, as if to say that **Rav Yosef's** statement that he is deemed credible **since** it is in his power to divorce her **is gone** due to Rabbi Yoḥanan's statement.

אִינִי? וְהָא אָמַר רַבִּי חִיָּיא בַּר אָבִין אָמַר רַבִּי יוֹחָנָן: בַּעַל שֶׁאָמַר ״גֵּרַשְׁתִּי אֶת אִשְׁתִּי״ – נֶאֱמָן!

The Gemara asks: **Is that so?** Did Rabbi Yoḥanan actually say that? **But doesn't Rabbi Ḥiyya bar Avin say that Rabbi Yoḥanan says: A husband who says: I have divorced my wife,** is **deemed credible?**

לָא קַשְׁיָא: כָּאן לְמַפְרֵעַ,

The Gemara answers: That is **not difficult. Here,** in the statement that the husband is not deemed credible, Rabbi Yoḥanan was referring to **a retroactive** testimony. For example, in a case where he testified that he divorced her on a certain date, and it is discovered that she engaged in sexual intercourse with another man after that date, his testimony is not accepted concerning whether the woman is liable to receive punishment; she is not considered to have been divorced at the time. This is because it is not in the husband's power to divorce her retroactively.

כָּאן לְהַבָּא.

By contrast, the statement **there,** where Rabbi Yoḥanan said that the husband's testimony is deemed credible, refers to testimony **for the future,** e.g., where he says that he divorced her on that same day, or without specifying a date, in which case his statement is relevant only for the future. Since it was in his power to divorce her at that time, his testimony is deemed credible; if he dies, she is exempt from levirate marriage, and if she engages in sexual intercourse with another man, she is not considered to have committed adultery.

אִיבַּעְיָא לְהוּ: אֲמַר לְמַפְרֵעַ, מַהוּ לְהֵימוּנֵיהּ לְהַבָּא?

A dilemma was raised before the Sages: If the husband **said** that he divorced his wife on a certain date, as **a retroactive** testimony, **what is** the *halakha* **concerning** his testimony being **deemed credible** and accepted **with regard to the future,** rendering her divorced from that time onward, despite the fact that his claim is not accepted with regard to the past?

NOTES

A husband who said: I have divorced my wife, is not deemed credible – בַּעַל שֶׁאָמַר גֵּרַשְׁתִּי אִשְׁתִּי אֵינוֹ נֶאֱמָן: The Rashbam explains that divorce is usually known to the public, or at least rumors circulate concerning divorce. Therefore although the husband should be deemed credible since he could have made a more advantageous claim [*miggo*], as he had the ability to divorce her, this *miggo* runs counter to testimony, i.e., the circumstantial evidence that he did not divorce her. Therefore, his statement is not deemed credible. If the husband claims that he has a child, his wife is exempt from levirate marriage, as he could have divorced her.

מִי פָּלְגִינַן דִּבּוּרָא, אוֹ לָא פָּלְגִינַן דִּבּוּרָא? רַב מָארִי וְרַב זְבִיד, חַד אָמַר: פָּלְגִינַן, וְחַד אָמַר: לָא פָּלְגִינַן.

The dilemma is based on the following fundamental question: **Do we divide the** husband's **statement,** accepting that he divorced his wife inasmuch as she is considered divorced from that time onward, since it is in his power to divorce her now, even though his claim that he divorced her in the past is not accepted? **Or do we not divide the statement,** and say instead that his claim is rejected altogether, since his claim concerning the past cannot be accepted? **Rav Mari and Rav Zevid** engaged in a dispute with regard to this issue. **One says** that **we divide** the husband's statement, **and one says** that **we do not divide** it.

מַאי שְׁנָא מִדְּרָבָא, דְּאָמַר רָבָא: "אִישׁ פְּלוֹנִי בָּא עַל אִשְׁתִּי" – הוּא וְאַחֵר מִצְטָרְפִין לְהוֹרְגוֹ, לְהוֹרְגוֹ וְלֹא לְהוֹרְגָהּ?

The Gemara asks: In **what** way **is** this case **different from Rava's** statement? **As Rava says** that if a man says: **So-and-so engaged in sexual intercourse with my wife,**[H] the husband **and another** witness **combine to kill him,** i.e., to have him sentenced to death for adultery. The Gemara infers: He combines with another witness **to kill him, but not to kill her.** The wife is not sentenced to death based on this testimony, even if they testified that she engaged in sexual intercourse willingly, as a husband is disqualified from bearing witness concerning his wife. Evidently, the husband's testimony is divided; his testimony concerning the man is accepted even though the testimony concerning his wife's part in the same action is rejected.

בִּתְרֵי גּוּפֵי פָּלְגִינַן, בְּחַד גּוּפָא לָא פָּלְגִינַן.

The Gemara answers: **With regard to two** separate **bodies**[N] **we divide** the statement. Therefore the husband's testimony is accepted with regard to the man but rejected with regard to his wife. **With regard to one body we do not divide** it. That is why one Sage holds that a husband's claim that he divorced his wife in the past cannot be divided, so that his claim that he divorced her would be accepted while his claim as to when he divorced her would be rejected.

HALAKHA

So-and-so engaged in sexual intercourse with my wife – אִישׁ פְּלוֹנִי בָּא עַל אִשְׁתִּי: If a man states: So-and-so engaged in sexual intercourse with my wife, he and one other witness can combine to testify concerning the man, thereby having him sentenced to death; but he may not testify concerning his wife. In the present, when there is no court-imposed capital punishment, they can combine to render the man disqualified from bearing witness. This is because the husband's testimony is divided so that only his testimony with regard to the man is accepted, as one's wife is as oneself, and he is disqualified from giving testimony concerning her (Rambam *Sefer Shofetim, Hilkhot Edut* 12:2; *Shulḥan Arukh, Ḥoshen Mishpat* 34:26).

NOTES

With regard to two bodies – בִּתְרֵי גּוּפֵי: The Rashbam explains that the testimony relates to two different people, the wife and the man who engaged in sexual intercourse with her. By contrast, the Ritva interprets the expression: Two bodies, as referring to two independent elements of the testimony. Testimony that includes two independent elements can be accepted partially, as it can be treated as two separate testimonies. That is the case in Rava's statement, as the testimony that this man engaged in sexual intercourse with the wife is independent from the testimony that she engaged in sexual intercourse willingly.

Perek **VIII**
Daf **135** Amud **a**

הַהוּא דַּהֲוָה קָא שָׁכֵיב, אָמְרוּ לֵיהּ: אִתְּתֵיהּ לְמַאן? אָמַר לְהוּ: חֲזְיָא לְכַהֲנָא רַבָּה.

The Gemara relates: There was **a certain** man, who was presumed to have brothers but no children, **who was dying.** His wife was therefore presumed to be obligated in levirate marriage. Those with him **said to him: To whom** may **his wife,** i.e., your wife, be married?[N] Is she required to enter into levirate marriage, or is she permitted to marry whomever she wishes? **He said to them: She is fit to** marry even **a High Priest.**[N] She is not required to enter into levirate marriage.

NOTES

To whom may his wife be married – אִתְּתֵיהּ לְמַאן: The Rashbam explains that the people asked him whether she was obligated in levirate marriage. Rabbeinu Ḥananel explains that they were certain that she was obligated in levirate marriage, and they asked him which brother he preferred to have enter into levirate marriage with her.

She is fit to marry even a High Priest – חֲזְיָא לְכַהֲנָא רַבָּה: The reference to a High Priest was clearly an exaggeration, as it is prohibited for a High Priest to marry a widow. Furthermore, there was no High Priest at the time of this incident. There is a discussion among the commentaries as to whether the husband meant that she was permitted to marry a common priest. The Rashbam explains that the husband meant that his wife is not obligated to enter into levirate marriage because he had divorced her, and he exaggerated concerning this as well, as it is prohibited for a common priest to marry a divorcée (Rashbam). Others explain that the husband did not mean that she is exempt from levirate marriage because he divorced her, but because he now had a child. Therefore, it would be permitted for her to marry a common priest after his death (Rabbeinu Gershom Meor HaGola). In addition, there are versions of the text that read: Even a priest, not: Even a High Priest, according to which he may not have exaggerated at all.

אָמַר רָבָא: מַאי נֵיחוּשׁ לָהּ? הָא אָמַר רַב חִיָּיא בַּר אַבָּא אָמַר רַבִּי יוֹחָנָן: בַּעַל שֶׁאָמַר ״גֵּרַשְׁתִּי אֶת אִשְׁתִּי״ – נֶאֱמָן. אֲמַר לֵיהּ אַבַּיֵי: וְהָא כִּי אֲתָא רַבִּי יִצְחָק בַּר יוֹסֵף, אָמַר רַבִּי יוֹחָנָן: בַּעַל שֶׁאָמַר ״גֵּרַשְׁתִּי אֶת אִשְׁתִּי״ – אֵינוֹ נֶאֱמָן! אֲמַר לֵיהּ, וְלָאו מִי לָא שַׁנִּינְהוּ: כָּאן לְמַפְרֵעַ וְכָאן לְהַבָּא?

Rava said: With what possibility need we be concerned with regard to her? Doesn't Rabbi Ḥiyya bar Abba say that Rabbi Yoḥanan says: A husband who says: I have divorced my wife, is deemed credible,[N] and she is exempt from levirate marriage? Therefore, this woman will be exempt as well. Abaye said to him: But when Rav Yitzḥak bar Yosef came from Eretz Yisrael, he said that Rabbi Yoḥanan says: A husband who says: I have divorced my wife, is not deemed credible.[H] Rava said to him: But didn't we resolve the contradiction, concluding that here Rabbi Yoḥanan was referring to a retroactive testimony and there he was referring to testimony for the future? Therefore, according to both versions of Rabbi Yoḥanan's statement, the husband should be deemed credible in this case.

וְאַשִּׁנּוּיֵי נֵיקוּם וְלִסְמוֹךְ? אֲמַר לֵיהּ רָבָא לְרַב נָתָן בַּר אַמִּי: חוּשׁ לָהּ.

Abaye responded: But shall we arise and rely on answers in a halakhic ruling? Although the contradiction can be resolved in this manner, there is no guarantee that this resolution is correct. Therefore Rav Yitzḥak bar Yosef's statement should still be taken into consideration. Rava subsequently said to Rav Natan bar Ami: Be concerned about it.[N] There may be a dispute with regard to this issue, as the resolution cannot be relied upon.

הַהוּא דַּהֲוָה מוּחְזַק לָן דְּלֵית לֵיהּ אַחֵי, וַאֲמַר בִּשְׁעַת מִיתָה דְּלֵית לֵיהּ אַחֵי. אֲמַר רַב יוֹסֵף: מַאי לֵיחוּשׁ לָהּ? חֲדָא, דְּמוּחְזַק לָן דְּלֵית לֵיהּ אַחִין; וְעוֹד, הָא אֲמַר בִּשְׁעַת מִיתָה דְּלֵית לֵיהּ. אֲמַר לֵיהּ אַבַּיֵי: הָא אָמְרִי דְּאִיכָּא עֵדִים בִּמְדִינַת הַיָּם דְּיָדְעִי דְּאִית לֵיהּ אַחֵי!

The Gemara relates: There was a certain man who was presumed by us, i.e., the court, to have no brothers,[H] and he said at the time of his death that he has no brothers. Rav Yosef said: With what possibility need we be concerned with regard to his wife, in terms of her requiring levirate marriage? For one, he is presumed by us to have no brothers, and furthermore, he said at the time of his death that he has none. Abaye said to him: But don't people say[N] that there are witnesses overseas who know that he has brothers? Therefore, we should be concerned that this report is accurate.

הַשְׁתָּא מִיהַת הָא לֵיתְנְהוּ קַמָּן; לָאו הַיְינוּ דְּרַבִּי חֲנִינָא, דְּאָמַר רַבִּי חֲנִינָא: עֵדִים בְּצַד אִסְתָּן וְתֵאָסֵר?

Rav Yosef responded: In any event, now the witnesses are not present before us, so this possibility does not need to be taken into account. Isn't this the same as Rabbi Ḥanina's ruling in a case where women who were captured and subsequently liberated claimed that they were not raped in captivity (*Ketubot* 23a)? As although people said there were witnesses elsewhere who could testify that they were raped, Rabbi Ḥanina says that they were permitted to marry a priest, reasoning: Just because there may be witnesses in the north [*istan*],[L] i.e., in a distant place, will the woman be forbidden?[H]

HALAKHA

I have divorced my wife, is not deemed credible – גֵּרַשְׁתִּי אֶת אִשְׁתִּי אֵינוֹ נֶאֱמָן: If a husband claims that he divorced his wife, his claim is not accepted; rather, it is considered uncertain whether he actually divorced her. Therefore, if his wife engages in sexual intercourse with another man, it is uncertain if her children have the status of *mamzerim*; if the husband dies, she must perform *ḥalitza* and not levirate marriage. This is the *halakha* whether he claimed to have divorced her on that very day or previously, in accordance with Abaye's ruling according to the statement of Rav Yitzḥak bar Yosef in the name of Rabbi Yoḥanan. Abaye was not willing to rely on the Gemara's resolution to the contradiction between the two statements in Rabbi Yoḥanan's name, and Rava accepted this claim (Rambam *Sefer Nashim*, *Hilkhot Geirushin* 12:5; *Shulḥan Arukh*, *Even HaEzer* 152:1).

Presumed by us to have no brothers – מוּחְזַק לָן דְּלֵית לֵיהּ אַחִין: If a husband dies without children, and there is no presumption that he has brothers, but a rumor circulates that there are witnesses overseas who know that he has brothers, the woman must take this into consideration and wait until the witnesses return and are examined by the court before she remarries, even if the husband said on his deathbed that he has no brothers, in accordance with Rava's ruling. In *Beit Shmuel* it is added that according to the Rambam, the woman must take the rumor into consideration even if it was not discussed in court (Rambam *Sefer Nashim*, *Hilkhot Yibbum VaḤalitza* 3:3; *Shulḥan Arukh*, *Even HaEzer* 157:8).

There may be witnesses in the north, will she be forbidden – עֵדִים בְּצַד אִסְתָּן וְתֵאָסֵר: If a woman says that she was taken captive but was not raped, even if it is rumored that there are witnesses who can testify that she was raped, she is permitted to marry a priest unless the witnesses testify in court that she was raped, as the *halakha* is to be lenient concerning a captive woman (Rambam *Sefer Kedusha*, *Hilkhot Issurei Bia* 18:23; *Shulḥan Arukh*, *Even HaEzer* 7:7).

LANGUAGE

The north [*istan*] – אִסְתָּן: In Aramaic, this term refers to the north wind. It apparently derives from Assyrian, where it means north.

NOTES

I have divorced my wife, is deemed credible – גֵּרַשְׁתִּי אֶת אִשְׁתִּי נֶאֱמָן: The explanation of Rava's proof depends on the interpretation of the husband's claim. According to the interpretation that he meant that he divorced her, Rabbi Yoḥanan's statement provides explicit support for Rava's lenient ruling. Those who explain that he meant that she is exempt from levirate marriage because he has a child explain here that Rabbi Yoḥanan's statement provides proof that a husband's power to divorce his wife gives him credibility with regard to the consequences of divorce, such as exemption from levirate marriage. Therefore his claim that he has children or does not have brothers is accepted.

Be concerned about it – חוּשׁ לָהּ: The Rashbam explains that the contradiction between the two versions of Rabbi Yoḥanan's statement cannot be ignored, so the woman should not be permitted to marry. The Ramah adds that according to this reasoning, she must perform *ḥalitza*, not levirate marriage, as the status of her levirate bond is uncertain. Others interpret Rava's statement to mean that the case must be investigated further, as the husband's statement should not be relied upon alone (Rabbeinu Barukh; Rabbeinu Yona). A third interpretation is cited by Rabbeinu Gershom Meor HaGola: Treat the resolution to the contradiction strictly and deem the wife exempt from levirate marriage.

Don't people say, etc. – הָא אָמְרִי וכו׳: There are several versions and several interpretations of this statement. Rabbi Avraham *Av Beit Din* explains that there was a rumor that he had brothers who were overseas. Another explanation is that he was rumored to have had brothers, and the possibility was raised that there may be witnesses overseas who could clarify the matter. Others explain that it was known that there were witnesses overseas who could testify as to whether or not he had brothers (see Rabbi Yitzḥak Karkusha). By contrast, the majority of the early commentaries maintain that there was a rumor that there were witnesses overseas that he had brothers. The Ramban adds that the rumor must have been established in court; the Rambam apparently disagrees.

אֲמַר לֵיהּ אַבַּיֵי: אִם הֵקַלְנוּ בִּשְׁבוּיָה מִשּׁוּם דִּמְנַוְּולָא נַפְשָׁהּ לְגַבֵּי שַׁבַּאי, נָקֵל בְּאֵשֶׁת אִישׁ? אֲמַר לֵיהּ רָבָא לְרַב נָתָן בַּר אַמִי: חוּשׁ לָהּ.

Abaye said to him: If we were lenient with regard to a captive woman, due to, among other reasons, the fact that **she makes herself repulsive**[N] **before the captor** so that he will not want to rape her, and we assume that she was not raped, **should we be lenient with regard to a married woman? Rava said to Rav Natan bar Ami: Be concerned about it.**[N] Do not permit this woman to remarry until the matter is clarified.

״זֶה אָחִי – אֵינוֹ נֶאֱמָן״. וְאִידָךְ מַאי קָאָמְרִי? אִי קָאָמְרִי ״אָחוּנָא הוּא״, אַמַּאי יִטּוֹל עִמּוֹ בְּחֶלְקוֹ וְתוּ לָא? אֶלָּא דְּקָא אָמְרִי ״לָאו אָחִינוּ הוּא״;

§ The mishna teaches that one who says: **This is my brother,** is **not deemed credible** with regard to his other brothers' share of their father's inheritance. Rather, the man in question receives a portion only from the portion of the one who testified concerning him. The Gemara clarifies: **And what do the other brothers say? If they say: He is our brother, why** does the man in question **take** a portion of the inheritance only **with** the one who testified, **from his portion, and nothing more?** If the other brothers admit that he is their brother, they should give him a share of their portions as well. **Rather, they are saying: He is not our brother.**

אֵימָא סֵיפָא: נָפְלוּ לוֹ נְכָסִים מִמָּקוֹם אַחֵר – יִירְשׁוּ אֶחָיו עִמּוֹ, הָא אָמְרִי לֵיהּ ״לָאו אָחוּנָא הוּא״!

The Gemara questions this: **Say the last clause** of the mishna: If **property came into** the possession of the man in question **from somewhere else,** and he died, **the brothers of** the one who testified **shall inherit** the man in question's property **with him.** Why should they inherit with him? **Didn't they say to him: He is not our brother?**

לָא צְרִיכָא, דְּקָא אָמְרִי ״אֵין אָנוּ יוֹדְעִין״.

The Gemara answers: **No,** it is **necessary** to state this ruling only in a case **where they say: We do not know** if he is our brother. Therefore, they are not obligated to give him a portion of their inheritance, as he cannot prove to them that he is their brother. Nevertheless, they can claim a portion of his inheritance after his death, on the basis of their brother's testimony.

אֲמַר רָבָא, זֹאת אוֹמֶרֶת: ״מָנֶה לִי בְּיָדְךָ״, וְהַלָּה אוֹמֵר ״אֵינִי יוֹדֵעַ״ – פָּטוּר.

Rava says: That is to say that if one says to another: **I have one hundred dinars in your possession,**[H] **and the other** person **says: I do not know,** he is **exempt,** similar to this case, where the brothers who claim that they do not know if this person is their brother are not obligated to share their inheritance with him.

אַבַּיֵי אֲמַר:

Abaye said:

Perek **VIII**
Daf **135** Amud **b**

לְעוֹלָם אֵימָא לָךְ: חַיָּיב, וְשָׁאנֵי הָכָא, דְּכִ״מָנֶה לְאַחֵר בְּיָדְךָ״ דָּמֵי.

Actually, I will say to you that one who responds to a claim that he does not know if he owes the one hundred dinars is **obligated** to pay; **but here,** in the case of the brothers, it **is different.** The brothers are not obligated to share their portion with the man in question **because** the brother who testified **is like** one who claims: **Another** person **has one hundred dinars in your possession.** Since the claimant is not the one who is owed the money, the other party can reject his claim by merely answering that he does not know whether he owes him.

״מֵת – יַחְזְרוּ נְכָסִים לִמְקוֹמָן״. בָּעֵי רָבָא: שֶׁבַח שֶׁשָּׁבְחוּ נְכָסִים מֵאֲלֵיהֶם, מַהוּ?

§ The mishna teaches: If the man in question **dies,** the **property** he received from the father's inheritance **shall return to its place,** i.e., to the possession of the brother who testified on his behalf, and if the man in question received property from elsewhere, it is inherited by all the brothers equally. **Rava raises a dilemma:** With regard to **the enhancement of the property** received by the man in question from the portion of the brother who testified, **where** its **enhanced** value was the result of an enhancement that **happened naturally,** as opposed to one that resulted from exertion, **what is the** *halakha*? Who inherits it?

NOTES

She makes herself repulsive, etc. – דִּמְנַוְּולָא נַפְשָׁהּ וכו׳: This reason for the leniency is not written in the Rashbam's version of the text. He holds that the main distinction between the cases where the possibility of there being witnesses was raised is that a captive woman has the presumptive status of being permitted to marry a priest, and even if it is prohibited for her to marry a priest, her prohibition is relatively minor. This is in contrast to the case here, where the woman was rumored to be obligated in levirate marriage while she was a married woman, and had the presumptive status of being forbidden to engage in sexual intercourse with another man, a more severe prohibition (see Rabbeinu Yona). The version of the text before the *ge'onim* and the Rif includes the reason that she makes herself repulsive, and the Ramban maintains that this is, in fact, the main distinction between the cases.

Be concerned about it – חוּשׁ לָהּ: In this case too, the interpretations of this statement vary: The woman is permitted to remarry only following *ḥalitza* (Rashbam); the court should wait for the witnesses to return (Rid); or the court should investigate whether the husband had brothers overseas (Rabbi Avraham *Av Beit Din*).

HALAKHA

I have one hundred dinars in your possession, etc. – מָנֶה לִי בְּיָדְךָ וכו׳: If one claims that another owes him one hundred dinars, whether as result of a loan, a deposit, or theft, and the other claims that he has no knowledge of the debt, the latter takes an oath of inducement that he does not know and is exempt from payment. If he wishes to fulfill his obligation toward Heaven, he must pay (Rambam *Sefer Mishpatim*, *Hilkhot To'en VeNitan* 1:8; *Shulḥan Arukh*, *Ḥoshen Mishpat* 75:9).

בְּשֶׁבַח הַמַּגִּיעַ לִכְתֵפַיִם לָא תִּיבָּעֵי לָךְ, דְּכִי נָפְלוּ לוֹ נְכָסִים מִמָּקוֹם אַחֵר דָּמֵי. כִּי תִּיבָּעֵי לָךְ – בְּשֶׁבַח שֶׁאֵינוֹ מַגִּיעַ לִכְתֵפַיִם, כְּגוֹן דִּיקְלָא וְאָלִים, אַרְעָא וְאַסְקָא שִׂרְטוֹן, מַאי? תֵּיקוּ.

The Gemara elaborates: **With regard to enhancement that reaches shoulders,**[HN] i.e., ripe produce that needs only to be harvested from the field, **do not raise the dilemma, as it is** considered **like property that came into his possession from elsewhere.** It is not considered part of the land that was given to him by the brother who testified, and it is therefore divided among all the brothers. Rather, **let the dilemma be raised with regard to enhancement that does not reach shoulders,** and is not considered separate from the ground, **such as a palm tree that thickened,** or **land that yielded silt. What is the** *halakha* in this case? Is the enhancement included in the property itself, or is it considered separate property? The Gemara comments: The dilemma **shall stand** unresolved.

מתני׳ מִי שֶׁמֵּת וְנִמְצֵאת דַּיְיתִיקֵי קְשׁוּרָה עַל יְרֵיכוֹ – הֲרֵי זוֹ אֵינָהּ כְּלוּם. זִיכָּה בָּהּ לְאַחֵר, בֵּין מִן הַיּוֹרְשִׁין בֵּין שֶׁאֵינָן מִן הַיּוֹרְשִׁין – דְּבָרָיו קַיָּימִין.

MISHNA With regard to **one who died, and a will written by a person on his deathbed** [***dayetikei***][L] **is found bound to his thigh,**[H] which clearly indicates that it was written by him and was not forged, **this is nothing.**[N] The will is not valid, as he did not give it to anyone, and he may have reconsidered. If **he transferred ownership of** the will to the designated recipient **through another** person, **whether one of the heirs**[N] or **whether not one of the heirs, his statement stands.**

גמ׳ תָּנוּ רַבָּנַן: אֵיזֶה הִיא דַּיְיתִיקֵי? כָּל שֶׁכָּתוּב בָּהּ: ״דָּא תְּהֵא לְמֵיקָם וּלְהְיוֹת״; וְאֵיזֶה הִיא מַתָּנָה? כָּל שֶׁכָּתוּב בָּהּ: ״מֵהַיּוֹם וּלְאַחַר מִיתָה״.

GEMARA The Sages taught (*Tosefta* 8:10): **Which** deed is considered **a** ***dayetikei***, and is collected by the designated recipient after the death of the giver? **Any** deed **in which it is written: This will be to stand and exist**[N] after my death. **And which** type is considered a deed of **gift? Any** deed **in which it is written: From today and after** my **death.**[N]

אֶלָּא ״מֵהַיּוֹם וּלְאַחַר מִיתָה״ הוּא דְּהָוְיָא מַתָּנָה, ״מֵעַכְשָׁיו״ לָא הָוְיָא מַתָּנָה? אֲמַר אַבַּיֵי, הָכִי קָאָמַר: אֵיזוֹ הִיא מַתְּנַת בָּרִיא שֶׁהִיא כְּמַתְּנַת שְׁכִיב מְרַע, דְּלָא קָנֵי אֶלָּא לְאַחַר מִיתָה? כָּל שֶׁכָּתוּב בָּהּ: ״מֵהַיּוֹם וּלְאַחַר מִיתָה״.

The Gemara asks: **Is it** considered a deed of **gift only** if the expression: **From today and after** my **death,** is written, whereas if it is written only: **From now,** it is not considered a deed of **gift? Abaye said** that **this** is what the *baraita* **is saying: Which** deed **of gift of a healthy person is** considered **like** the deed of **gift of a person on his deathbed,**[H] in **that** the recipient **acquires** it **only after the death** of the giver? **Any** deed **in which it is written: From today and after** my **death.**

NOTES

With regard to enhancement that reaches shoulders, etc. – בְּשֶׁבַח הַמַּגִּיעַ לִכְתֵפַיִם וכו׳: The Rashbam explains that this refers to enhancement caused by the shoulders, i.e., physical labor, of the man in question. Accordingly, the ultimate dilemma is not only with regard to enhancement that cannot be separated from the property itself, but also to enhancement that did not involve effort on his part. The examples mentioned, namely a palm tree that thickened and land that yielded silt, lend support to this explanation.

By contrast, almost all of the other commentaries interpret the expression: Enhancement that reaches shoulders, to refer to ripe produce that can be harvested and carried on one's shoulders; since it no longer needs the earth, it is not considered part of it. Since a palm tree that thickened or land that yielded silt do not serve as counterexamples to produce that is ready to be harvested, it is apparent that these commentaries did not have the version of the text that provides the examples mentioned in the standard version of the Gemara (Ri Migash; see Ritva and Ran).

This is nothing – הֲרֵי זוֹ אֵינָהּ כְּלוּם: The Rashbam explains that a will has the legal status of a deed of transfer, but it does not enable the designated recipient to acquire the property before he receives the deed. Since the recipient did not receive it during the person's lifetime, and the deed is not effective after his death, the deed is meaningless. The Rashbam adds that the *halakha* that the will of a person on his deathbed has the legal status of a transferred deed is a rabbinic ordinance that applies only to his oral instructions and not to a written document. Other commentaries disagree, maintaining that a written will has the same status as an oral one, but in this case it is invalid because the person did not transfer the deed to anyone or tell anyone that he desires that it be fulfilled. Therefore, there is concern that he reconsidered after writing it (Ri Migash; see Rabbi Avraham *Av Beit Din*).

Whether one of the heirs, etc. – בֵּין מִן הַיּוֹרְשִׁין וכו׳: The Rashbam explains that the case is where the person on his deathbed instructs another to acquire the property mentioned in the will on behalf of a third party, regardless of whether that third party is the one mentioned in the will. Others explain that even if the one who is asked to transfer the will is one of the legal heirs, and is instructed to perform an act of acquisition for another person, the acquisition is valid, and the deed is considered to have left the giver's possession and acquired by the person mentioned in the will (Ra'avad; see Rashba and *Tosefot Yom Tov*).

This will be to stand and exist – דָּא תְּהֵא לְמֵיקָם וּלְהְיוֹת: *Dayetikei* is interpreted as an acronym for *da tehe lemeikam*, meaning: This will stand. The Rashbam interprets this statement as a confirmation of the will (see also Ri Migash; Rambam's Commentary on the Mishna). Rabbeinu Tam, citing the *Tosefta* (8:10), explains that the one writing the will declares that he is writing it with the intention of recovering and continuing to live, and not out of resignation to death.

From today and after my death – מֵהַיּוֹם וּלְאַחַר מִיתָה: Rabbeinu Gershom Meor HaGola explains that this means: The gift will enter your possession today, but the transfer will be completed only after my death. The Rashbam, citing the Gemara (136a), explains that the recipient acquires the item itself immediately and its profits after the death of the giver. Rabbeinu Tam, cited in *Tosafot*, explains the expression to mean: This gift is hereby yours from today, if I do not change my mind until my death. He adds that in different places in the Talmud the phrase has different meanings (see *Sefer HaYashar*).

HALAKHA

With regard to enhancement that reaches shoulders – בְּשֶׁבַח הַמַּגִּיעַ לִכְתֵפַיִם: In a case of two brothers, Reuven and Shimon, where Reuven claims that Levi is their brother and Shimon does not concede, the *halakha* is that Levi receives a portion of their father's inheritance from Reuven's portion, and if Levi then dies his portion returns to Reuven. In this case, if Levi's portion appreciated before his death due to enhancement that reaches shoulders, e.g., grapes that are ready for harvesting, the enhanced value is divided between Reuven and Shimon, just like the property of Levi that he received from elsewhere. This is the *halakha* whether Levi had to expend effort to grow the grapes, or whether the enhanced value of the grapes happened naturally without Levi's involvement, in accordance with the version of the Gemara accepted by the Rambam and *Shulḥan Arukh* (see *Sma*). If the grapes are not yet ready for harvesting, they belong to Reuven. The *Maggid Mishne* explains that since the Gemara's dilemma remained unresolved, Reuven has the advantage, since he makes a definite claim and Shimon makes a questionable claim, and in the laws of inheritance the definite claim has the advantage (Rambam *Sefer Mishpatim*, *Hilkhot Naḥalot* 4:8; *Shulḥan Arukh*, *Ḥoshen Mishpat* 280:3).

One who died, and a ***dayetikei*** **is found bound to his thigh, etc.** – מִי שֶׁמֵּת וְנִמְצֵאת דַּיְיתִיקֵי קְשׁוּרָה עַל יְרֵיכוֹ וכו׳: If one dies and a deed of gift is found bound to his thigh, the deed is disregarded, even if it was signed by witnesses who performed an act of acquisition to enhance the power of the recipient (see *Sma*), as the person may have reconsidered before his death. If he transferred the deed to another person, it is effective, whether or not the recipient of the deed is one of his heirs, according to the principle that the instruction of a person on his deathbed is heeded (Rambam *Sefer Kinyan*, *Hilkhot Zekhiya UMattana* 9:24; *Shulḥan Arukh*, *Ḥoshen Mishpat* 250:25).

Which deed of gift of a healthy person is considered like the deed of gift of a person on his deathbed – אֵיזוֹ הִיא מַתְּנַת בָּרִיא שֶׁהִיא כְּמַתְּנַת שְׁכִיב מְרַע: If the phrase: From today and after my death, is written in a deed of gift by a healthy person, though he cannot renege on the gift, the property is acquired by the recipient only after the death of the giver, in accordance with Abaye's interpretation of the *baraita* (see Rashbam). As explained by Rabbeinu Tam, if it is written that the transaction takes effect: From today unless I change my mind before my death, the gift is treated like that of a person on his deathbed in its entirety; the giver can renege on the gift even with regard to the property itself (Rambam *Sefer Kinyan*, *Hilkhot Zekhiya UMattana* 12:14; *Shulḥan Arukh*, *Ḥoshen Mishpat* 257:6).

LANGUAGE

Will written by a person on his deathbed [*dayetikei*] – דַּיְיתִיקֵי: From the Greek διαθήκη, *diathēkē*, meaning will.

יָתֵיב רַבָּה בַּר רַב הוּנָא בְּאַכְסַדְרָא דְּבֵי רַב, וְיָתֵיב וְקָאָמַר מִשְּׁמֵיהּ דְּרַבִּי יוֹחָנָן: שְׁכִיב מְרַע שֶׁאָמַר ״כִּתְבוּ וּתְנוּ מָנֶה לִפְלוֹנִי״ וּמֵת – אֵין כּוֹתְבִין וְנוֹתְנִין, שֶׁמָּא לֹא גָּמַר לְהַקְנוֹתוֹ אֶלָּא בִּשְׁטָר, וְאֵין שְׁטָר לְאַחַר מִיתָה.

§ **Rabba bar Rav Huna was sitting in the balcony of Rav's study hall, and sat and said in the name of Rabbi Yoḥanan:** If there is **a person on his deathbed who says: Write** a deed of transfer, granting property of mine to another, **and give** with it **one hundred dinars to so-and-so, and he then died,**[N] **one does not write and give** it. This is because **perhaps he resolved to transfer it** to him **only with a deed** of transfer, **and since the** deed was not written in his lifetime it cannot be written after his death, as **a deed** of transfer is **not** effective **after the death** of the owner.

אֲמַר לְהוּ רַבִּי אֶלְעָזָר: אִיזְדַּהֲרוּ בָּהּ. רַב שֵׁיזְבִי אֲמַר: רַבִּי אֶלְעָזָר אֲמָרָהּ, וַאֲמַר לְהוּ רַבִּי יוֹחָנָן: אִיזְדַּהֲרוּ בָּהּ.

Rabba bar Rav Huna continued that when Rabbi Yoḥanan stated this *halakha*, **Rabbi Elazar said to** the other Sages: **Heed this** *halakha*; it is correct. **Rav Sheizevi said:** That is not what happened; **Rabbi Elazar** is the one who **said this** *halakha*, **and** it was **Rabbi Yoḥanan** who **said to them: Heed this** *halakha*.

אֲמַר רַב נַחְמָן בַּר יִצְחָק: כְּוָתֵיהּ דְּרַב שֵׁיזְבִי מִסְתַּבְּרָא; אִי אָמְרַתְּ בִּשְׁלָמָא רַבִּי אֶלְעָזָר אֲמָרָהּ – אִצְטְרִיךְ רַבִּי יוֹחָנָן לְאַסְהוֹדֵי עֲלֵיהּ דְּרַבִּי אֶלְעָזָר. אֶלָּא אִי אָמְרַתְּ רַבִּי יוֹחָנָן אֲמָרָהּ, אִצְטְרִיךְ רַבִּי אֶלְעָזָר לְאַסְהוֹדֵי עֲלֵיהּ דְּרַבִּי יוֹחָנָן רַבֵּיהּ?

Rav Naḥman bar Yitzḥak said: It is reasonable to say that the incident was **in accordance with** the version presented **by Rav Sheizevi. Granted, if you say** that **Rabbi Elazar said** the *halakha*, **Rabbi Yoḥanan needed to affirm** the ruling **of Rabbi Elazar. But if you say** that **Rabbi Yoḥanan** was the one who **said it, did Rabbi Elazar need to affirm** the ruling **of Rabbi Yoḥanan, his teacher?**

וְעוֹד, תָּא שְׁמַע דְּרַבִּי אֶלְעָזָר אֲמָרָהּ, דְּשָׁלַח רָבִין מִשְּׁמֵיהּ דְּרַבִּי אַבָּהוּ, הֱווּ יוֹדְעִים שֶׁשָּׁלַח רַבִּי אֶלְעָזָר לַגּוֹלָה מִשּׁוּם רַבֵּינוּ: שְׁכִיב מְרַע שֶׁאָמַר ״כִּתְבוּ וּתְנוּ מָנֶה לִפְלוֹנִי״ וּמֵת – אֵין כּוֹתְבִין וְנוֹתְנִין, שֶׁמָּא לֹא גָּמַר לְהַקְנוֹתוֹ אֶלָּא בִּשְׁטָר, וְאֵין שְׁטָר לְאַחַר מִיתָה, וְרַבִּי יוֹחָנָן אָמַר: תִּיבָּדֵק.

And furthermore, come and hear proof **that Rabbi Elazar** was the one who **said** this *halakha*, from another statement of his, **as Ravin sent** a message **in the name of Rabbi Abbahu: Know that Rabbi Elazar sent** a ruling **to the exile in the name of our teacher,** stating that if there is **a person on his deathbed who says: Write** a deed of transfer **and give** with it **one hundred dinars to so-and-so, and he then died, one does not write and give** it. This is because **perhaps he resolved to transfer it only with a deed** of transfer, **and** since the deed was not written in his lifetime it cannot be written after his death, as **a deed** of transfer is **not** effective **after the death** of the owner. **And Rabbi Yoḥanan says:** This ruling is correct; however, the wording of the deed **should be examined.**

מַאי תִּיבָּדֵק? כִּי אֲתָא רַב דִּימִי אָמַר: דַּיְיתִיקֵי מְבַטֶּלֶת דַּיְיתִיקֵי. שְׁכִיב מְרַע שֶׁאָמַר ״כִּתְבוּ וּתְנוּ מָנֶה לִפְלוֹנִי״ וּמֵת, רוֹאִין: אִם כִּמְיַיפֶּה אֶת כֹּחוֹ – כּוֹתְבִין, וְאִם לָאו – אֵין כּוֹתְבִין.

The Gemara asks: **What** did Rabbi Yoḥanan mean by saying that the wording **should be examined?** The Gemara answers: **When Rav Dimi came** from Eretz Yisrael to Babylonia, **he stated** two *halakhot*. The first was that **a** ***dayetikei*** **cancels** a previous ***dayetikei***.[H] The second explains the examination to which Rabbi Yoḥanan was referring: If there is **a person on his deathbed who said:**[H] **Write a** deed of transfer **and give** with it **one hundred dinars to so-and-so, and** he then **died,** the court must **see** what his intention was in instructing the other person to write a deed of transfer; **if** it was **to enhance** the recipient's **power** by writing a document proving that he was given the gift, **one writes** the document even after his death, as he intended to give the money anyway. **But if not,** rather it was the giver's intention to transfer the gift specifically through a deed of transfer, **one does not write** it and give the money, as a deed of transfer is not effective after the death of the owner.

מְתִיב רַבִּי אַבָּא בַּר מֶמֶל: בָּרִיא שֶׁאָמַר ״כִּתְבוּ וּתְנוּ מָנֶה לִפְלוֹנִי״ וּמֵת – אֵין כּוֹתְבִין וְנוֹתְנִין, הָא שְׁכִיב מְרַע – כּוֹתְבִין וְנוֹתְנִין! הוּא מוֹתִיב לַהּ, וְהוּא מְפָרֵק לַהּ: בִּמְיַיפֶּה אֶת כֹּחוֹ.

Rabbi Abba bar Memel raises an objection from a *baraita*: If there is **a healthy person who said:**[NH] **Write** a deed of transfer **and give with it one hundred dinars to so-and-so, and he then died, one does not write and give** it. Rabbi Abba bar Memel inferred: **But if a person on his deathbed** states this request, **one writes and gives** it. **He raises the objection and he resolves it:** The ruling of that *baraita* is **in** a case where **he was enhancing** the recipient's legal **power** by writing him a document of proof.

הֵיכִי דָּמֵי מְיַפֶּה אֶת כֹּחוֹ?

The Gemara explains: **What are the circumstances** under which it is apparent that **he was enhancing his** legal **power?**

NOTES

And he then died – וּמֵת: According to the Rashbam and the Rambam, if the deed was written and given before his death, the transfer is effective. Other early commentaries claim that since the gift was meant as a will, it cannot be transferred with a deed of transfer, as property given through a will is acquired by the recipient only after the death of the giver, whereas a deed of transfer is effective only if given in the giver's lifetime. These commentaries reason that one who orders that a deed of transfer be written is clearly not concerned that he will die before it is written (Rabbi Avraham *Av Beit Din*) and that the rabbinic ordinance that the bidding of a person on his deathbed is equivalent to a deed of transfer was instituted only so that he will not become distressed as a result of the concern that his affairs will not be settled (Ritva).

A healthy person who said, etc. – בָּרִיא שֶׁאָמַר וכו׳: A healthy person certainly intended to transfer the property with the deed of transfer, as his instruction cannot cause his property to be transferred after his death, as it would for a person on his deathbed. Therefore, if he dies, the deed may not be written (Rashbam).

HALAKHA

A *dayetikei* cancels a *dayetikei* – דַּיְיתִיקֵי מְבַטֶּלֶת דַּיְיתִיקֵי: If a person on his deathbed wills his property to a certain person, and subsequently wills it to another, the latter acquires it. A person on his deathbed can change his will several times before he dies (Rambam *Sefer Kinyan, Hilkhot Zekhiya UMattana* 9:15; *Shulḥan Arukh, Ḥoshen Mishpat* 250:13).

A person on his deathbed who said, etc. – שְׁכִיב מְרַע שֶׁאָמַר וכו׳: If a person on his deathbed instructs that his property be given to a specific person and that a deed be written for the gift, and he dies before the deed was written, one may not write the deed or give the property to the designated recipient, as the deceased may have resolved to transfer it to him only with a deed of transfer, which is not effective after the death of the owner (see Ra'avad). If the owner merely meant to enhance the power of the recipient by giving him a written document, e.g., if he said: Give him the property and write a deed for him as well, it is given to him even if the owner died before the deed was written, in accordance with Rav Dimi's statement. The *Sma* notes that if the deed was given to the recipient before the death of the giver, he thereby acquires the property in any event (Rambam *Sefer Zekhiya UMattana* 8:12; *Shulḥan Arukh, Ḥoshen Mishpat* 250:18).

A healthy person who said, etc. – בָּרִיא שֶׁאָמַר וכו׳: If a healthy person said: Write a deed of transfer and give with it one hundred dinars to so-and-so, and he then died, one may not write and give it, even if, by requiring the deed of transfer, he merely meant to enhance the recipient's legal power. Some authorities rule that if he did not request the writing of a deed of transfer, but rather merely said: Give one hundred dinars to so-and-so, and died, the money should be given to the designated recipient, as it is a mitzva to fulfill the statement of the dead (Rabbeinu Yona). The Ramah rules that it is not a mitzva in this case, unless the giver deposited the money with another on the recipient's behalf (*Shulḥan Arukh, Ḥoshen Mishpat* 250:23).

כִּדְאָמַר רַב חִסְדָּא: ״וְקָנֵינָא מִינֵּיהּ מוֹסִיף עַל מַתְּנְתָּא דָּא״, הָכָא נַמִי – דְּאָמַר: ״אַף כְּתוֹבוּ וַחֲתוֹמוּ וְהָבוּ לֵיהּ״.

It is as **Rav Ḥisda says** that if it is written in the will: **And we acquired it from him** through an act of acquisition **in addition to this gift,** this formulation does not cancel the will's power to take effect after the person's death, as the intention of referring to it as a gift is merely to enhance the legal power of the recipient by confirming the transfer through an act of acquisition. **Here too,** in a case **where** he **says: Write and sign** a document **as well, and give** it **to him,** it is apparent that his request is to enhance the legal power of the recipient by writing a document in addition to transferring the gift itself.

אִיתְּמַר: רַב יְהוּדָה אָמַר שְׁמוּאֵל, הֲלָכָה: כּוֹתְבִין וְנוֹתְנִין. וְכֵן אָמַר רָבָא אָמַר רַב נַחְמָן, הֲלָכָה: כּוֹתְבִין וְנוֹתְנִין.

It was stated that **Rav Yehuda** says that **Shmuel says** that the ***halakha*** is that **one writes** a document **and gives** the money in this case. **And Rava says similarly** that **Rav Naḥman says** that the ***halakha*** is that **one writes** a document **and gives** the money in this case.

מַתְנִי׳ הַכּוֹתֵב נְכָסָיו לְבָנָיו – צָרִיךְ שֶׁיִּכְתּוֹב ״מֵהַיּוֹם וּלְאַחַר מִיתָה״, דִּבְרֵי רַבִּי יְהוּדָה; רַבִּי יוֹסֵי אוֹמֵר: אֵינוֹ צָרִיךְ.

MISHNA A healthy person **who writes** a document granting **his property to his sons**[H] in his lifetime, but wishes to continue to derive benefit from it until his death, **must write:** I give the property **from today and after** my **death.**[N] This is **the statement of Rabbi Yehuda. Rabbi Yosei says: He need not** write: From today and after my death; it is sufficient for him to write that the transfer will take effect after he dies.

הַכּוֹתֵב נְכָסָיו לִבְנוֹ לְאַחַר מוֹתוֹ – הָאָב אֵינוֹ יָכוֹל לִמְכּוֹר, מִפְּנֵי שֶׁהֵן כְּתוּבִין לַבֵּן, וְהַבֵּן אֵינוֹ יָכוֹל לִמְכּוֹר, מִפְּנֵי שֶׁהֵן בִּרְשׁוּת הָאָב.

If **one writes** a document granting **his property to his son** from today and **after his death,**[H] **the father cannot sell** the property **because it is written** as granted **to the son, and the son cannot sell** it **because it is** still **in the possession of the father** with regard to using the property and consuming its produce.

מָכַר הָאָב – מְכוּרִים עַד שֶׁיָּמוּת, מָכַר הַבֵּן – אֵין לַלּוֹקֵחַ בָּהֶן כְּלוּם עַד שֶׁיָּמוּת הָאָב.

If **the father sold** the property, **it is sold** to the purchaser inasmuch as he may use it and consume its produce **until** the father **dies,** at which point it belongs to the son. If **the son sold** it during his father's lifetime, **the purchaser has no** right to use it **until the father dies.**

גְּמָ׳ וְכִי כָּתַב ״מֵהַיּוֹם וּלְאַחַר מִיתָה״ מַאי הָוֵי? הָא תְּנַן: ״מֵהַיּוֹם וּלְאַחַר מִיתָה״ – גֵּט וְאֵינוֹ גֵּט, וְאִם מֵת – חוֹלֶצֶת וְלֹא מִתְיַיבֶּמֶת!

GEMARA And if he wrote: I give the property **from today and after** my **death, what of it? Didn't we learn** in a mishna (*Gittin* 72a): If a husband said to his wife: This is your bill of divorce from **today and after** my **death,** it is **a bill of divorce but not** a complete **bill of divorce,**[HN] and therefore **if he dies** without children his wife **performs the ritual through which a woman is freed of her levirate bonds** [***ḥalitza***],[B] as perhaps the bill of divorce is invalid and she is bound by the levirate bond and may not remarry without first performing *ḥalitza*. **But she does not enter into levirate marriage,** as perhaps the bill of divorce is valid, and it is forbidden for a divorcée to marry her former husband's brother.

HALAKHA

Who writes a document granting his property to his sons – הַכּוֹתֵב נְכָסָיו לְבָנָיו: With regard to a deed of gift of a healthy person in which it is written that a certain individual will receive a property after the death of the giver, the *halakha* depends on the circumstances. If the date is written in the deed, whether at the beginning or the end (*Sma*), and the giver was still alive at the time, the gift is valid, as the mention of the date proves that the giver's intention is to transfer the ownership immediately, even if the act of acquisition is not mentioned. It is considered as though the phrase: From today and after my death, is written in the deed.

The Rema, citing the Ramah, writes that if it is written that the recipient will receive the property thirty days after the writing of the deed, the mention of the date does not prove that the giver intends to transfer ownership immediately, as it serves only to indicate the date on which the transfer will be completed. Therefore, if the owner dies within the thirty days the transaction does not take effect, unless the phrase: From today and after my death, is written (Rambam *Sefer Kinyan, Hilkhot Zekhiya UMattana* 12:15; *Shulḥan Arukh, Ḥoshen Mishpat* 258:1, and 258:2 in the comment of Rema).

If one writes a document granting his property to his son after his death – הַכּוֹתֵב נְכָסָיו לִבְנוֹ לְאַחַר מוֹתוֹ: If one writes a document granting his property to his son after his death, the son attains ownership of the property itself on the date mentioned in the document, and the rights to the produce belong to the father until his death. During the father's lifetime, neither can sell the property on his own, due to the share of the other; but they can sell it together (*Be'er HaGola*, citing Rashbam). If the father does try to sell it, he sells only the produce of the land, even if he then reacquires his son's portion (Rema, citing *Nimmukei Yosef*). From the time the father dies, the son or his heirs can repossess the produce from the purchaser. If the son sells the property, the purchaser receives it only after the death of the father (Rambam *Sefer Kinyan, Hilkhot Zekhiya UMattana* 12:13; *Shulḥan Arukh, Ḥoshen Mishpat* 257:1, 3–4; see 211:5).

From today and after my death, it is a bill of divorce but not a complete bill of divorce – מֵהַיּוֹם וּלְאַחַר מִיתָה גֵּט וְאֵינוֹ גֵּט: If a husband said to his wife: This is your bill of divorce from today and after my death, or: From now and after my death, and he dies, it is uncertain whether she is divorced. She must perform *ḥalitza* and not levirate marriage, as perhaps by saying: After my death, the husband intended to retract his declaration that she is divorced immediately, and divorce cannot take effect after the husband's death (Rambam *Sefer Nashim, Hilkhot Geirushin* 9:14; *Shulḥan Arukh, Even HaEzer* 145:3).

BACKGROUND

Performs *ḥalitza* – חוֹלֶצֶת: *Ḥalitza* is the ceremony that frees the widow of a man who died without children from the obligation to marry one of her deceased husband's brothers and allows her to remarry (see Deuteronomy 25:7–10). The term *ḥalitza* is derived from the central element of this ceremony, which involves the removal by the widow of a special sandal from the foot of one of her deceased husband's brothers, described in the verse with the words "and remove [*veḥaletza*] his shoe"(Deuteronomy 25:9). *Ḥalitza* must be performed in the presence of a rabbinical court. The *halakhot* governing this ceremony are discussed in detail in tractate *Yevamot*.

NOTES

From today and after my death – מֵהַיּוֹם וּלְאַחַר מִיתָה: If one writes: After my death, the deed is not effective, as once he dies the property belongs to his legal heirs, and he no longer has the power to give it to someone else. The gift of a person on his deathbed is an exception, as the Sages gave him the legal power to transfer his property after his death.

A bill of divorce but not a complete bill of divorce – גֵּט וְאֵינוֹ גֵּט: It is uncertain whether the husband's intention was for the bill of divorce to take effect today and is therefore a valid bill of divorce, in which case the wife has no levirate bond and is forbidden to marry her brother-in-law, or if his intention was that it should take effect after his death and is therefore invalid. In such a case, after he dies the wife is a widow and has a levirate bond. Therefore, she may not enter into levirate marriage, but must perform *ḥalitza* to release herself of the possible levirate bond.

הָתָם מְסַפְּקָא לָן אִי תְּנָאָה הָוֵי אִי חֲזָרָה הָוֵי, אֲבָל הָכָא הָכִי קָאָמַר לֵיהּ: גּוּפָא קְנֵי מֵהַיּוֹם, פֵּירָא – לְאַחַר מִיתָה.

The Gemara answers: **There, we are uncertain**[N] **if** the expression: And after my death, **is** meant as **a condition,** i.e., if I die you will be divorced retroactively from today, **or if it is a retraction** of the statement: From today, meaning that the divorce would take effect only after his death, which would render it invalid. **But here,** in the case of a deed of gift, there is no contradiction in the statement, as **this is what** the father **is** presumably **saying to him: Acquire** the property **itself today,** and **the produce after** my **death.**

״רַבִּי יוֹסֵי אוֹמֵר: אֵינוֹ צָרִיךְ״. רַבָּה בַּר אֲבוּהּ חָלַשׁ, עָל לְגַבֵּיהּ רַב הוּנָא וְרַב נַחְמָן; אֲמַר לֵיהּ רַב הוּנָא לְרַב נַחְמָן, בְּעֵי מִינֵּיהּ: הֲלָכָה כְּרַבִּי יוֹסֵי אוֹ אֵין הֲלָכָה כְּרַבִּי יוֹסֵי? אֲמַר לֵיהּ: טַעְמֵיהּ דְּרַבִּי יוֹסֵי לָא יָדַעְנָא, הֲלָכָה אִיבְּעֵי מִינֵּיהּ? אֲמַר לֵיהּ: אַתְּ בְּעֵי מִינֵּיהּ אִי הֲלָכָה אִי לָא, וְטַעְמֵיהּ אֲנָא אֵמִינָא לָךְ.

§ The mishna teaches: **Rabbi Yosei says** that **he need not** write: From today and after my death. The Gemara relates: **Rabba bar Avuh was sick,** and **Rav Huna and Rav Naḥman entered** to visit **him. Rav Huna said to Rav Naḥman: Ask him**[N] whether the ***halakha*** **is in accordance with the opinion of Rabbi Yosei or** the ***halakha*** **is not in accordance with the opinion of Rabbi Yosei.** Rav Naḥman **said to** Rav Huna: **I do not know Rabbi Yosei's reasoning; can I ask him** about the ***halakha***? Rav Huna **said to** Rav Naḥman: **You ask him if** the ***halakha*** is in accordance with his opinion **or not, and I will tell you his reasoning** afterward.

בְּעָא מִינֵּיהּ. אֲמַר לֵיהּ, הָכִי אָמַר רַב: הֲלָכָה כְּרַבִּי יוֹסֵי. בָּתַר דִּנְפַקוּ, אֲמַר לֵיהּ: הַיְינוּ טַעְמֵיהּ דְּרַבִּי יוֹסֵי – דְּאָמַר: זְמַנּוֹ שֶׁל שְׁטָר מוֹכִיחַ עָלָיו. תַּנְיָא נָמֵי הָכִי, רַבִּי יוֹסֵי אוֹמֵר: אֵינוֹ צָרִיךְ, מִפְּנֵי שֶׁזְּמַנּוֹ שֶׁל שְׁטָר מוֹכִיחַ עָלָיו.

Rav Naḥman **asked** Rabba bar Avuh. Rabba bar Avuh **said to him** that **this** is what **Rav says:** The ***halakha*** is **in accordance with** the opinion of **Rabbi Yosei. After they left,** Rav Huna **said to** Rav Naḥman that **this is Rabbi Yosei's reasoning: He says** that writing: From today and after my death, is unnecessary because **the date** written **in a document proves** when **it** takes effect. The Gemara adds: **That is also taught** in a *baraita* (*Tosefta, Ketubot* 8:4): **Rabbi Yosei says** that **he need not** write: From today and after my death, **because the date** written **in a document proves** when **it** takes effect.

בְּעָא מִינֵּיהּ רָבָא מֵרַב נַחְמָן: בְּהַקְנָאָה, מַהוּ? אֲמַר לֵיהּ: בְּהַקְנָאָה אֵינוֹ צָרִיךְ.

§ **Rava asked Rav Naḥman: In** a case where the father performed an act of **transfer,** transferring his property to his son after his death, **what is the** *halakha*?[NH] Is it still necessary to write: From today and after my death? Rav Naḥman **said to him: In** a case where he performed an act of **transfer, he need not** write: From today and after my death.

רַב פַּפִּי אָמַר: אִיכָּא אַקְנָיְתָא דְּצָרִיךְ, וְאִיכָּא אַקְנָיְתָא דְּלָא צָרִיךְ; ״אַקְנְיֵיהּ וְקָנֵינָא מִינֵּיהּ״ – לָא צָרִיךְ, ״קָנֵינָא מִינֵּיהּ וְאַקְנְיֵיהּ״ – צָרִיךְ.

Rav Pappi said: There is a case of **transfer where** he **needs** to write: From today and after my death, **and there is** a case of **transfer where** he does **not need** to do so. If it is written in the deed that **he transferred it to him and we,** the witnesses, **acquired** it **from him,**[N] he does **not need** to write: From today and after my death. But if the statement is written in the opposite order: **We acquired** it **from him and he transferred** it **to him,** he still **needs**[N] to write: From today and after my death.

מַתְקִיף לַהּ רַב חֲנִינָא מִסּוּרָא: מִי אִיכָּא מִידֵּי דַּאֲנַן לָא יָדְעִינַן וְסָפְרֵי יָדְעִי? שַׁאֲלוּנְהוּ לְסָפְרֵי דְּאַבָּיֵי – וְיָדְעִי, וּלְסָפְרֵי דְּרָבָא – וְיָדְעִי.

Rav Ḥanina of Sura objects to this distinction: **Is there anything that we,** the Sages, **do not know, and the scribes know?** The distinction between the two opposite orderings of the above statement was unknown to the Sages. The Gemara relates that the Sages **asked Abaye's scribes and they knew** the distinction, **and** they asked **Rava's scribes and they** also **knew** the distinction.

רַב הוּנָא בְּרֵיהּ דְּרַב יְהוֹשֻׁעַ אָמַר: בֵּין ״אַקְנְיֵיהּ וְקָנֵינָא מִינֵּיהּ״, בֵּין ״קָנֵינָא מִינֵּיהּ וְאַקְנְיֵיהּ״ – לָא צָרִיךְ, וּבְ״דוּכְרַן פִּתְגָּמֵי דַּהֲוֵי בְּאַנְפָּנָא״ – פְּלִיגִי.

Rav Huna, son of Rav Yehoshua, said: Whether the wording is **he transferred** it **to him and we acquired** it **from him,** or **whether** it is **we acquired** it **from him and he transferred** it **to him,** he **need not** write: From today and after my death, as the act of transfer is mentioned in any event. **And** Rabbi Yehuda and Rabbi Yosei in the mishna **disagree** whether the phrase: From today and after my death, is necessary only **with regard to** a case where the deed merely states: This is **a record of the proceedings that took place in our presence,** without any mention of an act of transfer.

NOTES

There we are uncertain – הָתָם מְסַפְּקָא לָן: Since a divorce cannot take effect in stages, the statement: From today and after my death, is considered self-contradictory and is therefore treated as a divorce of uncertain status. Concerning a transfer of property, the ownership and the right of use can be transferred in separate stages, so there is no contradiction.

Ask him – בְּעֵי מִינֵּיהּ: Even though Rav Naḥman was much younger than Rav Huna and was his student, since Rabba bar Avuh was ill Rav Huna did not want to ask him the question. Therefore, he asked Rav Naḥman, who was loved by Rabba bar Avuh and may even have been his son-in-law, to ask the question instead.

In a case of transfer, what is the *halakha* – בְּהַקְנָאָה מַהוּ: The Rashbam and other commentaries maintain that this dilemma is raised according to Rabbi Yehuda's opinion, although the *halakha* is in accordance with Rabbi Yosei's opinion. Other commentaries (Rabbeinu Tam; Rabbeinu Yitzḥak) explain that it is raised according to Rabbi Yosei's opinion as well, in a case where the date is not written in the deed.

The reason it might be unnecessary to write: From today and after my death, in this case is that an act of transfer indicates that the transfer is intended to take effect immediately (Ri Migash; see Ramban).

He transferred it to him and we acquired it from him – אַקְנְיֵיהּ וְקָנֵינָא: Some commentaries explain that the two statements are written sequentially to emphasize the significance of the act of transaction. The Rashbam rejects this interpretation, reasoning that if the two statements are written together, the order is inconsequential. He explains that the statement: He transferred it to him, is written at the beginning of the deed, indicating that the owner instructed that an act of acquisition be performed, and the statement: And we acquired it from him, is written at the end, meaning that the act was performed. The combination of the two statements emphasizes the significance of this act.

We acquired it from him and he transferred it to him, he needs – קָנֵינָא מִינֵּיהּ וְאַקְנְיֵיהּ צָרִיךְ: The Meiri explains that this is not the standard formulation, so the significance of the act of transfer is uncertain. The Rashbam explains that when the statements are written in this order, the statement that the owner transferred it to him is merely a statement that the acquisition was performed, and does not serve to emphasize the importance of the act.

HALAKHA

In a case of transfer, what is the *halakha* – בְּהַקְנָאָה מַהוּ: If one writes a deed of gift to take effect after his death and performs an act of transfer, the recipient attains ownership of the property itself immediately, even if the deed of gift does not mention the date. This is in accordance with Rava's statement in the name of Rav Naḥman, according to the explanation that it applies to Rabbi Yosei's opinion as well, in the case of a deed of gift in which the date is not written (*Shulḥan Arukh, Ḥoshen Mishpat* 258:2).

אֲמַר רַב כָּהֲנָא: אֲמַרִיתָהּ לִשְׁמַעְתָּא קַמֵּיהּ דְּרַב זְבִיד מִנְּהַרְדְּעָא, וַאֲמַר לִי: אַתּוּן הָכִי מַתְנִיתוּ לַהּ, אֲנַן הָכִי מַתְנִינַן לַהּ, אָמַר רָבָא אָמַר רַב נַחְמָן: בְּהַקְנָאָה – אֵינוֹ צָרִיךְ; בֵּין ״אַקְנְיֵיהּ וְקָנֵינָא מִינֵּיהּ״, בֵּין ״קָנֵינָא מִינֵּיהּ וְאַקְנְיֵיהּ״ – לָא צָרִיךְ; בְּ״דוּכְרַן פִּתְגָּמֵי דַּהֲווֹ בְּאַנְפָּנָא״ – פְּלִיגִי.

Rav Kahana said: I stated this *halakha* **in the presence of Rav Zevid of Nehardea, and he said to me: You teach it like this,** i.e., as a question and answer followed by a dispute; **we teach it like this,** i.e., as a single, unbroken statement: **Rava says** that **Rav Naḥman says** that **in** a case where **transfer** is mentioned in the deed, the owner **need not** write: From today and after my death. This is the *halakha* **whether** the wording is **he transferred** it **to him and we acquired** it **from him,** or **whether** the wording is **we acquired** it **from him and he transferred** it **to him;** he **need not** write: From today and after my death. They **disagree** only **with regard to** a case where the wording is: This is **a record of the proceedings that took place in our presence.**

״הַכּוֹתֵב נְכָסָיו לִבְנוֹ לְאַחַר מוֹתוֹ״. אִיתְּמַר: מָכַר הַבֵּן בְּחַיֵּי הָאָב, וּמֵת הַבֵּן בְּחַיֵּי הָאָב,

§ The mishna teaches that if **one writes** a document granting **his property to his son** from today and **after his death,** neither he nor the son can sell the property. **It was stated** that in a case where **the son sold** the property **during the father's lifetime, and** then **the son died during the father's lifetime,** after which the father died as well,

Perek **VIII**
Daf **136** Amud **b**

אָמַר רַבִּי יוֹחָנָן: לֹא קָנָה לוֹקֵחַ, וְרֵישׁ לָקִישׁ אָמַר: קָנָה לוֹקֵחַ.

Rabbi Yoḥanan says: The purchaser did not acquire[N] the property, **and Reish Lakish says: The purchaser acquired**[H] the property.

רַבִּי יוֹחָנָן אָמַר לֹא קָנָה לוֹקֵחַ, קִנְיַן פֵּירוֹת כְּקִנְיַן הַגּוּף דָּמֵי;

The Gemara explains their reasoning: **Rabbi Yoḥanan says** that **the purchaser did not acquire** the property because he holds that **ownership of** the rights to use an item and the **profits** it engenders **is considered** to be **like ownership of the item itself.** Even though the property itself did not belong to the father, it is as though the father owned the property, because all of the produce belonged to him in practice. Therefore, the son's sale can take effect only after the father's death. If the son dies first, since he never attained ownership, his sale can never come to fruition.

וְרֵישׁ לָקִישׁ אָמַר קָנָה לוֹקֵחַ, קִנְיַן פֵּירוֹת לָאו כְּקִנְיַן הַגּוּף דָּמֵי.

And Reish Lakish says: The purchaser acquired the property, because he holds that **ownership of** the rights to use an item and the **profits** it engenders **is not considered** to be **like ownership of the item itself.** Therefore, the father's rights do not prevent the son, who owns the property itself, from selling it, and eventually the purchaser receives full rights to it.

וְהָא אִיפְלִיגוּ בָּהּ חֲדָא זִימְנָא! דְּאִיתְּמַר: הַמּוֹכֵר שָׂדֵהוּ לְפֵירוֹת – רַבִּי יוֹחָנָן אָמַר: מֵבִיא וְקוֹרֵא, וְרֵישׁ לָקִישׁ אָמַר: מֵבִיא וְאֵינוֹ קוֹרֵא.

The Gemara asks: **But didn't they** already **engage in a dispute** concerning **this** issue **one time? As it was stated:** With regard to **one who sells his field for** just its **produce,** meaning that he retains ownership over the field itself and he sells the rights to all of its produce to someone else, **Rabbi Yoḥanan says:** The purchaser **brings** first fruits from this field to the Temple **and recites** the verses in the Torah associated with the bringing of the first fruits,[N] in which he thanks God for: "The land that You, Lord, have given me" (Deuteronomy 26:10). **And Reish Lakish says:** The purchaser **brings** the first fruits, **but he does not recite**[NH] the verses, since it is not his field.

NOTES

The purchaser did not acquire – לֹא קָנָה לוֹקֵחַ: According to the opinion of Rabbi Yoḥanan, who inherits the property after the father's death? The Rashbam holds that even though the sale did not take effect, the son lost his right to the property when he sold it, and it is inherited by the father's other sons, not the heirs of that son. Other early commentaries maintain that he did not lose his right, and all the sons inherit the property, including the heirs of that son (see *Tosafot*).

The recitation of the first fruits – מִקְרָא בִּכּוּרִים: It is a mitzva by Torah law to bring to the Temple the first fruits from the seven species for which Eretz Yisrael was praised (Deuteronomy 26:1–11). The *halakhot* of this mitzva are detailed in tractate *Bikkurim*. At the Temple, a ceremony takes place in which a priest lifts the basket with the fruit, the Levites sing, and the one who brought the fruit recites the verses in the Torah pertaining to this occasion. It was established that the verses are recited only if the wording is an accurate representation of the situation of the one reciting them. There are several types of people who are obligated to bring the first fruits to the Temple but do not recite the verses, e.g., a woman, a *tumtum*, a steward, and an agent. According to the opinion of Reish Lakish, one who sells the rights only to the produce of his field falls into this category.

Brings but he does not recite – מֵבִיא וְאֵינוֹ קוֹרֵא: The Rashbam holds that he does not recite the verses because the expression "The land that You, the Lord, have given me" (Deuteronomy 26:10) does not apply to him; but he is obligated to bring the fruit to the Temple because the definition of the mitzva, namely, "You shall take of the first of all the fruit of the ground, which you shall bring in from your land" (Deuteronomy 26:2), does apply to him. *Tosafot* counter that this is a contradiction; if the former verse does not apply to him neither does the latter, as both refer to his land. Therefore, they claim, by Torah law this person is exempt from the mitzva entirely, and he is obligated only due to a rabbinic ordinance. The Sages instituted that he should bring the fruit without reciting the verses because the verse (Deuteronomy 26:10) does not apply to him, or in order to emphasize that by Torah law these are not considered first fruits, and one is obligated to tithe them (see 82a).

HALAKHA

The purchaser acquired – קָנָה לוֹקֵחַ: If one writes a document granting his property to his son, specifying that the son attain full ownership of it after his death, and the son sells it during his father's lifetime, and the son predeceases the father, the purchaser receives the property after the father's death, as the father owns only the rights to the produce of the property and is not considered the owner of the property itself (see *Sma*). The Gemara in tractate *Yevamot* (36b) rules in accordance with the opinion of Reish Lakish (Rambam *Sefer Kinyan*, *Hilkhot Zekhiya UMattana* 12:13; *Shulḥan Arukh*, *Ḥoshen Mishpat* 257:5).

Brings but he does not recite – מֵבִיא וְאֵינוֹ קוֹרֵא: If one sells the rights to the produce of his field, the purchaser brings its first fruits but does not recite the verses associated with the first fruits, as ownership of the rights to the produce is not considered like ownership of the land itself; he therefore cannot recite: "The land that You, the Lord, have given me" (Deuteronomy 26:10). This is in accordance with the opinion of Reish Lakish (Rambam *Sefer Zera'im*, *Hilkhot Bikkurim* 4:6).

רַבִּי יוֹחָנָן אָמַר מֵבִיא וְקוֹרֵא, קָסָבַר: קִנְיַן פֵּירוֹת כְּקִנְיַן הַגּוּף דָּמֵי; וְרֵישׁ לָקִישׁ אָמַר מֵבִיא וְאֵינוֹ קוֹרֵא, קִנְיַן פֵּירוֹת לָאו כְּקִנְיַן הַגּוּף דָּמֵי!

The Gemara explains the reason behind the dispute: **Rabbi Yoḥanan says he brings** the first fruits **and recites** the verses because **he maintains** that **ownership of** the rights to use an item and the **profits** it engenders **is considered** to be **like** the **ownership of the item itself.** Even though the field itself does not belong to him, it is as if he acquired the field because all of the produce belongs to him in practice. **And Reish Lakish says** that **he brings** the first fruits **and does not recite** the verses **because** he holds that **ownership of** the rights to use an item and the **profits** it engenders **is not considered** to be **like** the **ownership of the item itself.** Why was it necessary for them to engage in a dispute concerning this issue twice?

אָמַר לָךְ רַבִּי יוֹחָנָן: אַף עַל גַּב דִּבְעָלְמָא קִנְיַן פֵּירוֹת כְּקִנְיַן הַגּוּף דָּמֵי, הָכָא אִצְטְרִיךְ; סָלְקָא דַּעְתָּךְ אָמִינָא: אַבָּא לְגַבֵּי בְּרֵיהּ אַחוּלֵי אַחֵיל, קָא מַשְׁמַע לַן.

The Gemara answers: It was necessary for the dispute to be stated also in the context of one who sells his father's property and then dies. This is because **Rabbi Yoḥanan** could have **said to you** that **although in general ownership of** the rights to use an item and the **profits** it engenders **is considered** to be **like** the **ownership of the item itself, here it was necessary** to emphasize this principle, because it might **enter your mind to say** that **with regard to a father and son,** the father presumably **waived** his rights in the property itself. Rabbi Yoḥanan **teaches us** that even in this case, the father's ownership of the rights to use an item and the profits it engenders is considered to be like the ownership of the item itself.

וְרַבִּי שִׁמְעוֹן בֶּן לָקִישׁ אָמַר: אַף עַל גַּב דִּבְעָלְמָא קִנְיַן פֵּירוֹת לָאו כְּקִנְיַן הַגּוּף דָּמֵי, הָכָא אִצְטְרִיךְ; סָלְקָא דַּעְתָּךְ אָמִינָא: כׇּל לְגַבֵּי נַפְשֵׁיהּ, אֲפִילּוּ בִּמְקוֹם בְּרֵיהּ – נַפְשֵׁיהּ עֲדִיפָא לֵיהּ, קָא מַשְׁמַע לַן.

And Rabbi Shimon ben Lakish could have **said** that **although in general ownership of** the rights to use an item and the **profits** it engenders **is not considered** to be **like** the **ownership of the item itself,** as one who sells the produce of his field retains full ownership of the land itself, **here it was necessary** to emphasize this principle, as it might **enter your mind to say** that in **any** sale **concerning oneself, even vis-à-vis his son, one grants preference to himself.** Accordingly, if one grants the property itself to his son, reserving the rights to the produce for himself, he retains the rights to the property itself as well. Reish Lakish **teaches us** that he does not retain the rights to the property.

אֵיתִיבֵיהּ רַבִּי יוֹחָנָן לְרֵישׁ לָקִישׁ: ״נְכָסַי לָךְ, וְאַחֲרֶיךָ יִירַשׁ פְּלוֹנִי, וְאַחֲרָיו יִירַשׁ פְּלוֹנִי״, מֵת רִאשׁוֹן – קָנָה שֵׁנִי, מֵת שֵׁנִי – קָנָה שְׁלִישִׁי,

Rabbi Yoḥanan raised an objection to the opinion of **Reish Lakish** from a *baraita* (*Tosefta* 8:4): If one states: **My property** will go **to you** after my death for your use during your lifetime, **and after you** die, **so-and-so will inherit** the property, **and after** the one who inherits after you dies, **so-and-so will inherit** the property, in this case, when **the first** recipient **dies, the second acquires** it, and when **the second dies, the third acquires** it.

מֵת שֵׁנִי בְּחַיֵּי רִאשׁוֹן – יַחְזְרוּ נְכָסִים לְיוֹרְשֵׁי רִאשׁוֹן;

If **the second dies during the lifetime of the first, the property returns** after his death **to the heirs of the first,** and does not go to the third designated recipient, as his right was to inherit it from the second, who never received it.

וְאִם אִיתָא, לְיוֹרְשֵׁי נוֹתֵן מִיבָּעֵי לֵיהּ!

And if it is so that ownership of the rights to use an item and the profits is not considered to be like ownership of the item itself, the *baraita* **should have** stated that the property returns **to the heirs of the giver,** as the first and second recipients received only the right to use the property and enjoy its profits during their lifetimes, after which it was designated to be transferred to others. Therefore, in a case where the transfer does not apply, the property should return to the possession of the one who owns the property itself, namely the giver and his heirs.

אֲמַר לֵיהּ, כְּבָר תִּרְגְּמָהּ רַב הוֹשַׁעְיָא בְּבָבֶל: ״אַחֲרֶיךָ״ שָׁאנֵי. וְכֵן רְמֵי רַבָּה בַּר רַב הוּנָא קַמֵּיהּ דְּרַב, וַאֲמַר: ״אַחֲרֶיךָ״ שָׁאנֵי.

Reish Lakish **said to him: Rav Hoshaya already interpreted in Babylonia** that a case of **after you,** i.e., where the owner said to the recipient: After you die so-and-so will inherit the property, **is different,**[N] as the giver intended to grant full ownership of the property to the first recipient as well, including both the rights to the produce and the property itself. **And Rabba bar Rav Huna also raised this contradiction before Rav, and Rav said** in response: **After you, is different.**

וְהָתַנְיָא: יַחְזְרוּ לְיוֹרְשֵׁי נוֹתֵן!

The Gemara asks: **But isn't it taught** in another *baraita* that if the second designated recipient dies before the first, after the death of the first the property **returns to the heirs of the giver?**[N]

NOTES

After you, is different – **אַחֲרֶיךָ שָׁאנֵי:** The expression: After you die, can be understood to mean: What you leave after you die. In other words, the first receives full ownership of the property, with the qualification that if the asset is not sold, it enters the possession of the second after the death of the first, as explained on 137a.

But isn't it taught that the property returns to the heirs of the giver – **וְהָתַנְיָא יַחְזְרוּ לְיוֹרְשֵׁי נוֹתֵן:** The Rashbam explains this as an objection to Rabbi Yoḥanan's statement: If there is an opinion among the *tanna'im* that even in a case of: After you, the owner of the rights to the produce is not considered the owner of the property, certainly in other cases where one owns the rights to the produce but not the property itself, he is not considered the owner of the property.

תַּנָּאֵי הִיא; דְּתַנְיָא: ״נְכָסַי לְךָ וְאַחֲרֶיךָ לִפְלוֹנִי״, וְיָרַד רִאשׁוֹן וּמָכַר וְאָכַל – הַשֵּׁנִי מוֹצִיא מִיַּד הַלָּקוֹחוֹת, דִּבְרֵי רַבִּי; רַבָּן שִׁמְעוֹן בֶּן גַּמְלִיאֵל אוֹמֵר: אֵין לַשֵּׁנִי אֶלָּא מַה שֶּׁשִּׁיֵּיר רִאשׁוֹן.

The Gemara answers: The *halakha* in this case **is** a dispute between *tanna'im*; **as it is taught** in a *baraita*: With regard to one who said: **My property** is given **to you, and after you, to so-and-so,**[H] and the **first** recipient **entered** the property **and sold** it **and consumed**[N] the profits, **the second** recipient **repossesses** the property **from the purchasers,** as the property belongs to him after the death of the first recipient; **this is the statement of Rabbi** Yehuda HaNasi. **Rabban Shimon ben Gamliel says: The second** recipient receives **only that which the first** beneficiary **left,** since his sale is valid.

וּרְמִינְהִי: ״נְכָסַי לְךָ וְאַחֲרֶיךָ לִפְלוֹנִי״ – יוֹרֵד רִאשׁוֹן וּמוֹכֵר וְאוֹכֵל, דִּבְרֵי רַבִּי; רַבָּן שִׁמְעוֹן בֶּן גַּמְלִיאֵל אוֹמֵר: אֵין לָרִאשׁוֹן אֶלָּא אֲכִילַת פֵּירוֹת בִּלְבַד.

And the Gemara **raises a contradiction** from another *baraita* (*Tosefta* 8:4): If one says: **My property** is given **to you, and after you, to so-and-so, the first one may enter** the property **and sell** it **and consume** the profits; this is **the statement of Rabbi** Yehuda HaNasi. **Rabban Shimon ben Gamliel says: The first one has only** the right of **consumption of the produce.**

קַשְׁיָא דְּרַבִּי אַדְּרַבִּי, וּדְרַבָּן שִׁמְעוֹן בֶּן גַּמְלִיאֵל אַדְּרַבָּן שִׁמְעוֹן בֶּן גַּמְלִיאֵל!

This statement **of Rabbi** Yehuda HaNasi **is difficult** as it is contradicted by the other statement **of Rabbi** Yehuda HaNasi, **and** this statement **of Rabban Shimon ben Gamliel is difficult** as it is contradicted by the other statement **of Rabban Shimon ben Gamliel.** Their opinions in the latter *baraita* seem to be the opposite of those in the former *baraita.*

דְּרַבִּי אַדְּרַבִּי לָא קַשְׁיָא: הָא לְגוּפָא, הָא לְפֵירָא; דְּרַבָּן שִׁמְעוֹן בֶּן גַּמְלִיאֵל אַדְּרַבָּן שִׁמְעוֹן בֶּן גַּמְלִיאֵל לָא קַשְׁיָא: הָא לְכַתְּחִלָּה, הָא דִּיעֲבַד.

The Gemara answers: The apparent contradiction between one statement **of Rabbi** Yehuda HaNasi and the other statement **of Rabbi** Yehuda HaNasi is **not difficult; this** ruling that the first one cannot sell it is referring **to the** property **itself,** and **that** ruling that he can sell it is referring **to the produce.** The apparent contradiction between one statement **of Rabban Shimon ben Gamliel** and the other statement **of Rabban Shimon ben Gamliel** is **not difficult** either; **this** statement, that the first has only the right to consume the produce, is referring to his rights ***ab initio***, whereas **that** statement, that if he sold the property the second one gets nothing, is referring to the *halakha* **after the fact.**

אָמַר אַבָּיֵי: אֵיזֶהוּ רָשָׁע עָרוּם? זֶה הַמַּשִּׂיא עֵצָה לִמְכּוֹר בִּנְכָסִים כְּרַבָּן שִׁמְעוֹן בֶּן גַּמְלִיאֵל.

Abaye says: Who is a cunning wicked person? This is one who provides advice[N] **to sell property in accordance with** the ruling **of Rabban Shimon ben Gamliel.** Although Rabban Shimon ben Gamliel holds that the sale is valid, he does not permit one to do so *ab initio*, as that would deprive the second designated recipient of the property. Therefore, one who advises the first recipient to do so is considered a cunning wicked person.

אָמַר רַבִּי יוֹחָנָן: הֲלָכָה כְּרַבָּן שִׁמְעוֹן בֶּן גַּמְלִיאֵל; וּמוֹדֶה, שֶׁאִם נְתָנָן בְּמַתְּנַת שְׁכִיב מְרַע – לֹא עָשָׂה כְּלוּם.

Rabbi Yoḥanan says: The ***halakha*** **is in accordance with** the opinion of **Rabban Shimon ben Gamliel; but** Rabban Shimon ben Gamliel **concedes that if** the first recipient **gave** the property to another **as the gift of a person on his deathbed,**[H] in which case no formal act of acquisition is required, **he has done nothing;** the second recipient can repossess the property from the one to whom it was given.

מַאי טַעְמָא? אָמַר אַבָּיֵי: מַתְּנַת שְׁכִיב מְרַע לֹא קָנֵה אֶלָּא לְאַחַר מִיתָה, וּכְבָר קָדְמוֹ ״אַחֲרֶיךָ״.

What is the reason? Abaye says: The recipient of **the gift of a person on his deathbed acquires** it **only after** the person's **death, and** in this case, the acquisition of the recipient resulting from the statement of: **After you,** i.e., the second designated recipient, **has already preceded** the acquisition of the first one.

וּמִי אָמַר אַבָּיֵי הָכִי? וְהָא אִיתְּמַר: מַתְּנַת שְׁכִיב מְרַע מֵאֵימָתַי קָנֵה? אַבָּיֵי אָמַר: עִם גְּמַר מִיתָה, וְרָבָא אָמַר: לְאַחַר גְּמַר מִיתָה!

The Gemara asks: **But did Abaye** actually **say this,** that the gift of a person on his deathbed takes effect only after his death? **But wasn't it stated** in an amoraic dispute concerning the matter: **From when does** the recipient of **the gift of a person on his deathbed acquire** it?[H] **Abaye says: With the completion of death,** i.e., at the moment he dies; **and Rava says: After the completion of death.**

HALAKHA

My property is given to you, and after you, to so-and-so, etc. – **נְכָסַי לְךָ וְאַחֲרֶיךָ לִפְלוֹנִי וכו׳**: If one on his deathbed says: My property is given to so-and-so, and after he dies, to so-and-so, the second one receives only what remains of the property after the first dies. The first may not sell the property or give it away; rather, he may enjoy the benefits of the property until he dies, and then the second receives it. If the first sold the property or gave it away anyway, the second cannot repossess it from the purchasers, as he does not have any fundamental right to the property, other than his right to receive what remains after the first dies. Anyone who advises the first to sell the property or give it away is considered a wicked person. This is in accordance with the opinion of Rabban Shimon ben Gamliel, which was accepted by Rabbi Yoḥanan (Rambam *Sefer Kinyan*, *Hilkhot Zekhiya UMattana* 12:8–9; *Shulḥan Arukh*, *Ḥoshen Mishpat* 248:3, and see *Beur HaGra* there).

That if he gave the property as the gift of a person on his deathbed – **שֶׁאִם נְתָנָן בְּמַתְּנַת שְׁכִיב מְרַע**: If the first recipient gave the property to another person as the gift of a person on his deathbed, the gift is invalid, as the gift of a person on his deathbed takes effect only after his death, and by that time the second recipient had already acquired the property. This is in accordance with the statements of Rabbi Yoḥanan and Abaye (Rambam *Sefer Kinyan*, *Hilkhot Zekhiya UMattana* 12:10; *Shulḥan Arukh*, *Ḥoshen Mishpat* 248:4).

From when does the recipient of the gift of a person on his deathbed acquire it – **שְׁכִיב מְרַע מֵאֵימָתַי קָנֵה**: The gift of a person on his deathbed is acquired by the recipient only after the person's death, whether it is a gift of real estate or movable property, in accordance with Rava's statement (Rambam *Sefer Kinyan*, *Hilkhot Zekhiya UMattana* 8:8, 12:10; *Shulḥan Arukh*, *Ḥoshen Mishpat* 248:4, 252:1).

NOTES

And sold and consumed – **וּמָכַר וְאָכַל**: The Rashbam explains that the first recipient sold the property and then consumed, i.e., expended, the profits. The Ritva explains that he used the property in a manner that left nothing for the second one, either by selling it or, in the case of movable property, by using it in a way that consumes it.

One who provides advice, etc. – **הַמַּשִּׂיא עֵצָה וכו׳**: The Rashbam explains that he is considered wicked because he causes the recipient to contravene the will of the giver, and is considered cunning because his advice is beneficial, as the sale is effective. He adds that only the one who provides the advice is considered wicked, as he causes an inappropriate effect without deriving any benefit from it; the seller himself is not considered evil, even though his action is inappropriate.

הֲדַר בֵּיהּ אַבַּיֵי מֵהַהִיא. מִמַּאי דְּמֵהַהִיא הֲדַר בֵּיהּ? דִּלְמָא מֵהָא הֲדַר בֵּיהּ!

The Gemara answers: **Abaye retracted that** latter statement. The Gemara asks: **From where** is it known **that he retracted that** statement? **Perhaps he retracted this,** i.e., the statement that the recipient acquires it only after the person's death, and his conclusion is that he acquires it at the moment of his death.

לָא סָלְקָא דַּעְתָּךְ, דִּתְנַן: "זֶה גִּיטֵּךְ אִם מַתִּי", "זֶה גִּיטֵּךְ מֵחוֹלִי זֶה", "זֶה גִּיטֵּךְ לְאַחַר מִיתָה" – לֹא אָמַר כְּלוּם.

The Gemara answers: That possibility **should not enter your mind, as we learned** in a mishna (*Gittin* 72b): If a man on his deathbed says to his wife: **This is your bill of divorce if I die,**[H] or: **This is your bill of divorce** if I die **from this illness,** or: **This is your bill of divorce after I die, he has said nothing.**[N] The divorce does not take effect after his death. Evidently, when one gives instructions on his deathbed, his intention is for them to be effective after he dies.

אָמַר רַבִּי זֵירָא אָמַר רַבִּי יוֹחָנָן: הֲלָכָה כְּרַבָּן שִׁמְעוֹן בֶּן גַּמְלִיאֵל, וַאֲפִילּוּ הָיוּ בָּהֶן עֲבָדִים וְהוֹצִיאָן לְחֵירוּת.

Rabbi Zeira says that **Rabbi Yoḥanan says:** The *halakha* **is in accordance with** the opinion of **Rabban Shimon ben Gamliel** that if the first recipient sells the property, the sale is valid, **and this** is the *halakha* **even if there were** Canaanite **slaves** included **in the** property[H] **and** the first recipient **emancipated them.**

פְּשִׁיטָא! מַהוּ דְּתֵימָא, אָמַר לֵיהּ: לְמֶיעֱבַד אִיסּוּרָא לָא יַהֲבִינַן לָךְ, קָא מַשְׁמַע לַן.

The Gemara asks: Isn't that **obvious?** The Gemara answers: **Lest you say** that the giver **would have said to him: I did not give you** my Canaanite slaves **to transgress a prohibition,**[N] as it is prohibited to emancipate Canaanite slaves, Rabbi Yoḥanan **teaches us** that he has the legal right to do so.

אָמַר רַב יוֹסֵף אָמַר רַבִּי יוֹחָנָן: הֲלָכָה כְּרַבָּן שִׁמְעוֹן בֶּן גַּמְלִיאֵל, וַאֲפִילּוּ עֲשָׂאָן תַּכְרִיכִין לְמֵת. פְּשִׁיטָא! מַהוּ דְּתֵימָא: לְשַׁוִּינְהוּ אִיסּוּרֵי הֲנָאָה לָא יְהַבִי לָךְ, קָא מַשְׁמַע לַן.

Rav Yosef says that **Rabbi Yoḥanan says:** The *halakha* **is in accordance with** the opinion of **Rabban Shimon ben Gamliel even if he made** the gift into **shrouds for a corpse.** The Gemara asks: Isn't that **obvious?** The Gemara answers: **Lest you say** that the giver would have said to him: **I did not give you** my possessions **to render them into items from which** deriving **benefit is prohibited,** but rather so that you may use and enjoy them, and Rabbi Yoḥanan **teaches us** that he may do so.

דָּרַשׁ רַב נַחְמָן בַּר רַב חִסְדָּא: "אֶתְרוֹג זֶה נָתוּן לְךָ בְּמַתָּנָה וְאַחֲרֶיךָ לִפְלוֹנִי", נְטָלוֹ רִאשׁוֹן וְיָצָא בּוֹ – בָּאנוּ לְמַחְלוֹקֶת רַבִּי וְרַבָּן שִׁמְעוֹן בֶּן גַּמְלִיאֵל.

§ **Rav Naḥman bar Rav Ḥisda taught:** If one said to another: **This** *etrog* **is given to you as a gift, and after you** die, **to so-and-so,** and **the first** recipient then **took it and fulfilled** his obligation of taking the four species on the first day of *Sukkot* **with it,**[N] when one is obligated to take species that belong to him, in this case, **we have arrived at the dispute between Rabbi** Yehuda HaNasi **and Rabban Shimon ben Gamliel** as to the nature of the ownership of the first recipient. According to Rabbi Yehuda HaNasi's opinion that he cannot sell the *etrog*, it is not considered entirely his, and he does not fulfill his obligation by taking it. According to the opinion of Rabban Shimon ben Gamliel, who holds that he can sell it, he fulfills his obligation.

מַתְקִיף לָהּ רַב נַחְמָן בַּר יִצְחָק: עַד כָּאן לָא פְּלִיגִי רַבִּי וְרַבָּן שִׁמְעוֹן בֶּן גַּמְלִיאֵל הָתָם, אֶלָּא דְּמָר סָבַר: קִנְיַן פֵּירוֹת כְּקִנְיַן הַגּוּף דָּמֵי, וּמָר סָבַר: קִנְיַן פֵּירוֹת לָאו כְּקִנְיַן הַגּוּף דָּמֵי. אֲבָל הָכָא,

Rav Naḥman bar Yitzḥak objects to this statement, reasoning that **Rabbi** Yehuda HaNasi **and Rabban Shimon ben Gamliel disagree only there,** in the case of: After you, with regard to the nature of the recipient's ownership; **as one Sage,** Rabban Shimon ben Gamliel, **holds** that **ownership of** the rights to use an item and the **profits** it engenders **is considered like ownership of the item itself, and** the other **Sage,** Rabbi Yehuda HaNasi, **holds** that **ownership of** the rights to use an item and the **profits** it engenders **is not considered like ownership of the item itself. But here,** with regard to the *etrog*,

HALAKHA

This is your bill of divorce if I die, etc. – זֶה גִּיטֵּךְ אִם מַתִּי וכו׳: If a husband says to his wife: This is your bill of divorce if I die, or: This is your bill of divorce if I die from this illness, or: This is your bill of divorce after I die, the Rambam rules that it is not a valid divorce. The Ramban and other authorities rule that it is uncertain if it is a divorce, as it is unclear, in their opinion, whether Rabbi Yosei's opinion that the date written in a document proves when it takes effect (see 136a) is accepted in this context (Rambam *Sefer Nashim, Hilkhot Geirushin* 9:12; *Shulḥan Arukh, Even HaEzer* 145:1).

There were slaves included in the property, etc. – הָיוּ בָּהֶן עֲבָדִים וכו׳: If the first recipient sold the property, even if by doing so he committed a transgression, e.g., there were Canaanite slaves included in the property and he emancipated them, or there were clothes and he used them as shrouds for a corpse (see *Sma*), his actions are effective (Rambam *Sefer Kinyan, Hilkhot Zekhiya UMattana* 12:3; *Shulḥan Arukh, Ḥoshen Mishpat* 248:3).

NOTES

He has said nothing – לֹא אָמַר כְּלוּם: The Rashbam explains that the reason for the mishna's ruling applies here as well: Just as the husband presumably does not wish to divorce his wife until after his death, so too, a person on his deathbed does not wish to part with his property until after his death.

To transgress a prohibition – לְמֶיעֱבַד אִיסּוּרָא: One who emancipates his Canaanite slave transgresses the positive mitzva: "Of them you take as your bondmen forever" (Leviticus 25:46). Therefore, one might assume that by doing so, the recipient contravenes the intention of the one who gave him the slaves and he has no right to do so.

And fulfilled with it – וְיָצָא בּוֹ: On the first day of *Sukkot* one is obligated by Torah law to fulfill the mitzva of taking the four species. One fulfills the obligation only by taking his own four species. This *halakha* is derived from the fact that the verse states: "And you shall take for you on the first day the fruit of a beautiful tree" (Leviticus 23:40), and the Sages interpreted the phrase "for you" to mean: From your own.

אִי מֵיפַּק לָא נָפֵיק בֵּיהּ, לְמַאי יְהָבֵיהּ נִיהֲלֵיהּ?

if he does not fulfill[N] his obligation **with it, for what** purpose **did** the owner **give it to him?**

אֶלָּא, מֵיפַּק – דְּכוּלֵּי עָלְמָא לָא פְּלִיגִי דְּנָפֵיק בֵּיהּ, מְכָרָהּ אוֹ אֲכָלָהּ – בָּאנוּ לְמַחֲלוֹקֶת רַבִּי וְרַבָּן שִׁמְעוֹן בֶּן גַּמְלִיאֵל.

Rather, with regard to **fulfilling** his obligation, **everyone agrees that he fulfills** his obligation **with it.** It is only in a case where the first recipient **sold it or consumed it,** that **we have arrived at the dispute between Rabbi** Yehuda HaNasi **and Rabban Shimon ben Gamliel.** According to Rabbi Yehuda HaNasi, if he sold it, the second recipient can repossess the *etrog* from the purchaser, and if he consumed it he must pay the second recipient its value, whereas according to Rabban Shimon ben Gamliel, he owes nothing to the second recipient, as the *etrog* belongs to him.

אָמַר רַבָּה בַּר רַב הוּנָא: הָאַחִין שֶׁקָּנוּ אֶתְרוֹג בִּתְפוּסַת הַבַּיִת, נְטָלוֹ אֶחָד מֵהֶן וְיָצָא בּוֹ, אִם יָכוֹל לְאוֹכְלוֹ – יָצָא, וְאִם לָאו – לֹא יָצָא;

Rabba bar Rav Huna says: In a case of **brothers who acquired an *etrog*** with money from the jointly **held** property **of the estate,**[H] and **one of them took it** on *Sukkot* **and** attempted to **fulfill** his obligation **with it,** the *halakha* depends on the limits of his ownership of the *etrog*: **If he may eat it,** i.e., his brothers allow him to do so, **he has fulfilled** his obligation to perform the mitzva, **and if not, he has not fulfilled**[N] his obligation.

וְדַוְקָא דְּאִיכָּא אֶתְרוֹג לְכָל חַד וְחַד, אֲבָל פָּרִישׁ אוֹ רִמּוֹן – לָא.

And this is **specifically** in a case **where there is an *etrog* for each and every one**[N] of the brothers; **but** if the other brothers get merely **a quince or a pomegranate,**[N] he has **not** fulfilled his obligation even if he has the right to eat it.

אָמַר רָבָא: ״אֶתְרוֹג זֶה נָתוּן לְךָ בְּמַתָּנָה עַל מְנָת שֶׁתַּחֲזִירֵהוּ לִי״, נְטָלוֹ וְיָצָא בּוֹ, הֶחֱזִירוֹ – יָצָא, לֹא הֶחֱזִירוֹ – לֹא יָצָא. קָא מַשְׁמַע לָן: דְּמַתָּנָה עַל מְנָת לְהַחֲזִיר שְׁמָהּ מַתָּנָה.

Rava says: If one person said to another: **This *etrog* is given to you as a gift on the condition that you return it to me,**[H] and the recipient **took it** on *Sukkot* **and** attempted to **fulfill** his obligation **with it,** if he ultimately **returned it, he has fulfilled** his obligation; if he **did not return it, he has not fulfilled** his obligation, as he did not fulfill the condition, thereby retroactively invalidating the gift. The Gemara explains that Rava **teaches us that a gift** given **on the condition that it be returned**[H] **is considered** a valid **gift.**

NOTES

If he does not fulfill, etc. – אִי מֵיפַּק לָא נָפֵיק וכו׳: Even according to the opinion of Rabbi Yehuda HaNasi, who holds that the first one receives only the right to use the property and not the ownership of the property itself, he fulfills the mitzva by taking the *etrog*, as fulfillment of the mitzva is the purpose for which the *etrog* was given to him. The Rashbam adds that the exclusive right to use the *etrog* is sufficient for it to be considered his with regard to fulfillment of the mitzva. By contrast, the Rosh maintains that it can be considered his only if he has full ownership of it. He explains that since the purpose of the gift was in order to enable the recipient to fulfill the mitzva, it is interpreted as a gift given on the condition that it be returned, which grants the recipient full ownership of the *etrog*.

He has not fulfilled – לֹא יָצָא: Apparently this refers to the first day of *Sukkot*, on which one fulfills his obligation to take the four species only with those that belong to him. Rabbeinu Gershom Meor HaGola maintains that this *halakha* applies on the other days of *Sukkot* as well, as using another's *etrog* is considered theft, and one does not fulfill his obligation with a stolen *etrog* on any day of *Sukkot*.

The early commentaries derive from here that the *etrog* must belong exclusively to the one performing the mitzva; if there are other partners, he does not fulfill his obligation with it. This raises a problem, as many Jewish communities, particularly those in Europe, where *etrogim* were difficult to obtain, would acquire one *etrog* for the entire community. The Rashbam and other authorities conclude that each resident must transfer his share to the one taking the *etrog* at the time he picks it up, so that when each member uses it he will be considered to have full ownership and will therefore fulfill the mitzva. This transfer need not be explicit, as it is the presumed intention of all residents. The Rashba asserts that the intention of the community at the time of the purchase is that every resident will own the *etrog* exclusively at the time he takes it for the mitzva, according to the principle of retroactive designation, that the status of an item can be finalized after the fact. Therefore, it is unnecessary to execute an explicit transfer each time.

And specifically where there is an *etrog* for each and every one, etc. – וְדַוְקָא דְּאִיכָּא אֶתְרוֹג לְכָל חַד וְחַד וכו׳: The Rashbam deletes this sentence, considering it a superfluous and unintelligible interpretation. Most early commentaries keep it in the text and attempt to interpret it. *Tosafot* say that this is an explanation of the case where one of the brothers can eat the *etrog*, i.e., where every one of the brothers has his own *etrog*. The Rambam understands this as an additional condition, i.e., even if the other brothers do not mind if he eats it, he does not fulfill his obligation with it unless every one of them has an *etrog* (see *Leḥem Mishne*). The Ri Migash explains that if every brother has an *etrog*, he has the right to eat it even if the other brothers protest.

A quince or a pomegranate – פָּרִישׁ אוֹ רִמּוֹן: The Ramah explains that even if a quince or a pomegranate is worth more than an *etrog*, it is necessary for each brother to have an *etrog* on *Sukkot*. Rabbeinu Gershom Meor HaGola explains that this is not a case where the brothers have actual *etrogim*, but rather where they have sufficient funds to purchase *etrogim* for each and every one. If there is only enough of the common money to purchase a quince or a pomegranate for each brother, he does not fulfill his obligation.

HALAKHA

Brothers who acquired an *etrog* with money from the jointly held property of the estate, etc. – הָאַחִין שֶׁקָּנוּ אֶתְרוֹג בִּתְפוּסַת הַבַּיִת וכו׳: In a case where brothers acquired *etrogim* with money from their common property, if one of the brothers took one of the *etrogim* on *Sukkot* to fulfill his obligation with it, the *halakha* depends on the limits of his ownership of the *etrog*. If the brothers would protest his eating it, he has not fulfilled the mitzva unless they relinquished their shares of the *etrog*. If they would not protest, he has fulfilled the mitzva. His ability to fulfill the mitzva with it in the event that the brothers would not protest is limited to a case where the brothers have at least one other *etrog*, even if it is inferior as far as the *halakhot* of an *etrog* are concerned. If they do not, even if they acquired other fruit in addition to the *etrog* and they would agree to his eating the *etrog*, the brother who took the *etrog* has not fulfilled the mitzva, unless the other brothers relinquished their shares of the *etrog* (Rambam *Sefer Zemanim*, *Hilkhot Shofar VeSukka VeLulav* 8:11 and *Maggid Mishne* there; *Shulḥan Arukh*, *Oraḥ Ḥayyim* 658:8 and *Beur HaGra* there).

This *etrog* is given to you as a gift on the condition that you return it to me – אֶתְרוֹג זֶה נָתוּן לְךָ בְּמַתָּנָה עַל מְנָת שֶׁתַּחֲזִירֵהוּ לִי: If one takes an *etrog* that he received on the condition that he return it to its previous owner for the mitzva of *lulav* on *Sukkot*, he has fulfilled the mitzva if he returns it, as a gift given on the condition that it is returned is considered a valid gift. If he does not return it, he has not fulfilled his obligation, even if he cannot return it due to circumstances beyond his control, and even if he pays for it. If he returns it after the holiday, the *halakha* depends on the wording of the condition: If the one who gave it to him stipulated: On the condition that you return it, the recipient has fulfilled his condition even if he returns it after the holiday. If he stipulated: On the condition that you return it to me, the recipient has not fulfilled his obligation unless he returns it during the holiday (Rambam *Sefer Zemanim*, *Hilkhot Shofar VeSukka VeLulav* 8:10 and *Sefer Kinyan*, *Hilkhot Zekhiya UMattana* 3:9; *Shulḥan Arukh*, *Oraḥ Ḥayyim* 658:4–5 and *Ḥoshen Mishpat* 241:6).

A gift given on the condition that it be returned – מַתָּנָה עַל מְנָת לְהַחֲזִיר: If one gives another a gift on the condition that it be returned, whether immediately or by a specific time, or upon the death of the giver or the recipient, the gift is valid, and the recipient may enjoy its use for the entire period of the gift, on the condition that it is indeed returned at the specified time. If he does not return it, the gift is nullified retroactively, and he must return the profits he enjoyed. The Rema adds that if the time by which the gift should be returned is not specified, the recipient may return it whenever he wishes, unless it is obvious that the giver intended that it be returned at a specific time. For example, one who gives another an *etrog* on *Sukkot* clearly intends that it be returned to him during the holiday, so that he, the owner, may continue to use it for the mitzva (Rambam *Sefer Zemanim*, *Hilkhot Shofar VeSukka VeLulav* 8:10 and *Sefer Kinyan*, *Hilkhot Zekhiya UMattana* 3:9; *Shulḥan Arukh*, *Oraḥ Ḥayyim* 658:4–5 and *Ḥoshen Mishpat* 241:6, 9).

הַהִיא אִיתְּתָא דַּהֲוָה לַהּ דִּיקְלָא בְּאַרְעָא דְּרַב בֵּיבַי בַּר אַבָּיֵי. כׇּל אֵימַת דַּהֲוָת אָזְלָא לְמִיגְזְרֵיהּ, הֲוָה קָפֵיד עִילָּוַהּ. אַקְנִיתֵיהּ נִיהֲלֵיהּ כׇּל שְׁנֵי חַיָּיו, אֲזַל אִיהוּ אַקְנְיֵיהּ נִיהֲלֵיהּ לִבְנוֹ קָטָן;

§ The Gemara relates: There was a **certain woman who had a palm tree on the land of Rav Beivai bar Abaye. Whenever she would go to harvest** the produce from **it, he would get angry at her** for trampling on his crops. Since she did not wish to anger him, **she** decided to temporarily waive her right to the tree's produce, and **transferred** ownership **of it to him for all the years of his life,** so that after his death she would once again be able to harvest the produce. **He** then **went and transferred it to his minor son,**[N] so that it would remain in his family even following his death.

אֲמַר רַב הוּנָא בְּרֵיהּ דְּרַב יְהוֹשֻׁעַ: מִשּׁוּם דְּאָתוּ מִמּוּלָאֵי אָמְרִיתוּ מִילֵּי מוּלְיָאתָא? אֲפִילּוּ רַבָּן שִׁמְעוֹן בֶּן גַּמְלִיאֵל לָא קָאָמַר אֶלָּא לְאַחֵר, אֲבָל לְעַצְמוֹ לָא.

Rav Huna, son of Rav Yehoshua, said to Rav Beivai bar Abaye: Is it **because you descend from truncated** [*mula'ei*] people,[N] as Rav Beivai's family traced their lineage to Eli, all of whose descendants were condemned to premature death (see I Samuel 2:31), that **you speak truncated** [*mulyata*] and unsound **matters? Even Rabban Shimon ben Gamliel,** who holds that in a case where one says: My property is given to you, and after you, to so-and-so, if the first recipient sells the property the sale is valid, **says** so **only** in a case where it was to be given **to another** person; **but** if the giver said that it will return **to himself,** he did **not**[HN] say that the first recipient can sell it, as the giver clearly intended to maintain his ownership of the property. Accordingly, Rav Huna, son of Rav Yehoshua, held that Rav Beivai's sale did not take effect.

אָמַר רָבָא אָמַר רַב נַחְמָן: ״שׁוֹר זֶה נָתוּן לָךְ בְּמַתָּנָה עַל מְנָת שֶׁתַּחֲזִירֵהוּ לִי״, הִקְדִּישׁוֹ וְהֶחֱזִירוֹ – הֲרֵי זֶה מוּקְדָּשׁ וּמוּחְזָר.

§ **Rava says** that **Rav Naḥman says:** If one said to another: **This ox is given to you as a gift on the condition that you return it to me,** and the recipient **consecrated it and** then **returned it**[H] to him, **it is consecrated and returned.** The consecration takes effect, and although the owner may not use it, nevertheless it is considered returned and the condition is fulfilled.

אֲמַר לֵיהּ רָבָא לְרַב נַחְמָן: מַאי אַהְדְּרֵיהּ? אֲמַר לֵיהּ: וּמַאי חַסְרֵיהּ? אֶלָּא אָמַר רַב אַשִׁי: חָזֵינַן, אִי אֲמַר לֵיהּ ״עַל מְנָת שֶׁתַּחֲזִירֵהוּ״ – הָא אַהְדְּרֵיהּ, אִי אֲמַר לֵיהּ ״עַל מְנָת שֶׁתַּחֲזִירֵהוּ לִי״ – מִידֵּי דַּחֲזֵי לֵיהּ קָאָמַר לֵיהּ.

Rava said to Rav Naḥman: What did he return to him? The ox was not returned to the possession of the giver, as it is consecrated. Rav Naḥman **said to him: And what did he cause him to lose?**[N] He returned the ox. **Rather, Rav Ashi said:** We must rule in this case based on what **we see. If** the giver **said to** the recipient: **On the condition that you return it,** it is considered returned, as **he returned it.** But **if he said to him: On the condition that you return it to me, he was** effectively **saying to him** that he must return **something fit for him** to use. Consequently, the consecration prevents the condition from being fulfilled, and both the gift and the consecration are retroactively nullified.

HALAKHA

To himself he did not – לְעַצְמוֹ לָא: The *halakha* that when property is transferred to two recipients one after the other, the first one can sell or give the property to another person, does not pertain to transferring the property to one of his heirs. In that case, the sale or gift is invalid (see *Sma*), in accordance with the statement of Rav Huna, son of Rav Yehoshua (Rambam *Sefer Kinyan, Hilkhot Zekhiya UMattana* 12:10; *Shulḥan Arukh, Ḥoshen Mishpat* 248:4).

Consecrated it and returned it – הִקְדִּישׁוֹ וְהֶחֱזִירוֹ: If one gives another an ox as a gift and stipulates: This ox is given to you on the condition that you return it, and the recipient consecrates the ox before returning it, the consecration takes effect. If the wording of the condition was: On the condition that you return it to me, the consecration does not take effect, as the giver intended for the recipient to return it to him in suitable condition. This is in accordance with the statement of Rav Ashi (Rambam *Sefer Kinyan, Hilkhot Zekhiya UMattana* 3:10; *Shulḥan Arukh, Ḥoshen Mishpat* 241:7).

NOTES

He went and transferred it to his minor son – אֲזַל אִיהוּ אַקְנְיֵיהּ נִיהֲלֵיהּ לִבְנוֹ קָטָן: The Rashbam explains that Rav Beivai understood that since the woman gave him the tree for his entire lifetime and did not state that it would be transferred to another's possession afterward, she clearly intended that it be entirely his and that he should have the right to do with it as he pleased. He then transferred it to his son so that the woman would not be able to claim it back, in accordance with the opinion of Rabban Shimon ben Gamliel, that in the case of a gift to two people, one after the other, if the first one sells it, the second does not then acquire it. The Rashbam adds that he sold it specifically to his minor son so that he could enjoy the profits during his lifetime, as his son was supported by him.

In addition, according to the Rashbam (137a), only one who advises another to take advantage of the opinion of Rabban Shimon ben Gamliel is considered a cunning, wicked person. One who does so for his own benefit, enjoying his legal right to sell the property, is not considered wicked.

Because you descend from truncated [*mula'ei*] people – מִשּׁוּם דְּאָתוּ מִמּוּלָאֵי: The Rashbam explains that Rav Beivai's family came from the village of Mamla, whose residents were descendants of Eli. Rabbeinu Gershom Meor HaGola interprets the word *mula'ei* to mean truncated, as Eli's descendants were condemned to premature death. Rashi (tractate *Yevamot* 75b) says that the word derives from *umelal*, meaning wretched, as Rav Beivai descended from a wretched family. An alternative understanding is that *mula'ei* means important people who speak in a superior manner. In other words, since he comes from a distinguished family, Rav Beivai permits himself to speak without examining his words carefully (*Arukh*).

To himself he did not – לְעַצְמוֹ לָא: The Rashbam explains that the recipient acquires ownership of the property itself only if it is designated to be transferred to a second recipient, as the owner has relinquished ownership of the property, but not if it is designated to be returned to the owner. Rabbeinu Ḥananel maintains that the recipient cannot sell the property to himself, i.e., to his sons or other heirs, as that is tantamount to keeping it in his possession indefinitely. A third approach is that this refers specifically to selling the property to his son whom he provides for, as this enables him to enjoy the profits of the property even after the sale (see Rashba).

What did he cause him to lose – מַאי חַסְרֵיהּ: The Ritva explains that the owner can redeem the ox from the Temple treasury, which would enable him to use it. Therefore it is considered returned. This statement of Rav Naḥman's is omitted in some versions, as the recipient certainly caused him to lose money (see *Tosefot HaRosh* and Maharshal).

אָמַר רַב יְהוּדָה אָמַר שְׁמוּאֵל: הַכּוֹתֵב נְכָסָיו לְאַחֵר, וְאָמַר הַלָּה ״אִי אֶפְשִׁי בָּהֶן״ – קָנָה, וַאֲפִילּוּ עוֹמֵד וְצוֹוֵחַ; וְרַבִּי יוֹחָנָן אָמַר: לֹא קָנָה.

§ **Rav Yehuda says that Shmuel says: If one writes** a document granting **his property to another, and the other** person **says: I do not want it,** he **acquires** it, **and** this is the *halakha* **even** if he is **standing and shouting** in protest that he does not want it. **And Rabbi Yoḥanan says** that he **does not acquire** it.

אָמַר רַבִּי אַבָּא בַּר מֶמֶל, וְלָא פְּלִיגִי.

Rabbi Abba bar Memel said: And they do not disagree with each other:

Perek **VIII**
Daf **138** Amud **a**

כָּאן בְּצוֹוֵחַ מֵעִיקָּרָא, כָּאן בְּשׁוֹתֵק מֵעִיקָּרָא וּלְבַסּוֹף צוֹוֵחַ.

Here, in Rabbi Yoḥanan's statement, it is a case **where he is shouting** in protest **at the outset.**[NH] As soon as he is given the deed of gift he states that he does not want it. In this case, he does not receive the property. **There,** in Shmuel's statement, it is a case **where he is initially silent** when he receives the deed of gift, **and is ultimately shouting**[N] in protest that he does not want it. In this case he acquires the gift before he protests, so it is his.

אָמַר רַב נַחְמָן בַּר יִצְחָק: זִיכָּה לוֹ עַל יְדֵי אַחֵר, וְשָׁתַק וּלְבַסּוֹף צָוַח – בָּאנוּ לְמַחְלוֹקֶת רַבָּן שִׁמְעוֹן בֶּן גַּמְלִיאֵל וְרַבָּנַן;

Rav Naḥman bar Yitzḥak says that if the owner **transfers ownership** of the property **to him through another**[H] person, who performs an act of acquisition for this other party in his presence, **and he was initially silent,** i.e., when the act of acquisition is performed, **but ultimately shouted** in protest when the property is actually given to him, **we have arrived at the dispute between Rabban Shimon ben Gamliel and the Rabbis.**

דְּתַנְיָא: הַכּוֹתֵב נְכָסָיו לְאַחֵר וְהָיוּ בָּהֶן עֲבָדִים, וְאָמַר הַלָּה ״אִי אֶפְשִׁי בָּהֶן״, אִם הָיָה רַבָּן שֵׁנִי כֹּהֵן – הֲרֵי אֵלּוּ אוֹכְלִין בִּתְרוּמָה; רַבָּן שִׁמְעוֹן בֶּן גַּמְלִיאֵל אוֹמֵר: כֵּיוָן שֶׁאָמַר הַלָּה ״אִי אֶפְשִׁי בָּהֶן״ – כְּבָר זָכוּ בָּהֶן יוֹרְשִׁין;

This is **as it is taught** in a *baraita* (*Tosefta* 8:1): **If one wrote** a document granting **his property to another, and there were slaves**[H] among his property, **and the other** person **said: I do not want them, if their second master,** i.e., the recipient, **was a priest, they partake of** ***teruma***,[B] the portion of the produce designated for the priest, as his protest is ignored. **Rabban Shimon ben Gamliel says: Once the other** person **said: I do not want them,** the giver or his **heirs have already acquired them,** and they are the slaves' owners.

NOTES

Where he is shouting at the outset – בְּצוֹוֵחַ מֵעִיקָּרָא: The Rashbam explains that a gift cannot be given to a person against his will, because a gift is somewhat to one's detriment, as indicated in the verse: "One who hates gifts shall live" (Proverbs 15:27). The status of the property at this stage is subject to a dispute among the early commentaries. The Rashbam, Rav Hai Gaon, and others hold that the property becomes ownerless, and anyone can take possession of it, based on the Gemara in tractate *Karetot* (24a). The majority of the early commentaries maintain that in this case the property remains in the possession of the giver, and it becomes ownerless only in a case where the recipient protests the giving of the gift after he already received it, as his later response is perceived as a renouncement of his ownership of the property (*Tosafot*; Rashi on *Karetot* 24a). This opinion is the accepted *halakha*.

And is ultimately shouting – וּלְבַסּוֹף צוֹוֵחַ: The Rashbam explains that the recipient protested after he already received the deed of gift. By contrast, the Rif and other commentaries assume that this is a case of a gift of a person on his deathbed, where a deed of gift is unnecessary. Therefore, the Ramah explains that the protest was voiced after the time required to say a short phrase (see Meiri, citing *Tosafot*). The Meiri explains that he protested after the gift was finished being discussed; if he protests beforehand, he does not acquire the property.

BACKGROUND

Teruma – תְּרוּמָה: Whenever the term *teruma* appears without qualification, it is referring to the great *teruma*. The verse states that: "The first fruit of your grain, of your wine, and of your oil" (Deuteronomy 18:4; see Numbers 18:12), should be given to the priest. The Sages extended the scope of this mitzva to include all produce. This mitzva applies only in Eretz Yisrael. After the first fruits have been separated, a certain portion of the produce must be separated for priests. *Teruma* is sacred and may be eaten only by a priest and his household while they are in a state of ritual purity (see Leviticus 22:9–15). If *teruma* becomes ritually impure, it may no longer be eaten and must be burned. Nevertheless, it remains the property of the priest and he may benefit from its burning. Today, *teruma* is not given to the priests, because they can provide no definite proof of their priestly lineage. Nevertheless, the obligation to separate *teruma* remains. Only a small portion of the produce is separated.

HALAKHA

Here where he is shouting at the outset, etc. – כָּאן בְּצוֹוֵחַ מֵעִיקָּרָא וכו׳: If a person gives another a gift and the latter protests, stating that he does not want the gift, he does not acquire it, and it remains in the possession of the owner. If the recipient does not protest upon receiving the gift and protests only later, stating: I do not want it, or: I do not accept it, or: The gift is null, or: I detect a clearly visible flaw in it (see *Maggid Mishne*), the gift is still valid in that the item does not return to its previous owner. Rather, it is rendered ownerless, and anyone can take possession of it. This is also the *halakha* in the case of the gift of a person on his deathbed, where the recipient does not protest when the item is willed to him, and protests only later: Even if he did not yet receive the item, his protest can no longer nullify the gift. The Rema adds that if the recipient owes money to someone, the creditor can collect the item as payment (see *Sma* and *Netivot HaMishpat*). The Rema also writes that if the recipient claims that he never intended to accept the gift in the first place, his claim is deemed credible even if he did not protest at the time he received the gift, and even if by making this claim he is incurring liability for his creditor (Rambam *Sefer Kinyan, Hilkhot Zekhiya UMattana* 4:1, 9:13–14; *Shulḥan Arukh, Ḥoshen Mishpat* 245:10–11).

Transfers ownership to him through another, etc. – זִיכָּה לוֹ עַל יְדֵי אַחֵר וכו׳: If one gives another a gift by conferring on him possession of it via a third person, and the recipient does not protest upon hearing of the gift, but protests later, stating that he does not wish to receive it, in this case, it is uncertain who owns the item, as the *halakha* is subject to a dispute between Rabban Shimon ben Gamliel and the Rabbis (*Maggid Mishne*). Therefore, if another person takes possession of the item, the court does not appropriate it from him, since the recipient may have effectively renounced ownership of it after accepting the gift. Despite this, if the previous owner seizes it from the one who took possession of it, the court does not appropriate it from him either (see *Sma*), as the recipient may have not accepted the gift at all, according to which it never left the possession of the previous owner. According to the Rosh, if it is the gift of a person on his deathbed, and the recipient did not protest upon hearing of it, the recipient has acquired the gift even if he protested later. The Rema holds that he acquires it even if it is the gift of a healthy person, as he rules in accordance with the opinion of the Rabbis (Rambam *Sefer Kinyan, Hilkhot Zekhiya UMattana* 4:2; *Shulḥan Arukh, Ḥoshen Mishpat* 245:11, and see *Sma, Shakh*, and *Taz* there).

One wrote a document granting his property to another, and there were slaves, etc. – הַכּוֹתֵב נְכָסָיו לְאַחֵר וְהָיוּ בָּהֶן עֲבָדִים וכו׳: If one wrote a document granting his property to another and conferred possession of it on him via a third person, and the property included slaves, and the recipient did not protest at the time, and only later claimed that he does not accept the gift, it is uncertain who owns the slaves, as the case is subject to a dispute between Rabban Shimon ben Gamliel and the Rabbis. Therefore, whether the giver is a priest and the recipient a non-priest, or vice versa, the slaves do not partake of *teruma* (Rambam *Sefer Zera'im, Hilkhot Terumot* 9:6).

וְהָוֵינַן בָּהּ: וְתַנָּא קַמָּא, אֲפִילּוּ עוֹמֵד וְצוֹוֵחַ?!

And we discussed the *baraita*: And does the first *tanna* hold that he acquires them **even** if **he is standing and shouting** in protest that he does not want them? That is not reasonable.

אֲמַר רָבָא, וְאִיתֵּימָא רַבִּי יוֹחָנָן: בְּצוֹוֵחַ מֵעִיקָּרוֹ – דְּכוּלֵּי עָלְמָא לָא פְּלִיגִי דְּלָא קָנֵי, שָׁתַק וּלְבַסּוֹף צָוַוח – דְּכוּלֵּי עָלְמָא לָא פְּלִיגִי דְּקָנֵי,

Rava says, and some say it was **Rabbi Yoḥanan** who says: **In a** case **where he is shouting** in protest **at the outset,** when he is given the gift, **everyone agrees that he did not acquire** them. In a case where **he was silent** at the time **and ultimately shouted** in protest, **everyone agrees that he acquired** them.

כִּי פְּלִיגִי – שֶׁזִּיכָּה לוֹ עַל יְדֵי אַחֵר וְשָׁתַק וּלְבַסּוֹף צָוַוח, דְּתַנָּא קַמָּא סָבַר: מִדִּשְׁתֵיק – קָנֵינְהוּ, וְהַאי דְּקָא צָוַוח – מִהֲדַר הוּא דְּקָא הָדַר בֵּיהּ,

When they disagree it is in a case **when he transfers ownership to him through another** person, and the recipient was there **and was silent, and ultimately,** when he actually receives the slaves, he **shouted** in protest. **As the first *tanna* holds** that **once he was** initially **silent, he acquired them, and** the fact **that he is shouting** indicates that **he is retracting** his initial acceptance of the gift. His acquisition cannot be canceled in this manner. If he does not want to own the slaves, he can sell them, give them away, or emancipate them.

וְרַבָּן שִׁמְעוֹן בֶּן גַּמְלִיאֵל סָבַר: הוֹכִיחַ סוֹפוֹ עַל תְּחִלָּתוֹ, וְהַאי דְּלָא צָוַוח עַד הָשְׁתָּא – דְּסָבַר: כִּי לָא מְטוּ לִידַי מַאי אֶצְוַוח.

And Rabban Shimon ben Gamliel holds that **his ultimate** actions **prove** the nature of **his initial** intent; he never intended to acquire the slaves. **And** the reason **that he did not shout** in protest **until now** is **that he reasoned: As long as they did not enter my possession,** to **what** end **will I shout?**

תָּנוּ רַבָּנַן: שְׁכִיב מְרַע שֶׁאָמַר ״תְּנוּ מָאתַיִם זוּז לִפְלוֹנִי, וּשְׁלֹשׁ מֵאוֹת לִפְלוֹנִי, וְאַרְבַּע מֵאוֹת לִפְלוֹנִי״ – אֵין אוֹמְרִין: כָּל הַקּוֹדֵם בַּשְּׁטָר זוֹכֶה. לְפִיכָךְ, יָצָא עָלָיו שְׁטַר חוֹב – גּוֹבֶה מִכּוּלָּם;

§ **The Sages taught** (*Tosefta* 9:6): If **a person on his deathbed said: Give two hundred dinars**[H] **to so-and-so, and three hundred to so-and-so, and four hundred to so-and-so,** in this case one **does not say** that **whoever appears first in the deed acquires** his money first. **Therefore, if a promissory note emerged against** the one who gave the gifts, and it becomes clear that the money given was pledged to a creditor, then the creditor **collects from all of them.**

אֲבָל אָמַר ״תְּנוּ מָאתַיִם זוּז לִפְלוֹנִי, וְאַחֲרָיו לִפְלוֹנִי, וְאַחֲרָיו לִפְלוֹנִי״ – אוֹמְרִין: כָּל הַקּוֹדֵם בַּשְּׁטָר זוֹכֶה. לְפִיכָךְ, יָצָא עָלָיו שְׁטַר חוֹב – גּוֹבֶה מִן הָאַחֲרוֹן, אֵין לוֹ – גּוֹבֶה מִשֶּׁלְּפָנָיו, אֵין לוֹ – גּוֹבֶה מִשֶּׁלִּפְנֵי פָנָיו.

But if a person on his deathbed **said: Give two hundred dinars to so-and-so, and after him, to so-and-so, and after him, to so-and-so,** then one **says: Anyone who appears first in the deed gains. Therefore, if a promissory note emerged against** the giver, the creditor first **collects from the last** one of the recipients. If **he does not have** enough in his portion to repay the debt, **he collects from the previous** recipient. If **he does not have** enough in his portion to repay the debt, **he collects from** the recipient listed **before the previous** recipient.

תָּנוּ רַבָּנַן: שְׁכִיב מְרַע שֶׁאָמַר ״תְּנוּ מָאתַיִם זוּז לִפְלוֹנִי בְּנִי בְּכוֹר כָּרָאוּי לוֹ״ – נוֹטְלָן וְנוֹטֵל אֶת בְּכוֹרָתוֹ. אִם אָמַר ״בִּבְכוֹרָתוֹ״ – יָדוֹ עַל הָעֶלְיוֹנָה, רָצָה נוֹטְלָן, רָצָה נוֹטֵל בְּכוֹרָתוֹ;

The Sages taught in a *baraita*: If there was **a person on his deathbed who said: Give two hundred dinars to so-and-so, my firstborn son,**[H] **as is appropriate for him,**[N] the firstborn **takes** the two hundred dinars **and takes his portion as a firstborn** as well. **If he said:** Give my firstborn son two hundred dinars **for his portion as a firstborn,** he does not receive both, but **he has the advantage;** if **he wants, he takes** the two hundred dinars, and if **he wants, he takes his portion as a firstborn.**

וּשְׁכִיב מְרַע שֶׁאָמַר ״תְּנוּ מָאתַיִם זוּז לִפְלוֹנִית אִשְׁתִּי כָּרָאוּי לָהּ״ – נוֹטַלְתָּן וְנוֹטֶלֶת אֶת כְּתוּבָּתָהּ. אִם אָמַר ״בִּכְתוּבָּתָהּ״

The *baraita* continues: **And** similarly, if there was **a person on his deathbed who said: Give two hundred dinars to so-and-so, my wife, as is appropriate for her, she takes** the two hundred dinars **and takes** payment of **her marriage contract** as well. **If he said:** Give her two hundred dinars as payment **for her marriage contract,**

HALAKHA

If a person on his deathbed said, give two hundred dinars, etc. – **שְׁכִיב מְרַע שֶׁאָמַר תְּנוּ מָאתַיִם זוּז וכו׳**: If a person on his deathbed said: Give two hundred dinars to so-and-so, and three hundred to so-and-so, and four hundred to so-and-so, without pausing in between (Rema; see *Sma*), the order in which the recipients were mentioned is immaterial. If the person left nine hundred dinars after his death, the sum is divided in accordance with his directive. If a promissory note emerges against him, the creditor collects from each recipient in proportion to the size of his gift. For example, if the debt was four hundred and fifty dinars, the debt is divided into nine parts of fifty. The one who received two hundred dinars pays two parts, or one hundred dinars; the one who received three hundred pays three parts, or one hundred and fifty dinars; and the one who received four hundred pays four parts, or two hundred dinars.

The Rema writes that in a case where a healthy person confers ownership of his money to several people via a third party, the *halakha* is the same (see *Sma*). He adds, citing *Tosafot*, the Rosh, and the *Tur*, that if the person gave two hundred dinars to each recipient, they receive the money in the order that they were mentioned, as the fact that the giver did not simply will them six hundred dinars collectively shows that the order was intentional. Others disagree (*Maggid Mishne*, citing Rashbam).

If a person on his deathbed said: Give two hundred dinars to so-and-so, and after him, three hundred dinars to so-and-so, and after him, four hundred dinars to so-and-so, they receive in the order that they were mentioned. Therefore, if a promissory note emerges against him, the creditor collects from the last recipient. If his share is not sufficient to pay the debt, the creditor collects from the one before him, and if that is not enough, he collects from the one before him as well (Rambam *Sefer Kinyan*, *Hilkhot Zekhiya UMattana* 10:13–14; *Shulḥan Arukh*, *Ḥoshen Mishpat* 253:9).

Give two hundred dinars to so-and-so my firstborn son, etc. – **תְּנוּ מָאתַיִם זוּז לִפְלוֹנִי בְּנִי בְכוֹר וכו׳**: If a person on his deathbed says: Give two hundred dinars to so-and-so, my son, as is appropriate for him, referring to his firstborn son, or if he says: Give two hundred dinars to my wife, as is appropriate for her, in this case the recipient receives two hundred dinars from the estate, in addition to the firstborn's portion or the payment of the wife's marriage contract. If he says: Give my son two hundred dinars for his portion as a firstborn, or: Give my wife two hundred dinars for her marriage contract, the recipient receives two hundred dinars, and if the firstborn's portion or the marriage contract is more than two hundred dinars, the recipient receives the full amount, as he has the advantage. The *Tur*, citing the Rashbam, writes that this is the *halakha* in a case where the owner mentions neither the phrase: As is appropriate for him or her, or: For his portion as a firstborn, or: For her marriage contract. Other authorities maintain that the *halakha* where he mentions neither is as it is in the first case, where the recipient receives two hundred dinars in addition to his or her portion or marriage contract (Ramah; Rosh). If he says: Give my firstborn son, these authorities concede that it is as if he added the phrase: For his portion as a firstborn. The Rema, citing the Rivash, comments that if he says: Give two hundred dinars to so-and-so as a gift, his intention is for the recipient to receive two hundred dinars in addition to his portion or her marriage contract (Rambam *Sefer Kinyan*, *Hilkhot Zekhiya UMattana* 11:16–18; *Shulḥan Arukh*, *Ḥoshen Mishpat* 253:8 and *Even HaEzer* 109:1–3).

NOTES

As is appropriate for him – **כָּרָאוּי לוֹ**: As the Gemara will soon explain, this phrase is interpreted to mean that the gift is in addition to his portion as a firstborn. It does not mean: As is appropriate for him, being a firstborn, rather: As is appropriate for him for treating me lovingly and devotedly (Meiri). With regard to a wife, it is interpreted in a similar manner.

יָדָהּ עַל הָעֶלְיוֹנָה, רָצָה – נוֹטַלְתָּן, רָצָה – נוֹטֶלֶת כְּתוּבָּתָהּ;

she has the advantage; if **she wants, she takes** the two hundred dinars, and if **she wants, she takes** payment of **her marriage contract.**

וּשְׁכִיב מְרַע שֶׁאָמַר ״תְּנוּ מָאתַיִם זוּז לִפְלוֹנִי בַּעַל חוֹבִי כָּרָאוּי לוֹ״ – נוֹטְלָן וְנוֹטֵל אֶת חוֹבוֹ, וְאִם אָמַר ״בְּחוֹבוֹ״ – נוֹטְלָן בְּחוֹבוֹ.

The *baraita* continues: **And** if there was **a person on his deathbed who said: Give two hundred**[H] **dinars to so-and-so, my creditor, as is appropriate for him,** the creditor **takes** the two hundred dinars **and takes** payment of the **debt** as well. **But if he said:** Give him two hundred dinars as payment **for the debt, he takes** the two hundred dinars as payment **for the debt.**[N]

מִשּׁוּם דְּאָמַר ״כָּרָאוּי לוֹ״, נוֹטְלָן וְנוֹטֵל אֶת חוֹבוֹ? וְדִלְמָא ״כָּרָאוּי לוֹ בְּחוֹבוֹ״ קָאָמַר!

The Gemara asks: **Because he says: As is appropriate for him, he takes** the two hundred dinars **and takes** payment of the **debt** as well? **But perhaps he was saying: As is appropriate for him** as payment **for the debt,** and meant only to specify the amount of the debt.

אֲמַר רַב נַחְמָן, אֲמַר לִי הוּנָא: הָא מַנִּי? רַבִּי עֲקִיבָא הִיא, דְּדָיֵיק לִישָּׁנָא יְתֵירָא;

Rav Naḥman said: Rav Huna said to me: In accordance with whose opinion **is this? It is** in accordance with the opinion of **Rabbi Akiva,**[N] **who expounds superfluous language.** Rabbi Akiva holds that if one uses unnecessary words, he apparently intended to add a matter.

דִּתְנַן: וְלֹא אֶת הַבּוֹר וְלֹא אֶת הַדּוּת – אַף עַל פִּי שֶׁכָּתַב לוֹ ״עוּמְקָא וְרוּמָא״, וְצָרִיךְ לִיקַּח לוֹ דֶּרֶךְ, דִּבְרֵי רַבִּי עֲקִיבָא.

As we learned in a mishna (64a): One who sells a house without specification has sold **neither the pit nor the cistern** [*dut*][L] with it, **even if he writes for** the buyer in the bill of sale: With **its depth and its height.** This is because anything that is not part of the house, like pits and cisterns, must be explicitly mentioned in the contract or else they remain in the seller's possession. **And** therefore the seller **must purchase for himself a path** through the buyer's domain to reach whatever remains his, because he has sold the area of the house along with the house itself, and he no longer has permission to walk there. This is **the statement of Rabbi Akiva.**

וַחֲכָמִים אוֹמְרִים: אֵינוֹ צָרִיךְ לִיקַּח לוֹ דֶּרֶךְ. וּמוֹדֶה רַבִּי עֲקִיבָא בִּזְמַן שֶׁאָמַר לוֹ ״חוּץ מֵאֵלּוּ״ שֶׁאֵינוֹ צָרִיךְ לִיקַּח לוֹ דֶּרֶךְ.

And the Rabbis say: The seller **need not purchase for himself a path** through the buyer's domain, as this is certainly included in what he has withheld for himself from the sale. **And Rabbi Akiva concedes that when** the seller **says to** the buyer in the bill of sale: I am selling you this house **apart from** the pit and the cistern, **he need not purchase for himself a path** through the buyer's domain. Since the seller unnecessarily emphasized that the pit and the cistern are not included in the sale, he presumably intended to reserve for himself the right of access to them.

אַלְמָא, כֵּיוָן דְּלָא צְרִיךְ וְקָאָמַר – לְטַפּוּיֵי מִלְּתָא קָאָתֵי, הָכָא נַמִי, כֵּיוָן דְּלָא צְרִיךְ וְקָאָמַר – לְטַפּוּיֵי מִלְּתָא קָא אָתֵי.

Apparently, according to Rabbi Akiva, **since he did not need** to state: Apart from the pit and the cistern, **and stated** it anyway, the seemingly superfluous statement **was coming to add a matter.** Since the seller unnecessarily stressed that the pit and cistern are not included in the sale, he must have intended to thereby reserve for himself the right of access. **Here too,** with regard to the gift given by a person on his deathbed to his creditor, **since he did not need** to say: As is appropriate for him, **and said** it anyway, this phrase **was coming to add a matter,** i.e., that the two hundred dinars are in addition to the debt.

תָּנוּ רַבָּנַן: שְׁכִיב מְרַע שֶׁאָמַר ״מָנֶה יֵשׁ לִי אֵצֶל פְּלוֹנִי״ – הָעֵדִים כּוֹתְבִין אַף עַל פִּי שֶׁאֵין מַכִּירִין, לְפִיכָךְ, כְּשֶׁהוּא גּוֹבֶה – צָרִיךְ לְהָבִיא רְאָיָה, דִּבְרֵי רַבִּי מֵאִיר; וַחֲכָמִים אוֹמְרִים: אֵין כּוֹתְבִין אֶלָּא אִם כֵּן מַכִּירִין, לְפִיכָךְ, כְּשֶׁהוּא גּוֹבֶה – אֵין צָרִיךְ לְהָבִיא רְאָיָה.

§ **The Sages taught** (*Tosefta* 8:18): If there was **a person on his deathbed who said: I have one hundred dinars** owed to me **by so-and-so,**[H] **the witnesses** that hear this **may write** his statement in a document **even if they do not know** whether the statement is true. **Therefore, when** the person's heir **collects** the debt, **he must bring proof** of the debt, as the document written by these witnesses is not regarded as proof. This is **the statement of Rabbi Meir. And the Rabbis say:** The witnesses **may not write** the document **unless they know** for a fact that the statement is true. **Therefore, when** the heir **collects** the debt, **he need not bring proof** other than the document written by the witnesses, as it has the status of a promissory note.

HALAKHA

And a person on his deathbed who said, give two hundred, etc. – **וּשְׁכִיב מְרַע שֶׁאָמַר תְּנוּ מָאתַיִם וכו׳:** If a person on his deathbed says: Give two hundred dinars to my creditor, as is appropriate for him, the creditor receives two hundred dinars in addition to the amount of the debt. If he says: Give my creditor two hundred dinars for the debt, without adding: As is appropriate for him, the creditor receives only the amount of the debt, since, if he receives more than that, it will be perceived as interest (*Sma*). If the owner adds neither the phrase: As is appropriate for him, nor: For the debt, the creditor has the advantage, and he can collect either the amount of the debt or the two hundred dinars. The *Sma* explains that since the debt was not mentioned by the owner, it will not be perceived as interest. According to the Rema, citing the *Tur* (and see *Sma*), in this case the debtor's intention is for the creditor to receive the two hundred dinars in addition to the amount of the debt (Rambam *Sefer Kinyan*, *Hilkhot Zekhiya UMattana* 11:19; *Shulḥan Arukh*, *Ḥoshen Mishpat* 253:8).

A person on his deathbed who said, I have one hundred dinars owed me by so-and-so – **שְׁכִיב מְרַע שֶׁאָמַר מָנֶה יֵשׁ לִי אֵצֶל פְּלוֹנִי:** If a person on his deathbed says in the presence of two witnesses: I am owed one hundred dinars by so-and-so, and the witnesses do not know the statement to be true, they should write a document with the following wording: So-and-so stated that he is owed two hundred dinars by so-and-so. Consequently, when the person's heirs claim the debt, they will have to furnish proof supporting their claim. This is in accordance with Rabbi Meir's opinion (*Shulḥan Arukh*, *Ḥoshen Mishpat* 255:1).

NOTES

But if he said, for the debt, he takes for the debt – **וְאִם אָמַר בְּחוֹבוֹ נוֹטְלָן בְּחוֹבוֹ:** The *baraita* as recorded in the *Tosefta* (7:14) states: He receives only payment of the debt. In other words, if the debt is less than two hundred dinars, he receives only the amount of the debt. This version appears in the Gemara as well according to several commentaries. In *Sefer Hashlama* it is explained that in contrast to the case of one's son or wife, in this case the recipient does not have the advantage, because only when there is a close relationship is it assumed that the owner intended to give the recipient the greater sum. Other commentaries explain that giving him more than the amount of the debt would entail a transgression of the prohibition of interest (Ramah). In a case where the owner says: As is appropriate for him, there is no such problem, as the gift is not considered to be related to the debt (Ritva). There is another version of the text that states: He has the advantage. According to this version, there is no concern about interest, as the giver must have been referring to other debts (Ramah).

It is the opinion of Rabbi Akiva, etc. – **רַבִּי עֲקִיבָא הִיא וכו׳:** The Rabbis in the mishna cited from 64a agree with the principle that superfluous language should be expounded, such as with regard to the phrase: As is appropriate for him. Rabbi Akiva is mentioned only because the principle is explicit in his statement in that mishna.

LANGUAGE

Cistern [*dut*] – **דּוּת:** This word, *dut*, appears in ancient Aramaic and Arabic in the form of *hadut*. It refers to a place built for gathering water or produce. A pit and a cistern serve the same purpose, but a pit is dug into the ground or rock, whereas a cistern is a stone structure built above the ground.

אָמַר רַב נַחְמָן, אָמַר לִי הוּנָא: תָּנָא, רַבִּי מֵאִיר אוֹמֵר: אֵין כּוֹתְבִין, וַחֲכָמִים אוֹמְרִים: כּוֹתְבִין. וְאַף רַבִּי מֵאִיר לֹא אָמַר אֶלָּא מִשּׁוּם בֵּית דִּין טוֹעִין. אָמַר רַב דִּימִי מִנְּהַרְדְּעָא, הִלְכְתָא: אֵין חוֹשְׁשִׁין לְבֵית דִּין טוֹעִין.

Rav Naḥman says: Rav Huna told me that the opposite is **taught** in another *baraita*: **Rabbi Meir says** that the witnesses **may not write** his statement in a document unless they know for a fact that the statement is true, **and the Rabbis say** that **they may write** it even if they do not know whether the statement is true; **and even Rabbi Meir said** that they may not write it **only due to** the concern that it might be presented before **a court that errs** and allows the heirs to collect without furnishing additional proof. **Rav Dimi of Neharde'a says: The *halakha*** is that **there is no** concern about the possibility of **a court that errs.**[H]

וּמַאי שְׁנָא מִדְּרָבָא, דְּאָמַר רָבָא: אֵין חוֹלְצִין אֶלָּא אִם כֵּן מַכִּירִין, וְאֵין מְמָאֲנִין אֶלָּא אִם כֵּן מַכִּירִין, לְפִיכָךְ כּוֹתְבִין גֵּט חֲלִיצָה וְגֵט מֵיאוּן וְאַף עַל פִּי שֶׁאֵין מַכִּירִין;

The Gemara asks: **And in what** way **is** this case **different from Rava's statement? As Rava says:** A court **may not** supervise ***ḥalitza*** **unless** the judges **recognize**[H] the *yavam* and *yevama*. **And** a court **may not** supervise a declaration of the **refusal**[N] of a girl upon her reaching majority to remain married to the man to whom her mother or brothers married her as a minor after the death of her father, **unless they recognize**[H] the girl. **Therefore,** another court **may write a document** attesting to the performance **of *ḥalitza***[H] **or a document** stating that a declaration **of refusal** was made in a court elsewhere based on the testimony of witnesses **even if** the judges **do not recognize** these people, relying on the presumption the first court would not have allowed the act to be performed had they not been sure of the identities of the parties.

מַאי טַעֲמָא? לָאו מִשּׁוּם דְּחוֹשְׁשִׁין לְבֵית דִּין טוֹעִין?

What is the reason Rava said that the court must recognize the participants in these actions? Is it **not due to the concern that a court that errs** might write such a document based on the testimony of witnesses without verifying that the participating parties were recognized by the court where the *ḥalitza* or refusal took place?

לָא, בֵּית דִּינָא בָּתַר בֵּית דִּינָא – לָא דָּיְיקִי, בֵּית דִּינָא בָּתַר עֵדִים דָּיְיקִי.

The Gemara answers: The two issues are **not** the same. **A court does not** normally **examine**[H] the act of **another court,** so there is concern that the court where the document is written might assume that the court where the act took place recognized the participating parties. But **a court does** normally **examine** the statement of **witnesses.** Therefore, there is no concern that it will rely on a statement written by witnesses without their knowledge of its accuracy.

מתני׳ הָאָב תּוֹלֵשׁ וּמַאֲכִיל לְכָל מִי שֶׁיִּרְצֶה, וּמַה שֶּׁהִנִּיחַ תָּלוּשׁ – הֲרֵי הוּא שֶׁל יוֹרְשִׁין.

MISHNA In continuation of the case discussed in the previous mishna of a father who wrote a document granting his property to his son but reserved the rights to the produce during his lifetime, the mishna states that **the father may detach** produce from the land **and feed**[H] the produce **to whomever he wishes, and what he left detached** at the time of his death **belongs to** all the father's **heirs,** not only to this son.

גמ׳ תָּלוּשׁ – אִין, מְחוּבָּר – לָא;

GEMARA The mishna indicates that what the father left **detached, yes,** it is inherited by all the heirs; but the produce that is **connected** to the ground at the time of his death, **no,** it is not inherited by them. Rather, it belongs to the son who received the property.

HALAKHA

There is no concern about a court that errs – אֵין חוֹשְׁשִׁין לְבֵית דִּין טוֹעִין: If a court writes in a promissory note: We were in a panel of three and the note was ratified in our presence, the note is considered to be ratified, even if the court did not specify on what grounds it was ratified, as there is no concern that the court erred, in accordance with Rav Dimi's ruling. Nevertheless, the court normally records the basis for its ratification. The *Shakh* writes that the current practice is not to record the basis for its ratification (Rambam *Sefer Shofetim, Hilkhot Edut* 6:4; *Shulḥan Arukh, Ḥoshen Mishpat* 46:8).

A court may not supervise *ḥalitza* unless the judges recognize, etc. – אֵין חוֹלְצִין אֶלָּא אִם כֵּן מַכִּירִין וכו׳: A court may not supervise *ḥalitza* unless the judges recognize the *yavam*, the *yevama*, and her late husband. Therefore, two men who witnessed *ḥalitza* may write for the woman a document attesting to the *ḥalitza* even if they do not recognize them, as they may rely on the court (Rambam *Sefer Nashim, Hilkhot Yibbum VaḤalitza* 4:29; *Shulḥan Arukh, Even HaEzer* 169:56).

And a court may not supervise refusal unless they recognize, etc. – וְאֵין מְמָאֲנִין אֶלָּא אִם כֵּן מַכִּירִין וכו׳: A minor orphan who was married off by her mother or brother and now wishes to refuse her husband must make a declaration of refusal in the presence of two men who recognize her and her husband. Therefore, anyone who witnessed the declaration of refusal may write her a document attesting to the refusal, even one who does not know her, as he may rely on the witnesses in whose presence she declared her refusal (Rambam *Sefer Nashim, Hilkhot Geirushin* 11:10; *Shulḥan Arukh, Even HaEzer* 155:8).

Document of *ḥalitza* – גֵּט חֲלִיצָה: Although there is no requirement for the *ḥalitza* to be documented, it was nevertheless customary for the court to grant her a document as proof that she performed *ḥalitza* and that it is now permitted for her to marry a man from the general public. There was a standard formulation for this document. In some places it is not customary to write a document of *ḥalitza*, but the preferred custom is to write one (Rambam *Sefer Nashim, Hilkhot Yibbum VaḤalitza* 4:30; *Tur, Even HaEzer* 169; *Shulḥan Arukh, Even HaEzer* 169:56, and see *Be'er Heitev* there).

Does not examine, etc. – לָא דָּיְיקִי וכו׳: A court never examines the act of another court, as the judges in any court are presumed to be knowledgeable and to not err. The court does examine the statement of witnesses (Rambam *Sefer Shofetim, Hilkhot Edut* 6:5).

The father may detach and feed, etc. – הָאָב תּוֹלֵשׁ וּמַאֲכִיל וכו׳: If one writes a document granting his property to his son during his lifetime for him to receive it after his death, while the father continues to benefit from the property in his lifetime (see 136a), and he dies, leaving produce connected to the ground, the produce belongs to the son, as a person's disposition is favorable toward his son. If the produce was detached, or even if it was connected but was ready to be harvested, it belongs to all the father's heirs, in accordance with the opinion of the Rosh, which is contrary to the Rashbam's opinion (Rambam *Sefer Kinyan, Hilkhot Zekhiya UMattana* 12:13; *Shulḥan Arukh, Ḥoshen Mishpat* 257:2, and see *Shakh* there).

NOTES

Refusal – מֵיאוּן: A girl under the age of twelve can be married off by her father. If her father is no longer alive, then by Torah law she cannot marry while still a minor. Nevertheless, the Sages ordained that her mother or brothers may marry her off with her consent. Since her consent is not legally valid until she reaches the age of maturity, i.e., the age of twelve, the girl may terminate this marriage once she reaches that age by performing an act of refusal, which entails her declaring that she does not desire this marriage. In such cases, no bill of divorce is necessary. When a girl performs an act of refusal, the marriage is nullified retroactively, and it is considered as though she had never been married at all. This act of refusal need not be performed in the presence of the husband or even in court. Only two witnesses are necessary to attest to the refusal. Some authorities require three witnesses *ab initio*. It is implicit here that the norm was to perform the act of refusal in court.

וְהָא תַּנְיָא: שָׁמִין אֶת הַמְחוּבָּרִין לַלּוֹקֵחַ!

But isn't it taught in a *baraita* (*Tosefta, Ketubot* 8:5) that in a similar case, the court **appraises the** produce still **connected** to the ground **for the purchaser**[NH] of the land, who must pay the seller's heirs for it? Accordingly, the connected produce also belongs to the heirs.

אָמַר עוּלָּא, לָא קַשְׁיָא: כָּאן בִּבְנוֹ, כָּאן בְּאַחֵר, הוֹאִיל וְדַעְתּוֹ שֶׁל אָדָם קְרוֹבָה אֵצֶל בְּנוֹ.

Ulla said that this is **not difficult; here,** in the mishna, the *halakha* is stated **with regard to his son,** who receives the connected produce after the father's death. **There,** in the *baraita*, the *halakha* is stated **with regard to another** person who purchased the land from the son. **Since a person's disposition is favorable toward his son,** the father certainly intended to bequeath the connected produce to his son together with the property itself. When the son sold it to another person, there was no such intention.

מַתְנִי׳ הִנִּיחַ בָּנִים גְּדוֹלִים וּקְטַנִּים – אֵין הַגְּדוֹלִים מִתְפַּרְנְסִין עַל יְדֵי הַקְּטַנִּים, וְלֹא הַקְּטַנִּים נִזּוֹנִין עַל הַגְּדוֹלִים, אֶלָּא חוֹלְקִין בְּשָׁוֶה.

MISHNA If a person died and **left adult and minor sons, the adults are not provided for by** using funds of **the minors, and the minors are not sustained,**[H] i.e., they do not receive food, **by** using funds **of the adults. Rather, they receive a share** of the inheritance **equally,** and each son sees to his needs from his own share.

נָשְׂאוּ הַגְּדוֹלִים – יִשְׂאוּ הַקְּטַנִּים, וְאִם אָמְרוּ קְטַנִּים: הֲרֵי אָנוּ נוֹשְׂאִין כְּדֶרֶךְ שֶׁנְּשָׂאתֶם אַתֶּם – אֵין שׁוֹמְעִין לָהֶם, אֶלָּא מַה שֶּׁנָּתַן לָהֶם אֲבִיהֶם נָתַן.

If the adults married,[H] **the minors marry,** as the Gemara will explain. **But if the minors say: We are marrying in the same manner that you** adults **married** during our father's lifetime, the court **does not listen to them. Rather, whatever their father gave** the adults in his lifetime **he gave** them, and the minors do not have the right to receive more than their share of the inheritance.

הִנִּיחַ בָּנוֹת גְּדוֹלוֹת וּקְטַנּוֹת – אֵין הַגְּדוֹלוֹת מִתְפַּרְנְסוֹת עַל יְדֵי הַקְּטַנּוֹת, וְלֹא הַקְּטַנּוֹת נִזּוֹנוֹת עַל הַגְּדוֹלוֹת, אֶלָּא חוֹלְקוֹת בְּשָׁוֶה.

Similarly, if the father **left adult and minor daughters**[H] but no sons, in which case his daughters inherit the estate, **the adults are not provided for by** using funds **of the minors, and the minors are not sustained by** using funds **of the adults. Rather, they receive a share** of the inheritance **equally,** and each daughter sees to her needs from her share.

נָשְׂאוּ גְּדוֹלוֹת – יִשְׂאוּ קְטַנּוֹת, וְאִם אָמְרוּ קְטַנּוֹת: הֲרֵי אָנוּ נוֹשְׂאוֹת כְּדֶרֶךְ שֶׁנְּשָׂאתֶם אַתֶּם – אֵין שׁוֹמְעִין לָהֶן.

If the adult daughters **married,**[H] **the minor** daughters **marry,** as the Gemara will explain. **But if the minors say: We are marrying in the same manner that you** adults **married** during our father's lifetime, the court **does not listen to them.**

NOTES

Appraises the produce still connected to the ground for the purchaser – שָׁמִין אֶת הַמְחוּבָּרִין לַלּוֹקֵחַ: The Rashbam, *Tosafot*, and most other commentaries explain that this *baraita* is addressing a case where the son sold the property in his father's lifetime. After the father's death, when the purchaser receives the right to use the property, he must pay the father's heirs for the produce that is connected to the ground. The Rif and Ri Migash explain the *baraita* differently: It is addressing a case where, after writing a document granting his field to his son but reserving his rights to the produce, the father sold to a third party his rights to the produce. When the father dies and the son collects the field from the purchaser, the court appraises the surplus value of the field due to the produce still connected to the ground, and the son pays this amount to the purchaser.

HALAKHA

Appraises the produce still connected to the ground for the purchaser, etc. – שָׁמִין אֶת הַמְחוּבָּרִין לַלּוֹקֵחַ וכו׳: If one writes a document granting his field to his son for him to receive it after his death and the father then sells the property, the son or his heirs appropriate the field from the purchaser after the father's death. If there is produce in the field that is still connected to the ground, the son receives the produce, but the court appraises it and the son pays the purchaser for it. If the produce is detached from the field, or if it is ready to be harvested, it belongs to the purchaser. This is the ruling of the Rambam and *Shulḥan Arukh*, in accordance with the Rif's interpretation of the *baraita*.

The Rema, citing the *Tur*, rules that if the son sells his right to the property, then when the father dies, the purchaser does not receive any of the produce, even if it is connected and is not ready to be harvested. Rather, it belongs to the father's heirs, and the purchaser pays them its value at the time of the father's death or waits for it to grow and be harvested by the heirs. This is in accordance with the Rashbam's interpretation of the *baraita*. According to this opinion, in the former case, where the father sells his rights to the produce, the son appropriates the connected produce from the purchaser and is not obligated to pay him for it, as he would if the father had not sold it (Rambam *Sefer Kinyan, Hilkhot Zekhiya UMattana* 12:13; *Shulḥan Arukh, Ḥoshen Mishpat* 257:2–3).

The adults are not provided for…and the minors are not sustained, etc. – אֵין הַגְּדוֹלִים מִתְפַּרְנְסִין...וְלֹא הַקְּטַנִּים נִזּוֹנִין וכו׳: If one dies, leaving children of different ages, although the elder children have greater clothing expenses and the younger ones have greater food expenses, neither is paid for from the common inheritance. Rather, the property is shared equally, and each child sees to his own needs. The Rashba rules that this *halakha* pertains only to a case where the children protest each other's expenditures from the common inheritance. If there is no protest, they presumably allow each other to purchase their necessities from the common inheritance, as partners normally do. The Rid holds that this *halakha* pertains even to a case where there is no protest, and that the children can later demand payment from each other for their expenditures from the common inheritance (Rambam *Sefer Mishpatim, Hilkhot Naḥalot* 9:12; *Shulḥan Arukh, Ḥoshen Mishpat* 286:1).

The adults married, etc. – נָשְׂאוּ הַגְּדוֹלִים וכו׳: If the elder siblings married after the father's death and paid for their weddings with money from the common inheritance, the younger siblings may do the same, and the remainder of the inheritance is shared equally. If the elder siblings married during their father's lifetime, the younger ones do not have the right to pay for their weddings from the common inheritance (Rambam *Sefer Mishpatim, Hilkhot Naḥalot* 9:12; *Shulḥan Arukh, Ḥoshen Mishpat* 286:3).

Left adult and minor daughters, etc. – הִנִּיחַ בָּנוֹת גְּדוֹלוֹת וּקְטַנּוֹת וכו׳: If one dies, leaving only adult and minor daughters, the court does not sustain the minors until they reach majority and then give each daughter a share of the inheritance. Rather, each receives an equal share immediately, as is the *halakha* with regard to sons (Rambam *Sefer Nashim, Hilkhot Ishut* 19:22; *Shulḥan Arukh, Ḥoshen Mishpat* 286:1 and *Even HaEzer* 112:18).

If the adults married, etc. – נָשְׂאוּ גְּדוֹלוֹת וכו׳: If one dies, leaving a son and a single daughter, the court estimates the sum of money that the father would have given his daughter for her dowry and gives it to her from his estate. If the court is not capable of estimating the amount, the daughter is given one-tenth of the estate. If he left several single daughters in addition to a son, the eldest receives one-tenth of the estate, and each of the other daughters receives one-tenth of the remaining property after her older sisters receive their shares. If the father left only daughters and no sons, the property is divided equally among all the daughters, as the Sages did not institute the provision for dowries in this case (*Shulḥan Arukh, Even HaEzer* 113:1, 4, 9).

זֶה חוֹמֶר בְּבָנוֹת מִבְּבָנִים, שֶׁהַבָּנוֹת נִזּוֹנוֹת עַל הַבָּנִים וְאֵין נִזּוֹנוֹת עַל הַבָּנוֹת.

This following *halakha* **is a stringency with regard to daughters'** inheritance[N] **vis-à-vis sons'** inheritance: **The** *halakha* is **that the daughters are sustained by** using funds **of the sons,**[H] as stipulated in their mother's marriage contract, **but they are not sustained by** using funds **of the** other **daughters.**

גמ׳ אָמַר רָבָא: הַאי גָּדוֹל אָחִי דִּלְבַשׁ וְאִיכַּסֵּי מִבֵּיתָא – מַאי דַּעֲבַד עֲבַד.

GEMARA **Rava says:** With regard **to this eldest of the brothers who wears**[H] garments **and covers himself from** the common property of **the house, what he did is done,**[N] and the other brothers cannot subtract from his share of the inheritance as a result.

וְהָא אֲנַן תְּנַן: אֵין הַגְּדוֹלִים מִתְפַּרְנְסִין עַל הַקְּטַנִּים! מַתְנִיתִין בְּשַׁרְכָא.

The Gemara asks: **But didn't we learn** in the mishna that **the adults are not provided for by** using funds **of the minors?** The Gemara answers: **The mishna** is referring **to an unemployed person** [*bisherakha*],[N] whereas Rava was referring to the brother who handles the finances of the entire family. Therefore it is in the interest of all the brothers for him to wear appropriate attire.

שַׁרְכָא, פְּשִׁיטָא! מַהוּ דְּתֵימָא: נִיחָא לְהוּ דְּלָא נִינְווֹל, קָא מַשְׁמַע לָן.

The Gemara asks: If the mishna is referring to an **unemployed person,** isn't it **obvious** that he may not take from the common inheritance of all the brothers? The Gemara answers: **Lest you say** that it is **preferable for them** that he dress appropriately so **that he will not be repulsive,** thereby dishonoring the family name, the mishna **teaches us** that he does not have the right to take money for clothing from the common inheritance, and if he does so, the brothers can subtract from his share of the inheritance as a result.

״נָשְׂאוּ גְּדוֹלִים יִשְׂאוּ קְטַנִּים״. מַאי קָאָמַר?

§ The mishna teaches that if **the adults married, the minors marry.** The Gemara asks: **What is it saying?** What does this mean?

אָמַר רַב יְהוּדָה, הָכִי קָאָמַר: נָשְׂאוּ גְּדוֹלִים לְאַחַר מִיתַת אֲבִיהֶן – יִשְׂאוּ קְטַנִּים לְאַחַר מִיתַת אֲבִיהֶן. אֲבָל נָשְׂאוּ גְּדוֹלִים בְּחַיֵּי אֲבִיהֶן, וְאָמְרוּ קְטַנִּים לְאַחַר מִיתַת אֲבִיהֶן: הֲרֵי אָנוּ נוֹשְׂאִין כְּדֶרֶךְ שֶׁנְּשָׂאתֶם אַתֶּם – אֵין שׁוֹמְעִין לָהֶן, אֶלָּא מַה שֶּׁנָּתַן לָהֶן אֲבִיהֶן נָתַן.

Rav Yehuda says that **this** is what **it is saying:** If **the adults married after their father's death** and used the common inheritance to pay for their weddings, **the minors** that **marry after their father's death** may also pay for their weddings from the common inheritance. **But if the adults married during their father's lifetime, and the minors said after their father's death: We will marry in the same manner that you married,** the court **does not listen to them. Rather, whatever** sum **their father gave** the adults to pay for their weddings in his lifetime **he gave** them, and the minors do not have the right to demand that same sum from the inheritance.

״הִנִּיחַ בָּנוֹת גְּדוֹלוֹת וּקְטַנּוֹת״. שְׁלַח לֵיהּ אֲבוּהּ בַּר גְּנִיבָא לְרָבָא, יְלַמְּדֵנוּ רַבֵּינוּ: לָוְותָה וְאָכְלָה וְעָמְדָה וְנִשֵּׂאת, בַּעַל לוֹקֵחַ הָוֵי אוֹ יוֹרֵשׁ הָוֵי?

§ The mishna teaches that if the father **left adult and minor daughters,** and the adults married, the minors marry. **Avuh bar Geneiva sent** a question **to Rava: Our teacher, instruct us:** If a woman **borrowed** money **and consumed** it, **and** before repaying the debt **she arose and married,**[NH] bringing her property into the marriage, what is the *halakha*? **Is the husband** considered **a purchaser** of her property **or is** he considered **an heir**[N] to her property?

NOTES

This *halakha* is a stringency with regard to daughters' inheritance, etc. – **זֶה חוֹמֶר בְּבָנוֹת וכו׳**: It is stipulated in a marriage contract that after the husband's death, his sons are obligated to sustain the daughters from the inheritance. This does not apply in a case where the daughters inherit the estate. Therefore, the adult daughters are not obligated to sustain the minor daughters from their share (Rashbam).

What he did is done – **מַאי דַּעֲבַד עֲבַד**: The Rashbam maintains that the eldest brother may not take from the common property to purchase clothing *ab initio*; but if he did so, he is not liable to return the amount he took. By contrast, the Rid holds that if he supervises the family's affairs he is allowed to do so *ab initio*, unless his brothers protest at the outset.

An unemployed person [*sherakha*] – **שַׁרְכָא**: The Rashbam interprets this term as referring to an unemployed person, from whom the family derives no benefit. *Tosafot* cite the *Arukh*, which has a version of the text that reads *shedakha*, meaning quiet, i.e., an unemployed person who sits quietly without doing anything. The early commentaries cite proof for this interpretation from Onkelos's translation of the phrase: "A cunning hunter" (Genesis 25:27), as *nahshirekhan*, which means one who knows only how to hunt and who is not capable of engaging in commerce (see *Tosafot* and Rid).

Another explanation is that *sherakha* refers to a fancy garment of silk or purple wool. According to this explanation, the Gemara means that although the eldest brother may purchase suitable clothing to represent the family respectably, he may not buy fancy clothing from the family's money, as that is unnecessary (Rabbeinu Ḥananel; see Rif).

And she arose and married – **וְעָמְדָה וְנִשֵּׂאת**: According to Rabbeinu Asher of Lunel, the dilemma pertains only to a case where the woman borrowed the money before her betrothal. If she borrowed it after her betrothal, her husband is certainly liable to repay her debt (see Meiri). *Tosafot* comment that the dilemma is relevant only if the creditor demands payment from the husband after the wife's death. If he demands payment from the woman in her lifetime, he can collect the debt from her usufruct property, which is considered her personal property even while she is married. Other commentaries infer from the Gemara that it makes no difference whether he demands payment during her lifetime or after her death (Rid; Rabbi Yitzḥak Karkusha).

Is the husband a purchaser or is he an heir – **בַּעַל לוֹקֵחַ הָוֵי אוֹ יוֹרֵשׁ הָוֵי**: According to *Piskei HaRid*, the dilemma pertains only to the wife's usufruct property; with regard to her guaranteed property the husband is certainly considered a purchaser, as he is liable to return its full value to her if he dies or divorces her.

HALAKHA

The daughters are sustained by funds of the sons, etc. – **הַבָּנוֹת נִזּוֹנוֹת עַל הַבָּנִים וכו׳**: If one dies, leaving both sons and daughters, the sons inherit the property, and they are obligated to sustain their sisters until they either reach majority or get married. If there is not enough of the estate for both the inheritance of the sons and the sustenance of the daughters, the daughters are sustained, and the sons beg for their own sustenance (Rambam *Sefer Nashim*, *Hilkhot Ishut* 19:17; *Shulḥan Arukh*, *Even HaEzer* 112:11).

This eldest of the brothers who wears, etc. – **הַאי גָּדוֹל אָחִי דִּלְבַשׁ וכו׳**: Although the elder brothers may not spend money from the common inheritance on their clothing, if the younger brothers would benefit from the eldest brother wearing respectable clothing, e.g., if he handles the family's finances and it is to their benefit that people with whom he deals treat him with respect, he may pay for these clothes from the common inheritance. His brothers have the right to protest his doing so. This is in accordance with the Rosh's explanation, as opposed to the Rashbam's explanation, of Rava's statement (Rambam *Sefer Mishpatim*, *Hilkhot Naḥalot* 9:15; *Shulḥan Arukh*, *Ḥoshen Mishpat* 286:2).

If a woman borrowed money and consumed it and she arose and married – **לָוְותָה וְאָכְלָה וְעָמְדָה וְנִשֵּׂאת**: If a woman marries after taking a loan by oral agreement, the creditor cannot collect the debt from her husband, as a husband is considered a purchaser with regard to his wife's property, and one does not collect from purchasers a loan by oral agreement. This is in accordance with the Rif's opinion that the Gemara's dilemma was not resolved. The *Shakh* explains that the creditor is considered at fault for his loss, as he knew that the woman was likely to marry and should have lent her the money with a promissory note. It is added there that if the creditor seizes payment from the husband, the court does not appropriate it from him, as he has the right to act based on the ruling of Rabbeinu Ḥananel and the Rashbam that the husband is considered his wife's heir in this context, due to the creditor's loss, and the husband is liable to pay. The Rema states that if the actual money that was given to the woman was not yet spent, the husband is liable to return it (Rambam; Rabbeinu Yitzḥak; Mordekhai). He adds that the creditor can demand that the woman not marry until she repays him, even if the debt is not yet due (Rambam *Sefer Mishpatim*, *Hilkhot Malve VeLoveh* 26:12,17 and *Sefer Kinyan*, *Hilkhot Zekhiya UMattana* 12:12; *Shulḥan Arukh*, *Even HaEzer* 91:2, and see *Ḥoshen Mishpat* 112:5, 132:2, 4).

NOTES

This incident occurred with me – עַל יָדִי הָיָה מַעֲשֶׂה: Rabbeinu Gershom Meor HaGola explains that this means that the incident was presented before him. Rabbi Yitzḥak Karkusha explains the phrase to mean that it happened to him, i.e., Rav Yehuda's wife was the daughter in the case, and he asked the Sages whether he is obligated to sustain the widow.

These do not return in the Jubilee, the portion of the firstborn – אֵלּוּ הֵן שֶׁאֵין חוֹזְרִין בַּיּוֹבֵל הַבְּכוֹרָה: This is because only sold property returns to its original owner in the Jubilee Year, whereas the portion of the firstborn is considered a gift that he is granted by the Torah (Rashbam; Rabbeinu Gershom Meor HaGola).

HALAKHA

The portion of the firstborn – הַבְּכוֹרָה: Brothers who divided their father's inheritance are considered like purchasers and are obligated to return their portions to the common estate in the Jubilee Year. They need not divide the property again; rather, they can exchange their shares (see *Kesef Mishne*; Radbaz). Similarly, the firstborn is obligated to return his additional portion, and he receives a new additional portion. This is in accordance with the opinion of the Rabbis mentioned in the mishna in *Bekhorot* 52b (Rambam *Sefer Zera'im*, *Hilkhot Shemitta VeYovel* 11:20).

לוֹקֵחַ הָוֵי, וּמִלְוָה עַל פֶּה אֵינוֹ גּוֹבֶה מִן הַלָּקוֹחוֹת. אוֹ דִּלְמָא יוֹרֵשׁ הָוֵי, וּמִלְוָה עַל פֶּה גּוֹבֶה מִן הַיּוֹרְשִׁין?

The halakhic ramification of this dilemma is as follows: **Is he** considered **a purchaser, and** the creditor therefore cannot collect his wife's premarital debt from him, as **one does not collect from the purchasers a loan by oral** agreement? **Or perhaps he is** considered her **heir, and one collects from the heirs a loan by oral** agreement.

אֲמַר לֵיהּ, תְּנֵינָא: נָשְׂאוּ גְּדוֹלוֹת – יִשְּׂאוּ קְטַנּוֹת; מַאי לָאו נָשְׂאוּ גְּדוֹלוֹת לַבַּעַל – יִשְּׂאוּ קְטַנּוֹת מִבַּעַל?

Rava **said to him: We learned** the answer to this question in the mishna: If **the adult** daughters **married, the minor** daughters **marry. What, is it not** teaching that if **the adult** daughters **married,** each one of them transferring money from the common inheritance **to** her **husband** to cover the wedding expenses, **the minor** daughters also **marry,** paying for the wedding **from** the money that each elder sister transferred to her **husband?** Clearly, although the money the elder daughters took from the inheritance for their weddings has the status of a loan by oral agreement, their husbands are liable to return it. This proves that the husbands are considered heirs.

לָא, נָשְׂאוּ גְּדוֹלוֹת לַבַּעַל – יִשְּׂאוּ קְטַנּוֹת לַבַּעַל.

The Gemara answers: **No,** the mishna is teaching that if **the adults married** and each one transferred money **to** her **husband, the minors** also **marry,** and each one may transfer money from the common inheritance **to** her **husband** for the wedding expenses. They cannot collect money from what was already transferred by their sisters to their husbands.

אִינִי? וְהָא תָּנֵי רַבִּי חִיָּיא: נָשְׂאוּ גְּדוֹלוֹת לַבַּעַל – יִשְּׂאוּ קְטַנּוֹת מִבַּעַל!

The Gemara asks: **Is that so? But didn't Rabbi Ḥiyya teach** that if **the adults married** and transferred money **to the husband, the minors marry** and collect money **from the husband** of each elder sister?

דִּלְמָא שָׁאנֵי פַּרְנָסָה, דְּאִית לַהּ קָלָא.

The Gemara answers: Even according to this interpretation, there is no proof from the mishna with regard to the case of a loan by oral agreement. **Perhaps** the provision of wedding **expenses** for the daughters **is different, as it generates publicity.** Since it is well known that a specific portion of a person's estate is liened to the future wedding expenses of his single daughters, it has the status of a loan with a promissory note. Therefore, the younger daughters can collect from the husbands of the elder daughters even if the status of the husbands is that of purchasers.

אֲמַר לֵיהּ רַב פַּפָּא לְרָבָא, לָאו הַיְינוּ דִּשְׁלַח רָבִין בְּאִגַּרְתֵּיהּ: מִי שֶׁמֵּת וְהִנִּיחַ אַלְמָנָה וּבַת – אַלְמְנָתוֹ נִזּוֹנֶת מִנְּכָסָיו. נִשֵּׂאת הַבַּת – אַלְמְנָתוֹ נִזּוֹנֶת מִנְּכָסָיו. מֵתָה הַבַּת – אָמַר רַב יְהוּדָה בֶּן אֲחוֹתוֹ שֶׁל רַבִּי יוֹסֵי [בֶּן חֲנִינָא], עַל יָדִי הָיָה מַעֲשֶׂה וְאָמְרוּ: אַלְמְנָתוֹ נִזּוֹנֶת מִנְּכָסָיו;

Rav Pappa said to Rava: Is this not identical to the *halakha* that **Ravin sent in his letter** from Eretz Yisrael? That *halakha* states that with regard to **one who died and left a widow and a daughter, his widow is sustained from his property.** If **the daughter** then **married, the widow** is still **sustained from his property,** although it is now in the possession of the daughter's husband, as she had inherited the property from her father. With regard to a case where **the daughter** then **died** and her husband inherited from her, **Rav Yehuda, son of the sister of Rabbi Yosei ben Ḥanina, says:** This **incident occurred with me,**[N] and the Sages **said** that the late man's **widow is** still **sustained from his property** although it is fully owned by his daughter's husband.

אִי אָמְרַתְּ בִּשְׁלָמָא יוֹרֵשׁ הָוֵי, מִשּׁוּם הָכִי אַלְמְנָתוֹ נִזּוֹנֶת מִנְּכָסָיו. אֶלָּא אִי אָמְרַתְּ לוֹקֵחַ הָוֵי, אַמַּאי נִזּוֹנֶת מִנְּכָסָיו?

Rav Pappa explains: **Granted, if you say** the husband **is** considered **an heir,** it is **due to that** reason that **his** father-in-law's **widow is sustained from his property;** it is still liened to her sustenance. **But if you say** that a husband **is** considered **a purchaser** of his wife's property, **why** is his father-in-law's widow **sustained from his property?** The purchasers of inherited property are not obligated to sustain the widow.

אֲמַר אַבָּיֵי: אִי לָאו דִּשְׁלַח רָבִין, אֲנַן לָא יָדְעִינַן? וְהָא תְּנַן, אֵלּוּ הֵן שֶׁאֵין חוֹזְרִין בַּיּוֹבֵל: הַבְּכוֹרָה,

Abaye said: If **Ravin had not sent** this letter, **would we not have known** that the husband has the status of a purchaser? **But didn't we learn** in the mishna (*Bekhorot* 52b): **These** properties **do not return** to their original owners **in the Jubilee** Year (see Leviticus 25:13–24): The portion of **the firstborn,**[NH] i.e., it does not return to the common ownership of the brothers to be shared equally like the rest of the inheritance, but rather remains in the possession of the firstborn;

וְהַיּוֹרֵשׁ אֶת אִשְׁתּוֹ!

and one who inherits the property of **his wife**[H] after her death, i.e., the property is not returned to her family. Evidently, the husband does not have the status of a purchaser, as a purchaser must return the property to its original owner in the Jubilee Year.

אֲמַר לֵיהּ רָבָא: וְהַשְׁתָּא דִּשְׁלַח מִי יָדְעִינַן? הָאָמַר רַבִּי יוֹסֵי בְּרַבִּי חֲנִינָא: בְּאוּשָׁא הִתְקִינוּ, הָאִשָּׁה שֶׁמָּכְרָה נִכְסֵי מְלוֹג בְּחַיֵּי בַעְלָהּ וּמֵתָה – הַבַּעַל מוֹצִיא מִיַּד הַלָּקוֹחוֹת!

Rava said to him: And now that Ravin **sent** the letter, **do we** in fact **know** that the husband has the status of an heir? **Doesn't Rabbi Yosei, son of Rabbi Ḥanina, say: In Usha they instituted** an ordinance that in the case of **a woman who sold her usufruct property,**[HB] i.e., property that she alone owns and her husband benefits only from the profits, **in her husband's lifetime and** then **died, the husband repossesses it from the purchasers?** Apparently the husband's status is that of a purchaser, as a purchaser can appropriate his purchase from a later purchaser, whereas an heir does not inherit property that the person sold before he died.

אֶלָּא אָמַר רַב אָשֵׁי: בַּעַל – שַׁוְיוּהוּ רַבָּנַן כְּיוֹרֵשׁ וְשַׁוְיוּהוּ רַבָּנַן כְּלוֹקֵחַ, וְהֵיכָא דְּטָבָא לֵיהּ עֲבַדוּ לֵיהּ; גַּבֵּי יוֹבֵל שַׁוְיוּהוּ רַבָּנַן כְּיוֹרֵשׁ מִשּׁוּם פְּסֵידָא דִּידֵיהּ, גַּבֵּי דְּרַבִּי יוֹסֵי בְּרַבִּי חֲנִינָא שַׁוְיוּהוּ רַבָּנַן כְּלוֹקֵחַ מִשּׁוּם פְּסֵידָא דִּידֵיהּ, גַּבֵּי דְּרָבִין מִשּׁוּם פְּסֵידָא דְּאַלְמָנָה שַׁוְיוּהוּ רַבָּנַן כְּיוֹרֵשׁ.

Rather, Rav **Ashi says** that **the Sages equated the husband with an heir, and the Sages equated him with a purchaser. And they deemed him** as **whichever is better for him,** based on the circumstances of the case. **With regard to** the **Jubilee** Year, **the Sages equated him with an heir,**[N] **due to his** potential **loss** were he to be equated with a purchaser, as he would be obligated to return the property to his wife's heirs. **With regard to** the case **of Rabbi Yosei, son of Rabbi Ḥanina,** where the wife sold the property, **the Sages equated him with a purchaser, due to his** potential **loss** were he to be equated with an heir. **With regard to Ravin's** *halakha*, concerning the sustenance of the husband's father-in-law's widow, **due to the** potential **loss of the widow, the Sages equated him with an heir.**[H]

NOTES

With regard to the Jubilee the Sages equated him with an heir – **גַּבֵּי יוֹבֵל שַׁוְיוּהוּ רַבָּנַן כְּיוֹרֵשׁ**: The Gemara in *Bekhorot* (52b) infers that the *tanna* of this mishna clearly holds that a husband is considered an heir by Torah law, as, if by Torah law he is considered a purchaser and is obligated to return his wife's property in the Jubilee Year, the Sages would not equate him with an heir, thereby canceling this obligation. Accordingly, the Gemara here means that the Sages did not change his status as an heir (*Tosafot*). By contrast, the Rambam maintains that a husband inherits from his wife only by rabbinic law, and nevertheless he is not obligated to return the property in the Jubilee Year, as the Sages reinforced this ordinance, giving it the force of Torah law.

HALAKHA

And one who inherits the property of his wife – **הַיּוֹרֵשׁ אֶת אִשְׁתּוֹ**: A husband who inherits from his wife need not return the inheritance to her family in the Jubilee Year. Although the *halakha* that a husband inherits his wife is by rabbinic law, the Sages reinforced this ordinance, giving it the force of Torah law (Rambam *Sefer Zera'im*, *Hilkhot Shemitta VeYovel* 11:21).

A woman who sold her usufruct property, etc. – **הָאִשָּׁה שֶׁמָּכְרָה נִכְסֵי מְלוֹג וכו׳**: If a married woman sold her usufruct property, the husband owns the rights to the profits and usage of the property during her lifetime, and after her death he appropriates the property from the purchasers, owing them no compensation. The Rema, citing the Rosh and the *Tur*, rules that the husband can appropriate the property even during his wife's lifetime (Rambam *Sefer Nashim*, *Hilkhot Ishut* 22:7; *Shulḥan Arukh*, *Ḥoshen Mishpat* 90:9).

Due to the potential loss of the widow the Sages equated him with an heir – **מִשּׁוּם פְּסֵידָא דְּאַלְמָנָה שַׁוְיוּהוּ רַבָּנַן כְּיוֹרֵשׁ**: If one dies, leaving a widow and a daughter, the widow is sustained from the estate, and the daughter begs for her sustenance. Even if the daughter marries, bringing the inheritance into the marriage, the widow is still sustained from the property, even after the daughter's death. This is because the Sages equated the daughter's husband with an heir, so that the widow does not lose her sustenance. The *Beit Shmuel* notes that if the daughter brings property into the marriage not as usufruct property but as guaranteed property, the husband is considered a purchaser and owes nothing to the widow (Rambam *Sefer Nashim*, *Hilkhot Ishut* 20:11; *Shulḥan Arukh*, *Even HaEzer* 93:4).

BACKGROUND

Usufruct property – **נִכְסֵי מְלוֹג**: A married woman's property is divided into two categories, usufruct property and guaranteed property. Usufruct property is the property that a wife brings to the marriage from her father's home and that is not included in her marriage contract, and property that she inherits or receives as a gift after her marriage. All this property remains hers even after she is married, and her husband is not permitted to sell it, although he is entitled to benefit from its profits. The husband must care for this property, although he is not responsible if it decreases in value, provided that the loss was not intentionally caused by him. The property is returned to the wife if the husband dies or divorces her, and any increase or decrease in its value at that time by comparison with its value at the beginning of the marriage is her profit or loss. If she dies during the lifetime of her husband, he inherits the property. Before marriage, a couple can form any agreement they wish with regard to usufruct property.

וְהָא גַּבֵּי דְּרַבִּי יוֹסֵי בְּרַבִּי חֲנִינָא דְּאִיכָּא פְּסֵידָא לַלָּקוֹחוֹת, וְשַׁוְיוּהוּ רַבָּנַן כְּלוֹקֵחַ!

The Gemara asks: **But with regard to** the case **of Rabbi Yosei, son of Rabbi Ḥanina, there is a loss to the purchasers,** from whom the husband appropriates the property, **and** nevertheless, **the Sages equated him with a purchaser.**

הָתָם אִינְהוּ אַפְסִידוּ אַנַּפְשַׁיְיהוּ, כֵּיוָן דְּאִיכָּא בַּעַל, לָא אִיבָּעֵי לְהוּ לְמִיזְבַּן מֵאִיתְּתָא דְּיָתְבָא תּוּתֵי גַּבְרָא.

The Gemara answers: **There,** the purchasers **caused their own loss.**[N] **Since** they knew **that there is a husband, they should not have purchased** property **from a wife living under** the authority of **her husband,** removing it from the husband and his heirs.

הדרן עלך יש נוחלין

NOTES

The purchasers caused their own loss – אִינְהוּ אַפְסִידוּ אַנַּפְשַׁיְיהוּ: The conclusion with regard to the case at the center of the discussion, i.e., a woman who borrowed money and then got married, is subject to a dispute between the early commentaries. Rabbeinu Ḥananel maintains that the creditor can collect payment from the husband. The Rashbam explains that this is because the creditor is not to blame for his loss. Other commentaries hold that the creditor cannot collect payment; he is at fault for lending the woman money without a promissory note. The Rif maintains that the *halakha* in this case remains uncertain, and in practice, payment cannot be appropriated from the husband.

Summary of **Perek VIII**

The order in which relatives inherit formulated in the Talmud includes both the *halakhot* stated in the Torah and *halakhot* that are not explicit in the Torah. Precedence is granted to one's offspring, i.e., to one's sons or daughters and their descendants. If a man has no descendants, his paternal family members inherit from him, starting with his father, and if his father is deceased then his father's descendants inherit from him. If his father has no descendants, the inheritance goes to his paternal grandfather and his descendants, or to his paternal great-grandfather and his descendants, and so forth. In all cases, sons and their descendants precede daughters and their descendants.

An exception is that a husband takes precedence with regard to his wife's inheritance despite the fact that they are not blood relatives. Although there are different opinions as to whether a husband's inheritance of his wife's property is by Torah or rabbinic law, even those who hold that it is by rabbinic law concede that it takes precedence over that of other heirs.

In principle, an heir does not lose his right to the inheritance after his death; if the heir is dead, his heirs receive it. Nevertheless, a husband does not inherit property inherited by his wife after her death, nor do brothers inherit property inherited by their brother after his death.

A firstborn son receives a double portion of the property his father possessed at the time of his death, but not of the property that was due to be paid to the deceased. He does not receive a double portion of his mother's inheritance. The definition of a firstborn is a son who is the first viable offspring of his father. Whether he is his mother's firstborn is immaterial. If the firstborn was born by caesarean section, he does not receive a double share, nor does the following son. If there are twins, the midwife's attestation at the time of their birth as to which baby was born first is deemed credible. The mother's testimony during the first seven days after their birth is also deemed credible. The father's testimony that a specific son of his is the firstborn is deemed credible at any time.

One cannot bequeath his estate to one who is not his heir by Torah law. Despite this, one can apportion his estate to his heirs unevenly, with the exception of the firstborn's double portion, which may not be reduced. This principle is relevant only with regard to inheritance; if one distributes his property to others during his lifetime, even if he reserves the rights of usage until after his death, he can distribute the property to whomever he wishes. The Sages are displeased with one who distributes his entire property to people other than his heirs.

Although one's sons take precedence with regard to inheritance, a wife's marriage contract guarantees her and her daughters sustenance from the estate. This right precedes the sons' right to receive their inheritance.

As long as the inheritance has not yet been divided between the children, each child must keep an account of his expenditures from the inheritance, as no child may take more than the others. Money that was spent on the children during their father's lifetime is not taken into consideration.

Several *halakhot* that have only historical significance are also discussed in the chapter, i.e., the distribution of Eretz Yisrael among the tribes in the days of Joshua, and a particular *halakha* that pertained to that period with regard to the transfer of inheritance from the possession of members of one tribe to the possession of members of another.

Image **Credits**

תלמוד בבלי

— מהדורת נאה —

בבא בתרא חלק ו

Steinsaltz
Center

ירושלים

KOREN

Please note that the number ranges that appear at the bottom of each daf of the Vilna pages indicate the corresponding pages of the Koren Talmud Bavli translation and commentary.

תלמוד בבלי

הוצאת קורן ירושלים

— מהדורת נאה —

מסכת בבא בתרא
דף קח. עד דף קלט:

COMMENTARY BY
Rabbi Adin Even-Israel Steinsaltz

EDITOR-IN-CHIEF
Rabbi Dr Tzvi Hersh Weinreb

EXECUTIVE EDITOR
Rabbi Joshua Schreier

STEINSALTZ CENTER
KOREN PUBLISHERS JERUSALEM

כְּדֵי שֶׁלֹּא תְּהֵא חַיָּה קוֹפֶצֶת. וְלַעֲבֵיד חָרִיץ וְלָא לַעֲבֵיד בֵּן חָרִיץ! אַיְּדֵי דְּרָווּחַ, קַיְימָא בְּגַוֵּיהּ וְקָפְצָה. וְלַעֲבֵיד בֵּן חָרִיץ וְלָא לַעֲבֵיד חָרִיץ! אַיְּדֵי דְּקָטִין, קַיְימָא אַשְּׂפְתֵיהּ וְקָפְצָה. וְכַמָּה בֵּין חָרִיץ לְבֶן חָרִיץ? טֶפַח.§

הדרן עלך בית כור

א)יֵשׁ נוֹחֲלִין וּמַנְחִילִין, וְיֵשׁ נוֹחֲלִין וְלֹא מַנְחִילִין, מַנְחִילִין וְלֹא נוֹחֲלִין, לֹא נוֹחֲלִין וְלֹא מַנְחִילִין. וְאֵלּוּ נוֹחֲלִין וּמַנְחִילִין: אהָאָב אֶת הַבָּנִים, וְהַבָּנִים אֶת הָאָב, וְהָאַחִין מִן הָאָב — נוֹחֲלִין וּמַנְחִילִין. הָאִישׁ אֶת אִמּוֹ, וְהָאִישׁ אֶת אִשְׁתּוֹ, וּבְנֵי אֲחָיוֹת — נוֹחֲלִין וְלֹא מַנְחִילִין. הָאִשָּׁה אֶת בָּנֶיהָ, וְהָאִשָּׁה אֶת בַּעְלָהּ, וַאֲחֵי הָאֵם — מַנְחִילִין וְלֹא נוֹחֲלִין. וְהָאַחִין מִן הָאֵם לֹא נוֹחֲלִין וְלֹא מַנְחִילִין.§ **גמ'** מַאי שְׁנָא דְּקָתָנֵי "הָאָב אֶת הַבָּנִים" בְּרֵישָׁא? לִיתְנֵי "הַבָּנִים אֶת הָאָב" בְּרֵישָׁא! חֲדָא, ב)דְּאַתְחוּלֵי בְּפוּרְעָנוּתָא לָא מַתְחֲלִינַן, וְעוֹד

רשב"ם

כְּדֵי שֶׁלֹּא תְּהֵא חַיָּה קוֹפֶצֶת. עַל הַגָּדֵר, אִיצְטְרִיךְ חָרִיץ וּבֶן חָרִיץ. וְלַעֲבֵיד חָרִיץ. דְּהַשְׁתָּא נַמִי לֹא קָפְלָה, שֶׁהֶחָרִיץ מַרְחִיקָהּ מִן הַגָּדֵר. אַיְּדֵי דְּרָווּחַ. שְׁשָּׁה טְפָחִים, נִכְנֶסֶת לְתוֹכוֹ, וּמַמְשֶׁכֶת מְעַט לַאֲחוֹרֶיהָ וְקוֹפֶצֶת. קַיְימָא אַשְּׂפְתֵיהּ. הַתִּיצוֹנָה. הָכִי גָּרְסִינַן: כַּמָּה בֵּין חָרִיץ לְבֶן חָרִיץ טֶפַח. וּמַסְקָנָא דִבְרַיְיתָא הוּא.

הדרן עלך בית כור

יֵשׁ. קְרוֹבִים שֶׁנּוֹחֲלִין אֶת קְרוֹבֵיהֶם כְּשֶׁמֵּתִים, וְגַם אִם הֵם מֵתִים — מַנְחִילִין לָהֶם אֶת מָמוֹנָם, דְּהַיְינוּ שֶׁשְּׁנֵיהֶם נוֹחֲלִין זֶה אֶת זֶה. וְהַאי דְּלָא קָתָנֵי "יֵשׁ נוֹחֲלִין זֶה אֶת זֶה" — הַיְינוּ מִשּׁוּם דְּבָעֵי לְמִיתְנֵי סֵיפָא "נוֹחֲלִין וְלֹא מַנְחִילִין", תָּנָא נַמִי רֵישָׁא "נוֹחֲלִין וּמַנְחִילִין". וְיֵשׁ שֶׁנּוֹחֲלִין. אֶת קְרוֹבֵיהֶם, אֲבָל אִם יָמוּתוּ הֵם — אֵין מַנְחִילִין לְאוֹתָן קְרוֹבִים שֶׁהֵן מוֹרִישֵׁיהֶן. מַנְחִילִין וְלֹא נוֹחֲלִין. הֵם אוֹתָם דְּאָמְרוּ בְּהוּ "נוֹחֲלִין וְלֹא מַנְחִילִין", מִכְּלָל דְּאִיפְּךָ שֶׁאֵלּוּ נוֹחֲלִין אוֹתָם וְלֹא מַנְחִילִין לָהֶן — מִיקְּרוּ "מַנְחִילִין וְלֹא נוֹחֲלִין". וּבַגְּמָ' מְפָרֵשׁ לְמַאי אִיצְטְרִיכוּ הָנֵךְ תְּרֵי בָּבֵי, דְּהָא חֲדָא נָפְקָא מִכְּלַל חֲבֶירְתָּהּ. **הָאָב.** נוֹחֵל אֶת הַבָּנִים, וְגַם מַנְחִיל לָהֶם. וּכְגוֹן שֶׁאֵין לְאוֹתָן הַבָּנִים זֶרַע — אָז נוֹחֵל אוֹתָן הָאָב, אֲבָל אִם יֵשׁ לָהֶם בָּנִים — הֵם קוֹדְמִין לִזְקֵנָם, כִּדְמְפָרֵשׁ בַּגְּמָ'. **וְהַבָּנִים אֶת הָאָב.** נוֹחֲלִין וּמַנְחִילִין. **וְהָאַחִין מִן הָאָב.** כְּגוֹן רְאוּבֵן וְיוֹסֵף בְּנֵי יַעֲקֹב, אע"פ שֶׁהֵן מִלֵּאָה וּמֵרָחֵל — יוֹרְשִׁים זֶה אֶת זֶה, בִּשְׁבִיל שֶׁהֵן אַחִין. וּכְגוֹן שֶׁמֵּת יַעֲקֹב אֲבִיהֶן, אֲבָל אִם יַעֲקֹב קַיָּים — הוּא קוֹדֵם, וּכְגוֹן שֶׁאֵין לָהֶם בָּנִים. וְדַוְקָא אַחִין מִן הָאָב, דְּמִשְׁפַּחַת אָב קְרוּיָה מִשְׁפָּחָה, כִּדְיָלְפִינַן כו'. **הָאִישׁ נוֹחֵל אֶת אִמּוֹ.** אֲבָל לֹא מַנְחִיל, שֶׁהֲרֵי קְרוֹבֵי הָאָב יוֹרְשִׁין אוֹתוֹ, דְּמִשְׁפַּחַת אֵם אֵינָהּ קְרוּיָה מִשְׁפָּחָה. **וְהָאִישׁ אֶת אִשְׁתּוֹ.** נוֹחֵל אוֹתָהּ, כִּדְנָפְקָא לָן בַּגְּמָ'. ה"ג בְּסֵדֶר הַמִּשְׁנָה: **וּבְנֵי אֲחָיוֹת נוֹחֲלִין וְלֹא מַנְחִילִין.** דְּבֵן נוֹחֵל אֶת אֲחוֹת אִמּוֹ. שֶׁהֲרֵי הוּא בָּא מִכֹּחַ הָאֵם, וְאִילּוּ מֵתָה דּוֹדָתוֹ בְּחַיֵּי אִמּוֹ — יוֹרַשְׁתָּהּ, וְגַם הוּא יוֹרֵשׁ אֶת אִמּוֹ, נִמְצָא שֶׁבָּאוּ לְיָדוֹ נִכְסֵי דּוֹדָתוֹ. **וְלֹא מַנְחִילִין.** דִּכְשֶׁמֵּת הַבֵּן — אֵינוֹ מַנְחִיל לַאֲחוֹת אִמּוֹ אֶלָּא לִקְרוֹבֵי אָבִיו, דְּמִשְׁפַּחַת אֵם אֵינָהּ קְרוּיָה מִשְׁפָּחָה. וְעוֹד, דַּאֲחוֹת אִמּוֹ הֵיאַךְ תִּירָשֶׁנּוּ? הֲלֹא הִיא בָּאָה מִכֹּחַ אֲחוֹתָהּ שֶׁהִיא אִמּוֹ שֶׁל זֶה, וְלֹא הָאֵם יְכוֹלָה לְיוֹרְשׁוֹ, כִּדְאָמְרַן: הָאִישׁ אֶת אִמּוֹ נוֹחֵל וְלֹא מַנְחִיל, קַל וָחוֹמֶר שֶׁהִיא לֹא תִּירַשׁ אֶת בֶּן אֲחוֹתָהּ. וּבַאֲחָיוֹת מִן הָאָב מַיְירֵי, אֲבָל אֲחָיוֹת מִן הָאֵם — אֵין נֶכְדָּהּ בֶּן אֲחוֹתָהּ יוֹרֵשׁ אוֹתָהּ, דְּמִמִּשְׁפַּחַת אֵם הוּא. ל"א: וּבְנֵי אָחוֹת — בְּנֵי אֲחוֹתוֹ שֶׁל רְאוּבֵן, כְּגוֹן בְּנֵי דִּינָה — נוֹחֲלִין אוֹתוֹ, שֶׁהֲרֵי דִּינָה יוֹרֶשֶׁת אֶת רְאוּבֵן אָחִיהָ, וּבָנֶיהָ בָּאִין מִכֹּחָהּ. אֲבָל לֹא מַנְחִילִין לִרְאוּבֵן — שֶׁהֲרֵי רְאוּבֵן מִכֹּחַ אֲחוֹתוֹ דִּינָה בָּא לִירַשׁ אוֹתָן, וַהֲלֹא דִּינָה עַצְמָהּ אֵין יוֹרַשְׁתָּן, כִּדְאָמְרַן דְּהָאֵם אֵינָהּ נוֹחֶלֶת אֶת בְּנָהּ, אֶלָּא קְרוֹבֵי בַּעְלָהּ שֶׁל דִּינָה יוֹרְשִׁין אֶת בָּנֶיהָ, דְּמִשְׁפַּחַת אָב יוֹרֶשֶׁת וְלֹא מִשְׁפַּחַת אֵם. וְזֶה נִרְאֶה בְּעֵינַי, מִשּׁוּם דְּקָתָנֵי סֵיפָא: הָאִשָּׁה אֶת בְּנָהּ וְהָאִשָּׁה אֶת בַּעְלָהּ וַאֲחֵי הָאֵם — מַנְחִילִין וְלֹא נוֹחֲלִין, וְכָל הָנֵךְ תְּלָתָא שָׁמְעִינַן לְהוּ מֵהָנֵךְ תְּלָת דְּהַךְ בָּבָא דְּנוֹחֲלִין וְלֹא מַנְחִילִין, כִּדְאָמְרִינַן בַּגְּמָ' דְּהַיְינוּ הַךְ, דְּקָפָרֵיךְ בַּגְּמָ': דַּאֲחֵי הָאֵם הַיְינוּ דִּבְנֵי אָחוֹת. וְהִלְכָּךְ גָּרְסִי' "בְּנֵי אָחוֹת", דְּהַיְינוּ נַמִי דַּאֲחֵי הָאֵם מַנְחִילִין אֶת בֶּן אֲחוֹתָם וְלֹא נוֹחֲלִין. וְאִי נַמִי גָּרְסִינַן "בְּנֵי אֲחָיוֹת" (א) — אִיכָּא לְפָרוּשֵׁי בִּבְנֵי אֲחָיוֹת, כְּלוֹמַר בְּנֵי אַחְיוֹתָיו שֶׁל אָדָם נוֹחֲלִין אוֹתוֹ אֲבָל לֹא מַנְחִילִין, דְּהוּא אֵינוֹ יוֹרְשָׁן. **הָאִשָּׁה אֶת בָּנֶיהָ וְהָאִשָּׁה אֶת בַּעְלָהּ כו'.** בַּגְּמָ' פָּרֵיךְ דְּהַיְינוּ נַמִי הַךְ בָּבָא דְ"נוֹחֲלִין וְלֹא מַנְחִילִין", דְּמֵהַהִיא שָׁמְעִינַן לָהּ, דְּהַיְינוּ הַךְ. **לֹא נוֹחֲלִין וְלֹא מַנְחִילִין.** זֶה לָזֶה, אֶלָּא קְרוֹבֵי אָבִיו שֶׁל זֶה וְאָבִיו שֶׁל זֶה יוֹרְשִׁין אוֹתוֹ. וְכָל הָנֵךְ קְרוֹבִים דְּקָתָנֵי שֶׁיּוֹרְשִׁים זֶה אֶת זֶה — הנ"מ כְּשֶׁאֵין קָרוֹב לַמֵּת יוֹתֵר מִזֶּה. גַּם הָנְהוּ קְרוֹבִים דְּקָתָנֵי בְּהֶן: לֹא נוֹחֲלִין וְלֹא מַנְחִילִין, כְּגוֹן קְרוֹבִים שֶׁמִּצַּד הָאֵם — הָנֵי מִילֵּי שֶׁיֵּשׁ קְרוֹבִים מִצַּד הָאָב הַיּוֹרְשִׁין אוֹתוֹ, וּקְרוֹבִים לוֹ יוֹתֵר מִקְּרוֹבֵי הָאֵם, וְאע"פ שֶׁגַּם אִמּוֹ מִמִּשְׁפַּחַת אָבִיו. אֲבָל אֵם אִמּוֹ קְרוֹבָה לוֹ מִצַּד מִשְׁפַּחַת אָבִיו, וְאֵין לוֹ קָרוֹב מֵאָבִיו שֶׁקָּרוֹב לוֹ כְּמוֹ אִמּוֹ — אָז הָאֵם יוֹרֶשֶׁת אֶת הַבֵּן. וְאִם אֵין הָאֵם בַּחַיִּים — קְרוֹבֵי הָאֵם יוֹרְשִׁין אוֹתוֹ, דַּהֲוֵי לֵיהּ מִשְׁפַּחַת אָב, דְּמִכֹּחַ קוֹרֶבֶת אָבִיו בָּאִין לְיוֹרְשׁוֹ. כְּגוֹן רְאוּבֵן שֶׁנָּשָׂא סֶרַח בַּת אָשֵׁר, וְיָלְדָה לוֹ נַפְתָּלִי, וּמֵת נַפְתָּלִי בְּלֹא בָּנִים — הֲרֵי רְאוּבֵן אָבִיו יוֹרְשׁוֹ. וְאִם אֵין לוֹ אָב — "וּנְתַתֶּם אֶת נַחֲלָתוֹ לְאֶחָיו" שֶׁל נַפְתָּלִי, וְאִם אֵין לוֹ אַחִין — "וּנְתַתֶּם נַחֲלָתוֹ לַאֲחֵי אָבִיו", דְּהַיְינוּ אָשֵׁר, אֲבִי אִמּוֹ. וְאִם אֵין לוֹ אַחִין לְאָבִיו, דְּאֵין אָשֵׁר קַיָּים — "וּנְתַתֶּם אֶת נַחֲלָתוֹ לַקָּרוֹב אֵלָיו". נִמְצֵאת סֶרַח, דְּהַיְינוּ בְּנֵי אָשֵׁר, אוֹ בְּנוֹת אָשֵׁר אִם אֵין לוֹ בָּנִים דְּהַיְינוּ סֶרַח, יוֹרֶשֶׁת אֶת בְּנָהּ. **גמ' מַאי שְׁנָא דְּתָנֵי.** בְּרֵישָׁא דְּמַתְנִי' הָאָב נוֹחֵל אֶת הַבֵּן וּמַנְחִיל? וַהֲלֹא בְּעֵת שֶׁנּוֹחֵל הָאָב לִבְנוֹ — נִמְצָא שֶׁמֵּת הַבֵּן בְּחַיֵּי הָאָב, וְלֹא הִנִּיחַ הַבֵּן הַהוּא זֶרַע לְיוֹרְשׁוֹ, לְפִיכָךְ אָבִיו יוֹרְשׁוֹ. וְזוֹ קְלָלָה הִיא כְּשֶׁאָדָם מֵת בְּלֹא בָּנִים, וְגַם כְּשֶׁהָאָב רוֹאֶה בְּמִיתַת בְּנוֹ, וְהָיָה לוֹ לַתַּנָּא דְּמַתְנִיתִין לִפְתּוֹחַ: הַבֵּן נוֹחֵל אֶת הָאָב, שֶׁזֶּה בְּרָכָה שֶׁיָּמוּת הָאָב וְיִקְבְּרֶנּוּ בְּנוֹ, כְּדִכְתִיב (בראשית מו): "וְיוֹסֵף יָשִׁית יָדוֹ עַל עֵינֶיךָ" — הִבְטִיחוֹ שֶׁיִּקְבְּרֵהוּ בְּנוֹ.

וְעוֹד

תוספות

יש נוחלין. ואלו נוחלין ומנחילין. איכא דוכתי דנקיט אדסליק מיניה, ואיכא אדפתח ביה. ובמס' נדרים (דף ג,) מפרש לה. **האב** את הבנים והבנים את האב. תימה: "והאב את הבנים" — היינו "בנים את האב", שאם האב נוחל את בנו — אם כן בנו מנחילו, ואם הוא מנחיל לבנו — א"כ בנו *נוחלו! ואור"י, דאייתר למידק מיניה: בנים ולא בנות. אע"ג דקתני לה בהדיא בסמוך — מכל מקום תנא ליה הכא אגב אורחיה, ולקמן נמי (ב) תניא למנות סדר נחלות. וכן משמע בגמ', דקאמר: הבנים את האב מנלן? אמר קרא "ובן אין לו", הא יש לו בן — בן קודם לבת. משמע דמתני' לאקדומי בן לבת איצטריך. אבל מרישא דקתני: "האב את הבנים" — ליכא למידק הכי דהאב מנחיל בנים ולא בנות, דהא לא מייתר. ואם תאמר: דקתני "בני אחיות", ודייק בגמ' עלה: ולא בנות אחיות, אע"ג דלא מייתר, ומתוך כך צריך לומר דמתני' איני יודע מי שנאה — לימא דבנים לאו דוקא, אלא הוא הדין בנות, ואתיא שפיר כרבי זכריה בן הקצב. אע"ג דתנא בגמ' בני אחיות ולא בנות אחיות — [יש] לומר דברייתא פליגא אמתניתין, ויודע מי שנאה! ואור"י: דקים ליה דברייתא נשנית על המשנה, לפיכך דייק מינה. ועוד אומר ר"י: דכיון ד"בנים את האב" אייתר למידק בנים ולא בנות, אית לן למימר דכולהו "בנים" דמתני' דוקא — ולא בנות, לקדוש. **ואחין** מן האב. הקשה ר"י אמאי לא קתני: "אחי האב נוחלין ומנחילין"? שהן כתובין נמי בפרשה! ותירץ: משום דאחי האב וכל שאר אב נפקי מהנך: "האב את הבנים והבנים את האב, והאחין מן האב". דכיון שנודע שהבנים קודמין, ואחר הבנים האב, ואחר האב אחין — הרי אחי האב נפקי מכלל זה על ידי משמוש. דאם היה האב קיים — היה יורש, (ג) ועכשיו שאינו קיים — הרי הוא יורש בקבר, להנחיל לבנו שהוא *(אחי אביו) של מת. ומשמוש שמעינן מדתנן בסמוך בני אחות, שמנחילה בקבר נכסי אחיה לבנה. וא"ת: אם כן, "אחין מן האב" נמי לא ליתני, דשמעינן ליה מ"האב את הבנים" על ידי משמוש נחלה, שהאב יורש את בנו להנחיל לשאר בניו הקיימין, שהן אחי המת! ויש לומר, דנקט (ד) אגב דבעי למיתני: אחים מן האם לא נוחלין ולא מנחילין. דההוא איצטריך למיתני אע"ג דתנא האשה אינה נוחלת את בנה; סד"א: נהי דאינו יורש אחיו מן האם מכח אמו, מכח אח הוה אמינא דיורש, דכתיב "ונתתם את נחלתו לאחיו" לא שנא מן האב ולא שנא מן האם. וכי תימא: דמכל מקום לא איצטריך למיתני, דשמעי' מרישא דקתני אחין מן האב דוקא, ולא אחין מן האם! איצטריך, דהוה אמינא אחין מן האב לרבותא נקט, אף על פי שאין כל כך ודאין כמו אחין מן האם. ואם תאמר: אם כן, אחי האב נמי ליתני אגב אחי האם דסיפא! ויש לומר: דאי הוי תני אחי האב תו לא הוה צריך למיתני אחי האם, דמכלל אחי האב שמעינן להו. ועוד: דלא שייך למיתני אגב אחי האם, דהיא גופה משנה דלא צריכא היא, כדדייקינן בגמ' דהיינו בני אחות.

יבול

א) [נדרים ב: נזיר ב.] ב) [לעיל יד:]

רבינו גרשום

אידי דרויח החריץ ו' טפחים ממשכת עצמה בתוך החריץ לאחריה וקופצת חוץ א)סמוך לגדר ומשום הכי צריך בן חריץ עדיין שמעכב: אידי דקטין. ג' טפחים קיימא החיה אשפתיה וקופצת לעבר אחר הלכך צריכי תרוייהו כדי שלא תקפוץ:

הדרן עלך האומר לחבירו בית כור

יש נוחלין. שנוחלין אחרים והן עצמן מנחילין ממונם ליורשין: האב את הבנים. שהאב יורש את הבנים והבנים יורשין את האב: ליתני הבנים יורשין את האב תחלה. משום דתרי טעמי איכא דהוה ליה למיתני הבנים את האב חדא משום דאתחולי לא ב) מתחלינן בפורענותא הוא שהבנים מתים בחיי אביהן והאב יורשן שמנהג העולם שהבן יורש האב ולא האב את

א) לכאורה נ"ל וקופצת מתוך על הגדר וכו'. או הנ"ל וקופצת מתרין על הגדר.

ב) נראה דצ"ל לאתחולי בפורענותא לא מתחלינן דהאב את הבנים פורענותא הוא שהבנים וכו'.

עין משפט נר מצוה

א א מיי' פ"א מהל' נחלות הל' א סמג עשין נו טוש"ע ח"מ סי' רעו סעיף א:

[עי' לקמן קיד: רשב"ם סד"ה אף.

ס"א אחיו

הגהות הב"ח

(א) רשב"ם ד"ה ולא מנחילין וכו' ואי נמי גרסינן בני אחיות. נ"ב אבל לקמן בדף קיד ראש ע"ב פירש בע"א: (ב) תוס' ד"ה האב וכו' ולקמן נמי תנא ליה למנות: (ג) ד"ה ואחין וכו' היה יורש לבנו ועכשיו שאינו קיים הרי הוא יורש בקבר להנחיל לאחיו שהוא אחי אביו: (ד) בא"ד דנקט לה אגב:

וְעוֹד, כְּדִכְתִיב: °"אִישׁ כִּי יָמוּת וּבֵן אֵין לוֹ"! וְתַנָּא, אַיְּדֵי דְּאָתְיָא לֵיהּ א)מִדְּרָשָׁא חֲבִיבָא לֵיהּ. וּמַאי דְּרָשָׁא? דְּתַנְיָא: "שְׁאֵרוֹ" – זֶה הָאָב, מְלַמֵּד אשֶׁהָאָב קוֹדֵם לָאַחִין; יָכוֹל יְהֵא קוֹדֵם לַבֵּן? בת"ל: °"הַקָּרוֹב" – (א) קָרוֹב קָרוֹב קוֹדֵם. ב)וּמָה רָאִיתָ לְרַבּוֹת אֶת הַבֵּן וּלְהוֹצִיא אֶת הָאָח? מְרַבֶּה אֲנִי אֶת הַבֵּן, שֶׁכֵּן גקָם תַּחַת אָבִיו לְיַעֲדָה דוְלִשְׂדֵה אֲחוּזָּה. אַדְּרַבָּה, מְרַבֶּה אֲנִי אֶת הָאָח, שֶׁכֵּן הקָם תַּחַת אָחִיו לְיִבּוּם! כְּלוּם יֵשׁ יִבּוּם ואֶלָּא בְּמָקוֹם שֶׁאֵין בֵּן, הָא בְּמָקוֹם שֶׁיֵּשׁ בֵּן – אֵין יִבּוּם. טַעֲמָא דְּאִיכָּא הַאי פִּירְכָא, הָא לָאו הָכִי – הֲוָה אָמֵינָא אָח עֲדִיף; תֵּיפוֹק לֵיהּ דְּהָכָא

תורה אור: במדבר כז; שם

ועוד כדכתיב ואיש כי ימות ובן אין לו וגו'. הא יש לו בן – בנו יורשו. וכי היכי דפרשת נחלות פתחה בירושת הבן לאביו – כך היה לו לתנא לפתוח. חדא דאתחולי כו'. מסקנא דקושיא היא. דאתיא ליה מדרשא. שהאב נוטל את בנו. דתניא ונתתם את נחלתו לשארו הקרוב אליו זה האב. של מת. ואשמעינן קרא שהאב פעמים שיורש את בנו, דשארו היינו אביו, כדכתיב (ויקרא יח): "שאר אביך הוא" כדלקמן. וכתיב נמי: "כי אם לשארו הקרוב אליו לאמו ולאביו" וגו'. מלמד שהאב. של מת, קודם לאחיו של מת. כגון, שאם מת ראובן בלא בנים – יעקב יורשו ולא שמעון אחיו יורשו. ולקמיה מפרש ואזיל היאך למידין אנו מכאן שקודם לאחין ולא לבנים ובנות של מת. ולקמן פרכינן: והא קראי לאו הכי כתיבי? ומשני: קראי שלא כסדרן כתיבי. דמאי דכתיב "הקרוב אליו" דמשמע הקרוב קרוב קודם – אתא לגלויי על *(פי') סדר נחלות דשלא כסדרן כתיבי, אלא הקרוב קרוב תקדים לירש. וכן תסדר אותן: איש כי ימות ובן אין לו והעברתם את נחלתו לבתו, ואם אין לו בת ונתתם את נחלתו לשארו הקרוב, ואח"כ ונתתם וגו' לאחיו. כלומר, שאם אין לו שאר – ונתתם את נחלתו לאחיו, ואם אין לו אחים – ונתתם את נחלתו לאחי אביו, ואם אין אחין לאביו – הקרוב אליו ממשפחתו וירש אותה. יכול. יהא יעקב קודם לחנוך בן ראובן, דאפי' היכא דהניח ראובן זרע – יירש יעקב, ולעולם לא יירש בן ראובן אלא היכא דאין יעקב קיים. ונסדר הפסוק כן: איש כי ימות ונתתם את נחלתו לשארו, ובן אין לו והעברתם את נחלתו לבתו וגו'. כלומר, אם אין לו שאר, וגם בן אין לו שיירש במקום שאין שאר – והעברתם את נחלתו לבתו. הקרוב קרוב. למת יותר, הוא קודם בנחלה ליורשו. והבן של מת, כגון חנוך בן ראובן, קרוב הוא לראובן יותר מיעקב אביו, שהרי קם תחת אביו ליעדה ולשדה אחוזה, כדלקמן, אבל האב לא מצינו שיהא קם תחת בנו לכלום. ומשום דמילתא דפשיטא הוא, לא חשש הגמרא להקשות: ומה ראית לרבות את הבן ולהוציא את האב, כי היכי דפריך לקמיה "ומה ראית לרבות את הבן ולהוציא את האח". דבשלמא גבי אח אשכחן שום קורבה – שקם תחת אחיו ליבום, אבל באב לא מצינו כלל. ומה ראית לרבות את הבן. של מת, שיהא קודם לאחי המת, וכל שכן שקודם לאחי המת היכא דליכא אב. ולהוציא את האח, ולומר שהאב קודם לאח, וכל שכן שהבן שקודם לאב קודם לאח? אדרבה, מרבה אני את האח, כדלקמיה. מרבה אני את הבן. חנוך בן ראובן, שיקום תחת אביו לנחלה טפי משמעון אחי ראובן, שהרי קם חנוך תחת אביו ראובן ליעוד. שאם קנה ראובן אמה העבריה – יכול ליעדה לו כשירצה בכסף מקנתה שנתן לאביה זה ימים, וכבר ניתנו להוצאה, ואין צריך ליתן קדושין אחרים, אלא כך יאמר: "הרי את מיועדת לי". כדכתיב (שמות כא): ו"אם רעה בעיני אדוניה אשר לא יעדה" וגו' – מכלל שיכול לייעדה, וגם לבנו יכול לייעדה – כדכתיב: "ואם לבנו ייעדנה" וגו'. אבל לאדם אחר אין יכול לייעדה אלא א"כ יקדשנה האיש קדושין גמורין, ואפי' לאחיו אין יכול לייעדה. ולשדה אחוזה. דדרשינן בערכין בפרק "אין מקדישין", ותניא נמי בתורת כהנים: "ואם לא יגאל את השדה" – בעליו שהקדישו, "ואם מכר את השדה" – הגזבר מכרה, "לאיש אחר" – לאיש אחר ולא לבנו של מקדיש, "והיה השדה בצאתו ביובל קודש" וגו' – שיוצאה לכהנים ביובל. אבל אם לא פדאו איש אחר אלא בנו – חוזרת לאביו ביובל. אבל אם אחיו של מקדיש פדאו – יוצאה לכהנים, כדכתיב: "לאיש אחר" דהיינו אחיו, אבל בנו לאו "אחר" הוא. והתם נמי פרכינן: מה ראית לרבות את הבן כו' (ג) כי הכא, שכן קם תחת אביו כו'. אבל לא מצי למימר: שבן קודם את אחי המת לנחלה, כמו שסדור בפרשה: "ואם אין לו בן והעברתם את נחלתו לבתו ואם אין לו בת ונתתם את נחלתו לאחיו". דכיון דקראי לאו כסדרן כתיבי, כדמוכח קרא, כדכתב: "הקרוב" – קרוב קודם, ונימא דאח קודם בין לאב בין לבן. אדרבה מרבה אני את האח כו'. ומהפכינן קרא כי האי גוונא: איש כי ימות ונתתם את נחלתו לאחיו, ואם אין לו אחים ונתתם את נחלתו לבנו. אי נמי, ואם אין לו אחים ובן אין לו – והעברתם את נחלתו לבתו. ואם אין לו בת – ונתתם את נחלתו לשארו, ואם אין לו שאר – ונתתם נחלתו לאחי אביו, ואם אין אחים לאביו – הקרוב אליו ממשפחתו וירש. ליבום. כדכתיב (דברים כה): "כי ישבו אחים יחדו ומת אחד מהם ובן אין לו" וגו'. אבל הבן אינו מייבם את אמו. ומשני: כלום יש יבום כו' הא יש בן אין יבום. אלמא, אפילו לגבי יבום קם הבן תחת אביו טפי מאחי אביו, שהרי פוטר אותה ממנו. דהכא

יכול יהא קודם לבן. פריב"ס: יהא קודם לבן ולא לאח, כדמסיק בתר הכי: דאדרבה, מרבה אני את האח שכן קם תחת אחיו ליבום. ולא פריך השתא שיקדום ג)אב לבן – דהא פשיטא ליה להאי תנא שאין להקדימו אלא לאחד מהן, או לאח או לבן, ולא לתרוייהו. דהא אי לאו נכתב "שארו" – לא היינו מקדימין אפי' לאחד, (ד) שהרי האב אינו קם תחת בנו לשום דבר, ולכך, השתא דכתב "שארו" – די אם נקדימנו לאחד מהן, ובזה נושא ונותן איזה מהן קרוב יותר אח או בן, ונקדימנו למרוחק שבהן. ואין נראה פירושו כלל, דכיון דאין סברא להקדימו אלא לאחד מהן – מה צריך לדרשא דהקרוב קרוב? מסברא יש לי להקדימו לאח יותר מלבן, כדמסיק: כלום יש יבום אלא במקום שאין בן! ונראה לפר"ס, דהשתא קאמר: יכול יקדום אף לבן, דמדכתב "שארו" להקדים אקדמיה לכל הכתוב בפרשה – תלמוד לומר "הקרוב אליו" דקרוב קודם. ומה ראית דמוקמת "הקרוב" לבן, ו"שארו" להקדים לאח? אימא איפכא! **יכול** יהא קודם לבן. ואם תאמר: אם כן, לא יירשו בן ובת ואח לעולם, פס האב קודם לבן. שהרי האב יורשו בקבר, ואם יקדום אחי המת לבנו ולבתו ולאחיו – יקדום אחריו אבי אביו, דנחלה ממשמשת והולכת עד ראובן, כדנפקא ליה לקמן (דף קטו:)! ויש לומר: דאיכא לאוקומי לקרא דיורשין בן ובת ואח בבן דגר, ובבן בנו של גר, כדי לקיים שיירשנו אחי אביו. אי נמי, היכא דאיכא בן ובת או אח – לא נאמר דממשמשת והולכת, כיון דדריש מקרא לקמן (דף קט:) שאין לך מעביר נחלה משבט לשבט אלא בת, הואיל ובנה ובעלה יורשה. דאם כן – נמצא כל נחלות מעבירות משבט לשבט, דממשמשת נחלה עד יעקב אבינו ומוריש לכל ישראל, כיון שהאבות קודמין לבן ולבת ולאח. רשב"א. ואם תאמר: אחי אביו דכתב רחמנא, למה לי? תיפוק לי מ"אין לו" – עיין עליו, דדרשי' מינה לקמן (דף קטו.) דנחלה ממשמשת ובאה! ותירץ ריב"ס: דכתביה לאשמועינן דקראי שלא כסדרן כתיבי. דאי לא כתב אחי אביו – הוי אמינא דכסדרן כתיבי, ואחי המת קודמין לאב, אבל השתא דכתב אחי אביו – על כרחך לא נכתב "שארו" אלא להקדימו לאחין, דלהקדימו לאחי האב – לא איצטריך, כדאמרינן לקמן. וקשיא לר"י: התינח למאן דאמר קראי לאו כסדרן כתיבי, אלא למאן דאמר כסדרן כתיבי, אמאי כתב אחי האב? ועוד קשיא לרשב"א: דאפילו למאן דאמר שלא כסדרן כתיבי – לא איצטריך למכתב אחי האב, דעל כרחך לא נכתב "שארו" אלא להקדימו לאחיו, דבע"א למאי כתבי' רחמנא? דאי לאשמועינן דהיכא דליכא בן ובת ואח שהוא יורש – פשיטא, אלא מאן לירת? אטו בר קשא דמתא לירת?! כדאמרינן לקמן (דף קי.). וליכא למימר: אי לאו דכתב אחי האב הוה אמינא דאיצטריך "שארו" לאשמועינן שהאחין קודמין לאב, דאי לא הוה כתב "שאר" הוה אמינא דאב קודם לאחיו. דאי היינו (ד) אומרים דאב קודם לאחיו – לא לכתוב רחמנא לא אב ולא אחי האב. ועוד, דכולה שמעתין אנו דוחקין למצוא פסוק מנא לן דאב קודם לאחיו, משום דמסברא אית לן למימר דאחיו קדמי. ואור"י: דמ"אין לו" לא הוה שמעינן נחלה ממשמשת לכעלה אלא למטה, כגון בן הבן ובת הבן ובן בת הבן. אע"ג דעלה אמר לקמן דנחלה הולכת וממשמשת עד ראובן, דהיינו למעלה, אהאי קרא דאחי אביו סמיך. וא"ת: ואחין דכתב רחמנא למה לי? כיון דנחלה ממשמשת עד ראובן – ירש האב בקבר להנחיל לבניו הנותרים! וי"ל: דאי לא כתב אחין, ה"א שהאב קודם לבת, דאית לן לאקדומי אב לחד מהנך דכתיבי בהדיא בקרא.

שכן קם תחת אביו ליעדה ולשדה אחוזה. ה"ה דה"מ למנקט נמי: ולעבד עברי. **כלום** יש יבום אלא במקום שאין בן. אין לפרש דלא עדיף לענין יבום בן מאב, אלא כלומר, הן שוין לענין יבום, וא"כ – הכי נמי עדיף בן מאח, משום דקם תחת אביו ליעדה ולשדה אחוזה. דעל כרחך לקמן גבי בת לא אפשר לפרש כן, דאמרינן: כיון דלענין יבום כי הדדי נינהו לענין נחלה נמי כי הדדי ניהו. כלומר, ותהא עדיפא בת מאח, שיקדום אב לאח ולא לבת. ואי לא עדיפא מאח לענין יבום – היכי עדיפא מיניה לענין נחלה? אלא ודאי מהאי טעמא: דכלום יש יבום אלא במקום שאין בת, דהיא עדיפא מאח, דבת מקימה שם, ואח אינו מקים שם אלא צריך לייבם. כיון

עין משפט נר מצוה

ב א ב מיי' פ"א מהל' נחלות הלכה ג סמג עשין צו טוש"ע ח"מ סי' רעו סעיף א:

ג ג מיי' פ"ד מהל' עבדים הלכה ז סמג עשין פו:

ד ד מיי' פ"ד מהל' ערכין הלכה כ סמג עשין קלא:

ה ה ו מיי' פ"א מהל' יבום הלכה א סמג עשין נב טור וש"ע אה"ע סי' קנו סעי' א:

רבינו גרשום

הבן ועוד כדקאמר קרא הוה ליה למיסמך כדכת' איש כי ימות ובן אין לו והעברתם את נחלתו לבתו אלמא דאב מיית מקמי הבן וצריך למיעבר נחלתיה אי לית ליה בן. ומשני תנא דמתני' משום הכי נקט למיתני ברישא האב את הבנים דאיידי דאתיא ליה מדרשא חביבא ליה: ומאי דרשא דתניא שארו זה האב שמהפכין קראי דלא כתיבי כסדרן וכדבעי למימר לקמן והכי מהפכינן להו איש כי ימות ובן אין לו והעברתם את נחלתו לבתו ואם אין לו בת ונתתם את נחלתו לשארו ואם אין לו שאר ונתתם את נחלתו לאחיו ואם אין לו אחים ונתתם את נחלתו לאחי אביו ואם אין אחים לאביו ונתתם את נחלתו לקרוב אליו ולא אמרינן הכא לשארו דהא דרשי' ליה שהוא קודם לאחיו של מת מלמד שהאב של מת קודם לאחין של מת ה"נ מהפכי' א) של מת וכדמהפכי' לעיל קראי: יכול יהא. האב של מת קודם לבנו של מת דכי היכי דמהפכי' לקראי שהאב קודם לאחין של מת הכי נמי מהפכי' שהאב של מת קודם לבן של מת ליורשו ת"ל דלא דכתי' הקרוב אליו הקרוב קרוב קודם והבן קרוב הוא לירש את אביו שמת יותר מאביו של מת ומשום דאתא מדרשא שהאב קודם לאחיו של מת חביבא ליה למיתני האב יורש את הבנים אע"פ שפורענ' הוא ג)דמצטר' דהיכא דמת הבן בחיי האב ואין לו לבן לא בן ולא בת אביו יורשו קודם לאחיו של מת: ג)והא מצינן למימר כי היכי דמהפכת קרא לרבות את הבן ולהוציא את האח דהבן קרוב מן האב וכל הקרוב קרוב קודם אימא איפכא שאח קרוב למת אין האב של מת מקודם בירושה אבל לבן של מת מקדים דהואיל דלא כתיבי קראי כסידרן מצית [להקדים] האב של מת בין המת ובין הבן של מת ואימא איש כי ימות ונתתם את נחלתו לשארו ואם אין לו שאר ונתתם את נחלתו לבנו. ומשני בדין הוא דמרבה אני את הבן של מת קודם לאביו של מת שכן אית ביה בבן מה שאין בכולהו קרובים שבן קם תחת אביו ליעדה באמה העבריה וכדאמרי' במס' קדושין ואם לבנו ייעדנה ולא לאחר דהוא קם תחת אביו דכי היכי דאיהו מייעד ליה לדידיה ה"נ מצי ליעדה לבריה ולא לאחיו וכדדרשינן התם והכי נמי לשדה אחוזה כדאמר במס' ערכין הקדישה לשדהו וגאלה אינה יוצאה מידו ביובל גאלה בנו חוזר אביו וגואלה ממנו דבנו קם תחת אביו וכגופו דמי גאלה אחר וכו' ואמרי' בגמ' ת"ר אם לא יגאל את השדה הבעל' אם מכר גזבר את השדה לאיש אחר לאחר ולא לבן אתה אומר לאחר ולא לבן או אינו אלא לאחר ולא לאח אלמא דלא כצי מייעד לאמה העבריה אלא לבנו ד) אלא מצי למיפרך שדה אחוזה דתיהדר למרה לאחר היובל אלא הבן לחוד דאימא דדרך הבן למהדר לאביו ומשום הכי דין הוא דבן של מת קודם מכל קרובים בירושה. ומקשינן אדרבה מרבה אני את האח של מת שיהא קודם לאביו של בן ומוצא אני את הבן שכן קם תחת אחיו לייבום מה שאין כן בבן. ומשני ליה כלום יש יבום אלא במקום שאין בן הא יש בן אין יבום אלמא דמכח הבן קא גרע לאחיו מייבום הלכך מרבה אני את הבן ומוצא אני את האח: ולמה לי לתרוצי כלום יש יבום כו' ותיפוק דהכא

מסורת הש"ס

א) יבמות כ: וש"נ. ב) ערכין כה: קידושין יז: ג) [צ"ל אף רש"ל]:

הגהות הב"ח

(א) גמ' ת"ל הקרוב הקרוב קרוב קודם. נ"ב ע"ל דף קי ע"ב כתב הרשב"ם דהיינו ה"א דהקרוב קדריש דומיא דהשולה ע"ש: (ב) רשב"ם ד"ה ולשדה אחוזה וכו' לרבות את הבן כו' ופרקינן כי הכא מרבה אני את הבן שכן קם תחת: (ג) תום' ד"ה יכול וכו' אפילו לאחד מהן שהרי וכו' הקרוב אליו הקרוב קרוב קודם ומה: (ד) ד"ה יכול וכו' דאי היינו אמרינן מסברא דאב קודם וכו' ועוד דכולה שמעתין וכו' לא הוה שמעינן דנחלה ממשמשת:

א) נראה דצ"ל ה"נ מהפכינן במתני' האב של מת מקודם. או דצ"ל וע"כ דמהפכינן לשאר של מת מקודם וכדמהפכינן וכו'. ב) אולי צ"ל דמצטריך לאשמעינן. ג) נראה דצ"ל ומה ראית לרבות את הבן. והא מצינן למימר וכו'. ד) נראה דזהו הג"ה מאיזה מפרש דמשדה אחוזה אינו ראיה וצ"ל ומיהו מצינן למיפרך דשאני שדה אחוזה דמש"ה לא תהדר למרה לאחר היובל אלא אם גאלה הבן לחוד וכו' וצ"ע.

דהכא תרתי והכא חדא! שדה אחוזה גופה מהאי טעמא הוא דקא קיימא ליה לתנא: כלום יש יבום אלא במקום שאין בן, הא יש בן – אין יבום. (א) אימא: "שארו" – זה האב, מלמד שהאב קודם לבת; יכול יקדים לבן? ת"ל: "הקרוב" – קרוב קרוב קודם! כיון דלענין יבום – בן ובת כי הדדי נינהו, אלענין נחלה נמי – בן ובת כי הדדי נינהו. ואימא: "שארו" – זה האב, מלמד שהאב קודם לאחי האב; יכול יקדים לאחין? תלמוד לומר: "הקרוב" – קרוב קרוב קודם! אחי האב לא צריכי קרא; אחי האב מכח מאן קא אתו? מכח אב, קאי אב קא ירתי אחי האב?! והא קראי לאו הכי כתיבי, דכתיב: (במדבר כז) °"ואם אין אחים לאביו" וגו'! קראי שלא כסדרן כתיבי. והאי תנא מייתי לה מהכא: דתניא, את זו דרש רבי ישמעאל ברבי יוסי: (שם) °"איש כי ימות ובן אין לו" וגו' – במקום בת אתה מעביר נחלה מן האב, בואי אתה מעביר נחלה מן האב במקום אחין. ואימא: במקום בת אתה מעביר נחלה מן האחין, ואי

דהכא תרתי. יעידה ושדה אחוזה. והכא חדא. יבום. והוה מלי לתרוצי הנך נפישי. ומשני: משום דשדה אחוזה גופה לא קיימא לן במס' ערכין שיהא הבן במקום האב טפי מאחיו אלא מהך פירקא, דפרכינן התם: כלום יש יבום כו'. דאמרי' נמי התם: מה ראית לרבות את הבן ולהוציא את האח? מרבה אני את הבן שכן קם תחת אביו ליעדה כו'. אדרבה, מרבה אני את האח שכן קם תחת אחיו ליבום. ומשני: כלום יש יבום כו'. שהרי לא מצינו כתוב בפירוש שיהא הבן קם תחת אביו טפי מאחיו אלא ליעדה, שגם האח קם תחתיו ליבום. ונמצא דהכא חדא והכא חדא הוא. ושאר דברים שהבן קם תחת אביו טפי מאחיו, כגון שדה אחוזה ועבד עברי במסכת קידושין, וקדימת הבן לאח בנחלה – כולהו מייתינן להו מדין יעידה לחוד, שכ' בפירוש שהבן קם תחת אביו. ואי לא דמשנינן דאפי' לגבי יבום אין האח קם תחתיו כמו בנו, דכלום יש יבום אלא במקום שאין בן – לא הוה מלינן לרבויי בן שיקום תחת אביו לכלום טפי מאחיו, דליהוי הכא חדא והכא חדא. ולקמיה פרכינן: דבן ובת ואח כמו שסדורין בפרשה ליקדמו כולהו לאב, שהרי כולם קרובים למת טפי מאביו, שהם קמים תחתיו ליעידה וליבום, אבל האב אינו קם תחתיו לכלום. מלמד שהאב קודם לבת. דהא אינה קמה תחת אביה לכלום כבנו וכאחיו. וסדר את הפסוקים כן: איש כי ימות ובן אין לו – ונתתם את נחלתו לשארו, ואם אין לו שאר – ונתתם את נחלתו לאחיו, ואם אין לו אחים – והעברתם את נחלתו לבתו, ואם אין לו בת – ונתתם את נחלתו לאחי אביו, ואם אין אחין לאביו – הקרוב אליו ממשפחתו וירש. בן ובת כי הדדי נינהו. כדכתיב: "ובן אין לו" – עיין עליו. נמצאת גם הבת פוטרת את האחין מן היבום. אבל אבי המת אינו פוטר את אשת בנו מן היבום, נמצאת הבת קמה תחת אביה טפי מאבי המת ואחי המת. קודם לאחי האב. של מת. ולא לאחין, משום דקרובים למת יותר מאביו, שהרי קמים תחתיו ליבום. אבל אביו אין קם תחתיו לכלום. וסדר המקרא כך הוא: ונתתם את נחלתו לאחיו, ואם אין לו אחים – ונתתם את נחלתו לשארו, ואם אין לו שאר – ונתתם את נחלתו לאחי אביו, ואם אין אחים לאביו – הקרוב אליו ממשפחתו וירש. ומשני: אחי האב לא צריכי קראי. לא היה צריך לכתוב לבסוף "שארו" לקדם את אחי האב, דסברא הוא דקודם האב לאחיו שלו לירש את בנו. דאחי האב מכח מאן קאתו לירש את נכדם בן אחיהן – פשיטא דמכח אבי המת, שהוא אחיהם, אתו. והלכך, למה לי קרא? מאחר שכתוב למעלה שאחי האב יורשין את נכדם – מי איכא למימר דהיכא דקאי אב ירתי אחים של אב? בתמיה. הלכך לא נכתב "שארו" אלא לקדם אחיו של מת, דלקדם אחי האב – כבר שמעינן ליה מתאי דאמר "ואם אין לו אחים ונתתם את נחלתו לאחי אביו" – הרי הוא כמי שכתב: ואם אין לו אחים ונתתם את נחלתו לאביו, ואם אין לו אב ונתתם את נחלתו לאחי אביו. הלכך, לא נכתב "שארו" אלא לחדש ולומר שיקדום לאחד מהני דכתב לעיל, ומנו – אחי המת, שהן בניו. דלקדם אחי האב לא שדינן ליה, דהא לא צריך, כדפרישית. ולקדם את בנו ואת בתו של מת – לא אמרי', שהרי קרובים למת יותר מן האחין כדאמרן. הלכך, שדינן ליה באחין של מת, לקדם האב לבניו לירש את בנו. דסד"א יקדמוהו הם, שהרי קמים תחת אחיהן ליבום, מה שאין כן באב. והא קראי לאו הכי כתיבי. ד"שארו" לבסוף כתב, אחר אחי האב, והוה לן למימר דגזירת הכתוב הוא שאחי האב של מת קודמין לאביו. קראי שלא כסדרן כתיבי. דהא כתיבי אחי האב, ואח"כ שאר אב, ובעל כרחך אב קדים להו, כדאמרן: דהא מכח אב קאתו. דלא דקדק הכתוב בסדרן, משום דסמך אמאי דכתב "הקרוב" – קרוב קודם, ומעצמך תסדר אותם כפי קורבתן. ואם תאמר: כיון דאין אנו הולכין אחר הסדר – לשתוק קרא מיניה, וליכתוב "איש כי ימות ונתתם את נחלתו לקרוב אליו ממשפחתו" וגו'! איכא למימר דקרא אריכא טובא, כדלקמן בפירקין (דף קטו.): "ובן אין לו" – עיין עליו, "ואם אין לו בת" – עיין עליה. וכן כולן. הכי גרסינן: והאי תנא מייתי לה מהכא. דהאב קודם לאחין. והעברת. משמע: תעביר מקרוב זה שהוא קיים, כדי לתת לזה. והעברת מן האב כדי לתת לבת. במקום אחין. שאין למת בן ובת, אלא אחין. ובסיפרי מסיים לה הכי: ומנין שהאב יורש – אמרת קל וחומר כו'. איכא. דהאי "והעברת" אאחין דקיימי קמן קאי, וקאמר: והעברת מן האחין לתת לבת. הא אין בת – אחין יורשין אותו. ואכתי אב מנלן דירית מקמי אח? (ג) ואי משום דדייקינן: ואי אתה מעביר נחלה מן האב ואפי' במקום בת – הך דיוקא לאו מ"והעברת" שמעינן לה, דאדרבה מ"והעברת" איכא למידק: אתה מעביר נחלה מן האב במקום הבת. אם כן. דלגלויי אתא האי "והעברת", דאחין ירתי במקום שאין בת – לא ליכתוב "והעברת", דממילא שמעינן לה מדכתב "ואם אין לו בת ונתתם את נחלתו לאחיו". דהא להאי תנא קראי כסדרן כתיבי, דהא לא דריש "שארו" לאב, דנימא שלא כסדרן כתיבי.

ואי

כיון דלענין יבום בן ובת כי הדדי נינהו. וא"ת: מנא לן דבת פוטרת מן היבום? אי מדכתיב "ובן אין לו" – עיין עליו, הא אילטריך לאיתויי ממזר, כדאמר בפ' שני דיבמות (דף כב: ושם ד"ה בן)! וי"ל: דשקולין, ויבאו שניהן. ואע"ג דבפ' "אלמנה לכ"ג" (שם דף ע.) גבי "וזרע אין (ג) לו" דבת כהן שניסת לישראל, משמע דלא דרשינן מיניה תרתי, דקאמר: אין לי אלא זרעה, זרע זרעה מנין – ת"ל "וזרע אין לה", מ"מ. אין לי אלא זרע כשר, זרע פסול מנין – ת"ל "וזרע אין לה", מ"מ. ופריך: והא אפיקתי' לזרע זרעה! היינו משום דקמרבי התם זרע פסול – היינו זרע זרעה פסול. דאילו זרע פסול – תיפוק ליה דנבעלה לפסול לה. ולהכי פריך שפיר, דאי אילטריך קרא לזרע זרעה כשר – היכי תו יליף זרע זרעה פסול? אי נמי, יש לרבות בת שפוטרת מן היבום מ"לא ימחה" – פרט לזה שאין שמו מחוי. דכי האי גוונא דריש ביבמות (כד.). אבל ממזר אילטריך ריבוי, משום דבזרע פסול אכתי הוי שמו מחוי. וא"ת: הא דתניא בפ"ק דקידושין (דף יז:): עבד עברי עובד את הבן ואינו עובד את הבת. ואמאי? נימא: מדלענין יבום בן ובת כי הדדי נינהו – הכי נמי לענין עבד עברי, כדאמרינן הכא לענין נחלה. ומדכתיב "ועבדך שש שנים" דמשמע: לך ולא ליורש – לא נמעט אלא את דוקא! ואור"י: משום דדרשינן "ועבדך" – לך ולא לאחר, כל שהוא אחר לגבי בן. ובת נמי לגבי בן כאחר דמיא לענין נחלה, שהבן קודם לבת. וכה"ג אמרי' בפרק "אין מקדישין" (ערכין דף כה:) גבי שדה אחוזה, דבת אינה מעמדת שדה לאביה, משום דכי היכי דלגבי נחלה בת לגבי בן כאחר דמיא – לענין שדה אחוזה נמי כאחר דמיא.

במקום בת אתה מעביר נחלה מן האב. פריב"ס: מדלא כתיב "ונתתם" גבי בת כדכתיב בכולהו. ד"והעברתם" משמע לשון העברה, שמעבירין נחלה ממקום הראוי לירש מן הדין, למקום שאינו ראוי. והשתא נושא ונותן מי הוא הקרוב שהיה ראוי להקריבו לבת, ומוקי לה באב, לפי שהמת יוצא ירכו ואין לך קרוב יותר ראוי ממנו. ובדידיה מיסתבר לאוקומי, אפי' שלא נכתב בפירוש אלא ע"י אחי האב, דממילא "והעברתם" עליה קאי, לדרוש ולקבוע בו מקום. ואע"ג דאי לא כתיב "והעברתם" לא הייתי אומר שהאב קרוב אפי' מן האח, שאינו קם תחת הבן לכלום, מיהו השתא דכתיב "והעברתם" בבת – משמע שמעבירים הנחלה ממקום הראוי – מוקי לה באב.

*(רש"ל הד"א) **ואי** אתה מעביר נחלה (ד) ממקום האב במקום האחין. כלומר, מדלא כתיב אלא "והעברתם" אחד – אין לנו לעשות אלא העברה אחת ולא שתים, ומכאן ואילך הקרוב קרוב קודם. דהשתא דכתיב "והעברתם" – משמע שהיה האב ראוי לקדום לבת – כ"ש שראוי לקדום לאח, שהבת קרובה מן האח, שהיא יוצאת ירכו של מת. ועוד, דאין יבום במקום בת. לפיכך אין להעביר נחלה מן האב אלא במקום בת לחודה, כיון דכתיב בבת העברה, ולא במקום אחין.

ואימא

רבינו גרשום

דהכא גבי בן איכא תרי מילי שכן קם תחת אביו ליעדה ולשדה אחוזה משום הכי דין הוא דמרבינן ליה: והכא. גבי האח ליכא אלא חדא שכן קם תחת אחיו לייבום ולא איצטריך ליה לתרוצי כלום יש ייבום: ומשני גבי בן נמי ליכא אלא חדא דהיינו יעידה דשדה אחוזה גופה מהאי פירכא הוא דקיימא ליה לתנא. כלומר מכח קושיא זו דקא מקשינן ליה כלום יש ייבום אלא במקום שאין בן מעמיד שדה אחוזה שקם בן תחת אביו ולא אח וכדאמרינן נמי כי האי גוונא במסכת ערכין דמקשי' להיכא דמוקים שדה אחוזה בידא דבן ומפיק ליה מידא דאח מה ראית לרבות את הבן ולהוציא את האח מרבה אני את הבן שכן קם תחת אביו ליעדה ולעבד עברי כדאמרינן במסכת קדושין עבד עברי עובד את הבן ואינו עובד את האח ומפיק לה התם מדרשא דקרא אדרבה מרבה אני את האח שקם תחת אחיו לייבום כלום יש ייבום אלא במקום שאין בן הא יש בן אין ייבום ותיפוק ליה דהכא תרי והכא חדא משום דעבד עברי מהא פירכא הוא דנפיק מכלום יש יבום אלא במקום כו' וכי האי גוונא מקשי' ומפקי' במס' קידושין בעבד עברי ועיקר תירוץ מלתייהו ליכא אלא מדמתרצי כלום יש ייבום אלא במקום שאין בן ואמטול הכי לא חשיב גבי בן אלא חדא דהיינו יעידה ושדה אחוזה לא מצינן לאוקמה בידא דבן אלא משום דקא מתרץ ליה הכי: ומקשי' ואמאי חזית דמוקמת שארו זה האב של מת קודם לאחי של מת וכדמהפכת קרא ואימא שארו זה האב וכדמוקמת הכי מצינו לאוקמי מלמד שהאב קודם לבת דמהפכי לקרא הכי ואיש כי ימות ושאר אין לו ונתתם את נחלתו לבתו הא שאר יש לו ונתתם את נחלתו לו ואוקמי' לקרא כי היכי דמקדמי' אביו של מת לאחין של מת ה"נ מקדמי' האב של מת לבתו של מת הואיל דלא כתבו כסדרן ויכול יהא קודם לבן של מת דאמרינן בהאי כדאמרי' באידך ואמר ליה דאמר קרא הקרוב דכל הקרוב קודם והבן קרוב למת מאביו של מת ואביו של מת מבת ומאחיו. ומשני הא ליכא למימר דמקדמינן אב של מת מקמי בתו של מת משום דכיון דלענין ייבום בן ובת כי הדדי נינהו דכי היכי דהיכא דאית לה בן אינה זקוקה לייבום ה"נ אם אית לה בת אינה זקוקה לייבום ולענין נחלה נמי בן ובת כי הדדי נינהו דלא מקדמי' אב מקמי בת כי היכי דלא מקדמי גבי בן: והשתא דדרשת שארו זה האב ובעית לאקדומי מקמי אחין של מת ואימא לעולם אחין של מת קודמין לאב והאי דאוקמת שארו זה האב להכי ללמד שהוא קודם לאחין שלו של אב עצמו והכי מוקמי' לקראי ואם אין לו בת ונתתם את נחלתו לאחיו ואם אין לו אחים למת ונתתם את נחלתו לשארו דהיינו אביו של מת ואם אין לו שאר ונתתם את נחלתו לאחיו של אביו ואם אין אחים לאביו ונתתם את נחלתו לקרוב אליו וגו' יכול יהא קודם האב לאחיו של מת ת"ל הקרוב לו ואחיו קרוב טפי מאביו שקם תחתיו לייבום. והיכי מצינן לאוקמי ולהקדים אביו לאחיו דמאי חזית דמהפכת לקראי הכי אפכינהו הכי. ומשני משום אחי האב לא צריך קרא למעוטינהו במקום אב דודאי דאב קדים דהיכי שבקי' אב ולירש אחי אב דאתיין מכח אב אלא ודאי למאי אתא קרא לאקדומי לאחין של מת. והא קראי לאו הכי כתיבי דמקדמי' אביו של מת מקמי שאר קרובים דשארו אחר כולהו קרובים כתיב. ומשני קראי שלא כסידרן כתיבי והכי צריכי למיכתבינהו כדמוקמינא להו לעיל: והאי תנא. דאמרינן לקמן: מייתי לה. דאביו של מת קודם לאחיו של מת: מהכא דתניא את זו דרש ר' ישמעאל בר' יוסי. מוהעברתם דקא משני הכתוב [לכתוב והעברתם] בבת להכי דבמקום שיש בת אתה מעביר נחלה מן האב של מת ואי אתה מעביר נחלה וכו' ומקשי' מאי חזית דאמרת הכי אימא לצד אחר הכי במקום בת אתה מעביר נחלה מן אחיו של מת

ואי

ו א ב מיי' פ"א מהל' נחלות הלכה ג סמג עשין צו טוש"ע ח"מ סימן רעו סעיף א:

הגהות הב"ח

(א) גמ' ואימא שארו: (ב) רשב"ם ד"ה אימא דהאי והעברת וכו' מקמי אח הס"ד ואחר כך מ"ה אם כן לגלויי וכו' שלא כסדרן כתיבי ואי משום דדייקינן וכו' במקום הבת והאי דקאמר ואי אתה מעביר נחלה מן האב אפילו במקום בת הך לא משתמעא מקרא מידי אלא ה"ק מהאי וכו' דלא מיירי קרא באב אלא באחין אבל לעולם אימא לך דאב כנ"ל והד"א: (ג) תוס' ד"ה כיון וכו' גבי וזרע אין לה דבת וכו' היינו משום דמאי דקא מרבינן התם זרע פסול היינו זרע זרעה: (ד) ד"ה ואי אתה מעביר נחלה מן האב:

ז א מיי' פ"א מהל' נחלות הלכה ו סמג שם טור ש"ע ח"מ סימן רעו ס"ל:
ח ב מיי' פכ"א מהל' איסורי ביאה הל' לב סמג לאוין קכו טוש"ע אה"ע סימן ב סעיף ו:

וְאִי אַתָּה מַעֲבִיר נַחֲלָה מִן הָאָב אֲפִילּוּ בִּמְקוֹם בַּת! אִם כֵּן, לֹא נִכְתּוֹב רַחֲמָנָא "וְהַעֲבַרְתֶּם"! וּלְמַאן דְּנָפְקָא לֵיהּ מִ"וְהַעֲבַרְתֶּם", הַאי "שְׁאֵרוֹ" מַאי עָבֵיד לֵיהּ? מִיבָּעֵי לֵיהּ לְכִדְתַנְיָא: א)"שְׁאֵרוֹ" — זוֹ אִשְׁתּוֹ, מְלַמֵּד שֶׁהַבַּעַל יוֹרֵשׁ אֶת אִשְׁתּוֹ. וּלְמַאן דְּנָפְקָא לֵיהּ מִ"שְּׁאֵרוֹ", הַאי "וְהַעֲבַרְתֶּם" מַאי עָבֵיד לֵיהּ? מִיבָּעֵי לֵיהּ לְכִדְתַנְיָא, ב)רַבִּי אוֹמֵר: בְּכוּלָּן נֶאֱמַר בָּהֶן נְתִינָה, וְכָאן נֶאֶמְרָה בָּהֶן הַעֲבָרָה — שֶׁאֵין לְךָ שֶׁמַּעֲבִיר נַחֲלָה מִשֵּׁבֶט לְשֵׁבֶט אֶלָּא בַּת, הוֹאִיל וּבְנָהּ וּבַעְלָהּ יוֹרְשִׁין אוֹתָהּ. וּמִמַּאי דִּ"שְׁאֵרוֹ" זֶה הָאָב? דִּכְתִיב: °"שְׁאֵר אָבִיךָ הוּא" (ויקרא יח), אֵימָא: "שְׁאֵרוֹ" — זוֹ הָאֵם, דִּכְתִיב: °"שְׁאֵר אִמְּךָ הִיא" (שם)! אָמַר רָבָא, אָמַר קְרָא: °"מִמִּשְׁפַּחְתּוֹ וְיָרַשׁ אוֹתָהּ" (במדבר כז) — ג)מִשְׁפַּחַת אָב קְרוּיָה מִשְׁפָּחָה, אמִשְׁפַּחַת אֵם אֵינָהּ קְרוּיָה מִשְׁפָּחָה, דִּכְתִיב: °"לְמִשְׁפְּחוֹתָם לְבֵית אֲבוֹתָם" (שם א). ימִשְׁפַּחַת אֵם אֵינָהּ קְרוּיָה מִשְׁפָּחָה? וְהָא כְּתִיב: °"וַיְהִי נַעַר מִבֵּית לֶחֶם יְהוּדָה מִמִּשְׁפַּחַת יְהוּדָה וְהוּא לֵוִי וְהוּא גָר שָׁם" (שופטים יז); הָא גּוּפָא קַשְׁיָא, אָמַרְתְּ (א) "וְהוּא לֵוִי" — אַלְמָא מִלֵּוִי אָתֵי, "מִמִּשְׁפַּחַת יְהוּדָה" — אַלְמָא מִיהוּדָה אָתֵי; אֶלָּא לָאו דַּאֲבוּהּ מִלֵּוִי וְאִימֵּיהּ מִיהוּדָה, וְקָאָמַר: "מִמִּשְׁפַּחַת יְהוּדָה"! אָמַר רָבָא בַּר רַב חָנָן: לָא, גַּבְרָא דִּשְׁמֵיהּ לֵוִי. אִי הָכִי, הַיְינוּ דְּקָאָמַר מִיכָה: °"עַתָּה יָדַעְתִּי כִּי יֵיטִיב ה' לִי כִּי הָיָה לִי הַלֵּוִי לְכֹהֵן" (שם יז)? אִין, דְּאִיתְרְמִי לֵיהּ גַּבְרָא דִּשְׁמֵיהּ לֵוִי. וְכִי לֵוִי שְׁמוֹ? וַהֲלֹא יְהוֹנָתָן שְׁמוֹ, שֶׁנֶּאֱמַר: °"וִיהוֹנָתָן בֶּן גֵּרְשֹׁם בֶּן מְנַשֶּׁה הוּא וּבָנָיו הָיוּ כֹהֲנִים לְשֵׁבֶט הַדָּנִי" (שם יח)! (ב) אָמַר לֵיהּ: וְלִיטַעְמִיךְ, וְכִי בֶּן מְנַשֶּׁה הוּא? וַהֲלֹא בֶּן מֹשֶׁה הוּא, דִּכְתִיב: °"בְּנֵי מֹשֶׁה גֵּרְשֹׁם וֶאֱלִיעֶזֶר" (דה"א כג)! אֶלָּא, מִתּוֹךְ שֶׁעָשָׂה מַעֲשֵׂה מְנַשֶּׁה — תְּלָאוֹ הַכָּתוּב בִּמְנַשֶּׁה; הָכָא נַמִי, מִתּוֹךְ שֶׁעָשָׂה מַעֲשֵׂה כִּמְנַשֶּׁה דְּאָתֵי מִיהוּדָה — תְּלָאוֹ הַכָּתוּב בִּיהוּדָה. אָמַר רַבִּי יוֹחָנָן מִשּׁוּם רַבִּי שִׁמְעוֹן בֶּן יוֹחַי: מִכָּאן שֶׁתּוֹלִין אֶת הַקַּלְקָלָה בִּמְקוּלְקָל. רַבִּי יוֹסֵי בַּר חֲנִינָא אָמַר, מֵהָכָא: °"וְגַם הוּא טוֹב תֹּאַר מְאֹד וְאוֹתוֹ יָלְדָה אַחֲרֵי אַבְשָׁלוֹם" (מ"א א), וַהֲלֹא אֲדֹנִיָּה בֶּן חַגִּית וְאַבְשָׁלוֹם בֶּן מַעֲכָה! אֶלָּא, מִתּוֹךְ שֶׁעָשָׂה מַעֲשֵׂה אַבְשָׁלוֹם דְּמָרַד בַּמַּלְכוּת — תְּלָאוֹ הַכָּתוּב בְּאַבְשָׁלוֹם; (ה"נ, מִתּוֹךְ שֶׁעָשָׂה מַעֲשֵׂה מְנַשֶּׁה — תְּלָאוֹ הַכָּתוּב בִּמְנַשֶּׁה.) אָמַר רַבִּי אֶלְעָזָר: בלְעוֹלָם יִדָּבֵק אָדָם בְּטוֹבִים, שֶׁהֲרֵי מֹשֶׁה שֶׁנָּשָׂא בַּת יִתְרוֹ — יָצָא מִמֶּנּוּ יְהוֹנָתָן, אַהֲרֹן שֶׁנָּשָׂא בַּת עַמִּינָדָב — יָצָא מִמֶּנּוּ פִּנְחָס. וּפִנְחָס לָאו מִיִּתְרוֹ אָתֵי? וְהָא כְּתִיב: °"וְאֶלְעָזָר בֶּן אַהֲרֹן לָקַח לוֹ מִבְּנוֹת פּוּטִיאֵל לוֹ לְאִשָּׁה" (שמות ו), מַאי לָאו (ג) דְּאָתֵי מִיִּתְרוֹ שֶׁפִּיטֵּם עֲגָלִים לַעֲ"ז? לָא, דְּאָתֵי מִיּוֹסֵף שֶׁפִּטְפֵּט בְּיִצְרוֹ. וַהֲלֹא ד)שְׁבָטִים מְבַזִּים אוֹתוֹ וְאוֹמְרִים: רְאִיתֶם בֶּן פּוּטִי זֶה, בֶּן שֶׁפִּיטֵּם אֲבִי אִמּוֹ עֲגָלִים לַעֲ"ז, יַהֲרוֹג נְשִׂיא שֵׁבֶט מִיִּשְׂרָאֵל?! אֶלָּא

ואימא במקום בת אתה מעביר נחלה מן האחין ואי אתה כו'. כלומר, השתא דמשמע לך מ"והעברתם" אתא לקבוע מקום לאב — אדרשנו כך שאפילו לבת יקדום. וה"ה דהוה מצי למימר דבמקום בת אתה מעביר נחלה מן האחין, אבל אי אתה מעביר מן האחין במקום אב, ונימא שאח יקדום לאב. אלא לפי משמעות הברייתא, דאב חשוב יותר מכולם, נקיט. **א"כ** לא לכתוב רחמנא "והעברתם" — כלומר, לא תוכל לדרוש: במקום בת אתה מעביר נחלה מן האחין — דאין זו העברה, שהבת קרובה למת יותר מאח, לפי שהיא יוצאת ירכו. ולענין יבום לא הוה ליה למכתב. אלא על כרחך יש לדרוש: במקום בת אתה מעביר נחלה כו'. אנא ק"ק: דהשתא משמע דלא שייך העברה מאחין לבת, דפשיטא דקרובה יותר מאחין, אבל מן האב ובת ניחא ליה דשייך העברה. ובכולה שמעתין מספקא לן אי אב קרוב טפי מאח או לא! ולרשב"א נראה לפרש: א"כ לא ליכתוב רחמנא "והעברתם", כלומר, אי לא אתי למדרש אלא דבמקום בת (אי) אתה מעביר נחלה מן האחין ולא מן האב — א"כ לא הוה ליה למכתב "והעברתם" אלא "ונתתם", והוה ידעינן דבת אינה יורשת במקום אב, דהוה דרשינן מיתורא ד"ונתתם את נחלתו לבתו" — דוקא מן האחין אתה מעביר נחלה במקום בת, ולא מן האב. דהא לגופה לא איצטריך, שהרי מ"וכל בת יורשת נחלה" שמעינן דבת ירושה היא, וממילא ידעינן שהיא קודמת לאח, שהרי היא קרובה יותר, שהיא מקימה שם, ולא אינו מקים שם אלא צריך ליבם. ואי להקדים בן לבת — הא מ"והתנחלתם אותם לבניכם" נפקא לן לקמן. ומדכתי' "והעברתם" אתא למימר דבמקום בת אתה מעביר נחלה מן האב.
אלא

ואי אתה מעביר נחלה מן האב אפי' במקום בת. הָךְ לָאו דַּוְקָא מִקְּרָא: מֵהַאי קְרָא לָא תֵּילַף דְּבַת קוֹדֶמֶת לָאָב, דְּלָא מַיְירֵי קְרָא בְּאָב אֶלָּא בְּאַחִיו. אֶלָּא לְעוֹלָם אֵימָא לָךְ דְּאָב קוֹדֵם לְבַת, דְּהוּא קָרוֹב טְפֵי. **שְׁאֵרוֹ זוֹ אִשְׁתּוֹ.** כִּדְכְתִיב: "וְהָיוּ לְבָשָׂר אֶחָד" (בראשית ב), וְכָתַב נַמִי: "שְׁאֵרָהּ כְּסוּתָהּ וְעוֹנָתָהּ לֹא יִגְרָע" (שמות כא). **יוֹרֵשׁ אֶת אִשְׁתּוֹ.** דְּקָסָבַר: גּוֹרְעִין וּמוֹסִיפִין וְדוֹרְשִׁין, וּקְרֵי הָכִי: וּנְתַתֶּם אֶת נַחֲלַת שְׁאֵרוֹ לוֹ. וְהָכִי מְפָרְשִׁינַן לָהּ לְקַמָּן בְּפִירְקִין, וְיָלֵיף לָהּ מִ"וְיָרַשׁ אוֹתָהּ" לְשׁוֹן נְקֵבָה. **הַאי וְהַעֲבַרְתֶּם מַאי עָבֵיד לֵיהּ.** לִכְתּוֹב "וּנְתַתֶּם"! **מִשֵּׁבֶט לְשֵׁבֶט.** נַחֲלַת שֵׁבֶט רְאוּבֵן לְשֵׁבֶט שִׁמְעוֹן. **הוֹאִיל וּבְנָהּ וּבַעְלָהּ יוֹרְשִׁין אוֹתָהּ.** כְּגוֹן סֶרַח בַּת אָשֵׁר שֶׁנְּשׂוּאָה לַחֲנוֹךְ בֶּן רְאוּבֵן, וּמֵת אָשֵׁר בְּלֹא בָּנִים זְכָרִים, וִירֵשַׁתּוּ סֶרַח בִּתּוֹ. וּמֵתָה סֶרַח, וִירָשָׁהּ בְּנָהּ אוֹ בַּעְלָהּ שֶׁהֵם מִשֵּׁבֶט רְאוּבֵן — נִמְצָא שֶׁהוּסְּבָה נַחֲלַת שֵׁבֶט אָשֵׁר לְשֵׁבֶט רְאוּבֵן. וְאַשְׁמְעִינַן קְרָא שֶׁהַבַּעַל אוֹ הַבֵּן יוֹרֵשׁ אֶת אִשְׁתּוֹ וְאֶת אִמּוֹ. וְאִיכָּא דְּדָרֵישׁ לְקַמָּן יְרוּשַּׁת הַבֵּן אֶת אִמּוֹ מִקְּרָא אַחֲרִינָא, וְרַבִּי דָּרֵישׁ לָהּ מֵהָכָא. **אֵימָא שְׁאֵרוֹ זוֹ הָאֵם.** וְנֵילַף מִכָּאן דְּבֵין אָבִיו בֵּין אִמּוֹ יוֹרְשִׁין אוֹתוֹ. **מִמִּשְׁפַּחְתּוֹ.** הַיְינוּ הַקְּרוֹבִים לוֹ מִצַּד אָבִיו. **וַיְהִי נַעַר וגו'.** בְּסֵפֶר שׁוֹפְטִים כְּתִיב, בְּפָרָשַׁת פִּסְלוֹ שֶׁל מִיכָה. וְקָא מְתַמַּהּ גְּמָרָא: מִמִּשְׁפַּחַת יְהוּדָה. אַלְמָא מִיהוּדָה קָאָתֵי, וּכְתִיב "וְהוּא לֵוִי" אַלְמָא מִלֵּוִי קָאָתֵי. קַשְׁיָין אַהֲדָדֵי. **אֶלָּא לָאו דַּאֲבוּהּ מִלֵּוִי.** לְהָכִי קָרוּ לֵיהּ "לֵוִי", שֶׁהַלְוִיִּם לְמַטֵּה אֲבוֹתָם נִקְרָאִים לְוִיִּם. וְהַאי דְּקָאָמַר "מִמִּשְׁפַּחַת יְהוּדָה" — עַל שֵׁם שֶׁאִמּוֹ מִשֵּׁבֶט יְהוּדָה. וּמְשַׁנֵּי: **לָא גַּבְרָא דִּשְׁמֵיהּ לֵוִי.** הַאי דִּכְתִיב "וְהוּא לֵוִי" — כְּלוֹמַר, כָּךְ שְׁמוֹ. וְלֹא מִשֵּׁבֶט לֵוִי הוּא, אֶלָּא מִשֵּׁבֶט יְהוּדָה, כִּדְכְתִיב "מִמִּשְׁפַּחַת יְהוּדָה", דְּמִשְׁפַּחַת אָב קְרוּיָה מִשְׁפָּחָה. **הַיְינוּ דְּקָאָמַר מִיכָה כו'.** בִּתְמִיָּה. שֶׁהָיָה מִתְגָּאֶה בְּעַצְמוֹ עַל שֶׁנִּזְדַּמֵּן לוֹ אִישׁ לֵוִי לְכֹהֵן לַעֲ"ז, וְאִי מִשֵּׁבֶט יְהוּדָה הוּא — מִמָּה הָיָה מִשְׁתַּבֵּחַ לְעַצְמוֹ? אֶלָּא וַדַּאי מִשּׁוּם דְּמִשֵּׁבֶט לֵוִי הוּא, שֶׁבָּהֶם בָּחַר הַקָּדוֹשׁ בָּרוּךְ הוּא לְשָׁרְתוֹ. וּלְעוֹלָם אֲבוּהּ מִלֵּוִי וְאִימֵּיהּ מִיהוּדָה, וְהָדְרָא קוּשְׁיָין לְדוּכְתָּהּ. וּמְשַׁנֵּי: **דְּאִתְרְמֵי לֵיהּ גַּבְרָא שֶׁשְּׁמֵיהּ לֵוִי.** בְּכָךְ הָיָה מִשְׁתַּבֵּחַ, כְּאִילּוּ הֲוָה מִשֵּׁבֶט לֵוִי. וּלְעוֹלָם לָאו לֵוִי הוּא, אֶלָּא מִשֵּׁבֶט יְהוּדָה. **וַהֲלֹא יוֹנָתָן שְׁמוֹ.** בְּעַל כָּרְחָךְ הַאי דְּקָרֵי לֵיהּ לֵוִי — הַיְינוּ דְּמִשֵּׁבֶט לֵוִי הֲוֵי, וְקָרֵי לֵיהּ "מִשְׁפַּחַת יְהוּדָה". אַלְמָא מִשְׁפַּחַת הָאֵם קְרוּיָה מִשְׁפָּחָה. **בֶּן מְנַשֶּׁה.** הַנּוּ"ן תְּלוּיָה, לְפִי שֶׁהִיא יְתֵירָה, דְּבֶן מֹשֶׁה (ד) הוּא. "וִיהוֹנָתָן בֶּן גֵּרְשֹׁם" כו' בְּהַהִיא פָּרָשָׁתָא כְּתִיב, בְּגָלוּ שֵׁבֶט הַדָּנִי פִּסְלוֹ שֶׁל מִיכָה, וְהַלֵּוִי הָלַךְ עִמָּהֶם לִהְיוֹת לָהֶם לְכֹהֵן. וּמְשַׁנֵּי: **וְכִי בֶּן מְנַשֶּׁה הוּא? וַהֲלֹא בֶּן מֹשֶׁה הוּא** — דִּלְכָךְ הַנּוּ"ן תְּלוּיָה. וְגַם מִדְּקָרֵי לֵיהּ לֵוִי, שֶׁהָיָה מִשֵּׁבֶט לֵוִי, וּכְדִכְתִיב בְּדִבְרֵי הַיָּמִים: "בְּנֵי מֹשֶׁה גֵּרְשׁוֹם וֶאֱלִיעֶזֶר". **אֶלָּא מִתּוֹךְ שֶׁעָשָׂה מַעֲשֵׂה מְנַשֶּׁה.** בֶּן חִזְקִיָּה מֶלֶךְ יְהוּדָה, שֶׁעָבַד ע"ז — תְּלָאוֹ הַכָּתוּב בִּמְנַשֶּׁה. **הָכָא נַמִי,** לְעוֹלָם מִשֵּׁבֶט לֵוִי הוּא כִּדְקָאָמְרַתְּ, וְהַאי דְּקָרֵי לֵיהּ "מִמִּשְׁפַּחַת יְהוּדָה" — לָאו מִשּׁוּם דְּאָתֵי מִיהוּדָה, לֹא אָבִיו וְלֹא אִמּוֹ, אֶלָּא מִתּוֹךְ שֶׁעָשָׂה מַעֲשֵׂה מְנַשֶּׁה בֶּן חִזְקִיָּה כו'. **מִכָּאן.** מִדְּקָרֵי לֵיהּ בֶּן מְנַשֶּׁה "מִמִּשְׁפַּחַת יְהוּדָה". **הַקַּלְקָלָה.** דְּהָךְ פָּרָשָׁתָא מַיְירֵי שֶׁנַּעֲשָׂה כֹּהֵן לַע"ז. **בִּמְקוּלְקָל.** מְנַשֶּׁה. **יָלְדָה אַחֲרֵי אַבְשָׁלוֹם.** מַשְׁמַע שֶׁמֵּאֵם אַחַת הָיוּ. **וַהֲלֹא אֲדֹנִיָּה.** הָיָה בֶּן חַגִּית. **יָצָא מִמֶּנּוּ יְהוֹנָתָן.** בֶּן בְּנוֹ שֶׁל מֹשֶׁה. **פִּנְחָס.** בֶּן בְּנוֹ שֶׁל אַהֲרֹן. וּמַתְמְהִינַן: **פִּנְחָס וַהֲלֹא מִיִּתְרוֹ קָאָתֵי.** מִבַּת יִתְרוֹ, אַלְמָא קָרוֹב הָיָה לְיִתְרוֹ יוֹתֵר מִיהוֹנָתָן בֶּן גֵּרְשׁוֹם, וַאֲפִי' הָכִי חָסִיד הָיָה. וְאֵין לִלְמוֹד מִכָּאן שֶׁיִּדָּבֵק אָדָם בְּטוֹבִים, שֶׁהֲרֵי אֶלְעָזָר אֲבִי פִּנְחָס לָקַח בַּת יִתְרוֹ וְיָצָא מִמֶּנָּה פִּנְחָס, וְאִם אַהֲרֹן דָּבַק בְּטוֹבִים — אֶלְעָזָר בְּנוֹ לֹא דָּבַק בְּטוֹבִים! **מַאי לָאו.** מִבְּנוֹת יִתְרוֹ כו', כְּלוֹמַר בַּת יִתְרוֹ מַמָּשׁ, אַחַת מִבְּנוֹתָיו. **מִבְּנוֹת יוֹסֵף.** כְּלוֹמַר, מִשֵּׁבֶט יוֹסֵף. **שֶׁפִּטְפֵּט.** מַתְרִים וְנִלְחָם כְּנֶגֶד יִצְרוֹ, כִּדְאָמְרִי' לְקַמָּן בְּפִירְקִין (דף קטו:): חוּץ מִזָּקֵן אֶחָד שֶׁהָיָה מְפַטְפֵּט כְּנֶגְדּוֹ. וּפָרְכִינַן: **וַהֲלֹא שְׁבָטִים מְבַזִּין אוֹתוֹ כו'.** בְּסַנְהֶדְרִין בְּפֶרֶק "אֵלּוּ הֵן הַנִּשְׂרָפִין": הִתְחִילוּ שְׁבָטִים מְבַזִּין אוֹתוֹ כו'. **שֶׁפִּיטֵּם.** כִּדְכְתִיב: "כֹּהֵן אוֹן" (בראשית מא) — כּוֹמֶר.
אֶלָּא

רבינו גרשום

ואי אתה מעביר נחלה מן האב אפי' במקום בת. שהאב קודם לבתו. ומשני אם כן לא לכתוב רחמנא והעברתם אלא ונתתם את נחלתו לבתו כדכתב באינך. אלא מדשני רחמנא וכתב והעברתם משמע דאפי' במקום אב דהוא קדים לאחין צריך להעביר נחלה מן האב וליתנה לבת: ולמאן דנפקא ליה מוהעברתם. דמקדמי' אב לאחין האי לשארו מאי עביד ליה: שארו זו אשתו. דגורעין ומוסיפין ודורשין לו כלומר א) דהכי' נחלת שארו לו. וירש אותה דגורעין ו' מנחלתו ול' מלשארו ומצרפין אהדדי ודורשין לו כלומר דיהבין נחלת שארו דהיינו אשתו לו: בכולן. של קרובים נאמר בהן נתינה וגבי בת כתיב העברה לומר לך ב) מי שמעביר נחלה משבט לשבט אלא הבת שהוא משבט ראובן והיו לה אחין הראויין לירש את אביה ונשאת לאחר משבט שמעון ולאחר שנשאת מת אחיה ולא היה להן יורש אלא זו ועכשיו מעברת משבט לשבט הואיל שכשמתה בנה או בעלה שהן משבט שמעון יורשין אותה: וממאי דהאי שארו אב הוא. דמצית למדרש מיניה מלמד שהאב קודם לאחין משום דאב איקרי שאר דכתיב שאר אביך הוא דלמא שאר זו האם דכתיב שאר אמך היא ואימא שהאם קודמת לאחין של מת. ומאי חזית דאמרת הכי אימא הכי ואכתי שהאב קודם לאחין מנא לך. אמר רבא לא מצית למימר שהאם קודמת לאחין ולא האב משום דבתר האב אזלינן דאמר קרא ממשפחתו של אב ולא ממשפחתה של אם וירש אותה נחלה ומשפחת אב קרויה משפחה דכתיב ויתילדו על משפחותם לבית אבותם ולעולם אב של מת קודם לאחיו של מת: וקרו לה משפחה. אלמא דמשפחת אם קרויה משפחה: כי היה לי הלוי לכהן. ואי שמיה לוי מאי הטבה איכא אלא משום דמשבט לוי הוה דיצאו ממנו כהנים להכי קאמ' כי ייטיב דאית ביה צד כהונה. ומשני לא לעולם לוי שמו ומשבט יהודה היה ומשום דשמו היה לוי ג): לשבט הדני. היינו מיכה: מעשה מנשה. ששימש לע"ז תלאו הכתוב ביהודה ולעולם משבט לוי הוה ולעולם משפחת אם אינה קרויה משפחה: ואותו ילדה אחרי אבשלום. משמע דבני אם אחת היו והלא אדוניה בן חגית וכו': שפטפט ביצרו. שכבשו: דיקא

א) [לקמן קיא:] ב) שם קמז: ג) [שם קיז: יבמות נד:] ד) סנהדרין פב: [וסוטה מג.]

הגהות הב"ח

(א) גמ' הא גופא קשיא אמרת ממשפחת יהודה אלמא מיהודה אתי והוא לוי אלמא מלוי אתי אלא לאו דאבוה: (ב) שם כהנים לשבט הדני וכי בן מנשה כו"ל ותיבות א"ל וליטעמיך נמחק: (ג) שם מאי לאו מבנות יתרו שפיטם עגלים לע"ז לא מבנות יוסף שפטפט: (ד) רשב"ם ד"ה בן מנשה וכו' בן משה היה הס"ד:

א) אולי צ"ל ונתתם נחלת וכו'. ב) צ"ל לומר לך שאין לך מי שמעביר. ג) אולי צ"ל ובשום דשמו היה לוי לפיכך קאמר והוא לוי.

אֶלָּא, אִי אֲבוּהָ דְּאִמֵּיהּ מִיּוֹסֵף — אִמָּהּ דְּאִמֵּיהּ מִיִּתְרוֹ, אִי אֲבוּהָ דְּאִמֵּיהּ מִיִּתְרוֹ — אִמָּהּ דְּאִמֵּיהּ מִיּוֹסֵף. דַּיְקָא נַמִי, דִּכְתִיב: "מִבְּנוֹת פּוּטִיאֵל", תַּרְתֵּי, שְׁמַע מִינַּהּ. אָמַר רָבָא: הַנּוֹשֵׂא אִשָּׁה צָרִיךְ שֶׁיִּבְדּוֹק בְּאַחֶיהָ, שֶׁנֶּאֱמַר: °"וַיִּקַּח אַהֲרֹן אֶת אֱלִישֶׁבַע בַּת עַמִּינָדָב אֲחוֹת נַחְשׁוֹן", מִמַּשְׁמַע שֶׁנֶּאֱמַר "בַּת עַמִּינָדָב", אֵינִי יוֹדֵעַ שֶׁאֲחוֹת נַחְשׁוֹן הִיא? מַה תַּלְמוּד לוֹמַר "אֲחוֹת נַחְשׁוֹן"? מִכָּאן, שֶׁהַנּוֹשֵׂא אִשָּׁה צָרִיךְ שֶׁיִּבְדּוֹק בְּאַחֶיהָ. תָּנָא: [א]רוֹב בָּנִים דּוֹמִין לַאֲחֵי הָאֵם. °"וַיָּסוּרוּ [ב](שָׁמָּה וַיֹּאמֶר) מִי הֱבִיאֲךָ הֲלֹם וּמָה אַתָּה עוֹשֶׂה בָּזֶה וּמַה לְּךָ פֹה", אָמְרוּ לוֹ: לָאו מִמֹּשֶׁה קָא אָתֵית, דִּכְתִיב בֵּיהּ: °"אַל תִּקְרַב הֲלֹם"? לָאו מִמֹּשֶׁה קָא אָתֵית דִּכְתִיב בֵּיהּ: °"מַה זֶּה בְיָדֶךָ"? לָאו מִמֹּשֶׁה קָא אָתֵית דִּכְתִיב בֵּיהּ: °"וְאַתָּה פֹּה עֲמֹד עִמָּדִי"? תֵּעָשֶׂה כֹּהֵן לַעֲ"ז?! אָמַר לָהֶן, כָּךְ מְקוּבְּלַנִי מִבֵּית אֲבִי אַבָּא: [א]לְעוֹלָם יַשְׂכִּיר אָדָם עַצְמוֹ לַעֲ"ז וְאַל יִצְטָרֵךְ לַבְּרִיּוֹת. וְהוּא סָבַר: לַעֲ"ז מַמָּשׁ; וְלָא הִיא, [ב]אֶלָּא ע"ז — עֲבוֹדָה שֶׁזָּרָה לוֹ, [ג]כְּדַאֲמַר לֵיהּ רַב לְרַב כָּהֲנָא: [ד)ג]נְטוֹשׁ נְבֵילְתָא בְּשׁוּקָא וּשְׁקוֹל אַגְרָא, וְלָא תֵּימָא: גַּבְרָא רַבָּא אֲנָא וְזִילָא בִּי מִילְּתָא. כֵּיוָן שֶׁרָאָה דָּוִד שֶׁמָּמוֹן חָבִיב עָלָיו בְּיוֹתֵר, מִינָּהוּ עַל הָאוֹצָרוֹת, שֶׁנֶּאֱמַר: °"וּשְׁבוּאֵל בֶּן גֵּרְשׁוֹם בֶּן [ה)]מְנַשֶּׁה נָגִיד עַל הָאוֹצָרוֹת". וְכִי שְׁבוּאֵל שְׁמוֹ? וַהֲלֹא יְהוֹנָתָן שְׁמוֹ! א"ר יוֹחָנָן: שֶׁשָּׁב לָאֵל בְּכָל לִבּוֹ.§ "וְהַבָּנִים אֶת הָאָב".§ מְנָלַן? דִּכְתִיב: °"אִישׁ כִּי יָמוּת" וגו', טַעְמָא דְּאֵין לוֹ בֵּן, הָא יֵשׁ לוֹ בֵּן — בֵּן קוֹדֵם. אֲמַר לֵיהּ רַב פַּפָּא לְאַבַּיֵי, אֵימָא: אִי אִיכָּא בֵּן — לֵירוֹת בֵּן, אִיכָּא בַּת — תֵּירוֹת בַּת, אִיכָּא בֵּן וּבַת — לָא הַאי לֵירוֹת וְלָא הַאי לֵירוֹת! וְאֶלָּא

מַאן

תורה אור: שמות ו; שופטים יח; שמות ג; שם ד; דברים ה; דה"א כו; במדבר כז

רש"י

אֶלָּא אִי אֲבוּהּ דְּאִמֵּיהּ כו'. אֶלָּא לְעוֹלָם לָאו מִבַּת יִתְרוֹ מַמָּשׁ נוֹלַד פִּנְחָס, שֶׁהֲרֵי גַּם מִיּוֹסֵף הָיָה, כִּדְדָרְשִׁינַן לְקַמָּן: "פּוּטִיאֵל" – שְׁנֵי פִּיטְפּוּטִין מַשְׁמַע, מִיּוֹסֵף שֶׁפִּיטְפֵּט בְּיִצְרוֹ וּמִיִּתְרוֹ שֶׁפִּיטֵּם עֲגָלִים, וְהִלְכָּךְ אִי אֶפְשָׁר שֶׁתְּהֵא אִמּוֹ בַּת יִתְרוֹ מַמָּשׁ, דְּמָה עִנְיַן בַּת יִתְרוֹ אֵצֶל שֵׁבֶט יוֹסֵף? אֶלָּא ה"ק: וְאֶלְעָזָר לָקַח לוֹ אִשָּׁה מִבְּנוֹת פּוּטִיאֵל, כְּלוֹמַר שֶׁאִשְׁתּוֹ נוֹלְדָה מִיִּתְרוֹ וּמִיּוֹסֵף. וּמֵהַשְׁתָּא מָצִינַן לְמֵימַר שֶׁדּוֹר רְבִיעִי אוֹ דּוֹר חֲמִישִׁי הָיָה פִּנְחָס לְבַת יִתְרוֹ, וְלֹא הָיָה קָרוֹב לְיִתְרוֹ כִּיהוֹנָתָן בֶּן גֵּרְשֹׁם, וּלְהָכִי אַהֲנֵי מַה שֶּׁדָּבַק אַהֲרֹן בַּטּוֹבִים. וְאוֹתוֹ זְקֵינוֹ שֶׁל פִּנְחָס מִצַּד הָאֵם, שֶׁדָּבַק בְּיִתְרוֹ וְאעפ"כ יָצָא מִמֶּנּוּ פִּנְחָס – לֵיכָּא לְאַקְשׁוּיֵי מִינֵּיהּ לְמַאי דְּבָעֵינַן לְמֵילַף מִמֹּשֶׁה שֶׁיָּצָא מִמֶּנּוּ יְהוֹנָתָן, שֶׁהֲרֵי פִּנְחָס הָיָה רָחוֹק מִיִּתְרוֹ יוֹתֵר מִיהוֹנָתָן. **אֲבוּהּ דְּאִמֵּיהּ מִיּוֹסֵף.** וְאִמֵּיהּ דְּאִמֵּיהּ נָפְקָא מִיִּתְרוֹ – כְּגוֹן מִבָּנָיו שֶׁל יִתְרוֹ, אוֹ מִבְּנֵי בָנָיו. וְלֵיכָּא לְמֵימַר "אִמָּהּ דְּאִמֵּיהּ מִיִּתְרוֹ" – בַּת יִתְרוֹ מַמָּשׁ, דְּאִם כֵּן קָרוֹב הוּא לְיִתְרוֹ כִּיהוֹנָתָן, וְלָא יָלְפִינַן מִמֹּשֶׁה וּמֵאַהֲרֹן מִידֵּי. **אֲבוּהּ דְּאִמֵּיהּ מִיִּתְרוֹ.** מִבְּנוֹת יִתְרוֹ. *וְנִרְאֶה בְּעֵינַי דְּה"ג: אֶלָּא אִי אֲבוּהּ דְּאִמֵּיהּ מִיּוֹסֵף כו', וְאַמָּהּ שֶׁל אֵם פִּנְחָס קָאֵי. וְה"ק: אִי אֲבִי אִמָּהּ שֶׁל אֵשֶׁת אֶלְעָזָר מִיּוֹסֵף כו', דְּהַשְׁתָּא הֲוָה לֵיהּ לְפִנְחָס דּוֹר אֶחָד רָחוֹק מִיִּתְרוֹ יוֹתֵר מִיהוֹנָתָן. **פּוּטִיאֵל תַּרְתֵּי מַשְׁמַע.** מִדְּלָא כְּתַב "פּוּטְאֵל" בְּלֹא יו"ד, הִלְכָּךְ שְׁנֵי פִּיטּוּיִים דָּרְשִׁינַן: שֶׁפִּיטְפֵּט וְשֶׁפִּיטֵּם. אִי נַמִי מִדִּכְתִיב "מִבְּנוֹת" – דְּמַשְׁמַע מִשְּׁתֵּי בָּנוֹת שֶׁל פִּיטְפּוּט וּפִיטּוּם, מִדְּלָא כְּתִיב "בַּת פּוּטִיאֵל", כֵּן נִרְאֶה בְּעֵינַי. **שֶׁיִּבְדּוֹק בְּאַחֶיהָ.** שֶׁהַבָּנִים דּוֹמִין לַאֲחֵי הָאֵם, כִּדְלְקַמָּן. מְלַמֵּד שֶׁבָּדַק בְּאָחִיהָ. לְפִי שֶׁהָיְתָה אֲחוֹת נַחְשׁוֹן, שֶׁהָיָה נָשִׂיא לְמַטֵּה יְהוּדָה מִתּוֹךְ חֲשִׁיבוּתוֹ, לְכָךְ לְקָחָהּ. **וַיָּסוּרוּ שָׁם וגו'.** בִּיהוֹנָתָן בֶּן גֵּרְשֹׁם מַיְירֵי, בְּפָרָשַׁת מִיכָה. **וַיֹּאמְרוּ לוֹ.** שֵׁבֶט הַדָּנִי שֶׁבָּאוּ שָׁם. **יַשְׂכִּיר עַצְמוֹ כו'.** אֶלָּא שֶׁלֹּא יְהֵא לִבּוֹ לַעֲ"ז. **שֶׁהִיא זָרָה לוֹ.** הוּא חָשׁוּב וְהַמְּלָאכָה נִמְבְּזָה וּמְכוֹעֶרֶת, אֶלָּא שֶׁאֵין בָּהּ אִיסּוּר. **נְטוֹשׁ.** הַפְשֵׁט. **וְטוֹל אַגְרָא.** כְּלוֹמַר, הַפְשִׁיטֶנָּה בְּשָׂכָר, בַּשּׁוּק לְעֵין כֹּל, וְאֵין כָּאן חִילּוּל הַשֵּׁם כְּלָל. וְלָא קָרֵינָא בֵּיהּ: "וּמְשַׂנְאַי אָהֲבוּ מָוֶת", דְּדָרְשִׁינַן לֵיהּ בְּמַסֶּכֶת שַׁבָּת (דף קיד.) [א] בְּתַלְמִידֵי חֲכָמִים שֶׁיֵּשׁ רְבָב עַל בִּגְדוֹ, אֲבָל לַעֲשׂוֹת מְלָאכָה לְהִתְפַּרְנֵס – אֵין כָּאן גְּנַאי. ה"ג: **וְלָא תֵּימָא גַּבְרָא רַבָּא אֲנָא.** וְאִית [ב] דְּגָרְסִינַן נַמִי: "וְלָא תֵּימָא כָּהֲנָא אֲנָא" כֹּהֵן אֲנִי וְחָשׁוּב, וּגְנַאי לִי הַדָּבָר. **וַהֲלֹא יְהוֹנָתָן שְׁמוֹ.** שֶׁלֹּא הָיָה לוֹ לְגֵרְשֹׁם בָּנִים כִּי אִם זֶה בִּלְבַד, כִּדְכְתִיב בְּדִבְרֵי הַיָּמִים: "וּבְנֵי גֵרְשֹׁם שְׁבוּאֵל הָרֹאשׁ". **שֶׁשָּׁב לָאֵל בְּכָל לִבּוֹ.** עַכְשָׁיו, שֶׁהָיָה לוֹ מָמוֹן הַרְבֵּה. וְאִי מִשּׁוּם דִּכְתִיב: "וִיהוֹנָתָן בֶּן גֵּרְשֹׁם בֶּן מְנַשֶּׁה הוּא וּבָנָיו כֹּהֲנִים לְשֵׁבֶט הַדָּנִי עַד יוֹם גְּלוֹת הָאָרֶץ", וְאָמְרִינַן בְּסֵדֶר עוֹלָם: עַד יוֹם שֶׁגָּלָה מַטֵּה דָן וּפִסְלוֹ שֶׁל מִיכָה עִמּוֹ – כָּךְ מְפוֹרָשׁ בְּפֶרֶק בַּתְרָא דִּבְרָכוֹת יְרוּשַׁלְמִי: מְתִיבִין לֵיהּ: וְהָכְתִיב "עַד יוֹם גְּלוֹת הָאָרֶץ"! אָמְרֵי: כֵּיוָן שֶׁמֵּת דָּוִד עָמַד שְׁלֹמֹה, וְהֶחֱלִיף כָּל הַסַּנְקְלִיטִין, וְהֶחֱלִיפוּ עִמָּהֶן – חָזַר לְקִלְקוּלוֹ הָרִאשׁוֹן. הה"ד "וְנָבִיא אֶחָד זָקֵן יוֹשֵׁב בְּבֵית אֵל" אָמְרִין: הוּא הֲוָה. וְקָבְעֵי הָתָם: כֹּהֵן לַעֲ"ז וְהֶאֱרִיךְ יָמִים? אָמְרֵי: ע"י שֶׁהָיְתָה עֵינוֹ צָרָה בַּעֲ"ז שֶׁלּוֹ. כֵּיצַד? הֲוָה בַּר נָשׁ מַיְיתֵי לֵיהּ תּוֹר אוֹ אִימַּר אוֹ גְּדִי לַעֲ"ז, וַהֲוָה א"ל: פַּיְּיסֵיהּ עֲלָוֵי. וְהוּא אָמַר: מַה מוֹעִילָה לָךְ? לֹא אָכְלָה וְלֹא שׁוֹתָה לֹא מְטִיבָה וְלֹא מְרִיעָה. א"ל: וּמָה נַעֲבֵיד? א"ל: זִיל אַיְיתֵי לִי חֲדָא פִּינָךְ דְּסֹלֶת, וְעֶשֶׂר בֵּיעִין עֲלוֹי, וַאֲנָא מְפַיֵּיס לָהּ עֲלָךְ. וְכֵיוָן דְּאָזַל לֵיהּ – אָכִיל לוֹן. אֲתָא חַד בַּר פַּחִין, וַאֲמַר לֵיהּ כֵּן. אֲמַר לֵיהּ: אִם אֵינָהּ מוֹעִילָה כְּלוּם מָה אַתְּ עָבֵיד הָכָא? אֲמַר לֵיהּ: בְּגִין חַיֵּי. וְכֵיוָן שֶׁעָמַד דָּוִד כו'. **וְהַבָּנִים אֶת הָאָב מְנָלַן.** דְּהַבָּנִים קוֹדְמִים לַבָּנוֹת? מִדְּלָא קָתָנֵי "הַבָּנִים וְהַבָּנוֹת אֶת הָאָב". וּמִיהוּ, בָּנוֹת נוֹטְלוֹת עִישּׂוּר נְכָסִים כְּתַקָּנַת חֲכָמִים בְּמַסֶּ' כְּתוּבּוֹת (דף סח.). **דִּכְתִיב אִישׁ כִּי יָמוּת וּבֵן אֵין לוֹ וגו'.** וַהֲוָה לֵיהּ לְמִכְתַּב: "אִישׁ כִּי יָמוּת וּבֵן וּבַת אֵין לוֹ", אִי נַמִי: "אִישׁ כִּי יָמוּת וְהַעֲבַרְתֶּם אֶת נַחֲלָתוֹ לְבִתּוֹ וְלִבְנוֹ". **טַעְמָא דְּאֵין לוֹ בֵּן.** עִם הַבַּת, הָא יֵשׁ לוֹ בֵּן וּבַת – הַבֵּן קוֹדֵם. **א"ל רַב פַּפָּא לְאַבַּיֵי אֵימָא.** דְּהָכִי אַשְׁמוֹעִינַן קְרָא: אִיכָּא בֵּן בְּלֹא בַּת – לֵירוֹת בֵּן, אִיכָּא בַּת בְּלֹא בֵּן – תֵּירוֹת בַּת, אִיכָּא תַּרְוַיְיהוּ בֵּן וּבַת – לָא הַאי לֵירוֹת כו', כִּדְמְפָרֵשׁ לְקַמֵּיהּ: לָא הַאי לֵירוֹת כּוּלּוֹ וְלָא הַאי לֵירוֹת כּוּלּוֹ, אֶלָּא כְּאַחַת יִרְתּוּן. דְּה"ק קְרָא: אִישׁ כִּי יָמוּת וּבֵן אֵין לוֹ עִם הַבַּת שֶׁיִּירְשׁוּ שְׁנֵיהֶן כְּאַחַת, אֶלָּא בַּת יְחִידִית בְּלֹא בֵּן יֵשׁ לוֹ – וְהַעֲבַרְתֶּם אֶת הַנְּכָסִים לְבִתּוֹ. הָא אִיתְנְהוּ – תַּרְוַיְיהוּ יֵירְתוּן כְּאַחַת.

מַאן

תוספות

אלא אי אבוה דאמיה מיוסף אמה דאמיה מיתרו. וא"ת: א"כ היאך פנחס בן טובים טפי מיהונתן? שהרי אימיה דאמיה דפנחס מיתרו אתיא, כי היכי דאמיה דאבוה דיהונתן מיתרו אתיא! וי"ל: משום שיהונתן היה מצד האב, שהיה אביו בן בת יתרו, ופנחס מצד האם.

נשוט נבילתא גרסינן בערוך. והוי כמו "פשוט", כי ההיא ד"חלק" (סנהדרין דף ק:): לא תנטוש גילדנא מאוניה דלא ליזיל משכיה לחבלא. פירוש: דג ששמו גילדנא אל תתחיל לפשטו מאזנו, פן ילך העור לאיבוד. ואע"ג דהתם נטוש והכא נשוט — רוב פעמים מתחלפין האותיות בענין זה, כמו (פסחים דף ל:): אין טשין התנור באליה, דהוי כמו "אין שטין". כמו "וטח את הבית" ומתרגם בירושלמי: [ו]"וישוטון ית ביתא" (ויקרא יד). **ולא** תימא כהנא אנא. מפר"ת: ולא תימא אני רב כהנא שאני חשוב. ולא מפני שהיה כהן, דלאו כהן הוה, כדאמרינן ב"הזרוע" (חולין דף קלב. ושם ד"ה רב): רב כהנא הוה אכל בשביל אשתו. ובפ' "אלו עוברין" (פסחים דף מט. ושם) אמר רב כהנא: אי לאו דנסיבי כהנתא — לא גלאי. אמרו לו תלמידיו: והא למקום תורה גלית — אמר להו: לא גלאי כדגלו אינשי, שגלה ע"י דשמטיה לקועיה דההוא גברא. וכן מפר"ת ההיא ד"ערבי פסחים" (דף קיג. ושם): לא תדור במתא דרישא אסי. כלומר, שאתה בעצמך תהיה ראש, שסמך רב אסי, שלא תתבטל מחמת צרכי צבור. ולא כמו שפירש רבינו שמואל דרישא אסי — רופא.

ושבואל בן גרשם בן משה. ה"ג: משה. שאין לקרותו על שם מנשה, שהרי כבר שב בכל לבו. ויש דגרס "בן מנשה", וטעמא לפי שחזר לקלקולו, כדפ"ה.

טעמא דאין לו בן הא יש לו בן [בן] קודם. נראה לרשב"א דכל הסוגיא אליבא דמ"ד שלא כסדרן כתיבי. מדפריך רב פפא בתר הכי [ז](ולמ"ד כסדרן כתיבי ואימא אי איכא בן) למה יש לנו לשנות קראי מכי היכי דכתיבי? ועוד, דקאמר ליה אביי: איצטריך קרא לאשמועינן דמאן דלית ליה אלא וכו'. ופ"ה: ואמאי כתב "ובן אין לו והעברתם את נחלתו"? פשיטא, ולשתוק מיניה. והכי איבעי למכתב: איש כי ימות וזרע אין לו וגו'. ואי אליבא דמ"ד דכסדרן כתיבי — היכי נשתוק קרא ולא ליכתוב "והעברתם את נחלתו לבתו"? הא איצטריך למידרש: במקום בת אתה מעביר נחלה מן האב. וליכא למימר דאביי דייק מדלא כתיב ואיש כי ימות והעברתם את נחלתו לבתו — דא"כ מאי פריך ודלמא קמ"ל דבת נמי בת ירושה היא — דמ"מ הכי הוה מצי למכתב, ולא ליכתוב "ובן אין לו". אלא ודאי אליבא דמ"ד שלא כסדרן כתיבי אתיא, דלדידיה לא איצטריך "והעברתם". ואע"ג דמוקי "והעברתם" לכדרבי, שאין לך מעביר נחלה כו' — אין זה צורך שום דרשה, ולא אשמועינן שום חידוש. אלא דלגבי בת שייך לשון העברה. ור"י אומר: דאפילו למ"ד דכסדרן כתיבי אתיא, ואביי דריש מדלא כתיב: איש כי ימות והעברתם את נחלתו לבנו, דהוה מצי למידרש: במקום בן אתה מעביר נחלה מן האב כו', והוה ידעינן דבן ובת שוין, הואיל ומצינו במקום אחר שהיא בת ירושה.

ודלמא

מסורת הש"ס

א) [מס' סופרים פט"ו ה"י]: ב) [נ"ל שם ויאמרו לו]: ג) פסחים קיג. ע"ש: ד) לפ גי' התוס' נ"ל נשוט: ה) [בכל הכתובים איתא משה]: ו) בנוסחאות שלפנינו איתא ויטשון וכן איתא במתורגמן ולע"ק: ז) [נ"ל ואימא אי איכא בן ולמ"ד כסדרן כתיבי]:

הגהות הב"ח

(א) רשב"ם ד"ה וטול וכו' בתלמיד חכם שיש: (ב) ד"ה ה"ג ולא וכו' ואית דגרסי נמי:

עין משפט נר מצוה

ט א ב ג מיי' פ"י מהל' מתנות עניים הלכה יח טוש"ע י"ד סי' רנה סעיף א:

רבינו גרשום

דיקא נמי. דמתרוייהו אתא מיוסף ויתרו: דכתיב פוטיאל. מלא שני פוטיאל דפוטי משמע תרתי מיוסף ומיתרו. ואית דמפקי מבנות דמשמע תרתי: מאי היא דקאמ' ליה לאותו לוי מי הביאך הלום ומה אתה עושה בזה ומה לך פה כלומר כולי האי למה להו למישאל בחדא סגי אלא לאו הכי קאמרי ליה וכו': נשוט. כמו פשוט: מינהו. לאותו לוי: פים' אלא הואיל דלא האי לירות

גמרא

מאן (א) [א]כו' לירות? אטו בר קשא דמתא לירות?! הכי קא אמינא: איכא בן ובת – לא האי לירות כוליה, ולא האי לירות כוליה, אלא כי הדדי לירתו! א"ל אביי: ואצטריך קרא לאשמועינן היכא דלית ליה אלא חד ברא לירתינהו לכולהו נכסי? ודלמא הא קמ"ל, דבת נמי בת ירושה היא! ההיא, מ"וכל בת יורשת נחלה" (במדבר לו) נפקא. רב אחא בר יעקב אמר, מהכא: "למה יגרע שם אבינו מתוך משפחתו כי אין לו בן" (שם כז), טעמא דאין לו בן, הא יש לו בן – בן קודם. ודלמא בנות צלפחד הוא דקאמרן הכי, [ב]ניתנה תורה ונתחדשה הלכה! אלא, מחוורתא כדשנין מעיקרא. רבינא אמר, מהכא: "הקרוב אליו" (שם), הקרוב – קרוב קודם. ומאי קורבה דבן מבת, שבן קם תחת אביו ליעדה ולשדה אחוזה? יעדה – בת לאו בת יעדה היא, שדה אחוזה נמי – מהאי פירכא גופה הוא, דהא קיימא ליה לתנא: כלום יש יבום אלא במקום שאין בן! אלא, מחוורתא כדשנין מעיקרא. ואי בעית אימא, מהכא: "והתנחלתם אותם לבניכם אחריכם" (ויקרא כה), בניכם – ולא בנותיכם. אלא מעתה, "למען ירבו ימיכם וימי בניכם" (דברים יא), ה"נ בניכם ולא בנותיכם? [ג]ברכה שאני. § [א]"והאחין מן האב נוחלין ומנחילין" וכו'. § מנלן? [ד]אמר רבה: אתיא אחוה אחוה מבני יעקב, מה להלן מן האב ולא מן האם, אף כאן מן האב ולא מן האם. ולמה לי? "ממשפחתו וירש אותה" (במדבר כז) כתיב; [ה]משפחת אב קרויה משפחה, משפחת אם אינה קרויה משפחה! אין הכי נמי, וכי איתמר דרבה – לענין יבום איתמר. § "והאיש את אמו" וכו'. § מנא הני מילי? דתנו רבנן:

וכל

רשב"ם

מאן [ו] כו'. אם לא קרוביו הקרובים לו יותר. בר [ז] קשא. מושל העיר. א"ל אביי לרב פפא. אי איתא דאמר רחמנא דכחדא ירתון – נמצא שאין הבן ראוי לירושה יותר מן הבת, ובן ובת כשני בנים דמו. וכי איצטריך קרא לאשמועינן דמאן דלית ליה אלא חד ברא לירתינהו לכולהו נכסי דאב? בתמיה. ואמאי כתב "ואם אין לו בן והעברתם את נחלתו לבתו"? פשיטא, לישתוק קרא מיניה. והכי איבעי ליה למכתב: איש כי ימות וזרע אין לו ונתתם את נחלתו וגו' – וממילא ידענא דאם אין לו בן הבת תירש את הכל, מאחר ששניהן שוין בנחלה! אלא ודאי לאשמועינן אתא דבן קודם לבת. ואיצטריך לאשמועינן דאע"ג דאין הבת יורשת במקום שיש בן, וסד"א היכא דלית (ב) בן – ונתתם את נחלתו לאחיו, אבל לא לבתו. דכי היכי דאין אמו יורשתו, דמשפחת אם אינה קרויה משפחה – הכי נמי אין בתו יורשתו, דאין משפחת נשים קרויה משפחה, לא למעלה דידיה כגון אמו, ולא למטה דידיה כגון בתו, קמ"ל "והעברתם את נחלתו לבתו". אמר ליה רב פפא לאביי. אימא להכי כתב רחמנא כי האי גוונא "ובן אין לו והעברתם", ולא כתב: ונתתם את נחלתו לבנו ולבתו – דהא קא משמע לן: דבת נמי, בלא בן, בת יורשת הויא. דסד"א בן ובת ירתון כחדא, אבל היא לבדה – איכא למימר דלא תירות מידי, קמ"ל "והעברתם את נחלתו לבתו", וכל שכן שתירש עם הבן. כל רבותי מפרשין כן. ולא נהירא, דכיון דא"ל אביי: איצטריך קרא לאשמועינן דמאן דלית ליה אלא חד ברא כו' – אלמא פשיטא ליה הך סברא, דכיון דכחדא ירתון היא שקולה כבן, ופשיטא דתירות כל הנכסים כי ליכא בן בהדה. ואין זו שיטת גמרא שיכחיש המקשה סברת המתרץ בלא טענה אחרת, אלא אם כן מקשה לו מצד אחר. ונראה בעיני דה"פ: ודלמא הא קמ"ל האי "והעברתם" – דבת נמי כמו בן, בת ירושה הויא, שישנה בכלל ירושת אב. דסד"א לא תירש בת כלל, לא עם הבן ולא בלא בן, דבזכרים קפיד רחמנא, כדכתב "ונתתם את נחלתו לאחי אביו", וכתב נמי "ממשפחתו" – משפחת אב קרויה משפחה, קא משמע לן דיורשת הויא. והלכך, כי איכא בן – נמי תפלוג בהדיה, דמהיכא ממעטינן לה? דלמא ה"ק קרא: איש כי ימות ובן אין לו שיירש עם הבת – והעברתם את כל הנחלה לבתו. כלומר, אז עוברת כל הנחלה משבט לשבט על ידי בתו, כדרבי. אבל היכא דאיכא בן בהדה – אין כל הנחלה נעקרת משבט זה. ומשום דאתא קרא לאשמועינן כדרבי – לא הוה מצי למכתב "לבנו ולבתו"! ומשני: ההוא מוכל בת יורשת נחלה נפקא. דמיניה שמעינן דבת יורשת כל נכסי אביה כי ליכא בן בהדה, דבבת בלא בן מיירי קרא. וללשון האחרון שפירשתי שמעינן מיהת דבת ישנה בכלל ירושה, וה"מ למכתב: איש כי ימות וזרע אין לו ונתתם את נחלתו לאחיו, ולא איצטריך "ובן אין לו" אלא להקדים בן לבת. רב אחא בר יעקב אמר מהכא. נפקא דבן קודם לבת, דקאמרי בנות צלפחד למשה: "למה יגרע שם אבינו מתוך משפחתו" שלא ליטול כלום בנחלה בשביל שאין לו בן, ולא תעשה לנו תקנה ליטול במקום בן, מאחר דליכא בן. שאילו היה לאבינו בן – היינו שותקות ולא היינו תובעות נחלה, שהרי לא היה נגרע שם אבינו, אבל עתה כי אין לו בן – "תנה לנו נחלה" וגו'. דקאמרן הכי. שהיו סבורות שיהיה הדין כן. ניתנה תורה. לאחר דברי בנות צלפחד, שלאחר דבריהן נאמרה פרשת נחלות, ונתחדשה הלכה דברא וברתא ירתון כחדא, ולא כשהיו סבורות. כדשנין מעיקרא. מ"איש כי ימות ובן אין לו". רבינא אמר מהכא. [נפקא] בן קודם לבת. הקרוב. יש מפרשין דהקרוב דריש, כדאמר רבא (פסחים דף נח:): ד"העולה" – עולה ראשונה, ואמרינן נמי (חולין דף לא.): "הירך" – המיומנת שבירך. הכא נמי: "הקרוב" – קרוב קודם, מי שקרוב יותר קודם לחבירו, ובן קרוב מבת, כדמפרש ואזיל. ופרכינן: ומאי קורביה דבן. לאב כפי מבת? אם תאמר שבן קם תחת אביו ליעדה ולשדה אחוזה, מה שאין כן בבת – הא לאו מילתא היא, דאי משום יעדה – אינו קרוב יותר, אלא מפני שהבת אינה בת יעדה, שאי אפשר לאשה להנשא לאשה אחרת. וגבי שדה אחוזה נמי – איכא למימר דקמה תחת אביה. דמהך פירכא ד"כלום יש יבום אלא במקום שאין בן" קיימא ליה לתנא דהבן קם תחת אביו לשדה אחוזה ולא האח, והכי נמי איכא למימר גבי בת. ואע"ג דבמס' ערכין פרק "אין מקדישין" (דף כה:) ממעט לה לבת משדה אחוזה, מדכתב "אם מכר את השדה לאיש אחר", ותנא דבי ר' ישמעאל: כל שהוא אחר במקום בן, ובת נמי במקום בן כי אחר דמיא – הני מילי דחשבינן לה כי אחר לגבי בן משום דדרשינן "איש כי ימות ובן אין לו" וגו' שהבן קודם לבת, אבל אי לא הך דרשה ד"איש כי ימות" וגו' – הוה אמינא: בין לגבי ירושה בין לגבי שדה אחוזה כי הדדי נינהו. אלא מחוורתא כו'. ומהשתא איכא למידרש מיניה גבי שדה אחוזה דבת במקום בן כאחר דמיא, כדאשכחן גבי ירושה. לבניכם אחריכם. הוה מצי למכתב "לזרעכם". ולא בנותיכם. במקום שיש בן. ברכה שאני. דלכל ישראל מברך, ולא איצטריך למכתב "זרעכם". דסברא היא, דבין אבנים בין אבנות קאי, דאין ברכה לחצאין. אבל גבי ירושה, אם איתא דבנות יורשות במקום בן – הוה ליה למכתב "זרעכם". אחוה אחוה. כתיב הכא: "ונתתם את נחלתו לאחיו", וכתיב התם (בראשית מב): "שנים עשר עבדיך אחים אנחנו בני איש אחד" וגו'; "בני איש" מיותר הוא, לדרוש דהתם אחין אינן אלא מן האב. למה לי. גזרה שוה גבי ירושה? הא נפקא לן מדכתיב "ממשפחתו", ואחין מן האם אינן ממשפחתו! לענין יבום. "כי ישבו אחים יחדו ומת אחד מהם ובן אין לו" וגו' (דברים כה) דאחיו מאביו מייבם את אשתו, ולא אחיו מאמו. מה"מ. דהאיש יורש את אמו ולא הבת את אמה, דבן קודם לבת בנכסי האם? דכי כתיב בן קודם לבת – בנכסי האב הוא דכתיב: "איש כי ימות ובן אין לו והעברתם" וגו', אבל אשה כי תמות – מנלן דירית לה בן, וגם מנלן שיקדום לבת?

וכל

תוספות

ודלמא הא קמ"ל דבת נמי בת ירושה. דסד"א דלאו בת ירושה היא, משום דמסבת נחלה, דבנה ובעלה יורשין אותה.

ושדה אחוזה נמי מהאי פירכא הוא דקיימא לן. אוריב"ס: דל"ג "כלום יש יבום אלא במקום שאין בן". דהלשון משמע שהוא מודה שהבת אינה קמה לשדה אחוזה מהאי טעמא, כי ההיא דלעיל גבי אח, דמסיק בהאי לישנא. ופ"ה דחוק הוא מאד, דמפרש דה"ק: ושדה אחוזה נמי איכא למימר דקמה תחת אביה, ומייתי סייעתא למילתיה, (ג) דהך פירכא דכלום יש יבום כו' קיימא ליה לתנא שהבן קם תחת אביו לשדה אחוזה ולא האח, וה"נ איכא למימר גבי בת. דמה לו לתלות הטעם בפירכא שהיא גבי אח? ולא היה לו לומר אלא: בת נמי תיקום לשדה אחוזה! ולכך נראה לו דלא גרסינן, (ד) אלא הכי גרסינן ליה: שדה אחוזה נמי מהאי פירכא הוא דקיימא ליה. וה"פ: והלא שדה אחוזה גופה, מה שאין בבת כבן – זהו מטעם שהבן קודם לנחלה מן הבת. וכל כמה דלא קיימא לן שהבן קודם לנחלה מן הבת – מעמדת הבת שדה לאביה כמו הבן. דהכי אמר בפ' "אין מקדישין" (ערכין דף כה:): בעא מיניה רבה בר אבוה: בת מהו שתעמיד שדה אחוזה לאביה? כיון דלענין יבום כי הדדי נינהו – מוקמינן, או דלמא כיון דלענין נחלה בת במקום בן כי אחר דמיא, לא מוקמינן? ופשיט ליה דכי אחר דמיא, מהך טעמא. **האיש** את אמו מנא הני מילי כו'. אומר ריב"ס: דבשאר ירושות של נשים, כגון בתו או אחותו – פשיטא ליה דיורשת אביה או אחיה, כיון שאין הירושה נעקרת ממשפחת אב. ופשיטא שהזכרים והנקבות שוין, בין לירש בין להוריש. דמה לי זכרים ומה לי נקבות, דאטו נכסי נשים יהיו הפקר? ודוקא בן בנכסי האם צריך למילף, לפי שניסבת נחלה ממטה אביה ע"י הבן.

קל

רבינו גרשום

ולא האי לירות בר קשא דמתא לירות. בלשון תמיה כלומר הממונה על העיר יירשנו: אלא כי הדדי לירתו. דהכי משמע והעברתם את נחלתו לבתו הא איכא בן ובת תרויהו לירתו. ואכתי בן קודם לבת מנלן. אמר ליה האי דכתיב ובן אין לו הא יש לו יורש וכי איצטרי' קרא לאשמוע' דמאן דלית ליה אלא חד ברא לירשינהו לכולהו נכסי ודאי הא לא אתי לאשמועינן דברא ירית אלא מאי אתא לאשמוע' להיכא דאית ליה בן ובת דבן קודם לבת. ודלמא קרא לא אתא אלא משום סיפא דכתיב והעברתם את נחלתו לאשמועינן להיכא דלית בן ירתא בתו א) אימא לירתו בהדדי. ומשני היכ' דלית בן לא איצטריך לאשמעינן מהאי קרא דבת בת ירושה היא דההיא מוכל בת יורשת נחלה נפקא והאי קרא ואיש כי ימות לא אתי לאשמעינן אלא היכא דאיכא בן ובת דהבן קודם: ורב אחא בר יצחק אמר מהכא. מצינן למידק דבן קודם לבת דכתיב למה יגרע וכו'. ודלמא בנות צלפחד אינהו דקאמרי הכי ולאו משום דהכי דינא ואח"כ נתנה תורה ונתחדשה הלכה ודדייקינן מואיש כי ימות דאי איכא בן ובת לא האי ירית כולה ולא האי ירית כולה ואלא תרוייהו כי הדדי והיינו חידוש הלכה: אלא מחוורתא כדשנינן מעיקרא. דאי אמרינן הכי איכא למיפרך כדפרכינן אמר ליה איצטריך קרא לאשמועי' דכיון דלית ליה וכו' אלא הא אתא לאשמועינן דבן קודם לבת: ומאי קורביה דבן מבת. משום דאיכא למימר שבן קם תחת אביו ליעדה ולשדה אחוזה מה שאין כן בבת ב) מש"ה אינה קמה תחת אביה ליעדה דלאו בת יעוד היא שדה נמי איכא למימר דהיא קמה תחת אביה דאם היא פרקה אותו שדה הדרא לאביה ביובל דכגוף של אביה דמיא כבן עצמו ומהאי טעמא דקי"ל לתנא דשדה אחוזה אי פריק לי' הבן חוזר לאביו ביובל מצינן למימר נמי דאי פרקא לה איהי הוה חוזרת לאביה משום דלענין ייבום בן ובת כי הדדי נינהו וכי היכי דאיכא למיפרך כלום יש ייבום אלא במקום שאין בן הכא נמי איכא למיפרך מבת כלום יש ייבום במקום בת ומאי קורביה דבן מבת אלא מחוורתא כו': ואיבעית אימ' מהכא. איכא למשמע דבן קודם לבת: אמר ליה ברכה שאני. דכולל להו אהדדי אבל בעלמא לא אמרי' הכי: **פים'** האחין מן האב נוחלין ממונן של בנים בני אחין והם עצמן מנחילין ממונם לבנים דהיינו נבדיהן: ומנלן. דבתר אחי מן האב שייכי: אמר רבא אתיא אחוה אחוה מבני יעקב. כתיב הכא ונתתם את נחלתו לאחיו וכתיב ביעקב שנים עשר אחים אנחנו בני אבינו: למה לי. למשמע מהכא. ממשפחתו שלו אמר רחמנא של אב: אין הכי נמי. מדכא עיקר: לענין יבום אתמר. דאחיו מן האם אין זקוק ליבום אלא אחין מן האב חולצין ומייבמין: **פים'** והאיש את אמו נוחל

א) נראה דל"ל אבל היכא דאיכא בן ובת אימא דלירתו בהדדי. ב) אולי דל"ל ופרכינן דלמא מש"ה כו' ליעדה משום דלאו כו'.

עין משפט נר מצוה

י א מיי' פ"א מהלכות נחלות הלכה ג סמג עשין צו טוש"ע ח"מ סי' רעו סעיף א:

מסורת הש"ס

א) ס"א בו. רש"ל: ב) [שבת קלה.]: ג) [שם קה:]: ד) יבמות יז: כב.: ה) [לעיל קטו: וש"נ]: ו) ס"א בו רש"ל: ז) [ורשב"ם בפסחים קיא: כתב בר קשא פי' שוטר העיר]:

הגהות הב"ח

(א) גמ' מאן לירות כל"ל ותיבת כו' נמחק: (ב) רשב"ם ד"ה א"ל אביי וכו' דלית ליה בן: (ג) תוס' ד"ה ושדה וכו' דמהך פירכא דכלום: (ד) בא"ד דלא גרסינן ליה אלא הכי גרסי' שדה וכו' מה שאין הבת כבן:

יא א מיי' פ"א מהל' נחלות הלכה ג סמג עשין צו טוש"ע ח"מ סי' רעו סעיף ז:

"וְכָל בַּת יוֹרֶשֶׁת נַחֲלָה מִמַּטּוֹת בְּנֵי יִשְׂרָאֵל" — הֵיאָךְ בַּת יוֹרֶשֶׁת שְׁנֵי מַטּוֹת? אֶלָּא זוֹ שֶׁאָבִיהָ מִשֵּׁבֶט אֶחָד וְאִמָּהּ מִשֵּׁבֶט אַחֵר, וּמֵתוּ, וִירֵשַׁתָּן. וְאֵין לִי אֶלָּא בַּת, בֵּן מִנַּיִן? אָמַרְתָּ קַל וָחוֹמֶר: וּמַה בַּת שֶׁהוּרַע כֹּחָהּ בְּנִכְסֵי הָאָב — יָפֶה כֹּחָהּ בְּנִכְסֵי הָאֵם, בֵּן שֶׁיָּפֶה כֹּחוֹ בְּנִכְסֵי הָאָב — אֵינוֹ דִּין שֶׁיָּפֶה כֹּחוֹ בְּנִכְסֵי הָאֵם? וּמִמָּקוֹם שֶׁבָּאתָ: מַה לְּהַלָּן בֵּן קוֹדֵם לְבַת, אַף כָּאן בֵּן קוֹדֵם לְבַת. ר' יוֹסֵי בְּר' יְהוּדָה וְר"א בְּר' יוֹסֵי אָמְרוּ מִשּׁוּם רַבִּי זְכַרְיָה בֶּן הַקַּצָּב: אֶחָד הַבֵּן וְאֶחָד הַבַּת שָׁוִין בְּנִכְסֵי הָאֵם. מַאי טַעְמָא? דַּיּוֹ לַבָּא מִן הַדִּין לִהְיוֹת כַּנִּדּוֹן. וְתַנָּא קַמָּא לָא דָרֵישׁ "דַּיּוֹ"? וְהָא "דַּיּוֹ" דְּאוֹרַיְיתָא הוּא! דְּתַנְיָא: א)מִדִּין קַל וָחוֹמֶר כֵּיצַד? °"וַיֹּאמֶר ה' אֶל מֹשֶׁה וְאָבִיהָ יָרֹק יָרַק בְּפָנֶיהָ הֲלֹא תִכָּלֵם שִׁבְעַת יָמִים", קַל וָחוֹמֶר לַשְּׁכִינָה אַרְבָּעָה עָשָׂר! אֶלָּא דַּיּוֹ לַבָּא מִן הַדִּין לִהְיוֹת כַּנִּדּוֹן! בְּעָלְמָא דָּרֵישׁ "דַּיּוֹ", וְשָׁאנֵי הָכָא, דְּאָמַר קְרָא: "מִמַּטּוֹת", מַקִּישׁ מַטֵּה הָאֵם לְמַטֵּה הָאָב, מַה מַּטֵּה הָאָב — בֵּן קוֹדֵם לְבַת, אַף מַטֵּה הָאֵם — בֵּן קוֹדֵם לְבַת. רַב נִיתַּאי סָבַר לְמֶעֱבַד עוֹבְדָא כְּר' זְכַרְיָה בֶּן הַקַּצָּב, אֲמַר לֵיהּ שְׁמוּאֵל: כְּמַאן, כִּזְכַרְיָה? אֶפֶס זְכַרְיָה. רַבִּי טַבְלָא עֲבַד עוֹבְדָא כְּרַבִּי זְכַרְיָה בֶּן הַקַּצָּב, א"ל רַב נַחְמָן: מַאי הַאי? א"ל, דְּאָמַר רַב חִינָּנָא בַּר שֶׁלֶמְיָא מִשְּׁמֵיהּ דְּרַב: הֲלָכָה כְּרַבִּי זְכַרְיָה בֶּן הַקַּצָּב. אֲמַר לֵיהּ: זִיל אַהֲדַר בָּךְ, וְאִי לָא — מַפֵּיקְנָא לָךְ רַב חִינָּנָא בַּר שֶׁלֶמְיָא מֵאוּנָיךְ. רַב הוּנָא בַּר חִיָּיא סָבַר לְמֶעֱבַד עוֹבְדָא כְּרַבִּי זְכַרְיָה בֶּן הַקַּצָּב, אֲמַר לֵיהּ רַב נַחְמָן: מַאי הַאי? אֲמַר לֵיהּ, דְּאָמַר רַב הוּנָא אָמַר רַב: הֲלָכָה כְּר' זְכַרְיָה בֶּן הַקַּצָּב. אֲמַר לֵיהּ: ב)אֶשְׁלַח לֵיהּ? אִיכְסִיף. אֲמַר לֵיהּ: הַשְׁתָּא כִּי נָח נַפְשֵׁיהּ דְּרַב הוּנָא, אִיתְרִיסַתְּ לְקִבְלִי. וְאִיהוּ כְּמַאן סְבָרָהּ? כִּי הָא דְּרַב וּשְׁמוּאֵל דְּאָמְרִי תַּרְוַיְיהוּ: אֵין הֲלָכָה כְּר' זְכַרְיָה בֶּן הַקַּצָּב. מִיסְתַּמֵּיךְ וְאָזֵיל רַבִּי יַנַּאי אַכַּתְפָּא דְּרַבִּי שִׂמְלַאי שַׁמָּעֵיהּ, וְאָתֵי ר' יְהוּדָה נְשִׂיאָה לְאַפַּיְיהוּ. א"ל: בַּר אֱנָשׁ דְּאָתָא לְקִיבְלָנָא, הוּא יָאֵי וְגוּלְתֵיהּ יָאֵי. כִּי מְטָא לְגַבֵּיהּ גְּשָׁשֵׁהּ, אֲמַר לֵיהּ: דֵּין שִׁיעוּרֵיהּ כַּשַּׂק. ג)בְּעָא מִינֵּיהּ: א)מִנַּיִן לְבֵן שֶׁקּוֹדֵם לְבַת בְּנִכְסֵי הָאֵם? אֲמַר לֵיהּ, דִּכְתִיב: "מַטּוֹת", מַקִּישׁ מַטֵּה הָאֵם לְמַטֵּה הָאָב, מַה מַּטֵּה הָאָב — בֵּן קוֹדֵם לְבַת, אַף מַטֵּה הָאֵם — בֵּן קוֹדֵם לְבַת. א"ל: אִי מַה מַּטֵּה הָאָב — בְּכוֹר נוֹטֵל פִּי שְׁנַיִם, אַף מַטֵּה הָאֵם — בְּכוֹר נוֹטֵל פִּי שְׁנַיִם!

אֲמַר

(תורה אור: במדבר לו; שם יב)

רשב"ם

וכל בת יורשת נחלה ממטות וגו'. סיפא דקרא: "לאחד ממשפחת מטה אביה תהיה לאשה", כדי שלא תסוב נחלה ממטה למטה אחר. ומיהו, לא נהג אלא באותו הדור, כדלקמן בפירקין (דף קכ.). ולקמן (א) מפרשינן: כיון דיורשת שני מטות והיא נשאת למטה אביה — הרי מכל מקום סובבת נחלת האם למטה אחר! ולקמן מתרצינן לה. בת יורשת נחלה ממטות. משמע שבת אחת מקבלת נחלה משני מטות, ואי אתה מוצא קרובים לה שתתקבל נחלה מהם יותר מאביה ואמה. וכגון שאביה משבט ראובן ואמה משבט שמעון, וכשנישאת אמה לאביה היו לה אחין לאמה של בת זו שירשו נחלת אביהן, דליכא הסבת נחלת אם לאב בשעת נישואין. דלא קפיד קרא אלא שבשעת נישואין לא תהא ראויה לירש נכסי אביה. ומיהו, אחרי כן מתו אחיה, ואחר כך מת אביה, וירשה אותו. ומתו האם והאב, ולא היה להם כי אם בת זו, וירשתן. נמצאת יורשת שני מטות: נחלת אמה ממטה שמעון, ונחלת אביה ממטה ראובן. בן מנין. שיורש את אמו? דאיכא למימר בהכי קפיד קרא: הבן יירש את האב, והבת תירש את האם. שהורע כחה בנכסי האב. דבן קודם לה. יפה כחה בנכסי האם. דיורשת את האם. אינו דין שיפה כחו בנכסי האם. שיירש כמו הבת? אבל עדיין לא למדנו שיקדום לבת. והיינו דקאמר: וממקום שבאת, וממקום שהתחלת ללמוד, דהיינו מנכסי האב — חזור ולמד עוד מה להלן כו'. ולקמיה פריך, לימא: דיו לבא מן הדין להיות כנדון. שוין. דירתון כחדא. מדין קל וחומר כו'. בריש תורת כהנים תניא: רבי ישמעאל אומר, בשלש עשרה מדות התורה נדרשת בהן: מקל וחומר, ומגזירה שוה, ומבנין אב כו'. והדר מפרש להו חדא חדא. מקל וחומר כיצד — באיזה ענין אנו דורשין דבר מדבר ע"י קל וחומר. ויאמר ה' כו'. כלומר, לא להחמיר (ב) על החמור מבקל, הואיל ובא ללמוד מן הקל, אלא דיו ללמד שיהא כמלמד. כלומר, דיו לבא מן הדין כו', לפיכך תסגר שבעת ימים כו'. מקיש מטה האם כו'. מאחר דאתא בן בקל וחומר דיורש את אמו כבת, והוקשו המטות בתיבה אחת, דלא כתב שני מטות — הלכך דרשינן: מה מטה האב כו'. ולקמיה פרכינן: אי מה מטה האב בכור נוטל בה פי שנים כו'. ניתאי. שם חכם. כר' זכריה בן הקצב. דהבן והבת יחלקו בשוה בנכסי האם. אפס זכריה. כמו "כי אפס כסף" (בראשית מז) כלומר, בטלו, שאין הלכה כמותו.

מפיקנא לך כו'. משמתינא לך, ולא יסייע לך רב חיננא בר שלמיא. דאמר רב הונא אמר רב כו'. רב הונא בר חייא מהדר הכי לרב נחמן. אמר ליה. רב נחמן לרב הונא בר חייא. אשלח ליה. לרב הונא ואודיעו שאתה אומר כן משמו, ואדע אם אמת הוא שאמר רב הונא כן. איכסיף. דשמא חזר בו רב הונא, או לא היה סומך בשמועתו. איתריסת לקבלי. ולא היית חוזר בך. ואיהו. רב נחמן. רבי ינאי. זקן היה, והחלו עיניו כהות. א"ל. שמעיה דר' ינאי. בר אינש דאתי לקיבלנא הוא יאי. אדם חשוב בא כנגדנו. וגולתיה יאי. כלומר, טלית של תלמידי חכמים. אי נמי — נאה ממש, כדמוכח לקמיה, דקאמר: דין שיעוריה כשק. גששה. רבי ינאי לגולתיה דרבי יהודה נשיאה. דין שיעוריה כשק. בגד עב וגרוע, ושיעורו לקבל טומאה ד' טפחים על ד' טפחים כשק. כדתנן: השק ד' על ד', הבגד ג' על ג', במסכת שבת (דף עו.) ובמסכת סוכה (דף יז:). אמר ליה. רבי יהודה נשיאה לרבי ינאי: (ג) בן קודם לבת כו'. אמר ליה. רבי יהודה נשיאה לרבי ינאי: אי מה מטה האב כו'.

אמר

תוספות

קל וחומר לשכינה י"ד. אור"ת: דלכך נקט י"ד, משום דאמר ב"המפלת" (נדה דף לא.): שלשה שותפין יש באדם; הקדוש ברוך הוא אביו ואמו, ונותן בו הקב"ה כנגד שניהן. אבל קשה קצת: דאם כן אין זה קל וחומר, דמן הדין יש להיות כנגד שניהן! ועוד אמר בספרי בתוספתא: קל וחומר למלך וכהן י"ד. פירוש: משה רבינו שהיה מלך וכהן גדול, ששימש שבעת ימי המילואים. ואמשה רבינו אמאי נקט י"ד? ודוחק לומר דמלך היינו הקדוש ברוך הוא, וכהן — משה.ד) ורבינו חיים כהן מפרש: קל וחומר לשכינה יותר מעט מז' וכיון דאפיקתיה מז' דהיינו הסגר — אוקמה אשני הסגרות, וכן משמע (ד) באבותח). דין שיעוריה כשק. ואם תאמר: וכי גרע ממטלניות דפרק "לא יחפור" (לעיל דף כ. ושם) דאוקימנא כעין ו) [רסקא], ואפילו הכי שיעורייהו בג' על ג'? וי"ל: דהתם לא מוקי לה כעין שקא אלא לענין דלא חזו לאומנא לקנח הדם, אבל האי — קשה יותר מדאי. מקיש מטה האם למטה האב וכו'. תימה לרשב"א: אמאי איצטריך לאשמועינן דבן קודם לבת בנכסי האם מהיקשא דמטות? תיפוק ליה מ"וירש אותה" דאמר לקמן (דף קיג:): מקיש ירושה שניה לירושה ראשונה, מה ירושה ראשונה בן קודם לבת — אף ירושה שניה בן קודם לבת. דמיניה ילפינן לקמן דבני אחות קודמין לבנות אחות לירש בנכסי אחי האם ובנכסי אבי האם, דמה ירושה ראשונה דהיינו בנכסי האב בן קודם לבת — אף ירושה שניה, כגון בן הבת קודם לבת הבת בנכסי אבי האם! ואומר רשב"א: דבן בנכסי האם היינו נמי ירושה ראשונה הבאה מכח האם. ואי לאו דנפקא לן מהיקשא דמטות דבן קודם לבת בנכסי האם — היכי הוה שמעינן דקודם בנכסי אבי האם? דלא אתי אלא מכח היקשא דירושה ראשונה. הלכך איצטריך הכא למילף מעיקרא דבן קודם לבת בנכסי האם, שהיא ירושה ראשונה הבאה מכח האם. ושוב נפקא לן מהיקשא דלקמן, דמקיש ירושה שניה לירושה ראשונה, בין ירושה שניה דאב בין ירושה שניה דאם. ור"י אומר: דאע"ג דנפקא לן לקמן דבן קודם לבת בנכסי אבי האם — היינו משום דמכח אבוה דאימיה קאתי, ולא שמעינן מינה דקודם בנכסי האם עצמן. ואין נראה לרשב"א, דהא מכח דאבוה דאם לא ירית אלא ע"י משמוש, דנפלו לפני האם והוא יורש את אמו. וא"ת: כיון דמהכא שמעינן דמהיקש דמטות דבן קודם לבת בנכסי האם, אמאי איצטריך כל הנך קראי, ד"לא תסוב נחלה" דאיירי בסיבת הבן, וקרא ד"אם אין לו בת", דאמר לקמן: בן הבת ובת הבת מנין? ת"ל: "אם אין לו" — עיין עליו, דמשמע דאתא לאשמועינן דבן יורש את אמו? ומיהו, ההוא ד"ואם אין לו בת" איצטריך טובא, דלא הוה ידעינן שהיה בן הבת יורש כלל ע"י משמוש, והא דדרשינן נמי מ"וירש אותה" להקיש ירושה שניה לראשונה — הוה מוקמינן *בבת הבן דוקא.ז) ו"לא תסוב" נמי איצטריך ללאו בסיבת הבן, ו"לא תסוב" שני בסיבת הבעל.

ולמאן

רבינו גרשום

נוחל ממון שלה ואינה נוחלת היא את ממון בנה דבהכי משפחת האב רמינן נחלת הבן: מנהני מילי. דבן יורש את אמו וקודם לבת הוא: דכתיב רחמנא וכל בת יורשת נחלה ממטות בני ישראל היאך וכו' שאביה משבט אחד ואמה משבט אחר. והיו אחין לאמה הראוין לירש את אביה דהא מציא למעבד שפיר דליכא משום לא תסוב נחלה הואיל דאחיה קיימין ולאחר שנישאת אמה של זו מת אחיה ונפלה ירושתן לאמה והיה לה בת זו ומתו אביה ואמה וירשתן בת זו שלא היה להן בן אלמא דבת יורש את אמה היא: ואין לי: דיורשת את אמה: אלא בת. כדכתיב וכל בת יורשת וכו': בן מנין אמרת ק"ו ומה בת שהורע כחה בנכסי האב. שבמקום בן לא ירתא בת. יפה כחה בנכסי האם. וכדאמרינן הכא דהא אשכחן מיהא מן קרא דבת יורשת נכסי האם. בן שיפה כחו בנכסי האב אינו דין וכו': וממקום שבאת. כלומר מאותו ק"ו מצי למידרש נמי דבן קודם לבת בנכסי האם דמה להלן גבי נכסי האב בן קודם לבת כדאמרי' לעיל טעמא דאין לו בן הא יש לו בן קודם לבת אף כאן נמי גבי נכסי האם בן קודם לבת: איכא למימר דהא ק"ו דבא מן הדין של ק"ו להיות כנדון דהבן דלירת בנכסי האם מק"ו של בת קאתי ומש"ה בדין הוה דלהוי שוין בן ובת בנכסי האם: ותנא דמתני' דיליף לה מברייתא ואמר דבן קודם לבת לא דרש דיו: והא דיו דאורייתא הוא דתניא מדין ק"ו כיצד. אחד מי"ג מדות שהתורה נדרשת בהן: הלא תכלם שבעת ימים: כדין מצורע שהמצורע היה מצטרע משום שהי' מוציא שם רע וזו דברה כלפי שכינה. ק"ו שהיא טעונה י"ד יום הסגר דכל מצורע ז' ימים היה טעון הסגר: אלא דיו לבא מן הדין להיות כנדון. ושכינה מאדם ילפינן אלמא דאורייתא היא: ומשני ודאי בעלמא דריש דיו ושאני הכא דלא דרש דיו ואמר דבן קודם לבת דאמר קרא וכו': אפס זכריה. כלומר אין הלכה כמותו. כלומר לא תיהדר מפיק לך ר' חנניא ב"ר שלמיה דאמר הלכה כר' זכריה מאונך. כלומר משלך אוציא בעל ברחך ואהדר ליה: אשלח ליה לרב הונא דאמרת משמי' הלכה כר' זכריה אם אמר הכי אי לא. ואיכסף ר' הונא בר חייא. דאיהו לא הוה אמר הכי משמיה דרב הונא אלא כדי להעמיד דבריו ותלה בגברא רבא כרב הונא: איתרסת לקבלי. כלומר היית מקנטר בדבריך כנגדי: אינהו. שמואל דאמר אפס זכריה ורב ושמואל דאמרי תרווייהו וכו': מסתמיך ואזיל ר' ינאי אכתפיה דר' שמלאי שמעיה. משום דמחמת שיבה הוה סגי נהור וכהה מאורו: אמר ליה שמעיה בר אינש דאתי לקבלנא הוא יאה וגולתיה יאה. כלומר יפה במעשים טובים וטליתו נאה: גששיה. משמש ר' ינאי לטלית של ר' יהודה: אמר ליה. לשמעיה אמרת לי דגולתיה יאה דין שיעוריה כשק הוא כלומר שיעורו של טלית זו כשק הוא שאין דבר חשוב ואין מקבל טומאה עד שיהא בו ד' על

מסורת הש"ס

א) ב"ק כה. זבחים סט: ב) [ע"ז לו.] ג) גי' רש"ל אמר ליה: ד) [עי' תוס' זבחים סט: ותוס' ב"ק כה. ד"ה ק"ו] ה) [לא ידעתי מקומו. ועי' דבתוס' ב"ק כה. כתבו וכן מוכח בתוספ' דאבות וכן העתיק התוי"ט בפ"ב מ"ה דב"ק ד"ה דיו וכו' לשון התוס' וכן מוכח בתוספתא דאבות ע"ש והנה לפנינו לא נמצא שום תוספתא על מס' אבות וחפשתי באבות דר' נתן ולא מצאתי אלא בפ"ט תניא בזה"ל א"ל הקב"ה אילו אביה ירק בפניה לא היתה נכלמת ז' ימים אני מלך מלכי המלכים על אחת כמה וכמה לא דין הוא שתכלם י"ד ימים אלא דיו לבא מן הדין להיות כנדון ע"כ] ו) ג"ה דסקלא: ז) גליון ולכאורה אמאי איצטריך אין לו דבת למשמע ניחא לי' מממשות בבן הבת בהיקשא דמטות:

הגהות הב"ח

(א) רשב"ם ד"ה וכל בת וכו' ולקמן פרכינן כיון דיורשת: (ב) ד"ה ויאמר וכו' להחמיר בחמור מבקל: (ג) ד"ה א"ל רבי יהודה נשיאה לר' ינאי מנין לבן שקודם לבת: (ד) תוס' ד"ה קל וחומר וכו' וכן משמע בתוספתא באבות:

עין משפט נר מצוה

יב א מיי' פ"ב מהלכות נחלות הלכה ח סמג עשין לו טוש"ע ח"מ סי' רעח סעיף א:

יג ב מיי' פ"א שם הלכה ח ופכ"ב מהל' אישות הלכה א סמג שם וסי' מח טור וש"ע אה"ע סי' צ סעיף א וסי' נז:

יד ג מיי' פ"א מהלכות נחלות הלכה ח סמג שם:

אֲמַר לֵיהּ לְשַׁמָּעֵיהּ: גּוּד, לֵית דֵּין צָבֵי דְּמֵילַף. וְטַעְמָא מַאי? אֲמַר אַבַּיֵי, אָמַר קְרָא: "בְּכֹל אֲשֶׁר יִמָּצֵא לוֹ", לוֹ — וְלֹא לָהּ. וְאֵימָא: הָנֵי מִילֵּי בָּחוּר שֶׁנָּשָׂא אַלְמָנָה, אֲבָל בָּחוּר שֶׁנָּשָׂא בְּתוּלָה ה"נ דְּשָׁקֵיל! א"ר נַחְמָן בַּר יִצְחָק, אָמַר קְרָא: "רֵאשִׁית אוֹנוֹ", אוֹנוֹ — וְלֹא אוֹנָהּ. הַהוּא מִבַּעְיָא לֵיהּ לְבָא אַחַר נְפָלִים דְּלֶהֱוֵי בְּכוֹר לְנַחֲלָה — מִי שֶׁלִּבּוֹ דָּוֶה עָלָיו, יָצָא זֶה שֶׁאֵין לִבּוֹ דָּוֶה עָלָיו! אִם כֵּן, לֵימָא קְרָא כִּי הוּא "רֵאשִׁית אוֹן", מַאי "אוֹנוֹ"? שְׁמַע מִינָּהּ תַּרְתֵּי. וְאַכַּתִּי אֵימָא: הָנֵי מִילֵּי אַלְמוֹן שֶׁנָּשָׂא בְּתוּלָה, אֲבָל בָּחוּר שֶׁנָּשָׂא בְּתוּלָה הָכִי נַמִי דְּשָׁקֵיל! אֶלָּא אֲמַר רָבָא, אָמַר קְרָא: "לוֹ מִשְׁפַּט הַבְּכוֹרָה". מִשְׁפַּט הַבְּכוֹרָה לָאִישׁ, וְלֹא מִשְׁפַּט הַבְּכוֹרָה לָאִשָּׁה.§ "וְהָאִישׁ אֶת אִשְׁתּוֹ" וכו'.§ מְנָהָנֵי מִילֵּי? דְּתָנוּ רַבָּנַן: "שְׁאֵרוֹ" — זוֹ אִשְׁתּוֹ, מְלַמֵּד שֶׁהַבַּעַל יוֹרֵשׁ אֶת אִשְׁתּוֹ. יָכוֹל אַף הִיא תִּירָשֶׁנּוּ? תַּלְמוּד לוֹמַר: "וְיָרַשׁ אוֹתָהּ", הוּא יוֹרֵשׁ אוֹתָהּ, וְאֵין הִיא יוֹרֶשֶׁת אוֹתוֹ. וְהָא קְרָאֵי לָאו הָכִי כְּתִיבִי! אֲמַר אַבַּיֵי, תָּרֵיץ הָכִי: "וּנְתַתֶּם אֶת נַחֲלָתוֹ לַקָּרוֹב אֵלָיו, שְׁאֵרוֹ וְיָרַשׁ אוֹתָהּ". אֲמַר רָבָא: סַכִּינָא חֲרִיפָא מְפַסְקָא קְרָאֵי? אֶלָּא אֲמַר רָבָא, הָכִי קָאָמַר: "וּנְתַתֶּם אֶת נַחֲלַת שְׁאֵרוֹ לוֹ". קָא סָבַר: גּוֹרְעִין וּמוֹסִיפִין וְדוֹרְשִׁין. וְהַאי תַּנָּא מַיְיתֵי לָהּ מֵהָכָא, דְּתַנְיָא: "וְיָרַשׁ אוֹתָהּ" — מְלַמֵּד שֶׁהַבַּעַל יוֹרֵשׁ אֶת אִשְׁתּוֹ, דִּבְרֵי ר"ע. רַבִּי יִשְׁמָעֵאל אוֹמֵר: אֵינוֹ צָרִיךְ, הֲרֵי הוּא אוֹמֵר: "וְכָל בַּת יוֹרֶשֶׁת נַחֲלָה מִמַּטּוֹת בְּנֵי יִשְׂרָאֵל לְאֶחָד מִמִּשְׁפַּחַת" וגו', בַּהֲסִבַּת הַבַּעַל הַכָּתוּב מְדַבֵּר; וְאוֹמֵר: "וְלֹא תִסֹּב נַחֲלָה לִבְנֵי יִשְׂרָאֵל מִמַּטֶּה אֶל מַטֶּה"; וְאוֹמֵר: "וְלֹא תִסֹּב נַחֲלָה מִמַּטֶּה לְמַטֶּה אַחֵר"; וְאוֹמֵר: "וְאֶלְעָזָר בֶּן אַהֲרֹן מֵת וַיִּקְבְּרוּ אוֹתוֹ בְּגִבְעַת פִּנְחָס בְּנוֹ", וְכִי מִנַּיִן לְפִנְחָס שֶׁלֹּא הָיָה לוֹ לְאֶלְעָזָר? אֶלָּא, מְלַמֵּד שֶׁנָּשָׂא פִּנְחָס אִשָּׁה וּמֵתָה וִירֵשָׁהּ; וְאוֹמֵר: "וּשְׂגוּב הוֹלִיד אֶת יָאִיר וַיְהִי לוֹ עֶשְׂרִים וְשָׁלֹשׁ עָרִים בְּאֶרֶץ הַגִּלְעָד", וְכִי

ולמאן דדריש בעל מ"שארו" איצטריך לעבור עליו בשני לאוין. ומיהו, קשה לרשב"א: דאמאי איצטריך הכא היקשא דמטות? כיון דשמעינן מ"ואם אין לו בת" ומ"לא תסוב" דבן יורש את אמו, תיפוק ליה מקל וחומר דבן קודם לבת. והשתא לא אמר דיו, כיון דמפריך ק"ו. ומיהו, פלוגתא היא ב"כילד הרגל" (ב"ק דף כה.), דאיכא מ"ד אפילו היכא דמיפרך ק"ו אמר דיו. ומיהו, אפילו למ"ד לא אמר דיו — איכא למימר דמילתא דאתיא בק"ו טרח וכתב לה קרא.

לו משפט הבכורה. השתא לא שייך למיפרך, אפילו בלא הנך קראי דלעיל: ואימא ה"מ בבחור שנשא אלמנה. מדכתיב "משפט הבכורה" משמע דלא שייך משפט הבכורה אלא באיש, וקרא דלעיל אתי לדרשה אחריתי[ח].

הוא יורש אותה. משמע ליה מיעוטא, מדלא כתיב "וירשה", ומדכתיב "אותה" — משמע כיעוט, דאין היא יורשת אותו. ועוד: דלגמרי "וירש אותה" מיותר, ד"משארו" שמעי' תרתי, דכיון שהיא יורשת אותו מטעם שהיא שארו — גם הוא ירשנה מטעם שארו. ומיהו, קשה: דאמאי איצטריך כלל מיעוט? דמקפיד בסיבת הבעל ולא קפיד בסיבת האשה — משמע דאינה יורשת אותו!

מנין

אמר ליה רבי ינאי לשמעיה גוד. משוך אותי ונלך. לית דין רוצה למילף. אלא להקשות דברים שאינן צריכין. כלומר, דדבר קל הוא לתרץ, כדלקמן. ואימא הני מילי. דאין נוטל. בבחור שנשא אלמנה. שהיו לה בנים מאיש אחר, הילכך "לו" ולא לה, דהוי ראשית אונו ולא ראשית אונה. אבל בחור שנשא בתולה, דהוי אונו ואונה — הכי נמי דשקיל בנכסי האם פי שנים! אונו ולא אונה. דמצי למיכתב "ראשית און" כדלקמן, והלכך אפילו בבתולה דהוי ראשית אונה — לא שקיל חלק בכורה. ומקשינן: האי ראשית אונו. איצטריך לדרשא אחרינא, לאשמועינן דהבא אחר נפלים — שילדה אמו לפניו הרבה נפלים, כגון נולדו מתים, או בן ח' חיים, וזה נולד אחריהם — הוי בכור לנחלה. דאע"ג דלא הוי בכור לכהן, דבפטר רחם תלא רחמנא, וזה לא פטר את הרחם — אפילו הכי הוי בכור לנחלה. דבולד ראשון שלבו דוה עליו אם ימות תלא רחמנא, וזה שנולד אחר הנפלים — הוא ראשון שלבו דוה עליו אם ימות, דבן קיימא הוא. אבל נפלים קמאי — אין לבו דוה עליהן. יצא נפל שאין לבו דוה עליו. ולא יהא קרוי בכור לנחלה, לעשות פשוט אותו הבא אחריו. ואימא הני מילי. דממעט קרא דקאמר "אונו" ולא אונה — ה"ק: אם הוא בחור שנשא אלמנה, דראשית אונו נוטל פי שנים בכל אשר ימצא לו. אבל לא אונה, שאם הוא אלמון שנשא בתולה, דאיכא אונה לחוד — אינו נוטל בה פי שנים. אבל היכא דהוי גם אונו, כגון בחור שנשא בתולה, אימא: מגו דשקיל פי שנים בשלו — שקיל נמי פי שנים בשלה, דהוי בכור לנחלה בין לאב בין לאם. דליכא לאוקמי מיעוטא דאונו ולא אונה אלא במאי דדמי למעוטי טפי, כגון היכא דליכא ראשית און משני לדדין. לו משפט הבכורה. האי "לו" דריש ליה לגבי אב, לימר שמשפט הבכורה בנכסי האיש ולא בנכסי האשה. והכא ליכא למימר: הני מילי בבחור שנשא אלמנה, כדלעיל. דמדקאמר "משפט הבכורה" — כלל הוא, שכלל דיני בכורה בנכסי איש, ולא בנכסי אשה. והאיש יורש את אשתו. אפילו היכא דאיכא בן. שהרי הבעל אינו קרוב לה כשאר קרובים שלה שקרובים לה ממשפחתה, ואפילו הכי אמרינן שהוא יורש את אשתו, הלכך ודאי לקדם כל קרובים שלה הוא, דאמרינן דבעל יורש ולא הם. מנהני מילי. דהאיש נוחל את אשתו ולא מנחיל. שארו. "ונתתם את נחלתו לשארו" — זו אשתו, כדכתיב (בראשית ב): "והיו לבשר אחד". ולאו אדכתיב לעיל מיניה: "ואם אין אחים לאביו" קאי, אלא מילתא באנפי נפשה היא. והאי דכתיב: "הקרוב אליו" — מסקנא דמילתא דההוא קרא הוא, דכתיב: "ואם אין אחים לאביו". דעיקר פשטיה הכי משמע: "ונתתם את נחלתו לשארו" — לאשתו, ונדרשיה לקרא הכי: ונתתם את נחלתו אם ימות לשארו, וירש. כלומר, וגם הוא יירש שארו אם תמות היא. ת"ל וירש אותה. דמצי למיכתב "וירש" בלא "אותה", דהוה שמעינן מקרא דהוא ירשה והיא יורשתו, כדפרישית: "ונתתם את נחלתו לשארו וירש", קרי ביה: ונתתם נחלתו לשארו, וקרי ביה נמי: שארו יורש, שהוא יורש את אשתו. הלכך כתב רחמנא "אותה", למעוטי שהיא לא תירשנו, ואתא לגלויי אדרשא דקרא, דכתיב: "ונתתם את נחלתו לשארו", דמיבעי לן לפרושי דבעל יורשה, כדלקמן. והא קראי לאו הכי כתיבי. דכתיב: "ונתתם את נחלתו לשארו" — דמשמע שהאשה יורשת את בעלה! ונתתם את נחלתו להקרוב אליו. דהקרוב כרוב קודם. שארו וירש אותה. מילתא אחריתי היא, דאשתו יירשנה בעלה. מפסקא קראי. שאתה מסרס התיבות לעשות "שארו" המוקדם מאוחר, ו"הקרוב אליו" שהוא מאוחר — אתה עושה מוקדם ז). אלא אמר רבא ה"ק ונתתם את נחלת שארו לו כסבר גורעין ומוסיפין ודורשין. גרע וי"ו מ"נחלתו" ולמ"ד מ"לשארו" ומוסיפין שתי אותיות הללו זו על גב זו, לעשותו תיבה אחת, והיא "לו", ודרוש הכי: ונתתם את נחלת שארו לו. ולאו דוקא מגרע ומוסיף, דאם כן רבא נמי סכינא חריפא הוא. אלא פשטיה דקרא איכא לפרושי כאילו גורעין ומוסיפין ודורשין, דהכי משמע: "ונתתם את נחלתו" כלומר, תתנוה לזה האיש שתהיה נחלתו. לשארו. — לשארו לאותו האיש שאשה זאת שארו. כלומר, על מי מצוה אני ונתתם את הירושה להיות נחלתו — לשארו. כלומר, נחלת האשה תתנו לבעל. אי נמי, איכא למימר דלא חשיב פיסוק קראי אלא בהקדמת תיבות שלימות, להקדים "הקרוב" לשארו, אבל בשינוי אותיות — ליכא פיסוקי קראי. והרי הוא כמו שכתוב: "ונתתם את נחלת שארו לו וירש אותה"; אהני "לו" לאשמועינן דיורש את אשתו, ואהני "אותה" למעוטי אשה שאינה יורשת לבעלה, ומילתא שמעינן דצריך לגרוע ולהוסיף ולדרוש ראשו של פסוק כמו שאמרנו, דלא תקשי ראשו לסופו. והאי תנא. (א) דבי ר' ישמעאל. מייתי לה. לבעל שיורש את אשתו. וירש אותה. משום דעיקר דרשא נפקא לן לעיל מ"וירש אותה", הלכך נקט ליה, דאיהו מגלי עליה דרישיה דקרא לפרושי שהבעל יורש את אשתו. אינו צריך. דלית ליה גורעין ומוסיפין ודורשין. ומוקי לה ב"שארו" זה האב, כדאמר בריש פירקא. בסיבת הבעל הכתוב מדבר. כלומר, בשביל הסבת נחלה ממטה למטה על ידי הבעל, שיורש את אשתו והוא משבט אחר, ונמלא שהוסבה משבט לשבט — בכך דבר הכתוב, והקפיד שלא תנשא למטה אחר אלא לאחד ממשפחת מטה אביה. כיצד? אם תנשא אשה מבנות שבט ראובן לאחד משבט שמעון והיא יורשת, שלא הניח אביה בן אלא אותה הבת, לכשתמות יירשנה בעלה, ונמצאת נחלת שבט ראובן הוסבה לשבט שמעון. לפיכך הזהירה תורה שלא תנשא בת יורשת אלא לאחד ממשפחת מטה אביה. מכאן שהבעל יורש את אשתו. ולקמיה פריך: ודלמא בסיבת הבן הכתוב מדבר, שהבן יירש את אמו והוא מתייחס אחר מטה אביו, ונמצא שעל ידו הוסבה נחלה אם תנשא לשבט אחר. אבל הבעל — איכא למימר דלא ירית, ואינו מיסב הנחלה לשבט שלו, ובשביל סיבת הבעל לא הזהיר רחמנא להנשא לשבט שלה, אלא בשביל סיבת בנה! [ואומר]. נקמיה מפרש מאי "ואומר". בגבעת פנחס בנו. מכלל דלא היתה של אלעזר. מנין היה לו לפנחס. שום קרקע אלא אם כן ירשה מאביו? וירשה. ולקמיה פריך: דלמא זבן מיזבן! ויהי לו. ליאיר ולא לשגוב, דכתיב לעיל מיניה "ותלד לו את שגוב", והכא הוה ליה למכתב "ויהי לו" וגו'. אלא ליאיר קאי. ועוד, דכתיב בתריה "ויקח גשור וארם את חות יאיר מאתם" וגו'.

וכי

רבינו גרשום

על ד' מה שאין כן בשאר בגדים: אמר ליה ר' יהודה לר' ינאי מנין שבן קודם לבת (א) כלומר אף ממטה האם בכור נוטל פי שנים בנכסי האם: אמר ליה לשמעיה גוד. כלומר ב)עבור זה רוצה ללמוד שאני אומר לו דבר של טעם והוא מקנתר כנגדי (אמר ליה) אעפ"כ טעמא מאי אינו נוטל פי שנים בנכסי האם וכו': הכי נמי דשקיל. הואיל דבכור מן האב הוא: ואימא (הוא) הני מילי באלמון שנשא בתולה דקרינן ביה דבכור שלו שהיה לו קודם לכן נוטל פי שנים דאונו בעינן ולא אונה אבל בחור שנשא בתולה דאונו ואונה הוא הכי נמי דשקיל פי שנים בנכסיה: לאיש ולא לאשה. משום הכי אין נוטל מנכסי האם פי שנים:

פיסקא האיש את אשתו יורש אבל היא אינה יורשת אותו. והא קראי לאו הכי כתיבי כי אם ונתתם את נחלתו לשארו דמשמע דאשתו יורשתו ואין הוא יורש אותה: אמר אביי תריץ. לקראי הכי ונתתם את נחלתו לקרוב אליו ואת שארו הוא יורש אותה דמשמע הוא יורשה: אמר רבא כמה סכינא חריפא מפסקי קראי. כלומר היכי מצינן לפסוקי קראי דכתיבי אלא גורעין ו' דנחלתו ול' דלשארו ומוסיפין אהדדי ודורשין לו דמשמע הוא יורשה: והאי תנא מייתי ליה מהכא. מסיפיה דקרא דבעל יורש את אשתו: וירש אותה כו' ר' ישמעאל אומר אינו צריך. לאפוקי מהכא דהבעל יורש את אשתו משום דמדוכתא אחריתי מצינן למידרש. הרי הוא אומר וכל בת יורשת נחלה ממטות בני ישראל לא' ממשפחת מטה אביה תהיה לאשה. היאך בת אחת יורשת שני מטות אלא שהיתה משבט ראובן ובשעת נישואיה שנישאת לשבט שמעון היו לה אחין הראוין לירש את אביה דאי לא הוו לה אחי לא מציא לאינסובי לשבט אחר משום דכתי' לא תסוב נחלה ממטה למטה אחר. והשתא לאחר נישואיה איתרמי דמת אחיה בלא בנים ונפלה לה נחלת אביה בירושה והוה לה בת אח' משבט ראובן ומשבט שמעון ולא בן ומת אבי' וירשתו הבת ועכשיו הנכסים עדיין בחזקת שבט שמעון כל זמן שלא נישאת ולפיכך הזהירה תורה שלא להנשא לשבט אחר כי

א) נדה כג: ב) בכורות נב: ג) לעיל קטו: ד) [מנחות מח. ערכין כו.] ה) [יומא מח. זבחים כה. בכורות מח: עי' בערוך ערך גרע א' שכתב ביאור יפה בשם רבינו חננאל] ו) ב"ק מב:

הגהות הב"ח

(א) רשב"ם ד"ה והאי תנא ר' ישמעאל כצ"ל ותיבת דבי נמחק:

אם למשפחת מטה אביה לפי שאם תנשא לאחד משבט אחר היתה ממטה למטה לפי שאם תמות יורשה בעלה משום הכי תנשא לאחד משבט אביה כי היכי דיירש לאשתו וקיימי נכסים בחזקת שבט אביה. ואיכא למישמע מהכא דמשום הכי הזהיר שלא להינשא לשבט אחר דבהסיבת הבעל הכתוב מדבר דכיון דבעל יורש את אשתו היה נסבת נחלה ותפשוט לך מהא דבעל יורש את אשתו: או אינו אלא בהסיבת הבן. כלומר או אינו אומר הכתוב לאחד ממטה אביה לאו משום דבעל יורשה אלא משום דבנה יורשה ובנה משבט אחר הוא והיתה נסבת נחלה: לא ס"ד דבהסיבת הבן לחוד מיירי ובעל לא ירית. דכשהוא אומר לא תסוב נחלה לבני ישראל ואומר לא תסוב נחלה ממטה. תלתא קראי כתיבי בהסיבה למה לי אלא או לאשמועינן דבעל יורש את אשתו: ואומר ואלעזר בן אהרן מת כו' וירשה פנחס. משום דהבעל יורש את אשתו: מאי

א) נ"ל מנין שבן קודם לבת כלומר אף ממטה האם ה"ל או מה מטה האב וכו'. ב) נראה דצ"ל עבור מזה שאינו רוצה ללמוד וכו'.

וְכִי מִנַּיִן לְיָאִיר שֶׁלֹּא הָיָה לוֹ לִשְׂגוּב? מְלַמֵּד שֶׁנָּשָׂא יָאִיר אִשָּׁה וּמֵתָה וִירָשָׁהּ. מַאי "וְאוֹמֵר"? וְכִי תֵּימָא: בְּסִבַּת הַבֵּן קָא קָפֵיד קְרָא, אֲבָל בַּעַל לָא יָרֵית — תָּא שְׁמַע: "וְלֹא תִסּוֹב נַחֲלָה לִבְנֵי יִשְׂרָאֵל מִמַּטֶּה לְמַטֶּה"; וְכִי תֵּימָא: לַעֲבוֹר עָלָיו בְּלָאו וַעֲשֵׂה — ת"ש: "לֹא תִסּוֹב נַחֲלָה מִמַּטֶּה לְמַטֶּה אַחֵר"; וְכִי תֵּימָא: לַעֲבוֹר עָלָיו בִּשְׁנֵי לָאוִין וַעֲשֵׂה — תָּא שְׁמַע: "וְאֶלְעָזָר בֶּן אַהֲרֹן מֵת" וגו'; וְכִי תֵּימָא: אֶלְעָזָר הוּא דְּנָסֵיב אִיתְּתָא, וּמֵתָה וְיָרְתָהּ פִּנְחָס — תָּא שְׁמַע: "וּשְׂגוּב הוֹלִיד אֶת יָאִיר" וגו'. וְכִי תֵּימָא: הָתָם נַמִי הָכִי הוּא — אִם כֵּן תְּרֵי קְרָאֵי לָמָּה לִי? אֲמַר לֵיהּ רַב פָּפָּא לְאַבָּיֵי: מִמַּאי? דִּלְמָא לְעוֹלָם אֵימָא לָךְ: בַּעַל לָא יָרֵית, וּקְרָאֵי בְּסִבַּת הַבֵּן כִּדְשַׁנֵּינָן, וְיָאִיר — דִּזְבֵין מִיזְבַּן, וּפִנְחָס נַמִי — דִּזְבֵין מִיזְבַּן! א"ל: פִּנְחָס דִּזְבֵין מִיזְבַּן לָא מָצֵית אָמְרַתְּ, דְּאִם כֵּן, נִמְצֵאת שָׂדֶה חוֹזֶרֶת בַּיּוֹבֵל, וְנִמְצָא צַדִּיק קָבוּר בְּקֶבֶר שֶׁאֵינוֹ שֶׁלּוֹ. אֶלָּא אֵימָא: דְּנָפְלָה לֵיהּ מִשְּׂדֵה חֲרָמִים! אֲמַר אַבָּיֵי: סוֹף סוֹף הָא קָא מִתְעַקְּרָא נַחֲלָה מִשִּׁבְטָא דְּאִימָּא לְשִׁבְטָא דְּאַבָּא. וּמִמַּאי? וְדִלְמָא שָׁאנֵי הָתָם, שֶׁכְּבָר הוּסַבָּה! (א) א"ל: שֶׁכְּבָר הוּסַבָּה לָא אָמְרִינַן. א"ל רַב יֵימַר לְרַב אַשִׁי: *אִי אָמְרַתְּ בִּשְׁלָמָא שֶׁכְּבָר הוּסַבָּה, הַיְינוּ דְּמִתּוֹקְמָא קְרָא בֵּין בְּסִבַּת הַבֵּן בֵּין בְּסִבַּת הַבַּעַל, אֶלָּא אִי אָמְרַתְּ לָא אָמְרִינַן שֶׁכְּבָר הוּסַבָּה, כִּי מִינַּסְבָא לְאֶחָד מִמִּשְׁפַּחַת מַטֵּה אָבִיהָ מַאי הֲוָה? הָא מִתְעַקְּרָא נַחֲלָה מִשִּׁבְטָא דְּאִימָּא לְשִׁבְטָא דְּאַבָּא! דְּמַנְסְבִינַן לָהּ לְגַבְרָא, דַּאֲבוּהִי מִשִּׁבְטָא דַּאֲבוּהָ וְאִימֵּיהּ מִשִּׁבְטָא דְּאִימָּהּ. אִי

וְכִי תֵּימָא. לֹא מִפְּנֵי שֶׁהַבַּעַל יוֹרֵשׁ אֶת אִשְׁתּוֹ, אֶלָּא מִפְּנֵי בֵּן שֶׁתֵּלֵד, וְהוּא יוֹרְשָׁהּ, וְהוּא נִקְרָא עַל שֵׁבֶט אָבִיו. וְעַל סִיבַּת הַבֵּן הַתּוֹרָה מַקְפֶּדֶת, שֶׁהֲרֵי הוּא קָרוֹב לָהּ מִן הַבַּעַל. **תָּא שְׁמַע.** מִקְרָא אַחֲרִינָא: "לֹא תִסּוֹב" וגו' — הָא תּוּ לָמָּה לִי? אֶלָּא לָאו לְסִיבַּת הַבַּעַל אֲתָא, לְאַשְׁמוּעִינַן שֶׁהַבַּעַל יוֹרֵשׁ. **וְכִי תֵּימָא לַעֲבוֹר עָלָיו בְּלָאו וַעֲשֵׂה.** דְּתַרְוַיְיהוּ בְּסִיבַּת הַבֵּן. וּמַה שֶּׁשָּׁנָה הַכָּתוּב — לֹא נִתְכַּוֵּין אֶלָּא לְהַתְרוֹת שֶׁלֹּא תִּנָּשֵׂא לְשֵׁבֶט אַחֵר, כְּדֵי לְהִתְחַיֵּיב מַלְקוּת. דְּמִקְרָא קַמָּא לָא שָׁמְעִינַן אֶלָּא עֲשֵׂה, דִּכְתִיב בֵּיהּ: "לְאֶחָד מִמִּשְׁפַּחַת מַטֵּה אָבִיהָ תִּהְיֶה לְאִשָּׁה" אֲבָל לֹא לְמַטֶּה אַחֵר, וְלָאו הַבָּא מִכְּלַל עֲשֵׂה — עֲשֵׂה. **וְכִי תֵּימָא אֶלְעָזָר הוּא דְּנָסֵיב אִיתְּתָא.** וּמֵתָה בְּחַיֵּי אֶלְעָזָר, וִירָשָׁהּ פִּנְחָס בְּנָהּ וְלֹא אֶלְעָזָר, דְּאֵין הַבַּעַל יוֹרֵשׁ אֶת אִשְׁתּוֹ אֶלָּא בְּנָהּ יוֹרְשָׁהּ, וַאֲתָא לְאַשְׁמוּעִינַן דְּהַבֵּן יוֹרֵשׁ אֶת אִמּוֹ. דְּמֵהָנֵי קְרָאֵי דִּלְעֵיל דְּמַיְירֵי בְּסִיבַּת הַבֵּן אִיכָּא לְמֵימַר דְּנְסִיבַּת הַבַּת הוּא דְּמַיְירֵי, כִּדְאַשְׁכְּחַן לְעֵיל בְּהֶדְיָא שֶׁהַבַּת יוֹרֶשֶׁת אֶת אִמָּהּ, וְאִיצְטְרִיכוּ הָנֵי קְרָאֵי לִשְׁנֵי לָאוִין וַעֲשֵׂה, כְּדַאֲמָרַן. אֲבָל לֹא אַשְׁכַּחַן דְּהַבֵּן יוֹרֵשׁ אֶת אִמּוֹ בְּהֶדְיָא אֶלָּא מִקַּל וָחוֹמֶר פְּרִיכָא, דְּאִיכָּא לְמִיפְרַךְ "דַּיּוֹ", וְהַשְׁתָּא אֲתָא הַאי קְרָא דְּפִנְחָס לְאַשְׁמוּעִינַן דְּבֵן יוֹרֵשׁ אֶת אִמּוֹ. וְלָא אַיְירֵי בְּסִיבַּת הַבַּעַל כְּלָל. **תָּא שְׁמַע.** מִפָּסוּק חֲמִישִׁי: "וּשְׂגוּב הוֹלִיד אֶת יָאִיר". **וְכִי תֵּימָא הָתָם נַמִי הָכִי הוּא.** כִּדַאֲמָרַן גַּבֵּי פִּנְחָס, שֶׁהָיְתָה לוֹ לִשְׂגוּב אִשָּׁה וּמֵתָה, וִירָשָׁהּ יָאִיר. **תְּרֵי קְרָאֵי לָמָּה לִי.** לְאַשְׁמוּעִינַן שֶׁהַבֵּן יוֹרֵשׁ אֶת אִמּוֹ כְּמוֹ הַבַּת. **וְיָאִיר דִּזְבַן מִזְבַּן.** לָקַח בַּכֶּסֶף הָנְהוּ עֲיָירוֹת. וְלֹא אָתָא קְרָא לְאוֹרוּיֵי לָן מִידֵּי, אֶלָּא עָשְׁרוֹ שֶׁל יָאִיר מַרְאֶה לָנוּ, כְּמוֹ שֶׁמָּלֵינוּ בְּהַרְבֵּה מְקוֹמוֹת בַּנְּבִיאִים. וְלֹא מִבַּעְיָא קָאָמַר; לָא מִבַּעְיָא דְּאִם בִּירוּשׁוֹת מַיְירֵי כִּדְקָאָמְרַן, דְּלֵיכָּא לְמִיפְרַךְ: תְּרֵי קְרָאֵי לָמָּה לִי, שֶׁהַפְּסוּקִים לֹא בָּאוּ לְלַמֵּד לָנוּ אֶלָּא עָשְׁרָם, וְסִיפּוּר דְּבָרִים בְּעָלְמָא הוּא, וְאִיכָּא לְמֵילַף מִינַּיְיהוּ מִיהָא סִיבַּת הַבֵּן. אֶלָּא גְּדוֹלָה מִזּוֹ יֵשׁ לְהַקְשׁוֹת לָךְ: דְּאִיכָּא לְמֵימַר דִּקְרָאֵי לָא אַיְירֵי בִּירוּשָּׁה כְּלָל, וְלָא תִּשְׁמַע מִינֵּיהּ לֹא סִיבַּת הַבֵּן וְלֹא סִיבַּת הַבַּעַל, אֶלָּא תַּרְוַיְיהוּ זְבִין מִזְבַּן, וְסִיפּוּר דְּבָרִים בְּעָלְמָא הוּא. (ב) וְהַתַּנָּא עַצְמוֹ לֹא נִתְכַּוֵּין לִדְרוֹשׁ יִתּוּר קְרָאֵי, אֶלָּא הָכִי קָאָמַר: מִנַּיִן הָיָה לוֹ לְפִנְחָס כו'. וְאִיכָּא לְאַקְשׁוּיֵי: יָכוֹל לִהְיוֹת לוֹ מִמְּקָח וּמִמְכָּר. וּפִנְחָס נַמִי דִּזְבַן מִזְבַּן. רְבוּתָא הוּא דְּקָפָּרֵיךְ, דִּבְלָאו הַאי פִּירְכָא נַמִי לָא הֲוָה מָצֵי לְמֵילַף מִינֵּיהּ סִיבַּת הַבַּעַל, כִּדְפָרְכִינַן לְעֵיל: וְכִי תֵּימָא אֶלְעָזָר הוּא דְּנָסֵיב כו'. (ג) כְּלוֹמַר, וַאֲפִילּוּ פִּנְחָס נַמִי, דְּסָלְקָא דַּעְתָּךְ מֵעִיקָּרָא לְמֵילַף מִינֵּיהּ יְרוּשַּׁת הַבַּעַל — אִיכָּא לְמֵימַר דְּלָא אַיְירֵי בְּשׁוּם יְרוּשָּׁה בָּעוֹלָם. וּמְשַׁנֵּי. הַךְ רְבוּתָא דְּקָפָּרְכַתְּ מִפִּנְחָס — לֵיתָא, דְּלֵיכָּא לְמֵימַר גַּבֵּיהּ דִּזְבַן מִיזְבַּן, דְּאִם כֵּן לֹא הָיָה קוֹבֵר בָּהּ אֶת אָבִיו, דְּנִמְצֵאת חוֹזֶרֶת כו'. וּמִיהוּ, אִיכָּא לְאַקְשׁוּיֵי הָנָךְ קוּשְׁיוֹת דִּלְעֵיל, דִּבְלָאו הַךְ קוּשְׁיָא אִיכָּא פִּירְכָא אַחֲרִיתִי דִּלְעֵיל, דְּלָא מָצֵינוּ לְמֵילַף מִינֵּיהּ יְרוּשַּׁת הַבַּעַל. **מִשְּׂדֵה חֲרָמִים.** כִּדְכְתִיב (במדבר יח): "כָּל חֵרֶם בְּיִשְׂרָאֵל לְךָ יִהְיֶה". אִי נַמִי, הַהוּא דִּכְתִיב (ויקרא כז): "וְהָיָה הַשָּׂדֶה בְּצֵאתוֹ בַיֹּבֵל קֹדֶשׁ לַה' כִּשְׂדֵה הַחֵרֶם" שֶׁמִּתְחַלֵּק לַכֹּהֲנִים. וְהָווּ הָתָם חֲרָמִים טוּבָא, וְנָטַל אֶלְעָזָר חֶלְקוֹ בְּהָנְהוּ חֲרָמִים, וּלְחֵלֶק פִּנְחָס נָפְלָה הַהִיא גִּבְעָה. יֵשׁ שֶׁגּוֹרְסִין כֵּן: **א"ל אַבָּיֵי אִי סָלְקָא** דַּעְתָּךְ דְּבַעַל לָא יָרֵית סוֹף סוֹף כִּי מִינַּסְבָא כו'. וְאִי אֶפְשָׁר לְיַישְּׁבָהּ. וְעוֹד: מַה תֵּירוּץ מְתָרֵץ אַבָּיֵי לְרַב פָּפָּא דְּאַקְשֵׁי לֵיהּ דְּמִקְּרָאֵי דְּבָרַיְיתָא לָא מַשְׁמַע לֵיהּ יְרוּשַּׁת הַבַּעַל, דְּקָאָתֵי אַבָּיֵי לִיתֵּן טַעַם מִצַּד אַחֵר שֶׁהַבַּעַל יוֹרֵשׁ אֶת אִשְׁתּוֹ? מ"מ בָּרַיְיתָא לָא מִיתָּרְצָא, וּקְרָאֵי לָא מִיתָּרְצֵי. שֶׁהַתַּנָּא שֶׁאָמַר כָּל הָנֵי "וְאוֹמֵר" הוֹכִיחַ שֶׁאֵין לִלְמוֹד אֶלָּא מִן הָאַחֲרוֹן, וְגַם בְּאוֹתוֹ פָּרִיכְנָא לְעֵיל, וְאַבָּיֵי מַה בָּא לְפָרֵשׁ? וְא"ת: לֹא נִתְכַּוֵּין אַבָּיֵי לְתָרֵץ הַבָּרַיְיתָא, אֶלָּא לְהוֹדִיעַ לְרַב פָּפָּא שֶׁהַבַּעַל יוֹרֵשׁ אֶת אִשְׁתּוֹ — הֲלֹא רַב פָּפָּא עַצְמוֹ הָיָה יוֹדֵעַ דְּוַדַּאי בַּעַל יוֹרֵשׁ אֶת אִשְׁתּוֹ מִקְּרָאֵי טוּבָא, דִּלְקַמָּן בִּשְׁמַעְתִּין וּבְפִירְקִין דִּלְעֵיל! אֶלָּא ה"ג: וְכֵן נִמְצָא בִּתְשׁוּבַת רַבֵּינוּ גֵּרְשׁוֹם מְאוֹר עֵינֵי הַגּוֹלָה זַ"ל: אָמַר אַבָּיֵי סוֹף סוֹף הָא קָמִתְעַקְּרָא נַחֲלָה מִשִּׁבְטָא דְּאִימָּא לְשִׁבְטָא דְּאַבָּא. מִמַּאי? דִּלְמָא שָׁאנֵי הָתָם שֶׁכְּבָר הוּסַבָּה. וְדִלְמָא שֶׁכְּבָר הוּסַבָּה לָא אָמְרִינַן. אָמַר לֵיהּ רַב יֵימָר לְרַב אַשִׁי: אִי אָמְרַתְּ בִּשְׁלָמָא אָמְרִינַן שֶׁכְּבָר הוּסַבָּה — שַׁפִּיר, אֶלָּא אִי אָמְרַתְּ לָא אָמְרִינַן שֶׁכְּבָר הוּסַבָּה — הָא מִתְעַקְּרָא נַחֲלָה מִשִּׁבְטָא דְּאִימָּא לְשִׁבְטָא דְּאַבָּא! דְּמַנְסְבִינַן לָהּ לְגַבְרָא דַּאֲבוּהִי מִשִּׁבְטָא דַּאֲבוּהּ וְאִימֵּיהּ מִשִּׁבְטָא דְּאִימָּהּ.

מנין ליאיר שלא היה לשגוב. תימה לרשב"א: אי לבאי הארץ נתחלקה הארץ, אמאי לא היה ליאיר שלא היה לשגוב? **וכי** תימא לעבור עליו בשני לאוין. תימה: הא היכא דאיכא למידרש — לא מוקמינן בלאוי יתירי! *)וכי תימא דהכי קאמר: דאפילו אי מוקמת להו בלאוי יתירי איכא למילף שהבעל יורש את אשתו — דלא משמע הכי בסמוך, דקאמר: לעולם קראי בסיבת הבן, כדשנינן. **אם** כן תרי קראי למה לי. אע"ג דקרא קמא נמי שלא לצורך, דכבר שמעינן מתורת משה סיבת הבן — מ"מ בזה אינו מקפיד אי אשמועינן יהושע נמי סיבת הבן. אבל תרי זימני לית ליה לאשמועינן. רשב"א. **אימא** דנפלה ליה משדה חרמים. תימה לרשב"א: דלמה דוחק כל כך? כיון דבעא למימר דאתא קרא להראות עשרם, הוה ליה למימר דפנחס ויאיר ירשו מאמם או מאבי אמם! (ד) ונראה לר"י גירסת הספרים, דגרסינן: א"ל אביי אי סלקא דעתך דבעל לא ירית כו'. ולא גרסינן הכא: בין למ"ד בסיבת הבן בין למ"ד בסיבת הבעל, אלא גבי "אי אמרת בשלמא" דרב יימר בסמוך גרסינן ליה. ואמאי דאקשי רב פפא: דלמא קראי בסיבת הבן — מהדר אביי לשנויי הכי, וקאמר: אי אמרת בשלמא דבעל ירית וקרא אסיבת הבעל קפיד — אתי שפיר הא דמשמע דאתי קרא למיעבד תקנתא אפילו לנחלת האם שלא תסוב, מדכתיב ירושת שני מטות גבי איסור הסבה. אע"פ שכבר הוסבה נחלת האם — מ"מ קפיד קרא שלא תסוב יותר על ידי נישואי הבת. ובסיבת הבעל איכא תקנתא, דמנסבין לה גברא דאבוהי משבטא דאבוה ואימיה משבטא דאימה, דהשתא לא מתעקר ע"י סיבת הבעל יותר ממה שהוסבה כבר. ואע"פ כשימות בעל ויירשנו בנו מתעקרא נחלת האם משבטא דאימא לשבטא דאבא, שהרי הבן אביו ואמו מתיחסים על שבט אביהן, או שמת הבעל לא יירשנה כלל, שתתאלמן או תתגרש, ויירשנה הבן — הא לא איכפת ליה, לפי שאי אפשר לעשות תקנה לדבר זה. אלא אי אמרת דבעל לא ירית, וקראי במסיבת הבן כדקא פרכת, כי קא מינסבא נמי לגברא דאבוהי משבטא דאבוה ואימיה משבטא דאימה — מתעקרא נחלת האם על ידי הבן, כדפרי'. אלא ודאי בסיבת הבעל משתעי. ולהכי קים ליה לתנא דקרא ד"וכל בת יורשת נחלה" בסיבת הבעל כתיב, מדכתיב ביה ירושת שני מטות — משמע דלנחלת האם נמי עבדינן תקנתא שלא תסוב יותר. והכי פירושא דברייתא: הרי הוא אומר "וכל בת יורשת נחלה", ובסיבת הבעל הכתוב מדבר, דמהניא תקנתא לנחלת האם. וכי תימא בסיבת הבן משתעי, וקרא לא אתא למעבד תקנתא אלא לנחלת האב — תא שמע "לא תסוב נחלה", ומיתורא דקראי שמעינן דחד בסיבת הבן וחד בסיבת הבעל. ואם כן, ההוא דכתב ביה ירושת שני מטות, דמשמע דבעי תקנתא לנחלת האם — בסיבת הבעל כתב, דאשכחינן ביה תקנתא. **אמר** ליה רב פפא לאביי דלמא שאני התם שכבר הוסבה. אע"ג דכתיב ביה ירושת שני מטות — לא קפיד קרא אנחלת האם שכבר הוסבה. ולעולם קאי בסיבת הבן, אע"ג דליכא תקנתא לנחלת האם. א"ל: שכבר הוסבה לא אמרינן — אין סברא לומר שלא הקפיד הכתוב אנחלת אם אע"פ שכבר הוסבה, דכיון דכתיב ירושת שני מטות — משמע דבנחלת האם עבדינן נמי תקנתא. **אמר** ליה רב יימר לרב אשי אי אמרת בשלמא שכבר הוסבה היינו דמתוקמי קראי בין בסיבת הבן בין בסיבת הבעל כו'. רב יימר לא הוה יודע דאביי כי הוה מוקי לקרא בסיבת הבעל מפרש לקרא דמנסבין לה גברא דאבוהי משבטא דאבוה ואימיה משבטא דאימה, ולהכי קשיא ליה: אמאי ניחא ליה לאוקומי בסיבת הבעל טפי מבסיבת הבן? ובין הכי ובין הכי כי

*) [כדאיתא פסחים כח:]

רבינו גרשום

מאי ואומר. דכתב הכא: וכי תימא. דליכא למישמע מהכא מוכל בת יורשת נחלה דבעל יורש את אשתו אלא משום כך הזהירה תורה שלא תנשא לשבט אחר שהבן שיהיה לה ממנו יורש אותה ובנה נחשב אחר משפחת אביו שהוא משבט אחר והיינו הסבת נחלה ת"ש דהבעל יורש אתתיה דכתיב לא תסוב נחלה לבני ישראל ממטה אל מטה משמע דבהסבת הבעל הכתוב מדבר כי היכי דלא לירית לה בעל שהוא משבט אחר דאי בהסבת הבן הכתוב מדבר. תרתי קראי בהסבת הבן למה לי. וכי תימא להכי כתיבי תרי קראי בהסבת הבן דאי נסבה ממטה אחר עובר' עליו בלאו דכתיב לא תסוב נחלה ממטה למטה ועשה כדכתיב וכל בת יורשת נחלה ממטות בני ישראל לאחד ממשפחת מטה אביה תהיה לאשה ולא לאחר ולאו הבא מכלל עשה עשה. ת"ש דבעל ירית דכתיב ולא תסוב נחלה וגו' משמע דבסבת בעל הכתוב מדבר דאי בהסבת הבן כל הני קראי למה לי: וכי תימא לעולם בעל לא ירית אלא בהסבת הבן הכתוב מדבר. דאלעזר הוא דנסיב איתתא ומתה וירשה פנחס דהיינו בהסבת הבן. ת"ש דבעל יורש את אשתו דכתיב ושגוב הוליד את יאיר וגו'. וכי תימא הכי הוה מעשה כדפנחס דשגוב לקח אשה שהי' לה כ"ג ערים ומתה וירשה בנו יאיר ולעולם בעל לא ירית. אם כן תרי קראי דאתיין להא דרשה למה לי. אלא ש"מ חד בסיבת הבן וחד בסיבת הבעל: וקראי בסיב' הבן כדשנין. לעבור עליו בב' לאוין ועשה. והרי קרא דיאיר דאמרת מהיכן היו לו כ"ג ערים דזבן מיזבן שקנה אותן ולא משום הסבה דבן [וכן] פנחס ולעולם בעל לא ירית. ומשני פנחס דזבין מיזבן לא מצית למימר דאם כן שקנאה נמצאת שדה חוזרת לבעלים ביובל ונמצא אותו צדיק אלעזר קבור בקבר שאינו שלו: אלא אימא ודאי. דיאיר מזבן זבן ולפנחס הית' אותה שדה משדה חרמים. שבאותו פרק היה משמר של פנחס שהיה מכהן במשמרתו וכתיב אך כל חרם אשר יחרים איש לה' מכל אשר לו מאדם ובהמה ומשדה אחוזתו לא ימכר ולא יגאל כל חרם קדש קדשים הוא לה' דסתם שדה חרמים לכהן שנאמר כל חרם בישראל לך יהיה ואם נפשך לומר א"כ מה ת"ל קדש קדשים [הוא] אלא א) מלמד שחל על קדשים קלים כעל קדשים חמורי' שהכל לכהן וכה"ג אמרי' במס' ערכין (דף כח ע"ב) דהשתא לא הדרא ארעא ביובל ולעולם בעל לא ירית: אמר ליה אביי לרב פפא אי ס"ד כדקאמרת דבעל לא ירית ולהכי אזהר רחמנא וכל בת יורשת נחלה ממטות בני ישראל לא' ממשפחת מטה אביה תהיה לאשה לפי שאם היה משבט אחר ומתה והיתה לה בן היה יורשה והיתה מסבת נחלה אבל כשתנשא למשפחת מטה אביה ליכא הסבת נחלה [דהוא] נמי הוי משבט אביה ואמר ל' אביי סוף סוף מאי הוי מועיל הא מיתעקרא נחלה משבטא דאימא דהאי אתתא דהואי משבט שמעון ונפלה ביד בנה של זו שהוא שבט אביה (כל כך) מן ראובן דבתר אבא שייך הבן ואיכא הסבת נחלה שנופלת נחלת אימא שהיתה משבט שמעון ביד שבט ראובן. ומשני רב פפא לעולם בעל לא ירית וקראי בהסבת הבן כתיבי

כתיבי ודקא קשיא לך כי מתנסבא לשבטא אבוה מאי הוי מתעקרא נחלה משבטא דאימא לשבטא דאבא. הא לא קשיא דהא הסבה דהשתא דשבט אימא לשבט אביה על ידי בנה לא חשיבא הסבה גמורה דשאני התם דאמרינן שכבר הוסבה נחלה מתחלה מנשואין הראשונים של אביה ואמה של בת להיכא דנודוונו מטות אהדדי אע"ג דנודוונו בהיתר שבשעת נישואיה עדיין אחיה קיימין הראויין לירש את אביה הכי הוסבה נחלה מחמת הנהו נישואין הלכך השתא כשבנה יורשה דמתעקרא נחלה משבטא דאימא לשבטא דאבא לא חשיב [הסבה] גמורה שכבר הוסבה מתחלה: אמר ליה רב אשי. האי לאו תירוצא הוא דאמרת שכבר הוסבה מנשואין ראשונים הוסבה בהיתר דאחיה דאימא הוו קיימין אבל הא בת אע"ג דמתנסבא לאחר ממטה אבוה כשירשה בנה דשייך בתר אביה השתא הויא הסבה דאיסורא דאין לה יורש אלא (אוקלא) בנה שאין לה אחין וקא מתעקרא נחלה דשבטא דאימא לשבט אבוה הלכך לא מצינן לאוקמי בהסבת הבן כלל דאי יורשה בנה מתעקרא נחלה משבטא דאימא לשבטא דאבא ולא מצינן למעבד תקנה בהסבת הבן אלא ש"מ דבעל ירית ובהסבת הבעל איכא תקנה לא נסבה לחד דאבוה משבטא דאביה ואמיה משבטא דאימה דהדרי הוא כוותה ואי ירית אבוה לא מיעקרא נחלה דאימא דהא בעל נמי אמיה משבטא דאימה ונכסים דקיימי קיימי: אמר ליה רב יימר לרב אשי. אפי' לאביי דאמר לעיל דבעל ירית קרא בהסבת הבעל כתיבי בעל כרחו שכבר הוסבה אמרינן דאי לאו הכי מיתוקמי קראי שפיר דאי אמרת בשלמא דאמרינן שכבר הוסבה היינו דמיתוקמי קראי וכל בת יורשת נחלה ממטות בני ישראל וגו' ולא תסוב נחלה ממטה למטה אחר וגו'. מתוקמי שפיר בין בסיבת הבן בין בסיבת הבעל בסיבת הבן כדאמרן דההיא עקירה נחלה דאימא דהויא על ידי בן לא הוי עקירה דכבר הוסבה מנשואין קמאי וכן בסיבת הבעל הואיל ודמתנסבא לאחר ממשפחת אביה אי לא אמר' שכבר הוסבה שעל ידי בן לא הויא עקירה דבר אבתי מיעקרא נחלה משבטא דאימא לשבטא דאבא משום דבעלה בתר משפחת בית אבא שייך אלא כיון דאמרי' שכבר הוסבה ניחא לן דעקירה דהשתא לא חשיבא עקירה אלא אי אמרת דלא אמרינן שכבר הוסבה ובעל ירית אפי' כי מנסבא לאחר ממטה אביה מאי הוי סוף סוף קא מיעקרא נחלה משבטא דאימא לשבטה דאבוה ואי אפשר בתוכם ולרב יימר דמקשה הכא לא הוה משמע ליה דמינסבא לבעל דאימ' משבטא דאימה משום הכי מקשה ליה הכי דלא קיימי נכסים בדוכתייהו. ומשני ליה רב אשי לאביי לעולם אימא לך שכבר הוסבה לא אמר' ואפי' הכי דבעל ירית מתוקמי קראי שפיר ודקשיא לך הא מיתעקרא נחלה תרין הכי דמנסבינן לה לבעל דמתיליד אבוהי משבטא דאבוה ואימי' משבטא דאימה דהשתא קיימי נכסים כדמעיקרא בחזקת שבט ראובן ושבט שמעון וליכא סיבת נחלה כלל ואם לחשך אדם לומר כיון דבעל ירית וקראי בסיבת בעל כתיבי

א) נראה דל"ל מלמד שחל על קדשי קדשים כעל קדשים קלים שהכל לכהן וכו'.

הגהות הב"ח (א) גמ' שכבר הוסבה ולדלמא שכבר הוסבה לא אמרינן: (ב) רשב"ם ד"ה ויאיר וכו' וסיפור דברים בעלמא הוא ואפי' אח"ל דהתנא עצמו לא: (ג) ד"ה ופנחס נמי כו' דנסיב כו' אלא כלומר: (ד) תוס' ד"ה אימא וכו' ונראה לר"י. נ"ב זהו דיבור בפני עצמו:

אי הכי, האי "לאחד ממשפחת מטה אביה ואמה" מיבעי ליה! אי כתיב הכי, הוה אמינא אפילו איפכא, קא משמע לן. תניא בסבת הבן, ותניא בסבת הבעל. (א) תניא בסבת הבן: "ולא תסב נחלה לבני ישראל ממטה אל מטה" (במדבר לו) – בסבת הבן הכתוב מדבר; אתה אומר: בסבת הבן, או אינו אלא בסבת הבעל? כשהוא אומר "ולא תסב נחלה ממטה למטה אחר" (שם) – הרי בסבת הבעל אמור, הא מה אני מקיים "ולא תסוב נחלה לבני ישראל ממטה אל מטה" – בסבת הבן הכתוב מדבר.

תניא

אי הכי האי לאחד כו'. וה"פ: לאביי, האי קרא ד"וכל בת יורשת נחלה" מספקא ליה אי דווקא קאמר "לאחד ממשפחת מטה אביה תהיה לאשה", אבל לשבט דאמה דידה – לא חיישינן. או דלמא בעינן נמי שיהא ממשפחת אמה, והאי דקאמר משפחת אביה – לאו דווקא, דהוא הדין דבעינן שיהא ממשפחת אמה, כדלקמן במסקנא. והכי קמבעיא ליה: האי קרא ד"וכל בת יורשת נחלה ממטות" – הא אוקימנא ביורשת שני מטות, שהיה אביה משבט ראובן ואמה משבט שמעון, ומתו, וירשתן זו הבת, ואמרה תורה: "לאחד ממשפחת מטה אביה תהיה לאשה" והוא שבט ראובן. עכשיו, משתנשא לאחד משבט ראובן ותלד בן ויירשנה בנה, או תמות ויירשנה בעלה – הלא הבן ההוא או הבעל ההוא לשבט ראובן מתייחסים, למשפחת אביו, והנה נמלאת הנחלה שירשה מאמה שהיתה משבט שמעון – הוסבה משבט שמעון לשבט ראובן, והכתוב הזהיר לנו "ולא תסוב נחלה", כלומר הזהרו בכל נשואי נשים שבשעת נישואין לא יוכלו לבא לידי הסבת נחלה, לא שנא הסבת נחלת אב של אשה, לא שנא הסבת נחלת אמה – בתרוייהו איכא למימר דקפיד קרא שלא תסוב למטה אחר. ולקמיה פריך: הא בעל כרחך קרא קאמר "למשפחת מטה אביה" וגו' – אבל למשפחת אמה לא חייש, וכיון דלא (ב) שייך – שמעינן מינה דהאי "לא תסוב" לא קפיד אלא אנחלה שיורשת מאב! ולאביי משנינן לה לקמן דאיכא למימר דמנסבין לה גברא דדמי לה, שאביו מראובן ואמו משמעון. ומשנינן: דלמא שאני התם שכבר הוסבה. כלומר, לעולם אימא לך דקרא לא קפיד אם מוסבת נחלת אם למטה אחר, שהרי בעל כרחך כבר הוסבה משעה שנפלה ירושת האם שמשבט שמעון לזו הבת, שאביה משבט ראובן והיא מתייחסת למטה אביה. נמלא שמעלמא הוסבה הנחלה של שמעון לשבט ראובן בלא נישואי הבת, הלכך, כי מנסבינן לה לאחד ממשפחת מטה אביה – שפיר דמי, ולא קפיד קרא אלא אנחלה שהיא יורשת מאביה, שלא תוסב למטה אחר. דההיא שיורשת מאביה – כדקיימא קיימא, דאכתי בחזקת שבט ראובן איתא לנחלה, שהבת על שם שבט ראובן מתייחסת. ואביי פריך: ודלמא שכבר הוסבה לא אמרינן. כלומר, בשביל שהוסבה קצת – אין לנו לומר: לא חיישי תו אי מתעקרא לגמרי, ומנסבינן לה לגברא דהוא משבט ראובן מאביו ומאמו, ומתעקרא נחלת אם שירשה בת זו שהיא מנחלת מטה שמעון – אין לנו לומר כן, שהרי "לא תסוב" כתיב, דמשמע: לא תסוב על ידי נישואין כלל. שאע"פ שהוסבה קצת – לא נוסיף להסיבה יותר ולעקרה לגמרי, אלא נעשה לה תקנה שלא תעקר לגמרי, כדלקמן. לפי שהיה יודע אביי שאפשר לעשות תקנה שלא תעקר נחלת האם, כדלקמן, הלכך פריך הכי: ודלמא שכבר הוסבה לא אמרינן, שאפשר בתקנה. או דלמא קרא לא חייש להיות הסבה, דלא קפיד אלא שתנשא לאחד ממטה אביה, אבל לאמה לא חייש. א"ל רב יימר לרב אשי. אמאי מספקא ליה לאביי אי אמרינן שכבר הוסבה או לא אמרינן? הא ודאי מקרא שמעינן דאמרי שכבר הוסבה, דהא לא קפיד קרא אי מיעקרא נחלה דאימא, כדכתיב: "לאחד ממשפחת מטה אביה" וגו' – ולאמה לא חייש. דאי אמרת בשלמא אמרינן שכבר הוסבה – שפיר, דהא לא קפיד קרא אי מיעקרא נחלה דאימא, כדכתיב: "לאחד ממשפחת מטה אביה", דהא השתא ודאי מיעקרא לגמרי נחלת אימא. אלא אי אמרת לא אמרינן דכבר הוסבה, כדקאמר אביי, והלא כשניסת לאחד ממשפחת אביה כדכתב בקרא – הא ודאי מיעקרא נחלה משבטא דאימא לשבטא דאבא! אלא לאו שמע מינה דאמרינן שכבר הוסבה. והלכך, כי אמר רחמנא "לא תסוב" – אירושת אב קאי, אבל ירושה דאימא – כבר הוסבה, ולא חיישינן אם תעקר לגמרי. דמנסבינן לה כו'. אליבא דאביי קא משני, דהכי קמיבעיא ליה: מי אמרינן שכבר הוסבה, כדמוכח קרא כדכתיב: "ממשפחת מטה אביה תהיה לאשה", דהשתא מיעקרא נחלה דאימא, וכי כתיב "לא תסוב" – אנחלת אב קא מזהר רחמנא, ולא אנחלת אם. או דלמא "לא תסוב" דווקא, דאפילו בנחלת אם מזהר לן רחמנא, ולא אמרינן שכבר הוסבה. והאי דכתיב: "מטה אביה" – לאו דווקא, אלא דמנסבינן לה לגברא שהוא דומה לה מכל וכל, שאביו משבט ראובן כמותה ואמו משבט שמעון דוגמת האשה הזאת. דהשתא ליכא עקירת נחלה כלל, דבודאי נחלתה מאביה לא מיעקרא כלל, דמשבט ראובן היתה והשתא נמי של שבט ראובן היא, דבין בנה ובין בעלה מתייחסין על שבט ראובן. ואע"ג דמעיקרא היתה משבט ראובן לגמרי, והשתא נהפכה לאיש שמקצת משמעון – אין זו הוסבה, שהרי לא חסר הכתוב ליקח לאיש משבט ראובן אשה משבט שמעון כדי שלא יירש הבן שהוא משבט אחר מצד אמו. ואע"פ שנהפכה נחלת איש שכולו מראובן לבנו שמשבט שמעון מצד אמו. ונחלת אמה של בת זו שמשבט שמעון לא מיעקרא כלל, דאי ירית לה בעל שהוא משמעון מצד אמו ואביו מראובן, או בנו, נמצאת גם עתה הנחלה בחזקת איש שמקצת מאב ומקצת מאם כמו שהיתה בחזקתה, שהיא מראובן ומשמעון. אי הכי. דאשה היורשת ב' מטות בעינן נמי שתנשא לאיש שנולד מהנהו ב' מטות – "ממשפחת מטה אביה ואמה" מיבעי ליה. אלא מדכתב "מטה אביה" לחוד – שמעינן דלא קפיד קרא אעקירת נחלת אם, לפי שכבר הוסבה, ואכתי מאי איבעיא ליה לאביי? ומשני: אי כתב. רחמנא הכי, "מטה אביה ואמה" – הוה אמינא אפילו איפכא – אביו משמעון ואמו מראובן, ואע"פ שאביה מראובן ואמה משמעון. דסד"א: לא קפיד קרא אלא שיהא הוא נמי מאותן שני מטות שלה, בין באותו ענין בין למפרע, דהשתא נמי לא מיעקרא לא נחלת אב ולא נחלת אם לגמרי, דהא בהאי בעל איכא חד צד מראובן וחד צד משמעון, ונמצאו שני הנחלות של שבט שמעון וראובן בחזקתן קיימי, קמ"ל: דווקא "ממשפחת מטה אביה" יהא עיקר הייחס של בעלה, שיהא נמי אביו משבט ראובן. שאילו היה אביו משמעון, אע"פ שאמו מראובן, הרי הוסבה נחלת ראובן למטה שמעון, שעיקר יחס הבן אחר אביו, והבת אחר אביה. ומדכתב "לא תסוב" – ממילא שמעינן דמנסבינן לה גברא דאימיה נמי משבטא דאימא של זו, כדי שלא תעקר נחלת האם יותר. והיינו דמספקא ליה מעיקרא: סוף סוף הא קא מתעקרא כו'. אם לא תרצה לומר דמנסבינן לה גברא דאימיה משבטא דאימה ואבוהי משבטא דאבוה, משום דקשיא לך: מטה אביה ואמה מיבעי ליה, ול"לא תסוב" לא חיישת, דלא איירי קרא בהסבת נחלת אם משום דכבר הוסבה. אדרבה, "לא תסוב" דווקא הוא, ולא אמרינן שכבר הוסבה, אבל "מטה אביה" לאו דווקא, דהאי דלא כתב "מטה אביה ואמה" – משום דהוה אמינא אפילו איפכא, ולעולם מנסבינן לה לגברא דהוא נמי משבטא דאימה, ולא מיעקרא נחלה דאימא. וכיון דאיכא למימר הכי – לא אמרינן שכבר הוסבה. תניא בסיבת הבן תניא בסיבת הבעל. כלומר, אע"ג דאוקמינן להני תרי קראי – "לא תסוב נחלה לבני ישראל ממטה אל מטה" ו"לא תסוב נחלה ממטה למטה אחר" – תרוייהו בסיבת הבן, ולשני לאוי, כדקתני "ואומר", אפילו הכי אשכחן ברייתות דמוקי לקמא בסיבת הבן, ולתנייא בסיבת הבעל. וקדייק לה לקמן מדכתב ביה "למטה אחר", ובן לאו אחר הוא, אלא בבעל מיירי, ומדבתרא בסיבת הבעל – קמא בסיבת הבן. ושני הברייתות תנו בסיבת הבן ותנו נמי בסיבת הבעל, דבשני הברייתות מפרש להני תרי קראי, ומוקי חד בסיבת הבן וחד בסיבת הבעל. ה"ג: תניא בסיבת הבן ותניא בסיבת הבעל לא תסוב נחלה לבני ישראל ממטה אל מטה בסיבת הבן הכתוב מדבר אתה אומר בסיבת הבן או אינו אלא בסיבת הבעל כשהוא אומר לא תסוב נחלה ממטה למטה אחר הרי הסבת הבעל אמור הא מה אני מקיים לא תסוב נחלה לבני ישראל ממטה אל מטה בסיבת הבן הכתוב מדבר.

תניא

כי מינסבא לשבטא דאבוה — מתעקרא נחלת האם משבטא דאימא לשבטא דאבא, כיון דלא אמר שכבר הוסבה! ומשני: דמנסבינן לה וכו'. ועל פ"ה יש לתמוה: שאין זה שיטת גמרא, דרב פפא אקשי לאביי אברייתא, ואביי לא מהדר מידי, ועושה בעיא שלו בלשון קושיא. ועוד, דמסיק אביי: שכבר הוסבה לא אמרינן, ולפירושו הוה ליה למימר "ודלמא", דהא מספקא ליה, ואין בספרים "ודלמא". ועוד: דבכל הספרים גרסינן "אמר ליה אביי" דמשמע דאקושיא דאקשי ליה רב פפא מהדר לשנויי. ה"ג ר"ת: תניא בסיבת הבעל לא תסוב נחלה לבני ישראל ממטה למטה (ג) (אחר) — הרי בסיבת הבעל הכתוב מדבר. אתה אומר בסיבת הבעל, או אינו אלא בסיבת הבן? כשהוא אומר "לא תסוב נחלה ממטה למטה אחר" — הרי בסיבת הבעל הכתוב מדבר. דכמו שזה בסיבת הבעל גם זה בסיבת הבעל. דלפירוש הקונטרס לא אתי שפיר אמאי קרי הך בסיבת הבן והך בסיבת הבעל — והא תרוייהו איירי בין בסיבת הבן ובין בסיבת הבעל. וזהו דוחק לומר דמשום דהאי תנא פתח בקרא דסיבת הבן, והאי תנא פתח בקרא דסיבת הבעל, קאמר הכי. ולגירסת רבינו תם אתי שפיר הא דתניא בסיבת הבעל, דתרי קראי מוקי להו בסיבת הבעל. ותניא בסיבת הבן דקרא קמא מוקי בסיבת הבן. ועוד, דלפ"ה הוה מצי למימר נמי דכ"ע מיהת קרא קמא בסיבת הבן מאי משמע.

תרוייהו

כתיבי אפי' בר בריה ירית ליה לאב ואיכא סיבת נחלה משבטא דאמא לשבטא דאבא והבן שייך בתר האב לחודיה. תריץ הכי דלא מזהר קרא דכי תסוב אלא בשעת נישואין דבשעת נישואין מזהיר דמנסבין לה כי היכי דלא תסוב אבל מן הבן והיורשין לא מזהיר הואיל דנישאת למשפחת אביה. ומקשי רב יימר אי הכי כדמוקמת לה האי דכתב בקרא לאחד ממשפחת אביה ואמה מיבעי ליה ומשני אע"ג דלא כתב בקרא ממשפחת מטה אביה ואמה משמע הכי דכי האי גוונא קיימי נכסים כדקיימי קיימי וגלי רחמנא ממשפחת מטה אביה והוא הדין למשפחת אמה דאי כתב רחמנא לאחד ממשפחת מטה אביה ואמה הוה אמינא אפי' איפכא דאבא של בעל ממשפחת אמה של בת ואמו של בעל ממשפחת אביה של בת דהשתא מתעקרא נחלה משום דבעל שייך אחר אביו קמ"ל דאיפכא לא אלא אביו משבט אביה ואמו משבט אמה כי היכי דמתוקמי קראי שפיר: תנא בסבת הבן. ולא תסוב נחלה לבני ישראל ממטה למטה בסיבת הבן הכתוב מדבר כו'. ובהאי לישנא איכא למשמע בין בסיבת הבן בין בסיבת הבעל אבל באידך לישנא ליכא למשמע מינה כי אם בסיבת הבעל לחוד

(א) גמ' ותניא בסיבת הבעל ולא תסוב כצ"ל ותיבות תניא בסיבת הבן נמחק: (ב) רשב"ם ד"ה אי הכי וכו' וכיון דלא חייש שמעינן מינה: (ג) תוס' ד"ה ה"ג ר"ת וכו' ממטה למטה בסיבת הבעל כצ"ל ותיבות אחר הרי נמחק ונ"ב כך היא גירסת ר"ת תניא בסיבת הבן תניא בסיבת הבעל תניא בסיבת הבן ולא תסוב נחלה ממטה וכו' תניא בסיבת הבעל ולא תסוב נחלה לבני ישראל ממטה למטה בסיבת הבעל הכתוב מדבר אתה אומר כו' כשהוא אומר לא תסוב נחלה ממטה למטה אחר הרי בסיבת הבעל הכתוב מדבר:

תַּנְיָא אִידָךְ לֹא תִסּוֹב נַחֲלָה מִמַּטֶּה לְמַטֶּה אַחֵר בְּסִיבַּת הַבַּעַל הַכָּתוּב מְדַבֵּר אַתָּה אוֹמֵר בְּסִיבַּת הַבַּעַל אוֹ אֵינוֹ אֶלָּא בְּסִיבַּת הַבֵּן כְּשֶׁהוּא אוֹמֵר לֹא תִסּוֹב נַחֲלָה לִבְנֵי יִשְׂרָאֵל מִמַּטֶּה אֶל מַטֶּה הֲרֵי סִיבַּת הַבֵּן אָמוּר הָא מָה אֲנִי מְקַיֵּים מִמַּטֶּה לְמַטֶּה אַחֵר בְּסִיבַּת הַבַּעַל הַכָּתוּב מְדַבֵּר. וּמַשְׁמָעוּת דּוֹרְשִׁין אִיכָּא בֵּינַיְיהוּ; תַּנָּא דְּבָרַיְיתָא קַמַּיְיתָא פְּשִׁיטָא לֵיהּ דִּקְרָא בַּתְרָא, דְּהַיְינוּ "מִמַּטֶּה לְמַטֶּה אַחֵר" – בְּסִיבַּת הַבַּעַל מַיְירֵי, כִּדְמְפָרֵשׁ לְקַמֵּיהּ, מִדִּכְתִיב בֵּיהּ "אַחֵר", וְהִלְכָּךְ מוֹקֵי לְקַמָּא בְּסִיבַּת הַבֵּן, דִּתְרֵי קְרָאֵי בְּסִיבַּת הַבַּעַל לָמָּה לִי? וּסְבִירָא לֵיהּ לְהַאי תַּנָּא כִּדְאָמְרִינַן בְּעָלְמָא (פסחים כד.) דְּכָל הֵיכָא דְּאִיכָּא לְמִידְרַשׁ – דָּרְשִׁינַן, וְלָא מוֹקְמִינַן בְּלָאוֵי יְתֵירֵי. וְתַנָּא בַּתְרָא לָא סְבִירָא לֵיהּ הַךְ דְּרָשָׁא דְּאַחֵר דִּלְקַמָּן, וּמוֹקֵי מִסְּבָרָא לִקְרָא קַמָּא בְּסִיבַּת הַבֵּן, דְּקָרֵיב לֵיהּ טְפֵי מִבַּעַל, וּמִתּוֹךְ כָּךְ אִיַּיתַּר לֵיהּ קְרָא תִּנְיָנָא לְסִיבַּת הַבַּעַל. כֵּן נִרְאֶה בְּעֵינַי, וְעִיקָּר. דְּכוּלֵּי עָלְמָא מִיהַת. אֲפִילּוּ תַּנָּא דְּבָרַיְיתָא קַמַּיְיתָא, סְבִירָא לֵיהּ דְּהַאי "מִמַּטֶּה לְמַטֶּה אַחֵר" – בְּסִיבַּת הַבַּעַל מַיְירֵי. מַאי מַשְׁמַע. לְתַנָּא קַמָּא קָבָּעֵי לֵיהּ. דְּבִשְׁלָמָא לְבָרַיְיתָא בַּתְרַיְיתָא – קְרָא קַמָּא סְבִירָא לֵיהּ בְּסִיבַּת הַבֵּן, מִשּׁוּם דְּקָרוֹב לְאִמּוֹ טְפֵי מִבַּעַל, אִיַּיתַּר "מִמַּטֶּה לְמַטֶּה אַחֵר" לְסִיבַּת הַבַּעַל. וְלָאו מִמַּשְׁמָעוּתָא מוֹקֵי לֵיהּ הָכִי, אֶלָּא מִיַּיתּוּרָא. אֶלָּא לְת"ק דְּאָמַר דְּהַאי "מִמַּטֶּה לְמַטֶּה אַחֵר" פְּשִׁיטָא לֵיהּ דִּבְסִיבַּת הַבַּעַל מַיְירֵי, וְאִיהוּ מְגַלֵּי אַאִידָךְ קְרָא דִּבְסִיבַּת הַבֵּן מַיְירֵי, מְנָא מַשְׁמַע לֵיהּ סִיבַּת הַבַּעַל? **אָמַר קְרָא אִישׁ.** דְּמַשְׁמַע בַּעַל, כְּמוֹ "אִישׁ נָעֳמִי" (רות א), כְּלוֹמַר, בְּסִיבַּת הַבַּעַל קָפֵיד קְרָא. סֵיפָא דְּהַאי קְרָא דְּ"מִמַּטֶּה לְמַטֶּה אַחֵר" – "כִּי אִישׁ בְּנַחֲלָתוֹ יִדְבְּקוּ מַטּוֹת בְּנֵי יִשְׂרָאֵל", כְּלוֹמַר, הַבַּעַל בְּנַחֲלָתוֹ יִדְבַּק, וְלֹא בְּנַחֲלַת שֵׁבֶט אַחֵר. תַּרְוַיְיהוּ נַמֵי **אִישׁ** כְּתִיב בְּהוּ. דִּכְתִיב בִּקְרָא קַמָּא: "מִמַּטֶּה אֶל מַטֶּה כִּי אִישׁ בְּנַחֲלַת מַטֵּה אֲבוֹתָיו יִדְבְּקוּ בְּנֵי יִשְׂרָאֵל", וְאִי "אִישׁ" מַשְׁמַע לֵיהּ סִיבַּת הַבַּעַל – תַּרְוַיְיהוּ נַמֵי בְּסִיבַּת הַבַּעַל! וּמִיהוּ, גַּם הַמְתָרֵץ הָיָה יוֹדֵעַ דִּבְהַאי קְרָא "אִישׁ" כְּתִיב, דְּזִיל קְרִי בֵּי רַב הוּא. וְאַמַּאי דְּבָעֵינַן לְעֵיל: מְנָא מַשְׁמַע דְּהַאי קְרָא "מִמַּטֶּה לְמַטֶּה אַחֵר" בְּסִיבַּת הַבַּעַל מַיְירֵי, אָתָא אִיהוּ לְמֵימַר דְּשַׁפִּיר מַשְׁמַע דִּבְסִיבַּת הַבַּעַל מַיְירֵי, דְּהָא כְּתִיב בֵּיהּ "אִישׁ", וּתְמַהּ עַל עַצְמְךָ: לָמָּה גַּם הָרִאשׁוֹן אֵינוֹ מְדַבֵּר בְּסִיבַּת הַבַּעַל כֵּיוָן דִּכְתִיב בֵּיהּ "אִישׁ"? אֶלָּא מִתּוֹךְ שֶׁמְּיוּתָּר – מוֹקֵי לֵיהּ בְּסִיבַּת הַבֵּן, וְהַהוּא "אִישׁ" דִּקְרָא קַמָּא לִדְרָשָׁא בְּעָלְמָא אָתָא. וְגַם הַמַּקְשֶׁה מֵשִׁיב: תַּרְוַיְיהוּ נַמֵי "אִישׁ" כְּתִיב בְּהוּ, וּמָה רָאִיתָ שֶׁיְּהֵא אַחֲרוֹן דַּוְקָא וְקַמָּא לִדְרָשָׁא? אַדְּרַבָּה, קַמָּא לְגוּפֵיהּ לְסִיבַּת הַבַּעַל, וּבַתְרָא לִדְרָשָׁא, וְאַכַּתִּי מַאי מַשְׁמַע דְּבַתְרָא בְּסִיבַּת הַבַּעַל? **יִדְבְּקוּ.** אֵין לְשׁוֹן דֶּבֶק אֶלָּא בֵּין אִישׁ לְאִשָּׁה, כִּדְכְתִיב: "וְדָבַק בְּאִשְׁתּוֹ" (בראשית ב), דְּכֵיוָן דִּמְפוֹרָשׁ כָּל כָּךְ, דִּכְתִיב בֵּיהּ לְשׁוֹן דְּבִיקָה – וַדַּאי בְּסִיבַּת בַּעַל מַיְירֵי. וּמֵהָכָא הוּא דַּהֲוָה פְּשִׁיטָא לֵיהּ לְתַנָּא. וְאַע"ג דִּבְקְרָא קַמָּא נַמֵי "יִדְבְּקוּ" כְּתִיב – תֵּיתֵי לִדְרָשָׁא בְּעָלְמָא. **מַטּוֹת.** מַשְׁמַע בַּעַל, דִּדְבִיקַת מַטּוֹת עַל יְדֵי בַּעַל הוּא. תַּרְוַיְיהוּ נַמֵי מַטּוֹת כְּתִיב בְּהוּ. לָא גָּרַס. **רַב אַשִׁי אָמַר.** הָכִי מַשְׁמַע קְרָא: לֹא תִסּוֹב נַחֲלָה מִמַּטֵּה הָאִשָּׁה לְמַטֶּה אַחֵר, שֶׁיִּירָשֶׁנָּה בַּעְלָהּ אִם תִּנָּשֵׂא לוֹ, שֶׁהוּא אַחֵר לְגַבָּהּ. אֲבָל אִם נוֹסֶבֶת הַנַּחֲלָה עַל יְדֵי בְּנָהּ שֶׁיּוֹרְשָׁהּ – אֵינוֹ אַחֵר מַמָּשׁ לְגַבָּהּ, דְּיוֹרֵשׁ כַּרְעֵיהּ דְּאִמֵּיהּ הוּא. **בְּרָאוּי.** כְּגוֹן שֶׁמֵּתָה אִשְׁתּוֹ, וְאַחַ"כ מֵת אָבִיהָ, דְּנַחֲלָה זוֹ רְאוּיָה לָהּ אִילּוּ הָיְתָה קַיֶּימֶת – מִנַּיִן שֶׁלֹּא יִירַשׁ, אֶלָּא קְרוֹבֶיהָ מִצַּד הָאָב, אוֹ בְּנָהּ יִירָשֶׁנָּה? שֶׁהַבֵּן יוֹרֵשׁ אֶת זְקֵנוֹ, כִּדְכְתִיב: "וְאִם אֵין לוֹ בַּת" – עַיֵּין עָלֶיהָ, שֶׁכֵּן הַבַּת יוֹרֶשֶׁת אָבִיהָ. **בְּבַמּוּחְזָק.** יְרוּשָּׁה שֶׁהִיא מוּחְזֶקֶת כְּבָר קוֹדֶם מִיתָתָהּ, כְּגוֹן שֶׁמֵּת אָבִיהָ וְאַחַר כָּךְ מֵתָה הִיא. וּמִנַּיִן שֶׁלֹּא יִירַשׁ? דְּסַד"א: כֵּיוָן דְּבַעַל קוֹדֵם לִבְנָהּ לִירָשָׁהּ – וְה"נ כְּשֶׁמֵּתָה וְאַחַר כָּךְ נָפְלָה לָהּ יְרוּשָּׁה יַקְדִּים הָאָב לִבְנוֹ. דְּק"ו הוּא: כֵּיוָן דִּבְמָקוֹם בֵּן הוּא קוֹדֵם לִיטּוֹל בְּמוּחְזָק – בְּרָאוּי נַמֵי הוּא יוֹרֵשׁ, ק"ו מִבֵּן שֶׁיּוֹרֵשׁ בְּרָאוּי. **וִירָשָׁהּ יָאִיר.** וְלֹא שְׂגוּב אָבִיו, לְפִי שֶׁאֵין הַבַּעַל נוֹטֵל בְּרָאוּי. דְּאִילּוּ הָיָה נוֹטֵל בְּרָאוּי – הוּא הָיָה יוֹרְשָׁהּ וְלֹא יָאִיר בְּנָהּ, שֶׁהָאָב קוֹדֵם לִבְנוֹ בִּירוּשַּׁת אִשְׁתּוֹ. וִירָשָׁהּ יָאִיר. לְאִשְׁתּוֹ. **נַחֲלָה הָרְאוּיָה לוֹ וִירָשָׁהּ בְּנוֹ.** מֵ"אֲשֶׁר נִיתַּן לוֹ בְּהַר אֶפְרָיִם" קָדָיֵיק, דְּמַשְׁמַע שֶׁבָּאוּ לַדִּין אֶלְעָזָר וּפִנְחָס עַל עֵסֶק יְרוּשָּׁה זוֹ, לְפִי שֶׁהָיְתָה רְאוּיָה לְאֶלְעָזָר וְנָתְנָה בֵּית דִּין לְפִנְחָס בְּנוֹ, לְפִי שֶׁאֵין הַבַּעַל נוֹטֵל בְּרָאוּי. וְרַבֵּינוּ חֲנַנְאֵל פֵּירֵשׁ דְּדָיְיקִינַן מִדִּכְתִיב בְּהַאי קְרָא "בְּנוֹ", וְכִי אִילּוּ כָּתַב "בְּגִבְעַת פִּנְחָס" וְלֹא אָמַר "בְּנוֹ" – הֲלֹא יָדוּעַ שֶׁפִּנְחָס בֶּן אֶלְעָזָר הוּא, וּמִפְּנֵי מָה כָּתַב "בְּנוֹ"? לְלַמֵּד כִּי זוֹ הַגִּבְעָה הָיְתָה רְאוּיָה לְאֶלְעָזָר, וִירָשָׁהּ פִּנְחָס בְּנוֹ. דְּ"בְנוֹ" מִיעוּט מַשְׁמַע – בְּנוֹ וְלֹא הוּא, מִכְּלָל שֶׁהָיְתָה רְאוּיָה לְאֶלְעָזָר. וְהִלְכָּךְ לֵיכָּא לְמֵימַר דְּנָפְלָה לֵיהּ מִשְּׂדֵה חֲרָמִים, שֶׁחֵלֶק פִּנְחָס לֹא הָיָה רָאוּי לְאֶלְעָזָר. כֵּן כָּתוּב בְּפֵירוּשֵׁי רַבֵּינוּ חֲנַנְאֵל. **וּבְנֵי אֲחוֹת.** יוֹרְשִׁין אֲחֵי אִמָּן. **תָּנָא בְּנֵי אֲחוֹת וְלֹא בְּנוֹת אֲחוֹת.** וּכְדִמְפָרְשִׁינַן לְקַמֵּיהּ.

לְמַאי

תורה אור

(במדבר לו) תַּנְיָא אִידָךְ: "וְלֹא תִסּוֹב נַחֲלָה מִמַּטֶּה לְמַטֶּה אַחֵר" – בְּסִיבַּת הַבַּעַל הַכָּתוּב מְדַבֵּר; אַתָּה אוֹמֵר: בְּסִיבַּת הַבַּעַל, אוֹ אֵינוֹ אֶלָּא בְּסִיבַּת הַבֵּן? (שם) כְּשֶׁהוּא אוֹמֵר: "וְלֹא תִסּוֹב נַחֲלָה לִבְנֵי יִשְׂרָאֵל מִמַּטֶּה אֶל מַטֶּה" – הֲרֵי הַסִיבַּת הַבֵּן אָמוּר, הָא מָה אֲנִי מְקַיֵּים "וְלֹא תִסּוֹב נַחֲלָה מִמַּטֶּה לְמַטֶּה אַחֵר" – בְּסִיבַּת הַבַּעַל הַכָּתוּב מְדַבֵּר. דְּכוּלֵּי עָלְמָא מִיהַת, "מִמַּטֶּה לְמַטֶּה אַחֵר" – בְּסִיבַּת הַבַּעַל הַכָּתוּב מְדַבֵּר, מַאי מַשְׁמַע? [א]סִימָן אָמַר רַבָּה בַּר רַב שֵׁילָא, אָמַר קְרָא: "אִישׁ". תַּרְוַיְיהוּ "אִישׁ" כְּתִיב בְּהוּ! אֶלָּא אָמַר רַב נַחְמָן בַּר יִצְחָק, אָמַר קְרָא: "יִדְבְּקוּ". תַּרְוַיְיהוּ "יִדְבְּקוּ" כְּתִיב בְּהוּ! אֶלָּא אָמַר רָבָא, אָמַר קְרָא: "יִדְבְּקוּ מַטּוֹת". רַב אַשִׁי אָמַר, אָמַר קְרָא: "מִמַּטֶּה לְמַטֶּה אַחֵר", וּבֵן לָאו אַחֵר הוּא. א"ר אַבָּהוּ אָמַר ר' יוֹחָנָן אָמַר רַבִּי יַנַּאי אָמַר רַבִּי, וּמָטוּ בָּהּ מִשְּׁמֵיהּ דְּרַבִּי יְהוֹשֻׁעַ בֶּן קָרְחָה: מִנַּיִן [ב]לַבַּעַל [א]שֶׁאֵינוֹ נוֹטֵל בְּרָאוּי כִּבְמוּחְזָק? (דה"א ב) שֶׁנֶּאֱמַר: "וּשְׂגוּב הוֹלִיד אֶת יָאִיר וַיְהִי לוֹ עֶשְׂרִים וְשָׁלֹשׁ עָרִים בְּאֶרֶץ הַגִּלְעָד", מִנַּיִן לְיָאִיר שֶׁלֹּא הָיָה לוֹ לִשְׂגוּב? אֶלָּא, מְלַמֵּד שֶׁנָּשָׂא שְׂגוּב אִשָּׁה וּמֵתָה בְּחַיֵּי מוֹרִישֶׁיהָ, וּמֵתוּ מוֹרִישֶׁיהָ וִירָשָׁהּ יָאִיר; וְאוֹמֵר: (יהושע כד) "וְאֶלְעָזָר בֶּן אַהֲרֹן מֵת וַיִּקְבְּרוּ" וגו', מִנַּיִן לְפִנְחָס שֶׁלֹּא הָיָה לוֹ לְאֶלְעָזָר? מְלַמֵּד שֶׁנָּשָׂא אֶלְעָזָר אִשָּׁה וּמֵתָה בְּחַיֵּי מוֹרִישֶׁיהָ, וּמֵתוּ מוֹרִישֶׁיהָ וִירָשָׁהּ פִּנְחָס. וּמַאי "וְאוֹמֵר"? וְכִי תֵּימָא: יָאִיר דַּהֲוָה נְסֵיב אִיתְּתָא וּמֵתָה (א) וְיָרְתָהּ – תַּלְמוּד לוֹמַר: "וְאֶלְעָזָר בֶּן אַהֲרֹן מֵת"; וְכִי תֵּימָא: דִּנְפָלָה לֵיהּ בִּשְׂדֵה חֲרָמִים – אָמַר קְרָא: "בְּנוֹ", נַחֲלָה הָרְאוּיָה לוֹ, וִירָשָׁהּ בְּנוֹ.§ "וּבְנֵי אֲחוֹת".§ [ג]תָּנָא: בְּנֵי אֲחוֹת, וְלֹא בְּנוֹת אֲחוֹת.

לְמַאי

תרווייהו נמי ידבקו כתיב בהו. פעמים שלא היו בקיאין בפסוקים. וכן מלינו בסוף "שור שנגח את הפרה" (ב"ק דף נה.): מפני מה לא נאמר בדברות הראשונות "טוב" כו'. א"ל: עד שאתה שואלני כו', שאיני יודע אם נאמר בהן "טוב" או לאו, כלך אצל ר' תנחום כו'. ומיהו, הכא תימה, דמדאקשי ליה: תרווייהו "איש" כתיב בהו – משמע דידע פסוקים, ולא היה לו לתרץ: אמר קרא "ידבקו", כיון דתרווייהו נמי "ידבקו" כתיב! ובקונטרס פי' יפה: וקמא נמי ידע דתרווייהו "איש" כתיב בהו, ואתא לשנויי הא דקא בעי: מאי משמע, דשפיר משתמעי תרווייהו דאיירי בסיבת הבעל, מדכתב בהו "איש", אלא דמוקי תנא "איש" דקרא קמא לדרשא אחרינא. והוא דקאמר אמר קרא "ידבקו" – לא משמע ליה מ"איש" מידי, דדריש מ"ידבקו", ו"ידבקו" דקרא קמא דריש לדרשא אחרינא. **ומטו** בה משמיה דרבי יהושע בן קרחה. אומר ר"י: דקרחה הוא רבי עקיבא, שהיה קרח, כדאיתא בפרק בתרא דבכורות (דף נח. ושם ד"ה חוץ), דקאמר בן עזאי: כל חכמי ישראל דומין לפני כקליפת השום חוץ מן הקרח הזה. והיה לו בן ששמו יהושע, כדאמרינן בשבועות (דף ו.): א"ל רבי יהושע בנו של רבי עקיבא לר"ע. ואין נראה לרבינו תם, דנהי דבן עזאי הוא דקאמר ליה הכי בלשון בדיחותא – חס ושלום שהיה להעלות לו שם על שום קרחות, דגנאי הוא, כמו "עלה קרח" (מלכים ב ב). ובפרק "שואל" (שבת דף קנב.) דאמר ליה ההוא גוזאה לרבי יהושע: מהכא לקרחינאה כמה הוי כו' – שהיה מגנה אותו על שהיה קרח. ועוד, דאמרינן בפרק בתרא דמגילה (דף כח.): שאל רבי את רבי יהושע בן קרחה: במה הארכת ימים כו'. א"ל: רבי, ברכני. א"ל: יהי רצון שתגיע לחצי שנותי. ואי קרחה הוא ר' עקיבא – הלא לא נשא בת כלבא שבוע עד שקבל עליו ללמוד, ואז היה כבר בן ארבעים שנה, כדתניא (ספרי פ' הברכה): ארבעים שנה עסק בפרקמטיא, וארבעים שנה למד, וארבעים שנה לימד, וכל ימיו ק"כ שנה. ואפילו נולד ר' יהושע בנו מיד כשנשאה – אכתי לא היה כי אם בן פ' כשנולד רבי, דאמר בפרק בתרא דקידושין (דף עב:): עד שלא מת רבי עקיבא נולד רבינו הקדוש. ופחות ממאה וארבעים לא היה ר' יהושע כשבירך את רבי, דבפחות משבעים לא היה מברכו. וכבר היה רבי בן ששים שנה, ומה ברכה היא זו לברכו בעשר שנים? ועוד, דסברא שלא נולד עד שחזר ר' עקיבא מבי רב אחר כ"ד שנה, א"כ כשהיה ר' יהושע בן ק' וארבעים כבר היה רבי בן פ"ד, שהוא יותר מחצי ימיו. ועוד: שפי' רבינו נסים במגלת סתרים שמצא בבראשית רבה ד"חוץ מן הקרח" היה רבי אלעזר בן עזריה. אלא אומר ר"ת דקרחה הוא שם אדם, כמו קרח[ד]. **מתה** בחיי מורישיה (ב) וירשה יאיר. וא"ת: דבן יורש בראוי נכסי אמו, ובעל אינו יורש, מנלן דבעל קודם לבן? וי"ל: כיון שהבעל אינו יורש מחמת קורבה אלא מחמת שאירות, שהן חשובין כבשר אחד – אם כן כמו שהוא קודם לשאר קרובים, כך הוא קודם לבן, דמאי לי האי ומאי לי האי.

וירש

רבינו גרשום

וה"ג לה לא תסוב נחלה לבני ישראל ממטה אל מטה בסיבת הבעל הכתוב מדבר אתה אומר בסיבת הבעל או אינו אלא בסיבת הבן כשהוא אומר לא תסוב ממטה למטה אחר הוי אומר בסיבת הבעל הכתוב מדבר. דילפינן סתום ממפורש וליכא למשמע מהכא כי אם בסיבת הבעל: דכולי עלמא מיהת. בין תנא קמא בין תנא בתרא: ממטה למטה אחר בסיבת הבעל הכתוב מדבר כו': אמר קרא איש. איש כתיב ביה דכתיב איש בנחלתו ידבקו וגו' ואיש היינו סיבת הבעל. ומקשינן תרוייהו נמי איש כתיב בהו דהכי נמי כתיב באידך לא תסוב נחלה לבני ישראל ממטה אל מטה כי איש בנחלת אבותיו: ידבקו כתיב. דמשמע בסיבת הבעל דכתיב ודבק באשתו: אמר קרא ידבקו מטות. דמשמע הסיבת הבעל וכדאמר לעיל וכל בת יורשת נחלה ממטות וגו' ודביקת מטות על ידי בעל הוא: ובן לאו אחר הוא. דשייך בתר האם: מנין לבעל שאין יורש את אשתו מה שראוי לבוא לידה. כגון ירושת אביה אם אין לו בן ומתה בחיי האב ואחר כך מת אביה שאינו יורש ירושה זו אלא מה שמוחזק בידיה בחייה הוא יורשה: ומתה בחיי מורישיה. היינו חמיו וחמותו של שגוב ואח"כ מתו הן ועכשיו ראוי היה לו לשגוב אילו מת חמיו ואחר [היתה] מתה אשתו היה מוחזק בהן שגוב לפי שבאו לו מאשתו ועכשיו שמתה אשתו ואחר מתו הן להכי חוזרת הירושה לבן אשת שגוב והיינו יאיר בנו והכי נמי יתפרש אידך דפנחס: מאי ואומר. הואיל דשמעינן מיאיר דאין הבעל נוטל בראוי כבמוחזק אמאי איצטריך קרא דפנחס להכי אצטריך דכי תימא מעשה דיאיר לא הוה כדאמרי' אלא הכי הוה שיאיר נשא אשה שהיו לה ל"ג ערים ומתה וירשה בעלה יאיר ומהכא ליכא למשמע דאין הבעל נוטל בראוי כבמוחזק ת"ש מפנחס וכי תימא פנחס נמי ירש את אשתו וא"כ תרי קראי לחד מלתא למה לי אלא ודאי פנחס ירש את אמו משום דאין הבעל נוטל בראוי וכי תימא מפנחס לא שמעינן דההיא גבעה משדה חרמים נפלה לו כדאמרי' לעיל ת"ש מלישנא דקרא דכתיב אשר נתן לו להכי כתב אשר נתן לו דב"ד נטלה מאלעזר ונתנוה לפנחס בנו משום דאין הבעל נוטל בראוי כבמוחזק כדאמרינן: **פיס'** ובני אחיות נוטלין כל אחד ממון אחות אמו אם אין לה לא בן ולא בת. ולא מנחילין ממון לאחות אמן משום דאין מכח אמן דכשם דאמן יורשת אחותה בשאין לה בנים כך בניה יורשין ממון אחות אמן אם אין אמן קיימת בשעת מיתת אחותה אבל אם מתו בניה של זו אין אחיות אמן יורשות אותן הואיל דאין האם עצמה יורשת את בניה כך אחות האם אין יורשת את אחותה. ואית דמפרשי בני אחיות הכי בני אחיות נוחלין ממון אחי אמן משום דאשה יורשת אחיה ואין אחי האם יורש את בן אחותו דכשם שהאם אינה יורשת את בנה כך אין אחיה יורש

מסורת הש"ס: א) י"ל שהוא סם אמורא: ב) [לקמן קטז. ב"ק מב:], ג) [לקמן קטו:], ד) [ועי' תוס' שבת קנ ע"א ד"ה וריב"ק ותוס' בכורות נח ע"א ד"ה חוץ ותוס' פסחים קיב. ד"ה עיה].

עין משפט נר מצוה: טו א מיי' פ"א מהל' נחלות הלכה יא סמג עשין לו טוש"ע ח"מ סי' ל סעיף א: טז ב מיי' שם הלכה ג וסמג שם טוש"ע ח"מ סי' רעו סעיף א:

הגהות הב"ח: (א) גמ' ומתה וירשה תלמוד לומר: (ב) תוס' ד"ה מתה בחיי מורישיה ומתו מורישיה וירשה יאיר וא"ת כיון דבן יורש בראוי כנכסי.

לְמַאי הִלְכְתָא? (א)אָמַר רַב שֵׁשֶׁת: (א)לְקַדֵּם. תָּנֵי רַב שְׁמוּאֵל בַּר רַב יִצְחָק קַמֵּיהּ דְּרַב הוּנָא: "וְיָרַשׁ" – (ב)מַקִּישׁ יְרוּשָּׁה שְׁנִיָּה לִירוּשָּׁה רִאשׁוֹנָה, מַה יְרוּשָּׁה רִאשׁוֹנָה – בֵּן קוֹדֵם לְבַת, אַף יְרוּשָּׁה שְׁנִיָּה – בֵּן קוֹדֵם לְבַת. (ב)תָּנֵי רַבָּה בַּר חֲנִינָא קַמֵּיהּ דְּרַב נַחְמָן: "וְהָיָה בְּיוֹם הַנְחִילוֹ אֶת בָּנָיו" (דברים כא) – בַּיּוֹם אַתָּה מַפִּיל נְחָלוֹת, וְאִי אַתָּה מַפִּיל נְחָלוֹת בַּלַּיְלָה. א"ל אַבַּיֵי: אֶלָּא מֵעַתָּה, דְּשָׁכֵיב בִּימָמָא הוּא דְּיָרְתִי לֵיהּ בְּנֵיהּ, מַאן דְּשָׁכֵיב בְּלֵילְיָא לָא יָרְתִי לֵיהּ בְּנֵיהּ?! (ג)דִּלְמָא דִּין נְחָלוֹת קָא אָמְרַתְּ, דְּתַנְיָא: "וְהָיְתָה לִבְנֵי יִשְׂרָאֵל לְחֻקַּת מִשְׁפָּט" (במדבר כז) – אוֹרְעָה כָּל הַפָּרָשָׁה כּוּלָּהּ לִהְיוֹת דִּין; וּכְדְרַב יְהוּדָה. (ג) דְּאָמַר רַב יְהוּדָה: (ד)שְׁלֹשָׁה שֶׁנִּכְנְסוּ לְבַקֵּר אֶת הַחוֹלֶה – רָצוּ כּוֹתְבִין, רָצוּ עוֹשִׂין דִּין, (ה)שְׁנַיִם – כּוֹתְבִין וְאֵין עוֹשִׂין דִּין; וְאָמַר רַב חִסְדָּא: (ו)לֹא שָׁנוּ אֶלָּא בַּיּוֹם, אֲבָל

ויורש אותה מקיש כו'. אע"ג דאיצטריך לכדאמר לעיל, הכא לא דריש אלא מוי"ו, כדפירש בקונטרס. **מקיש** ירושה שניה לראשונה. פי' בקונטרס: ראשונה – בן ובת, דהך ירושה כתב בירושה ברישא. ומה בההיא בן קודם לבת – אף בשניה, דהיינו אחין קודמין לאחות לירש בנכסי האח. ואין נראה לר"י דמשמעו הכי, דא"כ מירושה שניה לא שמעינן דבני אחות קודמין לבנות אחות! אלא נראה לר"י: דירושה שניה היינו בן הבן ובת הבן, בן הבת ובת הבת. דהיקשא קאי אכל הנך דכתיבי בקרא, והנך דרשינן להו לקמן (דף קטו.) מ"אין לו" – עיין עליו. ומה שפירש נמי בקונטרס דאחות האב קודמין לבני אחי האב – (ג) אגב חורפיה לא עיין בה, דהא תנן: (שם) כל הקודם לנחלה יוצאי יריכו קודמין. **אורעה** כל הפרשה כולה להיות דין. פי' בקונטרס: לענין זה שצריך שלשה לחלוקת נחלה כמו בדין. וקשה לפירושו: דא"כ, אמאי מייתי דרב יהודה? והא רב יהודה לא איירי בחלוקה, אלא מיירי בדבר שייך בו דין גמור! ועוד, דהוה ליה למימר: חלוקת נחלות קא אמרת? לא, דין נחלות. אלא מפר"י: אורעה כל הפרשה כולה להיות דין – לענין שעל ברחם של בנים נעשים דיינים אותם העומדים שם בשעת צואה, ועושין דין, ולא מצי האי למימר: איני רוצה לדון לפניכם אלא לפני ב"ד הגדול או לפני ב"ד חשוב שבעירי, אלא על כרחו מקבל אותן בדיינין. ולא איירי במתנת שכיב מרע – דהא לא הוו דבריו ככתובין וכמסורין אלא מדרבנן, אלא מיירי כשנותן בקנין גמור במתנת בריא מעכשיו אם ימות. וקרי לה נחלה, לפי שהיא כעין נחלה, שאינו קונה אלא לאחר מיתה. ולר' יוחנן בן ברוקה אתי שפיר אפילו בלא קנין, דאמר במתניתין (לקמן דף קל.): אם אמר על מי שראוי ליורשו – דבריו קיימין מן התורה. וא"ת: הא דאמר פרק "אחד דיני ממונות" (סנהדרין דף לד:): ור"מ דמקיש ריבים לנגעים, מה נגעים ביום – אף ריבים ביום, האי "ביום הנחילו" מאי עביד ליה? מיבעי ליה לדתני רבה בר חנינא. והשתא, אי מיירי בדבר שייך בו דין גמור – הא שמעינן ליה מהיקשא דריבים לנגעים, ואמאי איצטריך "ביום הנחילו"? ולפירוש הרשב"ם אתי שפיר, דאיצטריך לחלוקה בעלמא, ולא הייתי מצריך "ביום", דומיא דחלוקת שותפות בעלמא. ואומר ר"י: דלפי' נמי איצטריך, דס"ד כיון דמשונה משאר דיינין שדנין בעל כרחו – ה"א דדנין אפילו בלילה.

אבל

למאי הלכתא. ממעט להו? הא ודאי יורשות אחי אמן, שהרי הבת יורשת אמה, ובמקום אמה עומדת לירש אחי אמה. שהרי האשה יורשת את אחיה במקום שאין אח, כדלקמן בסמוך, דמקיש ירושה שניה לירושה ראשונה כו'. **לקדם.** שיקדמו הבנים לבנות לירש את דודיהן, דילפינן לקמן מירושה ראשונה דהבן קודם לבת. ה"ג: דתני רב שמואל כו' **וירש אותה.** הכי נמי הוה מצי למינקט: "ואם אין לו בת ונתתם את נחלתו לאחיו", דהיינו ירושה שניה. אלא סיפא דכולהו נקט, וכ"ש ירושה שניה ושלישית דסמיכי לירושה ראשונה. **ירושה ראשונה** – הכתובה תחלה וקודמת לכל היורשין, שהבן קודם לכל יורשין שבעולם. **מקיש.** דכתיב: "ואם אין לו בת" "ואם אין לו אחים", וכן כולם, בוי"ו מוסיף על ענין ראשון. **אף ירושה שניה.** והוא הדין לעשירית, דבן קודם לבת. דאחין קודמין לאחות לירש בנכסי האח, והאחות קודמת לאחי האב של מת, ואחי האב קודמין לאחות האב, ואחות האב קודמת לבני אחי האב, ובני אחי האב קודמין לבנות אחי האב אחיותיהן. אבל אם יש שני אחי האב, ולזה בנים ולזה בנות – אלו יורשין חלק אביהן, ואלו יורשות חלק אביהן. וכן הלכה. **ביום הנחילו.** הוה מצי למכתב "בהנחילו". **ביום אתה מפיל נחלות.** לקמיה מפרש לה. **א"ל אביי** כו'. סבור היה דהאי מפיל נחלות, כלומר: מת ביום – מפילין הנחלות ליורשין, שאם מת ביום – יירשו בניו נכסיו. **דלמא דין נחלות קאמרת.** שאין דנין אותן אלא ביום כשאר דיני ממונות, דכתיב בהו (ירמיהו כא): "בית דוד דינו לבקר משפט". דהא כל שאר נחלות נמי מיקרו משפט, כדתניא, דכתיב בסוף פרשת נחלות: "והיתה לבני ישראל לחוקת משפט", מדקרי להו משפט – ש"מ כל שאר נחלות נמי ביום. ואי משום דכתיב: "ושפטו את העם בכל עת" – הא אוקמיה רבא בסנהדרין בפרק "אחד דיני ממונות" (דף לד:) לגמר דין, אבל תחלת דין – ביום, דלהכי כתיב "ביום הנחילו". והיינו דתנן: דיני ממונות דנין ביום וגומרין אף בלילה. **דתניא** כו'. כלומר, דהכי נמי אשכחן בברייתא אחריתי דמשוי להו לכל נחלות דין. דסד"א חילוק נחלות הרי הוא כחלוקת שותפין בעלמא, ולא חשיב דין, קמ"ל. ומיהו, תרוייהו קראי צריכי; "ביום הנחילו" איצטריך לתחלת דין דביום, "וחוקת משפט" אצטריך לרבויי כל שאר נחלות דליהוו דין. דהאי "ביום הנחילו" לא איירי אלא בבן היורש אביו לחוד. **אורעה.** לשון מאורע, לשון "ויקר מקרה" (רות ב). כלומר, נסתייעה להיות דין, וצריך ג' וביום. וילפינן נמי מינייהו לכל דיני ממונות, להיות דנין תחלתן ביום, כנחלות דכתיב בהו "ביום הנחילו". **וכדרב יהודה.** אתא לאשמועינן רבה בר חנינא, דצריך ג' לחלק נחלות כדין, וביום. **ג' שנכנסו לבקר את החולה רצו כותבין** כו'. נראה בעיני דדוקא נקט שנכנסו לבקר, הלכך, רצו – יעידו, רצו – יהיו דיינים. אבל אם נכנסו להעיד, שזימנום לשם והביאום לשמוע כדי להעיד – הרי הם עדים, ואין עד נעשה דיין. דדמי לנכנסו בלילה, דחשיב להו עדים לקמן, הואיל ומתחלה לא היו ראוין לדין, דלילה לאו תחלת דין הוא. וכ"ש הכא, דאם באו לשם עדות – אין עד נעשה דיין. וראיה לדבר בפ"ק דמכות (דף ו.), דקחשיב להו רבי יוסי התם עדים לפסול את השאר אם ראו עמהן את המעשה והן פסולין לעדות, וחשיב לה עדות שנמצא אחד מהן קרוב או פסול, ותבטל עדות כולן. ורבי פליג עליה, ואמר: מה יעשו שני אחין שראו באחד שהרג את הנפש? ואמרינן בגמ' דרבי נמי מודה דהוו להו עדים בראייה בעלמא, אם באו לראות כדי להעיד. דאמר רבא: כי אמרינן להו: למיחזי אתיתו, או לאסהודי אתיתו? כלומר, כשבאתם לראות את המעשה, לאיזה דעת באתם, לראות או להעיד? אי אמרי לאסהודי אתינן, נמצא אחד מהן קרוב או פסול – עדותן בטילה, ואי אמרי למיחזי אתינן – מה יעשו שני אחין כו'. ואמר רב נחמן התם: הלכה כרבי. וקי"ל הלכה כרב נחמן בדיני. נמצינו למדין שהבא לראות מעשה כדי להעיד – חשבינן ליה עד, ואפילו לפסול כל חביריו לבטל עדותן אם הוא פסול, וכל שכן היכא דזימנוהו לבוא לראות צוואת שכיב מרע כדי להעיד, דשוב אינו עושה דין. והדתנן בראש השנה (דף כה:): ראוהו ג' והם בית דין יעמדו שנים ויושיבו מחבריהם אצל היחיד – התם הוא, שלא באו מתחלה כדי לראותו על מנת להעיד, דא"כ שוב אין היחיד יכול להיות דיין, דאין עד נעשה דיין. אלא כשראוהו מעצמם בלכתם בשוק, או שהיו יושבין במקום אחד ומשם ראוהו. וסייג מצאתי לדברי מתשובת רבינו שלמה זקני מ"כ שכתב בה כן. (א) ועוד, מדרב יהודה שמעינן דאין צריך לומר "אתם עדי" בשכיב מרע. דאמר רב יהודה: ג' שנכנסו לבקר את החולה, רצו – כותבין, רצו – עושין דין. שנים – כותבין ואין עושין דין. ופירש רב חסדא: לא אמרן אלא ביום, אבל בלילה – כותבין ואין עושין דין. כיון דליליא לא חזי לדינא, עדים הוא דשוינהו, ואין עד נעשה דיין. והאי ביום היכי דמי? אי דאמר להו "הוו עדים" – מי מצי למימר רצו עושין דין? הא בהדיא סהדי שוינהו! אלא לאו דלא אמר להו "הוו עלי עדים", וקתני: רצו כותבין. **רצו כותבין.** את העדות כמו ששומעין מפי החולה היאך מנחיל נכסיו. **רצו עושין דין.** דהא שלשה נינהו, ודנין. ואומרים: כך הדין, שפלוני יטול חלק זה ופלוני חלק זה, שדמיהן מכוונין בשוה. וכותבין להם פסק דין, שלא יוכלו עוד לערער זה על זה כלום. ואע"ג דאין כאן אדם שמעיד בפניהם כלום – הא פרכינן בר"ה: לא תהא שמיעה גדולה מראייה. וכיון דהן רואין את החולה שמחלק נכסיו בפניהם – הודאת בעל דין כמאה עדים דמי, ולצורך מה יעידו עדים בפניהם? והני מילי דאם רצו עושין דין, דמשמע שאפילו החולה אינו יכול לחזור בו – כגון מתנת שכיב מרע במקצת, ודאיכא קנין, דתו לא מצי הדר ביה, כדאמרן לקמן בפרק "מי שמת" (דף קנא:). אבל בלא קנין, כיון דיכול לחזור – אין עושין דין, כדמוכח לקמן שאין להן לדיינין לעשות דין בדבר שאפשר להבטל. ואם דנו – אין דיניהן דין, דעדיין לא דנו עד שימות האב, שמא יחזור בו. **רצו עושין דין.** אם לא כתבו. אבל אם כתבו – שוב אין עושין דין, שהרי הכניסו עצמם בתורת עדות, ואין עד נעשה דיין. **לא שנו.** הא דאם רצו עושין דין – אלא שנכנסו לבקר את החולה ביום. דכיון דשמעו מפי החולה – הרי הועד בפניהן, ולא תהא שמיעה גדולה מראייה, ויכולין היו לעשות דין באותה שעה, דיום הוא. וכיון דנתרצו להיות דיינין בדבר כששמעו את העדות מפי החולה – יכולין לדון היום או למחר, כבית דין ששמעו עדות ואחר כך הולכין לבתיהן ונושאין ונותנין בדבר ופוסקין את הדין כפי מה שעיניהם רואות. אבל אם נכנסו לבקר את החולה בלילה, שבאותה שעה לא היו ראוין להיות דיינין, ועדות שהועד בפניהם מפי החולה בלילה – לא בפני בית דין הוא, דבההיא שעתא אינן יכולין להיות דיינין, (ב) והויא ראייה דידהו אינה כשמיעת ב"ד ששומעין עדות מפי עדים, אלא הן עצמן עדים הם במה ששומעין מפי החולה.

אפילו

עין משפט נר מצוה

יז א ב מיי' פ"א מהל' נחלות הלכה ד סמג עשין נו טוש"ע ח"מ סי' רעו סעיף ג ד:
יח ג ד ה ו מיי' פ"ג מהלכות סנהדרין הלכה ה ו סמג שם טור ש"ע ח"מ סי' רנג ס"א:

רבינו גרשום

יורש את בנה תנא בני אחיות יורשין אחות אמן: קא בעי למאי הלכתא. קא תני ולא בנות אחיות וכי אם אין להם אחים אמאי לא ירית בנות: אמר רב ששת לקדם קתני. כלומר ודאי יורשות בנות אחיות היכא דלית לה אחי אבל אם אית להו אחי הם קודמין לירש ולא בנות וכי היכי דגבי אמן הבנים קודמין לבנות הכי נמי גבי אחיות: וירש אותה מקיש ירושה שניה. דכל המאוחר מן קרובים שבפרשה שני הוא לגבי חבירו שלמעלה ממנו: מקיש שניה. דהיינו ירושה של שאר קרובים לירושה ראשונה דבת דאם יש לו בן שהבן קודם לבת: ודלמא דיני נחלות. אי אתה דן בלילה: אורעה כמו מאורע. כל הפרשה כולה של נחלות להיות דין וכדרב יהודה כו' והאי קרא בסוף פרשת נחלות כתיב: שלשה שנכנסו לבקר את החולה ולא נכנסו לא על שם עדי צוואה ולא להיות דיינין כי אם לבקר: רצו כותבין. עדות צוואת אותו שכ"מ שחילק נכסיו ליורשין: רצו עושין דין. שאם נתן למי שלא היה ראוי לירש או שהניח להן אביהן ירושה ולא רצה אחד מהן לחלוק עם אחיו או לא נתן לבכור פי שנים כדין תורה יכולין לעשות כדין וכופין אותו עד שיחלוק דהואיל דג' נינהו עושין דין דג' דנין [דיני] ממונות: ב' כותבין. ומקבלי עדות נינהו ואין רשאין לדין דאין בית דין פחות מג': לא שנו. דרצו כותבין רצו עושין דין: אלא באם שנכנסו לבקר

מסורת הש"ס

א) [לקמן קטו.]: ב) סנהדרין לד:: ג) שם ע"ש:

הגהות הב"ח

(א) רשב"ם ד"ה ג' שנכנסו וכו' שכתב בה כן מדרב יהודה כנ"ל ותיבת ועוד נמחק: (ב) ד"ה לא שנו וכו' אינן יכולין להיות דיינין דלא מצינו למימר לא תהא שמיעה גדולה מראיה והויא ראיה דידהו אינה: (ג) תוס' ד"ה מקיש וכו' לבני אחי האב אף כאן אגב חורפיה:

אבל בלילה, אפילו שלשה — כותבין ואין עושין דין; מאי טעמא? דהוו להו עדים, א)ואין עד נעשה דיין. אמר ליה: אין, הכי נמי קאמינא.§ איתמר: קנין, עד אימתי חוזר? רבה אמר: כל זמן שיושבין; רב יוסף אמר: ב)כל זמן שעוסקין באותו ענין. אמר רב יוסף: כוותי דידי מסתברא, דאמר רב יהודה: שלשה שנכנסו לבקר את החולה — רצו כותבין, רצו עושין דין; ואי סלקא דעתך כל זמן שיושבין, ליחוש דלמא הדר ביה! אמר רב אשי: אמריתה לשמעתא קמיה דרב כהנא: ולרב יוסף מי ניחא? וליחוש דלמא הדר ביה! אלא מאי אית לך למימר? דיסליקו מעניינא

אפילו הן שלשה כותבין ואין עושין דין. למחר, אפילו לא כתבו, אלא אם כן יבואו אחרים ויעידו בפניהם. כדאמר בראש השנה: ראוהו שלשה והן בית דין — יושיבו מחבריהם אצל היחיד, אחד מהשלשה, ויעידו השנים בפניהן, ויאמרו השלשה "מקודש". ופרכינן התם: ולוקמו בדוכתייהו וליקדשו! ומוקמינן כשראוהו בלילה. הלכך, הן עצמן אינם יכולין לקדש למחר, שהרי בלילה עדים היו ולא דיינין, ולמחר — אין עד הרואה בדבר נעשה דיין על פי עדות עצמו, אלא אם כן יעיד אחר בפניו, דהשתא אינו עושה הדין על פי עדות עצמו. והלכך, אחד מן השלשה שראו החדש, כשמושיבין שנים אצלו להיות דיינין, ושנים הרואין מעידין בפניהם — יכול הוא להיות דיין אע"פ שראוהו בלילה עמהן, שהרי ע"פ עדות אחרים שמעידין לפניו הוא דן את הדין ולא על פי ראיית עצמו, דאין לנו לפסול דיינין בשביל שראו בדבר כל זמן שלא העידו. אלא שהוא עצמו לא ידון את הדין על פי ראיית עצמו, דאין עד נעשה דיין. וכגון שראה בשעה דאינו יכול להיות דיין, אבל אם ביום ראה, דבההיא שעתא מצי לדון את הדין, דלא תהא שמיעה גדולה מראייה — מה לי אם ידון עכשיו מה לי אם ידון למחר? והכא נמי, מהאי טעמא, משום דהוו להו עדים בראיית הלילה, דלא מצי למימר לא תהא שמיעה גדולה מראייה. דההיא ראייה לא חשבינן לה כעדות שהועד בפניהן אלא היכא דראו בשעה שיכולין לעשות הדין, אבל היכא דראו בשעה שאין יכולין להיות דיינין, כגון בלילה — ההיא ראייה ראיית עדים היא שרואין בדבר, ולא ראיית דיינין היא, והלכך, ע"פ ראייתן, דהיינו כאילו הם עדים — אין יכולין הן עצמן להיות דיינים על פי ראיית עצמן, דאין עד נעשה דיין. ומיהו, ב"ד שהעידו לפניהם עדות בלילה — עדות גמורה היא ויכולין לדון למחר ביום, אבל ראייה דידהו שרואין בלילה — לא חשבינן כאילו הועד לפניהם בלילה. דכיון דלא חזו בההיא שעתא לדינא — ראייה דידהו אינה כשמיעה ממש ששמעו מפי עדים בלילה, אלא הן עצמן נעשו עדים, ושוב לא יהו דיינין בעדות עצמן, אא"כ יעידו אחרים בפניהם. והכי הלכתא. וכי הא סוגיא אשכחן בב"ק בפ' "החובל" (דף צ:) גבי התוקע לחבירו. ואין עד נעשה דיין. המעיד על הדבר אין נעשה עוד דיין באותו דבר. וגם אם ראה את הדבר ונעשה עד — אין נעשה עליה עוד דיין בעדות עצמו, אלא אם כן מעידין אחרים בפניו. ונראה בעיני דגזירת הכתוב היא, דכתיב: "ועמדו שני האנשים" וגו' — בעדים הכתוב מדבר (שבועות דף ל.), "לפני ה'" — היינו לפני הדיינין, אשמועינן קרא דצריך להעיד שנים לפני הדיינין, אבל העדים אינן חוזרין ויושבין ודנין. ה"ג: קנין עד אימתי יכול לחזור. וכ"כ בפירושי רבינו חננאל. ובין מתנת בריא, ובין מתנת שכיב מרע במקצת דאית ביה קנין, מיירי. וקבעי: עד אימתי יכול לחזור בו מקנינו ולבטלו? דהא לא גמר ומקני מיד אלא לדעת לקיים לו תנאים שיפרש אחרי כן, או אם ירצה לחזור בו מיד שיוכל לחזור. דקים להו לרבנן דאדעתא דהכי מקני איניש, שיתן לבו אחרי כן וידע אם אפשר לו בקנין זה, לעשותו קנין גמור. כל זמן שיושבין. דאדעתא דהכי מקני ליה, ע"מ שאם לא יחזור בו באותו מעמד. אבל אם יחזור בו — יבטל. באותו ענין. של אותה מתנה. שלשה שנכנסו כו'. במתנת שכיב מרע במקצת ובקנין מיירי, דאינו יכול לחזור בו. ליחוש דלמא הדר ביה. ואמאי קאמר: רצו עושין דין, דמשמע: באותו מעמד, אע"פ שעדיין יושבין — עושין דין גמור. ואמאי? הא כיון דיכול לחזור בו ויבטל הדין — לא הוי דין! אמריתה לשמעתא כו'. נתווכחתי בדבר לפניו, והקשיתי לו. (א) ולרב יוסף מי ניחא כו'. והכי גרסינן: אמריתה לשמעתא קמיה דרב כהנא.

אבל בלילה אפילו שלשה כותבין ואין עושין דין. דההיא ראייה כמו עדות, ואין מקבלין עדות בלילה, כדמוכח פרק "ראוהו בית דין" (ר"ה דף כה: ושם) דקבלת עדות כתחלת דין. והיום דראוי לקבלת עדות — יכולין לדון על פי ראיית יום, דלא תהא שמיעה גדולה מראייה. ולא כמו שפירש הקונטרס דאמר: קבלו עדות שהעידו לפניהם בלילה — דנין למחר ע"פ אותו עדות, ואין צריכין לחזור ולהעיד בפניהם ביום. ומה שפירש הקונטרס: דוקא שנכנסו לבקר, אבל הזמינום להעיד שוב אין יכולין לדון אפילו יעידו אחרים, דהוו להו עדים ואין עד נעשה דיין. והביא ראיה מפ"ק דמכות (דף ו.), דרבי יוסי סבר נמצא אחד מהן קרוב או פסול — עדות כולן בטלה, ולרבי נמי, כי אמרי "לאסהודי אתינא" — עדותן בטלה, ופסיק רב נחמן דהלכתא כוותיה דרבי, וקיימא לן כרב נחמן בדיני. והביא דר"ה, דמושיבין מחבריהן אצל היחיד, איירי שלא הלכו מתחלה ע"מ לראות, דא"כ אין שוב היחיד יכול להיות דיין. והביא ראיה נמי מתשובת רש"י זצ"ל, שהיה מדקדק מכאן שאין צריך לומר "אתם עדי", דאי אמר להו "ליהוי עלי סהדי" אמאי רצו עושין דין? הא בהדיא שוינהו סהדי! ואע"פ שפ"ה שיכול להיות דיין כשראו בלילה כיון שיש עדים מעידים בפניו, כשמתכוין להעיד גרע טפי. ואין להקשות: כי פריך בפ' "ראוהו ב"ד" (ר"ה דף כה:): מושיבין מחבריהן. לוקמו בדוכתייהו וליקדשו, דלא תהא שמיעה גדולה מראייה! אמאי לא משני: כגון שנתכוונו להעיד, דאין יכולים להיות דיינין? דהא אי נתכוונו — לא היה היחיד נעשה דיין. ומיהו, אין נראה פי'. דטעם דאין עד נעשה דיין הוי או משום דהויא עדות שאי אתה יכול להזימה, דכיון שהן עצמן עדים ודיינין לא יקבלו הזמה על עצמן, או משום דבעינן "ועמדו שני האנשים" — אלו העדים, "לפני ה'" — אלו דיינין, אבל העדים עצמן אין חוזרין ויושבין ודנין. ומהני טעמי אין לפסול המתכוין להעיד, אלא דוקא עד המעיד. ומההיא דמכות שהביא — אין ראיה, דהתם גזירת הכתוב הוא דמקיש ג' לשנים, דאפילו הן מאה אם נמצא אחד מהן קרוב או פסול — עדותן בטלה. ועוד קשה לר"י: לפירושו, דמדמה אין עד נעשה דיין לנמצא אחד מהן קרוב או פסול, א"כ לרבי יוסי, דאית ליה דבראייה בעלמא בלא כוונת עדות נמצא אחד מהן קרוב או פסול עדותן בטלה — כמו כן לא יעשה שוב דיין, א"כ לית ליה שלא תהא שמיעה גדולה מראייה. והשתא בר"ה פריך בפשיטות: ולא תהא שמיעה גדולה מראייה, ומשמע דליכא מאן דפליג! ועוד: קשה דרב יהודה אדרב יהודה, דרב יהודה פסיק במכות (דף ו.) כרבי יוסי דבראייה בעלמא נעשה עד, ואין עד נעשה דיין, ב)וא"ת: היכי קאמר רב יהודה רצו עושין דין? הלא נעשו עדים אע"פ שלא נתכוונו! אלא ודאי אומר ר"י דאין לדמותו. ועוד אומר ר"י: דהתם נמי, בכוונה לחודה, שנתכוונו להעיד בשעת ראייה — לא היתה עדותן בטלה, אלא כשהעידו אח"כ בב"ד. דאי לא תימא הכי — אין לך גט כשר כשנותנין בפני קרובין או קדושין אם נתכוונו להעיד. והא דקאמר: ומה יעשו שני אחין שראו באחד שהרג את הנפש, אע"פ שאין עדותן בטלה אלא כשמעידין בפני ב"ד — מ"מ פעמים שאין האח זה יודע שכבר העיד אחיו, ומעיד. ומיהו, מעיקרא הוה בעי למימר התם דבראייה בעלמא בלא העדאה נפסלין כשנמצא אחד מהם קרוב או פסול, מדפריך: הרוג יציל, נרבע יציל, הורג ורובע יצילו. אבל לפי המסקנא דבעי למימר, ומסיק רבא: אמר קרא "יקום דבר" במקיימי דבר הכתוב מדבר, דהיינו עדים, שהדבר מתקיים על ידיהן — אין נפסלין עד שיעידו בבית דין ויקיימו דבר. **ואין** עד נעשה דיין. היינו עד המעיד, כדפרישית. ודוקא בדאורייתא, אבל בדרבנן — נעשה דיין, כדמוכח בפ"ק דגיטין (דף ה:) ובפ"ב דכתובות (דף כא: ושם). ורבי עקיבא דאמר ב"החובל" (ב"ק דף צ: ושם): כולן עדים הן, ואפילו עד הרואה אין נעשה דיין — היינו דוקא בדיני נפשות, כדמוכח בפ' "ראוהו ב"ד" (ר"ה כו.), דמפרש טעמא: כיון דחזו דקטל — תו לא מצו חזו ליה בזכותיה. [נ"ל דבפ"ב] ואם תאמר (דבפרק קמא) דמכות (דף יב. ושם) מפרש טעמא אחרינא, דקאמר ר' עקיבא: מנין לסנהדרין שראו כו' שאין ממיתין אותו עד שיעמוד בב"ד — שנאמר "עד עמדו לפני העדה למשפט" — עד שיעמוד בב"ד אחר. וי"ל: דההיא דרשא דמכות עיקר, וההיא דר"ה (דף כו. ושם) לא קאמר אלא דמההיא טעם לא גמרינן שאר דינים מהתם, דדוקא בדיני נפשות אין עד הרואה נעשה דיין, משום "והצילו העדה".

ניחוש דלמא הדר ביה. קשה לר"י: דא"כ כל מתנת שכיב מרע בכולה, או מצוה מחמת מיתה, ניחוש דלמא הדר ביה! וכי תימא הכי נמי, וצריך עדים שלא חזר בו עד שמת, דהא בסוף פ"ק דב"מ (דף יט:) אמר: קמא ובתרא — בתרא קני, קמא לא קני. משמע: ואי ליכא בתרא — קמא קני

רבינו גרשום

ביום אבל בלילה אפי' שלשה כותבין. משום עדות: ואין עושין דין. דאין דין נוהג בלילה כדגרסינן בסנהדרין דיני ממונות דנין ביום וגומרין אף בלילה אבל אין מתחילין בלילה דכתיב והיה ביום הנחילו את בניו הא כיצד יום לתחלת דין לילה לגמר דין: מאי טעמא. כשנכנסו בלילה אין עושין דין. משום דהוו עדים ואין עד נעשה דיין: אין ה"נ קאמינא דין נחלות: איתמר קנין. שקני משכיב מרע או מיד אחר אם רצה לחזור מאותו קנין עד אימתי יכול לחזור: רבה אמר כל זמן שיושבין. אע"פ שאין עוסקין באותו ענין: רב יוסף אמר כל זמן שעוסקין באותו ענין אע"פ שאין יושבין: ואי סלקא דעתך כל זמן שיושבין יכול לחזור אם כן אמאי אם רצו עושין דין מיד לאלתר כשצווה ומורידין כל אחד לירושתו וליחוש דלמא הדר ביה אותו שכיב מרע מצואתו עד שהן יושבין א) ודברי שכיב מרע אין צריכין קנין וחשוב כקנין דכתובין וכמסורין דמי כל זמן שקנין חוזר יכול הוא נמי לחזור בו אלא הואיל דכל זמן דעסוקין באותו ענין לא הדר ביה תו לא מצי הדר בי' הואיל דסלקי מההוא ענינא: אלא מאי אית לך למימר. לרב יוסף דמצי למיעבד דין משום דבר סליק

א) אולי צ"ל ואף שדברי שכ"מ וכו' וככתובין וכמסורין דמו מ"מ כל זמן שקנין חוזר וכו'.

עין משפט נר מצוה

יט א מיי' פ"ה מהל' עדות הלכה ח סמג עשין קט טוש"ע ח"מ סי' ז סעיף ה:

כ ב מיי' פ"ה מהלכות מכירה הלכה י סמג עשין פג טוש"ע ח"מ סי' קכה סעיף ו:

מסורת הש"ס

א) ר"ה כו. גיטין ה: כתובות כח: ב"ק ל: סנהדרין לז: ב) נ"ו וח"כ:

הגהות הב"ח

(א) רשב"ם ד"ה אמריתה וכו' והקשיתי לו הס"ד ואחר כך מ"ה וה"ג אמריתה לשמעתא קמיה דרב כהנא ולרב יוסף מי ניחא כו':

מֵעִנְיָנָא לְעִנְיָנָא, ה"נ — דְּקָמוּ וַהֲדַר יָתִיבוּ. א)וְהִלְכְתָא כְּוָותֵיהּ דְּרַב יוֹסֵף: בְּשָׂדֶה, עִנְיָן, וּמֶחֱצָה.§ "הָאִשָּׁה אֶת בְּנָהּ" וכו'.§ הָא תּוּ לָמָּה לִי? הָא תְּנָא לֵיהּ רֵישָׁא: הָאִישׁ אֶת אִמּוֹ וְהָאִישׁ אֶת אִשְׁתּוֹ! (א) הָא קָא מַשְׁמַע לָן, דְּאִשָּׁה אֶת בְּנָהּ דּוּמְיָא דְּאִשָּׁה אֶת בַּעְלָהּ: מָה אִשָּׁה אֶת בַּעְלָהּ — ס״א אֵין הַבַּעַל יוֹרֵשׁ אֶת אִשְׁתּוֹ בַּקֶּבֶר, אַף אִשָּׁה אֶת בְּנָהּ — ג)ב אֵין הַבֵּן יוֹרֵשׁ אֶת אִמּוֹ בַּקֶּבֶר לְהַנְחִיל לָאַחִין מִן הָאָב. אָמַר רַבִּי יוֹחָנָן מִשּׁוּם רַבִּי יְהוּדָה (ב) בֶּן ר' שִׁמְעוֹן: דְּבַר תּוֹרָה — הָאָב יוֹרֵשׁ אֶת בְּנוֹ וְאִשָּׁה יוֹרֶשֶׁת אֶת בְּנָהּ, שֶׁנֶּאֱמַר: "מַטּוֹת", מַקִּישׁ מַטֵּה הָאֵם לְמַטֵּה הָאָב, מַה מַּטֵּה הָאָב — אָב יוֹרֵשׁ אֶת בְּנוֹ, אַף מַטֵּה הָאֵם — אִשָּׁה יוֹרֶשֶׁת אֶת בְּנָהּ.

אֵיתִיבֵיהּ

רשב"ם

מֵעִנְיָנָא לְעִנְיָנָא. שֶׁפָּסְקוּ מֵאוֹתוֹ עִנְיָן, וְדִבְּרוּ בְּעִנְיָנִים וּבְמַעֲשִׂים אֲחֵרִים, וְאָז, אִם רָצוּ — עוֹשִׂין דִּין. אֲבָל כָּל זְמַן שֶׁעֲסוּקִין בְּאוֹתוֹ עִנְיָן — אֵין עוֹשִׂין דִּין. **וְהִלְכְתָא** כְּוָותֵיהּ דְּרַב יוֹסֵף בְּשָׂדֶה. בְּפ"ק (לעיל דף יג:) אָמַר רַב יוֹסֵף: מַאי אָמַר לֵיהּ "מַעֲלֵינָא לָךְ כִּנְכְסֵי דְּבַר מַרְיוֹן". עִנְיָן. הָא דַּאֲמָרַן. וּמֶחֱצָה. לְקַמָּן, בְּ"מִי שֶׁמֵּת" (דף קמג.): הַהוּא דְּאָמַר לִדְבֵיתְהוּ "נִכְסַי לִיךְ וְלִבְרִיךְ", אֲמַר רַב יוֹסֵף: קַנְאִי פַּלְגָא. דְּדָרֵישׁ: "וְהָיְתָה לְאַהֲרֹן וּלְבָנָיו" — מֶחֱצָה לְאַהֲרֹן וּמֶחֱצָה לְבָנָיו. הָאִשָּׁה אֶת בְּנָהּ לָמָּה לִי. לְמִיתְנָא: מַנְחֶלֶת וְלֹא נוֹחֶלֶת? הַיְינוּ רֵישָׁא, דְּקָתָנֵי: הָאִישׁ אֶת אִמּוֹ — נוֹחֵל וְלֹא מַנְחִיל. וְהָאִשָּׁה אֶת בַּעְלָהּ נַמִי, דְּקָתָנֵי מַנְחֶלֶת וְלֹא נוֹחֶלֶת — הַיְינוּ נַמִי רֵישָׁא: הָאִישׁ אֶת אִשְׁתּוֹ נוֹחֵל וְלֹא מַנְחִיל. וְכֵן אֲחֵי הָאֵם דְּקָתָנֵי דְּמַנְחִילִין לְנֶכְדָּם בְּנֵי אֲחוֹתָם וְלֹא נוֹחֲלִין — הַיְינוּ נַמִי רֵישָׁא דְּקָתָנֵי: בְּנֵי אֲחוֹת שֶׁל אִישׁ נוֹחֲלִין דּוֹדֵיהֶן וְלֹא מַנְחִילִין. וּלְמַאן דְּתָנֵי נַמִי בְּמַתְנִיתִין בְּנֵי אֲחָיוֹת — הַךְ סֵיפָא נַמִי הַיְינוּ בְּנֵי אֲחָיוֹת, דְּכִי הֵיכִי דְּהָאִישׁ נוֹחֵל אֶת דּוֹדוֹ וְאֵינוֹ מַנְחִיל — ה"נ נוֹחֵל אֶת דּוֹדָתוֹ וְאֵינוֹ מַנְחִיל. ה"ג: הָא קָא מַשְׁמַע לָן דְּהָאִשָּׁה כו'. וְלָא גָּרְסִינַן "אֶלָּא". כְּלוֹמַר, לְהָכִי תָּנָא בָּבָא יְתֵירָה, לְאַקּוּשֵׁי הָאִשָּׁה אֶת בְּנָהּ לְהָאִשָּׁה אֶת בַּעְלָהּ, דִּבְאוֹתוֹ עִנְיָן שֶׁהָאִשָּׁה מַנְחֶלֶת לְבַעְלָהּ — מַנְחֶלֶת נַמִי לִבְנָהּ. מָה הָאִשָּׁה אֶת בַּעְלָהּ. אֵינָהּ מַנְחֶלֶת לוֹ בָּרָאוּי לָהּ לְאַחַר מִיתָתָהּ, אֶלָּא בַּמּוּחְזָק. כִּדְאָמְרַן לְעֵיל, וְיָלְפִינַן מִקְּרָאֵי, דְּאֵין הַבַּעַל יוֹרֵשׁ אֶת אִשְׁתּוֹ בְּנַחֲלָה הַבָּאָה לָהּ מִמּוֹרִישֶׁיהָ כְּשֶׁהִיא בַּקֶּבֶר. אֶלָּא אוֹ בְּנָהּ אוֹ בִּתָּהּ יוֹרְשָׁהּ, וְאִם אֵין לָהּ בֵּן — הַקָּרוֹב לְמוֹרִישָׁהּ יוֹתֵר קוֹדֵם. **אַף הָאִשָּׁה אֶת בְּנָהּ.** אֵינָהּ מַנְחֶלֶת לוֹ בָּרָאוּי לוֹ לְאַחַר מִיתָתוֹ, כְּדֵי שֶׁיַּנְחִיל הוּא לִקְרוֹבָיו שֶׁמִּצַּד אָבִיו וְלֹא מִצַּד אִמּוֹ. כְּגוֹן שֶׁאִם מֵת הַבֵּן וְאַחַר כָּךְ מֵתָה אִמּוֹ — אֵין זֶה הַבֵּן, שֶׁהוּא כְּבָר מֵת וְנָתוּן בַּקֶּבֶר מִקּוֹדֶם מִיתַת אִמּוֹ, יוֹרֵשׁ עַתָּה אֶת אִמּוֹ לְהַנְחִיל אֶת אָחִיו מֵאָבִיו. אֶלָּא יוֹרְשֵׁי אָבִיהָ יוֹרְשִׁין אוֹתָהּ. וּסְבָרָא הוּא, דְּכֵיוָן דְּמֵת בְּנָהּ מִקַּמֵּי דִּידָהּ — פָּקַע לוֹ כֹּחוֹ בִּירוּשַּׁת אִמּוֹ. וּמִיהוּ, לְהָכִי אִיצְטְרִיךְ לְאַשְׁמוּעִינַן דְּלָא יָרֵית כְּשֶׁהוּא בַּקֶּבֶר אֶת אִמּוֹ, דְּס"ד אָמֵינָא: "לֹא תִסּוֹב" תְּרֵי זִימְנֵי כְּתִיב, וְתַרְוַיְיהוּ בְּסִבַּת הַבֵּן, חַד לְהֵיכָא דְּמֵתָה אִמּוֹ מִקַּמֵּיהּ דְּיָרֵית לָהּ, וְאִידָּךְ לְאַשְׁמוּעִינַן דַּאֲפִילּוּ הֵיכָא דְּמִית אִיהוּ בְּרֵישָׁא וּמֵתָה הִיא אַחֲרָיו, דְּהוּסְבָה נַחֲלָה לְאָבִיו אוֹ לִקְרוֹבָיו מִן הָאָב, קמ"ל מִשְׁנָה יְתֵירָה דְּלָא יָרֵית בָּרָאוּי. וּקְרָאֵי לִכְדִדְרְשִׁינְהוּ לְעֵיל. וְהַאי דְּקָתָנֵי אֲחֵי הָאֵם דְּלָא צָרִיךְ — אַגַּב גְּרָרָא דְּהָנָךְ נָקַט לֵיהּ. וְהַאי דְּקָתָנֵי בְּרֵישָׁא הָאָב אֶת הַבָּנִים וְהַבָּנִים אֶת הָאָב, וַהֲוָה מָצֵינוּ לְמִשְׁמַע סֵיפָא מֵרֵישָׁא, מִיהוּ כֵּיוָן דְּמִיתְנֵי לֵיהּ בְּתַרְוַיְיהוּ נוֹחֲלִין וּמַנְחִילִין — קָתָנֵי לְהוּ, דְּכָל נוֹחֲלִין וּמַנְחִילִין קָחָשֵׁיב. אֲבָל הַךְ בָּבָא דְּמַנְחִילִין וְלֹא נוֹחֲלִין — כּוּלָּהּ מְיוּתֶּרֶת הִיא, שֶׁהֲרֵי כְּבָר נִשְׁנֵית בַּבַּת נוֹחֲלִין וְלֹא מַנְחִילִין. (ג) יוֹרֵשׁ אֶת אִמּוֹ בַּקֶּבֶר. דָּמֵי לְהַהוּא בַּקֶּבֶר דִּלְעֵיל, שֶׁכְּשֶׁהָאִשָּׁה בַּקֶּבֶר אֵינָהּ יוֹרֶשֶׁת אָבִיהָ כְּדֵי לְהַנְחִיל לְבַעְלָהּ. וְהָכָא נַמִי, כְּשֶׁהַבֵּן בַּקֶּבֶר — אֵינוֹ יוֹרֵשׁ אֶת אִמּוֹ כְּדֵי לְהַנְחִיל לְאַחִין מִן הָאָב. מִשּׁוּם רַבִּי יְהוּדָה בְּרַבִּי שִׁמְעוֹן. מִשּׁוּם דְּלֹא הָיָה רַבּוֹ מוּבְהָק קָאָמַר "מִשּׁוּם", שֶׁלֹּא הוּרְגַּל ר' יוֹחָנָן לוֹמַר דְּבָרִים מִשְּׁמוֹ שֶׁל ר' יְהוּדָה בַּר' שִׁמְעוֹן. אֲבָל מֵרַבּוֹ יֹאמַר: אָמַר ר' יוֹחָנָן אָמַר ר' יַנַּאי (ד). דְּבַר תּוֹרָה. כְּלוֹמַר, מִן הַפָּסוּק יֵשׁ לִלְמוֹד. הָאָב יוֹרֵשׁ אֶת בְּנוֹ. וְה"ה לְבִתּוֹ, כִּדְיָלְפִינַן בְּרֵישׁ פִּירְקִין. יוֹרֶשֶׁת אֶת בְּנָהּ. וְה"ה גְּנֵבָתָהּ בְּמָקוֹם שֶׁאֵין הָאָב. אֲבָל אִם אָבִיו קַיָּים — הוּא קוֹדֵם, דִּלְהָכִי מִיהָא אַהֲנֵי מִשְׁפַּחַת אָב שֶׁקְּרוּיָה מִשְׁפָּחָה, לְהַקְדִּים שְׁאֵר הָאָב לִשְׁאֵר הָאֵם. מַטּוֹת. "וְכָל בַּת יוֹרֶשֶׁת נַחֲלָה מִמַּטּוֹת", וּבְיוֹרֶשֶׁת שְׁנֵי מַטּוֹת אוֹקִימְנָא.

אֵיתִיבֵיהּ

תוספות

קני קמא, ואע"ג דלא ידעינן אי הדר ביה. ואמר נמי: דייתיקי מבטלת דייתיקי. ומיהו, בקונטרס פי' דהכי פריך: כיון דיכול לחזור ויבטל — הדין לא הוי דין, ואע"ג דלא חזר — חיישינן שמא יחזור. ואין נראה לר"י, דא"כ הוה ליה למיפרך: והא מצי הדר ביה! ונראה לפרש: דאמאי עושים דין? ניחוש שמא יחזור, והוי כמו אטרוחי בי דינא בכדי.

והלכתא כוותיה דרב יוסף בשדה ענין ומחצה. אע"ג דבמחצה ליכא מאן דפליג עליה דרב יוסף, מ"מ הוצרך לפסוק הלכה כמותו משום דאביי מקשי עלה. ואע"ג דשני ליה ד)רב יוסף שפיר, סלקא דעתך משום דרב יוסף (ה) איעקר תלמודיה, ולא הוי שינוי דידיה עיקר — קמ"ל. ומכאן אין להוכיח דהלכתא כרבה לגבי רב יוסף בכולי גמרא, שסברי כאן פוסק אפילו בדבר דלא פליג עליה רבה. דמסתברא דלא אתי למימר: אין הלכה כמותו בכל מה שדבר בגמ' אלא במכילתין, דהנך ג' איתנהו במכילתין. אבל יש ראיה מפרק "מי שאחזו" (גיטין דף עה:) דקאמר: והא קי"ל הלכתא כרבה ה), ובהא אין הלכה כרשב"ג. ומדלא קאמר "והא קי"ל בהאי הלכתא כרבה" כדקאמר גבי רבן שמעון בן גמליאל — משמע דבכולי גמרא הלכתא כרבה. ובההיא דריש "הכונס" (ב"ק דף נו: ושם) דפליגי רבה ורב יוסף בשומר אבידה — אומר ר"י דהלכה כרבה, דהוי שומר חנם, ולא כמו שפוסקין כרב יוסף, ושם (ד"ה בההיא) פירשנו.

מה אשה את בעלה אין הבעל יורשה בקבר. פ"ה אינו מיושב, דמפרש "בקבר" אאשתו קאי, דאין הבעל יורשה אם נפלו לה נכסים כשהיא בקבר. דהא דומיא (ו) דזה ליכא לפרושי "אף אשה את בנה אין הבן יורש את אמו כשהיא בקבר". והא ליתא, שהר הבן יורש את אמו כשהיא בקבר, כשמתה בחיי מורישה, כדאמר לעיל. ולקמן נמי מרבינן בן הבת. ואם כפרש: (ז) יורש הבעל, כשהוא בקבר אין יורש את אשתו להנחיל לאחיו — הוה אתי שפיר, דאף האשה — אין הבן יורש את אמו כשהוא בקבר להנחיל לאחיו מן האב. אבל קימה: דאמאי פשיטא ליה בבעל טפי מבבן? דמה שפי' ריב"ס דלכך פשיטא ליה בבעל, משום דשאירות פקע ליה על ידי מיתה כמו ע"י גירושין — אין נראה, (ח) דאמר ב"הבא על יבמתו" (יבמות דף נה:) ו)דלאחר מיתה נמי מיקריא "שארו". ואומר ר"י: דהיינו טעמא — משום דאין אדם יורש בקבר להנחיל לקרובין, אלא ע"י מבמוש נפקא לן לקמן מ"ובן אין לו", דהיינו הנהו דיורשין מחמת קורבה. אבל בעל דלא ירית מחמת קורבה — לא אשכחת משמוש. ורשה לרשב"א: דא"כ אמאי איצטריך קרא לעיל דאין הבעל יורש אשתו בראוי, עד דיליף מפנחס? פיפוק ליה משום דלא אשכח משמוש בירושה הבאה מכח שאירות! תראה לו: שזהו סברתו של רשב"ס דנקט יורש אשתו — כשהאשה בקבר. דודאי כשהבעל בקבר הוה ליה למימר, והא דלא פירש הכי — שסובר דהיא גופה לא נפקא לן אלא ממאי דאשכח שאינו יורש את אשתו כשהאשה בקבר, כדילפינן לעיל מקרא דפנחס. דנהי דלא מבטל שאירות נגמרי כדאמר ביבמות, מ"מ מכח שאירות בקבר אשכחן דאינו יורש, הלכך אין לו לבעל לירש כשהוא עצמו בקבר. וה"נ בן, אע"ג דיורש אמו כשהיא בקבר מ"ואין לו" כתיב, מ"מ אינו יורשה כשהוא בקבר להנחיל לאחין מן האב, דיליף מבעל. ובסוף פ' "מי שמת" (לקמן דף קנט:) יליף לה מקרא אחרינא: נאמר סיבה בבן ונאמר סיבה בבעל כו'. וכופר האשה דלא ירית בעל — נפקא לן מקרא אחרינא, בפרק "שור שנגח ארבעה וחמשה" (ב"ק דף מב:), ומפרש התם טעמא — לפי שהוא ראוי, שאינו משתלם אלא לאחר מיתה. וכן נזקיה ומלוה שלה, למאן דחשיב ליה ראוי, אור"י: לפי שאינן ממורישי אשה (ט) הוי, לכן צריך לפסוק אחר. ובב"ק פי' דמכופר לא אתי שאר ראוי, דה"א: שאני כופר, דלעולם הוה ראוי. ומירושה לא שמעינן כופר, לפי שמחיים נעשה החבלה.

אף מטה האם האשה יורשת אר. בנה. הקשה ר"י: א"כ, ע"י איש נמי מסבת נחלה ממטה למטה; שאם ישא משבט אחר וימות, ויירשנו בנו, ואח"כ ימות הבן ותירשנו אמו שהיא משבט אחר. ואמאי אזהר רחמנא לאשה מ"וכל בת יורשת נחלה" טפי מלאיש? ועוד, דאם כשאין האב האשה יורשת — א"כ לא תהיה נחלה ממשמשת לקרובי האב, ולקמן מקרא נפקא לן משמוש נחלה. ואם שניהן יורשין יחד את הבן — הא משפחת אם אינה קרויה משפחה! ונראה לרבינו תם ולר"י: דבגזירות קאמר דיורשת את בנה, ונפקא מינה שלא יהיו נכסיו הפקר.

בן

עין משפט נר מצוה

כא א מיי' פ"א מהל' נחלות הלכה יב סמג עשין נו טוש"ע אה"ע סי' צ סעיף א:

כב ב מיי' שם הלכה יג ועי' בהשגות ובמגיד משנה סמג שם טוש"ע ח"מ סי' רעו סעיף ה:

רבינו גרשום

מאותו ענין ולא הדר בו והתחיל לדבר מענין אחר ומשום הכי עושין דין. שוב הכי נמי לרבה משום הכי עושין דין דקמו כבר אחר שצוה ולא הדר ביה והדר יתבי ועשו דין משום הכי לא מצי למיהדר ביה: והלכתא כוותיה דרב יוסף. בהני ג' הלכות א) דאיירינן בפירקא קמא דמעלינן לי' כנכסי דבר מריון וענין דהכא דאמר רב יוסף כל זמן שעוסקין באותו ענין ומחצה כדאמרי' באידך פירקין מי שמת ההוא דאמר לה לדביתהו נכסי לך ולבנך אמר ר' יוסף קנאי איתתא פלגא דדרש קרא דכתי' והיתה לאהרן ולבניו זכה מחצה לאהרן ומחצה לבניו: **פיס'** האשה את בנה והאשה את בעלה ואחי האם מנחילין ממונם האשה לבעלה והאשה לבנה ואחי האם לבני אחותו ואינם נוחלין את ממונם: האשה את בנה מורישה ממונה לבנה ואינה יורשת ממון של בנה היינו דקתני ברישא דמתני' האיש את אמו נוחל ואינן מנחילין ותרתי זימני ל"ל והאשה את בעלה מורשת ממונה לבעלה ואינה יורשת היינו דקתני ברישא האיש את אשתו נוחל ולא מנחיל ואחי האם מורישין ממון לבני אחות היינו דקתני ובני אחות נוחלין ולא מנחילין דמה לי אחי האם ומה לי אחות האם ותרתי זימנא ל"ל: אין הבעל יורש את אשתו בקבר. דלאחר מיתת אשתו אם נפלה לה ירושה אין הבעל יורש אותה ירושה כי אם הבנים לפי שאינו נוטל בראוי כבמוחזק: אף אשה את בנה אין הבן יורש את אמו בקבר. שאם נפלה לה ירושה לאחר מיתתה אין הבן יורש אותה כדי שיהא יכול להורישה לאחין מן האב אבל הוא עצמו יכול לירש אותה עד שהוא חי ואחריו לקרובי האב ואגב דאיצטריך למיתני הני תרי נקט ואחי האם ולא משום דדרשינן לה כלום

א) נ"ל בקצה דאיירינן וכו' וכמובן ערך סדום גרס הכא בסדום וכונו הך מימרא דרב יוסף לאמר התם דכופין על מדת סדום.

מסורת הש"ס

א) לקמן קמג: ב) [לקמן קנט:] ג) [שם] ד) [לפנינו לקמן קמג. לא מצינו שהשיב רב יוסף כלום על קושיית אביי ע"ש וצריך לפרש:] ה) [ועי' תוס' מנחות לב. ד"ה מנגע ובתוספות מגילה כט: ד"ה והלכתא וכו'] ו) [ע"ש בתוס' ד"ה לאחר]

הגהות הב"ח

(א) גמ' והאיש את אשתו אמר רב ששת הא קא משמע לן: (ב) שם ר' יהודה בר' שמעון: (ג) רשב"ם ד"ה אין הבן יורש את אמו בקבר: (ד) ד"ה משום וכו' אמר ר' ינאי. נ"ב לעיל בדף קיט ע"א: (ה) תוס' ד"ה והלכתא כו' דרב יוסף איעקר תלמודיה לא הוי שינוי: (ו) ד"ה מה וכו' דהא דומיא דהכי ליכא וכו' דהא ליתא: (ז) בא"ד ואם נפרש כירושת הבעל: (ח) בא"ד אין נראה דהא אמר בהבא: (ט) בא"ד שאינן ממורישין אשה הוא רעיה לפסוק אחר כצ"ל:

אֵיתִיבֵיהּ רַבִּי יוֹחָנָן לְרַבִּי יְהוּדָה (א) בֶּן שִׁמְעוֹן: הָאִשָּׁה אֶת בְּנָהּ, וְהָאִשָּׁה אֶת בַּעְלָהּ, וַאֲחֵי הָאֵם — מַנְחִילִין וְלֹא נוֹחֲלִין! אֲמַר לֵיהּ: מִשְׁנָתֵנוּ, אֵינִי יוֹדֵעַ מִי שְׁנָאָהּ. וְלֵימָא לֵיהּ: רַבִּי זְכַרְיָה בֶּן הַקַּצָּב הִיא, דְּלָא דָּרֵישׁ "מַטּוֹת"! לָא מִיתּוֹקְמָא מַתְנִיתִין כְּרַבִּי זְכַרְיָה בֶּן הַקַּצָּב. דְּקָתָנֵי: וּבְנֵי אָחוֹת; א)וְתָנָא: בְּנֵי אָחוֹת — וְלֹא בְּנוֹת אָחוֹת; וַאֲמַרִינַן: לְמַאי הִלְכְתָא? וַאֲמַר רַב שֵׁשֶׁת: לְקַדֵּם; וְאִי סָלְקָא דַּעְתָּךְ מַתְנִי' רַבִּי זְכַרְיָה בֶּן הַקַּצָּב הִיא, הָא אָמַר: אֶחָד הַבֵּן וְאֶחָד הַבַּת שָׁוִין בְּנִכְסֵי הָאֵם. וְתַנָּא דִּידָן, ממ"נ? אִי דָּרֵישׁ "מַטּוֹת" — אִשָּׁה נַמִי תִּירַשׁ אֶת בְּנָהּ, אִי לָא דָּרֵישׁ "מַטּוֹת" — בֵּן דְּקוֹדֵם לְבַת בְּנִכְסֵי הָאֵם מְנָא לֵיהּ? לְעוֹלָם דָּרֵישׁ "מַטּוֹת", וְשָׁאנֵי אהָכָא, דְּאָמַר קְרָא: °"וְכָל בַּת יוֹרֶשֶׁת נַחֲלָה", יוֹרֶשֶׁת — וְאֵינָהּ מוֹרֶשֶׁת.§ במדבר לו

מתני' סֵדֶר בנְחָלוֹת כָּךְ הוּא: °"אִישׁ כִּי יָמוּת וּבֵן אֵין לוֹ וְהַעֲבַרְתֶּם אֶת נַחֲלָתוֹ לְבִתּוֹ" — ב)בֵּן קוֹדֵם לַבַּת, כָּל יוֹצְאֵי יְרֵיכוֹ שֶׁל בֵּן קוֹדְמִין לַבַּת. בַּת קוֹדֶמֶת לָאַחִין, יוֹצְאֵי יְרֵיכָהּ שֶׁל בַּת קוֹדְמִין לָאַחִין. אַחִין קוֹדְמִין לַאֲחֵי הָאָב, יוֹצְאֵי יְרֵיכָן שֶׁל אַחִין קוֹדְמִין לַאֲחֵי הָאָב. זֶה הַכְּלָל: כָּל הַקּוֹדֵם בְּנַחֲלָה — יוֹצְאֵי יְרֵיכוֹ קוֹדְמִין. ג)וְהָאָב קוֹדֵם לְכָל יוֹצְאֵי יְרֵיכוֹ.§ שם כז

גמ' תָּנוּ רַבָּנַן: "בֵּן" — אֵין לִי אֶלָּא בֵּן; בֶּן הַבֵּן, אוֹ בַּת הַבֵּן, אוֹ בֶּן בַּת הַבֵּן, מִנַּיִן? תַּלְמוּד לוֹמַר: ד)"אֵין לוֹ" — ה)עַיֵּין עָלָיו. "בַּת" — אֵין לִי אֶלָּא בַּת; בַּת הַבַּת, וּבֶן הַבַּת, וּבַת בֶּן הַבַּת, מִנַּיִן? ת"ל: "אֵין לוֹ" — עַיֵּין עָלָיו.

הָא

תורה אור

איתיביה כו'. הכי נמי מצי למפרך מרישא, דקתני: האיש את אמו נוחל ולא מנחיל. אלמא: אין האם נוחלת את בנה. אלא דעדיפא ליה לאותוביה מסיפא, דקתני בהדיא: מנחלת ולא נוחלת, וקשיא ליה לרבי יהודה דאמר: יורשת. **משנתנו איני יודע מי שנאה.** דאינה עיקר. דהיא גופה קשיא, כדלקמן, דפרכינן: **ותנא** דידן מה נפשך כו'. והלכך, כיון דשמעינן ליה דדריש היקשא דמטות כדאמרינן לעיל בפירקין (ד' קיא.): להקדים הבן לבת בנכסי האם — הכי נמי הוה מצי לאקושי ולמימר דיורשת את בנה. **דלא דריש.** היקשא ד"מטות", כדאמרינן לעיל דאחד הבן ואחד הבת שוין בנכסי האם. דלא מקיש מטה האם למטה האב. **לא מיתוקמא** כרבי זכריה. דאיכא למשמע ממתני' דהבן קודם לבת בנכסי האם. **ותני** עלה **בני אחות ולא בנות אחות.** והא ברייתא אינה מוספת על המשנה אלא מפרשת היא, דדוקא נקט מתני' בני אחות — למימר שהבנים נוחלין את דודיהן, ולא הבנות, כל זמן שיש בן. לפי שהבנים באין לירש את דודיהן מכח אמם שהיתה אחותן, כדכתיב: "ואם אין לו אחים", ודרשינן לקמן: עיין עליו, דבן אחין במקום אחין קאי. וה"ה דבן אחותו במקום אחותו קאי, וכמי שאמם מוחזקת דמי, והן באין לירש מכחה. וסבירא ליה דבן קודם לבת בנכסי האם. אבל לר' זכריה בן הקצב — הבנים והבנות יירשו כאחד את דודיהם, דמכח אמם קא ירתי, וסבירא ליה דבן ובת כי הדדי ירתי בנכסי האם. **ותנא** דידן מה נפשך. כלומר, מה הוא דעתו, דסבירא ליה תרתי: בן קודם לבת בנכסי האם, כדקתני: האיש את אמו ולא הבת את אמה, ונפקא לן לעיל מהיקשא דמטות וסבירא ליה דאין האשה יורשת את בנה, דלהכי לא דריש היקשא דמטות מה נפשך דמקיש לחלאין? והלא אין היקש למחצה! לעולם דריש מטות. להיקשא שיקדים הבן לבת בנכסי האם. ומיהו, להכי לא דרשינן היקשא לומר שתירש האם את הבן — דאמר קרא: "וכל בת יורשת נחלה ממטות" וגו', והוה מצי למכתב "וכל בת נחלה", וכתיב "יורשת", למימרא: דוקא יורשת שני מטות, אבל אינה מורשת לשני מטות אם מתה היא, אלא אחד מהם, דהיינו אב, דאין האם יורשת. ורבינו חננאל דייק מ"ס ד"ממטות" — מקצת שני מטות הוא דיורשת ואינה מורשת. כגון אם, שאין האם יורשת בתה, והוא הדין לבנה. דעל כרחך האי מ"ס לדיוקא דידיה אתא, דאי לגופיה, לאשמועינן דבירושת אחד משני מטות מיירי — לשתוק קרא מיניה, ולא לכתוב לא "מטות" ולא מ"ס, והוה אמינא דלכל אשה אזהר רחמנא שלא תנשא לשבט אחר, בין שהיא יורשת מטה אחד, בין יורשת שני מטות. **מתני'** בן קודם לבת. ראובן קודם לדינה אחותו לירש את יעקב. וכן כל יוצאי יריכו של ראובן, אם מת ראובן — קודמין לדינה אחותו, לירש את יעקב. כגון מת ראובן — חנוך בנו קודם לדינה לירש נכסי יעקב, ובן של חנוך ובן בנו עד אלף דור — כולן קודמין לדינה. ובגמרא מפרש טעמא, מדכתיב: "אין לו" — עיין עליו. בת קודמת לאחין. ואם יש אב למת — גם לו קודמת. אחין קודמין לאחי האב. ואם יש להן אחות — הן קודמין לאחות, והאחות ויוצאי יריכה קודמין לאחי האב. כל הקודם בנחלה. ומת, יוצאי יריכו עומדין במקומו לירש אותה נחלה, ולא שאר קרובי המת יורשין אותו, אע"פ שקרובין למת יותר מיוצאי יריכו של זה. והאב קודם. לירש בנו או בתו שמתו, לכל יוצאי יריכו — דהיינו אחי המת. וכבר נפקא לן בריש פירקין מ"והעברתם" דהאב קודם לאחין. ודוקא מיוצאי יריכו, אבל יוצאי יריכו של בנו — קודמין לכל אדם. **גמ'** ובת הבן. במקום שאין שם בן הבן ובן של בת הבן. והוא הדין לבת של בת הבן, אבל לישנא קלילא הוא דנקט. **אין לו עיין עליו.** של מת, אם יש לו בן או הבא מכחו של בן, כגון יוצאי יריכו. ויו"ד יתירא קא דריש, דמצי למכתב "אן" בלא יו"ד, כדכתיב: "מאן בלעם". והכי מפרשינן בקידושין (דף ד.) גבי "ויצאה חנם אין כסף". עיין עליו. דהאי מת, אם יש לו בת כלל (ב) וכלל. וכיון דאיכא יוצאי יריכה — עובר ירך אמו הוא.

הא

בן הבן ובת הבן ובן בת הבן מנין תלמוד לומר אין לו עיין עליו. וא"ת: תיפוק ליה דבני בנים הרי הן כבנים, כדאמר בפ' "אלמנה" (יבמות דף ע.), דזרע זרעה לא צריך קרא, דבני בנים הרי הן כבנים! וי"ל: דהתם דכתיב "וזרע אין לה", מ"זרע" משמע בני בנים, כדמשמע בפ' "ד' מיתות" (סנהדרין דף סד: ושם) גבי מעביר בנו ובתו באש, דקאמר: אין לי אלא בנו ובתו, בן בנו ובן בתו מנין? ת"ל "ומזרעך". אלמא דמלשון "זרע" משמע בני בנים. וליכא למימר דהתם מיתורא דריש, דא"כ הוה ליה למדרש איפכא, דקרא "ומזרעך" כתוב ברישא, אבל מ"בנו ובתו" לא משמע ליה התם בני בנים. הלכך, הכא דכתיב "בן" — איצטריך לרבויי בנו ובתו. וממאי דכתיב (ויקרא יח) "ערות אשה ובתה לא תגלה את בת בנה" — אין ראיה מדאיצטריך לכתוב "בת בנה" דבני בנים לא הוו כבנים, דאיכא למימר דאי לא כתב "בת בנה" הוה אסרינן עד סוף כל הדורות, משום דבני בנים הרי הן כבנים. וא"ת: כיון דאין בני בנים כבנים, מנלן גבי יבום דפוטר בן הבן מיבום? וכי תימא דנפקא לן מ"אין לו" — הא איצטריך לרבות ממזר! וי"ל: דשקולים הם, ויבאו שניהם. אי נמי: דבן הבן נפקא לן מ"לא ימחה" — פרט לזה שאין שמו מחוי. וקשה לרשב"א: דאמאי איצטריך הכא קרא דבני בנים קודמין לאחין? תיפוק ליה מדלענין יבום בני בנים ובנים כי הדדי נינהו — לענין נחלה נמי כי הדדי נינהו! וי"ל: דהכא איצטריך, דבן הבן או בת הבן יורשין עם בני המת, או בת הבת עם הבנות. דמיבום לא הוה ידעינן (ג) אלא דעדיפא מאח. ולר"י נראה: הא דבני בנים כבנים גבי יבום — מנחלה הוא דקיימא לן, ולא מהנך טעמי דפרישית לעיל (דף קח.). ואם תאמר: ומנלן דממזר יורש את אביו, כדמשמע בקידושין (דף ד. ושם) (יבמות ד' כב:)? דהא גבי יבום צריך רבוי, וכן גבי בת כהן נמי איצטריך קרא לזרע פסול! וליכא למימר דנפקא לן מ"ואין לו" — דשקולין הם, או משום דיבום בנחלה תלא רחמנא, וגבי יבום איכא רבויא. דאי איצטריך דרשא להכי — אמאי פריך בפ' שני דיבמות (דף כב: ושם): יורשו ומטמא לו, פשיטא! ויש לומר: ד"זרע" משמע כשר, לכך איצטריך גבי בת כהן רבויא. אבל "בן" — משמע נמי פסול. והא דאיצטריך גבי יבום לרבויי בן פסול — היינו משום דה"א נילף אחוה אחוה מבני יעקב דכשרים ולא פסולים. דמהאי טעמא נמי אמר התם דה"א שאם פסול אינו זוקק ליבום, אי לאו משום דמלינו בקרא דבן פסול פוטר, ומדלענין מיפטר פוטר — מזקיק נמי זקיק. [ועי' תוס' לעיל קט. ד"ה כיון]:

אפילו

כג א מיי' פ"א מהל' נחלות הלכה ג סמג עשין צו טוש"ע ח"מ סי' רעו סעיף ז:

כד ב מיי' שם הלכה א ב ג טוש"ע שם ס"א:

רבינו גרשום

מנחילין ולא נוחלין. אלמא דהאשה אינה יורשת את בנה וקשיא לר' יהודה: איני יודע מי שנאה. דלא ידעינן תנאי דסבירא ליה כותיה: ולימא ר' זכריה בן הקצב היא דלא דריש מטות. כדאוקימנן לעיל: שוין בנכסי [האם]. דלא מקדמי' להו: ותנא דידן ממה נפשך. אמאי האשה אינה יורשת בנה: אי דקדריש מטות. בדין הוא דהאשה יורשת בנה כדאמר ר' יהודה לעיל אשה יורשת את בנה דבר תורה כו': ואי דלא דרש מטות בן קודם לבת בנכסי האם מנין. דהא לעיל נפקא לתנא דידן מהתם דאמרי' שני התם דאמר קרא מטות מקיש מטה כו': לעולם דריש מטות ואם כן אמאי אין אשה יורשת בנה דשני הכא דאמר קרא וכל בת יורשת נחלה. דהבת יורשת ממון אמה מה שנפל לה מן אמה ואינה מורשת ממונה לאמה הוא הדין נמי לבן דאינו מוריש את אמו: **פיסקא** סדר נחלות כך הוא כו' והעברתם את נחלתו לבתו. הא יש לו בן הוא קודם לבת וכל יוצאי יריכו של בן קודמין לבת. זה הכלל כל הקודם לנחלה והוא ליתיה קודמין הנחלה ליוצאי יריכו: תנו רבנן בן אין לי אלא בן דליהוי קודם לנחלה בן הבן דליהוי קודם לאבי אביו והכי נמי בת הבן ובן בת (הבת) של בן שיהא יורש אבי אמו מנין ת"ל אין לו כלומר מהאי אל"ף דאין לו עשה עי"ן כלומר עיי"ן עליו מכל צדדין הבאין מכח כחו א) לו יורשתו והכי נמי דרשי בת והוא הדין נמי לכל הני דקודמין לנחלה צריך לפשפש ולחקור ולעיין אחריהם אם יש להן יורשין מכל כחו ליתן להם נחלתו ואחיו נמי דקודמין לאחי האב צריך לעיין לכל הבאין מכח אחיו וליתן להן

א) נראה דצ"ל הבאין מכח כחו ליתן להם ירושתו.

א) [לעיל קיג.]: ב) [לקמן קכב: כתובות נ.]: ג) [יבמות מ.]: ד) [יבמות כב: וש"נ]: ה) [בערוך ערך אין איתא איין ועמ"ש הסמ"ע סי' רעו ס"ק א וע"ע בערך עין]:

הגהות הב"ח

(א) גמ' לר' יהודה ברבי שמעון: (ב) רשב"ם ד"ה עיין וכו' בת כלל וכיון כצ"ל ותיבת וכלל נמחק: (ג) תוס' ד"ה בן הבן וכו' דמיבום לא הוה ידעינן. נ"ב ע"ל בדף קח במ"ש התוס' בד"ה כלום יש יבום:

עין משפט נר מצוה

כה א מיי' פ"א מהל' נחלות הלכה ג סמג עשין צו טוש"ע ח"מ סי' רעו סעיף א:
כו ב מיי' שם הלכה ד טוש"ע שם סעיף ב:

הָא כֵּיצַד? ^א^נַחֲלָה מְמַשְׁמֶשֶׁת וְהוֹלֶכֶת עַד רְאוּבֵן. וְלֵימָא: עַד יַעֲקֹב! אֲמַר אַבַּיֵי: גְּמִירִי, דְּלָא כָּלֶה שִׁבְטָא. אָמַר רַב הוּנָא אָמַר רַב: ^ב^כָּל הָאוֹמֵר תִּירַשׁ בַּת עִם בַּת הַבֵּן, אֲפִילּוּ נָשִׂיא שֶׁבְּיִשְׂרָאֵל — אֵין שׁוֹמְעִין לוֹ, שֶׁאֵינָן אֶלָּא מַעֲשֵׂה צְדוֹקִין. דְּתַנְיָא: בְּאַרְבָּעָה וְעֶשְׂרִים בְּטֵבֵת תָּבְנָא לְדִינָנָא; שֶׁהָיוּ צְדוֹקִין אוֹמְרִין: תִּירַשׁ הַבַּת עִם בַּת הַבֵּן; נִטְפַּל לָהֶן רַבָּן יוֹחָנָן בֶּן זַכַּאי, אָמַר לָהֶם: שׁוֹטִים, מִנַּיִן זֶה לָכֶם? וְלֹא הָיָה אָדָם שֶׁהֶחֱזִירוֹ דָּבָר, חוּץ מִזָּקֵן אֶחָד שֶׁהָיָה מְפַטְפֵּט כְּנֶגְדּוֹ וְאוֹמֵר: ^א)^וּמַה בַּת בְּנוֹ הַבָּאָה מִכֹּחַ בְּנוֹ, תִּירָשֶׁנּוּ. בִּתּוֹ הַבָּאָה מִכֹּחוֹ, לֹא כָּל שֶׁכֵּן? קָרָא עָלָיו אֶת הַמִּקְרָא הַזֶּה: °"אֵלֶּה בְנֵי שֵׂעִיר הַחֹרִי יֹשְׁבֵי הָאָרֶץ לוֹטָן וְשׁוֹבָל וְצִבְעוֹן וַעֲנָה", וּכְתִיב: ב)°"אֵלֶּה בְנֵי צִבְעוֹן וְאַיָּה וַעֲנָה"! אֶלָּא, מְלַמֵּד שֶׁבָּא צִבְעוֹן עַל אִמּוֹ וְהוֹלִיד עֲנָה. וְדִלְמָא תְּרֵי עֲנָה הֲווּ! אָמַר ^ג)^רַבָּה: אָמֵינָא מִלְּתָא דְּלָא אֲמָרָהּ שָׁבוּר מַלְכָּא, וּמַנּוּ? (א) שְׁמוּאֵל; אִיכָּא דְּאָמְרִי, אָמַר רַב פַּפָּא: אָמֵינָא מִלְּתָא דְּלָא אֲמָרָהּ שָׁבוּר מַלְכָּא, וּמַנּוּ? ^ד)^רַבָּה; אָמַר קְרָא: °"הוּא עֲנָה" — הוּא עֲנָה דְּמֵעִיקָּרָא. אָמַר לֵיהּ: רַבִּי, בְּכָךְ אַתָּה פּוֹטְרֵנִי? אָמַר לוֹ: שׁוֹטֶה, וְלֹא

תורה אור: בראשית לו — שם — שם

רשב"ם

הָא כֵּיצַד. כְּלוֹמַר, (ג) וַדַּאי כִּי הֵיכִי דְּאָמְרִינַן עַיֵּין עָלָיו לְמַטָּה — הָכִי נַמִי אָמְרִינַן עַיֵּין עָלָיו לְמַעְלָה, שֶׁאִם כָּלָה זַרְעוֹ לִגְמָרֵי הַעֲבִירֶנָּה לְיוֹרְשֵׁי הָאָב לְמַעְלָה. הָא כֵּיצַד אַתָּה מוֹצֵא בְּכָל מָקוֹם "עַיֵּין עָלָיו"? נַחֲלָה מְמַשְׁמֶשֶׁת וְהוֹלֶכֶת עַד רְאוּבֵן. שֶׁאִם אֵין לוֹ אָב, וְלֹא אָח וְלֹא בֶּן אָח, וְלֹא אָחוֹת וְלֹא בֶּן אָחוֹת, וְלֹא בְּנֵי בְנֵיהֶן עַד עוֹלָם, וְלֹא אֲבִי הָאָב, וְלֹא אֲחֵי הָאָב וְלֹא בְּנֵי אֲחֵי הָאָב, וְלֹא אֲחוֹת הָאָב וְלֹא בְּנֵי אֲחוֹת הָאָב — מַחֲזִירִין לְמַטָּה וּלְמַעְלָה עַל קְרוֹבֵי אֲבוֹתָיו עַד רְאוּבֵן, וְלֹא יִתְּנוּהָ לִקְרוֹבֵי הָאֵם. שֶׁבּוֹדְקִין אַחַר (אֲחֵי) אֲבִי אֲבִי אָבִיו, וְאִם אֵין אֲבִי אֲבִי אָבִיו, לֹא הוּא וְלֹא בָּנָיו וְלֹא בְּנֵי בָנָיו — בּוֹדְקִין אַחַר אֲחֵי אֲבִי אֲבִי אָבִיו, אוֹ הוּא אוֹ יוֹצְאֵי יְרֵיכוֹ, דְּהַיְינוּ דּוֹד אֲבִי אָבִיו אוֹ בְּנֵי דּוֹד אֲבִי אָבִיו. אֲבָל הָאָבוֹת לְעוֹלָם קוֹדְמִין לַאֲחֵי הָאָבוֹת, כִּדְאָמְרִינַן לְקַמָּן: אֲבִי הָאָב וַאֲחֵי הָאָב, כְּגוֹן אַבְרָהָם וְיִשְׁמָעֵאל בְּנִכְסֵי עֵשָׂו — דְּאַבְרָהָם קוֹדֵם. וְכֵן יְהֵא הוֹלֵךְ וּבוֹדֵק עַד רְאוּבֵן, דַּאֲבִי אֲבִי אָב תְּחִלָּה, אוֹ הוּא אוֹ בָּנָיו. וְאִם אֵינוֹ — יִבְדּוֹק אַחֲרֵי כֵן בָּאַחִין, דְּהַיְינוּ אֲחֵי אֲבִי (ג) הָאָב, אוֹ הוּא אוֹ בָּנָיו, וְאִם אֵין — יִבְדּוֹק בַּאֲחוֹתוֹ אוֹ בְּבָנֶיהָ, דְּהַיְינוּ אֲחוֹת אֲבִי אָבִיו. וְאִם אֵינוֹ — עוֹלֶה עוֹד לְמַעְלָה דּוֹר אֶחָד, וְיִבְדּוֹק תְּחִלָּה בָּאָבוֹת, וְאַחַ"כ בַּאֲחֵיהֶם, וְאַחַר כָּךְ בְּאַחְיוֹתֵיהֶם, וְכֵן לְעוֹלָם, עַד רְאוּבֵן. כְּגוֹן: וּבְנֵי רְאוּבֵן חֲנוֹךְ וּפַלּוּא, וּבְנֵי פַלּוּא אֱלִיאָב, וּבְנֵי אֱלִיאָב נְמוּאֵל וְדָתָן. מֵת בְּנוֹ שֶׁל נְמוּאֵל בְּלֹא זֶרַע — נְמוּאֵל יוֹרְשׁוֹ, וְאִם אֵין נְמוּאֵל קַיָּים — אֶחָיו, בָּנָיו שֶׁל נְמוּאֵל, דְּהַיְינוּ בְּנֵי נְמוּאֵל יוֹרְשִׁין אוֹתוֹ. וְאִם אֵין לוֹ אַחִים — וְנִתְפַּס אֶת נַחֲלָתוֹ לַאֲחֵי אָבִיו, דְּהַיְינוּ דָּתָן דּוֹדוֹ, אוֹ הוּא אוֹ בָּנָיו. כָּלָה דָתָן — נוֹתְנִין לֶאֱלִיאָב אֲבִי אָבִיו שֶׁל מֵת, אוֹ לַאֲחֵי אֱלִיאָב, אוֹ לַאֲחוֹת אֱלִיאָב, לָהֶם וְלִבְנֵיהֶם וְלִבְנֵי בְנֵיהֶם. מֵת אֱלִיאָב בְּלֹא אַחִים וּבְנֵי אַחִים — חוֹזְרִין אֵצֶל פַּלּוּא, וְאִם מֵת — נוֹתְנִין לַחֲנוֹךְ וְחֶצְרוֹן וְכַרְמִי אוֹ לִבְנֵיהֶם, דְּהָווּ לְהוּ בְּנֵי אֲחֵי אֲבִי אֲבִי אָבִיו שֶׁל מֵת. וּבְעִנְיָן זֶה אִי אֶפְשָׁר שֶׁלֹּא יִמְצָא אֶחָד בַּשֵּׁבֶט הָרָאוּי לְנַחֲלָה, שֶׁאֵין הַשֵּׁבֶט כָּלֶה לִגְמָרֵי. כְּלָלָא דְּמִילְּתָא: אֲבִי הַמֵּת קוֹדֵם לַאֲחֵי הַמֵּת, וְכֵן אֲבִי אֲבִי הַמֵּת קוֹדֵם לַאֲחֵי אֲבִי הַמֵּת. אֲבָל אֲחֵי הַמֵּת קוֹדֵם לַאֲבִי אֲבִי הַמֵּת, וְכֵן אֲחֵי אֲבִי הַמֵּת קוֹדֵם לַאֲבִי אֲבִי אָבִיו שֶׁל מֵת, כִּדְאָמְרִינַן לְקַמָּן גַּבֵּי בְּעָיוֹת דְּרָמֵי בַּר חָמָא (ד). וְלֵימָא עַד יַעֲקֹב. שֶׁאִם מֵת רְאוּבֵן, הוּא וְכָל זַרְעוֹ — חוֹזְרִין אֵצֶל יַעֲקֹב, וְאִם אֵין יַעֲקֹב — שִׁמְעוֹן וְלֵוִי יוֹרְשִׁין אֶת הָרָאוּי לִרְאוּבֵן אֲחִיהֶם, דְּהָווּ לְהוּ אֲחֵי אֲבִי אֲבִי אַב אָבִיו! **אָמַר אַבַּיֵי.** אִם כֵּן נִמְצָא שֵׁבֶט אֶחָד כָּלֶה מִיִּשְׂרָאֵל, וּגְמִירִי דְּלָא כָּלֶה שִׁבְטָא. וּרְאָיָה לַדָּבָר בְּמַלְאָכִי: (ג) "כִּי אֲנִי ה' לֹא שָׁנִיתִי וְאַתֶּם בְּנֵי יַעֲקֹב לֹא כְלִיתֶם". בְּפר"ח: רְאוּבֵן דְּנָקַט לָאו דַּוְקָא, אֶלָּא מִפְּנֵי שֶׁהוּא שֵׁבֶט רִאשׁוֹן נְקָטוֹ. **אָמַר רַב הוּנָא אָמַר רַב כָּל.** דַּיָּין הָאוֹמֵר וּפוֹסֵק דִּין שֶׁתִּירַשׁ הַבַּת שֶׁל מֵת עִם בַּת הַבֵּן שֶׁל מֵת, מִקַּל וָחוֹמֶר דִּלְקַמָּן, אֲפִילּוּ הֲוֵה הַדַּיָּין נָשִׂיא בְּיִשְׂרָאֵל, שֶׁהַכֹּל נִמְנִין עִמּוֹ לָדוּן כְּמוֹתוֹ — אֵין שׁוֹמְעִין לוֹ, מִפְּנֵי שֶׁדִּין זֶה מַעֲשֵׂה צְדוֹקִין הוּא, כִּדְמְפָרֵשׁ לְקַמָּן. וּלְחַזֵּק אֶת הַדָּבָר אָמַר כֵּן, כְּעֵין דְּאָמְרִינַן (מנחות ד' לב.): אִם יָבֹא אֵלִיָּהוּ וְיֹאמַר — אֵין שׁוֹמְעִין לוֹ. וְיֵשׁ מְפָרְשִׁין: שְׁכִיב מְרַע שֶׁמְּצַוֶּה: "תִּירַשׁ הַבַּת בִּנְכָסַיי עִם בַּת בְּנִי", וְאַלִּיבָּא דְּר' יוֹחָנָן בֶּן בְּרוֹקָה דְּאָמַר לְקַמָּן בְּפִירְקִין: אִם אָמַר עַל מִי שֶׁרָאוּי לְיוֹרְשׁוֹ דְּבָרָיו קַיָּימִין — הָכָא אֵין שׁוֹמְעִין לוֹ, מִשּׁוּם דְּדָמֵי דְּמִכֹּחַ יְרוּשָּׁה בְּלֹא צַוָּאָה הִיא בָּאָה לִירַשׁ עִם בַּת הַבֵּן, כְּדִבְרֵי צְדוֹקִין, הִלְכָּךְ אָמוּר רַבָּנַן דְּאֵין שׁוֹמְעִין לוֹ. וְלָאו מִילְּתָא הִיא, דִּבְלָאו מַעֲשֵׂה צְדוֹקִין נַמִי אֵין שׁוֹמְעִין, דְּמַתְנֶה עַל מַה שֶּׁכָּתוּב בַּתּוֹרָה, שֶׁהֲרֵי הַבַּת אֵינָהּ רְאוּיָה לִירַשׁ כְּלָל עִם בַּת הַבֵּן. דַּאֲפִילּוּ ר' יוֹחָנָן בֶּן בְּרוֹקָה לֹא קָאָמַר אֶלָּא בְּבֵן בֵּין הַבָּנִים, אוֹ בַּת בֵּין הַבָּנוֹת, דִּבְלָאו הָכִי הֲוֵה רָאוּי לִירַשׁ קְצָת — הִלְכָּךְ רָאוּי גַּם לִירַשׁ לוֹ אֶת הַכֹּל. אֲבָל בַּת בֵּין הַבָּנִים, וְהוּא הַדִּין לְבַת אֵצֶל בַּת הַבֵּן — אֵין בִּדְבָרָיו כְּלוּם. וְהָכִי אָמְרִינַן לְקַמָּן בְּפִירְקִין. **כִּדְתַנְיָא.** בִּמְגִילַּת תַּעֲנִית, דְּקָחָשִׁיב אִילֵּין יוֹמַיָּא דְּלָא לְהִתְעַנָּאָה בְּהוֹן, וּמַיְירֵי בְּטֵבֵת, וְקָתָנֵי: בְּעֶשְׂרִים וְאַרְבָּעָה בּוֹ תָּבְנָא לְדִינָנָא — שַׁבְנוּ לְמִשְׁפָּטֵנוּ הָרִאשׁוֹן, שֶׁהוֹדוּ לָנוּ הַצְּדוֹקִין. **עִם בַּת הַבֵּן.** וּמִיהוּ, עִם בֶּן הַבֵּן מוֹדוּ דְּלֹא תִּירוֹת. צָדוֹק וּבַיְיתוֹס תַּלְמִידֵי אַנְטִיגְנוֹס אִישׁ סוֹכוֹ הָיוּ, וְהָיוּ שׁוֹנִין לְתַלְמִידֵיהֶן מַה שֶּׁקִּיבְּלוּ מֵאַנְטִיגְנוֹס: אַל תִּהְיוּ כַּעֲבָדִים הַמְשַׁמְּשִׁין כו'. וְטָעוּ הַתַּלְמִידִים בְּכָךְ, שֶׁהָיוּ סְבוּרִים דְּהָכִי קָאָמַר: עִבְדוּ לַמָּקוֹם וְאַל תְּקַבְּלוּ שָׂכָר. וְאָמְרוּ: כְּמוֹ שֶׁאֵין בּוֹ מַמָּשׁ בְּדָבָר זֶה — כֵּן כָּל דִּבְרֵי חֲכָמִים. וְטָעוּ וּפָקְרוּ בְּדִבְרֵי חֲכָמִים, וְנִקְרְאוּ צְדוֹקִין עַל שֵׁם צָדוֹק, וּבַיְיתוֹסִין עַל שֵׁם בַּיְיתוֹס, בְּאָבוֹת דְּרַבִּי נָתָן (פ"ה). **קָרָא עָלָיו מִקְרָא.** שֶׁאָנוּ לְמֵידִין מִמֶּנּוּ שֶׁעֲנָה בְּנוֹ שֶׁל צִבְעוֹן הָיָה, וְקָרָא לֵיהּ "בֶּן שֵׂעִיר", וְקָאָמַר נַמִי "יֹשְׁבֵי הָאָרֶץ", כְּלוֹמַר שֶׁעֲנָה יָרַשׁ אֶרֶץ שֵׂעִיר אֲבִי אָבִיו, וְנִמְצָא שֶׁבְּנֵי בָנִים יוֹרְשִׁין נַחֲלַת הָאָב כְּבָנִים עַצְמָן. וְהוּא הַדִּין לְבַת בְּנוֹ, וְהִלְכָּךְ לֹא תִּירַשׁ הַבַּת עִם בַּת הַבֵּן, כִּי הֵיכִי דְּאֵינָהּ יוֹרֶשֶׁת עִם הַבֵּן. **וּכְתִיב וְאֵלֶּה בְנֵי צִבְעוֹן וְאַיָּה וַעֲנָה וגו'.** אַלְמָא בְּנוֹ הֲוָה, וּלְעֵיל קָרֵי לֵיהּ אָחִיו. **אֶלָּא צִבְעוֹן בָּא עַל אִמּוֹ** וְהוֹלִיד מִמֶּנָּה עֲנָה. נִמְצָא שֶׁהוּא אָחִיו וּבְנוֹ. וְאֵין לוֹמַר דִּבְנוֹ שֶׁל צִבְעוֹן הָיָה, וְהַאי דְּקָרֵי לֵיהּ בֶּן שֵׂעִיר לֹא מִשּׁוּם שֶׁהָיָה אָחִיו שֶׁל צִבְעוֹן, אֶלָּא לְאַשְׁמוּעִינַן דִּבְנֵי בָנִים הֲרֵי הֵן כְּבָנִים — א"כ לָא לִכְתְּבֵיהּ גַּבֵּי צִבְעוֹן. (ה) אֶלָּא מִדְּקָאָמַר "צִבְעוֹן וַעֲנָה" — אַחִים הָיוּ. וּמִיהוּ מִדִּכְתִיב "יֹשְׁבֵי הָאָרֶץ" שָׁמְעִינַן מֵהָכָא דִּבְנֵי בָנִים הֲרֵי הֵן כְּבָנִים לְנַחֲלָה. **אָמַר רַבָּה אָמֵינָא כו'** וּמַנּוּ שְׁמוּאֵל. וּלְפִי שֶׁהֲלָכָה כְּמוֹתוֹ בְּדִינִים קָרֵי לֵיהּ הָכִי, וְהוּא שֵׁם שֶׁל מֶלֶךְ פָּרַס. **אִיכָּא דְּאָמְרִי אָמַר רַב פַּפָּא כו'.** רַבָּה נַמִי קָרֵי שָׁבוּר מַלְכָּא, מִשּׁוּם דְּהִלְכְתָא נַמִי כְּוָותֵיהּ, לְבַד מִשָּׂדֶה עִנְיָן וּמֶחֱצָה, דְּהִלְכְתָא כְּרַב יוֹסֵף (לעיל דף קיד:). **בְּכָךְ אַתָּה פּוֹטְרֵנִי.** בִּתְמִיָּה, הֲלֹא גַּם אֲנִי מוֹדֶה לְךָ דְּבֶן הַבֵּן יוֹרֵשׁ אֶת זְקֵנוֹ וַאֲפִילּוּ בִּמְקוֹם בַּת, אֲבָל בַּת הַבֵּן [הוּא] דְּאָמְרִינַן שֶׁתִּירַשׁ הַבַּת עִמָּהּ! לא

תוספות

אפילו נשיא שבישראל. שרוצה לתקן לפי צורך שעה. כעין שמצינו בבני בנימין, שהתנו שלא תירש בת הבן עם אחיו אין שומעין לו, משום צדוקין. **מלמד** שבא צבעון על אמו והוליד ממנה ענה. קשה לר"ת: דאמאי אהדר ליה מענה? דלמא בן הבן הוי כבנו, אבל בת בנו — לא תהיה כבנו, אלא כבתו! (ו) ונראה לר"ת דענה אשה היתה, כדמוכחי קראי. דכתיב "ואלה בני אהליבמה בת ענה בת צבעון" — אלמא אשה היתה. וליכא למימר דענה אחר היה, דהא אמר הכא דצבעון הוליד ענה. ועוד, דמייתי אחר קרא דמייתי הכא "הוא ענה אשר מצא" וגו' כתיב "אלה בני ענה דישן ואהליבמה בת ענה". והשתא אהדר להו שפיר ר' יוחנן בן זכאי דבת הבן חשובה כבן לירש עם שאר בנים, שהן קודמין לבת מדקרי ליה "יושבי הארץ", וכך היא קודמת לבת. ומכאן סותר לבסוף ק"ו שלהן. והא דכתיב "הוא ענה" בלשון זכר — היינו משום שירשה עם *אחי' צבעון כזכר. וא"ת: והיאך ירשה ענה? והלא היה לה אח, (ז) וכתיב "ובני צבעון איה וענה"! וי"ל: דמת איה. תדע, מדלא חשיב בני איה כדחשיב בני ענה. ורש"י פירש בפירוש חומש דאהליבמה היתה בת ענה ובת צבעון, וכי היכי דאמר הכא שבא צבעון על אמו והוליד ממנה ענה, ולכך חשיב ליה (ח) בני שעיר — הכי נמי בא ענה על אמו והוליד ממנה אהליבמה, ולהכי קרי לה אהליבמה בת ענה בת צבעון.

*בדפו"י אחי ופי' רשב"ם

כי

רבינו גרשום

ירושתן: הא כיצד נחלה ממשמשת והולכת עד ראובן. עד בנו של ראובן חנוך או פלוא ובני פלוא אליאב ובני אליאב נמואל דתן ואבירם ועכשיו אם מת אבירם בלא יורש יורש אליאב אביו ואם היה מת אליאב יורש נמואל ודתן אחיו ואם אין שכבר מתו תחזור ירושתו א) מכח אמם ואם כולן מתו תחזור הירושה לפלוא שהוא אבי אביו של מת ואם אין פלוא תחזור הירושה לבני פלוא או לבתו ואם אין לו בנים לפלוא תחזור לאחי פלוא דהיינו חנוך חצרון וכרמי: ומקשי' ולימא עד יעקב. כלומר סמוך ליעקב דתחזור ירושה לראובן ומ"ש דקאמר עד ראובן ולא ראובן ממש גמירי דלא כלה שבטא מראובן דמצי למירש: כל האומר תירש הבת. של אב עם בת הבן היכא דליכא בן אפי' נשיא כו': תבנא לדינא. חזרנו לדינו: מפטפט. מקנתר כנגדו להשיב לו דבור ומה בת בנו הבאה מכח בנו תירשנו וכו': קרא עליו המקרא הזה. כלומר שלא היה רוצה להחזיר להם תשובה אלא מתוך דבריהם רצה לנצחן שהן מודין שממזר אינו יורש את אביו אע"פ שבא מכחו: וצבעון וענה. אלמא דאחי הוו והדר כתיב אלה בני צבעון ואיה וענה אלמא דענה בן צבעון היה אלא מלמד שבא צבעון על אמו והוליד ממנה ענה דאחיו ובנו הוה ומדבריהן החזיר להן תשובה דממזר אינו יורש אע"פ שבא מכחו בת האב נמי אע"פ שבאה מכחו אינה יורשת במקום בת הבן ואמר לו אותו זקן רבי בכך פוטרני ומדחני שלא תירש בת האב עם בן הבת. אמר לו שוטה בדין הוא שאפטרך בכך

א) אינו מובן ואולי צ"ל דתחזור הירושה לאחיותיהם ואם כולן מתו וכו'.

מסורת הש"ס

א) [תוספתא ידים פ"ב ע"ש]: ב) פסחים נד. ע"ש: ג) [שם איתא רבא וע"ש ברש"י]: ד) [שם איתא רבא]:

הגהות הב"ח

(א) גמ' ומנו שמואל. נ"ב עי' בסוף מסכת ב"מ: (ב) רשב"ם ד"ה הא כיצד כלומר כי היכי כצ"ל ותיבת ודאי נמחק: (ג) ד"ה נחלה וכו' אח"כ באחין דהיינו אחי אבי אבי אבי האב וכו' אחות אבי אבי אבי אביו וכו' בני נמואל יורשין אותו ואם אין לו אחים או בני אחים או בנות אחים נותנים לאחותו או לבני אחותו שהיא בת נמואל ואם אין אח או אחות ונתפס את נחלתו לאחי אביו וכו' לאליאב אבי אביו של מת (או לאחי אליאב וכו' וחצרון וכרמי) תא"מ ונ"ב ס"א והוא עיקר ואם אין אליאב נותנין לבניו של אליאב דהיינו אחי אביו של מת מת אליאב בלא בנים ובני בנים חוזרים אצל פלוא ואם מת נותנים לראובן ואם אין ראובן נותנים לחנוך חצרון וכרמי כו': (ד) בא"ד דרמי בר חמא וכן הלכה הס"ד: (ה) ד"ה אלא צבעון בא וכו' א"כ לא לכתביה גבי צבעון. נ"ב כלומר אמאי כתביה לענה טפי מאיה והרי שניהם היו בניו של צבעון וכך מפורש בתוס' פרק מקום שנהגו בדף נד: (ו) תוס' ד"ה מלמד וכו' ונראה לר"ת. נ"ב כוונתו דריב"ז השיב לצדוקי גם מתחלה על פי האמת דענה אשה היתה למעטה מיפרך ק"ו שלכם והצדוקי לא הבין וסבר דענה זכר היה כפשוטו של מקרא ולכן א"ל רבי בכך אתה פוטרני גם אנחנו מודים דבן הבן [יורש זקנו וריב"ז השיב לו] האמת ואמר לו לא תהא תורה שלימה כו' כלומר לא היתה תשובתי שיחה בטילה כמו שהבנת [אלא אני] השבתיך דענה אשה היתה בת בנו של שעיר כדמוכח מבת ענה בת צבעון והיתה יורשת עם יושבי הארץ והשתא מיפרך ק"ו שלכם דמה לבת בנו כו' וז"ש ר"ת ומכאן סותר לבסוף ק"ו שלהן דזה היה בדעתו כשהשיב לו מתחלה ולפי פי' זה לא יהיה פי' לא תהא תורה שלימה כו' אני [צריך לחותך בקש כמו] שפרשב"ם דלא דחה אותו בקש כל עיקר ואי לאו פר"ת הייתי מפרש על פי דרכו [דלא מיפרך] ק"ו שלהם וא"ל דענה אשה היתה אלא לאחר שהצדוקי א"ל רבי בכך אתה פוטרני [אבל מתחלה היה סבור] דענה זכר היה וקרא דבת ענה בת צבעון אינה ראויה דיש לפרש דענה בא [על אמו אלא דלאחר שא"ל בכך אתה פוטרני] אז השיב לו ריב"ז לא תהא תורה שלימה כו' פי' אני צריך לחותך בקש: (ז) בא"ד דכתיב ובני צבעון וכו' שבא צבעון על אמו. נ"ב פי' אשת שעיר: (ח) בא"ד חשיב ליה בבני שעיר הכי נמי בא ענה על אמו. נ"ב פי' אשת צבעון שהיא אשת אביו ואמו לאו דוקא.

מסורת הש"ס

א) לקמן קמא.: ב) ברכות ה:: ג) מו"ק כז: ע"ש:

עין משפט נר מצוה

כז א מיי' פ"א מהל' נחלות הלכה ב סמג עשין נו טוש"ע ח"מ סי' רעו סעיף א:

תורה אור

ולא תהא תורה שלמה שלנו כשיחה בטלה שלכם; מה לבת בנו – שכן יפה כחה במקום האחין, תאמר בבתו – שהורע כחה במקום אחין! ונצחום, ואותו היום עשאוהו יום טוב. [שופטים כא] "ויאמרו ירושת פלטה לבנימן ולא ימחה שבט מישראל" – אמר רבי יצחק דבי רבי אמי: מלמד, שהתנו על שבט בנימין שלא תירש בת הבן עם האחין. א)אמר רבי יוחנן משום ר' שמעון בן יוחאי: כל שאינו מניח בן ליורשו – הקדוש ברוך הוא מלא עליו עברה. כתיב הכא: [במדבר כז] "והעברתם את נחלתו", וכתיב התם: [צפניה א] "יום עברה היום ההוא". [תהלים נה] "אשר אין חליפות למו ולא יראו אלהים" – רבי יוחנן ורבי יהושע בן לוי, חד אמר: כל שאינו מניח בן, וחד אמר: כל שאינו מניח תלמיד. תסתיים (א) רבי יוחנן דאמר תלמיד, דאמר ב)רבי יוחנן: דין גרמיה דעשיראה ביר, תסתיים דרבי יוחנן דאמר תלמיד. ומדרבי יוחנן אמר תלמיד, רבי יהושע בן לוי אמר בן? ג)והא רבי יהושע בן לוי לא אזיל לבי טמיא אלא לבי מאן דשכיב בלא בני, דכתיב: [ירמיה כב] "בכו בכה להולך", ואמר רב יהודה אמר רב: להולך בלא (ב) בן זכר! אלא, רבי יהושע בן לוי הוא דאמר תלמיד. ומדר' יהושע בן לוי הוא דאמר תלמיד, רבי יוחנן אמר בן; קשיא דרבי יוחנן אדרבי יוחנן! לא קשיא: הא דידיה, הא דרביה. § סימן: הדד עני וחכם § דרש רבי פנחס בן חמא, מאי דכתיב: [מלכים א יא] "והדד שמע במצרים כי שכב דוד עם אבותיו וכי מת יואב שר הצבא", מפני מה בדוד נאמרה בו שכיבה, וביואב נאמרה בו מיתה? דוד שהניח בן – נאמרה בו שכיבה, יואב שלא הניח בן – נאמרה בו מיתה. ויואב לא הניח בן? והכתיב: [עזרא ח] "מבני יואב עובדיה בן יחיאל"! אלא, דוד שהניח בן כמותו – נאמרה בו שכיבה, יואב שלא הניח בן כמותו – נאמרה בו מיתה. דרש ר' פנחס בן חמא: קשה עניות בתוך ביתו של אדם יותר מחמשים מכות, שנאמר: [איוב יט] "חנוני חנוני אתם רעי כי יד אלוה נגעה בי", וקא אמרי ליה חבריה: [שם לו] "השמר אל תפן אל און כי על זה בחרת מעוני". דרש ר' פנחס בר חמא: כל שיש לו חולה בתוך ביתו, ילך אצל חכם ויבקש עליו רחמים, שנא': [משלי טז] "חמת מלך מלאכי מות ואיש חכם יכפרנה". § "זה הכלל: כל הקודם בנחלה – יוצאי ירכו קודמין; והאב קודם לכל יוצאי ירכו". § בעי רמי בר חמא: אבי האב ואחי האב, כגון אברהם וישמעאל בנכסי עשו, איזה מהן קודם? אמר רבא, א)תא שמע: האב קודם לכל יוצאי ירכו. ורמי בר חמא? אגב

רש"י

לא תהא תורה שלמה שלנו כו'. איני צריך לדחותך בקש. ומיהו, מעיקרא לא היה חפץ לגלות לו טעמו של דבר, דאסור לגלות להם טעמי תורה. **כשיחה בטלה שלכם.** קל וחומר שאתם דנין מעצמכם, שיש עליו תשובה. מה לבת בנו שיפה כחה במקום אחין – שיורשת במקום אביה, כגון בנות צלפחד שירשו בנכסי חפר אבי אביהן עם בני חפר, שנאמר: "נתן תתן להם אחוזת נחלה בתוך אחי אביהן". **תאמר בבתו** שהורע כחה **אצל האחין.** כשם שאינה יורשת עם אחיה בנכסי אביה – כך אינה יורשת עם בת אחיה. בוא וראה שבנות צלפחד ירשו בנכסי חפר, ולא לקחו בני חפר ובנות חפר כל נכסי חפר. נמצאת בת הבן קודמת לבת, דהיינו בנות צלפחד שקדמו לבנות חפר. **ואותו היום.** שנצחום כ"ד בטבת היה. **שלא תירש בת הבן עם האחין.** של בן, אלא האחין יורשין כל נכסי האב, ואפילו חלק שהיה ראוי לאחיהן המת. לפי שבאותו מעשה דפילגש בגבעה מתו במלחמה כל שבט בנימין, ואפילו הנשים, כדכתיב: "מה נעשה לנותרים לנשים כי נשמדה מבנימין אשה". ולא נותר מהם כי אם שש מאות שנשאו נשים, ארבע מאות מבנות יבש גלעד, ומאתים שחטפו מבנות שילה. ונמצא כל ארץ בנימין לשש מאות איש. לפיכך, באותו העת מגיע (ג) מאד מן הנחלה לאשה אחת הבאה לירש, ואם תנשא לשבט אחר – נמצאת נגרעת נחלת שבט בנימין. לפיכך התקינו דהיכא דיש בנים יורשין את אביהם, דלא מיעקרא נחלה מבני המת – התנו שלא תירש בת הבן עמהן, דהפקר ב"ד הפקר. אבל אם לא הניח בנים אלא בנות *(לשם גם הבנות) – גם בת הבת תירש עמהן, דלא ניחא ליה למת שתעקר נחלתו מזרעו. אי נמי, היכא דאיכא בנות ובת הבן – תירש בת הבן את כל הנכסים. ומסתמא היו נזהרות שלא להנשא לשבט אחר, פן תסוב הנחלה לשבט אחר. והכי משמע קרא: "ויאמרו לתת הירושה לפלטת בנימין" – כלומר, לבנים, הנקראים על שבט בנימין, ולא לבת הבן, שיכולה להנשא לשבט אחר ונעקרה נחלה מבנימין. ה"ג: **מלא עליו עברה.** בפירוש רבינו חננאל: כלומר, שונא אותו. **חליפות.** חליפין, ממלא מקומו. **דין גרמא דעשיראה ביר.** נשאר אצלו שן אחד מבניו, ובו היה מנחם למרי נפש האבלים. שהשן של מת אינו טמא, דתנן באהלות פרק ג' (מ"ג): כל שבמת – טמא, חוץ מן השיניים והשער והצפורן, ובשעת חיבורן – הכל טמא. וכיון דרבי יוחנן לא הניח בן, אם איתא דסבירא ליה דמי שלא הניח בן נקרא לא ירא אלהים – לא היה אומר (ד) לבריות "דין גרמא דעשיראה ביר", דאמרינן בעלמא (ברכות דף לד:): חליף עלי מאן דמפרסם חטאיה, כדכתיב: "אשרי נשוי פשע כסוי חטאה". **לא הוה עייל לבי טמיא.** לבית המת להתאבל עליו, כדתנן (אהלות פ' טו מ"ג): בית מלא טמיא – מלא מתים, לפי שלא היה רוצה להתבטל מלמודו. **הא דידיה.** "דין גרמא" כו'. דסבירא ליה כר' יהושע בן לוי: זה שלא הניח תלמיד. **הא דרביה.** מאי דאמר: זה שלא הניח בן, ולא סבירא ליה. **קשה עניות כו'.** וצריך למיבעי רחמי. ואגב גררא דדרשות דר' פנחס בר חמא נקט ליה הכא. **כי יד אלוה וגו'.** היינו נ' מכות. שהרי במצרים דכתיב ביה: "אצבע אלהים הוא" (שמות ח) – לקו י' מכות, נמצא ליד שיש בה חמש אצבעות – חמשים מכות. **אל תפן אל און.** אל תהרהר אחר מדת הדין, כי יש מצירים יותר ממך. כי טוב לך זה החמשים מכות מעוני, והרי יש לך כסף וזהב וקרקעות, ועדיין הקב"ה מרחם עליך יותר מהרבה בני אדם שהן עניים. **חמת מלך.** היינו נער שבאה לו חימה מאת המקום. **מלאכי מות** – היינו חולה שנוטה למות. **יכפרנה.** יקנחנה. **בעי רמי בר חמא אבי אביו.** של מת, ואחי אביו של מת, איזה מהן קודם? ומשום דתרווייהו אתו לירש את המת מכח אבי המת קא בעי לה. **בנכסי עשו.** מיתה נקט בעשו שהוא רשע, ולא ביעקב. **האב קודם לירש את בנו לכל יוצאי ירכו.** נמצא אברהם יורש את יצחק מקמי ישמעאל. והלכך, כיון דתרווייהו מכח יצחק אתו – הרי הוא כאילו יורש יצחק את עשו, וחוזר אברהם ויורש את יצחק בנו, כדאמרן בריש פירקין, שהאב קודם לאחין. דכי היכי דדרשינן: "אין לו בן" – עיין עליו, הכי נמי דרשינן בכל קרובים. וגבי אבי המת נמי דרשינן: אם אין לו אב – ונתתם את נחלתו לאחיו, עיין עליו. שאם יש ליצחק שום יורש דראוי ליורשו – יבא במקומו, והיינו אברהם שקודם לישמעאל. וכן הלכה. אגב

תוספות

כי על זה בחרת מעוני. טוב לך במכות הללו ממה שהיית עני. דעשיר היה, דלא מצינו שהפסיד איוב אלא בהמות, אבל קרקעות וכסף וזהב – לא הפסיד. אע"ג דקאמר "ערום יצאתי מבטן אמי וערום אשוב שמה" (איוב א) – מתנחם היה על הפסדו. שלא היה לו לחוש שבמותו לא יוליך כלום עמו, כדכתיב בקהלת (ה) "ומאומה לא ישא בעמלו שיולך בידו". והא דכתיב (רישיה דקרא) (איוב מב) "ויתנו לו איש קשיטה אחת ונזם זהב אחד" – לא מפני שהיה עני, אלא דורון היו מביאין לו.

*__אבי__ האב ואחיו. כגון אברהם ויעקב בנכסי עשו, מהו? אמר רבא: תא שמע, האב קודם לבן, ש"מ שאברהם קודם. לפי טעותו לא היה בן יורש את אביו, אלא אב קודם כל שעה לבן, שהיה סבור שאברהם יורש כשימות עשו ויפלו הנכסים לפני יצחק. ולדבריו שהיה סבור שאברהם קודם ליעקב – אין בן יורש את אביו. ושהיה

רבינו גרשום

שלא תהא תורה שלמה שלנו כשיחה בטלה שלכם. אלא אותו ק"ו שאתם מבקשים ומביאין ראיה שתירש מופרך ומוקשה הוא משום דמה לבת בנו בדין הוא שתירש קודם לבת שכן יפה כחה במקום אחי אביה דהיא עומדת במקום אביה ויורשת עם אחי אביה. תאמר בבתו אע"ג דאתיא מכחו דתירשנו שכן הורע כחה במקום אחין שאינה נוטלת ירושה במקום אחיה דהבן קודם לבת. וכתיב במעשה בנימין כשנתפייסו אחיו עמו השבטים ואמרו ירושת פליטה לבנימין. מאי ירושת פליטה התקינו שלא תירש בת הבן עם האחין של אביה לפי שלא היו רוצין שלא יתמעט השבט ולא תסוב נחלתו משבט לשבט שאילמלי תירש והיתה רוצה לינשא לשבט אחר תסוב נחלתם לשבט אחר אע"פ שבהיתר היא עושה שכשהזהירה תורה לא תסוב נחלה ממטה למטה אחר לאותן שעמדו על הר סיני בלבד הזהירה ולא לדורות שכתוב בפרשה זה הדבר אשר צוה ה' לבנות צלפחד וגו' ואמר ולא תסוב וגו' מכלל דהוראת שעה היתה ולאו לדורות והכי קאמר לקמן בהאי פירקין ועכשיו התקינו לבנימין שלא תירש בת הבן עם האחין כדי שלא תסוב נחלה אבל אם רוצה לינשא לאחד משבטה תירש עם האחין: אשר אין חליפות למו זה שלא הניח תלמיד. תחתיו שלא רצה ללמד תורה לאחרים. דין גרמיה דעשיראה ביר. שהיה שומר (ונכנס המגיהמן) [השן] של בנו הקטן ומפני עגמת נפש. ואם איתא דר' יוחנן [הוא דאמר] שלא הניח בן היינו רשע הרי איהו לא הניח בן דכולן מתו בחייו ולא הוה קרי לנפשיה רשע אלא תסתיים דהוא דאמר זה שלא הניח תלמיד: לבי טמיא. לבית אבל נפיק מאטב"ח ומאלב"ם אבל: אלא למאן דשכיב בלא בני. מפני עגמת נפש אי הוה אמר דהוא רשע לא אזיל לבי טמיא רשע: הא דידיה. כלומר משמו היה אומר שלא הניח תלמיד. ומשמיה דרביה אמר זה שלא הניח בן: כי יד אלוה נגעה בי. דהיינו חמשים מכות דגמרי' יד דהכא מן וירא ישראל את היד הגדולה שבאצבע של הקב"ה לקו י' מכות ועל הים לקו נ' מכות דהתם ראו כל היד מתחלקת לנ' מכות. ומאי (אזהרו) [אהדרו] ליה חבריה לאיוב השמר אל תפן אל און. כלומר אם היית משמר עצמך ולא היית חוטא לא הוה מגיעך לך כל זה שעשה לך הקב"ה בחרת מעוני כלומר מוטב לך שתלקה בנ' מכות יותר מעוני: חמת מלך. מלכו של עולם היינו צער מלאך המות היינו חולה ילך אצל חכם והוא יכפרנה שמבקש רחמים והוא יצילנו: **פיסקא** האב קודם לכל יוצאי ירכו בנכסי בנו. היכא דאינן לבנו לא בן ולא בת הוא קודם לאחיו של מת. ובעי רמי בר חמא אבי האב ואחי האב כגון אברהם שהוא אבי אביו של עשו וישמעאל שהוא אחי יצחק אביו של עשו או ישמעאל אחי יצחק: אמר רבא ת"ש. ממתני' דקתני האב קודם לכל יוצאי ירכו (א) דיצחק וישמעאל מכח מאן קאתו מכח אברהם אביהן משום הכי דין הוא שיקדים אברהם היכא דליתיה ליצחק: אגב

הגהות הב"ח

(א) גמ' תסתיים דר' יוחנן הוא דאמר תלמיד דאמר וכו' ביר תסתיים דר' יוחנן הוא דאמר: (ב) שם להולך בלא בנים אלא ר' יהושע בן לוי: (ג) רשב"ם ד"ה שלא תירש וכו' מגיע הרבה מאד מן הנחלה: (ד) ד"ה דין גרמא וכו' לא היה אומר. נ"ב ובלאו הכי נמי יש לפרש דלא היתה נחמה איבעי ליה לנחומי לצורי קא מצערא ליה שמזכיר לפניו שאינו ירא אלהים וכ"כ תוס' בברכות דף ה ע"ב ע"ש:

א) ר"ל כיון דישמעאל נמי יוצאי ירכו של אברהם כמו יצחק ולפיכך אברהם קודם לאב קודם לכל יוצאי ירכו.

עין משפט נר מצוה

כח א מיי' פ"א מהל' נחלות הלכה ב סמג עשין נו טוש"ע ח"מ סי' רעו סעיף א:

א) אַגַּב חוּרְפֵיהּ לָא עַיֵּין בָּהּ. בָּעֵי רָמִי בַּר חָמָא: אֲבִי הָאָב וְאָחִיו, כְּגוֹן אַבְרָהָם וְיַעֲקֹב בְּנִכְסֵי עֵשָׂו, אֵיזֶה מֵהֶן קוֹדֵם? אָמַר רָבָא, א תָּא שְׁמַע: הָאָב קוֹדֵם לְכָל יוֹצְאֵי יְרֵיכוֹ. וְרָמִי בַּר חָמָא? יוֹצְאֵי יְרֵיכוֹ שֶׁלּוֹ, וְלֹא יוֹצְאֵי יְרֵיכוֹ שֶׁל בְּנוֹ. ה"נ מִסְתַּבְּרָא, דְּקָתָנֵי, זֶה הַכְּלָל: כָּל הַקּוֹדֵם בְּנַחֲלָה – יוֹצְאֵי יְרֵיכוֹ קוֹדְמִין; וְאִילּוּ אִיתֵיהּ לְיִצְחָק – יִצְחָק קוֹדֵם, הַשְׁתָּא נַמִי דְּלֵיתֵיהּ יִצְחָק – יַעֲקֹב קוֹדֵם, שְׁמַע מִינַּהּ.§ **מתני'** ב) בְּנוֹת צְלָפְחָד נָטְלוּ ג' חֲלָקִים בְּנַחֲלָה: חֵלֶק אֲבִיהֶן שֶׁהָיָה עִם יוֹצְאֵי מִצְרַיִם, וְחֶלְקוֹ עִם אֶחָיו בְּנִכְסֵי חֵפֶר, ג) וְשֶׁהָיָה בְּכוֹר נוֹטֵל שְׁנֵי חֲלָקִים.§ גמ'

אַגַּב חוּרְפֵיהּ. חֲרִיפוּתוֹ, שֶׁהָיָה טָרוּד בִּשְׁאֵלָה אַחֶרֶת דִּלְקַמָּן, דַּעֲדִיפָא מִינַּהּ. **אֲבִי הָאָב.** שֶׁל מֵת, וְהָאַחִין שֶׁל מֵת, דְּהַיְינוּ זְקֵנוֹ וְאַחִין, אֵיזֶה מֵהֶן קוֹדֵם? מִי לֵימָא: כֵּיוָן דְּיִצְחָק קוֹדֵם לְיַעֲקֹב לִירַשׁ אֶת עֵשָׂו, דְּהָאָב קוֹדֵם לָאָח – הֲרֵי הוּא כְּאִילּוּ יְרָשׁוֹ יִצְחָק לְעֵשָׂו, וְהִלְכָּךְ יָבֹא יַעֲקֹב וְיִירַשׁ אֶת יִצְחָק אָבִיו. אֲבָל אַבְרָהָם לֹא יִירָשֶׁנּוּ, שֶׁהַבֵּן שֶׁל מֵת קוֹדֵם לַאֲבִי הַמֵּת. אוֹ דִּלְמָא בְּנֵי בָנִים הֲרֵי הֵן כְּבָנִים, וְנִמְצָא עֵשָׂו בֶּן אַבְרָהָם, וְקוֹדֵם אַבְרָהָם לְיַעֲקֹב בְּנִכְסֵי עֵשָׂו, דְּהָאָב קוֹדֵם לָאַחִין. ת"ש הָאָב קוֹדֵם לְכָל יוֹצְאֵי יְרֵיכוֹ. וְיַעֲקֹב יוֹצֵא יְרֵיכוֹ שֶׁל אַבְרָהָם הָיָה, וְהִלְכָּךְ אַבְרָהָם קוֹדֵם לוֹ בְּנִכְסֵי עֵשָׂו. וְרָמִי בַּר חָמָא. אָמַר לָךְ: מִשּׁוּם הָכִי מְסַפְּקָא לִי, דְּאִיכָּא לְמֵימַר: "יוֹצְאֵי יְרֵיכוֹ" מַשְׁמַע יוֹצְאֵי יֶרֶךְ שֶׁלּוֹ, דְּהַיְינוּ בָּנָיו מֵאִשְׁתּוֹ, וְלֹא יוֹצְאֵי יֶרֶךְ בְּנוֹ. הָכִי נַמִי מִסְתַּבְּרָא. דְּיַעֲקֹב קוֹדֵם לְאַבְרָהָם בְּנִכְסֵי עֵשָׂו. דְּקָתָנֵי רֵישָׁא: כָּל הַקּוֹדֵם בַּנַּחֲלָה וְאֵינוֹ, כְּגוֹן יִצְחָק שֶׁקּוֹדֵם לְאַבְרָהָם בְּנִכְסֵי עֵשָׂו אִילּוּ הָיָה קַיָּים, הַשְׁתָּא דְּלֵיתֵיהּ לְיִצְחָק – יוֹצְאֵי יְרֵיכוֹ קוֹדְמִין, דְּהַיְינוּ יַעֲקֹב, שֶׁיּוֹרֵשׁ זְכוּת אָבִיו יִצְחָק. שֶׁכֵּן הוּא הַדִּין, שֶׁהֲרֵי אִם מֵת יִצְחָק אַחַר עֵשָׂו – הָיָה יַעֲקֹב יוֹרֵשׁ, וְלֹא אַבְרָהָם, דְּהַבָּנִים קוֹדְמִין לָאָב, כְּדַאֲמָרַן בְּרֵישׁ פִּירְקִין. הוּא הַדִּין כְּשֶׁמֵּת יִצְחָק מִקַּמֵּי עֵשָׂו – יַעֲקֹב יוֹרֵשׁ אֶת זְכוּתוֹ, וְלֹא אַבְרָהָם. וְכֵן הֲלָכָה. וְהַשְׁתָּא שְׁמַעִינַן מִפִּירְקִין שֶׁסֵּדֶר נַחֲלוֹת כָּךְ הוּא: רְאוּבֵן שֶׁמֵּת – חֲנוֹךְ וּפַלּוּא חֶצְרוֹן וְכַרְמִי בָּנָיו יוֹרְשִׁין אוֹתוֹ. וְאִם מֵת אֶחָד מִן הַבָּנִים קוֹדֵם רְאוּבֵן, וְהַהוּא בֵּן הִנִּיחַ בֵּן אוֹ בַּת, אוֹ בֶּן בַּת אוֹ בַּת בַּת, עַד מֵאָה דוֹרוֹת – יִירַשׁ בִּמְקוֹם אָבִיו בְּנִכְסֵי רְאוּבֵן. וְאִם אֵין לִרְאוּבֵן בָּנִים וְלֹא בְּנֵי בָנִים, וְאַף לֹא בְּנוֹת בָּנִים – הֵן יוֹרְשׁוֹת בְּנוֹת רְאוּבֵן אֶת רְאוּבֵן. וְאִם אֵין לִרְאוּבֵן בָּנוֹת וְלֹא בְּנֵי בָנוֹת וְלֹא בְּנוֹת בָּנוֹת אֲפִילּוּ בְּסוֹף הַדּוֹרוֹת – אָז יוֹרֵשׁ יַעֲקֹב אֶת רְאוּבֵן בְּנוֹ. וְאִם אֵין יַעֲקֹב קַיָּים – וְנוֹתְנִים אֶת נַחֲלַת רְאוּבֵן לְאֶחָיו בְּנֵי אָבִיו, שִׁמְעוֹן וְלֵוִי וִיהוּדָה וְיוֹסֵף וּבִנְיָמִין. וְאִם אֵינָם קַיָּימִין – תִּתְּנוּ נַחֲלַת רְאוּבֵן לִבְנֵי שִׁמְעוֹן יְלֵוִי. וְאִם אֵין לָהֶם בָּנִים וְלֹא בְּנֵי בָנִים – תִּתְּנוּ לִבְנוֹתֵיהֶן אוֹ לִבְנֵי בְנוֹתֵיהֶן אוֹ לִבְנוֹת בְּנוֹתֵיהֶן. דְּבכ"מ הַזָּכָר וְיוֹרְשָׁיו קוֹדְמִין לַנְּקֵבָה, כְּדַאֲמָרַן: מַקִּישׁ יְרוּשָּׁה שְׁנִיָּה לִירוּשָּׁה רִאשׁוֹנָה. וְאִם אֵין לוֹ אַחִים לִרְאוּבֵן, וְלֹא בְּנֵי בָנִים לָאַחִים, שֶׁמֵּתוּ אֶחָיו בְּלֹא בָּנִים, אוֹ שֶׁלֹּא הָיָה לוֹ אָח מֵעוֹלָם – וְנִכְתְּבִים אֶת נַחֲלָתוֹ לְבַת יַעֲקֹב, אֲחוֹתוֹ מִן הָאָב, אוֹ לְבָנֶיהָ וְלִבְנֵי בָנֶיהָ אוֹ לִבְנוֹתֶיהָ וְלִבְנוֹת בְּנוֹתֶיהָ עַד עוֹלָם. וְאִם אֵין לִרְאוּבֵן אָחוֹת וְלֹא בְּנֵי אָחוֹת מִן הָאָב – וְנִתְּנִים נַחֲלָתוֹ לַאֲבִי אָבִיו, דְּהַיְינוּ יִצְחָק. וְאִם אֵין יִצְחָק קַיָּים – וְנִתְּנִים נַחֲלָתוֹ שֶׁל רְאוּבֵן לְעֵשָׂו בֶּן יִצְחָק, שֶׁהוּא אֲחִי אָבִיו שֶׁל רְאוּבֵן. וְאִם אֵין עֵשָׂו קַיָּים – וְנִתְּנִים אֶת נַחֲלָתוֹ שֶׁל רְאוּבֵן לֶאֱלִיפַז בֶּן עֵשָׂו, אוֹ לְבָנָיו וּבְנֵי בָנָיו. וְאִם אֵין בָּנִים לְעֵשָׂו – וְנִתְּנִים אֶת נַחֲלַת רְאוּבֵן לִבְנוֹת עֵשָׂו וְלִבְנֵיהֶם וְלִבְנוֹת בְּנוֹתָיו. וְאִם אֵין אַחִין לְאָבִיו שֶׁל רְאוּבֵן – וְנִתְּנִים אֶת נַחֲלָתוֹ לִבְנוֹת יִצְחָק, דְּהַיְינוּ אֲחוֹת אָבִיו, אוֹ לִבְנֵיהֶן וְלִבְנֵי בְנֵיהֶן אוֹ לִבְנוֹתֵיהֶן וְלִבְנֵי בְנוֹתֵיהֶן. יאִם אֵין לְאָבִיו שֶׁל רְאוּבֵן לֹא אַחִים וְלֹא בְּנֵי אַחִים, לֹא אָחוֹת וְלֹא בְּנֵי אָחוֹת – וְנִתְּנִים אֶת נַחֲלַת רְאוּבֵן לְאַבְרָהָם אֲבִי אֲבִי אָבִיו. וְאִם אֵין אַבְרָהָם קַיָּים – וְנִתְּנִים לְיִשְׁמָעֵאל אֲחִי אֲבִי אָבִיו, אוֹ לְבָנָיו שֶׁל יִשְׁמָעֵאל וְלִבְנֵי בָנָיו אוֹ לִבְנוֹתָיו וְלִבְנֵי בְנוֹתָיו. וְאִם אֵין יִשְׁמָעֵאל וְלֹא בָּנָיו קַיָּימִין, וְגַם לֹא אֲחוֹתוֹ וּבְנֵי אֲחוֹתוֹ – וְנִתְּנִים נַחֲלָתוֹ לְתֶרַח אֲבִי אַבְרָהָם. וְאִם אֵין תֶּרַח – תִּתְּנוּ לְנָחוֹר וּלְהָרָן בָּנָיו, אוֹ לִבְנֵי בְנֵיהֶן אוֹ לְאַחְוֹתָם וּלְיוֹצְאֵי יְרֵיכָם. וְכֵן לְעוֹלָם עַד אָדָם הָרִאשׁוֹן, ד) הָאָב קוֹדֵם לְעוֹלָם (א) לַאֲחֵי ה) (הָאָב), וַאֲחֵי הָאָב קוֹדְמִין לַאֲחוֹת הָאָב, וַאֲחוֹת הָאָב קוֹדְמִין לַאֲבִי הָאָב, וַאֲבִי הָאָב קוֹדֵם לַאֲחֵי אֲבִי הָאָב (וְלַאֲחוֹתוֹ), וַאֲחֵי אֲבִי הָאָב [וְאַף] אֲחוֹתוֹ קוֹדְמִין לַאֲבִי אֲבִי הָאָב, וְכֵן לְעוֹלָם. וְגַם לָמַדְנוּ שֶׁהַבַּעַל יוֹרֵשׁ אֶת אִשְׁתּוֹ, וְאִם אֵין בַּעַל קַיָּים – בְּנָהּ יוֹרְשָׁהּ, וְאִם אֵין בְּנָהּ – בִּתָּהּ יוֹרַשְׁתָּהּ, בְּכָל הַסֵּדֶר הַזֶּה עַד אָדָם הָרִאשׁוֹן. **מתני'** בְּנַחֲלָה. בְּנַחֲלַת אֶרֶץ יִשְׂרָאֵל. וּמִשּׁוּם דַּאֲמָרַן לְעֵיל (דף קטו.): כָּל יוֹצְאֵי יְרֵיכוֹ שֶׁל בֵּן קוֹדֵם *לָאַחִין, דְּאַשְׁמוּעִינַן דְּבַת הַבֵּן נוֹחֶלֶת בִּמְקוֹם הַבֵּן – מִשּׁוּם הָכִי נְקַט לָהּ. שֶׁהֲרֵי בְּנוֹת צְלָפְחָד נָחֲלוּ חֵלֶק אֲבִיהֶן בְּנִכְסֵי חֵפֶר בִּמְקוֹם צְלָפְחָד אֲבִיהֶן. **חֵלֶק אֲבִיהֶן.** צְלָפְחָד, שֶׁהָיָה מִיּוֹצְאֵי מִצְרַיִם. שֶׁהַבֵּן הַנִּכְנָס לָאָרֶץ לֹא הָיָה נוֹטֵל בִּשְׁבִיל עַצְמוֹ חֵלֶק בָּאָרֶץ, הוֹאִיל וְלֹא יָצָא מִמִּצְרַיִם, כִּדְאָמַר בַּגְּמָ' דְּקָסָבַר הַאי תַּנָּא: לְיוֹצְאֵי מִצְרַיִם נִתְחַלְּקָה הָאָרֶץ וְלֹא לְבָאֵי הָאָרֶץ, וְנָפְקָא לָן מִקְּרָאֵי. וְאע"פ שֶׁיּוֹצְאֵי מִצְרַיִם לֹא נִכְנְסוּ לָאָרֶץ אֶלָּא מֵתוּ בַּמִּדְבָּר, וְלֹא נָטְלוּ חֵלֶק בָּאָרֶץ – מִיהוּ לְהָכִי הֲהֵנֵי, שֶׁאִם יָצָא רְאוּבֵן וְשִׁמְעוֹן מִמִּצְרַיִם וְנוֹלְדוּ לָהֶם בַּמִּדְבָּר בָּנִים שֶׁנִּכְנְסוּ לָאָרֶץ, לִרְאוּבֵן עֲשָׂרָה בָּנִים וּלְשִׁמְעוֹן בֵּן אֶחָד – יִטּוֹל בֶּן שִׁמְעוֹן חֵלֶק כְּנֶגֶד עֲשָׂרָה בְּנֵי רְאוּבֵן, שֶׁהֲרֵי לִרְאוּבֵן וְשִׁמְעוֹן נִתְחַלְּקָה הָאָרֶץ, וְזָכוּ בְּנֵי כָּל אֶחָד בְּנִכְסֵי אֲבִיהֶן. וּצְלָפְחָד יָצָא מִמִּצְרַיִם וּמֵת בַּמִּדְבָּר, לְפִיכָךְ נָטְלוּ בְּנוֹתָיו חֶלְקוֹ. וְכָל שְׁלֹשָׁה חֲלָקִים דְּמַתְנִי' נָפְקָא לָן בַּגְּמָרָא מִקְּרָאֵי, הִלְכָּךְ בָּעֵינַן לְפָרוּשֵׁי דִּבְרֵי הַאי גַּוְונָא הֲוָה מַעֲשֶׂה, דִּצְלָפְחָד יָצָא מִמִּצְרַיִם כְּשֶׁהוּא בֶּן עֶשְׂרִים, וְכֵן חֵפֶר אָבִיו, וְשֶׁהָיָה צְלָפְחָד בְּכוֹר – כָּל דְּבָרִים הַלָּלוּ יֵשׁ לְךָ לִלְמוֹד מִן הַפָּסוּק ד"נָתֹן תִּתֵּן לָהֶם" וגו' דְּיָלְפִינַן מִינֵּיהּ בַּגְּמָ' לְהָנֵי שְׁלֹשָׁה חֲלָקִים. וְחֶלְקוֹ עִם אֶחָיו בְּנִכְסֵי חֵפֶר. דְּחֵפֶר יָצָא מִמִּצְרַיִם, וְנָטְלוּ בָּנָיו חֵלֶק אֲבִיהֶן שֶׁהָיָה מִיּוֹצְאֵי מִצְרַיִם, לְבַד חֵלֶק עַצְמָן, שֶׁגַּם הֵם יָצְאוּ מִמִּצְרַיִם. וּבְנוֹת צְלָפְחָד קִבְּלוּ חֵלֶק אֲבִיהֶן (ב) מִנִּכְסֵי חֵפֶר בְּשָׁעָה שֶׁחָלְקוּ אֲחֵי צְלָפְחָד נַחֲלַת אֲבִיהֶן בֵּינֵיהֶן, דְּבַת הַבֵּן הֲרֵי הִיא בִּמְקוֹם הַבֵּן לִירַשׁ עִם הָאַחִין, כִּדְקָתָנֵי לְעֵיל: כָּל הַקּוֹדֵם בַּנַּחֲלָה יוֹצְאֵי יְרֵיכוֹ קוֹדְמִין. וְשֶׁהָיָה צְלָפְחָד בְּכוֹר. וְהָיָה רָאוּי לִיטּוֹל פִּי שְׁנַיִם עִם אֶחָיו בְּנִכְסֵי חֵפֶר. וְאע"ג שֶׁאֵין הַבְּכוֹר נוֹטֵל בְּרָאוּי כִּבְמוּחְזָק – אֶרֶץ יִשְׂרָאֵל מוּחְזֶקֶת הִיא לְיוֹצְאֵי מִצְרַיִם כִּדְאָמַר בַּגְּמָ', וּכְמִי שֶׁהֶחֱזִיק חֵפֶר בְּחֶלְקוֹ דָּמֵי. וַאֲפִילּוּ אִם מֵת צְלָפְחָד מִקַּמֵּי חֵפֶר נִמְצָא צְלָפְחָד יוֹרֵשׁ פִּי שְׁנַיִם בְּכָל אֲשֶׁר יִמָּצֵא לְחֵפֶר, כִּי הוּא רֵאשִׁית אוֹנוֹ. וְאע"ג דִּכְשֶׁמֵּת חֵפֶר לֹא הָיָה צְלָפְחָד קַיָּים – אֲפִילּוּ הָכִי בְּנוֹתָיו הָיוּ יוֹרְשׁוֹת חֵלֶק בְּכוֹרַת צְלָפְחָד בְּנִכְסֵי חֵפֶר, כִּי הֵיכִי דְּיוֹרְשׁוֹת חֵלֶק פְּשִׁיטוּתוֹ בְּנִכְסֵי חֵפֶר. כִּדְתַנְיָא בְּהֶדְיָא בַּתּוֹסֶפְתָּא דִּבְכוֹרוֹת (פ"ו): כֵּיצַד אֵין הַבְּכוֹר נוֹטֵל בְּרָאוּי כִּבְמוּחְזָק? מֵת אָבִיו בְּחַיֵּי אָבִיו – נוֹטֵל פִּי שְׁנַיִם (ג) מִנִּכְסֵי אָבִיו, וְאֵין נוֹטֵל פִּי שְׁנַיִם מִנִּכְסֵי אֲבִי אָבִיו. כְּגוֹן יַעֲקֹב שֶׁמֵּת בְּחַיֵּי יִצְחָק, הֲרֵי רְאוּבֵן הַבְּכוֹר נוֹטֵל בְּנִכְסֵי יַעֲקֹב פִּי שְׁנַיִם, אֲבָל לֹא בְּנִכְסֵי יִצְחָק זְקֵנוֹ, שֶׁהֲרֵי אֲפִילּוּ אִם הָיָה יַעֲקֹב קַיָּים כְּשֶׁמֵּת יִצְחָק – לֹא הָיָה יַעֲקֹב נוֹטֵל פִּי שְׁנַיִם, שֶׁהֲרֵי פָּשׁוּט הוּא, הִלְכָּךְ רְאוּבֵן הַבָּא לִירַשׁ מִכֹּחַ יַעֲקֹב בְּנִכְסֵי יִצְחָק – לֹא יִטּוֹל אֶלָּא חֵלֶק פְּשִׁיטוּתוֹ שֶׁל אָבִיו. וְאִם הָיָה אָבִיו בְּכוֹר – אַף הוּא נוֹטֵל פִּי שְׁנַיִם בְּנִכְסֵי אֲבִי אָבִיו, שֶׁאִם הָיָה יַעֲקֹב בְּכוֹר, אַף עַל פִּי שֶׁמֵּת בְּחַיֵּי יִצְחָק – הֲרֵי בָּא רְאוּבֵן וְנוֹטֵל חֵלֶק בְּכוֹרַת יַעֲקֹב אָבִיו בְּנִכְסֵי יִצְחָק, שֶׁהַבֵּן בִּמְקוֹם אָב עוֹמֵד, בֵּין לְחֵלֶק בְּכוֹרָה בֵּין לְחֵלֶק פְּשִׁיטוּת. וְהוּא הַדִּין לִבְנוֹת צְלָפְחָד בְּנִכְסֵי חֵפֶר, דְּאַף עַל פִּי שֶׁמֵּת צְלָפְחָד בְּחַיֵּי חֵפֶר – יוֹרְשׁוֹת חֵלֶק בְּכוֹרַת אֲבִיהֶן בְּנִכְסֵי חֵפֶר. וְה"נ תַּנְיָא בְּהֶדְיָא בִּגְמָרַת יְרוּשַׁלְמִי. וְאָמְרִינַן נַמִי הָתָם: רֵישׁ לָקִישׁ אָמַר בְּשֵׁם אַבָּא כֹּהֵן בַּרְדְּלָא: נֶאֱמַר מִשְׁפָּט לְעִנְיַן כְּפִילָה, וְנֶאֱמַר מִשְׁפָּט לְעִנְיַן פְּשִׁיטָה, מַה לְּעִנְיַן פְּשִׁיטָה אַתָּה רוֹאֶה אֶת הַבֵּן כְּאִילּוּ קַיָּים, לִיטּוֹל פְּשִׁיטוּת אָבִיו – אַף לְעִנְיַן כְּפִילָה אַתָּה רוֹאֶה אֶת הַבֵּן כְּאִילּוּ קַיָּים לִיטּוֹל כְּפִילַת אָבִיו. מִפֵּירוּשׁ רַבֵּינוּ חֲנַנְאֵל גָּאוֹן זֵכֶר צַדִּיק לִבְרָכָה לָמַדְתִּי זֹאת, וְכֵן הֲלָכָה. וּמִדְּאָמְרִינַן בַּגְּמָרָא: "וְהַעֲבַרְתָּ" – זוֹ חֵלֶק בְּכוֹרָה, יָלְפִינַן דִּצְלָפְחָד בְּכוֹר הָיָה. וְהַאי דִּכְתִיב בְּדִבְרֵי הַיָּמִים (א ז): "וְשֵׁם הַשֵּׁנִי צְלָפְחָד" – לָאו שֵׁנִי לָאַחִין קָאָמַר, דְּהָא לָא אַיְירֵי לְעֵיל בָּאַחִין כְּלָל, אֶלָּא בְּגִלְעָד

ושהיה בכור נוטל שני חלקים. כאן לא דקדק הקונטרס יפה, דפי': אע"ג דכשמת חפר לא היה צלפחד קיים — אפ"ה בנותיו נוטלות חלק בכורה של צלפחד בנכסי חפר, כדתניא בתוספתא דבכורות: כילד אין הבכור נוטל בראוי כבמוחזק? מת אביו בחיי אביו — נוטל פי שנים בנכסי אביו, ואינו נוטל פי שנים בנכסי אבי אביו. כגון יעקב שמת בחיי יצחק, (ד) היה ראובן בכור — נוטל פי שנים בנכסי יעקב, אבל לא בנכסי יצחק זקנו, שהרי [אפילו] אם היה יעקב קיים כשמת יצחק לא היה יעקב נוטל פי שנים, שהרי פשוט הוא. הלכך, ראובן הבא לירש מכח יעקב בנכסי יצחק — לא יטול אלא חלק פשיטות של אביו, ע"כ. ולא היה לו לפרש כן, דלא קרי "ראוי" כי האי גוונא מה שאין ראובן נוטל פי שנים מעשו בנכסי יצחק, אלא הא קרי "ראוי" — מה שאין ראובן נוטל פי שנים מאחיו בנכסי יצחק שלא הוחזק בהן מעולם יעקב, והוה ליה ראוי. ומחזירין

רבינו גרשום

אגב חורפיה. שהיה מחזיר תלמודו: לא עיין בה. במתני' שלא דקדק בה לפיכך היה שואל: האב קודם לכל יוצאי ירכו. ואברהם קודם משום דכל הני מכחו קאתו: ורמי בר חמא. דקא מיבעיא ליה הכי קאמר לך. הא דקתני האב קודם לכל יוצאי ירכו שלא יהא יצחק יורשו דהוא קודם מן האחין של בנו דהיינו ישמעאל אבל אין אבי האב קודם לכל יוצאי ירכו של בנו דלא מקדמינן ליה לאברהם מקמי יעקב בנכסי עשו אלא יעקב קודם: ה"נ מסתברא דקתני. סיפא דמתני' זה הכלל וכו': ואם איתיה יצחק שהוא אבי עשו יצחק קודם השתא דליתי' יעקב קודם לאברהם אע"ג דכל הני מכחו של אברהם קא אתיין הכא יעקב קודם משום דקרוב ליה טפי יעקב מאברהם שהוא אבי אביו ותו לא מידי דליכא לדקדק בדבר כלום: **פיסקא** בנות צלפחד נטלו ג' חלקים בנחלה חלק אביהן שהיה מיוצאי מצרים. דסבירא ליה לתנא דליוצאי מצרים נתחלקה הארץ אע"ג דמתו בניהן יורשין חלקן: וחלקו עם אחיו. של צלפחד: בנכסי חפר. שהיה נמי מיוצאי מצרים. ולפי שהיה צלפחד בכור נטלו שני חלקים בנכסי חפר אביו דהיינו שלשה חלקים:

מסורת הש"ס

א) [עירובין ל. ב"מ נו: נדה לג:]: ב) [לקמן קכב:]: ג) [שם]: ד) האב קודם לעולם לאחי האב מבניהם ואחי אחות האב קודמים לאבי אבי האב ואחי אבי האם לאחותו ואחי האב ואחותו קודמין לאבי אבי האב וכן לעולם וגם למדנו כו' כן מצאתי כ"א: ה) [כ"א המת רש"ל]:

[נ"ל לבת וכן העתיק התוי"ט]

הגהות הב"ח

(א) רשב"ם ד"ה הכי נמי וכו' האב קודם לעולם לאחין של מת ואחין ואחות קודמים לאבי האב ואבי האב לאחי האב ולאחותו ואחי האב ואחותו קודמין לאבי אבי אב וכן לעולם כל"ל: (ב) ד"ה וחלקו וכו' בנכסי: (ג) ד"ה ושהיה לצלפחד וכו' בנכסי אביו ואין נוטל פי שנים בנכסי אבי אביו וכו': (ד) תום' ד"ה ושהיה וכו' בחיי יצחק הרי ראובן הבכור נוטל:

גמ' תְּנַן כְּמַאן דְּאָמַר: לְיוֹצְאֵי מִצְרַיִם נִתְחַלְּקָה הָאָרֶץ; דְּתַנְיָא, ר' יֹאשִׁיָּה אוֹמֵר: לְיוֹצְאֵי מִצְרַיִם נִתְחַלְּקָה הָאָרֶץ, שֶׁנֶּא': °"לִשְׁמוֹת מַטּוֹת אֲבוֹתָם יִנְחָלוּ". אֶלָּא מָה אֲנִי מְקַיֵּים °"לָאֵלֶּה תֵּחָלֵק הָאָרֶץ בְּנַחֲלָה"? "לָאֵלֶּה" — כָּאֵלֶּה, לְהוֹצִיא אֶת הַטְּפָלִים; ר' יוֹנָתָן אוֹמֵר: לְבָאֵי הָאָרֶץ נִתְחַלְּקָה הָאָרֶץ, שֶׁנֶּאֱמַר: "לָאֵלֶּה תֵּחָלֵק הָאָרֶץ בְּנַחֲלָה". אֶלָּא מָה אֲנִי מְקַיֵּים "לִשְׁמוֹת מַטּוֹת אֲבוֹתָם יִנְחָלוּ"? מְשׁוּנָּה נַחֲלָה זוֹ מִכָּל נְחָלוֹת שֶׁבָּעוֹלָם, שֶׁכָּל נְחָלוֹת שֶׁבָּעוֹלָם — חַיִּין יוֹרְשִׁין מֵתִים, וְכָאן מֵתִים יוֹרְשִׁין חַיִּין. אָמַר רַבִּי: אֶמְשׁוֹל לְךָ מָשָׁל, לְמָה הַדָּבָר דּוֹמֶה? לִשְׁנֵי אַחִין כֹּהֲנִים שֶׁהָיוּ בְּעִיר אַחַת, לְאֶחָד יֵשׁ לוֹ בֵּן אֶחָד, וְאֶחָד יֵשׁ לוֹ שְׁנֵי בָנִים, וְהָלְכוּ לַגּוֹרֶן. זֶה שֶׁיֵּשׁ לוֹ בֵּן אֶחָד — נוֹטֵל חֵלֶק אֶחָד, וְזֶה שֶׁיֵּשׁ לוֹ שְׁנֵי בָנִים — נוֹטֵל שְׁנֵי חֲלָקִים. וּמַחֲזִירִין אֵצֶל אֲבִיהֶן, וְחוֹזְרִין וְחוֹלְקִין בְּשָׁוֶה. רַבִּי שִׁמְעוֹן בֶּן אֶלְעָזָר אוֹמֵר: לָאֵלּוּ

במדבר כו / שם

תורה אור

בגלעד אבי חפר ובמכיר אבי גלעד לעיל מינה איירי, ואיכא למימר דאגלעד קאי, ומאי "שני" – שני לגלעד, כלומר בן בנו, כדכתיב: "בן חפר בן גלעד". הרי ג' חלקים: ב' חלקי בכורה, וחלק לצלפחד עצמו שהיה מיוצאי מצרים. והאי דלא קחשיב במתני' ד' חלקים שהיה להם לבנות צלפחד, כדכתיב (יהושע יז): "ויפלו חבלי מנשה עשרה" – שיתא דשיתא בתי אבות, וארבע דידהו, דהוה להו חד אחא דאבא (א) ונטלו חלק בנכסיו, כדאמרי' בגמ' – היינו טעמא, דלא הוה משמע לן מידי, דהא כבר אשמועינן דבת הבן הרי היא במקום הבן ליטול עם האחין בנכסי חפר, דהוא הדין דהרי היא במקום הבן ליטול עם האחין בנכסי האב. ואי לאשמועינן דליוצאי מצרים נתחלקה הארץ – הא שמעינן לה מדנטלו חלק לצלפחד בשביל שהיה מיוצאי מצרים. אבל בהני ג' חלקים דקתני אשמועינן תלתא מילי: דליוצאי מצרים נתחלקה הארץ, ובת הבן היא כבן לירש עם האחין, וארץ ישראל מוחזקת היא ליוצאי מצרים ונטל בה בכור פי שנים. **גמ'** **ליוצאי מצרים** נתחלקה הארץ. כלומר, לבאי הארץ נתחלקה הארץ כפי חשבון של יוצאי מצרים, שנטלוה בתורת ירושה מאבותיהם. דלפי חשבון הראשון שנמנו בשנה שניה לצאתם ממצרים נתחלקה הארץ כאילו ירשוה הן עצמן, ומי שהיה לו עתה בביאת הארץ בן אחד – נטל כל חלקו, ומי שהיו לו עשרה בנים – נמי לא נטלו בין כולם אלא חלק אחד. **שנאמר.** בפנחס, בבאי הארץ, באותו מנין דערבות מואב דכתיב בהו "ובאלה לא היה איש מפקודי משה ואהרן" וגו'. **לשמות מטות אבותם.** של אלה שנמנו ביציאת מצרים, ינחלו אלו. דלאותן יחלקו הנחלה, ואלו אשר קמו תחתיהן יירשום. ולקמן מפרש מנלן דהאי "אבותם" – ביוצאי מצרים קאמר. **לאלה תחלק.** דכתיב לעיל: "אלה פקודי בני ישראל שש מאות אלף ואלף שבע מאות ושלשים" וסמיך ליה "וידבר ה' אל משה לאמר לאלה תחלק הארץ" – אלמא לבאי הארץ נתחלקה. **כאלה.** שהן בני עשרים. דלבני עשרים שיצאו ממצרים נתחלקה הארץ, אבל לא לטפלים שיצאו פחות מבן כ', שלא נטלו חלק בארץ לא הם ולא בניהם, אלא בזכות מורישיהן. ואם לא היה להם שום מוריש שיצא ממצרים, כגון שלא היה להם אב ולא דוד ואח שמתו במדבר בלא בנים – אז לא נטלו חלק בארץ. ובסיפרי כתב: מה ת"ל "לאלה תחלק הארץ" (ב) – מפני כשרים וקדושים. כלומר, לאפוקי רשעים שבהן שלא היה להן חלק בה, ואפילו בניהן אינן זוכין בה בשביל אביהן, אלא בזכות זקניהם אם היו מיוצאי מצרים, כדאמרינן לקמן: בני מרגלים ומתלוננים נטלו בזכות אבי אביהן ובזכות אבי אמותיהן. **לבאי הארץ** נתחלקה הארץ. ולא ליוצאי מצרים, דאין הולכין אחר היוצאין אלא אחר הנכנסים. דראובן ושמעון שיצאו ממצרים והולידו בנים במדבר, זה עשרה וזה אחד, אי הוה אזלינן בתר יוצאי מצרים – היה נוטל האחד כנגד כולן, אבל עכשיו – העשרה נוטלין י' חלקים, והאחד נוטל חלק אחד. **אלא מה אני מקיים לשמות מטות אבותם.** דמשמע דאחר יוצאי מצרים נמי יש לנו לחלק הנחלה. ומפרש ואזיל דלהכי אהני "לשמות מטות אבותם ינחלו" – דלאחר שנטלו בני ראובן ושמעון י"א חלקים בארץ מחלקין אותה ביניהן לפי חשבון מטות אבותם, כאילו ליוצאי מצרים, דהיינו ראובן ושמעון אבותם, נתחלקו הני י"א חלקים. וכגון דהנהו יוצאי מצרים היו בני עשרים, דומיא דבאי הארץ, דקפיד קרא לענין נחלת ארץ ישראל אבני כ', כדכתיב "לאלה". והבנים אינן כי אם שלוחים בעלמא להביא לשניהן י"א חלקים. וחוזרין ראובן ושמעון ומורישין לבניהן, בניו של ראובן נוטלין מחצה מי"א חלקים, ובנו של שמעון נוטל מחצה. והכי תניא בתוספתא (פ"ז) כיצד? שני אחין שהיו מיוצאי מצרים, לאחד יש לו ט' בנים ולאחד יש לו בן אחד, ולפניהם בית ה' כורין, דהיינו י' לתכין – תשעה נטלו לתך לתך ט' לתכין, והאחד נטל לתך. החזירום לאבותיהם וחזרו האבות והורישום לבניהן – ט' אחין נטלו מחצה שהן כוריים וחצי, ואחד נטל מחצה שהן כוריים וחצי. וזהו שאמרו בכל מקום חיין יורשין את המתים, וכאן המתים יורשין את החיים. וכך היא הצעה של ברייתא בסיפרי: שינה הכתוב נחלה זו מכל נחלות שבתורה, שכל נחלות שבתורה, חיין יורשין את המתים, וכאן המתים יורשין את החיים. אמר רבי: משל למה הדבר דומה – לשני אחין כהנים שהיו בעיר, לזה לו בן אחד ולזה לו ג' בנים, ויצאו לגורן, זה נטל סאה ואלו נטלו ג' סאין, והוליכו אצל אביהן, וחזרו וחלקו בשוה. כיוצא בו אתה אומר בבאי הארץ, זה נטל סאה ואלו נטלו ג' סאין, והורישו את אבותיהן, וירשו מתים את חיין, וחזרו וחלקו בשוה, כדפרישית לעיל. והשתא מתוקמי שני קראי; "לאלה תחלק הארץ" אשמועינן שיטול כל אחד חלק אחד, ואהני "לשמות מטות אבותם" לענין חלוקה, לחלוק ביניהן מה שנטלו כאילו ליוצאי מצרים אבותיהם נתחלקו הנהו חלקים שנטלו, ונוטל בן שמעון מאלו החלקים כנגד כל בני ראובן. **שני אחין** כהנים. והתנו ביניהן לחלוק כל התרומות והמתנות לשניהן בשוה. לאלו

ומחזירין אצל אביהן וחוזרין וחולקין בשוה. בפירוש חומש פרש"י דמחזירין אצל אבי אביהן. ורוצה לפרש: אדם שיצא ממצרים ולו שני בנים, ולאותן שני בנים לזה בן אחד ולזה שנים, והשתא כשמחזירין לאבי אביהן — יש לחזור ולחלוק בשוה, שמכחו באין, ואין לו לירש לזה יותר מלזה. שאם לא יצא אבי אביהן ממצרים אלא אבותיהן עצמן — למה יחלקו בשוה כשמחזיר כל אחד לאביו? הלא כל אב יחזיר ויוריש לבניו, ולא לבני אחיו! והא דקאמר הכא משל לב' אחים כהנים, ואין מזכיר אביהן — לא נקטינהו אלא למשל בעלמא. וקשה, דלפירוש זה היה למיכתב "לשמות מטות אבות אבותם", דכשאין אבי אבות אלא אבות לבדם — לא נפקא מינה מידי בחזרה! ועוד: בתוספתא שהביא רבינו שמואל לא קתני אלא: שני אחין שהיו מיוצאי מצרים לזה יש לו ט' וכו', ולא קתני: שני אחין ואביהן! ונראה לריב"א: דגזרת הכתוב הוא, כשמחזירין אצל אביהן שחולקין אותו שני אחין בשוה. אע"ג דבעלמא אין הדין כך — הכא גזרת הכתוב, מהנך שני מקראות. ודקאמר מתים יורשים את החיים — לאו כדין ירושה ממש, אלא כעין ירושה. וא"ת: מאי נפקא מינה, בין למאן דאמר ליוצאי מצרים נתחלקה הארץ, בין למאן דאמר לבאי הארץ נתחלקה? דהשתא כשמחזירין כל באי הארץ לאבותיהן כל מה שנטלו, והאבות יחלקו בשוה — הרי הוא כאילו ליוצאי מצרים נתחלקה! וי"ל: דדוקא כשהן אחין חוזרין וחולקין בשוה, אבל אם אינן אחין — לא, ואם לזה תשעה בנים ולזה אחד — זה נוטל ט' לתכים וזה נוטל לתך אחד. אבל למאן דאמר ליוצאי מצרים — כולן נוטלין בשוה. והא דפ"ה דראובן ושמעון שיצאו ממצרים והולידו בנים במדבר זה עשרה וזה אחד, אי אזלינן בתר יוצאי מצרים היה נוטל האחד כנגד כולן, אבל עכשיו י' נוטלים עשרה והאחד נוטל חלק אחד — לא איירי בראובן ושמעון אחים, דא"כ גם למ"ד לבאי הארץ היו חולקין בשוה, אלא נכרים הם. ור"ת מפרש: דכשהבנים מחזירין לאבותיהן — כל אבות ישראל חולקין בשוה. ונפקא מינה בין למ"ד ליוצאי מצרים בין למ"ד לבאי הארץ — לענין טפלים, שאם היו האבות בני עשרים מיוצאי מצרים ומתו במדבר, ובניהן כשנכנסו לארץ כולם טפלים או נשים, כבנות צלפחד, למאן דאמר ליוצאי מצרים נתחלקה — היו נוטלין, ולמ"ד לבאי הארץ — לא היו נוטלים כלום. או איפכא, אם יצאו ממצרים טפלים ולא אבות, וכשבאו לארץ היו בני עשרים, או הם או בניהם, למאן דאמר לבאי הארץ — נוטלין, ולמאן דאמר ליוצאי מצרים — אין נוטלין. וקשיא לפירושו: דאמאי נקט בתוספתא שני אחין? ועוד קשיא לריב"ם: ד"לשמות מטות אבותם" משמע אחין דוקא, דבכל מקום קוראין לאחין אבות, כגון "לא יומתו אבות על בנים" ומפקינן (סנהדרין דף כז:) דבן אחיו פסול לו לעדות. וגם מ"בנים לא יומתו על אבות" נפקא לן (שם) דאחי האב פסול. וגם משם יש להוכיח שיש להחזיר אצל האבות, ולא אצל אבי אביהן. ועוד

הגהות הב"ח

(א) רשב"ם ד"ה (בדף הקודם) ושהיה כו' חד אחא דאבא דמת ונטלו: (ב) ד"ה כאלה וכו' תחלק הארץ לכשרים כצ"ל ותיבת מפני נמחק:

לשמות מטות אבותם ינחלו. כלומר על שם אותן שיצאו ממצרים מחלקין ארץ ישראל וכיצד שאם הוציא אחד ממצרים י' בנים ומתו ה' במדבר בלא בן ונשתיירו ה' אותן ה' שנשתיירו יטלו י"א חלקים אחד בשביל אביהם וה' חלקים בשביל אחיהן שמתו וה' חלקים בשביל עצמן ואם יצא [עם] ה' ושוב נולדו לו ה' במדבר ונכנסו י' לארץ לא יטלו אלא ששה חלקים חלק חמשה בנים וחלק אביהן שיצאו ממצרים: אלא מה אני מקיים. הא דכתיב בפרשת פנחס לאחר שנמנו מבן עשרים שנה לאלה תחלק הארץ וגו'. דמשמע דלהני דלא יצאו ממצרים נתחלקה הארץ דהוו מבן כ' שנה ומעלה. הא אתא לאשמועינן לאלה כאלה. כשם שאלו שנמנו הן בני כ' שנה ומעלה כך הללו שיורשין שנוטלין בשביל יוצאי מצרים צריכין שיהו מבן כ' שנה: להוציא את הטפלים. קטנים שנכנסו לארץ שאין חולקים להם ולעולם ליוצאי מצרים נתחלקה הארץ ואי איתנייהו שקלי בשביל עצמן ואי אמרת היכי אמרת דאיתנייהו הא כתיב במדבר הזה יתמו יפלו פגריכם הא אמר לקמן דלא נגזרה גזירה לא על פחות מבן כ' ולא על יותר מבן ס' ואי דליתנייהו שקלי במקומן הנך דבן עשרים שנה ומעלה. ור' יונתן אמר לבאי הארץ. ממש לאותן שנכנסו לארץ נתחלקה הארץ דשקלי בשביל עצמן ולא שקלי בשביל אביהם או אחיהן שיצאו ממצרים שמתו שנאמר לאלה תחלק הארץ אלה דייק בשביל עצמו: אלא מה אני מקיים לשמות מטות אבותם. דמשמע דבשביל אבות שיצאו ממצרים נוחלין: אלא משונה נחלה זו. כדדרש במשל לשני כהנים אחין שעדיין לא חלקו בנכסי אביהן לאחד היה לו בן אחד ולאחד היה לו ב' בנים ומתו הללו שני אחין בגורן קודם שחלקו זה שהיה לו בן אחד נטל אותו בן חלק אחד מתרומה וזה שהיו לו שני בנים נטלו ב' חלקים ומחזירין אצל אביהן ברשות אביהן הואיל והחזירום ברשות אביהם קנאם אביהם ביחד בשוה אע"פ שמתו דומה כמו שיורשים מאביהם וחוזרין ומורישין אותם להם וחולקין אותן בשוה ומי שיש לו בן אחד נוטל אותו בן חלק ומחצה ואותן שני בנים נוטלין חלק ומחצה ואף כאן אילו היו ב' אחין שיצאו ממצרים ולא חלקו עדיין נכסי אביהם והיה לאחד ד' בנים ולאחד י' בנים ובאו הבנים לארץ ונתנו להם בשביל עצמן י"ד חלקים ועכשיו כל אותן י"ד חלקים חוזרין אצל אביהן שמתו וחוזרין הבנים ויורשין אותו מאביהן מי שהיו לו ד' בנים נוטלין ז' חלקים ואידך י' בנים נוטלין ז' חלקים והיינו לשמות מטות אבותם דאף על גב דשקלו כל אחד ואחד מבאי הארץ חלקו בשביל עצמו חוזרין וחולקים כמו שירשו מאבותם: ר' שמעון בן אלעזר אומר. בין ליוצאי מצרים בין לבאי הארץ נתחלקה הארץ כדי

תורה אור

לְאֵלּוּ וּלְאֵלּוּ נִתְחַלְּקָה הָאָרֶץ, כְּדֵי לְקַיֵּים שְׁנֵי מִקְרָאוֹת הַלָּלוּ; הָא כֵּיצַד? הָיָה מִיּוֹצְאֵי מִצְרַיִם — נוֹטֵל חֶלְקוֹ עִם יוֹצְאֵי מִצְרַיִם, הָיָה מִבָּאֵי הָאָרֶץ — נוֹטֵל חֶלְקוֹ עִם בָּאֵי הָאָרֶץ, מִכָּאן וּמִכָּאן — נוֹטֵל חֶלְקוֹ מִכָּאן וּמִכָּאן. מְרַגְּלִים — יְהוֹשֻׁעַ וְכָלֵב נָטְלוּ חֶלְקָם, מִתְלוֹנְנִים וַעֲדַת קֹרַח לֹא הָיָה לָהֶם חֵלֶק בָּאָרֶץ, הַבָּנִים נָטְלוּ בִּזְכוּת אֲבִי אֲבִיהֶן וּבִזְכוּת אֲבִי אִמּוֹתֵיהֶן. כַּאי מַשְׁמַע דְּהַאי °"לִשְׁמוֹת מַטּוֹת אֲבוֹתָם" בְּיוֹצְאֵי מִצְרַיִם כְּתִיב? דִּלְמָא לִשְׁבָטִים קָאָמַר לָהּ! דִּכְתִיב: °"וְנָתַתִּי אוֹתָהּ לָכֶם מוֹרָשָׁה אֲנִי ה'", יְרוּשָּׁה הִיא לָכֶם מֵאֲבוֹתֵיכֶם, וּלְיוֹצְאֵי מִצְרַיִם קָאָמַר לְהוּ.§ סִימָן: לָרַב צְלָפְחָד וְיוֹסֵף אִיכְפַּל מְנַשֶּׁה יַחְשֹׁב.§ אֲמַר לֵיהּ רַב פַּפָּא לְאַבַּיֵי: בִּשְׁלָמָא לְמ"ד לְיוֹצְאֵי מִצְרַיִם נִתְחַלְּקָה הָאָרֶץ, הַיְינוּ דִּכְתִיב: °"לָרַב תַּרְבֶּה נַחֲלָתוֹ וְלַמְעַט תַּמְעִיט נַחֲלָתוֹ", אֶלָּא

במדבר כו · שמות ו · במדבר כו

לאלו ולאלו. ליוצאי מצרים ולבאי הארץ. וחזרה לית ליה להאי תנא. ומתני' מתוקמא שפיר אליביה, דבנות צלפחד לדידיה נמי נטלו ג' חלקים, דהא אית ליה נמי ליוצאי מצרים נתחלקה הארץ. והיינו דאמרן לעיל: תנן כמאן דאמר ליוצאי מצרים נתחלקה הארץ. ולא אמרינן "מתניתין רבי יאשיה היא", משום דמתוקמא נמי כר' שמעון בן אלעזר. היה מיוצאי מצרים (ולא מבאי הארץ) כו'. הכי פירושו: אם היה מיוצאי מצרים ולא מבאי הארץ. כגון ראובן שיצא ממצרים והוא בן כ' והוליד בנים במדבר, ומת ראובן, ובניו היו טפלים בכניסתן לארץ, ואינן יכולין ליטול בשביל עצמן לפי שאינן בני עשרים — נוטלין בניהן חלק אחד בשביל ראובן שהיה מיוצאי מצרים. היה מבאי הארץ. ולא מיוצאי מצרים. כגון ראובן שהוליד בנים במצרים ומת במצרים, והבנים היו טפלים ביציאתן, וכשנכנסו לארץ היו בני עשרים — נוטלין כל אחד חלקו עם באי הארץ. א"נ, כשיצא ראובן ממצרים לא היה בן עשרים, והוליד בנים במדבר, ומת ראובן והבנים נכנסו לארץ — נוטלין חלקן בשביל שהן באי הארץ, אם הם י' — נוטלין י' חלקים. היה מכאן ומכאן. כגון ראובן שהיה בן כ' כשיצא ממצרים והוליד בנים במדבר ומת, והבנים היו בני כ' בכניסתן לארץ — נוטלין חלקן בשביל עצמן שהן באי הארץ, ונוטלין נמי חלק אחד בשביל אביהן שהיה מיוצאי מצרים. ויש מפרשים: היה מכאן ומכאן — באדם אחד איירי, שהיה מיוצאי מצרים ומבאי הארץ, כגון שיצא ממצרים יותר מבן ששים ונכנס לארץ, דאמרינן לקמן: לא נגזרה גזירה ביתר מבן ששים, דהוה ליה האי גברא עצמו מיוצאי מצרים ומבאי הארץ, הלכך יטול שני חלקים. ולאו מילתא היא, דמשום באי הארץ לא יטול, דהכי כתיב "לאלה תחלק הארץ" — אבני יוצאי מצרים הוא דכתיב, שלא היה בהן איש מפקודי משה ואהרן הכהן, ולא איוצאי מצרים עצמן קאי. ומיהו, יש ללמוד דנוטל שני חלקים, מדתני בתוספתא: וכן היה ר' שמעון אומר: יהושע וכלב נטלו ג' חלקים בנחלה, שהיו מיוצאי מצרים ומן העומדים בערבות מואב, ושנטלו חלקם של מרגלים. מרגלים. אף על פי שהיה (א) לבניהן שבאו לארץ ליטול חלק אביהן שהיו מיוצאי מצרים — אפילו הכי לא נטלו, אלא יהושע וכלב נטלו חלקן, כדכתיב: "חיו מן האנשים ההם" לקמן בשמעתין, שחיו בחלקן, שאמרה תורה: נתחייב רשע — יבא צדיק ויזכה בחלקו. דמקרא שמעינן שלא היה למרגלים ומתלוננים ועדת קרח חלק בארץ, מדקאמרי בנות צלפחד: "אבינו מת במדבר" (במדבר כז) "והוא לא היה בתוך העדה" — אלו מרגלים, "הנועדים על ה'" — אלו מתלוננים, "עדת קרח" — כמשמעו, "למה יגרע שם אבינו" מאחר דלא היה לא ממרגלים ולא ממתלוננים ועדת קרח. מכלל דכל הנך לא נטלו בניהן חלק בארץ בזכות אבותיהן. מתלוננים ועדת קרח. לקמן מפרש: מתלוננים שבעדת קרח, דהיינו חמשים ומאתים איש. ולא היה להם חלק בארץ, שלא נטלו בניהן את חלקן אע"פ שהיו מתלוננים מיוצאי מצרים, אלא כמאן דליתנהו דמו, וזכו כל השבטים בחלקם, כאילו נתחלקה ליוצאי מצרים בלא מתלוננים, ונתרבה חלק כל אחד ואחד פורתא. והאי תנא סבירא ליה ליוצאי מצרים נתחלקה הארץ. ואיכא למימר דמסקנא דמילתא דר' שמעון בן אלעזר היא, דאמר: לאלו ואלו נתחלקה הארץ. והבנים. של מרגלים ומתלוננים, שבאו לארץ ולא היו יכולין ליטול בשביל אביהן — יטלו בזכות אבי אביהן, אם היו מיוצאי מצרים. אבל חלק אביהן, שהיה ראוי להן ליטול בשביל אביהן עצמו, שהיה מיוצאי מצרים — אותו חלק ניתן ליהושע וכלב מן המרגלים, ושל מתלוננים ניתן לכל השבטים. ובזכות אבי אמותיהן. אם לא היה לאמותיהן אחין. ולקמן מוקי להך סיפא אפילו למאן דאמר לבאי הארץ נתחלקה. וכגון דלא היו בני עשרים כשנכנסו לארץ, דלא נטלו בשביל עצמן אלא נטלו ע"י חזרה, שהחזירו בני אבי אביהן ובני אבי אמותיהן נחלה שלקחו בניהן לזקניהן, כדכתיב: "לשמות מטות אבותם", וחזרו והורישו לבניהן ולבני המתלוננים עמהן, דבני בנים הרי הן כבנים. ממאי. דהאי "אבותם" על יוצאי מצרים קאמר, דילפינן מיניה ליוצאי מצרים נתחלקה הארץ? דלמא לשבטים קאמר, י"ב בני יעקב, להם נתחלקה הארץ, ולא ליוצאי מצרים קאמר! וליוצאי מצרים קאמר להו. דודאי להם נאמר פסוק זה. נראה בעיני דס"ג: בשלמא למ"ד ליוצאי מצרים נתחלקה הארץ היינו דכתיב לרב תרבה נחלתו ולמעט תמעיט נחלתו אלא

ועוד הקשה, דמאי פריך לקמן: אלא למאן דאמר לבאי הארץ אמאי לוותו בני יוסף? (לכן) [ולפי] פר"ת, כך שפיר לוותו למאן דאמר לבאי הארץ כמו למאן דאמר ליוצאי מצרים, דמ"מ לא נטלו אלא כפי מה שהיו האבות שיצאו ממצרים, כיון שכל אבות ישראל חולקין בשוה! אבל אם אין חולקין בשוה אלא אחין — אתי שפיר הא דפריך, ואע"פ שהיו אבות בני יוסף מועטין — הרי החזרו להן בניהן לפי מה שנתרבו. וצריך לומר לפר"ת שאין מחזירין אלא לאותן אבות שבאותו שבט, ולא לכל ישראל. והכי משמע "לשמות מטות אבותם ינחלו" — דוקא לאבות שבאותו מטה. ורבינו תם דחק לתרץ בענין אחר, ודוחק. מכאן ומכאן נוטל חלקו מכאן ומכאן. באדם א' איירי, שנוטל ב' חלקים בשביל עצמו, שהיה מיוצאי מצרים ומבאי הארץ, כדמוכח בתוספתא שהביא בקונטרס עצמו. דקתני, ר"ש אומר: אף נתחלקה ליוצאי מצרים. כילד? היה מיוצאי מצרים ולא מערבות מואב, מבאי הארץ ולא מיוצאי מצרים — נוטל חלק מכאן ומכאן וכו'. וכן היה ר' שמעון אומר: יהושע וכלב נטלו שלשה חלקים בארץ, שהיו מיוצאי מצרים, ומן העומדים בערבות מואב, ונטלו חלקם של מרגלים. ותימה: דא"כ יהושע וכלב מחמת ביאת הארץ נמנו בערבות מואב, דהא כתיב "לאלה תחלק הארץ", ואם כן בערבות (ב) נמנו יתרים מבני ס', דהא יהושע היה בן מאה ועשר ולא פרנס את ישראל אלא כ"ח שנה, וכן כלב היה נמי בן שמונים כדכתיב (יהושע יד) "בן ארבעים שנה אנכי בשלוח משה עבד ה'" וגו', ולא גמרינן מערכין, כדגמרינן לקמן (ג) דלא נגזרה על בן ס', מערכין. אע"ג דכתיב במנין של ישראל "מבן עשרים ומעלה" — לא גמרינן מעלה מערכין. ומדנמנו בערבות מואב יתרים מבני ס' — נמנו כמו כן במדבר סיני, וא"כ היכי כתיב במנין של ערבות מואב "ובאלה לא היה איש מפקודי משה וגו' ולא נותר מהם איש כי אם כלב בן יפונה ויהושע בן נון"? וכיון דנמנו יתרים מבני ס' — הלא נשאר יאיר בן מנשה ומכיר בן מנשה שנולדו בימי יעקב, ולא מתו עד שנכנסו לארץ, כדאמרינן לקמן, דלא נגזרה גזרה על פחות מבן עשרים ויתרים מששים! ונראה לרשב"א, דהכי קאמר קרא: ובאלה לא היה איש מפקודי משה ואהרן שהיו ראוין שתגזר עליהם גזירה, כי אם כלב בן יפונה ויהושע בן נון, דלא היו בני ס' במנין ראשון.

בשלמא למ"ד ליוצאי מצרים היינו דכתיב לרב תרבה נחלתו. כלומר, לרב ביציאת מצרים תרבה, אע"פ שהוא מועט בכניסתו לארץ. ולמעט ביציאת מצרים תמעיט, אע"פ שהוא עתה רב בכניסת הארץ. דהכי דריש בסיפרי, כמו שהביא בקונטרס, דתניא בהדיא: "לרב תרבה", הרי שיצאו כמו י' בנים ממצרים ובכניסתן לא נמצאו אלא חמשה — קורא אני עליהן "לרב תרבה". פירוש: שנוטלין חמשה שנשארו עשר חלקים, הרי נתרבה נחלתן. ומיהו, סיפא לא דמיא להא, דקתני: שיצאו עמו חמשה בנים ממצרים ובכניסתן נמצאו עשרה — קורא אני עליו "למעט תמעיט", דהשתא נחלת אותן חמשה לא נתמעטה במה שנמצאו עשר, דמ"מ נוטלין ה' חלקים, וחמשה

כדי לקיים ב' מקראות והא כיצד היו מיוצאי מצרים שהוציא ממצרים י' בנים ומתו במדבר נוטל אביהן חלקו ממצרים ונוטל י' חלקים בשביל בניו שיצאו ממצרים אע"פ שמתו במדבר היה מבאי הארץ שנולדו לו י' בנים במדבר והכניסן לארץ אע"ג דלא יצאו ממצרים נוטל חלקו וי' חלקים של בניו שהן באי הארץ היה מיכן ומיכן שהוציא י' בנים ממצרים והכניסן לארץ ישראל דבאי הארץ היה נוטל חלקו מיכן ומיכן מיוצאי מצרים י"א חלקים מבאי הארץ י"א חלקים. ומרגלים שיצאו ממצרים ומתו במדבר יהושע וכלב נטלו חלקן של מרגלים כדאמרינן לקמן חיו מן האנשים ההם שחיו בחלקן והא דתניא כר' יאשיה הוא דאמר לעיל ליוצאי מצרים נתחלקה הארץ והבנים של מתלוננים וכו' עדת קרח נטלו בזכות אביהן שיצאו ממצרים ובזכות אבי אמותם. ונתתי אותה לכם מורשה באותה פרשה כו' כתב בה ולא שמעו אל משה מקוצר רוח כתיב האי קרא: היינו דכתיב בין רב למעט דמשמע בין שהיה רב כשיצאו ממצרים שהיו לו י' בנים ומתו ה' אעפ"כ תנו לו י' חלקים לפי רובא שיצא ממצרים. למעט משיצא ממצרים היו לו ה' בנים ואחר כך נולדו לו ה' אחרים במדבר תנו לו כפי מיעוטו שיצא ממצרים.

כס"י ליתא

הגהות הב"ח

(א) רשב"ם ד"ה מרגלים אע"פ שהיה ראוי לבניהן וכו' האנשים ההם ואמרי' לקמן: (ב) תוס' ד"ה מכאן וכו' וא"כ בערבות מואב נמנו: (ג) בא"ד כדגמרינן לקמן בסוף דף קכא דלא נגזרה גזירה על יתרים מבני ס' מערכין:

א) [גיטין כב: וש"נ]. ב) גליון: ג) נ"ל דכספים:

תורה אור

אֶלָּא לְמַאן דְּאָמַר לְבָאֵי הָאָרֶץ, מַאי "לָרַב תַּרְבּוּ נַחֲלָתוֹ"? קַשְׁיָא. וַאֲמַר לֵיהּ רַב פַּפָּא לְאַבַּיֵי: בִּשְׁלָמָא לְמַאן דְּאָמַר לְיוֹצְאֵי מִצְרַיִם, הַיְינוּ דְּקָא צַוְוחָן בְּנוֹת צְלָפְחָד, אֶלָּא לְמ"ד לְבָאֵי הָאָרֶץ, אַמַּאי צַוְוחָן? הָא לֵיתֵיהּ דְּלִשְׁקוֹל! אֶלָּא לַחֲזָרָה וְלִיטּוֹל בְּנִכְסֵי חֵפֶר. בִּשְׁלָמָא לְמַאן דְּאָמַר לְיוֹצְאֵי מִצְרַיִם, הַיְינוּ דְּקָא צַוְוחָן בְּנֵי יוֹסֵף, דִּכְתִיב: °"וַיְדַבְּרוּ בְּנֵי יוֹסֵף", (יהושע יז) אֶלָּא לְמַאן דְּאָמַר לְבָאֵי הָאָרֶץ, מַאי קָא צָוְוחִי? כּוּלְּהוּ שְׁקוּל! מִשּׁוּם טְפָלִים דַּהֲווּ נְפִישִׁי לְהוּ. אֲמַר אַבַּיֵי, שְׁמַע מִינָּהּ: לָא הֲוָה חַד דְּלָא שָׁקֵיל, דְּאִי סָלְקָא דַּעְתָּךְ הֲוָה חַד דְּלָא שָׁקֵיל, אִיבָּעֵי לֵיהּ לְמִצְוַוח. וְכִי תֵּימָא: דִּצְוַוח וְאַהֲנֵי — כְּתָבֵיהּ קְרָא, דִּצְוַוח וְלָא אַהֲנֵי — לָא כְּתָבֵיהּ קְרָא, הָא בְּנֵי יוֹסֵף דִּצְוְוחִי וְלָא אַהֲנֵי וּכְתָבִינְהוּ קְרָא. הָתָם א)עֵצָה טוֹבָה קָא מַשְׁמַע לָן, דְּאִיבָּעֵי לֵיהּ לְאִינִישׁ לְאִיזְדַּהוּרֵי מֵעֵינָא בִּישָׁא. וְהַיְינוּ דְּקָאָמַר לְהוּ יְהוֹשֻׁעַ, דִּכְתִיב: °"וַיֹּאמֶר אֲלֵיהֶם יְהוֹשֻׁעַ אִם עַם רַב אַתָּה עֲלֵה לְךָ הַיַּעְרָה", (שם) אֲמַר לְהוּ: לְכוּ וְהַחְבְּאוּ עַצְמְכֶם בַּיְּעָרִים שֶׁלֹּא תִשְׁלוֹט בָּכֶם עַיִן רַע.

אֲמַרוּ

רשב"ם

אֶלָּא לְמַאן דְּאָמַר לְבָאֵי הָאָרֶץ נִתְחַלְּקָה מַאי לָרַב תַּרְבֶּה נַחֲלָתוֹ וגו' קַשְׁיָא. וְלָא גָּרְסִינַן מַאי "בֵּין (א) לָרַב לִמְעַט", דְּמֵהַהוּא לָא מָצֵי לְאַקְשׁוּיֵי מִידֵּי, דְּהָא אִיצְטְרִיךְ לְמִדְרַשׁ מִינֵּיהּ דְּא"י לִשְׁבָטִים אִיתְפַּלַּג, שֶׁלָּקְחוּ כָּל הַשְּׁבָטִים זֶה כָּזֶה ע"פ הַגּוֹרָל, שֵׁבֶט הַמּוּעָט כַּמְרוּבֶּה. דְּהָכִי מַשְׁמַע: "עַל פִּי הַגּוֹרָל תֵּחָלֵק נַחֲלָתוֹ" – בֵּין שֶׁהוּא רַב בֵּין שֶׁהוּא מְעַט, אוֹתוֹ הַשֵּׁבֶט מַה שֶּׁיְּזַכֵּהוּ הַגּוֹרָל יִקַּח, לְקַמָּן בְּפִירְקִין (דף קכב.). וְעוֹד דָּרְשִׁינַן מִינֵּיהּ דִּבְכְסָפִים נִתְחַלְּקָה הָאָרֶץ. אֲבָל מִ"לָּרַב תַּרְבֶּה נַחֲלָתוֹ" מַקְשֶׁה, דְּמַשְׁמַע: לְמִי שֶׁהָיָה רַב בִּיצִיאַת מִצְרַיִם, כִּדְכְתִיב בַּתְרֵיהּ: "לִשְׁמוֹת מַטּוֹת אֲבוֹתָם יִנְחָלוּ" אע"פ שֶׁעַכְשָׁיו נִתְמַעֵט בִּכְנִיסָתָן לָאָרֶץ – תַּרְבֶּה נַחֲלָתוֹ, וּלְאוֹתוֹ שֶׁהָיָה מְעַט בִּיצִיאַת מִצְרַיִם – תַּמְעִיט גַּם עַתָּה נַחֲלָתוֹ, אע"פ שֶׁנִּתְרַבָּה. וְהָכִי קָתָנֵי לָהּ בְּסִפְרֵי בְּהֶדְיָא: "לָרַב תַּרְבֶּה נַחֲלָתוֹ" וגו', הֲרֵי שֶׁיָּצְאוּ עִמּוֹ י' בָּנִים מִמִּצְרַיִם, וּבִכְנִיסָתָן לֹא נִמְצְאוּ אֶלָּא ה' – קוֹרֵא אֲנִי עָלָיו "לָרַב תַּרְבֶּה נַחֲלָתוֹ". הֲרֵי שֶׁיָּצְאוּ עִמּוֹ ה' בָּנִים מִמִּצְרַיִם וּבִכְנִיסָתָן נִמְצְאוּ עֲשָׂרָה – קוֹרֵא אֲנִי עָלָיו "וְלַמְעַט תַּמְעִיט נַחֲלָתוֹ". דְּסָלְקָא דַּעְתָּךְ אָמֵינָא נֵיזוּל בָּתַר הַשְׁתָּא, קָא מַשְׁמַע לָן. קַשְׁיָא. לְדִידָן קַשְׁיָא, דְּלָא יָדְעִינַן לְתָרוּצֵי קְרָא אַלִּיבָּא דְּהַהוּא תַּנָּא. דְּהָא לֵיכָּא לְמֵימַר: "לָרַב תַּרְבֶּה" – אוֹתוֹ שֶׁהוּא רַב עַכְשָׁיו תַּרְבֶּה נַחֲלָתוֹ, וְלַמְעַט – שֶׁהוּא מוּעָט עַכְשָׁיו תַּמְעִיט נַחֲלָתוֹ. דִּסְבָרָא הוּא, כִּדְכְתִיב לְעֵיל: "לָאֵלֶּה תֵּחָלֵק הָאָרֶץ", וְלָא צָרִיךְ קְרָא. וְגַם אֵין לְשׁוֹן "תַּרְבֶּה" וְ"תַמְעִיט" מַשְׁמַע אֶלָּא כְּשֶׁזֶּה נוֹטֵל הַרְבֵּה וְזֶה מְעַט, שֶׁחֵלֶק אִישׁ זֶה מְרוּבֶּה וְחֵלֶק חֲבֵירוֹ מוּעָט. אֲבָל כְּשֶׁכָּל הַחֲלָקִים שָׁוִים – אֵין זֶה "תַּרְבֶּה" וְ"תַמְעִיט", אֶלָּא הָכִי הו"ל לְמֵימַר: חֵלֶק כְּחֵלֶק יִנְחָלוּ. וּבַחֲזָרָה נַמִי לֵיכָּא לְאוֹקוּמֵיהּ, דְּמִ"לִּשְׁמוֹת מַטּוֹת אֲבוֹתָם" שָׁמְעִינַן לָהּ שַׁפִּיר אַלִּיבֵּיהּ דְּהַאי תַּנָּא. וְעוֹד: "תַּרְבֶּה" וְ"תַמְעִיט" מַשְׁמַע נְטִילָה רִאשׁוֹנָה שֶׁנּוֹטֵל כָּל אֶחָד חֶלְקוֹ קוֹדֶם שֶׁיַּחֲזִירוּ לַאֲבוֹתֵיהֶם, כִּדְכְתִיב בְּסֵיפֵיהּ דִּקְרָא: "אִישׁ לְפִי פְקוּדָיו יוּתַּן נַחֲלָתוֹ". הַיְינוּ דְּקָא צַוְוחָן בְּנוֹת צְלָפְחָד. לָמָּה יִגָּרַע שֵׁם אָבִינוּ מִתּוֹךְ מִשְׁפַּחְתּוֹ שֶׁזּוֹכָה בְּאֶרֶץ יִשְׂרָאֵל, כִּי אֵין לוֹ בֵּן. שֶׁאִילּוּ הָיָה לוֹ בֵּן הָיָה נוֹטֵל הַבֵּן חֶלְקוֹ שֶׁל אָבִיו שֶׁהָיָה מִיּוֹצְאֵי מִצְרַיִם, וְעַתָּה בִּשְׁבִיל שֶׁאֵין לוֹ בֵּן – לָמָּה לֹא נִירַשׁ אֶת חֶלְקוֹ? לָא הֲוָה. לִצְלָפְחָד נַחֲלָה בְּאֶרֶץ יִשְׂרָאֵל דְּלִישְׁקוֹל, לֹא הוּא וְלֹא יוֹצְאֵי יְרֵכוֹ בִּזְכוּתוֹ, שֶׁהֲרֵי לְבָאֵי הָאָרֶץ נִיתְּנָה! וַאֲפִילּוּ אִם הָיָה לוֹ בֵּן – לֹא הָיָה נוֹטֵל כְּלוּם בִּשְׁבִיל אָבִיו, וַאֲפִילּוּ בִּשְׁבִיל עַצְמוֹ אִם הוּא פָּחוֹת מִכ', וּמַאי הַאי דְּקָא צַוְוחָן בִּשְׁבִיל שֶׁאֵין לוֹ בֵּן? אֶלָּא לַחֲזָרָה וְלִיטּוֹל בְּנִכְסֵי חֵפֶר. דְּמַאן דְּאִית לֵיהּ לְבָאֵי הָאָרֶץ – אִית לֵיהּ חֲזָרָה, שֶׁמַּחֲזִירִין לַאֲבוֹתֵיהֶן כָּל מַה שֶּׁנָּטְלוּ, וְחוֹזְרִין וְיוֹרְשִׁין מֵאֲבוֹתֵיהֶן כַּמִּשְׁפָּט. וְהָכִי אָמְרֵי: לָמָּה יִגָּרַע שֵׁם אָבִינוּ לִצְלָפְחָד מִתּוֹךְ מִשְׁפַּחְתּוֹ, שֶׁהָיָה לוֹ לִזְכּוֹת עִם אֶחָיו בְּנִכְסֵי חֵפֶר זְקֵנֵנוּ אִילּוּ הָיָה לוֹ בֵּן – כְּשֶׁיִּטְּלוּ בְּנֵי חֵפֶר שֶׁהֵם אֲחֵי אָבִינוּ נַחֲלָה בְּא"י יַחֲזִירוּ אוֹתָהּ לְחֵפֶר אֲבִיהֶן, וְיוֹרִישׁ אוֹתָהּ לְכָל בָּנָיו, וְיִטּוֹל אָבִינוּ שֶׁהוּא בְּכוֹר ב' חֲלָקִים, אוֹ הוּא אוֹ בְּנוֹ שֶׁקָּם תַּחְתָּיו, כִּדְכְתִיב: "וְאִם אֵין לוֹ" – עַיֵּין עָלָיו. וְהַשְׁתָּא שֶׁאֵין בֵּן – לָמָּה לֹא נָקוּם תַּחַת אָבִינוּ לִירַשׁ נַחֲלָתוֹ הַבָּאָה לוֹ מֵחֵפֶר אָבִיו, ע"י חֲזָרָה שֶׁהֶחֱזִירוּהָ בָּנָיו אוֹ בְּנֵי בָּנָיו שֶׁהָיוּ מִבָּאֵי הָאָרֶץ? שֶׁהֲרֵי בַּת הַבֵּן יוֹרֶשֶׁת עִם הָאַחִין. וּלְקַמָּן נַמִי אָמְרִינַן: דַּרְשָׁנִיּוֹת הָיוּ, וְהָיוּ יוֹדְעוֹת שֶׁבַּת הַבֵּן תִּירַשׁ עִם הָאַחִין שֶׁלָּמְדוּ מִפָּרָשַׁת יְבָמִין, כִּדִלְקַמָּן (דף קיט:). הַיְינוּ דְּקָא צָוְוחִי בְּנֵי יוֹסֵף. שֶׁהָיוּ עַכְשָׁיו מְרוּבִּין, וְנִגְרְעוּ יוֹתֵר מִשְּׁאָר שְׁבָטִים, וְהֵן לֹא נָטְלוּ אֶלָּא לְחֶשְׁבּוֹן שֶׁל יוֹצְאֵי מִצְרַיִם, וְהָיְתָה נַחֲלַת כָּל אֶחָד מוּעֶטֶת מֵחֵלֶק כָּל אִישׁ וְאִישׁ מִיִּשְׂרָאֵל. כּוּלְּהוּ שְׁקוּל. בְּשָׁוֶה. וּמִיהוּ, לְקַמָּן אָמְרִינַן דְּאֶרֶץ יִשְׂרָאֵל לִשְׁבָטִים אִיתְפַּלַּג, וּבְדִין צָווּחוּ בְּנֵי יוֹסֵף, שֶׁלֹּא נָטְלוּ אֶלָּא כְּאֶחָד מִן הַשְּׁבָטִים אַף עַל פִּי שֶׁאֵין גָּדוֹל בְּכָל הַשְּׁבָטִים כַּשֵּׁבֶט שֶׁלָּהֶן. אֶלָּא מִשּׁוּם דְּמִבַּעְיָא לֵיהּ לְקַמָּן, לָא בָּעֵי לְתָרוּצֵי הָכִי. מִשּׁוּם טְפָלִים. יְתוֹמִים שֶׁלֹּא הָיוּ בְּנֵי עֶשְׂרִים בִּכְנִיסָתָם לָאָרֶץ, וְגַם לֹא הָיָה לָהֶם אָב הַנִּכְנָס לָאָרֶץ שֶׁיַּנְחִילֵם חֶלְקוֹ כְּשֶׁיָּמוּת. וְגַם לֹא הָיָה לָהֶם שׁוּם מוֹרִישׁ שֶׁיָּצָא מִמִּצְרַיִם, שֶׁיִּירְשׁוּ מִמֶּנּוּ עַל יְדֵי חֲזָרָה. שְׁמַע מִינָּהּ. מִצְּוָוחַת בְּנֵי יוֹסֵף וּבְנוֹת צְלָפְחָד, דְּלָא הֲוָה חַד בְּכָל הַשְּׁבָטִים דְּלָא שָׁקֵיל, אוֹ הוּא אוֹ אָבִיו. וְאַף עַל גַּב דַּהֲוָה מָצֵי מִתְרַמֵּי – דְּאַלִּיבָּא דְּמַאן דְּאָמַר לְיוֹצְאֵי מִצְרַיִם כָּל אוֹתָן שֶׁיָּצְאוּ פָּחוֹת מִבֶּן עֶשְׂרִים בְּלֹא אָב לֹא נָטְלוּ חֵלֶק בָּאָרֶץ, שֶׁהֲרֵי לֹא הֵן וְלֹא אֲבִיהֶן הָיוּ מִיּוֹצְאֵי מִצְרַיִם, דִּטְפָלִין שֶׁיָּצְאוּ לֹא נִתְחַלְּקָה לָהֶם – וַאֲפִילּוּ הָכִי לָא אִיתְרְמִי, שֶׁלֹּא יָצָא יָתוֹם מִמִּצְרַיִם פָּחוֹת מִבֶּן עֶשְׂרִים, וְאִם יָצָא – אִם כֵּן מֵת אֶחָד מִקְּרוֹבָיו בַּמִּדְבָּר שֶׁהָיוּ מִיּוֹצְאֵי מִצְרַיִם לְהוֹרִישׁוֹ חֶלְקוֹ. דּוּמְיָא דִּבְנוֹת צְלָפְחָד שֶׁלֹּא הָיוּ רְאוּיִן לִיטּוֹל חֵלֶק בָּאָרֶץ, כִּדְתַנְיָא בְּסִיפְרֵי: "אִישׁ לְפִי פְקוּדָיו" לְהוֹצִיא אֶת הַנָּשִׁים, דְּדָמוּ לִטְפָלִים, וַאֲפִילּוּ הָכִי יָרְשׁוּ חֵלֶק אֲבִיהֶן. וּלְמַאן דְּאָמַר לְבָאֵי הָאָרֶץ נַמִי, כָּל הַנִּכְנָסִין לָאָרֶץ פָּחוֹת מִבֶּן עֶשְׂרִים לֹא נָטְלוּ חֵלֶק בָּאָרֶץ אֶלָּא עַל יְדֵי חֲזָרָה, וּכְגוֹן שֶׁהָיוּ מוֹרִישָׁיו מִיּוֹצְאֵי מִצְרַיִם, וְאִם לָאו – לֹא יִטּוֹל, וַאֲפִילּוּ הָכִי לָא הֲוָה חַד דְּלָא שָׁקֵיל, דְּלָא אִיתְרְמִי מִילְּתָא, דְּכָל אוֹתָן שֶׁנִּכְנְסוּ לָאָרֶץ בְּנֵי עֶשְׂרִים – נָטְלוּ חֶלְקָם, וְהַטְּפָלִים, יְתוֹמִין הַפְּחוּתִים מִבֶּן עֶשְׂרִים – נָטְלוּ כּוּלָּן עַל יְדֵי חֲזָרָה כִּבְנוֹת צְלָפְחָד, וְאוֹתָן שֶׁהָיָה לָהֶם אָב וָאֵם, וְלֹא הָיוּ יְכוֹלִין לִיטּוֹל בַּחֲזָרָה לֹא מֵאֲבִי אֲבִיהֶן וְלֹא מֵאֲבִי אִמּוֹתֵיהֶן, שֶׁהֲרֵי אָבִיו וְאִמּוֹ קוֹדְמִין – הֲרֵי אֲבִיהֶן נוֹטֵל חֵלֶק בָּאָרֶץ מִשּׁוּם בָּאֵי הָאָרֶץ, וּכְמַאן דְּשָׁקֵיל אִיהוּ דָּמֵי, וְאֵין לוֹ לִצְעוֹק. אִיבָּעֵי לֵיהּ לְמִצְוַוח. כִּבְנוֹת צְלָפְחָד וּבְנֵי יוֹסֵף. וְגַם הַנָּבִיא הָיָה לוֹ לִכְתּוֹב, כִּדְכְתִיב בִּבְנוֹת צְלָפְחָד וּבְנֵי יוֹסֵף. דִּצְוַוח וְאַהֲנֵי. כְּגוֹן בְּנוֹת צְלָפְחָד. דִּצְוַוח וְלָא אַהֲנֵי. שֶׁלֹּא *יָכוֹל [בדפו"י שלא היה] לִגְזוֹל שְׁאָר שְׁבָטִים וְלִיתֵּן לָהֶם. וּמַה שֶּׁהֱשִׁיבָם: "עֲלֵה לְךָ הַיַּעְרָה" וגו' – לִדְרָשָׁה אִיצְטְרִיךְ, כִּדְלְקַמָּן, וְלָא כִּפְשָׁטֵיהּ שֶׁנָּתַן לָהֶם יְעָרוֹת לְהַרְחִיב נַחֲלָתָן. שֶׁאִם מִנַּחֲלַת שֵׁבֶט אַחֵר הֵן – אֵין הָרְשׁוּת בְּיָדוֹ, וְאִם שֶׁל מַטֵּה בְּנֵי יוֹסֵף הָיוּ – הָרְשׁוּת בְּיָדָם לִכְרוֹת הַיַּעַר (ג) וּלְגָרְשָׁם, וַעֲדַיִין לֹא נָתְנָה לָהֶם יְהוֹשֻׁעַ כְּלוּם. וּמְשַׁנֵּי: הָתָם עֵצָה טוֹבָה קָא מַשְׁמַע לָן. בִּשְׁבִיל שֶׁלְּמֵדִין אָנוּ מִמַּה שֶּׁהֱשִׁיב לָהֶם יְהוֹשֻׁעַ, דְּמִיבָּעֵי לֵיהּ לְאִינִישׁ לְהַטְמִין עַצְמוֹ, לְאִזְדַּהוּרֵי מֵעֵינָא בִּישָׁא – לְהָכִי כְּתָבֵיהּ קְרָא לִצְוָוחַת בְּנֵי יוֹסֵף. לְהוֹסִיף נַחֲלָה אִי אֶפְשָׁר, אַךְ עֵצָה טוֹבָה אֲנִי נוֹתֵן לָכֶם, שֶׁאִם עַם רַב אַתָּה – "עֲלֵה לְךָ הַיַּעְרָה" וגו' "וּבֵרֵאתָ" – כְּרוֹת הַיַּעַר, וְתִבְנֶה לְךָ שָׁם בֵּית מוֹשָׁב, כִּדְכְתִיב: "וּבָרֵא אוֹתְהֶן בְּחַרְבוֹתָם" (יחזקאל כג).

אֲמַרוּ

תוספות

וחמשה שנולדו חולקים בחלק אביהן עם החמשה הראשונים! ונראה לרשב"א: דרישא וסיפא מיירי כגון שמתו אותם שיצאו ממצרים בלא זרע, ולא נכנסו לארץ, דודאי מתו במדבר כל אותן שהיו בני עשרים כשיצאו ממצרים. ומיירי רישא שמתו העשרה שיצאו עמו, וחמשה בנים נולדו במדבר. ובסיפא מתו חמשה שיצאו עמו, ונולדו במדבר י'. והשתא הוי סיפא דומיא דרישא. ואתי נמי שפיר דנקט "שיצאו עמו", דמה לך ליציאת האב? אלא משום דבעי למימר שאותן מתו ונולדו אחרים במדבר. ולריב"ם קשה על פירוש הקונטרס: דהא מ"לרב תרבה" משמע שפיר טפי — למי שהוא רב עתה תרבה. ואי משום דהא כבר כתיב "לאלה תחלק הארץ" — אם כן למי שהיה רב ביציאת מצרים מ"לשמות מטות אבותם" נפקא! ונראה לו דגרס: היינו דכתיב "בין רב למעט", כמו שכתוב בספרים. וה"פ: בשלמא למ"ד ליוצאי מצרים, דאם הוו שני אחין מיוצאי מצרים, והוי להו עשרה בנים מבאי הארץ, ושני אחין אין להן כי אם שני בנים מבאי הארץ — הרי אותן עשרה לא נטלו, אע"פ שהן מרובין, כי אם כמו שני בנים שהן מועטין — היינו "בין רב למעט". אע"ג דלקמן דריש מהאי קרא דלשבטים איתפלג — השתא לא אסיק אדעתיה ההיא דרשא. תדע, דהא פריך בסמוך למ"ד לבאי הארץ אמאי קא צווחו בני יוסף? ואי לשבטים איתפלג — שפיר צווחו לכולי עלמא. אלא ודאי לא אסיק אדעתא ההיא דרשה, ב)(וההיא דרשה ג)(דספרי) הוי לפי המסקנא).

ולמאן

רבינו גרשום

אלא למאן דאמר לבאי הארץ. נתחלקה הארץ מאי בין רב למעט האי כל באי הארץ נוטל חלקו ולא יותר קשיא. ויש ספרים שכתוב בהן היינו דכתיב לרב תרבה נחלתו ומפרש נמי כדמפרש בין רב למעט: היינו דקא צווחן בנות צלפחד. משום דאבוהון מיוצאי מצרים היה ומבקשות לירש חלקו: אלא למ"ד לבאי הארץ. נתחלקה הארץ לא הוה להן למשקל מידי דהא מת במדבר: אלא לחזרה וליטול בנכסי חפר. צווחן כלומר דאפילו למאן דאמר לבאי הארץ נתחלקה משום הכי צווחן משום חזרה ליטול בנכסי חפר אביו של צלפחד שהיו לו בנים לחפר שנולדו במדבר ובאו לארץ ונטלו חלקם ואחר כך היה להם להחזיר אצל חפר אביהן ולחזור ולחלק בשוה עם בנות צלפחד שהן תחת אביהן ואמטו להכי צווחן: היינו דקא צווחן בני יוסף. דאבוהן מיוצאי מצרים נינהו וצווחן על חלק אבוהון: הא כולהו שקלי. כל אחד חלקו: ומשני לעולם לבאי הארץ הוי ומשום טפלים דאיתא בהו טפי משאר שבטים דכתיב בן פורת יוסף שהן פרין ורבין טפי וצווחן דלא שקלי לצורך טפלים ודחיקי להו דוכתייהו: אמר אביי. איכא למשמע מהא הלכה בין למאן דאמר ליוצאי מצרים כו' לא הוה חד דלא שקיל. אפי' טפלים דאליבא דת"ק דאמר ליוצאי מצרים נתחלקה ומוציא את הטפלים (אפי' הכי לא) [דלא] שקלי בזכות עצמן אפי' הכי שקלי בשביל אביהן שיצאו ממצרים ושקלו נחלת אביהן בארץ. ולאידך תנא נמי דאמר לבאי הארץ נתחלקה הארץ ומוציא את הטפלים אפי' הכי שקלו טפלים משום דחזרה נחלה אצל אביהן לירת מכח אביהם עם שאר אחיהם בשוה. ואי ס"ד דלא שקלי הוה להו למיצווח כדצווחי בני יוסף על הטפלים שלהן. וכי תימא ודאי צווחו אלא הני דצווחי ואהני דיהבו להו נחלה על שצווחו כת' ביה קרא אבל צווחו ולא אהנו צווחתם לא כתב. והא בני יוסף דצווחו ולא אהני להו אפי' הכי כתביה קרא. ומשני לעולם דצווחו ולא אהנו ומשום הכי לא כתבינהו קרא. ודקא קשיא לך הא בני יוסף דצווחו ולא אהנו ואפ' הכי כתבינהו התם לאו משום האי טעמא הוא

הגהות הב"ח

(א) רשב"ם ד"ה אלא וכו' בין רב למעט וכו' זה כזה. נ"ב ע"ל בריש דף קכב: (ב) ד"ה לצוות וכו' לכרות היער ולגור שם ועדיין:

אֲמַרוּ לֵיהּ: א)אֲנַן מִזַּרְעָא דְּיוֹסֵף דְּלָא שָׁלְטָא בֵּיהּ עֵינָא בִּישָׁא; דִּכְתִיב: °"בֵּן פֹּרָת יוֹסֵף בֵּן פֹּרָת עֲלֵי עָיִן", וְאָמַר רַבִּי אַבָּהוּ: אַל תִּקְרֵי "עֲלֵי עָיִן" אֶלָּא: עוֹלֵי עַיִן. ר' יוֹסֵי בְּרַבִּי חֲנִינָא אָמַר, מֵהָכָא: °"וְיִדְגּוּ לָרֹב בְּקֶרֶב הָאָרֶץ", מַה דָּגִים שֶׁבַּיָּם — מַיִם מְכַסִּים עֲלֵיהֶם וְאֵין הָעַיִן שׁוֹלֶטֶת בָּהֶם, אַף זַרְעוֹ שֶׁל יוֹסֵף — אֵין הָעַיִן שׁוֹלֶטֶת בָּהֶם.§ "מְרַגְּלִים — יְהוֹשֻׁעַ וְכָלֵב נָטְלוּ חֶלְקָם".§ מְנָהָנֵי מִילֵּי? אָמַר עוּלָּא, דְּאָמַר קְרָא: °"וִיהוֹשֻׁעַ בִּן נוּן וְכָלֵב בֶּן יְפֻנֶּה חָיוּ מִן הָאֲנָשִׁים הָהֵם", מַאי "חָיוּ"? אִילֵימָא חָיוּ מַמָּשׁ — וְהָא כְּתִיב קְרָא אַחֲרִינָא: °"וְלֹא נוֹתַר מֵהֶם אִישׁ כִּי אִם כָּלֵב בֶּן יְפֻנֶּה וִיהוֹשֻׁעַ בִּן נוּן"! אֶלָּא מַאי "חָיוּ"? שֶׁחָיוּ בְּחֶלְקָם.§ "מִתְלוֹנְנִין וַעֲדַת קֹרַח לֹא הָיָה לָהֶן חֵלֶק בָּאָרֶץ".§ וְהָתַנְיָא: מְרַגְּלִים, מִתְלוֹנְנִים וַעֲדַת קֹרַח — יְהוֹשֻׁעַ וְכָלֵב נָטְלוּ חֶלְקָם! לָא קַשְׁיָא: מָר מַקִּישׁ מִתְלוֹנְנִים לַמְרַגְּלִים, מָר לָא מַקִּישׁ מִתְלוֹנְנִים לַמְרַגְּלִים; דְּתַנְיָא: °"אָבִינוּ מֵת בַּמִּדְבָּר" — זֶה צְלָפְחָד, "וְהוּא לֹא הָיָה בְּתוֹךְ הָעֵדָה" — זֶה עֲדַת מְרַגְּלִים, "הַנּוֹעָדִים עַל ה'" — אֵלּוּ מִתְלוֹנְנִים, "בַּעֲדַת קֹרַח" — כְּמַשְׁמָעוֹ; מָר מַקִּישׁ מִתְלוֹנְנִים לַמְרַגְּלִים, וּמָר לָא ב)מַקִּישׁ מִתְלוֹנְנִים לַמְרַגְּלִים. וַא"ל רַב פַּפָּא לְאַבַּיֵי: וּלְמַאן דְּמַקִּישׁ מִתְלוֹנְנִים לַמְרַגְּלִים, אִיכְפּוּל יְהוֹשֻׁעַ וְכָלֵב וְיָרְתוּ לְכוּלָּהּ א"י? א"ל: מִתְלוֹנְנִים שֶׁבַּעֲדַת קֹרַח קָאָמְרִינַן. וַא"ל רַב פַּפָּא לְאַבַּיֵי: בִּשְׁלָמָא לְמ"ד לְיוֹצְאֵי מִצְרַיִם נִתְחַלְּקָה הָאָרֶץ, הַיְינוּ דִּכְתִיב: °"וַיִּפְּלוּ חַבְלֵי מְנַשֶּׁה עֲשָׂרָה", שִׁיתָּא דְּשִׁיתָּא בָּתֵּי אָבוֹת וְאַרְבָּעָה דִּידְהוּ — הָא עֲשָׂרָה. אֶלָּא לְמ"ד לְבָאֵי הָאָרֶץ — תְּמָנְיָא הוּא דַּהֲווּ, שִׁיתָּא דְּשִׁיתָּא בָּתֵּי אָבוֹת וּתְרֵי דִּידְהוּ, הָא תְּמָנְיָא! וְלִיטַעְמִיךְ, וּלְמ"ד לְיוֹצְאֵי מִצְרַיִם נִתְחַלְּקָה הָאָרֶץ, ט' הָווּ! אֶלָּא מַאי אִית לָךְ לְמֵימַר? חַד אַחָא דְּאַבָּא הֲוָה לְהוּ, ה"נ — תְּרֵי אַחֵי דְּאַבָּא הֲוָה לְהוּ; דְּתַנְיָא: °"נָתֹן תִּתֵּן לָהֶם" — זוֹ נַחֲלַת אֲבִיהֶן, "בְּתוֹךְ אֲחֵי אֲבִיהֶן" — זוֹ נַחֲלַת אֲבִי אֲבִיהֶן, "וְהַעֲבַרְתָּ אֶת נַחֲלַת אֲבִיהֶן לָהֶן" — זוֹ חֵלֶק בְּכוֹרָה; רַבִּי אֱלִיעֶזֶר בֶּן יַעֲקֹב אוֹמֵר: אַף חֵלֶק אֲחִי אֲבִיהֶם נָטְלוּ, שֶׁנֶּאֱמַר: "נָתֹן תִּתֵּן". וּלְמ"ד: תְּרֵי אַחֵי דְּאַבָּא הֲוָה לְהוּ, הַהוּא מֵ"אֲחֻזַּת נַחֲלָה" נָפְקָא. וַא"ל רַב פַּפָּא לְאַבַּיֵי: קְרָא מַאי קָא חָשֵׁיב? אִי טְפָלִים קָא חָשֵׁיב, טוּבָא הָווּ! אִי בָּתֵּי אָבוֹת קָחָשֵׁיב, שִׁיתָּא הָווּ!
לְעוֹלָם

(בראשית מט; שם מח; במדבר יד; שם כו; שם כז; יהושע יז; במדבר כז)

רשב"ם

אֲמַרוּ לוֹ [אֲנַן] מִזַּרְעָא דְּיוֹסֵף כו'. וְהַיְינוּ דִּכְתִיב: "וַיֹּאמְרוּ בְּנֵי יוֹסֵף לֹא יִמָּצֵא לָנוּ הָהָר" כְּלוֹמַר, אֵין אָנוּ חוֹשְׁשִׁין לְאוֹתוֹ הַר, הַיְינוּ יַעַר, כִּדִכְתִיב הָתָם: "הַר יִהְיֶה לָּךְ כִּי יַעַר הוּא". עוֹלֵי עָיִן. הֵן עוֹלִין עַל הָעַיִן וְשׁוֹלְטִין עָלָיו, וְאֵין הָעַיִן עוֹלָה עֲלֵיהֶן. וְהָכְתִיב קְרָא אַחֲרִינָא. וּתְרֵי קְרָאֵי לָמָּה לִי? נִרְאֶה בְּעֵינַי דְּהָכִי גָּרַס: לָא קַשְׁיָא מָר מַקִּישׁ מִתְלוֹנְנִים לַמְרַגְּלִים וּמָר לָא מַקִּישׁ מִתְלוֹנְנִים לַמְרַגְּלִים דְּתַנְיָא כו' וּלְקַמָּן מְפָרֵשׁ לָהּ. זֶה צְלָפְחָד. מִילְּתָא דִּפְשִׁיטָא הִיא, דְּהָא כְּתִיב לְעֵיל בְּנוֹת צְלָפְחָד, אֶלָּא אַגַּב גְּרָרָא דְּהָנָךְ קָאָמַר לָהּ. וְנִרְאֶה בְּעֵינַי שֶׁחָסֵר מִן הַסְּפָרִים, דְּהָכִי קָתָנֵי רֵישָׁא דְּהַךְ בָּרַיְיתָא בְּסִיפְרֵי: "אָבִינוּ מֵת בַּמִּדְבָּר", ר' עֲקִיבָא אוֹמֵר: נֶאֱמַר כָּאן "בַּמִּדְבָּר" וְנֶאֱמַר לְהַלָּן "מִדְבָּר", מַה מִּדְבָּר הָאָמוּר כָּאן צְלָפְחָד — אַף מִדְבָּר הָאָמוּר לְהַלָּן צְלָפְחָד. דְּמִינָהּ שָׁמְעִינַן דְּהַיְינוּ מְקוֹשֵׁשׁ. "וְהוּא לֹא הָיָה בְּתוֹךְ הָעֵדָה" כו' כִּי הָכָא. זוֹ עֲדַת מְרַגְּלִים. דִּכְתִיב בְּהוּ: "עַד מָתַי לָעֵדָה הָרָעָה הַזֹּאת אֲשֶׁר הֵמָּה מַלִּינִים עָלַי" (במדבר יד) אֶת הַשְּׂאָר. אֵלּוּ מִתְלוֹנְנִים. כִּדְמְפָ': מִתְלוֹנְנִים שֶׁבַּעֲדַת קֹרַח, דִּכְתִיב בְּהוּ: "לָכֵן אַתָּה וְכָל עֲדָתְךָ הַנּוֹעָדִים עַל ה'". וְהַאי דְּקָאָמַר: עֲדַת קֹרַח, כְּמַשְׁמָעוֹ — מַסְקָנָא דְּמִילְּתֵיהּ הִיא. מָר מַקִּישׁ. הוֹאִיל וְנִכְתְּבוּ בְּפָסוּק אֶחָד, וְכִי הֵיכִי דְּיָרְשׁוּ הַמְרַגְּלִים — יָרְשׁוּ נַמִי הַמִּתְלוֹנְנִים. וּמָר לָא מַקִּישׁ. לָא חָשֵׁיב לֵיהּ הֶיקֵּשׁ, כֵּיוָן דְּלָא כְּתִיב בֵּיהּ וָי"ו "בְּתוֹךְ הָעֵדָה וְהַנּוֹעָדִים". לְכוּלָּהּ אַרְעָא דְּיִשְׂרָאֵל. לָאו דַּוְקָא כּוּלָּהּ, אֶלָּא רוּבָּהּ, כִּדִכְתִיב: "וַיִּלֹּנוּ הָעָם עַל מֹשֶׁה לֵאמֹר מַה נִּשְׁתֶּה". דְּבִשְׁלָמָא לְמ"ד דְּלָא מַקִּישׁ — הֲרֵי כָּל שֵׁבֶט וְשֵׁבֶט נָחֲלוּ חֵלֶק קְרוֹבֵיהֶם מִתְלוֹנְנִים שֶׁבַּשְּׁבָטִים. אֶלָּא לְמַאן דְּמַקִּישׁ — נִגְרְעָה כָּל נַחֲלַת שֵׁבֶט וְשֵׁבֶט טוּבָא, וַאֲנַן קַיְימָא לָן, וּמִקְּרָאֵי אִיכָּא לְמֵילַף, דַּאֲפִילּוּ חֵלֶק אֶחָד מֵאֱלֶף לֹא נָטְלוּ! הַיְינוּ דִּכְתִיב. בִּיהוֹשֻׁעַ, אַחַר שֶׁנָּטְלוּ בְּנוֹת צְלָפְחָד, "וַיִּפְּלוּ חַבְלֵי מְנַשֶּׁה עֲשָׂרָה", דְּהַיְינוּ שִׁיתָּא דְּשִׁיתָּא בָּתֵּי אָבוֹת הַכְּתוּבִים לְמַעְלָה, וְד' דִּידְהוּ — הֲרֵי עֲשָׂרָה. דִּכְתִיב לְעֵיל: "וַיְהִי לִבְנֵי מְנַשֶּׁה הַנּוֹתָרִים לְמִשְׁפְּחוֹת לִבְנֵי אֲבִיעֶזֶר וְלִבְנֵי חֵלֶק וְלִבְנֵי אַשְׂרִיאֵל וְלִבְנֵי שֶׁכֶם וְלִבְנֵי חֵפֶר וְלִבְנֵי שְׁמִידָע, אֵלֶּה בְּנֵי מְנַשֶּׁה בֶּן יוֹסֵף הַזְּכָרִים לְמִשְׁפְּחוֹתָם. וְלִצְלָפְחָד בֶּן חֵפֶר וגו' וַיִּתֵּן לָהֶן יְהוֹשֻׁעַ נַחֲלָה עַל פִּי ה' בְּתוֹךְ אֲחֵי אֲבִיהֶן וַיִּפְּלוּ חַבְלֵי מְנַשֶּׁה עֲשָׂרָה" — בֵּין נְטִילַת שִׁשָּׁה בָּתֵּי אָבוֹת וְאַרְבָּעָה דִּבְנוֹת צְלָפְחָד: חֵלֶק צְלָפְחָד שֶׁהָיָה מִיּוֹצְאֵי מִצְרַיִם. וּשְׁנֵי חֲלָקִים מִנִּכְסֵי חֵפֶר, וְחַד אַחָא דְּאַבָּא, שֶׁהָיָה מִיּוֹצְאֵי מִצְרַיִם וְנָטְלוּ חֵלֶק הָרָאוּי לִצְלָפְחָד בְּנַחֲלַת אָחִיו כִּדְלְקַמָּן. וּלְקַמָּן פָּרֵיךְ: קְרָא מַאי קָחָשֵׁיב כו'. וּתְרֵי דִּידְהוּ. שְׁנֵי חֲלָקִים בְּנִכְסֵי חֵפֶר, בְּתוֹרַת חֲזָרָה. שֶׁנָּטְלוּ בְּנֵי חֵפֶר אִישׁ אִישׁ חֶלְקוֹ בָּאָרֶץ, אוֹתָן שֶׁהָיוּ בָּאֵי הָאָרֶץ, אוֹ הֵם אוֹ (א) בְּנֵי חֵפֶר, כִּדִכְתִיב: "לָאֵלֶּה תֵּחָלֵק הָאָרֶץ" וגו', וְהֶחֱזִירוּ כּוּלָּן נַחֲלָתָן לְמוֹרִישׁ שֶׁלָּהֶן, דְּהַיְינוּ חֵפֶר שֶׁהָיָה מִיּוֹצְאֵי מִצְרַיִם. דְּאֵינָן אֶלָּא שְׁלוּחָיו, כִּדִכְתִיב: "לִשְׁמוֹת מַטּוֹת אֲבוֹתָם יִנְחָלוּ", וְנִמְצָא כְּאִילּוּ זָכָה וְהוּחְזַק חֵפֶר בְּכָל חֲלָקִים הַלָּלוּ, וּכְשֶׁמֵּת חֵפֶר — יָרְשׁוּ מִמֶּנּוּ כָּל בָּנָיו. בְּנוֹת צְלָפְחָד יָרְשׁוּ שְׁנֵי חֲלָקִים לְפִי שֶׁהוּא בְּכוֹר, וְכָל אֶחָיו אִישׁ אִישׁ חֵלֶק אֶחָד — הֲרֵי לִבְנוֹת צְלָפְחָד שְׁנֵי חֲלָקִים שֶׁל אָבִיו בְּנִכְסֵי חֵפֶר. וְגַם כְּשֶׁמֵּתוּ שְׁנַיִם מֵאַחֵי צְלָפְחָד כִּדְלְקַמָּן, יָרְשׁוּ אַחֵי צְלָפְחָד אוֹתָן שֶׁבַּחַיִּים, וְגַם בְּנוֹת צְלָפְחָד בִּמְקוֹם אֲבִיהֶן יָרְשׁוּ אוֹתָן אַחִין הַמֵּתִים, וְזָכוּ בַּחֵלֶק שֶׁהָיָה לָהֶם לִיטּוֹל בְּנִכְסֵי חֵפֶר כְּשֶׁהֶחֱזִירוּ לוֹ בָּנָיו שֶׁבָּאוּ לָאָרֶץ, וְהוּא חָזַר וְהוֹרִישׁ לָהֶם, כִּדְפָרֵישִׁית. אֲבָל חֵלֶק צְלָפְחָד עַצְמוֹ לֹא נָטְלוּ, שֶׁהֲרֵי לֹא לְיוֹצְאֵי מִצְרַיִם נִתְחַלְּקָה הָאָרֶץ. וַחֲזָרָה לָא שַׁיָּיךְ בֵּיהּ, שֶׁהֲרֵי לֹא הָיוּ לוֹ בָּנִים הַנִּכְנָסִין לָאָרֶץ שֶׁיַּחֲזִירוּ לוֹ נַחֲלָה. תִּשְׁעָה הָווּ. שִׁיתָּא דְּשִׁיתָּא בָּתֵּי אָבוֹת, וּתְלָתָא דִּידְהוּ הַשְּׁנוּיִין בְּמַתְנִיתִין. ה"נ תְּרֵי אַחֵי דְּאַבָּא כו'. וְהָנְהוּ תְּרֵי אַחֵי מֵתוּ אַחֲרֵי מוֹת חֵפֶר אֲבִיהֶן, וְזָכוּ קוֹדֶם מִיתָתָן בְּנִכְסֵי חֵפֶר שֶׁהֶחֱזִירוּ לוֹ בָּנָיו שֶׁבָּאוּ לָאָרֶץ, כִּדְפָרֵישִׁית לְעֵיל. כְּגוֹן שֶׁהָיוּ לְחֵפֶר ח' בָּנִים, הַשְּׁנַיִם מֵתוּ בַּמִּדְבָּר וְגַם צְלָפְחָד עִמָּהֶם, וְהַחֲמִשָּׁה בָּאוּ לָאָרֶץ וְנָטְלוּ ה' חֲלָקִים, הֶחֱזִירוּם לְחֵפֶר אֲבִיהֶם. מֵת חֵפֶר — יְרָשׁוּהוּ שְׁמוֹנָה בָּנָיו, צְלָפְחָד נָטַל שְׁנֵי חֲלָקִים כִּי הוּא הַבְּכוֹר, וְז' אַחִין נָטְלוּ ז' חֲלָקִים. מֵת צְלָפְחָד — נָטְלוּ בְּנוֹתָיו שְׁנֵי חֲלָקִים שֶׁלּוֹ שֶׁיָּרַשׁ מִנִּכְסֵי חֵפֶר. מֵתוּ שְׁנֵי אֶחָיו בְּלֹא בָּנִים — בָּאוּ חֲמִשָּׁה הָאַחִין וּבְנוֹת צְלָפְחָד בִּמְקוֹם צְלָפְחָד אֲבִיהֶם וִירָשׁוּם. נִמְצְאוּ בְּנוֹת צְלָפְחָד נוֹטְלוֹת אַרְבָּעָה חֲלָקִים: ב' חֲלָקִים גְּדוֹלִים בְּנִכְסֵי חֵפֶר, וּב' חֲלָקִים קְטַנִּים בְּנִכְסֵי שְׁנֵי אֲחֵי אֲבִיהֶן. וּמִיהוּ, הַמַּקְשֶׁה לָא הֲוָה סְבִירָא לֵיהּ תְּרֵי אַחֵי, אֶלָּא חַד אַחָא דְּאַבָּא, כִּדְאַשְׁכְּחַן בְּבָרַיְיתָא. נָתֹן תִּתֵּן. קְרָאֵי יְתֵירֵי דָּרֵישׁ, דְּמָצֵי לְמִכְתַּב "יִנְחֲלוּ בְּנוֹת צְלָפְחָד" וְתוּ לָא. זוֹ נַחֲלַת אֲבִיהֶן. שֶׁהָיָה מִיּוֹצְאֵי מִצְרַיִם, וְקָסָבַר: לְיוֹצְאֵי מִצְרַיִם נִתְחַלְּקָה הָאָרֶץ. בְּתוֹךְ אֲחֵי אֲבִיהֶן זוֹ נַחֲלַת חֵפֶר. אֲבִי אֲבִיהֶן, שֶׁנָּטַל בָּהּ צְלָפְחָד חֵלֶק כְּאֶחָד מֵאֶחָיו. וְהַעֲבַרְתָּ זוֹ חֵלֶק בְּכוֹרָה. כִּדִכְתִיב: "וְהַעֲבַרְתָּ כָל פֶּטֶר רֶחֶם" (שמות יג) — שֶׁנָּטַל צְלָפְחָד בְּנִכְסֵי חֵפֶר חֵלֶק אֶחָד יוֹתֵר עַל אֶחָיו בִּשְׁבִיל שֶׁהָיָה בְּכוֹר. וּמִיהוּ, סְבִירָא לֵיהּ נַמִי לְהַאי תַּנָּא כְּר' אֱלִיעֶזֶר, דְּחַד אַחָא דְּאַבָּא הֲוָה לְהוּ, וְנָפְקָא לֵיהּ מִיַּיתּוּר דַּ"אֲחֻזַּת נַחֲלָה" כִּדְאָמְרִינַן לְקַמָּן. דְּאִי לֵית לֵיהּ — לָא מַשְׁכַּחַתְּ לָהּ חַבְלֵי מְנַשֶּׁה עֲשָׂרָה. אֲבָל מִ"נָּתֹן תִּתֵּן" אֵינוֹ רוֹצֶה לִדְרוֹשׁ מִכְּפַל הַמִּקְרָא כְּרַבִּי אֱלִיעֶזֶר, דְּס"ל דִּבְּרָה תּוֹרָה כִּלְשׁוֹן בְּנֵי אָדָם. וּכְה"ג הָוְיָא פְּלוּגְתָּא דְּתַנָּאֵי בְּקִידּוּשִׁין (דף יז:) גַּבֵּי "הַעֲנֵיק תַּעֲנִיק לוֹ" וּבְכַמָּה מְקוֹמוֹת בַּגְּמָ'. מֵאֲחֻזַּת נַחֲלָה. דְּמָצֵי לְמִיכְתַּב: נָתֹן תִּתֵּן לָהֶם נַחֲלָה בְּתוֹךְ אֲחֵי אֲבִיהֶן. קְרָא. דִּכְתִיב: "חַבְלֵי מְנַשֶּׁה עֲשָׂרָה", מַאי קָחָשֵׁיב? טוּבָא הָווּ. כָּל אַחִין שֶׁבְּמַטֵּה מְנַשֶּׁה שֶׁנָּטְלוּ חֵלֶק אֲבִיהֶן הָיָה לוֹ לַחְשׁוֹב, כִּדְקָחָשֵׁיב חֶלְקֵי בְּנוֹת צְלָפְחָד. שִׁיתָּא הָווּ. דְּהָא בְּנוֹת צְלָפְחָד עַל שֵׁם מִשְׁפַּחַת הַחֶפְרִי נִקְרָאִין, כְּכָל בְּנֵי חֵפֶר, וְכֵיוָן דְּקָחָשֵׁיב בֵּית אָב שֶׁל חֵפֶר — לָמָּה לִי לְמִיתְנֵי חֶלְקֵי בְּנוֹת צְלָפְחָד?
לְעוֹלָם

תוספות

וּלְמַאן דאמר לבאי הארץ תרי אחי דאבא הוו להו. משמע כולה סוגיא דלמאן דאמר לבאי הארץ שלא נטלו כלום מחמת צלפחד עצמו, אלא מחמת חפר אבי אביהן. ותימה: אם כן מאי קאמר "והוא לא היה בתוך העדה הנועדים" וגו'. מאי נפקא מינה שלא היה בעדתם? אפילו היה — היו נוטלין על ידי חזרה, דהא אמרינן לעיל בני מרגלים ובני מתלוננים נחלו בזכות אבי אביהן, ובזכות אבי אמותיהן! ואין לפרש (א) דנ"מ לענין חלק בכורה, דהא כי היכי דשקלי חלק פשיטות, אע"ג דבא להן מכח אביהן — ה"נ יטלו חלק בכורה. ועוד קשה לרשב"א: למ"ד לבאי הארץ, היכי קאמר לעיל: מרגלים יהושע וכלב נטלו חלקם? והלא לא היה להם חלק בארץ כלל לכל אותן שלא באו בארץ! וכ"ת: נטלו מה שהגיע להן על ידי חזרה מבניהם שבאו לארץ — הא ליתא, דאמרינן לקמן דבניהן שהיו בני עשרים נטלו בזכות עצמן! ורשב"ם פי': דלמ"ד לבאי הארץ לא נטלו מידי יהושע וכלב מחלק מרגלים, ומפרש "חיו מן האנשים" — ממש חיו, כפשטיה.

וּלְמַאן דאמר תרי אחי דאבא הוו להו ההוא מאחוזת נחלה נפקא. קשיא לריב"א: אפילו למאן דאמר חד אחא דאבא הוה להו נמי מ"אחוזת נחלה" נפקא לרבנן, דלא דרשי "נתון תתן". ולר"א דדריש "נתון תתן" — לא צריך ל"אחוזת נחלה" אפילו למאן דאמר תרי אחי דאבא הוו. דהא למאן דאמר לבאי הארץ הוא דאית ליה דתרי אחי דאבא הוו, והוא לא דריש "נתון תתן להם נחלה" לחלק אביהם, דלדידיה לא היה שום חלק. ולדרוש מיניה חד אחא, ואידך מ"נתון תתן" כדדריש ראב"י!
ובזכות

רבינו גרשום

דמצית למימר דלא הוה דלא שקיל דודאי הוה ולגבי בני יוסף משום הכי כתבינהו דעצה טובה קמ"ל וכו' אבל אי לאו הכי לא כתבינהו: שחיו בחלקיהן. שירשו חלקן המגיען: מאן דמקשי מתלוננים למרגלים בחד קרא סבירא ליה דהוה להו חלק בארץ דכי היכי דלגבי מרגלים יהושע וכלב נטלו חלקם כדאמרי' הכי נמי נטלו חלק [של] מתלוננים. מאן דלא מקיש מתלוננים למרגלים סבירא ליה דלא הוה להן חלק בארץ כלל. דתניא אבינו מת במדבר והוא לא היה בתוך כל הני וכל הני מדברייתא מקיש מתלוננים למרגלים. משום הכי יהושע וכלב נטלו חלקם כדגמרינן הכא. ותנא קמא לא מקיש: איכפול יהושע וכלב. לאורתה לכל ארץ ישראל דהא כל ישראל שמתו במדבר מתלוננים הוו: אותן מתלוננים שבעדת קרח. אותן מאתים וחמשים איש קאמרי' דיהושע וכלב נטלו חלקם ולא מאחריני: היינו דכתיב ויפלו חבלי מנשה עשרה שיתא דשיתא בתי אבות וארבעה דידהו הא עשרה הכי פירושא שיתא דשיתא בתי אבות לבני אביעזר לבני חלק לבני אפרים לבני שכם לבני חפר ולבני שמידע הא שיתא דכל הני מיוצאי מצרים הוו וארבעה דידהו של בנות צלפחד שהוא היה מיוצאי מצרים ותנן במתני' בנות צלפחד נטלו ג' חלקים חלק אביהן שהיה מיוצאי מצרים וחלקו עם אחיו בנכסי חפר ונטלו ב' חלקים לפי שצלפחד היה בכור. תשעה. אותו חלק עשירי מקשינן לקמן ומתרץ חד אחא דאבא הוה להו ומית ונטלו חלק אחד מירושתו שהיה האח מיוצאי מצרים הרי חבלי מנשה י' חלקים: אלא למאן דאמר לבאי הארץ. נתחלקה תמניא הוו שיתא דשיתא בתי אבות שהיתה חוזרת נחלה ותרתי דידהו פי שנים של בכור שנטלו בנכסי חפר בחזרת נחלה הרי תמניא וחלק צלפחד עצמו לא נטלו לפי שמת במדבר ולא היה מבאי הארץ: אמר ליה ולטעמיך למאן דאמר ליוצאי מצרים נתחלקה ט' הוו. שיתא דשיתא בתי אבות ותלת דידהו דמתני' הרי ט': אלא מאי אית לך למימר. דליהוו עשרה חד אחא הוה ליה לצלפחד דמית בלא בנים ונטלו חלקו הרי י'. תריץ לה נמי למאן דאמר לבאי הארץ תרתי אחי הוו ליה לצלפחד ומתו ונטלו בנותיו חלקן הרי י': זו נחלת אביהן. ממש: בתוך אחי אביהן. ירשו בנכסי חפר אבי אביהן: והעברת זו חלק בכור שהעבירו מחלק אחי אביהן ונתנו להן: דכתיב נתון תתן. יתירא הוא ומיניה דייק אחי אביהן: ולמאן דאמר תרי אחי דאבא. מפיק ליה מתתן ונחלה דיתורי דלא צריך למכתב: קרא. דכתיב ויפלו חבלי מנשה עשרה אי בתי אבות גופיהו קא חשיב שיתא הוו ותו לא ואמאי קא חשיב בנות צלפחד למיהוי עשרה ואי טפלים שיצאו מהם קא חשיב משום הכי חשיב בנות צלפחד מאי טעמא אמר חבלי מנשה עשרה הא הוו כמה אלפים. אמר ליה לעולם

מסורת הש"ס

א) ברכות כ. נה: ב"מ פד. סוטה לו: ב) [עי' פרש"י דסוכה לא. ד"ה לא מקשינן ובתוספות ד"ה ורבי יהודה]:

הגהות הב"ח

(א) רשב"ם ד"ה ותרי וכו' או הם או בני בני חפר: (ב) תוס' ד"ה ולמ"ד לבאי וכו' ואין לפרש דלענין חלק בכורה קאמרי הכי דהא כי היכי:

לְעוֹלָם בָּתֵּי אָבוֹת קָא חָשֵׁיב, וְהָא קָא מַשְׁמַע לָן, דִּבְנוֹת צְלָפְחָד נָטְלוּ חֵלֶק בְּכוֹרָה. אַלְמָא: א"י מוּחְזֶקֶת הִיא. אָמַר מָר: וְהַבָּנִים נָטְלוּ בִּזְכוּת אֲבִי אֲבִיהֶם וּבִזְכוּת אֲבִי אִמּוֹתֵיהֶן. וְהָתַנְיָא: בִּזְכוּת עַצְמָן! לָא קַשְׁיָא: הָא — כְּמַאן דְּאָמַר לְיוֹצְאֵי מִצְרַיִם, הָא — כְּמַאן דְּאָמַר לְבָאֵי הָאָרֶץ. וְאִיבָּעֵית אֵימָא: הָא וְהָא לְבָאֵי הָאָרֶץ, וְלָא קַשְׁיָא: הָא — דַּהֲוָה בֶּן עֶשְׂרִים, הָא — דְּלָא הֲוָה בֶּן עֶשְׂרִים.§ "וְשֶׁהָיָה בְּכוֹר נוֹטֵל שְׁנֵי חֲלָקִים".§ וְאַמַּאי? רָאוּי הוּא, א)וְאֵין הַבְּכוֹר נוֹטֵל בְּרָאוּי כִּבְמוּחְזָק! אָמַר רַב יְהוּדָה אָמַר שְׁמוּאֵל: בִּיתֵדוֹת אֹהָלִים. מְתִיב רַבָּה, רַבִּי יְהוּדָה אוֹמֵר: בְּנוֹת צְלָפְחָד נָטְלוּ ד' חֲלָקִים, שֶׁנֶּאֱמַר °"וַיִּפְּלוּ חַבְלֵי מְנַשֶּׁה עֲשָׂרָה"! אֶלָּא אָמַר רַבָּה: אֶרֶץ יִשְׂרָאֵל מוּחְזֶקֶת הִיא. מֵיתִיבֵי, אָמַר רַבִּי חִידְקָא: שִׁמְעוֹן הַשִּׁקְמוֹנִי הָיָה לִי חָבֵר מִתַּלְמִידֵי רַבִּי עֲקִיבָא, וְכָךְ הָיָה רַבִּי שִׁמְעוֹן הַשִּׁקְמוֹנִי אוֹמֵר: יוֹדֵעַ הָיָה מֹשֶׁה רַבֵּינוּ שֶׁבְּנוֹת צְלָפְחָד יוֹרְשׁוֹת הֵן, אֲבָל לֹא הָיָה יוֹדֵעַ אִם נוֹטְלוֹת חֵלֶק בְּכוֹרָה אִם לָאו, ב)וּרְאוּיָה הָיְתָה פָּרָשַׁת נְחָלוֹת לִיכָּתֵב עַל יְדֵי מֹשֶׁה, אֶלָּא שֶׁזָּכוּ בְּנוֹת צְלָפְחָד וְנִכְתְּבָה עַל יָדָן. ג)וְיוֹדֵעַ הָיָה מֹשֶׁה רַבֵּינוּ שֶׁהַמְקוֹשֵׁשׁ בְּמִיתָה, שֶׁנֶּאֱמַר: °"מְחַלְלֶיהָ מוֹת יוּמָת", אֲבָל לֹא הָיָה יוֹדֵעַ בְּאֵי זוֹ מִיתָה הוּא יָמוּת, ד)וּרְאוּיָה הָיְתָה פָּרָשַׁת מְקוֹשֵׁשׁ שֶׁתִּכָּתֵב ע"י מֹשֶׁה, אֶלָּא שֶׁנִּתְחַיֵּיב מְקוֹשֵׁשׁ וְנִכְתְּבָה עַל יָדוֹ; לְלַמֶּדְךָ, שֶׁמְּגַלְגְּלִים

תורה אור: יהושע יז | שמות לא

רש"י

לְעוֹלָם בָּתֵּי אָבוֹת קָא חָשֵׁיב. וְלָא טְפָלִים. חוּץ מִבְּנוֹת צְלָפְחָד דְּקָחָשֵׁיב ד' חֲלָקִים שֶׁלָּהֶן, וְאַשְׁמוּעִינַן דְּדָרְשִׁינַן הַאי קְרָא דְ"נָתֹן תִּתֵּן" דְּמִינֵּיהּ נָפְקָא לָן ד' חֲלָקִים עַל יְדֵי שֶׁאָנוּ דּוֹרְשִׁין: "וְהַעֲבַרְתָּ" זוֹ חֵלֶק בְּכוֹרָה. אַלְמָא אַשְׁמוּעִינַן דְּא"י מוּחְזֶקֶת הִיא לָהֶן מִיצִיאַת מִצְרַיִם וְאַף עַל פִּי שֶׁעֲדַיִין לֹא נִכְנְסוּ בָּהּ. הָא. דְּקָתָנֵי: בִּזְכוּת אֲבִיהֶן, אֲבָל לֹא בִּזְכוּת עַצְמָן. כְּמַאן דְּאָמַר לְיוֹצְאֵי מִצְרַיִם. נִתְחַלְּקָה הָאָרֶץ, וְלֹא לְבָאֵי הָאָרֶץ. הָא. דְּקָתָנֵי: בִּזְכוּת עַצְמָן — כְּמ"ד לְבָאֵי הָאָרֶץ, וּכְגוֹן דַּהֲווּ בְּנֵי כ' כְּשֶׁנִּכְנְסוּ לָאָרֶץ. הָא וְהָא לְבָאֵי הָאָרֶץ. דְּאַע"ג דְּרֵישָׁא דְּהַהִיא בָּרַיְיתָא דִּלְעֵיל לֵיכָּא לְאוֹקוֹמַהּ אֶלָּא לְמַאן דְּאָמַר לְיוֹצְאֵי מִצְרַיִם, דְּקָתָנֵי: מְרַגְּלִים יְהוֹשֻׁעַ וְכָלֵב נָטְלוּ חֶלְקָם — אִיכָּא לְמֵימַר: מַסְקָנָא דְּר' שִׁמְעוֹן בֶּן אֶלְעָזָר הִיא, דְּאִית לֵיהּ לְיוֹצְאֵי מִצְרַיִם וּלְבָאֵי הָאָרֶץ. הָא. דְּקָתָנֵי: בִּזְכוּת עַצְמָן — דַּהֲווּ בְּנֵי עֶשְׂרִים כְּשֶׁבָּאוּ לָאָרֶץ. הָא. דְּקָתָנֵי: בִּזְכוּת אֲבִי אֲבִיהֶן. דְּלָא הָווּ בְּנֵי עֶשְׂרִים. כְּשֶׁבָּאוּ לָאָרֶץ. וּבִבְנֵי בְּנֵי הַמִּתְלוֹנְנִים קָמַיְירֵי, שֶׁמֵּתוּ לָהֶן אֲבִיהֶן שֶׁהָיוּ בְּנֵי הַמִּתְלוֹנְנִים מַמָּשׁ בַּמִּדְבָּר, וְהֵם נִשְׁאֲרוּ טְפָלִים וְלֹא נָטְלוּ לְעַצְמָן, שֶׁעֲדַיִין לֹא הִגִּיעוּ לְכ'. וּבִזְכוּת אֲבִיהֶן מַמָּשׁ, בְּנֵי הַמִּתְלוֹנְנִים וְאֵין לָהֶם לִיטּוֹל, שֶׁהֵן מִמִּצְרַיִם לֹא יָצְאוּ וְלָאָרֶץ לֹא בָּאוּ, אֶלָּא בִּזְכוּת אֲבִי אֲבִיהֶן, דְּהַיְינוּ אֲבוֹת הַמְרַגְּלִים שֶׁיָּצְאוּ מִמִּצְרַיִם. וְכֵיוָן דְּהַךְ בָּרַיְיתָא כְּרַבִּי שִׁמְעוֹן בֶּן אֶלְעָזָר מוֹקְמִינָא לָהּ, דְּאִית לֵיהּ תַּרְתֵּי, נִמְצְאוּ אֵלּוּ בְּנֵי בְנֵיהֶן יוֹרְשִׁין אוֹתָן כִּבְנוֹת צְלָפְחָד שֶׁיָּרְשׁוּ בְּנִכְסֵי חֵפֶר זְקֵנָם וְאַע"ג דַּחֲשִׁיבִי כִּטְפָלִים דְּעָלְמָא. דִּלְעִנְיַן יְרוּשַּׁת אֲבִיהֶן שֶׁהָיוּ מִיּוֹצְאֵי מִצְרַיִם לָא בָּעֵינַן בְּנֵי כ' בִּכְנִיסָתָן לָאָרֶץ. וַחֲזָרָה לֵיכָּא לְמֵימַר, דְּהָא רַבִּי שִׁמְעוֹן בֶּן אֶלְעָזָר לֵית לֵיהּ חֲזָרָה, דְּמֵהֵיכָא תֵּיתֵי? הָא מַשְׁמַע לֵיהּ קְרָאֵי תַּרְוַיְיהוּ לְגוּפַיְיהוּ. וַאֲפִילּוּ אִם תִּמְצֵי לוֹמַר דְּהָא סֵיפָא לָאו ר' שִׁמְעוֹן הִיא, אִיכָּא לְאוֹקוֹמַהּ דְּנָטְלוּ בִּזְכוּת אֲבִי אֲבִיהֶן ע"י חֲזָרָה. כְּגוֹן שֶׁהָיוּ לָהֶם לַמִּתְלוֹנְנִים אַחִים שֶׁלֹּא הָיוּ בְּנֵי כ' בִּשְׁעַת הַגְּזֵירָה, וְלֹא מֵתוּ בַּמִּדְבָּר, דְּהָא לֹא נִגְזְרָה גְּזֵירָה עַל פָּחוֹת מִבֶּן כ'. וּכְשֶׁנָּטְלוּ חֶלְקָם בָּאָרֶץ, הֶחֱזִירוּ אֵצֶל (אֲבִי) אֲבִיהֶן. מֶה עָשׂוּ הָאָבוֹת? חָזְרוּ וְהוֹרִישׁוּ נִכְסֵיהֶן לְכָל יוֹצְאֵי יְרֵיכָן, בֵּין לַאֲחֵי הַמִּתְלוֹנְנִים בֵּין לִבְנֵי בְּנֵי הַמִּתְלוֹנְנִים, דְּכוּלָּן יוֹצְאֵי חֲלָצֵיהֶן הָיוּ, וְחוֹלְקִים אֲחֵי הַמִּתְלוֹנְנִים עִם בְּנֵי נֶכְדֵיהֶן בְּשָׁוֶה. דְּאַע"ג דִּטְפָלִים לָא שָׁקְלִי בְּאַנְפֵּי נַפְשַׁיְיהוּ — יְרוּשַּׁת אָבוֹת מִיהָא קָשָׁקְלִי, כִּדְאָמַר בִּבְנוֹת צְלָפְחָד, דַּהֲווּ לְהוּ כִּטְפָלִים שֶׁאֵין לָהֶן חֵלֶק לְעַצְמָן, וְחָלְקוּ עִם אֲחֵי אֲבִיהֶן בְּנִכְסֵי חֵפֶר. וְהַבָּנִים דְּקָתָנֵי — הַיְינוּ בְּנֵי הַבָּנִים, דְּבֶן בְּנוֹ שֶׁל אָדָם קָרוּי בְּנוֹ, כִּדְאָמְרִינַן לְקַמָּן בְּ"מִי שֶׁמֵּת" (דף קמג:), וַאֲבִי אֲבִיהֶן קָרֵי לֵיהּ אֲבִי אֲבִיהֶן. דְּבִבְנֵי הַמִּתְלוֹנְנִים עַצְמָן לֵיכָּא לְמֵימַר דְּלָא הָווּ בְּנֵי עֶשְׂרִים, דְּקַיְימָא לָן בְּשָׁנָה שְׁנִיָּה שָׁלַח מֹשֶׁה מְרַגְּלִים, וְתַנְיָא בְּסֵדֶר עוֹלָם: אַחַר בִּיאַת מְרַגְּלִים הָיְתָה בְּלִיעָתוֹ שֶׁל קֹרַח, וּבוֹ בַּיּוֹם נִשְׂרְפוּ הַמִּתְלוֹנְנִים. נִמְצְאוּ שֶׁבְּנֵיהֶן כְּשֶׁבָּאוּ לָאָרֶץ הָווּ בְּנֵי ל"ח שָׁנָה, שֶׁכֵּן עָמְדוּ יִשְׂרָאֵל בַּמִּדְבָּר אַחֲרֵי כֵן. (ת'. וּלְפִי הַאי לִישָּׁנָא בַּתְרָא לֵית לְהַאי תַּנָּא דְּבָרַיְיתָא דִּלְעֵיל דִּיהוֹשֻׁעַ וְכָלֵב נָטְלוּ כְּלָל חֵלֶק בִּשְׁבִיל מְרַגְּלִים, וְהַאי קְרָא דְּ"חָיוּ מִן הָאֲנָשִׁים" לָא דָּרֵישׁ לֵיהּ אֶלָּא כִּפְשָׁטֵיהּ. ת'). רְאוּיָה הָיָה. לְחֵפֶר וְלִצְלָפְחָד מִשֶּׁמֵּתוּ בַּמִּדְבָּר, אֲבָל לֹא הוּחְזְקוּ בָּהּ מֵעוֹלָם, שֶׁהֲרֵי לֹא בָּאוּ לָאָרֶץ! וְאֵין הַבְּכוֹר נוֹטֵל בְּרָאוּי. לְקַמָּן בְּפִרְקִין (דף קכד:). בִּיתֵדוֹת אֹהָלִים. כְּלוֹמַר, בְּמִטַּלְטְלִין שֶׁהָיָה לָהֶם בַּמִּדְבָּר, כְּגוֹן יְתֵדוֹת שֶׁתּוֹקְעִין בָּהֶן אָהֳלֵיהֶם, וּשְׁאָר מִטַּלְטְלִין שֶׁהֵן מוּחְזָקִין בָּהֶן. וְלְהָכִי נָקַט יְתֵדוֹת אֹהָלִים, דְּוַדַּאי לְכוּלָּן הָיוּ אֹהָלִים, וְאֵין אָדָם בַּמִּדְבָּר בְּלֹא אֹהֶל. אֲבָל בְּנַחֲלַת אֶרֶץ יִשְׂרָאֵל לֹא נָטַל חֵלֶק בְּכוֹרָה. וְכָל שְׁלֹשָׁה חֲלָקִים דְּמַתְנִיתִין, בֵּין בְּמִקַּרְקְעֵי בֵּין בְּמִטַּלְטְלֵי מַיְירֵי, לְבַד מֵחֵלֶק בְּכוֹרָה דְּמַיְירֵי בְּמִטַּלְטְלֵי. חַבְלֵי מְנַשֶּׁה. הַיְינוּ קַרְקַע, שֶׁחוֹלְקִין בַּחֶבֶל. וְחֵלֶק בְּכוֹרָה מֵאֵלּוּ אַרְבַּע חֲבָלִים הָיָה. מוּחְזֶקֶת הִיא. לְיוֹצְאֵי מִצְרַיִם, כְּדִכְתִיב: "וְנָתַתִּי אוֹתָהּ לָכֶם מוֹרָשָׁה" כְּלוֹמַר, אֲנִי נְתַתִּיהָ לָכֶם יְרוּשָּׁה. יוֹדֵעַ הָיָה מֹשֶׁה רַבֵּינוּ שֶׁבְּנוֹת צְלָפְחָד יוֹרְשׁוֹת הֵן. כְּמוֹ בֵּן. שֶׁהֲרֵי דִּינִין נִצְטַוּוּ בְּמָרָה, כִּדְאָמְרִינַן בְּסַנְהֶדְרִין (דף נו.) וּכְדִכְתִיב: "שָׁם שָׂם לוֹ חֹק וּמִשְׁפָּט", וּמַעֲשֶׂה דִּבְנוֹת צְלָפְחָד בְּעַרְבוֹת מוֹאָב בְּסוֹף הַמ' שָׁנָה. וְעוֹד, דְּאִיכָּא לְמֵילַף מִפָּרָשַׁת יְבָמִין שֶׁהַבַּת כַּבֵּן, כִּדְכְתִיב: "וּמֵת אַחַד מֵהֶם וּבֵן אֵין לוֹ" עַיֵּין עָלָיו. דְּהָא בְּנוֹת צְלָפְחָד מִשָּׁם לָמְדוּ, כִּדְלְקַמָּן: אִם כְּבֵן אָנוּ — נִירַשׁ, וְאִם לָאו — תִּתְיַיבֵּם אִמֵּנוּ. וְלֹא תֹּאמַר: אִם לֹא דִּבְּרוּ בְּנוֹת צְלָפְחָד וְלֹא נִתְחַיֵּיב מְקוֹשֵׁשׁ הָיוּ שְׁתֵּי פָּרָשִׁיּוֹת הַלָּלוּ חֲסֵרִין מִן הַתּוֹרָה, וְהָכִי נַמִּי אִיכָּא לְמֵימַר שֶׁהַרְבֵּה מִצְוֹת חֲסֵרִים מִן הַתּוֹרָה לְפִי שֶׁלֹּא אֵירְעוּ הַמַּעֲשִׂים. וּרְאוּיָה הָיְתָה וְכוּ'. שֶׁמְּקוֹשֵׁשׁ בְּמִיתָה. וְאַף עַל גַּב דִּכְתִיב: "כִּי לֹא פוֹרַשׁ מַה יֵּעָשֶׂה לוֹ" — הַיְינוּ שֶׁלֹּא הָיָה יוֹדֵעַ אִם בִּסְקִילָה חֲמוּרָה אִם בְּחֶנֶק הַקַּל, כִּדְמְפָרֵשׁ וְאָזֵיל.

תוספות

ובזכות אבי אמותיהן. וכגון שלאבי אמותיהן לא היו בנים כי אם בנות, דאם לא כן היו בנים יורשין. וא"ת: ומי החזיר להן? וי"ל: כגון שהיו אחים לאבי אמותיהן שהיו להם בנים, והחזירום בנים לאבותיהם וחלקו בשוה. **הא** דהוו בני עשרים כו'. בבניהם אי אתה מוצא שלא היו בני עשרים, כמו שפירש בקונטרס דבליעת קרח נמי היתה מיד אחר המרגלים, כמו שהביא מסדר עולם, דקתני: אחר ביאת מרגלים היתה בליעת קרח, ואם לא שסמוך היה מאי קא משמע לן. וכן משמע נמי מדאמרי "הן גוענו (א) כולנו אבדנו" (במדבר יז) ומתרגם: הא מיננא קטלית חרבא, הא מיננא בליעת ארעא, הא מיננא מתו במותנא. שפלשה מעשים הללו היו רצופין, מדמדכרי להו אהדדי, ו"קטלת חרבא" היינו מעשה מרגלים, כדכתיב (שם יד) "ויכום ויכתום" וגו'. ואין להקשות: אמאי הוצרך לומר בזכות אבי אביהן? לימא בזכות אביהן ממש, דהיינו בני מרגלים ובני המתלוננים עצמן! דהאי תנא אתא לאשמועינן דאפילו אותן שלא נטלו מחמת עצמן, שלא היו בני כ' כשבאו לארץ, ולא נטלו נמי בזכות אבותיהן ממש, כגון שמתו במדבר, ולא נטלו נמי ע"י חזרה, שלא נולדו להן שום בן שהיה בן עשרים — אפילו הכי נטלו בזכות אבי אביהן, אע"פ שבא להן מחמת מרגלים ומתלוננים. וא"ת, אמאי לא קאמר: הא והא ליוצאי מצרים, והא — כשהיו אביהן ממש, בני מרגלים ומתלוננים — בני עשרים כשיצאו ממצרים, דהיינו מחמת עצמן, שלא בא להן מכח מרגלים ומתלוננים. והא דקאמר בזכות אבי אביהן — שלא היו אבותיהן בני עשרים ביציאת מצרים? ובשלמא אי הוה אמר דבניהן ממש של מרגלים ושל מתלוננים עצמן מיירי הכא שבאו לארץ — הוה אתי שפיר, דלא הוה מצי למימר: הא והא ליוצאי מצרים והא (ב) והא דהוו בני עשרים כשיצאו, דאם כן איך באו לארץ? דבני עשרים כולן מתו במדבר! ויש לומר: דהשתא נמי דאיירי בבני בניהם — לא מצי לשנויי הכי, דמשמע נמי דבאי הארץ נטלו בזכות עצמן, ולא שאבותיהן נחלו והורישו להן. **מתיב** רבה רבי יהודה אומר בנות צלפחד נטלו ארבעה חלקים שנאמר ויפלו חבלי מנשה עשרה. וקרא ע"כ לא איירי ביתדות ואהלים אלא בחלוקה. וליכא למימר: דלמא תלתא אחי דאבא הוו להו. דאז לא הוו בהו שום חדוש, דהא חלק בכורה לא נטלו, וא"כ לא הוה ליה לקרא לאשמועינהו, אלא דבתי אבות גרידא, כדפריך רב פפא לעיל: אי טפלים קא חשיב — טובא הוו. **יודע** היה משה שבנות צלפחד יורשות הן. אע"פ שלא נאמרה פרשת נחלה, יודע היה משה, מטעם דלקמן: אם כבן אנו נירש אם כבת תתייבם אמנו. **שנאמר** מחלליה מות יומת אבל לא היה יודע באיזו מיתה נהרג. ואם תאמר: למה היה מסתפק? היה לו לדונו בחנק, דכל מיתה האמורה בתורה סתם חנק! ויש לומר: דמסברא היה נראה לו שנדון בסקילה כעובד ע"ז, דבכל דוכתא (חולין ה.) אמר דדומה שבת לע"ז, דהיינו מחלל שבת בפרהסיא לעובד ע"ז. וצריך לומר דסבר כרבנן ולא כר"י, דאי כר' יהודה דאמר ב"אלו הן הנשרפין" (סנהדרין דף פ:): עד שיודיעוהו באיזו מיתה הוא נהרג, דלדידיה אמר התם דהוראת שעה היתה, ה)(דאם) כן לא ידע משה שדינו במיתה. אילו

עין משפט נר מצוה

כט א מיי' פ"ג מהל' נחלות הלכה א סמג עשין צו טוש"ע ח"מ סי' רעה סעיף ג:

רבינו גרשום

לעולם בתי אבות קחשיב. וכדין הוא דלא הוה ליה למיחשב אלא שיתא ואמאי קא חשיב בנות צלפחד משום האי חידוש שנטלו חלק בכורה. אלמא ארץ ישראל מוחזקת היה להם ולא ראויה דאי ראויה הא קי"ל דאין הבכור נוטל בראוי כבמוחזק: למאן דאמר ליוצאי מצרים נתחלקה. נטלו בזכות אביהן: הא דהוו בר עשרים כשבאו לארץ נטלו בשביל עצמן. אבל אי לא הוו עשרים דאכתי טפלים נינהו נטלו בזכות אביהן בתורת נחלה: ביתדות אהלים. שהיה מוחזק בידן מטלטלין שהיו רוצין לקבען לארץ מהן נטלו שני חלקים ולא בגופה של קרקע מפני שראויה היא: ויפלו חבלי מנשה עשרה. דמשמע דבארץ גופה נטלו חלק בכורה:

מסורת הש"ס

א) [לעיל נה. לקמן קכג: קכה: קמה: יבמות כד: בכורות נא:]: ב) סנהד' ח.: ג) שם עח: [ע"ש]: ד) שם ח.: ה) [צ"ל ואם]:

הגהות הב"ח

(א) תוס' ד"ה הא דהוו וכו' הן גוענו אבדנו כולנו: (ב) בא"ד הא והא ליוצאי מצרים והא דהוו כצ"ל ותיבת והא נמחק:

א)שֶׁמְּגַלְגְּלִים זְכוּת עַל יְדֵי זַכַּאי וְחוֹבָה עַל יְדֵי חַיָּיב; וְאִי סָלְקָא דַּעְתָּךְ אֶרֶץ יִשְׂרָאֵל מוּחְזֶקֶת, מַאי קָא מִסְתַּפְּקָא לֵיהּ? הִיא גּוּפָהּ קָא מִסְתַּפְּקָא לֵיהּ, דִּכְתִיב: "וְנָתַתִּי אוֹתָהּ לָכֶם מוֹרָשָׁה אֲנִי ה'" (שמות ו) יְרוּשָּׁה הִיא לָכֶם מֵאֲבוֹתֵיכֶם, אוֹ דִּלְמָא שֶׁמּוֹרִישִׁין וְאֵינָן יוֹרְשִׁין? וּפַשְׁטוּ לֵיהּ: תַּרְוַיְיהוּ — ב)יְרוּשָּׁה לָכֶם מֵאֲבוֹתֵיכֶם, וּמוֹרִישִׁין וְאֵינָן יוֹרְשִׁין. וְהַיְינוּ דִּכְתִיב: "תְּבִאֵמוֹ וְתִטָּעֵמוֹ בְּהַר נַחֲלָתְךָ" (שמות טו), תְּבִיאֵנוּ לֹא נֶאֱמַר, אֶלָּא "תְּבִאֵמוֹ", מְלַמֵּד שֶׁמִּתְנַבְּאִין וְאֵינָן יוֹדְעִין מָה מִתְנַבְּאִין. "וַתַּעֲמֹדְנָה לִפְנֵי מֹשֶׁה וְלִפְנֵי אֶלְעָזָר הַכֹּהֵן (במדבר כז) וְלִפְנֵי הַנְּשִׂיאִם וְכָל הָעֵדָה" — אֶפְשָׁר עָמְדוּ לִפְנֵי מֹשֶׁה כו' וְלֹא אָמְרוּ לָהֶן דָּבָר, וְעָמְדוּ לִפְנֵי הַנְּשִׂיאִם וְכָל הָעֵדָה? אֶלָּא סָרֵס הַמִּקְרָא וְדָרְשֵׁהוּ, דִּבְרֵי רַבִּי יֹאשִׁיָּה; אַבָּא חָנָן אָמַר מִשּׁוּם רַבִּי אֱלִיעֶזֶר: בְּבֵית הַמִּדְרָשׁ הָיוּ יוֹשְׁבִין, וְהָלְכוּ וְעָמְדוּ לָהֶן לִפְנֵי כּוּלָּן. בְּמַאי קָמִיפַּלְגִי? מָר סָבַר: ג)חוֹלְקִין כָּבוֹד לְתַלְמִיד בִּמְקוֹם הָרַב, וּמָר סָבַר: אאֵין חוֹלְקִין. וְהִלְכְתָא: חוֹלְקִין. וְהִלְכְתָא: אֵין חוֹלְקִין. קַשְׁיָא הִלְכְתָא אַהִלְכְתָא! הִלְכְתָא אַהִלְכְתָא לָא קַשְׁיָא: בהָא — דְּפָלֵיג לֵיהּ רַבֵּיהּ יְקָרָא, הָא — דְּלָא פָּלֵיג לֵיהּ רַבֵּיהּ יְקָרָא. תָּנָא: בְּנוֹת צְלָפְחָד חַכְמָנִיּוֹת הֵן, דַּרְשָׁנִיּוֹת הֵן, צַדְקָנִיּוֹת הֵן. חַכְמָנִיּוֹת הֵן — שֶׁלְּפִי שָׁעָה דִּבְּרוּ, דְּאָמַר רַב שְׁמוּאֵל בַּר רַב יִצְחָק: מְלַמֵּד שֶׁהָיָה מֹשֶׁה רַבֵּינוּ יוֹשֵׁב וְדוֹרֵשׁ בְּפָרָשַׁת יְבָמִין, שֶׁנֶּאֱמַר: "כִּי יֵשְׁבוּ אַחִים יַחְדָּו" (דברים כה), אָמְרוּ לוֹ: אִם כְּבֵן אָנוּ חֲשׁוּבִין — תְּנָה לָנוּ נַחֲלָה כְּבֵן, אִם לָאו — תִּתְיַבֵּם אִמֵּנוּ! מִיָּד: "וַיַּקְרֵב מֹשֶׁה אֶת מִשְׁפָּטָן לִפְנֵי ה'" דַּרְשָׁנִיּוֹת הֵן — שֶׁהָיוּ אוֹמְרוֹת: אִילּוּ הָיָה [לוֹ] בֵּן, לֹא דִּבַּרְנוּ. וְהָתַנְיָא: בַּת! אָמַר ר' יִרְמְיָה: סַמֵּי מִכָּאן בַּת. אַבָּיֵי אָמַר: אֲפִילּוּ הָיָה בַּת לַבֵּן, לֹא דִּבַּרְנוּ. צַדְקָנִיּוֹת הֵן — שֶׁלֹּא נִישְּׂאוּ אֶלָּא לְהָגוּן לָהֶן. תָּנֵי רַבִּי אֱלִיעֶזֶר בֶּן יַעֲקֹב: אֲפִילּוּ קְטַנָּה שֶׁבָּהֶן לֹא נִשֵּׂאת פְּחוּתָה מֵאַרְבָּעִים שָׁנָה. אִינִי? וְהָא אָמַר רַב חִסְדָּא: נִיסֵּת פְּחוּתָה מִבַּת עֶשְׂרִים — יוֹלֶדֶת עַד שִׁשִּׁים, בַּת עֶשְׂרִים — יוֹלֶדֶת עַד אַרְבָּעִים, בַּת אַרְבָּעִים — שׁוּב אֵינָהּ יוֹלֶדֶת! אֶלָּא, מִתּוֹךְ שֶׁצִּדְקָנִיּוֹת הֵן נַעֲשָׂה לָהֶן נֵס כְּיוֹכֶבֶד, דִּכְתִיב: "וַיֵּלֶךְ אִישׁ מִבֵּית לֵוִי וַיִּקַּח אֶת בַּת לֵוִי" (שמות ב),

אֶפְשָׁר

שמגלגלים זכות. שהבנים והקרובים יירשו את קרוביהם. **על ידי זכאי.** בנות צלפחד. **וחובה.** היינו סקילה שאמורה, דנוח הוא לאדם לדון בחנק. **על ידי חייב.** מקושש. **היא גופה.** קמבעיא ליה, מה דפשיטא לן השתא דארץ ישראל מוחזקת היא, קמספקא ליה. ואנן דפשיטא לן — היינו מאי דפשט ליה הקב"ה: "והעברת" — זה חלק בכורה. דכתיב ונתתי אותה לכם מורשה. והאי "מורשה" לשון ירושה משמע, כמו "למורש קפוד" (ישעיה יד), מועד מופת מוצא מורד. וגם לשון מוריש לאחרים, מדלא כתיב "ירושה". וקא מיבעיא ליה: האי "מורשה" דקאמר רחמנא, פשיטא לי דמורישין ואינן יורשין הוא, מדכתיב "מורשה" ולא כתיב ירושה, ועוד שהרי כבר מתו כולן במדבר. אלא הכי קמבעיא ליה: מי איכא למימר נמי דהכי קאמר: ירושה היא לכם מאבותיכם, ונוטל בה הבכור חלק בכורה? דכיון דכתיב "לכם מורשה" — ירושה היא לכם נמי בעי למימר. **או דלמא** מורישין ואינן יורשין. לחוד קאמר, אבל אינה ירושה להם, ולא יטול בה הבכור חלק בכורה. **ופשטו ליה.** משמיא, דתרווייהו משמע. מדקאמר ליה רחמנא: "והעברת" זה חלק בכורה — ש"מ דירושה היא לכם מאבותיכם נמי קאמר רחמנא, אבל מורישין ואינן יורשין — ממילא הוה ידע, כדפרישית. והאי דפשט ליה תרווייהו — לא קאי אמורישין ואינם יורשין, אלא א"ירושה היא לכם מאבותיכם" קאי, וממילא ידע דתרווייהו קאמר רחמנא, דכתיב "מורשה" ולא כתיב ירושה. ועוד, שכבר מתו מתי מדבר. כן נראה בעיני, ועיקר. **כיוצא בדבר אתה אומר.** דכי היכי דהאי "מורשה" אתא להתנבאות עליהן דמורישין ואינן יורשין, ואע"ג שלא חטאו עדיין חטא דמרגלים, ולא נגזרה גזירה — כך אנו מוצאים פסוק אחר שנתנבאו שלא יכנסו לארץ, ואע"פ שעדיין לא נגזר עליהן שלא ליכנס. **תביאמו.** לאחרים משמע. **אפשר** עמדו לפני משה ולא **אמר** להן כלום. והלכו אחרי כן לפני אלעזר? משה לא ידע, אלעזר מנין לו? ואפשר שאלעזר לא אמר כלום, והלכו אחרי כן לפני הנשיאים, ואח"כ לפני העדה? ה"ג: והלכו לפני הנשיאים וכל העדה **אלא סרס את המקרא** כו'. ולא גרסינן: ולא אמרו כלום. **ודרשהו.** כלומר, דרשהו כאילו כתוב למפרע: ותעמדנה לפני משה, ומקמי משה עמדו לפני אלעזר, ומקמי אלעזר עמדו לפני הנשיאים, ומקמי הנשיאים עמדו לפני העדה. והאי דלא כתב "ותעמדנה לפני העדה ולפני הנשיאים ולפני אלעזר ולפני משה" היינו לפי שאינו רוצה להקדים בפסוק תלמיד לרב, אלא ראשון ראשון חשוב. **בבית המדרש היו יושבין.** משה ואלעזר ונשיאי העדה, ועמדו לפני כולן, ששאלו לכולן כאחד, וחלקו כבוד לתלמידים במקום רבותיהם. **אבא חנן סבר חולקין.** דכל זה חשיבותו של רב הוא, וניחא ליה. **רבי יאשיה סבר אין חולקין.** הלכך מסרס המקרא. **הא דפליג ליה רביה.** לתלמיד יקרא, ודאי ניחא ליה שיחלקו לו גם אחרים כבוד. ומשה רבינו הוה פליג יקרא לכל ישראל, וכן זה לזה. **חכמניות הן.** בדרך ארץ. **שלפי שעה דברו.** שכשמצאו פתח לדבריהם באו בעלילה ובטענה מעלייתא לבית דין, כדמפרש ואזיל. **בפרשת יבמין.** "ובן אין לו" — עיין עליו. **אם כבן אנו** (א). לפטור אמנו מיבום, שהרי היבם קם על שם אחיו לנחלה, כדדרשינן ביבמות (דף כד.), והבן מונעו מלייבם את אמו ומלירש את אביו, ופוטר הוא את אמו ויורש את אביו — ואף הבת כן. וסברא בעלמא הוא. **אילו היה לו בן.** כדכתיב: "כי אין לו בן". וכבר היה ידוע (ב) שהבן יורש את אביו, שהרי היו יודעות פרשת נחלות, כדאמרן לעיל, דלא הוה מספקא להו אלא אי נוטלות חלק בכורה אם לאו. ונמצא שהיו יודעות לדרוש דהאי דכתיב: "ובן אין לו והעברתם" וגו' — הא יש לו בן הוא קודם לבת, ולא כדאמר רב פפא לאביי לעיל בפרקין (דף קי.): אימא בן ובת לא האי לירש בו ולא האי לירש בו. הגה"ה. ואם לאו, שאין הנקבות חשובות זרע — תתייבם אמנו לאחד מאחי אבינו, והוא יירש נחלת אבינו, והבן היוצא ממנו לאמנו יירש אחריו נכסי אבינו. ע"כ תוס'). **והתניא.** "אילו היתה בת לא דברנו". והמקשה עצמו אינו יודע לפרשה. **שאפילו** היה בת לבן **לא** דברנו. שהיו יודעות לדרוש שהבת אינה יורשת עם בת הבן, כדאמרן לעיל. **שלא נישאו אלא להגון להן.** כדאמרן לקמן: בנות צלפחד הותרו להנשא לכל מי שירצו, כדכתיב: "לטוב בעיניהן" וגו', אלא מה אני מקיים "למשפחת מטה אביהן תהיינה לנשים" — עצה טובה השיאן הכתוב, שלא ינשאו אלא להגון להן. אלמא משפחת מטה אביהן הגונין היו. ואשכחן שנישאו להם, כדכתיב: "ותהיינה מחלה ונועה חגלה ומלכה ותרצה לבני דודיהן לנשים", דאף על גב דהותרו לטוב בעיניהן — לא רצו להדבק אלא בהגונים. **לא נישאת פחותה מארבעים.** שהיו מצפות להגון להן. **שוב אינה יולדת.** ואם נתעכבו עד ארבעים שנה לא היה אדם נושא אותן, והן נמי לא היה להן להתעכב עד ארבעים שנה, מאחר שלא ילדו עוד. ומשני: מתוך שצדקניות היו. בטוחות בצדקתן שיעשה להם נס כיוכבד, ולכך נתעכבו עד ארבעים שנה בשביל להנשא להגון, כיוכבד שילדה אחר ארבעים. ומיהו, נישואיה איכא למימר דהיו קודם ארבעים.

אפשר

אילו היה לו בן לא דברנו. כ"ה: שכבר היו יודעות פרשת נחלות. וקשה: דהא אכתי לא נאמרה, כדאמרינן לעיל: שזכו בנות צלפחד ונכתבה על ידן! ועוד: דאפילו ידעות פרשת נחלות דבן ובת יורשין, היאך יודעות דבן קודם לבת? הא אכתי לא נאמר "וכל בת יורשת נחלה", ואם כן איכא למימר כדפריך רב פפא לעיל לאביי: איכא בן ובת לא האי לירות כו'! ועוד: אם היו יודעות פרשת נחלות — למה הוצרכו לדבר מכח פרשת יבמין? ונראה לרשב"א: דהיו יודעות מ"והתנחלתם לבניכם" ולא לבנותיכם. א"נ, מסברא, משום דבת (ג) מעכבת נחלה ולא בן. אי נמי, מדכתיב "לאלה תחלק (את) הארץ" — היינו זכרים. ועוד קשיא לן, דקאמר: אילו היה בת לבן לא דברנו — והא אכתי לא נאמר משמוש נחלה! ונראה לפרש "לא דברנו" — לפי שלא היה להן אז שום כח לדבר, אבל עכשיו שאין [בת] בן — יש ד)(להן כח) מפרשת יבמין. **אפילו** קטנה שבהן **לא נשאת פחות מארבעים** שנה. נראה לרשב"א דסבר לה כמ"ד (שבת דף נו:): צלפחד היינו מקושש, ומעשה המקושש היה בתחלת ארבעים מיד אחר מעשה מרגלים. דאמר במדרש דלשם שמים נתכוין, שהיו אומרים ישראל כיון שנגזר עליהן שלא ליכנס לארץ ממעשה מרגלים — שוב אין מחוייבין במצות, עמד וחילל שבת כדי שיהרג ויראו אחרים. ולא נשאו עד סוף ארבעים שנה, כדמוכחי קראי.

מתיב

רבינו גרשום

ומאי קמיבעיא ליה למשה. אם נוטלות חלק בכורה אם לאו הואיל דמוחזק הוא הרי ידע דודאי נוטלות והא לא אצטריך וקשיא לרבא דאמר ארץ ישראל מוחזקת היא. ומשני לעולם מוחזקת היא ודקא קשיא לך מאי קא מיבעיא ליה. היא גופה קא מיבעיא ליה אי מוחזקת היא כי היכי דנוטלות חלק בכורה אי לאו וכהאי גוונא דכתיב ונתתי אותה לכם מורשה אני ה' דאמר להו ליוצאי מצרים ומשום הכי מספקא ליה האי דקאמר הכי משמע ירושה היא לכם מאבותיכם ממש ולא לבניכם ותטלו חלק בכורה (ולא לבניכם) או דלמא הכי קאמר מורשה משמע אתם מורישין אותה לבניכם דנוטלין בה פי שנים אבל אתם אין יורשין אותה משום דבמדבר יפלו פגריכם משום דמספקא ליה אי אמרי' הכי אי הכי קא (מיבעיא) [פשטו] לי' ב"ד של מעלה תרוייהו ירושה היא לכם מאבותיכם ותטלו בה פי שנים דכבר מוחזקת היא לכם מאבותיכם אבל מורישין אתם אותה לבניכם ואין אתם יורשין אותה. והיינו דקאמר בהאי לישנא מורשה כלומר להוריש ולא לירש: ומתנבאין ואינן יודעין מה מתנבאין. כלומר שניבאו על עצמן שלא יכנסו לארץ אלא בניהם ולא נתכוונו לכך: אפשר עמדו לפני משה ולא אמר להם כלום וכו'. אם משה שהיה רבם לא היה יודע להשיב להן כל שכן אידך ומאי קא בעיין קמייהו תו: אלא סרס. הפך את המקרא הקדם המאוחר ודרוש ותעמודנה לפני העדה ולפני הנשיאים ולפני אלעזר הכהן ולפני משה: מר סבר. ר' יאשיה: חולקין כבוד לתלמיד במקום הרב. דשואלין לתלמיד תחלה אפי' במקום הרב ואבא חנן סבר אין חולקין אלא למשה שאלו הלכו ועמדו כולם לפני משה לידע מה משיב להן: הא דפליג ליה רביה יקרא. שמכבדו ונושאו כבוד חולקין: שלפי שעה דברו. כלומר המתינו עד שנזדמנה שעה טובה לדבר בשעה שפוסק משה בפרשת יבמין ואמרו אם כבן אנו נחשבין נירש כבן כדאמרינן בריש פירקין כיון דלענין ייבום בן ובת כי הדדי נינהו לענין נחלה נמי בן ובת כי הדדי ליהוי. ואי לאו דהוי כמאן דלית לאבינו יורש תתייבם אמנו וחכמה היא זו: דרשניות היו. שהיו יודעות לדרוש דבת במקום בן אינה ירשת מדקאמרי ובנים לא היו לו מכלל דאם היו לו קודמין: והתניא בת. כלומר דאית ברייתא דאמר שאלמלי היה בת לא דברנו: סמי מיכן בת. דהאי ברייתא לאו דוקא דהנהו גופייהו בנות הוו: שאפי' היה לאבינו בת לבן והבן מת בחייו לא דברנו שהיינו יודעין שבת הבן קודמת לנו והיינו דקאמר דרשניות היו שהיו יודעין לדרוש כן: לא נישאת פחותה ממ' שנה. שהמתינו להגון להם:

אפשר

ל א ב מיי' פ"ה מהל' ת"ת הלכה ח סמג עשין יג טוש"ע י"ד סי' רמב סעיף כא [וברב אלפס קדושין פ"א דף רכח:]

א) [שבת לב. וש"נ: ב) ע"ז נג:]: ג) [יומא סט. סוטה מ: מג:]: ד) רש"ל להוכיח.

הגהות הב"ח

(א) רשב"ם ד"ה אם כבן אנו תשובות לפטור אמנו מייבום נ"ב שהרי: (ב) ד"ה אילו וכו' ידוע להן שהבן: (ג) תום' ד"ה אילו בן וכו' דבת מעכבת נחלה ולא בן וכו' דקאמר אפילו היה בת.

אֶפְשָׁר בַּת מֵאָה וּשְׁלֹשִׁים שָׁנָה וְקָרָא לָהּ "בַּת"? דְּאָמַר ר' חָמָא בַּר חֲנִינָא: זוֹ יוֹכֶבֶד שֶׁהוֹרָתָהּ בַּדֶּרֶךְ וְנוֹלְדָה בֵּין הַחוֹמוֹת, דִּכְתִיב: "אֲשֶׁר יָלְדָה אוֹתָהּ לְלֵוִי בְּמִצְרָיִם", לֵידָתָהּ בְּמִצְרַיִם וְהוֹרָתָהּ שֶׁלֹּא בְּמִצְרַיִם. וְאַמַּאי קָרוּ לָהּ "בַּת"? אָמַר רַב יְהוּדָה בַּר זְבִידָא: מְלַמֵּד שֶׁנּוֹלְדוּ בָּהּ סִימָנֵי נַעֲרוּת, נִתְעַדֵּן הַבָּשָׂר, נִתְפַּשְּׁטוּ הַקְּמָטִין, וְחָזַר הַיּוֹפִי לִמְקוֹמוֹ. "וַיִּקַּח" – "וַיַּחֲזוֹר" מִיבָּעֵי לֵיהּ! אָמַר רַב יְהוּדָה בַּר זְבִידָא: מְלַמֵּד שֶׁעָשָׂה לָהּ מַעֲשֵׂה לִקּוּחִין, הוֹשִׁיבָהּ בְּאַפִּרְיוֹן, וְאַהֲרֹן וּמִרְיָם מְשׁוֹרְרִים לְפָנֶיהָ, וּמַלְאֲכֵי שָׁרֵת אוֹמְרִים: "אֵם הַבָּנִים שְׂמֵחָה". לְהַלָּן מְנָאָן הַכָּתוּב דֶּרֶךְ גְּדוּלָּתָן וְכָאן דֶּרֶךְ חָכְמָתָן. מְסַיְּיעָא לֵיהּ לְרַבִּי אַמִי, דְּא"ר אַמִי: בִּישִׁיבָה הַלֵּךְ אַחַר חָכְמָה, בִּמְסִיבָּה הַלֵּךְ אַחַר זִקְנָה. א"ר אַשִׁי: וְהוּא דְּמַפְלִיג בְּחָכְמָה, וְהוּא דְּמַפְלִיג בְּזִקְנָה. תָּנָא דְּבֵי רַבִּי יִשְׁמָעֵאל: בְּנוֹת צְלָפְחָד שְׁקוּלוֹת הָיוּ, שֶׁנֶּאֱמַר: "וַתִּהְיֶינָה", הֲוָיָה אַחַת לְכוּלָּן. אָמַר רַב יְהוּדָה אָמַר שְׁמוּאֵל: בְּנוֹת צְלָפְחָד הוּתְּרוּ לְהִנָּשֵׂא לְכָל הַשְּׁבָטִים, שֶׁנֶּאֱמַר: "לַטּוֹב בְּעֵינֵיהֶם תִּהְיֶינָה לְנָשִׁים", אֶלָּא מָה אֲנִי מְקַיֵּים "אַךְ לְמִשְׁפַּחַת מַטֵּה אֲבִיהֶם תִּהְיֶינָה לְנָשִׁים"? עֵצָה טוֹבָה הִשִּׂיאָן הַכָּתוּב, שֶׁלֹּא יִנָּשְׂאוּ אֶלָּא לְהָגוּן לָהֶן. מוֹתִיב רַבָּה: "אֱמוֹר אֲלֵיהֶם" – לְאוֹתָן הָעוֹמְדִים עַל הַר סִינַי, "לְדוֹרוֹתֵיכֶם" – אֵלּוּ דּוֹרוֹת הַבָּאִים. אִם נֶאֱמַר אָבוֹת לָמָּה נֶאֱמַר בָּנִים, וְאִם נֶאֱמַר בָּנִים לָמָּה נֶאֱמַר אָבוֹת? מִפְּנֵי שֶׁיֵּשׁ בָּאָבוֹת מַה שֶּׁאֵין בַּבָּנִים, וְיֵשׁ בַּבָּנִים מַה שֶּׁאֵין בָּאָבוֹת; בָּאָבוֹת הוּא אוֹמֵר: "וְכָל בַּת יוֹרֶשֶׁת נַחֲלָה", וְהַרְבֵּה מִצְוֹת נִצְטַוּוּ בָּנִים שֶׁלֹּא נִצְטַוּוּ אָבוֹת; הָא מִפְּנֵי שֶׁיֵּשׁ בָּאָבוֹת שֶׁאֵין בַּבָּנִים, וְיֵשׁ בַּבָּנִים מַה שֶּׁאֵין בָּאָבוֹת – הוּצְרַךְ לוֹמַר אָבוֹת הוּצְרַךְ לוֹמַר בָּנִים. קָתָנֵי מִיהַת: בָּאָבוֹת הוּא אוֹמֵר: "וְכָל בַּת יוֹרֶשֶׁת נַחֲלָה"! הוּא מוֹתִיב לָהּ, וְהוּא מְפָרֵק לָהּ: לְבַר מִבְּנוֹת צְלָפְחָד. אָמַר מָר: בָּאָבוֹת הוּא אוֹמֵר "וְכָל בַּת יוֹרֶשֶׁת נַחֲלָה". בָּאָבוֹת – אִין, בַּבָּנִים – לָא, מַאי מַשְׁמַע? אָמַר רָבָא, אָמַר קְרָא: "זֶה הַדָּבָר", דָּבָר זֶה לֹא יְהֵא נוֹהֵג אֶלָּא בְּדוֹר זֶה. אָמַר לֵיהּ רַבָּה זוּטֵי לְרַב אַשִׁי: אֶלָּא מֵעַתָּה, "זֶה הַדָּבָר" דִּשְׁחוּטֵי חוּץ, הָכִי נַמִי דְּלֹא יְהֵא נוֹהֵג אֶלָּא בְּדוֹר זֶה?! שָׁאנֵי הָתָם, דִּכְתִיב: "לְדוֹרוֹתָם".

זה

רשב"ם

אֶפְשָׁר בַּת מֵאָה וְל' שָׁנָה. כִּדְלְקַמָּן, וְקָרֵי לָהּ "בַּת"? אִשָּׁה הֲוָה לֵיהּ לְמִיכְתַּב! וּמְנָלַן דְּבַת מֵאָה וּשְׁלֹשִׁים הָיְתָה? דְּאָמַר ר' חָמָא בַּר חֲנִינָא. לְקַמָּן בְּפִירְקִין. דְּמִבָּעֲיָא לָן, דְּבִכְלָלָן אַתָּה מוֹצֵא שִׁבְעִים, וּבִפְרָטָן אִי אַתָּה מוֹצֵא אֶלָּא שִׁבְעִים חָסֵר אַחַת, וְעַל זוֹ א"ר חָמָא בַּר חֲנִינָא: זוֹ יוֹכֶבֶד כו', וּ"בַת לֵוִי" דְּקָאָמַר קְרָא הַיְינוּ בַּת לֵוִי מַמָּשׁ, בִּתּוֹ שֶׁל לֵוִי, וְהָא דְּלָא קָחָשֵׁיב לָהּ בְּהֶדְיָא – לְפִי שֶׁלֹּא בָּאָה לְמִצְרַיִם אֶלָּא בְּבֶטֶן אִמָּהּ. וְלֵידָתָהּ בֵּין הַחוֹמוֹת – כְּלוֹמַר בְּתוֹךְ מִצְרַיִם, וּמִשּׁוּם דְּקָאָמַר "בַּדֶּרֶךְ" גַּבֵּי הוֹרָתָהּ, קָאָמַר נַמִי "בֵּין הַחוֹמוֹת" גַּבֵּי לֵידָתָהּ. אֲשֶׁר יָלְדָה. קְרָא יְתֵירָא הוּא, דְּהָא כְּבָר כְּתִיב "בַּת לֵוִי". וְיִשְׂרָאֵל עָמְדוּ בְּמִצְרַיִם מָאתַיִם וָעֶשֶׂר שָׁנָה, שֶׁכֵּן רָמַז יַעֲקֹב לְבָנָיו: רְד"וּ שָׁמָּה. וּבְסֵדֶר עוֹלָם יָלֵיף מִקְּרָא: נֶאֱמַר לְאַבְרָהָם בִּבְרִית בֵּין הַבְּתָרִים: "כִּי גֵר יִהְיֶה זַרְעֲךָ בְּאֶרֶץ לֹא לָהֶם", אֵיזֶה זֶרַע – זֶה יִצְחָק, שֶׁנֶּאֱמַר: "כִּי בְיִצְחָק יִקָּרֵא לְךָ זָרַע". בְּיִצְחָק הוּא אוֹמֵר: "וְיִצְחָק בֶּן שִׁשִּׁים שָׁנָה בְּלֶדֶת אוֹתָם", וְיַעֲקֹב אָבִינוּ אָמַר לְפַרְעֹה: "יְמֵי שְׁנֵי מְגוּרַי שְׁלֹשִׁים וּמְאַת שָׁנָה", הֲרֵי ס' דְּיִצְחָק וְק"ל דְּיַעֲקֹב – הֲרֵי מֵאָה וְתִשְׁעִים. וּמָאתַיִם וְי' עָמְדוּ בְּמִצְרַיִם – הֲרֵי ד' מֵאוֹת שָׁנָה שֶׁנֶּאֶמְרוּ לְאַבְרָהָם. וְכָל ד' מֵאוֹת שָׁנָה הָיוּ בְּמִצְרַיִם – אִי אֶפְשָׁר לוֹמַר, שֶׁהֲרֵי קְהָת מִיּוֹרְדֵי מִצְרַיִם הָיָה, כִּדְכְתִיב: "וּבְנֵי לֵוִי גֵּרְשׁוֹן קְהָת וּמְרָרִי", וּשְׁנֵי חַיֵּי קְהָת שָׁלֹשׁ וּשְׁלֹשִׁים וּמְאַת שָׁנָה, וּשְׁנֵי חַיֵּי עַמְרָם שֶׁבַע וּשְׁלֹשִׁים וּמְאַת שָׁנָה, וּפ' שָׁנָה שֶׁל מֹשֶׁה – הֲרֵי ש"נ. א"כ מַה ת"ל "וַעֲבָדוּם וְעִנּוּ אוֹתָם אַרְבַּע מֵאוֹת שָׁנָה"? (א) כ"ז שֶׁזַּרְעֲךָ בְּאֶרֶץ לֹא לָהֶם ת' שָׁנָה. נִמְצֵאת יוֹכֶבֶד בַּת ק"ל שָׁנָה, שֶׁהֲרֵי בִּתְחִלַּת בִּיאַת מִצְרַיִם נוֹלְדָה, וּמֹשֶׁה בֶּן פ' שָׁנָה הָיָה בְּצֵאתָם – נִשְׁתַּיְּירוּ ק"ל מִמָּאתַיִם וָעֶשֶׂר. נִתְעַדֵּן הַבָּשָׂר. הֶחֱלִיק כְּנַעַר קָטָן. וַיַּחֲזוֹר מִיבָּעֵי לֵיהּ. שֶׁהֲרֵי עָבְרוּ יָמִים רַבִּים שֶׁלְּקָחָהּ, שֶׁהֲרֵי כְּבָר נוֹלְדוּ אַהֲרֹן וּמִרְיָם! אֶלָּא שֶׁפֵּירַשׁ עַמְרָם מִמֶּנָּה מִפְּנֵי הַגְּזֵירָה שֶׁהָיוּ מַשְׁלִיכִין הַזְּכָרִים לַיְאוֹר, וְעַכְשָׁיו הֶחֱזִירָהּ מִפְּנֵי מִרְיָם שֶׁנִּתְנַבְּאָה לוֹ שֶׁעָתִיד בֵּן לָצֵאת מִמֶּנּוּ שֶׁיּוֹשִׁיעַ אֶת יִשְׂרָאֵל. כִּדְנַפְקָא לָן (סוטה דף יב:) מִדִּכְתִיב: "מִרְיָם הַנְּבִיאָה אֲחוֹת אַהֲרֹן", בְּעוֹד שֶׁהִיא אֲחוֹת אַהֲרֹן – וְלֹא אֲחוֹת מֹשֶׁה, שֶׁעֲדַיִין לֹא נוֹלַד – הָיְתָה הִיא נְבִיאָה, שֶׁנִּתְנַבְּאָה עַל מֹשֶׁה שֶׁעָתִיד לְהִוָּלֵד. מְשׁוֹרְרִין. מִתּוֹךְ שִׂמְחָה, שֶׁהָיָה עָתִיד מֹשֶׁה רַבֵּינוּ לָצֵאת מֵהֶן. וְהַיְינוּ דִּכְתִיב: "לְדֵעָה מַה יֵּעָשֶׂה לוֹ" – מַה יִּהְיֶה סוֹף נְבוּאָתָהּ, כִּדְאִיתָא בְּסוֹטָה (דף יג.). לְהַלָּן. כְּשֶׁנִּישְּׂאוּ בְּנוֹת צְלָפְחָד, מְנָאָן הַכָּתוּב דֶּרֶךְ גְּדוּלָּתָן, דִּכְתִיב: "וַתִּהְיֶינָה מַחְלָה תִרְצָה חָגְלָה וּמִלְכָּה וְנוֹעָה בְּנוֹת צְלָפְחָד לִבְנֵי דוֹדֵיהֶן לְנָשִׁים", וּמְסַתֵּבֵר דְּכָךְ נוֹלְדוּ, כִּדְכְתִיב "לֹא יֵעָשֶׂה כֵן בִּמְקוֹמֵנוּ לָתֵת הַצְּעִירָה לִפְנֵי הַבְּכִירָה" (בראשית כט). וְכָאן. כְּשֶׁעָמְדוּ לִפְנֵי מֹשֶׁה – דֶּרֶךְ חָכְמָתָם, כְּסֵדֶר שֶׁהֵן חֲכָמוֹת זוֹ יוֹתֵר מִזּוֹ, הִקְדִּימָן הַכָּתוּב "מַחְלָה נוֹעָה חָגְלָה מִלְכָּה וְתִרְצָה". וּמִסְּבָרָא אָמְרִי' הָכִי, דְּלָא לִיקְשׁוּ קְרָאֵי אַהֲדָדֵי. בִּישִׁיבָה. בֵּין לְדִין, בֵּין לִשְׁאָר יְשִׁיבוֹת שֶׁל תּוֹרָה – מוֹשִׁיבִין אֶת הֶחָכָם לְמַעְלָה מִן הַזָּקֵן. וּכְדִמְפָרֵשׁ לְקַמֵּיהּ, שֶׁהֶחָכָם מוּפְלָג מִכָּל חֲבֵירָיו בְּחָכְמָה, שֶׁחָכָם הוּא מְאֹד. אֲבָל בִּשְׁבִיל שֶׁהוּא חָכָם מְעַט מִן הַזָּקֵן – אֵין מְכַבְּדִין אוֹתוֹ יוֹתֵר מִן הַזָּקֵן שֶׁהוּא חָכָם קְצָת. וּמִבְּנוֹת צְלָפְחָד אִיכָּא לְמֵילַף דְּגַבֵּי שְׁאֵלַת הַדִּין מַקְדִּים הַכָּתוּב חָכְמָה תְּחִלָּה. בִּמְסִיבָּה. שֶׁל מִשְׁתֶּה, וְה"ה לְנִישּׂוּאִין (ב). וְהוּא דְּמַפְלִיג. הֶחָכָם בְּחָכְמָה, אָז הַלֵּךְ אַחַר הַחָכְמָה וְלֹא אַחַר זִקְנָה. וְהוּא דְּמַפְלִיג בְּזִקְנָה. שֶׁזָּקֵן מְאֹד, אָז חוֹלְקִין לוֹ כָּבוֹד בְּבֵית הַמִּשְׁתֶּה יוֹתֵר מִן הֶחָכָם, וְאע"ג דְּמוּפְלָג הַהוּא חָכָם בְּחָכְמָה. וּכְגוֹן שֶׁהַזָּקֵן חָכָם קְצָת, אֲבָל אִם אֵינוֹ מוּפְלָג בְּזִקְנָה – הֶחָכָם שֶׁהוּא מוּפְלָג קוֹדֵם לִכְבוֹדוֹ. שָׁמְעִינַן מֵהָכָא, דְּחָכָם מוּפְלָג, וְזָקֵן מוּפְלָג שֶׁאֵינוֹ חָכָם כָּל כָּךְ כְּבָחוּר – בִּישִׁיבָה הַלֵּךְ אַחַר חָכְמָה, לְהוֹשִׁיב הֶחָכָם בָּרֹאשׁ וּלְדַבֵּר תְּחִלָּה, בִּמְסִיבָּה הַלֵּךְ אַחַר זִקְנָה. וְהֵיכָא דְּחָכָם הָוֵי מוּפְלָג בְּחָכְמָה, וְהַזָּקֵן אֵינוֹ מוּפְלָג בְּזִקְנָה – בְּכ"מ הַלֵּךְ אַחַר חָכְמָה, אֲפִילּוּ בִּמְסִיבָּה. וְהֵיכָא דְּהַזָּקֵן הָוֵי מוּפְלָג בְּזִקְנָה וְהֶחָכָם אֵינוֹ מוּפְלָג בְּחָכְמָה – בְּכָל מָקוֹם הַלֵּךְ אַחַר זִקְנָה, וַאֲפִילּוּ בִּישִׁיבָה, הוֹאִיל וְהַזָּקֵן חָכָם קְצָת, אע"פ שֶׁהַבָּחוּר חָכָם יוֹתֵר מִמֶּנּוּ. וְהֵיכָא דְּלֹא מוּפְלָג לֹא הַאי בְּחָכְמָה וְלֹא הַאי בְּזִקְנָה – נִרְאֶה בְּעֵינַי דִּבְכָל מָקוֹם הַלֵּךְ אַחַר זִקְנָה. מִדְּקָאָמַר רַב אַשִׁי: וְהוּא דְּמוּפְלָג בְּחָכְמָה וְהוּא דְּמוּפְלָג בְּזִקְנָה, דְּהֵיכָא דְּהָווּ תַּרְוַיְיהוּ מוּפְלָגִין הוֹלְכִים בִּישִׁיבָה אַחַר הֶחָכָם, וּבִמְסִיבָּה אַחַר הַזָּקֵן – מִכְּלָל דְּהֵיכָא דְּלָא הָווּ תַּרְוַיְיהוּ מוּפְלָגִין לָא הַאי וְלָא הַאי, הוֹלְכִין בְּכָל מָקוֹם אַחַר אֶחָד מֵהֶן, וּמִדְּלָא פֵּירֵשׁ – אִיכָּא לְמֵימַר דְּמִסְתַּמָּא הוֹלְכִין אַחַר הַזָּקֵן, דְּבִשְׁבִיל שֶׁהַבָּחוּר חָכָם קְצָת יוֹתֵר מִמֶּנּוּ אֵין לָנוּ לְבַיֵּישׁ אֶת הַזָּקֵן, וְהֶחָכָם אֵינוֹ בּוֹשׁ בְּכָךְ, מֵאַחַר שֶׁזָּקֵן מִמֶּנּוּ יוֹדֵעַ הוּא שֶׁבִּשְׁבִיל זִקְנָתוֹ חוֹלְקִין לוֹ כָּבוֹד. שְׁקוּלוֹת הָיוּ. וּלְכָךְ פְּעָמִים שֶׁהִקְדִּים זוֹ לָזוֹ וּפְעָמִים אִיפְּכָא, כִּדְדָרְשִׁינַן נַמִי ה) (מגילה דף יג): "הוּא אַהֲרֹן וּמֹשֶׁה" "הוּא מֹשֶׁה וְאַהֲרֹן" – מְלַמֵּד שֶׁשְּׁקוּלִין הָיוּ. וְלָא תְּסַיְּיעֵיהּ לְר' אַמִי. וַתִּהְיֶינָה. מְיוּתָּר הוּא, דְּמָצֵי לְמִכְתַּב: בְּנוֹת צְלָפְחָד לִבְנֵי דוֹדֵיהֶן לְנָשִׁים. הוּתְּרוּ. אע"פ שֶׁשְּׁאָר בַּת יוֹרֶשֶׁת נַחֲלָה נֶאֶסְרָה. עֵצָה טוֹבָה. וְאֵינָהּ מִצְוַת עֲשֵׂה. אֱמוֹר אֲלֵיהֶם לְדוֹרוֹתֵיכֶם כָּל אִישׁ אֲשֶׁר יִקְרַב מִכָּל זַרְעֲכֶם אֶל הַקֳּדָשִׁים אֲשֶׁר יַקְדִּישׁוּ בְנֵי יִשְׂרָאֵל לַה' וְטֻמְאָתוֹ עָלָיו. אֱמוֹר אֲלֵיהֶם. הַיְינוּ לְאוֹתָן הָעוֹמְדִין עַל הַר סִינַי נִשְׁנָה פָּסוּק זֶה. וּמִכָּאן תַּלְמוּד לִשְׁאָר מִצְוֹת הָאֲמוּרוֹת בַּתּוֹרָה סְתָם, שֶׁנֶּאֶמְרוּ בֵּין לָאָבוֹת בֵּין לַדּוֹרוֹת הַבָּאִין. וְכָל בַּת וגו'. לְיוֹצְאֵי מִצְרַיִם נֶאֱמַר, כִּדְמְפָרֵשׁ לְקַמֵּיהּ. אֲבָל לַדּוֹרוֹת הַבָּאִין לֵיכָּא אִיסּוּר הַסַּבַּת נַחֲלָה. נִצְטַוּוּ בָּנִים. מִצְוֹת הַתְּלוּיוֹת בָּאָרֶץ, תְּרוּמָה וּמַעֲשֵׂר חַלָּה עָרְלָה וְרִבְעִי לֶקֶט שִׁכְחָה וּפֵאָה, וְכֵן הַרְבֵּה. הוּצְרַךְ לוֹמַר לָאָבוֹת וְהוּצְרַךְ לוֹמַר לַבָּנִים. שֶׁאִם נִכְתַּב סְתָם וְלֹא פֵּירֵשׁ לֹא אָבוֹת וְלֹא בָּנִים – הֲוָה אוֹקִימְנָא לֵיהּ בָּאָבוֹת, מִדְּלָא כְּתַב "כִּי תָבוֹאוּ" כִּדְכְתַב בִּשְׁאָר מִצְוֹת הָאֲמוּרוֹת לַבָּנִים. אִי נַמִי, הֲוֵי יָלְפִינַן אוֹ בִּגְזֵירָה שָׁוָה אוֹ בְּבִנְיַן אָב אוֹ בְּקַל וָחוֹמֶר מֵאַחַת מִמִּצְוֹת הַמְפוֹרָשׁוֹת לַבָּנִים אוֹ לָאָבוֹת, וַהֲוֵי אוֹקִימְנָא לֵיהּ בְּאַחַת מֵהֶן. לְהָכִי כְּתִיבִי תַּרְוַיְיהוּ, וּמֵהַשְׁתָּא נֵילַף מֵהָכָא לְכָל מִצְוֹת הַסְּתוּמוֹת, שֶׁנּוֹהֲגוֹת בֵּין בַּבָּנִים בֵּין בָּאָבוֹת, עַד שֶׁיְּפָרֵט לְךָ הַכָּתוּב "כִּי תָבוֹאוּ" אוֹ יִכְתּוֹב לְךָ "זֶה הַדָּבָר" לְהַעֲמִידוֹ בַּדּוֹר הַזֶּה, כִּדְלְקַמָּן. לְבַר מִבְּנוֹת צְלָפְחָד. דְּהַאי "וְכָל בַּת יוֹרֶשֶׁת נַחֲלָה" לָאו אַבְּנוֹת צְלָפְחָד קָאֵי, דְּהָא גָּלֵי לְהוּ קְרָא "לַטּוֹב בְּעֵינֵיהֶם תִּהְיֶינָה לְנָשִׁים". מַאי מַשְׁמַע. דְּהַאי קְרָא לָא מִשְׁתָּעֵי אֶלָּא בְּאוֹתוֹ הַדּוֹר. זֶה הַדָּבָר. "אֲשֶׁר צִוָּה ה' לִבְנוֹת צְלָפְחָד וגו' וְלֹא תִסּוֹב נַחֲלָה". וְעַל כָּרְחָךְ הַאי "זֶה" לָאו אַבְּנוֹת צְלָפְחָד קָאֵי, אֶלָּא אַ"וְכָל בַּת יוֹרֶשֶׁת נַחֲלָה" דִּכְתִיב בַּתְרֵיהּ, "וְלֹא תִסּוֹב נַחֲלָה". זֶה הַדָּבָר אֲשֶׁר צִוָּה ה' דִּשְׁחוּטֵי חוּץ. "זֶה הַדָּבָר אֲשֶׁר צִוָּה ה' אִישׁ אִישׁ מִבְּנֵי יִשְׂרָאֵל אֲשֶׁר יִשְׁחַט שׁוֹר אוֹ כֶשֶׂב אוֹ עֵז בַּמַּחֲנֶה", דְּהָכִי נַמִי דְּלֹא הוּזְהֲרוּ עַל שְׁחוּטֵי חוּץ אֶלָּא אוֹתוֹ דּוֹר בִּלְבַד? שָׁאנֵי הָתָם. דִּכְתִיב: "חוּקַּת עוֹלָם תִּהְיֶה זֹּאת לָהֶם לְדוֹרוֹתָם".

זה

תורה אור

אשר ילדה אותה ללוי במצרים (במדבר כו) | אם הבנים שמחה (תהלים קיג) | לטוב בעיניהם תהיינה לנשים (במדבר לו) | אך למשפחת מטה אביהם תהיינה לנשים (שם) | אמור אליהם (ויקרא כב) | וכל בת יורשת נחלה (במדבר לו) | זה הדבר (שם) | זה הדבר (ויקרא יז) | לדורותם (שם)

תוספות

מתיב רבה אמור אליהם לדורותיכם וגו'. תימה לרשב"א: דמה לריך להקשות מברייתא? מקרא הוה ליה לאקשויי, דכתיב "לא תסוב נחלה"! ואומר ר"י: דה"א עלה טובה קמ"ל.

שהפרת

מסורת הש"ס

א) סוטה יב.: ב) לקמן קכג.: ג) [יבמות עח.]: ד) [לקמן קכא. תענית ל:]: ה) [לא נמלא בכל הש"ס אלא בתוספתא סוף כריתות]:

עין משפט נר מצוה

לא א ב טוש"ע י"ד סי' רמד סעי' יח [ברב אלפס קידושין פ"א ד' רכא]:

הגהות הב"ח

(א) רשב"ם ד"ה אשר ילדה וכו' שנה אלא כל זמן: (ב) ד"ה במסיבה וכו' לנישואין כבנות צלפחד הס"ד:

רבינו גרשום

אפשר בת מאה ושלשים וקרי לה בת. ומנלן דבת הכי הואי דאמר ר' חמא בר חנינא לקמן (קכג:) זו יוכבד שהשלימה מנין שבעים נפש שהורתה היתה בדרך שירדו למצרים ולידתה בין החומות כלומר בתוך חומות של מצרים ישראל משעה שנכנסו למצרים ועד שיצאו רד"ו שנה ובאותו פרק נגאלו ישראל טול ממאתים ועשר שמונים שנה נשתיירו מאה ושלשים שנה ונמצא שבשעה שנולד משה היתה אמו בת מאה ושלשים: ויקח ויחזור מיבעי ליה. שקודם לכן ילדה מרים ואהרן וגרשה כשגזר פרעה כל הבן הילוד: להלן. כשנשאו לבעל בנות צלפחד: מנאן הכתוב דרך גדולתן. כדרך שנולדו כדכתי' ותהיינה מחלה תרצה חגלה ומלכה ונועה: וכאן. כשעמדו לפני משה: מנאן הכתוב דרך חכמתן. כדכתיב ותקרבנה בנות צלפחד ואלה שמות בנותיו מחלה ונועה חגלה ומלכה ותרצה: בישיבה. בבית המדרש היו יושבין לפי חכמתן אע"פ שהוא בחור והושיבו למעלה: במסיבה. בסעודה: והוא דמופלג בחכמה ובזקנה. יותר מן האחרים: כולם שקולות. בחכמה: אלא להגון להם. שהוא חשוב במשפחת אביהן: מתיב רבא. האי קרא דכתיב גבי טומאת מקדש וקדשיו אמור אליהם לדורותיכם אלו הבנים משום הכי איצטריך למימר להו לתרוייהו מפני שיש מצות שנצטוו אבות ולא נצטוו בנים: באבות הוא אומר וכל בת יורשת נחלה. שלא היה נוהג אלא באותו דור כדאמרי' לקמן: והרבה מצות נצטוו בנים ולא אבות. כגון חלה ותרומה ומעשר וכל מצות הנוהגות בארץ מה שלא היו יכולין לקיים במדבר משום הכי הוצרך להזהיר אבות ובנים על טומאת מקדש וקדשיו: קתני מיהת באבות הוא אומר וכל בת יורשת נחלה וגו'. אלמא דבנות צלפחד לא הותרו לינשא אלא למשפחת אביהם ולא לכל מי שירצו וקשיא לרב יהודה: לבר מבנות צלפחד. דהותרו: אלא מעתה זה הדבר דכתיב גבי שחוטי חוץ. זה הדבר אשר צוה ה' לאמר איש איש מבני ישראל אשר ישחט שור

°"זֶה א)הַדָּבָר" דְּרָאשֵׁי הַמַּטּוֹת, הָכִי נַמִּי דְּלֹא יְהֵא נוֹהֵג אֶלָּא בְּדוֹר זֶה? א"ל: הַהוּא יָלֵיף "זֶה" "זֶה" מֵהָתָם. הַאי נַמִּי לֵילַיף "זֶה" "זֶה" מֵהָתָם! הַאי מַאי? בִּשְׁלָמָא הָתָם אִיצְטְרִי' ב)לִגְזֵרָה שָׁוָה, הָכָא לְמַאי אִיצְטְרִיךְ? לִשְׁתּוֹק קְרָא מִינֵּיהּ וַאֲנָא יָדַעְנָא דִּלְדוֹרוֹת הוּא. מַאי ג"ש? דְּתַנְיָא: ג)נֶאֱמַר כָּאן "זֶה הַדָּבָר" וְנֶאֱמַר לְהַלָּן °"זֶה הַדָּבָר", מַה לְהַלָּן אַהֲרֹן וּבָנָיו וְכָל יִשְׂרָאֵל, אַף כָּאן אַהֲרֹן וּבָנָיו וְכָל יִשְׂרָאֵל; וּמַה כָּאן רָאשֵׁי הַמַּטּוֹת, אַף לְהַלָּן רָאשֵׁי הַמַּטּוֹת. אָמַר מָר: מַה לְהַלָּן אַהֲרֹן וּבָנָיו וְכָל יִשְׂרָאֵל, אַף כָּאן אַהֲרֹן וּבָנָיו וְכָל יִשְׂרָאֵל. לְמַאי הִלְכְתָא? אָמַר רַב אַחָא בַּר יַעֲקֹב: לוֹמַר, אשֶׁהֲפָרַת נְדָרִים בִּשְׁלֹשָׁה הֶדְיוֹטוֹת. וְהָא "רָאשֵׁי הַמַּטּוֹת" כְּתִיב בֵּיהּ! ד)כִּדְאָמַר רַב חִסְדָּא אָמַר רַבִּי יוֹחָנָן: בְּיָחִיד מוּמְחֶה, ה"נ בבְּיָחִיד מוּמְחֶה.(א) "וּמַה כָּאן רָאשֵׁי הַמַּטּוֹת, אַף לְהַלָּן רָאשֵׁי הַמַּטּוֹת". לְמַאי הִלְכְתָא? אָמַר רַב שֵׁשֶׁת: לוֹמַר, גשֶׁיֵּשׁ שְׁאֵלָה בְּהֶקְדֵּשׁ. וּלְב"ש דְּאָמְרִי: ה)אֵין שְׁאֵלָה בְּהֶקְדֵּשׁ, דִּתְנַן, ו)ב"ש אוֹמְרִים: הֶקְדֵּשׁ טָעוּת הֶקְדֵּשׁ, דוּב"ה אוֹמְרִים: ראֵינוֹ הֶקְדֵּשׁ, הַאי "זֶה" וְ"זֶה" מַאי עָבְדִי לֵיהּ? "זֶה הַדָּבָר" דִּשְׁחוּטֵי חוּץ מִיבְּעֵי לֵיהּ: ז)עַל הַשּׁוֹחֵט הוּא חַיָּב, הוְאֵינוֹ חַיָּב עַל הַמּוֹלֵק; "זֶה הַדָּבָר" דְּרָאשֵׁי הַמַּטּוֹת מִיבְּעֵי לֵיהּ ח)לְחָכָם מַתִּיר וְאֵין בַּעַל מַתִּיר. בַּעַל מֵפֵר יוְאֵין חָכָם מֵפֵר. וּלְבֵית שַׁמַּאי דְּלֵית לְהוּ גְּזֵרָה שָׁוָה, הֲפָרַת נְדָרִים בִּשְׁלֹשָׁה הֶדְיוֹטוֹת מְנָא לְהוּ? נָפְקָא לְהוּ מִדְּתַנְיָא: °"וַיְדַבֵּר מֹשֶׁה אֶת מוֹעֲדֵי ה' אֶל בְּנֵי יִשְׂרָאֵל" — ר' יוֹסֵי הַגְּלִילִי אוֹמֵר: מוֹעֲדֵי

במדבר ל | ויקרא יז | שם כג

תורה אור

רשב"ם

זה הדבר דראשי המטות. דִּכְתִיב: "וַיְדַבֵּר מֹשֶׁה אֶל רָאשֵׁי הַמַּטּוֹת לִבְנֵי יִשְׂרָאֵל לֵאמֹר זֶה הַדָּבָר אֲשֶׁר צִוָּה ה' אִישׁ כִּי יִדֹּר נֶדֶר" וגו', ה"נ לֹא יְהֵא נוֹהֵג דִּין הֲפָרַת נְדָרִים אֶלָּא בַּדּוֹר הַזֶּה? בִּתְמִיָּה. יליף זה. דַּהֲפָרַת נְדָרִים, מִ"זֶּה" דִּשְׁחוּטֵי חוּץ דִּכְתִיב בֵּיהּ דּוֹרוֹת, ה"נ דּוֹרוֹת. וּפָרְכִינַן: ה"נ. לְעִנְיַן הֲסָבַת נַחֲלָה, נֵילַף "זֶה" דִּידֵיהּ מִ"זֶּה" דִּשְׁחוּטֵי חוּץ לְדוֹרוֹת! בשלמא התם. בִּשְׁחוּטֵי חוּץ וּבִנְדָרִים, לְהָכִי כְּתַב "זֶה", דְּהָא אִיצְטְרִיךְ לְהַךְ גְּזֵרָה שָׁוָה דְּבָעֵינַן לְמֵימַר בְּסָמוּךְ, וְהִלְכָּךְ דָּרְשִׁינַן לֵיהּ נַמִּי לְהָא גְּזֵרָה שָׁוָה דַּאֲמָרַן, דְּקַיְימָא לָן: אֵין גְּזֵרָה שָׁוָה לְמֶחֱצָה. אבל הכא. בַּהֲסִיבַּת נַחֲלָה, לָא אִיצְטְרִיךְ הַאי "זֶה" לְשׁוּם גְּזֵרָה שָׁוָה אַחֲרִיתִי, דְּנִדְרְשֵׁיהּ נַמִּי לְמֵילַף "זֶה" מִ"זֶּה" דִּשְׁחוּטֵי חוּץ לְדוֹרוֹת. וּלְהָא גְּזֵרָה שָׁוָה לְחוּד לֵיכָּא לְמֵימַר דִּלְהָכִי אִיצְטְרִיךְ לְמֵילַף מִשְּׁחוּטֵי חוּץ לְדוֹרוֹת, דְּהָא לָא צְרִיךְ קְרָא — לִישְׁתּוֹק קְרָא מִינֵּיהּ, דְּלָא נִכְתְּבֵיהּ כְּלָל, וַאֲנָא יָדַעְנָא דְּוַדַּאי הֲסָבַת נַחֲלָה נוֹהֶגֶת לְדוֹרוֹת, מִידֵּי דַּהֲוָה אַשְּׁאָר מִלֵּי דְּעָלְמָא, דְּלָא גָּרַע הַאי לָאו מִשְּׁאָר לָאוִין שֶׁבַּתּוֹרָה שֶׁהָיוּ נוֹהֲגִין לְעוֹלָם. אֶלָּא מִדִּכְתַבֵיהּ — ש"מ לְמַעוּטֵי אָתָא, דְּאֵינָהּ נוֹהֶגֶת אֶלָּא בַּדּוֹר הַזֶּה. מאי גזירה שוה. דְּיָלְפִי' "זֶה" דִּנְדָרִים וְ"זֶה" דִּשְׁחוּטֵי חוּץ מֵהֲדָדֵי. מה להלן. בִּשְׁחוּטֵי חוּץ, כְּתִיב בְּהוּ: "דַּבֵּר אֶל אַהֲרֹן וְאֶל בָּנָיו וְאֶל כָּל בְּנֵי יִשְׂרָאֵל" — אַף בִּנְדָרִים, אַהֲרֹן וּבָנָיו כְּאִילּוּ כְּתִיב בָּהֶם "וְכָל יִשְׂרָאֵל", כִּדְמְפָרֵשׁ לְקַמָּן לְמַאי הִלְכְתָא. מה כאן ראשי המטות אף להלן. בִּשְׁחוּטֵי חוּץ — רָאשֵׁי הַמַּטּוֹת. וּבְסָמוּךְ מְפָרֵשׁ לָהּ. למאי הלכתא. בָּעֵינַן גַּבֵּי נְדָרִים אַהֲרֹן וּבָנָיו וְכָל יִשְׂרָאֵל? לומר שהפרת נדרים בשלשה הדיוטות. דִּכְתִיב: "לֹא יַחֵל דְּבָרוֹ" — הוּא אֵינוֹ מֵיחֵל, אֲבָל אֲחֵרִים מַתִּירִין לוֹ, כְּגוֹן שְׁלֹשָׁה דַּהֲווּ בֵּית דִּין, כִּדְאָמְרִינַן בְּסַנְהֶדְרִין (דף ג.). וַאֲפִי' לִשְׁמוּאֵל דְּאָמַר הָתָם: שְׁנַיִם שֶׁדָּנוּ דִּינֵיהֶן דִּין, אֶלָּא שֶׁנִּקְרָאוּ ב"ד חָצוּף — הָנֵי מִילֵּי דִּינֵי מָמוֹנוֹת, אֲבָל לְמִישְׁרֵי אִיסּוּר נֶדֶר — לָא סַגִּי בְּפָחוֹת מִג'. וּלְהָכִי אֲהַנֵי גְּזֵרָה שָׁוָה, כְּאִילּוּ נִכְתַּב בִּנְדָרִים אַהֲרֹן וּבָנָיו וְכָל יִשְׂרָאֵל, לוֹמַר לְךָ שֶׁשְּׁקוּלִין כָּל יִשְׂרָאֵל לְהַתִּיר נְדָרִים, וַאֲפִי' הֶדְיוֹטוֹת, כְּאַהֲרֹן וּבָנָיו. הא ראשי המטות כתיב. דְּמַשְׁמַע מוּמְחִין! כדאמר רב חסדא. לְקַמָּן בִּשְׁמַעְתִּין. ה"נ ביחיד מומחה. בָּקִי בַּתַּלְמוּד. כְּלוֹמַר, רַב מוּבְהָק. וְהַאי דִּכְתַב "רָאשֵׁי" לְשׁוֹן רַבִּים — מוּמְחִין דְּעָלְמָא קָאָמַר. למאי הלכתא. צָרִיךְ רָאשֵׁי הַמַּטּוֹת גַּבֵּי שְׁחוּטֵי חוּץ. שיש שאלה בהקדש. כְּמוֹ שֶׁיֵּשׁ שְׁאֵלָה בִּנְדָרִים. דִּבִנְדָרִים כְּתִיב: "לֹא יַחֵל דְּבָרוֹ", וְהוּא הַדִּין לְכָל הֶקְדֵּשׁוֹת. שֶׁאִם שָׁחַט קָדָשִׁים בַּחוּץ וְנִתְחַיֵּיב כָּרֵת, וְאַח"כ הָלַךְ אֵצֶל חָכָם לְהַתִּיר לוֹ הֶקְדֵּשׁוֹ, וּמָצָא לוֹ פֶּתַח שֶׁל חֲרָטָה, וְעָקַר אֶת הַהֶקְדֵּשׁ מֵעִיקָּרוֹ, וַעֲבָדֵיהּ כְּהֶקְדֵּשׁ טָעוּת — אִיגַּלַּאי מִילְּתָא לְמַפְרֵעַ דְּלָא הֲוָה הֶקְדֵּשׁ מֵעוֹלָם, וּפָטוּר מִכָּרֵת. וְהוּא הַדִּין לְכָל דָּבָר הַקָּדוֹשׁ בְּמוֹצָא שְׂפָתָיו, כְּגוֹן תְּרוּמוֹת וּמַעַשְׂרוֹת, דְּאִי בָּעֵי מִיתְשִׁיל עֲלַיְיהוּ וְהוֹזְרִי' לְטִיבְלָן, כִּדְאָמְרִי' בִּנְדָרִים בִּשִׁילְהֵי פֶּרֶק "הַנּוֹדֵר מִן הַיָּרָק" (דף נט.). ולב"ש דאמרי אין שאלה בשום הקדש. בְּעוֹלָם, דַּאֲפִי' כְּשֶׁיִּמְצָא לוֹ הֶחָכָם פֶּתַח שֶׁל חֲרָטָה — אֵינוֹ יָכוֹל לְהַתִּירוֹ. דְּאע"ג דְּשׁוּקַר אֶת הַנֶּדֶר מֵעִיקָּרוֹ וְעוֹשֵׂהוּ נֶדֶר שֶׁל טָעוּת, אֲפִי' הָכִי גַּבֵּי הֶקְדֵּשׁ לָא אָמְרִי ב"ש הָכִי. דַּאֲפִי' כְּשֶׁנַּעֲשָׂה הַהֶקְדֵּשׁ בְּטָעוּת הַיָּדוּעַ לַמַּקְדִּישׁ חָשְׁבִי לֵיהּ הֶקְדֵּשׁ גָּמוּר — כ"ש הֵיכָא דְּהוּקְדַּשׁ בְּלֹא טָעוּת, שֶׁלֹּא יוֹעִיל פֶּתַח הַחֲרָטָה שֶׁיִּמְצָא לוֹ הֶחָכָם לְהַתִּירוֹ. דתנן ב"ש אומרים כו'. תְּחִלַּת הַפֶּרֶק הוּא בְּמַסֶּכֶת נָזִיר. הקדש טעות. כִּדִמְפָרֵשׁ הָתָם: כֵּיצַד? אָמַר "שׁוֹר שָׁחוֹר שֶׁיֵּצֵא מִבֵּיתִי רִאשׁוֹן הֲרֵי הוּא הֶקְדֵּשׁ", וְיָצָא לָבָן, ב"ש אוֹמְרִים: הֶקְדֵּשׁ, וּבֵית הִלֵּל אוֹמְרִים: אֵינוֹ הֶקְדֵּשׁ. וְאָמְרִינַן בַּגְּמָרָא: מַאי טַעֲמַיְיהוּ דב"ש — דְּיָלְפִי תְּחִלַּת הֶקְדֵּשׁ מִסּוֹף הֶקְדֵּשׁ, מַה תְּמוּרָה אֲפִי' בְּטָעוּת — אַף הֶקְדֵּשׁ אֲפִי' בְּטָעוּת. וּבֵית הִלֵּל סָבְרִי: ה"מ תְּמוּרָה, אֲבָל אֲחוּתֵי הֶקְדֵּשׁ בְּטָעוּת לָא מַחְתִּינַן. הקדש טעות הקדש. וְכֵיוָן דִּסְבִירָא לְהוּ דְּהָוֵי הֶקְדֵּשׁ אֲפִי' בְּטָעוּת, כ"ש דִּסְבִירָא לְהוּ דְּכָל הֶקְדֵּשׁ שֶׁהוּקְדַּשׁ בְּלֹא טָעוּת, כְּגוֹן "שׁוֹר זֶה הֶקְדֵּשׁ", דְּלֹא יוּכַל הֶחָכָם לַעֲשׂוֹתוֹ חוּלִּין עַל יְדֵי שׁוּם חֲרָטָה. דְּחָכָם נַמִּי הֶקְדֵּשׁ טָעוּת מְשַׁוֵּי לֵיהּ, וְהֶקְדֵּשׁ שֶׁטָּעוּתוֹ יָדוּעַ לַמַּקְדִּישׁ, לְבֵית הִלֵּל אֲפִי' שְׁאֵלָה אֵין צָרִיךְ, שֶׁהֲרֵי הוּא עַצְמוֹ יוֹדֵעַ שֶׁלֹּא נִתְכַּוֵּין לְהַקְדִּישׁ אֶת זֶה. וְכֵיוָן דְּחָשְׁבִי לֵיהּ בֵּית שַׁמַּאי הֶקְדֵּשׁ גָּמוּר — אַלְמָא שְׁאֵילַת חָכָם אֵין מוֹעִיל. וב"ה אומרים כו' וַאֲפִילּוּ שְׁאֵלָה אֵינוֹ צָרִיךְ. האי זה מאי עבדי ליה. "זֶה" דִּשְׁחוּטֵי חוּץ וְ"זֶה" דְּרָאשֵׁי הַמַּטּוֹת, מַאי דָּרְשֵׁי בְּהוּ? דְּכֵיוָן דְּלֵית לְהוּ שְׁאֵלָה בְּהֶקְדֵּשׁ — לֵית לְהוּ גְּזֵרָה שָׁוָה דְ"זֶה" "זֶה" כְּלָל, וַאֲפִי' לְמֵילַף נְדָרִים מִשְּׁחוּטֵי חוּץ לְאַהֲרֹן וּלְבָנָיו וּלְכָל בְּנֵי יִשְׂרָאֵל, דְּאֵין גְּזֵרָה שָׁוָה לְמֶחֱצָה. וּלְקַמָּן בָּעֵי לְהוּ: הֶדְיוֹטוֹת מְנָא לְהוּ. על השחיטה. בַּחוּץ, חַיָּיב כָּרֵת. דַּאֲפִילּוּ הַשּׁוֹחֵט עוֹף קָדָשִׁים בַּחוּץ, כִּדְנָפְקָא לָן בְּתוֹרַת כֹּהֲנִים וּבִזְבָחִים (דף קז.) מֵ"אוֹ אֲשֶׁר יִשְׁחַט", וְאֵינוֹ חַיָּיב עַל הַמְּלִיקָה שֶׁל עוֹף בַּחוּץ. (ג) מַשְׁמַע דְ"זֶה" — כָּעִנְיָן שֶׁמְּפוֹרָשׁ בַּפָּרָשָׁה חַיָּיב, כִּדִכְתִיב "כִּי יִשְׁחַט" וְלֹא כִּי יִמְלוֹק. ה"ג בְּתוֹרַת כֹּהֲנִים וּבִנְדָרִים בְּפֶרֶק "נַעֲרָה הַמְאוֹרָסָה": עַל הַשְּׁחִיטָה חַיָּיב, וְאֵינוֹ חַיָּיב עַל הַמְּלִיקָה. וּלְב"ה דְּדָרְשֵׁי לֵיהּ לג"ש נָפְקָא לְהוּ מֵהֵיכָא דְּנָפְקָא לָן בְּת"כ ת"ל "אֲשֶׁר יִשְׁחָט" — עַל הַשְּׁחִיטָה חַיָּיב, וְאֵין חַיָּיב עַל הַמְּלִיקָה. חכם מתיר. בִּלְשׁוֹן "מוּתָּר לָךְ". כִּדִכְתִיב: "לֹא יַחֵל דְּבָרוֹ" — הוּא דְּלֹא יַחֵל, אֲבָל אֲחֵרִים מוֹחֲלִין לוֹ. וּלְשׁוֹן הֶיתֵּר מַשְׁמַע לְהוּ לְרַבָּנַן הַאי "לֹא יַחֵל". וְטַעַם יֵשׁ לַדָּבָר, לְפִי שֶׁהֶחָכָם אֵינוֹ מַתִּיר בְּיוֹם שָׁמְעוֹ כְּמוֹ בַּעַל, בְּלֹא טַעֲנָה, אֶלָּא ע"י שֶׁמּוֹצֵא לוֹ חֲרָטָה וְעָקַר אֶת הַנֶּדֶר מֵעִיקָּרוֹ. הִלְכָּךְ לָא שַׁיָּיךְ בֵּיהּ לְשׁוֹן הֲפָרָה, אֶלָּא לְשׁוֹן הַתָּרָה, שֶׁהִתִּיר לוֹ אִיסּוּר ע"י הוֹרָאָה וְטַעֲנָה גְּמוּרָה. אֲבָל בַּעַל מֵיפֵר לְאִשְׁתּוֹ בְּיוֹם שָׁמְעוֹ בְּלֹא חֲרָטָה, מִגְּזֵירַת הַכָּתוּב, כְּמוֹ: "וְהֵפֵר אֶת בְּרִיתִי" (דברים לא). כָּל דְּבַר קִיּוּם הַנֶּעֱקָר וּמִתְבַּטֵּל בְּלֹא טַעַם — קָרוּי הֲפָרָה. ואין חכם מפר. שֶׁאִם אָמַר "מוּפָר לָךְ" — לֹא אָמַר כְּלוּם. דְּהָכִי מַשְׁמַע: "זֶה הַדָּבָר" — זֶה הַדִּבּוּר כְּמוֹ שֶׁכָּתוּב בַּפָּרָשָׁה — מְעַכֵּב, לָזֶה לְשׁוֹן הַתָּרָה וְלָזֶה לְשׁוֹן הֲפָרָה. וְהָכִי אָמְרִי' בְּהֶדְיָא בְּפֶרֶק "נַעֲרָה הַמְאוֹרָסָה" (נדרים דף עז:), א"ר יוֹחָנָן: חָכָם שֶׁאָמַר בִּלְשׁוֹן בַּעַל, וּבַעַל שֶׁאָמַר בִּלְשׁוֹן חָכָם — לֹא אָמַר כְּלוּם. דְּתַנְיָא: "זֶה הַדָּבָר" — חָכָם מַתִּיר וְאֵין בַּעַל מַתִּיר, שֶׁיָּכוֹל כו'. וְתַנְיָא אִידָךְ: "זֶה הַדָּבָר" — בַּעַל מֵיפֵר וְאֵין חָכָם מֵיפֵר, שֶׁיָּכוֹל כו'. וּלְב"ה נָפְקָא לְהוּ מִסְּבָרָא, כִּדְפָרֵישִׁית לְעֵיל, דִּבְחָכָם שַׁיָּיךְ לוֹמַר לְשׁוֹן הֶיתֵּר וּבְבַעַל לְשׁוֹן הֲפָרָה. הפרת נדרים בג'. הַיְינוּ הַתָּרַת חָכָם, דְּבָעֵינַן ב"ד ג' הֶדְיוֹטוֹת, אוֹ יָחִיד מוּמְחֶה דְּהָוֵי כְּב"ד. אֲבָל הֲפָרָה מַמָּשׁ סַגִּי בְּבַעַל לְחוּדֵיהּ, וַאֲפִי' הֶדְיוֹט. וְהַיְינוּ דְּאָמְרִינַן בְּשִׁילְהֵי מַסֶּכֶת שַׁבָּת (דף קנז.) דִּשְׁאֵלָה צְרִיכָה ב"ד, הֲפָרָה אֵינָהּ צְרִיכָה ב"ד. וַהֲפָרָה לְדוֹרוֹת נָפְקָא לְהוּ לְב"ש מִידֵּי דַּהֲוָה אַשְּׁאָר מִצְוֹת, דְּהַאי "זֶה" כֵּיוָן דְּאִיכָּא לְמִידְרְשֵׁיהּ לְמַעוּטֵי הֲפָרַת חָכָם וְהַתָּרַת בַּעַל — לָא מְמַעֲטִינַן (ג) נַמִּי דּוֹרוֹת.

מועדי

תוספות

שהפרת נדרים בשלשה הדיוטות. פי' ריב"ס: דמדכתיב "ראשי" — שנים משמע, ואין ב"ד שקול, מוסיפין עליהן עוד אחד. ואין נראה, דאדרבה מ"ראשי המטות" דרשינן יחיד מומחה, ו"ראשי" היינו ראשי דעלמא, כדפ"ה, והיכי נדרוש מיניה דבעינן שלשה? אלא נראה לר"י: דבלא קרא ידעינן, דהא מדבעינן יחיד מומחה — אם כן בהדיוטות לא סגי בחד, ובעינן שנים, ואין ב"ד שקול, מוסיפין עליהן עוד אחד.

דתנן ב"ש אומרים הקדש טעות הקדש. תימה: אדרבה, מכאן יש להוכיח שיש שאלה בהקדש, דהא מוקמינן התם מילתייהו דבית שמאי דכי אמר "שור שחור שיצא מביתי יהא קדוש" ויצא לבן, (ד) כגון דאמר: אילו הייתי יודע שיצא לבן לא הייתי אומר שחור, אלא לבן. ואומרים ב"ש: הקדש, משום דדעתו ומחשבתו מבטלת אמירתו. וה"נ כי נשאל על הקדש, כי אמר "אדעתא דהכי לא קדשי" — נתיר לו, כיון דאזלי ב"ש בתר מחשבה! ותירץ ר"ת: כיון דאמרי ב"ש מחשבתו מבטלת אמירתו למיהוי הקדש — כ"ש שתבטל אמירתו את מחשבתו, שאומר אדעתא דהכי לא נדר.

מיבעי להו חכם מתיר ואין בעל מתיר. פ"ה דלבית הלל נפקא להו מסברא. תימה: וכי ר' יוחנן סבר כב"ש? דבפ' "נערה" בנדרים (דף עז:) משמע דנפקא ליה מ"זה הדבר". דאמרינן התם, א"ר יוחנן: חכם שאמר בלשון בעל, ובעל שאמר בלשון חכם — לא אמר ולא כלום, דתניא: "זה הדבר" — חכם מתיר ואין הבעל מתיר! וי"ל: דלר' יוחנן לא נפקא מקרא אלא מסברא, ולא מייתי ראיה מדתניא אלא דלא אמר ולא כלום, ולא משום דנפקא ליה מ"זה הדבר". א"נ: מ"זה הדבר" דריש. ואע"ג דאיצטריך להכי — דרשי גזירה שוה, כיון דליכא למיפרך מידי.

ושבת

רבינו גרשום

וגו': אמר ליה. התם גבי הפרת נדרים לא מצית למימר דלא יהא נוהג אלא בדור זה דיליף זה זה משחוטי חוץ מה זה דשחוטי חוץ לדורות דכתיב ביה לדורותיכם אף זה דהפרת נדרים לדורותיכם: ומקשינן האי נמי. הפרת נדרים ליגמר זה הדבר מזה הדבר דבנות צלפחד דאזהרה דבנות צלפחד אינה נוהגת אלא ההוא דור ואף הכא הפרת נדרים לא יהא נוהג אלא בדור זה ולא לדורות. ומאי חזית דמקשת ליה הכי אקיש ליה הכי: האי מאי. כלומר הא לא מצית למימר דבשלמא התם גבי זה הדבר דהפרת נדרים איצטריך לגזירה שוה לאקושי לזה הדבר דשחוטי חוץ והואיל דאיצטריך לגזירה שוה להכי מדמינן ליה לדורות כשחוטי חוץ אבל הכא בבנות צלפחד מאי גזירה שוה מצינן למילף מיניה משום הכי לא ילפינן מיניה: מאי גזירה שוה. נאמר בשחוטי חוץ זה הדבר וגו' ונאמר גבי הפרת נדרים זה הדבר מה להלן בשחוטי חוץ אהרן ובניו וכל ישראל מוזהרין דכתיב דבר אל אהרן ואל בניו ואל כל בני ישראל זה הדבר וגו': אף כאן. גבי הפרת נדרים: אהרן ובניו וכל ישראל מצו להפר ומשום האי גזירה שוה ילפי' ליה מכל וכל משחוטי חוץ ולדורות משא"כ בבנות צלפחד: לומר שהפרת נדרים בג' הדיוטות. דומיא דכל ישראל כל דהו ישראל: והא ראשי המטות כתיב. בהפרת נדרים דמשמע דבעינן מומחין ולא הדיוטות: ומשני כדאמ' רב חסדא. לקמן גבי מועדי ה' דביחיד מומחה סגיא לקדושי זמנים הכא נמי הפרת נדרים ביחיד מומחה ואם אין מומחה בג' הדיוטות: לומר שיש שאלה בהקדש. שאם אמר שור שחור שיצא מביתי תחלה יהא הקדש ויצא לבן מטעם שלא שלא חישב בלבו שיצא אלא שחור ובא לחכם לישאל על טעותו אם הקדיש אותו שור שיצא לבן או לא ומחלוקת בית שמאי ובית הלל היא: ולבית שמאי דלית להו האי היקשא. האי זה הדבר דשחוטי חוץ ודהפרת נדרים מאי עביד ליה: ואינו חייב על המולק בחוץ. א)דשחיטה בעינן לפנים ומליקה בכל מקום כשירה ומשום הכי איצטריך זה הדבר: לחכם מתיר שאומר לו מותר לך נדרך כדכתיב לא יחל דברו הוא אינו מוחל אבל אחרים מוחלין לו אבל אינו יכול לומר לו מופר לך דבבעל תלא רחמנא הפרה כדכתיב ואם הפר יפר אותם ביום שמעו:

שבת

א) דברי רבינו צריך תיקון דהא אדרבה בפנים מנותו במליקה דוקא רק דבחוץ גזה"כ הוא דאינו חייב רק על השחיטה.

עין משפט נר מצוה

לב א ב מיי' פ"ד מהל' נדרים הל' ה סמג לאוין רמב טוש"ע י"ד סי' רכח סעיף ח:

לג ג מיי' שם הל' ז סמג שם:

לד ד מיי' פ"ו מהל' ערכין הל' לד ופ"ט מהל' נזירות הלכה ח:

לה ה מיי' פי"ח מהל' מעשה הקרבנות הלכה יח:

לו ו ז מיי' פי"ג מהל' נדרים הלכה ב ועיין בכ"מ ופ"ו מהל' שבועות הל' ה) סמג לאוין רמב טוש"ע י"ד סי' רלד סעיף לו [וסי' רכח סעיף ג]:

מסורת הש"ס

א) נדרים עח: ב) [זבחים קז.]: ג) [נדרים עח. כל הסוגיא]: ד) [לקמן קכא. יבמות כה: נדרים עח: ע"ש בכורות לו.] ה) [נזיר ט.] ו) נזיר לא: ערכין כג.: ז) [זבחים קז.]: ח) [נדרים עז:]:

הגהות הב"ח

(א) גמ' ביחיד מומחה אמר מר ומה כאן: (ב) רשב"ם ד"ה על וכו' של עוף בחוץ לזה משמע כענין שמפורש בפרשה זו חייב: (ג) ד"ה הפרת וכו' לא ממעטינן מינה דורות: (ד) תוס' ד"ה דתנן וכו' ויצא לבן הוי הקדש כגון דאמר:

תורה אור

מועדי ה' נאמרו, שבת בראשית לא נאמרה; בן עזאי אומר: מועדי ה' נאמרו, הפרת נדרים לא נאמרה. ר' [א]יוסי בר נתן (א) גמיר לה להא מתניתא ולא ידע ליה לפרושה, אזל בתריה דרב ששת לנהרדעא ולא אשכחיה, אזל בתריה למחוזא, אשכחיה, אמר ליה: מאי "מועדי ה' נאמרו, שבת בראשית לא נאמרה"? אמר ליה: [א]מועדי ה' צריכין קידוש בית דין, שבת בראשית אינה צריכה קידוש בית דין; סלקא דעתך אמינא: הואיל וכתיבי גבי מועדות, תיבעי קידוש בית דין כמועדות, קא משמע לן. מאי "מועדי ה' נאמרו, הפרת נדרים לא נאמרה"? מועדי ה' צריכין מומחין, הפרת נדרים אינה צריכה מומחין. והא "ראשי המטות" כתיב! [ב]אמר רב חסדא אמר רבי יוחנן: ביחיד מומחה. [ג]תנן התם, אמר רבן שמעון בן גמליאל: לא היו ימים טובים לישראל כחמשה עשר באב וכיום הכפורים, שבהן בנות ירושלים יוצאות בכלי לבן שאולין, שלא לבייש את מי שאין לו. [ד]בשלמא יום הכפורים — יום סליחה ומחילה, יום שניתנו בו לוחות אחרונות, אלא חמשה עשר באב מאי היא? אמר רב יהודה אמר שמואל: יום שהותרו שבטים לבא זה בזה. מאי דרוש? °"זה הדבר" (במדבר לו) — [ה]דבר זה לא יהא נוהג אלא בדור זה. רבה בר בר חנה אמר רבי יוחנן: יום שהותר שבט בנימן לבא בקהל, דכתיב: °"ואיש ישראל נשבע במצפה לאמר איש ממנו לא יתן בתו לבנימן לאשה" (שופטים כא). מאי דרוש? "ממנו" — ולא מבנינו. רב דימי בר יוסף אמר רב נחמן: יום שכלו בו מתי מדבר, דאמר מר: עד שלא כלו מתי מדבר —

לא

רשב"ם

מועדי ה' נאמרו. כולה מפרש לקמיה. מועדי ה' צריכין קידוש. שהיו מקדשין את החדש על פי הראייה ומתוך כך מתקדש מועד בזמנו, שלפי עיבור השנה ועיבור החדשים המועדים מתעכבין. אבל המועדים עצמן לא היו מקדשין, כי אם החדשים, כדתנן בר"ה (דף כד.) לגבי קידוש החדש, שאב בית דין אומר "מקודש" וכל העם עונין אחריו "מקודש מקודש", שנאמר: "אשר תקראו אותם" קרי ביה "אתם". ותרי זימני "מקודש, מקודש" נפקא לן מדכתיב "מקראי קדש", (ב) שהיו מקדשין את החדש על פי הראייה, וזהו תיקון המועדות וקדושתן. שבת בראשית אינה צריכה קידוש. כעין שמקדשין המועדות על ידי קידוש ראשי חדשים. אין מקדשין אחד בשבת להיות שביעי שלו שבת, אלא לעולם יום שביעי שבת הוא, בלא קידוש בית דין. ונפקא ליה מדכתיב "מועדי ה'" יתירא, דמצי למיכתב "אלה אשר תקראו אותם מקראי קדש". "שבת בראשית" קרי לשבת משום דכל מועדות נמי כתיב בהו "שבת שבתון", הלכך קרי ליה שבת בראשית, שמקודשת ובאה מששת ימי בראשית, דבשבת ראשונה כתיב בו ב"ויכולו" "ויקדש אותו". גבי מועדות. בפרשת "שור או כשב" (ויקרא כג). מועדי ה' צריכין מומחין. ולא מקדשי בג' הדיוטות כהפרת נדרים, ולא ביחיד מומחה כהפרת נדרים, אלא בשלשה מומחין, כדילפינן בראש השנה: אין לך מומחה בישראל יותר ממשה רבינו, וקאמר ליה רחמנא: עד דאיכא אהרן בהדך, דכתיב: "ויאמר ה' אל משה ואל אהרן וגו' החדש הזה לכם" — ככם, מומחין. ואין בית דין שקול, ומוסיפין עליהם עוד אחד. תנן התם. במס' תענית. ומשום דקאמר לקמן "יום שהותרו שבטים" כו' נקט לה. השאולין. שאפי' מי שיש לה היתה שואלת, שלא לבייש את השואלת מחמת שאין לה. כדאמרי' במסכת תענית (דף לא.): בת מלך שואלת מבת כהן גדול כו'. יום שנתנו בו לוחות האחרונות. כדתניא בסדר עולם: משה עלה *בששה בסיון לקבל לוחות הראשונות, וירד בי"ז בתמוז, דהיינו בסוף ארבעים יום. עלה בי"ח ובקש רחמים בשביל עון העגל, שנא': "ואתנפל לפני ה' את ארבעים היום ואת ארבעים הלילה אשר התנפלתי כי אמר ה' להשמיד אתכם" (דברים ט), ובאותה שעה נתרצה הקב"ה לישראל ואמר לו למשה: "פסל לך שני לוחות אבנים כראשונים". וירד בכ"ח באב, ופסל שני לוחות אבנים, כדכתיב: "ויפסול שני לוחות אבנים כראשונים וישכם משה בבקר", ועלה בכ"ט באב, ועשה עוד מ' יום (ג) מל' באב עד י' בתשרי, שנאמר: "ואנכי עמדתי בהר כימים הראשונים ארבעים" וגו'. בי' בתשרי הוא יום הכפורים נתרצה המקום בשמחה לישראל, ואותו היום ירד משה והלוחות בידו. יום שהותרו שבטים. הכי הוה קים להו. לבא זה בזה. שהותרו הסבת נחלה, שפסק אותו דור של באי הארץ שנאסר להם הסבת נחלה. והשתא מיהא, אם נשתיירו עדיין בני אדם שהיו באותו הדור — הכתי באיסורייהו קיימי, אבל שאר בני אדם שלא היו באותו הדור — מותרין. ויש מפרשים: יום שהותרו שבטים — שהרי בט"ו באב כלו מתי מדבר, כדלקמן. וטעות הוא בידם, שהרי לא לדור המדבר נאמר, אלא לבאי הארץ, בערבות מואב בסוף המ' שנה. יום שהותר שבט בנימן. כל הנך אמוראי לא פליגי, אלא מר גמיר האי מרביה, ומר גמיר האי מרביה. שכלו בו מתי מדבר. במדרש איכה: יום שבטל בו החפר. דאמר ר' לוי: כל ערב תשעה באב היה כרוז יוצא: "הכל יצאו לחפור", חופרין וישנין בהן. ובשחרית הכרוז יוצא: "יבדלו החיים מן המתים", והיו בודקין אותן, ונמצאו ט"ו אלף ופרוטרוט חסרין בכל שנה. וכך עשו מ' שנה, יום לשנה יום לשנה, הרי מ' שנה. בשנה אחרונה עשו כן, בדקו עצמן ונמצאו שלמים. אמרו: שמא טעינו בחשבון, וכן בי' בו, וכן בי"א, וכן בי"ב, וכן בי"ג, ובי"ד, עד דאיתמלי סיהרא. כיון דאיתמלי סיהרא — אמרו: ביטל הקב"ה אותה גזירה קשה מעלינו, ועשו משתה ושמחה ויו"ט. דאמר מר כו'. ולכך עשו ימי משתה ושמחה על הדיבור שחזר למשה.

ס"א בשבעה

לא

תוספות

ושבת בראשית אינה צריכה קידוש בית דין. ואם תאמר: דבסוף פרק קמא דקידושין (דף לז:) נפקא לן מדכתיב "מושבותיכם". דאמרינן התם: מושבות דכתב רחמנא גבי שבת למה לי? איצטריך, ס"ד אמינא הואיל ובעניינא דמועדות כתיבא — תיבעי קידוש ב"ד כמועדות, קמ"ל! ויש לומר: דרשא דהתם אתיא כבן עזאי, דדריש הכא: מועדי ה' נאמר, הפרת נדרים לא נאמר. אי נמי, אפי' לרבי יוסי הגלילי צריכין תרי קראי, דאי לא כתיב אלא חד לא הוה ממעטינן אלא מומחין — כתב קרא אחרינא למעוטי אפי' הדיוטות.

יום סליחה ומחילה. פירשתי בסוף "מרובה" (ב"ק דף פג. ד"ה כדי).

יום שכלו בו מתי מדבר. בשנה אחרונה נמי מתו. וידעו שכבר כלתה גזרה, כי כבר מתו כל בני כ', ולפי שהיו אבלים עד מקצת יום של ט"ו — לא חזר הדיבור, שאין השכינה שורה לא מתוך עצלות ולא מתוך עצבות, כדאשכחן גבי יעקב (תנחומא פ' וישב), שכל אותן ימים שנתאבל על יוסף לא שרתה עליו שכינה, כדאמר [בשבת (דף ל.)]. ולכך, כל ימי אבילתן של ישראל לא חזר הדיבור, שבזכותן היה מדבר עם משה, כדאמרי' בריש מכילתא: "לאמר", ר' יעקב אומר: לא ואמור להם שבזכותן אני מדבר עמך. שכל אותן שלשים ושמונה שנה שהיה כועס על ישראל — לא היה מדבר עם משה ואהרן, שנאמר "ויהי כאשר תמו" וכו'. וממדרש איכה שהיה רבינו שמואל מביא ראיה, קשיא טובא, שאם לא מתו בשנה אחרונה — למה נתעכב הדיבור שנה ויותר שלא חזר? ועוד, ט"ו אלף ופרוטרוט היה (ד) למות כל שנה. ולפי מדרש איכה היו מתין חמשה עשר אלף ופרוטרוט בכל שנה! ועוד: למאן דאמר בירושלמי במועד קטן שכולן בני ששים מתו — חידוש גדול הוא זה, שצריך לומר שחמש עשרה אלפים ופרוטרוט נולדו במצרים בכל שנה, זה קודם זה. ועוד, שלא היתה שמחה (ה) מפני הדיבור שחזר, [אלא] שאז כי איתמלי סיהרא ידעו שפסקה גזרה מעליהם! ועוד: מה שמחה היא שקדמו למות מאשתקד? והכתיב (שמות כג) "את מספר ימיך אמלא"! ועוד, אם מיהרו למות מאשתקד — א"כ לא מתו בני ששים אותן שהושלמו להן עשרים שנה בשעת יציאתם, שלכך תלה בכ' שנה, לפי שהיו בני כ' בנמנום! ונראה לר"ת (ו) לפי מדרש איכה שלא מיהרו למות, אלא בשנה אחרונה ביטל מהן הגזרה, ונשארו מהן ט"ו אלף ופרוטרוט, אותן שהיו ראוין למות בשנה אחרונה. כמו שמצינו בחזקיהו דכתיב (מלכים ב כ) "צו לביתך כי מת אתה" והאריך לו הרבה. [*והא דכתיב (במדבר כו) "ולא נותר מהם איש כי אם כלב בן יפונה ויהושע בן נון" — היינו מאותן שראוין למות קודם שנתבטלה הגזרה. דכלב ויהושע היו בני ארבעים בשלוח מרגלים, כדפרישית לעיל (ד' קיז: ד"ה מכאן). אי נמי, בתחלה נגזר אפי' על בני כ' בנמנום, ולבסוף ריחם עליהם הקב"ה ולא מתו אלא אותן שהיו בשעת גזרה לכל הפחות בני עשרים וחדש, שחדש בשנה אחרת חשוב שנה ולא יום אחד, כדאמרי' (מסכת פרה פ"א מ"ג) גבי פלגס, שכל חדש שלם אינו לא שה ולא איל, ונשארו בשנה אחרונה כל אותן שהיו בני כ' בנמנום]. הכי נמי אשכחן בדילוג קץ, זכו — "כי גר יהיה זרעך" מיצחק, לא זכו — "ועבדום וענו אותם" וכו'. והשתא אתי שפיר, דמשום חמשה עשר אלפים ופרוטרוט לשנה לא נתייחד הדיבור עד חמשה עשר באב של שנה אחרונה, שהיו ראוין למות, והיו עליבין בכך עד דאיתמלי סיהרא. ומה שהקשה ר"ת לפירוש הקונטרס: למה נשתהה הדיבור שנה ויותר? י"ל נמי שאין השכינה שורה לא מתוך עצבות, והן היו עליבין לפי שהיו סבורין למות באותה שנה. והאי דנקט נמי חמשה עשר אלפים ופרוטרוט — לאו על כל שנה ושנה קאמר, אלא רוב השנים. ומיהו, קשה על פירוש רבינו שמואל: דלמה חפרו קברים בשנה אחרונה? כיון שמאשתקד מתו כל אותן שהיו ראוין למות, שכל אחד היה יודע בעצמו שלא היה מבן עשרים ועד ששים מפקודי משה ואהרן!

גליון ... ע"כ

שבעה

מסורת הש"ס

א) [בנדרים עח. איתא רב אסי]: ב) [לעיל קכ: וש"נ]: ג) תענית כו: ד) שם ל: [ע"ש כמה שינויים]: ה) [לעיל קכ.]:

עין משפט נר מצוה

לז א מיי' פ"א מהל' קידוש החדש הל' א:

רבינו גרשום

שבת בראשית לא נאמר'. משום הכי קרי לה שבת בראשית כדכתיב וישבות ביום השביעי ומשמה של שבת זו א) שבת בראשית ויש שבתות אחרות כדכתיב ביום הראשון שבתון ועוד כתיב והיתה שבת הארץ וגו' ושבת של יום הכפורים ועוד כמה שבתות לפי עניינן אבל שבת בראשית היתה לכל השבתות: מועדי ה' צריכין קדוש בית דין. דכתיב אשר תקראו אותם מועדי קדש שמעברין את החודש ואת השנים ומקדשין זמנים: שבת בראשית אינה צריכה קידוש. משום דבכל שבעה ושבעה ימים שבת היא: מועדי ה' צריכין מומחה. לקדשן: ביחיד מומחה. הא אין מומחה בג' הדיוטות: יום שנתנו בו לוחות האחרונות. חשוב מיום שנשתברו הלוחות הן ארבעים וארבעים יום עד יום הכפורים: מאי דרוש. והתירו לבוא זה בזה והכתיב לא תסוב נחלה: ב) קודם מתי מדבר.

א) אולי צ"ל ומשמה של שבת זו נקראו כל השבתות שבת בראשית: ב) נראה דצ"ל עד שלא כלו מתי מדבר לא היה דיבור עם משה פה אל פה וכמו דכתיב פה כו':

הגהות הב"ח

(א) גמ' רבי יוסי בר נתן הוה גמיר: (ב) רשב"ם ד"ה מועדי ה' וכו' מדכתיב מקראי קדש וזהו תיקון המועדות וקדושתן כשהיו מקדשין את החדש על פי הראיה הס"ד: (ג) ד"ה יום שנתנו וכו' עשה עוד מ' יום ומ' לילה מלמ"ד באב: (ד) תום' ד"ה יום שכלו וכו' ט"ז אלף ופרוטרוט היה ראוי למות בכל שנה: (ה) בא"ד שלא היתה שמחה לפני הדיבור אלא כשחזר שאף כי לא אתמלי סיהרא ידעו: (ו) בא"ד ונראה לר"ת לפרש לפי מדרש:

לח א מיי' פ"ב מהל' ברכות הל' א [טור א"ח סי' קפט]:

לא היה דיבור עם משה, שנאמר: (דברים ב) °"ויהי כאשר תמו כל אנשי המלחמה למות מקרב העם", וסמיך ליה: "וידבר ה' אלי לאמר" — אלי היה הדיבור. עולא אמר: יום שביטל בו הושע בן אלה א)פרדסאות ב)שהושיב ירבעם על הדרכים שלא יעלו ישראל לרגל. רב מתנה אמר: יום שנתנו הרוגי ביתר לקבורה; ג)דאמר רב מתנה: אותו היום שנתנו הרוגי ביתר לקבורה — אתקנו ביבנה "הטוב והמטיב", "הטוב" — שלא הסריחו, "והמטיב" — שנתנו לקבורה. רבה ורב יוסף דאמרי תרוייהו: יום שפוסקין בו מלכרות עצים למערכה. ד)תניא, רבי אליעזר הגדול אומר: כיון שהגיע חמשה עשר באב תשש כחה של חמה, ולא היו כורתין עצים למערכה. אמר רב מנשה: וקרו ליה יום תבר מגל. מכאן ואילך, דמוסיף — יוסיף, שאינו מוסיף — יסיף. מאי "יסיף"? תני רב יוסף: תקבריה אמיה. תנו רבנן, שבעה קפלו את כל העולם כולו: מתושלח ראה אדם, שם ראה מתושלח, יעקב ראה את שם, עמרם ראה את יעקב, אחיה השילוני ראה את עמרם, אליהו ראה את אחיה השילוני ועדיין קיים. ואחיה השילוני ראה את עמרם? והא כתיב: (במדבר כו) °"ולא נותר מהם איש כי אם כלב בן יפונה ויהושע בן נון"! אמר רב המנונא: לא נגזרה גזרה על שבטו של לוי, דכתיב: (שם יד) °"במדבר הזה יפלו פגריכם וכל פקודיכם לכל מספרכם מבן עשרים שנה ומעלה", מי שפקודיו מבן עשרים, יצא שבטו של לוי שפקודיו מבן שלשים. ומשאר שבטים לא עייל? והתניא: יאיר בן מנשה ומכיר בן מנשה נולדו בימי יעקב, ולא מתו עד שנכנסו ישראל לארץ, שנאמר: (יהושע ז) °"ויכו מהם אנשי העי כשלשים וששה איש", ה)ותניא: שלשים וששה ממש, דברי ר' יהודה. אמר לו רבי נחמיה: וכי נאמר שלשים וששה? והלא לא נאמר אלא "כשלשים וששה"! אלא זה יאיר בן מנשה, ששקול כרובה של סנהדרין! אלא אמר רב אחא בר יעקב: לא נגזרה גזירה לא על פחות מבן עשרים ולא על יתר מבן ששים; לא על פחות מבן עשרים — דכתיב: "מבן עשרים שנה ומעלה", ולא על יתר מבן ששים — גמר "ומעלה", (ויקרא כז) °"ומעלה" מערכין, מה להלן יתר מבן ששים כפחות מבן כ', אף כאן יתר מבן ששים כפחות מבן עשרים. איבעיא להו: ארץ ישראל לשבטים איפלוג, או דלמא לקרקף גברי איפלוג? תא

שבעה קפלו כל העולם. האי תנא סבר דאליהו לא הוה פנחס. ז)דאי הוה פנחס — בצליר משבעה הוה מצי לאשכוחי, דיאיר ראה יעקב וראה פנחס. וסבר נמי האי תנא דסרח בת אשר אינה חיה לשלם. זבולון

לא היה דיבור עם משה. פה אל פה כבתחלה. אבל אם הוצרכו לדיבור, כגון במעשה דקרח שהיה אחר מעשה המרגלים — היה מדבר על ידי מלאך, או באורים ותומים. אי נמי, לא היה מדבר עמו אלא על ידי צורך מעשה הצריך להם. אלי היה הדיבור. דמצי למכתב: ויאמר ה' אלי, כדכתיב לעיל: "ויאמר ה' אלי אל תצר את מואב". אי נמי, מדסמכו ל"ויהי כאשר תמו" קדריש הכי, ולא ממשמעותא דקרא, אלא מייתורא ד"ויהי כאשר תמו", דקרא יתירא הוא. יום שביטל הושע בן אלה פרדסאות. שומ"ים. כדתניא בסדר עולם: כשראה הושע בן אלה שגלו עגלי הזהב, עמד (תורה אור) והעביר פרדסאות שהושיב ירבעם בן נבט שלא יעלו ישראל לרגל. ו) שבכל מלכי ישראל הוא אומר: "וילך בדרך ירבעם בן נבט ובחטאתו אשר החטיא את ישראל", אבל בהושע כתיב: "רק לא כמלכי ישראל אשר היו לפניו". הרוגי ביתר. במס' גיטין (דף נז.). דאמר רב מתנה כו'. ולכך שמחו, שזכו לקבורה ושלא הסריחו. ברכת הטוב והמטיב. שבברכת המזון, תקנו באותו היום. דמן התורה אינה אלא שלש ראשונות, כדנפקא לן מהאי קרא:(א) "וברכת את ה' אלהיך על הארץ" וגו'. מניסן ועד ט"ו באב היו כורתים עצים לצורך המערכה לכל השנה. מכאן ואילך תשש כח החמה, ויש בעצים לחלוחית, ומעלין עשן, וגם יגדל תולעת. וכדאמרינן במדרש איכה, רבי יעקב בר אחא בשם רבי יוסי אומר: שבו כלה זמן קילה למזבח. שכל עץ שנמצא בו תולעת פסול למזבח, וכל עץ שהוא נקלן אינו עושה מאכולת. ואותו יום שפסקו היו שמחים, לפי שבאותו יום היו משלימין מצוה גדולה כזאת. יום תבר מגל. שנשברו הקרדומות, שאין צורך עוד בהן לחטוב עצים. מט"ו באב ואילך דמוסיף. מן הלילה על היום לשנות — יוסיף ימים, כדכתיב: "כי הוא חייך" (דברים ל), וכתיב (משלי ג): "כי אורך ימים ושנות חיים [ושלום] יוסיפו לך". שמתוך שהלילות מאריכין והימים מתקצרין — צריך לעסוק בלימודו גם בלילה. ודלא מוסיף יסיף. מאי יסיף תני רב יוסף תקבריה אימיה. שימות בחצי ימיו, כמו (אסתר ט): "וזכרם לא יסוף מזרעם" — לשון כליה. ולא גרסי' "יאסף", דא"כ מאי קבעי תלמודא? הא מילתא דפשיטא היא ד"יאסף" לשון מיתה, כדכתיב (במדבר כ): "יאסף אהרן אל עמיו". ת"ר שבעה כו'. ברייתא היא בסדר עולם (ספ"א). ומשום דמיירי בכלב ויהושע לקמיה נקט ליה. אי נמי, משום דאיירי לעיל דמוסיף יסיף, ובא להודיענו שאלו שבעה, מתוך שצדיקים היו ועסקו בתורה — חיו כל כך. קפלו את כל העולם. סיבבוהו והקיפוהו, שנתקפל העולם ביניהם. וכל אלו השבעה שמשו זה את זה, כדקתני לעיל מינה בסדר עולם: נמצאת אומר שימש יעקב את שם נ' שנה, שימש שם את מתושלח צ"ח שנה, שימש מתושלח את אדם הראשון רמ"ג שנה. ומחשבון שנות הדורות הכתובין בפרשה דור אחר דור יש ללמוד כל זה. מתושלח לא מת עד תיכף למבול, כדאמר בחלק (סנהדרין דף קח:): "ויהי לשבעת הימים ומי המבול היו" — אלו שבעה ימי אבלו של מתושלח הצדיק. וכבר היה שם בן צ"ח שנה, כדכתיב: "שם בן מאת שנה ויולד את ארפכשד שנתים אחר המבול". ולמך נמי ראה את אדם ואת שם, אלא לצדיקים גמורים קחשיב, כמו ששימשו זה את זה, כדפרישית לעיל. והאי תנא לא ס"ל חנוך זה מטטרון, דהוה ליה למימר: שמנה קפלו את כל העולם. דהאי תנא דסדר עולם הוא, וס"ל דהאי "ואיננו כי לקח אותו אלהים" — היינו שמת בחצי ימיו, וכדקתני התם: חנוך קבר את אדם ואת (ב) *שם וחיה אחריו נ"ז שנה, מתושלח הוציא שנותיו עד המבול. עמרם ראה את יעקב. סברא הוא, שהרי קהת אביו מיורדי מצרים היה, כדכתיב: "ובני לוי גרשון וקהת" (בראשית מו) "ויחי יעקב בארץ מצרים שבע עשרה שנה", ובאותן י"ז שנה נולד עמרם לקהת, שהרי בנו הראשון היה, כדכתיב: "ובני קהת עמרם ויצהר". אחיה השילוני ראה את עמרם ואליהו ראה את אחיה. גמרא. והאי תנא לא סבירא ליה אליהו זה פנחס. דאם איתא — לימא: משה ראה עמרם, ופנחס ראה משה, ועדיין הוא קיים, ולא איצטריך ליה אחיה כלל. והא כתיב ולא נותר מהם. ואחיה השילוני נתנבא בימי ירבעם. ואם איתא דראה את עמרם במצרים — היאך יצא ממדבר ובא לו לארץ? והלא כל ימי יעקב במצרים י"ז שנה, ועמרם ראה את יעקב יום אחד לכל הפחות, ושני חיי עמרם קל"ז שנה — הרי קנ"ד, ואחיה ראה את עמרם. כמה פשו להו ממאתים ועשר אחר מות עמרם — נ"ו שנה, נמצא אחיה השילוני בן נ"ו שנה כשיצא ממצרים לכל הפחות, ושמא יותר, כגון שנולד בחיי עמרם הרבה. אחיה השילוני. לוי היה, כדכתיב בדברי הימים (א, כו): "והלוים אחיה על אוצרות בית אלהים". שפקודיו מבן שלשים. יום. שהיו הלוים נמנין מבן חדש ומעלה לפדות עליהן הבכורות, כדכתיב בפרשת "במדבר סיני": "מבן חדש ומעלה תפקדם". ולא נהירא לי, דא"כ הוה ליה למימר: יצא שבטו של לוי שפקודיו מבן חדש. אלא האי שלשים — היינו שלשים שנה, כדכתיב: "בני גרשון קהת ומררי מבן שלשים שנה ומעלה ועד בן חמשים שנה". וההוא חשבון נקט, שאותו חשבון כנגד חשבון של ישראל הוא, דביוצאי צבא קפיד רחמנא, דבישראל כתיב: "כל יוצא צבא", ובלוים כתיב: "מבן שלשים שנה וגו' כל הבא לצבא לעבוד" וגו'. ומשאר שבטים לא עייל. מיוצאי מצרים לארץ? בתמיה. ואמאי דחקת לתרוצי דמשום דלוי היה אחיה לכך בא לארץ? נולדו בימי יעקב. גמרא. ולא מתו כו'. לא יליף מקרא אלא חד מינייהו. סנהדרין היו ע"א, נמצא רובן שלשים וששה. ולא על יתר מבן ששים. ונהי נמי דאחיה ישראל הוה, הרי ראה את עמרם ה' שנים, וה"ל בן ס"א בצאתו ממצרים. יתר על ששים. בערכין אינו שוה לבן כ' שנה ומעלה, שהרי ערכו מועט יותר, כדכתיב בפרשת ערכין. כפחות מב'. שמועט ערכו נמי מבן כ' ומעלה. ואע"ג דאין ערך פחות מבן עשרים ויתר על בן ס' שוין זה לזה, מיהו בהכי שוים, ששניהם מועטין מערך יתר מבן כ' ומוחלקין מדינו של יתר מבן כ', וה"נ כי היכי דמוחלק פחות מבן עשרים מן הגזרה של יתר מבן כ' — ה"ה ליתר על בן ששים, ואיכא למימר נמי דלא נמנו בההוא חשבון. לשבטים איתפלג. שנתחלקה לשנים עשר חלקים שוין, ואח"כ כל שבט ושבט מתחלק לפי אנשיו, שהיו יוצאי מצרים, או לפי באי הארץ, למר כדאית ליה ולמר כדאית ליה. לקרקף גברי. לראשי אנשים. שכל אחד מיוצאי מצרים לרבי יאשיה, או לבאי הארץ לרבי יונתן, היה נוטל חלקו בארץ בפני עצמו, והיו כולם שוין בחלוקה.
תא

רבינו גרשום

פה אל פה אדבר בו: יום שפסקו מלכרות עצים למערכה. ולפי שעה שהיו עסוקים לכרות עצי המערכה היו מתבטלין בתלמוד תורה אבל אותו יום פסקו ועשאוהו יום טוב שמיכן ואילך היו עוסקין בתורה: תבר מגל. שהיה פוסק מגל מלכרות עצים למערכה: דמוסיף. מן הלילות על הימים ללמוד תורה: מוסיף. ימים לעולם הבא שמשם והלאה הלילות מאריכין: קיפלו. סבבו את העולם שראו זה את זה: ואחיה השילוני. שהיה משילו ראה את עמרם. משמע דעמרם ראה אחיה בשילה והכ' לא נותר מהם איש אלא לא יתכן לומר כך שעמרם לא ראה מעולם אחיה השילוני בשילה. לפי כי עמרם לא היה מעולם אלא קל"ז שנה וישראל עמדו במצרים ר"י שבע עשרה בימיו והשאר עמדו בגלותם נמצא שעמרם לא יצא ממצרים. אלא הכי מתרץ שאחיה השילוני שהיה בשילה ראה את עמרם במצרים ואחיה השילוני ממשפחת לוי הי' שפקודיו מבן שלשים שנה ומעלה כשנכנס לעבודה ולא מת במדבר וראה את עמרם במצרים: מה להלן גבי ערכין א) ערכך חמשים שקלים וכי היכי דיותר מבן ששים לא יהיב נ' שקלים וה"נ לגבי מתי מדבר [כמו] דלא נגזרה על פחות מבן עשרים ולא איענש למעלה מששים נמי לא איענש: לשבטים איתפלג. שנתחלקה לי"ב חלקים: אי לקרקף גברי איתפליג. ונתחלקה לפי האנשים שהיו בישראל כל אחד ואחד היה נוטל

א) נ"ל גבי ערכין דכתיב ואם מבן ששים שנה ומעלה יותר מבן ששים לא יהיב נ' שקלים וכו'.

ס"א חוה

מסורת הש"ס

א) [גיר' הערוך פרוזדאות ועי' תענית כח.]: ב) [גיטין פח.]: ג) ברכות מח: תענית לא.: ד) [נ"ל דתניא כך איתא בע"י]: ה) סנהדרין מד.: ו) [וכן אי' בגיטין פח.]: ז) [ב"מ קיד: וברש"י ד"ה לאו כהן מר]:

הגהות הב"ח

(א) רשב"ם ד"ה ברכת הטוב וכו' מהאי קרא ואכלת ושבעת וברכת: (ב) ד"ה קיפלו וכו' את אדם ואת חוה וחיה אחריו כצ"ל ותיבת שם נמחק:

תָּא שְׁמַע: °"בֵּין רַב לִמְעָט". וְעוֹד תַּנְיָא: עֲתִידָה אֶרֶץ יִשְׂרָאֵל שֶׁתִּתְחַלֵּק לִשְׁלֹשָׁה עָשָׂר שְׁבָטִים, שֶׁבַּתְּחִלָּה לֹא נִתְחַלְּקָה אֶלָּא לִשְׁנֵים עָשָׂר שְׁבָטִים. וְלֹא נִתְחַלְּקָה אֶלָּא בְּכֶסֶף, שֶׁנֶּאֱמַר: "בֵּין רַב לִמְעָט"; אָמַר רַבִּי יְהוּדָה: סְאָה בִּיהוּדָה שָׁוָה חָמֵשׁ סְאִין בַּגָּלִיל. וְלֹא נִתְחַלְּקָה אֶלָּא בְּגוֹרָל, שֶׁנֶּאֱמַר: °"אַךְ בְּגוֹרָל". וְלֹא נִתְחַלְּקָה אֶלָּא [א]בְּאוּרִים וְתוּמִּים, שֶׁנֶּאֱמַר: "עַל פִּי הַגּוֹרָל", הָא כֵּיצַד? [ב]אֶלְעָזָר מְלוּבָּשׁ אוּרִים וְתוּמִּים, וִיהוֹשֻׁעַ וְכָל יִשְׂרָאֵל עוֹמְדִים לְפָנָיו, וְקַלְפֵּי שֶׁל שְׁבָטִים וְקַלְפֵּי שֶׁל תְּחוּמִין מוּנָּחִין לְפָנָיו, וְהָיָה מְכַוֵּין בְּרוּחַ הַקֹּדֶשׁ וְאוֹמֵר: "זְבוּלֻן עוֹלֶה — תְּחוּם עַכּוֹ עוֹלֶה עִמּוֹ", טָרַף בַּקַּלְפֵּי שֶׁל שְׁבָטִים וְעָלָה בְּיָדוֹ זְבוּלֻן, טָרַף בַּקַּלְפֵּי שֶׁל תְּחוּמִין וְעָלָה בְּיָדוֹ תְּחוּם עַכּוֹ; וְחוֹזֵר וּמְכַוֵּין בְּרוּחַ הַקֹּדֶשׁ וְאוֹמֵר: "נַפְתָּלִי עוֹלֶה וּתְחוּם גִּינוֹסַר עוֹלֶה עִמּוֹ", טָרַף בַּקַּלְפֵּי שֶׁל שְׁבָטִים וְעָלָה בְּיָדוֹ נַפְתָּלִי, טָרַף בַּקַּלְפֵּי שֶׁל תְּחוּמִין וְעָלָה בְּיָדוֹ תְּחוּם גִּינוֹסַר. וְכֵן כָּל שֵׁבֶט וְשֵׁבֶט. וְלֹא כַּחֲלוּקָּה שֶׁל עוֹלָם הַזֶּה חֲלוּקָּה שֶׁל עוֹלָם הַבָּא; הָעוֹלָם הַזֶּה, אָדָם יֵשׁ לוֹ שְׂדֵה לָבָן — אֵין לוֹ שְׂדֵה פַּרְדֵּס, שְׂדֵה פַּרְדֵּס — אֵין לוֹ שְׂדֵה לָבָן; לָעוֹלָם הַבָּא, אֵין לְךָ [ג]כָּל אֶחָד וְאֶחָד שֶׁאֵין לוֹ בָּהָר וּבַשְּׁפֵלָה וּבָעֵמֶק, שֶׁנֶּאֱמַר: °"שַׁעַר רְאוּבֵן אֶחָד שַׁעַר יְהוּדָה אֶחָד שַׁעַר לֵוִי אֶחָד"; הַקָּדוֹשׁ בָּרוּךְ הוּא מְחַלֵּק לָהֶן בְּעַצְמוֹ, שֶׁנֶּאֱמַר: °"וְאֵלֶּה מַחְלְקוֹתָם נְאֻם ה'". קָתָנֵי מִיהַת: "שֶׁבַּתְּחִלָּה לֹא נִתְחַלְּקָה אֶלָּא לִשְׁנֵים עָשָׂר שְׁבָטִים", שְׁמַע מִינַּהּ לִשְׁבָטִים אִיפְּלוּג, שְׁמַע מִינַּהּ. אָמַר מָר: עֲתִידָה אֶרֶץ יִשְׂרָאֵל שֶׁתִּתְחַלֵּק לִשְׁלֹשָׁה עָשָׂר שְׁבָטִים. אִידָךְ לְמַאן? אָמַר רַב חִסְדָּא: [א]לַנָּשִׂיא, דִּכְתִיב: °"וְהָעוֹבֵד הָעִיר יַעַבְדוּהוּ מִכֹּל שִׁבְטֵי יִשְׂרָאֵל". אָמַר לֵיהּ רַב פַּפָּא לְאַבַּיֵי, אֵימָא: [ד]רוֹנְגַר בְּעָלְמָא! לָא סָלְקָא דַּעְתָּךְ, דִּכְתִיב: °"וְהַנּוֹתָר לַנָּשִׂיא מִזֶּה וּמִזֶּה לִתְרוּמַת הַקֹּדֶשׁ וְלַאֲחֻזַּת הָעִיר". וְלֹא נִתְחַלְּקָה אֶלָּא לִכְסָפִים, שֶׁנֶּאֱמַר: "בֵּין רַב לִמְעָט". לְמַאי? אִילֵימָא לְשׁוּפְרָא וְסַנְיָא — אַטּוּ [ה]בְּשׁוּפְטָנֵי עָסְקִינַן? אֶלָּא, לִקְרוֹבָה וּרְחוֹקָה. כְּתַנָּאֵי; רַבִּי אֱלִיעֶזֶר אוֹמֵר: בִּכְסָפִים הָעֲלוּהָ, רַבִּי יְהוֹשֻׁעַ אוֹמֵר: בְּקַרְקַע הָעֲלוּהָ. וְלֹא נִתְחַלְּקָה אֶלָּא בְּגוֹרָל, שֶׁנֶּאֱמַר: "אַךְ בְּגוֹרָל". תָּנָא: "אַךְ בְּגוֹרָל" — יָצְאוּ יְהוֹשֻׁעַ וְכָלֵב. לְמַאי? אִילֵימָא דְּלָא שְׁקוּל כְּלָל, הַשְׁתָּא דְּלָאו דִּידְהוּ שְׁקוּל, דִּידְהוּ מִיבַּעְיָא? אֶלָּא, שֶׁלֹּא נָטְלוּ בְּגוֹרָל, אֶלָּא ע"פ ה'; יְהוֹשֻׁעַ — דִּכְתִיב: °"עַל פִּי ה' נָתְנוּ לוֹ אֶת הָעִיר אֲשֶׁר שָׁאַל אֶת תִּמְנַת סֶרַח בְּהַר אֶפְרָיִם". כְּתִיב

במדבר כו | סס | יחזקאל מח | סס | סס | סס | יהושע יט | תורה אור

רשב"ם

תָּא שְׁמַע בֵּין רַב לִמְעָט. עַל פִּי הַגּוֹרָל תֵּחָלֵק הָאָרֶץ, נַחֲלָתָן שֶׁל יִשְׂרָאֵל, שֶׁיִּקַּח כָּל שֵׁבֶט וְשֵׁבֶט מַה שֶּׁיִּתֵּן לוֹ הַגּוֹרָל, בֵּין שֶׁהָיָה מַגִּיעַ לוֹ חֵלֶק מְרוּבֶּה — כְּגוֹן שֵׁבֶט שֶׁיֵּשׁ בּוֹ אֲנָשִׁים מְעַט, בֵּין שֶׁהָיָה לוֹ חֵלֶק מוּעָט — כְּגוֹן שֶׁיֵּשׁ לוֹ אֲנָשִׁים הַרְבֵּה. דְּכֵיוָן דְּכָל הַשְּׁבָטִים לוֹקְחִין בְּשָׁוֶה, שֵׁבֶט הַקָּטָן כְּשֵׁבֶט הַגָּדוֹל — נִמְצְאוּ חֶלְקֵי בְּנֵי שֵׁבֶט הַקָּטָן מְרוּבֶּה מֵחֵלֶק שֵׁבֶט בְּנֵי הַגָּדוֹל. וְאִי לְקַרְקֵף גַּבְרֵי — מַאי בֵּין רַב לִמְעָט? וַהֲלֹא נָטְלוּ כּוּלָּן בְּשָׁוֶה. **וְעוֹד תַּנְיָא.** בְּהֶדְיָא דְּלִשְׁבָטִים אִיתְפְּלַג. וּמִשּׁוּם דְּאִיכָּא לְמִידְרַשׁ נַמִי הַאי "בֵּין רַב לִמְעָט" לִכְדִלְקַמָּן בְּבָרַיְיתָא, אִיצְטְרִיךְ נַמִי הַאי. **וְעוֹד תַּנְיָא** כו'. שֶׁתִּתְחַלֵּק לֶעָתִיד לָבֹא לְי"ג שְׁבָטִים, כְּלוֹמַר לְי"ג חֲלָקִים שָׁוִין. וּלְקַמָּן מְפָרֵשׁ מַאי נִיהוּ אוֹתוֹ חֵלֶק דְּטָפֵי הָתָם, דְּאִי מִשּׁוּם לֵוִי דְּנָקֵיט נַחֲלָה כִּשְׁאָר שְׁבָטִים, כִּדְכְתִיב הָתָם: "שַׁעַר לֵוִי אֶחָד" — הָא מְנַשֶּׁה וְאֶפְרַיִם נַמִי לֹא יִטְּלוּ אֶלָּא חֵלֶק אֶחָד, כִּדְכְתִיב הָתָם: "שַׁעַר יוֹסֵף אֶחָד". נִמְצְאוּ י"ב שְׁבָטִים נוֹטְלִין י"ב חֲלָקִים, וְהַי"ג לַנָּשִׂיא, כִּדְלְקַמָּן. **שֶׁבַּתְּחִלָּה.** כְּשֶׁבָּאוּ לָאָרֶץ. **לֹא נִתְחַלְּקָה אֶלָּא לְי"ב שְׁבָטִים.** שֶׁלֵּוִי לֹא הָיָה לוֹ חֵלֶק בָּאָרֶץ, אֶלָּא שֶׁכָּל שֵׁבֶט וְשֵׁבֶט נָתְנוּ לוֹ עָרִים לָשֶׁבֶת בָּהֶן לִהְיוֹת עָרֵי מִקְלָט, אֲבָל מְנַשֶּׁה וְאֶפְרַיִם נָטְלוּ שְׁנֵי חֲלָקִים, כִּדְכְתִיב: "אֶפְרַיִם וּמְנַשֶּׁה כִּרְאוּבֵן וְשִׁמְעוֹן יִהְיוּ לִי" (בראשית מח). **בִּכְסָפִים.** קס"ד הַשְׁתָּא: מִי שֶׁהָיָה לוֹ חֵלֶק יָפֶה הָיָה נוֹתֵן דָּמִים לְמִי שֶׁהִגִּיעַ לוֹ חֵלֶק כָּחוּשׁ מַאי דְּבֵינֵי בֵּינֵי, שֶׁנֶּאֱמַר: "בֵּין רַב לִמְעָט" — כְּלוֹמַר, וְצָרִיךְ לְדַקְדֵּק בֵּין רַב לִמְעָט, לְהוֹסִיף דָּמִים הָרַב לַמְּעַט. שֶׁהַזִּיבּוּרִית קָרֵי לֵיהּ מְעַט, וְהָעִידִּית קָרֵי רַב. שֶׁכָּךְ אָמַר ר' יְהוּדָה: סְאָה בִּיהוּדָה שָׁוָה ה' סְאִין בַּגָּלִיל, וְהָיָה מַעֲלֶה דָּמִים זֶה שֶׁנָּפַל חֶלְקוֹ בִּיהוּדָה לְמִי שֶׁנָּפַל לוֹ חֶלְקוֹ בַּגָּלִיל. הָכִי גָּרְסִינַן: **אָמַר ר' יְהוּדָה כו'.** וְלֹא בָּא לַחֲלוֹק, מִדְּלָא קָתָנֵי "רַבִּי יְהוּדָה אוֹמֵר". **וְלֹא נִתְחַלְּקָה אֶלָּא בְּגוֹרָל.** מַסְקָנָא דְּמִילְּתֵיהּ דְּתַנָּא קַמָּא הִיא. **עַל פִּי.** מַשְׁמַע עַל פִּי אוּרִים וְתוּמִּים. **הָא כֵּיצַד.** אִם אוּרִים לָמָּה גּוֹרָל, וְאִם גּוֹרָל לָמָּה אוּרִים, וְשֶׁמָּא מַכְחִישִׁין זֶה אֶת זֶה? **אֶלְעָזָר מְלוּבָּשׁ כו'.** כִּדְכְתִיב (במדבר כז): "וְלִפְנֵי אֶלְעָזָר הַכֹּהֵן יַעֲמוֹד וְשָׁאַל לוֹ בְּמִשְׁפַּט הָאוּרִים לִפְנֵי ה' עַל פִּיו יֵצְאוּ" וגו'. **וְקַלְפֵּי שֶׁל שְׁבָטִים.** אַרְגָּז שֶׁמּוּנָּחִים בּוֹ י"ב פְּתָקִים שֶׁכָּתוּב בָּהֶן י"ב שְׁבָטִים, וְקַלְפֵּי שֶׁל תְּחוּמִין — אַרְגָּז שֶׁמּוּנָּחִין בּוֹ י"ב פְּתָקִין שֶׁל י"ב חֲלָקִים שֶׁל אֶרֶץ יִשְׂרָאֵל. **וְהָיָה מְכַוֵּין בְּרוּחַ הַקּוֹדֶשׁ.** כְּלוֹמַר בְּאוּרִים וְתוּמִּים, שֶׁשּׁוֹאֲלִים תְּחִלָּה בְּאוּרִים וְתוּמִּים קוֹדֶם שֶׁיִּטְרוֹף הַמְּמוּנֶּה בַּקַּלְפֵּי. וּבְכָךְ מִתְקָרְרָה דַּעְתָּן שֶׁל יִשְׂרָאֵל, שֶׁרוֹאִין שֶׁהַגּוֹרָל הָיָה עוֹלֶה כְּמוֹ שֶׁנִּתְנַבֵּא תְּחִלָּה וְיוֹדְעִים שֶׁחֲלוּקָה יְשָׁרָה הִיא, וְלֹא הָיוּ מִרְנָנִים בְּדָבָר הַשְּׁבָטִים מְרוּבִּים. וּשְׁנֵי קַלְפֵּי הָיוּ צְרִיכִין, אֶחָד לִשְׁבָטִים וְאֶחָד לִתְחוּמִין, וְלָא סַגִּי בְּחַד דִּתְחוּמִין, וְלֵימָא: עַכְשָׁיו אֲנִי נוֹטֵל מַה שֶּׁיַּעֲלֶה בְּיָדִי לְצוֹרֶךְ רְאוּבֵן — דְּאִ"כ אֵין כָּל הַחֲלוּקָה עֲשׂוּיָה בְּגוֹרָל, וּקְרָא קָאָמַר "אַךְ בְּגוֹרָל" וגו' — בְּלֹא הוֹצָאַת דִּיבּוּר מִפִּיו. **וְאוֹמֵר זְבוּלֻן עוֹלֶה.** עַכְשָׁיו יָבֹא לִידֵי הַטּוֹרֵף בַּקַּלְפֵּי כְּתַב שֶׁל זְבוּלֻן. וְהַאי דְּנַקְטִינְהוּ שֶׁלֹּא כַּסֵּדֶר — לְפִי שֶׁאֵין עוֹלֶה שׁוּם גּוֹרָל עַל הַסֵּדֶר, אֶלָּא עַל יְדֵי מִקְרֶה. **טָרַף.** עִירְבֵּב הַמְּמוּנֶּה לְכָךְ אֶת הַשְּׁטָרוֹת יָפֶה, שֶׁלֹּא יֹאמְרוּ: מִדַּעַת לָקַח אֶת זוֹ, שֶׁהָיָה יוֹדֵעַ מַה כָּתוּב בָּהּ. כְּמוֹ בֵּילִים טְרוּפוֹת בְּקַעֲרָה (עדיות פ"ג מ"ד). **שַׁעַר רְאוּבֵן אֶחָד.** שָׁוֶה, דְּכָל מַה שֶּׁיֵּשׁ לָזֶה יֵשׁ לָזֶה. **נְאוּם ה'.** הוּא עַצְמוֹ יֹאמַר לְכָל אֶחָד לִיטּוֹל חֵלֶק פְּלוֹנִי וּפְלוֹנִי. **אִידָךְ לְמַאן.** חֵלֶק י"ג לְמִי? דְּהָא י"ב שְׁבָטִים לְחוּד הוּא דְּשָׁקְלֵי, כִּדְכְתִיב בִּיחֶזְקֵאל. **לַנָּשִׂיא.** לְמֶלֶךְ הַמָּשִׁיחַ. **הָעוֹבֵד הָעִיר.** הַיְינוּ נָשִׂיא. דְּעוֹל רַבִּים מוּטָּל עָלָיו, כִּדְכְתִיב בִּרְחַבְעָם: "אִם הַיּוֹם תִּהְיֶה עֶבֶד לָעָם הַזֶּה" (מלכים א יב). **יַעַבְדוּהוּ.** יִתְּנוּ לוֹ נַחֲלָה מִכָּל שִׁבְטֵי יִשְׂרָאֵל. **רוֹנְגַר.** שְׂכִירִים בְּעָלְמָא, לַעֲבוֹד לוֹ כְּתַלְמִידִים לָרַב, אֲבָל לֹא יוֹתֵן לוֹ מִנַּחֲלָתָם. וְרַבֵּינוּ חֲנַנְאֵל פֵּירֵשׁ: (ב) רוֹן גַּר, "רוֹן" בִּלְשׁוֹן פָּרַס — יוֹם, וְגַר — שָׂכִיר, כְּלוֹמַר שְׂכִיר יוֹם. **וְהַנּוֹתָר מִזֶּה וּמִזֶּה.** מַשְׁמַע שֶׁנּוֹטֵל חֵלֶק מִזֶּה וּמִזֶּה. **לִתְרוּמַת הַקֹּדֶשׁ.** לְבַד מְקוֹמוֹ שֶׁל בֵּית הַמִּקְדָּשׁ. **וְלַאֲחֻזַּת הָעִיר.** וּלְבַד מְקוֹם הָעִיר. וּכְתִיב בְּסֵיפֵיהּ דִּקְרָא כְּאֶחָד הַחֲלָקִים. **וְלֹא נִתְחַלְּקָה כו'.** כְּמוֹ "אָמַר מָר". **לְמַאי הִלְכְתָא.** קָאָמַר שֶׁיְּהוּ מַעֲלִין כְּסָפִים זֶה לָזֶה? **אִילֵימָא בְּשׁוּפְרָא וְסַנְיָא.** מַה שֶּׁהָיְתָה זוֹ יָפָה מִזּוֹ וְזוֹ רָעָה מִזּוֹ, דְּמַסְּלֵיק לֵיהּ בִּדְמֵי מַאן דְּאִית לֵיהּ שׁוּפְרָא לְמַאן דְּאִית לֵיהּ סַנְיָא. **אַטּוּ בְּשׁוּפְטָנֵי עָסְקִינַן.** דְּמַסְּלְקֵי מִנַּחֲלָתָם בְּזוּזֵי? אֶלָּא וַדַּאי בַּגָּלִיל נוֹטֵל ה' סְאִין כְּנֶגֶד סְאָה בִּיהוּדָה. **לִקְרוֹבָה וּרְחוֹקָה.** הַקַּרְקָעוֹת הָיוּ חוֹלְקִין בְּשָׁוֶה, מִי שֶׁלּוֹקֵחַ מִן הַכָּחוּשׁ נוֹטֵל יוֹתֵר עַד כִּדְמֵי הַיָּפֶה. אֲבָל מִי שֶׁעוֹלֶה לוֹ גוֹרָלוֹ בְּקָרוֹב לִירוּשָׁלַיִם — מַעֲלֶה מָעוֹת לְמִי שֶׁעָלָה גוֹרָלוֹ בְּרָחוֹק מִירוּשָׁלַיִם. שֶׁהָרָחוֹק גָּרוּעַ הוּא מִפְּנֵי שְׁנֵי דְבָרִים: אֶחָד מִפְּנֵי שֶׁרָחוֹק מִבֵּית הַמִּקְדָּשׁ, וְאֶחָד מִפְּנֵי שֶׁקָּרוֹב הוּא לְאֶרֶץ הָעַמִּים, וְיֵשׁ לוֹ לִדְאֹג מֵהֶן. וְרַבִּי יְהוּדָה מִילְּתָא בְּאַפֵּי נַפְשַׁהּ קָאָמַר, דְּמִי שֶׁנָּפַל גּוֹרָלוֹ בַּגָּלִיל נוֹטֵל ה' סְאִין כְּנֶגֶד סְאָה שֶׁחֲבֵירוֹ נוֹטֵל בִּיהוּדָה. אִי נַמִי, מִשּׁוּם דְּקָאָמַר תַּנָּא קַמָּא דִּקְרוֹבָה וּרְחוֹקָה מְסַלְּקִין בִּכְסָפִים, אֲתָא אִיהוּ לְסַיּוֹעֵיהּ וּלְמֵימַר דִּסְאָה בִּיהוּדָה שָׁוֶה חָמֵשׁ סְאִין בַּגָּלִיל, בִּשְׁבִיל שֶׁיְּהוּדָה קָרוֹב לִירוּשָׁלַיִם וְגָלִיל רָחוֹק יוֹתֵר, וְצָרִיךְ לְהַעֲלוֹת כַּסְפִּין שָׁוֶה ד' סְאִין לִסְאָה שֶׁבַּגָּלִיל. **בִּכְסָפִים הָעֲלוּהָ.** לַהֲסוּא בֵּינֵי דִּקְרוֹבָה וּרְחוֹקָה. וּסְבָרָא הוּא. וּמִ"בֵּין רַב לִמְעָט" לָא נָפְקָא לֵיהּ, דְּמִקְרָא לָא שָׁמְעִינַן אֶלָּא הַעֲלָאָה, לָא שְׁנָא בִּכְסָפִים לָא שְׁנָא בְּקַרְקַע. **דְּלָאו דִּידְהוּ.** חֵלֶק מְרַגְּלִים, כִּדַּאֲמַרַן בְּפִירְקִין דִּלְעֵיל (דף קיח:).

כְּתִיב

תוספות

זבולן עולה תחום עכו עולה [עמו]. לאו עכו ממש, דעכו מחלק אשר, דכתיב (שופטים א) "ואשר לא הוריש יושבי עכו", אלא כלומר, תחום שבלד עכו. **העולם** הזה יש לו פרדס ואין לו שדה לבן. תימה: דבשלהי "מרובה" (ב"ק דף פא: ושם ד"ה אין) אמרינן מחלוקת ארץ ישראל: אין לך מישראל שאין לו בהר ובשפלה ונגב. ומיהו, אית דגרס: אין לך שבט ושבט מישראל. אבל הכא גרסינן: אין לך אחד מישראל לעולם הבא, ומשמע לו: "שער ראובן אחד" — היינו לכל אחד ואחד. אי נמי, בעולם הזה אין להם בשוה מזה כמו מזה, אלא מזה מעט ומזה הרבה, אבל לעולם הבא יש לו מן הכל שיעור שוה. **ואידך** למאן. אע"ג דכתיב "שער לוי אחד" — הא כתיב נמי "שער יוסף אחד", דלא מנו שבט יוסף אלא כאחד. **לא** סלקא דעתך דכתיב הנותר לנשיא וגו' ובב"ר בפר"ב דריש מהכא דגבעוני אינו מתרפא לעתיד לבא, מדכתיב "והעובד העיר" וגו'. ואיתא להא ואיתא להא, ומדאפקיה בלשון עובד — דרוש ביה נמי גבעוני. או שמא פליגי.

סתם

רבינו גרשום

חלקו: ת"ש בין רב למעט. בין היה השבט רב בין היה השבט מעט נוטל זה כגון זה דאי לקרקף גברי איתפלג מישתכח דכולהו כי הדדי נסבי אלא ש"מ לשבטים איתפלג: ולא נתחלקה אלא בכספים. כדאמר לקמן בקרובה ורחוקה ודכתיב בין רב למעט כולם היו שוין בנחלתם שאותו שהיה זיבורית או במקום רחוק מירושלים הי' מעלין לו דמים כדי שיקח במקום רחוק או כדי שיקח בזיבורית וכדאמר רב יהודה סאה ביהודה כו'. הנוטל ביהודה מוסיף דמים לנוטל בגליל: דכתיב על פי ה'. היינו אורים ותומים דכתיב על פיו יצאו: קלפי שבה שמות השבטים וקלפי שבה שמות התחומין מונחין לפניו והיה אלעזר מכוין ברוח הקדש. ואם אמר זבולן עולה שבולטין אותיות באבני אורים ותומים תחום עכו יהא עולה לחלקו אחר שהיה בולט שם זבולן טרף בקלפי ששמות שבטים בה עלה בידו שם זבולן וטרף בקלפי תחומים ועלה בידו תחום עכו היינו על פי אורים ותומים ועל פי הגורל וכן היה עושה לכל שבט ושבט: שדה פרדס. אילנות: שדה לבן. תבואה: שנא' שער ראובן אחד שער שמעון אחד. שכולן יהו חלוקין בשוה בהר ובשפלה ובנגב שאין זה צריך לזה: ואידך למאן. חלק שלשה עשר למאן: לנשיא דכתיב העובד את העיר. מלך שהוא משמר את העיר יעבדו אותו כל שבטי ישראל שכל שבט ושבט מצמצמין מנחלתו עד שעושין לו חלק אחד והיינו חלק י"ג: ודלמא רונגר בעלמא. שלא יתנו לו שיעור שבט כי אם עיר אחת או פלך אחד ואכתי אידך למאן: והנותר לנשיא היינו שבא מזה ומזה. כלומר אותו מותר שיהו מצמצמין משבט זה ומשבט זה ומייתרין לו בשיעור חלק אחד שלהן אותו מותר יחיד הקדש לאחוזת העיר כלומר למלך שאוחז העיר בידו: למאי אילימא בשופרא וסניא. כלומר שבשביל שנטל זה עידית וזה נטל זיבורית יעלה בעל עידית לבעל זיבורית כספים עד שיהו שוים בנחלה: וכי בשופטני עסקי'. דהניח לזה ליטול עידית והוא נוטל זיבורית: אלא בקורבא ורוחקא. שאם נטל זה ברחוק מירושלים יעלה לו זה בדמים שנפל חלקו בקרוב ויתן לזה שהוא ברחוק: בכספים העלוה. לארץ ישראל שהי' נותן לו דמים בשביל קריבת ירושלים. ור' יהודה אומר בקרקע העלוה שהיו נותנין יותר קרקע לאותו שברחוק יותר ממי שהוא בקרוב: דלאו דידהו שקלי. שנטלו חלק מרגלים ומתלוננים: דומין

מסורת הש"ס

א) [סנהדרין עז.]: ב) [עי' תוס' סנהדרין עז. ד"ה מה]: ג) ב"ק פא: ד) עי' יבמות עט. תוס' ד"ה רונגר גרסי': ה) [עמ"ש ב"ק פה. על נידון] ליתא לפנינו:

עין משפט נר מצוה

לט א מיי' פ"ד מהל' מלכים הל' ח:

הגהות הב"ח

(א) רשב"ם ד"ה רונגר וכו' ורבינו חננאל פי' רוזגר רוז בלשון פרס. נ"ב עיין לעיל ד' ל ע"ב:

עין משפט נר מצוה

מ א מיי' פי"ט מהל' איסורי ביאה [?] הל' י סמג עשין מח טוש"ע אה"ע סי' קיב סעיף א:

מא ב מיי' פ"ב מהל' נחלות הלכה ז סמג עשין נו טוש"ע ח"מ סי' רעו סעיף ג וסי' רעז סעיף טו:

מב ג מיי' שם הל' ח סמג עשין נו טוש"ע ח"מ סי' רעח סעיף א:

מג ד מיי' שם הלכה א סמג שם טוש"ע ח"מ סי' רעז סעיף א:

כְּתִיב: "סֶרַח", וּכְתִיב: "חֶרֶס"! אָמַר ר' אֶלְעָזָר: בַּתְּחִלָּה פֵּירוֹתֶיהָ כְּחֶרֶס, וּלְבַסּוֹף פֵּירוֹתֶיהָ מַסְרִיחִין; וְאִיכָּא דְּאָמְרִי: בַּתְּחִלָּה מַסְרִיחִין, וּלְבַסּוֹף כְּחֶרֶס. כָּלֵב — דִּכְתִיב: "וַיִּתְּנוּ לְכָלֵב אֶת חֶבְרוֹן כַּאֲשֶׁר דִּבֶּר מֹשֶׁה וַיּוֹרֶשׁ מִשָּׁם אֶת שְׁלֹשָׁה בְּנֵי הָעֲנָק". [א]חֶבְרוֹן עִיר מִקְלָט הֲוַאי! אָמַר אַבַּיֵי: פַּרְוָורָהָא, דִּכְתִיב: "וְאֶת שְׂדֵה הָעִיר וְאֶת חֲצֵרֶיהָ נָתְנוּ לְכָלֵב בֶּן יְפֻנֶּה בַּאֲחֻזָּתוֹ".§

תורה אור: שופטים א; שם; יהושע כא

מתני' אֶחָד הַבֵּן וְאֶחָד הַבַּת בְּנַחֲלָה, אֶלָּא [ב]שֶׁהַבֵּן נוֹטֵל פִּי שְׁנַיִם בְּנִכְסֵי הָאָב וְאֵינוֹ נוֹטֵל פִּי שְׁנַיִם בְּנִכְסֵי הָאֵם, [א]וְהַבָּנוֹת נִזּוֹנוֹת מִנִּכְסֵי הָאָב וְאֵינָן נִזּוֹנוֹת מִנִּכְסֵי הָאֵם.§ **גמ'** מַאי "אֶחָד הַבֵּן וְאֶחָד הַבַּת לְנַחֲלָה"? אִילֵימָא דְּיָרְתִי כִּי הֲדָדֵי — הָא תְּנַן: [ג]בֵּן קוֹדֵם לְבַת, כָּל יוֹצְאֵי יְרֵיכוֹ שֶׁל בֵּן קוֹדְמִין לְבַת! (סִימָן: נַפְשָׁם) אָמַר רַב נַחְמָן בַּר יִצְחָק, הָכִי קָאָמַר: אֶחָד הַבֵּן וְאֶחָד הַבַּת נוֹטְלִין בְּרָאוּי כִּבְמוּחְזָק. הָא נַמִּי תְּנֵינָא: [ד]בְּנוֹת צְלָפְחָד נָטְלוּ שְׁלֹשָׁה חֲלָקִים בְּנַחֲלָה, חֵלֶק אֲבִיהֶן שֶׁהָיָה מִיּוֹצְאֵי מִצְרַיִם, וְחֶלְקוֹ עִם אֶחָיו בְּנִכְסֵי חֵפֶר! וְעוֹד, מַאי "אֶלָּא"? אֶלָּא אָמַר רַב פַּפָּא, הָכִי קָאָמַר: [ב]אֶחָד הַבֵּן וְאֶחָד הַבַּת נוֹטְלִין חֵלֶק בַּבְּכוֹרָה. הָא נַמִּי תְּנֵינָא: [ה]וְשֶׁהָיָה בְּכוֹר נוֹטֵל שְׁנֵי חֲלָקִים! וְעוֹד, מַאי "אֶלָּא"? אֶלָּא אָמַר רַב אַשִׁי, הָכִי קָאָמַר: אֶחָד בֵּן בֵּין הַבָּנִים וְאֶחָד בַּת בֵּין הַבָּנוֹת, אִם אָמַר "יִירַשׁ כָּל נְכָסַי" — דְּבָרָיו קַיָּימִין. כְּמַאן, כְּר' יוֹחָנָן בֶּן בְּרוֹקָא? הָא קָתָנֵי לַהּ לְקַמָּן, [ו]ר' יוֹחָנָן בֶּן בְּרוֹקָא אוֹמֵר: אִם אָמַר עַל מִי שֶׁרָאוּי לְיוֹרְשׁוֹ — דְּבָרָיו קַיָּימִין, עַל מִי שֶׁאֵינוֹ רָאוּי לְיוֹרְשׁוֹ — אֵין דְּבָרָיו קַיָּימִין! וְכִי תֵּימָא: קָא סָתֵם לַן כְּרַבִּי יוֹחָנָן בֶּן בְּרוֹקָא — סְתָם וְאַחַר כָּךְ מַחֲלוֹקֶת הִיא, וּסְתָם וְאַחַר כָּךְ מַחֲלוֹקֶת — אֵין הֲלָכָה כִּסְתָם! וְעוֹד, מַאי "אֶלָּא"? אֶלָּא אָמַר מָר בַּר רַב אַשִׁי, הָכִי קָאָמַר: אֶחָד הַבֵּן וְאֶחָד הַבַּת שָׁוִין בְּנִכְסֵי הָאֵם וּבְנִכְסֵי הָאָב, [ג]אֶלָּא שֶׁהַבֵּן נוֹטֵל פִּי שְׁנַיִם בְּנִכְסֵי הָאָב, וְאֵינוֹ נוֹטֵל פִּי שְׁנַיִם בְּנִכְסֵי הָאֵם. ת"ר: "לָתֶת לוֹ פִּי שְׁנַיִם" (דברים כא) — [ד]פִּי שְׁנַיִם כְּאֶחָד. אַתָּה אוֹמֵר: פִּי שְׁנַיִם כְּאֶחָד, אוֹ אֵינוֹ אֶלָּא פִּי שְׁנַיִם בְּכָל הַנְּכָסִים? וְדִין הוּא: חֶלְקוֹ

רשב"ם

כתיב סרח. ביהושע. וכתיב חרס. בשופטים. בתחלה. קודם שבאת ליד יהושע, פירותיה דומין לחרס – יבשין ורעים כחרס היבש בלי שומן. ולבסוף. כשבאת לידו – פירותיה מסריחין מרוב שמנן, כשמשמרין אותן יותר מדאי, ומעליותא היא משום שומן, וזכותו של יהושע גרם. ואיכא דאמרי בתחלה פירותיה מסריחין. מרוב שמנן, ולא היו משתמרין, וגריעותא היא. ולבסוף פירותיה דומין לחרס, כלומר, שלא היו שמנין יותר מדאי אלא במדה, שיכולין להכניסם לאוצר ומתקיימין טובא, ומעליותא היא. כאשר דבר משה. והיכן דבר – דכתיב: "ולו אתן את הארץ אשר דרך בה ולבניו" וזו היא חברון שדרך בה, כדדרשינן באגדה: "ויבא עד חברון" – מלמד שנשתטח כלב על מערת קברי צדיקים שבחברון והתפלל שם לפני המקום שיצילהו מעצת מרגלים, שלא יכשל (א) בהן עמהן. עיר מקלט הואי. כדכתיב ביהושע: "ולבני אהרן הכהנים נתנו את עיר מקלט הרוצח את חברון ואת מגרשיה". פרוורהא. כפרים ושדות שסביב לעיר, חוצה למגרש. **מתני'** אחד הבן ואחד הבת כו'. כולה מפרש בגמרא. אלא שהבן כו'. בגמ' מפרש מאי "אלא". ואינו נוטל פי שנים בנכסי האם. כדדרשינן לעיל (דף קיא:): "לו משפט הבכורה" – משפט הבכורה לאיש, אבל לא לאשה. והבנות נזונות כו'. בנכסים מועטים, ולא הבנים. כדתנן לקמן בתחלת "מי שמת" (דף קלט:): מי שמת והניח בנים ובנות, בזמן שהנכסים מרובין – הבנים יירשו והבנות יזונו, נכסים מועטין – הבנות יזונו, והבנים ישאלו על הפתחים. ואינן נזונות מנכסי האם. לא במרובין ולא במועטין במקום בנים, שהבנים יורשין את הכל. אבל גבי נכסי אב – נזונות בתנאי כתובה, שכך כתב לאשתו: "בנן נוקבן דיהוון ליכי מינאי יהון מתזנן מנכסאי עד דתלקחן לגוברין". **גמ'** דירתון כי הדדי. בת במקום בן תירש עם הבן. והתנן. דלא ירתון כי הדדי. בן קודם לבת כו'. והכא לא גרסי' "ועוד מאי אלא", דהא טובא קא פריך ליה, ולא שייך למימר "ועוד" אלא היכא דפירכא בתרייתא עדיפא מקמייתא. א"ר נחמן בר יצחק הכי קאמר אחד הבן ואחד הבת. במקום שאין בן, שוין בנחלה ליטול מה שהיה ראוי לאביהן כאילו היה מוחזק לו. דבן בנו או בת בתו של אדם יורשין אותו, שעומדין בני בנים במקום בנים לירש את הזקן, כדנפקא לן מ"ובן אין לו" – עיין עליו, "ואם אין לו בת" – עיין עליה, אלמא, הבן או הבת יורשין את מה שהיה ראוי אביהן לירש אילו היה קיים. הא נמי תנינא. דבנות צלפחד נטלו חלק הראוי לצלפחד אביהן בנכסי חפר. ואע"ג דהוה ליה ראוי גבי צלפחד אביהן, דאפי' אם מת בחיי חפר קאמרי' דנטלו בנותיו חלק הראוי לו אילו היה קיים, דהא לא מפליג תנא דמתני' מידי. אלמא, בת יורשת את הראוי לאביה במקום שאין בן. והוא הדין דהוה מצי למימר: הא נמי תנינא (לעיל דף קטו.): וכל יוצאי ירכו של בן קודמין לבת. דמהתם שמעינן דאפי' בת הבן יורשת בנכסי זקן, דהיינו ראוי לאביה, שהרי מת אביה בחיי זקינה ואפ"ה יורשת זקינה במקום אביה. אלא מעובדא דבנות צלפחד ניחא ליה לאקשויי, דמעשה רב. ועוד. אפי' תאמר דמשום סיפא קתני רישא, שרוצה לתת חילוק ביניהן בסיפא, מאי "אלא"? היאך מוסב על הראשון? הא לא קתני ברישא דנכסי האב ונכסי האם שוין, דליתני בסיפא "אלא", שבדבר זה יש חילוק בין נכסי האב לנכסי האם שהבן כו'. וכיון דרישא קאמר דבן ובת שוין – לא היה לו לשנות בסיפא חילוק דאב ואם, אלא חילוק בין בן לבת. והכי ה"ל למיתני: אלא שהבן נוטל פי שנים אבל לא הבת. והבת ניזונת מן הנכסים אבל לא הבן. ה"ג: ועוד מאי אלא אלא אמר רב פפא כו'. וכן בכולהו גרסי' תרי זימני "אלא". אלא אמר רב פפא כו'. לרב פפא נמי קשיא ליה "אלא" כדלקמן. ואיהו לא בא לתרץ האי "אלא", אבל קושיא קמייתא "הא נמי תנינא" אתא לתרוצי, ולאוקמה בענין אחר, דלא תקשי מהאי מתני' דלעיל. ומההיא מתני' דלקמן דמקשינן לרב פפא מינה – אכתי לא הוה מסיק אדעתיה. וכן כולם. אחד הבן ואחד הבת. במקום שאין בן, נוטלין חלק בכרת אביהן, אע"פ שמת בחיי זקינם. דכי היכי דירתי חלק פשיטותו – הכי נמי ירתי חלק בכורתו, וכדפרישית בפירקין דלעיל (דף קטז: ד"ה ושהיה) גבי מתני' דבנות צלפחד. והבאתי ראיה מברייתא דבכורות, ומתלמוד ירושלמי. הא נמי תנינא. שהיה צלפחד בכור, ואע"פ שמת בחיי חפר – נטלו בנותיו חלק בכורתו עם חלק פשיטותו. וכשמת חפר ואח"כ צלפחד לא היה צריך להשמיענו אחד הבן ואחד הבת נוטלין חלק בכורה, דכיון דמת הזקן תחלה – מיד ירש הבכור חלק בכורתו, דאין כאן ראוי כלל, וכשמת הבכור אחרי כן – פשיטא דירשוהו בניו, הן חלק פשיטותו הן חלק בכורתו. ועוד מאי אלא. מי דבר עדיין למעלה בנכסי האם, דקתנא לאיפלוגי בסיפא בין נכסי האב לנכסי האם? אחד בן בין הבנים. דאיהו יכול לעשותו יורש, דמתנה הוא על מה שכתוב בתורה, ועד שיתן לו בלשון מתנה לא קני, כדתנן בפירקין (דף קל.) ולא אחר בין הבנים. בת בין הבנות. ובן אין לו. אם אמר יירש כל נכסי דבריו קיימין. הואיל ובר ירושה הוא במקצת. ונפקא לן מ"ביום הנחילו את בניו" – שמנחיל לבניו כל מה שירצה. והיינו דקתני: אחד הבן ואחד הבת דינן שוה, שיכול האב להנחיל כל הנכסים לאחד מן האחין, או לאחת מן האחיות היכא דאין בן. ופרכינן: כמאן כרבי יוחנן כו' ועוד מאי אלא. דאפי' אם תאמר שהרבה יש סתם ואח"כ מחלוקת בגמרא, שבתחלה ראה את דברי התנא ההוא וסתמן, ואח"כ חזר בו ופירשו, ומשנה ראשונה לא זזה ממקומה – מאי "אלא"? אחד הבן ואחד הבת. שאין חילוק בין נכסי האם לנכסי האב, בין לענין ירושת הבנים בין לענין הבנות, חוץ משני דברים שיש חילוקין בין נכסי האם לנכסי האב, דהיינו בכורה ומזון, כדמפרש ואזיל: אלא שהבן הזכר נוטל פי שנים בנכסי האב ולא בנכסי האם. דלענין ירושת הבן יש חילוק בין נכסי האב לנכסי האם, אבל לענין ירושת הבת – אין חילוק בין נכסי האב לנכסי האם, דאין בת נוטלת בכורה, כדדרשינן בסיפרי: "וילדו לו בנים" – הבנים בתורה הזאת, ואין הבנות בתורה הזאת. ועוד חילוק אחר: שהבת ניזונת כו'. ומיהו, הבן שוה לענין מזונות בשניהן, שהרי יורש הכל. והיכא דאין לו מה לירש – אפילו מזונות אין לו, כגון בנכסים מועטין דאב. פי שנים כאחד. כנגד אחד מן האחין נוטל פי שנים, שאם היו חמשה אחין – חולקין הנכסים בששה חלקים ונוטל הבכור פי שנים (ב) מהן. בכל הנכסים. שנוטל פי שנים בכולן. ודין הוא. דפי שנים כאחד, שחלקו יהא עם ה' אחין דומה כחלקו עם אחד. כשאין שם אלא בכור ופשוט נוטל פי שנים (ג) בכל הנכסים, ממה נפשך, דפי שנים כאחד הוא, וגם פי שנים בכל הנכסים. והיה

תוספות

סתם ואחר כך מחלוקת הוא ואין הלכה כסתם. תימה: נהי נמי דלא חשיב סתם גמור, מ"מ אהני הא (ד) דחשיב כרבים, וחשיב רבי יוחנן כרבים לגבי רבים, ויכול להיות הלכה כמותו. דהא בריש מסכת ביצה (דף ב. ושם) אמרי': גבי שבת סתם לן תנא כר"ש, דתנן: מחתכין את הדלועין כו', אע"ג דסתם ואחר כך מחלוקת הוא, דפליג עליה רבי יהודה. דקתני, רבי יהודה אומר: אם לא היתה נבלה מערב שבת — אסורה. אלמא דלכל הפחות חשיב ההוא (ה) כרבים לגבי יחיד! ושמא גרע טפי כשאין מחלוקת בסמוך, דאיכא למימר דהדר ביה רבי מן הסתם ממה שסתם[ז]. תיומה

רבינו גרשום

דומין לחרס. שהיו יבשין: ולבסוף. בזכותו דומין לחרס והיו משתמרים ואינם נרקבים: כאשר דבר משה. ולא דבר ממש אלא כמו שכתוב בספר משה ויעלו בנגב ויבוא עד חברון זה היה כלב שפירש מעצת מרגלים והיה הולך לחברון לקברי אבות להתפלל לשם: פרוורהא. הכפרים שסביב חברון נתן לו ולא חברון ממש לפי שהיא היתה עיר מקלט: **פים'** אחד הבן ואחד הבת לנחלה. כדאמר בגמ': אלא שהבן נוטל פי שנים וכו' והבנות ניזונות מנכסי האב והבנים יחזרו על הפתחים. משום דהכי כתב לה בנן נוקבן דיהוון ליכי מינאי וכו': אילימא דירתו כהדדי. בשוה: והתנן בן קודם לבת. ועוד קושיא אחרת דאפי' כי הדדי ירתיהא דקתני מתני' אלא שהבן נוטל פי שנים היכי מיתוקם הא אמרת אחד הבן ואחד הבת לנחלה דכי הדדי נינהו וליכא להאי טפי מהאי: אמר רב נחמן הכי מיתרצת מתני' אחד הבן ואחד הבת. במקום דליכא בן נוטלת בראוי לאביה כבמוחזק לאביה: הא נמי תנינא. במתני' בנות צלפחד נטלו ג' חלקים חלק אביהן שהיה מיוצאי מצרים [ואע"ג] דאכתי חפר לא היה מוחזק בהני נכסי' ותרתי זמני למה לי. ועוד אפי' מצית למימר דאתא לאשמוע' דבת נוטלת בראוי כבמוחזק הא דקתני מתני' אלא שהבן נוטל פי שנים היכי מיתרץ והא בת במקום דלית בן נוטל פי שנים: אמר רב פפא הכי תריץ. אחד הבן של מת ואחד הבת של מת במקום שאין בן נוטלין בחלק בכורה תחת אביהן: והא נמי תנינא ושהיה בכור נוטל ב' חלקים. ובמקום דלא היה לצלפחד בן נוטלו' הבנות ועוד מאי האי דקתני מתני' אלא שהבן וכו' והא בת נמי אי לית בן נוטלת שני חלקים כבן: אמר רב אשי הכי קאמר מתני' אחד הבן בין הבנים. שאם היו לו י' בנים ואמר מאחד מהן איש פלוני בני יירש כל נכסי הכי נמי לבת בין הבנות אם אמר תירש פלונית כל נכסיי אע"פ שמונע בנות אחרות מירושתו דבריו קיימין הא היינו אחד הבן ואחד הבת שוין בהאי: כמאן. אמרת להא מילת':

כר' יוחנן בן ברוקה. דאמר אם אמר על מי שראוי ליורשו פלוני יטול כל נכסי דבריו קיימין אבל אמר דנכרי יירש כל נכסי במקום בנים לא אמר כלום. והואיל דאמרה ר' יוחנן חדא זימנא למה לך לשנויי מילתא זימנא אחריתא. וכי תימא משום הכי אצטריך למימר דקא סתם לן תנא דמתני' אחד הבן ואחד הבת לנחלה (א)וכן מוקים לה רב אשי לסתומי דהלכתא כר' יוחנן בן ברוקה והא סתם ואחר כך מחלוקת היא דרבנן פליגי עליה דר' יוחנן בן ברוקה וכל סתם ואחר כך מחלוקת אין הלכה כסתם. ועוד אפי' מצית למימר דסתם לן תנא הלכה כר' יוחנן בן ברוקה הא דקתני אלא שהבן נוטל היכי נפיל בהא מילתא: מר בר רב אשי אמר הכי קאמר מתני' אחד הבן ואחד הבת. במקום שאין בן שוין בנכסי האם (ב)כדאמר לעיל בכל אשר ימצא לו ולא לה: לתת לו. לבכור: פי שנים כאחד שאם היו לו י' בנים וחלקו הנכסים בי"א חלקים נוטל הבכור ב' חלקים היינו פי שנים כאחד: אתה אומר פי שנים כאחד או אינו אלא פי שנים בכל הנכסים. דמצי למיטען הבכור פי שנים בכל הנכסים של אבא הבו לי בין בקרקע בין בשאר נכסים: ודין הוא. דלא יהבינן ליה אלא פי שנים כאחד משום

(א) נראה דל"ל ואחד הבת לנחלה לפי מה דאוקים רב אשי כו'. ב) חסר כאן וצ"ל ואינו נוטל פי שנים בנכסי האם. כדאמר לעיל וכו'

מסורת הש"ס

א) מכות י.: ב) [בכורות נא:]: ג) [לעיל קטו. כתובות נ.]: ד) [לעיל קטז:]: ה) [שם]: ו) דף קל.: ז) [בבילה תירצו כמ"ש רשב"ם כאן וע"ע תוס' יבמות מב. ד"ה ולמאי]:

הגהות הב"ח

(א) רשב"ם ד"ה כאשר דבר וכו' שלא יכשל עמהן כצ"ל ותיבת בהן נמחק: (ב) ד"ה פי שנים וכו' פי שנים כאחד מהן: (ג) ד"ה ודין הוא וכו' ופשוט נוטל פי שנים כאחד הס"ד ואח"כ מ"ה פי שנים בכל הנכסים: (ד) תוס' ד"ה סתם וכו' מ"מ אהני הא סתמא לחשיב: (ה) בא"ד דלכל הפחות חשיב ההוא סתמא כרבים:

א) ס"א רבא: ב) כ"א איש יודע ציד: ג) מגילה יג: ע"ש: ד) מהגאון ר' חייקי נ"א לה מקמאי: ה) [בפרקי דר"א פרק ל"ו ובב"ר פ' ויקב]

חֶלְקוֹ עִם אֶחָד וְחֶלְקוֹ עִם חֲמִשָּׁה, מַה חֶלְקוֹ עִם אֶחָד — פִּי שְׁנַיִם כְּאֶחָד, אַף חֶלְקוֹ עִם חֲמִשָּׁה — פִּי שְׁנַיִם כְּאֶחָד; אוֹ כְּלָךְ לְדֶרֶךְ זוֹ: חֶלְקוֹ עִם אֶחָד וְחֶלְקוֹ עִם ה', מַה חֶלְקוֹ עִם אֶחָד — פִּי שְׁנַיִם בְּכָל הַנְּכָסִים, אַף חֶלְקוֹ עִם ה' — פִּי שְׁנַיִם בְּכָל הַנְּכָסִים! ת"ל: "וְהָיָה בְּיוֹם הַנְחִילוֹ אֶת בָּנָיו", הַתּוֹרָה רִיבְּתָה נַחֲלָה אֵצֶל אַחִין, הָא אֵין עָלֶיךָ לָדוּן כַּלָּשׁוֹן הָאַחֲרוֹן אֶלָּא כַּלָּשׁוֹן הָרִאשׁוֹן; וְאוֹמֵר: "וּבְנֵי רְאוּבֵן בְּכוֹר יִשְׂרָאֵל כִּי הוּא הַבְּכוֹר וּבְחַלְּלוֹ יְצוּעֵי אָבִיו נִתְּנָה בְּכוֹרָתוֹ לִבְנֵי יוֹסֵף בֶּן יִשְׂרָאֵל וְלֹא לְהִתְיַחֵשׂ לַבְּכוֹרָה"; וְאוֹמֵר: "כִּי יְהוּדָה גָּבַר בְּאֶחָיו וּלְנָגִיד מִמֶּנּוּ וְהַבְּכוֹרָה לְיוֹסֵף", נֶאֶמְרָה בְּכוֹרָה לְיוֹסֵף וְנֶאֶמְרָה בְּכוֹרָה לְדוֹרוֹת, מַה בְּכוֹרָה הָאֲמוּרָה לְיוֹסֵף — פִּי שְׁנַיִם כְּאֶחָד, אַף בְּכוֹרָה הָאֲמוּרָה לְדוֹרוֹת — פִּי שְׁנַיִם כְּאֶחָד; וְאוֹמֵר: "וַאֲנִי נָתַתִּי לְךָ שְׁכֶם אַחַד עַל אַחֶיךָ אֲשֶׁר לָקַחְתִּי מִיַּד הָאֱמוֹרִי בְּחַרְבִּי וּבְקַשְׁתִּי", וְכִי בְּחַרְבּוֹ וּבְקַשְׁתּוֹ לָקַח? וַהֲלֹא כְּבָר נֶאֱמַר: "כִּי לֹא בְקַשְׁתִּי אֶבְטָח וְחַרְבִּי לֹא תוֹשִׁיעֵנִי"! אֶלָּא, "חַרְבִּי" — זוֹ תְּפִלָּה, "קַשְׁתִּי" — זוֹ בַּקָּשָׁה. מַאי "וְאוֹמֵר"? וְכִי תֵּימָא: הַאי לְכִדְר' יוֹחָנָן בֶּן בְּרוֹקָא הוּא דַּאֲתָא — ת"ש: "וּבְנֵי רְאוּבֵן בְּכוֹר יִשְׂרָאֵל"; וְכִי תֵּימָא: בְּכוֹרָה מִ"בְּכוֹרָתוֹ" לָא גָּמְרִינַן — ת"ש: "וְהַבְּכוֹרָה לְיוֹסֵף"; וְכִי תֵּימָא: יוֹסֵף גּוּפֵיהּ, מִמַּאי דְּפִי שְׁנַיִם כְּאֶחָד הֲוָה? תָּא שְׁמַע: "וַאֲנִי נָתַתִּי לְךָ שְׁכֶם אַחַד עַל אַחֶיךָ". א"ל רַב פַּפָּא לְאַבַּיֵי, אֵימָא: דִּיקְלָא בְּעָלְמָא! א"ל, עָלֶיךָ אָמַר קְרָא: "אֶפְרַיִם וּמְנַשֶּׁה כִּרְאוּבֵן וְשִׁמְעוֹן יִהְיוּ לִי". § בְּעָא מִינֵּיהּ ר' חֶלְבּוֹ מֵרַבִּי שְׁמוּאֵל בַּר נַחְמָנִי: מָה רָאָה יַעֲקֹב שֶׁנָּטַל בְּכוֹרָה מֵרְאוּבֵן וּנְתָנָהּ לְיוֹסֵף? מָה רָאָה?! "וּבְחַלְּלוֹ יְצוּעֵי אָבִיו" כְּתִיב! אֶלָּא, מָה רָאָה שֶׁנְּתָנָהּ לְיוֹסֵף? אֶמְשׁוֹל לְךָ מָשָׁל, לְמָה הַדָּבָר דּוֹמֶה? לְבַעַל הַבַּיִת שֶׁגִּידֵּל יָתוֹם בְּתוֹךְ בֵּיתוֹ, לְיָמִים הֶעֱשִׁיר אוֹתוֹ יָתוֹם וְאָמַר: אַהֲנֵיהוּ לְבַעַל הַבַּיִת מִנִּכְסַי. א"ל: וְאִי לָאו דַּחֲטָא רְאוּבֵן, לָא מַהֲנֵי לֵיהּ לְיוֹסֵף וְלָא מִדַּעַם? אֶלָּא, ר' יוֹנָתָן רַבָּךְ לֹא כָּךְ אָמַר: רְאוּיָה הָיְתָה בְּכוֹרָה לָצֵאת מֵרָחֵל, דִּכְתִיב: "אֵלֶּה תּוֹלְדוֹת יַעֲקֹב יוֹסֵף", אֶלָּא שֶׁקְּדָמַתָּה לֵאָה בְּרַחֲמִים, וּמִתּוֹךְ צְנִיעוּת שֶׁהָיְתָה בָּהּ בְּרָחֵל הֶחֱזִירָהּ הקב"ה לָהּ. מַאי קְדָמַתָּה לֵאָה בְּרַחֲמִים? דִּכְתִיב: "וְעֵינֵי לֵאָה רַכּוֹת", מַאי "רַכּוֹת"? אִילֵימָא רַכּוֹת מַמָּשׁ, אֶפְשָׁר? בִּגְנוּת בְּהֵמָה טְמֵאָה לֹא דִּבֵּר הַכָּתוּב, דִּכְתִיב: "מִן הַבְּהֵמָה הַטְּהוֹרָה וּמִן הַבְּהֵמָה אֲשֶׁר אֵינֶנָּה טְהוֹרָה", בִּגְנוּת צַדִּיקִים דִּבֵּר הַכָּתוּב?! אֶלָּא א"ר אֶלְעָזָר: שֶׁמַּתְּנוֹתֶיהָ אֲרוּכּוֹת. א)רַב אָמַר: לְעוֹלָם רַכּוֹת מַמָּשׁ, וְלֹא גְּנַאי הוּא לָהּ, אֶלָּא שֶׁבַח הוּא לָהּ; שֶׁהָיְתָה שׁוֹמַעַת עַל פָּרָשַׁת דְּרָכִים בְּנֵי אָדָם שֶׁהָיוּ אוֹמְרִים: שְׁנֵי בָנִים יֵשׁ לָהּ לְרִבְקָה, שְׁתֵּי בָנוֹת יֵשׁ לוֹ לְלָבָן, גְּדוֹלָה לְגָדוֹל וּקְטַנָּה לְקָטָן. וְהָיְתָה יוֹשֶׁבֶת עַל פָּרָשַׁת דְּרָכִים וּמְשַׁאֶלֶת: גָּדוֹל מַה מַּעֲשָׂיו? ב)אִישׁ רַע הוּא, מְלַסְטֵם בְּרִיּוֹת. קָטָן מַה מַּעֲשָׂיו? "אִישׁ תָּם יוֹשֵׁב אֹהָלִים", וְהָיְתָה בּוֹכָה עַד שֶׁנָּשְׁרוּ רִיסֵי עֵינֶיהָ. וְהַיְינוּ דִּכְתִיב: "וַיַּרְא ה' כִּי שְׂנוּאָה לֵאָה", מַאי שְׂנוּאָה? אִילֵימָא שְׂנוּאָה מַמָּשׁ, אֶפְשָׁר? בִּגְנוּת בְּהֵמָה טְמֵאָה לֹא דִּבֵּר הַכָּתוּב, בִּגְנוּת צַדִּיקִים דִּבֵּר הַכָּתוּב?! אֶלָּא רָאָה הקב"ה שֶׁשְּׂנוּאִין מַעֲשֵׂה עֵשָׂו בְּפָנֶיהָ — "וַיִּפְתַּח אֶת רַחְמָהּ". ג)וּמַאי צְנִיעוּת הָיְתָה בָּהּ בְּרָחֵל? דִּכְתִיב: "וַיַּגֵּד יַעֲקֹב לְרָחֵל כִּי אֲחִי אָבִיהָ הוּא וְכִי בֶּן רִבְקָה הוּא", וַהֲלֹא בֶּן אֲחוֹת אָבִיהָ הוּא! אֶלָּא, אֲמַר לָהּ: מִינַּסְבַתְּ לִי? אֲמָרָה לֵיהּ: אִין, מִיהוּ אַבָּא רַמָּאָה הוּא וְלָא יָכְלַתְּ לֵיהּ. אֲמַר לָהּ: מַאי רַמָּאוּתֵיהּ? אֲמָרָה לֵיהּ: אִית לִי אַחְתָּא דְּקַשִּׁישָׁא מִינַּאי, וְלָא מְנַסְּבָא ד)לִי מִקַּמַּהּ. אֲמַר לָהּ: אָחִיו אֲנִי בְּרַמָּאוּת. [א"ל:] וּמִי שָׁרֵי לְהוּ לְצַדִּיקֵי לְסַגּוּיֵי בְּרַמָּאוּתָא? אִין, "עִם נָבָר תִּתָּבָר וְעִם עִקֵּשׁ תִּתַּפָּל". מָסַר לָהּ סִימָנִין. כִּי קָא מְעַיְּילִי לָהּ לְלֵאָה, סְבָרָה: הָשְׁתָּא מִיכַּסְפָא אַחְתַאי. מְסַרְתִּינְהוּ נִיהֲלָהּ. וְהַיְינוּ דִּכְתִיב: "וַיְהִי בַבֹּקֶר וְהִנֵּה הִיא לֵאָה", מִכְּלָל דְּעַד הָשְׁתָּא לָאו לֵאָה הִיא?! אֶלָּא, מִתּוֹךְ סִימָנִים שֶׁמָּסַר לָהּ יַעֲקֹב לְרָחֵל וּמְסַרְתָּה לְלֵאָה, לָא הֲוָה יָדַע לָהּ עַד הַהִיא שַׁעְתָּא. בְּעָא מִינֵּיהּ אַבָּא חֲלִיפָא קְרוֹיָא מֵר' חִיָּיא בַּר אַבָּא: בִּכְלָלָן אַתָּה מוֹצֵא שִׁבְעִים, בִּפְרָטָן אַתָּה מוֹצֵא שִׁבְעִים חָסֵר אֶחָד! אֲמַר לֵיהּ: תְּאוֹמָה הָיְתָה עִם דִּינָה, דִּכְתִיב: "וְאֵת דִּינָה בִתּוֹ". אֶלָּא מֵעַתָּה, תְּאוֹמָה הָיְתָה עִם בִּנְיָמִן, דִּכְתִיב: וְאֵת

תיומה היתה עם בנימין. ובעלמא ה)אמרינן: תיומה היתה עם כל השבטים. היתה

וְהָיָה בְּיוֹם הַנְחִילוֹ אֶת בָּנָיו וגו'. כּוּלֵּיהּ קְרָא יְתֵירָא הוּא, דְּהָא כְּתִיב בָּתְרֵיהּ: "כִּי אֶת הַבְּכוֹר בֶּן הַשְּׂנוּאָה יַכִּיר לָתֶת לוֹ פִּי שְׁנַיִם" וגו'. רִיבְּתָה נַחֲלָה. שֶׁלֹּא יִטּוֹל פִּי שְׁנַיִם בְּכָל הַנְּכָסִים הֵיכָא דְּאִיכָּא שְׁנַיִם וג' אַחִים מִלְּבַדּוֹ. וְאוֹמֵר. לְקַמָּן מְפָרֵשׁ מַאי "וְאוֹמֵר". תָּנֵי קְרָאֵי בְּדִבְרֵי הַיָּמִים כְּתִיבִי. וְלֹא לְהִתְיַחֵשׂ עַל הַבְּכוֹרָה. לֹא שֶׁיִּקָּרֵא בְּכוֹר נִיתְּנָה לוֹ בְּכוֹרָה, דִּלְעוֹלָם רְאוּבֵן קָרֵי בְּכוֹר יִשְׂרָאֵל, אֶלָּא לִיטּוֹל שְׁנֵי חֲלָקִים כִּבְכוֹר, כִּדְכְתִיב: "אֶפְרַיִם וּמְנַשֶּׁה כִּרְאוּבֵן וְשִׁמְעוֹן יִהְיוּ לִי" (בראשית מח). בְּכוֹרָה לְדוֹרוֹת. "לוֹ מִשְׁפַּט הַבְּכוֹרָה" (דברים כא). מַה בְּכוֹרָה הָאֲמוּרָה לְיוֹסֵף פִּי שְׁנַיִם כְּאֶחָד. כִּדִלְקַמָּן. שְׁכֶם אַחַד עַל אַחֶיךָ. שְׁנֵי חֲלָקִים כְּנֶגֶד שְׁנֵי אַחִין, כִּדִלְקַמָּן. זוֹ תְּפִלָּה. שֶׁהִתְפַּלֵּל יַעֲקֹב עַל בָּנָיו, וְשֶׁזָּכָה לִקְנוֹת הַבְּכוֹרָה מֵעֵשָׂו בִּתְפִלָּתוֹ. ת"ש וּבְנֵי רְאוּבֵן בְּכוֹר יִשְׂרָאֵל. וּכְתִיב בְּהַאי קְרָא: "נִיתְּנָה בְּכוֹרָתוֹ", וְיָלְפִינַן בְּבִנְיַן אָב "בְּכוֹרָה" מִ"בְּכוֹרָתוֹ" דְּנְהִי דְּדִבְרֵי תוֹרָה מִדִּבְרֵי קַבָּלָה לָא יָלְפִינַן — גִּלּוּיֵי מִילְּתָא בְּעָלְמָא הוּא, דְּלָא הָיִינוּ יוֹדְעִין מַהוּ חֵלֶק בְּכוֹרָה, וְשָׁמְעִי' מֵהָתָם דְּפִי שְׁנַיִם כְּאֶחָד. כִּדְאָמְרִי' נַמִי בְּעָלְמָא (מו"ק דף ה.): דָּבָר זֶה מִתּוֹרַת מֹשֶׁה רַבֵּינוּ לֹא לָמַדְנוּ, עַד שֶׁבָּא יְחֶזְקֵאל וּפֵירֵשׁ "וְכָל בֶּן נֵכָר וגו' לֹא יָבֹא אֶל מִקְדָּשִׁי" וגו', וְאָמְרִינַן: עַד דַּאֲתָא יְחֶזְקֵאל מַאן אֲמָרָהּ? אֶלָּא גְּמָרָא הֲווּ גְּמִירִי לָהּ, וַאֲתָא יְחֶזְקֵאל וְאַסְמְכָהּ אַקְּרָא. וְהוּא הַדִּין לִבְכוֹרָה. אֵימָא דִּיקְלָא. קַרְקַע מוּעָט הוֹסִיף לוֹ יַעֲקֹב לְיוֹסֵף בִּשְׁבִיל בְּכוֹרָה! וְה"ה דַּהֲוָה מָצֵי לְמִיפְרַךְ: פִּי שְׁנַיִם בְּכָל הַנְּכָסִים, אֶלָּא מִשּׁוּם דְּהָא קָא חָזִינַן דְּלָא הֲוַאי לְהוּ נַחֲלָה כּוּלֵּי הַאי, דְּהָא קָלָווֹתֵי בְּנֵי יוֹסֵף. כִּרְאוּבֵן וְשִׁמְעוֹן. כְּנֶגֶד שְׁנֵי שְׁבָטִים, וּכְדַאֲמָרַן לִשְׁבָטִים אִיתְפַּלַּג — דְּהַיְינוּ פִּי שְׁנַיִם כְּאֶחָד. וְהַאי דְּלָא קָאָמַר בַּבָּרַיְיתָא: וְאוֹמֵר "כִּרְאוּבֵן וְשִׁמְעוֹן יִהְיוּ לִי" — הַיְינוּ מִשּׁוּם דְּמִילְּתָא דִּפְשִׁיטָא לֵיהּ לְתַנָּא יוֹתֵר מִדְּהַאי דְּהַאי "שְׁכֶם אֶחָד עַל אַחֶיךָ" אַהַהוּא קְרָא קָאֵי דִּכְתִיב לְעֵיל מִינֵּיהּ "כִּרְאוּבֵן וְשִׁמְעוֹן יִהְיוּ לִי", וּפֵירוּשָׁא דְּהַהוּא קְרָא הוּא, הִלְכָּךְ לֹא חָשׁ לְהַזְכִּיר, דְּזִיל קְרֵי בֵּי רַב הוּא. לְבַעַל הַבַּיִת. יוֹסֵף. יָתוֹם. יַעֲקֹב, דִּכְתִיב: "וַיְכַלְכֵּל אֶת אָבִיו" וגו' (בראשית מז). לְסוֹף הֶעֱשִׁיר. יַעֲקֹב, שֶׁבָּאָה לְיָדוֹ בְּכוֹרַת רְאוּבֵן עַל יְדֵי שֶׁחִילֵּל יְצוּעֵי אָבִיו, וְהָיָה יָכוֹל לִיתְּנָהּ לְכָל מִי שֶׁיִּרְצֶה. וְאִי לָאו דְּחָטָא רְאוּבֵן לָא הֲוָה מְהַנֵּי לֵיהּ לְיוֹסֵף. בִּתְמִיָּה. כְּלוֹמַר, מַה נָּתַן יַעֲקֹב לְיוֹסֵף? שֶׁהֲרֵי מֵחֵלֶק שְׁאָר אַחִין הוֹסִיף לוֹ, אֲבָל מִשֶּׁלּוֹ לֹא נָתַן לוֹ כְּלוּם, דְּמִשֶּׁלּוֹ הֲוָה לוֹ לְהַהֲנוֹתוֹ וְלֹא מִשֶּׁל אֲחֵרִים! אֶלָּא וַדַּאי מִשֶּׁלּוֹ נָתַן לוֹ, הֵן מָמוֹנוֹ הֵן בְּרָכוֹת שֶׁבֵּירְכוֹ (א) מְכוּוָּן, כְּגוֹן בְּרָכָה שֶׁבֵּירְכוֹ לְאֶפְרַיִם וּמְנַשֶּׁה "וְיִדְגּוּ לָרֹב" וגו' שֶׁאֵין עַיִן רָעָה שׁוֹלֶטֶת בָּהֶן, וּכְגוֹן "מֵאֵל אָבִיךָ וְיַעְזְרֶךָּ" וגו' "תִּהְיֶיןָ לְרֹאשׁ יוֹסֵף" וגו'. הִלְכָּךְ, מַה שֶּׁנָּתַן בְּכוֹרַת רְאוּבֵן לְיוֹסֵף — טַעַם אַחֵר יֵשׁ בַּדָּבָר. אֶלָּא ר' יוֹנָתָן רַבָּךְ לֹא כָּךְ אָמַר. כִּדְאָמְרִי' בְּכָל דּוּכְתָּא: א"ר שְׁמוּאֵל בַּר נַחְמָנִי א"ר יוֹנָתָן. לָצֵאת מֵרָחֵל. שֶׁתֵּלֵד רָחֵל אֶת יוֹסֵף קוֹדֶם שֶׁתֵּלֵד לֵאָה אֶת רְאוּבֵן, דְּלֶיהֱוֵי יוֹסֵף רֵאשִׁית אוֹנוֹ דְּיַעֲקֹב. שֶׁקְּדָמַתָּה לֵאָה בְּרַחֲמִים. בִּתְפִלָּה, לְקַמֵּיהּ מְפָרֵשׁ. צְנִיעוּת דְּרָחֵל. לְקַמֵּיהּ מְפָרֵשׁ. רַכּוֹת מַמָּשׁ. עֵינֶיהָ נוֹטְפוֹת דִּמְעָה. אֶפְשָׁר. לוֹמַר כֵּן? וַהֲלֹא בִּגְנוּת בְּהֵמָה טְמֵאָה. לֹא רָצָה הַכָּתוּב לְדַבֵּר, אֶלָּא עִיקֵּם שְׁמוֹנֶה אוֹתִיּוֹת, דִּכְתִיב: "אֲשֶׁר אֵינֶנָּה טְהוֹרָה", דְּאִיכָּא י"ג אוֹתִיּוֹת, וַהֲוָה מָצֵי לְמִיכְתַּב "הַטְּמֵאָה" דְּלֵיכָּא אֶלָּא ה' אוֹתִיּוֹת. בִּגְנוּתָן שֶׁל צַדִּיקִים דִּבֵּר הַכָּתוּב. בִּתְמִיָּה. אֶלָּא אָמַר רַבִּי אֶלְעָזָר כו'. תֵּלֵיכָּא דְּר' אֶלְעָזָר לָא אַשְׁכְּחַן שֶׁקְּדָמַתָּה לֵאָה בְּרַחֲמִים, אֶלָּא אַלִּיבָּא דְּרַב. אֲרוּכּוֹת. גְּדוֹלוֹת בִּכְהוּנָּה וּלְוִיָּה. (ב) דְּלֵוִי יָצָא מִמֶּנָּה, שֶׁמִּמֶּנּוּ כֹּהֲנִים וּלְוִיִּם, וּמַלְכוּת מִיהוּדָה. וַיִּפְתַּח אֶת רַחְמָהּ. הַיְינוּ שֶׁזָּכְתָה לִבְכוֹרָה. מָסַר לָהּ. יַעֲקֹב סִימָנִין לְרָחֵל, שֶׁתֹּאמַר לוֹ בַּלַּיְלָה בִּשְׁכִיבָה. בְּעָא מִינֵּיהּ אַבָּא חֲלִיפָא קְרוֹיָא מֵר' חִיָּיא כו'. מִשּׁוּם דְּאַיְירֵי לְעֵיל בִּבְעָיָא דִּקְרָאֵי דְּיַעֲקֹב וּבָנָיו, נָקַט נַמִי לְהַךְ בְּעָיָא הָכָא. בִּכְלָלָן. שֶׁל יִשְׂרָאֵל כְּשֶׁבָּאוּ לְמִצְרַיִם, אַתָּה מוֹצֵא כָּתוּב "כָּל הַנֶּפֶשׁ (הַבָּאָה לְיַעֲקֹב) מִצְרַיְמָה שִׁבְעִים", וּבִפְרָטָן — כְּשֶׁהוּא מוֹנֶה אוֹתָן אֶחָד אֶחָד לְמַעְלָה בַּפָּרָשָׁה, אִי אַתָּה מוֹצֵא אֶלָּא שִׁשִּׁים וְתֵשַׁע עִם יוֹסֵף וּשְׁנֵי בָנָיו, וּכְדִכְתִיב בְּהֶדְיָא: "כָּל נֶפֶשׁ שִׁשִּׁים וָשֵׁשׁ". וּמִבְּנֵי לֵאָה חָסֵר, דִּכְתִיב בִּכְלַל דִּידָהּ שְׁלֹשִׁים וג' וּבִפְרָטָם אִי אַתָּה מוֹצֵא אֶלָּא ל"ב. תְּיוֹמָה. שֶׁנּוֹלְדוּ לְלֵאָה שְׁתֵּי בָנוֹת בְּכֶרֶס אֶחָד. וְאֵת

[נ"ל לבית יעקב הבאה]

משום דחלקו עם אחד א) מן האחין דכי היכי דאי הוה חלק בין ה' אחין פי שנים כאחד או כלך לדרך זו וכו' דחלקו עם אחד היינו פי שנים בכל הנכסים השתא איכא למימר הכי דנוטל פי שנים כאחד ואיכא למימר דנוטל פי שנים בכל הנכסים משום הכי אצטריך למימר והיה ביום הנחילו את בניו דמצי למימר בקרא לחוד לא יוכל לבכר את בן האהובה וגו' כי את הבכור יכיר וגו' למה לי דכתב והיה ביום הנחילו את בניו וגו'. אלא התורה ריבתה נחלה אצל האחין כלומר דרוב הנחלה תהא אצל האחין ואי הוי שקיל בכור פי שנים בכל הנכסים נמצא רוב הנחלה אצל בכור השתא דאיכא למימר הכי ואיכא למימר הכי אין עליך לדון כלשון האחרון אלא כלשון הראשון דפי שנים כאחד בעינן: ולא להתייחש לבכורה. דאי דליהוי בכור ממש דהא לא אפשר אלא כדי ליתן לו פי שנים: ולנגיד ממנו והבכורה ליוסף נאמר בכורה ליוסף. דכתב ניתנה בכורה ליוסף: ונאמר בכורה לדורות. ולו משפט הבכורה: מה בכורה ליוסף פי שנים כאחד. דארץ ישראל לי"ב חלקים נתחלקה וכתיב אפרים ומנשה כראובן ושמעון יהיו לי היינו חלק בכורה אלמא פי שנים כאחד נקט יוסף ולא בכל הנכסים: מאי ואומר. דקאמר לעיל ואומר ובני ראובן בכור ישראל והא כבר דרשי' שפיר מוהיה ביום הנחילו דנוטל פי שנים כאחד. וכי תימא משום הכי אצטריך האי דאי הוה כתב ביום הנחילו את בניו לדרשא אחרינא הוא דאתא כדר' יוחנן בן ברוקא דאמר לקמן מאי טעמא דר' יוחנן בן ברוקא דאמר קרא והיה ביום הנחילו את בניו התורה נתנה רשות לאב להנחיל לכל מי שירצה ומשום הכי איצטריך למימר ובני ראובן בכור ישראל נאמר בכורה ליוסף וכו' וכי תימא בכורה מבכורתו לא ילפינן דבכורה לחוד ובכורתו לחוד. ת"ש והבכורה ליוסף דילפי' בכורה מבכורה וכי תימא יוסף כו'. ת"ש אמר ליה רב פפא לאביי ממאי מצית למימר דפי שנים כאחד יהיב ליה אימא דיקלא בעלמא יהיב ליה טפי מאחיו ולא פי שנים. אמר ליה עלך נאמר קרא כראובן ושמעון יהיו לי דנוטלין ב' חלקים כראובן ושמעון: אמר אהנה לבעל הבית מנכסי. הכי נמי עשה יעקב ליוסף לפי שיוסף גידל את יעקב אבינו ובניו בארץ מצרים כדכתי' ויכלכל יוסף את אחיו וגו' ולבסוף כשהעשיר יעקב שחילק נכסיו ובירך את בניו ההנהו ליוסף שנתן לו חלק הבכורה: אמר ליה ר' חלבו לר' שמואל בר נחמני ר' יונתן רבך לא אמר כן: ארוכות. בכהונה לעולם דכתיב ברית כהונת עולם. והכי נמי לויה. וארוכות במלכות בית דוד לו ולזרעו עד עולם. ריסי עיניה. שערות עפעפיה: בכללן. של ישראל כשנכנסו במצרים כתיב כל הנפש לבית יעקב הבאה מצרים שבעים: ובפרטן. שמחשב כל אחד בפני עצמו אתה מוצא שבעים שלמין הן ותאומה היתה עם דינה דכתיב ואת דינה בתו. לרבות תאומתה: אלא מעתה תאומה היתה עם בנימין דכתיב ואת

הגהות הב"ח

(א) רשב"ם ד"ה ואי לאו וכו' שבירכו יותר מכולן: (ב) ד"ה ארוכות וכו' ולויה ומלכות דלוי:

(בראשית מג) °"ואת בנימין אחיו בן אמו"! א)אמר: מרגלית טובה היתה בידך ואתה מבקש לאבדה ממני, הכי ב)אמר ר' חמא בר חנינא: זו יוכבד, שהורתה בדרך ילידתה בין החומות, שנאמר: (במדבר כ) °"אשר ילדה אותה ללוי במצרים", לידתה במצרים ואין הורתה במצרים. בעא מיניה ר' חלבו מר' שמואל בר נחמני, כתיב: (בראשית ל) °"ויהי כאשר ילדה רחל את יוסף" וגו', מאי שנא כי אתיליד יוסף? אמר ליה: ראה יעקב אבינו שאין זרעו של עשו נמסר אלא ביד זרעו של יוסף, שנאמר: (עובדיה א) °"והיה בית יעקב אש ובית יוסף להבה ובית עשו לקש" וגו'. איתיביה: (שמואל א ל) °"ויכם דוד מהנשף ועד הערב למחרתם"! אמר ליה: דאקריך נביאי לא אקריך כתובי, דכתיב: (דה"א יב) °"בלכתו אל צקלג נפלו עליו ממנשה עדנה ויוזבד וידיעאל ומיכאל ויוזבד ואליהוא וצלתי ראשי האלפים אשר למנשה". מתיב רב יוסף: (שם ד) °"ומהם מן בני שמעון הלכו להר שעיר אנשים חמש מאות ופלטיה ונעריה ורפיה ועזיאל בני ישעי בראשם, ויכו את שארית הפלטה לעמלק וישבו שם עד היום הזה". אמר רבה בר שילא: ישעי מבני מנשה אתי, דכתיב: (שם ה) ג)°"ובני מנשה חפר וישעי". תנו רבנן: ד)אהבכור נוטל פי שנים בזרוע ובלחיים ובקיבה, ובמוקדשין, ובשבח ששבחו נכסים לאחר מיתת אביהן. כיצד? בהניח להן אביהן פרה מוחכרת ומושכרת ביד אחרים, או שהיתה רועה באפר, וילדה — בכור נוטל פי שנים. אבל בנו בתים ונטעו כרמים — אין בכור נוטל פי שנים. האי הזרוע והלחיים והקיבה היכי דמי? אי דאתי לידי אבוהון פשיטא, ואי דלא אתי לידי אבוהון — ראוי הוא, ה)ואין הבכור נוטל בראוי כבמוחזק! גהכא במכירי כהונה עסקינן, ודאשתחיט בחיי דאבוהון, וקסבר: ו)דמתנות שלא הורמו כמי שהורמו דמו. מוקדשין — לאו דידיה נינהו! בקדשים קלים, ואליבא דרבי יוסי הגלילי דאמר: ממון בעלים הוא; ז)דתניא: (ויקרא ה) °"ומעלה מעל בה'" — לרבות קדשים קלים שהן ממון בעלים, דברי רבי יוסי הגלילי. הניח להן אביהן פרה מוחכרת ומושכרת ביד אחרים, או שהיתה רועה באפר, וילדה — בכור נוטל בה פי שנים. השתא מוחכרת ומושכרת דלאו ברשותא דמרה דידהו קיימא, אמרת: שקיל, רועה באפר מיבעיא? הא קא משמע לן, דמוחכרת ומושכרת דומיא דרועה באפר, מה רועה באפר — שבחא דממילא קא אתי, ולא קא חסרי בה מזונא,

אף

היתה מוחכרת או מושכרת ביד אחרים בכור נוטל פי שנים. לקמן מוקי לה כרבי, דלרבנן אין הבכור נוטל פי שנים בשבח ששבחו נכסים לאחר מיתת אביהן. אע"ג דבכור ופשוט שהניח להן אביהן עבד או בהמה טמאה עובד לזה יום אחד ולזה שני ימים, ה"נ אי אמר הבכור: או תחלקו או אטול פי שנים בשבח — הרשות בידו. והא דלא נקט חכרוה ושכרוה היתומין — משום דהשתא אשמעינן חידוש טפי, דאע"ג שהיתה חכורה ושכורה בחיי האב — לא חשבינן להפרה ראוי, ויטול פי שנים. **הכא** במכירי כהונה (ולויה) עסקינן. בכל דוכתא עביד מכירי כהונה מוחזק, בפרק "כל הגט" (גיטין דף ל.): המלוה מעות את הכהן והלוי. והיינו טעמא: שזהו מתנה מועטת, ואסור לחזור בו ואפי' בדברי' בעלמא. ואע"פ שאם רצה יכול לחזור בו, מכל מקום כל כמה דלא הדר — הוי כמוחזק. ודוקא דאשתחיט בחיי אבוהון, הא לאו הכי — לא, כיון דמת מי יזכה? **וקסבר** מתנות שלא הורמו כמי שהורמו דמו. תימה: דבסמוך מוקי לה כרבי, ובסוף פ"ב דקידושין (דף נח.) אית ליה ח)דלאו כמי שהורמו דמי! וי"ל: דתנא דהכא לא סבר ליה כרבי אלא בהא דבכור שקיל פי שנים בשבח. אי נמי, דוקא במתנות דתרומת מעשר אית ליה לרבי דלאו כמי שהורמו דמי, אבל מתנות דהכא, דזרוע ולחיים, שהן ניכרות — אית ליה כמי שהורמו דמיין.

אף

ואת. ריבוי הוא. מרגלית טובה. טעם יקר בעיני כמרגלית, שלא הייתי רוצה לגלות. ומעיקרא לחדודי הוא דבעי. לאבדה ממני. כלומר, לגלותה לאחרים. ולהכי הטעם היה אומר כן. זו יוכבד. ולכך לא פרט בה, שהרי עדיין לא יצאה לאויר העולם, אלא עובר במעי אמה היתה

תורה אור

בכניסת' למצרים. מאי שנא. דלא רצה לשוב לבית אביו עד שנולד יוסף? ויכם דוד. בעמלק, כשפשטו על צקלג ונהגו נשי דוד מיירי, בספר שמואל. והלא דוד מיהודה הוה ולא מיוסף, ונפל זרעו של עשו בידו, דעמלק היה בן אליפז בן עשו, ואתה אמרת שאינו נמסר אלא ביד זרעו של יוסף. והלא גם ביד שאר שבטים נמסר, ואמאי קאמר קרא: "ובית יוסף להבה" טפי משבט יהודה? דכתיב. בדברי הימים: "בלכתו אל צקלג" להלחם בעמלק. נפלו עליו כו'. "ראשי האלפים אשר למנשה". לפי שנשתתפו עמו ממנשה, דהיינו משבט יוסף, לכך נפלו בידו. מבני שמעון וגו'. "ויכו את שארית הפלטה לעמלק" — אלמא ביד בני שמעון נמי נפלו, ואתה אמרת שאין נמסר אלא ביד זרעו של יוסף. בכור. בן כהן. נוטל (א) בזרוע פי שנים כו'. לקמן מפרש לה. ובמוקדשים. לקמן מפרש לה. ששבחו. מעצמן, כיצד? הניח כו'. מוחכרת. למחצית שכר. מושכרת. בדבר קצוב עד זמן פלוני. באפר. אחו, דלא חסרי מזוני, כדלקמן. וילדה בכור נוטל פי שנים. בהאי ולד, הואיל ושבחא דממילא הוא, ודמי כאילו הוחזק בו אביהן. אבל בנו בתים. דהאי שבחא על ידי היתומים עצמן הוא, ולאו ממילא — לא קא שקיל פי שנים. ראוי הוא. דלא דמי לשבחא שהשביחו הנכסים. דכיון דהוי אבוהון מוחזק בנכסים, והן עצמן הושבחו — כמי שהוחזקו בשבח דמי. אבל הני מתנות לא זכה (ב) אביהן כלום מחיים, וכולן הוו שבח. ה"ג: במכירי כהונה עסקינן. שאנשי העיר קרוביו ומכיריו של כהן זה, ומזכין לו זיכוי גמור במתנות בהמותיהן מיד כשנשחטו, קודם שהופרשו מן הבהמה. ודאשתחיט בחיי אבוהון. ודמי כמאן דאתו לידיה בטבלייהו, דאמרי' ב"שחיטת חולין" בפ' "הזרוע" (דף קל.) דקני להו כהן אי אתו לידיה בטבלייהו. דמתנות שלא הורמו – כמי שהורמו דמיין, כדנפקא לן התם מ"וזה יהיה משפט הכהנים" – מלמד שהמתנות דינן להוציאן בדיינין אי אתו לידיה בטבלייהו, כדמפרש התם. וה"נ כיון דאשתחיט בחיי אבוהון, והן מכירין של כהן זה ומרעיו ואוהביו, אע"פ שעדיין לא הופרשו – הרי הם כאילו באו לידו. שאלו אוהביו גמרו ומקנו לו המתנות כשהן עדיין בתוך הבהמה, ודמי כמי שהוחזק בהן בחייו, דמתנות שלא הורמו כמי שהורמו דמיין, ויטול בהן בכור פי שנים. והשתא ליכא למיפרך "פשיטא", דהשתא אשמועינן טובא, דאע"פ שלא הורמו – כמי שהורמו דמיין. מוקדשין לאו דידיה נינהו. כגון חטאות ואשמות מחיים – קדשי ה' נינהו, ויש בהן מעילה כל זמן שלא נשחטו. אבל שלמים אין בהן מעילה, כדדרשינן: "קדשי ה'" – קדשים המיוחדים לשם, יצאו קדשים קלים שאין מיוחדים לשם. ומיהו אינם ממונו, דמיקדש מיהא קדשי, ולא קרינא ביהו "בכל אשר ימצא לו". ואפילו אם נשחטו, שיכול לאכלן – אינם שלו, כדתנן בפ"ב דקדושין: המקדש בחלקו, בין בקדשי קדשים בין בקדשים קלים – אינה מקודשת, דמשלחן גבוה קא זכו! ומשני: בקדשים קלים ומחיים, דהוי ממונו לרבי יוסי הגלילי. ומיהו, לאחר שחיטה – לא, כדאמרינן בפרק ראשון דב"ק: כי אמר ר' יוסי הגלילי – מחיים, אבל לאחר שחיטה, דכי קא זכו משלחן גבוה קא זכו – לא אמר. דאמר ממון בעלים הם. לכל דבר, אף לקדש את האשה. ומעלה מעל בה'. "וכחש בעמיתו בפקדון" וגו'. וכחש בה, ונשבע על שקר, וחזר והודה והביא את אשמו. לרבות קדשים קלים. להתחייב עליהם אשם גזילות אם כפר בהן ונשבע והודה, כשאר גזל ממון. שהרי ממונו הן, שהבשר והעור שלו, ואין לגבוה בהן אלא אימורים, ולכהן חזה ושוק. ו"בה'" ו"בעמיתו" קדריש, דהיינו שלמים, שהאימורים לשם והבשר לבעלים. והך מעילה דהכא אינו אלא לשון שינוי, וכן הוא אומר (דה"ב כו): "וימעל בה' אלהיו", וכן בסוטה הוא אומר (במדבר ה): "איש איש כי תשטה אשתו ומעלה בו מעל", בתורת כהנים. דהא מעילה ממש ליכא בשלמים, כדפריש"ת, דממעיט להו בתורת כהנים מדכתיב "קדשי ה'" – בנהנה מן ההקדש גבי מעילה. דלאו ברשותיה. דהב קיימא. רועה באפר. דהוי מוחזק מיבעיא. מה רועה באפר שבחא דממילא. מעשב השדה.

אף

עין משפט נר מצוה

מד א מיי' פ"ג מהל' נחלות הלכה ג סמג עשין נו טוש"ע ח"מ סימן רעח סעיף ה:

מה ב מיי' שם הלכה ב ועי' בהשגות ובמ"מ טוש"ע שם סעיף ד:

מו ג מיי' שם הל' ג טוש"ע שם סעיף ה:

מז ד מיי' פ"ה מהל' אישות הלכה ו:

רבינו גרשום

ואת בנימין אחי יוסף. א"כ היו להו טפי מן שבעים: אמר ליה מרגלית היתה בידי. כלומר טעם יפה שבידי: ואתה רוצה לאבדה ממני. מידי כלומר אתה רוצה שאומר לך וידעוהו הכל: איתיביה ויכם דוד. לאדומיים מהנשף ועד הערב אלמא דביד יהודה נמי נפלו. נפלו עליו. ונתחברו לדוד ממנשה דהוו ליה מיוסף ומשום הכי נצחום: אשר לעמלק. ועמלק מעשו היה דכתיב ותלד לאליפז את עמלק: בכור כהן שהניח להן אביהן מתנות הללו בכור נוטל פי שנים משום דכל אשר ימצא לו בשעת מיתתו אמרינן דיטול וכשהשביחו נכסי' לאחר מיתת אביהן שהוא התחיל להשביח כגון הניח להן אביהן פרה מוחכרת ששכרה אביהן לאחר לשנה בדמים קצובין. או מושכרת ששכרה לאחר שיתן לו מחצית השכר למחצה או לשליש או לרביע או שהניח להן אביהן באפר לרעות וילדה נוטל בכור באותו שבח פי שנים דדמי כמו שהשביחה ברשות אביהם אבל השביחום היתומים לאחר מיתת אביהן כגון שבנו בתים או נטעו כרמים אין נוטל פי שנים בהם: במכירי כהונה ולויה עסקי' שהיה לאבי' אוהבים מכירים שיהו שולחין לו מתנותיהם. ולא לאחרים והכי נמי מתנות לויה כגון מעשרו' ללוי מוסרן: ודאשתחיט הבהמה בחיי אבוהון ולא הספיק ליטול עד שמת. כמי שהורמו דמי. כבאו ליד אביו דמי דמכירין הן ומוחזק הוא ולא ראוי. ובמוקדשין אמאי נוטל פי שנים הא לאו דידיה דבר הקדש הוא: הכא בקדשים קלים עסקינן ואליבא דר' יוסי הגלילי דאמר ממון בעלים הן. במס' קדושין לקדש בהן אשה דתניא ומעלה מעל בה' וכחש בעמיתו שאם גנב מאחד מעשר או בכור אם נהנה מהם חייב קרבן מעילה לגבוה דכתיב ומעלה מעל בה' ואם כפר לו והודה ונשבע מביא אשם גזילות דכתיב וכחש בעמיתו ממון בעלים הוא ומשום הכי הבכור נוטל פי שנים: רועה באפר. וברשותו קיימא מיבעי': הא קמ"ל. דלא משום האי טעם שקיל דברשותי' קיימא דמוחכרת ומושכרת לא קיימא ברשות' אלא אבורינן מוחכרת ומושכרת לא חסרי בה יתמי מזוני דחוכר ושוכר יהבי להם מזוני משום הכי בכור נוטל בהן פי שנים: ומנו

מסורת הש"ס

א) [נ"ל אמר ליה]: ב) לעיל קכ. סוטה יב.: ג) לא מצאתי רק בדה"א ה' יש ואלה ראשי בית אבותם ועפר וישעי ועיין רש"א בח"א: ד) [תוספ' דבכורות פ"ו ע"ש]: ה) [לעיל נה. קיט. לקמן קכה: קמה: יבמות כד: בכורות נא:]: ו) [קדושין נב: נח: נדרים פה: חולין קל: בכורות יא. מכות כ.]: ז) קדושין נב: בכורות נג: זבחים קיד. תמורה ח. ב"ק יב:: ח) [בקדושין נח: נראה להדיא דס"ל לרבי דכמי שהורמו דמי ע"ש וע' סוגיא דנדרים פה. ובפי' רש"י והר"ן והרא"ש דהתם]:

הגהות הב"ח

(א) רשב"ם ד"ה נוטל פי שנים בזרוע כו': (ב) ד"ה ראוי וכו' לא זכה בהן אביהן:

א) [תוספ' בכורות פ"ו]: ב) [עיין תוס' כתובות לג. בד"ה רבי וכו']: ג) [בכורות נב:]: ד) [לעיל יב:]: ה) [לקמן קלה:]:

תורה אור

אף מוחכרת ומושכרת – שבחא דממילא קא אתי, דלא חסרי בה מזוני. מני? ר' היא; דתניא: א) אאין בכור נוטל פי שנים בשבח ששבחו נכסים לאחר מיתת אביהן; ב) רבי אומר, אומר אני: בכור נוטל פי שנים בשבח ששבחו נכסים לאחר מיתת אביהן, אבל לא בשבח שהשביחו יתומים לאחר מיתת אביהן. ירשו שטר חוב – בכור נוטל פי שנים, ביצא עליהן שטר חוב – בכור נותן פי שנים, ואם אמר: איני נותן ואיני נוטל – רשאי. מאי טעמייהו דרבנן? אמר קרא: °"לתת לו פי שנים", [דברים כא] ג) מתנה קרייה רחמנא, מה מתנה עד דמטיא לידיה, אף חלק בכורה – עד דמטיא לידיה. ורבי אומר, אמר קרא: "פי שנים", מקיש חלק בכורה לחלק פשוט, מה חלק פשוט אע"ג דלא מטא לידיה, אף חלק בכורה – אע"ג דלא מטא לידיה. ורבנן נמי, הכתיב: "פי שנים"! ההוא, גלמיתבא ליה ד) אחד מצרא. ורבי נמי, הכתיב: "לתת לו"! ההוא, שאם אמר: איני נוטל ואיני נותן – רשאי. א"ר פפא: ה) דדיקלא ואלים, ארעא ואסיק שירטון – דכ"ע לא פליגי דשקיל, כי פליגי – בחפורה והוה שובלי, שלופפי והוו תמרי, דמ"ס: שבחא דממילא, ומר סבר: האישתני.§ אמר רבה בר חנא אמר ר' חייא: עשה כדברי רבי – עשה, כדברי חכמים – עשה; מספקא

מספקא

רשב"ם

אף מוחכרת ומושכרת בשבחא דממילא. קמיירי, דאין מעלין לה היתומים מזונות. ואם תאמר: ליתני רועה בחפר, ואנא ידענא דהוא הדין למוחכרת ומושכרת היכא דלא מחסרי מזוני, ול"ל למיתני מוחכרת ומושכרת כלל, דאיצטריך תו רועה בחפר ללמד עליהם דבדלא חסרי מזונות מיירי? איצטריך, דס"ד כל מוחכרת ומושכרת לא שבחא דממילא הוא, אלא ע"י בני אדם שחורשין בה ועודרין בה, ולא לישקול בה בכור פי שנים, קמ"ל דכיון דהיתומין עצמן אין חורשין בהן ואין טורחין בהן, אלא אחרים – שבחא דממילא חשבינן לה, היכא דאין מעלין לה מזונות. הכי גרסינן: מני רבי היא. ולא גרסינן "ומני", דלא קמהדר אתירוצא דלעיל כלל, אלא מילתא באפי נפשה היא דקבעי גמרא. מני. הך ברייתא, דקתני דנוטל בכור בשבח ששבחו נכסים ממילא לאחר מיתת אביהן – רבי היא. בשבח ששבחו. ממילא. אבל כשהשביחו יורשין – הכל מודים דאינו נוטל פי שנים. ירשו שטר חוב. היינו מלוה בשטר – בכור נוטל פי שנים. דכיון דמוחזק בשטר ועל פי השטר גובין את המלוה – הרי הוא כאילו השטר השביח, דהיינו נכסים ששבחו ממילא. ומיהו, אליבא דרבנן אינו נוטל פי שנים, ומסקנא דמילתיה דרבי היא, והכי מוכח לקמן בשמעתין. ודוקא מלוה בשטר, אבל מלוה על פה, ואפי' בעדים, כיון דליכא שטרא ומצי למטען "פרעתיה לך", דהמלוה את חבירו בעדים אין צריך לפרעו בעדים אפי' רבי מודה דלא שקיל פי שנים, דהא אין מוחזקין מחוב זה כלל, דנימא הנכסים שבחו מעצמן. יצא עליהן שטר חוב. שחייב אביהם לאחרים. מילתא באנפי נפשה היא, ודברי הכל, ואפי' בלא ירשו שטר חוב מיירי. בכור נותן פי שנים. כי היכי דנוטל פי שנים, שאותן נכסים נשתעבדו כולן למלוה. ואם אמר איני נוטל. פי שנים מכל ירושת אבי, שהריני מוחל חלק בכורה ואטול חלק כפשוט, ולפיכך לא אשלם למלוה פי שנים, אלא כנגד מה שאני נוטל – רשאי, וכשתובעו זה המלוה לדין – אין בית דין יכולין לכופו לפרוע אלא כנגד חלק פשיטותו. ונפקא מינה שצריך זה המלוה לתבוע את אחיו של זה לדין, ואם אין יכול לכופם – מפסיד. או אם הלכו למדינת הים – אין מורידין לבע"ח בקרקע עד דשמעו ב"ד טענת האחין, דמה ידעינן איזה טענה יש להן? דשמא יטענו "פרענו", או "שטר פרוע הוא". דסלקא דעתך (א) כיון דבכור הוא – זכי ליה רחמנא פי שנים, ואינו יכול לומר איני חפץ שיהיו שלי, דבעל כרחו הרי הן שלו, דמשעה שמת אביו ירש פי שנים, עד שיפקירם או עד שימכרם או יתנם לאחרים, וצריך להגבות לזה המלוה כנגד פי שנים – קא משמע לן דבעל כרחו לא זכי ליה רחמנא, דכתב "לתת לו" – כעין מתנה, אם ירצה לקבלה. ואם ימחה שלא לקבל – אין מזכין לו לאדם בעל כרחו, דלא קרייה רחמנא ירושה אלא מתנה. אבל מחלק פשיטותו – אינו יכול לומר כן, שהרי יורש הוא בעל כרחו. ויש מפרשין: ואם אמר איני נוטל בשטר חוב שיש לאבי על אחרים פי שנים, וגם איני נותן בשטר חוב היוצא עליו פי שנים – רשאי. ושיבוש גמור הוא, שהרי השטר היוצא על אביהן – אינו דינו לגבות משטר שיש לאביהן על אחרים, דמטלטלי דיתמי לא משתעבדי לבעל חוב, אלא ממקרקעי הוא דקגבי. הלכך, אע"ג שמחל חלק בכורה מן השטרות של אביו, כיון דבקרקעות הוא נוטל פי שנים – חייב להחזיר למלוה פי שנים. מאי טעמייהו דרבנן. דאפי' בשבחא דממילא לא שקיל חלק בכורה. עד דמטיא לידיה. דנותן, ואינו יכול ליתנה לאחרים, דאין אדם מקנה דבר שלא בא לעולם. מקיש חלק בכורה לחלק פשוט. ד"פי שנים" היינו שני חלקים, חלק פשוט וחלק בכורה, והזכירם בתיבה אחת, דהוה מצי למכתב "חלק אחד על אחיו". מה חלק פשוט אע"ג דלא מטא לידיה. דכל ראוי שבעולם הבן יורש מאביו, דהא לא איקרייא ירושה מתנה, דנימא אינו נוטל חלק פשוט אלא במוחזק – אף חלק בכורה נמי. ומיהו, ראוי גמור, כגון שהשביחו יתומים – לא שקיל פי שנים, דלהכי אהני "בכל אשר ימצא לו". אחד מצרא. שני חלקים יטול במקום אחד, כחלק פשוט שהוא חלק אחד ונוטל במקום אחד. ונפקא מינה דכל מקום שנפל לו הגורל לחלק פשוט – יטול שם בלא גורל חלק בכורה. ואם הן שני אחין ושלש שדות – לא יפילו שלשה גורלות, שנים לבכור ואחד לפשוט, שהרי אם יפול חלק הפשוט בשדה האמצעי – לא יזכה בו, דאם כן נמצא נוטל הבכור בשני מקומות. אלא שני גורלות יפילו, ויטילום על שני שדות החיצונות, ואיזה שיעלה לבכור – יקח, ויטול גם האמצעי שאצלו עמו. ורבי, איכא למימר דהך סברא נמי דחד מצרא נפקא ליה מהיקשא. שאם אמר איני נוטל כו'. ורבנן נמי תרתי שמעת מינה; מדכתיב "לתת" שמעינן דמתנה קרייה רחמנא, ואינו יכול ליתן עד דאתיא לידיה דנותן. ומדכתיב "לו" שמעינן דלא זכה בה בכור עד שתבא לידו, שאם אמר "איני נוטל" – רשאי. שאם אמר איני נוטל ואיני נותן. האי "איני נותן" לאו דוקא נקט ליה הכא, דהא מקרא לא ילפינן ליה, אלא מסברא, דכיון דאין נוטל – ודאי לא יתן. וה"פ: ההוא שאם אמר "איני נוטל, לפי שאיני רוצה ליתן" – רשאי. ואורחא דמילתא נקט, שאין אדם רגיל לומר "איני נוטל" אלא מפני שצריך להחזיר מה שהוא נוטל לאחרים, דמה לו ולצרה ליטול כדי ליתן? דיקלא. קטן הניח להן אביהן. ואלים. שנתעבה אחרי כן. וכן הניח להן ארעא, ואסקא אחרי כן שירטון וזבל ונתייפתה בכך. דכ"ע. רבי ורבנן. דשקיל. דעדיין שמו עליו. בחפורה. שחת הניח להן, ונעשו אחרי כן שובלי. וכן שלופפי – דקלים שהפריחו פירות, ונעשו אחרי כן תמרים. בכי האי גוונא (ג) שבחא דממילא פליגי. ומר סבר. רבנן. אישתני. העשב להיות חטין, והפרחים להיות תמרים, דהוי דבר אחר ושם אחר. עשה. הדיין כדברי רבי. עשה. ולא נאמר: טעה בדבר משנה חוזר.

מספקא

תוספות

אף מוחכרת ומושכרת דלא חסרי בה מזוני. וא"ת: אדתנא "אבל בנו בתים" – ליפלוג וליתני בדידה, במוחכרת ומושכרת גופה: בד"א – דלא חסרי מזוני, אבל חסרי מזוני – אין הבכור נוטל פי שנים! ויש לומר: דהוה אמינא במוחכרת ומושכרת גופה דחסרי בה מזוני דוקא אין הבכור נוטל פי שנים, משום דהוי ראוי גמור, דאין השבח על גוף הפרה. אבל בנו בתים ונטעו כרמים, שהשבח על גוף הקרקע – אימא שאין זה ראוי, ויטול פי שנים, קא משמע לן. ואם אמר איני נוטל ואיני נותן רשאי. אומר ר"י: דנפקא מינה אם היתומין קטנים, דיכול לומר הבכור: איני נוטל פי שנים, וישאר הקרקע לפני היתומין, ולא יטול מהן, דאין נזקקין לנכסי יתומין אלא אם כן רבית אוכלת בהן. ולקמן מפיק מ"לתת לו" שיכול למחול לו בכורתו, משום דעדיין לא אתיא לידיה. ואפילו בלא קנין, כדמשמע לקמן, (ג) דאמר דויתר בכל הנכסים, דמדאחיל בהא אחיל בהא. אבל חלק פשיטות לא יוכל למחול ולסלק עצמו באמירה בעלמא, אם לא על ידי קנין. ורבינו תם מפרש: דאם אמר כשיצא עליו שטר חוב על הבכור עצמו, ולא על האחין: "איני נוטל ואיני נותן" – רשאי, ומפסיד בעל חוב, ואין לו על היתומין כלום, דלאו בעל דברים דידהו הוא. ולא הוי דומיא דרישא, דאיירי דיצא על כולן שטר חוב.

רבינו גרשום

מני. ברייתא זו דקתני הניח להם אביהם פרה וכו' דנוטל פי שנים: ר' היא דתנן אין הבכור נוטל פי שנים בשבח ששבחו נכסים לאחר מיתת אביהן. אפי' שבחו מאליהם דכל אשר ימצא לו בעינן: רבי אומר הבכו' נוטל פי שנים בשבח ששבחו נכסים לאחר מיתת אביהן. הואיל דשבחא ממילא קא אתי והכי נמי קתני ברייתא: ירשו שטר חוב. שהיה אחד חייב לאביהן: בכור נוטל פי שנים. משום דמלוה בשטר קלא אית ליה ומשום דמוחזקין בשטר כמאן דגביא דמי: והואיל דנוטל פי שנים בשטר חוב. פורע נמי פי שנים בחוב שמתחייב אביו בשטר (כולו). ואם אמר כו': מאי טעמא דרבנן. ת"ק דרבי: עד דמטיא לידיה. דנותן לא מצי יהיב ליה לאחריני. אף חלק בכורה עד דמטיא לידא דאבא לא מצי שקיל פי שנים: מקיש חלק בכורתו לחלק פשוט מה חלק פשוט אע"ג דלא מטא לידיה. דאבא אלא ראוי לו אפי' הכי שקיל דפשוט נוטל בראוי כבמוחזק. אף חלק בכורה נמי שקיל בשבחא דממילא אע"ג דלא מטי לידיה: ורבנן נמי הכתיב פי שנים. אמאי לא דרשי כרבי. ההוא דיהבינן ליה לבכור פי שנים: אחד מצרא. במקום אחד נוחלין לו חלק בכורתו סמוך לחלק פשוט שיהו ניכרים שהב' חלקים במקום אחד: דיקלא ואלים. שהי' קטן כשמת ושוב נתגדל. והכי נמי ארעא ומסקה שירטון. שנזדבלה מאליה שהרוח הפריח שם זבל משדות אחרות או הקשין שהיו שם בלו ונעשו זבל: כולי עלמא לא פליגי. דשקיל משום דכל אשר ימצא לו קרינן ביה: כי פליגי בחפירי והוי שובלי. שהניח להם אביהם חזיז ונתגדלו עד שנעשו שבלים. והכי נמי שלופפי והוו תמרי' שהניח להן אביהן תמרים מפריחין במקצתן ונעשים גדולים: דמר סבר. רבי שבחא ממילא אתי וכל אשר ימצא לו קרינן ביה: ומר סבר אשתני. מכמות שהניח להם אביהם ולא שקיל:

עין משפט נר מצוה

מח א מיי' פ"ג מהל' נחלות הלכה ד סמג עשין צו טוש"ע ח"מ סי' רעח סעיף ו:
מט ב טוש"ע שם ס"י:
נ ג מיי' שם הל' ח ופי"ב מהל' שכנים הל' ב סמג שם טוש"ע ח"מ סי' קעד סעיף ב:
נא ד ה מיי' פ"ג מהל' נחלות הלכה ד סמג עשין צו טוש"ע ח"מ סי' רעח סעיף ו:

הגהות הב"ח

(א) רשב"ם ד"ה ואם אמר וכו' דסלקא דעתך אמינא כיון: (ב) ד"ה בחפורה וכו' בכי האי גוונא פליגי כל"ל ותיבות שבחא דממילא נמחק. (ג) תוס' ד"ה ואם וכו' לקמן. נ"ב בדף קכו ע"ב:

מספקא ליה אי [א]הלכה כרבי מחבירו ולא מחביריו, או הלכה כרבי מחבירו ואפילו מחביריו. אמר רב נחמן אמר רב: אסור לעשות כדברי רבי; קא סבר: הלכה כרבי מחבירו ולא מחביריו. רב נחמן דידיה אמר: מותר לעשות כדברי רבי; קא סבר: הלכה כרבי מחבירו ואפילו מחביריו. אמר רבא: (א) אסור לעשות כדברי רבי, ואם עשה — עשוי; קא סבר: מטין איתמר. תני רב נחמן בשאר ספרי דבי רב: °"בכל אשר ימצא לו" — פרט לשבח שהשביחו יורשין לאחר מיתת אביהן; אבל שבח ששבחו נכסים לאחר מיתת אביהן — שקיל, ומני? רבי היא. תני רמי בר חמא בשאר ספרי דבי רב: "בכל אשר ימצא לו" — פרט לשבח ששבחו נכסים לאחר מיתת אביהן; וכל שכן שבח שהשביחו יורשין לאחר מיתת אביהן דלא שקיל, ומני? רבנן היא. אמר רב יהודה אמר שמואל: [א]אין בכור נוטל פי שנים במלוה. למאן? אילימא לרבנן? השתא שבחא דאיתיה ברשותיה אמרי רבנן לא שקיל, מלוה מבעיא? אלא לרבי. ואלא הא דתניא: ירשו שטר חוב — בכור נוטל פי שנים בין במלוה בין ברבית, מני? לא רבי ולא רבנן! לעולם לרבנן, ואצטריך; סלקא דעתך אמינא: מלוה, כיון דנקיט שטרא — כמאן דגביא דמיא, [ב]קא משמע לן. שלחו מתם: בכור נוטל פי שנים במלוה אבל לא ברבית. למאן? אילימא לרבנן, השתא שבחא דאיתיה ברשותיה אמרי רבנן דלא שקיל, מלוה מבעיא? אלא לרבי. ולרבי, ברבית לא? והתניא, רבי אומר: בכור נוטל פי שנים בין במלוה בין ברבית! לעולם רבנן היא, ומלוה כמאן דגביא דמיא. אמר ליה רב אחא בר רב לרבינא: איקלע אמימר לאתרין, ודריש: בכור נוטל פי שנים במלוה אבל לא ברבית. א"ל: נהרדעי לטעמייהו, [ב]דאמר (ב) רבה: גבו קרקע — יש לו, גבו מעות — אין לו; ורב נחמן אמר: גבו מעות — יש לו, גבו קרקע — אין לו. אמר ליה אביי לרבה: לדידך קשיא, לרב נחמן קשיא; לדידך קשיא: מאי

תורה אור: דברים כח

רשב"ם

מספקא ליה. הא דאמרי' בעירובין (דף מו:): הלכה כרבי מחבירו, אי אמרי' דוקא מחבירו — כשחולק יחיד עליו, אבל לא מחביריו, דבכל מקום הלכה כחביריו, והכא חביריו פליגי עליה. **ואפילו מחביריו.** בכל מקום, וה"ה להך. **אסור לעשות כדברי רבי.** אסור לדון כן, דקעבר א"לא תטה משפט", דהא אם עשה — אינו עשוי, כדמפ' לקמיה. **קסבר: הלכה כרבי** מחבירו ולא מחביריו. והאי דקאמר "אסור לעשות כן" ולא קאמר "אין הלכה כרבי", היינו משום דקאמר לעיל כי האי לישנא "עשה כדברי רבי עשה" — אמר איהו נמי "אסור לעשות". **אמר רבא** ג) (**הלכתא**) כרבי כו'. האי הלכתא לא סמכינן, אלא אהלכתא דרב פפא דהוא בתרא, לקמן בשמעתין (דף קכה:). **מטין איתמר.** כך נאמר בבית המדרש: מטין את הדין אחר דברי חכמים לדון כן לכתחלה. ומיהו, אי עבד כרבי — עבד, ולא מהדרינן עובדא. והכי מפרשינן לכל "מטין איתמר" שבגמרא. והכי אמרי' בהדיא במס' [כתובות] (דף פד:). **בשאר ספרי דבי רב.** "ספרא דבי רב" היינו תורת כהנים, ברייתא של ספר ויקרא. "שאר ספרי דבי רב" קרי למדרש של ספר במדבר מ"וישלחו מן המחנה" עד סוף הספר "אלה הדברי'" כו'. ומכילתא, דהיינו מדרש "אלה שמות" מ"החדש הזה לכם" עד סוף הספר — כולהו אקרי "שאר ספרי דבי רב". והיינו דאמרינן בעלמא (סנהדרין דף פו.): סתם מתני' רבי מאיר, סתם ספרא רבי יהודה, סתם ספרי רבי שמעון, סתם ד) סדר עולם ר' יוסי, ה) סתם תוספתא רבי נחמיה, וכולן אליבא דר' עקיבא. **פרט לשבח ששבחו.** ממילא. **שהשביחו.** כגון בנו בתים ונטעו כרמים, או חסרו מזוני או מעות בהוצאת נכסים להשביחן. **אין הבכור נוטל פי שנים במלוה.** אפי' במלוה בשטר. **אליבא דמאן.** כלומר, כמאן סבירא ליה, שהוצרך לומר כן? **שבחא דממילא.** כגון חפורה והוו שובלי, שמוחזק קצת באותן הנכסים. **מלוה.** דאינו מוחזק כלל במעות, אלא בשטר, דהוה ניירא בעלמא, מיבעיא? **לעולם אליבא דרבנן.** והך דקתני: ירשו שטר חוב — רבי היא. **במלוה.** של גוי. **אבל לא ברבית.** אע"פ שכתוב בשטר. ומלוה כמאן דגביא דמיא הואיל ונקיט שטרא, אבל רבית, אע"ג דנקיט שטר וכבר עבר הזמן משמת אביו — לא, דאין לך ראוי כזה, דבר שלא היה שלו מעולם. אבל מעות מלוה, דקשקיל מעות (ג) הלוהו ונמצא השטר מוחזק בידו במקום מעותיו, והרי הוא כמו משכון — ובזה הכל מודים דמלוה שהניח משכון עליה שקיל פי שנים, דבעל חוב קונה משכון. וכן פסק ר"ח. **הא דשלחו מתם.** פליגא אהך דרב יהודה אמר שמואל דלעיל, ותרווייהו אליבא דרבנן, מר משוי ליה מוחזק, כיון דנקיט שטרא. ומר לא חייש לשטרא, דניירא בעלמא הוא. וי"מ: דהא דשלחו מתם — במלוה של גוי, כדקתני: אבל לא ברבית. והך דרב יהודה אמר שמואל — במלוה של ישראל, ולא פליגי. והבל הוא בידם. דאדרבה, איפכא מסתברא, דבמלוה של ישראל הוי מוחזק טפי ממלוה של גוים, אשר פיהם דבר שוא. **נהרדעי לטעמייהו.** אמימר כרב נחמן סבירא ליה, דתרווייהו הוו מנהרדעא, כדאמר אמימר (לעיל ד' לא.): אנא מנהרדעא אנא וסבירא לי כו'. דתרווייהו סבירא להו דמעות שאדם חייב לחבירו הוי מוחזק בהן. **גבו קרקע.** בחוב מלוה אביהן — אין לו לבכור פי שנים, דמעות הלוהו ולא קרקע. אבל גבו מעות — יש לו, שהרי מעות הלוהו, ובמעות חשבינן ליה מוחזק אליבא דשלחו מתם. והיינו כאמימר, דדרש: בכור נוטל פי שנים במלוה, דהיינו מעות. ורב נחמן לפרושי אתא האי דשלחו מתם: בכור נוטל פי שנים במלוה. ול"נ: דהאי דאמרי' "נהרדעי לטעמייהו" לא בא למעט דברי רבה דאמר: גבו קרקע יש לו. דהא אמימר סתמא דרש: בכור נוטל פי שנים במלוה, לא שנא קרקע ולא שנא מעות. אלא למעוטי מדרב יהודה אמר שמואל אתא, דאמר לעיל אליבא דרבנן דאין הבכור נוטל פי שנים במלוה. ואמימר סבירא ליה כדשלחו מתם, וכרב נחמן ורבה דסבירא להו כדשלחו מתם. **גבו קרקע.** מבעל חוב, יש לו לבכור פי שנים. דהאי קרקע אשתעבד לאבוהון בחייו, וכמי שהיה לו במשכון דמי. וחשבינן ליה מוחזק ליטול הבכור פי שנים. **גבו מעות** אין לו. דמלוה להוצאה ניתנה. והני מעות אחריני נינהו, וכאילו לא הוחזק בם אביהן.

מ"ש

תוספות

מספקא ליה אי הלכה כרבי מחבירו ולא מחביריו או אפילו מחביריו. תימה: דבכולי גמרא אומר דאין הלכה כרבי מחביריו, והכא מספקא ליה! ותו, דרב נחמן דידיה אמר: אפי' כחביריו, וקיי"ל כרב נחמן בדיני. והא קיימא לן דאין הלכה כרבי כחביריו! ומפרש ר"ת: דדוקא הכא מספקא ליה, אבל בעלמא — לא, וכן לרב נחמן. אבל קלת קשה, דקאמר רב נחמן: מותר לעשות כדברי רבי, וכיון דסבירא ליה הכא שהלכה כרבי מחביריו — אמאי קאמר "מותר"? "חייב לעשות" הוה ליה למימר! ותו, דקאמר: קסבר רבא מטין איתמר. כלומר, מטין הדבר לעשות כרבנן לכתחלה. ובכל הגמרא לא קאמר "מטין" אלא על אותו שפסק הלכה כמותו, כדאמרי' ב"הכותב" (כתובות דף פד:) גבי הלכה כר"ע מחבירו, מר סבר: הלכה איתמר, ומר סבר: מטין איתמר. והכא לא הוזכרה הלכה אלא על רבי, ולא על רבנן! ונראה לר"י דהכי מספקא ליה: אי הלכה כרבי מחבירו ולא מחביריו, שפסקו כך בהדיא.

אין הבכור נוטל פי שנים במלוה. כרבנן מוקי לה, ובמלוה בשטר. מה שפירש הקונטרס לעיל גבי ירשו שטר חוב בכור נוטל פי שנים, שהשטר הוי הגוף, ומלוה הוי שבח — אין נראה. דא"כ, אמאי אמרי רבנן דאין הבכור נוטל פי שנים? דכיון שיחלקו שטרות, ויטול בשטרות פי שנים שהן הגוף — יטול גם השבח שיבא אח"כ, שהיא המלוה. דהא פשיטא דאחר שירלקו — כל השבח שיבוא מחלקו שהוא שלו.

נהרדעי לטעמייהו. לפירוש ר"ת דבסמוך, דפי' דרב נחמן אליבא דנפשיה אית ליה בין גבו קרקע בין גבו מעות יש לו — אתי שפיר הא דקאמר הכא: נהרדעי לטעמייהו. דאמימר נמי סתמא קאמר, דנוטל פי שנים במלוה בין גבו קרקע בין גבו מעות. אבל לפ"ה, דמפרש בסמוך דרב נחמן אליבא דנפשיה אית ליה בין גבו קרקע בין גבו מעות אין לו — לא יתכן הא דאמר "נהרדעי לטעמייהו".

גבו מעות יש לו. פי' הקונטרס: משום דמעות יהיב ומעות שקיל. ואין נראה, דבפרק "שור שנגח ד' וה'" (ב"ק דף מג.), דפריך אמאי דאוקי רבה ורב נחמן הא דאין בעל יורש [נזקי] אשתו לר"ע היינו דוקא בגרושה: ולוקמה לרבה כגון שגבו מעות, ולרב נחמן כגון שגבו קרקע, דהוה ליה ראוי. למה ליה למינקט קרקע? דגבו מעות נמי הוי ראוי, דהא דאמר הכא גבו מעות יש לו, והוי מוחזק — היינו משום דמעות יהיב מעות שקיל. אבל התם גבי נזק, דלא יהיב מעות — מודי רב נחמן דגבו מעות נמי הוי ראוי! ואין לפרש דהכי פריך: ולוקמה לרבה בגבו מעות ולרב נחמן אף בגבו קרקע. דהא לרבה נמי הוה מצי למינקט בין בגבו קרקע בין בגבו מעות, דהכי אית ליה בפ' "גט פשוט" (לקמן דף קעה:), אלא משום דלרב נחמן לא מצי למינקט אלא חדא, דהיינו בגבו קרקע נקט נמי לרבה חדא. אלא נראה: דטעמא דרב נחמן דאמר גבו מעות יש לו משום דדרך בע"ח לפרוע בחובם מעות ולא קרקע, והוי מוחזק בגבו מעות משום דסמיכי עלייהו. אבל קרקע, שאין דרך קרקע ליתן בחובם — לא סמכי עלה, ולא הוי מוחזק.

לטעמייהו

עין משפט נר מצוה

נב א ב מיי' פ"ג מהל' נחלות הלכה ה סמג עשין צו טוש"ע ח"מ סי' רעח סעיף ז:

רבינו גרשום

אלמא קסבר מטין אתמר. ולא דרשי' לה בפרקא ולכתחלה לא עבדינן כוותיה. אבל אי עבד לא מהדרינן: בשאר ספרי דרב. זו מכילתא וספרי דלא קרי ספרי דבי רב אלא תורת כהנים לחוד: ומני' [רבי] דהכי אמר לעיל: אמר רב יהודה אמר שמואל אין הבכור נוטל פי שנים במלוה. שאם חייב אדם לאביהן מלוה אין הבכור נוטל פי שנים משום דלא קרינן ביה בכל אשר ימצא לו: מלוה. דלא אתא לידיה מיבעיא. אלא אליבא דרבי דהאי מלוה לא אתא לידיה דאבוה: אלא הא דתניא. לעיל ירשו כו': לא לעולם רבנן. ודקא קשיא לך השתא שבחא דממילא אתי אמור רבנן כו'. אפי' הכי אצטריך למימר דאינו נוטל דסד"א מלוה כיון דנקיט שטרא בידיה כמאן דגביא דמי ונוטל פי שנים קמ"ל דאפי' הכי אינו נוטל: שלחו מתם. מארץ ישראל לבבל: בכור נוטל פי שנים במלוה. דכמאן דגביא דמיא: אבל לא ברבית. שחייב לו גוי משום דלא אתא לידיה: מלוה מבעיא. דהוא הדין דלא שקיל: אלא אליבא דרבי. נוטל במלוה פי שנים משום דמטא לידיה דאבוה אבל לא ברבית דלא אתא לידיה דאבוה: לעולם אליבא דרבנן. ומשום הכי שקיל פי שני' [דמלו'] כמאן דגביא דמיא: אמר ליה נהרדעי לטעמייהו. דאמימר ורב נחמן נהרדעי הוו: דאמר רב נחמן גבו קרקע. בחוב של אביהן אין לו לבכור פי שנים משום דהאי קרקע לא שבק אבוהון גבייהו אלא מעות של מלוה זו היא ברשות אביהם ושבק אבוהון גבייהו ומשום הכי בכור נוטל פי שנים במלוה והיינו (טעמא) נהרדעי לטעמייהו: רבה אמר גבו קרקע יש לו. משום דאחריות קרקע יש לו שכן כתוב בשטר דאי לא יהיב להו מעות טרפי מקרקע: אבל גבו מעות אין לו. משום דלאו הני מעות שבק אבוהון גביהון משום הכי אינו גובה: אמר לי' אביי לרבה לדידך. דאמרת גבו קרקע יש לו גבו מעות אין לו קשיא. ולרב נחמן בר פלוגתך קשיא: לדידך

הגהות הב"ח

(א) גמ' אמר רבא [אסור] לעשות וכו' עשוי תא"מ ונ"ב גירסת רשב"ם ותוס' היא אמר רבא הלכתא כרבי ואם עשה עשוי: (ב) שם נהרדעי לטעמייהו דאמר רב נחמן גבו קרקע אין לו גבו מעות יש לו ורבה אמר גבו מעות אין לו גבו קרקע יש לו כנ"ל: (ג) רשב"ם ד"ה אבל לא וכו' דקשקיל מעות שהלוהו:

מסורת הש"ס

א) [עירובין מו: פסחים כז. כתובות כח. נא.] ב) ב"ק מג. לקמן קנה: ג) [אסור לעשות כנ"ל] ד) [יבמות פכ:] ה) [סנהדרין פו.]

מַאי שְׁנָא מָעוֹת דְּלָא? דְּלָאו הָנֵי מָעוֹת שְׁבַק אֲבוּהוֹן, קַרְקַע נַמִּי — לָאו הָא קַרְקַע שְׁבַק אֲבוּהוֹן! וְעוֹד, (א) א)(הָא אַתְּ הוּא דַּאֲמַרְתְּ:) מִסְתַּבֵּר טַעֲמָא דִּבְנֵי מַעֲרָבָא, דְּאִי קָדֵים סַבְתָּא וְזַבְנָא — זְבִינָהּ זְבִינֵי! לְרַב נַחְמָן קַשְׁיָא: מַאי שְׁנָא קַרְקַע דְּלָא? דְּלָאו הָא קַרְקַע שְׁבַק אֲבוּהוֹן, מָעוֹת נַמִּי — לָאו הָנֵי מָעוֹת שְׁבַק אֲבוּהוֹן! וְעוֹד, הָא ב)אָמַר רַב נַחְמָן אָמַר רַבָּה בַּר אֲבוּהּ: איְתוֹמִים שֶׁגָּבוּ קַרְקַע בְּחוֹבַת אֲבִיהֶן — בַּעַל חוֹב חוֹזֵר וְגוֹבֶה מֵהֶן! אֲמַר לֵיהּ: לָא לְדִידִי קַשְׁיָא וְלָא לְרַב נַחְמָן קַשְׁיָא, טַעֲמָא דִּבְנֵי מַעֲרָבָא קָאָמְרִינַן, וְלָן לָא סְבִירָא לָן. מַאי סַבְתָּא? דְּהַהוּא דַּאֲמַר לְהוּ: נִכְסַי

רשב"ם

מ"ש מָעוֹת דְּלָא. שָׁקֵיל בְּהוּ בְּכוֹר פִּי שְׁנַיִם? וַדַּאי הַיְינוּ טַעֲמָא דִּידָךְ מִשּׁוּם דְּלָאו הָנֵי מָעוֹת כו'. לָאו הָא קַרְקַע שְׁבַק אֲבוּהוֹן. דְּאִי הֲוָה בָּעֵי לֹוֶה הֲוָה מְסַלֵּק לֵיהּ בְּזוּזֵי. וְעוֹד הָאָמַר [מָר]. רַבָּה, דְּאָמַר בָּעוּבְדָא דְּהַהִיא סַבְתָּא דַּהֲוְיָא לָהּ בַּת בֵּן בְּנָהּ הַנְּשׂוּאָה לְבַעַל, וּרְאוּיָה הָוְיָא הַהִיא בַּת לְיוֹרְשָׁהּ, מֵתָה הַהִיא בַּת וְאַחַ"כ מֵתָה הַסַּבְתָּא, וַאֲתָא בַּעַל וְקָא תָּבַע יְרוּשַּׁת הַזְּקֵנָה כְּאִילּוּ אִשְׁתּוֹ קַיֶּימֶת. וְשָׁלְחוּ מִתָּם, דְּהַיְינוּ בְּנֵי מַעֲרָבָא, שֶׁאֵין הַבַּעַל נוֹטֵל, מִשּׁוּם דַּהֲווּ הָנְהוּ קַרְקָעוֹת רְאוּיִן לְאִשְׁתּוֹ אִם תָּמוּת הַזְּקֵנָה בְּחַיֶּיהָ, וַהֲרֵי מֵתָה הִיא בְּחַיֵּי הַזְּקֵנָה, וְאֵין הַבַּעַל נוֹטֵל בָּרָאוּי כְּבַמּוּחְזָק. וְאָמַר רַבָּה: מִסְתַּבֵּר טַעֲמָא דִּבְנֵי מַעֲרָבָא דְּאֵין הַבַּעַל יוֹרֵשׁ, דַּהֲוָה לֵיהּ רָאוּי וְלֹא מוּחְזָק לַבַּת, שֶׁכָּל זְמַן שֶׁהַזְּקֵנָה בְּחַיֶּיהָ אֵין לַבַּת בָּהֶן כְּלוּם, שֶׁהֲרֵי אִם מָכְרָה הַזְּקֵנָה הַנְּכָסִים בְּחַיֵּי הַבַּת — מְכִירָתָהּ קַיֶּימֶת. כֵּן אֵלּוּ נִכְסֵי הַלֹּוֶה, אַע"פ שֶׁרְאוּיִם הֵן לִגְבּוֹת הַמַּלְוֶה חוֹבוֹ מֵהֶן, כֵּיוָן שֶׁלֹּא הִגִּיעוּ לִידֵי הַמַּלְוֶה מֵחַיִּים — רְאוּיִן הֵן, דְּהָא אִי הֲוָה בָּעֵי לֹוֶה — הֲוָה זָבֵין לְהוֹן, וּמְסַלֵּק לֵיהּ לַמַּלְוֶה בְּזוּזֵי אוֹ בְּקַרְקַע אַחֶרֶת חוּץ מִזּוֹ. הִלְכָּךְ, הָא קַרְקַע הֲוָה לֵיהּ רָאוּי, וְאֵין הַבְּכוֹר נוֹטֵל בָּרָאוּי פִּי שְׁנַיִם. וְעוֹד. קַשְׁיָא אַחֶרֶת לְרַב נַחְמָן, דְּחָשֵׁיב מָעוֹת מוּחְזָקוֹת טְפֵי מִקַּרְקָעוֹת: הָא אִיפְּכָא הֲוָה לֵיהּ לְמֵימַר, מִשּׁוּם דְּקַרְקַע שֶׁל זֶה הָוֵי מוּחְזָק טְפֵי לַמַּלְוֶה. דְּהָא הוּא דְּאָמַר מִשּׁוּם רַבָּה בַּר אֲבוּהּ: יְתוֹמִים בְּנֵי מַלְוֶה שֶׁגָּבוּ קַרְקַע מִן הַלֹּוֶה בְּחוֹבַת אֲבִיהֶן, בע"ח שֶׁל אֲבִיהֶן, שֶׁנִּתְחַיֵּיב לוֹ אֲבִיהֶן מָעוֹת — חוֹזֵר וְגוֹבֶה אוֹתָהּ מֵהֶן. וְאִם לֹא הָיָה מוּחְזָק בְּיַד אֲבִיהֶן בַּחַיִּים — הֵיאַךְ יָכוֹל בע"ח לִגְבּוֹתוֹ? וַהֲלֹא אִילּוּ קָנוּ הַיְּתוֹמִים אַחַר מִיתַת אֲבִיהֶן קַרְקַע מִי יָכוֹל לִגְבּוֹתוֹ? וַהֲלֹא מִשְׁנָה שְׁלֵמָה שָׁנִינוּ בִּבְכוֹרוֹת (דף נב.) שֶׁאֵין הָאִשָּׁה נוֹטֶלֶת כְּתוּבָּתָהּ בָּרָאוּי, וּבע"ח כַּיּוֹצֵא בּוֹ, וּמִטַּלְטְלֵי דְּיַתְמֵי לָא מִשְׁתַּעְבְּדֵי לְבע"ח. כֵּן כָּתוּב בְּפֵי' רַבֵּינוּ חֲנַנְאֵל. לְטַעֲמַיְיהוּ דִּבְנֵי **מַעֲרָבָא אָמְרִי'** וְלָן **לָא סְבִירָא** לָן. וְשִׁינּוּיָא הוּא דְּקָמְשַׁנֵּי רַבָּה: אֲנָא וְרַב נַחְמָן לָא סְבִירָא לָן דִּבְנֵי מַעֲרָבָא דְּשָׁלְחוּ מִתָּם כְּלָל, אֶלָּא כְּרַב יְהוּדָה אָמַר שְׁמוּאֵל, דְּאָמַר אַלִּיבָּא דְּרַבָּנַן: אֵין הַבְּכוֹר נוֹטֵל פִּי שְׁנַיִם בְּמִלְוֶה, וּכְדִפְסָקִי' נַמִּי הִלְכְתָא לְקַמָּן: לָא שְׁנָא גָּבוּ מָעוֹת לָא שְׁנָא גָּבוּ קַרְקַע אֵין הַבְּכוֹר נוֹטֵל פִּי שְׁנַיִם. וַאֲפִי' לְרַב נַחְמָן דְּאָמַר: יְתוֹמִים שֶׁגָּבוּ קַרְקַע בְּחוֹב אֲבִיהֶן, בע"ח חוֹזֵר וְגוֹבֶה אוֹתָהּ מֵהֶן — אַפ"ה מוֹדֶה, דִּלְגַבֵּי בְּכוֹרָה לָא חָשֵׁיב קַרְקַע הַלֹּוֶה מוּחְזָק לַמַּלְוֶה, וְלָא שָׁקֵיל בָּהּ בְּכוֹר פִּי שְׁנַיִם, כִּדְפָסְקִינַן הִלְכְתָא לְקַמָּן. וְהָכָא הַיְינוּ טַעֲמָא דְּרַב נַחְמָן, כִּדְמְפָרֵשׁ בִּפְסָחִים בְּפֶ' "כָּל שָׁעָה". דְּאִיתְּמַר: בע"ח, אַבַּיֵּי אָמַר: לְמַפְרֵעַ הוּא גּוֹבֶה, רָבָא אָמַר: מִכָּאן וּלְהַבָּא הוּא גּוֹבֶה, דְּלָא חָשֵׁיב מוּחְזָק אֶלָּא מִשְּׁעַת גְּבִיָּיה וְאֵילָךְ. וּכְדִמְפָרֵשׁ הָתָם טַעֲמָא דְּרָבָא: כֵּיוָן דְּאִילּוּ הֲוָה לֵיהּ זוּזֵי הֲוָה מְסַלֵּק לֵיהּ זוּזֵי — אִשְׁתַּכַּח דְּהַשְׁתָּא הוּא דְּקָא קָנֵי. וּמוֹתְבִינַן לְרָבָא מֵהָא דְּאָמַר רַב נַחְמָן אָמַר רַבָּה בַּר אֲבוּהּ: יְתוֹמִין שֶׁגָּבוּ קַרְקַע כו', אִי אָמְרַתְּ בִּשְׁלָמָא לְמַפְרֵעַ הוּא גּוֹבֶה — אַמְּטוּ לְהָכִי חוֹזֵר וְגוֹבֶה אוֹתָהּ מֵהֶן, דִּכְמַאן דְּגָבֵי לֵיהּ מֵחַיִּים דַּאֲבוּהוֹן דָּמֵי. אֶלָּא אִי אָמְרַתְּ מִכָּאן וּלְהַבָּא הוּא גּוֹבֶה — לָא יְהֵא אֶלָּא כְּזָבִין יַתְמֵי, וְאִילּוּ קָנוּ יַתְמֵי נִכְסֵי מִי מִשְׁתַּעְבְּדֵי לְבע"ח? וּמְשַׁנֵּי: שָׁאנֵי הָתָם דְּאָמַר לְהוּ בע"ח דַּאֲבוּהוֹן: כִּי הֵיכִי דְּמִשְׁתַּעְבַּד לֵיהּ הַהוּא לֹוֶה לַאֲבוּכוֹן — ה"נ מִשְׁתַּעְבַּד לְדִידִי מִדְּר' נָתָן כו'. וְהַהוּא שִׁינּוּיָא דְּסָמְכָא הוּא, דְּהָא רָבָא דְּהִלְכְתָא כְּוָותֵיהּ לְגַבֵּיהּ דְּאַבַּיֵּי הוּא מְשַׁנֵּי לְהָא דְּרַב נַחְמָן הָכִי. הִלְכָּךְ, אֲפִי' ר"נ לָא חָשֵׁיב לְקַרְקַע שֶׁל לֹוֶה מוּחְזָק לַמַּלְוֶה עַד שֶׁתָּבֹא לְיָדוֹ, מִשּׁוּם דְּאִי הֲוָה בָּעֵי הֲוָה מְזַבֵּין לֵיהּ עַד הַשְׁתָּא, דְּמִכָּאן וּלְהַבָּא הוּא גּוֹבֶה. וְהִלְכָּךְ, מַאי דְּא"ר נַחְמָן: גָּבוּ קַרְקַע אֵין לוֹ, גָּבוּ מָעוֹת יֵשׁ לוֹ — לְטַעֲמַיְיהוּ דִּבְנֵי מַעֲרָבָא קָאָמַר, דְּאָמְרִי אַלִּיבָּא דְּרַבָּנַן דְּנוֹטֵל בַּמִּלְוֶה פִּי שְׁנַיִם, דְּחָשְׁבִינַן לָהּ מוּחְזֶקֶת לְמִלְוֶה. וַאֲתָא רַב נַחְמָן לְמֵימַר: לְדִידִי, לָא שְׁנָא גָּבוּ קַרְקַע לָא שְׁנָא גָּבוּ מָעוֹת — אֵין לוֹ, דְּק"ו הוּא, כִּדַּאֲמָרַן לְעֵיל: שְׁבָתָא דְּמִמֵּילָא אָמְרֵי רַבָּנַן דְּלָא שָׁקֵיל, מִלְוֶה מִיבָּעֵי? אֶלָּא לְדִידְהוּ בְּקַרְקַע מוֹדוּ לִי מִיהָא דְּלָא שָׁקֵיל, דְּהַאי אַרְעָא לָא שְׁבַק לְהוּ אֲבוּהוֹן. כִּדְאָמְרִינַן לְקַמָּן: שָׁלְחוּ מִתָּם הִלְכְתָא כְּרַב עָנָן כִּדְפָרֵישׁ רַבָּה טַעֲמַיְיהוּ, דְּאִי קָדֵים סַבְתָּא כו'. דְּמֵהָתָם שָׁמְעִי' דְּלָא חָשְׁבִי בְּנֵי מַעֲרָבָא לְקַרְקַע שֶׁל לֹוֶה מוּחְזָק לַמַּלְוֶה. וְהִלְכָּךְ, הַאי שָׁלְחוּ מִתָּם דִּלְעֵיל — מִיבָּעֵי לָן לְאוֹקְמֵי בְּמָעוֹת וְלֹא בְּקַרְקַע, דְּלָא תִּקְשֵׁי דִּבְנֵי מַעֲרָבָא אַדִּבְנֵי מַעֲרָבָא, וּמִשּׁוּם הָכִי אָמַר רַב נַחְמָן: גָּבוּ קַרְקַע — אֵין לוֹ, גָּבוּ מָעוֹת — יֵשׁ לוֹ. וּמִיהוּ, לָא סְבִירָא לֵיהּ, אֶלָּא בֵּין קַרְקַע בֵּין מָעוֹת אֵין לוֹ, כִּדְפִרִישִׁי'. וְרַבָּה נַמִּי לְטַעֲמַיְיהוּ דִּבְנֵי מַעֲרָבָא קָאָמַר; לְדִידִי ל"ש מָעוֹת לָא שְׁנָא קַרְקַע אֵין לוֹ, כִּדְרַב יְהוּדָה אָמַר שְׁמוּאֵל, דְּהָא לֹא הָיָה אֲבוּהוֹן מוּחְזָק לָא בְּהַאי קַרְקַע וְלָא בְּהַאי מָעוֹת. מִיהָא, בְּנֵי מַעֲרָבָא, כֵּיוָן דַּחֲשִׁיבִי לֵי' מוּחְזָק בַּמִּלְוֶה, וְיִטּוֹל בָּהּ הַבְּכוֹר פִּי שְׁנַיִם — אִיכָּא לְמֵימַר דִּבְגָבוּ קַרְקַע הוּא דְּקָאָמְרִי דְּיֵשׁ לוֹ, דְּדָמֵי מוּחְזָק טְפֵי מִמָּעוֹת, דְּהָא אִשְׁתַּעְבַּד לֵיהּ מִיהָא בְּחַיָּיו. אֲבָל הָנֵי מָעוֹת לָא אִשְׁתַּעְבְּדוּ לֵיהּ כְּלָל, וּבְגָבוּ מָעוֹת מוֹדוּ לִי דְּאֵין לוֹ. וְהַאי דְּשָׁלְחוּ מִתָּם לְקַמָּן: הִלְכְתָא כְּרַב עָנָן כו', וּכְדִמְפָרֵשׁ רַבָּה: מִסְתַּבֵּר טַעֲמַיְיהוּ דִּבְנֵי מַעֲרָבָא כו' — הָתָם וַדַּאי בְּדִין הֲוָה דְּלָא יָרֵית בַּעַל, דְּה"ל רָאוּי לְגַמְרֵי, וְלָא אִשְׁתַּעְבַּד לָא לַבַּעַל וְלֹא לְאִשְׁתּוֹ הָנֵי נִכְסֵי דִּזְקֵנָה כְּלָל, שֶׁהֲרֵי לֹא לָוְותָה מִן הַבַּת וּמִן בַּעְלָהּ כְּלוּם, וְאִי קָדֵים סַבְתָּא וְזַבְנָה — זְבִינָהּ זְבִינֵי. אֲבָל נִכְסֵי דְּלֹוֶה, כֵּיוָן דְּמִשְׁתַּעְבְּדֵי לַמַּלְוֶה, וְאִי זַבֵּין לָא זְבִינֵי, וְיָכוֹל לִטְרוֹף מִן הַלָּקוֹחוֹת — הֲרֵי הֵן כְּמוּחְזָקִין בְּיָדוֹ, וְשָׁקֵיל בְּהוּ בְּכוֹר פִּי שְׁנַיִם. אֲבָל גָּבוּ מָעוֹת — וַדַּאי אֵין לוֹ.

נִכְסַאי

תוספות

לטעמייהו דבני מערבא קאמרי' ולא סבירא לן. פ"ה: דבין רב נחמן ובין רבה סברי תרווייהו אליבא דנפשייהו דבין גבו קרקע ובין גבו מעות אין לו. והא דקאמר רב נחמן דבע"ח חוזר וגובה אותה מהן — היינו כדתרלה *(רבה) משום דר' נתן. ולפירושו, הא דפסיק לעיל רב נחמן כרבי — היינו דוקא בשבח ולא במלוה. וקשה: דלרב נחמן עיקר התירוץ דמשני לדידיה חסר מן הספר, דלא משני מידי מההוא דיתומין שגבו בחובת אביהן. ועוד: דבפרק "שור שנגח ד' וה'" (ב"ק דף מג.) ה"ל למיפרך: ולוקמה בין לרבה בין לרב נחמן, בין גבו מעות בין גבו קרקע! ומיהו, זה י"ל: שהיה צריך להאריך, דלא דברו רבה ורב נחמן בהדיא בין גבו קרקע בין גבו מעות אין לו. (ג) דבפרק "גט פשוט" (לקמן דף קעה:) מוכח מההוא דסבר רבה שעבודא לאו דאורייתא קאמר, דסבר רבה אליבא דנפשיה דבין גבו קרקע בין גבו מעות אין לו. להכי מקשה בקוצר ובפשיטות ממה שדברו בהדיא רבה ורב נחמן. ור"ת מפרש: לטעמא דבני מערבא קאמרי', ולא סבירא לן הכי, אלא לדידי', בין גבו קרקע בין גבו מעות — אין לו, כדאמר גבי האי סבתא דאפי' גבו קרקע אין לו, כ"ש גבו מעות. וכן מוכיח בפ' "גט פשוט", דלרבה בין גבו קרקע בין גבו מעות אין לו, כיון דשעבודא לאו דאורייתא, והא דאמר גבו קרקע יש לו — אליבא דבני מערבא דאמרי הבכור נוטל פי שנים במלוה, ומסתבר ליה טפי לאוקמי בקרקע ולא במעות. והא דאמרי בני מערבא גבי סבתא דהוי ראוי, אע"ג דהוי קרקע — היינו משום שהבעל לא היה מוחזק מעולם, ולא היה לו ולאשתו שום חוב מעולם על הסבתא שישתעבד לו הקרקע, ולכך הוי ראוי, אבל גבי מלוה — הוי מוחזק אפי' לא יוכל לטרוף אם מכר, כגון אם שטר חוב הוי שלא באחריות, מ"מ היכא דלא מכר — הוי מוחזק, כיון שהיה משועבד לו בחובו. והא דקאמר רבה טעמא משום דאי קדמה סבתא וזבנא זבינה זביני — לאו אליבא דבני מערבא, (ג) דלדידהו לא תלה בהכי, כדפרישי'. אלא טעמא דנפשיה קאמר, דלדידי' אפי' במלוה הוי ראוי, משום דאי זבין הוי זביני. ועוי"ל: דלרבה, אפי' אי זבין לא הוי זביניה זביני — הוי ראוי. וגבי האי סבתא דוקא צריך להאי טעמא, משום דסבר רבה: כל האומר "אחריך" — כאומר "מעכשיו" דמי, והוי כאילו הוא מוחזק מעיקרא. אלא משום דאי קדמה וזבנא דהוי זבינה זביני — הוא דהוי ראוי. אבל בני מערבא לית להו: כדאמר "מעכשיו" דמי, מטעם דזבינה זביני לא הוי חשוב ראוי, כדאמר גבי מלוה. אלא סברי דלאו כאומר "מעכשיו" דמי, ולא הוחזק בו מעולם. ורב נחמן סבר: בין גבו קרקע בין גבו מעות — יש לו, כמו שהביא אביי מההוא דיתומין שגבו קרקע בחובת אביהן. ולדברי אביי קא"ל רבה, ולא לפי מה שתרלה רבא משום דר' נתן. דלרב נחמן אליבא דנפשיה — ודאי סבר דאפי' גבו קרקע יש לו. והא דקאמר: גבו קרקע אין לו — היינו אליבא דבני מערבא, דאמרי גבי סבתא דקרקע הוי ראוי. וא"ת: ומנא ליה לרב נחמן דלבני מערבא גבו קרקע אין לו? דלמא בני מערבא סבירא להו נמי גבו קרקע יש לו כרב נחמן, וגבי סבתא היינו טעמא — דלא נשתעבד לבעל הקרקע ולא הוחזק בו מעולם! וי"ל: דסבירא ליה לרב נחמן דמפלגי בני מערבא בין גבו קרקע לגבו מעות; מדלא קאמר: הבכור נוטל פי שנים במלוה בין גבו קרקע בין גבו מעות — מסתברא ליה לרב נחמן דטפי הוי מוחזק במעות מבקרקע. וא"ת: בפרק "שור שנגח ד' וה'" (ב"ק דף מג.), כי פריך: ולוקמה לרבה בגבו מעות ולר"נ בגבו קרקע. ומשני: ה"מ לבני מערבא, וכי קאמרי אינהו בגרושה כרבי, דחשיב מלוה מוחזק, לכך אוקמה בגרושה. והשתא, לפר"ת, לרבנן נמי צריך לאוקומי בגרושה לר"נ, דאית ליה בין גבו קרקע בין גבו מעות יש לו! וי"ל: דנקט כרבי משום רבה, דלדידיה דסבר בין גבו קרקע בין גבו מעות אין לו — א"א לאוקמי בגרושה אלא לרבי. והוה מצי לרבה לאוקמה בלא גרושה וכרבנן. [וכן לפ"ה הוה מצי בין רבה ובין ר"נ לאוקומי בלא גרושה וכרבנן] אלא דניחא ליה לישנה אפי' לרבי. ור' יעקב דאורליינ"ש תירץ: לפירוש הקונט' לא הוה מצי לאוקמי כרבנן, דרבה ור"נ אליבא דר"ל דאמר: לא אמר ר"ע דלא ירית לה בעל אלא בכופר, שאינו משתלם אלא לאחר מיתה, אבל שאר נזקין — ירית לה בעל. ואליבא דידיה איצטריכו ליה לשנויי האי דקתני: הכה אשה ויצאו ילדיה דלא ירית בעל — בגרושה כו'. ולא מצי לאוקמי כרבנן ובלא גרושה — דא"כ שום נזקין לא ירית בעל, דהא בין גבו קרקע בין לא גבו אין לו. ור"ל קאמר דשאר נזקין ירית — והיינו ע"כ כרבי.

לידתי

מסורת הש"ס

א) הא אמר מר כצ"ל רש"ל: ב) פסחים לא. (ב"ק מג.)כתובות לב. קי.:

רבינו גרשום

קשיא כו': ועוד. היכי מצית אמרת דקרקע יש לו: הא מר הוא דאמרת. בהאי מעשה דסבתא דלקמן מיסתבר טעמא דבני מערבא. דשלחו מתם וקבעו הלכ' כותיה דרב ענן דאמר לירתאי ולא לירתי ירתאי ובעל לא ירית משום דשכיבא איתתיה בחיי סבתא ואין הבעל נוטל בראוי כבמוחזק. ומשום הכי אמר רבא לקמן מיסתבר טעמייהו דבני מערבא דאי קדמא סבתא בחייה וזבנא זבינה זביני אלמא דלא מוחזק הוא ביד הבעל כל זמן דלא אתא לידיה הכי נמי להיכא דגבו קרקע בחוב אביהן אמאי נוטל בכור פי שנים והא אע"ג דאית להו שטר וכמאן דגבוי ההוא חוב דמי אפי' הכי אינה מוחזקת האי קרקע בידיה דאבוהון כלום דהא אי בעי בעל חוב מצי לזבוני לאחריני ולמיתן להו קרקע אחריתי. אי נמי מצי מסלק להו בזוזי ולא בקרקע והוה ליה הא קרקע ראוי ולא מוחזק ואין הבכור נוטל פי שנים בראוי כבמוחזק ואמאי אמרת להיכא דגבו קרקע יש לו פי שנים: ולרב נחמן קשיא מאי שנא כו' ועוד. קשיא אחריתי אמאי אינו נוטל בקרקע: האמ' רב נחמן אמר רבה בר אבוה יתומין שגבו קרקע בחובת אביהן. שהיה אחד חייב לאביהן: בעל חוב. שהיה אביהן חייב לו: חוזר וגובה אותה מהן. מן היתומים [כמו] דאי שביק להון אבוהון קרקע דמוחזקת בידם דגבי ליה בעל חוב של אביהן ה"נ אע"ג דלא שבקה לה אבוהון גבייהו אלא ראויה להו א) מיחייב אבוהון אפי' הכי גבי ליה מינייהו דלא מצי למיטען ליה מטלטלי דהיינו שטר שבק אבונא גבן ומטלטלי לבעל חוב לא משתעבדי אלא כיון דגבו קרקע דמי כמאן דמוחזקת בחיי אבוהון א"כ הכא נמי בכור אמאי גבו קרקע אין לו פי שנים הא כמוחזק דמיא. השתא קשיא דרב נחמן אדרב נחמן: אמר ליה לא לדידי קשיא ולא לרב נחמן קשיא. במילתין קיימינן והאי דאמינא לעיל גבו קרקע יש לו גבו מעות אין לו ורב נחמן נמי דאמר גבו קרקע אין לו גבו מעות יש לו אין טעמא דבני מערבא מפרשי' דשלחו מתם בכור נוטל פי שנים במלוה לדידי הכי שמיעא לי דסבירא להו גבו קרקע יש לו ורב נחמן שמיעה ליה דסבירא להו לבני מערבא דגבו מעות יש לו ולן לא סבירא לן כוותיהו דליהוי לבכור פי שנים במלוה לא בקרקע ולא במעות: מאי מעשה דסבתא. דההוא שכיב מרע דאמר להו

א) אולי צ"ל ראויה להו מבע"ח לאבוהון.

עין משפט נר מצוה

נג א מיי' פי"א מהל' מלוה ולוה הלכה ט סמג עשין לב טוש"ע ח"מ סימן קז סעיף א:

[צ"ל רבא]

רש"ל

הגהות הב"ח

(א) גמ' ועוד הא מר הוא דאמר מיסתבר: (ב) תום' ד"ה לטעמייהו וכו' אין לו אלא דבפרק גט פשוט: (ג) בא"ד דבני מערבא קאמר דלדידהו לא וכו' דאי זבין הוי זביניה זביני:

עין משפט נר מצוה

נד א ב ג מיי' פי"ב מהל' זכיה ומתנה הלכה יב טוש"ע ח"מ סימן רמח סעיף ט:

נה ד מיי' פ"א מהל' נחלות הל' יא סמג עשין צו טוש"ע אה"ע סי' צ סעיף א:

נו ה מיי' שם פ"ג הל' ח סמג שם טוש"ע ח"מ סימן רעח סעיף ג:

נז ו מיי' שם הל' ה טוש"ע שם סעיף ז:

"נכסי לסבתא ובתרה לירתאי", הויא ליה ברתא דהוה נסיבא, שכיבא בחיי בעלה ובחיי סבתא, בתר דשכיבא סבתא אתא בעל קא תבע; אמר רב הונא: "לירתי" – ואפי' לירתי ירתי, ורב ענן אמר: "לירתי" – ולא לירתי ירתי. שלחו מתם: הלכתא כוותיה דרב ענן, ולאו מטעמיה; [א]הלכת' כוותיה דרב ענן – דבעל לא ירית. ולאו מטעמיה – דאילו רב ענן סבר: אע"ג דהוה לי' ברא לברתיה לא ירית; [ב]ולא היא, דאילו הוה ליה ברא לברתיה – ודאי ירית, ובעל היינו טעמא דלא ירית, [ג]משום דהוה ליה ראוי, (א)ואין הבעל נוטל בראוי כבמוחזק. מכלל דרב הונא סבר: בעל נוטל בראוי כבמוחזק?! א"ר אלעזר, דבר זה נפתח בגדולים ונסתיים בקטנים: כל האומר "אחריך", כאומר "מעכשיו" דמי. אמר רבה: מסתברא טעמא דבני מערבא, דאי קדים סבתא וזבנא – זבינה זביני. אמר רב פפא, הלכתא: [ד]אין הבעל נוטל בראוי כבמוחזק, (ב)[ה]ואין הבכור נוטל בראוי כבמוחזק, [ו]ואין הבכור נוטל פי שנים במלוה – בין שגבו קרקע בין שגבו מעות.

ומלוה

תורה אור

רשב"ם

נכסאי לסבתא. לזקנתי אני נותן כל נכסי. אם אביו או אם אמו. ובתרה לירתאי. אחר מות זקנתי לא יירשו יורשין שלה, כגון בנה או בתה או אביה או אחיה, אלא יורשין שלי, כגון בני או בתי או אחי – הקרוב קרוב קודם. הויא ליה. לההוא גברא חדא ברתא. שכיבא. ההיא ברתא. בחיי בעלה ובחיי סבתא. ואח"כ שכיבא סבתא. ואתא בעלה וקתבע. לפי שבשעת צוואת המת היתה בתו קיימת, וכמי שאמר "נכסיי לסבתא ובתרה לבתי", דהיינו "ירתי", והיה רוצה לירש זכות אשתו. א"ר הונא. האי "ובתרה לירתאי" דקאמר ההוא גברא – לירתאי ולירתי ירתאי קאמר. (א) כיון שנתנה ליורש', והרי זכתה בהן הבת שהיתה יורשת שלה, כדמפרש טעמא לקמן, דכל האומר "אחריך" – כאומר "מעכשיו" דמי, וכיון דזכתה בהן מחיים – הרי הבעל יורש את אשתו, דהיינו ירתי ירתאי. והכי מפרש לה לקמיה. ומיהו, השתא לא ידעינן אכתי טעמא דרב הונא, אלא שרואין אנו שזיכה את הבעל. וטעמא לא ידעינן עד דמפרש ליה לקמיה. ורב ענן אמר לירתא ולא לירתי ירתאי. וה"ק: ובתרה לירתאי – לאותן יורשין שיהיו לי בעולם בשעת שתמות הזקנה אני נותן את נכסיי. כגון אם היתה בתו קיימת, או אחיו או אביו, דכל אלו אני קורא בהן "ירתאי". אבל לא בן בתו, כדמוכח לקמיה, דהיינו ירתי ירתאי, שמכח בתו הוא בא לירש אותו. ולא לבעלה, דאיהו נמי ירתי ירתאי. דירתאי דוקא קאמר – אותן הבאים מכחי, ולא לירתי ירתאי הבאין מכח כחי. והלכך, היכא דליכא ירתאי אחר מות הזקנה, אלא ירתי ירתאי – נשארו הנכסים ביד יורשי הזקנה. דדומה לאומר "נכסי לך ואחריך לפלוני", שאם מת אותו שני – יירשו יורשי ראשון, כדתנינן לקמן בפירקין (דף קלו:): ואם מת שני בחיי ראשון – יחזרו נכסים ליורשי ראשון. דבעל לא ירית. הכא, דראוי הוא. אע"ג דהוה ליה ברא לברתא. דהוה ליה ירתי ירתאי, קאמר רב ענן דההוא ברא לא ירית. כדקא דייק לישנא, דירתאי משמע, ולא ירתי ירתאי. ולא היא. דאילו הוה ליה ברא – ודאי ירית, הואיל והוא ראוי לירש את זה הנותן, שהרי הבת וכל יוצאי יריכה, במקום שאין בן – קודמין לכל יורשי האיש, דירתאי קרינא ביה, הואיל והוא קודם לכל יורשיו, ואע"פ שבא מכח כחו. ומעיקרא כי אמר "לירתאי" – לירתאי שיהא לי במות הזקנה קאמר, ובן בתו יורש אותו, וקודם לאביו ולאחיו ולאחותו. ואע"פ שהן קרוין ירתאי, והבן ההוא קרוי ירתי ירתאי – אפילו הכי קודם, דליורשיו הראוין ליורשו מן התורה רגיל לקרות ירתאי. וטעמא דבעל לא ירית – לא משום דהוי ירתי ירתאי, דאילו היה ראוי לירש נחלה זו מן התורה, ירתאי הוה קרינא ביה. אלא משום דאינו ראוי ליורשה, דהוה ליה האי ממון ראוי לאשה ולא מוחזק, שעדיין לא נפל בידה, ובעל אינו נוטל בראוי. אבל אי איכא בן דחזי למירתה – ודאי ירית, דבן ירית בראוי. ומקשינן: מכלל דרב הונא סבר כו'. מדאוקימנא טעם דבני מערבא דבעל לא ירית, היינו משום דחשבי להני נכסי ראוי, אם כן רב הונא דאמר ירית בעל ס"ל דבעל נוטל בראוי? אר"א. לפרושי טעמא דרב הונא קאתי. נפתח. התחיל. בגדולים. רב הונא. בקטנים. רבי אלעזר. ועצמו קרי קטן לגבי רב הונא. כאומר מעכשיו. וכיון דאמר "ובתרה לירתאי" דהיינו לבת – היינו נמי כמו שאמר: מיד אני נותן את גוף הקרקע לבתי, אלא שזקנתי תאכל פירות בחייה, ואחר כן תקח בתי או הבא מכחה את הנכסים. דחשיב לה רב הונא לגבי בת כמתנת "מהיום ולאחר מיתה", והלכך הויא לה זו הבת מוחזקת בחייה בהני נכסים, וכי קא ירית בעל – שפיר קא ירית במוחזק. מסתברא טעמייהו דבני מערבא. דחשבי להו ראוי לגבי בת, ולא מוחזק. דליכא למימר כאומר "מעכשיו" דמי, דהא אם קדמה הזקנה בחייה ומכרה לאחרים – זבינה זביני, וכשמתות הזקנה, אפי' אם תהיה הבת קיימת לא תטול כלום, כדאמרינן בכתובות ולקמן בפרקין (דף קלז.): "נכסי לך ואחריך לפלוני" אם קדם הראשון ומכר – מה שמכר מכר, ואין לשני אלא מה ששייר ראשון. ואם לא שייר כלום – לא שקיל מידי. והלכך, בעל לא ירית, דאשתו לא הויא הוחזקה כלל בהני נכסים בחייה, שהרי היתה הזקנה יכולה למכרן לגמרי, מה שאין כן במתנת "מהיום ולאחר מיתה". ונמצא שאף גוף הקרקע לא הוחזק לבת בחיי הזקנה, וגם כשמתה הזקנה אין הבת בחייה להוריש המוחזק לה לבעל. א"ר פפא הלכתא אין הבעל נוטל בראוי כבמוחזק. בראוי ממש, כגון לירש את אשתו בקבר בנחלה שנפלה לה לאחר מיתה, אתא רב פפא לאשמועינן דלא ירית. (ג) דהא כולי עלמא מודו דלא ירית, כדילפינן מקראי בפירקין דלעיל (ד' קיג.) מדכתיב: "בגבעת פנחס בנו". דרב הונא לא פליג אלא ב"אחריך" וכדפריש ר"א דכל האומר "אחריך" כאומר "מעכשיו" דמי, אבל בראוי דפליגי ביה רבי ורבנן, כגון חבורה והוי שובלי, שלופפי והוו תמרי – לא אתא לאשמועינן דאין הבעל נוטל. אלא ודאי הבעל נוטל, שהרי כשמתה יורש את כל נכסים שהיתה מוחזקת בהן, וכי גדלי פירי – ברשותיה גדלי. דנהי דפליגי רבנן בבכור – דהתם היינו טעמא כדאמרן לעיל (ד' קכד.): "לתת לו" – מתנה קרייה רחמנא, אבל גבי בעל ליכא למימר הכי. ועוד: דאפילו בכור כה"ג דליכא יורש אחר אלא הוא יורש כל נכסי אביו – הכל מודים שיירש הכל, ואפילו שבח הראוי, דהא כי אשבוח – ברשותיה אשבוח. ואין הבכור נוטל בראוי כבמוחזק. כרבנן, כגון דהוי שלופפי והוו תמרי, שנשתנה שמן על ידי שבח ששבחו אחר מיתת אביו. אבל דיקלא ואלים, ארעא ואסקא שירטון, שעדיין שם הראשון עליהם – הכל מודים דשקיל חלק בכורה. אבל עבדים וגרוס – לא שקיל בכור פי שנים אפי' לרבי, ואע"פ שעדיין לא נשתנה שמן, משום דשבח שהשביחו יתומים הכל מודים דלא שקיל. ומיהו, היכא דמת בכור בחיי אביו – בניו של בכור יורשין חלק בכורתו עם אחי האב, דומיא דבנות צלפחד, וכדפרישית לעיל בפירקין (ד' קטז: ד"ה ושהיה) כדתניא בתוספתא דבכורות, וכדאמרינן בהלכות גדולות. ובתלמוד ירושלמי יליף לה ריש לקיש: נאמר "משפט" לענין כפילה, ונאמר "משפט" לענין פשוטה כו', כדפרישית לעיל. ואין הבכור נוטל פי שנים במלוה. ואפילו בשטר, בין שגבו קרקע בין שגבו מעות. דלאו האי קרקע ולאו הני מעות שבק להון אבוהון, והוה ליה ראוי. ואי תפיס עלה משכון, אפי' לרב פפא בכור נוטל פי שנים, דקיימא לן (גיטין דף לז.): בעל חוב קונה משכון.

במלוה

תוספות

לירתי ולא לירתי ירתי. וא"כ: הא דאמר בפירקין לקמן (דף קלו:): "נכסיי לך ואחריך לפלוני ואחרי אחריך לפלוני", מת ראשון – קנה שני, ואם מת שני בחיי ראשון – יחזרו נכסים ליורשי הראשון. ולרב ענן דהכא דאמר ולא לירתי ירתי, אמאי נקט התם "אחרי אחריך לפלוני"? הא אפי' לא היה שלישי, אלא אמר "נכסיי לך ואחריך לפלוני" ותו לא, מת שני בחיי ראשון – יחזרו ליורשי ראשון! וי"ל: דאשמועינן דאם מת שני בחיי ראשון – לא יהא לשלישי. אמר רב פפא הלכתא דאין הבעל נוטל בראוי. אבל שבח נוטל, כדפירש הקונטרס. דכיון (ג) דאינו יורש, אלא הוא זוכה בנכסים מיד, וברשותו בא השבח. ולהכי לא חשיב במתניתין בפ' "יש בכור" (בכורות דף נב. ושם ד"ה ולא) גבי הנהו דאין נוטלין בראוי כבמוחזק, משום דבעל יש לו שבח. והוא הדין נמי דלא שקיל בעל במלות אשתו, אפי' במה שלותה אשתו מנכסי מלוג, דהא נמי הוי כנכסי מלוג, כדמוכח מתניתין ד"מציאת האשה" (כתובות דף סה:), ואפי' הכי משמע בפרק "שור שנגח ד' וה'" (ב"ק דף מב:) דלא ירית בעל. דלרבי דוקא הוצרך לאוקומי בגרושה, דלא חשיב מלוה ראוי בבכור, והוא הדין לגבי בעל. והאי דשביק בעל דאיירי בה, ונקט בכור שאינו נוטל פי שנים במלוה – היינו משום דלגבי בכור איפליגו אמוראי בשמעתין, אבל הוא הדין בעל, כדפרישי'. וליכא לאקשויי: דאמאי לא עריב ותני להו בהדי הדדי, דאין הבעל ובכור נוטלין בראוי כבמוחזק ונוטלין במלוה. משום דלגבי בכור משנה שלימה היא בבכורות (דף נא:) דאין נוטל בראוי, אבל בעל דאין נוטל בראוי – לא אשכח לא משנה ולא ברייתא, אלא מימרא דא"ר אבהו ומטו בה משמיה דרבי יהושע בן קרחה לעיל בפירקין (דף קיג.). ואין הבכור נוטל פי שנים במלוה. וכל שכן בשבח. והא דלא נקט שבח – משום דמשבח לא הוה שמעינן דמלוה הוה ראוי, דהא איכא למאן דאמר דאפי' לרבנן הוי מלוה מוחזק, דכמאן דגביא דמיא. ולהכי נקט רב פפא מלוה דאין הבכור נוטל פי שנים, דשמעינן מינה כל שכן שבח. ואע"ג דלגבי בעל ובכור חשבינן מלוה ראוי – לגבי כתובת אשה חשיבא מוחזקת, וגובה אשה כתובתה ממליה. אע"פ שאינה נוטלת לא מן השבח ולא מן הראוי, כדתנן בבכורות (דף נב. ושם) – אפי' הכי גביא כמלוה, כדתנן "הכותב" (כתובות פד.): מי שמת והניח אשה ובע"ח ויורשין, והיה לו פקדון או מלוה ביד אחרים, רבי טרפון אומר: ינתנו לכושל שבהן, רבי עקיבא אומר: ינתנו ליורשין. שכולן צריכין שבועה ואין היורשין צריכין שבועה. אלמא, אפילו לרבי עקיבא אי לא צריכה שבועה – היתה גובה, אבל לפי שצריכה שבועה – גובין היורשין, ותו לא תגבי האשה מהן, דהוו להו מטלטלי דיתמי ולא משתעבדי. ואם גבו

קרקע

רבינו גרשום

נכסי לסבתא. לזקינתי ובתרה לירתאי. ולא הוה ליה אלא חד בת אתא בעל לאחר מיתת הזקינה וקא תבע ירושת אשתו שהיתה ראויה לירש: אמר רב הונא. בדין הוא דיהבינן ליה דהכי משמע צוואת ההוא גברא כמאן דאמר ובתרה לירתאי אי ליכא ירתאי תיהוי לירתי ירתאי דהיינו בעל דיורש את אשתו: ורב ענן אמר לירתאי. פקיד ולא דייקי' מינה לירתי ירתאי ואין לבעל כלום אלא לאחי אשתו: והל' כוותיה דרב ענן. חדא דהואיל שמתה אשתו קודם שהיתה מוחזקת לא ירית בעל: מכלל דרב הונא. דאמר לירתאי ולירתי ירתאי סבר דבעל נוטל בראוי כבמוחזק בתמיה: אמר ר' אלעזר דבר זה. כלומר דין זה נפתח בגדולים כלומר רב הונא שהיה גדול אמר תחלה דבעל ירית: ונסתיים בקטנים. כלומר אם שאני קטן לגבי רב הונא אני אסיימו ואפרשו טעמא דרב הונא כל האומר אחריך כגון זה שאמר ובתרה לירתאי כאומר מעכשיו יהא בכח אחריך הלכך היא כמוחזקת ויורש אותה הבעל: אמר רבא מסתבר טעמייהו דבני מערבא. דקבעו הלכתא כרב ענן משום דלא היתה מוחזקת ביד אשתו לפיכך אי קדמא סבתא וזבין קודם מיתת אשתו זבינה זביני הואיל דראוי לבת ואינה מוחזקת: ואין הבכור נוטל פי שנים. במלוה בין שגבו קרקע בין שגבו מעות משום דלא מטא לידי.

מסורת הש"ס

א) [לעיל קיג. ב"ק מב:] ב) [לעיל קכג: וש"נ]

הגהות הב"ח

(א) רשב"ם ד"ה אמר רב הונא וכו' דכיון שנתנה לבת ליורשה והרי זכתה: (ב) ד"ה א"ר פפא וכו' דלא ירית דהא כ"ע מודו וכו' דאין הבעל נוטל דודאי הבעל כנ"ל ותיבת אלא נמחק: (ג) תוס' ד"ה אמר רב פפא וכו' דכיון דליכא יורש אחר אלא הוא זוכה בנכסים וכו' ולהכי לא חשיב בעל במתני' וכו' דאין נוטלין לשבח ולא בראוי כבמוחזק:

אוּמִלְוֶה שֶׁעִמּוֹ — פְּלִגִי. אָמַר רַב הוּנָא אָמַר רַב אַסִי: בבְּכוֹר שֶׁמִּיחָה — מִיחָה. אָמַר רַבָּה: מִסְתַּבֵּר טַעְמֵיהּ דְּרַב אַסִי — גבַּעֲנָבִים וּבְצָרוּם, זֵיתִים וּמְסָקוּם, אֲבָל דְּרָכוּם — לָא; וְרַב יוֹסֵף אֲמַר: אֲפִילּוּ דְּרָכוּם. דְּרָכוּם?! מֵעִיקָּרָא עִינְבֵי, הַשְׁתָּא חַמְרָא! כִּדְאָמַר רַב עוּקְבָא בַּר חָמָא: לִיתֵּן לוֹ דְּמֵי הֶיזֵּק עֲנָבָיו, ה"נ — נוֹתֵן לוֹ דְּמֵי הֶיזֵּק עֲנָבָיו. הֵיכָא אִיתְּמַר דְּרַב עוּקְבָא בַּר חָמָא? אַהָא דְּאָמַר רַב יְהוּדָה אָמַר שְׁמוּאֵל: בְּכוֹר וּפָשׁוּט שֶׁהִנִּיחַ לָהֶן אֲבִיהֶן עֲנָבִים וּבְצָרוּם, זֵיתִים וּמְסָקוּם — בְּכוֹר נוֹטֵל פִּי שְׁנַיִם, אֲפִילּוּ דְּרָכוּם. דְּרָכוּם?! מֵעִיקָּרָא עִינְבֵי הַשְׁתָּא חַמְרָא! אָמַר א)מָר עוּקְבָא בַּר חָמָא: לִיתֵּן לוֹ דְּמֵי הֶיזֵּק עֲנָבָיו.§ אָמַר רַב אַסִי: דבְּכוֹר שֶׁנָּטַל חֵלֶק כְּפָשׁוּט — וִיתֵּר. מַאי וִיתֵּר? רַב פַּפָּא מִשְּׁמֵיהּ דְּרָבָא אָמַר: וִיתֵּר בְּאוֹתָהּ שָׂדֶה, (א) רַב פַּפִּי מִשְּׁמֵיהּ דְּרָבָא אָמַר: וִיתֵּר הבְּכָל הַנְּכָסִים כּוּלָּן; רַב פַּפָּא מִשְּׁמֵיהּ דְּרָבָא אָמַר וִיתֵּר בְּאוֹתָהּ שָׂדֶה, קָא סָבַר: אֵין לוֹ לַבְּכוֹר קוֹדֶם חֲלוּקָּה, (וּמַה דַּאֲתָא לִידֵיהּ אַחֵיל, אִידָּךְ לָא אַחֵיל;) וְרַב פַּפִּי מִשְּׁמֵיהּ דְּרָבָא אָמַר וִיתֵּר בְּכָל הַנְּכָסִים כּוּלָּן, קָא סָבַר: יֵשׁ לוֹ לַבְּכוֹר קוֹדֶם חֲלוּקָּה, וּמִדְּאַחֵיל בְּהָא אַחֵיל בְּכוּלְּהוּ. ב)וְהָא דְּרַב פַּפִּי וְרַב פַּפָּא — ג)לָאו בְּפֵירוּשׁ אִיתְּמַר אֶלָּא מִכְּלָלָא אִיתְּמַר; דְּהַהוּא בְּכוֹר דַּאֲזַיל זַבֵּין נִכְסֵי דִּידֵיהּ וּדְפָשׁוּט, אֲזוּל יַתְמֵי בְּנֵי פָשׁוּט לְמֵיכַל תַּמְרֵי [מֵהַנְהוּ לָקוֹחוֹת, מַחוּנְהוּ;] רש"ל אָמְרֵי לְהוּ קְרוֹבִים: לָא מִיסְתַּיָּיא דִּזְבַנְתִּינְהוּ לְנִכְסַיְיהוּ, אֶלָּא מִימְחָא נַמִּי מַחִיתוּ לְהוּ? אֲתוּ לְקַמֵּיהּ דְּרָבָא, אֲמַר לְהוּ: לֹא עָשָׂה וְלֹא כְלוּם; מָר

בְּמִלְוֶה שֶׁעִמּוֹ. שֶׁהַבְּכוֹר נִתְחַיֵּיב לְאָבִיו. פְּלִגִי. חֵלֶק בְּכוֹרָה יַחְלְקוּ בֵּינֵיהֶן, אִיהוּ מְעַכֵּב פַּלְגָּא וְנוֹתֵן לְאָחִיו פַּלְגָּא, דְּהָוֵי לֵיהּ מָמוֹן הַמּוּטָּל בְּסָפֵק וְחוֹלְקִין. דְּאֵין יָדוּעַ אִי חָשֵׁיב מוּחְזָק לְאָבִיו, שֶׁהֲרֵי הַבְּכוֹר רוֹצֶה הוּא לְשַׁעְבֵּד נְכָסָיו לְאָבִיו לְגַמְרֵי, וּבָעֵין יָפֶה גָּמַר וּמַקְנֵי נְכָסָיו לְאָבִיו, כְּדֵי שֶׁיְּהֵא אָבִיו מוּחְזָק בְּהַךְ מִלְוֶה וְיִטּוֹל בָּהּ *אוֹתָן פִּי שְׁנַיִם, אוֹ דִּלְמָא לָא שְׁנָא מִשְּׁאָר מִלְוֶה. הִלְכָּךְ פְּלִגִי. יֵשׁ לְשׁוֹנוֹת אֲחֵרִים, וְלֹא נִתְיַישְּׁבוּ לְפִי הַלָּשׁוֹן הַכָּתוּב בַּסְּפָרִים. וְהָא דְּאָמְרִי': כָּל הָאוֹמֵר "אַחֲרֶיךָ" כְּאוֹמֵר "מֵעַכְשָׁיו" דָּמֵי — לָאו מִילְּתָא הִיא, אֶלָּא כְּשְׁלָחוּ מִתָּם, דְּאָמַר רַבָּה: מִסְתַּבֵּר טַעֲמָא דִּבְנֵי מַעֲרָבָא כו'. וְכָל הֵיכָא דְּאָמַר "נְכָסַיי לָךְ וְאַחֲרֶיךָ לְיוֹרְשַׁיי", מֵת רִאשׁוֹן — קָנוּ יוֹרְשֵׁי הַנּוֹתֵן אוֹ יוֹרְשֵׁי יוֹרְשִׁין הַקּוֹדְמִין לְיוֹרְשׁוֹ. אֲבָל בַּעַל לָא, דְּאֵין הַבַּעַל נוֹטֵל בָּרָאוּי. וְאִם נָתַן הַנְּכָסִים לַבַּת מֵהַיּוֹם וּלְאַחַר מִיתָה, אע"פ שֶׁמֵּתָה בְּחַיֵּי הַזְּקֵנָה — הַבַּעַל יוֹרְשָׁהּ, דְּהָוְיָא לָהּ מוּחְזֶקֶת בְּגוּף הַקַּרְקַע בְּחַיֵּי הַזְּקֵנָה. אָמַר רַב הוּנָא אָמַר רַב אַסִי. אע"ג דְּאוֹקִימְנָא לְדִבְרֵי הַכֹּל דְּאֵין הַבְּכוֹר נוֹטֵל פִּי שְׁנַיִם בְּשֶׁבַח שֶׁהִשְׁבִּיחוּ יְתוֹמִים לְאַחַר מִיתַת אֲבִיהֶן, מִיהוּ, אִם מִיחָה וְאָמַר: אַל תַּשְׁבִּיחוּ חֶלְקִי, אֶלָּא נַחֲלוֹק מִיָּד, וְאַשְׁבִּיחַ אֲנִי שְׁנֵי חֲלָקִים שֶׁלִּי, וְאֶטּוֹל כָּל שִׁבְחָן. וְהֵן נִתְיָיאֲשׁוּ מִלַּחֲלוֹק, וְהִשְׁבִּיחוּ הַנְּכָסִים — הֲרֵי מִיחָה בָּהֶן, וְיִטּוֹל פִּי שְׁנַיִם. דְּהָא פָּסְקִינַן לְקַמָּן: יֵשׁ לוֹ לַבְּכוֹר פִּי שְׁנַיִם קוֹדֶם חֲלוּקָה, מִשָּׁעָה שֶׁחָפֵץ לִזְכּוֹת בִּבְכוֹרָתוֹ. וַהֲרֵי חָפֵץ לִיטּוֹל חֶלְקוֹ לְאַלְתַּר, וְזוֹכֶה בְּחֵלֶק בְּכוֹרָתוֹ מִיָּד, כָּל מָקוֹם שֶׁהוּא, הִלְכָּךְ נְכָסִין דִּידֵיהּ אַשְׁבַּח. אָמַר רַבָּה מִסְתַּבְּרָא מִילְּתָא דְּרַב אַסִי. דְּיִטּוֹל הַבְּכוֹר פִּי שְׁנַיִם בְּשֶׁבַח שֶׁהִשְׁבִּיחוּ יְתוֹמִים, בִּשְׁבִיל מְחָאָתוֹ כְּשֶׁמִּיחָה — בַּעֲנָבִים מְחוּבָּרִים וּבְצָרוּם הַיְּתוֹמִים שֶׁלֹּא מִדַּעְתּוֹ. א"נ, מִדַּעְתּוֹ וּבְעַל כָּרְחוֹ, שֶׁלֹּא רָצוּ לַחֲלוֹק. אוֹ זֵיתִים הָיוּ מְחוּבָּרִין כְּשֶׁמִּיחָה בָּהֶן, וּמְסָקוּם וְהִשְׁבִּיחוּם יְתוֹמִים בִּבְצִירָה וּמְסִיקָה — בְּהַאי שֶׁבַח שָׁקֵיל בְּכוֹר פִּי שְׁנַיִם, שֶׁנּוֹטֵל שְׁנֵי חֲלָקִים מִן הָעֲנָבִים כְּמוֹת שֶׁהֵן בְּצוּרִים, וְלֹא יִתֵּן לָהֶם שְׂכַר בְּצִירָה. דַּעֲנָבִים הָיוּ וַהֲכַתֵּי עֲנָבִים נִינְהוּ, וַעֲנָבִים שֶׁל בְּכוֹר הוּא דְּאַשְׁבּוּ. וַהֲרֵי זֶה דּוֹמֶה לְגוֹזֵל פָּרָה וְהוֹקִירָה, דִּמְשַׁלֵּם אוֹתָהּ כְּמוֹת שֶׁהִיא, הוֹאִיל וְלֹא נִשְׁתַּנֵּית. אֲבָל דְּרָכוּם. ע"מ לִזְכּוֹת הֵן בְּשֶׁבַח דְּרִיכָה — לָא שָׁקֵיל בְּכוֹר פִּי שְׁנַיִם. כִּדְתְנַן: הַגּוֹזֵל עֵצִים וַעֲשָׂאָן כֵּלִים — מְשַׁלֵּם כִּשְׁעַת הַגְּזֵילָה, דְּקַנְיֵיהּ בְּשִׁינּוּי. ה"נ קַנְיֵינְהוּ יַתְמֵי לְהָנֵי עֲנָבִים בְּשִׁינּוּי. כָּךְ נִרְאֶה בְּעֵינַי. וְרַבֵּינוּ חֲנַנְאֵל פֵּירֵשׁ: בְּכוֹר שֶׁמִּיחָה וְאָמַר "אֵינִי מְוַותֵּר חֵלֶק בְּכוֹרָה" — דַּיּוֹ, וְא"צ לִמְחוֹת פַּעַם אַחֶרֶת. וְאָמַר רַבָּה: ה"מ כְּשֶׁמִּיחָה בַּעֲנָבִים וּבְצָרוּם, זֵיתִים וּמְסָקוּם — הוּא דְּאֵין צָרִיךְ לִמְחוֹת לוֹ פַּעַם אַחֶרֶת. אֲבָל אִם דְּרָכוּם וְחָלְקוּ וְלֹא מִיחָה — וִיתֵּר. וְלָא נְהִירָא לִי, חֲדָא: דַּאֲפִי' לֹא מִיחָה לֹא הִפְסִיד חֵלֶק בְּכוֹרָה עַד שֶׁיִּטּוֹל חֵלֶק בְּאַחַת מִן הַשָּׂדוֹת כְּפָשׁוּט, כִּדְלְקַמָּן, וְאָז וִיתֵּר חֵלֶק בְּכוֹרָה בְּכָל הַנְּכָסִים. וְעוֹד: הָא חַכַּתִּי לָא אַיְירִינַן לְעֵיל בְּשׁוּם וִיתּוּר, דְּנֵימָא מִכֵּיוָן שֶׁמִּיחָה מִיחָה, וְלֹא יְוַותֵּר עוֹד. וְרַב יוֹסֵף אָמַר אֲפִי' דְּרָכוּם. קס"ד הַשְׁתָּא דַּאֲפִי' דְּרָכוּם שָׁקֵיל בְּשֶׁבַח הַיַּיִן פִּי שְׁנַיִם. וְהַיְינוּ דְּקָא מְתַמֵּהּ גְּמָרָא: דְּרָכוּם, אַמַּאי שָׁקֵיל פִּי שְׁנַיִם? הָא מֵעִיקָּרָא עִנְבֵי וְהַשְׁתָּא חַמְרָא, וְקַנְיֵיהּ בְּשִׁינּוּי! כִּדְפְרֵישִׁית. וּמְשַׁנֵּי: כִּדְאָמַר רַב עוּקְבָא כו' לְקַמָּן, ה"נ נוֹתֵן לוֹ דְּמֵי הֶיזֵּק עֲנָבָיו. כְּלוֹמַר, הַאי דְּאָמַר רַב יוֹסֵף אֲפִי' דְּרָכוּם — לָא לִיטּוֹל שֶׁבַח הַיַּיִן הַיָּתֵר עַל הָעֲנָבִים קָאָמַר, דְּוַדַּאי לָא שָׁקֵיל אֶלָּא דְּמֵי עֲנָבִים. אֶלָּא הָכָא בְּמַאי עָסְקִינַן — שֶׁפָּחַת הַיַּיִן וְנִשְׁפַּךְ אוֹ נִתְקַלְקֵל, שֶׁאֵין שָׁוֶה כִּדְמֵי עֲנָבִים. וַאֲתָא רַב יוֹסֵף לְמֵימַר דַּאֲפִי' דְּרָכוּם וּפְחָתוּ — בְּכוֹר נוֹטֵל פִּי שְׁנַיִם בַּעֲנָבִים בְּצוּרִים כַּדָּמִים שֶׁהָיוּ שָׁוִין הָעֲנָבִים. דְּכֵיוָן דְּמִיחָה בָּהֶן — לָא הָווּ לְהוּ לִדְרוֹךְ עֲנָבִים שֶׁלּוֹ, וּמְשַׁלְּמִים לוֹ דְּמֵי עֲנָבָיו, הַכֹּל כִּשְׁעַת הַגְּזֵילָה. וּמָר אָמַר חֲדָא, וּמָר אָמַר חֲדָא וְלָא פְּלִיגִי; רַבָּה אַיְירֵי דְּאֵין נוֹטֵל בְּשֶׁבַח הַיַּיִן, וְרַב יוֹסֵף אֲתָא לְמֵימַר דְּה"נ לָא שָׁקֵיל בִּפְחִיתַת הַיַּיִן מִדְּמֵי עֲנָבִים. דְּאָמַר רַב יְהוּדָה אָמַר שְׁמוּאֵל בְּכוֹר וּפָשׁוּט כו' נוֹטֵל פִּי שְׁנַיִם. וּכְגוֹן שֶׁמִּיחָה. אָמַר רַב עוּקְבָא כו'. וְה"ק: וַאֲפִי' דְּרָכוּם — נוֹטֵל פִּי שְׁנַיִם בַּעֲנָבִים בְּצוּרִים כְּמוֹ שֶׁהֵן שָׁוִין קוֹדֶם דְּרִיכָה. בְּכוֹר שֶׁנָּטַל חֵלֶק. בְּאַחַת מִן הַשָּׂדוֹת כְּאֶחָד מֵאֶחָיו, חֵלֶק פְּשִׁיטוּת. וִיתֵּר. כְּלוֹמַר, הֲרֵי מָחַל חֵלֶק בְּכוֹרָה, כִּדְמְפָרֵשׁ לְקַמֵּיהּ אִי בְּהַאי שָׂדֶה אִי בְּכָל הַנְּכָסִים. וְטַעֲמָא — כִּדְאַמְרַן לְעֵיל: אִם אָמַר "אֵינִי נוֹטֵל וְאֵינִי נוֹתֵן" — רַשַּׁאי. דְּכֵיוָן דְּמַתָּנָה קָרְיֵיהּ רַחֲמָנָא, וְאִיהוּ לָא בָּעֵי לָהּ — לָא הָוְיָא מַתָּנָה, וְלֹא יִזְכֶּה בָּהּ עוֹד. קָסָבַר אֵין לוֹ לַבְּכוֹר. חֵלֶק בְּכוֹרָה, לֹא לָתֵת וְלֹא לִמְכּוֹר קוֹדֶם חֲלוּקָה, כִּדְכְתִיב: "לָתֶת לוֹ" — עַד דְּאָתְיָא לִידֵיהּ דִּמְקַבֵּל מַתָּנָה. הִלְכָּךְ, הַאי שָׂדֶה שֶׁבָּא לְיָדוֹ חֶלְקוֹ מִמֶּנָּה, וְהָיָה לוֹ לִזְכּוֹת בּוֹ חֵלֶק בְּכוֹרָה, דְּהָא שְׁעַת חֲלוּקָה הוּא וְקָרֵינַן בֵּיהּ "לָתֶת לוֹ" (ג) — הִלְכָּךְ מָצֵי מָחֵיל. אֲבָל בִּשְׁאָר נְכָסִים לָא מָצֵי מָחֵיל, דְּאֵין אָדָם מַקְנֶה דָּבָר שֶׁלֹּא בָּא לָעוֹלָם, דְּעַד שְׁעַת חֲלוּקָה לָא זָכֵי בְּהוּ. וְכ"ש בְּחֵלֶק פְּשִׁיטוּת דְּלָא זָכֵי קוֹדֶם חֲלוּקָה, שֶׁלֹּא הוּבְרַר חֶלְקוֹ. וּמִיהוּ, אִם מֵת קוֹדֶם חֲלוּקָה, ל"ש בְּכוֹר וְל"ש פָּשׁוּט — בְּנוֹ יוֹרֵשׁ עִם הָאַחִין, וְנוֹטֵל חֵלֶק אָבִיו כְּשֶׁיָּבֹאוּ לַחֲלוֹק. דְּלָא גָּרַע הֵיכָא דְּמֵת הָאָב וְאח"כ מֵת הַבֵּן, מֵהֵיכָא דְּמֵת הַבֵּן בְּחַיֵּי הָאָב, דְּבֵן בְּנוֹ יוֹרְשׁוֹ, כִּדְכְתִיב: "וּבֵן אֵין לוֹ" — עַיֵּין עָלָיו. אֲבָל קוֹדֶם חֲלוּקָה — אֵין יְכוֹלִין לִמְכּוֹר, לֹא הָאָב וְלֹא הַבֵּן. יֵשׁ לוֹ לַבְּכוֹר קוֹדֶם חֲלוּקָה. וְאע"ג דְּחֵלֶק פָּשׁוּט אֵין לוֹ. דְּהָא כְּתִיב "לָתֶת" — מִשְּׁעַת שֶׁמֵּת הָאָב הוּא רָאוּי לִיתֵּן לוֹ, הִלְכָּךְ בִּבְכוֹר תַּלְיָא מִילְּתָא, דְּבְשָׁעָה שֶׁיִּרְצֶה יִזְכֶּה בְּחֶלְקוֹ, וּכְדַאֲמָרַן לְעֵיל: בְּכוֹר שֶׁמִּיחָה מִיחָה, וְהִלְכָּךְ יֵשׁ כֹּחַ בְּיָדוֹ לִמְחוֹל כָּל שָׁעָה שֶׁיִּרְצֶה, דְּהַיְינוּ דָּבָר שֶׁבָּא לָעוֹלָם. וַאֲנַן סַהֲדֵי, דְּכִי הֵיכִי דְּאַחֵיל בְּהָא שָׂדֶה — אַחֵיל בְּכוּלְּהוּ. וְכֵיוָן דְּיֵשׁ כֹּחַ בְּיָדוֹ לִזְכּוֹת — יֵשׁ כֹּחַ נַמִּי בְּיָדוֹ לִיתֵּן וְלִמְחוֹל, וְהָוְיָא מְחִילָה. בְּנִכְסֵי דִּידֵיהּ וּדְפָשׁוּט. יֵשׁ מְפָרְשִׁין: בְּחֵלֶק בְּכוֹרָתוֹ וּבְחֵלֶק פְּשִׁיטוּתוֹ. וְאֵין זֶה לְשׁוֹן גְּמָרָא. וְעַל כָּרְחִי זָקוּק אֲנִי לְפָרֵשׁ שֶׁמָּכַר כָּל הַנְּכָסִים, שְׁנֵי חֲלָקִים שֶׁלּוֹ וְחֵלֶק פָּשׁוּט אָחִיו. מִקַּמֵּי דְּנִיפְלוּג בַּהֲדֵיהּ מָכַר כָּל הַשָּׂדֶה שֶׁלֹּא בִּרְשׁוּת אָחִיו, וּלְצוֹרֶךְ אָחִיו, לָתֵת לוֹ מָעוֹת שֶׁל חֶלְקוֹ. לְמֵיכַל תַּמְרֵי. מֵאוֹתוֹ שָׂדֶה, בִּשְׁבִיל חֵלֶק אֲבוּהוֹן. מַחוּנְהוּ. הִכּוּם. אָמְרוּ לְהוּ. לַלָּקוֹחוֹת, קְרוֹבַיְיהוּ דְּיַתְמֵי. דִּזְבַנְתִּינְהוּ לְנִכְסַיְיהוּ. שֶׁלֹּא מִדַּעְתָּם וְשֶׁלֹּא מִדַּעַת אֲבוּהוֹן. דְּהָא וַדַּאי חֵלֶק פָּשׁוּט אָחִיו לֹא הָיָה יָכוֹל לִמְכּוֹר. לֹא עָשָׂה. הַבְּכוֹר וְלֹא כְלוּם בִּמְכִירָה זוֹ. מָר

קרקע בחוב אביהן היא חוזרת וגובה מהן בשבועה, כדין בעל חוב, או אם פטרה מן השבועה — גובה ממלוה שהיא ביד אחרים, אפי' לר"ע ודלא כאבא שאול בן אימא מרים. ואין לומר דההוא כרבי אתיא, אבל לרבנן הוי מלוה ראוי — דהא לא משתמיט התם שום אמורא לאוקומי כרבי, משמע דליכא מאן דפליג, אלא כ"ע אית להו מלוה מוחזקת לגבי כתובה. ובזמן הזה דתקינו גאונים דגביא אשה ובעל חוב ממטלטלי דיתמי כמו ממקרקעי, יתומין שגבו בחובת אביהן בין מקרקעי בין מטלטלי — חוזרת אשה וגובה מהן. כי היכי דבמקרקעי משום דר' נתן חשיב כאילו גבאן אביהן מחיים — הכי נמי במטלטלי. וצריך עיון, דרב פפא סבר הכא בין גבו קרקע בין גבו מעות אין לו — אם כן סבר שעבודא לאו דאורייתא, דשילהי "גט פשוט" (לקמן ד' קעה:) מדמי להו אהדדי. ובפרק קמא דקדושין (ד' יג:) סבר רב פפא שעבודא דאורייתא. **ובמלוה** שעמו פלגי. לא משום דקי"ל ממון המוטל בספק חולקין. דהא לא קי"ל כסומכוס, כדפרישית לעיל (ד' לה. ד"ה ומ"ש). אלא תקנת חכמים היא הכא, ובמקום שמפורש בהדיא, דחולקין. **אבל** דרכום לא. לפי' הקונט', דטעמא משום דקנאום בשינוי — קשיא, דהיכי פריך: מעיקרא ענבים והשתא חמרא? הא איכא למ"ד ב"הגוזל קמא" (ב"ק ד' צה.): שינוי במקומו עומד! לא

א) [נ"ל רב עוקבא]: ב) (כאן שייך מ"ש לעיל ומה דאתא כו' רש"ל): ג) [ברכות ט. וש"נ]:

[נ"א איהו]

רבינו גרשום

דאבא: ובמלוה שעמו פליגי. שאם הבכור לוה מאביו ונשאר אותה מלוה בידו יטול ממנה חלק כדפשוט והחלק של הבכורה יטול המחצית בלבד וחצי האחר יחלוקו ביניהן האחים ומאי טעמא יטול מחצית ממנה חלק בכורה משום דלא דמי הא מלוה שעמו למלוה שישנה אצל אחרים דהתם לאו מוחזק הכא מוחזק והואיל ויש לה שם מלוה בדין הוא דלא שקיל מינה חלק בכור. אבל הואיל דמוחזק הוא מהני ליה דשקל פלג דבכורה: ל"א במלוה שעמו פליגי. כלומר אע"ג דפסיק רב פפא הלכת' הני מילי במלוה שישנה אצל אחרים אבל במלוה שעמו פליגי עליה בני מערבא א) דשקיל מיניה פי שנים: בכור שמיחה. ליתומים ואמר אין רצוני שתשביח נכסים של אבא עד שתתנו לי חלק בכורתי ולא רצו אלא השביחו אע"ג דאמרן לעיל אבל בנו בתים כו' השביחו נוטל פי שנים אף בשבח משום דמחאתו היה מחאה: בענבים ובצרום. הואיל שהיו משובחין בחיי אביהן ולא דרכום אלא בצרום בלבד ומיחה על הבצירה בצירה לא חשיב שבח כל כך אע"פ שטרחו ובצרום שקיל בכורה מענבים מובצרים ואינו מנכה להם כלום הואיל דמיחה וכן נמי בזיתים ומסקום אבל דרכום שכבר נשתנו שעכשיו הוא יין שטרחו בהן הרבה אע"פ שמיחה אינו נוטל פי שנים ביין: רב יוסף אמר אפי' דרכום אם מיחה מיחה ונוטל: ומקשי' הא הוו השתא חמרא שהשביחו יתומים ולא מטא לידא דאבוהון. נותן לו דמי היזק ענבים שאם דרכום הרבה אובדות מהם והרבה מתפזרות מהן אותו היזק ישלמו ליה ולא נוטל פי שנים: והא דרב עוקבא ב) דאמר בכור ופשוט שהניח כו' מוקים לה במיחה: חלק כפשוט. שלא נטל פי שנים: ויתר באותה שדה. ולא יהבינן ליה טפי באותה שדה כי אם כפשוט אבל בשאר [הנכסים] לא ויתר: ויתר בכל הנכסים. דבשאר נכסים נמי לא שקיל פי שנים. אין לבכור בנכסי אביו כלום קודם חלוקה כלומר לא ליתן ולא למכור. הלכך מה דאתא לידיה אותה שדה בלבד שחלק עם אחיו ולא נטל ממנה אלא כפשוט באותה שדה שבבר באתה לידו ויתר. אבל בכל הנכסים שעדיין לא באו לידו לא מחל חלק בכורה: זבין נכסיה דידיה ודפשוט. אחוה קודם שחלקו אתו לקמיה דרבא לדינא ואמר להו לא עשה ולא כלום אותו מכר: מר

נח א מיי' פ"ג מהל' נחלות הלכה ה סמג עשין לו טוש"ע ח"מ סי' רעח סעיף ז:

נט ב ג מיי' שם הל' ו ועיין בהשגות ובמגיד משנה טוש"ע שם סעיף ט:

ס ד ה מיי' שם טוש"ע שם סעיף ח:

הגהות הב"ח

(א) גמ' מאי ויתר רב פפא וכו' באותה שדה קא סבר אין לו לבכור קודם חלוקה ומה דאתא לידיה אחיל אידך לא אחיל רב פפי משמיה דרבא וכו' כולן קא סבר יש לו: (ב) רשב"ם ד"ה קסבר וכו' לתת לו מצי מחיל כצ"ל ותיבת הלכך נמחק:

א) לשון זה שכ' רבינו עולה שפיר לפי גירסתו ז"ל שגרס פלגי בלא יו"ד אבל לגי' הרשב"ם ז"ל שגרס פליגי בלא יו"ד אינו מיושב כ"כ. ונראה דלזה כוון הרשב"ם ז"ל במש"כ ויש כו' ולא נתיישבו לפי הלשון הכתוב בספרים ודו"ק. ב) נ"ל והא דרב עוקבא דאמר ליתן לו וכו': דאמר רב יהודה אמר שמואל בכור ופשוט שהניח וכו'.

מָר סָבַר: לֹא עָשָׂה כְּלוּם בְּפַלְגָּא, וּמָר סָבַר: בְּכוּלְּהוּ. שָׁלְחוּ מִתָּם: בְּכוֹר שֶׁמָּכַר קוֹדֶם חֲלוּקָּה — לֹא עָשָׂה כְּלוּם. אַלְמָא, אֵין לוֹ לַבְּכוֹר קוֹדֶם חֲלוּקָּה. [א]וְהִלְכְתָא: יֵשׁ לַבְּכוֹר קוֹדֶם חֲלוּקָּה. מָר זוּטְרָא מִדְּרִישְׁבָא פְּלַג בְּצַנָּא דְּפִלְפְּלֵי בַּהֲדֵי אַחִין בְּשָׁוֶה, אֲתָא לְקַמֵּיהּ דְּרַב אַשִׁי, אֲמַר לֵיהּ: הוֹאִיל וְיַתַּרְתָּה בְּמִקְצָת — וְיַתַּרְתָּה בְּכָל הַנְּכָסִים כּוּלָּן.§ **מתני'** [ב]הָאוֹמֵר: "אִישׁ פְּלוֹנִי בְּנִי בְּכוֹר לֹא יִטּוֹל פִּי שְׁנַיִם", "אִישׁ פְּלוֹנִי בְּנִי לֹא יִירַשׁ עִם אֶחָיו" — לֹא אָמַר כְּלוּם, שֶׁהִתְנָה עַל מַה שֶּׁכָּתוּב בַּתּוֹרָה. [א)ג]הַמְחַלֵּק נְכָסָיו (א) עַל פִּיו, רִיבָּה לְאֶחָד וּמִיעֵט לְאֶחָד, וְהִשְׁוָה לָהֶן אֶת הַבְּכוֹר — דְּבָרָיו קַיָּימִין, וְאִם אָמַר מִשּׁוּם יְרוּשָּׁה — לֹא אָמַר כְּלוּם. [ד]כָּתַב בֵּין בַּתְּחִלָּה בֵּין בָּאֶמְצַע בֵּין בַּסּוֹף מִשּׁוּם מַתָּנָה — דְּבָרָיו קַיָּימִין.§ **גמ'** לֵימָא, מַתְנִיתִין דְּלָא כְּר' יְהוּדָה, דְּאִי ר' יְהוּדָה, הָאָמַר: בְּדָבָר שֶׁל מָמוֹן תְּנָאוֹ קַיָּים! דְּתַנְיָא: [ב)]הָאוֹמֵר לְאִשָּׁה "הֲרֵי אַתְּ מְקוּדֶּשֶׁת לִי עַל מְנָת שֶׁאֵין לִיךְ עָלַי שְׁאֵר כְּסוּת וְעוֹנָה" — הֲרֵי זוֹ מְקוּדֶּשֶׁת, וּתְנָאוֹ בָּטֵל, דִּבְרֵי ר' מֵאִיר; ר' יְהוּדָה אוֹמֵר: [ה]בְּדָבָר שֶׁל מָמוֹן תְּנָאוֹ קַיָּים. אֲפִי' תֵּימָא ר' יְהוּדָה, הָתָם יָדְעָה וְקָא מַחֲלָה, הָכָא לָא קָא מָחֵיל. אָמַר רַב יוֹסֵף: [ו]אָמַר "אִישׁ פְּלוֹנִי בְּנִי בְּכוֹרִי הוּא" — נוֹטֵל פִּי שְׁנַיִם, "אִישׁ פְּלוֹנִי בְּכוֹר הוּא" — אֵינוֹ נוֹטֵל פִּי שְׁנַיִם, דִּלְמָא בּוּכְרָא דְּאִמָּא קָאָמַר. הַהוּא דַּאֲתָא לְקַמֵּיהּ דְּרַבָּה בַּר בַּר חָנָה, א"ל: מוּחְזְקַנִי בְּזֶה שֶׁהוּא בְּכוֹר. א"ל: מְנָא יָדְעַתְּ? דַּהֲוָה קָרֵי לֵיהּ אֲבוּהּ "בּוּכְרָא סִכְלָא". דִּלְמָא בּוּכְרָא דְּאִמָּא הוּא, דְּכָל בּוּכְרָא דְּאִמָּא נַמִי "בּוּכְרָא סִכְלָא" קָארוּ לֵיהּ. [ז]הַהוּא דַּאֲתָא לְקַמֵּיהּ דְּרַבִּי חֲנִינָא, אֲמַר לֵיהּ: מוּחְזְקַנִי בְּזֶה שֶׁהוּא בְּכוֹר. אֲמַר לֵיהּ: מְנָא יָדְעַתְּ? אֲמַר לֵיהּ: דְּכִי הָווּ אָתוּ לְגַבֵּי אֲבוּהּ, אֲמַר לְהוּ: זִילוּ לְגַבֵּי שִׁכְחַת בְּרִי, דְּבוּכְרָא הוּא וּמָסֵי רוּקֵיהּ. וְדִלְמָא בּוּכְרָא דְּאִמָּא הוּא! [ח]גְּמִירִי: בּוּכְרָא דְּאַבָּא — מָסֵי רוּקֵיהּ, בּוּכְרָא דְּאִמָּא — לָא מָסֵי רוּקֵיהּ. אָמַר ר' אַמִי: [ט]טוּמְטוּם שֶׁנִּקְרַע וְנִמְצָא זָכָר — אֵינוֹ נוֹטֵל פִּי שְׁנַיִם, דְּאָמַר קְרָא: °"וְהָיָה הַבֵּן הַבְּכוֹר לַשְּׂנִיאָה", עַד שֶׁיְּהֵא בֵּן מִשְּׁעַת הֲוָיָה. רַב נַחְמָן בַּר יִצְחָק אָמַר: [י]אַף אֵינוֹ נִידּוֹן כְּבֵן סוֹרֵר וּמוֹרֶה, דְּאָמַר קְרָא: °"כִּי יִהְיֶה לְאִישׁ בֵּן סוֹרֵר וּמוֹרֶה", עַד שֶׁיְּהֵא בֵּן מִשְּׁעַת הֲוָיָה. אַמֵימָר

דברים כא
שם

לא עשה כלום בפלגא. פירש הקונטרס: בחלק פשיטותו, וכל שכן בחלק פשיטות אחין. ואין נראה, דחלק פשיטותו — פשיטא דמכר, כדקאמר לעיל: מה חלק פשוט אע"ג דלא אתי לידיה! אלא נראה: דלא עשה ולא כלום בפלגא — היינו בחלק פשיטות אחין, אבל חלק בכורה — מכר, וכל שכן חלק פשיטותו. ומר סבר: לא עשה ולא כלום בכולהו — לא חלק בכורה ולא חלק פשיטות אחין. אך תימה: למאן דאמר לא עשה ולא כלום בפלגא, היינו בחלק פשיטות אחין — מאי קא משמע לן רבא? וכי על חלק אחין הוצרכו לישאל?
והלכתא יש לבכור קודם חלוקה. אע"ג דקיימא לן כרבנן, כדפסק רב פפא [ג)]דאין בכור נוטל פי שנים במלוה, כרבנן דאמרי: חלק בכורה עד דאתי לידיה — מודו רבנן דיש לו לבכור קודם חלוקה, כפ"ה, דהוי שפיר ראוי לתת לו, שמשעה שמת האב היה ראוי לתת לו. ומיהו, מכל מקום אין נוטל פי שנים בשבח, דלא מ"לתת לו" ממעטינן לה, אלא מ"ימצא לו" ממעטינן דבעי מלוי ומוחזק, למעוטי ראוי כלוה ושבח. ומ"לתת לו" גלי לן, מדקרייה מתנה דרשינן מ"ימצא לו" מלוי ומוחזק. ואי לא "ימצא לו" — לא הוה דרשינן מ"לתת לו" פרט לראוי. וכן משמע ההיא דספרי דבי רב [ד)]דמ"ימצא לו" ממעטינן שבח. ולעולם אית להו לרבנן דיש לו לבכור קודם חלוקה. והא דאמרינן: ואם אמר "איני נוטל ואיני נותן" רשאי — לא הוי טעמא משום דיש לו (ב) קודם חלוקה, דאפי' אין לו לבכור — יכול לומר "איני נוטל ואיני נותן". דלא משום שרוצה להסתלק מן הבכורה לגמרי שלא יוכל לחזור ולתבעה קאמר, אלא הכי קאמר להו: איני נוטל, וכל זמן שלא נטלתי — לא תוכלו לתבעני כנוס.
הרי זו מקודשת ותנאו בטל. מפירש בריש "אע"פ" (כתובות דף נו. ד"ה הרי). מדדרש

מָר סָבַר. רַב פַּפִּי. **לֹא עָשָׂה כְּלוּם בְּפַלְגָּא.** בְּחֵלֶק פְּשִׁיטוּתוֹ, וְכָל שֶׁכֵּן בְּחֵלֶק פָּשׁוּט אָחִיו. אֲבָל בְּחֵלֶק בְּכוֹרָה — יָפֶה מָכַר, דְּיֵשׁ לוֹ לַבְּכוֹר קוֹדֶם חֲלוּקָה. בְּכוּלְּהוּ. אֲפִי' בְּחֵלֶק בְּכוֹרָה. **וְהִלְכְתָא** יֵשׁ לוֹ לַבְּכוֹר קוֹדֶם חֲלוּקָה. וְאִם מָכַר, אוֹ מָחַל, אוֹ נָטַל חֵלֶק אֶחָד כְּפָשׁוּט — וִיתֵּר בְּכָל הַנְּכָסִים כּוּלָּן, מִשּׁוּם דְּמַתָּנָה קָרְיָיהּ רַחֲמָנָא, וּמִשֶּׁמֵּת אָב נְתוּנָה לַבְּכוֹר. **צַנָּא.** סַל מָלֵא פִּלְפְּלִין. **מתני'** הָאוֹמֵר **אִישׁ פְּלוֹנִי בְּנִי.** שֶׁהוּא בְּכוֹר, לֹא יִטּוֹל פִּי שְׁנַיִם. אִי נַמִי, אִישׁ [פְּלוֹנִי] בְּנִי פָּשׁוּט לֹא יִירַשׁ עִם אֶחָיו. **לֹא אָמַר כְּלוּם.** שֶׁהֲרֵי מַתְנֶה לַעֲקוֹר דָּבָר מִן הַתּוֹרָה, וּבְעַל כָּרְחוֹ שֶׁל זֶה יִירַשׁ עִם הָאַחִין. וְאֵינוֹ יָכוֹל לְסַלְּקוֹ מִירוּשָּׁה זוֹ אֶלָּא עַל יְדֵי שֶׁיִּתֵּן בִּלְשׁוֹן מַתָּנָה כָּל נְכָסָיו לִשְׁאָר בָּנָיו, אוֹ שֶׁיֹּאמַר: שְׁאָר בָּנַיי יִירְשׁוּ כָּל נְכָסַי, וְאַלִּיבָּא דְּרַבִּי יוֹחָנָן בֶּן בְּרוֹקָא. הַמְחַלֵּק נְכָסָיו עַל פִּיו. דִּלְוָואַת שְׁכִיב מְרַע אֵינָהּ צְרִיכָה קִנְיָן, וְלֹא שְׁטָר, וְלֹא מְשִׁיכָה, אֶלָּא בְּדִבּוּר פִּיו בְּעָלְמָא. וּכְגוֹן שֶׁמְּצַוֶּה מֵחֲמַת מִיתָה, כִּדְאָמַר לְקַמָּן בְּפֶרֶק "מִי שֶׁמֵּת". וְרִיבָּה לְאֶחָד. נָתַן לוֹ בְּמַתָּנָה כִּפְלַיִים, אוֹ שֶׁהִשְׁוָה לָהֶן הַבְּכוֹר בִּלְשׁוֹן מַתָּנָה. דְּבָרָיו קַיָּימִין. שֶׁיֵּשׁ כֹּחַ בָּאָדָם לִיתֵּן מָמוֹנוֹ בְּמַתָּנָה לְכָל מִי שֶׁיִּרְצֶה, וְאֵין כָּאן מַתְנֶה עַל מַה שֶּׁכָּתוּב בַּתּוֹרָה, שֶׁהֲרֵי לֹא נִשְׁאַר לוֹ אַחַר מִיתָתוֹ כְּלוּם לְהוֹרִישׁ לְבָנָיו בְּתוֹרַת יְרוּשָּׁה שֶׁיִּטְּלוּ הַפְּשׁוּטִים בְּשָׁוֶה וְהַבְּכוֹר פִּי שְׁנַיִם. וְאִם אָמַר מִשּׁוּם יְרוּשָּׁה לֹא אָמַר כְּלוּם. אִם רִיבָּה לְאֶחָד וּמִיעֵט לְאֶחָד בִּלְשׁוֹן יְרוּשָּׁה, שֶׁאָמַר "פְּלוֹנִי בְּנִי יִירַשׁ אוֹתוֹ שָׂדֶה בֵּית כּוֹר, וּפְלוֹנִי בְּנִי יִירַשׁ שָׂדֶה לֶתֶךְ", וְעַל בְּנוֹ בְּכוֹרוֹ אָמַר "פְּלוֹנִי בְּנִי יִירַשׁ שָׂדֶה פְּלוֹנִי, וּפְלוֹנִי בְּנִי יִירַשׁ שָׂדֶה פְּלוֹנִי הַגָּדוֹל כְּשֶׁל חֲבֵירוֹ" — לֹא אָמַר כְּלוּם, דְּמַתְנֶה עַל מַה שֶּׁכָּתוּב בַּתּוֹרָה, שֶׁאֵינוֹ יָכוֹל לַעֲשׂוֹתוֹ יוֹרֵשׁ אֶלָּא כְּמִשְׁפָּט הַכָּתוּב. וּדְלָא כְּר' יוֹחָנָן בֶּן בְּרוֹקָא, דְּאָמַר לְקַמָּן בְּמַתְנִיתִין (דף קל.): אִם אָמַר עַל מִי שֶׁרָאוּי לְיוֹרְשׁוֹ — דְּבָרָיו קַיָּימִין. וְהַךְ מִשְׁנָה דְּרַבָּנַן הִיא. וּרְבוּתָא הוּא דִּנְקַט רִיבָּה לְאֶחָד וּמִיעֵט לְאֶחָד מִשּׁוּם יְרוּשָּׁה לֹא אָמַר כְּלוּם, וְכָל שֶׁכֵּן הֵיכָא דְּעָקַר כָּל הַנַּחֲלוֹת מִן הָאַחִין וְהוֹרִישׁ לְאֶחָד מֵהֶן — לֹא עָשָׂה וְלֹא כְּלוּם. כָּתַב בֵּין בַּתְּחִלָּה כו' דְּבָרָיו קַיָּימִין. דְּכֵיוָן דְּאִיכָּא לְשׁוֹן מַתָּנָה בַּהֲדֵיהּ — מְהַנֵּי לֵיהּ דְּאַף לְשׁוֹן יְרוּשָּׁה קוֹנָה. **גמ'** לֵימָא מַתְנִי'. דְּקָתָנֵי: אֵין אָדָם מַתְנֶה, דְּלָא כְּרַבִּי יְהוּדָה. וַאֲנַן קַיְימָא לָן: רַבִּי מֵאִיר וְרַבִּי יְהוּדָה — הֲלָכָה כְּר' יְהוּדָה. שְׁאֵר. מָזוֹן. עוֹנָה. תַּשְׁמִישׁ. וּתְנָאוֹ בָּטֵל. דְּאֵין אָדָם מַתְנֶה עַל מַה שֶּׁכָּתוּב בַּתּוֹרָה, וַהֲוֵי קִידּוּשֵׁי, הַמַּעֲשֶׂה מַעֲשֶׂה, וְהַתְּנַאי כְּמַאן דְּלֵיתֵיהּ, דִּכְמַעֲשֶׂה בְּלָא תְּנַאי דָּמֵי. בְּדָבָר שֶׁל מָמוֹן. שְׁאֵר וּכְסוּת. אֲבָל עוֹנַת תַּשְׁמִישׁ — מִלְוָה הִיא, וְצַעֲרָא דְּגוּפָא הוּא. תְּנָאוֹ קַיָּים. הַקִּידּוּשִׁין קִידּוּשִׁין, וְיֵשׁ לָהּ עָלָיו עוֹנָה, אֲבָל לֹא שְׁאֵר וּכְסוּת. וּמַתְנִי' נַמִי — שֶׁל דְּבַר מָמוֹן הוּא. הָתָם קָא מָחֲלָה. שֶׁעַל מְנָת כֵּן קִבְּלָה קִידּוּשִׁין, וּבַהִיא הֲנָאָה דְּמְקַדֵּשׁ לָהּ מָחֲלָה לֵיהּ, וְכֵיוָן דְּקִבְּלָה לְקִידּוּשִׁין מִינֵּיהּ — נִתְרַצֵּית לִמְחוֹל. אֲבָל הָכָא מִי מָחֵיל? מָה הֲנָאָה יֵשׁ לוֹ לַבֵּן שֶׁיִּמְחוֹל? וְאַע"פ שֶׁשָּׁתַק הַבֵּן — אֵין זוֹ מְחִילָה, דְּאֵינוֹ רוֹצֶה לְהַכְעִיס אֶת אָבִיו. וְלָא גָּרְסִינַן: מִי יָדַע דְּמָחֵיל. הָאוֹמֵר **אִישׁ פְּלוֹנִי.** "הִנֵּה הוּא בְּנִי בְּכוֹרִי" — מְהֵימְנִינַן לֵיהּ לְאָב לִיטּוֹל פִּי שְׁנַיִם. דַּאֲפִי' רַבָּנַן דִּפְלִיגֵי אַדְּר' יְהוּדָה לְקַמָּן בִּשְׁמַעְתִּין, וְאָמְרִי: אֵינוֹ נֶאֱמָן — הָנֵי מִילֵּי בִּדְמוּחְזָק לָן דְּלָאו בְּכוֹר הוּא. אֲבָל בִּדְלָא מוּחְזָק לָן הֵי מִינַּיְיהוּ בְּכוֹר — מוֹדוּ דְּנֶאֱמָן, כִּדְאָמְרִינַן לְקַמָּן: אֶלָּא לְרַבָּנַן "יַכִּיר" לָמָּה לִי — בִּצְרִיךְ הֶיכֵּרָא. **אֲבָל אָמַר** יִירַשׁ פְּלוֹנִי בְּנִי הִנֵּה הוּא בְּכוֹר. וְלָא אָמַר "בְּכוֹרִי" — אָז לֹא יִטּוֹל פִּי שְׁנַיִם, דִּלְמָא בּוּכְרָא דְּאִמָּא קָאָמַר, וַהֲוֵי בְּכוֹר לְכֹהֵן אֲבָל לֹא לְנַחֲלָה, דְּלָא הָוֵי רֵאשִׁית אוֹנוֹ דִּידֵיהּ. וּמִסְפֵּיקָא לָא יָהֲבִינַן לֵיהּ פִּי שְׁנַיִם, וַאֲפִילּוּ אִם תָּפַס — מַפְּקִינַן מִינֵּיהּ, דְּלָא קָרֵינָא בֵּיהּ "יַכִּיר" לַאֲחֵרִים, דְּהָכָא מְסַפְּקָא לָן. מוּחְזָק אֲנִי בּוֹ. וְעֵד אַחֵר עִמּוֹ (כו'). **בּוּכְרָא סוּכְלָא.** בְּכוֹר שׁוֹטֶה. דְּכָל **בּוּכְרָא דְּאִמָּא** **בּוּכְרָא סוּכְלָא** קָרֵי לֵיהּ. וְלָא מִשּׁוּם שְׁטוּתוֹ, אֶלָּא לְפִי שֶׁאֵינוֹ בְּכוֹר גָּמוּר. כְּמוֹ "אָדָם שׁוֹטֶה", שֶׁאֵינוֹ כָּשֵׁר. מוּחְזָק **אֲנִי בְּזֶה שֶׁהוּא בְּכוֹר.** וְהָיָה עֵד אֶחָד עִמּוֹ. וְהַאי בְּכוֹר הָיָה שְׁמוֹ שִׁכְחַת, כִּדְלְקַמֵּיהּ. דְּכִי הָווּ אָתוּ. הַחוֹשְׁשִׁין בְּעֵינֵיהֶן. שִׁכְחַת בְּרִי. שֵׁם הַבְּכוֹר. וְלָאו הַיְינוּ בְּרֵיהּ דְּר"ח, דְּאָמְרִי' בְּ"לֹא יַחְפּוֹר" (לעיל דף כו.): אָמַר ר"ח: לֹא שָׁכִיב שִׁכְחַת בְּרִי אֶלָּא דְּקָץ תְּאֵינָתָא בְּלָא זִמְנַהּ. מָסֵי רוּקֵיהּ. לָעַיִן. **אָמַר ר' אַמִּי.** בְּכוֹר הַנּוֹלָד טוּמְטוּם, שֶׁאֵין נִיכָּר בּוֹ לֹא זַכְרוּת וְלֹא נַקְבוּת, וּלְאַחַר זְמַן נִקְרַע וְנִמְצָא זָכָר, שֶׁהָיָה גִּיד שֶׁלּוֹ וּבֵיצָיו טְמוּנִין בַּגּוּף. וּרְבוּתָא נָקַט, דְּאַף עַל גַּב שֶׁנִּמְצָא זָכָר גָּמוּר, וְכָל שֶׁכֵּן אַנְדְּרוֹגִינוֹס, שֶׁאֵין סְפֵיקוֹ עָתִיד לְהִוָּדַע. וְהָיָה. קְרָא יְתֵירָא הוּא. הֲוָיָה. לֵידָה.
אֲמֵימָר

ר' מאיר היא דאי ר' יהודה א) היינו דמתנה על מה שכתוב בתורה: ר' יהודה אומר בדבר של ממון תנאו קיים אבל עונה לא הואיל דלאו ממון הוא. עד כאן לא אמר ר' יהודה גבי אשה דבדבר של ממון תנאו קיים משום דידעה היא איתתא דלא בעי למיתן לה מזון וכסות אפי' הכא מקדשה ליה ומחלה ליה בההיא הנאה דמקדש לה ואית לה עונה ומחלה בממון וניחא לה בהנהו קדושין אבל הכא גבי מתנה מי ידע האי יורש דהוה בעי ממעט ליה חלקו דלימחול ליה משום הכי אפי' ר' יהודה מודה דתנאו בטל: בכורי הוא נוטל פי שנים. כיון דאמר בכורי משמע בכור של ראשית אונו. אבל אמר פלוני בכור לא יטול דדלמא בוכרא דאמו קאמר: בוכרא סכלא. כלומר בכור שוטה שאינו כל כך עיקר בכור כי הוא מן האם: בוכרא סכלא קראו ליה. דלא בכור ממש הוא ואינו נוטל: דכי הוו אתו אינשי דהוי להו שחין או מכה אתא לקמיה להתרפאות ומסי רוקו. כלומר שרוקו יפה לרפואה משום

א) נ"ל דאי ר' יהודה האמר בדבר של ממון תנאו קיים: ר"י אומר וכו'.

אמימר אמר אף אינו ממעט חלק בכורה. אותו טומטום שנקרע ונמצא זכר, אם הוא פשוט ואינו בכור, וכל נכסי האב תשעה מנים, והן שלשה בנים, בכור ופשוט וטומטום – חולקים הנכסים תחלה לשלשה חלקים כאילו אין כאן כי אם בכור ופשוט, והטומטום כמאן דליתיה. ומגיע לחלק הבכור ששה מנים שהן ב' חלקים, לפי שהבכור נוטל פי שנים בפשוט, נמצא חלק בכורה שלשה מנים. חוזרים וחולקים הששה מנים הנותרים בין שלשתן. נמצא הבכור נוטל חמשה מנים והטומטום והפשוט נוטלין כל אחד שני מנים. אבל אי הוה ממעט – לא היה נוטל הבכור אלא ארבעה וחצי מנים, פי שנים כנגד כל אחד. דנהי דאינו ממעט חלק בכורה – אבל חלק פשוט מיהא ממעט מכולן. **מאי טעמא** וילדו לו בנים. והיה הבן הבכור. מי שהוא בן בשעת לידה, חולק הבכור כנגדו חלק בכורה, וממעט לחלק בכורה מן הבכור. דהכי משמע קרא: כנגד הבנים משעת לידה יטול חלק בכורה, דהיינו חלק גדול, ולא נחשוב טומטום עמהם, שלא יטול הבכור אלא כנגד שנים מהם. דכשהן מרובין – ממעיט חלק בכורה. **אף אין אמו טמאה לידה.** שבעה, אם נקרע ונמצא זכר. וגם לא שבועיים אם נמצא נקבה, דכתיב: "וילדה זכר וטמאה", והכי נמי כתיב: "ואם נקבה תלד וטמאה שבועיים". יולדת טמאה היא אע"פ שאינה רואה דם. **אף אינו נימול לשמנה.** לדחות שבת, כדדרשינן (שבת דף קלג.): "וביום השמיני", "ביום" – אפילו בשבת. **המפלת טומטום.** וכל זמן שלא נקרע מספקינן ליה בזכר ובנקבה. **אנדרוגינוס.** שיש לו זכרות ונקבות. **תשב לזכר.** ימי טוהר דזכר, וימי טומאה דנקבה. שתטמא שבועיים משעת לידתה אפי' אם לא תראה דם, ומשבועיים ואילך תשב על דמי טהרה אם תראה דם עד ארבעים ללידתה, דהיינו ל"ג ימי טוהר דזכר חסר ז' ימים, שמנתה שבועיים לטומאה מספק. **תיובתא דרב שרביא.** דכלל כלל לא חשיב לה יולדת, לא לטומאה ולא לטהרה. **לימא תיהוי נמי תיובתא דרב שיזבי.** דאיהו נמי דריש לענין מילה: עד שיהא זכר משעת לידה, והוא הדין לגבי טומאת לידה. ואילו האי תנא חשיב ליה זכר לענין טומאת לידה, דקתני: תשב לזכר. **תנא.** דמסכת נדה, ספוקי מספקא ליה אי האי "וילדה זכר" להכי בעינן – דליהוי זכר משמע לידה בין לגבי טומאה בין לגבי מילה, ואזיל לחומרא ליתן עליו חומרי זכר, דשמא לא דרשינן האי "וילדה זכר" להכי דבעינן דליהוי זכר, אלא לכדאמרינן במסכת נדה (דף לא.): אשה מזרעת תחלה – יולדת זכר. ורב שיזבי נמי לחומרא קאמר, דלא דחייא מילתו שבת, דדלמא דרשינן: "וילדה זכר" – שיהא זכר משעת לידה. אבל רב שרביא לקולא דריש, דקא פטר לה מטומאת לידה. הלכך, אי לאו דפשיטא ליה – לא הוה דריש לקולא. הלכך הויא ו) (ברייתא) תיובתיה. **אי הכי.** דמספקא ליה היכא דנקרע ונמצא זכר, אם אמו טמאה לידה אי לאו, א"כ אמאי יהבינן ימי טוהר דזכר, כדקתני: לזכר ולנקבה – דהיינו ימי טוהר דזכר, וימי טומאה דנקבה? והלא שמא אם יקרע ימצא זכר, ושמא איכא למידרש: "וילדה זכר" – לטהר את אמו מדין לידה, ובין ימי טומאה בין ימי טהרה לית לה, ואמאי יהבינן לה ימי טוהר כלל? הכי הוה ליה למיתני: תשב לזכר ולנקבה ולנדה. וה"פ: תשב לנקבה – ימי טומאה דנקבה שבועיים, אפי' בלא ראיית דם, דלמא נקבה היא. ולנדה – לאחר שבועיים מיד אם תראה דם הויא טמאה נדה, (ג) מספיקא דלמא זכר הוה, ואית לן למידרש: עד שיהא זכר משעת לידה, ולית לה ימי טוהר כלל! במסכת נדה מקשינן: למה הוזכר זכר? כלומר, בכל מקום דקתני לנקבה ולנדה, למה לי למיתני לזכר בהדייהו? אם ליתן לה ימי טומאה דזכר – הא קתני: תשב לנקבה, וצריך שבועיים. ואם ליתן לה ימי טוהר דזכר – הא קתני: ולנדה, דמשמע דלא ניתיב לה ימי טוהר כלל! ומשנינן: נפקא מינה שאם תראה יום ל"ד ללידתה ותחזור ותראה יום מ"א – הויא מקולקלת למנינה, שמא לא הוה לה ימי טוהר והיתה תחלת נדה בראיית יום ל"ד, ובראיית מ"א הויא תחלת זיבה, ואם תראה שלשה רצופין – צריכה ז' נקיים וקרבן. או שמא זכר ילדה, וראיית יום ל"ד היו ימי טוהר, ועתה בראיית מ"א הויא תחלת נדה – הרי היא בספק זבה ונדה (ד) עד שתשב י"ז ימים נקיים, כדמפרש במס' ערכין (דף ח.), ואם ישבה לה י"ז נקיים (ה) ורואה יום י"ח – הרי היא תחלת נדה. וזו היא דינה: שאם תראה כל ז' ימים הללו, או אם לא תראה כי אם ראייה ראשונה – טובלת בליל שמיני ומשמשת עם בעלה. ואחר ז' ימים הללו באין י"א יום של ימי זיבה, שאם תראה בתחלתן או באמצעיתן או בסופן שלשה ימים רצופין – הויא זבה גדולה וצריכה ז' נקיים וקרבן, ולעולם לא תחזור לקדמותה להיות תחלת נדה עד אחר ז' נקיים. ואם לא ראתה בכל י"א יום הללו עד י"ב – הרי היא תחלת נדה בכל המשפט אשר פירשתי, ולכך נקראו י"א יום שבין נדה לנדה. **קשיא.** אבל תיובתא ממש איננה בשביל שחסר מן ז) (הברייתא) דמצי למימר: תני לזכר ולנקבה ולנדה. (הגה"ה: לכך הוזכר זכר, שאם תראה יום ל"ד ללידתה אמרינן טמאה היא, ואע"ג דאכתי משכי ימי טוהר דזכר, דמספקינן ליה בלא ולד ותשב לנדה. וכי הדר חזיא ליום מ"א שהוא ח' לראייתה, ותרצה להיות שומרת יום כנגד יום – אמרינן ולד הוה, וזכר הוה, וראייה דיום ל"ד דם טוהר הוה, והשתא הוא דהויא תחלת נדה. והשתא מקלקלינן לה, דלא טבלה עד מ"ח שהוא שמיני לראייה אחרונה. ואי לאו משום ספיקא דזכר – הוי טבלה למחר דיום מ"ב ממה נפשך, אי לאו ולד הוא – הרי היא שומרת יום כנגד יום, ואי ולד הוה ונקבה הוה – אכתי הוי דם טוהר עד שמונים, וספיקא דזכר מקלקלא לה. וכן לענין נקבה. כלומר, וספיקא דנקבה מקלקלא לה עד פ"ח דלא טבלה עד פ"ח ח) [אי ראתה ביום ע"ד], ואי הוה פשיטא לן דלא ולד הוא – הוה טבלה למחר ביום [פ"ב], דראיית פ"א בי"א יום שבין נדה לנדה היא, ומשום דמספקינן דלמא ולד הוה וראיית שבעים וארבעה דם טוהר, אמרינן דהשתא הוא דהויא תחלת נדה. כן פירשה רבינו שלמה זצ"ל, (נדה דף ל:) ע"כ הגה"ה). **בן.** "והיה הבן" – שיהא בן משעת לידה. **ולא טומטום.** ואע"פ שנקרע אחרי כן ונמצא זכר. **כדרבי אמי.** דטומטום שנקרע, אע"פ שנמצא זכר, אינו נוטל פי שנים. **אלא בכור ולא ספק לאפוקי מאי.** אי לאפוקי ספק בכור – פשיטא דלא שקיל חלק בכורה אא"כ מייתי ראיה שהוא הבכור! **לאפוקי מדדרש רבא.** דמסברא אית ליה, ואתי קרא למעוטיה. **שתי נשים.** של אדם אחד. **במחבא.** ואין ידוע איזה קדם להיות ראשית אונו. **כותבין הרשאה זה לזה.** ואתי חד מינייהו ותבע חלק בכורה מן האחין: אם בכור אני – תנו לי בשביל עצמי, ואם לאו – תנו לי בשביל אחי, שהרי נתן לי חלקו, ופסקינן לעיל: יש לו לבכור קודם חלוקה, ויכול למכור וליתן חלק בכורתו לכל מי שירצה. והך מילתא אתא קרא למעוטי, דאע"ג דמדינא אית ליה – גזירת הכתוב הוא שלא יתנו לו חלק בכורה מן הספק. **אמר ליה רב פפא לרבא.** כשדרש כן. **הוכרו.** בשעת לידה, אע"ג דלבסוף נתערבו כו', דהוה ליה בכור ודאי שעה אחת. וקרא לא אתא למעוטי אלא מאי דדמי טפי למעוטי, כגון דלא הוכרו כלל, דהוה ליה ספק בשעת לידה. דהכי משמע: "והיה הבן הבכור" – שיהא בן משעת לידה ולא טומטום, ושיהא בכור משעת הוייה ולא ספק. ושמעינן מהכא דהכי הלכתא – דאם הוכרו ולבסוף נתערבו מיהא כותבין הרשאה. **היו מוחזקין.** לאו בעדים שמעידין שראו שנולד קודם לאחיו, דאם כן – אין האב נאמן. אלא דקול בעלמא, כעין שאמרנו למעלה, דהוו קרי ליה בוכרא. **על אחד.** מן הבנים, מהו? מי מהימנינן לאב במקום חזקה שמכחשת דבריו, או לא?

תורה אור

אמימר אמר: [א]אף אינו ממעט חלק בכורה, שנא': (דברים כא) "וילדה לו בנים", עד שיהא בן בשעת לידה. [א] רב (א) [ב]שיזבי אמר: אף אינו נימול לשמנה, דאמר קרא: (ויקרא יב) "אשה כי תזריע וילדה זכר... וביום השמיני ימול", עד שיהא זכר משעת לידה. רב שרביא אמר: אף אין אמו טמאה לידה, דאמר קרא: "אשה כי תזריע וילדה זכר וטמאה שבעת ימים", עד שיהא זכר משעת לידה. מיתיבי:[ג] [ב]המפלת טומטום ואנדרוגינוס – תשב לזכר ולנקיבה; תיובתי' דרב שרביא! תיובתא. לימא, תיהוי תיובתא דרב שיזבי! תנא ספוקי מספקא ליה ולחומרא. אי הכי, תשב לזכר ולנקבה ולנדה מיבעי ליה! קשיא. אמר רבא, תניא כוותיה דר' אמי: "בן" – ולא טומטום, (ב) "בכור" – ולא ספק. בשלמא בן ולא טומטום – כדר' אמי, אלא בכור ולא ספק לאפוקי מאי? לאפוקי מדדרש רבא, דדרש רבא: שתי נשים שילדו ב' זכרים במחבא – כותבין הרשאה זה לזה. א"ל רב פפא לרבא, והא שלח רבין: דבר זה שאלתי לכל רבותי ולא אמרו לי דבר, ברם כך אמרו משום [ד]ר' ינאי: הוכרו ולבסוף נתערבו כותבין הרשאה זה לזה, לא הוכרו אין כותבין הרשאה זה לזה! הדר אוקי רבא אמורא עליה [ה]ודרש: דברים שאמרתי לכם טעות הן בידי, ברם כך אמרו משום ר' ינאי: [ג]הוכרו ולבסוף נתערבו – כותבין הרשאה זה לזה, לא הוכרו – אין כותבין הרשאה זה לזה. שלחו ליה בני אקרא דאגמא לשמואל, ילמדנו רבינו: היו מוחזקין בזה שהוא בכור, ואמר אביו על אחר "בכור הוא", מהו? שלח להו: כותבין הרשאה

זה

מדדרש רבא שתי נשים שילדו במחבא כותבין הרשאה זה לזה. ואם תאמר: הא רב [ט](פפי) משמיה דרבא אמר דאין לו לבכור קודם חלוקה, והיאך יבא ליטול בכורה מכח אידך? ואור"י: דאין זה בא אלא מכח שליחות, דהלכתא(ו) שליח שוויה.

כך

רבינו גרשום

משום דבכור הוא. טומטום בכור. שנקרע: עד שיהיה בכור בשעת הוי' משעת לידה וזה היה ספק קודם לכן אם זכר הוא אם לאו: אמימר אמר אף אינו ממעט בחלק. בשעה שאם היו שני אחים בכור ופשוט וזה טומטום שלישי כשיבואו לחלק בין נכסים כמאן דלית' דמי ויחלוק עם אחיו פי שנים בכל הנכסים. אבל אותן שני חלקים חלק פשוט של בכור וחלק אחיו פשוט יחלקו לג' ויקח טומטום חלק השלישי. מ"ט לא ממעט דכתיב וילדו לו בנים הנך דהוי' בנים בשעת לידה ממעטי והוא לאו בן הוא משעת לידה: רב שזבי אמר אף אינו נימול לשמנה. שאם חל שמיני שלו בשבת לא מחללינן עליה שבת דמחמרינן גבי שבת: רב שרביא אמר אף אין אמו טמאה לידה. משום דכל זכר מטמא שבעה ימים כימי נדתה אבל הוא אינו מטמא כלל: מיתיבי. קא תנא במס' נדה המפלת טומטום ואנדרוגינוס זה הוא זכר ונקבה. וטומטום הואיל דלא ידעינן מה הוא מחמרינן ותשב לזכר ולנקבה. כיצד יהבינן לזה ימי טהרה כזכר ארבעים יום ותו לא ומתוך אותן ארבעים תהא טמאה י"ד יום כדין יולדת נקבה אלמא דמחמרינן גבי טומאה. תיובתא דרב שרביא דאמר דאין אמו טמאה לידה כלל והא הכי מחמרי' בה לזכר ולנקבה. ולימא תיהוי תיובתא דרב שיזבי דאמר לעיל דלא דיינינן כזכר ודאי ואינו נימול לשמונה בשבת אע"ג דנקרע ונמצא זכר והא הכא דאמרינן דתשב לזכר ארבעים אף על פי שלא נקרע. ומשני לרב זביד לא הוי תיובתא משום דהאי תנא דאמר תשב לזכר ולנקבה ספוקי מספקא ליה אי זכר הוא או נקבה היא משום הכי אזיל לחומרא דתשב לתרווייהו לזכר ולנקבה והם הכי נמי אזיל רב שיזבי לחומרא הואיל דבשעת לידה מספקא ליה אם זכר אם נקבה אזלינן לחומרא ולא מהלינן לי' בשבת משום דבן ודאי בעינן משעת לידה והאי לאו הכי הוא ומשום הכי לא קשי' ליה דהכא נמי מחמיר: אי הכי הוא. דמשום חומרא הוא אמאי לא מחמרינן בה כל חומרות דמצינן למימר ונימא דתשב לזכר ולנקבה ולנדה. הכי פירושא אם ילדה זכר מטמא ז' ימים ומכאן ואילך לאחר מ' ימים כל דם שהיתה רואה סמוך לוסתה יושבת עליו ז' נקיים ואם ראתה באותן ל"ג (אפי' הכי) דם טוהר הוא. אבל אם חוזרה וראתה יום שמיני יושבת יום כנגד יום ואם ראתה ג' ימים רצופין בתוך י"א יום הרי זו זבה גמורה וצריכה נקיים. והאי דקאמרינן הכי תשב לזכר ולנקבה ולנדה כדאמר לא יהבינן לה ימי טוהר אלא אי חזי' ליום ט"ו הויא טמאה נדה. ומקשינן במס' נדה למה הזכיר זכר כיון דתני לנקבה ולנדה לא אצטריך למיתני זכר דאי לענין טמאה לידה הא קתני תשב לנקבה ולנדה לא איצטריך לטמאה לידה דזכר דהוי בכלל י"ד דנקבה. ואי לענין טהרה ימי טוהר קאמר לזכר הא קתני נדה כיון דקתני לנדה וש"מ דלית לה ימי טוהר אלא אי חזיא (ליום נ"א) הוי טמאה נדה אלא להכי תנא לזכר לחומרא דאע"ג דאין לה ימי טוהר יהבינן ליה דין דזכר להכי שאם תראה יום ל"ד ללידתה ביום ארבעים שלמו ז' ימי נדתה ואם תחזור ותראה ליום מ"א תהי' מקולקלת עד מ"ח די"ל ביום מ' שלמו ימי טוהר דזכר וכיון שראתה למחר יש לה שוב דין נדה ואינה טהורה עד מ"ח דאי לא תנא לזכר אמרינן בסוף מ' שלמו ימי נדתה ומה שראתה ביום מ"א היינו בתוך י"א יום דהויא שומרת יום כנגד יום וטובלת ביום מ"ב ומשמשת אלא להכי תנא לזכר דאסורה עד מ"ח. וכן לענין נקבה אם תראה ליום ע"ד ותחזור ותראה ליום פ"א תהיה מקולקלת עד פ"ח ומשום הכי איצטריך למיתני זכר. והכא נמי אי משום חומרא הוא ליתני לזכר ולנקבה ולנדה אלא ש"מ מדלא קתני הכי [ש"מ] דלאו משום חומרא הוא. וקשיא לרב שיזבי דמחמיר: שילדו שני זכרים במחבא. בלילה בהחבא בלא נר או ביום בחושך בלא אור ושתי הנשים היה להם בעל אחד בחור והיו מבכירות ואין ידוע אי זה מהן בכור ונולד לו שוב בנים אחרים כשיגדלו ויבואו לחלק ירוש' אביהן עם אחיהם יכתבו אחד מאלו שני ספיקי בכורות הרשאה לאחיו כדי ליטול פי שנים ויאמר לאחיו אם אני בכור תנו לי פי שנים בשביל עצמי ואם אחי הבכור ולא אני תנו לי פי שנים בשבילו שהרי בידי הרשאה שהרשני על חלק בכורתו ויחלקו הבכורה בינידם ולאפוקי מיהא אתי האי דרשא לשני זכרים שנולדו במחבא והוכרו מעיקרא איזה מהן בכור ולבסוף נתערבו ולא הוכרו כותבין הרשאה זה לזה משום דכתיב יכיר והרי הוכר מתחלה: בני אקרא דאגמא. כפר שעומד באגם: היו מוחזקין בו בני אדם. באחד שהוא בכור ואמר אביו על אחד מאחיו שהוא בכור מהו. מי אזלינן בתר דמוחזק לן שהוא בכור או בתר אביו אזלינן דאמר קים ליה בגויה: שלח להו כותבין הרשאה זל"ז משום ספיקא דלא אזלינן בתר חזקה א) דאבוה:

א) נ"ל דאבוה מכחיש ליה לחזקה.

מסורת הש"ס

א) [נ"ל וילדו]: ב) רש"ל גורס רב שרביא קודם: ג) נדה כח.: ד) [בכורות מז:]: ה) [שבת סג: וש"נ]: ו) [נ"ל משנה]: ז) [נ"ל המשנה]: ח) רש"ל: ט) [נ"ל פפא]:

הגהות הב"ח

(א) גמרא רב שרביא נ"ל קודם רב שזבי: (ב) שם בן ולא טומטום בכור ולא ספק. נ"ב נראה דרבא קודם חזרה היה מפרש ברייתא דה"ק בן ולא טומטום כלומר אילו נכתב בן ולא נכתב והיה הבן הייתי אומר אפי' טומטום השתא דכתיב והיה הבן שיהא בן משעת הויה ולא טומטום [בכור ולא ספק פירוש ואילו] נכתב והיה הבכור ולא נכתב והיה הבן הבכור הייתי אומר אפי' טומטום נמי וקרא דוהיה הבכור לא אתא אלא ללמד שיהא בכור משעת הויה דהיינו הוכרו ולבסוף נתערבו לאפוקי היכא שלא הוכרו כלל לכך כתב לך והיה הבן הבכור לאורויי דוהיה קאי אבן למימרא דבעינן בן משעת הויה ולא טומטום אבל לא בעינן בכור משעת הויה ולפיכך אפילו [לא הוכרו כלל כותבין] הרשאה זה לזה ובכור דקרא לגופיה אתא דלא אייתר כל עיקר ולבתר חזרה מההיא דר' ינאי קא מפרש רבא ברייתא דה"ק בן ולא טומטום כלומר אילו נכתב בן ולא נכתב והיה הבן כו' וכדפי' בכור ולא ספק פי' אילו נכתב והיה הבכור ולא נכתב והיה הבן הבכור לא הייתי ממעט אלא טומטום בלחוד וקרא הכי קאמר דבעינן [בכור משע' הויה ולא] טומטום השתא מיתורא דבן קא שמעינן תרתי כאילו נכתב והיה הבן והיה הבכור דוהיה אתרוייהו קאי דבעינן שיהא בן משעת הויה ולא טומטום ובכור [משעת הויה לאפוקי היכא] שלא הוכרו כלל ובזה מתיישבי כמה תמיהות בסוגיא זו גם לא נריך לפרש דקרא לא אתי למעוטי אלא מאי דדמי טפי למעוטי כגון דלא הוכרו כלל כו' [דמקרא לא שמעינן טפי] אלא שיהא בכור משעת הויה דהיינו הוכרו ולבסוף נתערבו וכיוצא בזה פירש רבינו אליהו דיכיר קאי נמי אבן השנואה לקמן בדף זה ע"ב בתוס' ד"ה כך: (ג) רשב"ם ד"ה אי הכי וכו' מספיקא דלמא זכר הוא. נ"ב ואף על פי דלעיל פי' אפילו כשנקרע ונמצא נקבה אינה מטמאה [משום לידה וכן] אין לה ימי טוהר אפשר לומר דנהי שכך הדין אליבא דרב שרביא מ"מ כאן דפריך עלויה ה"פ את"ל דלא [דרשינן הכי] אלא לגבי זכר אינה טמאה לידה אפילו הכי [ליתני ולנדה] דדלמא זכר הוא: (ד) בא"ד עד שתשב י"ז ימים נקיים. נ"ב כתב מהר"ש לוריא ז"ל לפום ריהטא קאמר הכי אבל לא דייקא אלא ע"ז נקיים בעי' מאחר דראתה ג' ימים ועם שתי ראיות האחרונות הוי י"ז ולא בעי' י"ז נקיים אלא בטועה ממש כדאיתא לקמן דלא ידענא באיזה פרק היא עומדת משום הכי בעי י"ז נקיים דשמא ב' ראיות הראשונות סוף זיבה הן וראייה השלישית התחלת נדה היא אבל הכא הראייה הראשונה ממ"נ או התחלת זיבה או התחלת נדה הלכך לא בעי בין הכל אלא י"ז ימים חוץ מיום ראשון דהיינו ראייה ראשונה ולא בעי' אלא ט"ו נקיים וה"ה אי ראתה כל ז' ימים לא בעי אלא י"א נקיים ודו"ק. עוד יש להקשות כשראתה ביום י"ח למה הוי תחלת נדה לימא שתחלת ראייה הוי זיבות וא"כ שלמו י"א ימי זיבה ואח"כ ז' ימי נדה וא"כ ביום י"ח חוץ מראייה הראשונה חזרה זיבות ול"ק מידי כי לעולם אינם מתחילין ימי נדות אחר שכלו כבר ימי זיבות אם לא שהיו כבר ימי נדות לעולם אין זיבות אלא אחר ימי נדות ולשם בערכין הבאתי דברי הרמב"ן שכ"כ להדיא: (ה) בא"ד וראתה יום י"ח. נ"ב פי' כשימנא ולאי זכר: (ו) תוס' ד"ה מדדרש וכו' דהלכתא שליח שוויה. נ"ב הכי אסיקנא ב"ק דף ע ע"א:

עין משפט נר מצוה

סח א מיי' פ"ב מהל' נחלות הל' ג סמג עשין צו טוש"ע ח"מ סי' רעז סעי' ז: [וע"ע י"ד סי' רסו סעי' י בהג"ה]

סט ב מיי' פ"י מהלכות איסורי ביאה הלכה יח סמג לאוין קיא טוש"ע י"ד סי' קצד סעיף ח:

ע ג מיי' פ"ב מהל' נחלות הלכה ו סמג עשין צו טוש"ע ח"מ סימן רעז סעיף יא.

עין משפט נר מצוה

עא א מיי' פ"ב מהלכות נחלות הל' יד סמג עשין צו טוש"ע ח"מ סי' רעז סעיף יב:

עב ב מיי' פט"ו מהלכות איסורי ביאה הל' טז סמג לאוין קטז טוש"ע אה"ע סי' ד סעיף כט:

עג ג מיי' פ"ב מהל' נחלות הל' טו סמג עשין צו טוש"ע ח"מ סימן רעז סעיף יג:

עד ד מיי' פ"ב מהלכות נחלות הל' ג סמג עשין צו טוש"ע ח"מ סי' רעט סעיף ג:

עה ה מיי' שם הל' ד טוש"ע שם סעיף ד:

עו ו מיי' שם הל' ג טור ש"ע שם סעיף ג:

מסורת הש"ס

א) יבמות מז. קדושין עד. [עח: כל הסוגיא], ב) [עיין תוספות בכורות מו: ד"ה מ"ט], ג) [לעיל עט: וש"נ], ד) רבנן וסיפא ר"י כל"ל רש"ל, ה) צ"ל משני, ו) צ"ל רבנן וסיפא ר"י. רש"ל:

זֶה לָזֶה. מַה נַּפְשָׁךְ? אִי כְּרַבָּנַן סְבִירָא לֵיהּ – לִישְׁלַח לְהוּ כְּרַבָּנַן, אִי כְּרַבִּי יְהוּדָה סְבִירָא לֵיהּ – לִישְׁלַח לְהוּ כְּרַבִּי יְהוּדָה! מְסַפְּקָא לֵיהּ אִי כְּרַבִּי יְהוּדָה אִי כְּרַבָּנַן. מַאי הִיא? דְּתַנְיָא: [א]°"יַכִּיר" – יַכִּירֶנּוּ לַאֲחֵרִים, מִכָּאן א"ר יְהוּדָה: [א]נֶאֱמָן אָדָם לוֹמַר "זֶה בְּנִי בְּכוֹר". וּכְשֵׁם שֶׁנֶּאֱמָן אָדָם לוֹמַר "זֶה בְּנִי בְּכוֹר", [ב]כָּךְ נֶאֱמָן אָדָם לוֹמַר "זֶה בֶּן גְּרוּשָׁה" וְ"זֶה בֶּן חֲלוּצָה"; וַחֲכָמִים אוֹמְרִים: אֵינוֹ נֶאֱמָן. א"ל רַב נַחְמָן בַּר יִצְחָק לְרָבָא: בִּשְׁלָמָא לְרַבִּי יְהוּדָה – הַיְינוּ דִּכְתִיב "יַכִּיר", אֶלָּא לְרַבָּנַן [ב]"יַכִּיר" לָמָּה לִי? בְּצָרִיךְ הֶיכֵּרָא. לְמַאי הִלְכְתָא – לְמֵיתְבָא לוֹ פִּי שְׁנַיִם; לֹא יְהֵא אֶלָּא אַחֵר, אִילּוּ בָּעֵי לְמֵיתְבָא לֵיהּ בְּמַתָּנָה מִי לָא יָהֵיב לֵיהּ?! לָא צְרִיכָא, בִּנְכָסִים שֶׁנָּפְלוּ לוֹ לְאַחַר מִכָּאן. וּלְר"מ דְּאָמַר: [ג]אָדָם מַקְנֶה דָּבָר שֶׁלֹּא בָּא לָעוֹלָם, "יַכִּיר" לָמָּה לִי? בִּנְכָסִים שֶׁנָּפְלוּ לוֹ כְּשֶׁהוּא גּוֹסֵס. § ת"ר: [ג]הָיוּ מוּחְזָקִין בּוֹ שֶׁהוּא בְּכוֹר, וְאָמַר אָבִיו עַל אַחֵר שֶׁהוּא בְּכוֹר – נֶאֱמָן; הָיוּ מוּחְזָקִין בּוֹ שֶׁאֵינוֹ בְּכוֹר, וְאָמַר אָבִיו בְּכוֹר הוּא – אֵינוֹ נֶאֱמָן; רֵישָׁא – [ד]רַבִּי יְהוּדָה, וְסֵיפָא – רַבָּנַן. א"ר יוֹחָנָן: [ד]אָמַר "בְּנִי הוּא", וְחָזַר וְאָמַר "עַבְדִּי הוּא" – אֵינוֹ נֶאֱמָן; "עַבְדִּי הוּא", וְחָזַר וְאָמַר "בְּנִי הוּא" – נֶאֱמָן, דִּמְשַׁמֵּשׁ לִי כְּעַבְדָּא קָאָמַר. וְחִילּוּפֵיהּ אַבֵּית הַמֶּכֶס: [ה]הָיָה עוֹבֵר עַל בֵּית הַמֶּכֶס וְאָמַר "בְּנִי הוּא", וְחָזַר וְאָמַר "עַבְדִּי הוּא" – נֶאֱמָן; אָמַר "עַבְדִּי הוּא", וְחָזַר וְאָמַר "בְּנִי הוּא" – אֵינוֹ נֶאֱמָן. מֵיתִיבֵי: הָיָה מְשַׁמְּשׁוֹ כְּבֵן, וּבָא וְאָמַר "בְּנִי הוּא", וְחָזַר וְאָמַר "עַבְדִּי הוּא" – אֵינוֹ נֶאֱמָן; הָיָה מְשַׁמְּשׁוֹ כְּעֶבֶד, וּבָא וְאָמַר "עַבְדִּי הוּא", וְחָזַר וְאָמַר "בְּנִי הוּא" – אֵינוֹ נֶאֱמָן! אר"נ בַּר יִצְחָק: [ו]הָתָם דְּקָארוּ לֵיהּ "עַבְדָּא מְצַר מְאָה". מַאי מְצַר מְאָה? מְצַר עַבְדָּא ק' זוּזֵי. שְׁלַח לֵיהּ ר' אַבָּא לְרַב יוֹסֵף בַּר חָמָא: הָאוֹמֵר לַחֲבֵירוֹ: "עַבְדִּי גְּנַבְתָּ", וְהוּא אוֹמֵר: "לֹא גְּנַבְתִּי". "מַה טִּיבוֹ אֶצְלְךָ"? "אַתָּה מְכַרְתּוֹ לִי,

אַתָּה

תורה אור
יכיר – דברים כא

תוספות

כך נאמן לומר זה בן גרושה כו'. תימה: לפי שנאמן לבכר יהא נאמן גם לפסול ולומר שהוא בן גרושה או בן חלוצה?! וי"ל לומר: כיון שנאמן לבכר – בכל ענין האמינו הכתוב, ואפילו על אחד מבניו הקטנים נאמן לומר שהוא בכור. ואם כן – עושה בניו הגדולים ממזרים, שמאיש אחר הם. והכי נמי נאמן לומר שהוא בן גרושה. ורבינו אליהו מפרש ד"יכיר" נמי קאי אבן השנואה, כלומר בן השנואה יכיר, דנאמן לומר שהוא בן שנואה – דהיינו שנואה בנישואיה, כדמפרש בפ"ב דיבמות (דף כג. ושם) כגון חייבי לאוין, שנשא כהן גרושה. ומיהו, "כשם שנאמן לומר" משמע דממה שנאמן לבכר יליף. אבל בירושלמי בפ' "עשרה יוחסין" משמע כפירוש רבינו אליהו. ופוסק בה"ג דהא דפסקינן לקמן הלכה כר' יהודה כדשלח ר' אבא – היינו דוקא כשפוסל ע"י הכרת בכורה, אבל אין הלכה כר' יהודה שיהא נאמן לומר "זה בן גרושה". ואין נראה לר"י, דאמר בפ' "החולץ" (שם דף מז.): ההוא דאתא לקמיה דרב יהודה, אמר ליה: נתגיירתי ביני לבין עצמי. אמר ליה: נאמן אתה לפסול עצמך, ואי אתה נאמן לפסול בניך. ופריך, והתניא: ר' יהודה אומר "יכיר"! ומשני, אמר רב נחמן בר יצחק דהכי קאמר: לדבריך גוי אתה, ואין עדות לגוי. ופסק התם הלכה כרב נחמן בר יצחק. משמע דאי לאו דאין עדות לגוי היה נאמן לפסול, אע"ג דליכא הכרת בכורה. **בנכסים** שנפלו כשהוא גוסס. הכי נמי הוה מצי לשנויי: (א) בנכסים דלא עבידי דאתו, אלא חדא מתרי טעמי נקט.

הכי

רשב"ם

זֶה לָזֶה. הַמּוּחְזָק וְאוֹתוֹ שֶׁאָמַר אָבִיו עָלָיו שֶׁהוּא בְּכוֹר. וְטַעֲמָא מְפָרֵשׁ וְאָזֵיל. [מַה נַּפְשָׁךְ]. כְּמַאן סְבִירָא לֵיהּ שְׁמוּאֵל. אִי כְּר' יְהוּדָה. לְקַמָּן. יַכִּיר. קְרָא יְתֵירָא הוּא. יַכִּירֶנּוּ לַאֲחֵרִים. רַבִּי יְהוּדָה קָאָמַר לָהּ. נֶאֱמָן אָדָם לוֹמַר. וְאַע"פ שֶׁמַּחֲזִיקִין אַחֵר בִּבְכוֹר. כָּךְ נֶאֱמָן לוֹמַר זֶה בֶּן גְּרוּשָׁה הוּא. לְאַחַר שֶׁגֵּרַשְׁתִּיהָ הֶחֱזַרְתִּיהָ, וְיָלְדָה לִי זֶה. אוֹ שֶׁנָּשָׂא אִשָּׁה גְּרוּשָׁה. וּסְבָרָא הוּא, מִדִּכְתִיב: "יַכִּיר" – מַה לִּי בְּכוֹר, מַה לִּי לְדָבָר אַחֵר. בֶּן גְּרוּשָׁה. וְחָלָל הוּא. בֶּן חֲלוּצָה – חָלָל מִדְּרַבָּנַן, גְּזֵירָה חֲלוּצָה אַטּוּ גְּרוּשָׁה. וְאַע"ג דִּנְפָקָא לָן בִּיבָמוֹת (דף כד.) מִדִּכְתִיב: "וְאִשָּׁה גְּרוּשָׁה" – הָא אָמְרִינַן הָתָם דִּקְרָא אַסְמַכְתָּא בְּעָלְמָא. וַחכ"א אֵינוֹ נֶאֱמָן. לֹא בִּבְכוֹר וְלֹא בְּחָלָל. וּכְגוֹן שֶׁמּוּחְזָקִין בְּאַחֵר שֶׁהוּא בְּכוֹר. וּקְרָא [ה] מוֹקֵי בְּצָרִיךְ הֶיכֵּרָא, כְּגוֹן שֶׁבָּאוּ מֵחָדָשׁ בְּכָאן וְאֵין מוּחְזָקִין בְּאֶחָד מֵהֶן מִי הַבְּכוֹר וּמִי הַפָּשׁוּט – הָתָם וַדַּאי אָב מְהֵימַן. לְמַאי הִלְכְתָא. אַדְּרַבָּנַן קָפָרֵיךְ, דְּאוֹקִימְנָא בְּצָרִיךְ הֶיכֵּרָא. דְּבִשְׁלָמָא לְרַבִּי יְהוּדָה – טוּבָא אַשְׁמוּעִינַן קְרָא, דִּמְהֵימְנִינַן לֵיהּ לְאָב אֲפִילּוּ בִּמְקוֹם חֲזָקָה וְיָהֲבִינַן לֵיהּ פִּי שְׁנַיִם. דְּסד"א: נֵיזִיל בָּתַר חֲזָקָה, וְנֵיתִיב פִּי שְׁנַיִם לַמּוּחְזָק לָנוּ. דְּלֵיכָּא לְמֵימַר גַּבֵּי אָב: מִגּוֹ דְּאִי בָּעֵי יָהֵיב לֵיהּ בְּמַתָּנָה פִּי שְׁנַיִם, כִּי אָמַר נַמִי עָלָיו שֶׁהוּא בְּכוֹר – נֶאֱמָן, דְּהָא קַיְימָא לָן דְּ"מַה לִּי לְשַׁקֵּר" בִּמְקוֹם עֵדִים לָא אָמְרִינַן. אֶלָּא לְרַבָּנַן, לְמַאי הִלְכְתָא כְּתַב "יַכִּיר"? לְצָרִיךְ הֶיכֵּרָא, שֶׁהָאָב נֶאֱמָן לְהַכִּירוֹ לַאֲחֵרִים. דְּאִי לְמֵיתְבָא לֵיהּ פִּי שְׁנַיִם – אַמַּאי צָרִיךְ קְרָא? סְבָרָא הוּא דְּנֶאֱמָן עַל יְדֵי מִגּוֹ, דְּלֹא יְהֵא הַאי בְּכוֹר אֶלָּא אָדָם נָכְרִי, וְאעפ"כ יָכוֹל הָיָה לִיתֵּן לוֹ בְּמַתָּנָה כָּל נְכָסָיו. הִלְכָּךְ מַה לּוֹ לְשַׁקֵּר בְּמַאי דְּאָמַר שֶׁהוּא בְּכוֹר – הָא בְּלָאו הָכִי יָכוֹל לִיתֵּן לוֹ פִּי שְׁנַיִם, שֶׁיֹּאמַר: הָבוּ לֵיהּ בְּמַתָּנָה מִנְּכָסַי. לָא צְרִיכָא. הָא דְּאַשְׁמְעִינַן קְרָא דִּמְהֵימְנִינַן לְאָב, אֶלָּא בִּנְכָסִים שֶׁאֵינוֹ יָכוֹל לִיתֵּן לוֹ בְּאוֹתָהּ שָׁעָה שֶׁאָמַר עָלָיו שֶׁהוּא בְּכוֹר, כְּגוֹן בִּנְכָסִים שֶׁנָּפְלוּ לוֹ לְאַחַר מִיכָּן, לְאַחַר שֶׁאָמַר "בְּנִי זֶה בְּכוֹרִי הוּא". דְּלֵיכָּא לְמֵימַר בְּהַהִיא שַׁעְתָּא "מִגּוֹ", דְּהָא אֵין אָדָם מַקְנֶה דָּבָר שֶׁלֹּא בָּא לָעוֹלָם. וּלְרַבִּי מֵאִיר דְּאָמַר כו'. דְּהָא רַבָּנַן דְּרַבִּי יְהוּדָה הַיְינוּ ר"מ דְּאָמַר: אָדָם מַקְנֶה, גַּבֵּי אוֹמֵר לְאִשָּׁה "הֲרֵי אַתְּ מְקוּדֶּשֶׁת לִי עַל מְנָת שֶׁאֶתְגַּיֵּיר" כו'. בִּנְכָסִים שֶׁנָּפְלוּ לוֹ כְּשֶׁהוּא גּוֹסֵס. דִּתְנַן בְּמַסֶּכֶת שְׂמָחוֹת (פ"א ה"א): הַגּוֹסֵס הֲרֵי הוּא כְּחַי לְכָל דְּבָרָיו, וּבַר יְרוּשָּׁה הוּא. וּלְהָנְהוּ נְכָסִים אִיצְטְרִיךְ "יַכִּיר" שֶׁיִּטּוֹל בָּהֶן הַבְּכוֹר פִּי שְׁנַיִם, דִּבְהָנְהוּ לֵיכָּא מִגּוֹ. דַּאֲפִי' לְר"מ דְּאָמַר: אָדָם מַקְנֶה דָּבָר שֶׁלֹּא בָּא לָעוֹלָם, הָנֵי מִילֵּי כְּגוֹן נְכָסִים שֶׁנּוֹפְלִים לוֹ בְּשָׁעָה שֶׁיֵּשׁ בּוֹ כֹּחַ לִיתְּנָם לַאֲחֵרִים, אֲבָל גּוֹסֵס אֵינוֹ יָכוֹל לְדַבֵּר וְאֵין בּוֹ כֹּחַ לִיתֵּן. וְהִלְכָּךְ לָא מָצֵי לְאַקְנוֹיְינְהוּ מִקַּמֵּי דְּאָתוּ לִידֵיהּ, דְּהָא אֲפִילּוּ בְּשָׁעָה שֶׁבָּאוּ לְיָדוֹ אֵין יָכוֹל לְהַקְנוֹתָן, וְכָל שֶׁכֵּן מִקּוֹדֶם לָכֵן. וּבִלְאַחַר מִיתָה לָא מָצֵי לְשַׁנּוּיֵי, דְּאֵין בְּכוֹר נוֹטֵל בְּרָאוּי. הָכִי גָּרְסִינַן: הָיוּ מוּחְזָקִין בּוֹ שֶׁאֵינוֹ בְּכוֹר וְאָמַר אָבִיו בְּכוֹר הוּא אֵינוֹ נֶאֱמָן. כְּרַבָּנַן, דִּבְמְקוֹם חֲזָקָה לָא מְהֵימְנִינַן לֵיהּ לְאָב. וְאָמַר אָבִיו עַל אַחֵר שֶׁהוּא בְּכוֹר נֶאֱמָן. כְּר' יְהוּדָה. רֵישָׁא [ו] ר' יְהוּדָה וְסֵיפָא רַבָּנַן. בְּנִיחוּתָא. וְחָזַר וְאָמַר עַבְדִּי הוּא. בֵּין בְּתוֹךְ כְּדֵי דִּיבּוּר, בֵּין לְאַחַר זְמַן אָמַר כֵּן, עַל אוֹתוֹ שֶׁאָמַר עָלָיו מִתְּחִלָּה "בְּנִי". אֵינוֹ נֶאֱמָן. בְּמַאי דְּאָמַר הַשְׁתָּא "עַבְדִּי". וְלֵיכָּא לְמֵימַר: הַאי דְּקָרֵי לֵיהּ מִתְּחִלָּה "בְּנִי" מִשּׁוּם דְּאוֹהֲבוֹ כִּבְנוֹ, דְּאֵין דֶּרֶךְ לִקְרוֹא לְעַבְדּוֹ בְּנוֹ. וְהִלְכָּךְ, אַחַר טַעֲנָה רִאשׁוֹנָה נֵלֵךְ, דְּהוֹאִיל וְזֹאת הָאַחֲרוֹנָה אֵינוֹ פֵּירוּשׁ כִּי אִם הַכְחָשָׁה – אֵין לָנוּ לֵילֵךְ אַחַר טַעֲנָה אַחֲרוֹנָה. דְּהוֹדָאַת פִּיו הֶאֱמִינָה תּוֹרָה בְּמַאי דְּאָמַר "בְּנִי", כְּדִכְתִיב "יַכִּיר", וְכֵיוָן שֶׁהִגִּיד – שׁוּב אֵינוֹ חוֹזֵר וּמַגִּיד. וְחָזַר וְאָמַר בְּנִי נֶאֱמָן. בְּמַאי דְּאָמַר הַשְׁתָּא "בְּנִי", דְּאֵינוֹ כּוֹתֵר דְּבָרָיו הָרִאשׁוֹנִים אֶלָּא מְפָרֵשׁ הוּא: "עַבְדִּי" דְּקָאָמְרִי – בְּנִי הוּא, וְהַאי דְּקָאָמַר "עַבְדִּי" – לְפִי שֶׁהוּא מְשַׁמְּשׁוֹ יוֹתֵר מִדַּאי, כְּאִילּוּ הוּא עַבְדּוֹ. אֲבָל בְּרֵישָׁא לָא שַׁיָּיךְ לְפָרוּשֵׁי הָכִי, דְּעַבְדּוֹ הוּא כִּדְאָמַר הַשְׁתָּא, וְהַאי דְּקָרֵי לֵיהּ מֵעִיקָּרָא "בְּנִי" לְפִי שֶׁאוֹהֲבוֹ כִּבְנוֹ. דְּאֵין דֶּרֶךְ הָאָדוֹן לְיַיחֵס לְעַבְדּוֹ וְלִקְרוֹתוֹ בְּנוֹ בִּשְׁבִיל שׁוּם חִיבָּה. אַבֵּית הַמֶּכֶס. לְשָׁם רָגִיל לִקְרוֹא לְעַבְדּוֹ בְּנוֹ, לְהַבְרִיחוֹ מִן הַמֶּכֶס. אֲבָל לִבְנוֹ לֹא יִקְרָא לְעוֹלָם עַבְדּוֹ, שֶׁהֲרֵי גּוֹרֵם לְעַצְמוֹ הֶפְסֵד עַל חִנָּם. וְאָמַר בְּנִי. אֵל הַמּוֹכְסִים. וְחָזַר וְאָמַר עַבְדִּי. כְּשֶׁעָבַר מִשָּׁם וָהָלְאָה. נֶאֱמָן. בְּמַאי דְּחָזַר וְאָמַר "עַבְדִּי". דְּוַדַּאי מֵעִיקָּרָא הֲוָה קָרֵי לֵיהּ "בְּנִי" בִּשְׁבִיל יִרְאַת הַמֶּכֶס. וְחָזַר וְאָמַר בְּנִי אֵינוֹ נֶאֱמָן. אֶלָּא וַדַּאי עַבְדּוֹ הוּא, כִּדְאָמַר מֵעִיקָּרָא. דְּאִילּוּ הָיָה בְּנוֹ – לֹא הָיָה אוֹמֵר לַמּוֹכְסִים שֶׁהוּא עַבְדּוֹ. ה"ג: מֵיתִיבֵי הָיָה מְשַׁמְּשׁוֹ כְּבֵן וּבָא וְאָמַר בְּנִי וְחָזַר וְאָמַר עַבְדִּי אֵינוֹ נֶאֱמָן הָיָה מְשַׁמְּשׁוֹ כְּעֶבֶד וְאָמַר עַבְדִּי וְחָזַר וְאָמַר בְּנִי אֵינוֹ נֶאֱמָן. וּמְסֵיפָא קָפָרֵיךְ לֵיהּ לְר' יוֹחָנָן. וְה"פ: הָיָה מְשַׁמְּשׁוֹ כְּבֵן, מַלְבִּישׁ וּמַנְעִיל מַכְנִיס וּמוֹצִיא, אֲבָל עֲבוֹדַת עֶבֶד לֹא. וּרְבוּתָא נָקַט, דְּאַף עַל גַּב דִּמְשַׁמְּשׁוֹ כְּבֵן, וְאִיכָּא לְמֵימַר הַאי דְּקָרֵי לֵיהּ בְּנוֹ מִשּׁוּם דִּמְשַׁמֵּשׁ לֵיהּ כְּבֵן, אֲפִי' הָכִי, כִּי חָזַר וְאָמַר "עַבְדִּי" – אֵינוֹ נֶאֱמָן בְּמַאי דְּקָאָמַר לְבַסּוֹף, אֶלָּא נֵלֵךְ אַחַר לָשׁוֹן רִאשׁוֹן, דְּוַדַּאי בְּנוֹ הוּא. דְּאֵין דֶּרֶךְ לִקְרוֹת לְעַבְדּוֹ בְּנוֹ אֲפִי' הֵיכָא דִּמְשַׁמֵּשׁ לֵיהּ כְּבֵן, שֶׁאֵין הָאָדוֹן מְחַבְּבוֹ כָּל כָּךְ לִקְרוֹתוֹ בְּנוֹ. הָיָה מְשַׁמְּשׁוֹ כְּעֶבֶד וְאָמַר עַבְדִּי וְחָזַר וְאָמַר בְּנִי אֵינוֹ נֶאֱמָן. בְּמַאי דְּקָאָמַר "בְּנִי", וְאַף עַל גַּב דְּאִיכָּא לְמֵימַר דְּמֵעִיקָּרָא קְרָאוֹ עַבְדּוֹ מִשּׁוּם דִּמְשַׁמְּשׁוֹ כְּעֶבֶד, וְלָאו מִשּׁוּם דְּעַבְדּוֹ הוּא. וְקַשְׁיָא לְר' יוֹחָנָן, דְּאָמַר: אָמַר "עַבְדִּי" וְחָזַר וְאָמַר "בְּנִי" – נֶאֱמָן. דְּר' יוֹחָנָן אֲפִילּוּ הֵיכָא דְּלָא חָזֵינַן דִּמְשַׁמְּשׁוֹ כְּעֶבֶד קָאָמַר דְּנֶאֱמָן בְּמַאי דְּקָאָמַר לְבַסּוֹף "בְּנִי", וְכָל שֶׁכֵּן הֵיכָא דְּחָזֵינַן דַּהֲוָה מְשַׁמְּשׁוֹ כְּעֶבֶד. וְאִילּוּ בְּבָרַיְיתָא, אֲפִילּוּ הֵיכָא דִּמְשַׁמְּשׁוֹ כְּעֶבֶד קָאָמַר דְּאֵינוֹ נֶאֱמָן בְּמַאי דְּקָאָמַר לְבַסּוֹף "בְּנִי", וְכ"ש הֵיכָא דְּלָא חָזֵינַן הֵיכָא מְשַׁמְּשׁוֹ, דְּאֵינוֹ נֶאֱמָן. וְקַשְׁיָא לְר' יוֹחָנָן דְּאָמַר נֶאֱמָן. הָתָם. בְּבָרַיְיתָא. דְּקָרֵי לֵיהּ עַבְדָּא מְצַר מְאָה. כְּלוֹמַר, עֶבֶד גָּמוּר הוּא לִי, שֶׁמַּעֲרִיכִים לוֹ עָלָיו מֵאָה דִּינָר בִּמְלַאכְתּוֹ שֶׁלּוֹ. כְּלוֹמַר, שֶׁשָּׁוֶה מֵאָה דִּינָר. וְהִלְכָּךְ, כִּי חָזַר אָמַר "עַבְדִּי מְצַר מְאָה" וְחָזַר וְאָמַר "בְּנִי" – אֵינוֹ נֶאֱמָן. דְּאִילּוּ הֲוָה בְּנוֹ – לָא הֲוָה קָרֵי לֵיהּ "עַבְדָּא מְצַר מְאָה", וְאַע"ג דִּמְשַׁמֵּשׁ לֵיהּ כְּעַבְדָּא, דְּאֵין קוֹרִין כֵּן אֶלָּא לְעֶבֶד. עַבְדָּא מְאָה זוּזֵי. שֶׁשָּׁוֶה מֵאָה זוּזֵי. שְׁלַח לֵיהּ ר' אַבָּא. כָּל הָנֵי לֵיהּ ר' אַבָּא לְרַב יוֹסֵף בַּר חָמָא נָקַט הָכָא, מִשּׁוּם דִּבְחַד מִינַּיְיהוּ קָא פָּסֵיק הִלְכְתָא כְּר' יְהוּדָה. וּבְכוּלְּהוּ הִלְכְתָא כְּדִשְׁלַח לֵיהּ ר' אַבָּא, כִּדְפָסְקִינַן בְּסֵיפָא דִּשְׁמַעְתִּין.

אַתָּה

רבינו גרשום

יכיר יכירנו. האב לאחרי: וחכמים אומרים אינו נאמן. דבתר חזק' אזלינן. אלא רבנן דאזלי בתר חזקה יכיר למה לי דהא משמע יכיר דאביו יכירנו לאחרים ונאמן. ומשני לעולם בתר חזקה אזלינן ולמאי הלכתא כתיב יכיר בצריך הכרה. שאם אין מוחזק לן מהאי אי בכור הוא או לא צריך אביו להכירו לאחרים אבל אי מוחזק הוא לן בתר חזקה דרבים אזלינן ולא בתר האב: למאי הלכתא. צריך להכירו למיתן ליה פי שנים לא יהא האי בן אלא אחר אם רוצה האב ליתן מתנה לאחר ואומר הבו ליה מי לא יהבינן ליה לאחר הא נמי מאי שנא: לא צריכא בנכסים שנפלו לו לאחר מיכן. שאם אמר תנו לאחר פלוני נכסים שאני עתיד להרויח לא יהבינן ליה כלל לאחר מכאן דאין אדם מקנה דבר שלא בא לעולם אבל אי עביד הכרה להאי בכור תנו לו פי שנים בנכסי שארויח יהבינן ליה מה שאין כן באחר: ולר' מאיר הא אמר אדם מקנה וכו' אפי' לאחר יכיר למה לי. אכתי איכא למפרך לא יהא אלא אחר: לא צריכא בנכסים שנפלו לו כשהוא גוסס. דאפי' ר"מ דאמר אדם מקנה דבר שלא בא לעולם הכא מודי הואיל דבגסיסתו נפלו לו לא יהבינן ליה. דלהכי אמר ר' מאיר אדם מקנה דבר שלא בא בעולם הכא מודי דאיהו [לא] מצי למיתן אבל גבי בכור אף על גב דאיהו גוסס יהבינן ליה היכא דהכירו מחיים ומשום הכי צריך הכרה להיכא דלא מוחזק לן אבל אי מוחזק לן בתר חזקה דידן אזלינן: רישא רבנן. דבתר חזקה דידן אזלינן: וסיפא ר' יהודה. דבתר אבוה אזלינן: מאי טעמא להיכא דאמר עבדי וחזר ואמר בני נאמן. דהאי דאמר עבדי משום דמשמש ליה כעבדא: וחילופיה אבית המכס. היכא דנותנין מכס מן העבדים וחוזר ואמר עבד נאמן. דהאי דקאמר בני כדי להבריח מן המכס קאמר. אמר עבדי לבית המכס הואיל דלאו להבריח קאמר וחוזר ואמר בני אינו נאמן הואיל דקא יהיב מכס. מיתיבי היה משמשו כעבד (א) ובא ואמר בני אינו נאמן ולא אמרינן משום הכי קרי ליה עבדא מעיקרא דמשמשו כעבד. וקשיא לר' יוחנן: לעולם נאמן והתם מ"ט אינו נאמן משום דקרו ליה אינשי עבדא מצר מאה משום הכי אינו נאמן כשחוזר ואמר בני. מצר מאה כלומר מצרו של עבד זה מאה זוזי. כלומר בטוח אדונו של זה שיכול ליקח ממנו מאה זוז שמאה זוז סמוכין לו בכל שעבד שם.

(א) אולי צ"ל כעבד ובא ומשמשו והולך וכו'.

הגהות הב"ח

(א) תוס' ד"ה בנכסים וכו' בנכסים דלא עבידי. נ"ב ע"ל בדף עט ע"ב.

אַתָּה נְתַתּוֹ לִי בְּמַתָּנָה, רְצוֹנְךָ הִשָּׁבַע וְטוֹל", וְנִשְׁבַּע — אאֵינוֹ יָכוֹל לַחֲזוֹר בּוֹ. מַאי קָא מַשְׁמַע לָן? תְּנֵינָא: א)אָמַר לוֹ: "נֶאֱמָן עָלַי אַבָּא", "נֶאֱמָן עָלַי אָבִיךָ", "נֶאֱמָנִין עָלַי שְׁלֹשָׁה רוֹעֵי בָקָר" — רַבִּי מֵאִיר אוֹמֵר: יָכוֹל לַחֲזוֹר בּוֹ, וַחֲכָמִים אוֹמְרִים: באֵינוֹ יָכוֹל לַחֲזוֹר בּוֹ! הָא קָא מַשְׁמַע לָן, דִּב"אֶתֵּן לְךָ" מַחֲלוֹקֶת, וַהֲלָכָה כְּדִבְרֵי חֲכָמִים.§ שְׁלַח לֵיהּ רַבִּי אַבָּא לְרַב יוֹסֵף בַּר חָמָא, ב)הֲלָכָה: גּוֹבִין מִן הָעֲבָדִים. וְרַב נַחְמָן אָמַר: גאֵין גּוֹבִין. שְׁלַח לֵיהּ ר' אַבָּא לְרַב יוֹסֵף בַּר חָמָא, דהֲלָכָה: שְׁלִישִׁי בְּשֵׁנִי — כָּשֵׁר. רָבָא אָמַר: האַף בְּרִאשׁוֹן. מָר בַּר רַב אַשִׁי אַכְשַׁר בְּאַבָּא דְאַבָּא. ווְלֵית הִלְכְתָא כְּמָר בַּר רַב אַשִׁי. שְׁלַח לֵיהּ רַבִּי אַבָּא לְרַב יוֹסֵף בַּר חָמָא: הָיָה יוֹדֵעַ לוֹ בְּעֵדוּת קַרְקַע עַד שֶׁלֹּא נִסְתַּמֵּא, וְנִסְתַּמֵּא — פָּסוּל. וּשְׁמוּאֵל אָמַר: כָּשֵׁר, אֶפְשָׁר דִּמְכַוֵּין מִצְרָנֵהָא, אֲבָל גְּלִימָא — לָא. וְרַב שֵׁשֶׁת אָמַר: אֲפִי' גְּלִימָא, אֶפְשָׁר דִּמְכַוֵּין מִדַּת אָרְכּוֹ וּמִדַּת רָחְבּוֹ, אֲבָל נַסְכָא — לָא. וְרַב פָּפָּא אָמַר: אֲפִי' נַסְכָא, אֶפְשָׁר דִּמְכַוֵּין מִדַּת מִשְׁקְלוֹתָיו. מֵיתִיבֵי: ג)זהָיָה יוֹדֵעַ לוֹ בְּעֵדוּת עַד שֶׁלֹּא נַעֲשָׂה חֲתָנוֹ וְנַעֲשָׂה חֲתָנוֹ, פִּיקֵּחַ וְנִתְחָרֵשׁ, פִּיתֵּחַ וְנִסְתַּמֵּא, שָׁפוּי וְנִשְׁתַּטָּה — פָּסוּל; חאֲבָל הָיָה יוֹדֵעַ לוֹ בְּעֵדוּת עַד שֶׁלֹּא נַעֲשָׂה חֲתָנוֹ וְנַעֲשָׂה חֲתָנוֹ וּמֵתָה בִּתּוֹ, פִּיקֵּחַ וְנִתְחָרֵשׁ וְחָזַר וְנִתְפַּקֵּחַ, פִּיתֵּחַ וְנִסְתַּמֵּא וְחָזַר וְנִתְפַּתֵּחַ, שָׁפוּי וְנִשְׁתַּטָּה וְחָזַר וְנִשְׁתַּפָּה — כָּשֵׁר; זֶה הַכְּלָל: טכָּל שֶׁתְּחִלָּתוֹ אוֹ סוֹפוֹ בִּפְסָלוּת — פָּסוּל, תְּחִלָּתוֹ וְסוֹפוֹ בְּכַשְׁרוּת — כָּשֵׁר;

תְּיוּבְתָּא

רשב"ם

אַתָּה נְתַתּוֹ לִי בְּמַתָּנָה. וְנֶאֱמָן הוּא בְּטַעֲנָה זוֹ. וְאַע"ג דַּאֲמַרַן בְּ"חֶזְקַת הַבָּתִּים" (לעיל דף לו.): הַגּוֹדְרוֹת אֵין לָהֶן חֲזָקָה – ה"מ לְאַלְתַּר, אֲבָל לְאַחַר ג' שָׁנִים – יֵשׁ לָהֶן חֲזָקָה. וְה"נ – כְּגוֹן שֶׁהֶחֱזִיק בּוֹ ג' שָׁנִים, אוֹ בְּקָטָן הַמּוּטָּל בַּעֲרִיסָה, דְּיֵשׁ לוֹ חֲזָקָה לְאַלְתַּר. אוֹ בְּעֶבֶד שֶׁלֹּא רָאָה אוֹתוֹ בְּעֵדִים זֶה הַמְעַרְעֵר בְּבֵיתוֹ שֶׁל זֶה. רְצוֹנְךָ הִשָּׁבַע וְטוֹל. רְבוּתָא הִיא, דְּקָא"ל הַאי מַחֲזִיק לַמְעַרְעֵר. שֶׁהֲרֵי פָּטוּר לְגַמְרֵי זֶה הַמַּחֲזִיק מִכָּל שְׁבוּעוֹת שֶׁבָּעוֹלָם, דְּקַיְ"ל: אֵין נִשְׁבָּעִין עַל הָעֲבָדִים, כִּשְׁבוּעוֹת (דף מב:), וְאֵינוֹ מְחוּיָּב בִּשְׁבוּעָה כְּלָל. וְגַם זֶה הַתּוֹבֵעַ אֵין שְׁבוּעָה מוֹעֶלֶת לִגְבּוֹת מִזֶּה, דְּכָל הַנִּשְׁבָּעִין שֶׁבַּתּוֹרָה נִשְׁבָּעִין וְלֹא מְשַׁלְּמִין, אִם לֹא מֵרְצוֹנוֹ שֶׁל זֶה שֶׁמַּטִּיל עָלָיו שְׁבוּעָה לִישָּׁבַע וְלִיטּוֹל. וְנִשְׁבַּע. זֶה הַתּוֹבֵעַ. אֵינוֹ יָכוֹל. זֶה הַמַּחֲזִיק לַחֲזוֹר בּוֹ, וְלוֹמַר: מְשַׁטֶּה הָיִיתִי בְּךָ. שֶׁהֲרֵי פָּטוּר הָיִיתִי, וְגַם לֹא נִתְחַיַּיבְתָּ לִי שְׁבוּעָה כְּדֵי לִישָּׁבַע וְלִיטּוֹל, דְּאֵין אָדָם נִשְׁבָּע וְנוֹטֵל, וְלֹא הִקְנֵיתִי לְךָ בְּקִנְיָן לָתֵת לְךָ הָעֶבֶד אִם תִּשָּׁבַע עָלָיו. אֶלָּא כֵּיוָן דְּעַל פִּיו נִשְׁבַּע וּבִנְוָוּאָתוֹ – צָרִיךְ לָתֵת לוֹ הָעֶבֶד. דְּכֵיוָן דְּהִטִּיל עָלָיו שְׁבוּעָה – הָא הֵימְנֵיהּ בִּשְׁבוּעָה, וּכְמַאן דְּאוֹדֵי לֵיהּ שֶׁהוּא עַבְדּוֹ שֶׁל זֶה הַנִּשְׁבָּע דָּמֵי. וְהַאי דְּנָקַט "עַבְדִּי גָּנַבְתָּ" – רְבוּתָא נָקַט, דְּלָא מִיבַּעְיָא שְׁאָר מִטַּלְטְלִין, שֶׁהַנִּתְבָּע חַיָּיב שְׁבוּעָה כְּדֵי שֶׁלֹּא יְשַׁלֵּם, וְהוּא הוֹפְכָהּ עַל שֶׁכְּנֶגְדּוֹ – דְּלָא מָצֵי הָדַר בֵּיהּ וּלְמֵימַר "אֶשָּׁבַע אֲנִי וְאֶפָּטֵר". אֶלָּא אֲפִי' עֲבָדִים, דְּלָא שַׁיְיכָא בְּהוּ שְׁבוּעָה כְּלָל – אפ"ה, כֵּיוָן דְּהִשְׁבִּיעוֹ לָא מָצֵי הָדַר בֵּיהּ. נֶאֱמָן עָלַי אַבָּא. לִהְיוֹת דַּיָּין. אַבָּא פָּסוּל מִן הַתּוֹרָה לְדוּנֵנוּ לֹא לִזְכוּת וְלֹא לְחוֹבָה, כִּדְנָפְקָא לָן בְּסַנְהֶדְרִין (דף כז:) מִ"לֹּא יוּמְתוּ אָבוֹת" וגו'. שְׁלֹשָׁה רוֹעֵי בָקָר. שֶׁאֵינָן בְּקִיאִין בַּדִּין. וְרוֹעֵי נָאן לָא נָקַט, מִשּׁוּם דִּרְשָׁעִים נִינְהוּ, דִּסְתַם רוֹעֵי בְּהֵמָה דַּקָּה גַּזְלָנִין נִינְהוּ, וּפְסוּלִין לְכָל דִּין שֶׁבָּעוֹלָם. אֲבָל אַבָּא וְאָבִיךָ – כְּשֵׁרִין מִיהָא לְדִינִין שֶׁל אֲחֵרִים. יָכוֹל לַחֲזוֹר בּוֹ. דִּדְבָרִים בְּעָלְמָא בְּלֹא קִנְיָן הוּא דְּקָא"ל. וַחכ"א אֵינוֹ יָכוֹל לַחֲזוֹר בּוֹ. וְה"ה לְגַבֵּי שְׁבוּעַת הַתּוֹבֵעַ, שֶׁנִּשְׁבַּע עַל הָעֶבֶד וְנוֹטֵל. דְּבַתְרַוַיְיהוּ, אַע"ג דְּלָא הָוֵי דִּינָא הָכִי, כֵּיוָן דְּקִיבֵּל עָלָיו – אֵינוֹ יָכוֹל לַחֲזוֹר בּוֹ. וּמְשַׁנֵּי: הָא קמ"ל ר' אַבָּא – דְּאָמַר "הִשָּׁבַע וְאֶתֵּן לְךָ" דְּאֵין יָכוֹל לַחֲזוֹר בּוֹ. דְּהָתָם נַמִי בְּ"אֶתֵּן לְךָ" פְּלִיגִי, שֶׁהַנִּתְבָּע אוֹמֵר לַתּוֹבֵעַ: נֶאֱמָן עָלַי אַבָּא, שֶׁאִם יְחַיְּיבוּנִי – אֶתֵּן לְךָ. וַאפ"ה אָמְרֵי רַבָּנַן דְּאֵינוֹ יָכוֹל לַחֲזוֹר, וְיִתֵּן. דְּהַיְינוּ דּוּמְיָא דְּר' אַבָּא, דִּלְאַחַר שֶׁנִּשְׁבַּע זֶה אֵין יָכוֹל לַחֲזוֹר בּוֹ, אֶלָּא יִתֵּן, דִּכְרַבָּנַן דְּהָתָם ס"ל. וְכ"ש הֵיכָא דְּקָאָמַר תּוֹבֵעַ: נֶאֱמָן עָלַי אַבָּא וְאָבִיךָ שֶׁאִם יִפְטְרוּךָ מָחוּל לָךְ, דְּכ"ע מוֹדוּ, אֲפִי' ר"מ, דְּאֵין יָכוֹל לַחֲזוֹר בּוֹ, שֶׁהֲרֵי מוּחְזָק וְעוֹמֵד, וּמְחִילָה דְּאִידָךְ – כְּקִנְיָן דָּמֵי. וְאִיכָּא לְמ"ד הָתָם בְּ"מָחוּל לָךְ" מַחֲלוֹקֶת, אֲבָל בְּ"אֶתֵּן לְךָ" – דִּבְרֵי הַכֹּל יָכוֹל לַחֲזוֹר בּוֹ. הִלְכָּךְ אִצְטְרִיךְ ר' אַבָּא לְאַשְׁמוּעִינַן דִּבְ"אֶתֵּן לְךָ" פְּלִיגִי, וַהֲלָכָה כְּדִבְרֵי חֲכָמִים, אַע"ג דְּמִסְתַּבֵּר טַעֲמָא דְּר"מ. גּוֹבִין מִן הָעֲבָדִים. בַּעַל חוֹב שֶׁמֵּת – גּוֹבֶה מֵעַבְדֵי יְתוֹמִים, דִּכְמִקַּרְקְעֵי דָּמֵי. וּבְהָא לְחוּד הוּא דְּלֵית הִלְכְתָא כְּר' אַבָּא. וּלְקַמָּן מְתָרְצִינַן לָהּ, וְאָמְרִי' הָכִי קָתָנֵי: אֵין גּוֹבִין, וְכֵן אָמַר ר"נ. וְר"נ **אָמַר אֵין גּוֹבִין.** דְּנְהִי דְּאִתְקַשׁ לְקַרְקָעוֹת, כְּדִכְתִיב (ויקרא כה): "וְהִתְנַחַלְתֶּם" – ה"מ לִדְבָרִים הַכְּתוּבִים בַּתּוֹרָה, כְּגוֹן לִקְנוֹתָן בְּכֶסֶף בִּשְׁטָר וּבַחֲזָקָה, וְשֶׁלֹּא לִישָּׁבַע עֲלֵיהֶן, וְשֶׁאֵין בָּהֶן אוֹנָאָה. אֲבָל לְעִנְיַן ב"ח – כְּמִטַּלְטְלֵי דָּמֵי. דְּאֵין ב"ח סוֹמֵךְ אֶלָּא עַל קַרְקָעוֹת שֶׁאֵין יְכוֹלִין לֵיאָבֵד וְלֹא לָזוּז מִמְּקוֹמָן, אֲבָל אַעֲבָדִים לָא סָמְכָא דַּעְתֵּיהּ, הִלְכָּךְ לָא מִשְׁתַּעְבְּדֵי לֵיהּ. שְׁלִישִׁי כָּשֵׁר. לְהָעִיד בִּקְרוֹבוֹ שֵׁנִי. כְּגוֹן בֶּן חֲנוֹךְ (א) שֶׁכָּשֵׁר לְהָעִיד בִּימוּאֵל בֶּן שִׁמְעוֹן, דִּבְנוֹ שֶׁל חֲנוֹךְ שְׁלִישִׁי לִרְאוּבֵן, וִימוּאֵל בֶּן שִׁמְעוֹן שֵׁנִי הוּא, וּרְאוּבֵן וְשִׁמְעוֹן רִאשׁוֹנִים. אֲבָל שֵׁנִי בְּשֵׁנִי – פָּסוּל, כְּגוֹן בֶּן רְאוּבֵן לְבֶן שִׁמְעוֹן, כִּדְנָפְקָא לָן בְּסַנְהֶדְרִין מִ"לֹּא יוּמְתוּ אָבוֹת עַל בָּנִים" דְּבָנִים לַהֲדָדֵי נַמִי מִיפַּסְלֵי. "אָבוֹת" – הַיְינוּ רְאוּבֵן וְשִׁמְעוֹן, וּ"בָנִים" – הַיְינוּ חֲנוֹךְ וִימוּאֵל. אֲבָל שְׁלִישִׁי בְּשֵׁנִי – לָא אַשְׁכְּחַן דְּפָסוּל. וּמִשּׁוּם דְּאִיכָּא לְמ"ד בְּפֶרֶק "זֶה בּוֹרֵר" בְּסַנְהֶדְרִין דִּשְׁלִישִׁי בְּשֵׁנִי פָּסוּל, לְהָכִי אִצְטְרִיךְ לְמֵימַר הָכָא דְּכָשֵׁר. **רָבָא אָמַר אַף בְּרִאשׁוֹן.** כְּגוֹן בְּנוֹ שֶׁל חֲנוֹךְ בֶּן רְאוּבֵן מֵעִיד לְשִׁמְעוֹן אֲחִי רְאוּבֵן. וְהָכִי הִלְכְתָא, מִדְּאָמְרִי' לְקַמָּן: מוֹסִיף הוּא. וּמִדְּפָסֵיק לְקַמֵּיהּ: וְלֵית הִלְכְתָא כְּמָר בַּר רַב אַשִׁי – מִכְּלָל דְּהִלְכְתָא מִיהָא כְּרָבָא. **בְּאַבָּא דְאַבָּא.** שֶׁיָּעִיד הַבֵּן לַאֲבִי אָבִיו, כְּגוֹן בֶּן חֲנוֹךְ מֵעִיד לִרְאוּבֵן, דְּהַיְינוּ שְׁלִישִׁי (ב) בְּרִאשׁוֹן. **וְלֵית הִלְכְתָא כְּמָר בַּר רַב אַשִׁי.** דִּבְנֵי בָנִים וּבְנֵי בְּנֵי בָנִים עַד אֶלֶף דּוֹרוֹת לֹא יָעִידוּ לַאֲבוֹתֵיהֶם, דְּבֶן יֶרֶךְ אָבִיו הוּא. **הָיָה יוֹדֵעַ.** אָדָם לַחֲבֵירוֹ בְּעֵדוּת קַרְקַע עַד הֵיכָן הִיא שֶׁלּוֹ, וְהִשִּׂיגוּ אֶת גְּבוּלוֹ, וְהֵבִיא אֶת זֶה וְעֵד אַחֵר עִמּוֹ לְהָעִיד עָלָיו. אע"פ שֶׁהָיָה יוֹדֵעַ יָפֶה בְּעֵדוּת זוֹ קוֹדֶם שֶׁלֹּא נִסְתַּמֵּא בְּעֵינָיו, שֶׁעֲדַיִין לֹא הָיָה סוּמָא, וְעַכְשָׁיו בִּשְׁעַת עֵדוּת נַעֲשָׂה סוּמָא, שֶׁכָּהָה מְאוֹר עֵינָיו – פָּסוּל לְהַאי עֵדוּת, דְּמֵאוֹמֶד הַדַּעַת אֵינוֹ יָכוֹל לְהָעִיד "עַד כָּאן תְּחוּם פְּלוֹנִי", וְלֹא נָחוּשׁ לְעֵדוּתוֹ. וְיֵשׁ לְשׁוֹנוֹת אֲחֵרִים בְּהַאי "נִסְתַּמֵּא" דְּלָא מְפָרְשֵׁי לְשׁוֹן עִוְּרוֹן עֵינַיִם, וְכוּלָּן הֶבֶל. **דִּמְכַוֵּין מִצְרָנֵהָא.** שֶׁיּוֹדֵעַ לְכַוֵּין הַמְּצָרִים, שֶׁיֵּשׁ לוֹ סִימָנִין בִּשְׁאָר שָׂדוֹת הַסְּמוּכִין לְד' רוּחוֹתֶיהָ. **אֲבָל גְּלִימָא.** טַלִּית אוֹ בֶּגֶד – אֵינוֹ יָכוֹל לְהָעִיד עָלֶיהָ אַחַר שֶׁנַּעֲשָׂה סוּמָא. דְּאַמִּדָּה לָא סָמְכִינַן, שֶׁהַרְבֵּה טַלִּיתוֹת מִדָּתָן שָׁוֹת. **נַסְכָא.** חֲתִיכַת כֶּסֶף אוֹ זָהָב. **וְנַעֲשָׂה חֲתָנוֹ.** וְנַעֲשָׂה פָּסוּל לְעֵדוּתוֹ בְּכָךְ, כִּדְאָמְרִינַן בְּסַנְהֶדְרִין בְּפֶרֶק "זֶה בּוֹרֵר" (דף כז:). **פִּיתֵּחַ.** עֵינָיו פְּקוּחוֹת, שֶׁרוֹאֶה יָפֶה. **שָׁפוּי.** חָכָם. **וְנִתְחָרֵשׁ.** מֵחֲמַת חוֹלִי. הַיְינוּ נַמִי נִשְׁתַּטָּה, דְּחֵרֵשׁ דּוּמְיָא דְּשׁוֹטֶה. א"נ, נִשְׁתַּתֵּק מֵחֲמַת חוֹלִי, וְהַתּוֹרָה אָמְרָה "מִפִּיהֶם" וְלֹא מִפִּי כְּתָבָם. וְרִאשׁוֹן נִרְאֶה בְּעֵינַי עִיקָּר, דְּאִי בְּנִשְׁתַּתֵּק מַיְירֵי – פְּשִׁיטָא, כֵּיוָן דְּאֵינוֹ יָכוֹל לְהָעִיד בְּפִיו – אֵין עֵדוּתוֹ עֵדוּת, וְלָא הֲוָה לֵיהּ לְמִיתְנְיֵיהּ בַּהֲדֵי הָנָךְ שֶׁיְּכוֹלִין לְהָעִיד אֶלָּא שֶׁפְּסוּלִין מֵחֲמַת דָּבָר אַחֵר, וְהַאי לָאו פְּסוּל עֵדוּת אִית בֵּיהּ, אֶלָּא שֶׁאֵין בּוֹ כֹּחַ לְהָעִיד. **וּמֵתָה בִּתּוֹ.** דְּהַיְינוּ קָרוֹב וְנִתְרַחֵק. וּכְגוֹן שֶׁאֵין לוֹ בָּנִים הֵימֶנָּה, כִּדְתְנַן בְּפ' "זֶה בּוֹרֵר" (שם). **וְחָזַר וְנִתְפַּתֵּחַ.** שֶׁחָזַר מְאוֹר עֵינָיו. **כָּל שֶׁתְּחִלָּתוֹ.** רְאִיַּית הַמַּעֲשֶׂה. **אוֹ סוֹפוֹ.** שְׁעַת הַגָּדַת עֵדוּת. **בִּפְסָלוּת.** כְּלוֹמַר, כָּל שֶׁתְּחִלָּתוֹ בִּפְסָלוּת שְׁעַת רְאִיַּית הָעֵדוּת, וְהַשְׁתָּא סוֹפוֹ בְּכַשְׁרוּת – פָּסוּל, דִּמְעִיקָּרָא לֹא הָיָה רָאוּי לְעֵדוּת זוֹ, וּקְרָא כְּתִיב (ויקרא ה): "וְהוּא עֵד אוֹ רָאָה" – דְּבִשְׁעַת רְאִיַּית הַמַּעֲשֶׂה יְהֵא רָאוּי לְעֵדוּת זוֹ. **אוֹ סוֹפוֹ.** אע"פ שֶׁתְּחִלָּתוֹ בְּכַשְׁרוּת.

תוספות

הכי גרסינן: ונשבע אינו יכול לחזור בו. פירוש: אם נשבע כבר — אינו יכול לחזור בו. אבל אם לא נשבע — יכול לחזור בו, כדאמרי' ב"זה בורר" (סנהדרין דף כד: ושם): מחלוקת לאחר גמר דין, אבל לפני גמר דין — דברי הכל (ג) היה יכול לחזור בו. והכא, אע"ג דאמר "השבע וטול" — יכול לחזור, כיון שעדיין לא נשבע הוי(ד) קודם גמר דין. וכן משמע בריש "המפקיד" (ב"מ דף לד: ושם): אמר "הריני משלם" וחזר ואמר "איני משלם", מהו? מי אמר מיהדר ביה? אלמא, דיכול לחזור בו, דהוי כמו קודם גמר דין. והא דאמר בריש "שבועת הדיינין" (שבועות דף לט. ושם): ואם אמר "איני נשבע" — פוטרין אותו מיד, אומר רבינו תם: היינו שמסלקין אותו, כדי שיתבייש מלחזור בו. אבל אם רוצה לחזור ולבא לב"ד ולישבע — הרשות בידו. אבל קלת קשה: מנא ליה הא דקאמר הכא דקסבר הלכה כחכמים? דלמא סבר דלפני גמר דין מחלוקת, אבל אחר גמר דין — דברי הכל אינו יכול לחזור בו. אבל רש"י פירש: אם אמר "איני נשבע" — פוטרין אותו מיד, דשוב אינו יכול לחזור בו. והכא גרס נשבע בלא וי"ו, שישבע בעל כרחו. וההוא דריש "המפקיד" (ב"מ דף לד: ושם) דקאמר: מי אמרי' מיהדר קא הדר ביה, אע"ג דאינו יכול לחזור בו, מ"מ כיון דדעתו לחזור ובעי לאטרוחי בי דינא — לא מקני ליה כפילא. דכה"ג אמר התם. אבל לפירוש זה לא אתי שפיר דפסיק בשמעתין ככל הני דשלח ר' אבא, וא"כ אפי' קודם גמר דין אינו יכול לחזור, וב"זה בורר" מסקינן דלפני גמר דין יכול לחזור בו. אם לא שנאמר הכא: אפי' קודם שבועה חשיב גמר דין כי אמר "רצונך השבע וטול".

מר בר רב אשי מכשר באבא דאבא. וא"ת: והלא אפי' שני בשני אמר בפרק "זה בורר" (סנהדרין דף כח. ושם ד"ה רב) דפסול, וכ"ש זקנו! ויש לומר: דאבא דאבא כשר טפי, דאיתפלג דרא. **לית** הלכתא כמר בר רב אשי. פירש בקונטרס דאפי' עד סוף כל הדורות פסול. ואין נראה לר"י, כיון דאתפלג דרא כ"כ. **פיתח** ונסתמא פסול. ואע"ג דגבי גט מכשירין, שאם היה בשעת כתיבה פיתח יכול לומר "בפני נכתב ובפני נחתם" לאחר שנסתמא — שאני התם, דאקילו רבנן להכשיר אפילו אשה וקרובים[ד].

נשבע

רבינו גרשום

רצונך השבע שלא מכרת לי וטול אינו יכול לחזור בו. המחזיק אע"פ שכל הנשבעין שבתורה נשבעין ולא משלמין מאחר שזה קיבל עליו שישבע התובע ויטול אין יכול לחזור בו: מאי קמ"ל תנינא נאמן עלי אביך בעדות זו נאמן עלי אבא אע"פ שאין כשרין להעיד עליו ונאמן עלי ג' רועי בקר לדין זה אע"פ שאין מומחין הואיל שקיבל עליו. ר' מאיר אומר יכול לחזור בו האי מוחזק אע"פ שדנו הואיל שאין ראויין. וחכמים אומרים אין יכול לחזור בו משעה שאמר ועשו מעשה. אלמא דהאי נמי מאחר שנשבע זה אינו יכול לחזור בו ומאי קמ"ל: הא קמ"ל. דקא מיבעיא במסכת סנהדרין על מחלוקת דר' מאיר ורבנן באתן לך פליגי. אבל השבע ויהא מחול לך דברי הכל אין יכול לחזור בו או דלמא איפכא. ומסקינן הלכתא באתן לך מחלוקת. והלכתא כדברי חכמים דאמרי אינו יכול לחזור בו ה"נ להיכא דאמר השבע וטול כאתן לך הוא. ואצטריך למימר דהלכה כחכמים: הלכה גובין מן העבדים. שאם הניח אביהן של יתומים עבדים גובה בעל חובו של אביהם את חובו מן העבדים כי היכי דהוי עביד מן הקרקע ולא מצו למטען ליה מטלטלי שבק אבון גבן משום דעבדא כמקרקע דמי: הלכתא שלישי בשני כשר. כגון ראובן ושמעון הם בניהם היינו ראשונים ובני בניהם היינו שניים ובני בני בניהם היינו דור שלישי של בן ראובן ודור שלישי של בן שמעון ודור שלישי של בן ראובן מותר להעיד לדור שני של בן שמעון: ורבא אמר אף שלישי מעיד בראשון. בבן שמעון עצמו דהיינו ראשון אע"פ שהוא קרוב לאביו. ובאחא דאבא שאדם יעיד לאחי אביו: ולית הלכתא כותי'. דקרוב ליה טפי: ונסתמא פסול. להעיד לו משום דעכשיו אינו יודע להראות עדותו באיזה מקום מגיע תחום קרקע שלו: ושמואל אמר כשר. אפשר דמכוין במצרנא מצר פלוני כך וכך סימן מצר פלוני כך: אבל גלימא לא. אם היה מכיר בגד של חבירו קודם שנסתמא ואחר שנסתמא אינו יכול להעיד זה בגדו של פלוני: אפשר דמכוין מדת ארכו ורחבו. שאמר אני יודע שכך היה ארכו ורחבו ונמצא כדבריו. וכן נמי אם נמצא משקל הנסכא כמו שהוא אמר כשר: מיתיבי היה יודע כו' קא תני מידת פיתח ונסתמא פסול להעיד שום עדות ותיובתא דכולהו תנאי דלעיל שמואל ורב פפא ורב ששת תיובתא: ומתה בתו. דרחוק ונתקרב ונתרחק הוא: כר'

עין משפט נר מצוה

עז א מיי' פ"ו מהלכות סנהדרין הלכה ג ועי' בכ"מ סמג עשין צז טור ושו"ע חו"מ סי' כב סעיף ג:

עח ב מיי' שם הלכה ב ועי' בכ"מ טוש"ע שם סעיף א:

עט ג מיי' פי"א מהל' מלוה הל' ח [ופי"א מהל' זכיה הלכה יג] סמג עשין לה טור שו"ע חו"מ סי' קז סעיף א [וטור שו"ע חו"מ סי' רמח ס"ז]:

פ ד ה ו מיי' פי"ג מהל' עדות הל' ו ז ח סמג לאוין ריד טור שו"ע חו"מ סי' לג סעיף ג [וברב אלפס עוד בסנהדרין פ"ג דף רכג]:

פא ז ח ט מיי' שם פ"ד הלכה ב סמג לאוין רטו טוש"ע שם סעיף יג וסימן לה סעיף יג [וברב אלפס שם]:

מסורת הש"ס

א) סנהדרין כד. ב) [כ"ק יא.] ג) [ערכין יז: ע"ש] ד) [וע"ע תוס' גיטין כג. ד"ה הוא הדין]:

הגהות הב"ח

(א) רשב"ם ד"ה שלישי וכו' כגון בן חנוך בן ראובן כשר להעיד בימואל: (ב) ד"ה באבא וכו' שלישי לראובן הראשון הס"ד: (ג) תוס' ד"ה הכי גרסי' וכו' דברי הכל יכול לחזור בו והכא נמי אע"ג ל ותיבת היה נמחק: (ד) בא"ד שעדיין לא נשבע הוי כמו קודם וכו' מיהדר קא הדר ביה אלמא:

תְּיוּבְתָּא דְּכוּלְּהוּ, תְּיוּבְתָּא. שְׁלַח ר' אַבָּא לְרַב יוֹסֵף בַּר חָמָא: הָאוֹמֵר עַל תִּינוֹק בֵּין הַבָּנִים — נֶאֱמָן; וְרַבִּי יוֹחָנָן אָמַר: אֵינוֹ נֶאֱמָן. מַאי קָאָמַר? אֲמַר אַבַּיֵי, הָכִי קָאָמַר: הָאוֹמֵר עַל תִּינוֹק בֵּין הַבָּנִים "יִירַשׁ כָּל נְכָסַי" — נֶאֱמָן, כְּרַבִּי יוֹחָנָן בֶּן בְּרוֹקָה; וְרַבִּי יוֹחָנָן אָמַר: אֵינוֹ נֶאֱמָן, כְּרַבָּנַן. מַתְקִיף לָהּ רָבָא: הַאי נֶאֱמָן וְאֵינוֹ נֶאֱמָן, יִירַשׁ וְלֹא יִירַשׁ מִבָּעֲיָא לֵיהּ! אֶלָּא אֲמַר רָבָא, הָכִי קָאָמַר: [א]דְּאוֹמֵר עַל תִּינוֹק בֵּין הַבָּנִים "בְּכוֹר הוּא" — נֶאֱמָן, כְּר' יְהוּדָה; וְר' יוֹחָנָן אָמַר: אֵינוֹ נֶאֱמָן, כְּרַבָּנַן.§ שְׁלַח לֵיהּ ר' אַבָּא לְרַב יוֹסֵף בַּר חָמָא: [ב]הָאוֹמֵר "תִּטּוֹל אִשְׁתִּי כְּאֶחָד מִן הַבָּנִים" — נוֹטֶלֶת כְּאֶחָד מִן הַבָּנִים. אָמַר רָבָא: [ג]וּבִנְכָסִים שֶׁל עַכְשָׁיו, [ד]וּבְבָנִים הַבָּאִין לְאַחַר מִכָּאן.§ שְׁלַח לֵיהּ רַבִּי אַבָּא לְרַב יוֹסֵף בַּר חָמָא: [ה]הַמּוֹצִיא שְׁטַר חוֹב עַל חֲבֵירוֹ, מַלְוֶה אוֹמֵר "לֹא נִפְרַעְתִּי כְּלוּם", וְלֹוֶה אוֹמֵר "פָּרַעְתִּי מֶחֱצָה", וְהָעֵדִים מְעִידִין שֶׁפָּרַע כּוּלּוֹ — הֲרֵי זֶה נִשְׁבָּע וְגוֹבֶה מֶחֱצָה מִנְּכָסִים בְּנֵי חוֹרִין, אֲבָל מִמְּשׁוּעְבָּדִין לָא, דְּאָמְרִי: אֲנַן אַעֵדִים סָמְכִינַן. וַאֲפִי' לְר' עֲקִיבָא דְּאָמַר: [א]מֵשִׁיב אֲבֵדָה הָוֵי — הָנֵי מִילֵּי הֵיכָא דְּלֵיכָּא עֵדִים, אֲבָל הֵיכָא דְּאִיכָּא עֵדִים — אִירְתּוּתֵי אִירְתַּת. מַתְקִיף לָהּ מָר בַּר רַב אַשִׁי: אַדְּרַבָּה, אֲפִי' לְר' שִׁמְעוֹן בֶּן אֶלְעָזָר דְּאָמַר: מוֹדֶה מִקְצָת הַטַּעֲנָה הָוֵי — הָנֵי מִילֵּי הֵיכָא דְּלֵיכָּא עֵדִים דְּקָא מְסַיְּיעִי לֵיהּ, אֲבָל הֵיכָא דְּאִיכָּא עֵדִים דְּקָא מְסַיְּיעִי לֵיהּ — וַדַּאי מֵשִׁיב אֲבֵדָה הָוֵי. דָּרַשׁ מָר זוּטְרָא מִשְּׁמֵיהּ דְּרַב שִׁימִי בַּר אַשִׁי: הִלְכְתָא בְּכָל הָנֵי שְׁמַעְתָּתָא כִּדְשְׁלַח לֵיהּ רַבִּי אַבָּא לְרַב יוֹסֵף בַּר חָמָא. אֲמַר לֵיהּ רָבִינָא לְרַב אַשִׁי: דְּר"נ מַאי? א"ל: "אֵין גּוֹבִין" מַתְנִינַן לָהּ, וְכֵן אר"נ. וְאֶלָּא הִלְכְתָא לְאַפּוּקֵי מַאי?

אי

רשב"ם

תְּיוּבְתָּא דְּכוּלְּהוּ. שְׁמוּאֵל וְרַב שֵׁשֶׁת וְרַב פַּפָּא. דְּכוּלָּן הִכְשִׁירוּ מִיהָא לְעֵדוּת קַרְקַע פִּיתֵּחַ וְנִסְתַּמֵּא, וְהָכָא קָא פָּסֵיל כּוּלְּהוּ עֵדִיּוֹת, מִדְּהַדַר וּתְנָא: זֶה הַכְּלָל, כָּל שֶׁתְּחִלָּתוֹ אוֹ סוֹפוֹ בִּפְסָלוּת — פָּסוּל. דְּהָא מֵרֵישָׁא שָׁמְעַתְּ מִינָּהּ דְּאִם סוֹפוֹ בִּפְסָלוּת פָּסוּל, וְלָמָּה לִי לְמֵהְדַּר וּלְמִתְנֵי בְּ"זֶה הַכְּלָל" אִי לָאו לְאַתּוּיֵי כָּל הָנֵי? הָאוֹמֵר עַל תִּינוֹק בֵּין הַבָּנִים נֶאֱמָן. לְקַמֵּיהּ מְפָרֵשׁ מַאי אָמַר עַל אוֹתוֹ תִּינוֹק. כְּרַבִּי יוֹחָנָן בֶּן בְּרוֹקָה. בְּמַתְנִיתִין. אִם אָמַר עַל מִי שֶׁרָאוּי לְיוֹרְשׁוֹ — דְּבָרָיו קַיָּימִים. וּפָסְקִינַן לְקַמָּן הִלְכְתָא כְּוָותֵיהּ. נֶאֱמָן. כְּר' יְהוּדָה. וְאַע"ג דְּמוּחְזָק לָן בְּאַחֵר שֶׁהוּא בְּכוֹר, אֲפִילּוּ הָכִי אָב נֶאֱמָן. וְהָכִי הִלְכְתָא, דְּהָא פָּסֵיק הָכִי לְקַמָּן דְּהִלְכְתָא בְּכוּלְּהוּ כִּדְשְׁלַח רַבִּי אַבָּא, וְאָמְרִינַן דִּלְאַפּוּקֵי [(א)]רַבִּי יוֹחָנָן אִצְטְרִיךְ, לְמִיפְסַק הִלְכְתָא כְּוָתֵיהּ דְּרַבִּי אַבָּא. וש"מ: אִם הוּחְזַק אֶחָד מִן הַבָּנִים בִּבְכוֹרָה בְּחַיֵּי הָאָב, אַף שֶׁלֹּא אָמַר הָאָב כִּי בְּנִי בְּכוֹרִי הוּא — נוֹטֵל פִּי שְׁנַיִם. שֶׁלֹּא נֶחְלְקוּ רַבִּי יְהוּדָה וַחֲכָמִים אֶלָּא בְּמוּחְזָק שֶׁאַחֵר בְּכוֹר, וְאָמַר אָבִיו עַל הַמּוּחְזָק בְּפָשׁוּט שֶׁהוּא בְּכוֹר, וְהָתָם אָמַר רַבִּי יְהוּדָה: נֶאֱמָן הָאָב לְבַטֵּל הַחֲזָקָה. אֲבָל אִם לֹא אָמַר הָאָב עַל הָאַחֵר שֶׁהוּא בְּכוֹר — הָתָם אֲפִילּוּ רַבִּי יְהוּדָה מוֹדֶה שֶׁהַחֲזָקָה קַיֶּימֶת. דְּאִי לָא תֵּימָא הָכִי — הֲוָה לֵיהּ לְרַבִּי יְהוּדָה לְמֵימַר הָכִי: רַבִּי יְהוּדָה אוֹמֵר: כָּל בְּכוֹר שֶׁלֹּא הִכִּירוֹ אָבִיו וְאָמַר "זֶהוּ בְּכוֹרִי" — אֵינוֹ נוֹטֵל פִּי שְׁנַיִם. אֶלָּא מִדְּלָא תָּנֵי הָכִי — שְׁמַע מִינָּהּ כִּדְאָמְרִינַן. אֵינוֹ נֶאֱמָן כְּרַבָּנַן. הוֹאִיל וּמוּחְזָק לָן בְּאַחֵר שֶׁהוּא בְּכוֹר. הָאוֹמֵר תִּטּוֹל אִשְׁתִּי כְּאֶחָד מִן הַבָּנִים. וְקִבְּלָה, שֶׁנִּתְרַצֵּית, כִּדְלְקַמָּן בְּפִירְקִין. אִי נַמִּי, לְבַר מִכְּתוּבָּתָהּ נָתַן לָהּ חֵלֶק בִּנְכָסָיו. וּבִשְׁכִיב מְרַע מַיְירֵי, דְּדְבָרָיו כִּכְתוּבִין וְכִמְסוּרִין. אִי נַמִּי, בְּבָרִיא וְעַל יְדֵי קִנְיָן. וּבִנְכָסִים שֶׁל עַכְשָׁיו. שֶׁאִם נִתְרַבּוּ הַנְּכָסִים בִּשְׁעַת חֲלוּקָה — אֵינָהּ נוֹטֶלֶת כִּי אִם בְּאוֹתָן שֶׁהָיוּ לוֹ בִּשְׁעַת אֲמִירָה, דְּאֵין אָדָם מַקְנֶה דָּבָר שֶׁלֹּא בָּא לָעוֹלָם. וַאֲפִילּוּ לְר' מֵאִיר דְּאָמַר אָדָם מַקְנֶה — הָנֵי מִילֵּי בִּמְפָרֵשׁ, אֲבָל בִּסְתָמָא — אֵין אָדָם מַעֲלֶה עַל דַּעְתּוֹ דָּבָר הָרָאוּי לוֹ לָבֹא לְהַקְנוֹתוֹ, אֶלָּא לְדָבָר שֶׁהוּא מוּחְזָק בּוֹ. וְהִלְכָּךְ, הַךְ אִשָּׁה — יָדָהּ עַל הַתַּחְתּוֹנָה, דְּמִסְתָמָא לֹא נָתַן לָהּ אֶלָּא נְכָסִים שֶׁהָיוּ לוֹ בְּאוֹתָהּ שָׁעָה. וּבְבָנִים הַבָּאִין לְאַחַר מִכָּאן. כְּלוֹמַר, לֹא לְפִי חֶשְׁבּוֹן הַבָּנִים שֶׁיֵּשׁ לוֹ עַכְשָׁיו לְבַד תַּחֲלוֹק לְאַחַר מוֹתוֹ וְתִטּוֹל חֵלֶק גָּדוֹל, אֶלָּא אַף לְפִי חֶשְׁבּוֹן כָּל הַבָּנִים שֶׁל שְׁעַת חֲלוּקָה נָתַן לָהּ. וְנִרְאֶה בְּעֵינַי דַּאֲפִילּוּ אִם הָיָה לוֹ בָּנִים מְרוּבִּים וְנִתְמַעֲטוּ בְּחַיֵּי הָאָב — דְּשָׁקְלָה חֵלֶק גָּדוֹל כְּחֶשְׁבּוֹן מִיעוּט הַבָּנִים הַבָּאִין לַחֲלוֹק בְּנִכְסֵי הָאָב לְאַחַר מִיתָתוֹ, דְּהָא תִּטּוֹל כְּאֶחָד מִכָּל הַבָּנִים קָאָמַר, וְלִשְׁעַת חֲלוּקָה אִיכַּוֵּין. דִּלְפִי חֲלוּקַת הַהִיא שַׁעְתָּא תִּטּוֹל, לָא שְׁנָא נִתְרַבּוּ וְלָא שְׁנָא נִתְמַעֲטוּ, דְּהָא נוֹטֶלֶת אִשְׁתּוֹ כְּאֶחָד מִן הַבָּנִים קָאָמַר רַבִּי אַבָּא. וְלֹוֶה אָמַר פָּרַעְתִּי מֶחֱצָה. וּמֶחֱצָה אֲנִי חַיָּיב, דַּהֲוָה לֵיהּ מוֹדֶה מִקְצָת הַטַּעֲנָה, וְיִשָּׁבַע, כִּדְמְפָרֵשׁ לְקַמֵּיהּ. וּכְגוֹן דְּמִקַּמֵּי דְּאַסְהִידוּ הָעֵדִים שֶׁפָּרַע לוֹ כּוּלּוֹ הוֹדָה לוֹ, דְּלָא הֲוָה מֵשִׁיב אֲבֵדָה. וְהָעֵדִים מְעִידִין. אַחַר דְּהוֹדָה מֶחֱצָה. נִשְׁבָּע. הַלֹּוֶה שֶׁפָּרַע, וְיִפָּטֵר מִלְּשַׁלֵּם מֶחֱצָה. וּמֶחֱצָה יְשַׁלֵּם, לְפִי שֶׁכְּבָר הוֹדָה, דְּהוֹדָאַת בַּעַל דִּין שָׁוֶה יוֹתֵר מֵהַעֲדָאַת עֵדִים. וְגוֹבֶה הַמַּלְוֶה מֶחֱצָה מִנְּכָסִים בְּנֵי חוֹרִין שֶׁיֵּשׁ לוֹ לַלֹּוֶה, אֲבָל לֹא מִמְּשׁוּעְבָּדֵי, דְּיָכְלֵי לָקוֹחוֹת לְמֵימַר: אַתּוּן קְנוּנְיָא עֲבִידְתּוּ אַהֲדָדֵי, אֲנַן אַעֵדִים סָמְכִינַן דְּמַסְהֲדֵי דְּפָרַע הַכֹּל. פְּלוּגְתָּא דְּרַבִּי עֲקִיבָא וְרַבִּי שִׁמְעוֹן בֶּן אֶלְעָזָר. בִּתְחִלַּת "שְׁנַיִם אוֹחֲזִין": שְׁטָר שֶׁכָּתוּב בּוֹ "סְלָעִין" אוֹ "דִּינָרִים", מַלְוֶה אוֹמֵר: חָמֵשׁ, וְלֹוֶה אוֹמֵר: שָׁלֹשׁ. רַבִּי שִׁמְעוֹן בֶּן אֶלְעָזָר אוֹמֵר: הוֹאִיל וְהוֹדָה מִקְצָת הַטַּעֲנָה — יִשָּׁבַע. רַבִּי עֲקִיבָא אוֹמֵר: אֵינוֹ אֶלָּא כְּמֵשִׁיב אֲבֵדָה, וּפָטוּר מִשְּׁבוּעָה. דִּסְלָעִין לָא מַשְׁמַע טְפֵי מִשְּׁנַיִם, דְּתָפַסְתָּ מְרוּבֶּה לֹא תָפַסְתָּ, וְיַד בַּעַל הַשְּׁטָר עַל הַתַּחְתּוֹנָה. וְעַל הַשְּׁלִישִׁי שֶׁהוֹדָה — הֲוָה מֵשִׁיב אֲבֵדָה, וּתְנַן: הַמּוֹצֵא מְצִיאָה לֹא יִשָּׁבַע, מִפְּנֵי תִּקּוּן הָעוֹלָם. וַאֲפִילּוּ לְר' עֲקִיבָא דְּאָמַר. הָתָם: מֵשִׁיב אֲבֵדָה הוּא בְּסֶלַע הַשְּׁלִישִׁי, דְּאִי הֲוָה בָּעֵי הֲוָה אָמַר אֵינָן אֶלָּא שְׁנַיִם, דִּסְלָעִין תְּרֵי מַשְׁמַע, וַהֲוָה מִיפְּטַר מִשְּׁבוּעָה כִּדְמְפָרֵשׁ הָתָם — מִשּׁוּם דְּקָא מְסַיֵּיעַ לֵיהּ שְׁטָרָא. הָנֵי מִילֵּי. דְּחָשְׁבִינַן לֵיהּ מֵשִׁיב אֲבֵדָה — הֵיכָא דְּלֵיכָּא עֵדִים, כִּי הָתָם, שֶׁעֵדֵי מַלְוֶה לֹא יָדְעוּ אֶלָּא מַה שֶּׁכָּתְבוּ, דִּסְלָעִין כָּתְבוּ סְתָם, וּפְחוֹת סְלָעִים — שְׁנַיִם. אֲבָל הֵיכָא דְּחָזֵינַן לְבַסּוֹף דְּאִיכָּא עֵדִים כְּאֶחָד מֵהֶם — אִיכָּא לְמֵימַר דְּזֶה הַלֹּוֶה הָיָה יוֹדֵעַ שֶׁרוֹצִין לְהָעִיד כְּאֶחָד מֵהֶן, וְאִירְתַּת שֶׁלֹּא יָבֹאוּ לְסַיֵּיעַ לַמַּלְוֶה, וּלְפִיכָךְ הוֹדָה כְּמֶחֱצָה. וַדַּאי מֵשִׁיב אֲבֵדָה הָוֵי. וְאַף עַל גַּב דְּלָא אָתוּ עֵדִים אֶלָּא בָּתַר הוֹדָאָתוֹ. וְהַךְ אַתְקַפְתָּא לָא חָיְישִׁינַן לָהּ, כִּדְלְקַמָּן. דְּרַב נַחְמָן מַאי. דִּפְלִיג עֲלֵיהּ גַּבֵּי עֲבָדִים, וְאָמַר: אֵין גּוֹבִין מִן הָעֲבָדִים, וְקַיְימָא לָן כְּרַב נַחְמָן בְּדִינֵי, וְקַשְׁיָא הִלְכְתָא אַהִלְכְתָא. אֵין גּוֹבִין מַתְנִינַן. כְּדְרַבִּי אַבָּא. וְאֶלָּא הִלְכְתָא לְאַפּוּקֵי מַאי. כֵּיוָן דְּלָא פְּלִיג, פְּשִׁיטָא דְּהָכִי הִלְכְתָא!

אי

תוספות

נשבע וגובה מחצה מנכסים בני חורין. נראה לר"י: דלהכי נאמן בשבועה — משום דחשיבא כמלוה על פה, שהרי עדים מעידין שהשטר פרוע. ואע"ג דלדבריו העדים פסולים, שהרי מכחישם, והומר שחייב מחלה — מכל מקום שטר אינו מתקיים אלא ע"י הודאתו, והא קאמר דפרע מחלה. ולא דמי למודה בשטר שכתבו שאין לריך לקיימו, ואינו נאמן לומר "פרעתי", וגובה מנכסים משועבדים אף ע"ג דאינו מקויים אלא על פיו. דהתם הוי שטר גמור, דעדים החתומים על השטר כמי שנחקרה עדותן בב"ד, אלא רבנן הוא דאלרכוהו קיום כי טעין בהדיא מזויף. אבל כשקיימו — הוי שטר גמור, ואין נאמן לומר "פרעתי".

ואפילו לרבי עקיבא דאמר משיב אבדה הוי. אומר ה"ר יעקב דאורליינ"ש: דלא גרס "רבי עקיבא", אלא "רבי יעקב" גרס. ואין להאריך[ב].

אבל היכא דאיכא עדים אירתותי מירתת. תימה לר"י: אמאי תלי טעמא משום מירתת במה שיש עדים שירא שמא יכחישוהו? הלא רק שלא יסייעוהו אינו יכול לכפור הכל ולהעיז פניו, דאין אדם מעיז פניו בפני בעל חובו לכפור הכל! ויש לומר: דכיון שהוא סבור שיבאו עדים לסייעו, שהרי מביאן, והגידו לו דעתן, ותו ליכא עזות אם יכפור הכל. ואי לאו שירא שמא יחזרו בהן ויכחישוהו — ה"ה לו מגו טוב, אבל לפי שירא שיכחישוהו — אין נוח לו לכפור הכל, שלא יראה שקרן יותר מדאי אם יכחישוהו.

הלכתא בכל הני שמעתתא. וא"ת: והא קיימא לן ד"הילך" פטור, כדפסק ר"ת בריש בבא מליעא (דף ד. ושם), והכא פסקינן דנשבע וגובה מחלה, והא הך שטרא כיון דקא מודה ביה "הילך" הוא! ויש לומר: דלא חשיב שטר "הילך" אלא שטר דגבי ביה ממשעבדי[ג].

אי

עין משפט נר מצוה

פב א מיי' פ"ב מהלכות נחלות הל' יד סמג עשין נו טוש"ע חו"מ סי' רעז סעיף יב:

פג ב ג ד מיי' פי"א מהל' זכיה ומתנה הלכה י ויא סמג עשין פב טוש"ע אה"ע סי' קח סעיף א:

פד ה מיי' פי"ד מהל' מלוה ולוה הלכה ד סמג עשין לב טוש"ע חו"מ סי' פב סעיף יג:

רבינו גרשום

כר' יוחנן בן ברוקה. דאמר כשאמר איש פלוני יירשני במקום שיש בת לא אמר כלום לדברי הת"ק וא"ר יוחנן אם על מי שראוי לירשו אם אותו פלוני שאמר יירשני במקום בת אם הוא ראוי ליורשו אם לא היה לו בת כגון שהוא אחיו כיון דהוה יורשו בשאין לו בת יורשו נמי במקום בת הכי נמי כשאמר על תינוק בין הבנים הואיל וראוי ליורשו אותו תינוק הכי מצי יהיב ליה כל נכסי' דהתורה נתנה רשות לאב להנחיל לכל מי שירצה מבניו כחפצו: ור' יוחנן אמר אינו נאמן. כרבנן ת"ק דר' יוחנן בן ברוקה: מתקיף לה רבא. לדברי' דמפרשת ליה הכי האי נאמן ואינו נאמן יירש ולא יירש מבעיא ליה. כר' יהודה דאמר לעיל יכיר יכירנו לאחרים: כרבנן דאמרי בתר חזקה אזלינן: תטול אשתי ירושה בין הבנים לבד מכתובתה נוטלת כאחד מן הבנים משום דמצי למיתן מתנה לכל מאן דבעי: אמר רבא ובנכסים שיש לו עכשיו. שהוא מוחזק בהן ונוטלת בהן כאחד מן הבנים הילדים לאחר מכן אבל מכל הנכסים הבאים לאחר מיכן אינה נוטלת לפי שאין אדם מקנה לגבי אשתו דבר שלא בא לעולם והיכי נוטלת חלקה מבנים שיולדו לאחר מיכן שנתן לה הבעל מתנה. משום דעם בניו ראשונים לחודייהו לא מציא למיטען תנו לי חלק עם הבנים שהי' באותה שעה בלבד דהא בשעת ירושה יש עוד בנים אחרים שיורשים אלא בעל כרחה אינה נוטלת חלק אלא באותן הנכסים שהיה לה באותה שעה ופלגי להן בין כל הבנים ונוטלת בהן חלק כאחד מן הבנים. והיינו בבנים הבאין לאחר מיכן דאית להו אחים הרבה ואינה יכולה לומר איני רוצה שיחלוקו אותן נכסים אלא לבנים שהי' לו באותה שעה ונוטלת אני כאחד מן הבנים לרבות חלקה אלא יחלקום בין כולם משום דכולהו יורשים הוו ונוטלת כאחד מהם באותן נכסים בלבד שהיו לו באותה שעה. אבל נכסים שבאו לו לאחר מיכן יורשין בנים ראשונים ואחרונים בלבד בשוה חוץ ממנה: והעדים מעידים אותו שפרעו כולו. הואיל והוא מודה שהוא חייב מחצה לא אזלינן בתר סהדותייהו דעדים אלא (א) נשבע המלוה שלא נפרע וגובה מחצה מנכסים בני חורין אבל מנכסים משועבדים שמכר או שמשכן אחר שלוד לא מצי למיגבי משום דמצו למימר לקוחות אנן כי זבינן אעדים דמסהדי דפרע כולו סמכינן ולית לך גבן כלום. וזה כלל גדול בדין בכל אותו ענין שהלוה רוצה לפטור את עצמו מן הפלוה כשתבעו במלוה שבעל פה באות ענין עצמו שיהיה לחייבו המלוה בשיש לו שטר חוב עליו כגון אם תובעו מלוה על פה וזה אמר אין לך בידי כלום דפטור אפי' משבועה דאין מודה לו כלום כך אחרי שכפר זה אם הוציא עליו שהוא חייב לו גובה ממנו אפי' בלא שבועה. ואם תבעו במלוה על פה וכפר במקצת והודה במקצת פורע לו מה שהודה ונשבע לו על מה שכפר כך כשכפר לו מקצת והוציא זה עליו שטר חוב שרייב לו וישבע המלוה על מה שכפר לו ונוטל על פה שכל הנשבעין שבתורה נשבעין ולא משלמין נשבע זה שהשטר בידו ונוטל. הלכך אמרינן הכא נשבע המלוה וגובה ממחצה שכופר לו הואיל והוציא עליו שטר. ואפי' לר' עקיבא דאמר בב"מ היכא דהוציא מלוה שטר על הלוה וכתוב ביה סלעים סתם מלוה אומר חמש הלויתי לו ולוה אומר שלש ר"ש אומר הואיל והודה במקצת הטענה דמודה עכשיו בסלע אחד יותר שהשטר משמע דבשטר כתב סלעים סתם ושנים נמי משמע סלעים השתא דאמר שלש מודה במקצת הטענה וישבע על השאר שטענו מלוה יותר ר' עקיבא אומר מאותו שליש שמודה לו על הכתוב בשטר אינו אלא כמשיב אבידה ופטור מן השבועה על השאר הואיל דמצי פטר נפשיה משנים האי נמי דאמר לא פרעתי אלא מחצה כמשיב אבידה הוא וכיון דעדים מעידין שפרע כולו והיינו להיות פטור משבועה והואיל וזה פטר עצמו משבועה בדין הוא שהמלוה שמוציא עליו שטר שצריך לבות בלא שבועה הואיל והלוה רוצה הוא לפטור את עצמו משבועה ומאי טעמא מחייב שבועה למלוה משום דאמרינן היכא אמר ר' עקיבא דהוה כמשיב אבידה ופטור הלוה היכא דליכא עדים כגון בשטר שכתוב בו סלעים סתם דלא ידעי' אי כדאמר מלוה אי כדאמר לוה אבל הכא דאיכא עדים על האי שטרא מירתת לוה מקמי עדים וחייש דלמא מסהדי עליה דלא פרעו כלל משום הכי קאמר לא פרעתי אלא מחצה ומודה במחצה הלכך לא הוי כמשיב אבידה אלא מודה במקצת הטענה הוי וחייב שבועה והואיל ויש שטר למלוה נשבע וגובה מחצה: מתקיף לה מר בר רב אשי. היכי מצית לחייבו שבועה על המלוה אדרבה אפי' לרבי שמעון בר פלוגתי' דר' עקיבא דאמר מודה במקצת הטענה ישבע הני מילי היכא דליכא עדים גבי לוה דקא מסייעי בהדיה אבל היכא דאיכא עדים דמסייעי בהדיה כי הכא בעדים מעידים אותו שפרע כולו ודאי הא דקאמר לא פרעתי אלא מחצה משיב אבידה הוי ופטור משבועה שכנגדו גבי מלוה אמאי נשבע וגובה מחצה הא בדין הוא דבלא שבועה יגבה: הלכתא בכל הני שמעתתא דאיירן לעיל כדשלח ליה רבה לר' יוסף בר חמא. הא דר"נ דאמר לעיל. אין גובין מתנינן וכן אמר רב נחמן. דיין מובהק הוה והלכתא כוותיה:

אימור

(א) כל דברי רבינו בכאן לריך ביאור והבנה ובסוף המסכת יבוא ביאור לדבריו אי"ה.

מסורת הש"ס

א) [ב"מ ז:]: ב) [ועי' תוס' ב"מ ז: ד"ה אין נשבעין הכ' ותוס' שבועות ז: ד"ה ר' עקיבא]: ג) [ועי' תוס' ב"מ ז. ד"ה ורב ששת]:

הגהות הב"ח

(א) רשב"ם ד"ה נאמן וכו' דלאפוקי מדר' יוחנן:

מסורת הש"ס

א) יבמות לו: ב) כתובות סט: תענית כח. [תוספ' כתובות פ"ו]:

עין משפט נר מצוה

פה א ב מיי' פ"ו מהל' נחלות הלכה ו סמג עשין נו טוש"ע ח"מ סי' רפא סעיף ז ועיין שם במ"מ ובהג"ה:

פו ג ד מיי' פי"א מהל' זכיה ומתנה הל' כג ופי"ב הלכה ו סמג עשין פב טור שו"ע חו"מ סי' רנג סעיף יז וסי' רמח סעיף ב:

אִי לְאַפּוּקֵי מִדְּרָבָא — מוֹסִיף הוּא, אִי (א) דְּמָר בַּר רַב אַשִׁי — לֵית הִלְכְתָא כְּמָר בַּר רַב אַשִׁי, אִי לְאַפּוּקֵי מִדִּשְׁמוּאֵל וְרַב שֵׁשֶׁת וְרַב פַּפָּא — הָא אִיתּוֹתְבוּ! אֶלָּא, לְאַפּוּקֵי מִדְּרַבִּי יוֹחָנָן וּמֵאַתְקַפְתָּא דְּמָר בַּר רַב אַשִׁי. § "הַמְחַלֵּק נְכָסָיו עַל פִּיו, רִיבָּה לְאֶחָד וּמִיעֵט לְאֶחָד" כו'. § הֵיכִי דָּמֵי מַתָּנָה בַּתְּחִלָּה, הֵיכִי דָּמֵי בָּאֶמְצַע, הֵיכִי דָּמֵי בַּסּוֹף? כִּי אֲתָא רַב דִּימִי אֲמַר רַבִּי יוֹחָנָן: "תִּנָּתֵן שָׂדֶה פְּלוֹנִית לִפְלוֹנִי וְיִירָשֶׁהָ" — זוֹ הִיא מַתָּנָה בַּתְּחִלָּה, "יִירָשֶׁהָ וְתִנָּתֵן לוֹ" — זוֹ הִיא מַתָּנָה בַּסּוֹף, "יִירָשֶׁהָ וְתִנָּתֵן לוֹ וְיִירָשֶׁהָ" — זוֹ הִיא מַתָּנָה בָּאֶמְצַע; וְדַוְקָא בְּאָדָם אֶחָד וְשָׂדֶה אַחַת, אֲבָל בְּאָדָם אֶחָד וּשְׁתֵּי שָׂדוֹת, שָׂדֶה אַחַת וּשְׁנֵי בְּנֵי אָדָם — לֹא. ר' אֶלְעָזָר אוֹמֵר: אֲפִי' אָדָם אֶחָד וּשְׁתֵּי שָׂדוֹת, שָׂדֶה אַחַת וּשְׁנֵי בְּנֵי אָדָם, אֲבָל בִּשְׁתֵּי שָׂדוֹת וּשְׁנֵי בְּנֵי אָדָם — לֹא. כִּי אֲתָא רָבִין אֲמַר: "תִּנָּתֵן שָׂדֶה פְּלוֹנִית לִפְלוֹנִי וְיִירַשׁ פְּלוֹנִי שָׂדֶה פְּלוֹנִית" — רַבִּי יוֹחָנָן אוֹמֵר: קָנָה, רַבִּי אֶלְעָזָר אוֹמֵר: לֹא קָנָה. אֲמַר לֵיהּ אַבָּיֵי לְרָבִין: אַנְחַתְּתְּ לָן חֲדָא וְאַתְקַפְתְּ לָן חֲדָא; בִּשְׁלָמָא דְּר' אֶלְעָזָר אַדְּרַבִּי אֶלְעָזָר לָא קַשְׁיָא: כָּאן בְּאָדָם אֶחָד וּשְׁתֵּי שָׂדוֹת, כָּאן בִּשְׁנֵי בְּנֵי אָדָם וּשְׁתֵּי שָׂדוֹת, אֶלָּא דְּר' יוֹחָנָן אַדְּרַבִּי יוֹחָנָן קַשְׁיָא! אֲמוֹרָאֵי נִינְהוּ וְאַלִּיבָּא דְּרַבִּי יוֹחָנָן. [א]וְרֵישׁ לָקִישׁ אָמַר: (ב) [א]לֹא קָנָה עַד שֶׁיֹּאמַר "פְּלוֹנִי וּפְלוֹנִי יִירְשׁוּ שָׂדֶה פְּלוֹנִית וּפְלוֹנִית שֶׁנְּתַתִּים לָהֶם בְּמַתָּנָה וְיִירָשׁוּם". בִּפְלוּגְתָּא; אָמַר רַב הַמְנוּנָא: לֹא שָׁנוּ אֶלָּא אָדָם אֶחָד וְשָׂדֶה אַחַת, אֲבָל אָדָם אֶחָד וּשְׁתֵּי שָׂדוֹת, שָׂדֶה אַחַת וּשְׁנֵי בְּנֵי אָדָם — לֹא; וְרַב נַחְמָן אָמַר: אֲפִילּוּ אָדָם אֶחָד וּשְׁתֵּי שָׂדוֹת, שָׂדֶה אַחַת וּשְׁנֵי בְּנֵי אָדָם, אֲבָל שְׁתֵּי שָׂדוֹת וּשְׁנֵי בְּנֵי אָדָם — לֹא; [ב]וְרַב שֵׁשֶׁת אָמַר: אֲפִי' שְׁתֵּי שָׂדוֹת וּשְׁנֵי בְּנֵי אָדָם. אָמַר רַב שֵׁשֶׁת: מְנָא אָמִינָא לָהּ? דְּתַנְיָא:(ב) [ג]הָאוֹמֵר "תְּנוּ שֶׁקֶל לְבָנַי בְּשַׁבָּת", וּרְאוּיִן לִיתֵּן סֶלַע — נוֹתֵן לָהֶן סֶלַע; וְאִם אָמַר "אַל תִּתְּנוּ לָהֶן אֶלָּא שֶׁקֶל" — אֵין נוֹתְנִין לָהֶן אֶלָּא שֶׁקֶל; [ד]וְאִם אָמַר "אִם מֵתוּ

יִירְשׁוּ

אי לאפוקי מדרבא. דאמר: אף בראשון – והלא מוסיף הוא על דברי ר' חמא דאמר שלישי בשני כשר, ואתא איהו למימר דאף בראשון, ואיכא למימר דאפי' ר' חמא מודה. והיא גופה אצטריך לר' חמא, לאשמועי' דשלישי בשני כשר, דאיכא למ"ד בסנהדרין פסול, בפרק "זה בורר" (דף כח.). ולאו למידק מיניה הא שלישי בראשון פסול, דדלמא עובדא הוה בשלישי בשני, ושלא ליה דכשר. **אי מדמר בר רב אשי.** דאכשר בחמא דחמא – הא כבר איפסיק דלית הלכתא כוותיה, כדאמרי' לעיל. והך דרשה דמר זוטרא בתר הכי הואי. והכי נמי הויא דמר בר רב אשי תוספת, אלא דעדיפא מיניה קא פריך. **לאפוקי מר' יוחנן.** דאמר: אינו נאמן, כרבנן. **ומאתקפתא דמר בר רב אשי.** דאתא למימר: ודאי משיב אבדה הוא. ולית הלכתא כוותיה. כיון דאכתי כשהודה לא העידו עדים, ולא קמסייעי ליה – איכא למימר דמירתת מינייהו, שאינו יודע מה בלבם, כרבי אבא. **המחלק נכסיו כו'.** כבר פירשתיה למעלה. **כתב בין בתחלה כו'.** אדם הנותן מתנה לאחר, או שנתן כל נכסיו לאחד מבניו, אם אמר לשון מתנה עם לשון ירושה – דבריו קיימין. דנהי דלא תפיס לשון ירושה, לפי שאין אדם מתנה על מה שכתוב בתורה, וכמו שלא אמר כלום דמי – לשון מתנה מיהא תפיס, והרי הוא כמי שאומר לשון מתנה לחוד, דקני. ובגמ' מפרש היכי דמי מתנה באמצע או בתחלה או בסוף. **תנתן שדה פלונית לפלוני ויירשה.** כלומר: ויירש אותה, לישנא דקרא (ג) "וירשוה" (ישעיהו לד), יירשנה ותנתן לו. **ודוקא באדם אחד ושדה אחת.** דבההוא שדה שנתן לאותו האיש איכא מתנה בהדי לשון ירושה. **אבל באדם אחד ושתי שדות.** כגון "יירש ראובן שדה פלונית שבמזרח, ותנתן לו לראובן שדה פלונית שבמערב" – ההוא דלשון מתנה קני, אבל ההוא דלשון ירושה – לא קני. דמתנה דהיאך לא מסייע לאידך, אלא זאת הוריש לו וזאת נתן לו. ובההיא דירושה הוי מתנה על מה שכתוב בתורה, ולא אמר כלום. וכן בשדה אחת ושני בני אדם, כגון "ראובן יירש חצי שדה זו, ותנתן חציה לשמעון" – שמעון קנה, ראובן לא קנה. וכ"ש ב' שדות וב' בני אדם, כגון "ראובן יירש שדה פלונית, ולשמעון תנתן שדה פלונית אחרת". **אפי' אדם אחד ושתי שדות** (ד) דכי היכי דנתכוין לזה ליתן במתנה – הכי נמי נתכוין לאידך, הואיל ובדבור אחד נתן לשניהן. **אבל שתי שדות ושני בני אדם.** דהוו אנשים מוחלקים ושדות מוחלקים – לא מהניא מתנה דהאי גברא ושדה שלו לאידך גברא ולאידך שדה. ובסברות בעלמא פליגי. **כי אתא רבין אמר יירש פלוני כו'.** היינו שתי שדות ושני בני אדם. ומילתא באנפי נפשה היא, ולא איתמר אמתני'. ומיהו, הכי נמי הוה מפרש למתני'. **לא קנה.** ההוא דירושה. **אנחתת לן חדא.** אחד מדבריך נוחה לנו, דלא קשיא לן מידי בגויה. **ואתקפת** (ה) **חדא.** אחד מדבריך קשה לנו. **כאן באדם אחד ושתי שדות.** ההיא דלעיל. והיא סיומא דמלתא דרבי אלעזר דאמרן לעיל: "אבל שתי שדות ושני בני אדם" – לא גמרא קאמר לה ולא רבי אלעזר, דא"כ מאי הולכך לומר דר' אלעזר אדר' אלעזר לא קשיא? הא בהדיא קאמר לעיל דבשתי שדות ושני בני אדם לא קנה. **אמוראי נינהו.** אנא ורב דימי. **וריש לקיש אמר לעולם לא קנה.** בשתי שדות ושני בני אדם ההוא דלשון ירושה, ואפי' כי אמר לשניהן ביחד "תנתן שדה פלונית לראובן ושדה פלונית לשמעון ויירשום". דכיון דגופין מוחלקין נינהו וכל אחד הוי מעשה בפני עצמו, ולא שייך זה בזה כלל, הלכך שתי לשונות של לשון מתנה וירושה – כנגד שני מעשים הן, לאחד לשון מתנה ולאחד לשון ירושה, על ראשון ראשון, ועל אחרון אחרון. הלכך לא קנו עד שיאמר ירושה בתחלה וירושה בסוף ומתנה באמצע דהשתא יליף לשון מתנה מלשון ירושה, דכי היכי דלשון ירושה נאמר לשניהם – גם המתנה שבאמצע נאמרה בעל כרחך לשניהן, דלמאי תרמייה? והלכך צריך לומר כן: "ראובן ושמעון יירשו שדה פלונית ופלונית שנתתי להם במתנה ויירשום". דעל כרחך "יירשו" קמא עולה על ראובן, ובתרא על שמעון. הלכך לשניהן נמי לשון מתנה קאמר, דאיכא תרתי זימני לשון מתנה, דכתב "שנתתי להם", דמיערב אלשון ירושה ואיכא תרי זימני לשון ירושה. אבל אם אמר "פלוני ופלוני יירשו שדה פלונית ופלונית ותנתן להם שדה פלונית ופלונית ויירשום" – הוה אמינא דהאי "ותנתן ויירשום" אשמעון קאי, ולא קנה ראובן, דכיון דשני מעשים הן – יש לחלק להם גם הלשונות. וכן אם אמר "פלוני ופלוני יירשו שדה פלונית ופלונית שנתתי להם במתנה" ולא אמר "ויירשום" לבסוף – אכתי הוה אמינא: לראשון לשון ירושה, ולשני לשון מתנה, דשתי לשונות כנגד שתי מתנות. **בפלוגתא.** דרב המנונא כרב דימי אמר רבי יוחנן, ורב נחמן כר"א, ורב ששת כרבין אליבא דרבי יוחנן. **האומר תנו שקל כו'.** כגון שכיב מרע. אי נמי בריא, וכגון שהלך למדינת הים וצוה ליתן להם כשיעור הזה עד שיכלה הממון כולו. שקל שבתלמוד היינו חצי סלע, שהוא שני דינרין. **נותנין להם סלע.** דלא אמר שקל אלא כדי לזונן בצמצום, שלא יתנו יותר מכדי צרכן. **אל תתנו.** היינו קפידא – אין נותנין להם אלא שקל. בשילהי "מציאת האשה" במס' כתובות מוקמינן לה כר"מ, דאמר: מצוה לקיים דברי המת. ומיהו, אמרי' התם, אמר רב חסדא אמר מר עוקבא: הלכתא, בין שאמר "תנו" בין שאמר "אל תתנו" – נותנין להן כל צרכן. ומקשינן: והא קי"ל כר"מ, דאמר מצוה לקיים דברי המת! ומשנינן: הני מילי – אחרנייתא, אבל בהא מינח ניחא ליה, ומאי דאמר – לזרוזינהו הוא דעבד.

יירשו

אי לאפוקי מדרבא מוסיף הוא. ואפשר דר' אבא נמי מודה לרבא (ו) כדפי' בקונטרס, שלישי בראשון כשר, דלא ממעט הלכתא מילתא דרבא. ואי לאפוקי מדשמואל ורב ששת ודרב פפא — הא איתותבו. אבל ר' אבא בר חמא לא איתותב. ואע"ג דנקט בעדות קרקע, ומשמע — אבל בהלואה כשר אף על גב דנסתמא, ובברייתא משמע דפסיל ליה לכל עדיות — מצינן למימר דהוא הדין בהלואה דפסיל רבי אבא. וקרקע סבירא ליה דמכוין בטוב, כדשמואל, והוי כהלואה, ואפ"ה פסיל ליה. ור"ת פסק בספר הישר דשלישי בראשון פסול. וכן פוסק ה"ג, אלא שהם אינם פוסלים אלא מדרבנן, והוא פוסל מן התורה כדפסיל רב ב"זה בורר". ומפרש הכי: לאפוקי מאי? אי לאפוקי מדרבא — מוסיף הוא על דברי רבי אבא, ואי אתא למפסק דדוקא שלישי בשני כשר ולא שלישי בראשון — א"כ הוה ליה למימר: אין הלכה כרבא. ואי לאפוקי ממר בר רב אשי, כלומר הא דלא קאמר "אין הלכה כרבא", אלא: הלכתא כרבי אבא, משום שרוצה לכלול בהדיא דאין הלכה כמר בר רב אשי — הא לית הלכתא כו'. ואי משום שמואל ורב ששת ורב פפא — אצטריך ליה למימר דהלכה כרבי אבא, שעתה ממעט כולהו ביחד? הא איתותבו, ולימא "אין הלכה כרבא" בהדיא, אי לאפוקי מדידיה לחוד אתא! אלא לאפוקי מר' יוחנן. דהשתא לא מצי למימר דאין הלכה כרבא, ואצטריך ליה למימר דהלכה כרבי אבא דממעט לכולהו, ומפיק נמי מדרבא, דדוקא שלישי בשני כשר. וקשה לר"י: דאי דייקינן ממילתיה דרבי אבא דוקא שלישי בשני — א"כ נידוק נמי דדוקא עדות קרקע, ובהלואה כשר. ובברייתא פוסל הכל.

ודוקא באדם אחד ושדה אחת. לא גרסינן "אמר רבי יוחנן". אלא הכל ממילתיה דרב דימי, ורבין פליג עליה בסמוך. ואמוראי נינהו אליבא דרבי יוחנן.

והלכתא

הגהות הב"ח

(א) גמ' אי מדמר בר רב אשי: (ב) שם וריש לקיש אמר לעולם לא קנה: (ג) רשב"ם ד"ה תנתן וכו' לישנא דקרא וירשוה. נ"ב כך הגיה מהרש"ל וכתב פסוק הוא בישעיה וירשוה קאת וקיפוד בסוף ל"ד: (ד) ד"ה אפילו אדם אחד ושתי שדות שדה אחת ושני בני אדם דכי היכי: (ה) ד"ה ואתקפת לן חדא אחד: (ו) תוס' ד"ה אי לאפוקי וכו' מודה לרבא דשלישי בראשון כשר וכפי' בקונטרס דלא ממעט וכו' אבל ר' אבא דשלא לרבי יוסף בר חמא לא איתותב:

רבינו גרשום

אימור רבא דאמר לעיל אף בראשון כשר מוסיף הוי דלא אתי כלום לגרועי ממילתא דרבה בריה דרב יוסף אלא מוסיף הוי על מלתי' ואתי הלכ' לאפוקי ממאן אי מדשמואל כו'. דפליגי לעיל גבי עדות סומא: אלא לאפוקי מדר' יוחנן. דאמר לעיל על תינוק דאינו נאמן כרבנן דלית הלכתא כותי' אלא כר' יהודה דהאב מהימן להכיר לאחרים. ולאפוקי נמי מאתקפתא דמר בר רב אשי דלית הלכת' כוותי' אלא מלוה ישבע וגובה מחצה וכדמתרצי' אליבא דר' עקיבא: **פיסקא** המחלק נכסיו על פיו. היינו שכיב מרע דלא צריך לא קנין ולא כתיבה כי אם באמירה בעלמא כו': זו היא מתנה בתחלה. דקאמר תחלה תנתן ואחר כך יירשה: אמר ר' יוחנן. דוקא דמסייע מתנה בין בסוף בין בתחלה בין באמצע. בשדה אחת שנתנה לאדם אחד אע"ג דקאמר יירשה קנה. אבל אם אמר לאדם אחד תהי' לך שדה זו במתנה ושדה אחרת בירושה או שדה אחת ושני בני אדם דאמר תהא חציה לאדם זה במתנה ולזה חציה בירושה אמרי' דלא קנה לא האי ולא האי משום דחדא הוא מודעא לחבירתה ומדהא דירושה לא קנה האי נמי דמתנה לא קנה: ור' אלעזר אומר אפי' באדם אחד ושתי שדות ושדה אחת ושני בני אדם קנה דלא הוה מודעא לחבירתה ומדהאי דמתנה קנה האי נמי דבירושה קנה. אבל אם אמר בשתי שדות ושני בני אדם לזה חדא בירושה ולזה אידך במתנה לא קנה דהוי מודעא חדא לחבירתה דכי האי דירושה לא קנה דאין ירושה אלא לאחר מיתה האי נמי דמתנה לא קנה: כי אתי רבין אמר. יירש פלוני שדה פלונית ותנתן לפלוני שדה פלונית אחרת דהיינו שתי שדות ושני בני אדם ר' אלעזר אומר לא קנה: אנחתת לן חדא ואתקפת לן חדא. כלומר חדא מהני לישני אתי בניחותא ואידך בלשון קושיא: בשלמא דר' אלעזר אדר' אלעזר לא קשיא. הא דלעיל דאמר קנה איכא לאוקמי דבאדם אחד ושתי שדות הואיל דאדם אחד לא הוי חדא מודעא לחבירתה וכי היכי דקני מתנה קני נמי ירושה. והא דכי אתא רבין אמר ר' אלעזר לא קנה היינו בשני בני אדם ושתי שדות דחד הויא מודעא לחבריה: אלא דר' יוחנן אדר' יוחנן קשיא. דלעיל אמר באדם אחד ושתי שדות לא קנה וכל שכן בשני בני אדם ושתי שדות דלא קנה אמאי אמר רבין דר' יוחנן אמר דקנה: אמוראי נינהו ואליבא דר' יוחנן. דחד אמר דר' יוחנן אמר דוקא שדה אחת ואדם אחד קנה וחד אמר אפי' בשתי שדות ושני בני אדם אמר ר' יוחנן דקנה. וריש לקיש אתי לפלוני על ר' יוחנן. והכי קאמר הא דאמרת דמשום הכי קנה דאמר מתנה בין באמצע בין בתחלה בין בסוף דוקא בשדה אחת ואדם אחד. וריש לקיש אמר אפי' בשני בני אדם ושתי שדות ולעולם לא קני עד שאמר פלוני ופלוני יירשו שדה פלונית ופלונית במתנה שנתתי להם דמשמע שנתתי להם כבר קודם ירושה וירושה אע"ג דכתב מתנה באמצע בתר ירושה כיון דאמר נתתי משמע שנתתי להם לשעבר קודם לכן. ובענין דתיהוי מתנה בכולה קודם ירושה. ורבנו שנתתי בתר דאמר יירשו דמשמע השתא דאמר להו מתנה בין קודם ירושה בין לאחר ירושה ובין באמצע. ובפלוגתא דר' יוחנן ור' אלעזר וריש לקיש פליגי הכא דרב המנונא סבירא ליה כר' יוחנן ור' נחמן ס"ל כר' אלעזר ורב ששת סבירא ליה כריש לקיש: שכיב מרע האומר תנו שקל לבני למזונות לשבת. לשבוע הואיל וראוין לתת להם סלע על שטיפולן מרובה נותנין להם סלע והא דקאמר תנו להם שקל לא אמר אלא בשביל לצמצם להם ממון שלא יפסידוהו. אבל אם (אמר) אין דיי להם בזה תנו להם יותר. ואם אמר אל תתנו להם כל עיקר אלא שקל. או שאמר תנו להם שקל ואם מתו בני

יירשו

פז א מיי' פי"ב מהל' זכייה ומתנה הלכה ז ועיין בהשגות ובמ"מ סמג עשין פב טוש"ע חו"מ סי' רמח סעיף ג:

פח ב מיי' שם הלכה ו ועי' בהשגות ובמ"מ טוש"ע שם סעיף א:

פט ג מיי' פ"ו מהלכות נחלות הלכה ו סמג עשין צו טוש"ע חו"מ סי' רפא סעיף ז:

צ ד מיי' שם ופ"ב מהלכות שבועות הל' יז ופ"כ מהל' עדות הל' ג ועי' בהשגות ובכ"מ ופ"ח מהל' אבל הלכה ח ופ"ב מהל' תמורה הל' ד סמג עשין צו וקז ולאוין רמא טוש"ע שם וסי' כט סעיף א וטוש"ע יו"ד סי' רלד סעיף לא לב לג וסי' שמ סעיף כד כה:

צא ה מיי' פ"ג מהל' עבודת כוכבים הל"ד:

יִירְשׁוּ אֲחֵרִים תַּחְתֵּיהֶם", בֵּין שֶׁאָמַר "תְּנוּ" בֵּין שֶׁאָמַר "אַל תִּתְּנוּ" — אֵין נוֹתְנִין לָהֶן אֶלָּא שֶׁקֶל; וְהָא הָכָא דִּכְשְׁתֵּי שָׂדוֹת וְכִשְׁנֵי בְּנֵי אָדָם דָּמֵי, וְקָתָנֵי דְּקָנֵי! הוּא מוֹתִיב לָהּ, וְהוּא מְפָרֵק לָהּ: בְּרָאוּי לְיוֹרְשׁוֹ, א)וְר' יוֹחָנָן בֶּן בְּרוֹקָה הִיא. אָמַר רַב אַשִׁי, תָּא שְׁמַע: ב)א"נְכָסַי לְךָ, וְאַחֲרֶיךָ יִירַשׁ פְּלוֹנִי, וְאַחֲרֵי אַחֲרֶיךָ יִירַשׁ פְּלוֹנִי", מֵת רִאשׁוֹן — קָנָה שֵׁנִי, מֵת שֵׁנִי — קָנָה שְׁלִישִׁי, וְאִם מֵת שֵׁנִי בְּחַיֵּי רִאשׁוֹן — יַחְזְרוּ נְכָסִים לְיוֹרְשֵׁי רִאשׁוֹן; וְהָא הָכָא דִּכְשְׁתֵּי שָׂדוֹת וּשְׁנֵי בְּנֵי אָדָם דָּמֵי, וְקָתָנֵי דְּקָנָה! וְכִי תֵּימָא: הָכָא נַמִּי בְּרָאוּי לְיוֹרְשׁוֹ, וְר' יוֹחָנָן בֶּן בְּרוֹקָה הִיא, אִי הָכִי, מֵת שֵׁנִי קָנָה שְׁלִישִׁי? הָא ג)שָׁלַח רַב אַחָא בְּרֵי' דְּרַב עַוְיָא: לְדִבְרֵי ר' יוֹחָנָן בֶּן בְּרוֹקָה, ב"נְכָסַי לְךָ וְאַחֲרֶיךָ לִפְלוֹנִי", וְרִאשׁוֹן רָאוּי לְיוֹרְשׁוֹ — אֵין לַשֵּׁנִי בִּמְקוֹם רִאשׁוֹן כְּלוּם, שֶׁאֵין זֶה לְשׁוֹן מַתָּנָה אֶלָּא לְשׁוֹן יְרוּשָּׁה, וִירוּשָּׁה אֵין לָהּ הֶפְסֵק! תְּיוּבְתָּא ד)דְכוּלְּהוּ. תְּיוּבְתָּא. לֵימָא נַמִּי תֶּיהֱוֵי תְּיוּבְתֵּיהּ דְּרֵישׁ לָקִישׁ! וְתִסְבְּרָא? ה)וְהָא אָמַר רָבָא: הִלְכְתָא כְּוָותֵיהּ דְּרֵישׁ לָקִישׁ בְּהָנֵי תְּלָת! לָא קַשְׁיָא: גכָּאן בְּתוֹךְ כְּדֵי דִבּוּר, כָּאן לְאַחַר כְּדֵי דִבּוּר. ו)דוְהִלְכְתָא: כָּל תּוֹךְ כְּדֵי דִבּוּר כְּדִבּוּר דָּמֵי, הלְבַר מֵעֲבוֹדָה זָרָה וְקִדּוּשִׁין.

והלכתא דתוך כדי דבור כדבור דמי. פי' ר"ת: דלך אמר כדבור דמי כדי שאילת תלמיד לרב, היינו "שלום עליך רבי", לפי שכשאדם עושה סחורה עם חבירו, ויראה רבו או גדול הימנו בחכמה — לא יתן לו שלום, שאם יתן לו שלום — לא יוכל לחזור בו ממקחו, לכך תקנו חכמים שכשיעור זה יכול לחזור. וקשה לר"י: בפ' בתרא דנדרים (דף פז.) תניא: מי שיש לו חולה בתוך ביתו ונתעלף, כמדומה לו שמת, וקרע, ואח"כ מת — לא יצא ידי קריעה. ואמר ר"ש בן פזי אמר ר"ש בן לוי: לא שנו אלא אחר כדי דבור, אבל תוך כדי דבור — אינו חוזר וקורע. והתם לא שייך האי טעמא! וי"ל: דלא פלוג רבנן[כ]. **חוץ** מעבודה זרה וקדושין. פי' רשב"ם: שאם התפיס או הקלה דבר לעבודה זרה, ובתוך כדי דבור חזר בו — אפ"ה נאסר. ואין נראה לר"י, דהתפסה לא שייכא בעבודה זרה, דאמרי' בפ' "כל הצלמים" (ע"ז דף מד:): האומר "בית זה לעבודה זרה" — לא אמר כלום, שאין הקדש לעבודה זרה. ואמרינן נמי בפ' "כל האסורין" (תמורה כח: ושם) דאי מוקצה לעבודה זרה אלא שבע שנים, שנא' (שופטים ו) "ואת הפר השני שבע שנים", ועד שימסרנו (ב) לעבודה זרה, ויאכילנה כרשיני עבודה זרה. והתם לא שייך תוך כדי דבר. ויש לפרש: דאם ימכרנו לכהנים של עבודה זרה ע"מ לפטמו שבע שנים — הוי מוקצה, ואפילו חזר בו תוך כדי דבור לא מהני. ור"י פי': עבודה זרה — שא"ל "אלי אתה" וחזר תוך כדי דבור, דלא מהני מיד. ויכול להיות שהוא גזירת הכתוב. ובפ' בתרא דנדרים (דף פז.) קאמר: והלכתא, תוך כדי דבור — כדבור דמי, לבר מעבודה זרה ומגדף ומקדש ומגרש. פירוש: מגדף — שאם גידף וחזר בו תוך כדי דבור לא מהני מידי. וגמרא קיצר כאן, משום דמגדף הוי בכלל עבודה זרה, ומגרש בכלל מקדש, כי טעם אחד להם.

הלכה

יירשו אחרים. פלוני ופלוני, ולא בני בניי, גלי אדעתיה דניחא ליה בגלמוס טפי, כי היכי דלישתייר מהנהו נכסי להנהו אחרים, ודווקא קאמר שקל. **והא הכא.** דקאמר לשון מתנה לבניו כדקתני "תנו שקל לבני", ולשון ירושה לאחרים כדקתני "יירשו אחרים", וקתני דקנו הנהו אחרים. דמשום הכי קאמר בסיפא: אין נותנין להם אלא שקל — כדי לשייר מן הנכסים להנהו אחרים. ואע"ג דכשתי שדות ושני בני אדם דמי, דלבניו נתן שקל בכל שבת כל ימי חייהם והמותר מוריש לאחרים תחתיהן, והיינו כעין ב' שדות וב' בני אדם — שאין זוכין זה בחיי זה כלל, הלכך שתי שדות נינהו. ואפ"ה קנו אחרים, דמהני לשון מתנה דהאי (א) ולשון ירושה דהיאך, כרב ששת. **הוא מותיב לה והוא מפרק לה.** דלא תקשי לחביריו: בראוי ליורשו. דהאי דקנו אחרים בלשון ירושה — לאו משום דמהני ליה לשון מתנה דאידך, אלא משום דהני אחרים הוו ראוים ליורשו, כגון בניו. והיכי דמי — כגון דלשנים מבניו צוה לתת שקל בשבת, ואם מתו — יירש אחד משאר בניו כל המותר. ואע"ג דאיכא עוד בנים אחרים, ואיכא נמי בנים להני שמתו. וכרבי יוחנן בן ברוקה, דאמר לקמן דאם אמר על בן בין הבנים "יירש כל נכסיי" — דבריו קיימין. והלכך, אין נותנין להם אלא שקל, דניחא ליה דישתייר קצת לזה שהוא אוהב ומתכוין להורישו הכל. ולמאי דאמרי' לקמן דפליגי רבנן עליה דר' ישמעאל בנו של ר' יוחנן בן ברוקה, ומוקמינן לפלוגתא דרבי יוחנן בן ברוקה באחר במקום בת, ובת במקום בן, דלר' יוחנן בן ברוקה יכול להוריש כל נכסיו לההוא הראוי ליורשו אחר מיתת בנו, וה"נ בראוי ליורשו, כגון אחר במקום בן, מיירי. וה"ק: דאם מתו בניי יירשו אחיי, הראוים ליורשי ז) תחתיהן. ה"ג: נכסיי לך ואחריך יירש פלוני ואחרי אחריך יירש פלוני מת ראשון קנה שני מת שני קנה שלישי ואם מת שני בחיי ראשון יחזרו נכסים ליורשי ראשון. והכי פירושו: "נכסיי לך" — היינו לשון מתנה, כלומר: נכסיי נתונים לך, "ואחריך יירש פלוני" — הרי לזה במתנה ולזה בירושה, וכשתי שדות דמי, שאין לשני בחיי ראשון כלום — הרי מתנות מוחלקין ומקבלי מתנות מוחלקין, ואפ"ה קתני: קנה שני. אלמא: לשון מתנה דראשון מהני לשני. **יחזרו נכסים ליורשי ראשון.** דהא מכח השני נתן לשלישי אחריו, וכיון דשני לא זכה — שלישי מנא ליה? וכ"ת ה"נ. האי שני — בראוי ליורשו, כגון בן בין הבנים, ואגב ריהטיה אשמועינן כר' יוחנן בן ברוקה דשני קני בלשון ירושה, הואיל וראוי ליורשו ולהכי מהני ביה לשון ירושה, כרבי יוחנן בן ברוקה — אמאי כשמת שני קנה שלישי מכחו? **הא שלח רב אחא כו'.** דירושה אין לה הפסק, וכיון דהאי שני בתורת ירושה באו לידו — אין כח ביד המת לעקור נחלה מיורשי יורשיו לתתה להאי שלישי, אלא יחזרו נכסים ליורשי שני. דכיון דעשאו להאי שני יורש, כי אמר נמי: בתריה דהאי יורש אני נותן לשלישי — ה"ל מתנה על מה שכתוב בתורה, דכתיב: "ובן אין לו" — עיין עליו, דאשמועינן קרא דכל הקודם בנחלה יוצאי ירכו קודמין. וכ"ש היכא דהוא עצמו יורש את הנחלה, שאין כח בידינו להעבירה מבניו. **לדברי ר' יוחנן בן ברוקה.** דס"ל דאב יכול להוריש בלשון ירושה לאחד מבניו כל נכסיו. **אם אמר לאחד מהם נכסי לך.** כדמפרש לקמיה. וראשון ראוי ליורשו, ולא פירש לא לשון ירושה ולא לשון מתנה — אין לשני במקום ראשון, או יורשי ראשון, כלום. שאין כאן לשון מתנה להאי ראשון, אלא מסתמא לשון ירושה איכוין הנותן במאי דאמר "נכסיי לך", הואיל וחזי לירש כל הנכסים מן התורה אם ירצה אביו. וכיון דירושה הויא להאי ראשון — אינו יכול להפסיקה, דאין ירושה לחצאין. ולקמן בפרקין פרכינן: הא אפסקיה כו'. ודווקא לר' יוחנן בן ברוקה. אבל לרבנן, כיון דאינו יכול להרבות ירושה בזה יותר מזה בלשון ירושה כלל, ודאי מאי דאמר "נכסיי לך" לראשון — לשון מתנה הוא, ויכול להפסיקה, ויקנה שלישי. **תיובתא דכולהו.** בר מרבין אליבא דר' יוחנן, ורב ששת. **תיובתיה דר"ל.** דאמר: לשון מתנה לזה לא מהני ללשון ירושה לזה. **האמר רבא.** בפרק "השולח" הלכתא כו', וזו אחת מהן. ואם איתא דהויא ברייתא תיובתיה — לא פסקינן הלכתא הכי. **לא קשיא.** הא דקתני: מתנה לזה וירושה לזה דקנו שניהן — לא קשיא לר"ל דאמר לא קנה; ברייתא — דקאמר "ואחריך יירש פלוני" תוך כדי דבור הראשון דקאמר "נכסיי לך", הלכך כהני מתנה דראשון גם לשני. והאי דקאמר ר"ל: לא קנה בשתי שדות ושני בני אדם — האי לשון ירושה היינו לאחר כדי דיבור, ולהכי לא מהני ליה לשון מתנה דהאי אלשון ירושה דאידך. וה"ק ר"ל: לעולם לא קנה בלאחר כדי דבור עד שיאמר פלוני ופלוני כו'. והלכך, כיון דקאמר לשון מתנה אתרווייהו, אפילו לאחר כדי דבור — שפיר דמי. ומיהו, רב דימי ור"א איתותבו לגמרי, דאמרי: לא קנה אלא בשדה אחת או אדם אחד, אבל שתי שדות ושני בני אדם לא. דלדידהו אפילו תוך כדי דבור אמרי לא קנה. דאם איתא דקנה בשתי שדות ושני בני אדם תוך כדי דבור — לישמעינן דקנה, וכ"ש שדה אחת ואדם אחד לרב דימי, ושתי שדות ואדם אחד או שני בני אדם בשדה אחת לר"א — אפילו לאחר כדי דבור. אלא מדלא ידעו למצוא דליהני לשון מתנה ללשון ירושה אלא באדם אחד ובשדה אחת — מכלל דבשתי שדות ושני בני אדם לעולם לא קנה, בין תוך כדי דבור בין לאחר כדי דבור. **תוך כדי דבור.** היינו כדי שאילת תלמיד לרב, כדאמר בפ"ק דמס' מכות (דף ו.) א"ל רב אחא מדפתי לרבינא: מכדי, תוך כדי דבור היכי דמי — כדי שאילת תלמיד לרב כו'. ושאילת תלמיד לרב — "שלום עליך רבי", כדאמרי' בפרק "מרובה" (ב"ק דף עג:): כי לית ליה לר' יוסי — כדי שאילת תלמיד לרב "שלום עליך רבי" כו'. **והלכתא** כל תוך כדי דבור כדבור דמי. כל שני דברים שאדם מוציא מפיו זה אחר זה, בתוך כדי דבור שסיים דבור הראשון התחיל דבור האחרון — לא חשבינן ליה נמלך, אלא הרי הוא כאילו אמר שני דברים ביחד. ואם שניהם יכולים לתפוס, כגון: ח)"הרי זו תמורת עולה תמורת שלמים" — תמכר, ויביא בדמי חציה עולה ובדמי חציה שלמים, דהא לשניהן איתכוין אלא שאין יכול להוציא שני דברים כאחד. ואם האחד יש בו כח לתפוס, והאחד אינו כלום — יתפוס האחד, והאחד כמאן דליתיה. כגון ירושה ומתנה לאחד — לשון ירושה בטל, ולשון מתנה קונה. ואם שניהם סותרין זה את זה, כי היכי דאמר בפ' "בית כור" (לעיל דף קד:), כגון "מדה בחבל הן חסר הן יתר", וכגון ט) "איסתרא מאה מעי", וכגון י) מעשה דשכירות מרחץ בי"ב זהובים לשנה בדינר זהב לחדש — יש מהן שאומר תפוס לשון ראשון, ויש שאומר שתפוס לשון אחרון, ויש שמספקא ליה ואומר יחלוקו, ויש שהולך אחר המוחזק. ושם פירשתי דיניהן. והיכא דהדר ביה בהדיא תוך כדי דבור, דאמר "חוזרני בי" — הכל מודים דהויא חזרה. **לבר מעבודה זרה.** שאם התפיס או הקלה דבר לעבודה זרה, ובתוך כדי דבור חזר בו — אפ"ה נאסרה, משום חומרא דעבודה זרה. וכדאמר' נמי בעבודה זרה: "שקץ תשקצנו", דאע"ג דאתי מדינא להיתרא — אסור. **וקדושין.**

רבינו גרשום

יירשו אחרים נכסי תחתיהן ולא בניהן משמע השתא דבעין רעה נותן להם. אין נותנין להם אלא שקל משום עין רעה ואחרים יירשו תחתיהן: והא הכא דכשתי שדות ושני בני אדם דמי. דלבניו אמר תנו להם שקל ולאידך אמר יירשו תחתיהן מה ששייר להן הויא לה לזה במתנה ולזה בירושה דומיא דשתי שדות ושני בני אדם וקתני דקנו בניו ואחרים וקשיא לר' יוחנן ור' אלעזר דסברי דשני בני אדם ושתי שדות לא קנו: בראוי ליורשו. שאותו שאמר יירשו אחרים תחתיהן אותם אחרים או אחיו או בתו היו דראוין הן ליורשו במקום שאין בנים אבל היכא דאין ראוי ליורשו לא קנה ור' יוחנן בן ברוקה הוא. דאמר במתני' אם אמר על מי שראוי ליורשו דבריו קיימין: ת"ש. שכיב מרע שאמר לאחר נכסי נתונות לך ואחריך יירש פלוני ואחריך כו' אין לראשון אלא פירות של קרקע ולאחרים יהי' הגוף לו והפירות. מת ראשון קנה שני כדאמר המצוה ומת שני בחיי ראשון דלא באו נכסים ברשות שני וכשימות הראשון אין נותנין הנכסים לשלישי דשלישי היה לו לירש השני אם באו ליד שני והואיל ולא באו ליד שני אין נותנין לשלישי כלום אלא יחזרו נכסים ליורשי ראשון כדקיימי: והא הכא כשתי שדות ושני בני אדם דמיין. מאי דיהיב לראשון פירות יהיב ליה בלשון מתנה ולאידך יהיב גוף הקרקע בירושה דקאמר ואחריך [יירש] היינו יורש ודומיא דב' שדות ושני בני אדם הן ואפי' הכי קתני דקנו: וכי תימא בראוי ליורשו האי שני להכי קני. אי הכי אם מת שני אמאי קני שלישי והא שלח רב אחא כו'. שאין חשוב לשון מתנה מה שנתן לו אלא לשון ירושה חשיב הואיל וראוי ליורשו הוא וירושה אין לה הפסק כלומר מי שראוי ליורשו אחרי שנתן לו בירושה שוב אינה פוסקת אותה ירושה מזרע זרעו ואין לאחרים במקום יורש כלום ולא יורש אחר. אלא לאו ש"מ האי ואחריך לאו בראוי ליורשו הוא וקתני דקנו: תיובתא דכולהו תנאי. דאמרי לעיל להיכא דאמר להאי שדה זו בירושה ולאידך שדה זו במתנה לא דהויא ירושה מודעא לחבירתה למתנה והכא איכא למישמע דקני: ולימא תהוי תיובתא דריש לקיש. דמהכא איכא למישמע מינה להיכא דאמר נכסיי לך ואחריך לפלוני מת ראשון קני שני [מת שני] קנה שלישי אע"ג דלא אמר מתנה אלא לחד מינייהו לראשון ולשני ולשלישי בירושה ואפ"ה קני וריש לקיש אמר לעיל דלא קני עד שאמר פלוני ופלוני יירשו שדה פלונית ופלונית שנתתי להם דמשמע דלכל חד וחד צריך נתינה: חדא הא דלעיל. אידך דקאמר פירות לאו כקנין הגוף דמי. ואידך אשה מעוברת א) אם חלצה כשרה אם סאו שמת בנה והלכתא כוותיה כי היכי דתניא במתני' דיבמות (דף לו.): לא קשיא הכא. בנכסיי לך ואחריך לפלוני אמאי קנו כולם אע"ג דלא אמר מתנה אלא לראשון בלבד היינו טעמא דקנו בתוך כדי דבור דאמר נכסיי לך אמר נמי מיד ואחריך לפלוני כיון בתוך כדי נתינה דראשון (דמי בניו) דשייכי הני תרי בנתינה דראשון להכי קנו כולן אבל אם אמר אחר כדי דבור ושהא ואמר אחריך לפלוני לא קנו דהויא חדא מודעא לחברתה: לבר מעבודה זרה וקדושין

א) נראה דצ"ל אשה מעוברת שחלצה אינה חליצה ואפי' הפילה אח"כ.

מסורת הש"ס

א) [לקמן קל.] ב) [שם קלג:] ג) [שם קלב:] ד) [ועי' תוס' כתובות מח: ד"ה תיובתא] ה) יבמות לו. חולין עו. ו) נדרים פז. ז) פי' של בני בניו רש"ל ח) [תמורה כו:] ט) [לעיל קה:] י) [שם עג:] כ) וע"ע תוס' ב"ק עג: ד"ה כי וכו' ובכ"ז נדרים פז. ד"ה והלכתא]

הגהות הב"ח

(א) רשב"ם ד"ה והא הכא וכו' לשון מתנה דהאי ולשון ירושה: (ב) תוס' ד"ה חוץ וכו' שימסרנו לכומרי ע"ז:

מסורת הש"ס

א) לעיל קכב: קכט: לקמן קלג. קמח: ב) [עי' תוס' יבמות לו: ד"ה ואמר]:

עין משפט נר מצוה

צב א מיי' פ"ז מהלכות אישות הלכה כב סמג עשין מח טוש"ע אה"ע סי' מט סעיף ג:

צג ב מיי' פ"ו מהל' נחלות הלכה ב סמג עשין צו טוש"ע חו"מ סי' רפא סעיף א:

צד ג מיי' שם ופי"ב מהל' זכיה ומתנה הל"א סמג שם טוש"ע שם:

(א) [א]וקדושין.§ **מתני'** [ב]האומר "איש פלוני יירשני" במקום שיש בת, "בתי תירשני" במקום שיש בן – לא אמר כלום, שהתנה על מה שכתוב בתורה; [א]ר' יוחנן בן ברוקה אומר: [ג]אם אמר על מי שראוי ליורשו – דבריו קיימין, ועל מי שאין ראוי לו ליורשו – אין דבריו קיימין.§

גמ' טעמא דאחר במקום בת ובת במקום בן, הא בן בין הבנים ובת בין הבנות – דבריו קיימין; אימא סיפא, רבי יוחנן בן ברוקה אומר: אם אמר על מי שראוי ליורשו – דבריו קיימין; היינו תנא קמא! וכי תימא: רבי יוחנן בן ברוקה אפילו אחר במקום בת ובת במקום בן קאמר – והתניא, רבי ישמעאל בנו של רבי יוחנן בן ברוקה אומר: לא נחלקו אבא וחכמים על אחר במקום בת ובת במקום בן, שלא אמר כלום. על מה נחלקו? על בן בין הבנים ובת בין הבנות, שאבא אומר: יירש, וחכמים אומרים: לא יירש! איבעית אימא: מדקאמר "לא נחלקו", מכלל דתנא קמא סבר נחלקו. איבעית אימא: כולה דרבי יוחנן בן ברוקה היא, וחסורי מחסרא והכי קתני: האומר "איש פלוני יירשני" במקום שיש בת, "בתי תירשני" במקום שיש בן – לא אמר כלום; הא בת בין הבנות ובן בין הבנים, אם אמר יירש כל נכסיו – דבריו קיימין, שר' יוחנן אומר: אם אמר על מי שראוי ליורשו – דבריו קיימין. אמר רב יהודה אמר שמואל: הלכה כרבי יוחנן בן ברוקה. וכן [ב]אמר רבא: הלכה כר' יוחנן בן ברוקה. אמר רבא: מאי טעמיה דרבי יוחנן בן ברוקה? אמר קרא: °"והיה ביום הנחילו את בניו", התורה נתנה רשות לאב להנחיל לכל מי שירצה. אמר ליה אביי: הא מ"לא יוכל לבכר" נפקא! ההוא מיבעי ליה לכדתניא, אבא חנן אמר משום רבי אליעזר: מה

דברים כא

רש"י

וקדושין. שאם קידש אשה בפני עדים, וחזר ואמר בתוך כדי דבור: ליהוי מתנה ולא ליהוי קדושין – אין שומעין לו, ומקודשת ואינה מקודשת. וחומרא דרבנן היא, משום לעז ממזרות אם תנשא לאחר בלא גט. **מתני'** האומר איש פלוני יירשני. אפי' אחיו, במקום שיש לההוא מלוה בת. או בתי תירשני. ויש לו בן. לא אמר כלום. שעקר את הירושה ממקומה. ודייקינן בגמרא: הא בן בין הבנים, דראוי לירש קצת – קנה גם הכל. ולפום הך דיוקא לא מתוקמא הך סיפא אליבא דההוא תנא דלעיל, דקתני גבי ריבה לאחד ומיעט לאחד שאם אמר משום ירושה – לא אמר כלום, דהיינו בן בין הבנים, ואפ"ה קתני רישא דלא קני. ובגמרא מתרלינן לה. אם אמר על מי שראוי ליורשו. השתא משמע לן – כגון שהוא ראוי ליורשו במקצת, כגון בן בין הבנים, והלכך דבריו קיימין אם אמר יירש הכל. ועל מי שאין ראוי ליורשו – כגון אחיו במקום בתו, או בתו במקום בנו. **גמ'** טעמא. דהוי מתנה על מה שכתוב בתורה – דקמוריש לאחר במקום בת, דלא חזי השתא למירת מידי. אימא סיפא אם אמר על מי שראוי ליורשו דבריו קיימין היינו תנא קמא. דהכי משמע: על מי שראוי ליורשו עכשיו, דהיינו בן בין הבנים, או בת בין הבנות במקום שאין בן. וכי תימא. קפליג ר' יוחנן עליה דת"ק אפי' אאחר במקום בת. דשמעי' לת"ק דחשיב ליה מתנה על מה שכתוב בתורה אפי' בנו בין הבנים או בת בין הבנות, כדקתני רישא גבי ריבה לאחד ומיעט לאחד, שאם אמר משום ירושה – לא אמר כלום, וכ"ש באחר במקום בת, כדקתני סיפא: האומר "איש פלוני יירשני" כו' ו"זו ואין צריך לומר זו" קתני. א"נ, להכי תנייה להך סיפא, לאשמועינן דאפי' באחר במקום בת אתא ר' יוחנן לאיפלוגי עליה דת"ק ולמימר דבריו קיימין. ורישא נמי רבותא קתני, דאפילו בבן בין הבנים אמרי רבנן אין דבריו קיימין. ונמלא רישא מיתניא להשמיענו כח דרבנן, דאפילו בבן בין הבנים אמרי לא אמר כלום, וסיפא מיתניא להשמיענו כח דר' יוחנן בן ברוקה, דאפילו באחר במקום בת פליג אדרבנן ואמר דבריו קיימין. ולא למידק מינה כדדייקינן לעיל: טעמא דאחר במקום בת כו', דהוא הדין נמי לבן בין הבנים דלא אמר כלום. אלא משום רבי יוחנן בן ברוקה נקטיה, דאתא רבי יוחנן בן ברוקה למימר: אם אמר על מי שראוי היום ולמחר ליורשו אחר שתמות בתו – דבריו קיימין, ואע"ג דהשתא מיהא לא חזי ליורשו. ואם אין ראוי ליורשו אחר בתו, כגון דודו, ויש לו אחין דאחין קודמין לאחי אביו – לא אמר כלום, הואיל ואין ראוי ליורשו עד שתמות בתו ואחיו. ומשנינן: מדקאמר רבי ישמעאל לא נחלקו מכלל דפליגי חבירייו עליו ואמרין נחלקו. ומתני' רבנן היא, דמוקמי לפלוגתייהו אפילו באחר במקום בת, ומתני' כולה כדפרישית. ואיבעית אימא. לא פליגי רבנן עליה דרבי ישמעאל, אלא דכולי עלמא מודו דלא פליגי באחר במקום בת, דודאי לא אמר כלום, אלא בבן בין הבנים הוא דפליגי רבנן ורבי יוחנן בן ברוקה. והאי דקאמר, רבי יוחנן בן ברוקה אומר: אם אמר על מי שראוי ליורשו דבריו קיימין – היינו בבן בין הבנים, דראוי השתא ליורשו. ודקאמר: רבי יוחנן בן ברוקה היינו ת"ק – תריץ: כולה מתני' דהך בבא בתרייתא – רבי יוחנן בן ברוקה היא, (ב) דשמעי' לת"ק דאמר גבי ריבה לאחד ומיעט לאחד דאם אמר משום ירושה לא אמר כלום, דהיינו בן בין הבנים, ואתא איהו למימר דיירית. והכי קתני: האומר "איש פלוני יירשני" במקום שיש בת, "בתי תירשני" במקום שיש בן – לא אמר כלום. שרבי יוחנן בן ברוקה אומר: אם אמר על מי שראוי ליורשו, כגון בן בין הבנים ובת בין הבנות – הוא דדבריו קיימין. אבל אמר על מי שאינו ראוי ליורשו, כגון שאמר "איש פלוני יירשני" במקום שיש בת, או "בתי תירשני" במקום שיש בן – לא אמר כלום. הלכה כרבי יוחנן בן ברוקה. וכדמשמע סתמא דמתניתין, דמשמע דבבן בין הבנים קאמר, כדדייקינן לעיל וכדאוקימנא דכולה רבי יוחנן בן ברוקה היא. ואיכא נמי למידק מדלא קאמר שמואל: הלכה כרבי יוחנן בן ברוקה אפי' אחר במקום בת וכת במקום בן. וטעמא דרבי יוחנן בן ברוקה דמפרש' לקמן, מ"ביום הנחילו את בניו", משמע נמי דבבן בין הבנים קאמר. ולעיל נמי הכי אמרינן, אמר אביי: הכי קאמר, האומר על תינוק בין הבנים "יירש כל נכסיי" – נאמן, כרבי יוחנן בן ברוקה. מכלל דהוה סבירא להו דלא פליג אלא בבן בין הבנים. הלכך, ל"ש אם אמר "פלוני בני יירש חצי נכסיי" לא שנא אם אמר "יירש כל נכסיי" – דבריו קיימין, ואפי' אם כתב כן, דלא שנא אם אמר ל"ש כותב, כדמוכח לקמן בפירקין (דף קלג.): א"ר הונא שכיב מרע שכתב כל נכסיו לאחר – רואין, אם ראוי ליורשו – נוטלן משום ירושה. וא"ל ר"נ: גנבי גנובי למה לך? אי סבירא לך כרבי יוחנן בן ברוקה – אימא: הלכתא כר' יוחנן בן ברוקה, דשמעתך כר' יוחנן בן ברוקה קא אזלא. והא דאמרינן לקמן, אמר שמואל: הכותב כל נכסיו לאשתו לא עשאה אלא אפוטרופא, ואמרינן: הוא הדין נמי לבנו, דאם כתב לו כל נכסיו לא עשאו אלא אפוטרופא – ה"מ כותב לשון מתנה, או אומר לשון מתנה, דלכבודו איכוין להקנות לו נכסיו. אבל לשון ירושה – קנה הכל, כדין תורה, כדנפקא לן מ"ביום הנחילו את בניו". דבשלמא לשון מתנה – איכא למימר דהקנה לו הני נכסים להיותן בחזקתו כדין אפוטרופא, שגם כשעשאו אפוטרופוס נתקיימה מתנתו, שיש נותן מתנה גמורה ויש שנותן מתנת אפוטרופוס. אבל ירושה – אינה יכולה להיות אלא אם כן קונה הנכסים קנין גמור. דלשון ירושה משמע שקם תחת המוריש לקנות נכסיו לגמרי, ולהיות מוחזק בהן להיות שלו כמורישו, אבל אם אינו אלא אפוטרופוס – נמצא שלא הוריש לו כלום. וגם בהלכות גדולות מצאתי סייג לדברי. והני מילי – כשאין בכור, אז יכול להנחיל כל נכסיו לאחד מהן. אבל אם יש בכור – אינו יכול להנחיל חלקו לאחד מהן, כדנפקא לן לקמן מ"לא יוכל לבכר". ביום הנחילו. והוה מצי למכתב: ביום שינחלו בניו. לכל מי שירצה. מבניו, הן להרבות לו מאחיו, הן להורישו הכל. ולשנויא קמא דמשנינן לעיל, דפליג רבי יוחנן בן ברוקה אפי' באחר במקום בת – איכא למימר נמי דמהכא נפקא ליה, ובניו לאו דוקא, אלא יורשיו, (ג) ואפי' הראוי ליורשו יורש קרינא ביה. מלא יוכל לבכר נפקא. דהכי משמע: בכורה לא יוכל להעביר מבכור ולהנחיל לאחרים, אבל שאר נכסיו בלא חלק בכורה – יכול להנחיל אחד מבניו.

לא

הלכה כר' יוחנן בן ברוקה. נראה דדוקא בן בין הבנים ובת בין הבנות, כפירוש רבינו שמואל. **האי** מלא יוכל לבכר נפקא. פירוש: מדקאמר רחמנא דחלק בכורה אין יכול לשנות – מכלל דחלק פשיטות יכול לשנות, ולמה לי קרא ד"ביום הנחילו את בניו"? והוה מצי למימר: ולטעמיך, לרבנן נמי יקשה: אמאי אינו יכול לשנות חלק פשיטות? הא כיון דכתיב "לא יוכל לבכר" – מכלל דחלק פשיטות יכול.

*שיכול. (ד) ל"ג והלא דין הוא.

* שייך לע"ב

תלמוד תורה אור

רבינו גרשום

וקדושין. שאם חישב על בהמה להקריב לעבודה זרה ואמר להקריבה וחזר בו לאלתר בתוך כדי דבור לא הויא חזרה ואסורה בהנאה וקדושין נמי אם קידש אשה ובתוך כדי דבור חזר בו אפ"ה תופסין בה קדושין וצריכה גט: **פיס'** ר' יוחנן [בן ברוקה] אומר אם אותו איש פלוני שאמר יירשני במקום שיש בת אם ראוי ליורשו הוא אם לא היתה בת כגון שהוא אחיו דבריו קיימין ויורש אפי' במקום בת: טעמא דאחר במקום בת. משום הכי אמר ת"ק דלא אמר כלום דמתעקרא נחלה מן הראוין לשאינם ראויים: הא בבן בין הבנים. כלומר אם רצה ליתן לבן אחד כל נכסיו ולא לשאר בנים הואיל ונותנו למי שהוא יורש גמור דבריו קיימין והוא הדין אם לא הי' לו בנים אלא בנות ורצה ליתן לבת אחת בין שאר הבנות: אימא סיפא וכו' וכי תימא בהא קמפלגי ר' יוחנן [בן ברוקה] מיקל טפי מתנא קמא דאפי' אמר על אחר דראוי ליורשו במקום שיש בת דקרובה ליה טפי דבריו קיימין. וכן בת במקום בן: והא תניא כו'. וכיון דקאמר ר' ישמעאל דלא נחלקו אבא וחכמים על דבר זה הדרן קושין לדוכתיה דדייקינן טעמא דאחר במקום בת כו' דר' יוחנן היינו ת"ק. איבעית אימא תריץ הכי מדקאמר ר' ישמעאל לא נחלקו מכלל דת"ק דר' ישמעאל סבר דנחלקו ור' יוחנן לאו היינו ת"ק. ואיבעית אימא תריץ הכי כולה מתני' ר' יוחנן בן ברוקה היא וחסורא מחסרא מתני'. והכי קתני לה האומ' איש פלוני יירשני וכו': התורה נתנה רשות לאב להנחיל לכל מי שירצה מבניו. כלומר הנחילו לרצונו משמע: הא מלא יוכל לבכ' נפקא. דסגי ליה כי את הבכור בן השנואה יכיר מאי האי דכתיב לא יוכל לבכר וגו' כלומר בכור אי אתה יכול ליתן חלקו לאחר הא לשאר בנים יכול ליתן חלקם לאחר: אלא ההוא לא יוכל לבכר מיבעי ליה לכדתניא אבא חנן כו' שיכול

הגהות הב"ח

(א) גמ' לבר מעבודה זרה וקדושין. נ"ב הג"ה לענין מהדר קא אמרי' דאי בעי למהדר הדר לבר מקדושין דאי בעי למהדר בתר דקדיש או הוא או היא לא יכלין ואע"פ שעוסקין באותו ענין אע"ג דקיימין עדים ותקרובת עבודה זרה נמי כיון דאיתפס דבר לעבודה זרה לאלתר איחייב ליה ואסור בהנאה עכ"ה: (ב) רשב"ם ד"ה ואיבעית אימא וכו' ר"י בן ברוקה היא דשמע לת"ק: (ג) ד"ה לכל מי וכו' ואפי' הראוי ליורשו. נ"ב ולפענ"ד נראה שזה פירוש רחוק דאי בניו לאו דוקא אלא יורשיו כל יורשיו במשמע אלא נראה דבניו דוקא ומ"מ מדכתב את בניו את מרבה נמי אחר כלאו יורשיו אבל שאינו ראוי ליורשו לכולה רבוי לא וק"ל: (ד) תד"ה שיכול וכו'. נ"ב בפ"ק דחולין כתבו התוס' וז"ל בדף נ"ב בסוס דוכתין ל"ג תרווייהו דיכול משמע שלא...

עין משפט
נר מצוה

צה א מיי' פ"ו מהל' נחלות הלכה ג סמג עשין נו טוש"ע חו"מ סי' רפא סעיף ז:

מסורת הש"ס

א) [שיכול ומה פשוט שיפה כנ"ל ת"ח]: ב) [שבת כא: וש"נ]: ג) נדה ז:: ד) [ברכות כז. וש"נ]: ה) חולין מח: נה: נז. עו.: ו) [נדה ז: ע"ש וברש"י שם]: ז) נ"א והמקשה: ח) [נ"ל בפ' שני דפאה]: ט) [לא נמצא מקומו]: י) [נ"ל בהמה המקשה עו.]:

(א) מה תלמוד לומר °"לא יוכל לבכר"? לפי שנאמר: "והיה ביום הנחילו את בניו", א)שיכול, והלא דין הוא: ומה פשוט שיפה כחו, שנוטל בראוי כבמוחזק – התורה נתנה רשות לאב להנחיל לכל מי שירצה, בכור שהורע כחו, שאינו נוטל בראוי כבמוחזק – לא כל שכן? א)תלמוד לומר: "לא יוכל לבכר". ויאמר: "לא יוכל לבכר", מה ת"ל "והיה ביום הנחילו את בניו"? שיכול, והלא דין הוא: ומה בכור שהורע כחו, שאינו נוטל בראוי כבמוחזק – אמרה תורה: "לא יוכל לבכר", פשוט שיפה כחו, שנוטל בראוי כבמוחזק – לא כל שכן? ת"ל: "והיה ביום הנחילו את בניו", התורה נתנה רשות לאב להנחיל לכל מי שירצה. א"ר זריקא א"ר אמי א"ר חנינא (ב) אמר רבי: הלכה כר' יוחנן בן ברוקה. אמר ליה ר' אבא: "הורה" איתמר. במאי קמיפלגי? מר סבר: הלכה עדיפא, ומר סבר: ב)מעשה רב. ג)תנו רבנן: אין למדין הלכה לא מפי למוד ולא מפי מעשה – עד שיאמרו לו ד)הלכה למעשה. שאל ואמרו לו הלכה למעשה – ילך ויעשה מעשה, ובלבד שלא ידמה. מאי "ובלבד שלא ידמה"? והא כל התורה כולה דמויי מדמינן לה! אמר רב אשי, הכי קאמר: ובלבד שלא ידמה בטרפות; דתניא: ה)אין אומרים בטרפות זו דומה לזו; ואל תתמה, שהרי חותכה מכאן ומתה, חותכה מכאן וחיתה. א"ל ר' אסי לר' יוחנן: כי אמר לן מר "הלכה הכי", נעביד מעשה? אמר: לא תעבידו עד דאמינא "הלכה למעשה". אמר להו רבא לרב פפא ולרב הונא בריה דרב יהושע: כי אתי פסקא דדינא דידי לקמייכו וחזיתו ביה פירכא – לא תקרעוהו עד דאתיתו לקמאי, אי אית לי טעמא – אמינא לכו, ואי לא – הדרנא בי. לאחר מיתה – לא מיקרע תקרעוהו, ומגמר נמי לא תגמרו מיניה; לא מיקרע תקרעיניה – דאי הואי התם, דלמא הוה אמינא לכו טעמא, מגמר

תורה אור
דברים כא

לא יוכל לבכר מה תלמוד לומר. והלא כתיב בתריה: "הבכור בן השנואה יכיר". לפי שנאמר והיה ביום הנחילו את בניו. דמשמע שיכול לתת לכל אחד מבניו מה שירצה, ויכול אני לדון שאף הבכורה יעביר מן הבכור לתת לכל מי שירצה, עם שאר נחלה; דמה פשוט שיפה כחו כו' שנוטל בראוי, דבחלק פשוט לא כתיב: "בכל אשר ימצא לו". ויאמר לא יוכל לבכר. ולא אצטריך "ביום הנחילו". כאביי, דהוה דייקינן: בכורה לא יוכל לבכר, אבל חלק פשוט ינחיל למי שירצה! הורה. כר' יוחנן בן ברוקה, איתמר. במאי קא מיפלגי. נהי דמר שמיע ליה הכי, ומר שמיע ליה הכי, מאי בינייהו? הלכה עדיפא. שפוסק הלכה לעשות כן. אבל כי אמרינן "הורה" – איכא למימר דטעה הרואה, דשמא אותו הדין לא נפסק כרבי יוחנן בן ברוקה, אלא על ידי טענות אחרות זיכה את כל הנכסים לאחד מן הבנים. כגון שאמר האב לשון מתנה עם לשון ירושה, דלדברי הכל דבריו קיימין. וכדאמרינן (לעיל דף קכו.) נמי: לאו בפירוש אתמר אלא מכללא אתמר, דההוא בכור דאזיל וזבין בנכסי דידיה כו'. דסבר הרואה דמשום האי טעמא נפסק כן, והמעשה משום טעמא אחרינא. אבל כיון דקבע הלכה – אז אין לפקפק בדבר. ומר סבר מעשה רב. כשמורין לעשות מעשה – אז יש לסמוך ולעשותו. אבל כשאומר "הלכה כפלוני" – אין סומכין לעשות כן עד שיאמרו הלכה למעשה, כדלקמן. דאי אמר "הלכה" – איכא למימר דדרך למודו אמר הכי, אבל אם בא מעשה לידו – הוה מדקדק יותר, כדאמרי' בסמוך: אין למדין הלכה מפי למוד. אבל משהורה לעשות – שוב אין לפקפק אחריו. אין למדין הלכה. כלומר, אין למדין לעשות. לא מפי תלמוד. שאם לומד הרב דרך לימודו, ואמר: מסתבר טעמא דפלוני חכם – אין תלמידיו למדין משם הלכה. דשמא אם יבא לידו מעשה ידקדק יותר, ויראה טעם אחר בדבר. ולא מפי מעשה. אם יראה רבו עושה מעשה – אל יקבע הלכה בכך. דשמא טעה בטעם של פסק דין של אותו המעשה. דהרבה טועין בדבר הלמוד, כדאמרי': "והא דפלוני לאו בפירוש אתמר אלא מכללא אתמר", וטעה בסברא. עד שיאמרו לו הלכה למעשה. דכיון ששאל ע"י מעשה, ואינן יודעין בדבר אלא מה שהוא אומר להם – אין לומר: טעם חזו ביה דלא ידע. ג) ובמקום אחר ו) אמרי' אין למדין הלכה מתוך משנה. כגון זה שכתב במשנה "והלכה כדבריו". כגון הא דתנן במסכת נדה (דף ז.) רבי אליעזר אומר: ארבע נשים דיין שעתן כו'. ז) והמשפה כמה תשפה ותהא זבה, גבי יולדת בזוב מעת לעת, דברי ר' אליעזר (נדה לו:). וזב וזבה שבדקו יום ראשון ומצאו טהורה וכו' (שם סח:). ובשלשתן תנן במשנה "הלכה כדבריו", ואפ"ה קבע שמואל הלכה כמותו בתלמוד, ואשמעי' דאין מורין הלכה מתוך משנה אי לאו דקבע הלכה כמותו. וביבמות (דף מט.) (ד) תנן: איזהו ממזר? שמעון התימני אומר: כל שחייבין עליו כרת והלכה כדבריו. ואי לאו דפסיק בתלמוד הלכה כמותו – לא סמכינן אפסק דמתניתין. אבל בהלכות הפסוקות בדברי האמוראין – ודאי סמכי', דכיון שפסקום וכתבום רב אשי ורבינא שהם סוף הוראה – ודאי עלייהו סמכי'. מצינו למדין: היכא דפליג יחיד אגל רבים כי הני – לא סמכי' אפסק הלכה של משנה, אלא א"כ פוסק בתלמוד, אבל אפסק דתלמוד – סמכי', דכולהו הוו הלכה למעשה. אלא שר' יוחנן לבדו היה מחמיר לעצמו, ואמר לתלמידיו כדלקמן שלא יעשו דבר עד שיאמר להם הלכה למעשה. והיינו טעמא – דדלמא הדר ביה מההוא פסק הלכה שפסק, ויראה לו טעם אחר בעיניו. ומיהו, לאחר פטירתו יש להם לעשות מה שפסק להם, דהא כל ימי חייו לא הדר ביה. וכל שכן שיש לנו לסמוך על הלכות הכתובות בתלמוד כמו שסידרן רב אשי, דהא קיימא לן בבבא מציעא (דף פו.): רב אשי ורבינא סוף הוראה, ולמי נשאל עוד בשעת מעשה, אם לא נסמוך על ההלכות הפסוקות בתלמוד כמו שסדרן רב אשי, דקתני: עד שיאמר לו הלכה למעשה? הא אין אדם רשאי לחדש דבר מעתה! אלא ודאי כמו שפסקו האחרונים כך נעשה. והכי אמרי' ח) (בתחלת פאה) ירושלמי: ר' זעירא בשם שמואל אמר: אין למדין לא מן ההלכות ולא מן ההגדות ולא מן התוספתות, אלא מן התלמוד, כלומר, מדברי האמוראין. ולא מפי מעשה הכתוב במשנה וברייתא, כגון דפליגי רבים עליה, עד שיאמרו הלכה למעשה, כלומר: כן הלכה, לך ועשה כן. אי נמי, שיאמרו לו הלכה כדי לעשות מעשה, כגון שבא ושאל לחכמים: מעשה בא לידי, היאך הלכה כדי לעשות כך? ואמרו לו: הלכה כפלוני. אע"פ שאמרו סתם – זהו הלכה למעשה. ילך ויעשה מעשה. כל ימיו יעשה עוד כן, ולא יהא צריך עוד לשאול לכל מעשה ומעשה שבא לידו. ובלבד שלא ידמה. לדון דבר מתוך דבר. הא כל התורה כולה וכו'. כדאמרי' בעירובין (דף כא:) גבי שלמה: ואסברא בדדמי. בטרפות. ללמד זו מזו. כגון טרפות הכבד מן הריאה, כדאמרי': ט) וחילופא בכבדא. שאין חיות האיברים שוה. אין אומרים בטרפות זו דומה לזו, שהרי חותכה מכאן – בצומת הגידין ומתה, דמיטרפא בכך. חותכה מכאן – למעלה מצומת הגידין, וחיתה. שחתך הבשר עד העצם כשרה, כדאמרי' ב"בהמה המקשה" (חולין דף עו.), ומקל וחומר היה לנו לומר שהיא טריפה. אי אמר מר הלכה הכי. בשעה שאנו למדין לפניו, מי עבדינן עובדא ע"פ אותה הוראה? עד דאמינא לכו הלכה למעשה. שאומר לכם הלכה בשעה שתשאלו לי על ידי מעשה. דבשעת מעשה אדם ירא לידון ומכוין לבו יותר. כדאמרן לעיל: אין למדין הלכה מפי תלמוד עד שיאמרו לו הלכה למעשה. פסקא דדינא. שפסקתיו ומסרתיו לאדם להיות לראיה בידו – אל תקרעוהו לבטל דברי. דאי הוה וכו'. ושמא גם אתם תמצאו תירוץ לקושייתכם. ואל

תלמוד לומר לא יוכל לבכר. וא"ת: ולרבנן, למה לי "לא יוכל לבכר"? דמהי תיתי שיוכל לשנות חלק בכורה, דאצטריך קרא למעוטי? ולר' יוחנן בן ברוקה נמי, למה לי "ביום הנחילו"? דעל כרחך ליכא למימר דמקל וחומר יליף שלא יוכל לשנות חלק פשיטות – דא"כ ליפתוק מ"לא יוכל לבכר", ומינה ידעינן שאין יכול לשנות לא חלק בכורה ולא חלק פשיטות, משום דהוי מתנה על מה שכתוב בתורה. ואם כן ע"כ "לא יבכר" לא אצטריך אלא למעוטי חלק פשיטות! ויש לומר: דאי לאו "לא יבכר" – הוה אמינא דיכול לשנות חלק בכורה, משום דהורע כחו שאינו נוטל בראוי. והשתא אצטריך שפיר "ביום הנחילו" לרבי יוחנן בן ברוקה, דלא נילף חלק פשיטות בקל וחומר מחלק בכורה דאין יכול לשנות. שהרי חותכה מכאן. אין לפרש כפי' רבינו שמואל: חותכה מכאן וחיה – דהיינו למעלה מצומת הגידין. דהא בפרק י)"אלו טרפות" (חולין דף נו) צומת הגידין גופא קאמר: תדע, שהרי חותכה מכאן כו'. אלא יש לפרש: כגון בטחול, דקיימא לן (שם דף נה:) ניקב בסומכיה – טריפה, בקולשיה – כשרה. ושמע

רבינו גרשום

שיכול והלא דין הוא. שיהא האב רשאי להנחיל א) בין בכור לפשוט: ויאמר לא יוכל לבכר. בלבד ולישמע מינה תרתי דלבכור לא יוכל לבכר אחר במקומו הא לפשוט יכול ליתן לאחר חלק חבירו. אצטריך למכתב והיה ביום הנחילו את בניו (תאמר הריני דן אחד) שיכול והלא דין הוא דאינו רשאי להנחיל לאחרים אפי' במקום פשוט: ומה בכור כו': הורה אתמר. שהורה הלכה למעשה (שהתורה נתנה רשות וכו'): מר סבר הלכה עדיפא (נוקים) שפוסק הלכה בתלמוד בבית המדרש עיקר ומר סבר הוראה על ידי מעשה עיקר: אין למדין הלכה לא מפי תלמוד. שאם רואה אדם בתלמוד הלכה כי האי תנא או כי האי ולא מפי מעשה שרואה כתוב בתלמוד דשמא יחידאה הוא עד שישאל בבית המדרש ויאמרו הלכה כן לעשות בו מעשה: ובלבד שלא ידמה. מדעתו מעשה אחר למעשה זה שהורו לו: וכל התור' כולה דמויי מדמינן לה. דמפיק דומה לדומה: שלא ידמה בטריפות. שלא יאמר כשם שאם נשברה למטה מן הארכובה כשירה כך נשברה למעלה מן הארכובה כשירה לפי שאין בטריפות זו דומה לזו: ואל תתמה. מפני מה שאין אומרין כן. לפי שחותכה מיכן למעלה מן הארכובה ומתה ולמטה מן הארכובה חיה. ואיכא דמפרש שכל אדם בטפחות שנא' טפחות נתתה ימי מתחיל לחשב ממעלה למטה אם חותך טפח העליון מן גולגלת חי שלא נגע במוח וטפח שני כנגד מוחו ומת וטפח שלישי למטה מן המוח חי וטפח רביעי כנגד הגרון ומת וטפח חמישי הוא למעלה מן הלב וששי כנגד הלב וכן כל הגוף: שאין

א) אולי צ"ל שיהא האב רשאי להנחיל חלק בכורה לפשוט.

פי' הרשב"ם העקרי

ד"ה עד שיאמרו לו הלכה למעשה כו' זב וזבה שבדקו עצמן יום ראשון ומצאו טהור כו' עד והלכה כדבריו וא"ר יהודה אמר שמואל הלכה כר' אליעזר בארבע והני תלתא מינייהו ואקשינן מאי אתא לאשמעינן בכולהי תנא הלכה כדבריו במתני' ופרקינן אין למדין הלכה מפי תלמוד ולולי שאמר שמואל הלכה כר"א בהני לא הוי מיתוקמא הלכתא ממתני' כיוצא בהן ביבמות איזהו ממזר שמעון התימני אומר כל שחייבין עליו כרת בידי שמי' והלכה כדבריו ולולי שאמרו בגמ' הלכתא כוותיה לא סמכינן אמאי דפסיק הלכה כדבריו במשנתינו נמצאו למדין דהיכא דפליג יחיד כו' (כבדפוס): הא כל התורה כו'. כדאמרי' בעירובין ואסברה בדדמי בשלמה המלך מיירי: בטרפות. ללמד טרפות הכבד מטרפות הריאה דהא אמרינן וחילופיו בכבדא שאין חיות האיברים דומה זה לזה יש כשר בזה ופסול בחבירו: שהרי חותכה מכאן. למעלה מן הארכובה מעט במקום צומת הגידין: ומתה. דמיטרפא ביה כדאמרי' בפ' בהמה המקשה: וחותכה מכאן. למעלה מצומת הגידין חותך הבשר עד העצם כשרה כדאמרינן התם ומק"ו היה לנו לומר שהיא טרפה: כי אמר לן מר הלכה. כפלוני: עד דאמינא לכו הלכה. כשיבא מעשה לידכם דבשעת מעשה אדם ירא לדון אלא הברור לו ומכוון את לבו יותר: והדר חזיתו. טעם אחר בדבר: פסקא דינא. שדנו הדין כך וכתבוהו להתקיים כן וכהלכה למעשה למילף מיניה: ולא תקרעוה. לבטל דברי: דאי הוה אנא וכו'. ושמא גם אתם היום או מחר תמצאו תירוץ לפרכא דידכו: ומיגמר לא תגמרו מיניה. לדון אלא כפי מה שנראה לכם: שאין לו לדיין אלא מה שעיניו רואות. כדתניא במס' נדה בשילהי פרק שני רבי ראה דם וטמא ראהו ביום וטהרו המתין שעה אחת וראהו וחזר וטמאו אמר אוי לי שמא טעיתי ומקשינן הא ודאי טעה דתניא לא יאמר חכם אילו היה כן לא היה טמא אלא מה שעיניו רואות כו' והוא הדין לגבי התלוי בסברא אלא אין לו לדיין אלא מה שעיניו רואות:

הגהות הב"ח

(א) גמ' לא יוכל לבכר מה ת"ל לפי שנאמר והיה: (ב) שם אמר ר' חנינא אמר רבי ינאי אמר רבי הלכה כרבי יוחנן: (ג) רשב"ם ד"ה עד שיאמרו כו' ובמקום אחר. נ"ב נראה דלעתו לכאן ודאי פי' לא מפי תלמוד כשפוסק הלכה דרך למודו אלא שבמקום אחר דאמרי' נמי אין למדין הלכה מפי תלמוד ולכם הוה פירושו מתוך משנה כו' ומביאו הרב כאן כדי לחלק בין משנה לאמוראים ולקבוע ההלכה כמ"ש מצינו למדין כו' לאפסק שפסקו האמוראים יש לנו לסמוך על כל פנים אלא שר' יוחנן החמיר כו' ואין זה אלא כשפוסק הלכה כפלוני בפירוש אבל דרך למודו שיאמר מסתבר טעמא דפלוני חכם אין תלמידיו למדין משם ואין חלוק בזה בין התנאים לאמוראים דבכל זמן נוהג דבר זה וק"ל ומהרש"ל בהגהותיו פירש דהרב ז"ל כונתו לומר דמאחר דבמקום אחר אמרינן דאין למדין הלכה מתוך משנה כו' א"כ לפי זה גם כאן פי' אין למדין הלכה מפי תלמוד היינו הלכה שכתוב בתלמוד במשנה או בברייתא: (ד) בא"ד וביבמות נמי תנן:

א) סנהדרין ו: נדה כ:: ב) כתובות נב: ג) [שם נג.]: ד) [שם]: ה) [לעיל עט: וש"נ]: ו) [ב"מ ו:]: ז) כתובות נב: ח) נ"ל לח: ט) [גי' רש"א ומ"מ]: י) איתו כפי' שלנו:

מִגְמַר נַמִי לָא תִגְמְרוּ מִינֵּיהּ — א)דְּאֵין לַדַּיָּין אֶלָּא מַה שֶּׁעֵינָיו רוֹאוֹת. בָּעֵי רָבָא: בְּבָרִיא הֵיאָךְ? כִּי קא"ר יוֹחָנָן בֶּן בְּרוֹקָה — בְּשכ"מ, דְּבַר אוֹרוּתֵי הוּא, אאֲבָל בְּבָרִיא — לָא. אוֹ דִּלְמָא אֲפִילּוּ בְּבָרִיא נַמִי? אֲמַר לֵיהּ רַב מְשָׁרְשִׁיָּא לְרָבָא: תָּא שְׁמַע, דְּאָמַר לוֹ רַבִּי נָתָן לְרַבִּי: שְׁנִיתֶם מִשְׁנַתְכֶם כְּר' יוֹחָנָן בֶּן בְּרוֹקָה, ב)דִּתְנַן: בלֹא כָּתַב לָהּ "בְּנִין דִּיכְרִין דְּיֶהֱוְיָן לִיךְ מִינַּאי, אִינּוּן יִרְתּוּן כְּסַף כְּתוּבָּתֵיךְ יוֹתֵר עַל חוּלְקֵיהוֹן דְּעִם אֲחוּהוֹן" — חַיָּיב, (א) גשֶׁתְּנַאי ב"ד הוּא! וְאָמַר לוֹ רַבִּי: ג)"יִסְבּוּן" תְּנַן. וְאָמַר רַבִּי: יַלְדוּת הָיְתָה בִּי וְהֶעֱזְתִּי פָּנַי בְּנָתָן הַבַּבְלִי; אֶלָּא דדְּקַיְימָא לָן: ד)בְּנִין דִּכְרִין לָא טָרְפָא מִמְּשַׁעְבְּדֵי, אִי סָלְקָא דַּעְתָּךְ "יִסְבּוּן" תְּנַן, אַמַּאי לָא טָרְפָא מִמְּשַׁעְבְּדֵי? אֶלָּא ש"מ: "יִרְתּוּן" תְּנַן. מַאן שָׁמַעְתְּ לֵיהּ דְּאִית לֵיהּ הַאי סְבָרָא — ר' יוֹחָנָן בֶּן בְּרוֹקָה, וּשְׁמַע מִינַּהּ: אֲפִי' בְּבָרִיא. אֲמַר לֵיהּ רַב פָּפָּא לְאַבָּיֵי: בֵּין לְמַאן דְּאָמַר "יִסְבּוּן", וּבֵין לְמַאן דְּאָמַר "יִרְתּוּן", הָא אֵין אָדָם מַקְנֶה דָּבָר שֶׁלֹּא בָּא לָעוֹלָם! ה)וַאֲפִי' לְר' מֵאִיר דְּאָמַר: אָדָם מַקְנֶה דָּבָר שֶׁלֹּא בָּא לָעוֹלָם, הָנֵי מִילֵּי לְדָבָר שֶׁיֶּשְׁנוֹ בָּעוֹלָם, אֲבָל לְדָבָר שֶׁאֵינוֹ בָּעוֹלָם לָא! אֶלָּא, תְּנַאי בֵּית דִּין שָׁאנֵי, הָכָא נַמִי — תְּנַאי בֵּית דִּין שָׁאנֵי! א"ל: מִשּׁוּם דְּקָא מַפֵּיק לָהּ בִּלְשׁוֹן "יִרְתּוּן". ו)הֲדַר אֲמַר אַבָּיֵי: לָאו מִילְּתָא הִיא דַּאֲמַרִי, ז)דִּתְנַן: הלֹא כָּתַב לָהּ "בְּנָן נוּקְבָן דְּיֶהֶוְיָין לִיכִי מִינַּאי יֶהֶוְיָין יָתְבָן בְּבֵיתִי וְיִתְזָנָן מִנִּכְסַאי עַד דְּתִילַּקְחָן לְגוּבְרִין" — חַיָּיב, שֶׁהוּא תְּנַאי ב"ד; וַהֲוָה לְזֶה בְּמַתָּנָה וְלָזֶה בִּירוּשָּׁה, וְכָל לָזֶה בִּירוּשָּׁה וְלָזֶה בְּמַתָּנָה — אֲפִי' רַבָּנַן מוֹדוּ. אֲמַר לֵיהּ רַב נַחוּמִי, וְאִית דְּאָמַר רַב חֲנַנְיָה בַּר מְנְיוּמִי לְאַבָּיֵי:

מַמַּאי

ואל תגמרו. לדון מיניה, אלא כפי שדעתכם נוטה. דאין לו לדיין אלא מה שעיניו רואות. כדתניא במס' נדה בשילהי פ"ב (דף כ:): רבי ראה דם בלילה וטימא, ראה ביום וטיהרו, המתין שעה אחת (ג) וראהו, חזר וטימא. אמר: אוי לי שמא טעיתי. ומקשינן: ודאי טעה, דתניא: לא יאמר חכם אילו היה ח) (לא) היה טמא, אלא אין לדיין אלא מה שעיניו רואות. (ג) והוא הדין לדבר התלוי בסברא, דאין לו אלא מה שלבו רואהו. ובפרק קמא דסנהדרין נפקא לן מ"ועמכם בדבר המשפט" — עמכם בדבר, עמכם במשפט, אין לו לדיין אלא מה שעיניו רואות. **בבריא היאך.** בריא שאמר "פלוני יירש שדה פלונית", מי אמר ר' יוחנן בן ברוקה דקני, כיון דראוי ליורשו? **בר אורותי.** ראוי להוריש מיד, שהולך למות, וקרינא ביה "ביום הנחילו את בניו". **דאמר ליה ר' נתן לרבי.** שסידר המשנה. **שניתם משנתכם.** אתם שבארץ ישראל. **כר' יוחנן בן ברוקה.** דאמר: אם אמר על מי שראוי ליורשו — דבריו קיימין. **ר' נתן.** בבלי היה. **ששניתם.** בכתובות: לא כתב לה לאשתו בכתובתה "בנין דיכרין דיהוו ליכי מינאי" — אם תמותי בחיי ואירש כתובתיך, בניי הזכרים שתלדי לי הם יירשוה לאחר מותי, יתר על חלקם שיחלקו עם אחיהם שיהיו לי מאשה אחרת. **שהוא תנאי בית דין.** שבית דין תקנו כתובת בנין דיכרין, כדאמרי' בכתובות, כדי שיקפוץ אדם ויתן לבתו כבנו, דאם נותן לבתו — אינו יוצא מזרעו אם בתו מתה קודם בעלה, שירשו בניה את כתובתה אחר מות אביהם. והוא שיהא שם מותר דינר, שלא תעקר נחלה דאורייתא, כדאמרינן התם. אלמא: מוריש האב לבן בין הבנים, כר' יוחנן בן ברוקה, והיה לכם לשנות משנתכם כדברי הכל, ולא אליבא דיחידאה! **ואמר ליה רבי יסבון תנן.** ודברי הכל היא. **הדר אמר רבי: ילדות** ושטות היה בי שהעיזותי פני בנתן הבבלי, ודחיתיו בדבר שאינו. דודאי "ירתון" תנן, דהא קיימא לן דכתובת בנין דיכרין לא טרפא ממשעבדי מה שמכר אביהן. ואם "יסבון" תנן, דמשמע לשון מתנה — הוה משמע מעכשיו, ואם מכר לאחד (מהן) הוי טורפא ממשעבדי. שהרי כל נכסיו משועבדים לכתובת אמן, ואי מההיא שעתא חלה מתנתו — הוה טורפא ממשעבדי. אלא משום הכי אמרינן לשון "ירתון", דלשון ירושה אינו אלא לאחר מיתה, משום הכי לא מטרפא ממשעבדי, דלא חלה עד לאחר מיתה. על כרחין "ירתון" תנן, ויפה הקשה לי ר' נתן. **מאן שמעת ליה דאית ליה האי סברא.** יתור לשון הוא דלא צריך. **ושמע מינה אפילו בבריא קאמר.** ואפילו תנינן "יסבון", ממילתיה דר' נתן דקאמר: שניתם כר' יוחנן — איכא לאוכוחי דבבריא קאמר ר' יוחנן, ומיפשטא בעיא דרבא לגמרי. ולא הוצרך כל כך אלא כדי לסיים דבריו של רבי. ור' נתן דהוה מקשה לרבי, איכא למימר דתני "יסבון", וסבירא ליה דטריף ממשעבדי. ורבי ששנאם כריב"ב — משום דהכי סבירא ליה, כדאמרינן לעיל: אמר ר' זריקא אמר ר' אמי אמר ר' חנינא א"ר ינאי אמר רבי: הלכה כר' יוחנן בן ברוקה. **האי סברא.** דריבה לאחד ומיעט לאחד בלשון ירושה כי הכא, שיורשין כתובת אמן והמותר של שתי כתובות חולקין. **אמר ליה רב פפא לאביי.** רב פפא לאו אבעיא דרבא קאי, דהא איפשיטא. אלא אמאי דקאמר ליה רבי לרבי נתן. וה"ק: למה ליה לרבי למימר לרבי נתן: "יסבון" תנן, לאוקומי מתני' לדברי הכל? וכי תנינן נמי "ירתון" — דברי הכל היא! דהא בין למ"ד "יסבון", בין למ"ד "ירתון" תנן, איכא לאקשויי: אמאי קנייא האי מתנה כלל? הא אין אדם מקנה דבר שלא בא לעולם, ובשעת נשואין לא באו הבנים לעולם שהוא מקנה להם כתובה. ואפילו לר' מאיר דאמר אדם מקנה כו' — הני מילי לדבר שישנו בעולם, דכיון דהמקבל בעולם — יכול הנותן לשעבד עצמו לו שיתן לו מה שיקנה לו. אבל הכא — לא מצי משעבד נפשיה. **אלא תנאי בית דין שאני.** דאלים תנאי ב"ד, משום דהפקר ב"ד הפקר, להקנות אפי' לדבר שלא בא לעולם. והכא נמי אלים תנאי ב"ד. ואע"ג דאמרי רבנן דלשון ירושה בעלמא לא קני — הכא קני, ואפילו כרבנן אתיא מתניתין. **א"ל משום דמפיק לה בלשון ירתון.** הא דלא קאמר ליה הכי, משום דהוה א"ל ר' נתן: ומפני מה הנחת' לשון "יסבון" ותנית' לשון "ירתון" — אלא משום דלבך נוטה אחר ר' יוחנן בן ברוקה. ומשום הכי א"ל "יסבון" תנן. והדר מתחרט רבי בעצמו, משום דכי הוה מקשי ליה אמאי שנית' "ירתון" — מצי אמר ליה: משום הכי שנינן "ירתון" — לומר דלא טרפא ממשעבדי. **לאו מילתא היא דאמרי.** דודאי לא היה צריך רבי לומר "יסבון" תנן, דבלא שום דיוק מתני' אפי' כרבנן אתיא. דהא קתני בסיפא דההיא משנה דכתובות: אע"פ שלא כתב לה "בנן נוקבן וכו' ומיתזנן מנכסיי אחר מיתתי", כדא"ר אלעזר בן עזריה לקמן. וזה לשון מתנה בסוף, אפילו רבנן מודו, כדתנן במתניתין: כתב לשון מתנה בין בתחלה בין באמצע בין בסוף — דבריו קיימין, ואוקימנא אפילו בשני בני אדם ושני שדות, ובלבד שיהא תוך כדי דבור. והכא, שתי תקנות הללו, כיון דבבת אחת תקנו — הוי כמו תוך כדי דבור. והאי דקתני לשון "ירתון" — לאשמועינן מתניתין דרבנן מודו אפילו בשני בני אדם ושתי שדות.

ממאי

ושמע מינה אפי' בבריא נמי. אפי' בלא תנאי ב"ד. דהכי משמע המשנה: לא כתב לה — חייב, מפני שהוא תנאי ב"ד. אבל כתב לה, אפי' בלא תנאי ב"ד — חייב, דבבריא נמי קאמר. אמר ליה: והא אין אדם מקנה דבר שלא בא לעולם. ואם כן, אפי' כתב לה, ע"כ לא קנו אלא משום תנאי ב"ד. וה"נ, אע"ג דבבריא לא קנו — הכא קנו, משום דהוי תנאי ב"ד! ומכל מקום שפיר קאמר ליה רבי נתן לרבי: שניתם משנתכם כר' יוחנן בן ברוקה, דאית לי' דמהני "ירתון" בשכ"מ, ולהכי הכא אפילו בבריא קנו, משום תנאי ב"ד. דאילו לרבנן, כיון דבעלמא לא מהני לישנא ד"ירתון" אפילו בשכ"מ, לא ה"ל למתני הכא "ירתון" אפילו משום תנאי ב"ד, אלא "יסבון מבני חרי". א"ל אביי: משום דקא מפיק ליה בלשון "ירתון". פירוש: אע"ג דלא קנו אלא משום תנאי ב"ד, לפי שאין אדם מקנה לדבר שלא בא לעולם, מ"מ יש להוכיח דבבריא נמי אמרינן. דאי לא אמר בעלמא בבריא — לא הוה ליה לתנא לאפוקי בלשון "ירתון" משום תנאי ב"ד, כיון דלא מהני בעלמא. אלא הוה ליה למיתני "יסבון" וליתקנו דליטרוף ממשעבדי, או יהיה תנאי ב"ד שלא יטרוף אלא מבני חרי. אלא ודאי בבריא נמי אמר. הדר אמר אביי: לאו מלתא היא דאמרי, דתנן כו' והוה ליה לזה בירושה ולזה(ד) במתנה, אפי' רבנן מודו. ולעולם ר' יוחנן בן ברוקה לא אמר בבריא בעלמא. ט) וא"כ שפיר קאמר [ר' נתן] לרבי: שניתם משנתכם כרבי יוחנן בן ברוקה. דלדידיה, כיון ד"ירתון" לחודיה מהני בשכ"מ — בבריא נמי תנן ליה במתנה וירושה. אבל לרבנן, דאמרי: לא מהני "ירתון" לחודיה בעלמא כלל, אפי' בשכ"מ — א"כ היכי תני "ירתון"? אף ע"ג דמהני "ירתון" משום דאיכא מתנה בהדיה, מ"מ לא הוה ליה למיתני,(ה) דלא מהני כלל לחודיה אלא עם המתנה. אלא "יסבון מבני חרי" הוה ליה למיתני. ולעולם בבריא לא אמר.

י) ובקונטרס פי': משום דמפיק בלשון "ירתון", ואין זה מקנה לדבר שאין בעולם, כיון שאין המתנה באה אלא לאחר מיתה — ואז הבנים כבר בעולם, ובלא תנאי בית דין קנו. ואין נראה, דבריש "מי שמת" (לקמן דף קמא:) אמר: אימור דשמעת ליה לרבי מאיר כו' לדבר שאין בעולם מי אמר? אף על גב דכשילדה כבר העובר בעולם.

דלמא

פי' הרשב"ם העקרי

בבריא היאך. מי אית ליה לר"י בן ברוקא בין בבריא בין בשכ"מ שמנחיל לבניו כל מה שירצה (המקום חלק כדי לכתוב בו שתי מלות וצ"ל [או רק בשכ"מ]) כדמורית קרוב למות וקרינא ביה ביום הנחילו את בניו שראוי להורישם לאלתר: דאמר לי' ר' נתן לרבי. שסידר את המשנה: שניתם משנתכם. אתם שבארץ ישראל ההיא משנה דכתובות דלקמיה וסתמתם כר' יוחנן בן ברוקא דאמר אם אמר על מי שראוי ליורשו שיירש נכסיו דבריו קיימין ויפסיד שאר בניו את חלקם ולא יפה עשיתם דשבקיתון רבנן ועבידתון כריב"ב ולפי שר' נתן עלה מבבל קאמר לרבי משנתכם: לא כתב לה. לאשתו בכתובתה בין ראשונה בין שניה: בנין דיכרין כו'. בנים זכרים שתלדי לי ירשו לאחר מותי את כתובתיך שאירש ממך אם תמותי בחיי והם ירושה ממני לבד חלק נחלה שירשו בנכסי הנותרים עם אחיהם שיש לי [צ"ל להם] אז שיהיו לי מאשה אחרת והיינו כתובת בנין דיכרין כדי שיקפוץ אדם ויתן לבתו כבנו שהרי אפי' תמות בחייו בעלה ירושה בניה אחר מות אביהם: חייב שהוא תנאי ב"ד. דתנאי ב"ד כאילו כתוב בשטר הכתובה דמי אלמא מוריש האב לבן בין הבנים יותר מכדי חלקו כר"י בן ברוקא דהא לרבנן תנן אם אמר משום ירושה לא אמר כלום ובכאן ירתון תנן: וא"ל לר' נתן: אנן יסבון תנן. דהיינו לשון מתנה ומשום הכי דבריו קיימין אבל ירתון לא תנן והיינו כרבנן: הדר אמר רבי ילדות ושטות היתה בי שהעזתי פני. להשיב תשובה שאינה לר' נתן שאמרתי לו יסבון תנן אלא ודאי ירתון תנן: דהא קי"ל כתובת בנין דיכרין לא טרפא ממשעבדי. משום דהך ירושה לא נפלה קמייהו עד לאחר מיתת אביהם ואינן יורשין מה שמכר אביהן בחייו: ואי ס"ד יסבון תנן. הא מתנה משעת נתינה הוא דקניא ואמאי לא טרפא ממשעבדי הא קדמא לכל מאן דזבין ויהבן אלא ש"מ ירתון תנן. ויפה הקשה ליה ר' נתן ואיכא למימר דר' נתן דהוה מקשה לרבי הוה תני יסבון וס"ל דטריף ממשעבדי ור' שסתם כריב"ב הא סבר דבלשון ירוש' ירבה לאחד וימעט לאחר כי הכא שיורשין כתובת אמם והמותר על שתי כתובות חולקין ביניהן דאילו היכא דליכא מותר דינר על

רבינו גרשום

שאין לו לדיין אלא מה שעיניו רואות. כלומר לפי מה שנראה לי באותה שעה התכתי שמא בשעה אחרת היה נראה לי בענין אחר: בעי רבא. הא דקאמר ר' יוחנן בן ברוקה אם אמר על מי שראוי ליורשו דבריו קיימין בשכיב מרע קאמר דבר אורותי הוא אבל בריא דלא בר אורותי הוא דאין נוהג ליתן ירושה כל זמן שהוא בריא לא אמרינן דבריו קיימין אלא על יורשו ממש: אמר ליה ר' נתן לרבי שניתם במשנה כר' יוחנן בן ברוקה. דבריא מורית מי שראוי ליורשו דתנן לא כתב לה בנין דיכרין דיהוון ליכי מינאי אינון ירתין כסף כתובתיך יותר על חולקיהן דאית להון (מאם אחרת) [דעם] אחוהון כו' והא בריא הוא וקאמר אינון ירתון יותר: אמר ליה רבי לר' נתן מהא לא תפשוט דאין ירתון תנן אלא יסבון תנן. דמשמע במתנה ומתנה מצי למיתן לכל מאן דבעי אפי' לנכרי אבל בלשון ירושה לא: והדר אמר רבי ילדות היתה בי כשהעזתי פני בנתן הבבלי. דאמינא ליה יסבון תנן. משום דלא מצינן למימר יסבון דהא קי"ל כו' אמאי לא טרפא ממשעבדי: בשלמא אי אמרינן ירתון משום הכי לא טרפא ממשעבדי דהא היה קודם שטר שעבוד לקוחות מהאי ירושה דאינו אלא לאחר מיתה. דאי ס"ד דיסבון תנן אמאי לא טרפא ממשעבדי דהא הוה מוקדם שטר מתנה זה משטר לקוחות ובדין הוא דטרפא. אלא ש"מ דירתון תנן וש"מ בריא נמי דמאן שמעת ליה דאית ליה כי האי סברא. אע"ג דלא כתב לה בנין דיכרין אינון ירתון יותר דמצי מורית בשכיב מרע ר' יוחנן בן ברוקה דאמר אם אמר על מי שראוי ליורשו דבריו קיימין וש"מ אפי' בבריא קאמר: הא אין אדם מקנה דבר שלא בא לעולם. כגון הני בנין דכרין דאכתי לא באו לעולם. אלא מאי

צו א מיי' פי"ב מהל' זכיה ומתנה הלכה ב ועי' במ"מ ופ"ו מהלכות נחלות הל' ד ועי' במ"מ סמג עשין צו טוש"ע חו"מ סי' רפא סעיף ה:

צז ב ג מיי' פי"ב מהל' אישות הלכה ב ופי"ט הלכה א סמג עשין מח טוש"ע אה"ע סי' סט סעיף א וסעיף ב וסי' קיא סעיף א:

צח ד מיי' שם פי"ט הלכה ט סמג שם טוש"ע אה"ע סי' קיא סעיף יג:

צט ה מיי' שם ופי"ט הל' י וסמג שם טוש"ע שם סי' סט סעיף א וסעי' ב וסי' קיב סעיף א:

שתי הכתובות לא תקנו כתובת בנין דיכרין כדאמרינן בכתובות משום דמיעקרא נחלה דאורייתא מיהו להכי אהני כתובת בנין דיכרין שאפילו אם הכתובה האחת כפלים בחברתה וגם לזו בן אחד ולזו בנים הרבה יירש היחיד אמו הגדולה ואלו בין כולם יירשו כתובת אמם הקטנה והמותר יחלקו חלק כחלק וש"מ אפי' בבריא נמי דהאי בריא הוה כי כתב לה דהא ירתון דמשעת נשואין הוא דאתני ליה הכי: א"ל רב פפא לאביי. לעולם לא תפשוט מהכא דאמר ריב"ב אף בריא דבין למ"ד כו': ובין למ"ד יסבון. ר' נתן: הא אין אדם מקנה לדבר שלא בא לעולם. והני בנים עדיין לא באו לעולם דהא בתחילת נשואין הוא דמתני לה הכי: הני מילי לדבר כו'. כדקתני הרי את מקודשת על מנת שאתגייר כו' דהאשה והאיש באו לעולם: אלא. להכי ירתי הנהו בנים בתנאי זה הקודם ללידתן: דתנאי ב"ד שאני. הפקר ב"ד גבי ממון הפקר: ה"נ. אפי' רבנן מודו דאע"ג [illegible]

אית לך למימר דלא תקשי אמאי מקנה לרבנן בנין דיכרין דלא באו לעולם הואיל ותנאי ב"ד הוא ושאני הכי מבעלמא דבית דין אית להו א) בחוב עלמא לא קנה דבר שלא בא לעולם. הכי נמי האי מצי אמר להני בנין דיכרין ירתון או יסבון יותר על חולקיהון הכא שאני משום דבית דין גורו הכי אבל בעלמא (לא) בבריא אחר לא ומהכא לא תפשוט עדיין דהל' כר' יוחנן בן ברוקה אפי' בבריא: אמר ליה אביי איכא למשמע מהכא דהלכתא כותיה מדקא מפיק ליה תנא בלשון ירתון דמצי למימר יסבון וקתני ירתון ש"מ אם אמר על מי שראוי ליורשו דבריו קיימין אפי' הבריא בלא כתובה והל' כר' יוחנן בן ברוקה. והדר אמר אביי לאו מילתא היא דאמרי הא דבעינא לתרוצי הא מתני' דבנין דיכרין כר' יוחנן בן ברוקה דאפי' כרבנן דפליגי עליה דר' יוחנן בן ברוקה מתוקמי מתני' דבנין דיכרין משום דקתני סיפא לא כתב לה בנין נוקבן כו'. הוי ליה לזה לבנין דיכרין בירושה דקאמר [illegible]

א) תוס' נ"ל דכ"ד אית לו רשות להקנות טפי אף דבעלמא לא קנה וכו'. ב) נ"ל דבלשון ירושה אפי' לרבנן וכו'.

הגהות הב"ח (א) גמ' חייב שהוא תנאי ב"ד ואמר לו: (ב) רשב"ם ד"ה ואל תגמרו מיניה וכו' המתין שעה אחת חזר כצ"ל ותיבת וראהו נמחק: (ג) בא"ד שעיניו רואות והוא הדין. נ"ב והתם משני מעיקרא אחזיקא בעלמא כו': (ד) תוס' ד"ה ושמע מינה וכו' ולזה במתנה ולזה בירושה ולזה במתנה אפילו רבנן מודו ולעולם וכו' בבריא בעלמא ואפ"ה שפיר קאמר לרבי: (ה) בא"ד לא הוה ליה למיתני ירתון כיון דלא מהני:

עין משפט
נר מצוה

ק א מיי' פ"ב מהלכות אישות הלכה יד סמג עשין מח טוש"ע אה"ע סי' עא סעיף א:
קא ב מיי' פ"ו מהל' זכיה ומתנה הל' ד סמג עשין פב טוש"ע ח"מ סי' רמו סעיף יב וטוש"ע אה"ע סי' קז סעיף א:
קב ג ד מיי' שם הל"ב וסמג שם טוש"ע חו"מ שם סעיף ד וטוש"ע אה"ע שם סעיף ז:
קג ה מיי' שם הל"ג וסמג שם טוש"ע חו"מ שם סעיף ט:
קד ו מיי' שם הלכה ז סמג שם טור שו"ע אה"ע שם סעיף ח:
קה ז מיי' שם הל"ה וסמג שם טוש"ע אה"ע סי' קז סעיף ב:
קו ח מיי' שם הלכה ג ועי' במ"מ ובכ"מ ובל"מ וסמג שם טור שו"ע חו"מ סי' רמו ס"ח:
קז ט מיי' שם הלכה ז ועי' בהג"ל וסמג שם טוש"ע אה"ע סי' קז ס"ה:

מסורת הש"ס

א) כתובות מט.: ב) לקמן קמד. קנ: גיטין יז.: ג) רש"ל מ"ז לפי' רשב"ם: ד) ז פירוש אחר רש"ל:

מִמַּאי דִּבְחַד בֵּי דִּינָא אִיתְּקוּן? דִּלְמָא בִּתְרֵי בֵּי דִּינָא אִיתְּכוּן! לָא סָלְקָא דַּעְתָּךְ, דְּקָתָנֵי רֵישָׁא, א)זֶה מִדְרָשׁ דָּרַשׁ ר' אֶלְעָזָר בֶּן עֲזַרְיָה לִפְנֵי חֲכָמִים בַּכֶּרֶם בְּיַבְנֶה: הַבָּנִים יִירְשׁוּ וְהַבָּנוֹת יִזּוֹנוּ, מָה הַבָּנִים אֵינָן יוֹרְשִׁין אֶלָּא לְאַחַר מִיתַת אֲבִיהֶם, אאַף בָּנוֹת לֹא יִזּוֹנוּ אֶלָּא לְאַחַר מִיתַת אֲבִיהֶן; אִי אָמְרַתְּ בִּשְׁלָמָא בְּחַד בֵּי דִּינָא אִיתְּקוּן, הַיְינוּ דְּיָלְפִינַן תַּקָּנָה מִתַּקָּנָה, אֶלָּא אִי אָמְרַתְּ בִּתְרֵי בֵּי דִּינָא אִיתְּקוּן, הֵיכִי יָלְפִינַן תַּקָּנָה מִתַּקָּנָה! מִמַּאי? דִּלְמָא לְעוֹלָם אֵימָא לָךְ: בִּתְרֵי בֵּי דִּינָא אִיתְּקוּן, וּבֵי דִינָא בַּתְרָא תִּיקּוּן כְּבֵי דִינָא קַמָּא, כִּי הֵיכִי דְּלָא תִּקְשֵׁה תַּקַּנְתָּא אַתַּקַּנְתָּא.§ ב)אָמַר רַב יְהוּדָה אָמַר שְׁמוּאֵל: בהַכּוֹתֵב כָּל נְכָסָיו לְאִשְׁתּוֹ – לֹא עֲשָׂאָהּ אֶלָּא אַפּוֹטְרוֹפָּא. גפְּשִׁיטָא, בְּנוֹ הַגָּדוֹל – לֹא עֲשָׂאוֹ אֶלָּא אַפּוֹטְרוֹפּוֹס; בְּנוֹ הַקָּטָן מַאי? אִיתְּמַר, רַב חֲנִילַאי בַּר אִידִי אָמַר שְׁמוּאֵל: דאֲפִילּוּ בְּנוֹ קָטָן הַמּוּטָּל בַּעֲרִיסָה. הפְּשִׁיטָא, בְּנוֹ וְאַחֵר – אַחֵר בְּמַתָּנָה וּבְנוֹ אַפּוֹטְרוֹפּוֹס. ג)(ואִשְׁתּוֹ וְאַחֵר – לְאַחֵר בְּמַתָּנָה וְאִשְׁתּוֹ אַפּוֹטְרוֹפּוֹס.) ואִשְׁתּוֹ אֲרוּסָה וְאִשְׁתּוֹ גְּרוּשָׁה – בְּמַתָּנָה. אִיבַּעְיָא לְהוּ: בַּת אֵצֶל הַבָּנִים, וְאִשָּׁה אֵצֶל הָאַחִים, וְאִשָּׁה אֵצֶל בְּנֵי הַבַּעַל, מַהוּ? אָמַר רָבִינָא, מִשְּׁמֵיהּ דְּרָבָא: בְּכוּלְּהוּ לֹא (א) קָנָה, לְבַר מֵאִשְׁתּוֹ אֲרוּסָה וְאִשְׁתּוֹ גְּרוּשָׁה; רַב עֲוִירָא מִשְּׁמֵיהּ דְּרָבָא אָמַר: חבְּכוּלְּהוּ קָנֵי, טלְבַר מֵהָאִשָּׁה אֵצֶל הָאַחִין וְאִשָּׁה אֵצֶל בְּנֵי הַבַּעַל.

בָּעֵי

דלמא בתרי בי דינא איתקון. פירוש: דספיקא הוי אי אמר בבריא אי לא. ולר"י נראה: דבבריא נמי אמר, מדאמר רבי נתן: שניתם משנתכם כר' יוחנן בן ברוקה.

למחצה

ממאי דבחד בי דינא איתקון. דליהוו בתוך כדי דבור? דלמא בתרי בי דינא איתקון, ולא קאי האי אהאי כלל, ולא מהני לשון מתנה דזה חזה! **לא** ס"ד. דבתרי בי דינא איתקון. **אף הבנות אינן ניזונות אלא לאחר מיתת אביהם.** ובחייו אין כופין אותו לזון את בניו, כדאמרי' בכתובות. אלא כפינן ליה אסיפא בליבורא, וליקו וליפא "עורבא בעי בני, והאי גברא לא בעי בני". **דילפי'** תקנה מתקנה. דכיון דבחד בי דינא תקון להו, ולא מפורש בתקנות חילוק בין זו לזו – מסתמא בחד ענין תקנינהו. אבל אי בתרי בי דינא איתקון – דלמא חד בי דינא קמי אמסיים, וחד אלאחר מיתה, והיכי ילפי האי מהאי? **לעולם אימא לך בתרי בי דינא איתקון.** ואין כאן תוך כדי דבור, ומשו"ה אצטריך למימר לר' "יכתבון" תנן. ומיהו, תקנתא מתקנתא ילפינן, דבי דינא בתרא מעין בי דינא קמא תקינו, דלא תקשי תקנתא אתקנתא, דלא לימרו: מ"ש תקנה זו דכתובת בנין דיכרין דלאחר מיתה קכתב בה "ירתון", ומ"ש זו דאיתקנא מחיים? ומיהו, בעיא דהכא איפשיטא ממילתיה דר' נתן, כדפרישית. ואע"ג דרבי כר' יוחנן בן ברוקה ס"ל כדאמרינן לעיל: א"ר זריקא אמר ר' חנינא א"ר ינאי אמר רבי: הלכה כר' יוחנן – אפ"ה קאמר "יכתבון", לאוקומי מתניתין דברי הכל. **הכותב כל נכסיו לאשתו.** בלשון מתנה. **לא עשאה אלא אפוטרופא.** דאומד הדעת הוא דאין אדם מניח את בניו ונותן את הכל לאשתו, ולא נתכוין אלא לעשותה אפוטרופא, כדי שיחלקו לה בניו כבוד משום דאוקי אבוהון נכסי ברשותה לפרנסם מהם כפי אומד דעתה, ויהיו כפופים לה. ולקמן אמי לה מהני תלת מילי דשוינהו רבנן כהלכתא בלא טעמא, דדברי נבואה הם, בפ' "מי שמת", לפי שאנו מניחין מה שכתוב בשטר בהדיא, שנתן לה הכל, ליילך אחר אומד דעתנו. ובשכיב מרע מיירי, ורבא בעי לקמן בבריא היאך, ומשו"ה נקט לה הכא. וכן הא ד"תנן התם" דלקמן נמי, משום דרבא בעי עלייהו נמי בבריא היאך. ודוקא כל נכסיו, דליכא שיור לא במקרקעי ולא במטלטלי, אבל אי איכא שיור – קנתה. ומיהו, הכותב נכסיו לאחר, שאין בו אומד הדעת, שאינו חש כל כך לכבודו – אמרי' לקמן דאם כתב לו כל נכסיו, אם מת – קנה הכל. דכיון דלא שייר מידי – נראה שכיב מרע היא זו, שהיה ירא למות, והוו דבריו ככתובין וכמסורין. ה"ג לה לכולה: **פשיטא בנו הגדול לא עשאו אלא אפוטרופוס בנו הקטן מאי א"ר חנילאי בר אידי אמר שמואל אפילו קטן המוטל בעריסה. פשיטא בנו ואחר אחר משום מתנה ובנו משום אפוטרופא, אשתו ארוסה ואשתו גרושה משום מתנה. איבעיא להו בת אצל הבנים ואשה אצל האחין ואשה אצל בני הבעל מהו. אמר רבינא משמיה דרבא בכולהו לא קנו לבר מאשתו ארוסה ואשתו גרושה. ורב עוירא משמיה דרבא אמר בכולהו קנו לבר מאשה אצל האחין ואשה אצל בני הבעל. בעי רבא בבריא היאך וכו'** והכי פירושו: פשיטא, בנו גדול שכתב לו כל נכסיו לא עשאו אלא אפוטרופא, דרוצה הוא שיחלקו לו אחיו כבוד, שהרי חייבין בכבודו, כדאמרינן (כתובות קג.): "ואת" – לרבות אחיך הגדול, ואומד הדעת הוא שלכבודו נתכוין. בנו (ב) קטן מי אמר כיון דקטן הוא אינו חש לכבודו, ולמתנה איכוין. או דלמא אף בנו קטן רוצה לכבדו? **אפילו** כמן המוטל בעריסה. רוצה הוא בכבודו, ולא עשאו אלא אפוטרופא. **פשיטא בנו ואחר כו'.** כלומר, פשיטא לי שהכותב כל נכסיו לבנו, שקרוב לו יותר מכל קרוביו ורוצה בכבודו יותר, או הכותב כל נכסיו לאחר דלא חייש לכבודו כלל – בהני תרי פשיטא לי. דאחר במקום בניו – משום מתנה, דלכבודו לא חייש אלא להקנותו לתת לו במתנה. דאם לעשותו אפוטרופא נתכוין, בשביל שאין בניו יודעין בטיב משא ומתן – היה לו לומר בפירוש: אני עושה אותו אפוטרופא, ולא היה לו לכתוב לשון מתנה. ובנו במקום הבנים – משום אפוטרופא. ולא גרסי': אשתו ובנו אשתו משום מתנה ובנו משום אפוטרופא. דהא שמואל אמר דהכותב כל נכסיו לאשתו לא עשאה אלא אפוטרופא, ובאשה במקום בנים הוא דמיירי. והא דלא קאמר נמי: אשתו פשיטא משום אפוטרופא – היינו משום דקאמר לה שמואל בהדיא. אבל בנו ואחר, וכל הני דלא מיירי בהו שמואל בהדיא – הדר נקיט לפרושינהו, כן נראה בעיני. וי"מ: בנו ואחר – שנתן להם ביחד לשניהן כל נכסיו. ואין נראה בעיני, דא"כ אמאי בנו משום אפוטרופא? והלא הוא נותן מחלה לזה ומחלה לזה, והאי אחר היאך יזכה בכל הנכסים, ובנו אמאי יהיה אפוטרופא? והלא לא כתב לו כל נכסיו! ואם יש לפרשה במתנה לשניהן ביחד – הכי מפרשינן: אחר משום מתנה, וזכה בחלי הנכסים שכתב לו, ובנו משום אפוטרופא לאחיו בההוא חלי נכסים שכתב לו. דכיון דליכא שיור לבנים, שהרי לאחר נתן חלי הנכסים ולא נשאר לפניו כי אם החלי שכתב לבנו – הרי הוא כמו שכתב לו כל נכסים שיש לו דמי, ולא עשאו אלא אפוטרופא. ומיהו, לא נהירא לי כלל, דלא דמי לסיפא דקאמרי' אשתו ארוסה ואשתו גרושה במתנה. דהתם ודאי או או קתני, וה"ה לסך רישא. **בנו ואשתו.** לא גרסי'. ומיהו, הדין כך נראה בעיני: כתב לאשתו במקום בנו – בההיא קאמר שמואל בהדיא: לא עשאה אלא אפוטרופא. כתב לבנו במקום אשתו, חזינן: אם יש לזה הבן אחין – לא עשאו אלא אפוטרופא, כדי שיכבדוהו אחין, כדאמרי' לעיל: אפילו קטן המוטל בעריסה, ואפילו במקום אשתו דהיינו אמם קאמרינן. ואם אין לו אחין – ודאי משום מתנה כתב לו. דליכא למימר משום אפוטרופסות, דאינו רוצה שתכבד האם את הבן. דאדרבה, הוא רוצה שהבן יכבדנה, כדאמרי': הכותב כל נכסיו לאשתו – לא עשאה אלא אפוטרופא. אשתו ארוסה או אשתו גרושה – מודה שמואל דבמתנה יהיב לה, דכיון דלא נייס בהו – לא חשש בכבודן, אלא מתנה הוא רוצה ליתן להן. ד) (ג)(הג"ה. בנו ואחר, כגון בנו ובן בנו שמת, שהוא ראוי ליורשו כמו בנו, והוא אחר אצל בנו. או כגון שקיבל עליו לזון את בן אשתו. אם כתב נכסיו לבנו – פשיטא דלא עשאו אלא אפוטרופא, דרוצה שיכבדו אותו בן בנו או בן אשתו. אבל אם כתב לבן בנו או לבן אשתו, וכל שכן לאחר בעלמא – אמרי' דלא חש לכבודו, ונתכוין למתנה. אשתו ואחר שהן בביתו, אם כתב לאשתו – משום אפוטרופא, דרוצה הוא שיכבדוה אחרים. אבל אם כתב לאחר – ודאי למתנה נתכוין, דאינו חש שתכבדנו אשתו. נ"ל: בנו ואשתו, אשתו – משום מתנה, ובנו – משום אפוטרופוס, דאדם רוצה שיכבדו בניו את אשתו אפילו אינה אמם, שהן חייבין בכבודה, דדרשינן (שם): "את אביך" – לרבות אשת אביך, וכ"ש זו שהיא אמם. אבל אשתו – אינו רוצה שתתבזה לכבד את בניו. **אשתו ארוסה ואשתו גרושה** במתנה. דאינו חושש לכבודן, זו מפני שגירשה וזו מפני שלא הכניסה עדיין. ע"כ). **בת אצל הבנים.** כיון דאנו רואין דחוששין לענין נכסים מועטין, דאמרי': הבנות יזונו והבנים יחזרו על הפתחים – אלמא דחיישינן ליקרא דבנות מיקרא דבנים, ואיכא למימר דעשאה אפוטרופא. או דלמא: הני מילי לענין חזרת פתחים, אבל כי האי גוונא שיכבדוה בניו – לא חש לכבודה. **ואשה אצל האחין.** שאין לו בנים ואב אלא אחין, וכיון דאחיו אינן חייבין בכבוד אשתו כלל – אינו חושש שיכבדוה, ומתנה הוא דיהב לה. או דלמא, כיון דאשתו כגופו דמיא – רוצה שיכבדוה, ואפוטרופא שויה. **ואשה אצל בני הבעל.** דלא הוו ליה בנים ממנה, דנימא: אפוטרופא שויה כדי שיכבדוה בניה, שחייבין בכבודה. אבל יש לו בנים מאשה אחרת, ואינן חייבין בכבודה כל כך אלא מיתורא דקרא: "את אביך" – לרבות אשת אביך, וכל מי שאינן חייבין בכבודו – אינו מקפיד אם אין מכבדין אותו, וגם היא לא תקפיד אם לא יכבדוה אלו. והלכך גם הבעל אינו חושש, ולמתנה איכוין. **אמר רבינא משמיה דרבא כולהו.** הנך חמש נשים לא קנו, לבד מאשתו ארוסה ואשתו גרושה. **ורב עוירא משמיה דרבא אמר כולהו.** הנך חמש נשים קנו, לבד מאשה אצל אחין ואשה אצל בני הבעל. ובסברות בעלמא פליגי. ובת אצל הבנים לבדה איכא בינייהו, לרבינא לא קניא לרב עוירא קניא.

בעי

פי' הרשב"ם העקרי

ירושה בבריא והא [צ"ל דהא] אפי' שכ"מ כה"ג לא קני שהרי עדיין לא באו לעולם אלא הכי קאמר לי' ר' נתן לר' נהי דמן הדין לא קנו הני בנים כתובת בנין דיכרין שהרי עדיין לא באו הבנים לעולם ועוד דבריא הוה ולא מהני לשון ירושה בבריא אפי' לריב"ב אלא בכח ב"ד הוא דקא קנו מיהו לא היה להם לדון דין לתקן תנאי שלהם לפי דברי ריב"ב ולהזכיר לשון ירתון בתנאי שלהם דדמי [אולי צ"ל דאי משום דלא] טרפא ממשעבדי יתקנו נמי בתנאי ב"ד דלא תטרוף [אולי צ"ל דתטרוף או דפי' דיאמרו יסבון ויאמרו בפירוש דלא תטרוף] ממשעבדי: א"ל אביי לעולם פשטינן מינה דאמר נמי ריב"ב בבריא כדאמרן מעיקרא ודקשיא לך הא אין אדם מקנה דבר שלא בא לעולם כו' ומתוך קושיא זו באת לומר תנאי ב"ד שאני ומתוך כך דחית דלא תפשוט מהכא הקושיא אינה קושיא והתירוץ אינו דלא שאני הכא משאר תנאין דעלמא דמשום דקא מפיק בלשון ירתון קא מקני להו אע"פ שלא באו לעולם דהא עכשיו לא מקני להו מידי אלא הכי קאמר בנים אשר יולדו לי הם יירשו נכסי לכשאמות וכשימות כבר ישנן בעולם וההיא שעתא הוא דאתי וליכא הכא שום שינוי וחידוש יותר משאר תנאים דנצטרך למימר תנאי ב"ד שאני אלא בבריא והאי דקתני מפני שהוא תנאי ב"ד לאו משום דתנאי ב"ד שאני אלא ה"ק אע"פ שלא כתב האי תנאי כמי שכתב דמי מפני שכן הוא תנאי ב"ד שצריך לכתוב ואם לא כתב לא הפסידה בכך ולעולם התנאי עשוי כהלכתו דקני לשון ירתון בבריא ולעולם בין בבריא בין בשכיב מרע מהני לשון ירושה: הדר אמר אביי לאו מילתא היא דאמרי. דודאי ליכא למפשט מהכא מידי דהאי דקתני ירתון בבריא לשון מתנה איכא בהדה כדמפרש ואזיל דתנן כו' והלכך קני לדברי הכל כדקתני מתני' כתב בין בתחלה בין בסוף מתנה דבריו קיימין אבל ירתון גרידא בבריא לא קני לא לרבנן ולא לריב"ב: דתנן לא כתב לה כו'. סיפא דהך משנה דלעיל היא וקס"ד דבפעם אחת נתקנו בב"ד תנאין הללו ירושת כתוב' בנין דיכרין ומתנת מזון הבנות דהוו לשון ירושה לזה ולשון מתנה לזה ומוקמינן לעיל דאפילו בשתי שדות ושני בני אדם בתוך כדי דבור קני: ומיתזנן מנכסי. לאחר מיתתי ולשון מתנה הוא זה שהרי אינן ראויות ליורשו אלא הבנים והבנות יזונו כדתנן לקמן במי שמת אבל מחיים אינו חייב לזון את בניו ואין כופין אותו אלא הכי אמרינן ליה ידור [נ"ל ירוד] ילדה אבני מתא שדייה בכתובות: [צ"ל לזה בירושה]. כתובת בנין דיכרין כדקתני ירתון: ולזה במתנה. לבנות: אפי' רבנן מודו. כדקתני מתני' כתב בין בתחלה בין בסוף בין באמצע וכו' ואוקמה רב ששת אפי' בשתי שדות ושני בני אדם ואוקמן כוותיה לעיל והלכך הך משנה דכתובת בנין דיכרין דבריא הוא ולעולם לא פשטינן מינה אי אמר ריב"ב בבריא או לא ור' נתן דהוה אמר שניתם משנתכם כריב"ב איכא למימר דאלישנא דירתון קא קפיד דכיון דבע"כ מתנה היא דהא איכא בהדיה לשון מתנה למה לי למיתני ירתון דדמיא מילתא דאליבא דריב"ב אתיא ומיהו לעולם אפי' ר' נתן מודה דדברי הכל היא דהאי ירתון לשון מתנה איכא בהדיה ומכל מקום אהני לשון ירתון לכמה דברים שלא יטלו כי אם לאחר מיתת האב ולא לטרפי ממשעבדי כדין ירושה: *) ממאי דבחד בי דינא. הנך תרי תנאי ב"ד כתובת בנין דיכרין ומזון הבנות דנימא דמהניא מתנה דהאי להאי דלמא בתרי בי דינא איתקון ומעיקרא איתקון כתובת בנין דיכרין בי דינא דמיתניא ברישא במתני' דכתובות ואע"ג דלא הוה בהנהו כתובות של אותו ב"ד הראשון אלא לשון ירושה אפ"ה הוו קנו וש"מ דר' יוחנן אפי' בבריא דבר וכדתרצת לעיל משום דקא מפיק לה בלשון ירתון: בכרם. בבהמ"ד היו יושבין שורות שורות כגפנים בכרם: הבנים יירשו והבנות יזונו. כלומר הני שתי תקנות התקינו חכמים הראשונים שהבנים ירשו

בנין

*) ע"כ שייך לע"א

רבינו גרשום

הוה כוליה בלשון ירושה: ממאי דבחד בי דינא בחד זימנא איתקין. הני תרתי תקנתי בנין דכרין ובנן נוקבן דמצית למימר להאי במתנה ולזה בירושה ובעית לאוקמי משנה זו אפי' כרבנן. דלמא בתרי בי דינא איתקון ולא בחד זימנא ומאן דתקין כתובת בנין דיכרין דירתון סבר משום דמצי לאורותי לכל מאן דבעי ולעולם הלכה כר' יוחנן בן ברוקה. והיכי ילפי' תקנתא מתקנתא דהאי איתקנא בהאי בי דינא ואידך בהאי בי דינא דלמא לעולם אימא לך בתרי בי דינא איתקון ובי דינא בתרא איתקון בנן נוקבן כעין דתקון בי דינא קמא לבנין דכרין. ולהכי ילפינן תקנתא מתקנתא ולהכי אצטריך לאוקמי בתרי בי דינא כי היכי דלא קשיא תקנתא לתקנתא. דאי אמרת בחד בי דינא איתקון הוי קושיא מאי שנא זו בירושה וזו במתנה. אבל כי מוקמינן בתרי בי דינא לא הויא קושיא דהני סברי הכי והני סברי הכי. ולעולם ר' יוחנן בן ברוקה היא ולא רבנן: הכותב כל נכסיו לאשתו. בלשון מתנה ודאי לאו משום דיהיבנא ניהלה אלא כדי לעשותה אפוטרופא מחמת קרובות וחביבות שהיה מחבבה עשה לה כן כדי שיחלקו לה כבוד היורשין ולא קנתה כי אם שיעור כתובתה וכי האי גוונא אם כתב לבנו הגדול פשיטא דלא עשאו אלא אפוטרופא שינהגו בו אחים כבוד. ולא קנה אלא כאחד מן היורשין: בנו קטן מאי. אם כתב לו כל נכסיו דליכא למימר לשום אפוטרופא דלאו בר הכי שינהגו לו כבוד מאי מי אמרינן דקנה או לא: פשיטא אם כתב כל נכסיו לבנו ולאחר ודאי בנו דקרוב דעתו אצלו עשאו אפוטרופא לאחר לשום מתנה הכי נמי מפרש' גבי אשתו ואחר: אשתו ובניו משום דאינו קרוב דעתו אצלו יותר א) מאותו: אשתו ארוסה ואשתו גרושה אשתו ארוסה לא קרובה דעתו גבה כולי האי דאכתי אין לבו גם בה. ואשתו גרושה כבר נתרחקה אם כתב לה כל נכסיו ודאי משום מתנה הוא וקני': אבעיא להו אי כתב כל נכסיו לבתו במקום שהיו לו בנים מהו. מי אמרינן משום חביבותא הוא דכתב לה כדי שיחלקו לה בנים כבוד ועשאה אפוטרופא ולא קנתה או דלמא משום מתנה כעליא הוא דיהבה ניהלה וקנתה והכי נמי אשה אצל האחין אם כתב לה כל נכסיו מהו. מי אמרינן אפוטרופא עשאה כדי שיחלקו לה האחים כבוד או דלמא הואיל דאין חייבין בכבודה משום מתנה יהיב לה: ואשה אצל בני הבעל דלאו אמן היא. מהו מי אמרינן הואיל דהני בנים לא מחייבי בכבודה כולי האי משום מתנה הוא יהיב לה וקנתה או דלמא הואיל וכל דהו שייכי בכבודה דכתי' כבד את אביך ואת אמך לרבות אשת אביך ודאי משום דינהגו לה יקרא עבד ועשאה אפוטרופא ולא קנתה: אמר רבא כולהו. הני נשי לא קנו משום דעשאן אפוטרופא משום שיש להן חביבות וקורבית דעת: לבר מאשתו ארוסה ואשתו גרושה. דלא יהיב דעתיה לגביהו כולי האי: ורב עוירא אמר משמיה דרבא כולהו קנו. לשום מתנה: לבר מאשה אצל הבנים. דחייבים בכבוד אמן ואיכא למימר משום אפוטרופא היא והכי נמי אשה אצל בני הבעל דשייכי כל דהו בכבודה:

א) נראה דל"ל אשתו ובנו אשתו משום מתנה ובנו משום אפוטרופא משום דאינו קרוב דעתו אצלה יותר מבנו וכו'.

הגהות הב"ח (א) גמ' בכולהו לא קנו לבר: (ב) רשב"ם ד"ה ה"ג לה וכו' בנו הקטן מאי מי אמר: (ג) ד"ה הג"ה פריסה אחרת מצאתי ויפה בעיני בנו ואחר כגון וכו' שתכבדנו אשתו ה"ג בנו ואשתו:

בָּעֵי רָבָא בְּבָרִיא. שֶׁכָּתַב כָּל נְכָסָיו לְאִשְׁתּוֹ, וּלְכָל הָנֵי דְּאַיְּירֵי שְׁמוּאֵל, אִם כָּתַב לָהֶם בְּמַתָּנָה מֵהַיּוֹם לְגַמְרֵי, אִי נַמִּי מֵהַיּוֹם וּלְאַחַר מִיתָה, מִי אָמְרִינַן מַתָּנָה גְּמוּרָה הִיא. דְּאִי מִשּׁוּם כְּבוֹדָהּ – הָא קָאֵי הוּא, וִיכַבְּדוּהָ מֵאֵימָתוֹ. דְּלִישְׁתַּמְּעוּן מִלָּה מֵהַשְׁתָּא. לְפִי שֶׁיּוֹדְעִין שֶׁעֲתִידִין לִהְיוֹת כְּפוּפִין לָהּ. הַכּוֹתֵב. בְּמַתָּנָה. פֵּירוֹת נְכָסָיו. שֶׁעַכְשָׁיו בְּעַיִן. אִי נַמִּי, דְּאַקְנֵי לָהּ קַרְקַע לְפֵירוֹתֶיהָ, דְּאַקְנֵי לָהּ בְּגוּפָא דְּאַרְעָא דְּקַנְיֵיהּ. גּוֹבָה. (ג) כָּל כְּתוּבָּתָהּ מִן הַקַּרְקַע, דִּבְשְׁבִיל מַתָּנָה זוֹ לֹא מָחֲלָה שִׁעְבּוּד כְּתוּבָּתָהּ שֶׁעַל הַקַּרְקַע. וְאִם כָּתַב לָהּ קַרְקַע וּפֵירוֹת לְגַמְרֵי, מַחֲצִיתָן אוֹ שְׁלִישׁ אוֹ רְבִיעַ – גּוֹבָה כְּתוּבָּתָהּ מִן הַשְּׁאָר. וְ"לֹא זוֹ אַף זוֹ" קָתָנֵי: כָּתַב לָהּ פֵּירוֹת, וַאֲפִי' קַרְקַע. וּמִיהוּ, הַאי דְּקָתָנֵי לְמֶחֱצָה לִשְׁלִישׁ וְלִרְבִיעַ בְּ"זוֹ וְאֵין צ"ל זוֹ" מִיפָּרְשָׁא, וְלָאו דַּוְקָא נָקַט כִּי הַאי סִידְרָא הָכָא, אֶלָּא מִשּׁוּם דִּבְכָל דּוּכְתָּא רָגִיל לוֹמַר כֵּן. כָּתַב כָּל נְכָסָיו לְאִשְׁתּוֹ. וְקָא סָלְקָא דַּעְתָּךְ הָשְׁתָּא אֲפִי' בִּמְקוֹם בָּנִים, דְּאָמַר שְׁמוּאֵל לְעֵיל: לֹא עֲשָׂאָהּ אֶלָּא אַפּוֹטְרוֹפָּא, וְהָכָא קָאָמַר דְּקַנְיָא. וְיָצָא עָלָיו שְׁטַר חוֹב. שֶׁקָּדַם לְמַתָּנָה זוֹ. וּמִיהוּ, לִכְתוּבָּתָהּ לֹא קָדַם. תִּקְרַע מַתְּנָתָהּ וְתַעֲמוֹד עַל כְּתוּבָּתָהּ. דִּלְיַיפּוֹת כֹּחָהּ נִכְתְּבָה מַתָּנָה זוֹ, לִזְכּוֹת בְּמוֹתַר נְכָסִים. אֲבָל הִיא לֹא מָחֲלָה שִׁעְבּוּד כְּתוּבָּתָהּ שֶׁעַל נְכָסִים הַלָּלוּ בִּשְׁבִיל מַתָּנָה זוֹ, שֶׁאִם תִּיבָּטֵל מַתָּנָה זוֹ בִּשְׁבִיל בַּעַל חוֹב הַקּוֹדֵם – תַּחֲזוֹר עֲלֵיהֶם מִכֹּחַ שִׁעְבּוּד כְּתוּבָּתָהּ, וְהִלְכָּךְ רוֹצָה הִיא שֶׁתִּקָּרַע מַתְּנָתָהּ. תִּקְרַע כְּתוּבָּתָהּ. לָאו דַּוְקָא, שֶׁהֲרֵי אֵינָהּ מוֹחֶלֶת כְּתוּבָּתָהּ בִּשְׁבִיל שׁוּם מַתָּנָה שֶׁנּוֹתֵן לָהּ בַּעַל. דְּאִי קָנָה נְכָסִים אַחֲרֵי כֵן – תִּגְבֶּה מֵהֶן כְּתוּבָּתָהּ, כִּדְאָמְרִינַן לְקַמָּן בִּשְׁמַעְתִּין: שֶׁהֲרֵי כָּךְ כָּתַב לָהּ: "דִּקְנָאִי וּדְעָתִיד אֲנָא לְמִיקְנֵי". אֲבָל מֵהָנֵךְ נְכָסִים דִּיהֵיב לָהּ – מָחֲלָה שִׁעְבּוּד כְּתוּבָּתָהּ, דְּמִינַּיְיהוּ לֹא תִּגְבֵּי כְּתוּבָּתָהּ, הוֹאִיל וּבְמַתְּנַת חִנָּם בָּאוּ לְיָדָהּ. דְּאֵינָהּ נוֹתֶנֶת אֶל לִבָּהּ שֶׁמָּא יָבֹא בַּעַל חוֹב וְיִטְרְפֵם בְּחוֹבוֹ. הִלְכָּךְ, תִּקְרַע כְּתוּבָּתָהּ לְגַבֵּי הָנֵי נְכָסִים, שֶׁלֹּא תִּטְרוֹף. וְתַעֲמוֹד עַל מַתְּנָתָהּ. אִם אֶפְשָׁר לָהּ לְהִתְקַיֵּים. הִלְכָּךְ, כֵּיוָן דְּלָא הָוְיָא מַתָּנָה – נִמְצֵאת קֵרַחַת מִכָּאן וּמִכָּאן. וּמִיהוּ, מְחִילָה בְּטָעוּת לֵיתָא, דְּהַהִיא מַתָּנָה גְּמוּרָה הָיְתָה בְּאוֹתָהּ שָׁעָה, דְּהָא אִי בָּעֵי בַּעַל – מָצֵי מְסַלֵּק לֵיהּ בְּזוּזֵי, וְכִדְאָמַר רָבָא בִּפְסָחִים בְּפֶרֶק "כָּל שָׁעָה" (דף ל:) דְּבַעַל חוֹב מִכָּאן וּלְהַבָּא הוּא גּוֹבֶה. בְּבַת אֲחוֹתִי כַּלָּה. כַּלָּתִי אֵשֶׁת בְּנִי. שֶׁכָּתַב לָהּ בְּנִי כָּל נְכָסָיו, וְאַחַר כָּךְ בָּא בַּעַל חוֹב דִּבְנִי לִגְבּוֹת חוֹבוֹ שֶׁקּוֹדֵם לַמַּתָּנָה וּמְאוּחָר לִכְתוּבָּתָהּ. קַנְיָא. וְלָא אָמְרִינַן עֲשָׂאָהּ אַפּוֹטְרוֹפָּא. אֶלָּא לָאו בְּבָרִיא. וּשְׁמַע מִינַּהּ דִּבְבָרִיא קַנְיָא, דְּלֵיכָּא לְמֵימַר אַפּוֹטְרוֹפָּא עֲשָׂאָהּ, דְּהָא קָאֵי הוּא. וּבִשְׁכִיב מְרַע אַיְּירֵי שְׁמוּאֵל, וְלָא בְּבָרִיא. רַב עֲוִירָא מוֹקֵי בְּכוּלְּהוּ. כִּדְאָמְרִינַן לְעֵיל: כּוּלְּהוּ קָנוּ – דְּהַיְינוּ בַּת אֵצֶל הַבָּנִים, וְאִשְׁתּוֹ אֲרוּסָה וְאִשְׁתּוֹ גְּרוּשָׁה. וְה"נ, הַךְ אִשְׁתּוֹ דְּקָתָנֵי – הַיְינוּ אִשְׁתּוֹ אֲרוּסָה וְאִשְׁתּוֹ גְּרוּשָׁה. וּמִיהוּ, בְּבַת אֵצֶל הַבָּנִים לֵיכָּא לְאוֹקוּמַהּ, דְּהָא אִשְׁתּוֹ קָתָנֵי. וְאִי קַשְׁיָא: הָא רָבִינָא נַמִּי בְּאִשְׁתּוֹ אֲרוּסָה וְאִשְׁתּוֹ גְּרוּשָׁה מוֹקֵי לָהּ, כִּדְמְפָרֵשׁ לְקַמֵּיהּ, וְא"כ אַמַּאי קָאָמַר גְּמָרָא: רַב עֲוִירָא מוֹקֵי לָהּ בְּכוּלְּהוּ? לֵימָא נַמִּי: רַב עֲוִירָא מוֹקֵי לָהּ בְּאִשְׁתּוֹ אֲרוּסָה וְאִשְׁתּוֹ גְּרוּשָׁה, דְּהָא לֵיכָּא בֵּינַיְיהוּ אֶלָּא בַּת אֵצֶל הַבָּנִים לְחוּד, כִּדְפָרֵישִׁית לְעֵיל. וּבְבַת אֵצֶל הַבָּנִים לֵיכָּא לְאוֹקוּמַהּ, דְּהָא אִשְׁתּוֹ קָתָנֵי! תָּרֵיץ: מִשּׁוּם דַּאֲמָרַן לְעֵיל: רַב עֲוִירָא מִשְּׁמֵיהּ דְּרָבָא אָמַר כּוּלְּהוּ קָנוּ כו' – הִילְכָּךְ נָקַט נַמִּי הָכָא כִּי הַהוּא לִישָּׁנָא דִּלְעֵיל. הָכִי גָּרְסִינַן: רָבִינָא מוֹקֵי לָהּ בְּאִשְׁתּוֹ אֲרוּסָה וְאִשְׁתּוֹ גְּרוּשָׁה. אָמַר ר"נ הֲלָכָה תִּקְרַע כְּתוּבָּתָהּ וְתַעֲמוֹד עַל מַתְּנָתָהּ. דְּלָא תִּטְרוֹף כְּתוּבָּה מֵהָנֵי נְכָסִים אע"פ שֶׁקְּדָמָה לְבַעַל חוֹב, שֶׁהֲרֵי מָחֲלָה שִׁעְבּוּד אֶלָּא מִשּׁוּם דְּבָאוּ לְיָדָהּ בְּמַתָּנָה. וּמִיהוּ, אִם קָנָה נְכָסִים אַחֲרֵי כֵן – תִּגְבֶּה מֵהֶן כְּתוּבָּתָהּ, כִּדְאָמְרִי' לְקַמָּן בִּשְׁמַעְתִּין. וְהָא דְּאִיצְטְרִיךְ ר"נ לִפְסוֹק הֲלָכָה כַּחֲכָמִים – הַיְינוּ מִשּׁוּם דְּאִיכָּא לְאַקְשׁוּיֵי דִּידֵיהּ אַדִּידֵיהּ, כִּדְמַקְשֵׁי וְאָזֵיל, וְאַשְׁמוּעִינַן ר"נ דְּשִׁינּוּיָא דְּקָא מְשַׁנֵּינַן דְּלָא תִּקְשֵׁי דִּידֵיהּ אַדִּידֵיהּ – שִׁינּוּיָא הוּא. וְאִם לֹא אָמַר הֲלָכָה כַּחֲכָמִים – הֲוָה אָמֵינָא דס"ל כר"א, כִּדְמוֹכְחָא הַךְ מִילְּתָא דִּלְקַמָּן. וּמְתַמְהִינַן: וְר"נ לָא אָזֵיל בָּתַר אוּמְדָּנָא. דְּהָא מֵאוֹמֶד הַדַּעַת יֵשׁ לָנוּ לוֹמַר דְּלֹא מָחֲלָה שִׁעְבּוּד הָנֵי נְכָסִים בִּשְׁבִיל הַמַּתָּנָה. מַתְּנָתוֹ מַתָּנָה. שֶׁהֲרֵי לֹא פֵּירֵשׁ בִּשְׁעַת מַתָּנָה: בִּשְׁבִיל שֶׁאֲנִי סָבוּר שֶׁמֵּת בְּנִי אֲנִי נוֹתֵן מַתָּנָה זוֹ. יוֹדֵעַ. הַיְינוּ אוּמְדָּנָא, אע"פ שֶׁלֹּא פֵּירֵשׁ נַמִּי – כְּמִי שֶׁפֵּירֵשׁ דָּמֵי. וּמְשַׁנֵּי. ה"נ בָּתַר אוּמְדָּנָא אָזֵיל ר"נ, דְּקָאָמַר תִּקְרַע כְּתוּבָּתָהּ – דְּנִיחָא לָהּ בְּהַךְ מַתָּנָה, מִשּׁוּם דְּתֵיפּוֹק קָלָא דְּאִיהִי מְהֵימְנָא וַחֲשׁוּבָה גַּבֵּי בַּעְלָהּ, וּמִשּׁוּם הָכִי כָּתַב לָהּ כָּל נְכָסָיו. וּבְהַהִיא הֲנָאָה מָחֲלָה שִׁעְבּוּד כְּתוּבָּתָהּ, וְאָמְרָה: אִי אָתֵי בַּעַל חוֹב וְטָרֵיף לְהָנֵי נִכְסֵי – לָא חָיְישִׁינָא. תְּנַן הָתָם. בְּמַסֶּ' פֵּאָה, בְּסוֹף פ"ג (משנה ז). וּמִשּׁוּם דְּבָעֵי עֲלָהּ רָבָא בְּבָרִיא הֵיאַךְ, נָקַט לָהּ נַמִּי הָכָא. הָכִי גָּרְסִי' לָהּ: הַכּוֹתֵב נְכָסָיו לְבָנָיו. וְלָא גָּרְסִינַן "כָּל". וְכָתַב לְאִשְׁתּוֹ קַרְקַע כָּל שֶׁהוּא. וְלֹא פֵּירֵשׁ אִם לְפֵרָעוֹן כְּתוּבָּתָהּ אִם לְשֵׁם מַתָּנָה. דְּאִי לְפֵרָעוֹן כְּתוּבָּתָהּ – הֲרֵי הוּא כְּמוֹ שֶׁפָּרַע לָהּ קְצָת כְּתוּבָּה, וְכ"ע מוֹדוּ דְּמַה שֶּׁנָּתַן לְבָנָיו אֵינוֹ כְּלוּם, דִּמְשׁוּעְבָּד הָיָה לִכְתוּבָּתָהּ. אִבְּדָה כְּתוּבָּתָהּ. לֹא אִבְּדָה אֲבֵדָה מַמָּשׁ, שֶׁאִם יִקְנֶה נְכָסִים אַחַר כָּךְ – תִּגְבֶּה מֵהֶן הַמּוּתָר, כִּדְלְקַמָּן, דְּהָא כָּתַב לָהּ "דִּקְנָאִי וְדַעֲתִיד אֲנָא לְמִיקְנֵי". אֶלָּא אִבְּדָה כְּתוּבָּתָהּ מֵהָנֵי נְכָסִים, שֶׁאִם לֹא יִקְנֶה הַבַּעַל נְכָסִים אֲחֵרִים – הֲרֵי הִפְסִידָה, שֶׁמֵּאַחַר שֶׁנָּתַן לְבָנָיו לֹא תִּגְבֶּה עוֹד, דְּנִתְרַצֵּית לָהֶם בְּמַתָּנָה זוֹ הוֹאִיל וְנָתַן גַּם לָהּ קַרְקַע כָּל שֶׁהוּא, וְכִדְמְפָרֵשׁ טַעְמָא וְאָזֵיל. וּכְגוֹן שֶׁחִלֵּק לָהֶן וְלָהּ כָּל נְכָסָיו. אֲבָל שִׁיֵּיר אֲפִילּוּ חַד דִּיקְלָא שֶׁלֹּא חִלֵּק אוֹתוֹ – אָמְרִינַן לְקַמָּן: מִגּוֹ דְּנָחֲתָא אַדִּיקְלָא נָחֲתָא נַמִּי אַכּוּלְּהוּ. וְקָא פָּרֵיךְ: מִשּׁוּם דִּכְתַב לָהּ קַרְקַע כָּל שֶׁהוּא כו'. בִּתְמִיָּה. אָמַר רַב בִּמְזַכֶּה לָהֶן עַל יָדָהּ. עָסְקִינַן, שֶׁנָּתְנָה לוֹ סוּדָר שֶׁלָּהּ לְהַקְנוֹת לַבָּנִים, כִּדְקַיְי"ל (ב"מ דף מז.) בְּכֵלָיו שֶׁל קוֹנֶה. דְּמוֹכְחָא מִילְּתָא, מִדְּקָא מִשְׁתַּדְּלָא בִּזְכִיַּית הַבָּנִים, וְגַם נָתַן לָהּ קַרְקַע כָּל שֶׁהוּא וְאֵינָהּ מְעַרְעֶרֶת כְּלוּם, כֵּיוָן דְּאִיכָּא תַּרְתֵּי – וַדַּאי נִתְרַצֵּית לָהֶם בְּלֵב שָׁלֵם לִהְיוֹת קוֹנִין מַתָּנָה זוֹ, שֶׁלֹּא תּוּכַל לִטְרוֹף מֵהֶן כְּתוּבָּתָהּ, וּמָחֲלָה לָהֶן הַשִּׁעְבּוּד שֶׁעַל הַנְּכָסִים הַלָּלוּ, וְהִפְסִידָה כְּתוּבָּתָהּ אִם לֹא תִּמְצָא מָקוֹם אַחֵר לִגְבּוֹת. וּשְׁמוּאֵל אָמַר. אֲפִילּוּ אֵין מְזַכֶּה לְהוּ עַל יָדָהּ, אֶלָּא שֶׁהָיְתָה לְשָׁם בְּשָׁעָה שֶׁכָּתַב נְכָסָיו לְבָנָיו וְהִיא שׁוֹתֶקֶת. דְּכֵיוָן דִּכְתַב לָהּ קַרְקַע כָּל שֶׁהוּא – נִתְרַצֵּית, וּשְׁתִיקָה כְּהוֹדָאָה דָּמְיָא. אֲבָל אִם לֹא נָתַן לָהּ כְּלוּם – שְׁתִיקָה אֵינָהּ אֶלָּא כְּדֵי לַעֲשׂוֹת נַחַת רוּחַ לְבַעְלָהּ. רַבִּי יוֹסֵי בְּרַבִּי חֲנִינָא אָמַר. אֲפִילּוּ לֹא הָיְתָה שָׁם, וְלֹא חָלַק בְּפָנֶיהָ, אֶלָּא שֶׁאָמַר לָשׁוֹן זֶה כְּשֶׁכָּתַב לָהּ הַהוּא קַרְקַע כָּל שֶׁהוּא: "טְלִי קַרְקַע זוֹ בִּכְתוּבָּתֵיךְ", וְהִיא לֹא עִרְעֲרָה – וַדַּאי מָחֲלָה שִׁעְבּוּדָהּ מִשְּׁאָר הַנְּכָסִים. וְאַחֲרוֹן אַחֲרוֹן מֵיקֵל.
וּמִקּוּלֵּי

בָּעֵי רָבָא: בְּבָרִיא הֵיאַךְ? בְּשכ"מ הוּא דְּנִיחָא לֵיהּ דְּלִישְׁתַּמְעוּן מִלָּהּ, אֲבָל בְּבָרִיא – הָא קָאֵי אִיהוּ. אוֹ דִּלְמָא [א]בָּרִיא נַמִּי נִיחָא לֵיהּ דְּלִישְׁתַּמְעוּן מִלָּהּ מֵהַשְׁתָּא? תָּא שְׁמַע: הַכּוֹתֵב פֵּירוֹת נְכָסָיו לְאִשְׁתּוֹ – גּוֹבָה כְּתוּבָּתָהּ מִן הַקַּרְקַע; לְמֶחֱצָה לִשְׁלִישׁ וְלִרְבִיעַ – גּוֹבָה כְּתוּבָּתָהּ מִן הַשְּׁאָר. כָּתַב כָּל נְכָסָיו לְאִשְׁתּוֹ, וְיָצָא עָלָיו שְׁטַר חוֹב – רַבִּי אֱלִיעֶזֶר אוֹמֵר: תִּקְרַע מַתְּנָתָהּ וְתַעֲמוֹד עַל כְּתוּבָּתָהּ, וַחכ"א: [ב]תִּקְרַע כְּתוּבָּתָהּ וְתַעֲמוֹד עַל מַתְּנָתָהּ, וְנִמְצֵאת קֵרַחַת מִכָּאן וּמִכָּאן; וְאָמַר רַבִּי יְהוּדָה הַנַּחְתּוֹם: מַעֲשֶׂה וְאֵירַע הַדָּבָר בְּבַת אֲחוֹתִי כַּלָּה, וּבָא מַעֲשֶׂה לִפְנֵי חֲכָמִים וְאָמְרוּ: תִּקְרַע כְּתוּבָּתָהּ וְתַעֲמוֹד עַל מַתְּנָתָהּ, וְנִמְצֵאת קֵרַחַת מִכָּאן וּמִכָּאן; טַעֲמָא דְּיָצָא עָלָיו שְׁטַר חוֹב, הָא לֹא יָצָא עָלָיו שְׁטַר חוֹב – קַנְיָא; וּבְמַאי? אִילֵימָא בְּשכ"מ – וְהָא אָמְרַתְּ: לֹא עֲשָׂאָהּ אֶלָּא אַפּוֹטְרוֹפּוֹס! אֶלָּא לָאו בְּבָרִיא. לְעוֹלָם בִּשְׁכִיב מְרַע, וְרַב עֲוִירָא מוֹקֵי לָהּ בְּכוּלְּהוּ, רָבִינָא מוֹקֵי לָהּ בְּאִשְׁתּוֹ אֲרוּסָה וְאִשְׁתּוֹ גְּרוּשָׁה. אָמַר רַב יוֹסֵף בַּר מַנְיוּמֵי אָמַר רַב נַחְמָן, הֲלָכָה: תִּקְרַע כְּתוּבָּתָהּ וְתַעֲמוֹד עַל מַתְּנָתָהּ, וְנִמְצֵאת קֵרַחַת מִכָּאן וּמִכָּאן. לְמֵימְרָא, דְּלָא אָזֵיל רַב נַחְמָן בָּתַר אוּמְדָּנָא? [א)] וְהָתַנְיָא: הֲרֵי שֶׁהָלַךְ בְּנוֹ לִמְדִינַת הַיָּם, וְשָׁמַע שֶׁמֵּת בְּנוֹ, וְעָמַד וְכָתַב כָּל נְכָסָיו לַאֲחֵרִים, וְאַחַר כָּךְ בָּא בְּנוֹ – מַתְּנָתוֹ מַתָּנָה; ר' שִׁמְעוֹן בֶּן מְנַסְיָא אוֹמֵר: [ג]אֵין מַתְּנָתוֹ מַתָּנָה, (א) שֶׁאִילּוּ הָיָה יוֹדֵעַ שֶׁבְּנוֹ קַיָּים לֹא כְּתָבָן; וְאָמַר רַב נַחְמָן: הֲלָכָה כְּרַבִּי שִׁמְעוֹן בֶּן מְנַסְיָא! [ד]שָׁאנֵי הָתָם, דְּנִיחָא לָהּ דְּתֵיפּוֹק עֲלָהּ קָלָא דִּכְתַבִינְהוּ נִיהֲלָהּ לְהַנְהוּ נְכָסִים. תְּנַן הָתָם: [ב)][ה]הַכּוֹתֵב נְכָסָיו לְבָנָיו, וְכָתַב לְאִשְׁתּוֹ קַרְקַע כָּל שֶׁהוּא – אִבְּדָה כְּתוּבָּתָהּ. מִשּׁוּם דִּכְתַב לָהּ קַרְקַע כָּל שֶׁהוּא אִבְּדָה כְּתוּבָּתָהּ? אָמַר רַב: בִּמְזַכֶּה לָהֶן עַל יָדָהּ. וּשְׁמוּאֵל אָמַר: בְּמַחֲלֵק לְפָנֶיהָ וְהִיא שׁוֹתֶקֶת. רַבִּי יוֹסֵי בְּר' חֲנִינָא אָמַר: בְּאוֹמֵר לָהּ "טְלִי קַרְקַע זוֹ בִּכְתוּבָּתֵיךְ".
וּמִקּוּלֵּי

תוספות

למחצה לשליש ולרביע גובה כתובתה מן השאר. תימה: מאי קמ"ל? פשיטא! ואומר ר"י: דרבותא קמ"ל, דכשנותן לה פירות שדה אחת שתי שנים או שלש – לא יוכלו היתומין לטעון ולומר שתטול כתובתה מאותה שדה שיש לה פירות. אלא גובה כתובתה משאר שדות שאין לה בהן כלום. לפי שרוצה ליטול כתובתה מיד, ובשדה שיש לה פירות אינה יכולה ליהנות מכתובתה עד שתי שנים או שלש, שהן זמן פירותיה.
מכלל

רבינו גרשום

בעי רבא. הא פשיטא לי דהאי דקאמר עשאה אפוטרופא בשכיב מרע הוא. אבל בבריא שכתב לה היאך. מי אמרינן שכיב מרע הוא דעשאה אפוטרופא משום דניחא ליה דלישתמעון מלה בתר דימות עלייהו דבנים דלינהגון בה יקרא אבל בריא הואיל דכתב לה ודאי משום מתנה הוא דכתב דאי משום דאפוטרופא הא קאים איהו בחיים ואי חזא דלא נהגו בה יקרא מצי לאכוחינהו אמאי לא תנהגו לה יקרא לאמכון. או דלמא בריא נמי ניחא ליה דלישתמעון מלה מהשתא מחיים כי היכי דניחא ליה דלאחר מיתתו ינהגו לה כבוד ועשאה אפוטרופא מעכשיו: ת"ש הכותב פירות נכסיו לאשתו. במתנה גובה מן הקרקע ששייר דהני פירות לא יהיב לה משום כתובתה אלא משום מתנה: כתב לה הני פירות למחצה או שליש או רביע. יהב לה במתנה גובה כתובתה מן שאר פירות. והכותב כל נכסיו קרקע ופירות לאשתו במתנה ויצא עליו שטר חוב ר"א אומר תקרע מתנתה ותעמוד על כתובתה וכתובה קודמת לשטר חוב ואמאי [לא] תעמוד על מתנתה דאזלינן בתר אומדן דעתיה דהאי דיהיב לה כל נכסיו משום הנאתה עבד. ולהרווחה סבר אי מציא למינקטינהו כולהו הרי מוטב ואם יבואו בעלי חובות שלי איני רוצה שיאמרו לה מחלת כתובתיך בשביל מתנתך ושטרותיו קודם למתנתך משום דהא נתכוון להרווחה א) כולה כשנתן לה מתנה ולא להפסידה הלכך אינה מועלת לה מתנה משום בעלי חובות של בעלה ולא תפסיד בשביל מתנתה. אלא תקרע מתנתה ותעמיד על כתובתה ותגבה כתובת' מן הנכסים משום דשטר כתובתה קודם לשטר חובו. וחכ"א לא אזלינן בתר אומדנא אלא תקרע כתובתה ותעמיד על מתנתה משום דאיכא למימר דמחלה כתובתה לבעל בשביל המתנה. ג)ואח"כ הוציא בעל חוב שטר חובו שקדם שיעבודו לשיעבוד מתנתה והוציא מידה הנכסים ונמצא קרחת מכאן ומכאן מכתובה וממתנה: מעשה ואירע דבר. כענין הזה בבת אחותו של ר' יהודה שהיתה כלה ועשה לה ארוס כתובה מן האירוסין ואחר כך כתב לה נכסיו במתנה ומת ובא מעשה לפני חכמים שהוציא בעל חובו של ארוס שטר חובו ואמרו חכמים תקרע כתובתה ותעמיד על מתנתה משום דאיכא למימר דמחלה כתובתה על אותה מתנה ותעמיד על מתנתה כו'. אלא לאו בבריא ואמרי' קניא משום דקאים ותפשוט מהכא בעיא: לא לעולם בשכיב מרע. ודקאמרת הא לא עשאה אלא אפוטרופא ולא קניא איכא דקניא ואיכא דלא קניא. ורב עוירא מוקים לה לעיל בכולה דקני משום מתנה לבד מאשה אצל הבנים ואשה אצל בני הבעל. ורבינא לא מוקים לה דקנו בכלהו אלא אשתו ארוסה ואשתו גרושה בלבד קנו כדפריש לעיל ולעולם בשכיב מרע ומהא לא תפשוט לבריא: למימרא דרב נחמן לא אזיל בתר אומדנא. דלא אמרינן מסתבר לפי אומד דעתו דהא מתנה כדי ליפות כחה נתנה חוץ מכתובתה ולא כדי להחליש כח כתובתה שתמחול כתובה בשביל מתנתה: והתניא. דאזיל בתר אומדנא: דתניא הרי שהלך בנו למדינת הים כו' ר"ש בן מנסיא אומר אין מתנתו מתנה. משום דאמידא דעתו למימר אילו היה יודע שבנו קיים לא היה כותבן לאחרים. ואמר רב נחמן הלכה כר"ש בן מנסיא אלמא דאזיל בתר אומדנא. ומשני ודאי אזיל בתר אומדנא והכא נמי בהא איתתא דקאמר הלכה תקרע כתובתה וכו' דקא סברת דלא אזיל בתר אומדנא אין ודאי אזיל בתר אומדן דעתה דידה (אזיל) דאמדינן דעתה למימר דניחא לה למירע ליה כתובתה בשביל כבוד שעושה לה דכותב לה כל נכסיו כדי שיצא לה קול שחשובה היא בעיניו כל כך ומחלה לה כתובתה בשביל מתנה הלכך תקרע כתובתה ותעמוד על מתנה: תנן התם. במס' פאה: וכתב לה קרקע כל שהוא. דוקא כתב אבל אי לא כתב לא אבדה כתובתה משום דאיכא למימר דלא בעיא לצעורי בעלה לא מיחה: במזכה להן על ידה. שתקבל לכל אחד חלקו שלא בפניהם היה וזכתה לכל אחד ולא מיחת אמרי' דמחלה כתובתה באותו קרקע כל שהוא: ושמואל אמר במחלק לפניה. כל נכסיו והיא שותקת מחלה.
ומקולי

עין משפט נר מצוה

קח א מיי' פ"ו מהל' זכייה הלכה ז סמג עשין פב טוש"ע אה"ע סי' קז סעי' א וטוש"ע ח"מ סי' רמו סעיף ד:
קט ב מיי' שם הל' ח וסמג שם טוש"ע אה"ע סי' קז סעיף ג:
קי ג מיי' שם הל' א וסמג שם טוש"ע ח"מ סי' רמו סעיף א:
קיא ד מיי' שם הל' ח וסמג שם טוש"ע אה"ע סי' קז סעיף ג:
קיב ה מיי' שם הלכה ט ועי' במ"מ וסמג שם טוש"ע אה"ע סי' קו סעיף א וטוש"ע ח"מ סי' רמו סעיף יג:

מסורת הש"ס

א) לקמן דף קמז: [תוספתא דכתובות פ"ז], ב) פאה פ"ג מ"ז [לקמן קנ:].

הגהות הב"ח

(א) גמ' אין מתנתו מתנה בידוע שאילו היה יודע: (ב) רשב"ם ד"ה גובה כתובתה מן הקרקע דבשביל כצ"ל ותיבת כל נמחק וכו' ע"ב כדף זה ע"ב פירש הרב דלאינה גובה כ"א מותר כתובתה וכו':

פי' הרשב"ם העקרי

בנין דיכרין והבנות ליהוו מיתזנן מניכסיה כדתנן בכתובות הלכך ילפי מהדדי מה הבנים כו' דהא יתתן תנן אף הבנות כו' כדמפרש לעיל דמהימים לא כפינן ליה לאב אלא אומרים לו יזוד (צ"ל יהוד) ילדה כו' ובי דינא בתרא מעין בי דינא קמא תקון דלא תקשי תקנתא אתקנתא. שיתמהו הבריות למה נשתנו זו מזו והשתא לא איפשוט לן אי איירי רב"ב בבריא או לא הלכך מספקא לן ומה שתפס תפס: הכותב כל נכסיו. כלומר הנותן במתנה ובשכ"מ מיירי ולקמן בעי בבריא היאך ומשום הכי נקט לה הכא והך נמי דאמרי' לקמן תנן התם הכותב כו' דבכולהו בעי רבא בבריא האיך: לא עשאה אלא אפוטרופא. דכיון דלא שייר לבניו מידי איכא למימר דלהכי כתב לה שיהו כל בניה חולקין לה כבוד משום דאוקי אבוהון נכסי ברשותה לפרנסם מהם כפי אומד דעתה ויהיו כפופין לה ומחדא מתלתא הלכתא בלא טעמא קא חשיב לה לדברי נבואה הם שאנו סותרין את המתנה מדעתו ולמימר דאפוטרופוס בעלמא שויה ודוקא כל נכסיו דליכא שיור לא במקרקעי ולא במטלטלי אבל איכא שיור קנתה ודוקא אשתו אבל אחד שכתב לו שכ"מ כל נכסיו קי"ל לקמן בפ' מי שמת קונה הכל דכיון דלא שייר מידי צוואת שכ"מ היא זו דבריו כתובין ומסורין: ה"נ לה לבוכרה כו' (בכרפים) עד והכי פירושא פשטא דאם כתב כל נכסיו לבנו גדול לא קנה דלא עשאו אלא אפוטרופוס. לכבודו נתכוון שיחלקו לו אחיו כבוד בשביל שיהא אפוטרופוס בנכסיהם: אפי' קטן המוטל בעריסה לא קנה דאפוטרופוס שוייה:

א) אולי צ"ל להרווחה דילה. ב) נראה דל"ל ואם אח"כ הוציא וכו' מוציא מידה הנכסים ונמצאת קרחת וכו'.

קיג א ב ג מיי׳ פ״ו מהל׳ זכייה ומתנה הל׳ ט ועי׳ במ״מ סמג עשין פב טוש״ע אה״ע סי׳ קו סעיף ח:

קיד ד מיי׳ שם הלכה י טוש״ע שם ס״ב:

א)וּמִקּוּלֵּי כְתוּבָּה שָׁנוּ כָּאן. תְּנַן, ב)ר׳ יוֹסֵי אוֹמֵר: אִם קִבְּלָה עָלֶיהָ, אע״פ שֶׁלֹּא כָּתַב לָהּ — אִבְּדָה כְּתוּבָּתָהּ; מִכְּלָל דְּת״ק סָבַר: כְּתִיבָה וְקַבָּלָה בָּעֵי! וְכִי תֵּימָא: כּוּלָּהּ ר׳ יוֹסֵי הִיא — וְהָא תַּנְיָא, אָמַר רַבִּי יְהוּדָה: אֵימָתַי? שֶׁהָיְתָה שָׁם וְקִבְּלָה עָלֶיהָ, אֲבָל הָיְתָה שָׁם וְלֹא קִבְּלָה עָלֶיהָ, קִבְּלָה עָלֶיהָ וְלֹא הָיְתָה שָׁם — לֹא אִבְּדָה כְּתוּבָּתָהּ! תְּיוּבְתָּא דְּכוּלְּהוּ. תְּיוּבְתָּא. אֲמַר לֵיהּ רָבָא לְרַב נַחְמָן: הָא רַב, הָא שְׁמוּאֵל, הָא ר׳ יוֹסֵי בַּר׳ חֲנִינָא, מַר מַאי סְבִירָא לֵיהּ? א״ל, שֶׁאֲנִי אוֹמֵר: אכֵּיוָן שֶׁעֲשָׂאָהּ שׁוּתָּף בֵּין הַבָּנִים — אִבְּדָה כְּתוּבָּתָהּ. אִיתְּמַר נַמִּי, אָמַר רַב יוֹסֵף בַּר מַנְיוּמֵי אָמַר רַב נַחְמָן: כֵּיוָן שֶׁעֲשָׂאָהּ שׁוּתָּף בֵּין הַבָּנִים — אִבְּ־ה כְּתוּבָּתָהּ. בָּעֵי רָבָא: בְּבָרִיא הֵיאַךְ? מִי אָמְרִינַן: בְּשְׁכִיב מְרַע הוּא דְּיָדְעָה דְּלֵית לֵיהּ וְקָמַחֲלָה, אֲבָל בְּבָרִיא סָבְרָה: הָדַר קָנֵי. אוֹ דִּלְמָא בהַשְׁתָּא מִיהַת לֵית לֵיהּ? תֵּיקוּ. הַהוּא דַּאֲמַר לְהוּ: "פַּלְגָא לִבְרַת, וּפַלְגָא לִבְרַת, וְתִילְתָּא לְאִיתַּת בְּפֵירֵי"; אִיקְּלַע רַב נַחְמָן לְסוּרָא, עוּל לְגַבֵּי רַב חִסְדָּא, אֲמַר לֵיהּ: כִּי הַאי גַּוְונָא מַאי? אֲמַר לֵיהּ, הָכִי אָמַר שְׁמוּאֵל: גאֲפִילּוּ לֹא הִקְנָה לָהּ אֶלָּא דֶּקֶל אֶחָד לְפֵירוֹתָיו — אִבְּדָה כְּתוּבָּתָהּ. אֲמַר לֵיהּ: אֵימוּר דַּאֲמַר שְׁמוּאֵל הָתָם — דְּאַקְנֵי לָהּ בְּגוּפָהּ דְּאַ־עָא, הָכָא פֵּירָא (א) הוּא! אֲמַר לֵיהּ: דמִטַּלְטְלֵי קָא אָמְרַתְּ? (ב) מִטַּלְטְלֵי וַדַּאי לָא קָא אָמִינָא. הַהוּא דַּאֲמַר לְהוּ: "תִּילְתָּא לִבְרַת, וְתִילְתָּא לִבְרַת, וְתִילְתָּא לְאִיתַּת", שְׁכִיבָא חֲדָא מִבְּנָתֵיהּ; סָבַר רַב פַּפִּי לְמֵימַר: לָא שָׁקְלָא אֶלָּא תִּילְתָּא, אֲמַר

ומקולי כתובה שנו כאן. אכולהו קאי. דשאר בעלי חובין לא אבדו בכך, עד שיאמרו בפירוש: אנו מוחלין השעבוד שעל הנכסים הללו. אבל בכתובה הקלו, כדאקילו גבה נמי לעיין זיבורית. וכדמפרש טעמא בכתובות (דף פו.): דיותר משהאיש רוצה לישא אשה רוצה לינשא, דניחא לה בכל דהו, כדריש לקיש: טב למיתב טן דו מלמיתב ארמלו. אבל שאר בעל חוב, שעושה טובה ללוה — לא מקילינן גביה, דבשביל שהוא עושה טובה אין לו לאבד בחנם. ה״ג: תנן רבי יוסי אומר **אם** קבלה עליה **אע״פ** שלא **כתב** לה **אבדה** כתובתה. וסיפא דהך היא במס׳ פאה. "כתב לה אע״פ שלא קיבלה" לא גרסינן. קבלה עליה — שמחלה להם השעבוד בפירוש. מכלל. דשמעיה רבי יוסי לת״ק דבעי קבלה גמורה עם הכתיבה. דאם איתא דכתיבה לחוד קאמר — הכי הוה ליה לרבי יוסי למימר: אף על פי שכתב לה לא אבדה כתובה אלא אם כן קיבלה עליה. וקשיא לכל הני דלעיל, דמוקי למילתיה בשותקת, שלא נתרצית בפירוש. דהכי הוה ליה לתרוצי: הכא במאי עסקינן — בשקיבלה עם הכתיבה, דיקא נמי דקתני סיפא: רבי יוסי אומר כו׳. וכי תימא **כולה ר׳ יוסי היא**. ואשמעינן רישא דבכתיבת קרקע כל שהוא לחוד אבדה כתובתה, ואשמועי׳ נמי בסיפא דאם קבלה אע״פ שלא כתב לה אבדה כתובה, דאו הא או הא בעי. ומשום דבכתיבה לחוד מיירי רישא — אילטריכו לתרוצי מה שתירצו.

אמר רבי יהודה אימתי כו׳. דברי תנא קמא אתא רבי יהודה לפרושי בברייתא, היכי דמי האי "כתב לה קרקע כל שהוא" דקאמר ת״ק אבדה כתובתה. ומוקי לה ר׳ יהודה בדאיכא קבלה, והיתה שם בשעה שחלק לבניו. דכיון דהיתה שם וקיבלה — חזקה אין אדם רוצה שנותנין ממונו בפניו ומחזיק את המתנה לקיימה, אא״כ עושה בלב שלם. וכדאמר בסנהדרין (דף כה.): "אימתי" דרבי יהודה — לפרש דברי חכמים. **אבל היתה שם ולא** קיבלה עליה. אלא היתה שותקת. קיבלה עליה ולא היתה שם. מצי׳ למימר: נחת רוח עשיתי לבעלי. אלמא, מדרבי יהודה שמעינן דת״ק כתיבה וקבלה בעי. שותף בין הבנים. שכתב לה נמי קרקע כל שהוא — מחלה. ולא מצרכינן לכל הנך כאות דאמרי הנך אמוראי לעיל, אלא בכתיבה בעלמא אבדה, כר׳ יוסי דסגי לה בחדא או קבלה או כתיבה. ומצאתי בתשובות רבינו שלמה זקני זצ״ל דרב נחמן קאי בשיטת שמואל רבו, דאוקמה במחלק לפניה והיא שותקת. ואע״ג דאותביניה לעיל — ה״מ משום דת״ק קבלה נמי בעי. מיהו, לרבי יוסי דסבר דסגי ליה בחדא, בכתיבה בלא קבלה, איכא למיפרך נמי כדלעיל: משום דכתב לה קרקע כל שהוא אבדה כתובתה? וצריך לשנויי לרבי יוסי במחלק לפניה והיא שותקת. ורב נחמן כר׳ יוסי ס״ל דסגי ליה או בכתיבה או בקבלה, וכיון דמחלק לפניה והיא שותקת — לפיכך מוחלת, שהרי עשאה שותף לחלקה חלק בפני עצמה בין הבנים. ומיגו דחשיבא ליה כאחד מבניו, לחלק נמי לה חלק כמו שמחלק לבניו — מתרצה לו, ומוחלת השעבוד מן הנכסים. ורב נחמן לפרש טעם לדברי שמואל אתא. **בבריא היאך.** בריא שכתב נכסיו לבניו, וכתב לאשתו קרקע כל שהוא, ועשאה שותף בין הבנים, מי אבדה כתובתה או לא? מי אמרינן: בשכ״מ הוא דאבדה שעבוד כתובתה שעל הנכסים הללו, דהא ידעה דלית ליה נכסים יותר, וגם לא יהיו לו עוד שהרי ימות, והלכך הוה לה לערער במתנה זו, וכיון דשתקה — ודאי נתרצית, וקנו. אבל בבריא לפיכך שותקת — סברה: הדר קני בעלי נכסים היום או למחר ואגבה מהם, כדכתיב בשטר הכתובה "ודעתיד אנא למיקני", ומה לי להכעיסו עכשיו, עד שאראה אם יקנה עוד נכסים. וכיון דמשום הכי שתקה — לא אבדה שעבוד כתובתה מהני נכסי, ותטרוף מהן היום או למחר. **או דלמא השתא מיהא הא** לית ליה. ולא מסקא אדעתה דלמא הדר קני. וכיון דלא מסקא אדעתה — הויה לה למחות. אלא ודאי מדאישתיקא — אודויי אודיא ליה, ונתרצית, וגמרה ומחלה להו שעבודה. ומיהו, אם יבואו לו נכסים היום ולמחר — תגבה מהן, כדלקמן, שהרי חוב כתובתה לא מחלה, אלא שעבוד כל הני נכסים שנתן לבניו מחלה, ואהני מחילה דידה דלא תטרוף עוד מהן. כן נראה בעיני, ועיקר, דרבא פשיטא ליה דאילו קני נכסים גביא מינייהו, כדלקמן. ואית דמפרשי דמבעיא (ג) אי גביא מנכסים דקני למחר או לא. וטעות, דמילתא דמיפשטא לקמן לרב כהנא לאו אורחא דגמרא למימר תיקו. והכי הוה ליה למימר: מילתא דמבעיא ליה לרבא פשיטא ליה לרב כהנא, דההוא דאמר להו תילתא לברת כו׳, כדלקמן. דכה״ג אמר בפ׳ "הגוזל עצים" (ב״ק קה:): בעי רבא נשבע עליו מהו מי אמרי׳ כו׳. מילתא דמיבעיא ליה לרבא פשיטא ליה לרבה, דאמר רבה: שורי גנבת כו׳. **ההוא.** שכיב מרע. **דאמר** להו **פלגא** לברת כו׳. שתי בנות היו, וחלק להן כל נכסיו מקרקעי, ותילתא דפירי נתן לאשתו. קס״ד השתא — פירות מחוברין, ולקמיה מוקי לה בתלושין. **בה״ג.** דלא כתב לאשתו קרקע כל שהוא, אלא פירות, מאי? מי מחלה שעבוד שיש לה על הנהו מקרקעי בשביל שעשאה שותף בין הבנות בחלוקת הפירות, שהבנות נטלו שני חלקים והיא חלק שלישי, או לא, הואיל ולא עשאה שותף בגוף הקרקע, ותחזור ותטרוף מותר הכתובה מן הבנות. ומיהו, כל כתובתה לא תחזור ותטרוף, דהני פירות חשבינן לה בכתובתה, כדאמרינן לקמן בפירקין (דף קלח.): "תנו מאתים זוז לפלונית אשתי כראוי לה" — נוטלתן ואת כתובתה. ומפרשינן התם, דמשום לישנא יתירא דקאמר "כראוי לה" נוטלתן לבד כתובתה. אבל לא אמר "כראוי לה" — ידה על העליונה, שאם אותן מאתים הוו יותר — נוטלתן בכתובתה, ואם כתובתה יתירה — נוטלת כתובתה בין הכל. **אלא** דקל **אחד.** לאכול פירותיו עד שייבש האילן, ושוב אין לה בקרקע כלום. והיינו דבר שלא לעולם אפי׳ לרבנן דפליגי אדר״מ, דהא אקני לה בגוף האילן. **אבדה** כתובתה. שהרי עשאה שותף בין הבנים בקרקע, דהא יניקת קרקע אקני לה, וה״ה לפירות מחוברין. והאי דקאמר אילן לפירותיו — לא למעט פירות מחוברין בלא אילן, אלא רבותא הוא, דאע״ג דגוף האילן אינו שלה לכשייבש, והשתא לית ביה פרי — אפ״ה כקרקע דמי. וכ״ש היכא דאקני לה פירות גופייהו, שגדלו כבר ומחוברין לקרקע. **והכא פירא בעלמא.** (ד) דהא פירות תלושין מיבעי לן. מטלטלי **לא** קאמינא. דאבדה בכך. דודאי לא אבדה כתובתה, דלא חשיבי לה. ובמתני׳ קתני "קרקע כל שהוא" ולא מטלטלי, אבל הייתי סבור דמחוברין בעית מינאי. **ההוא.** ש״מ. **דאמר** להו **תילתא** לברת **ותילתא** לבתי השניה **ותילתא** לאשתי. דהיינו עשאה שותף בין הבנות. ומן הדין אבדה כתובתה מהני תרי תילתי שנתן האב לבנות, שהרי מחלה להו שעבודה, ולא תטרוף עוד מחוב כתובתה כלום אלא אם כן יקנה בעלה נכסים אחרים אחרי כן, שהרי מנכסים הבאים לא מחלה שעבוד שלה. ואיתרמי מילתא דלא קנה נכסים אחרים, אלא מהני נכסים עצמן חזר וקנה, דשכיבא חדא מבנתא בחייו וחזר וירשה, שהאב יורש את בתו. סבר רב פפי למימר. לית לה לאיתתא אלא תילתא דיהב לה בעלה. דמהא תילתא דחזר וקנה — לית לה מידי, שהרי לא ממקום אחר בא לידו, אלא מאותן נכסים עצמן של בנות שכבר מחלה האשה שעבודה עליהם, והלכך לא הדרי משעבדי לה.

א״ל

מכלל דתנא קמא כתיבה וקבלה בעי. ובקבלה גרידא מצי למימר: נחת רוח עשיתי לבעלי. ואם תאמר: מנא ליה דבעי תרוייהו? דלמא דבכתיבה גרידא סגי. וי״ל: דאם כן, מאי "אע״פ" דקאמר ר׳ יוסי, דמשמע שבא להקל על דברי תנא קמא? דהא קבלה עדיפא מכתיבה, וא״כ רבי יוסי מחמיר טפי! אלא ודאי ת״ק תרוייהו בעי. וקשה: דאי קבלה עדיפא מכתיבה — אמאי איצטריך ר׳ יהודה למימר "היתה שם ולא קבלה", כיון דאמר "קבלה ולא היתה שם"? ורשב״ם נמי, שפירש דרב נחמן כשמואל, אלא ששמואל אליבא דרבנן, ורב נחמן אליבא דר׳ יוסי קאמר דמהניא כתיבה לחודה בלא קבלה — אם כן אמאי נקט רבי יוסי "קבלה אע״פ שלא כתב לה"? הוה ליה למימר "כתב לה אף על פי שלא קבלה", דהוי חידוש יותר! ואי הוה אמר דכתיבה וקבלה שוין הן — הוה אתי שפיר. ודייק: (ה) תנא קמא כתיבה וקבלה בעי, דאי מהניא כתיבה גרידא — מאי "אף על פי" דקאמר רבי יוסי, דמשמע דאתא להקל? הלא הן שוין!

עיליתא

רבינו גרשום

ומקולי כתובה שנו כאן. דכולהו הני תנאי מקילין בכתובה וכולהו הני תנאי סברי אע״ג דלא קבלה עליה קבול גמור אותה קרקע אפי׳ הכי אבדה כתובתה: מכלל דת״ק סבר כתיבה וקבלה מעליא בעי וכי תימא כולה. הא משנה דתנן התם ר׳ יוסי היא ומשום הכי דסגי בקבלה כל שהוא: והתניא א״ר יהודה אימתי. אבדה כתובתה בזמן שהיתה שם וקבלה עליה כו׳. אלמא דלאו כולה ר׳ יוסי היא ואתי הדר קושיין לדוכתה דאמרי׳ לעיל מכלל דת״ק כתיבה וקבלה מעליא בעי וקשיא לכולהו דאמרי דלא בעינן קבלה מעליא לדברי הכל: כיון שעשאה שותף בין הבנים. דבהדי כתיבה נכסיו לבניו כתב לה קרקע כל שהוא וקבלה עליה אבדה כתובתה: בעי רבא בבריא. אי כתב כל נכסיו לבניו וכתב לאשתו קרקע כל שהוא מהו. מי אמרינן שכיב מרע הוא דידעה דלית ליה נכסים אחרים לחוד מההיא קרקע קא מחלה על אותו קרקע אבל דבריא לא מחלה דסברה הדר קני נכסים אחרים ומצינא למגבא כולה מיניה או מיורשין. או דלמא השתא מיהת הא לית נכסים ומחלה מכל וכל תיקו: ההוא דהוה אמר תרתי ברתא אית לי ואמר פלגא מנכסי לחדא ברתא ופלגא לאידך ותילתא לאינתת בפרי כי האי גוונא מאי. מי אמרינן הואיל דלא יהיב לה בגוף של קרקע לא אבדה כתובתה או דלמא לא שנא: מי דמי התם היכא דהוא הקנה לה דקל חד לפירותיו מקנה לה בגופא דארעא דהא דקל בגופא דארעא הוא הכא תילתא לאיתת בפירי פירא בעלמא הוא א) כלומר מטלטלי לא אמינא דודאי לא איבדה כתובתה: תלתא. בריא הוה תלתא לברת תלתא לברת. היא מחלן להן גוף הקרקע: שכיבא חדא מבנתיה. בחיי אבוה: סבר רב פפא למימר. לית להא איתתא אלא דמעיקרא אע״ג דהדר קנה בעלה שירש את

א) נראה דל״ל אמר ליה מטלטלי לא אמינא וכו׳.

א) [כתובות קי: בכורות נב:]: ב) פאה פ״ג מ״ז:

הגהות הב״ח

(א) גמ׳ הכא פירא בעלמא הוא: (ב) שם מטלטלי ודאי. נ״ב עי׳ פ׳ מי שמת דף ק״נ: (ג) רשב״ם ד״ה או דלמא וכו׳ דמיבעיא ליה אי: (ד) ד״ה והכא פירא בעלמא הוא דהא: (ה) תוס׳ ד״ה מכלל וכו׳ ודייק דתנא קמא:

אֲמַר לֵיהּ רַב כָּהֲנָא: אאִילּוּ הָדַר קָנֵי, מִי לָא שָׁקְלָא? וְכֵיוָן דְּאִילּוּ הָדַר קָנֵי שָׁקְלָא, בהָשְׁתָּא נַמִי שָׁקְלָא. הַהוּא דְּפַלְגִינְהוּ לְנִכְסֵיהּ לְאִתְּתֵיהּ וְלִבְנֵיהּ, שַׁיֵּיר חַד דִּיקְלָא; סָבַר רָבִינָא לְמֵימַר: לֵית לַהּ אֶלָּא חַד דִּיקְלָא. אֲמַר לֵיהּ רַב יֵימַר לְרָבִינָא: אִי לֵית לָהּ, חַד דִּיקְלָא נַמִי לֵית לָהּ! אֶלָּא, גמִיגּוֹ דְּנָחֲתָא לְדִיקְלָא, נָחֲתָא נַמִי לְכוּלְּהוּ נִכְסֵי. אָמַר רַב הוּנָא: דשְׁכִיב מְרַע שֶׁכָּתַב כָּל נְכָסָיו לְאַחֵר – רוֹאִין: אִם רָאוּי לְיוֹרְשׁוֹ – נוֹטְלָן מִשּׁוּם יְרוּשָּׁה, וְאִם לָאו – נוֹטְלָן מִשּׁוּם מַתָּנָה. אֲמַר לֵיהּ רַב נַחְמָן: א)גַּנָּבָא גְּנוּבֵי לָמָּה לָךְ? אִי סְבִירָא לָךְ כְּרַבִּי יוֹחָנָן בֶּן בְּרוֹקָה, אֵימָא: הֲלָכָה כְּרַבִּי יוֹחָנָן בֶּן בְּרוֹקָה, דְּהָא שְׁמַעְתִּתִיךְ כְּר' יוֹחָנָן בֶּן בְּרוֹקָה הוּא דְּאָזְלָא! דִּלְמָא כִּי הָא קָאָמְרַתְּ; דְּהַהוּא דַּהֲוָה קָא שָׁכֵיב, וַאֲמַרוּ לֵיהּ: נִכְסֵיהּ לְמַאן, דִּלְמָא לִפְלָנְיָא? וַאֲמַר לְהוּ: אֶלָּא לְמַאן? וַאֲמַרְתְּ לַן עֲלַהּ: אִם רָאוּי לְיוֹרְשׁוֹ – נוֹטְלָן מִשּׁוּם יְרוּשָּׁה, וְאִם לָאו – נוֹטְלָן מִשּׁוּם מַתָּנָה? אֲמַר לֵיהּ: האִין, הָכִי (א) קָאָמִינָא. לְמַאי הִלְכְתָא? סָבַר רַב אַדָּא בַּר אַהֲבָה קַמֵּיהּ דְּרָבָא לְמֵימַר: אִם רָאוּי לְיוֹרְשׁוֹ – אַלְמָנָתוֹ נִזּוֹנֵית מִנְּכָסָיו, וְאִם לָאו – אֵין אַלְמָנָתוֹ נִזּוֹנֵית מִנְּכָסָיו. אֲמַר לֵיהּ רָבָא: ומִיגְרַע גָּרְעָא? הָשְׁתָּא בִּירוּשָּׁה דְּאוֹרַיְיתָא אָמְרַתְּ: אַלְמָנָתוֹ נִזּוֹנֵית מִנְּכָסָיו, ב)בְּמַתָּנָה דְּרַבָּנַן לֹא כָּל שֶׁכֵּן? אֶלָּא אֲמַר רָבָא: ג)זכִּדְשָׁלַח רַב אַחָא בַּר רַב עָוְיָא: לְדִבְרֵי רַבִּי יוֹחָנָן בֶּן בְּרוֹקָה, "נְכָסַי לָךְ וְאַחֲרֶיךָ לִפְלוֹנִי", אִם הָיָה רִאשׁוֹן רָאוּי לְיוֹרְשׁוֹ – אֵין לַשֵּׁנִי בִּמְקוֹם רִאשׁוֹן כְּלוּם, שֶׁאֵין (ב) לְשׁוֹן מַתָּנָה אֶלָּא לְשׁוֹן יְרוּשָּׁה, וִירוּשָּׁה אֵין לָהּ הֶפְסֵק. אֲמַר לֵיהּ רָבָא לְרַב נַחְמָן: וְהָא אַפְסְקַהּ! הוּא סָבַר: יֵשׁ לָהּ הֶפְסֵק, וְרַחֲמָנָא אָמַר: אֵין לָהּ הֶפְסֵק.

הַהוּא

א"ל רב כהנא אילו. קנה נכסים אחרים בתר הכי, לית לה לאשה? בתמיה, הא ודאי אית לה. דנהי דמחלה שעבודה לבנות בשביל שעשאה שותף ביניהן – חוב כתובתה מיהא לא מחלה. שאם תמצא מקום לטרוף, כגון שיקנה נכסים – טורפת מהם, וכדכתב "ודעתיד אנא למיקני" שנכסים העתידין לבא ישתעבדו לה. וכיון דאילו הדר קני מאדם אחר או ממורישיו אית לה לאשה, השתא נמי כי נפלו לו מאותן נכסים עצמן – אית לה. דמה לי אותן נכסים עצמן, מה לי אחרים, שאם נתרצית להקנות המתנה לבנות ולמחול להם שעבודה – לבעלה מיהא לא מחלה מידי, אם תמצא מקום לגבות. וכן הלכה. **ההוא דפלגינהו.** כל נכסיו חילק לבניו ולאשתו, ובצוואת שכיב מרע, דהיינו עשאה שותף בין הבנים. אלא ששייר דקל אחד שלא פירש למי. **סבר רבינא** למימר לית לה. ממותר כתובה אלא ההוא דיקלא. דהא אי לא שייר דיקלא – אבדה כתובתה מן הבנים, שמחלה להם שעבודה, משום דנעשית שותף ביניהן. והשתא נמי זכו הבנים, והיא תטרוף את הדקל. **א"ל רב יימר לרבינא אי לית לה.** כתובתה מחלק הבנים, משום דידעה דלית ליה נכסים אחריני ומחלה להו בשביל שעשאה שותף ביניהם – א"ה דיקלא נמי לית לה, דהא ידעת ליה להאי דקל ומחלה להו ליורשיו, דכל כתובתה מחלה מהני נכסים דאית ליה, משום דעשאה שותף, דמה לי למחול שעבודה מאותן שחלק לבנים, ומה לי מן אותו דקל שלא חלק. אלא מאי אית לן למימר, מאיזה טעם נחתא אדקל לטרוף ממנו – היינו משום דלא מחלה כתובתה, שהרי הניח לה מקום קלט לגבות הימנו, כגון האי דקל שלא רצה לחלוק לבניו, ומגו דנחתא אדקל – נחתא נמי אחלק הבנים. דהאי דשתקה ולא ערערה היינו לפי שהיה מניח לה הדקל, וסברה: למה אערער עכשיו עד שישומו ב"ד את הדקל ואטרפנו, והדר אערער על הבנים ואטרוף מהן המותר. דלא הויא שתיקה דידה מחילה אלא היכא דמחלק כל הנכסים ולא שביק לה מידי, דמשום האי טעמא מספקא לן לעיל (דף קלב:) גבי בריא, דדלמא כיון דאיכא למימר הדר קני, סברה: למה אערער עכשיו עד אשר אראה אם אמצא מקום לגבות מצד אחר. וכיון דמשום הכי שתקה – לא הויא שתיקותה הודאה, אלא תלויה ועומדת אם תערער על אלו אם לאו. וה"נ כיון דשבק לה מידי למיטרף – להכי שתקה, ואח"כ תצעוק על המותר. והשתא שמעינן מהכא דשכיב מרע הכותב כל נכסיו או מחלק לבניו בפני אשתו, וגם לה נתן קרקע כל שהוא, ושתקה ולא ערערה. והוא הדין אם כתב כל נכסיו לאחרים בפניה, ולה כתב קרקע כל שהוא – קנו, שהרי מחלה להן שעבודה, ולא תטרוף מהן. כרב נחמן, דאמר: הואיל ועשאה שותף בין הבנים – אבדה כתובתה. דבעשאה שותף תליא מילתא, ל"ש עם בניו ול"ש עם אחרים. והנ"מ כשחילק כל נכסיו לאשתו וליורשיו. אבל שייר אפילו דקל אחד, דהיינו קרקע כל שהוא שלא פירש למי, מגו דהדרא אדיקלא – הדרא ונחתא למגבי מכולהו נכסי, ולא מחלה מידי. ודוקא כשכתב לה קרקע כל שהוא, אבל אם נתן לה מטלטלים ולא קרקע – לא מקריא שותף בין הבנים, ולא מחלה מידי, ונחתא אכולהו נכסי. כדאמר רב נחמן: מטלטלי לא קאמרי'. וה"מ דאבדה כתובתה – מהנהו נכסי שכתב לבניו. אבל אי הדר בתר הכי וקני נכסי אחריני, ואפי' מהנהו נכסי עצמן שחלק לבניו, כגון שמת אחד מבניו בחייו – הדרא וגביא מינייהו מותר כתובתה, שכך כתב לה "דעתיד אנא למיקני". ודוקא שכיב מרע, כדאמרן לעיל, אבל בריא שחלק נכסיו לבניו, וכתב גם לה קרקע כל שהוא – הא איבעיא ליה לרבא אי מחלה להו שעבודה שעל אותן נכסים אם לאו, ואוקימנא בתיקו. והלכך, כיון דמספקא לן – אמרינן: המוציא מחבירו, דהיינו אשה, עליה להביא הראיה. דבכל דין תיקו מאן דתפיס – תפיס. ומיהו, אי הדר קני – אית לה. **אמר רב הונא שכיב מרע** (ג) שאמר כו'. משום דאליבא דר' יוחנן בן ברוקה מיירי, כדלקמן, נקיט שכיב מרע. דהא בבריא מיבעיא לן לעיל אי איירי ביה ר' יוחנן בן ברוקה אי לא. **שכתב כל נכסיו.** סתם, ולא פירש לא לשון מתנה ולא לשון ירושה, אלא סתמא "נכסי לפלוני". **רואין אם.** אותו מקבל מתנה ראוי ליורשו, כגון בן בין הבנים – נוטלן בתורת ירושה כר' יוחנן בן ברוקה, דכיון דראוי ליורשו – מסתמא להורישו נתכוין, הואיל ולא פירש לשון מתנה. אבל גבי ירושה א"צ לפרש, דממילא קא ירית, הלכך, כל היכא דאיכא לאוקומה בירושה דתפסה מן התורה – לא מקני ליה מסתמא במתנה, למיעקר נחלה דאורייתא. **ואם לאו.** דאינו ראוי לירש – בעל כרחך "נכסי נתונין לפלוני" קאמר, דאין אדם מוציא דבריו בטלין מפיו, ולמתנה איכוין ולא לירושה. ולכך נוטלן משום מתנה. ולקמן מפרש מאי נפקא לן מינה אם נוטלן משום ירושה או משום מתנה. **גנבא גנובי** למה לך. לסתום דבריך ולמימר: רואין כו'. **אי סבירא** לך כר' יוחנן בן ברוקה. דאמר: אם אמר על מי שראוי ליורשו דבריו קיימין, ולפיכך אתה אומר: רואין אם ראוי ליורשו כו' – אימא בהדיא דהלכתא כוותיה, ולא תסתיר דבריך לומר כר' יוחנן בן ברוקה, בענין שלא יבינו בני אדם. **דלמא כי הא אמרת.** כל זה אמר ליה רב נחמן לרב הונא: שמא אתה לא לכך נתכוונת, לומר דבריך בסתם ולהשמיענו כר' יוחנן, אלא עובדא הכי הוה בסתם, כדמפרש ואזיל. ועיקר דבריך באת להשמיענו חילוק בין נטילה משום מתנה לנטילה משום ירושה, כדמפרש ואזיל, ואגב אורחך מיהא שמעינן דסבירא לך כר' יוחנן. ומיהו, עיקר שיטה זו שתפסת לא לכך באתה, דא"כ היה לך לומר בפירוש: הלכה כר' יוחנן בן ברוקה. **דהוה קא שכיב.** היה נפטר לבית עולמו. **אלא למאן.** כלומר, מאן קא שקיל נכסיי אלא הוא. והוי כמאן דא"ל "נכסיי לך". והיינו "שכתב" דקאמרת, דמה לי כתב מה לי אמר. **ואמרת לן עלה.** דמכל מקום שקיל. מיהו, אם קרובו וראוי ליורשו – הוי ירושה, ואי לאו – הוי מתנה. ד"אלא למאן" וכן "נכסיי לך" – שתי לשונות משמע; כשהוא יורש – משמע לשון ירושה, וכשאין ראוי לירש – הוי לשון מתנה. ולקמן מפרש מאי נפקא לן מינה, למאי אתא לאשמועינן. **אין ה"נ קאמינא.** על הכותב נכסיו סתם באתי להורות, דזמנין הוי ירושה וזמנין הוי מתנה. **סבר רב אדא בר אהבה קמיה דרבא.** לפרושי למאי נפקא מינה, ומה בא רב הונא ללמדנו, אם ראוי ליורשו. להכי אמר רב הונא דהוי לשון ירושה, שתהא אלמנתו של מת ניזונת מנכסיו שהוריש לזה, כדתנן (כתובות דף נה:): אלמנה ניזונת מנכסי יתומים, כלומר יורשין. **ואם לאו.** נוטלן משום מתנה, ושוב אין אלמנתו ניזונת מהן, כדתנן (גיטין דף מח:): אין מוציאין למזון אשה והבנות מנכסים משועבדים, מפני תיקון העולם. משום דהוי מזונות דבר שאין לו קצבה, ואין יכולין לקוחות להזהר, ובין מתנה ובין מכר הוו משועבדים. **א"ל רבא.** וכי בשביל שנתנו במתנת שכיב מרע שאינה קונה אלא מדרבנן, שהרי אין מתנה לאחר מיתה, אלא תקנת חכמים היא שיהיו דבריו ככתובין וכמסורין כדי שלא תטרף דעתו עליו. **מיגרע גרעה.** בתמיה? וכי הורע כחה של אלמנתו בכך? השתא בירושה דאורייתא, דאלימא כח יורש אם ראוי ליורשו, שהתורה זיכתה לו, כדכתיב: "ביום הנחילו את בניו" אפ"ה אמרינן: אלמנה ניזונת מנכסי היורש. **מתנה דרבנן.** כי הך מתנת שכ"מ שאין בה קנין אלא מדרבנן, כדפרישית – לא כ"ש דניזונת מהן? ולעולם לאו להכי נפקא מינה חילוק שהשמיענו רב הונא בין נוטל משום ירושה ובין נוטל משום מתנה. ומהכא שמעינן דהא דקיימא לן דמזון האשה והבנות לא טרפא ממשעבדי – ה"מ מתנה גמורה בקנין או מכר גמור, אבל מתנת שכ"מ – אלמנתו ניזונת מנכסי מקבל מתנה, וה"ה לבנות. **אלא אמר רבא.** להכי נפקא מינה בין מתנה לירושה. **כדשלח רב אחא כו'.** שאם אמר האי שכ"מ "ואלא למאן, ואחריו לפלוני" – רואין: אם היה ראשון ראוי ליורשו – נוטלו משום ירושה, ואין לשני אחריו כלום. דכיון דעשאו יורש, וזכה בדין תורה, כי קאמר תו "ואחריו לפלוני" – הוי מתנה על מה שכתוב בתורה, דאינו יכול לעקור תורת ירושה מאותו שירש כבר. וגם אפי' אם פירש "אני מורישך ע"מ שיטול האי שני אחריך" – הוי נמי מתנה על מה שכתוב בתורה, והוי המעשה מעשה והתנאי בטל. **דהא ירושה אין לה הפסק.** אלא ממשמשת עד ראובן, כדנפקא לן מקראי בפירקין (דף קטו:). **לדברי ר' יוחנן כו'.** לעיל (ד) בשמעתין פרישית לה. **והא אפסקה.** דעל תנאי שיטול שני אחריו הוריש לראשון. **ורחמנא אמר אין לה הפסק.** והוי מתנה על מה שכתוב בתורה, והוי מעשה מעשה, והתנאי בטל. והכי הלכתא כדשלח רב אחא, דהא חזינא עובדא בסמוך כוותיה.

ההוא

מסורת הש"ס

א) [יבמות נא. כתובות יט.] ב) [ועי' תוס' כתובות מט: ד"ה הוא ולאשתו] ג) לעיל קכט:

הגהות הב"ח

(א) גמרא הכי נמי קאמינא: (ב) שם שאין זה לשון מתנה: (ג) רשב"ם ד"ה אמר רב הונא שכיב מרע כו' כצ"ל ותיבת שאמר נמחק: (ד) ד"ה לדברי ר' יוחנן כו' לעיל. נ"ב דף קכ"ט ע"ב:

עין משפט נר מצוה

קטו א ב מיי' פ"ו מהל' זכייה ומתנה הלכה יא סמג עשין פב טוש"ע אה"ע סי' קו סעיף א וסי' קז סעיף ג:

קטז ג מיי' שם הלכה י וסמג שם טוש"ע שם סי' קו סעיף ב:

קיז ד ה מיי' פ"ט מהל' זכייה ומתנה הלכה ה ו ועיין בהשגות ובמ"מ סמג עשין פב טוש"ע ח"מ סי' רנג סעיף ו:

קיח ו מיי' פי"ט מהל' אישות הלכה יג ועיין בהשגות ובמגיד משנה סמג עשין מח טוש"ע אה"ע סי' צג סעיף כ וטוש"ע ח"מ סי' רנב סעיף א:

קיט ז מיי' פי"ב מהל' זכייה ומתנה הלכה ד סמג עשין פב טוש"ע ח"מ סי' רנג סעיף י:

רבינו גרשום

את בתו: כיון דאילו הדר קנה לאחר שכתב לה ההוא תילתא בכתובתה אית לה שטר כתובה ה"נ כשירש בתו אית לה ההוא תילתא נמי לאחר מותו: שייר לעצמו חד דקלא וסבר רבינא למימר לית לה. ליטול כתובתה אלא מאותו דקל: אי לית לה. מחמת כתובה משאר נכסים שהניח לבניו. באותו דקל ששייר נמי לית לה משום כתובה משום דאיכא למימר דמחלה כתובתה על ההיא פלגא נכסים דיהיב לה בעלה עם בניה: אלא מגו כו': רואין אם ראוי ליורשו. כגון אחיו: נוטל משום ירושה ואם לאו נוטל משום מתנה. דרבותה קמ"ל דחזיין בין במתנה בין בירושה: דשמעתיך כר' יוחנן בן ברוקה אזלא. דאמר אם אמר על מי שראוי ליורשו דבריו קיימין: אמרו ליה נכסיה [לפלניא] אלא למאן. כלומר אם לא אתנה לזה למי אתנה שלא היה לו בנים: אין הכי קאמינא. שכיב מרע שכתב כל נכסיו לאחר בשלא היו לו בנים ואמרו ליה נכסי למאן ולא כר' יוחנן בן ברוקה דאיהו אמר אפי' במקום בת או בן: אם ראוי ליורשו זה שנכתבו לו: אלמנתו. של כותב: ניזונת מנכסיו. כשם שהאלמנה ניזונית משאר יורשין גמורין ואם לאו אינה ניזונית משום דמחמת מתנה קיבלה: אמר ליה מגרע גרעה. אלמנה זו שאינה ניזונית במקום מתנה כבמקום ירושה: השתא בירושה דאורייתא. היכא דבנים יורשין אביהן שקלה מזוני. מתנה דרבנן היא מתנת שכיב מרע דיהיב לאחריני לא אשכחן מדאוריית' דרבנן תקנוה כדי שלא תטרף דעתו עליו א) או אינו יכול לעשות חפצי כל שכן דאית לה מזוני: אלא אמר רבא. הא דקאמר רב הונא לעיל שכיב מרע שכתב כל נכסיו לאחרים רואין אם ראוין לירש כו' כי ראויין האי גוונא קאמר כדשלח רב אחא בר בר חנא לעיל אם ראשון ראוי ליורשו הוא נוטלו משום ירושה ואין לשני כלום דלא חשבי' מתנה עיקר דיהב לה כל ימי חייו אלא ירושה שהן ראויין לו עיקר וירושה אין לה הפסק מזרעו לעולם: והא אפסקה. להיכא דאמר ואחריך לפלוני אפסקה מראשון: אמר ליה. לאו כל כמיניה והאי אמר הכי סבר יש לה הפסק ולא היא:

שני

א) אולי צ"ל דיאמר אינו יכול לעשות חפצו.

עין משפט נר מצוה

קכ א מיי' פ"ו מהלכות נחלות הל' יא סמג עשין צו טוש"ע ח"מ סי' רפב:

קכא ב מיי' פ"ע מהל' מכירה הלכה א טוש"ע י"ד סי' רנח סעיף יג:

קכב ג מיי' פ"ו מהל' נחלות הלכה יא סמג עשין צו טוש"ע ח"מ סי' רפב:

גמרא

הַהוּא דַּאֲמַר לֵיהּ לְחַבְרֵיהּ: "נְכָסַי לָךְ וְאַחֲרֶיךָ לִפְלוֹנִי", וְרִאשׁוֹן רָאוּי לְיוֹרְשׁוֹ הֲוָה. שְׁכֵיב רִאשׁוֹן, אֲתָא שֵׁנִי קָא תָבַע; סָבַר רַב עִילִישׁ קַמֵּיהּ דְּרָבָא לְמֵיכַר: שֵׁנִי נַמִי שָׁקֵיל, א"ל: דַּיָּינֵי דַּחֲצַצְתָּא הָכִי דָּיְינִי, לָאו הַיְינוּ דִּשְׁלַח רַב אַחָא בַּר רַב עַוְיָא? אִכְסִיף. קָרֵי עֲלֵיהּ: °"אֲנִי ה' א)בְּעִתָּהּ אֲחִישֶׁנָּה".§ **מתני'** אהַכּוֹתֵב אֶת נְכָסָיו לַאֲחֵרִים וְהִנִּיחַ אֶת בָּנָיו — מַה שֶּׁעָשָׂה עָשׂוּי, אֶלָּא אֵין רוּחַ חֲכָמִים נוֹחָה הֵימֶנּוּ; רשב"ג אוֹמֵר: אִם לֹא הָיוּ בָּנָיו נוֹהֲגִים כַּשּׁוּרָה — זָכוּר לַטּוֹב.§ **גמ'** אִיבַּעְיָא לְהוּ: מִי פְּלִיגִי רַבָּנַן עֲלֵיהּ דְּרשב"ג, אִי לָא? ת"ש: דְּיוֹסֵף בֶּן יוֹעֶזֶר הָיָה לוֹ בֵּן שֶׁלֹּא הָיָה נוֹהֵג כַּשּׁוּרָה, הֲוָה לֵיהּ עִילִּיתָא דְּדִינָרֵי, קָם אַקְדְּשָׁהּ. אֲזַל נְסֵיב בַּת ב)גָּאדֵיל כְּלִילֵי דְּיַנַּאי מַלְכָּא, אוֹלִידָה דְּבֵיתְהוּ, זְבֵין לָהּ בִּינִיתָא, קְרָעָהּ אַשְׁכַּח בָּהּ מַרְגָּלִיתָא. אֲמַרָה לֵיהּ: לָא תַּמְטְיָיהּ לְמַלְכָּא, דְּשָׁקְלִי לָהּ מִינָּךְ בִּדְמֵי קַלִּילֵי, זִיל אַמְטְיָיהּ לְגַבֵּי גִּזְבָּרֵי. בוְלָא תְּשַׁיְּימָהּ אַתְּ, ג)דַּאֲמִירָתוֹ לַגָּבוֹהַּ כִּמְסִירָתוֹ לְהֶדְיוֹט, אֶלָּא לְשַׁיְּימוּהָ אִינְהוּ. אַמְטְיָיהּ, שָׁמוּהָ בִּתְלֵיסַר עִלָּיָאתָא דְּדִינָרֵי. אָמְרִי לֵיהּ: שְׁבַע אִיכָּא, שִׁית לֵיכָּא. אֲמַר לְהוּ: שְׁבַע הֲבוּ לִי, שִׁית הֲרֵי הֵן מוּקְדָּשׁוֹת לַשָּׁמַיִם. עָמְדוּ וְכָתְבוּ: "יוֹסֵף בֶּן יוֹעֶזֶר הִכְנִיס אַחַת, וּבְנוֹ הִכְנִיס שֵׁשׁ". וְאִיכָּא דְּאָמְרִי: "יוֹסֵף בֶּן יוֹעֶזֶר הִכְנִיס אַחַת, וּבְנוֹ הוֹצִיא שֶׁבַע"; מִדְּקָא אָמְרִי "הִכְנִיס", מִכְּלָל דְּשַׁפִּיר עֲבַד. אַדְּרַבָּה, מִדְּקָא אָמְרִי "הוֹצִיא", מִכְּלָל דְּלָאו שַׁפִּיר עֲבַד! ד)אֶלָּא מֵהָא לֵיכָּא לְמִשְׁמַע מִינָּהּ. מַאי הָוֵי עֲלָהּ? ת"ש, ה)דַּאֲמַר לֵיהּ שְׁמוּאֵל לְרַב יְהוּדָה: ו)שִׁינָּנָא, גלָא תֶּיהֱוֵי בֵּי עֲבוּרֵי אַחְסַנְתָּא, וַאֲפִילּוּ מִבְּרָא בִּישָׁא לִבְרָא טָבָא, וְכ"ש מִבְּרָא לִבְרַתָּא. ת"ר: מַעֲשֶׂה בְּאָדָם אֶחָד שֶׁלֹּא הָיוּ בָּנָיו נוֹהֲגִין כַּשּׁוּרָה, עָמַד וְכָתַב נְכָסָיו לְיוֹנָתָן בֶּן עוּזִּיאֵל. מֶה עָשָׂה יוֹנָתָן בֶּן עוּזִּיאֵל? מָכַר שְׁלִישׁ, וְהִקְדִּישׁ שְׁלִישׁ, וְהֶחֱזִיר לְבָנָיו שְׁלִישׁ. בָּא עָלָיו שַׁמַּאי בְּמַקְלוֹ וְתַרְמִילוֹ. א"ל: שַׁמַּאי, אִם אַתָּה יָכוֹל לְהוֹצִיא אֶת מַה שֶּׁמָּכַרְתִּי וּמַה שֶּׁהִקְדַּשְׁתִּי — אַתָּה יָכוֹל לְהוֹצִיא מַה שֶּׁהֶחֱזַרְתִּי, אִם

רש"י

ההוא דאמר לחבריה. הָרָאוּי לְיוֹרְשׁוֹ, כִּדְמְפָרֵשׁ לְקַמֵּיהּ. שֵׁנִי נַמִי שָׁקֵיל. שֶׁהֲרֵי לֹא נָתַן לָרִאשׁוֹן כִּי אִם כָּל יְמֵי חַיָּיו, וּמַתָּנָה אֵינָהּ מִתְקַיֶּימֶת כִּי אִם לְדַעַת הַנּוֹתֵן. דַּיָּינֵי דַּחֲצַצְתָּא. דַּיָּינֵי פְשָׁרָה, שֶׁאֵין בְּקִיאִין בַּדִּין, וְחוֹלְקִין מֶחֱצָה לָזֶה וּמֶחֱצָה לָזֶה, כְּדִין מָמוֹן הַמּוּטָּל בְּסָפֵק. וְרַבֵּינוּ חֲנַנְאֵל פֵּירֵשׁ: חֲלַלְתָּא — בֵּית הַקְּבָרוֹת. לָאו הַיְינוּ דִּשְׁלַח כו'. וְכֵיוָן דְּרִאשׁוֹן רָאוּי לְיוֹרְשׁוֹ — אֵין לַשֵּׁנִי אַחֲרָיו כְּלוּם. אִיכְּסִיף. רַב עִילִישׁ מֵרָבָא, פֶּן יֹאמַר רָבָא בְּלִבּוֹ: אִילּוּ לֹא הָיִיתִי בְּכָאן הָיָה דָּן דִּין שֶׁקֶר, וְכֵן כָּל דִּינִין שֶׁהוּא דָּן שֶׁלֹּא בְּפָנַי. קָרָא עָלָיו. רָבָא לְנַחֲמוֹ: "אֲנִי ה' בְּעִתָּהּ אֲחִישֶׁנָּה", בְּעֵת שֶׁהַצַּדִּיקִים צְרִיכִין לִישׁוּעָה הקב"ה מַמְצִיאָהּ לָהֶם. אַף אַתָּה, אֲנִי יוֹדֵעַ בְּךָ שֶׁמֵּעוֹלָם לֹא בָּאת (א) דִּין תַּקָּלָה עַל יָדְךָ, שֶׁהֲרֵי עַכְשָׁיו זִימְּנַנִי לִי הקב"ה קוֹדֶם שֶׁהִגַּעְתָּ לְהוֹרָאָה וְלֹא נִכְשַׁלְתָּ. **מתני'** מַה שֶּׁעָשָׂה עָשׂוּי. מִילְּתָא דִּפְשִׁיטָא הִיא, וּמִשּׁוּם סֵיפָא נָקַט לָהּ, דְּאָסוּר לַעֲשׂוֹת כֵּן. אֵין רוּחַ חֲכָמִים נוֹחָה הֵימֶנּוּ. אֵין לַחֲכָמִים נַחַת רוּחַ מִמַּעֲשָׂיו, אֶלָּא חָרוֹן אַף גּוֹרֵם לָהֶן, שֶׁכּוֹעֲסִין עָלָיו דְּקָא עָקַר נַחֲלָה דְּאוֹרַיְיתָא. רשב"ג. בַּגְּמָרָא מְפָרֵשׁ לָהּ אִי לְפָרוּשֵׁי אֲתָא אִי לְפְלוּגֵי. **גמ'** מִי פְּלִיגִי כו'. דַּאֲפִילּוּ אֵין בָּנָיו נוֹהֲגִים כַּשּׁוּרָה אֵין רוּחַ חֲכָמִים נוֹחָה הֵימֶנּוּ, דִּדִלְמָא נָפְקָא מִינֵּיהּ זַרְעָא מַעַלְיָא, כִּדְלְקַמָּן. בַּת גָּאדֵיל כְּלִילֵי דְּיַנַּאי. בַּת מִי שֶׁמְּקַלֵּעַ עֲטָרוֹת דְּיַנַּאי הַמֶּלֶךְ. וְזָבֵין לָהּ בִּינִיתָא. דָּג, לְצוֹרֶךְ אִשְׁתּוֹ שֶׁיָּלְדָה. לָא תַּמְטְיָיהּ לְבֵי מַלְכָּא. לְמָכְרוֹ לְצוֹרֶךְ עַטְרוֹת הַמֶּלֶךְ. בִּדְמֵי קַלִּילֵי. בְּזוֹל. לַגִּזְבָּר. שֶׁל הֶקְדֵּשׁ, וְיִקְחֶנָּה לְאַבְנֵי אֵפוֹד. דְּנְהִי דְּבָטְלִי אוּרִים וְתוּמִּים לִישָּׁאֵל בָּהֶן, כִּדְכְתִיב (עזרא ב): "עַד עֲמוֹד כֹּהֵן לְאוּרִים וְתוּמִּים" כְּאָדָם שֶׁאוֹמֵר לַחֲבֵירוֹ: עַד שֶׁיָּבֹא מָשִׁיחַ — אֵפוֹד וְחוֹשֶׁן מִיהָא לֹא בָּטְלוּ, דְּאֵין כֹּהֵן מְשַׁמֵּשׁ בְּלֹא שְׁמוֹנָה בְגָדִים. וְלָא תְּשַׁיְּימָהּ אַתְּ. שֶׁלֹּא תִּפְתַּח לוֹמַר "בְּכָךְ וְכָךְ אֶתְּנֶנָּה לְהֶקְדֵּשׁ". דְּכֵיוָן דְּשַׁיַּימְתְּ לָהּ בִּדְמֵי קַלִּילֵי — תּוּ לָא מָצֵית לְמִישְׁקַל מִינֵּהּ טְפֵי, דַּאֲמִירָתוֹ לַגָּבוֹהַּ כו', כִּדְכְתִיב (ויקרא כז): "וְאִישׁ כִּי יַקְדִּישׁ" [וגו'] (דברים כג), "מוֹצָא שְׂפָתֶיךָ תִּשְׁמוֹר" [וגו'], אֶלָּא הַגִּזְבָּר שֶׁהוּא בָּקִי יְשַׁיְּימֶנָּה לָךְ, וְיִרְאָה שָׁמַיִם הוּא, וְלֹא יָשׁוּם אוֹתָהּ בְּזוֹל. שְׁבַע אִיכָּא. מִן הַי"ג יֵשׁ שֶׁבַע לַהֶקְדֵּשׁ, אֲבָל הַשֵּׁשׁ אֵינָן. הֲרֵי הֵן מוּקְדָּשׁוֹת. כְּלוֹמַר, מַה שֶּׁשָּׁוָה הָאֶבֶן יוֹתֵר — אֲנִי מַקְדִּישׁ מִמֶּנָּה לַגָּבוֹהַּ. עָמְדוּ וְכָתְבוּ. נִרְאֶה בְּעֵינַי שֶׁהָיוּ כּוֹתְבִין חֶשְׁבּוֹנוֹת שֶׁל הֶקְדֵּשׁ כַּמָּה מַכְנִיסִין וְכַמָּה מוֹצִיאִין. וּמִיהוּ, מִלָּשׁוֹן "שֶׁכָּתְבוּ" דְּיָיקִינַן. וְאִיכָּא לְמֵימַר נַמִי דְּלְמֵילַף מִינָּהּ כָּתְבוּ כֵּן. הִכְנִיס אֶחָד. חֲדָא עִילִּיתָא דְּדִינָרֵי, וּבְנוֹ שֶׁהָיָה סָבוּר שֶׁלֹּא יִנְהוֹג כַּשּׁוּרָה — הִקְדִּישׁ שֵׁשׁ עֲלִיּוֹת. שֶׁזְּכוּת אָבִיו, שֶׁהִקְדִּישׁ אַחַת בִּשְׁבִיל שֶׁלֹּא הָיָה בְּנוֹ נוֹהֵג כַּשּׁוּרָה, גָּרַם לִבְנוֹ שֶׁהוּכְשַׁר לְהַקְדִּישׁ שֵׁשׁ. וּמֵהָכָא דְּיָיקִינַן לְקַמָּן: מִכְּלָל דְּשַׁפִּיר עֲבַד יוֹסֵף בֶּן יוֹעֶזֶר. אַלְמָא לָא פְּלִיגִי רַבָּנַן עֲלֵיהּ, דְּהָא "עָמְדוּ וְכָתְבוּ" קָתָנֵי, דְּהַיְינוּ כָּל חַכְמֵי הַדּוֹר. אִיכָּא דְּאָמְרִי. לִגְנַאי: וּבְנוֹ הוֹצִיא שֶׁבַע — שֶׁלֹּא הָיָה לוֹ לְקַבֵּל כָּל (כָּךְ) מָמוֹן הַהֶקְדֵּשׁ לְהִתְרוֹקֵן מִכֹּל וָכֹל, וְהָיָה לוֹ לְהָנִיחַ בַּהֶקְדֵּשׁ שְׁתַּיִם אוֹ אַחַת. אַף הוּא גִּלָּה דַּעְתּוֹ שֶׁאִם הָיוּ כָּל הַשְּׁלֹשׁ עֶשְׂרֵה עֲלִיּוֹת בַּהֶקְדֵּשׁ — הָיָה נוֹטֵל אֶת כּוּלָּן. וְקָדַיְיק: מִדְּקָתָנֵי. בְּרֵישָׁא: וּבְנוֹ הִכְנִיס שֵׁשׁ, שֶׁמְּשַׁבֵּחַ אֶת הַבֵּן — מִכְּלָל דְּהָאָב שַׁפִּיר עֲבַד, כְּרַבָּן שִׁמְעוֹן, וּכְדִפְרֵישִׁית. וְלְאִיכָּא דְּאָמְרֵי לָא מַסֵּיק הָשְׁתָּא אַדַּעְתֵּיהּ. וְאוֹרְחֵיהּ דִּגְמָרָא לְאַתּוּיֵי רְאָיָה בְּכָל דּוּכְתָּא מֵרֵישָׁא, וּמְהַדַּר לֵיהּ מִסֵּיפָא. אַדְּרַבָּה. לְאִיכָּא דְּאָמְרִי אִיכָּא לְמֵידַק דְּרַבָּנַן פְּלִיגִי עֲלֵיהּ. מִדְּכָתְבוּ (ב) כֵּן: "וּבְנוֹ הוֹצִיא", הָכִי קָאָמַר: לְפִי שֶׁיּוֹסֵף בֶּן יוֹעֶזֶר הִכְנִיס אֶחָד שֶׁלֹּא כַּדִּין, שֶׁלֹּא הָיָה לוֹ לְהַקְדִּישׁ כָּל נְכָסָיו, כְּרַבָּנַן דִּפְלִיגִי עַל ר"ש, לְפִיכָךְ נִתְגַּלְגְּלָה חוֹבָה וְהוֹצִיא בְּנוֹ שֶׁבַע, שֶׁרִיקֵּן כָּל אוֹצְרוֹת הֶקְדֵּשׁ. אֶלָּא מֵהָא לֵיכָּא לְמִשְׁמַע מִינָּהּ. דְּהָא תַּנָּאֵי הִיא דִּפְלִיגִי בְּהָכִי, תַּנָּא דְּרֵישָׁא ס"ל דְּלָא פְּלִיגִי, וְתַנָּא דְּא"ד ס"ל דִּפְלִיגִי, הִלְכָּךְ אַנַּן אַמַּאן נִסְמוֹךְ? ת"ש דא"ל שְׁמוּאֵל כו'. אַלְמָא פְּלִיגִי רַבָּנַן עֲלֵיהּ, מִדְּקָאָמַר שְׁמוּאֵל הָכִי. דְּאִי לָא תֵּימָא הָכִי — שְׁמוּאֵל דְּאָמַר כְּמַאן? וְהָכִי הִלְכְתָא כְּרַבָּנַן, דְּקָם שְׁמוּאֵל כְּוָתַיְיהוּ. וְאַע"ג (ג) דא"ר יוֹחָנָן: ז) הֲלָכָה כְּרשב"ג בְּכ"מ בְּמִשְׁנָתֵנוּ חוּץ מֵעָרֵב וְצַיְדָן וּרְאָיָה אַחֲרוֹנָה — שְׁמוּאֵל לֵית לֵיהּ הַאי כְּלָלָא. וְגַם רָבָא דְּקָאָמַר בְּמַסֶּכֶת ע"ז בְּפֶרֶק חֲמִישִׁי (דף סט:): הֲלָכָה כְּרשב"ג — לֵית לֵיהּ נַמִי הַאי כְּלָלָא. הִלְכָּךְ, כָּל כְּלָלוֹת שֶׁבַּגְּמָרָא כְּגוֹן הֲלָכָה כִּסְתָם מִשְׁנָה, הֲלָכָה כר"ע מֵחֲבֵירוֹ, כְּר' יוֹסֵי מֵחֲבֵירוֹ, כְּרשב"ג בְּמִשְׁנָתֵנוּ, ר"א וְר' יְהוֹשֻׁעַ הֲלָכָה כְּר' יְהוֹשֻׁעַ, ר' יְהוּדָה ור"ש הֲלָכָה כְּר' יְהוּדָה, וְכֵן ר"מ וְר' יְהוּדָה הֲלָכָה כר"י — כּוּלְּהוּ קי"ל הָכִי, בַּר מֵהֵיכָא דִּמְפָרֵשׁ גְּמָרָא דְּלֵית הִלְכְתָא הָכִי. בֵּי עֲבוּרֵי אַחְסַנְתָּא. מָקוֹם שֶׁמַּעֲבִיר הָאָב נַחֲלָה מִן הָרָאוּי לָהּ, וַאֲפִילּוּ לְהַרְבּוֹת לְאֶחָד וּלְמַעֵט לְאֶחָד. ה"ג. וְכ"ש מִבְּרָא לִבְרַתָּא. מָכַר שְׁלִישׁ. לְצָרְכּוֹ. וְהִקְדִּישׁ שְׁלִישׁ. וְאִיכָּא לְמֵימַר דִּלְהָכִי מָכַר וְהִקְדִּישׁ מֵעִיקָּרָא, כְּדֵי לְהוֹדִיעַ שֶׁמָּה שֶׁמַּחֲזִיר לְבָנָיו — מִשֶּׁלּוֹ הוּא מַחֲזִיר, כִּדְאַהֲדַר לֵיהּ לְשַׁמַּאי כִּדְלְקַמָּן. בְּמַקְלוֹ וּבְתַרְמִילוֹ. כְּלוֹמַר, לְהִתְוַוכֵּחַ עִמּוֹ עַל שֶׁעָבַר דִּבְרֵי הַמֵּת, שֶׁנִּתְכַּוֵּין לָתֵת לוֹ ע"מ שֶׁלֹּא יֵהָנוּ בָּנָיו מִנְּכָסָיו, דִּכְמַאן דְּא"ל הֲרֵינִי נוֹתֵן לְךָ נְכָסַי ע"מ שֶׁתִּמְכְּרֵם לְצָרְכְּךָ, דְּתֶהֱנֵי בִּדְמֵיהֶן, וְלֹא ע"מ שֶׁתַּתְּנֵם לְבָנַי. דְּאִיכָּא אוּמְדַּן דַּעְתָּא דִּלְהָכִי יְהֵיב לֵיהּ, וְאַע"פ שֶׁלֹּא פֵּירֵשׁ. וְהָכִי קָאָמַר לֵיהּ שַׁמַּאי לְיוֹנָתָן: חֲזָרָה שֶׁהֶחֱזַרְתָּ לְבָנָיו אֵינָהּ כְּלוּם, דְּא"כ לָא הָוְיָא מַתָּנָה. וַהֲוֵי כְּמִי שֶׁהִפְקִיד לְךָ נְכָסָיו ע"מ שֶׁלֹּא יֵהָנוּ בָּהֶן בָּנָיו, וַחֲזוֹר וְקַח אוֹתָן, דְּקי"ל מִצְוָה לְקַיֵּים דִּבְרֵי הַמֵּת. וְשַׁמַּאי הָיָה טוֹעֶה בְּמַעֲשֶׂה דְּבֵית חוֹרוֹן דִּלְקַמָּן, דְּקָאָמַר: לֹא נָתַתִּי לְךָ אֶת שֶׁלִּי עַל מְנָת שֶׁתַּקְדִּישֵׁם לַשָּׁמַיִם, וְאָמְרוּ חֲכָמִים דְּלָא הָוְיָא מַתָּנָה, הוֹאִיל וְעָבַר

תוספות

עיליתא דדינרי. נראה לר"ת דאין לפרש עיליתא — עליה ממש, וגוזמא קאמר, כי ההיא דתליסר גמלי ספיקי דטריפות (חולין נה:), כמו שפי' בקונטרס התם. דמדקאמר הוא הכניס אחת ובנו הכניס שש — ש"מ דלאו גוזמא קאמר, אלא דוקא. לכך נראה לו: עיליתא — כלי ששואבים בו יין ושמן, כדאמרינן ב"כילד מעברין" (עירובין דף נג: ושם ד"ה ענת): עלת נקפת בכד.ח). **ולא** תשיימה את דאמירה לגבוה כו'. וא"ת: הא דאמרינן בפ"ק דקדושין (דף כט. ושם): משך הקדש במאתים ולא הספיק לפדותו עד שעמד במנה — נותן מאתים, דלא יהא כח הדיוט חמור מכח הקדש, דמן ההדיוט קונה כיון שמשך. והשתא, אפי' לא משך נמי, כיון שאמר לפדותו במאתים, דאמירה לגבוה כמסירה להדיוט! ויש לומר: דהתם היינו טעמא שאינו מתחייב מאתים באמירה — משום דלא אמר לתת כלום להקדש, יאין כאן נדר, כי לא אמר לקנות רק שוה בשוה. אבל אם ויתר כלום משלו להקדש — צריך לקיים, דאמירה לגבוה כו'ט). **בא** עליו שמאי במקלו ותרמילו כו'. נראה לרשב"א, דההוא גברא דכתב נכסיו ליהונתן בן עוזיאל הדיר נכסיו מבנו (ד) בחייו ובמותו, והיה סבור שמאי שנתן ליהונתן ע"מ שיתן לבניו. והיה סבור שהחזיר הכל, ועל כן בא עליו, לומר שע"י מתנה זו לא הותרו בהן הבנים, כמו מעשה דבית חורון שלא הותר האב ע"י מתנת הבן. והשיב לו יהונתן: אינו כמו שאתה סבור, דהתם לא היתה מתנה גמורה — אבל זו מתנה גמורה למכור ולהקדיש. וכן משמע בירושלמי בנדרים, דקאמר: יהונתן בן עוזיאל הדירו אביו מנכסיו, עמד וכתבו לשמאי. מה עשה שמאי: מכר מקצתם, והקדיש מקצתם, והתן לו את השאר. אמר: כל מי שיבא ויערער על מתנה זאת — יוציא מן הלקוחות ומיד ההקדש, ואחר כך יוציא מיד זה. ושמא זה המעשה עצמו היה, והירושלמי מהפך לה. כל

רבינו גרשום

שני נמי שקיל. כלומר דיחלוקו בין ראשון לשני: אמר ליה רבא דייני דחצצתא. שאין יודעין עיקר הדין אלא עושין פשרה ומחצצין ביניהן לזה חצי ולזה חצי דייני הכי. ולאו היינו דשלח רבא בר עולא אם ראשון ראוי ליורשו אין לשני במקום ראשון כלום: איכסיף. רב עיליש: קרא עליה. רבא: אני ה' בעתה אחישנה. כלומר אל תתבייש הואיל שלא עשית עדיין מעשה כי בעתה של מעשה החשתי והקדמתי והזכרתיך: **פיס'** והניח את בניו. שלא הוריש כלום אלא נתנן לאחרים במתנה: מי פליגי רבנן עליה דרשב"ג. דאפילו אין נוהגין כשורה פליגי דאין רוח חכמים נוחה הימנו: בת גדיל כלילי. בתו של אותו שהיה מתקן כתרי דינאי ואשתו היתה חכמה הרבה. אמרה ליה זיל אמטייה לגזבר של בית המקדש דאיהו שמייה לך כמה הוא שוה ולא תשמייה את דאת שמייה בציר משומתיה ולא מצית למיהדר בך דאמרינן לגבוה קונה באמירה כמסירה להדיוט: אמרו ליה הגזברים שב. עיליתא דדנרי איכא השתא בלשכה ושית ליכא השתא דעדיין לא נגבו. א"ל הואיל וליכא ליהוי מוקדשין. עמדו הגזברים וכתבו יוסף בן יועזר שהכנים אחת. שהקדיש עיליתא דדנרי אחת כדאמרן ובנו הכנים שית שהקדישן: ובנו הוציא שבע. מן הלשכה אותם שנתנו לו: מדאמר יוסף בן יועזר הכנים אחת מכלל דשפיר עבד. דהכניסן משום דבנו לא היה נוהג כשורה ובשביל אותו זכות שהכנים יצא ממנו בן שהכנים שש אלמא דלא פליגי רבנן אר' שמעון בן גמליאל: אדרבה מדקאמר. באידך לישנא בנו הוציא שש מכלל דלאו שפיר עבד אע"ג דלא היה נוהג כשורה שהקדישן דמשום עון שנטל מבנו ירושתו והקדיש אירע לו שיצא ממנו בן שהוציא שבע אלמא דלאו שפיר עבד דהקדיש אביו: ובא עליו שמאי. הזקן במקלו ובתרמילו לקנתרו להתרים כנגדו על שהחזיר את השליש לבניו משום דאביו לא נתכוין אלא להבריח נכסים מבניו והשתא חזרת לבנים ועברת על דעת הנותן ונמצא דמתנה שנתן לו אינה מתנה: אמר ליה. יונתן שמאי אם אתה יכול להוציא מה שמכרתי ומה שהקדשתי ולא משלי מכרתי והקדשתי הכי נמי אתה יכול להוציא מה שהחזרתי דלא ממון שלי החזרתי להם אלא ממון של אביהם וא"כ הוא עברתי ודאי על דברי הנותן ואם

מסורת הש"ס

א) [כלומר עדיין לא הגעת להוראה בעתה תמצאנה. ערוך ערך חצצתא]: ב) גי' הערוך גדל: ג) קדושין כח: תמורה כט: ב"מ ו. [ע"ז סג. נדרים כט:] [תוס' דקדושין פ"א תוספתא ב"ק פ"ד תוספתא דערכין פ"ד]: ד) [ברכות כה. וש"נ]: ה) כתובות נג.: ו) [ברכות לו. וש"נ עמ"ש חגיגה טו:]: ז) [כתובות עז.]: ח) [ועי' רש"י ותוס' שבת קיט. ד"ה בתליסר]: ט) [וע"ע תוס' קדושין שם כט. ד"ה משכו ותוס' ב"מ נז. ד"ה ילא]:

הגהות הב"ח

(א) רשב"ם ד"ה קרא וכו' לא באת תקלה על ידך בדין שהרי: (ב) ד"ה אדרבה וכו' מלכתבו ובנו כנ"ל ותיבת כן נמחק: (ג) ד"ה ת"ש וכו' דא"ל רבי יוחנן. נ"ב לקמן בדף קמ"ע: (ד) תוס' ד"ה בא וכו' בחייו ובמותו. נ"ב דלכ"ל יהיו נכסים לאחר מותו משום ירושה:

א) נדרים מח: ב) סוכה כח. ג) [עי' סנהדרין יח. רש"ל מוחק זה] ד) פירוש והוא הוא רש"ל ה) [מגילה יז.]

אִם לָאו — אִי אַתָּה יָכוֹל לְהוֹצִיא מַה שֶּׁהֶחֱזַרְתִּי. אָמַר: הֵטִיחַ עָלַי בֶּן עוּזִּיאֵל! הֵטִיחַ עָלַי בֶּן עוּזִּיאֵל! (א) מֵעִיקָּרָא מַאי סָבַר? מִשּׁוּם מַעֲשֶׂה דְּבֵית חוֹרוֹן; דִּתְנַן: [א]מַעֲשֶׂה בְּבֵית חוֹרוֹן בְּאֶחָד שֶׁהָיָה אָבִיו מוּדָּר הֵימֶנּוּ הֲנָאָה, וְהָיָה מַשִּׂיא בְּנוֹ, וְאָמַר לַחֲבֵירוֹ: הֲרֵי חָצֵר וּסְעוּדָה נְתוּנִין לְךָ בְּמַתָּנָה, וְאֵינָן לְפָנֶיךָ [אֶלָּא כְּדֵי] שֶׁיָּבֹא אַבָּא וְיֹאכַל עִמָּנוּ בַּסְּעוּדָה. אָמַר לוֹ: אִם שֶׁלִּי הֵן — הֲרֵי הֵן מוּקְדָּשִׁין לַשָּׁמַיִם! אָמַר לוֹ: לֹא נָתַתִּי לְךָ אֶת שֶׁלִּי שֶׁתַּקְדִּישֵׁם לַשָּׁמַיִם! אָמַר לוֹ: לֹא נָתַתָּ לִי אֶת שֶׁלְּךָ אֶלָּא שֶׁתְּהֵא אַתָּה וְאָבִיךָ אוֹכְלִין וְשׁוֹתִין וּמְרַצִּין זֶה לָזֶה, וִיהֵא עָוֹן תָּלוּי בְּרֹאשׁוֹ! אָמְרוּ חֲכָמִים: [א]כָּל מַתָּנָה שֶׁאֵינָהּ שֶׁאִם הִקְדִּישָׁהּ מוּקְדֶּשֶׁת — אֵינָהּ מַתָּנָה.§ [ב]תָּנוּ רַבָּנַן: שְׁמוֹנִים תַּלְמִידִים הָיוּ לוֹ לְהִלֵּל הַזָּקֵן, שְׁלֹשִׁים מֵהֶן רְאוּיִם שֶׁתִּשְׁרֶה עֲלֵיהֶן שְׁכִינָה [ג]כְּמֹשֶׁה רַבֵּינוּ, שְׁלֹשִׁים מֵהֶן רְאוּיִם שֶׁתַּעֲמוֹד לָהֶן חַמָּה כִּיהוֹשֻׁעַ בִּן נוּן, עֶשְׂרִים בֵּינוֹנִיִּים. גָּדוֹל שֶׁבְּכוּלָּן יוֹנָתָן בֶּן עוּזִּיאֵל, קָטָן שֶׁבְּכוּלָּן רַבָּן יוֹחָנָן בֶּן זַכַּאי. אָמְרוּ עָלָיו עַל רַבָּן יוֹחָנָן בֶּן זַכַּאי, שֶׁלֹּא הִנִּיחַ מִקְרָא וּמִשְׁנָה, תַּלְמוּד, הֲלָכוֹת וְאַגָּדוֹת, דִּקְדּוּקֵי תוֹרָה וְדִקְדּוּקֵי סוֹפְרִים, וְקַלִּין וַחֲמוּרִין, וּגְזֵרוֹת שָׁווֹת, וּתְקוּפוֹת, וְגִמַטְרִיָּאוֹת, וּמִשְׁלוֹת כּוֹבְסִים וּמִשְׁלוֹת שׁוּעָלִים, שִׂיחַת שֵׁדִים וְשִׂיחַת דְּקָלִים, וְשִׂיחַת מַלְאֲכֵי הַשָּׁרֵת, וְדָבָר גָּדוֹל וְדָבָר קָטָן; דָּבָר גָּדוֹל — מַעֲשֵׂה מֶרְכָּבָה, וְדָבָר קָטָן — הֲוָיוֹת דְּאַבַּיֵּי וְרָבָא; (משלי ח) לְקַיֵּים מַה שֶּׁנֶּאֱמַר: °"לְהַנְחִיל אוֹהֲבַי יֵשׁ וְאוֹצְרוֹתֵיהֶם אֲמַלֵּא". וְכִי מֵאַחַר דְּקָטָן שֶׁבְּכוּלָּם כֵּן, גָּדוֹל שֶׁבְּכוּלָּם — עַל אַחַת כַּמָּה וְכַמָּה! אָמְרוּ עָלָיו עַל יוֹנָתָן בֶּן עוּזִּיאֵל, בְּשָׁעָה שֶׁיּוֹשֵׁב וְעוֹסֵק בַּתּוֹרָה — כָּל עוֹף שֶׁפּוֹרֵחַ עָלָיו נִשְׂרָף.§ **מתני'** [ג]הָאוֹמֵר "זֶה בְּנִי" — נֶאֱמָן, "זֶה אָחִי" — אֵינוֹ נֶאֱמָן, [ג]וְיִטּוֹל עִמּוֹ בְּחֶלְקוֹ. מֵת — יַחְזְרוּ נְכָסִים לִמְקוֹמָן. נָפְלוּ לוֹ נְכָסִים מִמָּקוֹם אַחֵר — יִירְשׁוּ אֶחָיו עִמּוֹ.§ **גמ'** "זֶה בְּנִי" נֶאֱמָן, לְמַאי הִלְכְתָא? אָמַר רַב יְהוּדָה אָמַר שְׁמוּאֵל: לְיוֹרְשׁוֹ, [ד]וְלִפְטוֹר אֶת אִשְׁתּוֹ מִן הַיִּבּוּם.

לְיוֹרְשׁוֹ

וְעָבַר עַל דַּעַת הַנּוֹתֵן, וְגַם הַהֶקְדֵּשׁ לֹא חָל. וְה"נ, כֵּיוָן שֶׁעָבַרְתָּ עַל דִּבְרֵי הַמֵּת — הַמַּתָּנָה אֵינָהּ מַתָּנָה וְהַחֲזָרָה אֵינָהּ חֲזָרָה, כִּי הָתָם, דְּמַתָּנָה בְּטֵילָה וְגַם הַהֶקְדֵּשׁ לֹא נִתְפָּס. וּמִיהוּ לָא דָּמוּ, דְּהָתָם פָּרֵישׁ לֵיהּ בְּהֶדְיָא: "וְאֵינָן לְפָנֶיךָ אֶלָּא ע"מ שֶׁיָּבֹא אָבִיו וְיֹאכַל בּוֹ", אֲבָל הָכָא — סְתָמָא קָיָהֵיב לֵיהּ לְיוֹנָתָן, וְלֹא פֵּירֵשׁ "ע"מ שֶׁתֶּהֱנֶה בָּהֶן אַתָּה וְלֹא בָּנַי", הִלְכָּךְ לְגַמְרֵי יָהֵב לֵיהּ לַעֲשׂוֹת בָּהּ כִּרְצוֹנוֹ. וְהַיְינוּ דְּקָאָמַר לֵיהּ: כְּשֵׁם שֶׁאִי אַתָּה יָכוֹל לְהַחֲזִיר מַה שֶּׁמָּכַרְתִּי, דְּהָתָם מִיהָא מוֹדֵית לִי, דְּהָא ע"מ לֵיהָנוֹת אֲנִי בָּהֶן נְתָנָם לִי — אִי אַתָּה יָכוֹל לְהַחֲזִיר מַה שֶּׁהֶחֱזַרְתִּי. דִּבְע"כ אֵין מַתָּנָה לַחֲלָאִין, דְּאִם אֵינִי יָכוֹל לִיתְּנָהּ לְבָנָיו — א"כ גַּם אֲנִי בְּעַצְמִי אֵינִי יָכוֹל לֵיהָנוֹת בָּהֶן. (רש"ל) כִּדְאָמַר גַּבֵּי מַעֲשֶׂה דְּבֵית חוֹרוֹן, דְּכֵיוָן דִּנְתָנָהּ לוֹ לֵיהָנוֹת ע"מ שֶׁלֹּא יַקְדִּישׁ לֹא הָוֵי מַתָּנָה כְּלָל — ה"נ, אִם אִיתָא דִּלְדַעַת כֵּן עָשָׂה, שֶׁלֹּא יְהֵא לִי רְשׁוּת לִיתֵּן לְבָנָיו אוֹ לְכָל מִי שֶׁאֶרְצֶה, א"כ גַּם אֲנִי לֹא אוּכַל לִמְכּוֹר לַאֲחֵרִים אוֹ לְהַקְדִּישׁ. אֶלָּא מַאי אִית לָךְ לְמֵימַר, אַמַּאי הָוְיָא מְכִירָתִי מְכִירָה וְהֶקְדֵּשִׁי הֶקְדֵּשׁ? מִשּׁוּם דְּלָא פֵּירֵשׁ מִידֵּי, וְה"נ גַּבֵּי חֲזָרָה — הָא לָא פֵּירֵשׁ מִידֵּי. אֲבָל גַּבֵּי מַעֲשֶׂה דְּבֵית חוֹרוֹן, כֵּיוָן דְּפֵירֵשׁ פֵּירֵשׁ. וְשַׁמַּאי לָא הֲוָה דָּיֵיק מֵעִיקָּרָא אַמְּכִירָה וְאַהֶקְדֵּשׁ דְּמָכַר יְהוֹנָתָן וְהִקְדִּישׁ. הֵטִיחַ עָלַי. כְּמוֹ: הֵטִיחַ דְּבָרִים כְּלַפֵּי מַעְלָה (תענית דף כה.). כְּלוֹמַר, הֶשִׂיבַנִי דֶּרֶךְ בִּזָּיוֹן, וְנִלְחֲמַנִי. וּמִלְּתָא דִּבְדִיחוּתָא הוּא. וְהוּא סָבוּר. שַׁמַּאי, כִּדְפָרֵישִׁית לְעֵיל. כֵּן נִרְאֶה בְּעֵינַי. וְי"מ: דְּאַיּוֹנָתָן קָאֵי, שֶׁמָּכַר וְהִקְדִּישׁ תְּחִלָּה וְלֹא רָצָה לְהַחֲזִיר לְבָנָיו, וְלָא נְהִירָא. וְאִיכָּא סְפָרִים דִּכְתַב בְּהוּ: ד) מֵעִיקָּרָא סָבַר. וְהָיָה מַשִּׂיא אֶת בְּנוֹ. וְהָיָה חָפֵץ לְזַמֵּן אֶת אָבִיו לִסְעוּדָתוֹ. וְאֵינָן לְפָנֶיךָ. וּבְמַסֶּכֶת נְדָרִים מְתָרְצִינַן: אֲפִי' הֵיכָא דְּקָא אָמַר לֵיהּ: "הֲרֵי הֵן לְפָנֶיךָ וְיָבֹא אַבָּא וְיֹאכַל עִמָּנוּ" נַמִי מַיְירֵי, וַאפ"ה לָא הָוְיָא מַתָּנָה, דְּמ"מ מוֹכִיחַ דְּבִשְׁבִיל שֶׁיֹּאכַל אָבִיו הוּא עוֹשֶׂה, וְלֹא נִתְכַּוֵּין לָתֵת לוֹ מַתָּנָה גְּמוּרָה. וְקָאָמְרִינַן הָתָם דִּכְלָלָא דְּסֵיפָא קָאָתֵי לְאֵתוּיֵי, דְּקָתָנֵי: כָּל מַתָּנָה שֶׁאֵינָהּ כו'. וִיהֵא עָוֹן תָּלוּי כו'. שֶׁעַל יְדֵי שֶׁאֲנִי מְקַבֵּל מַתָּנָה שֶׁלְּךָ, וְהִיא אֵינָהּ מַתָּנָה — נִמְצְאֶתֶם חוֹטְאִין, וְנֶהֱנֶה זֶה מִשֶּׁל זֶה, וְקָעָבְרִיתוּ אַ"לֹא יַחֵל". הָכִי גָּרְסִינַן: אָמְרוּ חֲכָמִים כָּל מַתָּנָה שֶׁאֵינָהּ שֶׁאִם הִקְדִּישָׁהּ מוּקְדֶּשֶׁת אֵינָהּ מַתָּנָה. כְּלוֹמַר, כָּל מַתָּנָה שֶׁאֵין דִּין זֶה נוֹהֵג בָּהּ, שֶׁתְּהֵא מוּקְדֶּשֶׁת אִם הִקְדִּישָׁהּ — אֵינָהּ מַתָּנָה, הוֹאִיל וְגִילָּה דַּעְתּוֹ שֶׁע"מ כֵּן נְתָנָהּ לוֹ שֶׁלֹּא יַקְדִּישֶׁנָּה. וּלְעֵיל נַמִי, גַּבֵּי הַהוּא שֶׁכָּתַב נְכָסָיו לִיהוֹנָתָן, כֵּיוָן שֶׁלֹּא הָיָה בְּנוֹ נוֹהֵג כַּשּׁוּרָה — ע"מ שֶׁלֹּא יַחֲזִיר לְבָנָיו נָתַן לוֹ. וְיוֹנָתָן סָבַר: כֵּיוָן דִּסְתָמָא יָהֵב — הָוְיָא מַתָּנָה, לַעֲשׂוֹת בָּהּ כְּכָל אֲשֶׁר יַחְפּוֹץ. רְאוּיִם שֶׁתִּשְׁרֶה. אֶלָּא שֶׁעֲוֹן הַדּוֹר גּוֹרֵם, וְאֵין הַדּוֹר רָאוּי לְכָךְ. שֶׁתַּעֲמוֹד לָהֶם חַמָּה כִּיהוֹשֻׁעַ. וּלְמֹשֶׁה נַמִי עָמְדָה חַמָּה, דִּנְפָקָא לָן בְּמַסֶּכֶת ע"ז (דף כה.): "אָחֵל", "אָחֵל". אֶלָּא מִשּׁוּם דְּאֵין חֲשׁוּבִין כָּל כָּךְ כְּמֹשֶׁה תְּלָאָן בִּיהוֹשֻׁעַ. גְּמָרָא. סְבָרַת הַמִּשְׁנָיוֹת, כְּעֵין שֶׁאָנוּ מְפָרְשִׁין עֲלֵיהֶן: לֹא שָׁנוּ כו', חַסּוּרֵי מִחַסְּרָא כו'. הֲלָכוֹת. הֲלָכָה לְמֹשֶׁה מִסִּינַי. הַגָּדוֹת. מִדְרְשֵׁי פָּסוּק, כְּגוֹן תַּנְחוּמָא וּב"ר וַיִּקְרָא רַבָּה. דִּקְדּוּקֵי תוֹרָה. וָי"ו דְּ"וְזֶה לָכֶם הַטָּמֵא" (ויקרא יא), דְּמְרַבֵּינַן מִינֵּיהּ ה) דַּם הַשֶּׁרֶץ. דִּקְדּוּקֵי סוֹפְרִים. כְּגוֹן גְּזֵירוֹת שֶׁגָּזְרוּ חֲכָמִים שֶׁלֹּא יָבֹא לִידֵי אִיסּוּר תּוֹרָה. וְקַלִּים וַחֲמוּרִים. שֶׁאָדָם דָּן מֵעַצְמוֹ. גְּזֵירוֹת שָׁווֹת. כְּגוֹן יָלֵיף "קִיחָה" "קִיחָה" מִשְּׂדֵה עֶפְרוֹן (קדושין דף ג.). תְּקוּפוֹת. מוֹלַד הַלְּבָנָה. וְגִימַטְרִיָּאוֹת. כְּגוֹן: "אָנֹכִי" – אֲנָא נַפְשִׁי כְּתָבִית יְהָבִית, "יָרֵט" – יָרְאָה רָאֲתָה נָטְתָה (שבת דף קה.). וּמִשְׁלוֹת כּוֹבְסִין. נוֹרֵךְ יֵשׁ בָּהּ לִלְמוֹד דִּבְרֵי תוֹרָה, כִּדְכְתִיב (קהלת יב): "תִּקֵּן מְשָׁלִים הַרְבֵּה", וּכְתִיב: "לְהָבִין מָשָׁל וּמְלִיצָה" (משלי א). שִׂיחַת שֵׁדִים. לְהַשְׁבִּיעָם. וְנַפְקָא מִינָּהּ לַעֲשׂוֹת קָמֵיעַ לִרְפוּאָה. וְשִׂיחַת דְּקָלִים. שֶׁבְּנֵי אָדָם רְגִילִים לְדַבֵּר עַל הַדְּקָלִים, כִּדְכְתִיב בִּשְׁלֹמֹה: "וַיְדַבֵּר עַל הָעֵצִים" (מלכים א ד). וְשִׂיחַת מַלְאֲכֵי הַשָּׁרֵת. לְהַשְׁבִּיעָם. מַעֲשֵׂה מֶרְכָּבָה. שֶׁבִּיחֶזְקֵאל. הֲוָיוֹת דְּאַבַּיֵּי וְרָבָא. שֶׁהִקְשׁוּ מִשְׁנָיוֹת וּבָרַיְיתוֹת טוּבָא, וְתֵירְצוּם. עוֹלָמוֹת. וְכָל כָּךְ לָמָּה – כִּי אוֹצְרוֹתֵיהֶם מְלֵאִים כָּל טוּב, דִּבְרֵי תוֹרָה וְחָכְמָה. לְהַנְחִיל אוֹהֲבַי יֵשׁ. גָּדוֹל שֶׁבְּכוּלָּם עַל אַחַת כַּמָּה וְכַמָּה. לְהָבִין דָּבָר מִתּוֹךְ דָּבָר יוֹתֵר וְיוֹתֵר. **מתני'** הָאוֹמֵר זֶה בְּנִי נֶאֱמָן. בַּגְּמָרָא מְפָרֵשׁ לְמַאי הִלְכְתָא. זֶה אָחִי אֵינוֹ נֶאֱמָן. לְהוֹרִישׁוֹ עִם אֶחָיו, שֶׁהֲרֵי אֵינָן מַכִּירִין אוֹתוֹ. וְיִטּוֹל עִמּוֹ בְּחֶלְקוֹ. כִּדְמְפָרֵשׁ בַּגְּמָרָא. כְּגוֹן אִם שְׁנַיִם הֵן לְבַד הַסָּפֵק, וְיֵשׁ לָהֶן לַחֲלוֹק ג' שָׂדוֹת – זֶה נוֹטֵל שָׂדֶה וּמֶחֱצָה וְזֶה נוֹטֵל שָׂדֶה וּמֶחֱצָה, וְנוֹתֵן זֶה הַמֵּעִיד עַל אָחִיו הַסָּפֵק שֶׁהוּא אָחִיו, הַחֲצִי שָׂדֶה. דְּהָכִי קָאָמַר לֵיהּ: וַדַּאי אָחִי אַתָּה, וְיֵשׁ לְךָ לִיטּוֹל שָׂדֶה אַחַת מִן הַשָּׁלֹשׁ. וַחֲצִי הַשָּׂדֶה שֶׁיֵּשׁ לִי מֶחֶלְקְךָ – אֶתֵּן לָךְ, וַחֲצִי הָאַחֵר בְּיַד אָחִי הוּא, הָבָא לָךְ רְאָיָה וְטוֹל. מֵת. הַסָּפֵק. יַחְזְרוּ הַנְּכָסִים. שֶׁנָּתַן לוֹ מֵחֶלְקוֹ. לִמְקוֹמָן. כְּלוֹמַר, לְמִי שֶׁנְּתָנָם לוֹ. אֲבָל שְׁאָר אַחִין אֵין יוֹרְשִׁים עִמּוֹ. דְּאָמַר לְהוּ הַאי: הֲרֵי הֶחֱזַקְתֶּם בַּנַּחֲלָה הָרְאוּיָה לוֹ לַסָּפֵק מֵאָבִינוּ – אוֹתָהּ טְלוּ לָכֶם, שֶׁהֲרֵי לֹא מָחַל לָכֶם חֶלְקוֹ. וְאַכַּתִּי עַד הַשְׁתָּא בְּתוֹרַת גָּזֵל יֶשְׁנָהּ בְּיֶדְכֶם, וְעַתָּה תִּירְשׁוּ אוֹתוֹ חֵלֶק מִן הַדִּין. וְגַם אֲנִי אִירַשׁ חֶלְקִי שֶׁנָּתַתִּי לוֹ כְּמוֹ כֵן, דְּנִמְצֵינוּ כּוּלָּנוּ שָׁוִין בְּנַחֲלָתוֹ. נָפְלָה לוֹ יְרוּשָּׁה. לַסָּפֵק בְּחַיָּיו מִמָּקוֹם אַחֵר, אוֹ קָנָה נְכָסִים וְעַכְשָׁיו מֵת – יִירְשׁוּ אֶחָיו שֶׁל מֵעִיד עִמּוֹ, דְּהָא קָא מוֹדֵי לְהוּ שֶׁאֲחִיהֶם הוּא. **גמ'** לְיוֹרְשׁוֹ

כל מתנה שאינה שאם הקדישה מוקדשת כו'. ואם תאמר: דאמר לקמן בפירקין (דף קלז:): "הא לך אתרוג במתנה ע"מ שתחזירהו לי", החזירו — יצא, אע"פ שלא היה יכול להקדישו. דכיון דאמר "לי" — מידי דחזי לי קאמר, כדקאמר לקמן! ויש לומר: דהתם יכול להקדישו כל זמן שהוא בידו שלא יהנו אחרים ממנו, אבל הכא לא היה יכול להקדישו כלל. ולר"י נראה דלא תליא מתנה בהקדש, דאפילו אינו יכול להקדיש — הויא מתנה. והכי פי': כל מתנה שאינה כו', כלומר שגרועה כזאת שלא נתנה אלא ע"מ שיאכל אביו. ולאו דוקא נקט "שאם הקדישה אינה מקודשת", שהרי לא היה יכול לעשות ממנה כלום, ולא נתנה כלל אלא ע"מ שיאכל אביו, כדאמרי' בנדרים (דף מח.) לחד לישנא דסעודתו מוכחת עליו. ולא נקט "שאם הקדישה" אלא משום דמעשה הכי הוה. אי להוא לישנא דמפרש [התם] משום דויתור אסור במודר הנאה. ובעלמא, אע"פ שאינו יכול להקדישה — הויא מתנה. וכן משמע בירושלמי, דקאמר אההיא דכל מתנה שאינה שאם הקדישה כו', ר' ירמיה בעי: מעתה אין אדם נותן מתנה לחבירו על מנת שלא יקדישנה כו'. וקאמר (ב) במתני': כל מתנה שהיא כמעשה בית חורון, שהיתה בה ערמה — אינה מתנה.

לִיוֹרְשׁוֹ

קכג א מיי' פ"ז מהלכות נדרים הל' טז סמג לאוין רמב טוש"ע יו"ד סי' רכא סעיף ע:
קכד ב מיי' פ"ד מהל' נחלות הל' ה סמג עשין צו טוש"ע חו"מ סי' רעט סעיף א:
קכה ג מיי' שם הל' ח וסמג שם טוש"ע חו"מ סי' רב סעיף ב:
קכו ד מיי' פ"ג מהלכות יבום הל' א סמג עשין נא טוש"ע אה"ע סי' קנו סעיף ו:

רבינו גרשום

ואם אין אתה יכול להוציא מה שמכרתי והקדשתי משום דממון שלי הוא דלהכי מכרתי והקדשתי תחלה כדי שתהא מוחזקת המתנה בידי כך אינך יכול להחזיר מה שנתתי להם דמאחר שהייתי מוחזק מה שנתתי להם משלי נתתי ולא משל אביהן ולא עברתי על דעת הנותן דכי היכי דהקדשתי ומכרתי משלי ה"נ החזרתי משלי: הטיח עלי. כלומר נצחני יונתן בן עוזיאל: מעיקרא מאי סבר. הכי בעי מאי שנא מכר והקדיש קודם שהחזיר. משום דחשש למעשה בית חורון: ויהא עון. ביטול הנדר דכתיב לא יחל דברו: אמרו חכמים כל מתנה שאינה שאם הקדישה מוקדשת אינה מתנה. וה"נ הכי סבירא ליה ליונתן בן עוזיאל אי הממון שלי שאני יכול למוכרן ולהקדישן כך מה שאני מחזיר משלי אני מחזיר להכי מכר והקדיש תחלה כדי שתהא מוחזקת בידו המתנה: גדול שבכולם. שבבינונים: תלמוד. זו הלכה: הלכות. אלו ברייתא כגון ספרי וספרא: הגדות. מדרשים: דקדוקי תורה. כגון חסרות ויתרות ומסורות: דקדוקי סופרים. כל חשבון שמנו חכמים כגון חמש עשרה נשים פוטרות כו' וחשבון השניות וכגון חמשה דברים נאמרו בנבלת עוף טהור: שיחת שדים. שהיה יודע ללוחשן ולהשביען בשם: ושיחת דקלים. שהיה יודע ללחוש דבר שתתמלא השדה דקלים ושיתעקרו: ושיחת מלאכי השרת. שהיה יודע להשביען בשם: הויות דאביי ורבא. היו יכולין לתרצן: **פיס'** האומר זה בני. נאמן לפטור את אשתו מן היבום כדמפר' בגמ': זה אחי אינו נאמן. שאם היו י' אחין ובא אחד ממדינת הים ואמר אחים אנחנו ואמר אחד מן האחים אני מכיר שאחינו הוא ויטול עמנו בנחלה אינו נאמן הואיל ושאר אחים אינם מכירים אותו לא ימעט להם בנחלה שלא יהיו מצמצמין לו מנחלתן. אבל אותו שמכירו ומודה שאחיו הוא יטול עמו בחלקו חצי: ואם מת. בלא יורש אותו אח שבא: יחזרו הנכסים למקומן. לזה האח בלבד שנתן לו חלקו: נפלו לו נכסים ממקום אחר. לאותו אח שבא ומת: יירשו אחיו עמו עם זה שהודה בו שהוא אחיהן הואיל והוא מודה שאחיהן היה: למאי הלכתא. קא תני האומר זה בני נאמן: יש

הגהות הב"ח

(א) גמ' בן עוזיאל (מעיקרא מאי סבר) תא"מ ונ"ב ס"א וכן פי' רשב"ם והוא מאי סבר: (ב) תוס' ד"ה כל וכו' וקאמר כיני מתניתין:

לְיוֹרְשׁוֹ, פְּשִׁיטָא! לִפְטוֹר אֶת אִשְׁתּוֹ מִן הַיִּבּוּם אִצְטְרִיכָא לֵיהּ. הָא נַמִי תְּנֵינָא: א)מִי שֶׁאָמַר בִּשְׁעַת מִיתָתוֹ "יֵשׁ לִי בָּנִים" — נֶאֱמָן, א"יֵשׁ לִי אַחִים" — אֵינוֹ נֶאֱמָן! הָתָם דְּלָא מוּחְזָק לָן בְּאָח, הָכָא — באַף עַל גַּב דְּמוּחְזָק לֵיהּ בְּאָח. אָמַר רַב יוֹסֵף אָמַר רַב יְהוּדָה אָמַר שְׁמוּאֵל: מִפְּנֵי מָה אָמְרוּ: "זֶה בְּנִי" — נֶאֱמָן? הוֹאִיל וּבַעַל שֶׁאָמַר "גֵּרַשְׁתִּי אֶת אִשְׁתִּי" — נֶאֱמָן. ב)א"ר יוֹסֵף: מָרֵיהּ דְּאַבְרָהָם, תָּלֵי תַּנְיָא בִּדְלָא תַּנְיָא! אֶלָּא אִי אִתְּמַר הָכִי אִיתְּמַר, (א) א"ר יְהוּדָה אָמַר שְׁמוּאֵל: מִפְּנֵי מָה אָמְרוּ: "זֶה בְּנִי" — נֶאֱמָן? הוֹאִיל וּבְיָדוֹ לְגָרְשָׁהּ. אֲמַר רַב יוֹסֵף, הָשְׁתָּא דְּאָמְרַתְּ: אָמְרִינַן "הוֹאִיל", בַּעַל שֶׁאָמַר "גֵּרַשְׁתִּי אֶת אִשְׁתִּי" — נֶאֱמָן, הוֹאִיל וּבְיָדוֹ לְגָרְשָׁהּ. גכִּי אֲתָא רַב יִצְחָק בַּר יוֹסֵף אָמַר רַבִּי יוֹחָנָן: בַּעַל שֶׁאָמַר "גֵּרַשְׁתִּי אֶת אִשְׁתִּי" — גאֵינוֹ נֶאֱמָן. ד)מְנַפַּח רַב שֵׁשֶׁת בִּידֵיהּ: אֵ"ל לֵיהּ "הוֹאִיל" דְּרַב יוֹסֵף. אֵינִי? וְהָא ה)א"ר חִיָּיא בַּר אָבִין אָמַר רַבִּי יוֹחָנָן: בַּעַל שֶׁאָמַר "גֵּרַשְׁתִּי אֶת אִשְׁתִּי" — נֶאֱמָן! לָא קַשְׁיָא: כָּאן לְמַפְרֵעַ, כָּאן לְהַבָּא. אִיבַּעְיָא לְהוּ: אָמַר לְמַפְרֵעַ, מַהוּ לְהֵימוֹנֵיהּ לְהַבָּא? מִי פָּלְגִינַן דִּבּוּרָא, אוֹ לָא פָּלְגִינַן דִּבּוּרָא? רַב מָארִי וְרַב זְבִיד, חַד אָמַר: פָּלְגִינַן, וְחַד אָמַר: לָא פָּלְגִינַן. מַאי שְׁנָא מִדְּרָבָא, ו)דְּאָמַר רָבָא: ד"אִישׁ פְּלוֹנִי בָּא עַל אִשְׁתִּי" — הוּא וְאַחֵר מִצְטָרְפִין לְהוֹרְגוֹ, לְהוֹרְגוֹ וְלֹא לְהוֹרְגָהּ? בִּתְרֵי גוּפֵי פָּלְגִינַן, בְּחַד גּוּפָא לָא פָּלְגִינַן.

הַהוּא

רשב"ם

לְיוֹרְשׁוֹ פְּשִׁיטָא. דְּמִגּוֹ דְּאִי בָּעֵי יָהֵיב לֵיהּ בְּמַתָּנָה, כִּי אָמַר נַמִי "בְּנִי הוּא וְיִירָשֵׁנִי" — נֶאֱמָן. וְאִי מִשּׁוּם נְכָסִים הַבָּאִים לְאַחַר מִיכָּן אֲתָא לְאַשְׁמוּעִינַן, דְּאַע"ג דְּאֵין יָכוֹל לְהַקְנוֹתָן נֶאֱמָן — הָא לָאו מִלְּתָא הִיא, דְּוַדַּאי אֵינוֹ נֶאֱמָן, דְּהָא לֵיכָּא לְמֵימַר מִגּוֹ. וְאַע"ג דְּדָרְשִׁינַן לְעֵיל (דף קכז:): "יַכִּיר" — בְּלָרִיךְ הֶיכֵּרָא, וְאוֹקְמִינַן דְּהָכָא נֶאֱמָן אֲפִילּוּ לַנְּכָסִים הַבָּאִים לְאַחַר מִיכָּן, אִי נַמִי, שֶׁנָּפְלוּ לוֹ כְּשֶׁהוּא גּוֹסֵס — ה"מ גַּבֵּי חֵלֶק בְּכוֹרָה, דְּיָדְעִינַן שֶׁהוּא בְּנוֹ אַךְ אֵינוֹ יָדוּעַ אִם בְּכוֹר הוּא אִם לָאו, וַאֲתָא קְרָא לְמֵימַר דְּכֵיוָן דְּיָדְעִינַן דִּבְנוֹ הוּא — נֶאֱמָן לוֹמַר "בְּכוֹרִי הוּא". אֲבָל הֵיכָא דְּלָא יָדְעִינַן אִי בְּנוֹ הוּא אוֹ לָאו — לָא מְהֵימְנִינַן לֵיהּ אֶלָּא לַנְּכָסִים שֶׁיֵּשׁ לוֹ עַכְשָׁיו, מִשּׁוּם דְּאִיכָּא לְמֵימַר מִגּוֹ. לִפְטוֹר אִשְׁתּוֹ מִן הַיִּבּוּם אִצְטְרִיכָא לֵיהּ. לְמַתְנִיתִין לְמִיתְנֵי: הָאוֹמֵר: "זֶה בְּנִי" — נֶאֱמָן. דְּסד"א לֹא תִּנָּשֵׂא לַשּׁוּק בְּלֹא חֲלִיצָה, כִּדְלְקַמָּן. הָא נַמִי תְּנֵינָא. בְּקִדּוּשִׁין פֶּרֶק "הָאוֹמֵר". בִּשְׁעַת מִיתָתוֹ. אוֹרְחָא דְּמִלְּתָא נָקַט. יֵשׁ לִי בָּנִים. וְאֵין אִשְׁתּוֹ זְקוּקָה לְיָבֵם — נֶאֱמָן, וְתִנָּשֵׂא לַשּׁוּק. וּלְקַמֵּיהּ מוֹקֵי לָהּ בִּדְלָא מוּחְזָק לָן לָא בְּאַחֵי וְלָא בִּבְנֵי. יֵשׁ לִי אַחִין. וּזְקוּקָה לְיָבֵם. אֵינוֹ נֶאֱמָן. לְאָסְרָהּ. וְטַעְמָא מְפָרְשִׁי' לְקַמֵּיהּ. וּמְשַׁנֵּי: הָתָם דְּלָא מוּחְזָק לָן. הַאי גַּבְרָא בִּשְׁעַת מִיתָה לָא בְּאַחֵי וְלָא בִּבְנֵי, וְקַיְימָא הַךְ אִתְּתָא בְּחֶזְקַת שֶׁאֵינָהּ זְקוּקָה לְיָבֵם. דִּסְפֵק סְפֵיקָא הוּא: שֶׁמָּא יֵשׁ לוֹ בָּנִים, וְאת"ל אֵין לוֹ — שֶׁמָּא גַּם אַחִין אֵין לוֹ, וּמוּתֶּרֶת לַשּׁוּק. דְּהָכִי מוּקְמִי' לָהּ הָתָם בְּקִדּוּשִׁין, מִשּׁוּם דְּבָעֵי לְאוֹקְמָהּ אֲפִי' כְּר' נָתָן, דְּאָמַר: נֶאֱמָן לְאָסְרָהּ, שֶׁאִם אָמַר "יֵשׁ לִי אַחִין" — נֶאֱמָן. וְהַהִיא דְּר' נָתָן מוֹקְמִינַן לָהּ הָתָם בְּמוּחְזָק לָן דְּאִית לֵיהּ אַחֵי וְלָא מוּחְזָק לָן בִּבְנֵי. אֲבָל מַתְנִי' דְּהָתָם דְּקָתָנֵי: "יֵשׁ לִי בָּנִים" נֶאֱמָן, "יֵשׁ לִי אַחִים" אֵינוֹ נֶאֱמָן — בִּדְלָא מוּחְזָק לָן לָא בְּאַחֵי וְלָא בִּבְנֵי, כִּדְפָרִישִׁית. הִלְכָּךְ, אָמַר "יֵשׁ לִי בָּנִים" — אַחְזָקָה קַמַּיְיתָא הוּא דְּמוֹקֵי לָהּ, הִלְכָּךְ נֶאֱמָן. וְנ"מ, דַּאֲפִי' אִי אָתֵי אָח לְאַחַר מִכָּאן וְאָמַר "אֲחוּהִי דְּמִיתְנָא הֲוֵינָא" (ג) — לָא כָּל כְּמִינֵיהּ דְּלַהֲנֵי דִּבּוּרֵיהּ [לְאַחֲזוּקֵי] לַחֲזָקָה. אָמַר "יֵשׁ לִי אַחִין וְאֵין לִי בָּנִים" — לָאו כָּל כְּמִינֵיהּ דְּמַפִּיק לָהּ מֵחֲזָקָה. הָכָא. אָתֵי לְאַשְׁמוּעִינַן, דְּאַע"ג דְּמוּחְזָק לָן בְּגַוֵּיהּ דְּאִית לֵיהּ אַחֵי, חֲזָקָה בְּעָלְמָא בְּלָא עֵדִים, ספ"ה, אִי אָמַר "זֶה בְּנִי" — נֶאֱמָן לְפָטְרָהּ מִיִּבּוּם, וּכְדִמְפָרֵשׁ טַעְמָא לְקַמָּן: מִגּוֹ דְּאִי בָּעֵי פָּטַר לָהּ בְּגֵט, וְהִלְכָּךְ מַה לּוֹ לְשַׁקֵּר. דְּסד"א: לָא אָתֵי "מַה לִּי לְשַׁקֵּר" וּמֵרַע לֵיהּ לַחֲזָקָה, קמ"ל נֶאֱמָן. וְהַאי דְּקָתָנֵי: "זֶה בְּנִי" נֶאֱמָן — ה"ה דְּאִי אָמַר "יֵשׁ לִי בָּנִים" נֶאֱמָן לְהַתִּירָהּ. אֶלָּא מִשּׁוּם סֵיפָא אִצְטְרִיךְ לֵיהּ לְמִיתְנֵי: "זֶה אָחִי" אֵינוֹ נֶאֱמָן, לְאַשְׁמוּעִינַן דְּלָאַת לוֹ מֵחֶלְקוֹ הוּא נֶאֱמָן, וְלֹא לִירַשׁ עִם שְׁאָר אַחִין — תְּנָא נַמִי רֵישָׁא: "זֶה בְּנִי". וּמִיהוּ, סֵיפָא דְּקָתָנֵי: "זֶה אָחִי" אֵינוֹ נֶאֱמָן — לָא בְּהֶיתֵּר וְלָא בְּאִיסּוּר שֶׁל שׁוּק מַיְירֵי, דְּהָא וַדַּאי אֲפִי' שָׁתַק אֲסוּרָה, כֵּיוָן דְּמוּחְזָק לָן בְּאַחֵי וְלָא בִּבְנֵי. אֶלָּא לְעִנְיַן לִירַשׁ עִם אֶחָיו קָאָמַר דְּאֵינוֹ נֶאֱמָן. א"נ, אִיכָּא לְמֵימַר דְּהָכִי קָאָמַר: הָאוֹמֵר "זֶה בְּנִי" — נֶאֱמָן, וְאַע"ג דְּמוּחְזָק לָן בְּאַחֵי. "זֶה אָחִי" — אֵינוֹ נֶאֱמָן לְאָסְרָהּ אִם הָיָה בְּחֶזְקַת מוּתֶּרֶת, כְּגוֹן דְּלָא מוּחְזָק לָן לָא בְּאַחֵי וְלָא בִּבְנֵי. הוֹאִיל וּבַעַל שֶׁאָמַר גֵּרַשְׁתִּי אֶת אִשְׁתִּי נֶאֱמָן. וְהִלְכָּךְ, מִגּוֹ דְּאִי בָּעֵי אָמַר "גֵּרַשְׁתִּי" וְתִפָּטֵר מֵהַיִּבּוּם, כִּי אָמַר נַמִי "יֵשׁ לִי בָּנִים" — נֶאֱמָן. וְטַעְמָא דְּבַעַל שֶׁאָמַר "גֵּרַשְׁתִּי אֶת אִשְׁתִּי" נֶאֱמָן — הַיְינוּ מִשּׁוּם דְּאִי בָּעֵי מְגָרֵשׁ לָהּ הָשְׁתָּא בְּפָנֵינוּ. רַב יוֹסֵף חָלָה וְשָׁכַח תַּלְמוּדוֹ, כִּדְאָמְרִי' בְּמַסֶּכֶת נְדָרִים (דף מא.). וּשְׁמוּעוֹת שֶׁשָּׁמַע מֵרַב יְהוּדָה רַבּוֹ קוֹדֶם חָלְיוֹ, וְעַכְשָׁיו מִתְקַשֶּׁה בָּהֶן, הָיָה נוֹתֵן אֶל לִבּוֹ וְתָמֵהַּ אִם שָׁמַע כֵּן, וְהָיָה מְתָרְגֵּן מִדַּעְתּוֹ. וה"ק: רבש"ע, אֶפְשָׁר שֶׁשָּׁמַעְתִּי מֵרַב יְהוּדָה שִׁיבּוּשׁ גָּדוֹל כָּזֶה, דְּתָלֵי תַּנְיָא — הַמִּשְׁנָה, דְּקָתָנֵי: "זֶה בְּנִי" נֶאֱמָן, תּוֹלֶה טַעְמָא בְּלָא תַּנְיָא — בְּדָבָר שֶׁאֵינוֹ בַּמִּשְׁנָה וּבַבָּרַיְיתָא, הַךְ דְּבַעַל שֶׁאָמַר "גֵּרַשְׁתִּי אֶת אִשְׁתִּי", דְּמֵימְרָא בְּעָלְמָא הִיא, וְגַם הִיא צְרִיכָה טַעַם אַחֵר, וְתוֹלֶה אֶת הָעִיקָּר בַּטָּפֵל לוֹ?! אֶלָּא אִי. אָמַר לִי רַב יְהוּדָה — הָכִי אֲמָרָהּ. אָמַר שְׁמוּאֵל הוֹאִיל וּבְיָדוֹ לְגָרְשָׁהּ. דְּמִגּוֹ דְּאִי בָּעֵי מְגָרֵשׁ לָהּ וּפָטַר לָהּ בְּגִיטָּא מִיִּבּוּם, כִּי אָמַר נַמִי "זֶה בְּנִי" — נֶאֱמָן. ה"ג: אֶלָּא אִי אִתְּמַר הָכִי אִתְּמַר אָמַר שְׁמוּאֵל הוֹאִיל וכו'. בַּעַל שֶׁאָמַר גֵּרַשְׁתִּי אֶת אִשְׁתִּי נֶאֱמָן. לְפָטְרָהּ מִיִּבּוּם. אֵינוֹ נֶאֱמָן. דְּאִם אִיתָא דְּגֵרְשָׁהּ — קָלָא אִית לָהּ לְמִלְּתָא. הִלְכָּךְ לָא אָמְרִי' "מַה לִּי לְשַׁקֵּר", דְּכִ"מַה לִּי לְשַׁקֵּר" בִּמְקוֹם עֵדִים דָּמֵי. וּמִיהוּ, כִּי אָמַר "זֶה בְּנִי" — נֶאֱמָן, דְּהָתָם וַדַּאי אִיכָּא לְמֵימַר: הוֹאִיל וּבְיָדוֹ לְגָרְשָׁהּ. מְנַפַּח בִּידֵיהּ. דֶּרֶךְ שְׂחוֹק, כְּאָדָם שֶׁמְּנַפֵּחַ קַשׁ מִתַּחַת יָדָיו וּמַשְׁלִיכוֹ לְאִבּוּד. כְּלוֹמַר, כָּזֶה הָרוּחַ שֶׁהָלַךְ כָּךְ אָבַד טַעֲמוֹ שֶׁל רַב יוֹסֵף. הוֹאִיל דְּרַב יוֹסֵף. דְּאָמַר: בַּעַל שֶׁאָמַר "גֵּרַשְׁתִּיהָ". וּמִיהוּ, "הוֹאִיל" דִּשְׁמוּאֵל אִיתֵיהּ, דְּהָא וַדַּאי מָצֵי מְגָרֵשׁ לָהּ. לְמַפְרֵעַ. אִם עָמַד לְפָנֵינוּ בְּאֶחָד בְּאִיָּיר, וְאָמַר "גֵּרַשְׁתִּי אֶת אִשְׁתִּי מֵאֶחָד בְּנִיסָן" — אֵינוֹ נֶאֱמָן לְהַחֲזִיקָהּ כְּמוֹ מְגוֹרֶשֶׁת לְמַפְרֵעַ. שֶׁאִם יָבוֹאוּ עֵדִים אַחֲרֵי כֵן שֶׁיֹּאמְרוּ "אָנוּ רְאִינוּהָ שֶׁזִּינְּתָה בְּט"ו בְּנִיסָן" — תִּדּוֹן בְּחֶנֶק כְּדִין אֵשֶׁת אִישׁ. דְּאֵין הַבַּעַל נֶאֱמָן לַעֲשׂוֹתָהּ מְגוֹרֶשֶׁת לְמַפְרֵעַ, שֶׁהֲרֵי אֵינוֹ יָכוֹל עַכְשָׁיו בְּאֶחָד בְּאִיָּיר לַעֲשׂוֹת לָהּ גֵּט שֶׁתִּתְגָּרֵשׁ בּוֹ לְמַפְרֵעַ מִקּוֹדֶם זְנוּת. כָּאן לְהַבָּא. אִם אָמַר "גֵּרַשְׁתִּי אֶת אִשְׁתִּי" סְתָם, א"נ "עַכְשָׁיו גֵּרַשְׁתִּי", דְּאֵינוֹ מֵעִיד עָלֶיהָ לְמַפְרֵעַ, וְלָא נָפְקָא מִינַּהּ אֶלָּא לְפָטְרָהּ מִכָּאן וּלְהַבָּא, בֵּין לִזְנוּת בֵּין לִיפָּטֵר מִיִּבּוּם, וְגַם לְהִנָּשֵׂא לְכָל כִּי שֶׁתִּרְצֶה בְּחַיֵּי בַּעְלָהּ. דְּמַה לּוֹ לְשַׁקֵּר? הָא אִי בָּעֵי — מְגָרֵשׁ לָהּ בְּפָנֵינוּ. וְאַכַּתִּי לָא אָזַל לָהּ "הוֹאִיל" דְּרַב יוֹסֵף לְגַמְרֵי, דִּלְהַבָּא מִיהָא אָמְרִינַן "הוֹאִיל". אִיבַּעְיָא לְהוּ אָמַר לְמַפְרֵעַ מַהוּ לְהֵימוֹנֵיהּ לְהַבָּא. כְּלוֹמַר, הָא פְּשִׁיטָא לָן דְּהֵיכָא דְּאָמַר לְמַפְרֵעַ — לָא מְהֵימַן לְגַבֵּי זְנוּת דְּמַפְרֵעַ, דְּהָא לֵיכָּא מִגּוֹ. וְאִם אָמַר "עַכְשָׁיו גֵּרַשְׁתִּי", דְּלָא נָפְקָא מִינַּהּ אֶלָּא לְהַבָּא — וַדַּאי מְהֵימְנִינַן לֵיהּ, דְּהָא אִי בָּעֵי מָצֵי מְגָרֵשׁ לָהּ, וּמַה לּוֹ לְשַׁקֵּר. אֲבָל הָא קָמִבַּעְיָא לָן: הֵיכָא דְּקָאָמַר לְמַפְרֵעַ, כְּלוֹמַר "זֶה ל' יוֹם שֶׁגֵּרַשְׁתִּי אֶת אִשְׁתִּי", מַהוּ לְהֵימוֹנֵיהּ לְפָטְרָהּ מִזְּנוּת דִּלְהַבָּא? דְּגַבֵּי לְהַבָּא אִיכָּא לְמֵימַר מִגּוֹ דְּמַה לּוֹ לְשַׁקֵּר, לְפָטְרָהּ לְהַבָּא בְּטַעֲנַת גֵּרוּשִׁין דִּלְמַפְרֵעַ, הָא אִי בָּעֵי — מָצֵי מְגָרֵשׁ לָהּ הָשְׁתָּא. מִי פָּלְגִינַן דִּבּוּרָא. דִּבְמַאי דְּאָמַר "גֵּרַשְׁתִּי" — מְהֵימְנִינַן לֵיהּ, וְתִפָּטֵר אִשְׁתּוֹ מִכָּאן וּלְהַבָּא. וּבְמַאי דְּאָמַר "זֶה ל' יוֹם", דְּהַיְינוּ לְמַפְרֵעַ — לָא מְהֵימְנִינַן לֵיהּ, דְּלֵיכָּא מִגּוֹ. אוֹ לָא פָּלְגִינַן דִּבּוּרָא. אֶלָּא, כֵּיוָן דְּלָא מְהֵימְנִינַן לֵיהּ בְּגֵירוּשֵׁי מַפְרֵעַ, מִשּׁוּם דְּאֵין בְּיָדוֹ לַעֲשׂוֹת וְלֵיכָּא מִגּוֹ — נִמְצָא שֶׁלֹּא גֵּירֵשׁ אִשְׁתּוֹ לְמַפְרֵעַ. וְהָשְׁתָּא נַמִי לָא גֵּירֵשׁ, דְּאִיהוּ לָא טָעֵין אֶלָּא גֵּירוּשֵׁי מַפְרֵעַ, אֲנַן טָעֲנִינַן לֵיהּ? בִּתְמִיָּה. וְהִלְכָּךְ, כָּל הֵיכָא דְּאָמַר בַּעַל "גֵּרַשְׁתִּי אֶתְמוֹל" — לָא מְהֵימְנִינַן לֵיהּ כְּלָל, דְּמִגּוֹ דְּלָא מְהֵימַן לְגַבֵּי מַפְרֵעַ — לָא מְהֵימַן לְהַבָּא, דְּלָא פָּלְגִינַן דִּבּוּרָא. וְלָא מַשְׁכַּחַתְּ לָהּ דִּמְהֵימַן אֶלָּא הֵיכָא דְּאָמַר כִּתְמָא "גֵּרַשְׁתִּי אֶת אִשְׁתִּי", א"נ "עַכְשָׁיו גֵּרַשְׁתִּי אֶת אִשְׁתִּי", דִּמְהֵימְנִינַן אַכּוּלֵּיהּ דִּבּוּרֵיהּ. דְּכֵיוָן דְּלָא נָפְקָא לָן מִמַּעֲשֶׂה דְּלְשֶׁעָבַר כְּלָל, אֶלָּא אַהֲנָיוּהוּ דִּלְהַבָּא — מַה לּוֹ לְשַׁקֵּר, הֲרֵי יָכוֹל לְגָרְשָׁהּ. כֵּן נִרְאֶה בְּעֵינַי. דְּאָמַר רָבָא. בַּעַל שֶׁאָמַר בִּפְנֵי ב"ד: פְּלוֹנִי בָּא עַל אִשְׁתִּי הוּא וְאַחֵר מִצְטָרְפִין לְהוֹרְגוֹ. לַבּוֹעֵל, וְלֹא לְהוֹרְגָהּ. דְּאֵצֶל אִשְׁתּוֹ פָּסוּל הוּא לְעֵדוּת. אַלְמָא: פָּלְגִינַן הַאי עֵדוּת, דְּלַבּוֹעֵל מְהֵימַן, לָאִשָּׁה לָא מְהֵימַן! בִּתְרֵי גוּפֵי. בּוֹעֵל וְאִשָּׁה פָּלְגִינַן, דִּלְגַבֵּי בּ"עַל אָנוּ מַאֲמִינִין כָּל הָעֵדוּת. בְּחַד גּוּפָא. לְמַפְרֵעַ וּלְהַבָּא בְּאִשָּׁה אַחַת.

הַהוּא

תוספות

לְיוֹרְשׁוֹ פשיטא. דאנכסים שנפלו לו כשהוא גוסס לא (ג) יהא נאמן. אע"ג דלענין בכורה נאמן — היינו משום שראוי ליורשו, שהרי בידוע שהוא בנו. אבל הכא, דלא ידעינן אם הוא ראוי ליורשו או לא — אינו נאמן. הואיל ובידו לגרשה. אע"ג דהאי מגו לא חשיבא, שאם היה מגרשה היה פוסלה מן הכהונה, והשתא שאומר "זה בני" לא פסיל לה, מ"מ חשיב מגו לפטרה מיבם. אזל ליה הואיל דרב יוסף. ולא אמרינן: הואיל ובידו לגרשה. דס"ד השתא דאין נאמן לומר "גרשתי אשתי עתה", דאפי' להבא אין נאמן לומר "גרשתי אשתי". וא"ת: א"כ מ"ט דמתני' ד"זה בני" נאמן? וי"ל: דדוקא לענין שאמר "גרשתי" לא אמר מגו הואיל ובידו לגרשה, משום דאם איתא דגרשה — אית לה קלא, ולכך אינו נאמן. אבל "זה בני" — נאמן במגו דהואיל ובידו לגרשה, דיכול להיות שיש לו בן ואין ידוע לעולם. למפרע אין נאמן. תימה: דמאי קמ"ל? פשיטא דאין נאמן לומר למפרע "גרשתי אשתי". שאם היה נאמן — מה הועילו חכמים בתקנה שתקנו זמן בגיטין, שלא יחפה על בת אחותו אם תזנה תחתיו (גיטין דף יז.)? דלעולם יחפה, שיאמר "גרשתיה קודם הזנות", ויהיה נאמן! בשלמא למ"ד בסמוך דלא פלגינן דבורא — אתי שפיר, דאצטריך לאשמועינן דאפי' מכאן ולהבא אין נאמן כשאומר "גרשתי מקודם". אבל למ"ד פלגינן דבורא, ונאמן מכאן ולהבא, אלא למפרע דוקא אין נאמן — קשה, דמלתא דפשיטא היא! פלוני בא על אשתי. מילתיה דרבא היא בפ"ק דסנהדרין (דף י. ושם), וקאמר התם: מהו דתימא אדם קרוב אצל עצמו אמרינן, אבל אצל אשתו — לא אמר, קמ"ל. וקשה לה"ר חיים: דפשיטא הוא דאדם קרוב אצל אשתו, כדתנן ב"זה בורר" (שם דף כז:)! ויש לומר: דאף על גב דפסול לעדות הוא להעיד על אשתו, כשאומר "פלוני בא על אשתי" הוה אמינא: מתוך שנאמן על פלוני נאמן נמי עליה.

חזיא

רבינו גרשום

יש לי בנים. במדינת הים: נאמן ומותרת אשתו להנשא: יש לי אחים אינו נאמן. לאוסרה לעלמא: התם. משום הכי איכא למימר דנאמן דלא מוחזק לן בגויה דאית ליה אח: הכא. במתני' אע"ג דאתחזק באחי ואיכא למימר משום הכי אמר זה בני דלא בעי דנפלה איתתיה קמייהו ליבום אפי' הכי נאמן: מריה דאברהם. מתמיה: תלי תניא בדלא תניא. דהא דקא תני במתני' האומר זה בני נאמן ושנויה היא תלי במימרא דהא דקאמר בעל שאמר גרשתי כו'. כלומר דלא תיהוי זקוקה ליבום מימרא בעלמא היא ולא משנה. והיכי תלי מימרא במשנה משום דרב יוסף חולה היה ושכח תלמודו באונס היה מתמיה בעצמו היאך תלה רב יהודה רבו תניא בדלא תניא. אלא ודאי לעולם לא אמר לי כי הא מלתא דלא תלה משנה במימר'. אלא הכי אתמר אמר רב יוסף אמר רב יהודה אמר שמואל כו' הואיל ובידו לגרשה. בפנינו דאינה זקוקה ליבם להכי אמר מתני' זה בני נאמן דאמרינן הואיל ובידו לגרשה ולפוטרה מה לו לשקר היכא דאמר זה בני וטעם של משנתנו משום הואיל הוא ולאו משום מימרא כשאמר בעל גירשתי דלא ידעי דקושטא קאמר. אי לאו משום דאמרי' הואיל ובידו לגרשה לפנינו: והואיל וטעם משנתנו דבאומר זה בני [נאמן] משום האי טעמא הואיל ובידו לגרשה. בעל נמי שאמר גרשתי דנאמן מטעם דמשנתנו הואיל ובידו לגרשה: מנפח רב ששת. מפיח בידיה: אזל ליה הואיל דרב יוסף. דאמר הואיל ובידו לגרשה אינה עיקר השתא דרב יצחק ב"ר שמואל קתני דאינו נאמן: לא קשיא כאן למפרע כאן להבא. הכי פירושא אם זינתה אשתו ובתר הכי קאמר גירשתיה קודם שזינתה כדי לפוטרה ממיתה אין נאמן דאיכא למימר מחפה הוא עליה. אבל אם קודם שזינתה אמר גרשתי את אשתי נאמן. אבל הא מיבעיא לן זינתה למפרע ואחר כך אמר גירשתי וחזרה וזינתה אחר כך מהו להימוניה להבא. לזנות קמא אינו נאמן דאיכא למימר כדי לחפות עליה קאמר אבל מי מהימנינן ליה דאמרינן דבזנות שני כבר היתה פנויה הואיל ואמר קודם לכן גירשתי. א) אבל בזנות ראשון דשוב אמר גירשתי אינו נאמן. או לא פלגינן דבורא הואיל ואין נאמן מזנות ראשון דלחפות קאמר כך אינו נאמן לגבי אשתו דקרוב לאשתו אלמא פלגינן דבורא לגבי נואף נאמן ולגבי אשתו אינו נאמן: ומשני נואף ואשתו תרי גופי נינהו. ומשום הכי פלגינן דבורא אבל בחד מלתא כי האי מלתא דלעיל דזינתה וזינתה לא פלגינן ואינו נאמן להבא הואיל ואינו נאמן למפרע ואמרי

לזנות שני: ואין מצטרפין להורגה. הוא. הבעל עצמו: ואחר. עד עמו: מצטרפין להורגו. לאותו נואף דהבעל רחוק הוא לגבי נואף ונאמן להעיד עליו עם עד שני: משני: הוא. הבעל עצמו: ואחר. עד עמו: מצטרפין להורגו.

א) נראה דל"ל ודוקא על זנות ראשון דשוב אמר וכו'.

עין משפט נר מצוה

קכז א ב מיי' פ"ג מהל' יבום הלכה ב ועי' במ"מ ובלח"מ סמג עשין נא טוש"ע אה"ע סי' קנז סעיף ו:

קכח ג מיי' פי"ב מהל' גירושין הלכה ה סמג עשין נ טוש"ע אה"ע סי' קנב סעיף א:

קכט ד מיי' פי"ב מהל' עדות הל' ב ועי' בהשגות ובכ"מ סמג לאוין ריד טוש"ע חו"מ סי' לד סעיף כו:

מסורת הש"ס

א) קדושין סד.: ב) כתובות כ. שבת כב. [ועירובין עה.]: ג) [לקמן קלג. ע"ש]: ד) [סנהדרין מג.]: ה) [גיטין סד.] ו) סנהדרין י.

הגהות הב"ח

(א) גמ' הכי אתמר אמר שמואל כצ"ל ותיבות אמר רבי יהודה נמחק: (ב) רשב"ם ד"ה ומשני התם וכו' לאו כל כמיניה דלהני דבוריה לאחזוקה. נ"ב פי' דבוריה דהאיך שאמר יש לי בנים: (ג) תוס' ד"ה ליורשו וכו' גוסס לא יהא נאמן:

ס"א לאחזוקה

ההוא דַּהֲוָה קָא שָׁכֵיב, אֲמַרוּ לֵיהּ: אִתְּתֵיהּ לְמַאן? אֲמַר לְהוּ: חַזְיָא לְכָהֲנָא רַבָּה. אֲמַר (א) רָבָא: מַאי נֵיחוּשׁ לָהּ? הָא אֲמַר רַב חִיָּיא בַּר אַבָּא אָמַר ר' יוֹחָנָן: בַּעַל שֶׁאָמַר "גֵּרַשְׁתִּי אֶת אִשְׁתִּי" — נֶאֱמָן. א"ל אַבַּיֵי: וְהָא [א]כִּי אֲתָא ר' יִצְחָק בַּר יוֹסֵף, אָמַר ר' יוֹחָנָן: בַּעַל שֶׁאָמַר "גֵּרַשְׁתִּי אֶת אִשְׁתִּי" — אֵינוֹ נֶאֱמָן! א"ל, וְלָאו מִי לָא שַׁנִּינְהוּ: כָּאן לְמַפְרֵעַ וְכָאן לְהַבָּא? [ב]וְאַשִּׁנּוּיֵי נֵיקוּם וְלִסְמוֹךְ? א"ל רָבָא לְרַב נָתָן בַּר אַמֵּי: [א]חוּשׁ לָהּ. הַהוּא דַּהֲוָה מוּחְזַק לָן דְּלֵית לֵיהּ אַחֵי, וַאֲמַר בִּשְׁעַת מִיתָה דְּלֵית לֵיהּ אַחֵי. אֲמַר רַב יוֹסֵף: מַאי לֵיחוּשׁ לָהּ? חֲדָא, דְּמוּחְזַק לָן דְּלֵית לֵיהּ אַחִין; וְעוֹד, הָא אֲמַר בִּשְׁעַת מִיתָה דְּלֵית לֵיהּ. אֲמַר לֵיהּ אַבַּיֵי: [ב]הָא אָמְרִי דְּאִיכָּא עֵדִים בִּמְדִינַת הַיָּם דְּיָדְעִי דְּאִית לֵיהּ אַחֵי! הָשְׁתָּא מִיהַת הָא לֵיתְנְהוּ קַמָּן; לָאו הַיְינוּ דְּר' חֲנִינָא, [ג]דְּאָמַר רַבִּי חֲנִינָא: עֵדִים בְּצַד אִסְתָּן וְתֵאָסֵר? אֲמַר לֵיהּ אַבַּיֵי: אִם הֵקַלְנוּ בִּשְׁבוּיָה (ב) (מִשּׁוּם דִּמְנַוְּולָא נַפְשָׁהּ לְגַבֵּי שַׁבַּאי), נָקֵל בְּאֵשֶׁת אִישׁ? א"ל רָבָא לְרַב נָתָן בַּר אַמֵּי: [ג]חוּשׁ לָהּ.§ "זֶה אָחִי — אֵינוֹ נֶאֱמָן".§ (ג) וְאִידָךְ מַאי קָאָמְרִי? אִי קָאָמְרִי "אָחוּנָא הוּא", אַמַּאי יִטּוֹל עִמּוֹ בְּחֶלְקוֹ וְתוּ לָא? אֶלָּא דְּקָא אָמְרִי "לָאו אָחִינוּ הוּא"; אֵימָא סֵיפָא: נָפְלוּ לוֹ נְכָסִים מִמָּקוֹם אַחֵר — יִירְשׁוּ אֶחָיו עִמּוֹ, [ד]הָא אָמְרִי לֵיהּ "לָאו אָחוּנָא הוּא"! לָא צְרִיכָא, [ה]דְּקָא אָמְרִי "אֵין אָנוּ יוֹדְעִין". אָמַר [ד]רָבָא, זֹאת אוֹמֶרֶת: [ו]"מָנֶה לִי בְּיָדְךָ", [ה]וְהַלָּה אוֹמֵר "אֵינִי יוֹדֵעַ" — פָּטוּר. אַבַּיֵי אָמַר: לְעוֹלָם

רש"י

ההוא דַּהֲוָה קָא שָׁכֵיב. וְהָיוּ לוֹ אַחִין וְלֹא בָּנִין, דְּמוּחְזָק לְיַבֵּם. **אֲמַרוּ** לֵיהּ אִתְּתֵיהּ לְמַאן. זְקוּקָה לְיִבּוּם, אוֹ מוּתֶּרֶת לַשּׁוּק? **חַזְיָא לְכָהֲנָא**. לָאו דַּוְקָא, אֶלָּא שֶׁמּוּתֶּרֶת לְכָל אָדָם וְאֵינָהּ זְקוּקָה לְיָבָם. וּמִיהוּ, לִכְהֻנָּה אֲסִירָה, דְּהָא ע"י (ד) מִגּוֹ, דְּבַעַל שֶׁאָמַר "גֵּרַשְׁתִּי אֶת אִשְׁתִּי" נֶאֱמָן, מְהֵימְנִינַן, (ה) כִּדְמְפָרֵשׁ וְאָזֵיל. **לְמַאי** נֵיחוּשׁ לָהּ. לְאָסְרָהּ לַשּׁוּק. **הא"ר חִיָּיא בַּר אַבָּא** כו'. וְהַאי נַמִי הָכִי קָאָמַר: גֵּרַשְׁתִּי אֶת אִשְׁתִּי וְחַזְיָא לְעָלְמָא. וּמִיהוּ לִכְהֻנָּה אֲסִירָה, דְּהָא לָא פָּטְרִינַן לָהּ אֶלָּא בְּטַעֲנַת "גֵּרַשְׁתִּי אֶת אִשְׁתִּי", וּגְרוּשָׁה פְּסוּלָה לְכֹהֵן. שֶׁהֲרֵי אֵינָהּ נִפְטֶרֶת בְּטַעֲנַת "יֵשׁ לִי בָּנִים", דְּהָא מוּחְזָק לָן בְּגַוֵּיהּ דְּאֵין לוֹ בָּנִים, וְאִיהוּ לָא טָעֵין "יֵשׁ לִי בָּנִים" דְּנִיהֶמְנֵיהּ ע"י מִגּוֹ דְּמָצֵי פָּטַר לָהּ בְּגֵט. הִלְכָּךְ, הָכִי קָאָמַר: גֵּרַשְׁתִּי אֶת אִשְׁתִּי. וְנֶאֱמָן הוּא, דְּאִי בָּעֵי מְגָרֵשׁ לָהּ. **וַאֲנַן אַשִּׁנּוּיֵי** כו'. דִּלְמָא אֲמוֹרָאֵי נִינְהוּ דִּפְלִיגֵי אַלִּיבָּא דְּר' יוֹחָנָן, וְאִיכָּא לְמַאן דְּאָמַר אֵינוֹ נֶאֱמָן אֲפִילּוּ לְהַבָּא, דְּלָא אָמְרִינַן מִגּוֹ, שֶׁהֲרֵי רַגְלַיִם יֵשׁ לַדָּבָר שֶׁלֹּא גֵּירְשָׁהּ, דְּאִם גֵּירְשָׁהּ — קָלָא הֲוָה לֵיהּ לְמִילְתָא, כִּדְאָמְרִינַן בְּ"הָאִשָּׁה שֶׁנִּתְאַרְמְלָה". חוּשׁ לָהּ. כְּאַבַּיֵי, וְתֵיאָסֵר לַשּׁוּק. וּמִשּׁוּם דְּאָמַר לְעֵיל "לְמַאי נֵיחוּשׁ", קָאָמַר הָכָא דְּוַדַּאי אִיכָּא לְמֵיחַשׁ. וּמֵהָכָא שָׁמְעִינַן דְּבַעַל שֶׁאָמַר "גֵּרַשְׁתִּי אֶת אִשְׁתִּי" — אֵינוֹ נֶאֱמָן. **ההוא** דַּהֲוָה מוּחְזָק לָן. בְּגַוֵּיהּ דְּלֵית לֵיהּ אַחֵי, חֲזָקָה בְּעָלְמָא בְּלֹא עֵדִים, וְיוֹדְעִין הָיוּ בְּוַדַּאי דְּאֵין לוֹ בָּנִים. וְאִי לָאו דְּמוּחְזָק לָן דְּלֵית לֵיהּ אַחֵי — הָיָה לָנוּ לְאָסְרָהּ לַשּׁוּק מִסָּפֵק, כֵּיוָן דְּוַדַּאי אֵין לוֹ בָּנִים. וְעוֹד הָאָמַר בִּשְׁעַת מִיתָה כו'. וְאַע"פ שֶׁאֵין לוֹ בָּנִים, כֵּיוָן דְּאָמַר "אֵין לִי אַחִים" — נֶאֱמָן לְהַתִּירָהּ. וְאַע"ג דְּמוּחְזָק לָן בְּאַחֵי — נֶאֱמָן לְהַתִּירָהּ, מִגּוֹ דְּאִי בָּעֵי פָּטַר לָהּ בְּגִיטָא, וּמַה לּוֹ לְשַׁקֵּר. כִּדְאָמְרִי' נַמִי לְעֵיל, דְּאַף עַל גַּב דְּמוּחְזָק לָן בְּאַחֵי וְאָמַר "זֶה בְּנִי" — נֶאֱמָן לְהַתִּירָהּ מִשּׁוּם מִגּוֹ, דְּאָתֵי מִגּוֹ וּמֵרַע לֵיהּ לַחֲזָקָה. **אֲמַר לֵיהּ אַבַּיֵי הָא אָמְרִי**. בְּנֵי הָעִיר הַזֹּאת דְּאִיכָּא עֵדִים, וּצְרִיכִין אָנוּ לָחוּשׁ לְדִבְרֵיהֶם וּלְהַמְתִּין עַד שֶׁנִּשְׁמַע מַה בְּפִי עֵדִים. וּמְשַׁנֵּי: **הָשְׁתָּא** מִיהַת **הָא** לֵיתְנְהוּ. וְאֵין לָנוּ אֶלָּא מַה שֶּׁעֵינֵינוּ רוֹאוֹת. **לָאו** הַיְינוּ. דְּמַקְשִׁינַן בִּכְתוּבּוֹת בְּפ' "הָאִשָּׁה שֶׁנִּתְאַרְמְלָה" גַּבֵּי בְּנָתֵיהּ דְּמָר שְׁמוּאֵל דְּאִשְׁתַּבְיָין וְאַסְּקִינְהוּ לְאַרְעָא דְּיִשְׂרָאֵל, וַאֲמַרוּ "נִשְׁבֵּיתִי וּטְהוֹרָה אֲנִי" וְשָׁרִינְהוּ רַבִּי חֲנִינָא לְהִנָּשֵׂא לְכֹהֲנִים. וְאָמְרִי': וְהָאִיכָּא עֵדִים בִּמְדִינַת הַיָּם שֶׁנִּטְמְאוּ! וְאָמַר ר' חֲנִינָא: עֵדִים בְּצַד אִסְתָּן — רוּחַ צְפוֹנִית — וְתֵאָסֵר? בִּתְמִיָּה. וּמְפָרֵשׁ הָתָם דְּעֵדֵי טוּמְאָה אִתְּמַר. **אִם הֵקֵילוּ בִּשְׁבוּיָה**. דְּהַרְבֵּה הֵקִילוּ בָּהּ חֲכָמִים בְּמַסֶּכֶת כְּתוּבּוֹת, דַּאֲפִי' אִשָּׁה וְעֵד אֶחָד נֶאֱמָנִין לוֹמַר טְהוֹרָה. וְטַעֲמָא, דְּבִשְׁבִיל שֶׁנִּתְיַיחֲדָה בֵּין הַשַּׁבָּאִין אֵין לָנוּ לְאָסְרָהּ, שֶׁהֲרֵי סְתָם אִשָּׁה מְשַׁמֶּרֶת עַצְמָהּ מִזְּנוּת, וְאוֹקְמָהּ אַחֶזְקָתָהּ, וְאִיסּוּר קַל הוּא אִם נִישֵּׂאת לְכֹהֵן. **נָקֵל בְּאֵשֶׁת אִישׁ**. בִּתְמִיָּה. דְּאִיכָּא (ו) אִיסּוּר חֶנֶק, וַהֲרֵי הִיא בְּחֶזְקַת אִיסּוּר עַד עַתָּה. וְאַל תַּתִּירֶנָּה מִסָּפֵק, כֵּיוָן דְּאָמְרִי אֱינָשֵׁי דְּאִיכָּא עֵדִים בִּמְדִינַת הַיָּם שֶׁזְּקוּקָה לְיָבָם. **דִּמְנַוְּולָא נַפְשָׁהּ** לְגַבֵּי שַׁבַּאי. לָא גָּרְסִינַן, וּפֵירוּשׁ הָיָה בַּסְּפָרִים. חוּשׁ לָהּ. כְּאַבַּיֵי, וְלֹא תִּנָּשֵׂא בְּלֹא חֲלִיצָה. **דְּקָאָמְרִי אָחִינוּ הוּא**. וּמִשּׁוּם הָכִי קָתָנֵי גַּבֵּי נָפְלוּ לוֹ נְכָסִים מִמָּקוֹם אַחֵר, דְּכוּלָּן יוֹרְשִׁין אוֹתוֹ. **וְתוּ לָא**. הֲלֹא עִם כָּל אֶחָיו יֵשׁ לוֹ לִיטּוֹל! **דְּקָאָמְרִי אֵין אָנוּ יוֹדְעִין**. הִלְכָּךְ לָא שָׁקֵיל מִינַּיְיהוּ מִידֵּי, דְּאָמְרִי לֵיהּ: אַיְיתִי רְאָיָה. וּכְשֶׁמֵּת הֵן יוֹרְשִׁין אוֹתוֹ מִכֹּחַ אֲחִיהֶן הַחַי, שֶׁמּוֹדֶה לָהֶן שֶׁאוֹתוֹ הַסָּפֵק אֲחִיהֶן הָיָה. **זֹאת אוֹמֶרֶת** כו'. וּפְלוּגְתָּא הִיא בְּכַמָּה מְקוֹמוֹת בַּגְּמָ' (ב"ק דף קיח.) דְּרַב הוּנָא וְרַב יְהוּדָה אָמְרִי חַיָּיב, וְר"נ וְר' יוֹחָנָן אָמְרִי פָּטוּר. וְקַיְימָא לָן דְּפָטוּר, דְּהִלְכְתָא כְּרַבִּי יוֹחָנָן מֵחֲבֵירוֹ, וּכְרַב נַחְמָן בְּדִינֵי. אֶלָּא שֶׁיִּשָּׁבַע שְׁבוּעַת הֶיסֵּת שֶׁאֵינוֹ יוֹדֵעַ. וּמַתְנִיתִין נַמִי, הָאָח הָאֶחָד טוֹעֵן בִּשְׁבִיל אָחִיו הַסָּפֵק: מָמוֹן יֵשׁ לְאָחִי בְּיֶדְכֶם, וְהֵן אוֹמְרִים: אֵין אָנוּ יוֹדְעִין. וְאָמְרִי' פְּטוּרִין, דְּאוֹקֵי מָמוֹנָא בְּחֶזְקַת מָרֵיהּ. לְעוֹלָם

תוספות

חזיא לכהנא רבה. יש מוחקים "רבה", משום דלכל הפחות אלמנה היא, ולא חזיא לכהן גדול. ואומר ר"י: דשפיר גרס "רבה", דהא אף לכהן הדיוט אסירה, דהא מטעם שאמר "גרשתיה" היה מתיר, ולא שהיה אומר שהיו לו בנים — דא"כ היה נאמן, כדתנן במתניתין ד"זה בני" — נאמן, ומאי הוי מייתי עלה מילתא דר' יוחנן? אלא הכי פירושו: דחזיא לכהנא רבה כלומר — אינה זקוקה ליבום, שגרשתיה. דמותרת לכל העולם, ואפי' לכהן גדול מטעם זיקת יבמין. וה"ר מנחם גרס: חזיא לכהונה. כלומר, אינה זקוקה ליבם, וחוזרת לכהונת בי נשא לאכול בתרומה.

ה"ג: **הא** אמרי דאיכא סהדי במדינת הים דידעי דאית ליה אחי. וה"פ: הא יצא קול הכא, שאומרים דאיכא עדים במדינת הים. ול"ג: והא איכא סהדי במדינת הים. דאי ודאי דאיכא עדים במדינת הים — א"כ מאי קאמר "השתא מיהא הא ליתנהו"? ואי בעי למימר שיש לנו לחוש שמא יש עדים — הא ודאי ליכא למיחש, דהא תנן: "יש לי בנים" — נאמן. וה"ה "אין לי אחים" — נאמן, דמגו דאי בעי פטר לה בגיטא. וכן בפרק שני דכתובות (דף כג. ושם) על בנתיה דמר שמואל דאישתביין, ופריך: הא אמרי איכא עדים במדינת הים. אבל אי ליכא קול — אין לנו לחוש מאלינו שמא יש עדים, דהא תנן התם: "נשביתי וטהורה אני" — נאמנת.

אביי אמר לעולם חייב. — (ז) וקשה דרב יהודה אדרב יהודה, דבריש "שור שנגח את הפרה" (ב"ק דף מו. ושם) אמר רב יהודה אמר שמואל: זו דברי סומכוס, אבל חכמים אומרים: זה כלל גדול בדין, המע"ה. ומפרש התם ד"זה כלל גדול" — אפי' ניזק אומר ברי ומזיק אומר שמא. אלמא לרב יהודה, ברי ושמא — לאו ברי עדיף! וי"ל: דוקא גבי מלוה אית ליה לרב יהודה דברי עדיף, דהוי ברי חשוב, דאם לא הלוהו לא היה מעיז פניו לומר "מנה לי בידך", שהרי הלוה יודע שלא הלוה ממנו כלום. ושמא של לוה גרוע, שהיה לו לידע אם הלוה או לא הלוה, ולכך חייב. אבל גבי שור שנגח את הפרה, דלא חשיב ברי של ניזק, משום דיודע שהמזיק אינו יודע מתי ילדה קודם נגיחה או לאחר נגיחה, לכך טוען ברי, שיודע שלא יכחישנו המזיק. ושמא של מזיק אינו גרוע, כי אין לו לידע, כי לא היה שם. אבל קשה, הא דאמר בפ"ק דכתובות (דף יב: ושם) אמר ליה אביי לרב יוסף: הא דרב יהודה, אמר "מנה לי בידך" והלה אומר "איני יודע" חייב — דשמואל היא, דפסיק התם כרבן גמליאל דנאמנת כשאמרה "משארסתני נאנסתי ונסתחפה שדהו". והשתא, הא אפילו רב יהודה מודה לשם דאינה נאמנת. לפי שהבעל אינו יודע מתי נאנסה — לא חשיב ברי שלה, כי ההיא דניזק ומזיק! (ומיהו, י"ל: (ח) דהוה מצי למימר "וליטעמיך") וכן בריש "הבית והעלייה" (ב"מ דף קטז: ושם) גבי אם היה מכיר מקצת אבניו — נוטלן, ומוקי לה דקאמר "איני יודע". וקאמר: לימא תיהוי תיובתא דר"נ ור' יוחנן, דאמרי: "מנה לי בידך" והלה אומר "איני יודע" — פטור. והשתא, הא לרב יהודה נמי הוי תיובתא, דמודה התם דפטור, דהוי ברי גרוע, משום דאידך אינו יודע אם היו שלו, לפי שהרבה אבנים דומות זו לזו! וי"ל: דאביי דהכא לא משוי חילוק בין ברי חשוב דמלוה לברי גרוע. דהא קאמר הכא: לעולם חייב, ושאני הכא דכי "מנה לאחר בידך" דמי. משמע דאם הוא עצמו היה אומר "אחיך אני" והוא אומר "איני יודע" — יטול בחלקו, אע"ג דהוי ברי גרוע, דהם אינן יודעים אם יש להם אח במדינת הים או לאו. והשתא אתי שפיר, דההיא דכתובות — אביי אמר לה. וההיא ד"הבית והעלייה" (שם) נמי דקאמר: לימא תהוי תיובתא דר"נ — משום דלאביי לא הוי תיובתא דרב יהודה. ו"זה כלל גדול בדין" דריש פרק "הפרה" — לא מוקי אביי לאיתויי אפילו ניזק אומר ברי ומזיק אומר שמא. אלא מוקי להכי דאמר התם: א"נ לכי הא דאיתמר (לעיל דף נג.): המוכר שור לחבירו ונמצא נגחן, דאזלינן בתר חזקה אפילו כנגד רובא. ואין להאריך כאן. כל

רבינו גרשום

ואמרי ליה איתתא למאן. כלומר דלא הוה ידעי אי הוה [לו] בן כדי שלא תהיה אשתו זקוקה ליבום אי לאו: אמר להו חזיא לכהנא רבא. לאו משום דוקא קאמר לכהנא רבא משום דאיהו דאסור באלמנה אלא לכל כהנא הדיוטות דאינה זקוקה ליבום דאית ליה בני: חוש לה. להתירה דנאמן דנסמוך אשנויי. ואיכא דאמרי חוש לה דאינו נאמן: לאו היינו דר' חנינא דאמר. במסכת כתובות האשה שאמרה נשבתי וטהורה אני נאמנת שהפה שאסר הוא הפה שהתיר שאין עדות אחרת אלא היא. ואמרי' והלא שמא יש לך עדים במדינת הים שנשבית ולא תהא נאמנת שאומרת טהורה אני. אמר להו ר' חנינא עדים בצד אסתן. עדיה בצד דרום לסוף העולם דליתנהו קמן ואנן אסרין לה. הכא נמי הואיל דליתנהו הני עדים לקמן דאסהדי דאית ליה אחי והוא אומר אין לו אחין וגם מוחזק לן דלית אחי נאמן: נקל באשת איש. לפוטרה בלא חליצה ויבום: חוש לה. להיתר ואיכא דאמרי חוש לה לאיסור: ותו לא. הא בכל הנכסים ראוי ליטול כאחד מהן: יירשו אחיו עמו. הואיל דקאמרי דלא הוי אחיהון ואמאי יירשו: לא צריכא דקאמרי אין אנו יודעין אם אחינו הוא אם לאו. ומשום הכי ירתי בנכסים שנפלו לו לאחר מיכן ומצו למימר להאי אנת מיהא מודה דאחינו הוא משום הכי נירות כותך. והאי דלא יהיבנא ליה מחלקן משום דאנן לא ידעין דאחינו היה: זאת אומרת. דיטול עמו בחלקו דהני דמודי לו ולא בחלקן דהני דאמרי אין אנו יודעין. הכי נמי בעלמא כשאמר אחד לחבירו מנה לי בידך והלה אומר איני יודע פטור אפי' משבועה: אין

עין משפט נר מצוה

קל א מיי' פי"ב מהלכות גירושין הל' ה סמג עשין נ טוש"ע אה"ע סי' קנב סעיף א:
קלא ב ג מיי' פ"ג מהל' יבום הלכה ג סמג עשין נא טוש"ע אה"ע סי' קנז סעיף ח:
קלב ד מיי' פ"ד מהל' נחלות הל' ח ועי' במ"מ סמג עשין נו טור שו"ע חו"מ סי' רפ ס"ד:
קלג ה מיי' שם טוש"ע שם סעיף ב:
קלד ו מיי' פ"א מהל' טוען הל' ז ועיין במ"מ סמג עשין לה טור ש"ע חו"מ סי' עה ס"ט:

מסורת הש"ס

א) [לעיל קלד:] ב) [יבמות לא:] ג) כתובות כג. קדושין יב: ד) [לפמ"ש תוס' גיטין כו. ד"ה התם וכו' צ"ל רבה]: ה) [ב"ק קיח. ב"מ לז: קטז: כתובות יב:] ו) [ושמא של מזיק]:

הגהות הב"ח

(א) גמ' אמר רבה מאי ניחוש: (ב) שם אם הקלנו בשבויה נקל כצ"ל ותיבו' משום דמנוולא נפשה לגבי שבאי נמחק: (ג) שם ואידך מאי קאמרי אי דקאמרי אחונא הוא: (ד) רשב"ם ד"ה חזיא וכו' על ידי שאמר כצ"ל ותיבות מגו דבעל נמחק: (ה) בא"ד מהימנינן ליה כדמפרש: (ו) ד"ה נקל באשת איש וכו' איסור חנק. נ"ב אע"ג דעכשיו אינה א"א וליכא חנק כי אם לאו דלא תהיה אשת המת החוצה מ"מ מאחר דקודם שמת בעלה היתה בחזקת א"א עדיין בחזקת אותו איסור עומדת וזהו איסור חנק לא חנק ממש רק איסור חנק שהיה בה לא נסתלק ממנה עד שנפטרה מזיקת יבמה: (ז) תוס' ד"ה אביי וכו' חייב וא"ת וקשה דרב יהודה: (ח) בא"ד ומיהו י"ל התם דהוה מצי:

עין משפט
נר מצוה

קלה א ב מיי' פ"ד מהל' נחלות הל' ח סמג עשין צו טוש"ע חו"מ סי' רפ סעיף ג וע"ש:
קלו ג ד מיי' פי"ב מהל' זכיה הלכה כד כה טוש"ע חו"מ סי' רנ סעיף כה:
קלז ה מיי' שם פי"ב הלכה יד סמג עשין פב טוש"ע חו"מ סי' רנז סעיף ו:
קלח ו מיי' שם פ"ח הלכה יב סמג שם טוש"ע חו"מ סי' רנ סעיף יח:
קלט ז מיי' שם פ"ט הלכה טו סמג שם טוש"ע שם סעיף יג:
קמ ח מיי' שם פ"ח הל' יג סמג עשין פב טוש"ע שם סעיף יח:
קמא ט י טוש"ע שם סעיף כג:

מסורת הש"ס

א) [עי' תוס' לעיל מב: ד"ה שבח]: ב) לעיל קכז. ג) ב"מ יט. ד) לקמן קנג. גיטין טו. ה) לעיל סה. ו) [גיטין עו: לקמן קנג.] ז) לקמן קנב:

לְעוֹלָם אֵימָא לָךְ: חַיָּיב, וְשָׁאנֵי הָכָא, דְּכִ"מָנֶה לְאַחֵר בְּיָדְךָ" דָּמֵי.§ (א) "מֵת – יַחְזְרוּ נְכָסִים לִמְקוֹמָן".§ א)בָּעֵי רָבָא: שֶׁבַח שֶׁשָּׁבְחוּ נְכָסִים מֵאֲלֵיהֶם, מַהוּ? אבְּשֶׁבַח הַמַּגִּיעַ לִכְתֵפַיִם לָא תִּיבָּעֵי לָךְ, דְּכִי נָפְלוּ לוֹ נְכָסִים מִמָּקוֹם אַחֵר דָּמֵי. כִּי תִּיבָּעֵי לָךְ – בְּשֶׁבַח שֶׁאֵינוֹ מַגִּיעַ לִכְתֵפַיִם, כְּגוֹן ב)דִּיקְלָא וְאָלִים, אַרְעָא וְאַסְקָא שִׁרְטוֹן, מַאי? בתֵּיקוּ.§

מתני' גמִי שֶׁמֵּת וְנִמְצֵאת דַּיְיתִיקֵי קְשׁוּרָה עַל יְרֵיכוֹ – הֲרֵי זוֹ אֵינָהּ כְּלוּם. דזִיכָּה בָּהּ לְאַחֵר, בֵּין מִן הַיּוֹרְשִׁין בֵּין שֶׁאֵינָן מִן הַיּוֹרְשִׁין – דְּבָרָיו קַיָּימִין.§

גמ' תָּנוּ רַבָּנַן: אֵיזֶה הִיא דַּיְיתִיקֵי? ג)כָּל שֶׁכָּתוּב בָּהּ: "דָּא תְּהֵא לְמֵיקָם וְלִהְיוֹת"; וְאֵיזֶה הִיא מַתָּנָה? כָּל שֶׁכָּתוּב בָּהּ: "מֵהַיּוֹם וּלְאַחַר מִיתָה". אֶלָּא "מֵהַיּוֹם וּלְאַחַר מִיתָה" הוּא דְּהָוְיָא מַתָּנָה, "מֵעַכְשָׁיו" לָא הָוְיָא מַתָּנָה? אָמַר אַבַּיֵי, הָכִי קָאָמַר: האֵיזוֹ הִיא מַתְּנַת בָּרִיא שֶׁהִיא כְּמַתְּנַת שְׁכִיב מְרַע, דְּלָא קָנֵי אֶלָּא לְאַחַר מִיתָה? כָּל שֶׁכָּתוּב בָּהּ: "מֵהַיּוֹם וּלְאַחַר מִיתָה". יָתֵיב רַבָּה בַּר רַב הוּנָא בְּאַכְסַדְרָא דְּבֵי רַב, וְיָתֵיב וְקָאָמַר מִשְּׁמֵיהּ דְּר' יוֹחָנָן: ד)שְׁכִיב מְרַע שֶׁאָמַר "כִּתְבוּ וּתְנוּ מָנֶה לִפְלוֹנִי" וּמֵת – ואֵין כּוֹתְבִין וְנוֹתְנִין, שֶׁמָּא לֹא גָּמַר לְהַקְנוֹתוֹ אֶלָּא בִּשְׁטָר, וְאֵין שְׁטָר לְאַחַר מִיתָה. אָמַר לְהוּ רַבִּי אֶלְעָזָר: ה)אִיזְדַּהֲרוּ בָּהּ. רַב שֵׁיזְבִי אָמַר: רַבִּי אֶלְעָזָר אֲמָרָהּ, וְאָמַר לְהוּ רַבִּי יוֹחָנָן: אִיזְדַּהֲרוּ בָּהּ. אָמַר רַב נַחְמָן בַּר יִצְחָק: כְּוָתֵיהּ דְּרַב שֵׁיזְבִי מִסְתַּבְּרָא; אִי אָמְרַתְּ בִּשְׁלָמָא רַבִּי אֶלְעָזָר אֲמָרָהּ – אִצְטְרִיךְ רַבִּי יוֹחָנָן לְאַסְהוֹדֵי עֲלֵיהּ דְּר' אֶלְעָזָר. אֶלָּא אִי אָמְרַתְּ רַבִּי יוֹחָנָן אֲמָרָהּ, אִצְטְרִיךְ רַבִּי אֶלְעָזָר לְאַסְהוֹדֵי עֲלֵיהּ דְּר' יוֹחָנָן רַבֵּיהּ? וְעוֹד, תָּא שְׁמַע דְּר' אֶלְעָזָר אֲמָרָהּ, ו)דְּשָׁלַח רָבִין מִשְּׁמֵיהּ דְּרַבִּי אַבָּהוּ, הֱווּ יוֹדְעִים שֶׁשָּׁלַח רַבִּי אֶלְעָזָר לַגּוֹלָה מִשּׁוּם רַבֵּינוּ: שְׁכִיב מְרַע שֶׁאָמַר "כִּתְבוּ וּתְנוּ מָנֶה לִפְלוֹנִי" וּמֵת – אֵין כּוֹתְבִין וְנוֹתְנִין, שֶׁמָּא לֹא גָּמַר לְהַקְנוֹתוֹ אֶלָּא בִּשְׁטָר, וְאֵין שְׁטָר לְאַחַר מִיתָה, וְר' יוֹחָנָן אָמַר: תִּיבָּדֵק. מַאי תִּיבָּדֵק? כִּי אֲתָא רַב דִּימִי אָמַר: ז)דַּיְיתִיקֵי מְבַטֶּלֶת דַּיְיתִיקֵי. שְׁכִיב מְרַע שֶׁאָמַר "כִּתְבוּ וּתְנוּ מָנֶה לִפְלוֹנִי" וּמֵת, חרוֹאִין: אִם כִּמְיַפֶּה אֶת כֹּחוֹ – כּוֹתְבִין, וְאִם לָאו – אֵין כּוֹתְבִין. מְתִיב ר' אַבָּא בַּר מָמֵל: טבָּרִיא שֶׁאָמַר "כִּתְבוּ וּתְנוּ מָנֶה לִפְלוֹנִי" וּמֵת – אֵין כּוֹתְבִין וְנוֹתְנִין, הָא שְׁכִיב מְרַע – כּוֹתְבִין וְנוֹתְנִין! הוּא מוֹתִיב לָהּ, וְהוּא מְפָרֵק לָהּ: יבִּמְיַפֶּה אֶת כֹּחוֹ. הֵיכִי דָּמֵי מְיַפֶּה אֶת כֹּחוֹ?

כִּדְאָמַר

כל שכתוב בה מהיום ולאחר מיתה. פירש בקונטרס: דהוי כמתנה בריא, שאין יכול לחזור בה. וקשה: דתנן בפרק קמא דב"מ (דף יט.): מלא דייתיקי מתנות ושוברים – הרי זה לא יחזיר, שאני אומר כו'. ודייק בגמרא: הא אמר "תנו" – נותנין. ומוקי לה בשכיב מרע, דליכא למיחש שמא נתנו לאחר, דאפי' נתנו לאחר – מלי הדר ביה. והשתא הא קתני מתנה, דהיינו "מהיום ולאחר מיתה", דהוי כמתנת שכיב מרע דלא קני עד לאחר מיתה. ואי אינו יכול לחזור בו – אמאי אם אמר "תנו" נותנין? ומפרש רבינו תם: "מהיום ולאחר מיתה" – היינו: מהיום אם לא אחזור בי עד לאחר מיתה. ומיירי כגון שפירש בפירוש: מהיום אם לא יחזור עד לאחר מיתה. דמסתמא אם אמר "מהיום ולאחר מיתה", הוי מהיום קני גופו, ולאחר מיתה קני פירות, כדמשמע במתני' בסמוך. ולע"ג דנקט הכא כלישנא דלקמן – מכל מקום לא איירי בחד גוונא. וה"נ אשכחנא בפרק "כל הגט" (גיטין דף כו: ושם ד"ה לכשאכניסנה): אמר ללבלר "כתוב (ד) לאשתי, לכשאכניסנה אגרשנה" – אינו גט, משום שמא יאמרו גיטה קודם לבנה. וביבמות פ' "ר"ג" (דף נב. ושם ד"ה לכשאכניסנה): "כתוב גט לארוסתי לכשאכניסנה אגרשנה" – הרי זה גט. ול"ל דבגיטין איירי שכתב זמן שעומד בו, וביבמות איירי שכתב זמן שלאחר נשואין, אע"פ שהלשון שוה. מיהו, התם י"ל דאינו גט לכתחלה – כלומר מדרבנן, אבל מדאורייתא הוי גט.

אקנייה

לעולם חייב. דברי ושמא – ברי עדיף. ושאני הכא, דהספק עצמו אינו יודע ואינו יכול לטעון טענת ודאי, וספק וספק הוא, והלכך אוקי ממונא בחזקת מריה. אבל הכא טוען בשביל הספק: מנה לאחי בידכם, הלכך אמרי ליה: לאו בעל דברים דידן את. בשבח המגיע לכתפים לא תיבעי לך. שנתן זה לספק קרקע ריקנית, וטרח בה זה הספק לחרוש ולזרוע, והרי היא עתה כשחוזרת לו לנותן מלאה פירות – לא תיבעי לך, דהא ודאי כולהו חולקים בהאי שבח. דכי נפלו לו נכסים ממקום אחר דמי, דהא לא קרינא ביה יחזרו נכסים למקומן, שהרי לא נתן לו פירות, אלא קרקע ריקנית. ואלים. דלא נשתנה שמו מכבתחלה. ואסקא שרטון. מעצמה, שלא זיבלה הספק ולא טרח בכך. **מתני'** דייתיקי. שטר צוואת שכיב מרע. כדדריש ליה בגמרא: דא תהא למיקם ולהיות. על יריכו. רבותא נקט, דליכא למימר: אחר כתב ונתנה לשם, כדי לזכות בנכסי המת. הרי זו אינה כלום. שאפי' אם החזיק אחר מיתה באותו השטר אותו שנכתבה לו המתנה – לא קני. דאע"ג דצוואת שכיב מרע קונה לאחר מיתה – הני מילי (ב) כדי שלא תטרף דעתו עליו. אבל כח השטר לא עדיף כצוואתו, שהרי לא גמר להקנותו אלא בקבלת השטר, ואין שטר לאחר מיתה. זיכה בה. השכיב מרע. לאחר. מחיים, אע"פ שלא נכתב לשם אותו האיש, אלא כך אמר לו: נכסים הכתובים בשטר זה אני מקנה לך בקבלת השטר שתקבל ממני – הרי זה קנה, דלא גרע מצוואת פיו. ורבותא קתני. (ג) "לאחר" גרסינן בסדר המשנה. דבריו קיימין. אע"ג דאין ראוי ליורשו – קני לאחר מיתה בלא קנין, דדברי שכיב מרע ככתובין וכמסורין דמו. **גמ'** איזו היא דייתיקי. איזו היא מתנת שכיב מרע שגופה לאחר מיתה, אע"ג דלא כתב בה "מהיום". דא תהא למיקם ולמהוי. אחר מיתתי. והיינו לשון "דייתיקי". ואיזו היא מתנת בריא שתקנה כל שכתוב בה מהיום כו'. דמשמע הכי: גופה קנוי לך מהיום, ופירי לאחר מיתה. אבל אי לא הוה כתב בה "מהיום" – אינו קונה, דאין מתנה לאחר מיתה, שהרי אין כח לאדם ליתן מקודם לכן דבר שלא יוכל להקנות באותו הזמן שהוא רוצה שתתקיים המתנה, ואחר מיתה היאך יכול אדם ליתן אחרי שמת ונקבר? ומתמהינן: טעמא דהויא מתנה – משום דכתב "לאחר מיתה" בהדי "מהיום", אבל אם כתב "מהיום" גרידא – לא הויא מתנה? והלא קל וחומר הוא דהוי מתנה גמורה מעכשיו, שהרי נתן לו גוף ופירות מהיום! דלא קני. פירות אלא לאחר מיתה, דומיא דמתנת שכיב מרע שאינו קונה אלא לאחר מיתה. ומיהו, בהכי עדיפא משכיב מרע; דמתנת שכיב מרע יכול לחזור בו וליתן לאחר, כדלקמן: דייתיקי מבטלת דייתיקי. אבל מתנת בריא ד"מהיום ולאחר מיתה" – אינו יכול למכור עוד הגוף כל ימי חייו, אלא פירות. כתבו ותנו מנה. מנכסי לפלוני. ומת השכיב מרע קודם שכתבו ונתנו לו את השטר למקבל מתנה – שוב אין כותבין ונותנין לו את המנה. שמא לא גמר כו'. והאי דנקט "כתבו ותנו" – לאו דוקא, דהוא הדין אם אמר "תנו וכתבו", כדמוכח לקמן, דלא חשיב ליה מייפה את כחו לקנות בלא שטר עד דאמר להו "תנו אף כתבו" כדלקמן. איזדהרו בה. שכן הלכה. **אצטריך** ר' יוחנן לאסהודי עליה דרבי **אלעזר**. תלמידו, שיאמינו בו. **אצטריך** רבי **אלעזר**. בתמיה. והלא דברי הרב ודברי תלמיד, דברי מי שומעין? משום רבינו. רב. ורבי יוחנן **אומר** תיבדק. לאו לאיפלוגי עליה דרבי אלעזר אתא, דהא אסהיד רבי יוחנן עליה דרבי אלעזר כדאמרינן לעיל. אלא לפרושי אתא, שצריך לבדוק היאך נוה האי שכיב מרע לכתוב שטר זה. משום דזמנין דכותבין ונותנין לך לאחר מיתה, כגון במייפה שכיב מרע כחו של מקבל מתנה, כדמפרש ואזיל, דאמר "תנו אף כתבו" וכו'. כי **אתא** רב דימי אמר. שני דברים, והשניה מפרשת להך בדיקה. דייתיקי מבטלת דייתיקי. שכיב מרע שכתב נכסיו לאחד, וחזר וכתב לאחר – שני קנה, ראשון לא קנה. שהרי שכיב מרע יכול לחזור במתנתו, כדאמרינן בפרק "מי שמת", וכיון שכתב לשני – חזר בו מן הראשון. ודוקא בכתיבה בלא זיכוי, כדאמרינן לקמן בפרקין ד"מי שמת": פשיטא, כתב לזה וכתב לזה – היינו דכי אתא רב דימי אמר: דייתיקי מבטלת דייתיקי. כתב וזיכה לזה, וכתב וזיכה לזה – רב אמר: ראשון קנה כו'. אבל גבי מתנת בריא, שאינו יכול לחזור בו – ראשון קנה, ולא שני. **אם במיפה את כחו** כו'. אם כדי ליפות כחו של מקבל מתנה נוה השכיב מרע לכתוב לו את השטר, להיות לו לעדות על מתנה זו, ולא לעכב המתנה נתכוין, דלא יקנה אלא בשטר – כותבין ונותנין אפי' לאחר מיתה. ולקמן מפרש היכי דמי, והיינו תיבדק דלעיל. דכי היכי דאמרינן גבי צוואת שכיב מרע דדבריו ככתובין וכמסורין דמו משום דלא תטרף דעתו עליו – ה"נ אמרינן גבי שטר אפילו לאחר מיתה, דיש שטר שלו, דכנכתב מחיים דמי. **והוא** מפרק לה. להך דוקיא – במייפה את כחו. ומיהו, בריא, אע"ג שמייפה את כחו כענין זיכוי שכיב מרע, דקאמר "תנו אף כתבו" – אפילו הכי אין כותבין ונותנין לאחר מיתה. דבבריא אמרינן: משום דדבריו אינן ככתובין – הולכך לזכות לו בשטר, ולא גמר להקנותו אלא בשטר, ואין שטר לאחר מיתה.

כדאמר

רבינו גרשום

אין. חייב לשלם ושאני הכי אמאי לא יהבי ליה בחלקו דמי אחר כמי שאמ' לחבירו הרי מנה לפלוני בידך ואותו אחד פלוני עצמו אין יודע אם מחויב לו אם לאו ואמר הלה איני יודע שאני חייב לו פטור וכל דאף הכי כמו זה אומר על זה אחיכם הוא וזה עצמו אינו יודע אם אחיהם הוא והללו אומרים אין אנו יודעין פטורין מליתן לו כלום: בשבח שהשביחו נכסים הללו. שנטל מחלקו של אח והשביחו מאליהן ומת מהו מי אמרינן דכי היכי דנפלו לו נכסים ממקום אחר דמי וירשו אחיו עמו בשוה או דלמא הואיל דהנהו נכסים הן שנטל מחלק האח שהיה מודה ליה ולא ירשו הני אחריני אלא יחזרו נכסים למקומן ליד זה הלבד שחלק לו: המגיע לכתפים. כגון תבואה לקצור וענבים לבצור: פיס' ונמצאת דייתיקי קשורה על יריכו. להכי קאמ' קשורה שאילו נמצאת על המטה בלבד שמא איכא למימר שמא אחר זרקה על המטה. ונמצא כתוב באותו דייתיקי מתנה מכל נכסיו לאחר מן היורשים הרי זה אינה כלום ואיכא למימר הואיל ולא נתנה מחיים חזר בו: זיכה בו לאחר בין מן היורשין כו': דייתיק. שטר צוואת שכיב מרע: מתנה של בריא כל שכתוב בה מהיום כו'. הא לאו הכי לא קנה והא כל מתנה איבעי למיתן ליה מעכשיו הרשות בידו: כל שכתוב בו מהיום. יתחיל מתנה זו שיהא ברשותך ומגמר לא תגמר אלא לאחר מיתתו: באכסדרה דבי רב. בבית המדרש: ומת. קודם שהספיקו לכתוב: ר' שיזבי אמר ר' אלעזר אמרה. להא מלתא ואמר להו ר' יוחנן הזהרו בה דהכי עיקר דלא גמר להקנות אלא בשטר ואין שטר לאחר מיתה: היינו דאצטריך ר' יוחנן לאסהודי עליה. לומר הזהרו בה כדי לקיים דברי ר' אלעזר תלמידו: אלא אי אמרת כו' ועוד ת"ש דר' אלעזר אמרה כו': שלח ר' אלעזר לגולה כו' משום רבינו. רב. אלמא דר' אלעזר אמרה: ור' יוחנן אמר תבדק. באיזה ענין אמר אותו שכיב מרע כדמפרש רב דימי: כי אתא רב דימי אמר תרתי דייתיקי מבטלת דייתיקי. שאם כתב לאחד שטר מתנה מכל נכסיו וחזר ונטלן מזה וכתבן לאחר זו מתנה שכתב לשני מבטלת מתנה של ראשון ושני קנה ראשון לא קנה: רואין. והיינו דקאמר תבדק: אם במיפה את כחו. כדאמר לקמן דאמר להו תנו אף כתבו וחתמו דהיינו יפוי כח דאמר תנו אף כתבו דבנתינה לחוד סגי וכתיבה לא הוי אלא יפוי כח ולא משמע דבכתיבה לחוד יקנה כותבין: ואם לאו. דלא אמר הכי אין כותבין משום דלא גמר להקנות אלא בשטר ואין שטר לאחר מיתה: בריא שאמר כתבו ותנו מנה לפלוני ומת אין כותבין ונותנין. דבריא בעי קנין ושטר לאחר מיתה: הא שכיב מרע. שאמר הכי כותבין ונותנין משום דבלאו הכי באמירה בעלמא קונה שכיב מרע: הוא מפרק לה. אם אמר שכיב מרע במיפה את כחו כותבין ונותנין:

כדאמר

הגהות הב"ח

(א) גמ' לאחר בידך דמי נפלו לו נכסים ממקום אחר ויירשו אחיו עמו כצי רבה שבח: (ב) רשב"ם ד"ה הרי זו אינה וכו' הני מילי וצוואת שכיב מרע בפיו כדי שלא תטרף: (ג) ד"ה לאחר מחיים וכו' לאחר הס"ד ואח"כ מ"ה לאחר גרסי': (ד) תד"ה כל וכו' כתוב גט לאשתי וכו' וביבמות אמרי' האומר כתוב גט לארוסתי:

עין משפט נר מצוה

קמב א מיי' פ"ח מהל' זכיה הלכה יג סמג עשין פב טוש"ע חו"מ סי' רנ סעיף יח:
קמג ב מיי' שם פי"ב הלכה טו סמג שם טוש"ע חו"מ סי' רנח סעיף א:
קמד ג מיי' שם הלכה יג וסמג שם טור שו"ע חו"מ סי' רנז סעיף ז:
קמה ד מיי' שם טוש"ע שם סעיף ג:
קמו ה מיי' שם טוש"ע שם סעיף ד:
קמז ו ז מיי' פ"א מהל' גירושין הלכה יד סמג עשין נ טוש"ע אה"ע סי' קמה סעיף ג:
קמח ח ט מיי' פ"ב מהל' זכיה ומתנה הלכה טו סמג עשין פב טוש"ע חו"מ סי' רנח ס"ח:

מסורת הש"ס

א) לקמן קנב: ב) [תוספ' כתובות פ"ח]: ג) יבמות לו: כ"ק פח: ד) גיטין עב. קדושין נט: ה) [תוספ' לגיטין פ"ה]: ה) גיטין עב.: ו) [תוספ' לכתובות פ"ח גיטין עב. וש"נ]: ז) [סנהדרין כט.]: ח) ב"ק פח: יבמות לו: ט) ס"א הכא.

א)כִּדְאָמַר רַב חִסְדָּא: "וְקָנֵינָא מִינֵּיהּ מוֹסִיף עַל מַתַּנְתָּא דָּא", ה"נ — אדְּאָמַר: "אַף כְּתוֹבוּ וַחֲתוֹמוּ וַהֲבוּ לֵיהּ". אִיתְּמַר: רַב יְהוּדָה אָמַר שְׁמוּאֵל, הֲלָכָה: כּוֹתְבִין וְנוֹתְנִין. וְכֵן אָמַר רָבָא אָמַר רַב נַחְמָן, הֲלָכָה: כּוֹתְבִין וְנוֹתְנִין.§

מתני' ב)הַכּוֹתֵב נְכָסָיו לְבָנָיו — צָרִיךְ שֶׁיִּכְתּוֹב "מֵהַיּוֹם וּלְאַחַר מִיתָה", דִּבְרֵי רַבִּי יְהוּדָה; רַבִּי יוֹסֵי אוֹמֵר: באֵינוֹ צָרִיךְ. ג)גהַכּוֹתֵב נְכָסָיו לִבְנוֹ לְאַחַר מוֹתוֹ — הָאָב אֵינוֹ יָכוֹל לִמְכּוֹר, מִפְּנֵי שֶׁהֵן כְּתוּבִין לַבֵּן, וְהַבֵּן אֵינוֹ יָכוֹל לִמְכּוֹר, מִפְּנֵי שֶׁהֵן בִּרְשׁוּת הָאָב. דמָכַר הָאָב — מְכוּרִים עַד שֶׁיָּמוּת, המָכַר הַבֵּן — אֵין לַלּוֹקֵחַ בָּהֶן כְּלוּם עַד שֶׁיָּמוּת הָאָב.§

גמ' וְכִי כָּתַב "מֵהַיּוֹם וּלְאַחַר מִיתָה" מַאי הָוֵי? הָא תְּנַן: ד)ו"מֵהַיּוֹם וּלְאַחַר מִיתָה" — גֵּט וְאֵינוֹ גֵּט, וְאִם מֵת — חוֹלֶצֶת וְלֹא מִתְיַיבֶּמֶת! הָתָם זמְסַפְּקָא לַן אִי תְּנָאָה הָוֵי אִי חֲזָרָה הָוֵי, אֲבָל הָכָא הָכִי קָאָמַר לֵיהּ: גּוּפָא קְנֵי מֵהַיּוֹם, פֵּירָא — לְאַחַר מִיתָה.§ "רַבִּי יוֹסֵי אוֹמֵר: אֵינוֹ צָרִיךְ".§ ה)רַבָּה בַּר אֲבוּהּ חֲלַשׁ, עַל לְגַבֵּיהּ רַב הוּנָא וְרַב נַחְמָן; אֲמַר לֵיהּ רַב הוּנָא לְרַב נַחְמָן, בְּעֵי מִינֵּיהּ: הֲלָכָה כְּרַבִּי יוֹסֵי אוֹ אֵין הֲלָכָה כְּר' יוֹסֵי? אֲמַר לֵיהּ: טַעְמֵיהּ דְּרַבִּי יוֹסֵי לָא יָדַעְנָא, הֲלָכָה אִיבְּעֵי מִינֵּיהּ? אֲמַר לֵיהּ: אַתְּ בְּעֵי מִינֵּיהּ אִי הֲלָכָה אִי לָא, וְטַעְמֵיהּ אֲנָא אֵימָא לָךְ. בְּעָא מִינֵּיהּ. אֲמַר לֵיהּ, הָכִי אָמַר רַב: הֲלָכָה כְּרַבִּי יוֹסֵי. בָּתַר דִּנְפַקוּ, אֲמַר לֵיהּ: הַיְינוּ טַעְמֵיהּ דְּרַבִּי יוֹסֵי — דְּאָמַר: ו)חזְמַנּוֹ שֶׁל שְׁטָר מוֹכִיחַ עָלָיו. תַּנְיָא נַמִי הָכִי, רַבִּי יוֹסֵי אוֹמֵר: אֵינוֹ צָרִיךְ, מִפְּנֵי שֶׁזְּמַנּוֹ שֶׁל שְׁטָר מוֹכִיחַ עָלָיו. בְּעָא מִינֵּיהּ רָבָא מֵרַב נַחְמָן: בְּהַקְנָאָה, מַהוּ? אֲמַר לֵיהּ: בְּהַקְנָאָה אֵינוֹ צָרִיךְ. רַב פָּפִּי אֲמַר: אִיכָּא אַקְנָיְתָא דְּצָרִיךְ, וְאִיכָּא אַקְנָיְתָא דְּלָא צָרִיךְ; "אַקְנְיֵיהּ וְקָנֵינָא מִינֵּיהּ" — לָא צָרִיךְ, "קָנֵינָא מִינֵּיהּ וְאַקְנְיֵיהּ" — צָרִיךְ. מַתְקִיף לָהּ רַב חֲנִינָא מִסּוּרָא: ז)מִי אִיכָּא מִידֵּי דַּאֲנַן לָא יָדְעִינַן וְסָפְרֵי יָדְעִי? שְׁאֵלוּנְהוּ לְסָפְרֵי דְּאַבַּיֵי — וְיָדְעִי, וּלְסָפְרֵי דְּרָבָא — וְיָדְעִי. רַב הוּנָא בְּרֵיהּ דְּרַב יְהוֹשֻׁעַ אֲמַר: טבֵּין "אַקְנְיֵיהּ וְקָנֵינָא מִינֵּיהּ", בֵּין "קָנֵינָא מִינֵּיהּ וְאַקְנְיֵיהּ" — לָא צָרִיךְ, וּבְ"דוּכְרָן פִּתְגָּמֵי דַּהֲוֵי בְּאַנְפָּנָא" — פְּלִיגִי. אֲמַר רַב כָּהֲנָא: אֲמַרִיתָהּ לִשְׁמַעְתָּא קַמֵּיהּ דְּרַב זְבִיד מִנְּהַרְדְּעָא, וַאֲמַר לִי: אַתּוּן הָכִי מַתְנִיתוּ לָהּ, אֲנַן הָכִי מַתְנִינַן לָהּ, אָמַר רָבָא אָמַר רַב נַחְמָן: בְּהַקְנָאָה — אֵינוֹ צָרִיךְ; בֵּין "אַקְנְיֵיהּ וְקָנֵינָא מִינֵּיהּ", בֵּין "קָנֵינָא מִינֵּיהּ וְאַקְנְיֵיהּ" — לָא צָרִיךְ; בְּ"דוּכְרָן פִּתְגָּמֵי דַּהֲווּ בְּאַנְפָּנָא" — פְּלִיגִי.§ "הַכּוֹתֵב נְכָסָיו לִבְנוֹ לְאַחַר מוֹתוֹ".§ ח)אִיתְּמַר: מָכַר הַבֵּן בְּחַיֵּי הָאָב, וּמֵת הַבֵּן בְּחַיֵּי הָאָב — אָמַר

כדאמר רב חסדא כו'. לְקַמָּן בְּפֶרֶק "מִי שֶׁמֵּת", דְּאָמַר רַב יְהוּדָה אָמַר שְׁמוּאֵל: שכ"מ שֶׁכָּתַב כָּל נְכָסָיו, אע"פ שֶׁקָּנוּ מִיָּדוֹ, אִם עָמַד — חוֹזֵר. וּמַשְׁמַע: הָא אִם מֵת מְקַבֵּל מַתָּנָה — קָנָה. וְאע"פ שֶׁכָּתוּב קִנְיָן בְּהַךְ מַתְּנַת שְׁכִיב מְרַע — לָא אָמְרִי' שֶׁמָּא לֹא גָּמַר לְהַקְנוֹתוֹ אֶלָּא בִּשְׁטָר, וְאֵין שְׁטָר לְאַחַר מִיתָה. וּמַקְשִׁינַן מִינָּהּ הָתָם לִשְׁמוּאֵל, דְּאָמַר: מַתְּנַת שְׁכִיב מְרַע שֶׁכָּתוּב בָּהּ קִנְיָן — לָא יָדַעְנָא מַאי אֵידוֹן בָּהּ, דְּשֶׁמָּא לֹא גָּמַר לְהַקְנוֹתוֹ אֶלָּא בִּשְׁטָר, וּשְׁטָר שֶׁל שְׁכִיב מְרַע אֵינוֹ קוֹנֶה עַד לְאַחַר מִיתָה, וְאֵין שְׁטָר לְאַחַר מִיתָה. וּמְשַׁנֵּי: הָתָם בִּמְיַפֶּה אֶת כֹּחוֹ, הַהוּא דְּרַב יְהוּדָה אָמַר שְׁמוּאֵל, וְאֵין הַקִּנְיָן מְגָרֵעַ כֹּחַ הַשְּׁטָר שֶׁל שְׁכִיב מְרַע, שֶׁלֹּא הִקְנָה לוֹ אֶלָּא לְיַפּוֹת אֶת כֹּחוֹ. וְאָמְרִינַן: הֵיכִי דָּמֵי מְיַפֶּה אֶת כֹּחוֹ? אָמַר רַב חִסְדָּא: "וְקָנֵינָא מִינֵּיהּ מוֹסִיף עַל מַתַּנְתָּא דָּא". כְּלוֹמַר, אֵינוֹ אֶלָּא תּוֹסֶפֶת בְּעָלְמָא לְיַפּוֹת אֶת כֹּחוֹ. הֲלָכָה כּוֹתְבִין וְנוֹתְנִין. לְאַחַר מִיתָה, בִּמְיַפֶּה אֶת כֹּחוֹ, כְּרַבִּי יוֹחָנָן דְּאָמַר תִּבָּדֵק. וְהָכִי מוֹקְמִינַן לֵיהּ בְּהֶדְיָא לְהָא דִּשְׁמוּאֵל בִּמְיַפֶּה אֶת כֹּחוֹ, לְקַמָּן בְּ"מִי שֶׁמֵּת".

מתני' הַכּוֹתֵב נְכָסָיו לְבָנָיו. בָּרִיא שֶׁרוֹצֶה לִישָּׂא אִשָּׁה, וְאֵינוֹ רוֹצֶה לְשַׁעְבֵּד נְכָסָיו לְאִשְׁתּוֹ, פֶּן יַפְסִידוּ בָּנִים שֶׁיֵּשׁ לוֹ מֵאִשְׁתּוֹ רִאשׁוֹנָה. וְרוֹצֶה לִכְתּוֹב לָהֶם נְכָסָיו לְאַחַר מוֹתוֹ, אֶלָּא שֶׁיֹּאכַל פֵּירוֹת בְּחַיָּיו — צָרִיךְ שֶׁיִּכְתּוֹב "מֵהַיּוֹם וּלְאַחַר מִיתָה", דְּמַשְׁמַע: מֵהַיּוֹם יְהֵא קָנוּי לְךָ הַגּוּף לְבַדּוֹ, וּלְאַחַר מִיתָה תְּהֵא נִגְמֶרֶת הַמַּתָּנָה, שֶׁתֹּאכַל גַּם הַפֵּירוֹת לְאַחַר מִיתָתִי. אֲבָל בְּלֹא "מֵהַיּוֹם" — לֹא נָתַן לָהֶם כְּלוּם, דְּאֵין מַתָּנָה לְאַחַר מִיתָה. דְּבַהִיא שַׁעְתָּא אֵין לוֹ חֵלֶק בָּהֶן שֶׁיּוּכַל לְהַקְנוֹתָן. ר' יוֹסֵי אוֹמֵר אֵינוֹ צָרִיךְ. לִכְתּוֹב "מֵהַיּוֹם". וְטַעֲמָא מְפָרֵשׁ בַּגְּמָרָא.

גמ' גֵּט וְאֵינוֹ גֵּט. דְּשֶׁמָּא כָּךְ אָמַר: מֵעַכְשָׁיו יְהֵא גֵּט אִם אָמוּת. אוֹ דִּלְמָא מַהְדַּר קָא הָדַר בֵּיהּ, וְאֵין גֵּט לְאַחַר מִיתָה. הִלְכָּךְ, הָוְיָא סְפֵק מְגוֹרֶשֶׁת, וְאִם פָּשְׁטָה יָדָהּ וְקִבְּלָה קִדּוּשִׁין מֵאַחֵר — צְרִיכָה גֵּט מִשְּׁנֵיהֶם. חוֹלֶצֶת. דִּלְמָא לָא הָוֵי גֵּט. וְאֵינָהּ מִתְיַיבֶּמֶת. דִּלְמָא הָוֵי גֵּט, וְנִמְצָא לוֹקֵחַ גְּרוּשַׁת אָחִיו, וְחַיָּיב כָּרֵת. וְהָכָא נַמִי הֲוָה לָן לְמֵימַר דְּמַתְּנַת סָפֵק הִיא, וְלֹא קָנוּ! וּמְשַׁנֵּי: הָתָם גַּבֵּי גֵּט לֹא שַׁיְיכֵי בֵּהּ שְׁתֵּי מַתָּנוֹת כִּי הָכָא, דְּנֵימָא מִקְצָת הַגֵּט מֵהַיּוֹם וּמִקְצָתוֹ לְאַחַר מִיתָה, כִּדְאָמַר גַּבֵּי מַתְּנַת קַרְקַע. הִלְכָּךְ מְסַפְּקָא לָן אִי תְּנָאָה הָוֵי כו', כִּדְפָרֵישִׁית. אֲבָל הָכָא — אִיכָּא לְאוֹקְמֵי תַּרְוַויְהוּ שַׁפִּיר, דְּהָכִי קָאָמַר לֵיהּ: גּוּפָא מֵהַיּוֹם, וּפֵירֵי לְאַחַר מִיתָה. וְכֵיוָן דְּאִיכָּא לְמֵימַר הָכִי — לֹא נִתְכַּוֵּין לֹא לִתְנַאי וְלֹא לַחֲזָרָה, דְּהָכִי מַשְׁמַע טְפֵי. זְמַנּוֹ שֶׁל שְׁטָר. שֶׁכָּתַב בִּתְחִלָּתוֹ: "בְּכָךְ וְכָךְ בְּשַׁבָּת אָמַר לָנוּ פְּלוֹנִי הֱווּ עָלַי עֵדִים וּקְנוּ מִמֶּנִּי לִפְלוֹנִי בְּנִי לְאַחַר מִיתָתִי". מוֹכִיחַ עָלָיו. שֶׁמֵּאוֹתוֹ זְמַן הִתְחִילָה הַמַּתָּנָה. דְּאִי לֹא תֵּימָא הָכִי, זְמַן שֶׁנִּכְתַּב בַּשְּׁטָר — בְּחִנָּם נִכְתַּב. אֶלָּא וַדַּאי לְהַקְנוֹת מֵאוֹתוֹ הַיּוֹם נִכְתַּב. וְהָכִי הִלְכְתָא כְּרַבִּי יוֹסֵי, דְּאִם כָּתַב "לְאַחַר מִיתָה" — קָנָה אע"ג דְּלֹא כָּתַב "מֵהַיּוֹם", דְּהָא אָמַר רַב: הֲלָכָה כְּר' יוֹסֵי. וְאע"ג דְּאָמַר בְּפֶרֶק "הַמְגָרֵשׁ" (גיטין דף פה:): אַתְקֵין רַב בְּגִיטִּין "מִן יוֹמָא דְּנַן", לְאַפּוֹקֵי מִדְּר' יוֹסֵי דְּאָמַר: זְמַנּוֹ שֶׁל שְׁטָר מוֹכִיחַ עָלָיו. הוֹאִיל וְלֹא אִיתְּמַר בְּהֶדְיָא הָתָם בְּגִיטִּין "הָדַר בֵּיהּ רַב מֵהָא דְּאָמַר הֲלָכָה כְּרַבִּי יוֹסֵי", אֶלָּא "אַתְקִין", אִית לָן לְמֵימַר: לְגַבֵּי גֵּט אִשָּׁה, הוֹאִיל וְאֵין בּוֹ דְּבַר קִנְיָן — מִשּׁוּם הָכִי הוּא דְּאַתְקִין, לְרַוְוחָא דְּמִילְּתָא, מִשּׁוּם חוּמְרָא דַּעֲרָיוֹת. אֲבָל גַּבֵּי מָמוֹנָא — הֲלָכָה כְּר' יוֹסֵי, כִּי י"ל, כִּי לֹא אָמַר רַב הֲלָכָה כְּר' יוֹסֵי אֶלָּא בִּשְׁטָר שֶׁיֵּשׁ בּוֹ קִנְיָן. וְרָאִיתִי בְּדִבְרֵי הַגְּאוֹנִים ז"ל שֶׁאָמְרוּ: הָכִי נְהִיגֵי בְּמְתִיבְתָּא כְּר' יְהוּדָה אֲפִילּוּ בְּמָמוֹן, כְּתַקָּנַת רַב בְּגִיטִּין. וְאִילּוּ הָיְתָה קַבָּלָה בְּיָדָם כִּי הֲלָכָה כְּר' יְהוּדָה — לֹא הָיוּ מַנִּיחִין הֲלָכָה וּמְפָרְשִׁין מִנְהָג. (וְעוֹד) שֶׁלֹּא אָמְרוּ כִּי הֲלָכָה אֲפִילּוּ בְּמָמוֹן כְּתַקָּנַת רַב בְּגִיטִּין, אֶלָּא "נָהֲגוּ". וְי"ל, דְּכֵיוָן דְּחָזוּ דְּסוּגְיָא דִּשְׁמַעְתָּא לְקַמָּן כְּר' יְהוּדָה — נָהֲגוּ כְּוָותֵיהּ. כֵּן פֵּי' רַבֵּינוּ חֲנַנְאֵל גָּאוֹן. וּתְפוֹס דִּבְרֵי רַבִּי יוֹסֵי גַּבֵּי מָמוֹן, דְּהָא ר"נ דְּהִלְכְתָא כְּוָתֵיהּ בְּדִינֵי הוּא דְּבָעָא מֵרַבָּה בַּר אֲבוּהּ, אַלְמָא סְבִירָא לֵיהּ לְר"נ הָכִי. בְּהַקְנָאָה מַהוּ. בִּשְׁטָר שֶׁכָּתוּב בּוֹ קִנְיָן, מִי פָּלֵיג ר' יְהוּדָה וּמַצְרִיךְ לְמִכְתַּב "מֵהַיּוֹם"? וּמִשּׁוּם הָכִי קָמִבַּעְיָא לֵיהּ, דְּאִיכָּא לְמֵימַר דְּבִשְׁטָר מַתָּנָה בְּלֹא קִנְיָן פְּלִיגִי, כְּגוֹן שֶׁכָּתַב "שָׂדִי נְתוּנָה לְךָ לְאַחַר מִיתָה" וּמָסַר לוֹ אֶת הַשְּׁטָר, וְכִדְקַיְימָא לָן דְּקַרְקַע נִקְנֵה בְּכֶסֶף אוֹ בִּשְׁטָר אוֹ בַּחֲזָקָה. **אקנייה וקנינא מיניה לא צריך.** זֶהוּ שֶׁכּוֹתְבִין בְּכָל שְׁטָר שֶׁכָּתוּב בּוֹ קִנְיָן שְׁנֵי קִנְיָנִין: אֶחָד בִּתְחִלַּת הַשְּׁטָר — "וְכָךְ אָמַר לָנוּ הֱווּ עָלַי עֵדִים וּקְנוּ מִמֶּנִּי וְכִתְבוּ וְחִתְמוּ", וְהַיְינוּ "אַקְנְיֵיהּ", שֶׁהִקְנָה לְעֵדִים בְּקִנְיָן סוּדָר לִזְכּוֹת לוֹ לִמְקַבֵּל מַתָּנָה. וְאֶחָד בְּסוֹף הַשְּׁטָר: "וְקָנֵינָא מִן פְּלוֹנִי לִפְלוֹנִי כְּכָל מַה דִּכְתוּב וּמְפוֹרָשׁ לְעֵיל" כו', כִּדְאָמַר לְקַמָּן בְּ"גֵט פָּשׁוּט" (דף קסא:): צָרִיךְ שֶׁיַּחֲזוֹר מֵעִנְיָנוֹ שֶׁל שְׁטָר בְּשִׁיטָה אַחֲרוֹנָה. וְהִלְכָּךְ, אִם כָּתוּב בְּרֹאשׁ הַשְּׁטָר "אַקְנְיֵיהּ", וּבְסֵיפָא כָּתוּב "וְקָנֵינָא" — הַיְינוּ יִיפּוּי כֹּחַ, דְּמַשְׁמַע שְׁנֵי קִנְיָנִין: הוּא הִקְנָה, וְגַם אָנוּ קָנִינוּ מִמֶּנּוּ. וְקִנְיָן יְתֵירָא הוּא יִיפּוּי כֹּחַ לִקְנוֹת מֵהַיּוֹם. אֲבָל אִם כָּתַב בְּרֹאשׁ הַשְּׁטָר "וְקָנֵינָא", וּבְסוֹפוֹ "אַקְנְיֵיהּ" — מַשְׁמַע קִנְיָן אֶחָד, דְּפָרוּשֵׁי קָא מְפָרֵשׁ: וְקָנֵינָא מִינֵּיהּ, וְהֵיאַךְ — שֶׁהֲרֵי הִקְנָה לָנוּ וְאָמַר "כָּךְ וְכָךְ אֲנִי נוֹתֵן לִפְלוֹנִי". כֵּן נִרְאֶה שִׁיטָה זוֹ בְּעֵינַי, וְעִיקָּר. וְאֵין לְפָרֵשׁ שֶׁכָּתַב בַּשְּׁטָר שְׁנֵי דְּבָרִים הַלָּלוּ בְּיַחַד, "דְּאַקְנְיֵיהּ וְקָנֵינָא מִינֵּיהּ" דְּא"כ אַמַּאי מַשְׁוֶה חִילּוּק בֵּין "אַקְנְיֵיהּ וְקָנֵינָא מִינֵּיהּ" לְ"קָנֵינָא מִינֵּיהּ וְאַקְנְיֵיהּ"? לִישְׁוֵי חִילּוּק בֵּין הֵיכָא דְּכָתַב שְׁנֵי לְשׁוֹנוֹת קִנְיָן לְהֵיכָא דְּלֹא כָּתַב אֶלָּא אֶחָד. דַּאֲנַן לָא יָדְעִינַן. אֵין רוֹב חֲכָמִים בְּקִיאִין בְּחִילּוּק לָשׁוֹן זֶה. וְסָפְרֵי יָדְעֵי. בִּתְמִי', דְּאָמְרִי: לְכָךְ נִתְכַּוְּונוּ, וְלֹא צָרִיךְ לְמִכְתַּב "מֵהַיּוֹם". וּבְדוּכְרָן פִּתְגָּמֵי. הַיְינוּ שְׁטַר עֵדוּת בְּלֹא קִנְיָן, זִכְרוֹן דְּבָרִים וְלֹא זִכְרוֹן קִנְיָן. וְהַיְינוּ כְּר"נ, דְּאָמַר: הַקְנָאָה אֵינוֹ צָרִיךְ. **אתון הכי מתניתו** לָהּ. בִּלְשׁוֹן בָּעְיָא, כְּדַאֲמָרַן לְעֵיל: בָּעֵי רָבָא מר"נ כו'. וְהָכִי קַיְימָא לָן, דַּאֲפִילּוּ לְרַבִּי יְהוּדָה לֹא צָרִיךְ לִכְתּוֹב "מֵהַיּוֹם" בִּשְׁטָר שֶׁיֵּשׁ בּוֹ קִנְיָן.

מתני' הַכּוֹתֵב נְכָסָיו לִבְנוֹ. הוּא הַדִּין לְאַחֵר. לְאַחַר מוֹתוֹ. הַיְינוּ "מֵהַיּוֹם וּלְאַחַר מִיתָה". **הָאָב אֵינוֹ יָכוֹל לִמְכּוֹר.** לְאַחַר הַגּוּף וְהַפֵּירוֹת לְגַמְרֵי, מִפְּנֵי שֶׁכְּתוּבִין לַבֵּן הַגּוּף מֵעַכְשָׁיו וּפֵירוֹת לְאַחַר מִיתָה. הַבֵּן **אֵינוֹ** יָכוֹל לִמְכּוֹר. לְגַמְרֵי בְּחַיֵּי הָאָב. מִפְּנֵי שֶׁהֵן בִּרְשׁוּת הָאָב. לֶאֱכוֹל פֵּירוֹת. אֶלָּא בֵּין שְׁנֵיהֶן יְכוֹלִין לְמָכְרָן לְגַמְרֵי מֵעַכְשָׁיו, שֶׁהָאָב יִמְכּוֹר פֵּירוֹת וְהַבֵּן יִמְכּוֹר הַגּוּף. מָכַר הָאָב. סְתָמָא, מְכוּרִין לְפֵירוֹתֵיהֶן לַלּוֹקֵחַ עַד שֶׁיָּמוּת הָאָב. אֲבָל לִכְשֶׁיָּמוּת הָאָב — יִטּוֹל הַבֵּן גַּם גּוּף גַּם פֵּירוֹת, אוֹ הוּא אוֹ הַבָּא מִכֹּחוֹ, ל"ש מֵת הָאָב בְּחַיֵּי הַבֵּן וְל"ש מֵת הַבֵּן בְּחַיֵּי הָאָב. שֶׁהַפֵּירוֹת מָכַר הָאָב, אֲבָל הַגּוּף קָנוּי לְגַמְרֵי לַבֵּן מִשָּׁעָה שֶׁכָּתַב לוֹ הָאָב, וּכְשֶׁמֵּת הַבֵּן וְאח"כ הָאָב, וְיֵשׁ לוֹ בָּנִים לְאוֹתוֹ הַבֵּן — הֵן יוֹרְשִׁין אֶת כֹּחוֹ. מָכַר הַבֵּן. בְּחַיֵּי הָאָב — אֵין לַלּוֹקֵחַ פֵּירוֹת עַד שֶׁיָּמוּת הָאָב, שֶׁהֲרֵי הוּא כְּבֵן. אֲבָל כְּשֶׁיָּמוּת הָאָב יֵשׁ לוֹ מִיהַת לַלּוֹקֵחַ גּוּף וּפֵירוֹת. וּכְגוֹן שֶׁהַבֵּן קַיָּים, אֲבָל מֵת הַבֵּן וְאח"כ מֵת הָאָב — פְּלוּגְתָּא הִיא בַּגְּמָרָא אִם קָנָה לוֹקֵחַ אִם לָאו. **גמ'** לא

אקנייה וקנינא מיניה לא צריך. פי' בקונטרס: אחד בראש השטר ואחד בסוף השטר, כדאמר דצריך שיחזור מענינו של שטר בשיטה אחרונה. וקשה: דהא אין למדין משיטה אחרונה, והא (א) ט)א"כ למדין, דמשום הכי לא מצריכין לכתוב מהיום.

רבי

רבינו גרשום

כדאמר רב חסדא. בפרקין דלקמן היינו יפוי כח דכתב וקנינא מיניה מוסיף על מתנתא דא כלומר לבר מן המתנה שאני נותן מקנה אני בקנין כדי ליפות כחו: הכי נמי להכי כותבין דאמר אף כתובו כלומר ליפות כחו בעלמא כתבו לו שטר: הלכה כותבין ונותנין. גבי שכיב מרע אפי' לאחר מותו הואיל דבאמירה מקנה. הכותב. בריא כל נכסיו לבנו בין הבנים או לבניו וריבה לאחר ומיעט לאחר דבלשון מתנה רשאי ואינו רוצה שיהא שלו אלא לאחר מיתה צריך לכתוב מהיום ולאחר מיתה דאם לא כתב מהיום לא הוי שטר לאחר מיתה: ר' יוסי אומר אינו צריך. כדמפרש בגמ': והא תנן האומר לאשה הרי זה גיטך מהיום ולאחר מיתה אינו גט. דאין גט לאחר מיתה: ואם מת חולצת. דאינו גט: ולא מתייבמת. דאיכא למימר נפל עליה ריח גט. אלמא דבהאי גוונא לא הוי גט מתנה נמי הואיל דאמר ליה מהיום ולאחר מיתה אמאי קונה הא משתכח דההוא שטר מתנה אינה נגמרת אלא לאחר מיתה ואין שטר לאחר מיתה: אמר אביי לעולם מתנה היכא דאמר מהיום כו' והתם גבי גט משום הכי אינו גט משום דמספקא לן אי ההיא אמירה דקאמר (מהכי) מהיום אי תנאה הוי כלומר מהיום הוי גט. או חזרה הוי דאיכא למימר הואיל שאמר לאחר מיתה כלומר מהיום לאחר מיתה אני נותן לך גיטך כדי שתהא מותרת לאחר מיתתי. ואיכא למימר קודם מיתה חזר בו מאותו גט ואין גט לאחר מיתה ומשום דמספקא לן הכי גבי גט אזלינן לחומרא ואינו גט. אבל הכא גבי מתנה גופה של קרקע ושל נכסים קני ליה מהיום ופירא לאחר מיתה והשתא גובה מיתה מהיום והשתא נמי מתנה הוי וחשיבא מתנה: שזמנו של שטר מוכיח עליו. שכתב בו כך וכך לבריאת עולם בכך בחודש נתן פלוני לפלוני מתנה זו הואיל שהזמן על השטר ומכאן דהיכי מחיים הוא מתנה דמי ולא צריך למכתב מהיום: בעא מיניה רבא מרב נחמן אליבא דר' יהודה דאמר צריך למיכתב מהיום ולאחר מיתה בהקנאה מהו. כלומר אם הקנה לו בקנין מהיום מהו. מי אמרינן הואיל דהקנה לו מיכתב ליה מהיום ולאחר מיתה. או דלמא אע"ג דהקנה לו מחיים

רבינו גרשום

לא סגי דלאו הכי: אמר ליה אם הקנה לו מחיים לא צריך למיכתב ליה מהיום ולאחר מיתה: אקנייה וקנינא מיניה לא צריך. אקנייה שנתנה לו ושוב וקנינא מיניה משמע שתלה המתנה בקנין. כלומר כי היכי דקנינן מחיים אי כתב הכי לא צריך למיכתב מהיום ולאחר מיתה. אבל אי כתב ביה וקנינא מיניה ואקנייה שתלה הקנין במתנה דמשמע דלאחר הקנין היתה המתנה אי לא כתב ליה מהיום הוי משמע המתנה היתה לאחר מיתה ואין שטר לאחר מיתה: מי איכא מידי דאנן לא ידעינן. מה בין אקנייה וקנינא מיניה ומה בין וקנינא מיניה ואקנייה וספרי דכתבי שטרות ידעי. והא שום ספרא לא בקיאו בהני מילי: לא צריך. למיכתב מהיום ולאחר מיתה הואיל דכתב ביה קנין כל קנין מחיים הוא לדברי הכל. אלא אי לא כתב ביה קנין וכתב ביה דוכרן פתגמא דהוה באנפנא בכך וכך פליגי ר' יהודה ור' יוסי דר' יהודה סבר הואיל דלא כתב קנין אלא כתב כמנהג כל השטרות שכתוב בהן זכרון עדות לא סגי אי [לא] כתב בהו מהיום ולאחר מיתה משום דהוה שטר מתנה לאחר מיתה ואין שטר לאחר מיתה. ור' יוסי סבר הואיל דכתב ביה זכרון עדות בהדיא סגי משום דזמנו של שטר מוכיח עליו דמחיים הוה: אתון הכי מתניתו לה. בלשון בעיא בעא מיניה רבא מר"נ: אנן בלשון מימרא מתנינן ליה. אמר רב נחמן אם הקנה לו אינו צריך לכתוב מהיום ולאחר מיתה: הכותב נכסיו לבנו. שיהא שלו לאחר מיתה הגוף והפירות ועד שהאב חי הפירות של אב הבן והאב מכורים הפירות ללוקח עד שימות האב: מת הבן בחיי האב. דלא באו ליד הבן לא קרקע ולא פירות:

הגהות הב"ח

(א) תוס' ד"ה אקנייה וכו' וקשה וכו' משיטה אחרונה והא על כרחך למדין ממנה:

קמט א ב מיי' פי"ב מהל' זכיה ומתנה הל' יג סמג עשין פב טוש"ע חו"מ סי' רנז ס"ה:
קנ ג מיי' פ"ד מהלכות בכורים הלכה ו סמג עשין קמ:
קנא ד ה מיי' פי"ב מהל' זכיה ומתנה הל' ז ועי' בהשגות ובכ"מ סמג עשין פב טוש"ע חו"מ סי' רמח סעיף ג:

אָמַר רַבִּי יוֹחָנָן: לֹא קָנָה לוֹקֵחַ, וְרֵישׁ לָקִישׁ אָמַר: אקָנָה לוֹקֵחַ, רַבִּי יוֹחָנָן אָמַר לֹא קָנָה לוֹקֵחַ, א)קִנְיַן פֵּירוֹת כְּקִנְיַן הַגּוּף דָּמֵי; וְרֵישׁ לָקִישׁ אָמַר קָנָה לוֹקֵחַ, בקִנְיַן פֵּירוֹת לָאו כְּקִנְיַן הַגּוּף דָּמֵי. וְהָא אִיפְלִיגוּ בָּהּ חֲדָא זִימְנָא! ב)דְּאִיתְּמַר: הַמּוֹכֵר שָׂדֵהוּ לְפֵירוֹת – רַבִּי יוֹחָנָן אָמַר: מֵבִיא וְקוֹרֵא, וְרֵישׁ לָקִישׁ אָמַר: מֵבִיא וְאֵינוֹ קוֹרֵא. רַבִּי יוֹחָנָן אָמַר מֵבִיא וְקוֹרֵא, קָסָבַר: קִנְיַן פֵּירוֹת כְּקִנְיַן הַגּוּף דָּמֵי; וְרֵישׁ לָקִישׁ אָמַר גמֵבִיא וְאֵינוֹ קוֹרֵא, קִנְיַן פֵּירוֹת לָאו כְּקִנְיַן הַגּוּף דָּמֵי! אָמַר לָךְ ר' יוֹחָנָן: אַף עַל גַּב דִּבְעָלְמָא קִנְיַן פֵּירוֹת כְּקִנְיַן הַגּוּף דָּמֵי, הָכָא אִצְטְרִיךְ; סַלְקָא דַּעְתָּךְ אָמִינָא: אַבָּא לְגַבֵּי בְּרֵיהּ אַחוּלֵי אַחֵיל, קָא מַשְׁמַע לָן. וְרַבִּי שִׁמְעוֹן בֶּן לָקִישׁ אָמַר: אַף עַל גַּב דִּבְעָלְמָא קִנְיַן פֵּירוֹת לָאו כְּקִנְיַן הַגּוּף דָּמֵי, הָכָא אִצְטְרִיךְ; סַלְקָא דַּעְתָּךְ אָמִינָא: כָּל לְגַבֵּי נַפְשֵׁיהּ, אֲפִילּוּ בִּמְקוֹם בְּרֵיהּ – נַפְשֵׁיהּ עֲדִיפָא לֵיהּ, קָא מַשְׁמַע לָן. אֵיתִיבֵיהּ רַבִּי יוֹחָנָן לְרֵישׁ לָקִישׁ: ג)ד"נְכָסַי לָךְ, וְאַחֲרֶיךָ יִירַשׁ פְּלוֹנִי, וְאַחֲרָיו יִירַשׁ פְּלוֹנִי", מֵת רִאשׁוֹן – קָנָה שֵׁנִי, מֵת שֵׁנִי – קָנָה שְׁלִישִׁי, מֵת שֵׁנִי בְּחַיֵּי רִאשׁוֹן – היַחְזְרוּ נְכָסִים לְיוֹרְשֵׁי רִאשׁוֹן; וְאִם אִיתָא, לְיוֹרְשֵׁי נוֹתֵן מִיבָּעֵי לֵיהּ! אֲמַר לֵיהּ, כְּבָר תִּרְגְּמָהּ רַב הוֹשַׁעְיָא בְּבָבֶל: "אַחֲרֶיךָ" שָׁאנֵי. וְכֵן רָמֵי רַבָּה בַּר רַב הוּנָא קַמֵּיהּ דְּרַב, וַאֲמַר: "אַחֲרֶיךָ" שָׁאנֵי. וְהָתַנְיָא: יַחְזְרוּ לְיוֹרְשֵׁי נוֹתֵן! תַּנָּאֵי

רשב"ם

לֹא קָנָה לוֹקֵחַ. אֲפִילּוּ לִכְשֶׁיָּמוּת הָאָב אַחַר כָּךְ, שֶׁמֵּעוֹלָם לֹא הָיוּ רְאוּיִן לָבֹא לִידֵי הַבֵּן. אֶלָּא יַחְזְרוּ לִשְׁאָר יוֹרְשֵׁי הָאָב. וּמִיהוּ, אִם לֹא מְכָרָן הַבֵּן בְּחַיֵּי הָאָב – הָיָה מוֹדֶה רַבִּי יוֹחָנָן שֶׁאַף עַל פִּי שֶׁמֵּת הַבֵּן וְאַחַר כָּךְ מֵת הָאָב, אֲפִילּוּ הָכִי יוֹרְשֵׁי הַבֵּן יוֹרְשִׁין אֶת מַתְּנָתוֹ וְלֹא יוֹרְשֵׁי הָאָב. אֲבָל גַּבֵּי מְכִירָה, הֲרֵי סִילֵּק נַפְשׁוֹ מִשְּׁעַת מְכִירָה, וְגַם לֹא בָּא לְיָדוֹ שֶׁיּוּכַל הַלּוֹקֵחַ לִזְכּוֹת מֵאִתּוֹ. וּבְפֶרֶק "הַחוֹבֵל" בְּבָבָא קַמָּא מְפָרֵשׁ לִפְלוּגְתַּיְיהוּ הָכִי: רַבִּי יוֹחָנָן אָמַר לֹא קָנָה לוֹקֵחַ, אָמַר לָךְ: כִּי קָתָנֵי מַתְנִיתִין מָכַר הַבֵּן אֵין לַלּוֹקֵחַ עַד שֶׁיָּמוּת הָאָב, הָא כִּי מָיֵית אִית לֵיהּ לַלּוֹקֵחַ – דְּלֹא מֵת הַבֵּן בְּחַיֵּי הָאָב, דַּאֲתוּ לְהוּ לִידֵיהּ דְּבֵן. אֲבָל מֵת הַבֵּן בְּחַיֵּי הָאָב, דְּלָא אֲתוּ לִידֵיהּ דְּבֵן, כִּי מָיֵית אָב נַמִי לֵית לֵיהּ לַלּוֹקֵחַ. אַלְמָא קִנְיַן פֵּירוֹת כְּקִנְיַן הַגּוּף דָּמֵי, וְכִי זַבֵּין לָאו דִּידֵיהּ זַבֵּין. רֵישׁ לָקִישׁ אָמַר קָנָה לוֹקֵחַ, אָמַר לָךְ: כִּי קָתָנֵי מַתְנִי' מָכַר הַבֵּן אֵין לַלּוֹקֵחַ עַד שֶׁיָּמוּת הָאָב, כִּי מָיֵית מִיהָא אִית לַלּוֹקֵחַ – לָא שְׁנָא לֹא מֵת הַבֵּן בְּחַיֵּי הָאָב דַּאֲתוּ לִידֵיהּ דְּבֵן, לָא שְׁנָא מֵת הַבֵּן בְּחַיֵּי הָאָב דְּלָא אֲתוּ לִידֵיהּ דְּבֵן – קָנָה לוֹקֵחַ. אַלְמָא קִנְיַן פֵּירוֹת לָאו כְּקִנְיַן הַגּוּף דָּמֵי, וְכִי זַבֵּין דִּידֵיהּ זַבֵּין. קִנְיַן פֵּירוֹת. שֶׁיֵּשׁ לוֹ לָאָב – כְּאִילּוּ הַגּוּף קָנוּי לוֹ דָּמֵי, וְלֹא הָיָה הַבֵּן יָכוֹל לִמְכּוֹר אֶלָּא ע"מ דְּאָתוּ לִידֵיהּ, וְכֵיוָן דְּלָא אֲתוּ לִידֵיהּ – לָא קָנֵי לוֹקֵחַ. וּמִיהוּ, אִם לֹא מְכָרָן הַבֵּן וְלֹא סִילֵּק נַפְשׁוֹ מֵהֶם, וּמֵת הַבֵּן בְּחַיֵּי הָאָב – לִכְשֶׁיָּמוּת הָאָב, יִירַשׁ בֶּן הַבֵּן אֶת זְכוּת אָבִיו שֶׁהָיָה לוֹ בַּקַּרְקַע. וְקוֹרֵא. מִקְרָא בִּכּוּרִים, דְּקָרֵינָא בֵּיהּ: "הָאֲדָמָה אֲשֶׁר נָתַתָּה לִּי ה'" (דברים כו). מֵבִיא וְאֵינוֹ קוֹרֵא. שֶׁאֵינוֹ יָכוֹל לִקְרוֹת "הָאֲדָמָה אֲשֶׁר נָתַתָּה לִּי". וּמִיהוּ, בַּהֲבָאָה חַיָּיב, דִּכְתִיב: "אֲשֶׁר תָּבִיא מֵאַרְצְךָ", שֶׁהֲרֵי שִׁיעְבֵּד לוֹ יְנִיקַת הַקַּרְקַע לְפֵירוֹתָיו. אַחוּלֵי אַחֵיל לֵיהּ. גּוּפָא לְגַמְרֵי, וְקִנְיַן פֵּירוֹת דְּאִית לֵיהּ לָא לֶיהֱווּ קִנְיַן הַגּוּף. וְה"נ הֲוָה מָצֵי לְמֵימַר: דְּאִי אִיתְּמַר בְּהָא – בְּהָא קָאָמַר ר' יוֹחָנָן דְּקִנְיַן פֵּירוֹת כְּקִנְיַן הַגּוּף דָּמֵי, מִשּׁוּם דְּכָל לְגַבֵּי נַפְשֵׁיהּ, אֲפִילּוּ בִּמְקוֹם בְּרֵיהּ – נַפְשֵׁיהּ עֲדִיפָא לֵיהּ, וְכֵיוָן דְּעִכֵּב לְעַצְמוֹ פֵּירוֹת – שִׁייֵּר בְּקִנְיַן הַגּוּף לְעַצְמוֹ. אֲבָל לְגַבֵּי מוֹכֵר שָׂדֵהוּ לְפֵירוֹת – מוֹדֵי רַבִּי יוֹחָנָן לְרֵישׁ לָקִישׁ דְּקִנְיַן פֵּירוֹת שֶׁמַּקְנֶה לַאֲחֵרִים לָאו כְּקִנְיַן הַגּוּף דָּמֵי, דִּבְכָל דּוּכְתָּא נַפְשֵׁיהּ עֲדִיפָא לֵיהּ. וּמִשּׁוּם דְּשָׁמְעִינַן לָהּ מִתֵּירוּצֵיהּ דְּרֵישׁ לָקִישׁ לֹא חָשַׁשׁ הַגְּמָרָא לְפָרֵשׁ כֵּן. וּלְר"ל נַמִי, אִי אִיתְּמַר בְּהָא – בְּהָא קָאָמַר רֵישׁ לָקִישׁ, מִשּׁוּם דְּאַבָּא לְגַבֵּי בְּרֵיהּ אַחוּלֵי אַחֵיל, אֲבָל לְגַבֵּי מוֹכֵר שָׂדֵהוּ לְפֵירוֹת – אֵימָא מוֹדֵי לֵיהּ לְרַבִּי יוֹחָנָן דְּקִנְיַן פֵּירוֹת כְּקִנְיַן הַגּוּף דָּמֵי, קמ"ל. מֵת הַשֵּׁנִי. אַחֲרֵי הָרִאשׁוֹן, קָנָה שְׁלִישִׁי. יַחְזְרוּ נְכָסִים לְיוֹרְשֵׁי רִאשׁוֹן. כְּלוֹמַר, כְּשֶׁיָּמוּת הָרִאשׁוֹן – יוֹרְשָׁיו יוֹרְשִׁין מֵאִתּוֹ, שֶׁהֲרֵי לֹא זָכָה לַשְּׁלִישִׁי אֶלָּא מֵאֵת הַשֵּׁנִי, דְּהָא לָא קָאָמַר לָרִאשׁוֹן: נְכָסַי לְךָ וְאַחֲרֶיךָ לִפְלוֹנִי, וְאִם אֵין פְּלוֹנִי – יִתְּנוּ לִפְלוֹנִי הַשְּׁלִישִׁי. וְכֵיוָן דְּשֵׁנִי לֹא זָכָה – שְׁלִישִׁי נַמִי לֹא יִקְנֶה, אֶלָּא יוֹרְשֵׁי רִאשׁוֹן יִירְשׁוּ לְהָנֵי נְכָסִים. וְאַע"ג דְּלֹא הָיוּ קְנוּיִן לָרִאשׁוֹן אֶלָּא לֶאֱכוֹל פֵּירוֹתֵיהֶן כָּל יְמֵי חַיָּיו, דְּהָא קָאָמַר לֵיהּ "וְאַחֲרֶיךָ לִפְלוֹנִי" אֲפִי' הָכִי, כֵּיוָן דְּאֵין "אַחֲרֶיךָ" קַיָּים – זָכוּ יוֹרְשֵׁי רִאשׁוֹן בְּגוּף וּפֵירוֹת. אִי אָמְרַתְּ בִּשְׁלָמָא קִנְיַן פֵּירוֹת הָוֵי חָשׁוּב כְּקִנְיַן הַגּוּף – הִלְכָּךְ אִיכָּא לְמֵימַר יַחְזְרוּ לְיוֹרְשֵׁי רִאשׁוֹן, שֶׁהֲרֵי הַפֵּירוֹת קְנוּיִין לוֹ, וּכְקִנְיַן הַגּוּף דָּמֵי. דְּאַע"ג דְּהַמּוֹכֵר שָׂדֵהוּ לְפֵירוֹת לֹא קָנָה בַּעַל הַפֵּירוֹת אֶת הַגּוּף מִשּׁוּם קִנְיַן פֵּירוֹת כְּקִנְיַן הַגּוּף – הַיְינוּ מִשּׁוּם דִּבְהֶדְיָא פֵּירוֹת מָכַר לוֹ וְלֹא גּוּף, וַהֲרֵי הוּא כְּמִי שֶׁאָמַר לוֹ: וְאַחַר אוֹתוֹ זְמַן יְהֵא הַגּוּף וְהַפֵּירוֹת שֶׁלִּי. אֲבָל הָכָא לֹא שִׁייֵּר לְעַצְמוֹ כְּלוּם, אֶלָּא לַשְּׁלִישִׁי נָתַן אֶת הַגּוּף, וְלָרִאשׁוֹן וְלַשֵּׁנִי נָתַן אֶת הַפֵּירוֹת. וְכֵיוָן דְּאִיכָּא תַּרְתֵּי, שֶׁיֵּשׁ לָרִאשׁוֹן קִנְיַן פֵּירוֹת דִּכְקִנְיַן הַגּוּף דָּמֵי, וְגַם סִילֵּק הַנּוֹתֵן עַצְמוֹ מִגּוּף וּפֵירוֹת – הִלְכָּךְ יַחְזְרוּ לְיוֹרְשֵׁי רִאשׁוֹן. אֶלָּא אִי אִיתָא דְּלָאו כְּקִנְיַן הַגּוּף דָּמֵי – מֵאֵיזֶה טַעַם יַחְזְרוּ לָרִאשׁוֹן? יַחְזְרוּ לְיוֹרְשֵׁי נוֹתֵן מִיבָּעֵי לֵיהּ. שֶׁהֲרֵי לָרִאשׁוֹן נָתַן פֵּירוֹת, וְאֵין אַחֲרָיו אִישׁ שֶׁיְּקַבֵּל לֹא הַגּוּף וְלֹא פֵּירוֹת, הִלְכָּךְ יַחְזְרוּ לַנּוֹתֵן אוֹ לְיוֹרְשָׁיו! אַחֲרֶיךָ שָׁאנֵי. דְּמַשְׁמַע דְּגוּף וּפֵירוֹת נָתַן לָרִאשׁוֹן, דְּהָא בְּהֶדְיָא פֵּירֵשׁ: אַחֲרֶיךָ יִירַשׁ פְּלוֹנִי, וְהָא לֵיתֵיהּ דְּלִירַשׁ, הִלְכָּךְ יִשָּׁאֲרוּ בְּיַד יוֹרְשֵׁי רִאשׁוֹן. דְּהָכִי קָאָמַר לֵיהּ: כָּל יְמֵי חַיֶּיךָ יְהֵא הַכֹּל שֶׁלְּךָ הַפְּרִי וְהַגּוּף, וּמַה שֶּׁיִּשְׁתַּיֵּיר אַחֲרֶיךָ – יְקַבֵּל פְּלוֹנִי. וְאִם הָיָה רוֹצֶה רִאשׁוֹן – יָכוֹל לִמְכּוֹר הַגּוּף, כִּדְלְקַמָּן. וְהָתַנְיָא יַחְזְרוּ לְיוֹרְשֵׁי נוֹתֵן. לְר' יוֹחָנָן פָּרֵיךְ: אַע"ג דְּאִיכָּא לְמֵימַר "אַחֲרֶיךָ" שָׁאנֵי, אֲפִילּוּ הָכִי יַחְזְרוּ לְיוֹרְשֵׁי נוֹתֵן, דְּקִנְיַן פֵּירוֹת דְּרִאשׁוֹן לָאו כְּקִנְיַן הַגּוּף דָּמֵי, וְכ"שׁ קִנְיַן פֵּירוֹת דְּעָלְמָא דְּלָאו כְּקִנְיַן הַגּוּף דָּמֵי, כְּרֵישׁ לָקִישׁ. וְקַשְׁיָא לְרַבִּי יוֹחָנָן.

ה"ג

תוספות

רבי יוחנן סבר לא קנה לוקח. תימה: אם כן, אמאי אצטריך תקנת אושא, דאשה שמכרה בנכסי מלוג בחיי בעלה ומתה דלא עשתה ולא כלום (לקמן דף קלט:)? וי"ל: דמיירי כגון שכתב לה "דין ודברים אין לי בפירות נכסיך ובפירות פירותיך" ולא כתב "בנכסיך", דא"כ היה מכרה קיים, כדאמר ב"הכותב" (כתובות דף פג. ושם). אי נמי, התם קנין פירות דבעל דלא הוי אלא מדרבנן, ולא מצרכי לכתוב "מהיום", ולא הוי כקנין הגוף, לכך אצטריך תקנת אושא ד).

לא קנה לוקח. פי' ריב"ם: ויחזרו ליורשי הבן, ולא יוכלו לקוחות לומר: אביך זבין ואת מפקת? כדאמרינן בסוף "מי שמת" (לקמן דף קנט. ושם ד"ה ולימרו). דאף על גב דהכא לא שייך טעמא דלקמן משום שיאמר הבן "אנא מכח אבא דאבא קאתינא" – דא"כ יקחו אחי האב חלקם, כיון שאינו בא מכח אביו אלא מכח זקינו. אלא היינו טעמא שיחזרו ליורשי הבן – משום דבמיתת הבן נפלו נכסים לפני בנו, וכשמת זקינו – קנאם הבן בקבר ממילא, ואחר כך ירשם בן הבן. וקשה, דאמר בסמוך: מהו דתימא אביו אפילו לגבי בריה נפשיה כדיפא ליה, ולא יקחו הלקוחות במיתת האב. והלא אם המקח בטל – לא יחזרו לאב, כי אם ליורשי הבן! ויש לומר: דשפיר קרי ליה בן בנו "נפשיה" לגבי לוקח. ולא דמי ל"נכסיי לך ואחריך לפלוני ואחרי אחריך לפלוני", דאם מת שני בחיי ראשון יחזרו נכסים ליורשי ראשון, ולא אמר: כיון שהקנה הגוף לשלישי לבסוף הוי כנופל לפניו במיתת השני. שהרי לא הקנה לו כלום עד אחר שיזכה שני. ואפי' לרב ענן דאמר לעיל (דף קכה:): "לירתיי" ולא גירתי ירתיי, דלדידיה אם אמר "נכסיי לך ואחריך לפלוני" אם מת שני (א) לא יחזרו ליורשי שני – לא דמי להכא, דיותר יש לו לראשון בנכסים מלאב. דהתם אם מכר ראשון – כל הנכסים מכורים לעולם, דהלכתא כרבן שמעון בן גמליאל דאמר: אין לשני אלא מה ששייר ראשון, אבל הכא – אין האב יכול למכר אלא עד שימות. לכך יחזרו ליורשי הבן, והתם ליורשי ראשון.

מביא ואינו קורא. פי' בקונטרס: מביא – משום ד"אדמתך" קרינא ביה, ואינו קורא – דלא קרינא ביה "מן האדמה אשר נתתה לי". ותימה: דאי קרינא ביה "אדמתך" – קרינא ביה נמי "מן האדמה אשר נתתה לי"! ונראה שתקנו מדרבנן להביא, משום קנין פירות. אבל קריאה לא, מדאמרינן ב"המוכר את הספינה" (לעיל דף פב.) משום דמיחזי כשיקרא, או משום דאתי לאפקועי מתרומה ומעשר.

והתניא יחזרו נכסים ליורשי נותן. פירש בקונטרס: וקשה לר' יוחנן, דאמר קנין פירות כקנין הגוף דמי. ומשני: תנאי היא דפליגי בקנין פירות אי הוי כקנין הגוף או לא. ואין נראה, דהרבה תנאים מצינו דפליגי בקנין פירות. בהדיא יותר מאלו, גבי מוכר עבדו על מנת שישמשנו שלשים יום ב"חזקת הבתים" (לעיל דף נ. ושם). ועוד, (ב) דלדבריו לא גרסינן אלא: "אחריך" תנאי היא. ונראה, דלר"ל פריך, דשני: "אחריך" שאני. והכי פריך: אי אמרת בשלמא ד"אחריך" לא שאני, אלא ההיא דיחזרו ליורשי ראשון הוי טעמא משום דקסבר קנין פירות כקנין הגוף דמי, כר"י (ג) – א"ש, דמצינו הרבה תנאים דפליגי בהכי. אלא אי אמרת דההיא דיחזרו ליורשי ראשון סברא נמי בעלמא, דלאו כקנין הגוף דמי, והכא משום ד"אחריך" שאני – והתניא: יחזרו ליורשי נותן. והא אין סברא לומר דסבירא ליה ד"אחריך" לאו כלום, דלא מצינו פלוגתא בהכי! ומשני: אלא "אחריך" תנאי היא. כלומר, לעולם קמייתא נמי כריש לקיש, ו"אחריך" נמי תנאי היא, כדמייתי דפליגי רבי ורבן שמעון בן גמליאל ב"אחריך", דרבי סבר "אחריך" לאו כלום היא ולא הקנה לו אלא פירות, ורשב"ג סבר "אחריך" שאני, והשתא הוי כולהו כריש לקיש והלכתא כותיה. (גליון. נראה דמייתי שפיר תנאי, דע"כ ב"אחריך" פליגי אפי' לר"י, ולא בקנין פירות אי הוי כקנין הגוף אי לאו. דהא טעמא דרשב"ג אין לו לשני אלא מה ששייר הראשון – ע"כ משום דאמר "אחריך". דמשום קנין פירות גרידא – פשיטא דלא היה יכול למכור, כמו האב דאינו יכול למכור. ע"כ): (רש"א)

אבל

רבינו גרשום

קנין פירות שיש לאביו עד שהוא חי דמי כמו שגוף הקרקע יהא שלו ולא בא ליד בן הואיל שמת בחייו לפיכך לא קנה לוקח: לאו כקנין הגוף דמי. והגוף ברשות הבן היה להכי קנה לוקח: המוכר שדהו לפירות. ללוקח עד אותו זמן שהתנו: ר' יוחנן אמר מביא בכורים וקורא. מן האדמה אשר נתתה לי אע"ג דפירות בלבד שלו אותו קנין פירות כקנין הגוף של קרקע הוא שלו עד אותו הזמן דמי ויכול לקרות: ריש לקיש אמר מביא וכו'. ולמה להו לאפלוגי תרי זמנא בהכי: אמר לך ר' יוחנן אע"ג דגבי בכורים קנין פירות כקנין הגוף דמי אפ"ה אצטריך הכא לאשמועינן דלא קנה לוקח דסד"א ודאי קנה לוקח דאבא לגביה בריה מחיל ליה למכור אפילו בחייו וקנה לוקח קמ"ל דלא מחיל ולא קנה. וריש לקיש אמר דאע"ג לגבי בכורים בעלמא כו' הכא אצטריך דסד"א דלא קנה לוקח דקנין הגוף דמי דכל לגבי נפשיה אפי' לגבי בריה נפשיה עדיפא ליה מבריה ולא ניחא ליה למיזבן בחייו ולא קנה לוקח קמ"ל הכא דלגבי בריה מחיל ליה לזבוני שיהו מכורין במיתת האב וקנה לוקח: איתיביה ר' יוחנן לריש לקיש. אם אמר שכיב מרע נכסיי לך ואחריך לפלוני ואחריו לפלוני משמע שנתן לראשון ושני הפירות בחייהן והשלישי יהא יורש גוף הנכסים: מת שני. בחיי ראשון כיון שלא באו ליד השני אין לשלישי כלום ושלישי הוא בא מכח שני אלא יחזרו הנכסים ליורשי הראשון הואיל דליתא לאחריך ולשלישי לא מצינן למיתן ליה דהכי לא פקיד המצוה. ואם איתא לריש לקיש דקנין פירות שיהא לראשון לאו כקנין הגוף דמי. אמאי יחזרו ליורשי ראשון כיון דלא הוה ליה קנין הגוף הקרקע בשמת ראשון יחזרו אותו ליורשי אותו שנתן מתחל' מיבעי ליה. אלא מדקאמר ליורשי ראשון ש"מ דקנין פירות שיש לראשון כקנין הגוף דמי וקשיא לריש לקיש: תרגמא רב אושעיא. לעולם אימא לך בעלמא לאו כקנין הגוף דמי. והכא מאי טעמא יחזרו ליורשי ראשון דהיכא דאמר ליה נותן לראשון ואחריך לפלוני שאני דמשמע ואחריך לפלוני אחריך הן שלו ולא בחייך לפי שבחיים הכל שלך הגוף והפירות. והשתא דמת אחריך בחייך הכל שלך הוא. להכי יחזרו ליורשי ראשון ולא ליורשי נותן דנותן סליק עצמו מהן הואיל ואמר אחריך לפיכך קאמרינן בדעתו דלא חזרו עולמית לעצמו. ולעולם מהא לא תפשוט: והא תניא יחזרו ליורשי נותן. דמשמע דקנין פירות לאו כקנין הגוף דמי וקשיא לר' יוחנן דאמר כו'.
אלא

מסורת הש"ס

א) [שבת קלה. וש"נ]: ב) ב"מ נו. גיטין מז:: ג) [לעיל קכט:]: ד) [ועי' תוס' ב"ק פח: ד"ה באושא ותוס' כתובות נ. ד"ה הבעל ותוס' יבמות לו: ד"ה קנין]:

הגהות הב"ח

(א) תוס' ד"ה לא קנה וכו' אם מת שני בחיי ראשון לא יחזרו ליורשי שני: (ב) ד"ה והתניא וכו' דלדבריו לא גרסי'. נ"ב כלומר והוא תימה למחוק הגירסא שהיא ברוב הספרים: (ג) בא"ד כקנין הגוף דמי כר"י וההיא דיחזרו ליורשי נותן סבר לאו כקנין הגוף דמי כר"ל א"ש דמצינו הרבה תנאים:

א) [סוטה כה:] ב) לקמן קנט. [כתובות לה: סוטה כה: ערכין כג.] ג) גיטין עב. כתובות כב: ד) [שבת קלה: וש"נ]

תַּנָּאֵי הִיא; דְּתַנְיָא: א)"נְכָסַי לְךָ וְאַחֲרֶיךָ לִפְלוֹנִי", וְיָרַד רִאשׁוֹן וּמָכַר וְאָכַל — הַשֵּׁנִי מוֹצִיא מִיַּד הַלָּקוֹחוֹת, דִּבְרֵי רַבִּי; רַבָּן שִׁמְעוֹן בֶּן גַּמְלִיאֵל אוֹמֵר: אאֵין לַשֵּׁנִי אֶלָּא מַה שֶּׁשִּׁיֵּיר רִאשׁוֹן. וּרְמִינְהִי: "נְכָסַי לְךָ וְאַחֲרֶיךָ לִפְלוֹנִי" — יוֹרֵד רִאשׁוֹן וּמוֹכֵר וְאוֹכֵל, דִּבְרֵי רַבִּי; רַבָּן שִׁמְעוֹן בֶּן גַּמְלִיאֵל אוֹמֵר: באֵין לָרִאשׁוֹן אֶלָּא אֲכִילַת פֵּירוֹת בִּלְבַד. קַשְׁיָא דְּרַבִּי אַדְּרַבִּי, וּדְרשב"ג אַדְּרשב"ג! דְּרַבִּי אַדְּרַבִּי לָא קַשְׁיָא: הָא לְגוּפָא, הָא לְפֵירָא; דְּרשב"ג אַדְּרשב"ג לָא קַשְׁיָא: גהָא לְכַתְּחִלָּה, הָא דִּיעֲבַד. ב)אָמַר אַבַּיֵי: דאֵיזֶהוּ רָשָׁע עָרוּם? זֶה הַמַּשִּׁיא עֵצָה לִמְכּוֹר בִּנְכָסִים כְּרַבָּן שִׁמְעוֹן בֶּן גַּמְלִיאֵל. א"ר יוֹחָנָן: הֲלָכָה כְּרַבָּן שִׁמְעוֹן בֶּן גַּמְלִיאֵל; הוּמוֹדֶה, שֶׁאִם נְתָנָן בְּמַתְּנַת שְׁכִיב מְרַע — לֹא עָשָׂה כְּלוּם. מַאי טַעְמָא? אָמַר אַבַּיֵי: מַתְּנַת שְׁכִיב מְרַע לֹא קָנָה ואֶלָּא לְאַחַר מִיתָה, וּכְבָר קְדָמוֹ "אַחֲרֶיךָ". וּמִי אָמַר אַבַּיֵי הָכִי? וְהָא אִיתְּמַר: מַתְּנַת שְׁכִיב מְרַע מֵאֵימָתַי קָנָה? אַבַּיֵי אָמַר: עִם גְּמַר מִיתָה, וְרָבָא אָמַר: זלְאַחַר גְּמַר מִיתָה! הֲדַר בֵּיהּ אַבַּיֵי מֵהַהִיא. מִמַּאי דְּמֵהַהִיא הֲדַר בֵּיהּ? דִּלְמָא מֵהָא הֲדַר בֵּיהּ! לָא סָלְקָא דַּעְתָּךְ, דִּתְנַן: ג)ח"זֶה גִּיטֵּךְ אִם מַתִּי", "זֶה גִּיטֵּךְ מֵחוֹלִי זֶה", "זֶה גִּיטֵּךְ לְאַחַר מִיתָה" — לֹא אָמַר כְּלוּם. אָמַר רַבִּי זֵירָא א"ר יוֹחָנָן: הֲלָכָה כרשב"ג, טוַאֲפִילּוּ הָיוּ בָּהֶן עֲבָדִים וְהוֹצִיאָן לְחֵירוּת. פְּשִׁיטָא! מַהוּ דְּתֵימָא, (א) א"ל: לְמֶיעֱבַד אִיסּוּרָא לָא יַהֲבִינַן לָךְ, קָא מַשְׁמַע לָן. אָמַר רַב יוֹסֵף אָמַר רַבִּי יוֹחָנָן: הֲלָכָה כְּרַבָּן שִׁמְעוֹן בֶּן גַּמְלִיאֵל, יוַאֲפִי' עֲשָׂאָן תַּכְרִיכִין לְמֵת. פְּשִׁיטָא! מַהוּ דְּתֵימָא: לְשָׁוְינְהוּ אִיסּוּרֵי הֲנָאָה לָא יְהַבִי לָךְ, קָא מַשְׁמַע לָן. דָּרַשׁ רַב נַחְמָן בַּר רַב חִסְדָּא: "אֶתְרוֹג זֶה נָתוּן לְךָ בְּמַתָּנָה וְאַחֲרֶיךָ לִפְלוֹנִי", נְטָלוֹ רִאשׁוֹן וְיָצָא בּוֹ — בָּאנוּ לְמַחֲלוֹקֶת רַבִּי וְרשב"ג. מַתְקִיף לָהּ רַב נַחְמָן בַּר יִצְחָק: ע"כ לָא פְּלִיגִי רַבִּי וְרשב"ג הָתָם, אֶלָּא דְּמָר סָבַר: ד)קִנְיַן פֵּירוֹת כְּקִנְיַן הַגּוּף דָּמֵי, וּמָר סָבַר: קִנְיַן פֵּירוֹת לָאו כְּקִנְיַן הַגּוּף דָּמֵי. אֶלָּא הָכָא, אִי

רשב"ם

ה"ג: תַּנָּאֵי הִיא. וְלָא גָּרְסִי': "אֶלָּא אַחֲרֶיךָ נַמִי תַּנָּאֵי הִיא", דְּמַשְׁמַע דְּתֵירוּצָא דְּתָרְצִינַן לְעֵיל לְרֵישׁ לָקִישׁ "אַחֲרֶיךָ" שָׁאנֵי, לָאו תֵּירוּצָא הוּא. דְּהָא וַדַּאי לְרֵישׁ לָקִישׁ מְתָרְצִינַן "אַחֲרֶיךָ" שָׁאנֵי, כִּדְמִתָּרְצִי רַב וְרַבִּי הוֹשַׁעְיָא לְעֵיל, דְּהַשְׁתָּא קָיְימִי כּוּלְּהוּ בָּרַיְיתוֹת כְּרֵישׁ לָקִישׁ; בֵּין לְמַאן דְּאָמַר יַחְזְרוּ לְיוֹרְשֵׁי נוֹתֵן, בֵּין לְמַאן דְּאָמַר יַחְזְרוּ לְיוֹרְשֵׁי רִאשׁוֹן — כּוּלְּהוּ סְבִירָא לְהוּ דְּקִנְיַן פֵּירוֹת דְּעָלְמָא לָאו כְּקִנְיַן הַגּוּף דָּמֵי. דַּאֲפִילּוּ הַךְ דְּקָתָנֵי יַחְזְרוּ לְיוֹרְשֵׁי רִאשׁוֹן — הַיְינוּ מִשּׁוּם דְּ"אַחֲרֶיךָ" שָׁאנֵי. אֶלָּא לְרַבִּי יוֹחָנָן הוּא דִּמְתָרְצִינַן הָכִי: תַּנָּאֵי הִיא, כְּלוֹמַר: אִיכָּא תַּנָּאֵי דִּפְלִיגִי בְּקִנְיַן פֵּירוֹת דְּרִאשׁוֹן אִי כְּקִנְיַן הַגּוּף דָּמֵי אוֹ לָא, וַאֲנָא סְבִירָא לִי כְּמַאן דְּאָמַר כְּקִנְיַן הַגּוּף דָּמֵי. דְּתַנְיָא כו'. דְּרַבִּי ס"ל לָאו כְּקִנְיַן הַגּוּף דָּמֵי, וְהַךְ בָּרַיְיתָא דְּקָתָנֵי יַחְזְרוּ לְיוֹרְשֵׁי נוֹתֵן — רַבִּי הִיא. וְר"ש ס"ל כְּקִנְיַן הַגּוּף דָּמֵי, וְהַךְ דְּקָתָנֵי יַחְזְרוּ לְיוֹרְשֵׁי רִאשׁוֹן — ר"ש הִיא, וַאֲנָא ס"ל כְּר"ש, וְהַיְינוּ דְּפָסֵיק ר' יוֹחָנָן כְּר"ש. וּמִיהוּ, לְר"ל לָאו בְּקִנְיַן פֵּירוֹת כְּקִנְיַן הַגּוּף דָּמֵי פְּלִיגֵי. אֶלָּא לְכ"ע לָאו כְּקִנְיַן הַגּוּף דָּמֵי, וּבְהָא פְּלִיגֵי, רַבִּי סָבַר: "אַחֲרֶיךָ" נַמִי — קִנְיַן פֵּירוֹת בְּעָלְמָא הוּא דְּאִית לֵיהּ לָרִאשׁוֹן, וְהִלְכָּךְ שֵׁנִי מוֹצִיא מִיַּד הַלָּקוֹחוֹת. וְהֵיכָא דְּמֵת שֵׁנִי — יַחְזְרוּ לְיוֹרְשֵׁי נוֹתֵן, דְּקִנְיַן פֵּירוֹת לָאו כְּקִנְיַן הַגּוּף דָּמֵי. וְרשב"ג סָבַר: בְּעָלְמָא קִנְיַן פֵּירוֹת לָאו כְּקִנְיַן הַגּוּף דָּמֵי, וְהָכָא "אַחֲרֶיךָ" שָׁאנֵי, וְגוּף וּפֵירוֹת אַקְנֵי לָרִאשׁוֹן, הִלְכָּךְ אֵין לַשֵּׁנִי אֶלָּא מַה שֶּׁשִּׁיֵּיר רִאשׁוֹן, וְהֵיכָא דְּמֵת שֵׁנִי — יַחְזְרוּ לְיוֹרְשֵׁי רִאשׁוֹן. וְכֵן עִיקָּר, דְּהַשְׁתָּא לָא תִּקְשֵׁי הִלְכְתָא אַהִלְכְתָא, דְּהָא פָּסְקִינַן הִלְכְתָא כְּרֵישׁ לָקִישׁ בְּפֶ' "הַחוֹלֵץ" דְּקִנְיַן פֵּירוֹת לָאו כְּקִנְיַן הַגּוּף דָּמֵי, וּבְהָא דְּ"אַחֲרֶיךָ לִפְלוֹנִי" קַיְימָא לָן כְּרַבָּן שִׁמְעוֹן דְּאֵין לַשֵּׁנִי אֶלָּא מַה שֶּׁשִּׁיֵּיר רִאשׁוֹן, כִּדְפָסְקִינַן הִלְכְתָא לְקַמָּן, וְלָא פָּלֵיג רֵישׁ לָקִישׁ עַל הַהוּא פְּסַק דְּפָסֵיק רַבִּי יוֹחָנָן לְקַמָּן. וּמִדְּאַבַּיֵי נַמִי אִיכָּא לְמִשְׁמַע דְּהָכִי קַיְימָא לָן, דְּאָמַר אַבַּיֵי: אֵיזֶהוּ רָשָׁע עָרוּם כו'. וּלְקַמָּן נַמִי, בְּהַהִיא אִתְּתָא דַּהֲוָה לָהּ דִּיקְלָא בְּאַרְעָא דְּרַב בִּיבִי בַּר אַבַּיֵי, אֲזַל אִיהוּ אַקְנְיֵיהּ לִבְנוֹ קָטָן כְּרַבָּן שִׁמְעוֹן כו', עַד: אֲפִי' רַבָּן שִׁמְעוֹן לָא קָאָמַר כו' — דְּמֵהָתָם נַמִי שָׁמְעִינַן דְּהִלְכְתָא כְּרַבָּן שִׁמְעוֹן. וְהִלְכָּךְ בָּעֵינַן לְפָרוּשֵׁי דְּרַבָּן שִׁמְעוֹן ס"ל כְּר"ל דְּקִנְיַן פֵּירוֹת לָאו כְּקִנְיַן הַגּוּף דָּמֵי, וְהָכָא הַיְינוּ טַעְמָא: דְּאַחֲרֶיךָ שָׁאנֵי, וְלָא תִּקְשֵׁי הִלְכְתָא אַהִלְכְתָא. וְיָרַד הָרִאשׁוֹן וּמָכַר וְאָכַל. אוֹרְחָא דְּמִילְּתָא נָקַט, שֶׁמָּכַר וְהוֹצִיא הַמָּעוֹת בְּהוֹצָאָה. הַשֵּׁנִי מוֹצִיא מִיַּד הַלָּקוֹחוֹת. אַחַר שֶׁיָּמוּת הָרִאשׁוֹן. דְּקִנְיַן פֵּירוֹת דְּרִאשׁוֹן לָאו כְּקִנְיַן הַגּוּף דָּמֵי. וְ"אַחֲרֶיךָ שָׁאנֵי" לָא אָמְרִינַן אַלִּיבָּא דְּרַבִּי. אֶלָּא מַה שֶּׁשִּׁיֵּיר רִאשׁוֹן. וְאִם לֹא שִׁיֵּיר כְּלוּם — לֹא יִטּוֹל הַשֵּׁנִי כְּלוּם. דְּקִנְיַן פֵּירוֹת דְּרִאשׁוֹן כְּקִנְיַן הַגּוּף דָּמֵי לְר' יוֹחָנָן, וּלְרֵישׁ לָקִישׁ טַעְמָא — מִשּׁוּם דְּאַחֲרֶיךָ שָׁאנֵי. אֵין לָרִאשׁוֹן אֶלָּא אֲכִילַת פֵּירוֹת בִּלְבַד. קס"ד הַשְׁתָּא: פֵּירוֹת יָכוֹל לֶאֱכוֹל וְלִמְכּוֹר, אֲבָל לֹא הַגּוּף, וְאִם מָכַר — הַשֵּׁנִי מוֹצִיא מִיַּד הַלָּקוֹחוֹת. הָא לְגוּפָא. הָא קַמַּיְיתָא דְּקָאָמַר רַבִּי: הַשֵּׁנִי מוֹצִיא — הָנֵי מִילֵּי הֵיכָא דְּמָכַר הַגּוּף, שֶׁאֵין לוֹ לָרִאשׁוֹן אֶלָּא פֵּירוֹת. וְהַךְ בָּרַיְיתָא דְּקָאָמַר: יוֹרֵד רִאשׁוֹן וּמוֹכֵר — אַפֵּירוֹת קָאֵי. הָא לְכַתְּחִלָּה. קָאָמַר ר"ש: אֵין לוֹ לִמְכּוֹר לְכַתְּחִלָּה הַגּוּף, אֶלָּא אֲכִילַת הַפֵּירוֹת, כְּדֵי שֶׁיִּתְקַיֵּים דַּעְתּוֹ שֶׁל נוֹתֵן, דְּהָא גַּלֵּי דַּעְתֵּיהּ דְּנִיחָא לֵיהּ שֶׁיִּשְׁתַּיֵּיר קְצָת לַשֵּׁנִי אִם יִתְרַצֶּה הָרִאשׁוֹן לְשַׁיֵּיר אַחֲרָיו כְּלוּם. וְהָכִי קָתָנֵי: יוֹרֵד רִאשׁוֹן וּמוֹכֵר וְאוֹכֵל מִסְתָּמָא, דִּבְרֵי רַבִּי, שֶׁהֲרֵי אֵינוֹ יָכוֹל לִמְכּוֹר כ"א פֵּירוֹת. רשב"ג אוֹמֵר: אֵין לוֹ לָרִאשׁוֹן לֵירֵד וְלִמְכּוֹר מִסְתָּמָא, שֶׁהֲרֵי הַכֹּל מָכוּר, וְלֹא נִתְקַיְּימָה דַּעַת הַנּוֹתֵן. אֶלָּא אֲכִילַת פֵּירוֹת הוּא דְּאִית לֵיהּ לְכַתְּחִלָּה, אוֹ לְמָכְרָן, אֲבָל גּוּפָא — דִּיעֲבַד אִין, לְכַתְּחִלָּה לָא. וְהָא קַמַּיְיתָא — דִּיעֲבַד, אֵין לַשֵּׁנִי אֶלָּא מַה שֶּׁשִּׁיֵּיר רִאשׁוֹן. אֵיזֶהוּ רָשָׁע עָרוּם. (ב) גּוֹרֵם לַעֲבוֹר עַל דִּבְרֵי הַנּוֹתֵן. עָרוּם. דְּאַהֲנוּ מַעֲשָׂיו, וַהֲרֵי הוּא חוֹטֵא וְלֹא לוֹ. וּמִיהוּ, הַמּוֹכֵר עַצְמוֹ, דְּהַיְינוּ רִאשׁוֹן — לָא מִקְרֵי רָשָׁע, וְאַע"ג דִּלְכַתְּחִלָּה אָסוּר לַעֲשׂוֹת כֵּן, דְּלָא חֲמִיר אִיסּוּרֵיהּ, שֶׁהֲרֵי הִשְׁלִיטוֹ הַנּוֹתֵן בַּגּוּף וּפֵירוֹת לַעֲשׂוֹת בָּהֶן כִּרְצוֹנוֹ. זֶה הַמַּשִּׁיא עֵצָה. לָרִאשׁוֹן לִמְכּוֹר

תוספות

לִמְכּוֹר בִּנְכָסִים. דְּהָא קי"ל כְּר"ש דְּאֵין לַשֵּׁנִי אֶלָּא מַה שֶּׁשִּׁיֵּיר רִאשׁוֹן, וְלֹא נַעֲשָׂה נַחַת רוּחוֹ שֶׁל מֵת שֶׁאָמַר "אַחֲרֶיךָ לִפְלוֹנִי", דַּהֲוָה נִיחָא לֵיהּ אִם יִשְׁתַּיֵּיר. וּמִיהוּ, לָא אַקְפֵּיד קְפִידָא גְּמוּרָה שֶׁלֹּא יוּכַל הָרִאשׁוֹן לְמָכְרָן אִם יִרְצֶה. וּמוֹדֶה. ר"ש, אַע"ג דְּאָמַר: אֵין לַשֵּׁנִי אֶלָּא מַה שֶּׁשִּׁיֵּיר רִאשׁוֹן, אִם נְתָנוֹ אוֹתוֹ רִאשׁוֹן בְּמַתְּנַת שְׁכִיב מְרַע, כְּגוֹן דְּאָמַר "מֵהַיּוֹם וּלְאַחַר מִיתָה" — לֹא אָמַר כְּלוּם, וְהַשֵּׁנִי מוֹצִיא. אִי נַמִי, כְּשֶׁהָיָה שְׁכִיב מְרַע נְתָנָהּ. דִּשְׁתֵּי מַתָּנוֹת הַלָּלוּ שָׁווֹת, כִּדְאָמְרַן לְעֵיל: אֵיזֶהוּ מַתְּנַת בָּרִיא שֶׁהִיא כְּמַתְּנַת שְׁכִיב מְרַע כו'. ה"ג בַּהֲלָכוֹת גְּדוֹלוֹת וּבְפֵירוּשׁ רַבֵּינוּ חֲנַנְאֵל: מ"ט אָמַר אַבַּיֵי מַתְּנַת שְׁכִיב מְרַע אֵימַת הָוְיָא לְאַחַר מִיתָה וּכְבָר קְדָמוֹ אַחֲרֶיךָ. הַאי שֵׁנִי דְּקָאָמַר עָלֵיהּ הַנּוֹתֵן "אַחֲרֶיךָ לִפְלוֹנִי", קָדַם לָזֶה שֶׁנְּתָנוֹ לוֹ הָרִאשׁוֹן. דְּמִשָּׁעָה שֶׁהִתְחִיל הַאי רִאשׁוֹן לִטְרוֹף — קָנָה הַשֵּׁנִי. דְּ"אַחֲרֶיךָ" עִם גְּמַר מִיתָה מַשְׁמַע, דְּמִשָּׁעָה דְּאֵין הָרִאשׁוֹן צָרִיךְ לַנְּכָסִים הַלָּלוּ זִיכָּהוּ הַנּוֹתֵן לָזֶה הַשֵּׁנִי אַחֲרָיו מִיָּד. אֲבָל הַאי מְקַבֵּל מַתָּנָה מֵרִאשׁוֹן — לֹא קָנָה עַד לְאַחַר גְּמַר מִיתָה, דִּסְתָם אָדָם הַנּוֹתֵן מָמוֹנוֹ לְאַחַר מִיתָתוֹ אֵין רוֹצֶה לְהוֹצִיא מָמוֹנוֹ מִכֹּחוֹ עַד שֶׁתִּגָּמֵר מִיתָתוֹ. אֲבָל לְעֵיל, דְּנוֹתֵן סָלֵיק נַפְשֵׁיהּ מֵהָנֵי נְכָסִים, שֶׁהֲרֵי נְתָנוֹ לָרִאשׁוֹן — חָפֵץ הוּא שֶׁיִּזְכֶּה הַשֵּׁנִי עִם גְּמַר מִיתָתוֹ שֶׁל רִאשׁוֹן. וּמִי אָמַר אַבַּיֵי הָכִי. דְּמַתְּנַת שְׁכִיב מְרַע לְאַחַר גְּמַר מִיתָה? עִם גְּמַר מִיתָה. אַלְמָא, בַּהֲדֵי הֲדָדֵי קָנוּ, וְלָא שָׁמְעִינַן אַתָּא דְּחוֹלְקִין בְּשָׁוֶה. מֵהַהִיא. דְּעִם גְּמַר מִיתָה. לָא ס"ד. דְּמֵהַהִיא דִּלְאַחַר מִיתָה הֲדַר בֵּיהּ. דְּהָא וַדַּאי סְתָם שְׁכִיב מְרַע הַנּוֹתֵן לַאֲחֵרִים מָמוֹן שֶׁלּוֹ — אֵין בְּדַעְתּוֹ לְהוֹצִיאוֹ מֵרְשׁוּתוֹ עַד לְאַחַר גְּמַר מִיתָתוֹ. דְּאַשְׁכְּחַן נַמִי כְּה"ג גַּבֵּי אִשְׁתּוֹ כְּשֶׁהוּא מְגָרְשָׁהּ וּמַתִּירָהּ לַאֲחֵרִים, דְּלֹא גָּמַר לְהוֹצִיאָהּ מִכֹּחוֹ עַד לְאַחַר גְּמַר מִיתָתוֹ. דִּתְנַן הֲרֵי זֶה גִּיטֵּךְ אִם מַתִּי. כְּלוֹמַר, אִם אָמוּת — אָז יְהֵא גֵּט. זֶה גִּיטֵּךְ מֵחוֹלִי זֶה. לְאַחַר גְּמַר חוֹלִי, דְּהַיְינוּ לְאַחַר מִיתָה. זֶה גִּיטֵּךְ לְאַחַר מִיתָה לֹא אָמַר כְּלוּם. דְּלֹא גָּמַר לְגָרְשָׁהּ עַד לְאַחַר מִיתָה, וְאֵין גֵּט לְאַחַר מִיתָה. וּדְלָא כְּר' יוֹסֵי מוֹקְמִינַן לָהּ בְּגִיטִּין בְּפֶ' "מִי שֶׁאֲחָזוֹ קוּרְדְּיָיקוֹס". דְּאִי כְּרַבִּי יוֹסֵי — הָאָמַר: זְמַנּוֹ שֶׁל שְׁטָר מוֹכִיחַ עָלָיו, וּכְמַאן דְּאָמַר לָהּ "מֵהַיּוֹם וּלְאַחַר מִיתָה" דָּמֵי, דְּקָתָנֵי הָתָם: חוֹלֶצֶת וְלֹא מִתְיַיבֶּמֶת. וְגַבֵּי "אִם מַתִּי" נַמִי, דָּמֵי כְּמַאן דְּאָמַר "מֵהַיּוֹם אִם מַתִּי", דְּקָתָנֵי הָתָם: הֲרֵי זֶה גֵּט. מִיהוּ, שָׁמְעִינַן מִינַּהּ דִּלְאַחַר מִיתָה קָמְגָרֵשׁ לָהּ, וְה"ה לְמַתְּנָתוֹ, דְּאִי עִם גְּמַר מִיתָה — א"כ הָוֵי גֵּט, וְאַמַּאי קָתָנֵי לֹא אָמַר כְּלוּם? הָיוּ בָּהֶן עֲבָדִים כו'. כְּלוֹמַר, וְרַבָּן שִׁמְעוֹן קָאָמַר דְּמַה שֶּׁמָּכַר רִאשׁוֹן — הַכֹּל הָוֵי מָכוּר, וַאֲפִי' עֲבָדִים וְהוֹצִיאָם לְחֵירוּת. וְקָפָרֵיךְ: פְּשִׁיטָא, דְּכֵיוָן דְּאַקְנֵי גּוּף לָרִאשׁוֹן מָצֵי לְמֶעֱבַד בֵּיהּ כָּל מַה דְּבָעֵי! לְמֶיעֱבַד אִיסּוּרָא. דְּהַמְשַׁחְרֵר עַבְדּוֹ עוֹבֵר בַּעֲשֵׂה דְּ"לְעוֹלָם בָּהֶם תַּעֲבוֹדוּ" (ויקרא כה). תַּכְרִיכֵי הַמֵּת אֲסוּרִין בַּהֲנָאָה. וּבְפֶרֶק "נִגְמַר הַדִּין" (סנהדרין דף מז:) נָפְקָא לָן מִקְּרָאֵי. לְשָׁוְינְהוּ אִיסּוּר הֲנָאָה לָא יְהַבִינְהוּ נִיהֲלֵיהּ. אֶלָּא ע"מ לֵיהָנוֹת בָּהֶן בְּנֵי אָדָם, דְּנִיחָא לֵיהּ לְאִינִישׁ דְּלֵיהֲנוּ אֱינָשֵׁי מִמָּמוֹנֵיהּ וְלֹא יֵלֵךְ לְאִיבּוּד. אֶתְרוֹג זֶה נָתוּן לְךָ בְּמַתָּנָה. כָּל יָמֶיךָ. וְאַחֲרֶיךָ. אַחַר מִיתָתוֹ. לִפְלוֹנִי. לָצֵאת בּוֹ. וְגַם לְאָכְלוֹ אִם יִרְצֶה, דְּהָא לָא קָאָמַר "וְאַחֲרָיו לִפְלוֹנִי". נְטָלוֹ רִאשׁוֹן וְיָצָא בּוֹ. כְּלוֹמַר נְטָלוֹ לָצֵאת בּוֹ, וּבֵירֵךְ עָלָיו. בָּאנוּ לְמַחֲלוֹקֶת כו'. דִּלְרַבִּי לֹא יָצָא רִאשׁוֹן, דְּהָא לֵית לֵיהּ בְּגוּפֵיהּ אֶלָּא קִנְיַן פֵּירוֹת, שֶׁהֲרֵי אֵינוֹ יָכוֹל לְמָכְרוֹ, וְלָא קָרֵינָא בֵּיהּ "לָכֶם". וּלְר"ש רִאשׁוֹן יָצָא, דְּהָא אִי בָּעֵי הֲוָה אָכִיל לֵיהּ אוֹ מְזַבֵּין לֵיהּ, דְּהָא "אַחֲרֶיךָ" קָאָמַר: מַה שֶּׁיִּשְׁתַּיֵּיר אַחֲרֶיךָ. עַד כָּאן לֹא פְּלִיגֵי. רַבִּי וְר"ש בְּפֵירוֹת דְּרִאשׁוֹן, דְּוַדַּאי פֵּירוֹת אִית לֵיהּ. אֶלָּא בְּהָכִי פְּלִיגֵי, דְּר"ש סָבַר: קִנְיַן פֵּירוֹת שֶׁיֵּשׁ לוֹ לָרִאשׁוֹן — כְּקִנְיַן הַגּוּף דָּמֵי, אֲפִי' לְר"ל, דְּ"אַחֲרֶיךָ" שָׁאנֵי. וְרַבִּי סָבַר: לָאו כְּקִנְיַן הַגּוּף דָּמֵי, וְאִם מָכַר אֶת הַגּוּף — לֹא עָשָׂה וְלֹא כְּלוּם. אֲבָל בְּפֵירוֹת הַכֹּל מוֹדִים דְּאִית לֵיהּ. הִלְכָּךְ, גַּבֵּי אֶתְרוֹג נַמִי, יְלֵיאַת יְדֵי חוֹבָתוֹ לִיטְּלוֹ — הַיְינוּ פֵּירוֹתָיו, דַּאֲפִילּוּ לְרַבִּי יָצָא.

דְּאִי

עין משפט נר מצוה

קנב א ב ג ד מיי' פי"ב מהל' זכיה ומתנה הל' ח ט סמג עשין פב טוש"ע חו"מ סי' רמח סעיף ג:

קנג ה ו מיי' שם הלכה י טוש"ע שם ס"ד:

קנד ז מיי' שם ופ"ח שם הל' ח סמג שם טוש"ע חו"מ שם וסי' רנב סעיף א:

קנה ח מיי' פ"ט מהל' גירושין הלכה יב ועיין בהשגות ובמ"מ סמג עשין נ טוש"ע אה"ע סי' קמה סעיף א:

קנו ט י מיי' פי"ב מהל' זכיה ומתנה הל"ט סמג עשין פב טוש"ע ח"מ סי' רמח סעיף ג:

רבינו גרשום

אלא אחריך נמי אי דמי קנין פירות שלו בקנין הגוף או לא תנאי היא: השני. שהוא אחריך: מוציא מיד הלוקח. גוף הקרקע: דברי רבי. דס"ל דהראשון אין לו אלא הפירות וקנין פירות לאו כקנין הגוף דמי ולא מצי זבין הגוף. ורבי סבירא ליה כריש לקיש: ורבן שמעון בן גמליאל אומר אין לשני. מן הגוף: אלא מה ששייר ראשון. שלא מכר לפי שהיה רשאי למכור משום דקנין פירות כקנין הגוף דמי: א) והכא קאמר יורד ראשון מוכר ואוכל משום דקנין פירות כקנין הגוף דמי: ב) אכילת פירות בלבד ואינו רשאי למכור הגוף: דר' אדר' לא קשיא. הא דאמר ראשון מוכר ואוכל מפירי קאמר אבל גופה של קרקע אם מכר ואכל השני מוציא מיד הלוקח דקנין פירות לאו כקנין הגוף דמי: [הא] לכתחלה. אין לראשון אלא אכילת פירות דלאו כקנין הגוף דמי. אבל דיעבד אם מכר ואכל אין לשני בגוף קרקע אלא זה ששייר ראשון: איזהו רשע ערום. שהוא עושה רשע ג) מרשעו זה המשיא עצה שמתייעץ ומוכר נכסים שנתנו לו על מנת שאחריך לפלוני כרבן שמעון בן גמליאל דאמר דאי עבד אין לשני אלא מה ששייר ראשון דהכי קאמר הנותן נכסיי לך ולכל צרכך ואם תשאר כלום יהא אחריך לפלוני: ומודה. רבן שמעון בן גמליאל: שאם נתן ראשון במתנת ש"מ. כלומר מה שנתן במתנת בריא נותן אבל אם נתן במתנת שכיב מרע וכו': לאחר מיתה קונה וכבר קדמו אחריך. שהוא יורש וקנה בגמר מיתה עם שיצא נשמתו של ראשון. אביי אמר עם גמר מיתה: ודלמא הדר ביה [מהא] דאמר אחריך קונה בגמר מיתה: לא ס"ד. אלא ודאי סביר' דמתנת שכ"מ אינ' קונה אלא לאחר מיתה כדתנן הרי זה גיטך אם מתי הרי גיטך אם לא אחיה מחולי זה הרי זה גיטך לאחר מיתה לא אמר כלום. משום דהאי גט כמתנה הוא דקא יהיב ליה ומתנה אינה אלא לאחר מיתה נגמרת וקי"ל דאין גט לאחר מיתה. אלמא דלא הדר ביה מהא דאמר מתנה לאחר מיתה קונה: אפי' היו בהן. באותן נכסים עבדים והוציאן לחירות. מה שעשה עשוי ואין לשני אלא מה ששייר ראשון: פשיטא. מה לי עבדים מה לי שאר נכסים: מהו דתימא מצי אמר לי'. הנותן למיעבד איסורא לא יהבי לך. והאי דהוצאת עבדים לחירות איסור הוא דעובר בעשה דכתיב לעולם בהם תעבודו ואימא דלא עבד כלום. קמ"ל דמה שעשה עשה: תכריכין למת. איסורי הנאה נינהו: באנו למחלוקת רבי ורשב"ג. דלעיל אם יכול לצאת בו ידי חובתו דרבי דסבר קנין פירות לאו כקנין הגוף דמי סבירא ליה הואיל דהאי אתרוג לא יהבי נהליה כי אם לפירות לחודייהו דהיינו הברכה לאו כקנין הגוף של אתרוג דמי. ולא יצא דמשום דלא שלו הוא וקיימא לן יום טוב הראשון של חג אין אדם יוצא ידי חובתו בלולב של חבירו. ורשב"ג סבר דיצא משום דקנין פירות כקנין הגוף דמי: אבל הכא גבי אתרוג מאי קנין פירות איכא הכא:

למאי

הגהות הב"ח

(א) גמ' מהו דתימא מצי אמר ליה למיעבד איסורא לא יהבינהו לך: (ב) רשב"ם ד"ה איזהו רשע ערום רשע גורם:

א) נ"ל קשיא דרבי אדרבי דהכא קאמר וכו'. ב) נ"ל ורשב"ג אדרשב"ג דהכא קאמר דאין לראשון אלא אכילת פירות בלבד: ג) אולי נ"ל שהוא עושה רשע מערמתו.

אי מיפק לא נפיק ביה, למאי יהביה ניהליה? אלא, מיפק – דכולי עלמא לא פליגי דנפיק ביה, (א) מכרה או אכלה – באנו למחלוקת רב ורבן שמעון בן גמליאל. אמר רבה בר רב הונא: אהאחין שקנו אתרוג בתפוסת הבית, נטלו אחד מהן ויצא בו, אם יכול לאוכלו – יצא, ואם לאו – לא יצא: בודוקא דאיכא אתרוג לכל חד וחד, (ב) אבל פריש או רמון – לא. א)אמר רבא: ג"אתרוג זה נתון לך במתנה ע"מ שתחזירהו לי", נטלו ויצא בו, החזירו – יצא, לא החזירו – לא יצא. קא משמע לן: דמתנה על מנת להחזיר שמה מתנה. ההיא איתתא דהוה לה דיקלא בארעא דרב ביבי בר אביי. כל אימת דהות אזלא למיגזריה, הוה קפיד עילוה. אקניתיה ניהליה כל שני חייו, אזל איהו אקנייה יהליה לבנו קטן; אמר רב הונא בריה דרב יהושע: ב)משום דאתו ממולאי אמריתו מילי מולייתא? האפילו רשב"ג לא קאמר אלא לאחר, אבל לעצמו לא. אמר רבא אמר רב נחמן: "שור זה נתון לך במתנה על מנת שתחזירהו לי", הקדישו והחזירו – ה"ז מוקדש ומוחזר. אמר ליה רבא לרב נחמן: מאי אהדריה? (ג) אמר ליה: ומאי חסריה? אלא אמר רב אשי: יחזינן, אי אמר ליה "על מנת שתחזירהו" – הא אהדריה, אי א"ל "על מנת שתחזירהו לי" – מידי דחזי ליה קאמר ליה. ג)אמר רב יהודה אמר שמואל: הכותב נכסיו לאחר, ואמר הלה "אי אפשי בהן" – קנה, ואפילו עומד וצווח; ורבי יוחנן אמר: זלא קנה. אמר רבי אבא בר ממל, ולא פליגי: כאן

דאי מיפק לא נפיק ראשון, לרבי, למאי יהביה ניהליה? שהרי אין בו פירות אחרות, והגוף אינו יכול למכור ולאכול, ולא ניתן לראשון אלא לקיים בו מצות נטילה. ו"לכם" קרינן ביה, דאין לשני כח בו כל זמן שראוי לזה הראשון לצאת בו, דהא "אחריך" קאמר. ולא דמי לאתרוג השותפין שאין יוצא בו כדלקמן, דהתם כולהו מיהא הוו שותפין ביחד, אבל הכא אינו משועבד לשני כלל כל ימי חיי הראשון. (ד) מכרה או שאכלה. דלרבי צריך לשלם דמי אתרוג לשני, ולרבן שמעון אין לשני אלא מה ששייר ראשון. ולאשמועינן אתא, דכי היכי דפליגי בקרקעות – פליגי באתרוג. דלרבי יורד הראשון ומוכרו לצאת בו, דלפירי יהביה ניהליה – והיינו פירותיו. ולרבן שמעון אין לו לכתחלה אלא אכילת פירות, דהיינו לצאת בו, ואם מכר (ה) – מכור. ומשום דסד"א מכור, דאפי' רבי מודה דלגופו יהביה לראשון, דהא ליכא פירות – קא משמע לן דליטלו ולצאת בו היינו פירות שנתן לראשון, והגוף נתן לשני. שקנו אתרוג. ירשו מאביהן, או לקחו במעות ירושת אביהן בתפוסת הבית, כל זמן שלא חלקו. ונטלו אחד מן האחין בלא דעת חבירו, ויצא בו – רואין, אם אין האחין מקפידין זה על זה ויכול לאכלו בלא רשותם, כגון שיש אתרוגים הרבה בתפוסת הבית, או שימצאו הרבה אתרוגים בעיר, או שכבר יצאו ואין צריכין לו עוד. יצא. דקרינא ביה "לכם", שהרי כולו שלו הוא. ואם לאו לא יצא. דכתיב (ויקרא כג): "ולקחתם לכם" – משלכם, שיהא כולו שלו, ולא שמקנתו שלו. דאע"ג דדרשינן בשחיטת חולין בפ' "ראשית הגז" (דף קלה: קלו.): "בגדיכם" "עריסותיכם" "תרומותיכם" – לרבות טלית של שותפין ועיסת השותפין ותבואת השותפין, שחייבין בציצית ובחלה ובתרומה – ה"ה נמי אי הוה כתיב הכא: "פרי עץ הדרכס" אפי' של שותפות, אבל כיון דכתיב: "לכם" – צריך שתהא כולו שלו. והאי דלא כתיב "ולקחת לך" – היינו למדרש מיניה שתהא לקיחה לכל אחד ואחד, כדדרשינן במס' סוכה (דף מא:) ובתורת כהנים. ומנהג שלנו שנהגו לברך כל הקהל באתרוג אחד – דעתנו מסכמת לתת כל אחד במתנה את חלקו לחבירו, כדאמרינן גבי רבן גמליאל ור' יהושע במסכת סוכה (שם) ואע"ג דלא פריש – כמאן דפריש דמי. דלא גרע ממתנה ע"מ להחזיר, דלהכי מיהא דעת כל הקהל שוה – שיתן לכל אחד עד שיברך עליו, ואח"כ יחזיר. והני מילי ביו"ט ראשון. אבל ביו"ט שני, אמרי' מתוך שיוצא בשאול – יוצא בגזול. ומה שכתוב בספרים: ודוקא אתרוג אבל פריש ורמון לא – אריכות פירוש של שוטים הוא, ואינו מן הגמרא. כן נראה בעיני, וכשר. החזירו יצא. איגלאי מילתא למפרע דהויא מתנה מעיקרא, שהרי קיים עתה תנאי, שהמתנה היתה תלויה בתנאי ונתקיים. ואם לאו. אלא מכרו או אכלו – לא יצא, דאיגלאי מילתא דלא הויא מתנה. ואע"ג דלגבי גיטין קי"ל כר"מ דבעי תנאי כפול, כדאמר בפרק "מי שאחזו" (גיטין דף עה:): אתקין שמואל בגיטא דשכיב מרע כו – הני מילי לענין גיטין וקדושין הוא דבעינן תנאי כפול לכתחלה, לרווחא דמילתא, דילפינן מתנאי בני גד ובני ראובן. מיהא, לגבי דיני ממונות לא בעינן תנאי כפול, אלא גלויי דעתא בעלמא. וכיון דאמר "ע"מ שתחזירהו לי", ואע"ג דלא כפליה למימר "ואם לא תחזירהו לא תהא מתנה" אפ"ה לא הוי מתנה אא"כ נתקיים התנאי. דהא אפילו היכא דלא פירש כלום, והיכא דמיתלי באומדן דעתא – אזלינן בתר אומדן דעתא בפירקין לעיל גבי דיניס הרבה, כגון הכותב נכסיו לאשתו (דף קלא:) ולקמן בפרק "מי שמת" (דף קמח:) גבי שכיב מרע שכתב כל נכסיו לאחרים, וגבי מי ששמע שמת בנו וכתב נכסיו לאחרים ואח"כ בא בנו, דאמר בפרק "מי שמת" (לקמן דף קמו:) דלא הויא מתנה. אקניתיה ניהליה כל ימי חייו. ד"ב ביבי, ואחריו יחזור לה וליורשיה. אקנייה לבנו קטן. כרבן שמעון, דאמר: אין לשני אלא מה ששייר ראשון. ואע"ג דרבן שמעון לכתחלה אסר – הני מילי כשאמר לו נותן "אחריך לפלוני", דבעינן שישתייר לאותו פלוני אחריו רצה. אבל הך איתתא, כיון דיהבה ליה לגמרי כל ימי חייו, ולא פירשה לו לתת אחריו לאדם אחר, אלא לעצמו – לקורת רוחו של רב ביבי נתכוונה, ואפי' ליתנו לכתחלה לכל מי שירצה. והאי דאקני לבנו קטן – היינו כדי שלא תוכל האשה לחזור ולקנות ממנו. א"נ, לפי שסמוך על שלחנו, ויאכל רב ביבי הפירות תחת מזונות בנו. ונראה בעיני דלא גרס "לבנו קטן", אלא "לבנו" גרידא, וכן כתב בפירושי ר"ח, ואגב שיטפא דכתב הכי בגמרא בשאר מקומות כתבו נמי אף בכאן. ממולאי. כדאמר בר"ה (דף יח. ע"ש): רבה ואביי מדבית עלי קאתו. ועל שם מקומן נקראו בני עלי ממולאי, כדאמר בבראשית רבה בתחלת פרשה נ"ט: "ואברהם זקן" עטרת תפארת שיבה וגו' ר"מ אזל לממלא, ראה אותם שחורי ראש. אמר להם: שמא ממשפחת עלי אתם, דכתיב ביה: "וכל מרבית ביתך ימותו אנשים", אמרו: רבי, התפלל עלינו. אמר להם: לכו וטיפלו לצדקה ואתם זוכין לזקנה כו'. וה"נ אמר בר"ה (שם): "אם יתכפר עון בית עלי בזבח ומנחה" – בזבח ומנחה הוא דאין מתכפר, אבל מתכפר בתורה ובגמ"ח. אמריתו מילי מולייתא. דברים כרותים שאין בהם ממש, לשון "ימל קצירו" (איוב יח). א"נ: כגון מוליא במוליא, ב"חזקת הבתים" (לעיל דף נד.) – גבשושיות. כלומר, דברים בעלי מומין. ועל שם מקומם מגדפם, כדכתיב: "בתי אכזב לאכזב ועקרון תעקר" (מיכה א). אפי' רבן שמעון לא קאמר. דמה שמכר ראשון הוי מכור, אלא כשאמר "נכסי לך ואחריך לאחר". אבל כשאמר "ואחריך לעצמי", כי הך איתתא דלא אקניתיה לך אלא לימי חייך, ורוצה היא שאחריך יחזור לה – אפילו רשב"ג מודה דלא אקנייה לך אלא פירות, ומאי דאקנית לברך – לא אהני מידי, אלא לפירות כל ימי חייך. אמר רבא אמר רב נחמן שור זה כו'. נראה בעיני דהקמי הא עובדא דרב ביבי גרס לה, דדמיא להך דאמר רבא: אתרוג זה נתון לך במתנה ע"מ שתחזירהו לי. שור זה נתון לך במתנה עד זמן פלוני לעשות בו מלאכתך. על מנת שתחזירהו לי. אחר הזמן. הרי זה מוקדש ומוחזר. כלומר, הרי זה מוקדש, שהרי מותר הוא ונתקיים התנאי, דאיגלאי מילתא דהויא מתנה למפרע. ונראה בעיני דאם מת בתוך הזמן – דפטור מלשלם, דלא הוה שואל לאתחייב באונסין, ואף לא שומר להתחייב בגניבה ואבידה, אלא מקבל מתנה הוא, ולא נתחייב אלא בפשיעה. "ע"מ שתחזירהו לי" קאמר ליה, שיהא חזרתו לעצמו. מאי אהדריה. אבל כיון שהקדישו – אין זו כי אם חזרה להקדש! ה"ג: הכותב נכסיו לאחר. ולא גרס "כל". קנה ואפי' עומד צווח. איני חפץ במתנה זו. וטעמא מפרש לקמיה.

כאן

אבל פריש או רמון לא. פירש בקונטרס: לא גרסינן לה. ויש לפרש בדוחק: דוקא דיש לנותן אתרוג מלבד אות' שנטל מקבל מתנה, ואינו מקפיד אם יאכל הלה את האתרוג. אבל אי לית ליה לנותן אלא פריש או רמון – לא יצא, דמסתמא יקפיד אם יאכל הלה את האתרוג. ודוחק. לא החזירו לא יצא. וא"ת: אמאי לא יצא אפילו כי כפליה לתנאי? והא הוה תנאי ומעשה בדבר אחד, ואין זה כתנאי בני גד ובני ראובן, כדאמרינן ב"מי שאחזו" (גיטין דף עה. ושם): "ה"ז גיטך והנייר שלי" – אינה מגורשת, "על מנת שהנייר שלי" – מגורשת. ופריך: מאי שנא רישא ומאי שנא סיפא? אמר רבא: משום דהוי מעשה קודם לתנאי, ולכך התנאי בטל ומגורשת. ופריך רב אדא בר אהבה: טעמא דהוי מעשה קודם לתנאי, הא לאו הכי – לא? מכדי, כל תנאי גמרינן מתנאי בני גד ובני ראובן, מה התם לא הוי תנאי ומעשה בדבר אחד כו'! אלא אמר רב אדא בר אהבה: משום דהוי תנאי ומעשה בדבר אחד. ומיהו, יש לומר דרבא דהכא סבר דלא בעינן תנאי (ו) ומעשה בדבר אחד, דהא התם נמי לא בעי. אי נמי, רב אדא ס"ל דכל האומר "על מנת" לאו כאומר "מעכשיו" דמי, ולהכי הוי מעשה ותנאי בדבר אחד, שאינו מגרשה אלא כשתחזיר לו הנייר, ואיך תתגרש כשהגט בידו, ולהכי הוי מעשה ותנאי בדבר אחד ולא חשיב תנאי. אבל רבא סבר: כל האומר "על מנת" כאומר "מעכשיו" דמי, ולא הוי תנאי ומעשה בדבר אחד, ויכולים המעשה והתנאי להתקיים, ומגורשת מיד, ואחר כך תקיים התנאי. אי נמי, התם כרבי מאיר, והכא כרבנן ד).

באן

קנז א ב מיי' פ"ח מהל' לולב הלכה יא ועי' במ"מ סמג עשין מד טוש"ע א"ח סי' תרכח סעיף ח:

קנח ג מיי' שם הל' י טוש"ע שם סעיף ד וסעיף ה:

קנט ד מיי' שם ופ"ג מהל' זכיה ומתנה הל"ט סמג שם וסי' פב טוש"ע שם וטוש"ע חו"מ סי' רמא סעיף ו:

קס ה מיי' פי"ב מהל' זכיה ומתנה הלכה י ועי' בהגהות ובמ"מ סמג עשין פב טוש"ע חו"מ סי' רמח סעיף ד:

קסא ו מיי' שם פ"ג הלכה י סמג עשין פב טוש"ע חו"מ סי' רמא סעיף ז:

קסב ז מיי' שם פ"ט הלכה יג סמג שם טוש"ע חו"מ סי' רמה ס"י:

רבינו גרשום

למאי יהביה נהליה אלא למיפק ביה. ולהכי חשיב שלו ונפיק ביה והדר ביה לאחריך אלא אי דמי מחלוקת להא דמי. מכרו ראשון או אכלו. להאי אתרוג: באנו למחלוק' רבי ורשב"ג דר' דסבר קנין פירות לאו כקנין הגוף דמי. סבירא ליה דלא הקנה לו אלא הפירות לברכה והואיל שמכר הגוף השני מוציא מיד הלקוחות. ואם אכלו משלם ליה. ר' שמעון בן גמליאל סבר דאכלו או מכרו אין לשני כלום דקנין פירות כקנין הגוף דמי ומצי מזבין: בתפוסת הבית. דממון של אביהן קודם שנחלקו. נטלו אחד א) יכול ליקח לו אתרוג בזה יצא דדידיה הוא: ואם לאו לא יצא. משום דלולב הגזול הוי ופסול: ודוקא. אם נשתיירו שם כדי לקנות אתרוג לכל אחד. אבל אם אין שם אלא כדי לקנות פריש או רמון לכל אחד ואחד לא יצא: והחזירו יצא. לפי שקיים התנאי ולא הוי גזל: למיגזרא. פירי דקל: הוי קא קפיד עליה. אמר לה דושית עלוי הזרעים שלי את דורסת: אקניתה נהליה כל שנותיו דרב ביבי. אקנייה לבן קטן. משום דקטן קונה ואינו מקנה כדי שלא יוציאנה אדם מידו לא במתנה ולא במכר עד שיגדיל כדי שתהא תחת ידו עד זמן מרובה. משמע משום דסבר רב ביבי כרבן שמעון בן גמליאל דאמר אין לשני כלום אלא מה ששייר ראשון והא אתתא גופא דאקניתיה לפירא דיקלא או לקצוץ ממנה ענפים לר' ביבי כל ימי חייו איקנא ליה ואחריו של רב ביבי תחזור לידה דקל שלה וקדם רב ביבי עד שהוא בחיים והקנהו לבניו להוציאו מידה: אמר ליה רב [הונא ברי' דר"י] משום דאתו ממולאי. מבית עלי: אמריתו מילי מוליאתא. מקוצצו' ומקולקלו'. ואפי' רשב"ג לא אמר דאם קדם ראשון ומכר מכור אלא להיכא דאמר לו הנותן ואחריך ב) לי לעצמי כמו זו האשה שלא נתן אלא לימי חייו ומשמע דאחרי' תחזור דקל שלו לעצמה מי אמר ר' שמעון בן גמליאל דמצי זבין והאי דרב ביבי נמי לא מצי לאקנויי לבנו דהוא לא סילקה עצמה לגמרי אלא בחייו בלבד: הרי זה מוקדש ומוחזר. דאע"ג דמוקדש הוי מוחזר דאין חייב להחזיר לו אחר: מאי אהדריה. הא אסרו עליו בהנאה: אמר ליה ומאי חסריה. שור נתן לו שור החזיר לו ולעולם מוקדש ומוחזר הוא: אי א"ל ע"מ שתחזירהו לי מידי דחזי ליה קאמר ליה. והאי לאו ראוי לו שמוקדש הוא וחייב להעמיד לו אחר: ור' יוחנן אמר לא קנה. הואיל שאינו רוצה:

שותק

א) נראה דצ"ל אם יכול ליקח האתרוג ולאכלו יצא דכדידיה הוא. ב) נ"ל דאמר לו הנותן ואחריך לפלוני אבל אם אמר לו ואחריך לי לעצמי כמו זו האשה וכו'.

א) קדושין ו: סוכה מא:. ב) ערכין כה: ב"מ קט. לקמן קנא. יבמות עה: עו. כתובות פה.: ג) כריתות כד. גיטין לב.: ד) [וע"ע תוס' סוכה מא: ד"ה הילך ותוס' קדושין ו: ד"ה לא ודף מט: ד"ה לדברים ותוס' גיטין עה: ד"ה לתנאי]:

הגהות הב"ח

(א) גמ' מכרו או אכלו באנו למחלוקת: (ב) שם אתרוג לכל חד וחד אמר רבא כצ"ל ותיבות אבל פריש או רמון לא נמחק: (ג) שם מאי אהדריה (אמר ליה ומאי חסריה) תא"מ ונ"ב ס"א אינו: (ד) רשב"ם ד"ה מכרו או אכלו וכו' ומוכרו לצאת בו דלפירי יהביניה. נ"ב כלומר אבל גופו אינו מכור: (ה) בא"ד ואם מכר גופו מכור ומשום דסד"א גופו מכור לד"ה דאפילו רבי מודה: (ו) תום' ד"ה לא וכו' סבר דלא בעינן תנאי בדבר אחד ומעשה.

א) כריתות כד: חולין לט:: ב) גיטין נ:: ג) בס"י יחזור בו: ד) [עי' תוס' מנחות נח: ד"ה ואיכא]:

א כָּאן בְּצוֹוֵחַ מֵעִיקָּרָא, כָּאן בְּשׁוֹתֵק מֵעִיקָּרָא וּלְבַסּוֹף צוֹוֵחַ. אָמַר רַב נַחְמָן בַּר יִצְחָק: זִיכָּה לוֹ עַל יְדֵי אַחֵר, וְשָׁתַק וּלְבַסּוֹף צָוַוח — בָּאנוּ לְמַחְלוֹקֶת רַבָּן שִׁמְעוֹן בֶּן גַּמְלִיאֵל וְרַבָּנַן; דְּתַנְיָא: א) הַכּוֹתֵב נְכָסָיו לְאַחֵר וְהָיוּ בָּהֶן עֲבָדִים, וְאָמַר הַלָּה "אִי אֶפְשִׁי בָּהֶן", אִם הָיָה רַבָּן שֵׁנִי כֹּהֵן — הֲרֵי אֵלּוּ אוֹכְלִין בִּתְרוּמָה; ב רַבָּן שִׁמְעוֹן בֶּן גַּמְלִיאֵל אוֹמֵר: כֵּיוָן שֶׁאָמַר הַלָּה "אִי אֶפְשִׁי בָּהֶן" — כְּבָר זָכוּ בָּהֶן יוֹרְשִׁין; וְהָוֵינַן בָּהּ: וְת"ק, אֲפִילּוּ עוֹמֵד וְצוֹוֵחַ?! אָמַר רָבָא, וְאִיתֵּימָא רַבִּי יוֹחָנָן: בְּצוֹוֵחַ מֵעִיקָּרוֹ — דְּכוּלֵּי עָלְמָא לָא פְּלִיגִי דְּלָא קָנֵי, שָׁתַק וּלְבַסּוֹף צָוַוח — דְּכוּלֵּי עָלְמָא לָא פְּלִיגִי דְּקָנֵי, ג כִּי פְּלִיגִי — שֶׁזִּיכָּה לוֹ עַל יְדֵי אַחֵר וְשָׁתַק וּלְבַסּוֹף צָוַוח, דְּתַנָּא קַמָּא סָבַר: מִדִּשְׁתֵיק — קָנֵינְהוּ, וְהַאי דְּקָא צָוַוח — מֵהֲדַר הוּא דְּקָא הָדַר בֵּיהּ, וְרַבָּן שִׁמְעוֹן בֶּן גַּמְלִיאֵל סָבַר: הוֹכִיחַ סוֹפוֹ עַל תְּחִלָּתוֹ, וְהַאי דְּלָא צָוַוח עַד הַשְׁתָּא — דְּסָבַר: כִּי לָא מָטוּ לִידַי (א) מַאי אֶצְווַח. ב) תָּנוּ רַבָּנַן: ד שְׁכִיב מְרַע שֶׁאָמַר "תְּנוּ מָאתַיִם זוּז לִפְלוֹנִי, וּשְׁלֹשׁ מֵאוֹת לִפְלוֹנִי, וְאַרְבַּע מֵאוֹת לִפְלוֹנִי" — אֵין אוֹמְרִין: כׇּל הַקּוֹדֵם בַּשְּׁטָר זוֹכֶה. לְפִיכָךְ, יָצָא עָלָיו שְׁטַר חוֹב — גּוֹבֶה מִכּוּלָּם; ה אֲבָל אָמַר "תְּנוּ מָאתַיִם זוּז לִפְלוֹנִי, וְאַחֲרָיו לִפְלוֹנִי, וְאַחֲרָיו לִפְלוֹנִי" — אוֹמְרִין: כׇּל הַקּוֹדֵם בַּשְּׁטָר זוֹכֶה. לְפִיכָךְ, יָצָא עָלָיו שט"ח — גּוֹבֶה מִן הָאַחֲרוֹן, אֵין לוֹ — גּוֹבֶה מִשֶּׁלְּפָנָיו, אֵין לוֹ — גּוֹבֶה מִשֶּׁלִּפְנֵי פָנָיו. תָּנוּ רַבָּנַן: ו שְׁכִיב מְרַע שֶׁאָמַר "תְּנוּ מָאתַיִם זוּז לִפְלוֹנִי בְּנִי בְּכוֹר כָּרָאוּי לוֹ" — נוֹטְלָן וְנוֹטֵל אֶת בְּכוֹרָתוֹ. אִם אָמַר "בִּבְכוֹרָתוֹ" — יָדוֹ עַל הָעֶלְיוֹנָה, רָצָה נוֹטְלָן, רָצָה נוֹטֵל בְּכוֹרָתוֹ; ז וּשְׁכִיב מְרַע שֶׁאָמַר "תְּנוּ מָאתַיִם זוּז לִפְלוֹנִית אִשְׁתִּי כָּרָאוּי לָהּ" — נוֹטַלְתָּן וְנוֹטֶלֶת אֶת כְּתוּבָּתָהּ. אִם אָמַר "בִּכְתוּבָּתָהּ" —

יָדָהּ

כָּאן בְּצוֹוֵחַ מֵעִיקָּרָא. מִתְּחִלָּה, כְּשֶׁמָּסַר לוֹ זֶה אֶת הַשְּׁטָר, הִתְחִיל צוֹוֵחַ. הִלְכָּךְ לֹא קָנָה, שֶׁאֵין מְזַכִּין לוֹ לְאָדָם בְּעַל כָּרְחוֹ, דְּחוֹב הוּא לוֹ, דִּכְתִיב (משלי טו): "שׂוֹנֵא מַתָּנוֹת יִחְיֶה", וּכְדְאָמְרִינַן [בְּ"אֵלּוּ טְרֵיפוֹת"] (חולין ד' מד:). וְהַנּוֹתֵן עַצְמוֹ — לֹא (ג) תַּחֲזִיר לוֹ, שֶׁהֲרֵי סִילֵּק עַצְמוֹ מֵהֶם. אֶלָּא הֶפְקֵר הֵם, וְכׇל הַמַּחֲזִיק בָּהֶן זָכָה בָּהֶן, כִּדְאָמְרִינַן בִּכְרֵיתוֹת בִּתְחִלַּת פֶּרֶק "הַמֵּבִיא אָשָׁם תָּלוּי" (דף כד.), אָמַר רֵישׁ לָקִישׁ: הַנּוֹתֵן מַתָּנָה לַחֲבֵירוֹ וְאָמַר הַלָּה "אִי אֶפְשִׁי" (ג) — כׇּל הַמַּחֲזִיק בָּהּ זָכָה בָּהּ. וְאַסְּקִינַן הָתָם כְּרֵישׁ לָקִישׁ. **כָּאן בְּשָׁתַק וּלְבַסּוֹף צָוַוח.** קָנָה. כֵּיוָן דְּקִיבֵּל הַשְּׁטָר בִּשְׁתִיקָה — נִתְרַצָּה לִזְכּוֹת בַּמַּתָּנָה, וּמֵאַחַר שֶׁזָּכָה — אֵין מוֹעִיל כְּלוּם לְהוֹצִיאָהּ מֵרְשׁוּתוֹ (ג) מַה שֶּׁאָמַר "אִי אֶפְשִׁי בְּמַתָּנָה זוֹ", עַד שֶׁיִּתְנֶה בִּלְשׁוֹן מַתָּנָה לַאֲחֵרִים, אוֹ שֶׁיַּפְקִירֵם. **זִיכָּה לוֹ ע"י אַחֵר.** בְּפָנָיו, וְהוּא שָׁתַק כְּשֶׁמְּסָרוֹ אֶת הַשְּׁטָר אוֹ הִקְנוּ בְּקִנְיַן סוּדָר לַאֲחֵרִים לְצׇרְכּוֹ. וּכְשֶׁבָּאוּ לִמְסוֹר לוֹ הַשְּׁטָר — הִתְחִיל צוֹוֵחַ. **בָּאנוּ לְמַחְלוֹקֶת.** אִם קָנָה אִם לָאו. **וְהָיוּ בָּהֶן עֲבָדִים.** וּמִתּוֹךְ כָּךְ צָוַוח, שֶׁאֵינוֹ רוֹצֶה לָזוּן הָעֲבָדִים. דַּאֲפִי' לְמ"ד יָכוֹל הָרַב לוֹמַר לָעֶבֶד "עֲשֵׂה (ד) וְאֵינִי זָנְךָ", אֲפ"ה לָא נִיחָא לֵיהּ לַעֲשׂוֹת כֵּן. **רַבָּן שֵׁנִי.** מְקַבֵּל מַתָּנָה. **אוֹכְלִין בִּתְרוּמָה.** מֵחֲמַת הַשֵּׁנִי, דְּוַדַּאי קָנָה, וּכְתִיב "וְכֹהֵן כִּי יִקְנֶה נֶפֶשׁ קִנְיַן כַּסְפּוֹ הוּא יֹאכַל בּוֹ" (ויקרא כב). **יוֹרְשִׁין.** כְּלוֹמַר, רִאשׁוֹן אוֹ יוֹרְשָׁיו. (ה) וּלְרַבָּן שִׁמְעוֹן לָא סְבִירָא לֵיהּ הָא דְּרֵישׁ לָקִישׁ דְּאָמַר בִּכְרֵיתוֹת בְּפֶרֶק "הַמֵּבִיא": הַנּוֹתֵן מַתָּנָה לַחֲבֵירוֹ וְאָמַר הַלָּה "אִי אֶפְשִׁי בָּהּ" — כׇּל הַמַּחֲזִיק בָּהּ זָכָה בָּהּ. דִּסְבִירָא לֵיהּ לְרַבָּן שִׁמְעוֹן דְּאַדַּעְתָּא דְּהָכִי יָהֵיב לֵיהּ, דְּאִי לָא בָּעֵי מְקַבֵּל מַתָּנָה — תִּיהֲדַר לֵיהּ. וְהָכִי מְפָרֵשׁ בִּכְרֵיתוֹת. וּמִיהוּ, הִלְכְתָא כְּרֵישׁ לָקִישׁ. וּבְהַךְ פְּלוּגְתָּא נַמִי הִלְכְתָא כְּרַבָּנַן. דְּהָא דְּקי"ל "הֲלָכָה כרשב"ג בְּמִשְׁנָתֵנוּ" — הַיְינוּ מִשְׁנָה, אֲבָל בָּרַיְיתָא — לָא, אֶלָּא הֲלָכָה כְּרַבָּנַן. דְּ"מִשְׁנָתֵינוּ" — מַתְנִי' מַשְׁמַע, אֲבָל הֵיכָא דְּאָמְרִי' "מִשְׁנָה" — הַיְינוּ נַמִי בָּרַיְיתָא, כִּדְאָמְרִי' בְּעָלְמָא (גיטין דף סז.): מִשְׁנַת ר' אֱלִיעֶזֶר בֶּן יַעֲקֹב קַב וְנָקִי, וּמִשּׁוּ"ה קי"ל כְּוָתֵיהּ בֵּין בְּמִשְׁנָה בֵּין בְּבָרַיְיתָא. **הוֹכִיחַ סוֹפוֹ.** שֶׁצָּוַוח, עַל הַשְּׁתִיקָה שֶׁבַּתְּחִלָּה, דְּלָא נִתְרַצָּה בַּמַּתָּנָה. אֶלָּא לְהָכִי שָׁתַק, דִּגְנַאי הִיא לִצְווֹחַ כׇּל זְמַן שֶׁלֹּא הִגִּיעַ מַתָּנָה לְיָדוֹ. **תָּנוּ רַבָּנַן שְׁכִיב מְרַע כו'.** לְהָכִי נָקַט שְׁכִיב מְרַע, דִּבְדִידֵיהּ אִיכָּא לְאִיפְלוּגֵי בֵּין הֵיכָא דְּאָמַר "אַחֲרָיו לִפְלוֹנִי" לְהֵיכָא דְּלָא אָמַר, מִשּׁוּם דְּרָאוּי לְחַלֵּק כׇּל נְכָסָיו בְּדִבּוּר פִּיו, לָזֶה כָּךְ וְלָזֶה כָּךְ. אֲבָל בָּרִיא — רָגִיל לִיתֵּן לְכׇל אֶחָד בִּפְנֵי עַצְמוֹ, וְהַדָּבָר יָדוּעַ לְמִי מַקְנֶה תְּחִלָּה וּלְמִי לְבַסּוֹף. **שֶׁאָמַר תְּנוּ מָאתַיִם זוּז כו'.** וּכְגוֹן דְּלָא שִׁיֵּיר אַחֲרֵיהֶן כְּלוּם. דְּאִי שִׁיֵּיר מִידֵּי שֶׁלֹּא חָלַק לָהֶם, אע"ג דְּמִית — לֹא קָנוּ, אא"כ הִקְנָה לָהֶם בְּקִנְיַן סוּדָר, כְּדְפָסְקִינַן לְקַמָּן בְּ"מִי שֶׁמֵּת" (דף קנא:): מַתְּנַת שְׁכִיב מְרַע בְּמִקְצָת בָּעֵי קִנְיָן, וְאע"ג דְּמִית. **אִם יָצָא עָלָיו שט"ח.** קוֹדֶם שֶׁקִּבְּלוּ הַמָּעוֹת. אִי נַמִי, כְּגוֹן דְּהָנֵי מָאתַיִם זוּז וּשְׁלֹשׁ מֵאוֹת זוּז (ו) — שָׂדוֹת שֶׁשָּׁוּוֹת כָּךְ וְכָךְ דָּמִים. הִלְכָּךְ, אֲפִי' לְאַחַר שֶׁגָּבוּ — גּוֹבֶה בַּעַל חוֹב מֵהֶן, דִּמְקַבֵּל מַתְּנַת שְׁכִיב מְרַע *כְּיוֹרֵשׁ שַׁוְיוּהּ רַבָּנַן לְקַמָּן בְּ"מִי שֶׁמֵּת", וּמְקַרְקְעֵי דְּיַתְמֵי מִשְׁתַּעְבְּדֵי לְבַעַל חוֹב. **גּוֹבֶה מִכּוּלָּן.** שֶׁהֲרֵי לְכוּלָּם נִתְכַּוֵּין לִיתֵּן בְּיַחַד, אֶלָּא שֶׁאֵין אָדָם יָכוֹל לְהוֹצִיא שְׁנֵי דְבָרִים כְּאֶחָד. וּכְגוֹן שֶׁלֹּא שָׁתַק בֵּינְתַיִם, דְּהַיְינוּ נִמְלַךְ, לְקַמָּן בְּ"מִי שֶׁמֵּת". הִלְכָּךְ גּוֹבֶה מִכּוּלָּן, מִן הַמְּעַט יַמְעִיט וּמִן הָרַב יַרְבֶּה, כְּגוֹן אִם בָּא בַּעַל חוֹב לִטְרוֹף תֵּשַׁע דִּינָרִין — גּוֹבֶה מִן הַמָּאתַיִם ב' דִּינָר, וּמִן הַשְּׁלֹשׁ מֵאוֹת שְׁלֹשׁ דִּינָר, וּמִן הַד' מֵאוֹת אַרְבַּע דִּינָר. וְהָא דְּנָקַט הַאי סִידְרָא — רְבוּתָא הוּא דְּנָקַט, וּמִשּׁוּם סֵיפָא, דְּהֵיכָא דְּאָמַר "אַחֲרָיו וְאַחֲרָיו" — דְּאַחֲרוֹן אַחֲרוֹן נִפְסָד, וְאע"פ שֶׁאוֹהֲבוֹ הַשְּׁכִיב מְרַע יוֹתֵר לִיתֵּן לוֹ מַתָּנָה מְרוּבָּה. **אֵין לוֹ.** כְּדֵי הַחוֹב — גּוֹבֶה הַמּוֹתָר מִשֶּׁלְּפָנָיו. **לִפְלוֹנִי בְּכוֹרִי כָּרָאוּי לוֹ.** אָמְרִי' לְקַמָּן דְּהַאי "כָּרָאוּי לוֹ" לִישָּׁנָא יְתֵירָא הוּא, לְיִפּוּי כֹּחַ, שֶׁנָּתַן לוֹ הָנֵי מָאתַיִם זוּז לְבַד בְּכוֹרָתוֹ, הִלְכָּךְ נוֹטְלָן וְגַם אֶת בְּכוֹרָתוֹ. וְאִי לָא הֲוָה אָמַר "כָּרָאוּי לוֹ" — הָיָה נוֹטְלָן בִּבְכוֹרָתוֹ, רָצָה — בְּכוֹרָתוֹ נוֹטֵל, רָצָה — מָאתַיִם זוּז נוֹטֵל, דְּיָדוֹ עַל הָעֶלְיוֹנָה, כִּדְאָמְרִי' נַמִי לְקַמָּן גַּבֵּי הֵיכָא דְּאָמַר "בִּבְכוֹרָתוֹ" בְּהֶדְיָא. **רָצָה בְּכוֹרָתוֹ נוֹטֵל.** אִם הִיא יוֹתֵר מִמָּאתַיִם, שֶׁהֲרֵי אֵינוֹ יָכוֹל לִגְרוֹעַ מִבְּכוֹרָתוֹ אֲפִי' לְרַבִּי יוֹחָנָן בֶּן בְּרוֹקָה, כִּדְנַפְקָא לַן בְּפִרְקִין לְעֵיל (ז) מִ"לֹּא יוּכַל לְבַכֵּר". **רָצָה מָאתַיִם נוֹטֵל.** אִם בְּכוֹרָתוֹ פָּחוֹת מִמָּאתַיִם זוּז. וְה"ה אִם אָמַר "תְּנוּ מָאתַיִם זוּז לִפְלוֹנִי בְּנִי" סְתָמָא, וְלֹא אָמַר "בִּבְכוֹרָתוֹ" — דְּיָדוֹ עַל הָעֶלְיוֹנָה. כִּדְפָרְכִינַן לְקַמָּן: וְדִלְמָא כָּרָאוּי לוֹ בְּחוּטוֹ קָאָמַר! וּמְשַׁנֵּינַן: רַבִּי עֲקִיבָא הִיא, דְּדָיֵיק לִישָּׁנָא יְתֵירָא; (ח) אִם לֹא אָמַר "כָּרָאוּי לוֹ" הֲוָה אָמְרִינַן דְּבְחוּטוֹ אוֹ בִּבְכוֹרָתוֹ קָאָמַר דְּיִטּוֹל מָאתַיִם, וְהָא דְּנָקַט הָכָא "בִּבְכוֹרָתוֹ" — אֲתָא לְאַשְׁמוּעִינַן דְּאַף עַל גַּב דְּפָרֵישׁ בְּהֶדְיָא "בִּבְכוֹרָתוֹ" — אפ"ה יִטּוֹל כׇּל בְּכוֹרָתוֹ אִם הִיא יוֹתֵר מִמָּאתַיִם זוּז, דְּיָדוֹ עַל הָעֶלְיוֹנָה.

כירושה יעב"ץ

כאן בצווח מעיקרא. פי' בקונט': צווח מעיקרא לא קנה. ומ"מ הנותן סילק עצמו והם הפקר, כר"ל דאמר ב"המביא אשם תלוי" (כריתות דף כד.): הנותן מתנה לחבירו ואמר הלה "אי אפשי בה" — כל הקודם זכה. אבל בשתק ולבסוף צווח, כיון ששתק — לא הוי הפקר, וזכה בה בעל כרחו. ואע"ג דרבן שמעון בן גמליאל בסמוך, בזיכה לו ע"י אחר ושתק ולבסוף צווח עביד ליה כצווח מעיקרא, אפ"ה קאמר: יחזירו ליורשי נותן, ולא הוי הפקר — ריש לקיש לא סבר כותיה, אלא כרבנן. ובכריתות (שם ושם) דפריך אמילתיה דריש לקיש דאמר: "אי אפשי בה" כל הקודם זכה, מרב ששת דאמר: מקבל מתנה שאמר לאחר שבאת מתנה לידו "מתנה זו תבטל" "אי אפשי בה" — לא אמר ולא כלום, "בטילה היא" — דבריו קיימין. מאי לאו דבריו קיימין והדרא למרה? לפירושו הכי פריך: כי היכי ד"בטילה היא" דמהני אף לאחר שבאה לידו, והדרא למרה — הכי נמי הוה לן למימר ב"אי אפשי" קודם שבאה לידו — הדרא למרה. וריש לקיש אמר: כל הקודם בה זכה! ומשני: לא, דבריו קיימין ולא הדרא למרה. וקשה לר"י על פירושו: דהיכי פריך התם לריש לקיש מ"דין ודברים אין לי על שדה זו" דלא אמר כלום? לישני דמילתיה דריש לקיש בקודם שבאה לידו, ולכך הוי הפקר בסילק עצמו. אבל גבי "דין ודברים", שהנכסים שלו — אין יכול להסתלק בהאי לישנא! ועוד קשה: דהיכי פריך התם לריש לקיש מרבנן דהכא, דאמרי: הרי אלו אוכלין בתרומה? הא אוקמי' הכא מילתייהו דרבנן בשתק ולבסוף צווח, ומילתיה דריש לקיש בצווח מעיקרא. ואדרבה, מרשב"ג הוה ליה למיפרך! ועוד קשה: דעד כאן לא פליגי רבנן ורבן שמעון בן גמליאל הכא, אלא דהאי משוי ליה כשתק ולבסוף צווח, והאי משוי ליה כצווח מעיקרא. אבל אי צווח מעיקרא — לכולי עלמא כבר זכו יורשין, ולא הוי הפקר. וריש לקיש קאמר דהוי הפקר! ועוד קשה להר"ר פטר: דאמר ב"הגוזל" (ב"ק דף קטז.) גבי חמרא דרב ספרא, דאדעתא דאריא אפקריה, אדעתיה דכ"ע לא אפקריה. וא"כ, לריש לקיש קודם שבאה מתנה לידו — אמאי הוי הפקר? הוה ליה למימר שיחזירו לנותן, דאדעתא דליקבל מיניה קא יהיב, ולא שיהיה הפקר לכל! לכך נראה לפרש: דר"ל נמי איירי אחר שבאה מתנה לידו, דהיינו שתק ולבסוף צווח. והא דקאמר הכא דבשתק ולבסוף צווח קנה — היינו שלא יחזרו לנותן, אלא הפקר הן. ובצווח מעיקרא דלא קנה — יחזרו לנותן, דלא יהיב ליה אלא אדעתא דליקבל מיניה. והתם בכריתות גרס איפכא במילתיה דרב ששת: מקבל מתנה שאמר לאחר שבאה לידו "מתנה זו בטילה" — לא אמר כלום, "אי אפשי בה" "תבטל" — דבריו קיימין. מאי לאו דבריו קיימין והדרא למרה, אע"פ שבאה לידו מתנה? ומשני: דלא הדרא למרה. והשתא פריך נמי שפיר מ"דין ודברים", דאין יכול להסתלק הואיל והנכסים בידו, וכן ממילתייהו דרבנן דאמרי אוכלין בתרומה. ואיירי בשתק ולבסוף צווח, כמילתיה דריש לקיש. ומיהו בריש "השולח" (גיטין דף לב: ושם) גרסינן במילתיה דרב ששת להיפך, ד"לא אפשי" — לא אמר כלום, "בטילה היא" — דבריו קיימין, כדמוכח התם. והויא כ"איכא דאמרי". וכהנה רבות בגמרא[ד].

מאי

קסג א מיי' פ"ט מהל' זכיה ומתנה הל' י"ד סמג עשין פב טוש"ע חו"מ סי' רמה סעיף י:

קסד ב מיי' פ"ט מהל' תרומות הלכה ו:

קסה ג מיי' שם ופ"ד מהל' זכיה ומתנה הל"ג ועי' במ"מ סמג עשין פב טור שו"ע חו"מ סי' רמה סי"א:

קסו ד ה מיי' פ"י מהל' זכיה ומתנה הל' יג ויד סמג עשין פב לד טוש"ע חו"מ סי' רנג ס"ט:

קסז ו ז מיי' שם פי"א הל' טז יז יח סמג שם טוש"ע חו"מ סי' רנג סעיף ח:

רבינו גרשום

שותק ולבסוף צווח קנה. דכיון דשתק בשעת מתנה אודויי אודי ליה לקבל: זיכה לו. המתנה על ידי אחר: אם רבן שני כהן. זה שנכתב לו הנכסים: כבר זכו בהן יורשי נותן: והוינן בה ות"ק אפי' עומד וצווח. המקבל סבירא ליה דאוכלים בתרומה אמאי הא צווח דלא בעי להו: מיהדר קא הדר ביה. דלא בעי להו אבל כיון דשתק מעיקרא קננהו: הוכיח סופו על תחלתו. דמעולם לא היה דעתו לקבלו. והאי דלא צווח בשעה שזיכה לו על ידי אחר דסבר מאי איכפת ליה שזיכה אותו ע"י אחר כל זמן שלא בא לידו מאי אצווח: תנו מאתים זוז לפלוני וש' לפלוני ות' לפלוני אין אומרי' כל הקודם באותו שטר מתנה זכה. תחלה אלא כולם זכו כאחת שלא היה יכול להוציא שני שמות כאחד אם לא שיקדים זה לזה לפיכך זכה זה כזה. ולפיכך אם יצא עליו על זה הנותן שטר חוב שהיה חייב ממון גובה בעל חובו מכולן. דאין יכול לומר הראשון כי בעת שזכיתי אני במתנתי עדיין הנחתי לך מקום לגבות ממנו ולא השני יכול לומר לו כן לפי שכולם זכו כאחת: אבל אם אמר תנו מאתים זוז לפלוני ואחריו לפלוני. מדקאמר ואחריו הכא משמע דאם ישתייר כלום אחרי שיתנו לראשון יתנו לשני [ואם ישתייר משני] תנו לשלישי כל הקודם בשטר מתנה כעין שהן כתובים זכה תחלה. לפיכך אם יצא שטר חוב גובה מן האחרון שכל אחד מן הראשונים יכול לומר לו הנחתי לך מקום עדיין לגבות הימנו: אם אין לו. השלמת כל חובו מן האחרון: חוזר וגובה מן שלפניו. היינו אותו שזכה קודם האחרון: אין לו. עדיין השלמה: גובה משלפני פניו. מן הראשון: [כראוי לו]. האי דקאמר בראוי לו לטפויי מילתא קאתי דבלאו הכי היה נוטל בכורתו. אבל מדקאמר לישנא יתירא נוטלן ונוטל את בכורתו כדאמר לקמן הא מני ר"ע היא דדייק לישנא יתירא: אם אמר תנו לו. מאתים זוז בבכורתו ידו על העליונה. אם בכורתו יותר על מאתים יטול בכורתו ואם מאתים זוז יותר יטול מאתים. וכי האי גוונא מפרשי גבי אשתו וגבי בעל חובו:

הגהות הב"ח

(א) גמ' אמאי אצווח: (ב) רשב"ם ד"ה כאן בצווח וכו' אי אפשי בה כל: (ג) ד"ה כאן וכו' במה שאמר: (ד) ד"ה והיו וכו' עשה עמי ואיני: (ה) ד"ה יורשין וכו' יורשין שלו ולרבן: (ו) ד"ה אם יצא וכו' ושלש מאות זוז הן שדות: (ז) ד"ה רצה בכורתו וכו' לעיל מלא יוכל. נ"ב דף קל: (ח) ד"ה רצה מאתים וכו' לישנא יתירא אלמא דאם לא אמר.

עין משפט
נר מצוה

קסח א מיי' פי"א מהל' זכיה ומתנה הלי"ט סמג עשין פב טוש"ע חו"מ סי' רנג סעיף ח:
קסט ב טוש"ע חו"מ סי' רנה סעיף א:

רצתה. יעב"ץ

קע ג מיי' פ"ו מהל' עדות הל"ד טוש"ע חו"מ סי' מו ס"ח:
קעא ד מיי' פ"ד מהל' יבום הל' כט סמג עשין נא טוש"ע אה"ע סי' קסט סעיף נו:
קעב ה מיי' פי"א מהל' גירושין הל' י סמג עשין נ טוש"ע אה"ע סי' קנה סעיף ח:
קעג ו מיי' פ"ד מהל' יבום הל' כט סמג עשין נב טוש"ע אה"ע סי' קסט סעי' נו ופי' סדר חליצה סעיף לה בהג"ה:
קעד ז מיי' פי"א מהל' גירושין הלכה י סמג עשין נ טוש"ע אה"ע סי' קנה ס"ח:
קעה ח מיי' פ"ו מהל' עדות הלכה ה:
קעו ט מיי' פי"ב מהל' זכיה ומתנה הלי"ג סמג עשין פב טוש"ע חו"מ סי' רנז סעיף ב:

יָדָהּ עַל הָעֶלְיוֹנָה, רָצָה — נוֹטַלְתָּן, *רָצָה — נוֹטֶלֶת כְּתוּבָּתָהּ; א) אוּשְׁכִיב מְרַע שֶׁאָמַר "תְּנוּ מָאתַיִם זוּז לִפְלוֹנִי בַּעַל חוֹבִי כְּרָאוּי לוֹ" — נוֹטְלָן וְנוֹטֵל אֶת חוֹבוֹ, וְאִם אָמַר "בְּחוֹבוֹ" — נוֹטְלָן בְּחוֹבוֹ. מִשּׁוּם דְּאָמַר "כְּרָאוּי לוֹ", נוֹטְלָן וְנוֹטֵל אֶת חוֹבוֹ? וְדִלְמָא "כְּרָאוּי לוֹ בְּחוֹבוֹ" קָאָמַר! אֲמַר רַב נַחְמָן, אֲמַר לִי הוּנָא: הָא מַנִּי? רַבִּי עֲקִיבָא הִיא, דְּדָיֵיק לִישָּׁנָא יְתֵירָא; דִּתְנַן: ב) וְלֹא אֶת הַבּוֹר וְלֹא אֶת הַדּוּת — אַף עַל פִּי שֶׁכָּתַב לוֹ "עוּמְקָא וְרוּמָא", וְצָרִיךְ לִיקַּח לוֹ דֶּרֶךְ, דִּבְרֵי רַבִּי עֲקִיבָא, וַחֲכָמִים אוֹמְרִים אֵין צָרִיךְ לִיקַּח לוֹ דֶּרֶךְ. וּמוֹדֶה ר"ע, בִּזְמַן שֶׁאָמַר לוֹ "חוּץ מֵאֵלּוּ" — שֶׁאֵינוֹ צָרִיךְ לִיקַּח לוֹ דֶּרֶךְ; אַלְמָא, כֵּיוָן דְּלָא צְרִיךְ וְקָאָמַר — לְטַפּוּיֵי מִלְּתָא קָאָתֵי, הָכָא נַמִי, כֵּיוָן דְּלָא צְרִיךְ וְקָאָמַר — לְטַפּוּיֵי מִלְּתָא קָא אָתֵי.§ ת"ר: שְׁכִיב מְרַע שֶׁאָמַר "מָנֶה יֵשׁ לִי אֵצֶל פְּלוֹנִי" — ג) הָעֵדִים כּוֹתְבִין אַף עַל פִּי שֶׁאֵין מַכִּירִין, לְפִיכָךְ, כְּשֶׁהוּא גּוֹבֶה — צָרִיךְ לְהָבִיא רְאָיָה, דִּבְרֵי ר' מֵאִיר; וַחכ"א: אֵין כּוֹתְבִין אא"כ מַכִּירִין, לְפִיכָךְ, כְּשֶׁהוּא גּוֹבֶה — אֵין צָרִיךְ לְהָבִיא רְאָיָה. אָמַר רַב נַחְמָן, אָמַר לִי הוּנָא: תָּנָא, רַבִּי מֵאִיר אוֹמֵר: אֵין כּוֹתְבִין, וַחֲכָמִים אוֹמְרִים: כּוֹתְבִין. וְאַף רַבִּי מֵאִיר לֹא אָמַר אֶלָּא ג) מִשּׁוּם בֵּית דִּין טוֹעִין. אָמַר רַב דִּימִי מִנְּהַרְדְּעָא, ג הִלְכְתָא: אֵין חוֹשְׁשִׁין לְבֵית דִּין טוֹעִין. וּמַאי שְׁנָא מִדְּרָבָא, ד) דְּאָמַר רָבָא: ד אֵין חוֹלְצִין אֶלָּא אִם כֵּן מַכִּירִין, ה וְאֵין מְמָאֲנִין אֶלָּא אִם כֵּן מַכִּירִין, ו לְפִיכָךְ כּוֹתְבִין גֵּט חֲלִיצָה ז וְגֵט מֵיאוּן וְאע"פ שֶׁאֵין מַכִּירִין; ה) (מ"ט? לָאו) מִשּׁוּם דְּחוֹשְׁשִׁין לְבֵ"ד טוֹעִין? לָא, ח ב"ד בָּתַר בֵּית דִּינָא — לָא דָּיְיקִי, בֵּית דִּינָא בָּתַר עֵדִים דָּיְיקִי.§ **מתני'** ט הָאָב תּוֹלֵשׁ וּמַאֲכִיל לְכָל מִי שֶׁיִּרְצֶה, וּמַה שֶּׁהִנִּיחַ תָּלוּשׁ — הֲרֵי הוּא שֶׁל יוֹרְשִׁין.§ **גמ'** תָּלוּשׁ — אִין, מְחוּבָּר — לָא; וְהָא

רשב"ם

יָדָהּ עַל הָעֶלְיוֹנָה. וּכְגוֹן (א) שֶׁלֹּא מָחֲלָה לוֹ בְּכָךְ. **לא את הבור.** שֶׁבַּבַּיִת. **ולא את הדות.** שֶׁבַּבַּיִת, אֵינָן מְכוּרִין בִּכְלַל בַּיִת. (ב) דְּאַף עַל פִּי שֶׁכָּתַב לוֹ עוּמְקָא וְרוּמָא שֶׁל בַּיִת, דְּתַשְׁמִישׁ הֵן בִּפְנֵי עַצְמָן. וְלָא אַהֲנֵי "עוּמְקָא וְרוּמָא" אֶלָּא לְמִקְנֵי עוּמְקָא וְרוּמָא, כְּדַאֲמָרַן בְּפֶרֶק "הַמּוֹכֵר אֶת הַבַּיִת", דְּמִסְתָמָא לָא קָנֵי אִינִישׁ עוּמְקָא וְרוּמָא. וְצָרִיךְ לַמּוֹכֵר לִיקַּח לוֹ דֶּרֶךְ. לְבוֹרוֹ וּלְדוּתוֹ שֶׁשִּׁיֵּיר לְעַצְמוֹ, דְּמוֹכֵר בְּעַיִן יָפָה מוֹכֵר וְלֹא שִׁיֵּיר לְעַצְמוֹ דֶּרֶךְ. **שאין צריך.** דְּהָא "חוּץ מֵאֵלּוּ" לָא הֲוָה צָרִיךְ לְמֵימַר לְמַעוּטֵי בּוֹר וְדוּת, דְּהָא מִסְתָמָא לָא קָנֵי לְהוּ לוֹקֵחַ. אֶלָּא לְטַפּוּיֵי לוֹ שִׁיּוּר דֶּרֶךְ לְבוֹר וְדוּת עַצְמוֹ נִתְכַּוֵּין. וּמִיהוּ, רַבָּנַן נַמִי מוֹדוּ דְּכָל לִישָּׁנָא יְתֵירָא לְטַפּוּיֵי אָתֵי, הֵיכָא דְּאִיכָּא מִידֵי לְטַפּוּיֵי כִּי הָכָא בְּהַךְ בָּרַיְיתָא. וְהָא דַּאֲמָרַן: הָא מַנִּי רַבִּי עֲקִיבָא הִיא — לָאו דַּוְקָא, דְּהוּא הַדִּין לְרַבָּנַן, אֶלָּא מִשּׁוּם דְּאַשְׁכַּחַן בְּרַבִּי עֲקִיבָא בְּהֶדְיָא דְּדָרֵישׁ לִישָּׁנָא יְתֵירָא — מוֹקֵי לָהּ כְּר' עֲקִיבָא. **העדים כותבין.** מַה שֶּׁשּׁוֹמְעִין: "זִכָּרוֹן עֵדוּת שֶׁהָיְתָה בְּפָנֵינוּ, שֶׁאָמַר פְּלוֹנִי שְׁכִיב מְרַע שֶׁפְּלוֹנִי חַיָּיב לוֹ מָנֶה, וּמַה שֶּׁשָּׁמַעְנוּ כָּתַבְנוּ וְחָתַמְנוּ". **אע"פ שאין מכירין.** אֶת הַלֹּוֶה, אוֹ אִם נִתְחַיֵּיב לוֹ כְּלוּם אִם לָאו. **לפיכך.** שֶׁנָּתְנוּ חֲכָמִים רְשׁוּת לָעֵדִים לִכְתּוֹב מַה שֶּׁשָּׁמְעוּ, אַף עַל פִּי שֶׁאֵין יוֹדְעִין אִם אֱמֶת אִם שֶׁקֶר — צְרִיכִין הַיְּתוֹמִים לְהָבִיא רְאָיָה לִגְבּוֹת מֵאוֹתוֹ פְּלוֹנִי. דְּעֵדִים הַלָּלוּ — מַה שֶּׁשָּׁמְעוּ מִפִּי הַשְּׁכִיב מְרַע כָּתְבוּ, וְהֵם לֹא יָדְעוּ אִם מַמָּשׁ בִּדְבָרָיו אִם לָאו. **וחכמים אומרים אין כותבין וכו'.** דְּחָיְישִׁינַן לְבֵית דִּין טוֹעִין, שֶׁיִּרְאוּ שֶׁכָּתְבוּ הָעֵדִים, וִיהוּ סְבוּרִים שֶׁהָעֵדִים לֹא כָּתְבוּ צַוָּואַת שְׁכִיב מְרַע עַד שֶׁחָקְרוּ תְּחִלָּה הֵיטֵב וְיָדְעוּ שֶׁדְּבָרָיו אֱמֶת, כִּדְאָמַר רֵישׁ לָקִישׁ בִּכְתוּבּוֹת (דף יט.): אֵין הָעֵדִים חוֹתְמִין עַל הַשְּׁטָר אא"כ נַעֲשָׂה בְּגָדוֹל, וְאָמַר נַמִי: עֵדִים הַחֲתוּמִים עַל הַשְּׁטָר — נַעֲשָׂה כְּמִי שֶׁנֶּחְקְרָה עֵדוּתָן בְּב"ד, הִלְכָּךְ אֵין כּוֹתְבִין אֶלָּא אִם כֵּן מַכִּירִים שֶׁדְּבָרָיו אֱמֶת. **אינו צריך כו'.** שֶׁהֲרֵי לֹא כָּתְבוּ אֶלָּא אִם כֵּן הִכִּירוּ. (ג) וְאֵינוֹ צָרִיךְ לְהָבִיא רְאָיָה אַחֶרֶת, אֶלָּא שְׁטָר זֶה יִתְקַיֵּים בְּחוֹתְמָיו. **ואף ר' מאיר.** מִן הַדִּין הָיָה לוֹ לְהוֹדוֹת לְדִבְרֵי חֲכָמִים וְלוֹמַר כּוֹתְבִין, מִשּׁוּם דְּאֵין פְּנַאי לִשְׁכִיב מְרַע לִתְבּוֹעַ לַלֹּוֶה. אֶלָּא דְּחָיֵישׁ רַבִּי מֵאִיר לְבֵית דִּין טוֹעִין, דְּאִיהוּ סְבוּרִין שֶׁהָעֵדִים לֹא כָּתְבוּ אֶלָּא אִם כֵּן הִכִּירוּ, וְלֹא יַצְרִיכוּ לַיּוֹרְשִׁין לְהָבִיא רְאָיָה. **הלכתא אין חוששין לבית דין טועין.** אֶלָּא כּוֹתְבִין אע"פ שֶׁאֵין מַכִּירִין, כְּרַב נַחְמָן אַלִּיבָּא דְּרַבָּנַן. ה"ג: **מאי שנא מדרבא דאמר רבא אין חולצין כו'.** ול"ג: "דְּאָמַר רָבָא אָמַר רַב סְחוֹרָה אָמַר רַב הוּנָא". דְּאִינְהוּ חוֹלְצִין וּמְמָאֲנִין אע"פ שֶׁאֵין מַכִּירִין קָאָמְרִי, בְּפֶרֶק "מִצְוַת חֲלִיצָה". אֲבָל רָבָא דִּידֵיהּ אָמַר אֵין חוֹלְצִין כו'. וְאִי גָּרַס לְהוּ — הָכִי גָּרַס: וּמַאי שְׁנָא מִדְּרָבָא, דְּאָמַר רָבָא אָמַר רַב סְחוֹרָה אָמַר רַב הוּנָא חוֹלְצִין כו' וְרָבָא דִּידֵיהּ אָמַר אֵין חוֹלְצִין כו'. וְאַדְּרָבָא קָאֵי גְּמָרָא, וּפָרֵיךְ: מ"ש הַאי דְּפָסְקִינַן הִלְכְתָא אֵין חוֹשְׁשִׁין, מִדְּרָבָא דְּס"ל חוֹשְׁשִׁין. **אין חולצין אא"כ מכירין.** יָבָם וִיבָמָה שֶׁבָּאוּ לְפָנֵינוּ לַחֲלוֹץ, וְאֵין אָנוּ יוֹדְעִין שֶׁהוּא יְבָמָהּ — אֵין נִזְקָקִין לָהֶם ב"ד לַחֲלוֹץ, כִּדְמְפָרְשִׁי טַעְמָא לְקַמָּן, דְּחָיְישִׁינַן לְב"ד טוֹעִין. שֶׁאִם תָּבֹא לִינָּשֵׂא לְב"ד אַחֵר ע"י חֲלִיצַת ב"ד רִאשׁוֹן שֶׁחָלְצוּ לָהּ בְּלֹא הַכָּרָה — יַתִּירוּהָ ב"ד שֵׁנִי, לְפִי שֶׁיְּהוּ טוֹעִין לוֹמַר: לֹא חָלְצוּ לָהּ בֵּית דִּין רִאשׁוֹן אא"כ הִכִּירוּ שֶׁזֶּה יְבָמָהּ. וְלֹא יָדְעוּ הֲלָכָה זוֹ שֶׁחוֹלְצִין אע"פ שֶׁאֵין מַכִּירִין. הִלְכָּךְ תִּקְּנוּ דְּאֵין חוֹלְצִין אא"כ מַכִּירִין. וּכְה"ג אִיכָּא לְמֵימַר נַמִי אֵין מְמָאֲנִין — אֵין בֵּית דִּין נִזְקָקִין לְמֵיאוּן עַד שֶׁיַּכִּירוּ שְׁנֵיהֶם, כְּהַאי טַעְמָא גּוּפֵיהּ. **לפיכך.** כֵּיוָן שֶׁאֵין חוֹלְצִין אֶלָּא אִם כֵּן מַכִּירִין — כּוֹתְבִין עֵדִים גֵּט שֶׁל חֲלִיצָה וּמֵיאוּן לְהַתִּירָהּ אע"פ שֶׁאֵין מַכִּירִין, דְּהָא וַדַּאי ב"ד הִכִּירוּ כְּשֶׁחָלְצוּ וּמִיאֲנוּ. וְהִלְכָּךְ, אִם כָּתְבוּ לָהּ עֵדִים: רָאִינוּ שֶׁחָלְצָה וּמֵיאֲנָה מִפְּלוֹנִי, אֲפִילּוּ לֹא כָּתְבוּ בּוֹ "וְאִשְׁתְּמוֹדְעִינְהוּ" — נִיסֵּת בְּעֵדוּת זוֹ. **מאי טעמא.** אֵין חוֹלְצִין אֶלָּא אִם כֵּן מַכִּירִין? לָאו מִשּׁוּם דְּחוֹשְׁשִׁין לְבֵית דִּין טוֹעִין כִּדְפָרֵישִׁית, שֶׁאִם אַתָּה אוֹמֵר חוֹלְצִין בְּלֹא מַכִּירִין — יִטְעוּ בֵּית דִּין שֵׁנִי לְהַשִּׂיאָהּ בְּלֹא בְּדִיקָה, שֶׁיְּהוּ סְבוּרִין לֹא חָלְצוּ אֶלָּא אִם כֵּן הִכִּירוּ, שֶׁטּוֹעִין בַּהֲלָכָה זוֹ (וּסְבוּרִין חוֹלְצִין אע"פ שֶׁאֵין מַכִּירִין) וּלְעֵיל נַמִי נֵיחוּשׁ לְבֵית דִּין טוֹעִין, וְלֵימָא: אֵין כּוֹתְבִין, כְּרַבִּי מֵאִיר! וּמְשַׁנֵּי: **בי דינא בתר בי דינא לא דייקי.** כְּלוֹמַר, גַּבֵּי חֲלִיצָה וּמֵיאוּנִין — לְפִיכָךְ תִּקְּנוּ דְּאֵין חוֹלְצִין אֶלָּא אִם כֵּן מַכִּירִין, שֶׁאִם אַתָּה אוֹמֵר חוֹלְצִין אַף עַל פִּי שֶׁאֵין מַכִּירִין — הָתָם וַדַּאי חָיְישִׁינַן לְב"ד טוֹעִין, שֶׁיִּטְעוּ ב"ד שֵׁנִי לוֹמַר כִּי יָפֶה הִכִּירוּ ב"ד רִאשׁוֹן כְּשֶׁחָלְצוּ. דְּב"ד שֵׁנִי בָּתַר ב"ד רִאשׁוֹן לָא דָּיְיקִי, דְּכֵיוָן דַּחֲלִיצָה וּמֵיאוּנִין בְּג', כִּדְתְנַן בְּסַנְהֶדְרִין (דף ג.): קָמוּ ב"ד בְּמִילְּתָא, וְשַׁפִּיר עֲבוּד חֲלִיצָה וּמֵיאוּנִין. **בי דינא בתר עדים דייקי.** כְּגוֹן הָכָא, גַּבֵּי צַוָּואַת שְׁכִיב מְרַע — לֹא יִטְעוּ ב"ד לוֹמַר: לֹא כָּתְבוּ עֵדִים אֶלָּא אִם כֵּן הִכִּירוּ. אֶלָּא יְדַקְדְּקוּ אַחֲרֵי הָעֵדִים אִם הִכִּירוּ בַּדָּבָר אִם לָאו. וְהִלְכְתָא: אֵין חוֹשְׁשִׁין לְב"ד טוֹעִין, כִּדְפָסֵיק רַב דִּימִי. **מתני'** הָאָב תּוֹלֵשׁ וּמַאֲכִיל. אַהַכּוֹתֵב נְכָסָיו לִבְנוֹ לְאַחַר מוֹתוֹ קָאֵי, דְּאַקְנֵי לֵיהּ גּוּפָא מֵהַיּוֹם וּפֵירֵי לְאַחַר מִיתָה. וְהִלְכָּךְ מַאֲכִיל הָאָב בְּחַיָּיו פֵּירוֹת שֶׁתָּלַשׁ לְכָל מִי שֶׁיִּרְצֶה. אֲבָל מַה שֶּׁהִנִּיחַ מְחוּבָּר לַקַּרְקַע בִּשְׁעַת מִיתָתוֹ, אע"פ שֶׁעוֹמֵד לִתְלוֹשׁ — הֲרֵי הוּא שֶׁל בְּנוֹ מְקַבֵּל מַתָּנָה. וְדַוְקָא בְּנוֹ, אֲבָל הַכּוֹתֵב נְכָסָיו לְאַחֵר, אֲפִי' מַה שֶּׁהִנִּיחַ מְחוּבָּר לַקַּרְקַע בִּשְׁעַת מִיתָתוֹ — הֲרֵי הֵן שֶׁל יוֹרְשִׁים, שֶׁדַּעְתּוֹ שֶׁל אָדָם קְרוֹבָה אֵצֶל בְּנוֹ יוֹתֵר מֵאַחֵר. וְהָכִי מוּכַח בַּגְּמָרָא. **הֲרֵי הוּא שֶׁל יוֹרְשִׁין.** וְלֹא לִמְקַבֵּל מַתָּנָה לְבַדּוֹ. **גמ'** וּמַקְשִׁינַן: תָּלוּשׁ אִין. מַה שֶּׁהִנִּיחַ תָּלוּשׁ הֲרֵי הֵן שֶׁל יוֹרְשִׁין. אֲבָל הַמְחוּבָּר — הֲרֵי הוּא שֶׁל מְקַבֵּל מַתָּנָה. דִּכְגוּפָהּ שֶׁל קַרְקַע דָּמֵי, וְאַקְנְיֵיהּ נִיהֲלֵיהּ לְאַחַר מִיתָה.

ה"ג

תוספות

מאי שנא מדרבא דאמר רבא אין חולצין אלא אם כן מכירין משום דחיישינן לבית דין טועין. פירוש: אם היו חולצין אע"פ שלא הכירום, היו סבורין בית דין אחר שהכירום בית דין ראשון, ויתירוה לשוק על ידי אותה חליצה. ולא גרסי' "מאי שנא מדרבא אמר רב סחורה". ואי גרס — הוי ככו וכו'. וממילתיה דרבא קפריך, כפירוש רבינו שמואל. והכי איתא בפרק "מצות חליצה" (יבמות דף קו. ושם) בספרים ישנים: אמר רבא אמר רב סחורה אמר רב הונא: חולצין אע"פ שאין מכירין, ואין חוששין לבית דין טועין — כשיעידו בבית דין אחר שחלצה או במיאנה, שיתירוה ע"י חליצה ומיאון זה, שידעו שבית דין הראשון לא הכירום. ורבא דידיה אמר: אין חולצין אלא אם כן מכירין, דחוששין לבית דין טועין, כדפרישית. ור"י גרס בפרק "מצות חליצה" (שם) איפכא, בההיא דרב סחורה — דחוששין לבית דין טועין, ובההיא דרבא — אין חוששין. ופירש דקאי א"לפיכך אין כותבין", שאם כתבו לה עדים גט שחלצה או מיאנה, ולא כתבו "ואשתמודעינהו דאחוהי דמיתנא הוא" — חוששין שמא תראה גיטה לבית דין אחר, ויטעו ויסברו שבית דין ראשון לא חלצו אלא אם כן הכירו, לכך אין כותבין. ואין להקשות: דכי לא יכתבו נמי ניחוש שמא יעידו בב"ד אחר, ויטעו. דהא אם יבאו עדים עצמן — יוכלו ב"ד שני לברר על ידם אם הכירום ב"ד הראשון. ורבא אמר כו' לפיכך כותבין ואין חוששין לב"ד טועין, פי': הואיל ואין חולצין אא"כ מכירין — כותבין עדים שראו שחלצה (ד) אע"פ שאין מכירין, ולא חוששין שמא טעו בית דין הראשון בהלכה, וחלצו ואע"פ שלא הכירו. וקשה: דהשתא לא הוי ב"ד טועים דרב סחורה ודרבא שוין, דבית דין טועין דמילתיה דרב סחורה — היינו ב"ד אחר, ודרבא — היינו ב"ד הראשון! ועוד: דלפי גירסת רש"י צריך למיגרס הכא "מאי שנא מדרבא אמר רב סחורה", דממילתיה דרב סחורה פריך. ומיהו, יש ספרים דגרסי הכי. אבל אין נראה לר"י, אלא כמה שפירש, יכגירסת הספרים ישנים ד"מצות חליצה".

והתניא

רבינו גרשום

ודלמא בראוי לו בחובו קאמר ליה. והכי נמי בראוי לה בכתובתה והכי נמי בראוי לו בבכורתו ואמאי נוטלן ונוטל את חובו: דתנן המוכר את השדה סתם לא מכר לו את הבור ולא את הדות שבתוכה אע"פ שכתב לו עומקא ורומא וצריך ליקח לו מן הקונה דרך לילך לבור ולדות. שכשמכר לו את השדה לא שייר לעצמו שום דרך בשדה דמוכר בעין יפה מוכר דברי ר' עקיבא: וחכמים אומרים אינו צריך ליקח לו דרך. דמוכר בעין רעה מוכר: ומודה ר"ע בזמן שאמר לו. הריני מוכר לך עומקא ורומא חוץ מאלו בור ודות שאין צריך ליקח לו דרך. דאפילו לא אמר חוץ מאלו לא היו מכורין בור ודות. וכיון דאמר חוץ מאלו לטפויי מילתא אתא. דשייר לו דרך בורו. אלמא כל לישנא יתירא לטפויי מילתא קאתי: העדים. ששמעו הצואה: כותבין בלשון עדות. שכך צוה פלוני: אע"פ שאין מכירין. גוף המעשה אם אותו פלוני חייב לו מנה או לא: לפיכך. הואיל ויכולין לכתוב אע"פ שאין מכירין עיקר הדבר לפיכך כשבא היורש לגבות חובו אותו מנה מאותו פלוני. צריך להביא ראיה עדים שחייב לאביו שאלו עדים אינה ראיה שאין מעידין אלא על מה ששמעו מפי שכיב מרע: אינו צריך להביא ראיה. אחרת לפי שלא היו כותבין אלא אם היו מכירין שהוא חייב לו לפיכך אין צריך להביא ראיה אחרת אלא הן: אמר רב נחמן אמר לי הונא ר' מאיר אומר אין כותבין אלא אם כן מכירין וחכ"א כו'. והיינו איפכא מלישנא קמא: ואף ר' מאיר לא אמר. דאין כותבין אא"כ מכירין אלא משום דחוששין לב"ד טועין. דשמא יביאו היורשין כתב עדות הצוואה לפני ב"ד ולא ידקדקו ב"ד אם עדים הללו שחתומים על אותה צוואה אם לשום עדות צוואה בלבד חתמו או משום שהיו יודעין באמת שפלוני היה חייב לו יטעו ב"ד ויאמרו ודאי לא היו חותמין אא"כ היו יודעין שהוא חייב לו והם לא ידעו אלא עדות הצוואה בלבד ויחייבוהו ליתן בלא ראיה אחרת והיינו שלא כדין ומשום הכי אמרינן אין כותבין אא"כ יודעין החוב. ורבנן לא חיישי דליטעי ב"ד בהכי הלכך אין חוששין לב"ד טועין אלא כותבין אע"פ שאין מכירין וב"ד ידקדקו בדבר ולא יחייבו לו ליתן בלא שטר ראיה אחרת: ומאי שנא. מילתא דרב דימי מההיא דרבא: דאמר רבא אין חולצים. ב"ד ליבם אלא [א"כ] מכירין שזו יבמתו של זה. ומכירין נמי שזו ממאנת היא ארוסה של זה שממאנת בו לפיכך הואיל ואמרן דאין חולצין ולא ממאנין אא"כ מכירין אם לא כתבו אותו ב"ד שחלצו [בפניהם] גט חליצה או גט מיאון שלא הספיקו. ובאו עדים שהיו בארתה חליצה לפני ב"ד אחר ואמרו ב"ד לא הספיקו לכתוב גט חליצה כתבו לה אתם גט חליצה או גט מיאון כותבין לה זה ב"ד שני גט חליצה ומיאון אף ע"פ שאין מכירין היבם. מאי טעמא. אין חולצין ב"ד ראשון אא"כ מכירין לאו משום דחוששין לב"ד טועין. דאיכא למיחש דאי לא היו מכירין ב"ד ראשון סברי הללו ב"ד שני שלעולם לא היו נזקקין לחלוץ להם ב"ד אי לאו דמכירין אותן ויטעו בכך והיו כותבין גט חליצה. והכא נמי כרב דימי ליחוש לב"ד טועין. ומשני רב דימי בי דינא בתר בית דינא לא דייקי. הללו ב"ד שני לא ידקדקו על ב"ד ראשון אלא סבורין הן שלא חלצו אא"כ הכירו וסומכין הללו עליהן וכותבין [והלכך] אין חולצין אא"כ מכירין כדי שלא יטעו ב"ד שני אבל להיכא דאמר שכיב מרע יש לי מנה אצל פלוני העדים כותבין אע"פ שאין מכירין דאין חוששין לב"ד טועין דבתר כל עדים מדקדקי ב"ד עליהם אי ידעי גוף החוב אי לא ולא יוציאו האי מנה בלא ראיה גמורה הלכך אין חוששין כאן לב"ד טועין: פיס' האב תולש. מן פירות הקרקעות הללו שכתב לבנו אותן כל ימי חייו [ומאכיל] לכל מי שירצה. ומה שהניח תלוש בשעת מיתה. הרי הוא ליורשים כולם: ומקשינן מה שהניח תלוש בשעת מיתה הוי ליורשין. אבל פירות מחוברין שהניח בקרקע לא היו יורשין כולן אלא דהאי בן בלבד שכתב לו גוף הקרקע. כלומר ולא הוי

בכח

מסורת הש"ס

א) כתובות לג: ב) לעיל סג: סד. ערכין יט. [נזיר ז:]: ג) [לקמן קסז. יבמות קו. כתובות כא. סנהדרין ל.]: ד) יבמות קו: ה) [ולקמן תוספות ד"ה מ"ש מדרבא וכו' אא"כ מכירין משום דחיישינן לב"ד טועין ולא לעתוקיה מ"ט לאו נראה יפה דל"ג והדין עמהם כמבואר להמעיין]

הגהות הב"ח

(א) רשב"ם ד"ה ידה וכו' שלא מחלה. נ"ב כלומר לאפוקי היכא דעשאו שותף בין הבנים ושתקה דמחלה לו כתובה בכך כדלעיל דף קלב: (ב) ד"ה לא את הבור וכו' ואע"פ: (ג) ד"ה אינו צריך וכו' אא"כ הכירו ולהכי אינו צריך: (ד) תוס' ד"ה מאי שנא וכו' שראו שחלצה גט חליצה אע"פ שאין מכירין:

מסורת הש"ס

א) [תוספ' כתובות פ"ח] ב) [לקמן קמב.] ג) [עי' תוס' ב"מ קד. ד"ה הכי גרסינן] ד) כתובות מט: ה) [ע"ל ברבינו] ו) בכורות נב: ז) [ועי' תוס' בבא קמא נב: ד"ה לשרכין]

עין משפט נר מצוה

קעז א מיי' פי"ב מהל' זכיה ומתנה הל' יג סמג עשין פב טוש"ע חו"מ סי' רנז סעיף ב:
קעח ב מיי' פ"ע מהל' נחלות הל' יב ופי"ט מהל' אישות הל' כב סמג עשין נו טוש"ע חו"מ סי' רפו סעיף א:
קעט ג ד מיי' מהלכות נחלות שם טוש"ע שם סעיף ג:
קפ ה ו מיי' שם הל' טו טוש"ע שם ס"ב:
קפא ז מיי' שם הל' יב טוש"ע שם ס"ג:
קפב ח מיי' פכ"ו מהל' מלוה ולוה הלי"ב ופי"ב מהל' זכיה הלי"ב סמג עשין לד טוש"ע ח"מ סי' קיב סעיף ה וסי' קלב סעיף ב וטוש"ע אה"ע סי' נא ס"ב וס"ד:
קפג ט י מיי' פ"כ מהל' אישות הלי"א סמג עשין מח טוש"ע אה"ע סי' נג סעיף ד [וברב אלפס עוד בכתובות פד:]
קפד כ מיי' פי"א מהל' שמיטה ויובל הל' כ והלכה כא:

והא תניא: א)שמין את המחוברין ללוקח! אמר עולא, לא קשיא: א'כאן בבנו, כאן באחר, ב)הואיל ודעתו של אדם קרובה אצל בנו.§ **מתני'** ב'הניח בנים גדולים וקטנים — אין הגדולים מתפרנסין על ידי הקטנים, ולא הקטנים נזונין על הגדולים, אלא חולקין בשוה. ג'נשאו הגדולים — ישאו הקטנים, ואם אמרו קטנים: הרי אנו נושאין כדרך שנשאתם אתם — ד'אין שומעין להם, אלא מה שנתן להם אביהם נתן. הניח בנות גדולות וקטנות — אין הגדולות מתפרנסות על ידי הקטנות, ולא הקטנות נזונות על הגדולות, אלא חולקות בשוה. נשאו גדולות — ישאו קטנות, ואם אמרו קטנות: הרי אנו נושאות כדרך שנשאתם אתם — אין שומעין להן. זה חומר בבנות מבבנים, שהבנות נזונות על הבנים ואין נזונות על הבנות.§ **גמ'** אמר רבא: ה'האי גדול אחי דלבש ואיכסי מביתא — מאי דעבד עבד. והא אנן תנן: אין הגדולים מתפרנסין על הקטנים! מתני' ו'בשרכא. שרכא, פשיטא! מהו דתימא: ניחא להו דלא ניגוול, קמ"ל.§ "נשאו גדולים ישאו קטנים".§ מאי קאמר? אמר רב יהודה, ז'הכי קאמר: נשאו גדולים לאחר מיתת אביהן — ישאו קטנים לאחר מיתת אביהן. אבל נשאו גדולים בחיי אביהן, ואמרו קטנים לאחר מיתת אביהן: הרי אנו נושאין כדרך שנשאתם אתם — אין שומעין להן, אלא מה שנתן להן אביהן נתן.§ "הניח בנות גדולות וקטנות".§ שלח ליה אבוה בר גניבא לרבא, ילמדנו רבינו: ג)לוותה ואכלה ועמדה ונשאת, בעל לוקח הוי או יורש הוי? ח'לוקח הוי, ומלוה על פה אינו גובה מן הלקוחות. או דלמא יורש הוי, ומלוה על פה גובה מן היורשין? אמר ליה, תנינא: נשאו גדולות — ישאו קטנות; מאי לאו נשאו גדולות לבעל — ישאו קטנות מבעל? לא, נשאו גדולות לבעל — ישאו קטנות לבעל. איני? והא תני ר' חייא: נשאו גדולות לבעל — ישאו קטנות מבעל! דלמא שאני פרנסה, דאית לה קלא. א"ל רב פפא לרבא, לאו היינו דשלח רבין באגרתיה: ד)מי שמת והניח אלמנה ובת — ט'אלמנתו נזונת מנכסיו. נשאת הבת — אלמנתו נזונת מנכסיו. מתה הבת — אמר רב יהודה בן אחותו של ר' יוסי ה)(בן) חנינא, ע"י היה מעשה י'ואמרו: אלמנתו נזונת מנכסיו; אי אמרת בשלמא יורש הוי, משום הכי אלמנתו נזונת מנכסיו. אלא אי אמרת לוקח הוי, אמאי נזונת מנכסיו? אמר אביי: אי לאו דשלח רבין, אנן לא ידעינן? והא ו)תנן, כ'אלו הן שאין חוזרין ביובל: הבכורה, והיורש

והתניא שמין. גרסינן. דברייתא היא בתוספתא דכתובות, כמו שפירש ר"ש.

מתני' בשרכא. בכל הספרים כתוב "שרכא" בריש. ובערוך גרס "שדכא" בדלית. והוא לשון שקט, כמו "ותשקוט הארץ", ומתרגמינן: ושדיכת ארעא (שופטים ה) כלומר, אדם בטל ושקט אינו עוסק בכלום. וכן "יודע ציד איש שדה" ומתרגמינן: נחשדכן (בראשית כה) שהיה נח ושקט. וב"החובל" (ב"ק דף צב: ושם): מטייל ואזל דיקלא בישא לגבי קיני דשדכא ז).

והיורש

הגהות הב"ח

(א) רשב"ם ד"ה ואין נזונות הבנות כו' ותיבת מן נמחק:

ה"ג: והתניא שמין את המחוברין ללוקח. ובתוספתא דכתובות היא שנויה: מכר הבן ומת האב, אם יש בנכסים מחוברים לקרקעות — שמין לו. ולעיל מינה קתני: הכותב כל נכסיו לבנו צריך שיכתוב "מהיום ולאחר מיתה", ופירושה: הכותב כל נכסיו מהיום ולאחר מיתה לבנו, והלך אותו הבן ומכר הנכסים הללו בחיי אביו, ואחר זמן מת האב — זכה הלוקח במה שמכר לו בגופה של קרקע. ואם יש בנכסים פירות מחוברין — לא זכה הלוקח אלא בגופה של קרקע. אבל בפירות, אע"ג דמחוברים הן — ליורשין הן. לפיכך שמין אותן ללוקח, ונותן דמיהן ליורשין. ומשני: כאן בבנו. מתני' — שכתב לבנו, ולא מכרן לאחר בחיי האב. דדעתו של אדם קרובה אצל בנו, כדמפרש לקמיה, דלדעת בן אקני ליה גופא לאחר מיתה עם פירות המחוברין — דליזכי בהו איהו גופיה, ולא לדעת בן שיזכה בהן הלוקח מבנו בחייו. אי נמי, הבן עצמו לא אקני ללוקח, דהוא אחר, אלא הגוף ולא הפירות, אע"ג דמחוברין. כאן באחר. שמכרו הבן לאחר בחיי האב. וה"ה אם כתבו האב לאחר מהיום ולאחר מיתה, שאין לו חלק במחוברין. **מתני'** הניח בנים גדולים וקטנים. בדלא כתב נכסי' מיירי. מתפרנסין. לבוש וכסות. נזונין. מזונות ממש. ולפי שפרנסת הגדולים מרובין מפרנסת הקטנים, ומזון הקטנים וטפולן מרובה משל גדולים, לכך הוצרך לומר שהקטנים מעכבין על הגדולים מלהתפרנס, והגדולים מעכבין על הקטנים מליזון מתפוסת הבית. אלא חולקין בשוה, ויתפרנס ויזון כל אחד מחלקו. נשאו גדולים. נשים, ועשו צרכי חופה מתפוסת הבית, לאחר מיתת אביהן קודם חלוקה — ישאו גם הקטנים כמו כן, קודם חלוקה. ואם אמרו קטנים. לאחר מיתת אביהן: הרי אנו נושאים עתה כמו שנשאתם אתם בחיי אבינו. אין שומעין להם אלא מה שנתן להם אביהם. בחייו נתן, והכי מפרש לה בגמ'. הניח בנות. ולא בנים. גדולות וקטנות כו'. הכי מיפרשא כולה כדפרשינן גבי בנים. נשאו גדולות. לאחר מיתת האב — ישאו נמי קטנות. וזה חומר בבנות. היכא דבנות יורשות, מהיכא דבנים יורשין ואיכא נמי בנות בהדייהו. שהבנות נזונות מן הבנים בנכסים מרובין, כדתנן בריש פירקין דלקמן: הבנים יירשו והבנות נזונות, דהכי הוה תנאי כתובה: בנן נוקבן דיהוויין ליכי מינאי איהון מתזנן מנכסי כו'. ואין נזונות (א) מן הבנות. הקטנות מן הגדולות. דבמקום שהן יורשות כל הנכסים — ליכא תנאי כתובה דמזון בנן נוקבן. **גמ'** גדול אחי. שנושא ונותן בנכסים, ואיכא הנאה ליתמי כי מיכסי מלבושים נאים, כי היכי דלישתמעו מיליה. מאי דעבד עבד. ולא יטלו כנגדו. ומיהו, לכתחלה אין לבזבז בממון אחיו כל כך. בשרכא. אדם בטל, שאין להם ריוח בדבר. מאי קאמר. דמתני' לפי משמעותה קשיא רישא לסיפא, דקתני רישא: נשאו גדולים — ישאו קטנים, והדר תני: אם אמרו קטנים, דמשמע: לא ישאו קטנים. ועמדה וניסת. והכניסה כל נכסיה לבעלה, כדרך נשואה. בעל לוקח הוי. מי שויוהו רבנן בנכסי אשתו, בין בחייה בין לאחר מיתה, כדין לוקח או כדין יורש? ונפקא מינה לכל דינין החלוקין בין מקח לירושה, כי הנך לקמן בשמעתין. ישאו קטנות מבעל. חלקם המגיעם, אלמא יורש הוי. ישאו קטנות לבעל. מממון אביהן המונח ועומד עדיין בתפוסת הבית, כנגד אותו ממון שנטלה הגדולה. ומקשינן: והתני ר' חייא נשאו גדולות לבעל ישאו קטנות מבעל. אלמא מיד הבעל מוציאים. מכלל שהכניסה לו כל הממון, ואפי' חלק הקטנות. ושמע מינה, מדמוציאין מידו — דיורש הוה, דאי לוקח הוה — מלוה על פה הוא, ולא טריף ממשעבדי! ומשני: לעולם לוקח הוי. מיהו, מלוה בשטר היא האי פרנסת הקטנות, דשאני פרנסת נשואין דאית ליה קלא וכמלוה בשטר דמיא, הלכך טריפא ממשעבדי, ומוציאין אפי' מיד הלקוחות. דגרסינן בפ' "מציאת האשה": האחין שעשיעבדו — מוציאין אפי' מיד הלקוחות לפרנסה, ואין מוציאין למזונות, וכל שכן מן היורשין. ולעולם אימא לך לוקח הוי, ולענין לוותה ואכלה ונישאת — לא גבינן מבעל. אמר ליה רב פפא לרבא. דבעי למפשט מדרבי חייא יורש הוי. לאו היינו דשלח רבין כו'. ומהא איכא למפשט שפיר דיורש הוי. אלמנתו נזונת. בתנאי כתובתה, שכך כתב לה: ואת תהא יתבא בביתי ומיתזנא מנכסיי כל ימי מיגר ארמלותיך. ניסת הבת. והכניסה הנכסים לבעלה — אלמנתו נזונת מנכסיו. מתה הבת. וירשה בעל. אמר רב יהודה כו'. אמורא הוא. ואמרו אלמנתו נזונת. דלעולם היא נזונת, עד שתנשא, או שתתבע כתובתה, או שירצו היורשין ליתן לה כתובתה, כדאמרינן בכתובות. אי אמרת בשלמא. בעל בנכסי אשתו אפילו בחייה יורש הוי, משום הכי קתני: נישאת הבת — אלמנתו נזונת מנכסיו. דאע"ג דמזון האשה והבנות לא טרפא ממשעבדי, דהיינו לקוחות, מיורשין מיהא גביא. אלא אי אמרת לוקח הוי אמאי נזונת. והתנן ב"הנזקין" (גיטין ד' מח:): אין מוציאין למזון האשה והבנות מנכסים משועבדים, מפני תקון העולם! והא תנן. בבכורות. שאין חוזרין. לבעליהן, שאין חוזרין אלא ממכר. הבכורה. חלק בכורת הבכור, כדמפרש התם: מתנה קרייה רחמנא, "לתת לו פי שנים".

והיורש

רבינו גרשום

בכח האב שיהא יכול להורישן לשאר בניו אע"ג דגדלו הפירות בחייו: והתנן שמין את המחובר ללוקח. אדם שמכר שדה לחבירו. לסוף י' שנים ולא בתוך י' וכשהשלימו י' שנים היה תבואה של מוכר מחוברין לקרקע ועדיין לא נגמר בישולן אין אומרים דכגוף הקרקע דמיין ומכורין ללוקח אלא שמין אותן מחוברין ללוקח והוא קונה אותם משום דברשותיה דמוכר גדלו. ה"נ האי אב דהניח פירות מחוברים בחיי אביהן גדלו ואמאי לא הוה ברשותן אלא דהאי בן לחוד: כאן בבנו. הואיל ודעתו של אב קרובה אצל בניו כשכתב לו כל נכסים לאחר מותו מחל לו הפירות שבשעת מותו. אבל מוכר לאחר לא מחל לו הפירות לפיכך שמין. ואמר לן רבי א) דמשנה זו שמין את המחוברין ללוקח אין ידוע היכן הוא: **פיס'** הניח בנים גדולים וקטנים. והניח נכסים וקודם שחלקו הממון אין הגדולים מתפרנסין על הקטנים. כלומר אין קונין הגדולים מלבוש מתפושת הבית מפני שלא יתמעט חלקן של קטנים מפני שלגדולים צריכין יותר מלבוש מקטנים וקטנים צריכין יותר מזונות שאוכלין בכל שעה ביום לפיכך לא יזונו מחלקן של גדולים אלא חולקין הנכסים בשוה ויעשה כל אחד בחלקו מה שרוצה: האי גדול אחי שלבש וכסה עצמו. מתפושת הבית. מאי טעמא דמתני' דקתני דאין מתפרנסין דאפי' הוי גדול אחי: בשדכא עסקינן. כלומר אדם בטל שאין מרויח מן הנכסים כלום אבל אחר שמרויח מאי דעבד עבד: בשדכא פשיטא. דאין מתפרנסין הואיל דלית להו הנאה מיניה לא מחלי ליה: מהו דתימא. מחלי ליה משום דלא תזלזל שלא ילך ערום ויחף וקמ"ל דלא: נשאו גדולים מן הנכסים לצורך לישא נשים ינשאו קטנים מן הנכסים: אם אמרו קטנים כו': מאי קאמר. כלומר היכי מתרצי מתני' רישא קתני נשאו גדולים ישאו קטנים דמשמע דשוין אהדדי וסיפא קתני אם אמרו קטנים הרי אנו נושאין כדרך שאתם נשאתם אין שומעין להם דמשמע דלא שוין אהדדי: אמר ר' יהודה ה"ק נשאו גדולים. אשה מתפושת הבית ישאו קטנים נמי כנגדן מן הממון אבל אם נשאו בחיי אביהן ונתן להם אביהן ממון אם אמרו הקטנים לאחר מיתת אביהם הרי אנו נושאין עכשיו מתפושת הבית כדרך שנשאתם אתם בחיי אביהן אין שומעין להן אלא מחלקין הירושה: הניח בנות גדולות וקטנות כו'. כדמפ' גבי בנים הכי נמי מפרשינן גבי בנות. וכי היכי דמקשי' ומתרצי' גבי בנים ה"נ גבי בנות: וזה החומר בבנות מבנים. שהבנות נזונות מממון הבנים בנכסין מועטין והבנים ישאלו על הפתחים: ילמדנו רבינו. בתולה או אלמנה שלוותה ממון מאחרים ואכלה ואח"כ עמדה ונישאת לבעל קודם שתשלם והביאה לבעל נכסים מאי: בעל בנכסי אשתו (יש לו דין) לוקח הוי או יורש הוי. [לוקח הוי] ולא יפרע כלום משום דמלוה על פה אינה גובה מן הלקוחות דלית ליה קלא למלוה על פה. או דלמא יורש הוי וגובה כו': מאי לאו נשאו גדולות לבעל שלוו ונתפרנסו מממון הקטנות ונישאו לבעל הגדולות ישאו קטנות מה שלוו ואכלו אחיותיהן משלהן ישאו מממון הבעל אלמא דבעל בנכסי אשתו יורש הוי ויש לו דין יורש ומלוה על פה גובה מן היורשין. לא לעולם אימא לך לוקח הוי ומתני הכי נשאו גדולות לבעל מתפושת הבית הכי נמי כשנשאו קטנות לבעל יטלו כנגדן: והתני ר' חייא. בפירוש כמו דאמרן מעיקרא ומשמע דיורש הוי: לעולם לוקח הוי. והכא מ"ט גובות הקטנות מן הבעל הא לאו יורש [הוא] משום הכי גובה שאני פרנסה שנוטל ממון מן הקטנות דקלא אית ליה וכמלוה בשטר דמי ומלוה בשטר גובה מן הלקוחות: א"ל רב פפא לרבא לאו היינו דשלח רבין באגרתיה. דבעל יורש הוי: מי שמת והניח. אשתו ובת שיהא של שניהם ואין לה יורש אלא היא אלמנתו נזונת מנכסי בעלה לפי כי על היורשין ליתן לה לאלמנה מזונות: נישאת הבת. והכניסה הנכסים לבעלה שירשה מאביה שאלמנה זו ראויה ליזון מהן. אע"פ שנישאת לבעל אפ"ה אלמנה נזונת מנכסים של חתנה שהכניסה לו הבת: מתה הבת דהשתא לאו ברשותה נכסים קיימו: אמר ר' יהודה על ידי היה מעשה. שאירע כן ובאו לפניו לדין ואמרו חכמים דאפ"ה דמתה הבת הואיל שהנכסים שהכניסה לו בידו הן דין הוא דנזונת: אי אמרת בשלמא דהאי בעל יורש הוי. בנכסי אשתו משום הכי נזונת האלמנה דקדמה שטר כתובתה שנתחייב לה בעלה במזונותיה מקמי דנפלה ליה האי ירושה לבעל משום דאין יורש אלא לאחר מיתת אשתו ומשתכח דקדמה שעבוד אלמנה קודם שעבודו של בעל אלא אי אמרת לוקח הוי אמאי נזונת והא קיי"ל אין מוציאין למזון האשה והבנות מנכסים משועבדים מפני תקון העולם והני נכסים משועבדים הם לבעל משעה שהכניסתו לו אשתו. אלא לאו ש"מ יורש הוי ומשום הכי נזונית. ואם נפשך לומר הא קדם שטר כתובתה מן הבעל שהוא כלוקח ואיכא למימר בדין הוא דנזונת. אפ"ה דקדם אינה נזונת כדפרשי' לעיל מפני תקון העולם: אלו שאין חוזרין ביובל. דלא חשיב כזביני דהדרי משום דזכינהו רחמנא

אלמא

א) ונראה דלזה כוונו הרשב"ם והתוס' וכתבו והתניא גרסי' ור"ל לאפוקי מגי' רבינו.

וְהַיּוֹרֵשׁ אֶת אִשְׁתּוֹ! אֲמַר לֵיהּ רָבָא: וְהַשְׁתָּא דִּשְׁלַח מִי יָדְעִינַן? [א]הָאָמַר ר' יוֹסֵי בְּר' חֲנִינָא: בְּאוּשָׁא הִתְקִינוּ, הָאִשָּׁה שֶׁמָּכְרָה (א) נִכְסֵי מְלוֹג בְּחַיֵּי בַּעְלָהּ וּמֵתָה – הַבַּעַל מוֹצִיא מִיַּד הַלָּקוֹחוֹת! אֶלָּא אָמַר רַב אַשִׁי: בַּעַל – שַׁוְיוּהוּ רַבָּנַן כְּיוֹרֵשׁ וְשַׁוְיוּהוּ רַבָּנַן כְּלוֹקֵחַ, וְהֵיכָא דְּטָבָא לֵיהּ עֲבַדוּ לֵיהּ; גַּבֵּי יוֹבֵל שַׁוְיוּהוּ רַבָּנַן כְּיוֹרֵשׁ מִשּׁוּם פְּסֵידָא דִּידֵיהּ, גַּבֵּי דְּר' יוֹסֵי בְּר' חֲנִינָא שַׁוְיוּהוּ רַבָּנַן כְּלוֹקֵחַ מִשּׁוּם פְּסֵידָא דִּידֵיהּ, גַּבֵּי דְּרָבִין מִשּׁוּם פְּסֵידָא דְּאַלְמָנָה שַׁוְיוּהוּ רַבָּנַן כְּיוֹרֵשׁ. וְהָא גַּבֵּי דְּר' יוֹסֵי בְּר' חֲנִינָא דְּאִיכָּא פְּסֵידָא לַלָּקוֹחוֹת, וְשַׁוְיוּהוּ רַבָּנַן כְּלוֹקֵחַ! הָתָם אִינְהוּ אַפְסִידוּ אַנַּפְשַׁיְיהוּ, כֵּיוָן דְּאִיכָּא בַּעַל, לָא אִיבָּעֵי לְהוּ לְמִיזְבַּן מֵאִיתְּתָא דְּיָתְבָא תּוּתֵי גַּבְרָא.§

הדרן עלך יש נוחלין

רשב"ם

וְהַיּוֹרֵשׁ אֶת אִשְׁתּוֹ. מְפָרֵשׁ הָתָם: קָסָבַר יְרוּשַּׁת הַבַּעַל דְּאוֹרַיְיתָא. וְאִי לוֹקֵחַ הָוֵי מִשָּׁעָה שֶׁנִּשֵּׂאת – אֲפִילּוּ לְאַחַר מִיתָה לָא נָפְקָא מִכְּלַל מִקָּח וּמִמְכָּר, וְתֶהְדַּר בַּיּוֹבֵל! **בְּאוּשָׁא הִתְקִינוּ.** שֶׁגָּלְתָה סַנְהֶדְרִין לְשָׁם, כִּדְמְפָרֵשׁ בְּר"ה (ד' לא.). **הָאִשָּׁה שֶׁמָּכְרָה נִכְסֵי מְלוֹג בְּחַיֵּי בַּעְלָהּ.** שֶׁאִם יָמוּת בַּעְלָהּ יִזְכֶּה בָּהֶן, וְאִם תָּמוּת הִיא וְיִירָשֶׁהָ בַּעַל – יַפְסִידוּ. וְנִכְסֵי מְלוֹג הֵן נְכָסִים שֶׁנָּפְלוּ לָהּ מִבֵּית אָבִיהָ, אוֹ שֶׁהִכְנִיסָה קַרְקָעוֹת שֶׁלֹּא נִשּׁוּמוּ בִּכְתוּבָּתָהּ, וְלֹא קִיבֵּל בַּעַל עָלָיו אַחֲרָיוּת, וְאוֹכֵל פֵּירוֹתֵיהֶן בְּחַיֶּיהָ כְּתַקָּנַת חֲכָמִים תַּחַת פִּרְקוֹנָהּ. וּלְהָכִי מִיקְרֵי מְלוֹג – שֶׁמּוֹלְגָן וּמְחַסְּרָן בַּעַל, שֶׁאוֹכֵל הַפֵּירוֹת כִּמְלִיגַת הָרֹאשׁ. **אִי אָמְרַתְּ בִּשְׁלָמָא** לוֹקֵחַ שַׁוְיוּהוּ. רַבָּנַן, מִשָּׁעָה שֶׁנְּשָׂאָהּ, מִשּׁוּ"ה מַפֵּיק, דְּלוֹקֵחַ רִאשׁוֹן הָוֵי. אֶלָּא אִי אָמְרַתְּ בַּעַל בְּנִכְסֵי אִשְׁתּוֹ יוֹרֵשׁ הָוֵי מִשְּׁעַת נִשּׂוּאִין – אַמַּאי מַפֵּיק? לָמָּה תִּקְנוּ בְּאוּשָׁא שֶׁהַבַּעַל מוֹצִיא? וַהֲלֹא הָאִשָּׁה שֶׁהִיא מוֹרֶשֶׁת אוֹתוֹ מָכְרָה, וְאֵין כֹּחַ בַּיּוֹרְשִׁין לִירַשׁ מַה שֶּׁמָּכַר אֲבִיהֶן! אֶלָּא וַדַּאי מִדְּתִקְנוּ שֶׁהַבַּעַל מוֹצִיא, כָּךְ הָיָה עִיקַּר תַּקָּנַת אוּשָׁא – שֶׁיְּהֵא הַבַּעַל לוֹקֵחַ בִּנְכָסֶי' מִשָּׁעָה שֶׁנְּשָׂאָהּ, וְהִלְכָּךְ מוֹצִיא, שֶׁהֲרֵי קָדַם מִקָּחוֹ לְמִקָּחָן שֶׁל לָקוֹחוֹת. **אֶלָּא אָמַר רַב אַשִׁי כו'.** לְתָרֵץ עַל כָּל אֵלּוּ הַדְּבָרִים, שֶׁיֵּשׁ מְקוֹמוֹת שֶׁעֲשָׂאוּהוּ כְּיוֹרֵשׁ, וְיֵשׁ מְקוֹמוֹת שֶׁעֲשָׂאוּהוּ כְּלוֹקֵחַ. **וְהֵיכָא דְּטָבָא לֵיהּ כו'.** כִּדְמְפָרֵשׁ וְאָזֵיל. **גַּבֵּי יוֹבֵל כו' מִשּׁוּם פְּסֵידָא דִּידֵיהּ.** דְּלָא תֶּהְדַּר בַּיּוֹבֵל לְמִשְׁפַּחַת אִשְׁתּוֹ. **גַּבֵּי דְּרָבִין.** אע"ג דְּאִיכָּא פְּסֵידָא דִּידֵיהּ – חָיְישִׁי' לִפְסֵידָא דְּאַלְמָנָה, שֶׁמֵּאַחַר שֶׁקָּדַם תְּנַאי מְזוֹנוֹתֶיהָ לַנִּשּׂוּאִין – לֹא טוֹב לָנוּ לְהַפְסִידָהּ בְּיָדַיִם. **דְּאִיכָּא פְּסֵידָא** דְּלָקוֹחוֹת. אַמַּאי לָא חָיְישִׁינַן, כִּי הֵיכִי דְּחָיְישִׁינַן לִפְסֵידָא דְּאַלְמָנָה? **דְּיָתְבָא תּוּתֵי גַּבְרָא.** וְרָאוּי לְיוֹרְשָׁהּ כְּשֶׁתָּמוּת, וְאֵלּוּ הֶעֱרִימוּ לְהוֹצִיאָם מִיָּדוֹ – הִלְכָּךְ יַפְסִידוּ. וּלְעִנְיַן שְׁאֵילְתָא דִּשְׁאֵילְנָא, פֵּי' רַבֵּינוּ חֲנַנְאֵל, וְרוֹאֶה אֲנִי אֶת דְּבָרָיו: לָוְותָה וְאָכְלָה וְעָמְדָה וְנִיסֵּת – מִסְתַּבְּרָא דְּכְיוֹרֵשׁ הָוֵי, מִשּׁוּם פְּסֵידָא דְּמַלְוֶה. וְכֵן סוּגְיָא דִּשְׁמַעְתָּא, דְּכָל הֵיכָא דְּאִיכָּא פְּסֵידָא, כְּגוֹן פְּסֵידָא דְּאַלְמָנָה, דְּלֵיכָּא לְמֵימַר אִיהוּ דְּאַפְסֵיד אַנַּפְשֵׁיהּ – שַׁוְיוּהוּ רַבָּנַן כְּיוֹרֵשׁ.

הדרן עלך יש נוחלין

תוספות

והיורש את אשתו. פי' בקונטרס: ואי הוי לוקח מחיים – גם לאחר מיתה לא פקע, והוי לוקח. ואין נראה, דהא מחיים אין לו אלא פירות! ונראה לר"י לפרש: דמבעיא ליה אם בעל יורש הוי או לוקח הוי בין מחיים בין לאחר מיתה, מדלא מפליג מידי. ופשיט מדרבין, דלכל הפחות הוי יורש לאחר מיתה, כדקאמר: מתה הבת – אלמנתו נזונת מנכסיו, אע"פ שהבעל יורשה. אבל מחיים אין להוכיח מדבריו דהוי יורש אע"ג דקאמר: נשאת הבת – אלמנתו נזונת, דהא אפילו הוי לוקח מחיים קאמר שפיר דנזונת, שתוכל למכור הגוף מחיים והפירות לאחר מיתה, כיון דבעל יורש הוי לכל הפחות לאחר מיתה. ולהכי קא"ל אביי: ואי לאו דשלח רבין לא הוה ידעינן דהוי יורש לאחר מיתה? והתנן, אלו שאין חוזרים ביובל: הבכורה והיורש את אשתו, אלמא דיורש הוי לאחר מיתה. **גבי** יובל שויוהו רבנן כיורש. לאו דוקא נקט "שויוהו רבנן", דהא כיון דאית ליה דאינה חוזרת ביובל – אית ליה דירושת הבעל דאורייתא. דהכי אמר בבכורות (ד' נב:), וכן פי' בקונטרס. אלא "שויוהו רבנן" – בעי למימר: הניחוהו להיות יורש, ולא עשאוהו לוקח.

התם אינהו אפסידו אנפשייהו כו'. תימה: דבפרק "מי שהיה נשוי" (כתובות ד' נה:) אמר אביי: "נכסי לך ואחריך לפלוני", ומכרה ומתה – הבעל מוציא מיד הלקוחות, ו"אחריך" מיד בעל, ולוקח מיד "אחריך", ואוקימנא בידא דלוקח. ופריך התם: מאי שנא מהא דתנן דיעשו פשרה ביניהם? ומשני: התם אית להו פסידא לכולהו, הכא לוקח הוא דאית ליה פסידא. פי': וכיון דאיכא פסידא דלוקח – שויוהו רבנן (ג) בעל כיורש, ואין מוציא מיד לוקח. והשתא האמר הכא דאיהו דאפסיד אנפשיה, דלא ה"ל למיזבן מאתתא דיתבא תותי גברא, לפי שהבעל יוציא מידו! וכ"ת: התם לא אפסיד אנפשיה, שהוא סבור שלא יטול הבעל ממנו, לפי ש"אחריך" יוציא מידו – מ"מ הרי יודע דיחזרו אליה, ויצטרכו לעשות פשרה, וירויח הבעל! ואור"י: דהתם לא אפסיד אנפשיה, לפי שסבור שיעשה פשרה עם "אחריך" ולא יגבה הבעל כלום. וא"ת: מ"מ מהא דאמר התם לעיל: "נכסי לך ואחריך לפלוני" עמדה וניסת – בעל לוקח הוי ואין ל"אחריך" במקום בעל כלום. אלמא, אע"ג דאיכא פסידא ל"אחריך" הוי בעל לוקח! וי"ל: דמתנה שאני, דאין כל כך פסידא אם לא יקבל במתנה. וא"ת: דאמר בריש "המפקיד" (ב"מ ד' לה. ושם) שמו לה לאשה ואנסיבא, או שמו מינה (ד) ואנסיבא – בעל לוקח הוי ולא מיהדר כו', אע"ג דאיכא פסידא ללוה לא מיהדר ליה ארעא אע"פ דשומא הדרא לעולם! וי"ל: כיון דדין לא הדר, אלא משום "ועשית הישר והטוב" לא חשיב כל כך פסידא. עוד מקשים, דאמר ב"החובל" (ב"ק ד' פט. ושם): כי אתו רב פפא ורב הונא בריה דרב יהושע מבי רב אמרו: תקנת אושא מתני' היא: העבד והאשה פגיעתן רעה, אחרים שחבלו בהם חייבים והם שחבלו באחרים פטורין. ואי ס"ד ליתא לתקנת אושא תזבין נכסי מלוג ותיתיב ליה! משמע: הא איתא לתקנת אושא לא ליתיב ליה ולא מידי, ואמאי? הא לא תקנו רבנן דהוי לוקח אלא היכא דליכא פסידא לאחריני, אבל הכא איכא פסידא דנחבלים! וי"ל: דהוה מצי למפרך "ולטעמיך", אלא דבלאו הכי פריך שפיר. ולרשב"א נראה דלא קשה מידי, דהא כיון דתקינו רבנן דבעל מוציא מיד הלקוחות לטובתו היכא דליכא פסידא לאחריני – לא פלוג, ותקנו דבכ"מ שאשה מוכרת הבעל מוציא, אפילו במקום שחבלה באחרים דאיכא פסידא דאחריני. כיון דלא שכיחא מלתא שיהא פסידא דאחריני, לכך לא פלוג רבנן, ובכל מקום מוציא.

הדרן עלך יש נוחלין

רבינו גרשום

אלמא בעל בנכסי אשתו יורש הוי: נכסי מלוג. להכי קרי נכסי מלוג שכיון שלא קבל עליו הבעל אחריות מתחסרין והולכין כמו שמולגין את הראש שמתחסר השער להכי מקרי נכסי מלוג. אי אמרת בשלמא לוקח הוי משום הכי מפיק דקדם שעבוד לקיחתו משעה שהכניסה לו והלקוחות לא קנו עדיין אלא אי אמרת כיורש הוי הלא הוא אינו יורש בנכסי אשתו אלא לאחר מיתת אשתו והלקוחות קדם שעבודן קודם מיתתה אלא לאו ש"מ משום הכי מוציא הבעל בנכסי אשתו דלוקח הוי. אלמא אע"ג דשלח רבין באגרתיה דבעל יורש הוי ליכא למשמע מיניה דהשתא מצינן למשמע דלוקח הוי: משום פסידא דידיה דלא תיפוק מידיה ביובל ירושת אשתו דאי דיינינן ליה בלוקח נפקא מיניה ביובל כשאר לקוחות. גבי רבי יוסי ב"ר חנינא טבא עבדי ליה לבעל. דשוינהו כלוקח משום פסידא דידיה הוי דאי אמרת יורש הוי אם כן קדמה קניית לקוחות מירושתו שאין ירושה אלא לאחר מיתה אבל כי משוינן ליה לוקח קדמה קנייתו למכירתה משום הכי מוציא מיד הלקוחות גבי רבין דשלח באגרתיה דיורש הוי משום פסידא דאלמנה דתהוי נזונת מנכסי יורשין שויוהו רבנן כיורש כי היכי דתיקום שטר שעבוד כתובתה מירושתו של בעל שיורש הבת של זו דאי אמרינן דבעל כלוקח הוי אינה נזונת דאין מוציאין למזון האשה והבנות מנכסים משועבדים ללוקח מפני תקון העולם. ומקשי' משום פסידא דאלמנה אמרת שויוהו רבנן כיורש הא גבי מילתא דרבי יוסי ב"ר חנינא דאיכא פסידא ללוקח דבעל מוציא מידו ושויוהו רבנן לבעל כלוקח. ואי משום חששא דפסידא איבעי רבנן לשויוהו כיורש דהשתא לא קא מפסדי לקוחות דשעבודן הוי קדים מירושת הבעל. התם שאני הוא ובדין הוא דליפסדו מדידהו דהלקוחות הוא דאינהו דאפסידו אנפשייהו דלא איבעי להו למזבן כו'. אבל גבי אלמנה מאי הוי לה למיעבד משום הכי שויוהו רבנן כיורש דלא תפסיד אלמנה במזונותי':

הדרן עלך יש נוחלין

מסורת הש"ס

א) כתובות נ. עח: ב"ק פח: ב"מ לה. נו: לעיל נ.:

הגהות הב"ח

(א) גמ' בנכסי מלוג: (ג) תוס' ד"ה התם וכו' לבעל כיורש וכו' האמר הכא דאינהו דאפסדו אנפשייהו דלא הוה להו למיזבן: (ד) בא"ד או שמו מינה לאשה ואנסיבא ומתה בעל לוקח: